Codification of Statements on Auditing Standards

(Including Statements on Standards for Attestation Engagements)

Volume 1

> U.S. Auditing Standards – AICPA (Clarified) [AU-C]

> Attestation Standards [AT]

> Numbers 122 to 127

AS OF JANUARY 2013

10909-344

AICPA®

Reprinted from
AICPA *Professional Standards*
U.S. Auditing Standards—AICPA (Clarified) and Attestation Engagements Parts
(as of January 2013)

1 2 3 4 5 6 7 8 9 0 PrP 1 9 8 7 6 5 4 3

ISBN 978-1-93735-201-1

PREFACE

This set, issued by the Auditing Standards Board (ASB), is a codification of Statements on Auditing Standards (SASs) and the related auditing interpretations applicable to the preparation and issuance of audit reports for all nonissuers. Nonissuers are all entities other than issuers as defined by the Sarbanes-Oxley Act, or other entities who are required to be audited by a registered public accounting firm as prescribed by the rules of the Securities and Exchange Commission. Volume 1 contains the clarified codified auditing standards (SAS Nos. 122–127), which are effective for audits of financial statements for periods ending on or after December 15, 2012, as well as Statements on Standards for Attestation Services (SSAEs), and the related attestation interpretations. Volume 2 contains the codified auditing standards that were applicable for audits of financial statements for periods ending before December 15, 2012.

SASs are issued by the ASB, the senior technical body of the AICPA designated to issue pronouncements on auditing matters applicable to the preparation and issuance of audit reports for entities that are nonissuers. Rule 202, *Compliance With Standards* (AICPA, *Professional Standards*, ET sec. 202 par. .01), of the AICPA Code of Professional Conduct requires an AICPA member who performs an audit (the auditor) of the financial statements of a nonissuer to comply with standards promulgated by the ASB. An auditor is required to comply with an unconditional requirement in all cases in which the circumstances exist to which the unconditional requirement applies. An auditor is also required to comply with a presumptively mandatory requirement in all cases in which the circumstances exist to which the presumptively mandatory requirement applies; however, in rare circumstances, an auditor may depart from a presumptively mandatory requirement provided the auditor documents his or her justification for the departure and how the alternative procedures performed in the circumstances were sufficient to achieve the objectives of the presumptively mandatory requirement.

Auditing interpretations of SASs are *interpretive publications* pursuant to AU-C section 200, *Overall Objectives of the Independent Auditor and the Conduct of an Audit in Accordance With Generally Accepted Auditing Standards.* Interpretive publications are recommendations on the application of SASs in specific circumstances, including engagements for entities in specialized industries. Interpretive publications are issued under the authority of the ASB. An auditor should consider applicable interpretations in planning and performing an audit.

SSAEs are issued by senior technical bodies of the AICPA designated to issue pronouncements on attestation matters. Rule 202 of the AICPA Code of Professional Conduct requires an AICPA member who performs an attest engagement (a practitioner) to comply with such pronouncements. A practitioner is required to comply with an unconditional requirement in all cases in which the circumstances exist to which the unconditional requirement applies. A practitioner is also required to comply with a presumptively mandatory requirement in all cases in which the circumstances exist to which the presumptively mandatory requirement applies; however, in rare circumstances, a practitioner may depart from a presumptively mandatory requirement provided that the practitioner documents his or her justification for the departure and how the alternative procedures performed in the circumstances were sufficient to achieve the objectives of the presumptively mandatory requirement.

Attestation interpretations are recommendations on the application of SSAEs in specific circumstances, including engagements for entities in specialized industries, issued under the authority of AICPA senior technical bodies. An interpretation is not as authoritative as a pronouncement of the ASB; however, if a practitioner does not apply an attestation interpretation, the practitioner should be prepared to explain how he or she complied with the SSAE provisions addressed by such attestation guidance. The specific terms used to define professional requirements in the SSAEs are not intended to apply to interpretations because interpretations are not attestation standards. It is the ASB's intention to make conforming changes to the interpretations over the next several years to remove any language that would imply a professional requirement where none exists.

The Accounting and Review Services Committee and the ASB are the senior technical committees of the AICPA designated to issue enforceable standards under Rule 201, *General Standards*, and Rule 202 of the AICPA's Code of Professional Conduct concerning attest services in their respective areas of responsibility.

AUDITING STANDARDS BOARD
Bruce P. Webb, Chair
Charles E. Landes, Vice President—
Professional Standards and Services

WHAT'S NEW IN THIS EDITION

STANDARDS RECENTLY ISSUED

See volume 2 for Statement on Auditing Standards (SAS) Nos. 1–121.

Statement	Title	Issue Date	Section
SAS No. 126	*The Auditor's Consideration of An Entity's Ability to Continue as a Going Concern (Redrafted)*	June 2012	AU-C 570
SAS No. 127	*Omnibus Statement on Auditing Standard—2013*	January 2013	

ADDITIONAL CHANGES

Section	Change
AU-C 200	Revisions due to the issuance of SAS No. 126.
AU-C 230	Revisions due to the issuance of SAS No. 126.
AU-C 260	Revisions due to the issuance of SAS No. 126.
AU-C 315	Revisions due to the issuance of SAS No. 126.
AU-C 500	Revisions due to the issuance of SAS No. 126.
AU-C 540	Revisions due to the issuance of SAS No. 126.
AU-C 580	Revisions due to the issuance of SAS No. 122; addition of new exhibit C; revisions due to the issuance of SAS No. 126.
AU-C 600	Revisions due to the issuance of SAS No. 125, *Alert That Restricts the Use of the Auditor's Written Communication;* amended by SAS No. 127.
AU-C 706	Revisions due to the issuance of SAS No. 126.
AU-C 725	Revisions due to the issuance of SAS No. 122.
AU-C 800	Amended by SAS No. 127.
AU-C 805	Revisions due to the issuance of SAS No. 126.
AU-C 806	Revisions due to the issuance of SAS No. 126.
AU-C 930	Revisions due to the issuance of SAS No. 126.
AU-C 935	Revisions due to the issuance of SAS No. 126.
AT 101	Revisions due to the issuance of SAS Nos. 122–126; revisions due to the issuance of Statement on Quality Control Standards No. 8, *A Firm's System of Quality Control.*
AT 9101	Revisions due to the issuance of SAS Nos. 122–126.
AT 201	Revisions due to the issuance of SAS Nos. 122–126; revisions due to the issuance of Statement on Standards for Accounting and Review Services (SSARS) No. 19, *Compilation and Review Engagements.*

Section	Change
AT 301	Revisions due to the issuance of SAS Nos. 122–126; revisions due to the issuance of SSARS No. 19.
AT 401	Revisions due to the issuance of SAS Nos. 122–126; revisions due to the issuance of SSARS No. 19.
AT 501	Revisions due to the issuance of SAS Nos. 122–126.
AT 9501	Revisions due to the issuance of SAS Nos. 122–126.
AT 601	Revisions due to the issuance of SAS Nos. 122–126.
AT 701	Revisions due to the issuance of SAS Nos. 122–126.
AT 801	Revisions due to the issuance of SAS Nos. 122–126.

TABLE OF CONTENTS

ATTESTATION ENGAGEMENTS

HOW THIS VOLUME IS ORGANIZED

This volume is organized into three main sections.

The first section, "Applicability of AICPA Professional Standards and PCAOB Standards," provides guidance about standards applicable to nonissuers and standards applicable to issuers. Information about the Public Company Accounting Oversight Board's (PCAOB's) Interim Standards is included, as well as information about major differences between GAAS and PCAOB Standards.

The second section, "U.S. Auditing Standards—AICPA [Clarified]," contains the clarified codified auditing standards, which are effective for audits of financial statements for periods ending on or after December 15, 2012, and the related auditing interpretations.

The final section, "Attestation Standards," contains the codified attestation standards, and the related attestation interpretations.

These sections are described in more detail in the following sections.

U.S. Auditing Standards—AICPA [Clarified] [AU-C]

The AU-C sections comprise Statement on Auditing Standards (SAS) Nos. 122–127 and certain interpretations that the Auditing Standards Board retained and revised to reflect the issuance of SAS No. 122, *Statements on Auditing Standards: Clarification and Recodification*. Superseded portions have been deleted, and all applicable amendments have been included. The clarified SASs are effective for audits of financial statements for periods ending on or after December 15, 2012. The AU-C sections are arranged as follows:

AU-C Cross-References to SASs

Introduction

General Principles and Responsibilities

Risk Assessment and Response to Assessed Risks

Audit Evidence

Using the Work of Others

Audit Conclusions and Reporting

Special Considerations

Special Considerations in the United States

Exhibits

Appendixes

Topical Index

The AU-C Cross-References to SASs is a list of SASs issued since SAS No. 122 and a list of sources of sections in the current text.

The standards are divided into sections, each with its own section number. Each paragraph within a section is decimally numbered.

Auditing interpretations are numbered in the 9000 series with the last three digits indicating the section to which the interpretation relates. Interpretations immediately follow their corresponding section. For example, an interpretation related to section 230 is numbered 9230, which directly follows section 230.

There are two exhibits relating to auditing standards as follows:

Exhibit A provides a list of AU-C sections designated by SAS No. 122 cross referenced to a list of AU sections.

Exhibit B provides a list of retained interpretations.

There are five appendixes relating to auditing standards as follows:

Appendix A provides the historical background for the SASs.

Appendix B highlights substantive differences between International Standards on Auditing and Generally Accepted Auditing Standards.

Appendix C is reserved.

Appendix D lists AICPA Audit and Accounting Guides and Statements of Position.

Appendix E provides a schedule of changes that lists changes that are the result of SASs issued after SAS No. 122.

Appendix F provides a list of other auditing publications published by the AICPA that have been reviewed by the AICPA Audit and Attest Standards staff.

The AU-C topical index uses the keyword method to facilitate reference to the pronouncements. The index is arranged alphabetically by topic and refers the reader to major divisions, sections, and paragraph numbers.

Attestation Standards [AT Sections]

The AT sections include attestation standards issued through Statement on Standards for Attestation Engagements (SSAE) No. 17, *Reporting on Compiled Prospective Financial Statements When the Practitioner's Independence Is Impaired*. Superseded portions have been deleted, and all applicable amendments have been included. These sections are arranged as follows:

AT Cross-References to SSAEs

Defining Professional Requirements in Statements on Standards for Attestation Engagements

SSAE Hierarchy

Attest Engagements

Agreed-Upon Procedures Engagements

Financial Forecasts and Projections

Reporting on Pro Forma Financial Information

An Examination of an Entity's Internal Control Over Financial Reporting That Is Integrated With an Audit of Its Financial Statements

Compliance Attestation

Management's Discussion and Analysis

Reporting on Controls at a Service Organization

Topical Index

The AT Cross-References to SSAEs is a list of all issued SSAEs and a list of sources of sections in the current text.

The standards are divided into sections, each with its own section number. Each paragraph within a section is decimally numbered.

Attestation interpretations are numbered in the 9000 series with the last three digits indicating the section to which the interpretation relates. Interpretations immediately follow their corresponding section. For example, interpretations related to section 101 are numbered 9101, which directly follows section 101.

The AT topical index uses the key word method to facilitate reference to the statements and interpretations. The index is arranged alphabetically by topic with references to section and paragraph numbers.

Part I

Applicability of AICPA Professional Standards and Public Company Accounting Oversight Board Standards

Background

As a result of the passage of the Sarbanes-Oxley Act of 2002 (the act), auditing and related professional practice standards to be used in the performance of and reporting on audits of the financial statements of public companies are now established by the Public Company Accounting Oversight Board (PCAOB). Note that the term *public companies* is a general reference to the entities subject to the securities laws. The act more specifically defines these entities as *issuers*, the definition of which is provided in the section that follows.

Among other significant provisions, the act requires a public accounting firm that prepares or issues, or participates in the preparation or issuance of, any audit report with respect to any issuer to register with the PCAOB. Accordingly, public accounting firms registered with the PCAOB are required to adhere to all PCAOB standards in the audits of issuers. Moreover, the act authorizes the PCAOB to establish auditing and related attestation, quality control, ethics, and independence standards to be used by registered public accounting firms in the preparation and issuance of audit reports for issuers.

Who Is an Issuer?

As provided in Section 2 of the act, the term *issuer* means an issuer (as defined in Section 3 of the Securities Exchange Act of 1934 [15 U.S.C. 78c]), the securities of which are registered under Section 12 of that act (15 U.S.C. 78l) or that is required to file reports pursuant to Section 15(d) [15 U.S.C. 78o(d)], or that files or has filed a registration statement that has not yet become effective under the Securities Act of 1933 (15 U.S.C. 77a et seq.), and that it has not withdrawn.

Accordingly, nonissuers are those entities not subject to the act or the rules of the Securities and Exchange Commission (SEC). For audits of nonissuers, the preparation and issuance of audit reports must be conducted in accordance with the AICPA Code of Professional Conduct (AICPA Code) and the standards promulgated by the AICPA Auditing Standards Board (ASB). Audits of nonissuers remain governed by generally accepted auditing standards (GAAS) and the Statements on Quality Control Standards (SQCS) as issued by the ASB.

Standards Applicable to the Audits of *Nonissuers*

With the formation of the PCAOB, the ASB was reconstituted and its jurisdiction amended to recognize the ASB as the body authorized to promulgate auditing, attestation and quality control standards relating to the preparation and issuance of audit reports for nonissuers.

Failure to follow ASB standards in the audit of a nonissuer would be considered a violation of Rule 201, *General Standards*, and Rule 202, *Compliance With Standards* (ET sec. 201 par. .01 and ET sec. 202 par. .01), of the AICPA Code, or both.

As a caution to readers, pursuant to AU section 150, *Generally Accepted Auditing Standards*, interpretative publications are recommendations on the application of the Statements on Auditing Standards (SASs) in specific circumstances, including engagements for entities in specialized industries. Interpretative publications, which include auditing interpretations, auditing guidance in AICPA Audit and Accounting Guides, and auditing guidance found in Statements of Position (SOPs), are issued under the authority of the ASB. The auditor should identify interpretative publications applicable to his or her audit. If the auditor does not apply the auditing guidance included in an applicable interpretative publication, the auditor should be prepared to explain how he or she complied with the SAS provisions addressed by such auditing guidance.

The ASB continues to issue SASs and interpretative publications that relate to audits of nonissuers and auditors should be alert to those issuances.

Standards Applicable to the Audits of *Issuers*

Rule 3100, *Compliance With Auditing and Related Professional Practice Standards* (AICPA, *PCAOB Standards and Related Rules*, Select Rules of the Board), issued by the PCAOB (see PCAOB Release No. 2003-009, dated June 30, 2003) generally requires all registered public accounting firms to adhere to the PCAOB's standards in connection with the preparation or issuance of any audit report on the financial statements of an issuer. Rule 3100 requires registered public accounting firms and their associated persons to comply with all applicable standards. Accordingly, if the PCAOB's standards do not apply to an engagement or other activity of the firm, Rule 3100, by its own terms, does not apply to that engagement or activity.

Rule 3101, *Certain Terms Used in Auditing and Related Professional Practice Standards* (AICPA, *PCAOB Standards and Related Rules*, Select Rules of the Board), issued by the PCAOB (see PCAOB Release No. 2004-007, dated June 9, 2004) defines the degree of responsibility imposed on the auditor by the use of certain terms in the PCAOB's auditing and related professional practice standards, including the interim standards adopted in Rule 3200T, *Interim Auditing Standards*; Rule 3300T, *Interim Attestation Standards*; Rule 3400T, *Interim Quality Control Standards*; Rule 3500T, *Interim Ethics Standards*; and Rule 3600T, *Interim Independence Standards* (AICPA, *PCAOB Standards and Related Rules*, Select Rules of the Board) (further described in a later section). Effectively, Rule 3101 creates three categories of professional responsibilities:

1. *Unconditional responsibility*. The words *must*, *shall*, and *is required* indicate unconditional responsibilities. The auditor must fulfill responsibilities of this type in all cases in which the circumstances exist to which the requirement applies. Failure to discharge an unconditional responsibility is a violation of the relevant standard and Rule 3100.
2. *Presumptively mandatory responsibility*. The word *should* indicates responsibilities that are presumptively mandatory. The auditor must comply with requirements of this type specified in the PCAOB's standards unless the auditor demonstrates that alternative actions he or she followed in the circumstances were sufficient to achieve the objectives of the standard. Failure to discharge

a presumptively mandatory responsibility is a violation of the relevant standard and Rule 3100 unless the auditor demonstrates that, in the circumstances, compliance with the specified responsibility was not necessary to achieve the objectives of the standard.

3. *Responsibility to consider*. The words *may*, *might*, *could*, and other terms and phrases describe actions and procedures that auditors have a responsibility to consider. Matters described in this fashion require the auditor's attention and understanding. How and whether the auditor implements these matters in the audit will depend on the exercise of professional judgment in the circumstances consistent with the objectives of the standard.

Compliance With Standards Applicable to the Audits of *Issuers*

Any registered public accounting firm or person associated with such a firm that fails to adhere to applicable PCAOB standards in connection with an audit of the financial statements of an issuer may be the subject of a PCAOB disciplinary proceeding in accordance with Section 105 of the act. In addition, the act provides that any violation of the PCAOB's rules is to be treated for all purposes in the same manner as a violation of the Securities Exchange Act of 1934, 15 U.S.C. 78a et seq., or the rules and regulations issued thereunder, and any person violating the PCAOB's rules "shall be subject to the same penalties, and to the same extent, as for a violation of [the Exchange] Act or such rules or regulations."

Rule 201 and Rule 202 require a member who performs auditing and other professional services to comply with standards promulgated by bodies designated by the AICPA Council. The AICPA Council has designated the PCAOB as the body authorized to promulgate auditing and related attestation standards, quality control, ethics, independence and other standards relating to the preparation and issuance of audit reports for issuers.

The AICPA's Professional Ethics Division is able to hold an AICPA member who performs audits of the financial statements of issuers accountable under Rules 201 and 202 of the AICPA Code for complying with PCAOB's auditing and related professional practice standards when performing such audits.

PCAOB's Adoption of Interim Standards

The PCAOB is subject to SEC oversight. As such, rules and standards issued by the PCAOB must be approved by the SEC before they become effective.

Pursuant to PCAOB Release No. 2003-006, dated April 18, 2003, the PCAOB adopted, on an initial, transitional basis, five temporary rules that refer to professional standards of auditing, attestation, quality control, ethics, and independence in existence on that date (known collectively as the Interim Professional Auditing Standards). The SEC granted approval to these rules (see SEC Release No. 33-8222, dated April 25, 2003).

Essentially, the interim standards that the PCAOB adopted were the auditing standards, attestation standards, quality control standards issued by the ASB, certain former AICPA SEC Practice Section (SECPS) membership requirements, certain AICPA ethics and independence rules, and Independence Standards Board (ISB) rules as they existed on April 16, 2003. These interim standards will remain in effect while the PCAOB conducts a review of standards applicable to registered public accounting firms. Based on this review, the PCAOB may modify, repeal, replace, or adopt, in part or in whole, the interim standards. As reiterated in a succeeding paragraph, the PCAOB's interim independence standards are not to be interpreted to supersede the SEC's independence requirements. The PCAOB has also made certain conforming amendments to the interim standards to reflect the adoption of PCAOB standards.

If a provision of a PCAOB standard addresses a subject matter that also is addressed in the interim standards, the affected portion of the interim standard should be considered superseded or effectively amended.

The five rules that comprise the PCAOB's interim standards consist of Rules 3200T, 3300T, 3400T, 3500T, and 3600T, and are described in the paragraphs that follow.

Rule 3200T, *Interim Auditing Standards,* as Amended by PCAOB Release No. 2003-026

Rule 3200T provides that, in connection with the preparation or issuance of any audit report on the financial statements of an issuer, a registered public accounting firm shall comply with GAAS as described in AU section 150, as in existence on April 16, 2003, to the extent not superseded or amended by the PCAOB.

Rule 3300T, *Interim Attestation Standards,* as Amended by PCAOB Release No. 2003-026

Rule 3300T governs the conduct of engagements that (1) are described in the ASB's Statement on Standards for Attestation Engagements (SSAE) No. 10, *Attest Engagements* (AT sec. 101), and (2) relate to the preparation or issuance of audit reports for issuers. Registered public accounting firms involved in such engagements are required to comply with the ASB's SSAEs, and related interpretations and AICPA SOPs, as in existence on April 16, 2003, to the extent not superseded or amended by the PCAOB.

Rule 3400T, *Interim Quality Control Standards,* as Amended by PCAOB Release No. 2003-026

Rule 3400T sets forth minimum quality control standards with which registered public accounting firms must comply, in order to ensure that registered public accounting firms, and their personnel, comply with applicable accounting and auditing (and other professional) standards. Pursuant to Rule 3400T, the PCAOB has provisionally designated the SQCSs (QC sections 20–40) proposed and issued by the ASB and certain former AICPA SECPS [1] membership requirements, as they existed, and as they applied to SECPS members, on April 16, 2003, to the extent not superseded or amended by the PCAOB, as the PCAOB's Interim Quality Control Standards.

Because the PCAOB intends the Interim Quality Control Standards (QC sections 20–40) to preserve existing standards as they applied on April 16, 2003

---

[1] The Center for Audit Quality (CAQ) restructured and expanded the AICPA's Center for Public Company Audit Firms, which was the successor to the Securities and Exchange Commission Practice Section (SECPS). The CAQ, which began operating in January 2007, is an autonomous, nonpartisan, public policy organization affiliated with the AICPA and dedicated to enhancing investor confidence and public trust in the global capital markets by fostering high quality performance by auditors of public entities.

consistent with Section 103(a)(3) of the act, those Interim Quality Control Standards (QC sec. 20–40) adapted from the former AICPA SECPS requirements apply only to those firms that were members of the AICPA's SECPS on April 16, 2003.

Rule 3500T, *Interim Ethics Standards*, as Amended by PCAOB Release No. 2003-026

Rule 3500T sets forth ethical standards for registered public accounting firms and their personnel. Pursuant to Rule 3500T, the PCAOB has provisionally designated Rule 102, *Integrity and Objectivity*, and its interpretations (ET sec. 102 and .191) of the AICPA Code, and interpretations and rulings thereunder, as they existed on April 16, 2003, to the extent not superseded or amended by the PCAOB, as the PCAOB's Interim Ethics Standards.

Rule 3600T, *Interim Independence Standards*, as Amended by PCAOB Release No. 2003-026

Rule 3600T sets forth independence standards for registered public accounting firms and their personnel. Pursuant to Rule 3600T, the PCAOB has provisionally designated Rule 101, *Independence*, and its interpretations (ET sec. 101 and ET sec. 191) of the AICPA Code, and interpretations and rulings thereunder, as they existed on April 16, 2003, to the extent not superseded or amended by the PCAOB, and Standard Nos. 1, 2, and 3, and Interpretation Nos. 99-1, 00-1, and 00-2 of the ISB, to the extent not superseded or amended by the PCAOB, as the PCAOB's Interim Independence Standards (AICPA, *PCAOB Standards and Related Rules*, Interim Standards). In addition, the PCAOB requires compliance with the SEC's independence rules. The PCAOB's Interim Independence Standards are not to be interpreted to supersede the SEC's independence requirements. Therefore, to the extent that a provision of the SEC's rule or policy is more restrictive—or less restrictive—than the PCAOB's Interim Independence Standards, a registered public accounting firm must comply with the more restrictive requirement.

References to GAAS

Auditing Standard No. 1, *References in Auditors' Reports to the Standards of the Public Company Accounting Oversight Board* (AICPA, *PCAOB Standards and Related Rules*, Auditing Standards), changed the requirement in the PCAOB's interim standards that the auditors include in their reports a reference to auditing standards promulgated by the ASB, examples of which include GAAS, U.S. GAAS, auditing standards generally accepted in the United States of America, and standards established by the AICPA. Instead, it requires that auditor's reports on the financial statements of issuers that are issued or reissued after the effective date of Auditing Standard No. 1 include a statement that the engagement was conducted in accordance with "the standards of the Public Company Accounting Oversight Board (United States)."

Conforming amendments resulting from Auditing Standard No. 1 have not yet been reflected in the PCAOB's interim standards. Such conforming changes will be made after the PCAOB issues, and the SEC approves, such conforming amendments.

Standards Applicable If a Nonissuer's Financial Statements Are Audited in Accordance With Both GAAS and PCAOB Auditing Standards

Interpretation No. 18, "Reference to PCAOB Standards in an Audit Report on a Nonissuer," of AU section 508, *Reports on Audited Financial Statements* (AU sec. 9508 par. .89–.92), addresses the applicable standards, and references to those standards in the auditor's report, when an auditor is engaged to perform an audit of a nonissuer in accordance with GAAS and PCAOB auditing standards. The interpretation states that an auditor may indicate that the audit was conducted in accordance with GAAS and another set of auditing standards. If the auditor conducted the audit in accordance with GAAS and the auditing standards of the PCAOB, the auditor may indicate in the auditor's report that the audit was conducted in accordance with both sets of standards. The interpretation provides example report language.

Standards Applicable to an Integrated Audit of a Nonissuer's Financial Statements

In October 2008, the ASB issued SSAE No. 15, *An Examination of an Entity's Internal Control Over Financial Reporting That Is Integrated With an Audit of Its Financial Statements* (AT sec. 501), which establishes standards and provides guidance to practitioners performing an examination of a nonissuer's internal control over financial reporting in the context of an integrated audit (an audit of an entity's financial statements and an examination of its internal control). SSAE No. 15 supersedes extant AT section 501, *Reporting on an Entity's Internal Control Over Financial Reporting*, and converges the standards practitioners use for reporting on a nonissuer's internal control with PCAOB Auditing Standard No. 5, *An Audit of Internal Control Over Financial Reporting That Is Integrated with An Audit of Financial Statements* (AICPA, *PCAOB Standards and Related Rules*, Auditing Standards).

AICPA Standards and the Audits of Issuers

If a registered public accounting firm performs an audit of *an issuer* in accordance with PCAOB standards, the auditor does not need to follow standards promulgated by the ASB. However, AICPA members are required to comply with the AICPA Code in addition to the ethics and independence rules and standards required by the SEC and PCAOB.

AU-C

AU-C Cross-References to SASs

TABLE OF CONTENTS

AU-C Cross-References to SASs

Statements on Auditing Standards*

No.	*Date Issued*	*Title*	*AU-C Section*
122	October 2011	*Statements on Auditing Standards: Clarification and Recodification*	See exhibit A.
123	October 2011	*Omnibus Statement on Auditing Standards—2011*[1]	
124	October 2011	*Financial Statements Prepared in Accordance With a Financial Reporting Framework Generally Accepted in Another Country*	910
125	December 2011	*Alert That Restricts the Use of the Auditor's Written Communication*	905
126	June 2012	*The Auditor's Consideration of An Entity's Ability to Continue as a Going Concern* (Redrafted)	570
127	January 2013	*Omnibus Statement on Auditing Standards—2013*[2]	

* This table lists Statements on Auditing Standards (SASs) issued after SAS No. 122, *Statements on Auditing Standards: Clarification and Recodification*, was issued in October 2011. Refer to Cross-References to SASs (preceding the AU section) for SASs issued prior to SAS No. 122.

[1] SAS No. 123 has been integrated within sections 200.03, 200.15, 200.A17, 230.19, 260.12, 260.A27, 705.16, 705.A19, 720.10–.11, 720.A4, 915.09, 915.14, 935.30–.31, and 935.A41.

[2] SAS No. 127 has been integrated within sections 600.25–.26, 600.28, 600.32, 600.50, 600.A53–.A57, 600.A60, 600.A97, 800.01, 800.07, 800.11, 800.18, 800.20, 800.A4–.A5, 800.A8, 800.A24, and 800.A33.

Sources of Sections in Current Text

AU-C Section	*Contents*	*Source*
200–299	**General Principles and Responsibilities**	
200	*Overall Objectives of the Independent Auditor and the Conduct of an Audit in Accordance With Generally Accepted Auditing Standards*	SAS No. 122
210	*Terms of Engagement*	SAS No. 122
220	*Quality Control for an Engagement Conducted in Accordance With Generally Accepted Auditing Standards*	SAS No. 122
230	*Audit Documentation*	SAS No. 122
240	*Consideration of Fraud in a Financial Statement Audit*	SAS No. 122
250	*Consideration of Laws and Regulations in an Audit of Financial Statements*	SAS No. 122
260	*The Auditor's Communication With Those Charged With Governance*	SAS No. 122
265	*Communicating Internal Control Related Matters Identified in an Audit*	SAS No. 122
300–499	**Risk Assessment and Response to Assessed Risks**	
300	*Planning an Audit*	SAS No. 122
315	*Understanding the Entity and Its Environment and Assessing the Risks of Material Misstatement*	SAS No. 122
320	*Materiality in Planning and Performing an Audit*	SAS No. 122
330	*Performing Audit Procedures in Response to Assessed Risks and Evaluating the Audit Evidence Obtained*	SAS No. 122
402	*Audit Considerations Relating to an Entity Using a Service Organization*	SAS No. 122
450	*Evaluation of Misstatements Identified During the Audit*	SAS No. 122
500–599	**Audit Evidence**	
500	*Audit Evidence*	SAS No. 122
501	*Audit Evidence—Specific Considerations for Selected Items*	SAS No. 122
505	*External Confirmations*	SAS No. 122
510	*Opening Balances—Initial Audit Engagements, Including Reaudit Engagements*	SAS No. 122
520	*Analytical Procedures*	SAS No. 122
530	*Audit Sampling*	SAS No. 122
540	*Auditing Accounting Estimates, Including Fair Value Accounting Estimates, and Related Disclosures*	SAS No. 122
550	*Related Parties*	SAS No. 122
560	*Subsequent Events and Subsequently Discovered Facts*	SAS No. 122

AU-C Section	Contents	Source
570	*The Auditor's Consideration of An Entity's Ability to Continue as a Going Concern*	SAS No. 126
580	*Written Representations*	SAS No. 122
585	*Consideration of Omitted Procedures After the Report Release Date*	SAS No. 122
600–699	**Using the Work of Others**	
600	*Special Considerations—Audits of Group Financial Statements (Including the Work of Component Auditors)*	SAS No. 122
610	*The Auditor's Consideration of the Internal Audit Function in an Audit of Financial Statements*	SAS No. 65[3]
620	*Using the Work of an Auditor's Specialist*	SAS No. 122
700–799	**Audit Conclusions and Reporting**	
700	*Forming an Opinion and Reporting on Financial Statements*	SAS No. 122
705	*Modifications to the Opinion in the Independent Auditor's Report*	SAS No. 122
706	*Emphasis-of-Matter Paragraphs and Other-Matter Paragraphs in the Independent Auditor's Report*	SAS No. 122
708	*Consistency of Financial Statements*	SAS No. 122
720	*Other Information in Documents Containing Audited Financial Statements*	SAS No. 118[4]
725	*Supplementary Information in Relation to the Financial Statements as a Whole*	SAS No. 119[5]
730	*Required Supplementary Information*	SAS No. 120[6]

(continued)

[3] SAS No. 65, *The Auditor's Consideration of the Internal Audit Function in an Audit of Financial Statements*, is currently effective and codified as AU section 322. SAS No. 122 redesignates AU section 322 as AU-C section 610, which will be superseded when it is redrafted for clarity and convergence with ISA 610 (Revised), *Using the Work of Internal Auditors*, as part of the Clarification and Convergence Project of the ASB. Until such time, AU-C section 610 has been conformed to reflect updated section and paragraph cross references, but has not otherwise been subjected to a comprehensive review or revision.

[4] To address practice issues, SAS No. 118, *Other Information in Documents Containing Audited Financial Statements*, was issued in February 2010 as a SAS resulting from the Clarification and Convergence Project of the ASB, and is effective for audits of financial statements for periods beginning on or after December 15, 2010. SAS No. 118 was originally codified as AU section 550. SAS No. 122 redesignates AU section 550 as AU-C section 720 but does not supersede SAS No. 118. AU-C section 720 contains conforming changes necessary due to the issuance of SAS No. 122.

[5] To address practice issues, SAS No. 119, *Supplementary Information in Relation to the Financial Statements as a Whole*, was issued in February 2010 as a SAS resulting from the Clarification and Convergence Project of the ASB, and is effective for audits of financial statements for periods beginning on or after December 15, 2010. SAS No. 119 was originally codified as AU section 551. SAS No. 122 redesignates AU section 551 as AU-C section 725 but does not supersede SAS No. 119. AU-C section 725 contains conforming changes necessary due to the issuance of SAS No. 122.

[6] To address practice issues, SAS No. 120, *Required Supplementary Information*, was issued in February 2010 as a SAS resulting from the Clarification and Convergence Project of the ASB, and is effective for audits of financial statements for periods beginning on or after December 15, 2010. SAS No. 120 was originally codified as AU section 558. SAS No. 122 redesignates AU section 558 as AU-C section 730 but does not supersede SAS No. 120. AU-C section 730 contains conforming changes necessary due to the issuance of SAS No. 122.

AU-C Section	*Contents*	*Source*
800–899	**Special Considerations**	
800	*Special Considerations—Audits of Financial Statements Prepared in Accordance With Special Purpose Frameworks*	SAS No. 122
805	*Special Considerations—Audits of Single Financial Statements and Specific Elements, Accounts, or Items of a Financial Statement*	SAS No. 122
806	*Reporting on Compliance With Aspects of Contractual Agreements or Regulatory Requirements in Connection With Audited Financial Statements*	SAS No. 122
810	*Engagements to Report on Summary Financial Statements*	SAS No. 122
900–999	**Special Considerations in the United States**	
905	*Alert That Restricts the Use of the Auditor's Written Communication*	SAS No. 125
910	*Financial Statements Prepared in Accordance With a Financial Reporting Framework Generally Accepted in Another Country*	SAS No. 124
915	*Reports on Application of Requirements of an Applicable Financial Reporting Framework*	SAS No. 122
920	*Letters for Underwriters and Certain Other Requesting Parties*	SAS No. 122
925	*Filings With the U.S. Securities and Exchange Commission Under the Securities Act of 1933*	SAS No. 122
930	*Interim Financial Information*	SAS No. 122
935	*Compliance Audits*	SAS No. 117[7]

[7] To address practice issues, SAS No. 117, *Compliance Audits*, was issued in December 2009 as a SAS resulting from the Clarification and Convergence Project of the ASB, and is effective for compliance audits for fiscal periods ending on or after June 15, 2010. SAS No. 117 was originally codified as AU section 801. SAS No. 122 redesignates AU section 801 as AU-C section 935 but does not supersede SAS No. 117. AU-C section 935 contains conforming changes necessary due to the issuance of SAS No. 122.

AU-C Introduction

CONTENTS

AU-C Introduction

Foreword

Clarity Project

To address concerns over the clarity, length, and complexity of its standards, the Auditing Standards Board (ASB) has made a significant effort to clarify the Statements on Auditing Standards (SASs).[1] The ASB established clarity drafting conventions and undertook to redraft all of its SASs in accordance with those conventions, which include the following:

- Establishing objectives for each clarified SAS
- Including a definitions section, where relevant, in each clarified SAS
- Separating requirements from application and other explanatory material
- Numbering application and other explanatory material paragraphs using an A- prefix and presenting them in a separate section that follows the requirements section
- Using formatting techniques, such as bulleted lists, to enhance readability
- Including, when appropriate, special considerations relevant to audits of smaller, less complex entities within the text of the clarified SAS
- Including, when appropriate, special considerations relevant to audits of governmental entities within the text of the clarified SAS

Convergence

Consistent with the ASB's strategy to converge its SASs with International Standards on Auditing (ISAs) promulgated by the International Auditing and Assurance Standards Board while avoiding unnecessary conflict with standards of the Public Company Accounting Oversight Board,[2] clarified SASs have been developed using equivalent ISAs as a base, when applicable. Substantive differences in objectives, definitions, or requirements between a clarified SAS and the equivalent ISA are identified in AU-C appendix B, *Substantive Differences Between the International Standards on Auditing and Generally Accepted Auditing Standards*.

---

[1] The pamphlet *Clarification and Convergence* provides information about the Auditing Standards Board's (ASB's) Clarity Project and is available online at www.aicpa.org/Research/Standards/AuditAttest/ASB/DownloadableDocuments/Clarity/ASB_Clarity_%20and_Convergence_(8.5x11).pdf.

[2] The ASB's convergence paper is available online at www.aicpa.org/InterestAreas/FRC/AuditAttest/DownloadableDocuments/ASB_Convergence_Plan.pdf.

Issuance of Clarified SASs

SAS Nos. 117–120

In order to address practice issues timely, the following clarified SASs were issued in the clarity format and became effective before the issuance of SAS No. 122, *Statements on Auditing Standards: Clarification and Recodification*:

- SAS No. 117, *Compliance Audits* (issued December 2009; became effective June 15, 2010) (AU sec. 801)
- SAS No. 118, *Other Information in Documents Containing Audited Financial Statements* (issued February 2010; became effective December 15, 2010) (AU sec. 550)
- SAS No. 119, *Supplementary Information in Relation to the Financial Statements as a Whole* (issued February 2010; became effective December 15, 2010) (AU sec. 551)
- SAS No. 120, *Required Supplementary Information* (issued February 2010; became effective December 15, 2010) (AU sec. 558)

SAS No. 122 redesignates SAS Nos. 117–120 as follows and reissues the sections with conforming changes necessary due to the issuance of SAS No. 122:

- SAS No. 117 has been codified as AU-C section 935.
- SAS No. 118 has been codified as AU-C section 720.
- SAS No. 119 has been codified as AU-C section 725.
- SAS No. 120 has been codified as AU-C section 730.

Amendments are also made to SAS Nos. 117–118 due to the issuance of SAS No. 123, *Omnibus Statement on Auditing Standards—2011*.

SAS Nos. 122–127

The section *U.S. Auditing Standards—AICPA (Clarified)* incorporates all SASs issued beginning with SAS No. 122 and should be used for audits of financial statements for periods ending on or after December 15, 2012. The section *U.S. Auditing Standards—AICPA* should be used for audits of financial statements for periods ending before December 15, 2012.

SAS No. 122 contains 39 clarified SASs. SAS No. 122 supersedes all outstanding SASs through SAS No. 121 except the following:

- SAS No. 51, *Reporting on Financial Statements Prepared for Use in Other Countries* (AU sec. 534)
  - SAS No. 124, *Financial Statements Prepared in Accordance With a Financial Reporting Framework Generally Accepted in Another Country* (AU-C sec. 910), supersedes SAS No. 51.
- SAS No. 59, *The Auditor's Consideration of an Entity's Ability to Continue as a Going Concern*, as amended (AU sec. 341)
  - SAS No. 126, *The Auditor's Consideration of An Entity's Ability to Continue as a Going Concern* (Redrafted) (AU-C sec. 570), supersedes SAS No. 59.
- SAS No. 65, *The Auditor's Consideration of the Internal Audit Function in an Audit of Financial Statements* (AU sec. 322)

- SAS No. 87, *Restricting the Use of an Auditor's Report* (AU sec. 532)
  - — SAS No. 125, *Alert That Restricts the Use of the Auditor's Written Communication* (AU-C sec. 905), supersedes SAS No. 87.
- SAS Nos. 117–120

SAS No. 122 also withdraws SAS No. 26, *Association With Financial Statements*, as amended.

SAS No. 65 is currently being redrafted and will be issued as a separate SAS when finalized. However, SAS No. 122 redesignates SAS No. 65 as AU-C section 610 and reissues the section with conforming changes necessary due to the issuance of SAS No. 122.

SAS No. 127, *Omnibus Statement on Auditing Standards—2013*, amends SAS No. 122 section 600, "Special Considerations—Audits of Group Financial Statements (Including the Work of Component Auditors)," and SAS No. 122 section 800, "Special Considerations—Audits of Financial Statements Prepared in Accordance With Special Purpose Frameworks."

All auditing interpretations corresponding to a SAS have been considered in the development of a clarified SAS and incorporated accordingly, and have been withdrawn by the ASB except for certain interpretations that the ASB has retained and revised to reflect the issuance of SAS No. 122. The effective date of the revised interpretations aligns with the effective date of the corresponding clarified SAS.*

This section contains "AU-C" section numbers instead of "AU" section numbers. "AU-C" is a temporary identifier to avoid confusion with references to existing "AU" sections, which will remain in AICPA *Professional Standards* through 2013. The "AU-C" identifier will revert to "AU" in 2014, by which time substantially all engagements for which the "AU" sections were still effective are expected to be completed.

SAS No. 122 recodifies the AU section numbers as designated by SAS Nos. 1–121. AU-C section numbers for clarified SASs based on equivalent ISAs are the same as the equivalent ISA numbers. AU-C section numbers for clarified SASs with no equivalent ISAs have been assigned new numbers. The ASB believes that this recodification structure will aid firms and practitioners that use both ISAs and generally accepted auditing standards (GAAS). AU-C exhibit A, "List of AU-C Sections Designated by SAS No. 122, *Statements on Auditing Standards: Clarification and Recodification*, Cross Referenced to List of AU Sections," contains a complete, two-part cross-reference listing of AU-C and AU section numbers as designated by SAS No. 122.

SAS Nos. 122–127 are effective for audits of financial statements for periods ending on or after December 15, 2012. Refer to individual AU-C sections for specific effective date language.

Authority of the SASs

SASs are issued by the ASB, the senior committee of the AICPA designated to issue pronouncements on auditing matters applicable to the preparation and issuance of audit reports for entities that are nonissuers. Rule 202, *Compliance With Standards* (ET sec. 202 par. .01), of the AICPA Code of Professional Conduct requires an AICPA member who performs an audit (the auditor) of the

---

* See AU-C exhibit B, *Retained Interpretations*, for a list of these interpretations.

financial statements of a nonissuer to comply with standards promulgated by the ASB. An auditor is required to comply with an unconditional requirement in all cases in which the circumstances exist to which the unconditional requirement applies. An auditor is also required to comply with a presumptively mandatory requirement in all cases in which the circumstances exist to which the presumptively mandatory requirement applies; however, in rare circumstances, an auditor may depart from a presumptively mandatory requirement provided the auditor documents his or her justification for the departure and how the alternative procedures performed in the circumstances were sufficient to achieve the objectives of the presumptively mandatory requirement.

Exhibits and interpretations to SASs are *interpretive publications*, as defined in section 200, *Overall Objectives of the Independent Auditor and the Conduct of an Audit in Accordance With Generally Accepted Auditing Standards*. Section 200 requires the auditor to consider applicable interpretive publications in planning and performing the audit. Interpretive publications are not auditing standards. Interpretive publications are recommendations on the application of the SASs in specific circumstances, including engagements for entities in specialized industries. An interpretive publication is issued under the authority of the ASB after all ASB members have been provided an opportunity to consider and comment on whether the proposed interpretive publication is consistent with the SASs. Auditing interpretations of GAAS are included in AU-C sections. AICPA Audit and Accounting Guides and Auditing Statements of Position are listed in AU-C appendix D, "AICPA Audit and Accounting Guides and Statements of Position."

AUDITING STANDARDS BOARD
Bruce P. Webb, *Chair*
Charles E. Landes, Vice President—
Professional Standards and Services

AU-C Preface *

Principles Underlying an Audit Conducted in Accordance With Generally Accepted Auditing Standards

This preface contains the principles underlying an audit conducted in accordance with generally accepted auditing standards (the principles). These principles are not requirements and do not carry any authority.

The Auditing Standards Board has developed the principles to provide a framework that is helpful in understanding and explaining an audit. The principles are organized to provide a structure for the codification of Statements on Auditing Standards. This structure addresses the purpose of an audit (purpose), personal responsibilities of the auditor (responsibilities), auditor actions in performing the audit (performance), and reporting (reporting).

Purpose of an Audit and Premise Upon Which an Audit Is Conducted

.01 The purpose of an audit is to provide financial statement users with an opinion by the auditor on whether the financial statements are presented fairly, in all material respects, in accordance with the applicable financial reporting framework. An auditor's opinion enhances the degree of confidence that intended users can place in the financial statements.

.02 An audit in accordance with generally accepted auditing standards is conducted on the premise that management and, when appropriate, those charged with governance, have responsibility

a. for the preparation and fair presentation of the financial statements in accordance with the applicable financial reporting framework;

b. for the design, implementation, and maintenance of internal control relevant to the preparation and fair presentation of financial statements that are free from material misstatement, whether due to fraud or error; and

c. to provide the auditor with

i. access to all information of which management and, when appropriate, those charged with governance are aware that is relevant to the preparation and fair presentation of

---

* This section has been codified using an "AU-C" identifier instead of an "AU" identifier. "AU-C" is a temporary identifier to avoid confusion with references to existing "AU" sections, which will remain in AICPA *Professional Standards* through 2013. The "AU-C" identifier will revert to "AU" in 2014, by which time substantially all engagements for which the "AU" sections were still effective are expected to be completed.

the financial statements such as records, documentation, and other matters;

ii. additional information that the auditor may request from management and, when appropriate, those charged with governance for the purpose of the audit; and

iii. unrestricted access to persons within the entity from whom the auditor determines it necessary to obtain audit evidence.

Responsibilities

.03 Auditors are responsible for having appropriate competence and capabilities to perform the audit; complying with relevant ethical requirements; and maintaining professional skepticism and exercising professional judgment throughout the planning and performance of the audit.

Performance

.04 To express an opinion, the auditor obtains reasonable assurance about whether the financial statements as a whole are free from material misstatement, whether due to fraud or error.

.05 To obtain reasonable assurance, which is a high, but not absolute, level of assurance, the auditor

- plans the work and properly supervises any assistants.
- determines and applies appropriate materiality level or levels throughout the audit.
- identifies and assesses risks of material misstatement, whether due to fraud or error, based on an understanding of the entity and its environment, including the entity's internal control.
- obtains sufficient appropriate audit evidence about whether material misstatements exist, through designing and implementing appropriate responses to the assessed risks.

.06 The auditor is unable to obtain absolute assurance that the financial statements as a whole are free from material misstatement because of inherent limitations, which arise from

- the nature of financial reporting;
- the nature of audit procedures; and
- the need for the audit to be conducted within a reasonable period of time and so as to achieve a balance between benefit and cost.

Reporting

.07 Based on an evaluation of the audit evidence obtained, the auditor expresses, in the form of a written report, an opinion in accordance with the auditor's findings, or states that an opinion cannot be expressed. The opinion states whether the financial statements are presented fairly, in all material respects, in accordance with the applicable financial reporting framework.

AU-C Glossary [*]

Glossary of Terms [1, 2]

accounting and auditing practice.[3] A practice that performs engagements covered by QC section 10, *A Firm's System of Quality Control* (Redrafted), which are audit, attestation, compilation, review, and any other services for which standards have been promulgated by the AICPA Auditing Standards Board (ASB) or the AICPA Accounting and Review Services Committee (ARSC) under Rule 201, *General Standards* (ET sec. 201 par. .01), or Rule 202, *Compliance With Standards* (ET sec. 202 par. .01), of the AICPA Code of Professional Conduct. Although standards for other engagements may be promulgated by other AICPA technical committees, engagements performed in accordance with those standards are not encompassed in the definition of an *accounting and auditing practice*.

accounting estimate. An approximation of a monetary amount in the absence of a precise means of measurement. This term is used for an amount measured at fair value when there is estimation uncertainty, as well as for other amounts that require estimation. When section 540, *Auditing Accounting Estimates, Including Fair Value Accounting Estimates, and Related Disclosures*, addresses only accounting estimates involving measurement at fair value, the term *fair value accounting estimates* is used.

In the context of section 540, the term *accounting estimates* refers to those financial statement items that cannot be measured precisely but can only be estimated. Also see **auditor's point estimate or auditor's range, critical accounting estimates, fair value accounting estimates, management's point estimate,** and **outcome of an accounting estimate**.

accounting records. The records of initial accounting entries and supporting records, such as checks and records of electronic fund transfers; invoices; contracts; the general and subsidiary ledgers; journal entries and other adjustments to the financial statements that are not reflected in journal entries; and records, such as work sheets and spreadsheets, supporting cost allocations, computations, reconciliations, and disclosures.

accounts receivable (in the context of section 330, *Performing Audit Procedures in Response to Assessed Risks and Evaluating the Audit Evidence Obtained*). The entity's claims against customers that have

---

[*] This section has been codified using an "AU-C" identifier instead of an "AU" identifier. "AU-C" is a temporary identifier to avoid confusion with references to existing "AU" sections, which will remain in AICPA *Professional Standards* through 2013. The "AU-C" identifier will revert to "AU" in 2014, by which time substantially all engagements for which the "AU" sections were still effective are expected to be completed.

[1] Unless otherwise indicated, this glossary lists the terms defined for purposes of generally accepted auditing standards (GAAS) in AU-C sections as designated by Statement on Auditing Standards No. 122, *Statements on Auditing Standards: Clarification and Recodification*, and also lists certain terms included by the Auditing Standards Board. Terms defined for purposes of a specific AU-C section or for purposes of adapting GAAS to a compliance audit (section 935, *Compliance Audits*) are denoted as such. Terms may appear in more than one AU-C section.

[2] This glossary also lists terms defined in clarified QC section 10, *A Firm's System of Quality Control* (Redrafted), for purposes of the Statements on Quality Control Standards (SQCSs). Terms defined in AU-C sections and in QC section 10 are denoted as such.

[3] Term defined in paragraph .13 of QC section 10 for purposes of SQCSs.

arisen from the sale of goods or services in the normal course of business, and a financial institution's loans.

acknowledgment letter. See **awareness letter**.

advisory accountant. See **reporting accountant**.

analytical procedures. Evaluations of financial information through analysis of plausible relationships among both financial and nonfinancial data. Analytical procedures also encompass such investigation, as is necessary, of identified fluctuations or relationships that are inconsistent with other relevant information or that differ from expected values by a significant amount.

The use of analytical procedures as risk assessment procedures may be referred to as *analytical procedures used to plan the audit*. The auditor's use of analytical procedures as substantive procedures is referred to as *substantive analytical procedures*. Also see **risk assessment procedures, scanning,** and **substantive procedure**.

analytical procedures used to plan the audit. See **analytical procedures.**

applicable compliance requirements (in the context of adapting generally accepted auditing standards [GAAS] to a compliance audit). Compliance requirements that are subject to the compliance audit.

applicable financial reporting framework. The financial reporting framework adopted by management and, when appropriate, those charged with governance in the preparation and fair presentation of the financial statements that is acceptable in view of the nature of the entity and the objective of the financial statements, or that is required by law or regulation. The term also means the financial reporting framework that applies to the group financial statements. Also see **financial reporting framework**.

applied criteria (in the context of section 810, *Engagements to Report on Summary Financial Statements*). The criteria applied by management in the preparation of the summary financial statements.

appropriateness (of audit evidence). The measure of the quality of audit evidence (that is, its relevance and reliability in providing support for the conclusions on which the auditor's opinion is based). Also see **audit evidence**.

arm's length transaction. A transaction conducted on such terms and conditions between a willing buyer and a willing seller who are unrelated and are acting independently of each other and pursuing their own best interests.

assertions. Representations by management, explicit or otherwise, that are embodied in the financial statements as used by the auditor to consider the different types of potential misstatements that may occur.

audit documentation. The record of audit procedures performed, relevant audit evidence obtained, and conclusions the auditor reached (terms such as *working papers* or *workpapers* are also sometimes used). Also see **engagement documentation**.

audit evidence. Information used by the auditor in arriving at the conclusions on which the auditor's opinion is based. Audit evidence includes both information contained in the accounting records underlying the financial statements and other information. *Sufficiency of audit evidence* is the measure of the quantity of audit evidence. The quantity of the audit evidence needed is affected by the auditor's assessment of the risks of material misstatement and also by the quality of such audit evidence. *Appropriateness of audit evidence* is the measure of the quality of audit evidence; that is, its relevance and its reliability in providing support for the conclusions on which the auditor's opinion is based.

audit file. One or more folders or other storage media, in physical or electronic form, containing the records that constitute the audit documentation for a specific engagement.

audit findings (in the context of adapting GAAS to a compliance audit). The matters that are required to be reported by the auditor in accordance with the governmental audit requirement.

audit risk. The risk that the auditor expresses an inappropriate audit opinion when the financial statements are materially misstated. Audit risk is a function of the risks of material misstatement and detection risk.

Audit risk does not include the risk that the auditor might express an opinion that the financial statements are materially misstated when they are not. This risk is ordinarily insignificant. Further, *audit risk* is a technical term related to the process of auditing; it does not refer to the auditor's business risks, such as loss from litigation, adverse publicity, or other events arising in connection with the audit of financial statements. Also see **detection risk** and **risk of material misstatement**.

audit risk of noncompliance (in the context of adapting GAAS to a compliance audit). The risk that the auditor expresses an inappropriate audit opinion on the entity's compliance when material noncompliance exists. Audit risk of noncompliance is a function of the risks of material noncompliance and detection risk of noncompliance. Also see **detection risk of noncompliance** and **risk of material noncompliance**.

audit sampling (sampling). The selection and evaluation of less than 100 percent of the population of audit relevance such that the auditor expects the items selected (the sample) to be representative of the population and, thus, likely to provide a reasonable basis for conclusions about the population. In this context, *representative* means that evaluation of the sample will result in conclusions that, subject to the limitations of sampling risk, are similar to those that would be drawn if the same procedures were applied to the entire population.

audited financial statements. In the context of section 560, *Subsequent Events and Subsequently Discovered Facts*, reference to *audited financial statements* means the financial statements, together with the auditor's report thereon. In the context of section 810, the term *audited financial statements* refers to those financial statements audited by the auditor in accordance with GAAS and from which the summary financial statements are derived. Also see **financial statements**.

auditor. The term used to refer to the person or persons conducting the audit, usually the engagement partner or other members of the engagement team, or, as applicable, the firm. When an AU-C section expressly intends that a requirement or responsibility be fulfilled by the engagement partner, the term *engagement partner* rather than *auditor* is used. *Engagement partner* and *firm* are to be read as referring to their governmental equivalents when relevant. Also see **component auditor, engagement partner, experienced auditor, firm, predecessor auditor, service auditor,** and **user auditor**.

auditor's consent (in the context of section 925, *Filings With the U.S. Securities and Exchange Commission Under the Securities Act of 1933*). A statement signed and dated by the auditor that indicates that the auditor consents to the use of the auditor's report, and other references to the auditor, in a registration statement filed under the Securities Act of 1933 (the 1933 Act).

auditor's external specialist. See **auditor's specialist**.

auditor's inability to obtain sufficient appropriate audit evidence. See **limitation on the scope of an audit**.

auditor's internal specialist. See **auditor's specialist**.

auditor's point estimate or **auditor's range.** The amount or range of amounts, respectively, derived from audit evidence for use in evaluating the recorded or disclosed amount(s). Also see **accounting estimate**.

auditor's specialist. An individual or organization possessing expertise in a field other than accounting or auditing, whose work in that field is used by the auditor to assist the auditor in obtaining sufficient appropriate audit evidence. An auditor's specialist may be either an auditor's internal specialist (who is a partner or staff, including temporary staff, of the auditor's firm or a network firm) or an auditor's external specialist. *Partner* and *firm* should be read as referring to their governmental equivalents when relevant.

In the context of section 620, *Using the Work of an Auditor's Specialist*, an individual with expertise in applying methods of accounting for deferred income tax is not a specialist because this constitutes accounting expertise; a specialist in taxation law is a specialist because this constitutes legal expertise. Also see **engagement team** and **management's specialist**.

awareness letter (in the context of section 925). A letter signed and dated by the auditor to acknowledge the auditor's awareness that the auditor's review report on unaudited interim financial information is being used in a registration statement filed under the 1933 Act. This letter is not considered to be part of the registration statement and is also commonly referred to as an *acknowledgment letter*.

basic financial statements. Financial statements presented in accordance with an applicable financial reporting framework as established by a designated accounting standards setter, excluding required supplementary information. Also see **financial statements**.

business risk. A risk resulting from significant conditions, events, circumstances, actions, or inactions that could adversely affect an entity's ability to achieve its objectives and execute its strategies or from the setting of inappropriate objectives and strategies.

by-product report. An auditor's written communication that is based solely on matters identified by the auditor during the course of the audit engagement when identification of such matters is not the primary objective of the audit engagement.

capsule financial information (in the context of section 920, *Letters for Underwriters and Certain Other Requesting Parties*). Unaudited summarized interim financial information for periods subsequent to the periods covered by the audited financial statements or unaudited condensed interim financial information included in the securities offering. Capsule financial information may be presented in narrative or tabular form and is often provided for the most recent interim period and for the corresponding period of the prior year.

carve-out method. A method of reporting that excludes from the service auditor's report, when a service organization uses a subservice organization, the subservice organization's relevant control objectives and related controls in the service organization's description of its system and in the scope of the service auditor's engagement. Also see **inclusive method**.

cash basis. A basis of accounting that the entity uses to record cash receipts and disbursements and modifications of the cash basis having substantial support (for example, recording depreciation on fixed assets).

The cash basis of accounting is commonly referred to as an *other comprehensive basis of accounting*. In the context of section 800, *Special Considerations—Audits of Financial Statements Prepared in Accordance With Special Purpose Frameworks*, the cash basis of accounting is not a regulatory basis of accounting. Also see **other comprehensive bases of accounting** and **special purpose framework**.

change period (in the context of section 920). The period ending on the cut-off date and ordinarily beginning, for balance sheet items, immediately after the date of the latest balance sheet in the securities offering and, for income statement items, immediately after the latest period for which such items are presented in the securities offering.

closing date (in the context of section 920). The date on which the issuer of the securities or selling security holder delivers the securities to the underwriter in exchange for the proceeds of the offering.

comfort letter (in the context of section 920). A letter issued by an auditor in accordance with section 920 to requesting parties in connection with an entity's financial statements included in a securities offering.

comparative financial statements. A complete set of financial statements for one or more prior periods included for comparison with the financial statements of the current period. Also see **financial statements**.

comparative information. Prior period information presented for purposes of comparison with current period amounts or disclosures that is not in the form of a complete set of financial statements. Comparative information includes prior period information presented as condensed financial statements or summarized financial information. Also see **condensed financial statements** and **summary financial statements**.

comparison date and **comparison period (in the context of section 920).** The date as of which, and period for which, data at the cut-off date and data for the change period are to be compared.

competencies and capabilities.[4] The knowledge, skills, and abilities that qualify personnel to perform an engagement covered by QC section 10. Competencies and capabilities are not measured by periods of time because such a quantitative measurement may not accurately reflect the kinds of experiences gained by personnel in any given time period. Accordingly, for purposes of QC section 10, a measure of overall competency is qualitative rather than quantitative.

complementary user entity controls. Controls that management of the service organization assumes, in the design of its service, will be implemented

---

[4] Term defined in paragraph .A18 of QC section 10 for purposes of SQCSs.

by user entities, and which, if necessary to achieve the control objectives stated in management's description of the service organization's system, are identified as such in that description.

completion of the engagement quality control review. The completion by the engagement quality control reviewer of the requirements in section 220, *Quality Control for an Engagement Conducted in Accordance With Generally Accepted Auditing Standards.*[5] Also see **engagement quality control review**.

compliance audit (in the context of adapting GAAS to a compliance audit). A program-specific audit or an organization-wide audit of an entity's compliance with applicable compliance requirements.

compliance requirements (in the context of adapting GAAS to a compliance audit). Laws, regulations, rules, and provisions of contracts or grant agreements applicable to government programs with which the entity is required to comply.

component. An entity or business activity for which group or component management prepares financial information that is required by the applicable financial reporting framework to be included in the group financial statements.

In the context of section 600, *Special Considerations—Audits of Group Financial Statements (Including the Work of Component Auditors)*, an investment accounted for under the equity method constitutes a component. Investments accounted for under the cost method may be analogous to a component when the work and reports of other auditors constitute a major element of evidence for such investments. Also see **group** and **significant component**.

component auditor. An auditor who performs work on the financial information of a component that will be used as audit evidence for the group audit. A component auditor may be part of the group engagement partner's firm, a network firm of the group engagement partner's firm, or another firm.

In the context of section 600, auditors who do not meet the definition of a member of the group engagement team are considered to be component auditors. However, an auditor who performs work on a component when the group engagement team will not use that work to provide audit evidence for the group audit is not considered a component auditor. Also see **auditor**.

component management. Management responsible for preparing the financial information of a component. Also see **management**.

component materiality. The materiality for a component determined by the group engagement team for the purposes of the group audit.

components of internal control. The following five components, which provide a useful framework for auditors when considering how different aspects of an entity's internal control may affect the audit:

a. The control environment

b. The entity's risk assessment process

c. The information system, including the related business processes relevant to financial reporting and communication

---

[5] Paragraph .22 and, when applicable, compliance with paragraph .23 of section 220, *Quality Control for an Engagement Conducted in Accordance With Generally Accepted Auditing Standards.*

d. Control activities

e. Monitoring of controls

Also see **internal control**.

condensed financial statements. Historical financial information that is presented in less detail than a complete set of financial statements, in accordance with an appropriate financial reporting framework. Condensed financial statements may be separately presented as unaudited financial information or may be presented as comparative information. Also see **comparative information** and **financial statements**.

consolidation process. Reference to the *consolidation process* includes the following:

a. The recognition, measurement, presentation, and disclosure of the financial information of the components in the group financial statements by way of inclusion, consolidation, proportionate consolidation, or the equity or cost methods of accounting

b. The aggregation in combined financial statements of the financial information of components that are under common control

continuing accountant (in the context of section 915, *Reports on Application of Requirements of an Applicable Financial Reporting Framework*). An accountant who has been engaged to report on the financial statements of a specific entity or entities of which the specific entity is a component.

contractual basis. A basis of accounting that the entity uses to comply with an agreement between the entity and one or more third parties other than the auditor. Also see **special purpose framework**.

control risk. The risk that a misstatement that could occur in an assertion about a class of transaction, account balance, or disclosure and that could be material, either individually or when aggregated with other misstatements, will not be prevented, or detected and corrected, on a timely basis by the entity's internal control. Also see **risk of material misstatement**.

control risk of noncompliance (in the context of adapting GAAS to a compliance audit). The risk that noncompliance with a compliance requirement that could occur and that could be material, either individually or when aggregated with other instances of noncompliance, will not be prevented, or detected and corrected, on a timely basis by the entity's internal control over compliance. Also see **risk of material noncompliance**.

critical accounting estimates. Key assumptions and other sources of estimation uncertainty that have a significant risk of causing a material adjustment to the carrying amounts of assets and liabilities. Also may be referred to as *key sources of estimation uncertainty*. Also see **accounting estimate**.

current period. The most recent period upon which the auditor is reporting.

cut-off date (in the context of section 920). The date through which certain procedures described in the comfort letter are to relate.

date of approval of the financial statements. In some circumstances, final approval of the financial statements by governmental legislative bodies (or subsets of such legislative bodies) is required before the financial statements are issued. In these circumstances, final approval by such legislative bodies (or subsets of such legislative bodies) is not necessary for the auditor to conclude that sufficient appropriate audit evidence has been obtained. The date of approval of the financial statements is the earlier date on which those with the recognized authority determine that all the statements that the financial statements comprise, including the related notes, have been prepared and that those with the recognized authority have asserted that they have taken responsibility for them. Also see **financial statements**.

date of the auditor's report. The date that the auditor dates the report on the financial statements, in accordance with section 700, *Forming an Opinion and Reporting on Financial Statements*.

date of the financial statements. The date of the end of the latest period covered by the financial statements. Also see **financial statements**.

deficiency in design. A deficiency in design exists when a control necessary to meet the control objective is missing or an existing control is not properly designed so that, even if the control operates as designed, the control objective would not be met. Also see **deficiency in internal control** and **deficiency in internal control over compliance**.

deficiency in internal control. A deficiency in internal control exists when the design or operation of a control does not allow management or employees, in the normal course of performing their assigned functions, to prevent, or detect and correct, misstatements on a timely basis. A deficiency in *design* exists when (*a*) a control necessary to meet the control objective is missing, or (*b*) an existing control is not properly designed so that, even if the control operates as designed, the control objective would not be met. A deficiency in *operation* exists when a properly designed control does not operate as designed or when the person performing the control does not possess the necessary authority or competence to perform the control effectively. Also see **internal control**.

deficiency in internal control over compliance (in the context of adapting GAAS to a compliance audit). A deficiency in internal control over compliance exists when the design or operation of a control over compliance does not allow management or employees, in the normal course of performing their assigned functions, to prevent, or detect and correct, noncompliance on a timely basis. A deficiency in *design* exists when (*a*) a control necessary to meet the control objective is missing, or (*b*) an existing control is not properly designed so that, even if the control operates as designed, the control objective would not be met. A deficiency in *operation* exists when a properly designed control does not operate as designed or the person performing the control does not possess the necessary authority or competence to perform the control effectively. Also see **material weakness in internal control over compliance** and **significant deficiency in internal control over compliance**.

deficiency in operation. A deficiency in operation exists when a properly designed control does not operate as designed or the person performing the control does not possess the necessary authority or competence to perform the control effectively. Also see **deficiency in internal control** and **deficiency in internal control over compliance**.

degree of interaction. The extent to which a user entity is able to and elects to implement effective controls over the processing performed by the service organization.

designated accounting standards setter. A body designated by the Council of the AICPA to promulgate generally accepted accounting principles (GAAP) pursuant to Rule 202 and Rule 203, *Accounting Principles* (ET sec. 203 par. .01), of the AICPA Code of Professional Conduct.

detection risk. The risk that the procedures performed by the auditor to reduce audit risk to an acceptably low level will not detect a misstatement that exists and that could be material, either individually or when aggregated with other misstatements. Also see **audit risk** and **risk of material misstatement**.

detection risk of noncompliance (in the context of adapting GAAS to a compliance audit). The risk that the procedures performed by the auditor to reduce audit risk of noncompliance to an acceptably low level will not detect noncompliance that exists and that could be material, either individually or when aggregated with other instances of noncompliance. Also see **audit risk of noncompliance** and **risk of material noncompliance**.

disagreements with management (in the context of section 260, *The Auditor's Communication With Those Charged With Governance*). Disagreements that do not include differences of opinion based on incomplete facts or preliminary information that are later resolved.

documentation. See **audit documentation**.

documentation completion date. The date, no later than 60 days following the report release date, on which the auditor has assembled for retention a complete and final set of documentation in an audit file.

documents containing audited financial statements (in the context of section 720, *Other Information in Documents Containing Audited Financial Statements*). Refers to annual reports (or similar documents) that are issued to owners (or similar stakeholders) and annual reports of governments and organizations for charitable or philanthropic purposes that are available to the public that contain audited financial statements and the auditor's report thereon.

dual purpose test. Performing a test of controls and a test of details on the same transaction. Also see **substantive procedure** and **test of controls**.

effective date (in the context of section 920). The date on which the securities offering becomes effective.

effective date of the registration statement (in the context of section 925). The date on which the registration statement filed under the 1933 Act becomes effective for purposes of evaluating the auditor's liability under Section 11 of the 1933 Act.

element of a financial statement or **element (in the context of section 805, *Special Considerations—Audits of Single Financial Statements and Specific Elements, Accounts, or Items of a Financial Statement*).** Reference to this term means an element, account, or item of a financial statement.

emphasis-of-matter paragraph. A paragraph included in the auditor's report that is required by GAAS, or is included at the auditor's discretion, and that refers to a matter appropriately presented or disclosed in the financial statements that, in the auditor's professional judgment, is of such importance that it is fundamental to users' understanding of the financial statements. Also see **other-matter paragraph**.

engagement documentation.[6] The record of the work performed, results obtained, and conclusions that the practitioner reached (also known as *working papers* or *workpapers*). Also see **audit documentation**.

engagement partner.[7] The partner or other person in the firm who is responsible for the audit engagement and its performance and for the auditor's report that is issued on behalf of the firm and who, when required, has the appropriate authority from a professional, legal, or regulatory body. *Engagement partner*, *partner*, and *firm* refer to their governmental equivalents where relevant. Also see **auditor, firm, group engagement partner,** and **partner**.

engagement quality control review.[8] A process designed to provide an objective evaluation, before the report is released, of the significant judgments the engagement team made and the conclusions it reached in formulating the auditor's report. The engagement quality control review process is only for those audit engagements, if any, for which the firm has determined that an engagement quality control review is required, in accordance with its policies and procedures. Also see **completion of the engagement quality control review**.

engagement quality control reviewer.[9] A partner, other person in the firm, suitably qualified external person, or team made up of such individuals, none of whom is part of the engagement team, with sufficient and appropriate experience and authority to objectively evaluate the significant judgments that the engagement team made and the conclusions it reached in formulating the auditor's report.

engagement team.[10] All partners and staff performing the engagement and any individuals engaged by the firm or a network firm who perform audit procedures on the engagement. This excludes an auditor's external specialist engaged by the firm or a network firm. Also see **auditor's specialist** and **group engagement team**.

entity (in the context of section 920). The party whose financial statements are the subject of the engagement.

entity's risk assessment process. The entity's process for

a. identifying **business risks relevant to financial reporting objectives,**
b. estimating **the significance of the risks,**
c. assessing **the likelihood of their occurrence, and**
d. deciding **about actions to address those risks.**

estimation uncertainty. The susceptibility of an accounting estimate and related disclosures to an inherent lack of precision in its measurement.

evidence. See **audit evidence**.

exception. A response that indicates a difference between information requested to be confirmed, or contained in the entity's records, and information provided by the confirming party.

---

[6] See footnote 3.

[7] Term also defined in paragraph .13 of QC section 10 for purposes of SQCSs. Refer to QC section 10 for specific language.

[8] See footnote 7.

[9] See footnote 7.

[10] See footnote 7.

experienced auditor. An individual (whether internal or external to the firm) who has practical audit experience, and a reasonable understanding of

a. audit processes;
b. GAAS and applicable legal and regulatory requirements;
c. the business environment in which the entity operates; and
d. auditing and financial reporting issues relevant to the entity's industry.

Also see **auditor** and **practical audit experience**.

expertise. Skills, knowledge, and experience in a particular field.

extent of an audit procedure. Refers to the quantity of audit procedures to be performed (for example, a sample size or the number of observations of a control activity). Also see **nature of an audit procedure** and **timing of an audit procedure**.

external confirmation. Audit evidence obtained as a direct written response to the auditor from a third party (the confirming party), either in paper form or by electronic or other medium (for example, through the auditor's direct access to information held by a third party).

factual misstatements. Misstatements about which there is no doubt. Also see **judgmental misstatements, misstatement,** and **projected misstatements**.

fair presentation framework. See **financial reporting framework**.

fair value accounting estimates (in the context of section 540). Accounting estimates involving measurement at fair value. Also see **accounting estimate**.

financial reporting framework. A set of criteria used to determine measurement, recognition, presentation, and disclosure of all material items appearing in the financial statements; for example, U.S. GAAP, International Financial Reporting Standards promulgated by the International Accounting Standards Board, or a special purpose framework.

The term *fair presentation framework* is used to refer to a financial reporting framework that requires compliance with the requirements of the framework and

a. acknowledges explicitly or implicitly that, to achieve fair presentation of the financial statements, it may be necessary for management to provide disclosures beyond those specifically required by the framework; or
b. acknowledges explicitly that it may be necessary for management to depart from a requirement of the framework to achieve fair presentation of the financial statements. Such departures are expected to be necessary only in extremely rare circumstances.

A financial reporting framework that requires compliance with the requirements of the framework, but does not contain the acknowledgments in *a* or *b* is not a fair presentation framework. Also see **applicable financial reporting framework, general purpose framework,** and **special purpose framework**.

financial statements. A structured representation of historical financial information, including related notes, intended to communicate an entity's economic resources and obligations at a point in time or the changes therein for a period of time in accordance with a financial reporting framework. The related notes ordinarily comprise a summary of significant accounting policies and other explanatory information. The term *financial statements* ordinarily refers to a complete set of financial statements as determined by the requirements of the applicable financial reporting framework, but can also refer to a single financial statement.

In the context of section 700, reference to *financial statements* means a complete set of general purpose financial statements, including the related notes. In the context of section 800, reference to *financial statements* means a complete set of special purpose financial statements, including the related notes. Also see **audited financial statements, basic financial statements, comparative financial statements, condensed financial statements, date of approval of the financial statements, date of the financial statements, general purpose financial statements, group financial statements, historical financial information, special purpose financial statements,** and **summary financial statements**.

firm.[11] A form of organization permitted by law or regulation whose characteristics conform to resolutions of the Council of the AICPA and that is engaged in the practice of public accounting. Also see **auditor** and **engagement partner**.

fraud. An intentional act by one or more individuals among management, those charged with governance, employees, or third parties, involving the use of deception that results in a misstatement in financial statements that are the subject of an audit.

Although fraud is a broad legal concept, the auditor is primarily concerned with fraud that causes a material misstatement in the financial statements.

fraud risk factors. Events or conditions that indicate an incentive or pressure to perpetrate fraud, provide an opportunity to commit fraud, or indicate attitudes or rationalizations to justify a fraudulent action.

GAGAS. See ***Government Auditing Standards***.

general purpose financial statements. Financial statements prepared in accordance with a general purpose framework.

For audits of governmental entities, the term *general purpose financial statements*, in the context of section 700, would be considered or referred to as basic financial statements using the terms in the government's applicable financial reporting framework. Also see **financial statements**.

general purpose framework. A financial reporting framework designed to meet the common financial information needs of a wide range of users. Also see **financial reporting framework**.

generally accepted accounting principles (GAAP). Reference to *generally accepted accounting principles* in GAAS means generally accepted accounting principles promulgated by bodies designated by the Council of the AICPA pursuant to Rule 202 and Rule 203 of the AICPA Code of Professional Conduct.

generally accepted auditing standards (GAAS). Statements on Auditing Standards issued by the ASB, the senior committee of the AICPA designated to issue pronouncements on auditing matter for nonissuers. Rule 202 of the AICPA Code of Professional Conduct requires an AICPA member who performs an audit of a nonissuer to comply with standards promulgated by the ASB. Also see **nonissuer.**

---

[11] See footnote 7.

generally accepted government auditing standards. See ***Government Auditing Standards***.

Government Auditing Standards. Standards and guidance issued by the Comptroller General of the United States, U.S. Government Accountability Office for financial audits, attestation engagements, and performance audits. *Government Auditing Standards* also is known as generally accepted government auditing standards (GAGAS) or the Yellow Book.

government program (in the context of adapting GAAS to a compliance audit). The means by which governmental entities achieve their objectives. For example, one of the objectives of the U.S. Department of Agriculture is to provide nutrition to individuals in need. Examples of government programs designed to achieve that objective are the Supplemental Nutrition Assistance Program and the National School Lunch Program. Government programs that are relevant to section 935, *Compliance Audits*, are those in which a grantor or pass-through entity provides an award to another entity, usually in the form of a grant, contract, or other agreement. Not all government programs provide cash assistance; sometimes noncash assistance is provided (for example, a loan guarantee, commodities, or property).

governmental audit organization. A governmental entity, agency, or other department that is required or permitted by law or other authorization to audit other governmental entities, agencies, or departments.

governmental audit requirement (in the context of adapting GAAS to a compliance audit). A government requirement established by law, regulation, rule, or provision of contracts or grant agreements requiring that an entity undergo an audit of its compliance with applicable compliance requirements related to one or more government programs that the entity administers.

grantor (in the context of adapting GAAS to a compliance audit). A government agency from which funding for the government program originates.

group. All the components whose financial information is included in the group financial statements. A group always has more than one component. Also see **component** and **significant component**.

group audit. The audit of group financial statements. Also see **initial audit engagement, reaudit,** and **recurring audit**.

group audit opinion. The audit opinion on the group financial statements. Also see **modified opinion** and **unmodified opinion**.

group engagement partner. The partner or other person in the firm who is responsible for the group audit engagement and its performance and for the auditor's report on the group financial statements that is issued on behalf of the firm. When joint auditors conduct the group audit, the joint engagement partners and their engagement teams collectively constitute the group engagement partner and the group engagement team. *Group engagement partner* and *firm* refer to their governmental equivalents when relevant. Also see **engagement partner** and **partner**.

group engagement team. Partners, including the group engagement partner, and staff who establish the overall group audit strategy, communicate with component auditors, perform work on the consolidation process, and evaluate the conclusions drawn from the audit evidence as the basis for forming an opinion on the group financial statements. Also see **engagement team**.

group financial statements. Financial statements that include the financial information of more than one component. The term *group financial statements* also refers to combined financial statements aggregating the financial information prepared by components that are under common control. Also see **financial statements**.

group management. Management responsible for the preparation and fair presentation of the group financial statements. Also see **management**.

group-wide controls. Controls designed, implemented, and maintained by group management over group financial reporting.

historical financial information. Information expressed in financial terms regarding a particular entity, derived primarily from that entity's accounting system, about economic events occurring in past time periods or about economic conditions or circumstances at points in time in the past. Also see **financial statements** and **interim financial information**.

hypothetical transaction (in the context of section 915). A transaction or financial reporting issue that does not involve facts or circumstances of a specific entity.

included (in the context of section 920). References to information that is included in a document are to be read to also encompass information that is incorporated by reference in that document.

included or **the inclusion of (in the context of section 925).** References to *included* or *the inclusion of* in a registration statement means included or incorporated by reference in a registration statement filed under the 1933 Act.

inclusive method. A method of reporting that includes in the service auditor's report, when a service organization uses a subservice organization, the subservice organization's relevant control objectives and related controls in the service organization's description of its system and in the scope of the service auditor's engagement. Also see **carve-out method**.

inconsistency. Other information that conflicts with information contained in the audited financial statements. A material inconsistency may raise doubt about the audit conclusions drawn from audit evidence previously obtained and, possibly, about the basis for the auditor's opinion on the financial statements.

incorporated by reference. See **included** and **included or the inclusion of**.

independence.[12] Defined as:

a. *Independence of mind.* The state of mind that permits the performance of an attest service without being affected by influences that compromise professional judgment, thereby allowing an individual to act with integrity and exercise objectivity and professional skepticism.

b. *Independence in appearance.* The avoidance of circumstances that would cause a reasonable and informed third party, having

---

[12] Term defined in paragraph .06 of ET section 100-1, *Conceptual Framework for AICPA Independence Standards*.

knowledge of all relevant information, including safeguards applied, to reasonably conclude that the integrity, objectivity, or professional skepticism of a firm or a member of the attest engagement team had been compromised.

inherent risk. The susceptibility of an assertion about a class of transaction, account balance, or disclosure to a misstatement that could be material, either individually or when aggregated with other misstatements, before consideration of any related controls. Also see **risk of material misstatement**.

inherent risk of noncompliance (in the context of adapting GAAS to a compliance audit). The susceptibility of a compliance requirement to noncompliance that could be material, either individually or when aggregated with other instances of noncompliance, before consideration of any related controls over compliance. Also see **risk of material noncompliance**.

initial audit engagement. An engagement in which either (*a*) the financial statements for the prior period were not audited, or (*b*) the financial statements for the prior period were audited by a predecessor auditor. Also see **group audit, reaudit,** and **recurring audit**.

inputs. Refers, in some cases, to assumptions that may be made or identified by a specialist to assist management in making accounting estimates. Inputs may also refer to the underlying data to which specific assumptions are applied. Also see **observable inputs** (or equivalent) and **unobservable inputs** (or equivalent).

inspection.[13] A retrospective evaluation of the adequacy of the firm's quality control policies and procedures, its personnel's understanding of those policies and procedures, and the extent of the firm's compliance with them. Inspection includes a review of completed engagements.

interim financial information (in the context of section 930, *Interim Financial Information*). Financial information prepared and presented in accordance with an applicable financial reporting framework that comprises either a complete or condensed set of financial statements covering a period or periods less than one full year or covering a 12-month period ending on a date other than the entity's fiscal year end. Also see **historical financial information**.

internal control. A process effected by those charged with governance, management, and other personnel that is designed to provide reasonable assurance about the achievement of the entity's objectives with regard to the reliability of financial reporting, effectiveness and efficiency of operations, and compliance with applicable laws and regulations. Also see **components of internal control** and **deficiency in internal control**.

interpretive publications. Auditing interpretations of GAAS, exhibits to GAAS, auditing guidance included in AICPA Audit and Accounting Guides, and AICPA Auditing Statements of Position.

issuer.[14] An issuer (as defined in Section 3 of the Securities Exchange Act of 1934 [15 USC 78(c)]), the securities of which are registered under Section 12 of that act (15 USC 78(l)), or that is required to file reports under Section

---

[13] See footnote 3.

[14] Term defined in AU-C appendix B, *Substantive Differences Between the International Standards on Auditing and Generally Accepted Auditing Standards.*

15(d) (15 USC 78o(d)), or that files or has filed a registration statement that has not yet become effective under the 1933 Act (15 USC 77a et seq.), and that it has not withdrawn. Also see **nonissuer**.

judgmental misstatements. Differences arising from the judgments of management concerning accounting estimates that the auditor considers unreasonable or the selection or application of accounting policies that the auditor considers inappropriate. Also see **factual misstatements, misstatement,** and **projected misstatements**.

key sources of estimation uncertainty. See **critical accounting estimates.**

known questioned costs (in the context of adapting GAAS to a compliance audit). Questioned costs specifically identified by the auditor. Known questioned costs are a subset of likely questioned costs. Also see **likely questioned costs**.

legal counsel (in the context of section 501, *Audit Evidence—Specific Considerations for Selected Items*). The entity's in-house legal counsel and external legal counsel.

likely questioned costs (in the context of adapting GAAS to a compliance audit). The auditor's best estimate of total questioned costs, not just the known questioned costs. Likely questioned costs are developed by extrapolating from audit evidence obtained, for example, by projecting known questioned costs identified in an audit sample to the entire population from which the sample was drawn. Also see **known questioned costs**.

limitation on the scope of an audit. The auditor's inability to obtain sufficient appropriate audit evidence, which may arise from the following:

a. Circumstances beyond the control of the entity

b. Circumstances relating to the nature or timing of the auditor's work

c. Limitations imposed by management

Also may be referred to as a *scope limitation.*

management. The person(s) with executive responsibility for the conduct of the entity's operations. For some entities, management includes some or all of those charged with governance; for example, executive members of a governance board or an owner-manager.

In the context of section 210, *Terms of Engagement*, and section 580, *Written Representations*, references to *management* are to be read as "management and, when appropriate, those charged with governance" unless the context suggests otherwise. Also see **component management, group management,** and **those charged with governance**.

management bias. A lack of neutrality by management in the preparation and fair presentation of information.

management's point estimate. The amount selected by management for recognition or disclosure in the financial statements as an accounting estimate. Also see **accounting estimate**.

management's specialist. An individual or organization possessing expertise in a field other than accounting or auditing, whose work in that field is used by the entity to assist the entity in preparing the financial statements. Also see **auditor's specialist**.

material noncompliance (in the context of adapting GAAS to a compliance audit). In the absence of a definition of *material noncompliance* in the governmental audit requirement, a failure to follow compliance requirements or a violation of prohibitions included in the applicable compliance requirements that results in noncompliance that is quantitatively or qualitatively material, either individually or when aggregated with other noncompliance, to the affected government program.

material weakness. A deficiency, or a combination of deficiencies, in internal control, such that there is a reasonable possibility that a material misstatement of the entity's financial statements will not be prevented, or detected and corrected, on a timely basis. Also see **significant deficiency**.

material weakness in internal control over compliance (in the context of adapting GAAS to a compliance audit). A deficiency, or combination of deficiencies, in internal control over compliance, such that there is a reasonable possibility that material noncompliance with a compliance requirement will not be prevented, or detected and corrected, on a timely basis. In section 935, a reasonable possibility exists when the likelihood of the event is either reasonably possible or probable as defined as follows:

probable. The future event or events are likely to occur.

reasonably possible. The chance of the future event or events occurring is more than remote but less than likely.

remote. The chance of the future event or events occurring is slight.

Also see **deficiency in internal control over compliance** and **significant deficiency in internal control over compliance**.

misstatement. A difference between the amount, classification, presentation, or disclosure of a reported financial statement item and the amount, classification, presentation, or disclosure that is required for the item to be presented fairly in accordance with the applicable financial reporting framework. Misstatements can arise from fraud or error.

Misstatements also include those adjustments of amounts, classifications, presentations, or disclosures that, in the auditor's professional judgment, are necessary for the financial statements to be presented fairly, in all material respects. Also see **factual misstatements, judgmental misstatements, projected misstatements,** and **uncorrected misstatements**.

misstatement of fact. Other information that is unrelated to matters appearing in the audited financial statements that is incorrectly stated or presented. A material misstatement of fact may undermine the credibility of the document containing audited financial statements.

modified opinion. A qualified opinion, an adverse opinion, or a disclaimer of opinion. Also see **group audit opinion** and **unmodified opinion**.

monitoring.[15] A process comprising an ongoing consideration and evaluation of the firm's system of quality control, including inspection or a periodic review of engagement documentation, reports, and clients' financial statements for a selection of completed engagements, designed to provide the firm with reasonable assurance that its system of quality control is designed appropriately and operating effectively.

---

[15] See footnote 7.

nature of an audit procedure. Refers to the purpose (test of controls or substantive procedure) and type (inspection, observation, inquiry, confirmation, recalculation, reperformance, or analytical procedure) of an audit procedure. Also see **extent of an audit procedure** and **timing of an audit procedure**.

negative assurance (in the context of section 920). A statement that, based on the procedures performed, nothing has come to the auditor's attention that caused the auditor to believe that specified matters do not meet specified criteria (for example, that nothing came to the auditor's attention that caused the auditor to believe that any material modifications should be made to the unaudited interim financial information for it to be in accordance with GAAP).

negative confirmation request. A request that the confirming party respond directly to the auditor only if the confirming party disagrees with the information provided in the request. Also see **positive confirmation request**.

network.[16] An association of entities, as defined in ET section 92, *Definitions*.

network firm.[17] A firm or other entity that belongs to a network, as defined in ET section 92.

noncompliance (in the context of section 250, *Consideration of Laws and Regulations in an Audit of Financial Statements*). Acts of omission or commission by the entity, either intentional or unintentional, which are contrary to the prevailing laws or regulations. Such acts include transactions entered into by, or in the name of, the entity or on its behalf by those charged with governance, management, or employees. *Noncompliance* does not include personal misconduct (unrelated to the business activities of the entity) by those charged with governance, management, or employees of the entity.

nonissuer.[18] Any entity not subject to the Sarbanes-Oxley Act of 2002 or the rules of the U.S. Securities and Exchange Commission (SEC). Also see **generally accepted auditing standards (GAAS)** and **issuer**.

nonresponse. A failure of the confirming party to respond, or fully respond, to a positive confirmation request or a confirmation request returned undelivered.

nonroutine transactions. Transactions that are unusual, either due to size or nature, and that, therefore, occur infrequently.

nonsampling risk. The risk that the auditor reaches an erroneous conclusion for any reason not related to sampling risk.

nonstatistical sampling. See **statistical sampling**.

notes to financial statements. See **financial statements**.

observable. In the context of a fair value accounting estimate, the term *observable* refers to data that is readily available, such as published interest rate data or exchange-traded prices of securities.

observable inputs (or equivalent)**.** With respect to fair value accounting estimates, assumptions or inputs that reflect what market participants would

---

[16] See footnote 7.

[17] See footnote 7.

[18] See footnote 14.

use in pricing an asset or a liability, developed based on market data obtained from sources independent of the reporting entity. Also see **inputs** and **unobservable inputs** (or equivalent).

omitted procedure. An auditing procedure that the auditor considered necessary in the circumstances existing at the time of the audit of the financial statements but which was not performed.

opening balances. Those account balances that exist at the beginning of the period. Opening balances are based upon the closing balances of the prior period and reflect the effects of transactions and events of prior periods and accounting policies applied in the prior period. Opening balances also include matters requiring disclosure that existed at the beginning of the period, such as contingencies and commitments.

organization-wide audit (in the context of adapting GAAS to a compliance audit). An audit of an entity's financial statements and an audit of its compliance with the applicable compliance requirements as they relate to one or more government programs that the entity administers. Also see **program-specific audit**.

other auditing publications. Publications other than interpretive publications; these include AICPA auditing publications not defined as interpretive publications; auditing articles in the *Journal of Accountancy* and other professional journals; continuing professional education programs and other instruction materials, textbooks, guide books, audit programs, and checklists; and other auditing publications from state CPA societies, other organizations, and individuals.

other comprehensive bases of accounting. The cash, tax, and regulatory bases of accounting. Also see **cash basis, regulatory basis,** and **tax basis**.

other information. Financial and nonfinancial information (other than the financial statements and the auditor's report thereon) that is included in a document containing audited financial statements and the auditor's report thereon, excluding required supplementary information.

Other information does not encompass, for example, the following:

- A press release or similar memorandum or cover letter accompanying the document containing audited financial statements and the auditor's report thereon
- Information contained in analyst briefings
- Information contained on the entity's website

other-matter paragraph. A paragraph included in the auditor's report that is required by GAAS, or is included at the auditor's discretion, and that refers to a matter other than those presented or disclosed in the financial statements that, in the auditor's professional judgment, is relevant to users' understanding of the audit, the auditor's responsibilities, or the auditor's report. Also see **emphasis-of-matter paragraph**.

outcome of an accounting estimate. The actual monetary amount that results from the resolution of the underlying transaction(s), event(s), or condition(s) addressed by the accounting estimate. Also see **accounting estimate**.

owner-manager. The proprietor of a smaller entity who is involved in running the entity on a day-to-day basis.

partner.[19] Any individual with authority to bind the firm with respect to the performance of a professional services engagement. For purposes of this definition, *partner* may include an employee with this authority who has not assumed the risks and benefits of ownership. Firms may use different titles to refer to individuals with this authority. Also see **engagement partner** and **group engagement partner**.

pass-through entity (in the context of adapting GAAS to a compliance audit). An entity that receives an award from a grantor or other entity and distributes all or part of it to another entity to administer a government program.

performance materiality. The amount or amounts set by the auditor at less than materiality for the financial statements as a whole to reduce to an appropriately low level the probability that the aggregate of uncorrected and undetected misstatements exceeds materiality for the financial statements as a whole. If applicable, the term *performance materiality* also refers to the amount or amounts set by the auditor at less than the materiality level or levels for particular classes of transactions, account balances, or disclosures. Performance materiality is to be distinguished from tolerable misstatement. Also see **tolerable misstatement**.

performing initial procedures. On both client continuance and evaluation of relevant ethical requirements (including independence) at the beginning of the current audit engagement, performing initial procedures means that the procedures are completed prior to the performance of other significant activities for the current audit engagement. For continuing audit engagements, such initial procedures often begin shortly after (or in connection with) the completion of the previous audit.

personnel.[20] Partners and staff.

pervasive. A term used in the context of misstatements to describe the effects on the financial statements of misstatements or the possible effects on the financial statements of misstatements, if any, that are undetected due to an inability to obtain sufficient appropriate audit evidence. Pervasive effects on the financial statements are those that, in the auditor's professional judgment

- are not confined to specific elements, accounts, or items of the financial statements;
- if so confined, represent or could represent a substantial proportion of the financial statements; or
- with regard to disclosures, are fundamental to users' understanding of the financial statements.

population. The entire set of data from which a sample is selected and about which the auditor wishes to draw conclusions.

positive confirmation request. A request that the confirming party respond directly to the auditor by providing the requested information or indicating whether the confirming party agrees or disagrees with the information in the request. Also see **negative confirmation request**.

---

[19] See footnote 7.

[20] See footnote 7.

practicable (in the context of section 705, *Modifications to the Opinion in the Independent Auditor's Report*). The term *practicable*[21] means that omitted information is reasonably obtainable from management's accounts and records and that providing the information in the auditor's report does not require the auditor to assume the position of a preparer of financial information.

practical audit experience. Possessing the competencies and skills that would have enabled the auditor to perform the audit but does not mean that the auditor is required to have performed comparable audits. Also see **experienced auditor**.

preconditions for an audit. The use by management of an acceptable financial reporting framework in the preparation and fair presentation of the financial statements and the agreement of management and, when appropriate, those charged with governance, to the premise on which an audit is conducted.

predecessor auditor. The auditor from a different audit firm who has reported on the most recent audited financial statements or was engaged to perform but did not complete an audit of the financial statements. Also see **auditor**.

premise, relating to the responsibilities of management and, when appropriate, those charged with governance, on which an audit is conducted (the premise). Management and, when appropriate, those charged with governance have acknowledged and understand that they have the following responsibilities that are fundamental to the conduct of an audit in accordance with GAAS; that is, responsibility

a. for the preparation and fair presentation of the financial statements in accordance with the applicable financial reporting framework;

b. for the design, implementation, and maintenance of internal control relevant to the preparation and fair presentation of financial statements that are free from material misstatement, whether due to fraud or error; and

c. to provide the auditor with

  i. access to all information of which management and, when appropriate, those charged with governance are aware that is relevant to the preparation and fair presentation of the financial statements, such as records, documentation, and other matters;

  ii. additional information that the auditor may request from management and, when appropriate, those charged with governance for the purpose of the audit; and

  iii. unrestricted access to persons within the entity from whom the auditor determines it necessary to obtain audit evidence.

The premise, relating to the responsibilities of management and, when appropriate, those charged with governance, on which an audit is conducted may also be referred to as the *premise*.

---

[21] As used in the context of paragraphs .18 and .20c of section 705, *Modifications to the Opinion in the Independent Auditor's Report*.

prescribed guidelines. The authoritative guidelines established by the designated accounting standards setter for the methods of measurement and presentation of the required supplementary information.

presumptively mandatory requirements.[22] The category of professional requirements with which the auditor must comply in all cases in which such a requirement is relevant, except in rare circumstances discussed in section 200, *Overall Objectives of the Independent Auditor and the Conduct of an Audit in Accordance With Generally Accepted Auditing Standards*. GAAS use the word "should" to indicate a presumptively mandatory requirement. Also see **generally accepted auditing standards (GAAS)** and **unconditional requirements**.

private equity exchanges. Refers to entities that trade unregistered private equity securities on electronic trading platforms.

probable (in the context of adapting GAAS to a compliance audit). The future event or events are likely to occur. Also see **material weakness in internal control over compliance**.

professional judgment. The application of relevant training, knowledge, and experience, within the context provided by auditing, accounting, and ethical standards, in making informed decisions about the courses of action that are appropriate in the circumstances of the audit engagement.

professional skepticism. An attitude that includes a questioning mind, being alert to conditions that may indicate possible misstatement due to fraud or error, and a critical assessment of audit evidence.

professional standards.[23] Standards promulgated by the ASB or the ARSC under Rule 201 or Rule 202 of the AICPA Code of Professional Conduct, or other standards-setting bodies that set auditing and attest standards applicable to the engagement being performed and relevant ethical requirements.

program-specific audit (in the context of adapting GAAS to a compliance audit). An audit of an entity's compliance with applicable compliance requirements as they relate to one government program that the entity administers. The compliance audit portion of a program-specific audit is performed in conjunction with either an audit of the entity's or the program's financial statements. Also see **organization-wide audit**.

projected misstatements. The auditor's best estimate of misstatements in populations, involving the projection of misstatements identified in audit samples to the entire population from which the samples were drawn. Also see **factual misstatements, judgmental misstatements,** and **misstatement**.

purchase agreement. See **underwriter**.

purpose of an audit procedure. See **nature of an audit procedure**.

questioned costs (in the context of adapting GAAS to a compliance audit). Costs that are questioned by the auditor because (*a*) of a violation or possible violation of the applicable compliance requirements, (*b*) the costs are not supported by adequate documentation, or (*c*) the incurred

---

[22] Term also defined in paragraph .08 of QC section 10 for purposes of SQCSs. Refer to QC section 10 for specific language.

[23] See footnote 7.

costs appear unreasonable and do not reflect the actions that a prudent person would take in the circumstances.

readily available. Obtainable by a third-party user without any further action by the entity (for example, financial statements on an entity's website may be considered readily available, but being available upon request is not considered readily available).

reasonable assurance.[24] In the context of an audit of financial statements, a high, but not absolute, level of assurance.

reasonable period of time. A period of time not to exceed one year beyond the date of the financial statements being audited.

reasonably possible (in the context of adapting GAAS to a compliance audit). The chance of the future event or events occurring is more than remote but less than likely. Also see **material weakness in internal control over compliance**.

reaudit. An initial audit engagement to audit financial statements that have been previously audited by a predecessor auditor. Also see **group audit, initial audit engagement,** and **recurring audit**.

recurring audit. An audit engagement for an existing audit client for whom the auditor performed the preceding audit. Also see **group audit, initial audit engagement,** and **reaudit**.

reference to GAAP in GAAS. See **generally accepted accounting principles (GAAP)**.

regulatory basis. A basis of accounting that the entity uses to comply with the requirements or financial reporting provisions of a regulatory agency to whose jurisdiction the entity is subject (for example, a basis of accounting that insurance companies use pursuant to the accounting practices prescribed or permitted by a state insurance commission).

The regulatory basis of accounting is commonly referred to as *other comprehensive bases of accounting*. Also see **other comprehensive bases of accounting** and **special purpose framework**.

related notes. See **financial statements**.

related party. A party defined as a *related party* in GAAP.

relevant assertion. A financial statement assertion that has a reasonable possibility of containing a misstatement or misstatements that would cause the financial statements to be materially misstated. The determination of whether an assertion is a *relevant assertion* is made without regard to the effect of internal controls.

relevant ethical requirements.[25] Ethical requirements to which the engagement team and engagement quality control reviewer are subject, which consist of the AICPA Code of Professional Conduct together with rules of applicable state boards of accountancy and applicable regulatory agencies that are more restrictive.

remote (in the context of adapting GAAS to a compliance audit). The chance of the future event or events occurring is slight. Also see **material weakness in internal control over compliance**.

---

[24] See footnote 7.

[25] See footnote 7.

report on compliance. An auditor's report on an entity's compliance with aspects of contractual agreements or regulatory requirements, insofar as they relate to accounting matters, in connection with an audit of financial statements (commonly referred to as a *by-product report*). Also see **by-product report**.

report on management's description of a service organization's system and the suitability of the design of controls (referred to in section 402, *Audit Considerations Relating to an Entity Using a Service Organization*, as a *type 1 report*). A report that comprises the following:

a. Management's description of the service organization's system

b. A written assertion by management of the service organization about whether, in all material respects, and based on suitable criteria

i. management's description of the service organization's system fairly presents the service organization's system that was designed and implemented as of a specified date

ii. the controls related to the control objectives stated in management's description of the service organization's system were suitably designed to achieve those control objectives as of the specified date

c. A service auditor's report that expresses an opinion on the matters in *b*(i–ii)

report on management's description of a service organization's system and the suitability of the design and operating effectiveness of controls (referred to in section 402 as a *type 2 report*). A report that comprises the following:

a. Management's description of the service organization's system

b. A written assertion by management of the service organization about whether in all material respects and, based on suitable criteria

i. management's description of the service organization's system fairly presents the service organization's system that was designed and implemented throughout the specified period

ii. the controls related to the control objectives stated in management's description of the service organization's system were suitably designed throughout the specified period to achieve those control objectives

iii. the controls related to the control objectives stated in management's description of the service organization's system operated effectively throughout the specified period to achieve those control objectives

c. A service auditor's report that

i. expresses an opinion on the matters in *b*(i–iii)

ii. includes a description of the service auditor's tests of controls and the results thereof

report release date. The date the auditor grants the entity permission to use the auditor's report in connection with the financial statements.

reporting accountant (in the context of section 915). An accountant, other than a continuing accountant, in the practice of public accounting, as described in ET section 92, who prepares a written report or provides oral advice on the application of the requirements of an applicable financial reporting framework to a specific transaction or on the type of report that may be issued on a specific entity's financial statements.[26] (A reporting accountant who is also engaged to provide accounting and reporting advice to a specific entity on a recurring basis is commonly referred to as an *advisory accountant*.)

representative sample. See **audit sampling (sampling)**.

requesting party (in the context of section 920). One of the following specified parties requesting a comfort letter, which has negotiated an agreement with the entity:

- An underwriter
- Other parties that are conducting a review process that is, or will be, substantially consistent with the due diligence process performed when the securities offering is, or if the securities offering was, being registered pursuant to the 1933 Act, as follows:
    - — A selling shareholder, sales agent, or other party with a statutory due diligence defense under Section 11 of the 1933 Act
    - — A broker-dealer or other financial intermediary acting as principal or agent in a securities offering in connection with the following types of securities offerings:
        - Foreign offerings, including Regulation S, Eurodollar, and other offshore offerings
        - Transactions that are exempt from the registration requirements of Section 5 of the 1933 Act, including those pursuant to Regulation A, Regulation D, and Rule 144A
        - Offerings of securities issued or backed by governmental, municipal, banking, tax-exempt, or other entities that are exempt from registration under the 1933 Act
    - — The buyer or seller in connection with acquisition transactions in which there is an exchange of stock

required supplementary information. Information that a designated accounting standards setter requires to accompany an entity's basic financial statements. Required supplementary information is not part of the basic financial statements; however, a designated accounting standards setter considers the information to be an essential part of financial reporting for placing the basic financial statements in an appropriate operational, economic, or historical context. In addition, authoritative guidelines for the methods of measurement and presentation of the information have been established. Also see **supplementary information**.

retrospective application. An entity's application of a change in accounting principle to one or more prior periods that were included in previously issued financial statements, as if that principle had always been used.

risk assessment procedures. The audit procedures performed to obtain an understanding of the entity and its environment, including the entity's internal control, to identify and assess the risks of material misstatement,

---

[26] Paragraph .29 of ET section 92, *Definitions*.

whether due to fraud or error, at the financial statement and relevant assertion levels. Also see **analytical procedures**.

risk assessment process. See **entity's risk assessment process**.

risk of material misstatement. The risk that the financial statements are materially misstated prior to the audit. This consists of two components, described as follows at the assertion level:

inherent risk. The susceptibility of an assertion about a class of transaction, account balance, or disclosure to a misstatement that could be material, either individually or when aggregated with other misstatements, before consideration of any related controls.

control risk. The risk that a misstatement that could occur in an assertion about a class of transaction, account balance, or disclosure and that could be material, either individually or when aggregated with other misstatements, will not be prevented, or detected and corrected, on a timely basis by the entity's internal control.

Also see **audit risk** and **detection risk**.

risk of material misstatement at the overall financial statement level. Refers to risks of material misstatement that relate pervasively to the financial statements as a whole and potentially affect many assertions.

risk of material noncompliance (in the context of adapting GAAS to a compliance audit). The risk that material noncompliance exists prior to the audit. This consists of two components, described as follows:

inherent risk of noncompliance. The susceptibility of a compliance requirement to noncompliance that could be material, either individually or when aggregated with other instances of noncompliance, before consideration of any related controls over compliance.

control risk of noncompliance. The risk that noncompliance with a compliance requirement that could occur and that could be material, either individually or when aggregated with other instances of noncompliance, will not be prevented, or detected and corrected, on a timely basis by the entity's internal control over compliance.

Also see **audit risk of noncompliance** and **detection risk of noncompliance**.

sampling. See **audit sampling (sampling)**.

sampling risk. The risk that the auditor's conclusion based on a sample may be different from the conclusion if the entire population were subjected to the same audit procedure. Sampling risk can lead to two types of erroneous conclusions:

a. In the case of a test of controls, that controls are more effective than they actually are, or in the case of a test of details, that a material misstatement does not exist when, in fact, it does. The auditor is primarily concerned with this type of erroneous conclusion because it affects audit effectiveness and is more likely to lead to an inappropriate audit opinion.

b. In the case of a test of controls, that controls are less effective than they actually are, or in the case of a test of details, that a material misstatement exists when, in fact, it does not. This type of erroneous conclusion affects audit efficiency because it would usually lead to additional work to establish that initial conclusions were incorrect.

sampling unit. The individual items constituting a population.

scanning. A type of analytical procedure involving the auditor's exercise of professional judgment to review accounting data to identify significant or unusual items to test. Also see **analytical procedures**.

scope limitation. See **limitation on the scope of an audit**.

securities offerings (in the context of section 920). One of the following types of securities offerings:

- Registration of securities with the SEC under the 1933 Act
- Foreign offerings, including Regulation S, Eurodollar, and other offshore offerings
- Transactions that are exempt from the registration requirements of Section 5 of the 1933 Act, including those pursuant to Regulation A, Regulation D, and Rule 144A
- Offerings of securities issued or backed by governmental, municipal, banking, tax-exempt, or other entities that are exempt from registration under the 1933 Act
- Acquisition transactions in which there is an exchange of stock

service auditor. A practitioner who reports on controls at a service organization. Also see **auditor**.

service organization. An organization or segment of an organization that provides services to user entities that are relevant to those user entities' internal control over financial reporting. Also see **subservice organization** and **user entity**.

service organization's system. The policies and procedures designed, implemented, and documented by management of the service organization to provide user entities with the services covered by the service auditor's report. Management's description of the service organization's system identifies the services covered, the period to which the description relates (or in the case of a type 1 report, the date to which the description relates), the control objectives specified by management or an outside party, the party specifying the control objectives (if not specified by management), and the related controls.

significant component. A component identified by the group engagement team (*a*) that is of individual financial significance to the group, or (*b*) that, due to its specific nature or circumstances, is likely to include significant risks of material misstatement of the group financial statements. Also see **component** and **group**.

significant deficiency. A deficiency, or a combination of deficiencies, in internal control that is less severe than a material weakness yet important enough to merit attention by those charged with governance. Also see **material weakness**.

significant deficiency in internal control over compliance (in the context of adapting GAAS to a compliance audit). A deficiency, or a combination of deficiencies, in internal control over compliance that is less severe than a material weakness in internal control over compliance, yet important enough to merit attention by those charged with governance. Also see **deficiency in internal control over compliance** and **material weakness in internal control over compliance**.

significant risk. An identified and assessed risk of material misstatement that, in the auditor's professional judgment, requires special audit consideration.

single financial statement or **specific element of a financial statement (in the context of section 805).** Reference to this term includes the related notes. The related notes ordinarily comprise a summary of significant accounting policies and other explanatory information relevant to the financial statement or the specific element.

smaller, less complex entity. For purposes of specifying additional considerations to audits of smaller, less complex entities, this term refers to an entity that typically possesses qualitative characteristics, such as the following:

a. Concentration of ownership and management in a small number of individuals; and

b. One or more of the following:

   i. Straightforward or uncomplicated transactions
   ii. Simple record keeping
   iii. Few lines of business and few products within business lines
   iv. Few internal controls
   v. Few levels of management with responsibility for a broad range of controls
   vi. Few personnel, many having a wide range of duties

These qualitative characteristics are not exhaustive, they are not exclusive to smaller, less complex entities, and smaller, less complex entities do not necessarily display all of these characteristics.

special purpose financial statements. Financial statements prepared in accordance with a special purpose framework. Also see **financial statements**.

special purpose framework. A financial reporting framework other than GAAP that is one of the following bases of accounting:

a. **cash basis.** A basis of accounting that the entity uses to record cash receipts and disbursements and modifications of the cash basis having substantial support (for example, recording depreciation on fixed assets).

b. **tax basis.** A basis of accounting that the entity uses to file its income tax return for the period covered by the financial statements.

c. **regulatory basis.** A basis of accounting that the entity uses to comply with the requirements or financial reporting provisions of a regulatory agency to whose jurisdiction the entity is subject (for example, a basis of accounting that insurance companies use pursuant to the accounting practices prescribed or permitted by a state insurance commission).

d. **contractual basis.** A basis of accounting that the entity uses to comply with an agreement between the entity and one or more third parties other than the auditor.

The cash, tax, and regulatory bases of accounting are commonly referred to as *other comprehensive bases of accounting*. Also see **financial reporting framework**.

specialist. See **auditor's specialist.**

specific element of a financial statement. See **single financial statement**.

specific transaction (in the context of section 915). A completed or proposed transaction or group of related transactions or a financial reporting issue involving facts and circumstances of a specific entity.

specified parties. The intended users of the auditor's written communication.

staff.[27] Professionals, other than partners, including any specialists that the firm employs.

statistical sampling. An approach to sampling that has the following characteristics:

a. Random selection of the sample items

b. The use of an appropriate statistical technique to evaluate sample results, including measurement of sampling risk

A sampling approach that does not have characteristics *a* and *b* is considered nonstatistical sampling.

stratification. The process of dividing a population into subpopulations, each of which is a group of sampling units that have similar characteristics.

subsequent events. Events occurring between the date of the financial statements and the date of the auditor's report.

subsequently discovered facts. Facts that become known to the auditor after the date of the auditor's report that, had they been known to the auditor at that date, may have caused the auditor to revise the auditor's report.

subservice organization. A service organization used by another service organization to perform some of the services provided to user entities that are relevant to those user entities' internal control over financial reporting. Also see **service organization** and **user entity**.

substantive analytical procedures. See **analytical procedures** and **substantive procedure**.

substantive procedure. An audit procedure designed to detect material misstatements at the assertion level. Substantive procedures comprise

a. tests of details (classes of transactions, account balances, and disclosures) and

b. substantive analytical procedures.

Also see **analytical procedures, dual purpose test,** and **test of controls**.

successor auditor. See **auditor**.

sufficiency (of audit evidence). The measure of the quantity of audit evidence. The quantity of the audit evidence needed is affected by the auditor's assessment of the risks of material misstatement and also by the quality of such audit evidence. Also see **audit evidence**.

---

[27] See footnote 7.

suitably qualified external person.[28] An individual outside the firm with the competence and capabilities to act as an engagement partner (for example, a partner of another firm).

summary financial statements (in the context of section 810). Historical financial information that is derived from financial statements but that contains less detail than the financial statements, while still providing a structured representation consistent with that provided by the financial statements of the entity's economic resources or obligations at a point in time or the changes therein for a period of time. Summary financial statements are separately presented and are not presented as comparative information. Also see **comparative information** and **financial statements**.

supplementary information. Information presented outside the basic financial statements, excluding required supplementary information that is not considered necessary for the financial statements to be fairly presented in accordance with the applicable financial reporting framework. Such information may be presented in a document containing the audited financial statements or separate from the financial statements. Also see **required supplementary information**.

tax basis. A basis of accounting that the entity uses to file its income tax return for the period covered by the financial statements.

The *tax basis* of accounting is commonly referred to as an *other comprehensive basis of accounting*. In the context of section 800, the tax basis of accounting is not a regulatory basis of accounting. Also see **other comprehensive bases of accounting** and **special purpose framework**.

test of controls. An audit procedure designed to evaluate the operating effectiveness of controls in preventing, or detecting and correcting, material misstatements at the assertion level. Also see **dual purpose test** and **substantive procedure**.

those charged with governance. The person(s) or organization(s) (for example, a corporate trustee) with responsibility for overseeing the strategic direction of the entity and the obligations related to the accountability of the entity. This includes overseeing the financial reporting process. Those charged with governance may include management personnel; for example, executive members of a governance board or an owner-manager. Also see **management**.

threatened legal proceeding. A potential claimant has manifested to the auditor an awareness of, and a present intention to assert, a possible claim.

timing of an audit procedure. Refers to when an audit procedure is performed or the period or date to which the audit evidence applies. Also see **extent of an audit procedure** and **nature of an audit procedure**.

tolerable misstatement. A monetary amount set by the auditor in respect of which the auditor seeks to obtain an appropriate level of assurance that the monetary amount set by the auditor is not exceeded by the actual misstatement in the population.

Tolerable misstatement is also the application of performance materiality to a particular sampling procedure. Also see **performance materiality**.

tolerable rate of deviation. A rate of deviation set by the auditor in respect of which the auditor seeks to obtain an appropriate level of assurance that

---

[28] See footnote 7.

the rate of deviation set by the auditor is not exceeded by the actual rate of deviation in the population.

type 1 report. See **report on management's description of a service organization's system and the suitability of the design of controls**.

type 2 report. See **report on management's description of a service organization's system and the suitability of the design and operating effectiveness of controls**.

type of an audit procedure. See **nature of an audit procedure**.

unconditional requirements.[29] The category of professional requirements with which the auditor must comply in all cases in which such a requirement is relevant. GAAS use the word "must" to indicate an unconditional requirement. Also see **generally accepted auditing standards (GAAS)** and **presumptively mandatory requirements**.

uncorrected misstatements. Misstatements that the auditor has accumulated during the audit and that have not been corrected. Also see **misstatement**.

understanding of the entity. Obtaining an understanding of the entity and its environment, including the entity's internal control.

underwriter (in the context of section 920). As defined in the 1933 Act

> any person who has purchased from an issuer with a view to, or offers or sells for an issuer in connection with, the distribution of any security, or participates or has a direct or indirect participation in any such undertaking, or participates or has a participation in the direct or indirect underwriting of any such undertaking; but such term shall not include a person whose interest is limited to a commission from an underwriter or dealer not in excess of the usual and customary distributors' or sellers' commission. As used in this paragraph, the term "issuer" shall include, in addition to an issuer, any person directly or indirectly controlling or controlled by the issuer, or any person under direct or indirect common control with the issuer.

Except when the context otherwise requires, the word *underwriter* as used in section 920, refers to the managing, or lead, underwriter, who typically negotiates the underwriting agreement or purchase agreement (hereafter referred to as the *underwriting agreement*) for a group of underwriters whose exact composition is not determined until shortly before a securities offering becomes effective.

underwriting agreement. See **underwriter**.

unmodified opinion. The opinion expressed by the auditor when the auditor concludes that the financial statements are presented fairly, in all material respects, in accordance with the applicable financial reporting framework. Also see **group audit opinion** and **modified opinion**.

unobservable inputs (or equivalent)**.** With respect to fair value accounting estimates, assumptions or inputs that reflect the entity's own judgments about what assumptions market participants would use in pricing the asset or liability, developed based on the best information available in the circumstances. Also see **inputs** and **observable inputs** (or equivalent).

user auditor. An auditor who audits and reports on the financial statements of a user entity. Also see **auditor**.

---

[29] See footnote 22.

user entity. An entity that uses a service organization and whose financial statements are being audited. Also see **service organization** and **subservice organization**.

working papers or **workpapers.** See **audit documentation** and **engagement documentation**.

written report (in the context of section 915). Any written communication that provides a conclusion on the appropriate application of the requirements of an applicable financial reporting framework to a specific transaction or on the type of report that may be issued on a specific entity's financial statements.

written representation. A written statement by management provided to the auditor to confirm certain matters or to support other audit evidence. Written representations in this context do not include financial statements, the assertions therein, or supporting books and records.

Yellow Book. See ***Government Auditing Standards***.

AU-C Sections 200–299

GENERAL PRINCIPLES AND RESPONSIBILITIES

The following is a Codification of Statements on Auditing Standards (SASs) resulting from the Clarification and Convergence Project of the Auditing Standards Board (ASB), and related Auditing Interpretations. SASs are issued by the ASB, the senior committee of the AICPA designated to issue pronouncements on auditing matters. Rule 202, *Compliance With Standards* (ET sec. 202 par. .01), of the Code of Professional Conduct requires adherence to the applicable generally accepted auditing standards (GAAS) promulgated by the ASB. An auditor is required to comply with an unconditional requirement in all cases in which the circumstances exist to which the unconditional requirement applies. An auditor is also required to comply with a presumptively mandatory requirement in all cases in which the circumstances exist to which the presumptively mandatory requirement applies; however, in rare circumstances, an auditor may depart from a presumptively mandatory requirement provided the auditor documents justification for the departure and how the alternative procedures performed in the circumstances were sufficient to achieve the objectives of the presumptively mandatory requirement.

Exhibits in GAAS and auditing interpretations of GAAS are *interpretive publications*, as defined in section 200, *Overall Objectives of the Independent Auditor and the Conduct of an Audit in Accordance With Generally Accepted Auditing Standards*. Section 200 requires the auditor to consider applicable interpretive publications in planning and performing the audit. Interpretive publications are not auditing standards. Interpretive publications are recommendations on the application of GAAS in specific circumstances, including engagements for entities in specialized industries. An interpretive publication is issued under the authority of the ASB after all ASB members have been provided an opportunity to consider and comment on whether the proposed interpretive publication is consistent with GAAS. Auditing interpretations of GAAS are included in AU-C sections. AICPA Audit and Accounting Guides and Auditing Statements of Position are listed in AU-C appendix D, *AICPA Audit and Accounting Guides and Statements of Position*.

TABLE OF CONTENTS

AU-C Section 200 *

Overall Objectives of the Independent Auditor and the Conduct of an Audit in Accordance With Generally Accepted Auditing Standards

Source: SAS No. 122; SAS No. 123.

Effective for audits of financial statements for periods ending on or after December 15, 2012.

Introduction

Scope of This Section

.01 This section addresses the independent auditor's overall responsibilities when conducting an audit of financial statements in accordance with generally accepted auditing standards (GAAS). Specifically, it sets out the overall objectives of the independent auditor (the auditor) and explains the nature and scope of an audit designed to enable the auditor to meet those objectives. It also explains the scope, authority, and structure of GAAS and includes requirements establishing the general responsibilities of the auditor applicable in all audits, including the obligation to comply with GAAS.

.02 GAAS are developed and issued in the form of Statements on Auditing Standards (SASs) and are codified into AU-C sections. GAAS are written in the context of an audit of financial statements by an auditor. They are to be adapted as necessary in the circumstances when applied to audits of other historical financial information. GAAS do not address the responsibilities of the auditor that may exist in legislation, regulation, or otherwise, in connection with, for example, the offering of securities to the public. Such responsibilities may differ from those established in GAAS. Accordingly, although the auditor may find aspects of GAAS helpful in such circumstances, it is the responsibility of the auditor to ensure compliance with all relevant legal, regulatory, or professional obligations.

Association With Financial Statements

.03 An auditor is associated with financial information when the auditor has applied procedures sufficient to permit the auditor to report in accordance with GAAS. Statements on Standards for Accounting and Review Services address the accountant's considerations when the accountant prepares and presents financial statements to the entity or to third parties.†

---

* This section has been codified using an "AU-C" identifier instead of an "AU" identifier. "AU-C" is a temporary identifier to avoid confusion with references to existing "AU" sections, which will remain in AICPA *Professional Standards* through 2013. The "AU-C" identifier will revert to "AU" in 2014, by which time substantially all engagements for which the "AU" sections were still effective are expected to be completed.

† The proposed Statement on Standards for Accounting and Review Services (SSARS) *The Use of the Accountant's Name in a Document or Communication Containing Unaudited Financial Statements That Have Not Been Compiled or Reviewed*, which proposes to amend SSARS No. 19, *Compilation and*

(continued)

An Audit of Financial Statements

.04 The purpose of an audit is to provide financial statement users with an opinion by the auditor on whether the financial statements are presented fairly, in all material respects, in accordance with an applicable financial reporting framework, which enhances the degree of confidence that intended users can place in the financial statements. An audit conducted in accordance with GAAS and relevant ethical requirements enables the auditor to form that opinion. (Ref: par. .A1)

.05 The financial statements subject to audit are those of the entity, prepared and presented by management of the entity with oversight from those charged with governance. GAAS do not impose responsibilities on management or those charged with governance and do not override laws and regulations that govern their responsibilities. However, an audit in accordance with GAAS is conducted on the premise that management and, when appropriate, those charged with governance have acknowledged certain responsibilities that are fundamental to the conduct of the audit. The audit of the financial statements does not relieve management or those charged with governance of their responsibilities. (Ref: par. .A2–.A13)

.06 As the basis for the auditor's opinion, GAAS require the auditor to obtain reasonable assurance about whether the financial statements as a whole are free from material misstatement, whether due to fraud or error. Reasonable assurance is a high, but not absolute, level of assurance. It is obtained when the auditor has obtained sufficient appropriate audit evidence to reduce audit risk (that is, the risk that the auditor expresses an inappropriate opinion when the financial statements are materially misstated) to an acceptably low level. Reasonable assurance is not an absolute level of assurance because there are inherent limitations of an audit that result in most of the audit evidence, on which the auditor draws conclusions and bases the auditor's opinion, being persuasive rather than conclusive. (Ref: par. .A32–.A56)

.07 The concept of materiality is applied by the auditor when both planning and performing the audit, and in evaluating the effect of identified misstatements on the audit and uncorrected misstatements, if any, on the financial statements.[1] In general, misstatements, including omissions, are considered to be material if, individually or in the aggregate, they could reasonably be expected to influence the economic decisions of users that are taken based on the financial statements. Judgments about materiality are made in light of surrounding circumstances, and involve both qualitative and quantitative considerations. These judgments are affected by the auditor's perception of the financial information needs of users of the financial statements, and by the size or nature of a misstatement, or both. The auditor's opinion addresses the financial statements as a whole. Therefore, the auditor has no responsibility to plan and perform the audit to obtain reasonable assurance that misstatements, whether caused by fraud or error, that are not material to the financial statements as a whole, are detected. (Ref: par. .A14)

.08 GAAS contain objectives, requirements, and application and other explanatory material that are designed to support the auditor in obtaining reasonable assurance. GAAS require that the auditor exercise professional judgment

---

(footnote continued)

Review Engagements, to address the accountant's association with unaudited financial statements that the accountant has not compiled or reviewed, was issued for exposure in November 2010.

[1] See section 320, *Materiality in Planning and Performing an Audit*, and section 450, *Evaluation of Misstatements Identified During the Audit*.

and maintain professional skepticism throughout the planning and performance of the audit and, among other things,

- identify and assess risks of material misstatement, whether due to fraud or error, based on an understanding of the entity and its environment, including the entity's internal control.
- obtain sufficient appropriate audit evidence about whether material misstatements exist, through designing and implementing appropriate responses to the assessed risks.
- form an opinion on the financial statements, or determine that an opinion cannot be formed, based on an evaluation of the audit evidence obtained.

.09 The form of opinion expressed by the auditor will depend upon the applicable financial reporting framework and any applicable law or regulation.

.10 The auditor also may have certain other communication and reporting responsibilities to users, management, those charged with governance, or parties outside the entity, regarding matters arising from the audit. These responsibilities may be established by GAAS or by applicable law or regulation.[2]

Effective Date

.11 This section is effective for audits of financial statements for periods ending on or after December 15, 2012.

Overall Objectives of the Auditor

.12 The overall objectives of the auditor, in conducting an audit of financial statements, are to

a. obtain reasonable assurance about whether the financial statements as a whole are free from material misstatement, whether due to fraud or error, thereby enabling the auditor to express an opinion on whether the financial statements are presented fairly, in all material respects, in accordance with an applicable financial reporting framework; and

b. report on the financial statements, and communicate as required by GAAS, in accordance with the auditor's findings.

.13 In all cases when reasonable assurance cannot be obtained and a qualified opinion in the auditor's report is insufficient in the circumstances for purposes of reporting to the intended users of the financial statements, GAAS require that the auditor disclaim an opinion or withdraw from the engagement, when withdrawal is possible under applicable law or regulation.

Definitions

.14 For purposes of GAAS, the following terms have the meanings attributed as follows:

Applicable financial reporting framework. The financial reporting framework adopted by management and, when appropriate,

---

[2] For examples, see section 260, *The Auditor's Communication With Those Charged With Governance*; section 265, *Communicating Internal Control Related Matters Identified in an Audit*; and paragraph .42 of section 240, *Consideration of Fraud in a Financial Statement Audit*.

those charged with governance in the preparation and fair presentation of the financial statements that is acceptable in view of the nature of the entity and the objective of the financial statements, or that is required by law or regulation.

Audit evidence. Information used by the auditor in arriving at the conclusions on which the auditor's opinion is based. Audit evidence includes both information contained in the accounting records underlying the financial statements and other information. *Sufficiency of audit evidence* is the measure of the quantity of audit evidence. The quantity of the audit evidence needed is affected by the auditor's assessment of the risks of material misstatement and also by the quality of such audit evidence. *Appropriateness of audit evidence* is the measure of the quality of audit evidence; that is, its relevance and its reliability in providing support for the conclusions on which the auditor's opinion is based.

Audit risk. The risk that the auditor expresses an inappropriate audit opinion when the financial statements are materially misstated. Audit risk is a function of the risks of material misstatement and detection risk.

Auditor. The term used to refer to the person or persons conducting the audit, usually the engagement partner or other members of the engagement team, or, as applicable, the firm. When an AU-C section expressly intends that a requirement or responsibility be fulfilled by the engagement partner, the term *engagement partner* rather than *auditor* is used. *Engagement partner* and *firm* are to be read as referring to their governmental equivalents when relevant.

Detection risk. The risk that the procedures performed by the auditor to reduce audit risk to an acceptably low level will not detect a misstatement that exists and that could be material, either individually or when aggregated with other misstatements.

Financial reporting framework. A set of criteria used to determine measurement, recognition, presentation, and disclosure of all material items appearing in the financial statements; for example, U.S. generally accepted accounting principles, International Financial Reporting Standards (IFRSs) promulgated by the International Accounting Standards Board (IASB), or a special purpose framework.[3]

The term *fair presentation framework* is used to refer to a financial reporting framework that requires compliance with the requirements of the framework and

a. acknowledges explicitly or implicitly that, to achieve fair presentation of the financial statements, it may be necessary for management to provide disclosures beyond those specifically required by the framework; or

b. acknowledges explicitly that it may be necessary for management to depart from a requirement of the framework to achieve fair presentation of the financial statements. Such departures are expected to be necessary only in extremely rare circumstances.

---

[3] See section 800, *Special Considerations—Audits of Financial Statements Prepared in Accordance With Special Purpose Frameworks.*

A financial reporting framework that requires compliance with the requirements of the framework, but does not contain the acknowledgments in (*a*) or (*b*) is not a fair presentation framework.

Financial statements. A structured representation of historical financial information, including related notes, intended to communicate an entity's economic resources and obligations at a point in time or the changes therein for a period of time in accordance with a financial reporting framework. The related notes ordinarily comprise a summary of significant accounting policies and other explanatory information. The term *financial statements* ordinarily refers to a complete set of financial statements as determined by the requirements of the applicable financial reporting framework, but can also refer to a single financial statement.

Historical financial information. Information expressed in financial terms regarding a particular entity, derived primarily from that entity's accounting system, about economic events occurring in past time periods or about economic conditions or circumstances at points in time in the past.

Interpretive publications. Auditing interpretations of GAAS, exhibits to GAAS, auditing guidance included in AICPA Audit and Accounting Guides, and AICPA Auditing Statements of Position (SOP).

Management. The person(s) with executive responsibility for the conduct of the entity's operations. For some entities, management includes some or all of those charged with governance; for example, executive members of a governance board or an owner-manager.

Misstatement. A difference between the amount, classification, presentation, or disclosure of a reported financial statement item and the amount, classification, presentation, or disclosure that is required for the item to be presented fairly in accordance with the applicable financial reporting framework. Misstatements can arise from fraud or error.

Other auditing publications. Publications other than interpretive publications; these include AICPA auditing publications not defined as interpretive publications; auditing articles in the *Journal of Accountancy* and other professional journals; continuing professional education programs and other instruction materials, textbooks, guide books, audit programs, and checklists; and other auditing publications from state CPA societies, other organizations, and individuals.

Premise, relating to the responsibilities of management and, when appropriate, those charged with governance, on which an audit is conducted (the premise). Management and, when appropriate, those charged with governance have acknowledged and understand that they have the following responsibilities that are fundamental to the conduct of an audit in accordance with GAAS; that is, responsibility

a. for the preparation and fair presentation of the financial statements in accordance with the applicable financial reporting framework;

b. for the design, implementation, and maintenance of internal control relevant to the preparation and fair presentation of financial statements that are free from material misstatement, whether due to fraud or error; and

c. to provide the auditor with

i. access to all information of which management and, when appropriate, those charged with governance are aware that is relevant to the preparation and fair presentation of the financial statements, such as records, documentation, and other matters;

ii. additional information that the auditor may request from management and, when appropriate, those charged with governance for the purpose of the audit; and

iii. unrestricted access to persons within the entity from whom the auditor determines it necessary to obtain audit evidence.

The *premise, relating to the responsibilities of management and, when appropriate, those charged with governance, on which an audit is conducted* may also be referred to as the *premise.*

Professional judgment. The application of relevant training, knowledge, and experience, within the context provided by auditing, accounting, and ethical standards, in making informed decisions about the courses of action that are appropriate in the circumstances of the audit engagement.

Professional skepticism. An attitude that includes a questioning mind, being alert to conditions that may indicate possible misstatement due to fraud or error, and a critical assessment of audit evidence.

Reasonable assurance. In the context of an audit of financial statements, a high, but not absolute, level of assurance.

Risk of material misstatement. The risk that the financial statements are materially misstated prior to the audit. This consists of two components, described as follows at the assertion level:

Inherent risk. The susceptibility of an assertion about a class of transaction, account balance, or disclosure to a misstatement that could be material, either individually or when aggregated with other misstatements, before consideration of any related controls.

Control risk. The risk that a misstatement that could occur in an assertion about a class of transaction, account balance, or disclosure and that could be material, either individually or when aggregated with other misstatements, will not be prevented, or detected and corrected, on a timely basis by the entity's internal control.

Those charged with governance. The person(s) or organization(s) (for example, a corporate trustee) with responsibility for overseeing the strategic direction of the entity and the obligations related to the accountability of the entity. This includes overseeing the financial reporting process. Those charged with governance may include management personnel; for example, executive members of a governance board or an owner-manager.

Requirements

Ethical Requirements Relating to an Audit of Financial Statements

.15 The auditor must be independent of the entity when performing an engagement in accordance with GAAS unless (*a*) GAAS provides otherwise or (*b*) the auditor is required by law or regulation to accept the engagement and report on the financial statements. When the auditor is not independent and neither (*a*) nor (*b*) are applicable, the auditor is precluded from issuing a report under GAAS.

.16 The auditor should comply with relevant ethical requirements relating to financial statement audit engagements. (Ref: par. .A15–.A21)

Professional Skepticism

.17 The auditor should plan and perform an audit with professional skepticism, recognizing that circumstances may exist that cause the financial statements to be materially misstated. (Ref: par. .A22–.A26)

Professional Judgment

.18 The auditor should exercise professional judgment in planning and performing an audit of financial statements. (Ref: par. .A27–.A31)

Sufficient Appropriate Audit Evidence and Audit Risk

.19 To obtain reasonable assurance, the auditor should obtain sufficient appropriate audit evidence to reduce audit risk to an acceptably low level and thereby enable the auditor to draw reasonable conclusions on which to base the auditor's opinion. (Ref: par. .A32–.A56)

Conduct of an Audit in Accordance With GAAS

Complying With AU-C Sections Relevant to the Audit

.20 The auditor should comply with all AU-C sections relevant to the audit. An AU-C section is relevant to the audit when the AU-C section is in effect and the circumstances addressed by the AU-C section exist. (Ref: par. .A57–.A62)

.21 The auditor should have an understanding of the entire text of an AU-C section, including its application and other explanatory material, to understand its objectives and to apply its requirements properly. (Ref: par. .A63–.A71)

.22 The auditor should not represent compliance with GAAS in the auditor's report unless the auditor has complied with the requirements of this section and all other AU-C sections relevant to the audit.

Objectives Stated in Individual AU-C Sections

.23 To achieve the overall objectives of the auditor, the auditor should use the objectives stated in individual AU-C sections in planning and performing the audit considering the interrelationships within GAAS to (Ref: par. .A72–.A74)

a. determine whether any audit procedures in addition to those required by individual AU-C sections are necessary in pursuance of the objectives stated in each AU-C section; and (Ref: par. .A75) *b.* evaluate whether sufficient appropriate audit evidence has been obtained. (Ref: par. .A76)

Complying With Relevant Requirements

.24 Subject to paragraph .26, the auditor should comply with each requirement of an AU-C section unless, in the circumstances of the audit,

a. the entire AU-C section is not relevant; or

b. the requirement is not relevant because it is conditional and the condition does not exist. (Ref: par. .A77–.A78)

Defining Professional Responsibilities in GAAS

.25 GAAS use the following two categories of professional requirements, identified by specific terms, to describe the degree of responsibility it imposes on auditors:

- Unconditional requirements. The auditor must comply with an unconditional requirement in all cases in which such requirement is relevant. GAAS use the word "must" to indicate an unconditional requirement.
- Presumptively mandatory requirements. The auditor must comply with a presumptively mandatory requirement in all cases in which such a requirement is relevant except in rare circumstances discussed in paragraph .26. GAAS use the word "should" to indicate a presumptively mandatory requirement. (Ref: par. .A79)

.26 In rare circumstances, the auditor may judge it necessary to depart from a relevant presumptively mandatory requirement. In such circumstances, the auditor should perform alternative audit procedures to achieve the intent of that requirement. The need for the auditor to depart from a relevant presumptively mandatory requirement is expected to arise only when the requirement is for a specific procedure to be performed and, in the specific circumstances of the audit, that procedure would be ineffective in achieving the intent of the requirement. (Ref: par. .A80)

Interpretive Publications

.27 The auditor should consider applicable interpretive publications in planning and performing the audit. (Ref: par. .A81)

Other Auditing Publications

.28 In applying the auditing guidance included in an other auditing publication, the auditor should, exercising professional judgment, assess the relevance and appropriateness of such guidance to the circumstances of the audit. (Ref: par. .A82–.A84)

Failure to Achieve an Objective

.29 If an objective in a relevant AU-C section cannot be achieved, the auditor should evaluate whether this prevents the auditor from achieving the overall objectives of the auditor and thereby requires the auditor, in accordance with GAAS, to modify the auditor's opinion or withdraw from the engagement (when withdrawal is possible under applicable law or regulation). Failure to achieve an objective represents a significant finding or issue requiring documentation in accordance with section 230, *Audit Documentation.*[4] (Ref: par. .A85–.A86)

---

[4] Paragraph .08*c* of section 230, *Audit Documentation.*

Application and Other Explanatory Material

An Audit of Financial Statements

Scope of the Audit (Ref: par. .04)

.A1 The auditor's opinion on the financial statements addresses whether the financial statements are presented fairly, in all material respects, in accordance with the applicable financial reporting framework. Such an opinion is common to all audits of financial statements. The auditor's opinion, therefore, does not assure, for example, the future viability of the entity nor the efficiency or effectiveness with which management has conducted the affairs of the entity. In some circumstances, however, applicable law or regulation may require auditors to provide opinions on other specific matters, such as the effectiveness of internal control. Although GAAS include requirements and regarding such matters to the extent that they are relevant to forming an opinion on the financial statements, the auditor would be required to undertake further work if the auditor had additional responsibilities to provide such opinions.

Preparation and Fair Presentation of the Financial Statements (Ref: par. .05)

.A2 An audit in accordance with GAAS is conducted on the premise that management and, when appropriate, those charged with governance have acknowledged and understand that they have responsibility

a. for the preparation and fair presentation of the financial statements in accordance with the applicable financial reporting framework;

b. for the design, implementation, and maintenance of internal control relevant to the preparation and fair presentation of financial statements that are free from material misstatement, whether due to fraud or error; and

c. to provide the auditor with

  i. access to all information of which management and, when appropriate, those charged with governance are aware that is relevant to the preparation and fair presentation of the financial statements, such as records, documentation, and other matters;

  ii. additional information that the auditor may request from management and, when appropriate, those charged with governance for the purpose of the audit; and

  iii. unrestricted access to persons within the entity from whom the auditor determines it necessary to obtain audit evidence.

.A3 The preparation and fair presentation of the financial statements by management and, when appropriate, those charged with governance require

- the identification of the applicable financial reporting framework, in the context of any relevant laws or regulations.
- the preparation and fair presentation of the financial statements in accordance with that framework.
- the inclusion of an adequate description of that framework in the financial statements.

The preparation and fair presentation of the financial statements require management to exercise judgment in making accounting estimates that are reasonable in the circumstances, as well as in selecting and applying appropriate accounting policies. These judgments are made in the context of the applicable financial reporting framework.

.A4 The auditor may make suggestions about the form or content of the financial statements, or assist management by drafting them, in whole or in part, based on information provided to the auditor by management during the performance of the audit. However, the auditor's responsibility for the audited financial statements is confined to the expression of the auditor's opinion on them.

.A5 The financial statements may be prepared in accordance with the following:

- A general purpose framework (a financial reporting framework designed to meet the common financial information needs of a wide range of users); or
- A special purpose framework (a financial reporting framework, other than generally accepted accounting principles, which is a cash, tax, regulatory, or contractual basis of accounting).

.A6 The applicable financial reporting framework often encompasses financial accounting standards promulgated by an authorized or recognized standards-setting organization, or legislative or regulatory requirements. In some cases, the financial reporting framework may encompass both financial accounting standards promulgated by an authorized or recognized standards-setting organization and legislative or regulatory requirements. Other sources may provide direction on the application of the applicable financial reporting framework. In some cases, the applicable financial reporting framework may encompass such other sources, or may even consist only of such sources. Such other sources may include the following:

- The legal and ethical environment, including statutes, regulations, court decisions, and professional ethical obligations regarding accounting matters;
- Published accounting interpretations of varying authority issued by standards-setting, professional, or regulatory organizations;
- Published views of varying authority on emerging accounting issues issued by standards-setting, professional, or regulatory organizations;
- General and industry practices widely recognized and prevalent; and
- Accounting literature.

When conflicts exist between the financial reporting framework and the sources from which direction on its application may be obtained, or among the sources that encompass the financial reporting framework, the source with the highest authority prevails.

.A7 The requirements of the applicable financial reporting framework determine the form and content of the financial statements. Although the framework may not specify how to account for or disclose all transactions or events, it ordinarily embodies sufficiently broad principles that can serve as a basis for developing and applying accounting policies that are consistent with the concepts underlying the requirements of the framework.

.A8 The financial accounting standards promulgated by organizations that are authorized or recognized to promulgate standards to be used by entities for preparing financial statements in accordance with a general purpose framework include Financial Accounting Standards Board (FASB) *Accounting Standards Codification*™, issued by FASB; IFRSs, issued by the IASB; Statements of Federal Financial Accounting Standards, issued by the Federal Accounting Standards Advisory Board for U.S. federal government entities; and Statements of the Governmental Accounting Standards Board, issued by the Governmental Accounting Standards Board for U.S. state and local governmental entities.

.A9 The requirements of the applicable financial reporting framework also determine what constitutes a complete set of financial statements. In the case of many frameworks, financial statements are intended to provide information about the financial position, financial performance, and cash flows of an entity. For example, a complete set of financial statements might include a balance sheet, an income statement, a statement of changes in equity, a cash flow statement, and related notes. For some other financial reporting frameworks, a single financial statement and the related notes might constitute a complete set of financial statements. Examples of a single financial statement, each of which would include related notes, include the following:

- Balance sheet
- Statement of income or statement of operations
- Statement of retained earnings
- Statement of cash flows
- Statement of assets and liabilities
- Statement of changes in owners' equity
- Statement of revenue and expenses
- Statement of operations by product lines

.A10 Section 210, *Terms of Engagement*, establishes requirements and provides guidance on determining the acceptability of the applicable financial reporting framework.[5] Section 800, *Special Considerations—Audits of Financial Statements Prepared in Accordance With Special Purpose Frameworks*, addresses engagements in which the auditor issues a report in connection with financial statements prepared in accordance with a special purpose framework.

.A11 Because of the significance of the premise to the conduct of an audit, the auditor is required to obtain the agreement of management and, when appropriate, those charged with governance, that they acknowledge and understand that they have the responsibilities set out in paragraph .A2 as a precondition for accepting the audit engagement.[6]

Considerations Specific to Audits of Governmental Entities

.A12 The requirements for audits of the financial statements of governmental entities may be broader than those of other entities. As a result, the premise, relating to management's responsibilities, on which an audit of the financial statements of a governmental entity is conducted, may include additional responsibilities, such as the responsibility for the execution of transactions and events in accordance with law, regulation, or other authority. (See paragraph .A63.)

---

[5] Paragraph .06*a* of section 210, *Terms of Engagement*.

[6] Paragraph .06*b* of section 210.

.A13 In audits of governmental entities, auditors may have a responsibility under law, regulation, contract, or grant agreement to report to third parties, such as funding agencies or oversight bodies.

Materiality (Ref: par. .07)

Considerations Specific to Audits of Governmental Entities

.A14 For most state or local governmental entities, the applicable financial reporting framework is based on multiple reporting units, and therefore requires the presentation of financial statements for its activities in various reporting units. Consequently, a reporting unit, or aggregation of reporting units, of the governmental entity represents an opinion unit to the auditor. Generally, the auditor expresses or disclaims an opinion on a government's financial statements as a whole by expressing an opinion or disclaiming an opinion on each opinion unit. In this context, the auditor is responsible for the detection of misstatements that are material to an opinion unit within a governmental entity, but is not responsible for the detection of misstatements that are not material to an opinion unit.

Ethical Requirements Relating to an Audit of Financial Statements (Ref: par. .16)

.A15 The auditor is subject to relevant ethical requirements relating to financial statement audit engagements. Ethical requirements consist of the AICPA Code of Professional Conduct together with rules of state boards of accountancy and applicable regulatory agencies that are more restrictive.

.A16 The AICPA Code of Professional Conduct establishes the fundamental principles of professional ethics, which include the following:

- Responsibilities
- The public interest
- Integrity
- Objectivity and independence
- Due care
- Scope and nature of services

.A17 In the case of an audit engagement, it is in the public interest and, therefore, required by this section, that the auditor be independent of the entity subject to the audit. The concept of independence refers to both independence in fact and independence in appearance. The auditor's independence from the entity safeguards the auditor's ability to form an audit opinion without being affected by influences that might compromise that opinion. Independence enhances the auditor's ability to act with integrity, to be objective, and to maintain an attitude of professional skepticism. Independence implies an impartiality that recognizes an obligation to be fair not only to management and those charged with governance of an entity but also users of the financial statements who may rely upon the independent auditor's report. Guidance on threats to independence is set forth in the AICPA's *Conceptual Framework for AICPA Independence Standards* (ET sec. 100-1).

.A18 When the auditor is not independent but is required by law or regulation to report on the financial statements, section 705, *Modifications to the Opinion in the Independent Auditor's Report*, applies.

.A19 Due care requires the auditor to discharge professional responsibilities with competence and to have the appropriate capabilities to perform the audit and enable an appropriate auditor's report to be issued.

.A20 QC section 10, *A Firm's System of Quality Control*, sets out the firm's responsibilities to establish and maintain its system of quality control for audit engagements, and to establish policies and procedures designed to provide it with reasonable assurance that the firm and its personnel comply with relevant ethical requirements, including those pertaining to independence.[7] Section 220, *Quality Control for an Engagement Conducted in Accordance With Generally Accepted Auditing Standards*, addresses the engagement partner's responsibilities regarding relevant ethical requirements. These include remaining alert for evidence of noncompliance with relevant ethical requirements by members of the engagement team, determining, in consultation with others in the firm as appropriate, the appropriate action if matters come to the engagement partner's attention, through the firm's system of quality control or otherwise, that indicate that members of the engagement team have not complied with relevant ethical requirements, and forming a conclusion on compliance with independence requirements that apply to the audit engagement.[8] Section 220 recognizes that the engagement team is entitled to rely on a firm's system of quality control in meeting its responsibilities with respect to quality control procedures applicable to the individual audit engagement, unless the engagement partner determines that it is inappropriate to do so based on information provided by the firm or other parties.

Considerations Specific to Audits of Governmental Entities

.A21 In addition to the AICPA Code of Professional Conduct and GAAS, *Government Auditing Standards*, which may be required by law, regulation, contract, or grant agreement in audits of governmental entities and entities that receive government awards, set forth relevant ethical principles and auditing standards, including standards on auditor independence, professional judgment, competence, and audit quality control and assurance.

Professional Skepticism (Ref: par. .17)

.A22 Professional skepticism includes being alert to the following, for example,

- Audit evidence that contradicts other audit evidence obtained.
- Information that brings into question the reliability of documents and responses to inquiries to be used as audit evidence.
- Conditions that may indicate possible fraud.
- Circumstances that suggest the need for audit procedures in addition to those required by GAAS.

.A23 Maintaining professional skepticism throughout the audit is necessary if the auditor is, for example, to reduce the risks of

- overlooking unusual circumstances.
- over-generalizing when drawing conclusions from audit observations.

---

[7] Paragraphs .21–.25 of QC section 10, *A Firm's System of Quality Control*.

[8] Paragraphs .11–.13 of section 220, *Quality Control for an Engagement Conducted in Accordance With Generally Accepted Auditing Standards*.

- using inappropriate assumptions in determining the nature, timing, and extent of the audit procedures and evaluating the results thereof.

.A24 Professional skepticism is necessary to the critical assessment of audit evidence. This includes questioning contradictory audit evidence and the reliability of documents and responses to inquiries and other information obtained from management and those charged with governance. It also includes consideration of the sufficiency and appropriateness of audit evidence obtained in light of the circumstances; for example, in the case when fraud risk factors exist and a single document, of a nature that is susceptible to fraud, is the sole supporting evidence for a material financial statement amount.

.A25 The auditor may accept records and documents as genuine unless the auditor has reason to believe the contrary. Nevertheless, the auditor is required to consider the reliability of information to be used as audit evidence.[9] In cases of doubt about the reliability of information or indications of possible fraud (for example, if conditions identified during the audit cause the auditor to believe that a document may not be authentic or that terms in a document may have been falsified), GAAS require that the auditor investigate further and determine what modifications or additions to audit procedures are necessary to resolve the matter.[10]

.A26 The auditor neither assumes that management is dishonest nor assumes unquestioned honesty. The auditor cannot be expected to disregard past experience of the honesty and integrity of the entity's management and those charged with governance. Nevertheless, a belief that management and those charged with governance are honest and have integrity does not relieve the auditor of the need to maintain professional skepticism or allow the auditor to be satisfied with less than persuasive audit evidence when obtaining reasonable assurance.

Professional Judgment (Ref: par. .18)

.A27 Professional judgment is essential to the proper conduct of an audit. This is because interpretation of relevant ethical requirements and GAAS and the informed decisions required throughout the audit cannot be made without the application of relevant knowledge and experience to the facts and circumstances. In particular, professional judgment is necessary regarding decisions about the following:

- Materiality and audit risk
- The nature, timing, and extent of audit procedures used to meet the requirements of GAAS and gather audit evidence
- Evaluating whether sufficient appropriate audit evidence has been obtained, and whether more needs to be done to achieve the objectives of GAAS and thereby, the overall objectives of the auditor
- The evaluation of management's judgments in applying the entity's applicable financial reporting framework

---

[9] Paragraphs .07–.09 of section 500, *Audit Evidence*.

[10] Paragraph .10 of section 500 and paragraphs .10–.11 and .16 of section 505, *External Confirmations*.

- The drawing of conclusions based on the audit evidence obtained; for example, assessing the reasonableness of the estimates made by management in preparing the financial statements

.A28 The distinguishing feature of professional judgment expected of an auditor is that such judgment is exercised based on competencies necessary to achieve reasonable judgments, developed by the auditor through relevant training, knowledge, and experience.

.A29 The exercise of professional judgment in any particular case is based on the facts and circumstances that are known by the auditor. Consultation on difficult or contentious matters during the course of the audit, both within the engagement team and between the engagement team and others at the appropriate level within or outside the firm, such as those required by section 220, assists the auditor in making informed and reasonable judgments.[11]

.A30 Professional judgment can be evaluated based on whether the judgment reached reflects a competent application of auditing standards and accounting principles and is appropriate in light of, and consistent with, the facts and circumstances that were known to the auditor up to the date of the auditor's report.

.A31 Professional judgment needs to be exercised throughout the audit. It also needs to be appropriately documented. In this regard, the auditor is required to prepare audit documentation sufficient to enable an experienced auditor, having no previous connection with the audit, to understand the significant professional judgments made in reaching conclusions on significant findings or issues arising during the audit.[12] Professional judgment is not to be used as the justification for decisions that are not otherwise supported by the facts and circumstances of the engagement or by sufficient appropriate audit evidence.

Sufficient Appropriate Audit Evidence and Audit Risk (Ref: par. .19)

Sufficiency and Appropriateness of Audit Evidence

.A32 Audit evidence is necessary to support the auditor's opinion and report. It is cumulative in nature and is primarily obtained from audit procedures performed during the course of the audit. It may, however, also include information obtained from other sources such as previous audits (provided the auditor has determined whether changes have occurred since the previous audit that may affect its relevance to the current audit[13]) or a firm's quality control procedures for client acceptance and continuance. In addition to other sources inside and outside the entity, the entity's accounting records are an important source of audit evidence. Also, information that may be used as audit evidence may have been prepared by a specialist employed or engaged by the entity. Audit evidence comprises both information that supports and corroborates management's assertions and any information that contradicts such assertions. In addition, in some cases, the absence of information (for example, management's refusal to provide a requested representation) is used by the auditor, and, therefore, also constitutes audit evidence. Most of the auditor's work in forming the auditor's opinion consists of obtaining and evaluating audit evidence.

---

[11] Paragraph .20 of section 220.

[12] Paragraph .08 of section 230.

[13] Paragraph .10 of section 315, *Understanding the Entity and Its Environment and Assessing the Risks of Material Misstatement.*

.A33 The sufficiency and appropriateness of audit evidence are interrelated. *Sufficiency* is the measure of the quantity of audit evidence. The quantity of audit evidence needed is affected by the auditor's assessment of the risks of misstatement (the higher the assessed risks, the more audit evidence is likely to be required) and also by the quality of such audit evidence (the higher the quality, the less may be required). Obtaining more audit evidence, however, may not compensate for its poor quality.

.A34 *Appropriateness* is the measure of the quality of audit evidence; that is, its relevance and its reliability in providing support for the conclusions on which the auditor's opinion is based. The reliability of evidence is influenced by its source and by its nature, and is dependent on the individual circumstances under which it is obtained.

.A35 Whether sufficient appropriate audit evidence has been obtained to reduce audit risk to an acceptably low level, and thereby to enable the auditor to draw reasonable conclusions on which to base the auditor's opinion, is a matter of professional judgment. Section 500, *Audit Evidence*, and other relevant AU-C sections, establish additional requirements and provide further guidance applicable throughout the audit regarding the auditor's considerations in obtaining sufficient appropriate audit evidence.

Audit Risk

.A36 Audit risk is a function of the risks of material misstatement and detection risk. The assessment of risks is based on audit procedures to obtain information necessary for that purpose and evidence obtained throughout the audit. The assessment of risks is a matter of professional judgment, rather than a matter capable of precise measurement.

.A37 For purposes of GAAS, audit risk does not include the risk that the auditor might express an opinion that the financial statements are materially misstated when they are not. This risk is ordinarily insignificant. Further, audit risk is a technical term related to the process of auditing; it does not refer to the auditor's business risks, such as loss from litigation, adverse publicity, or other events arising in connection with the audit of financial statements.

Risks of Material Misstatement

.A38 The risks of material misstatement exist at two levels:

- The overall financial statement level
- The assertion level for classes of transactions, account balances, and disclosures

.A39 Risks of material misstatement at the overall financial statement level refer to risks of material misstatement that relate pervasively to the financial statements as a whole and potentially affect many assertions.

.A40 Risks of material misstatement at the assertion level are assessed in order to determine the nature, timing, and extent of further audit procedures necessary to obtain sufficient appropriate audit evidence. This evidence enables the auditor to express an opinion on the financial statements at an acceptably low level of audit risk. Auditors use various approaches to accomplish the objective of assessing the risks of material misstatement. For example, the auditor may make use of a model that expresses the general relationship of the components of audit risk in mathematical terms to arrive at an acceptable level of detection risk. Some auditors find such a model to be useful when planning audit procedures.

.A41 The risks of material misstatement at the assertion level consist of two components: inherent risk and control risk. Inherent risk and control risk are the entity's risks; they exist independently of the audit of the financial statements.

.A42 Inherent risk is higher for some assertions and related classes of transactions, account balances, and disclosures than for others. For example, it may be higher for complex calculations or for accounts consisting of amounts derived from accounting estimates that are subject to significant estimation uncertainty. External circumstances giving rise to business risks may also influence inherent risk. For example, technological developments might make a particular product obsolete, thereby causing inventory to be more susceptible to overstatement. Factors in the entity and its environment that relate to several or all of the classes of transactions, account balances, or disclosures may also influence the inherent risk related to a specific assertion. Such factors may include, for example, a lack of sufficient working capital to continue operations or a declining industry characterized by a large number of business failures.

.A43 Control risk is a function of the effectiveness of the design, implementation, and maintenance of internal control by management to address identified risks that threaten the achievement of the entity's objectives relevant to preparation and fair presentation of the entity's financial statements. However, internal control, no matter how well designed and operated, can only reduce, but not eliminate, risks of material misstatement in the financial statements, because of the inherent limitations of internal control. These include, for example, the possibility of human errors or mistakes, or of controls being circumvented by collusion or inappropriate management override. Accordingly, some control risk will always exist. GAAS provide the conditions under which the auditor is required to, or may choose to, test the operating effectiveness of controls in determining the nature, timing, and extent of substantive procedures to be performed.[14]

.A44 GAAS do not ordinarily refer to inherent risk and control risk separately, but rather to a combined assessment of the risks of material misstatement. However, the auditor may make separate or combined assessments of inherent and control risk depending on preferred audit techniques or methodologies and practical considerations. The assessment of the risks of material misstatement may be expressed in quantitative terms, such as in percentages or in nonquantitative terms. In any case, the need for the auditor to make appropriate risk assessments is more important than the different approaches by which they may be made.

.A45 Section 315, *Understanding the Entity and Its Environment and Assessing the Risks of Material Misstatement*, establishes requirements and provides guidance on identifying and assessing the risks of material misstatement at the financial statement and assertion levels.

Detection Risk

.A46 For a given level of audit risk, the acceptable level of detection risk bears an inverse relationship to the assessed risks of material misstatement at the assertion level. For example, the greater the risks of material misstatement the auditor believes exists, the less the detection risk that can be accepted and, accordingly, the more persuasive the audit evidence required by the auditor.

.A47 Detection risk relates to the nature, timing, and extent of the auditor's procedures that are determined by the auditor to reduce audit risk to an

---

[14] Paragraph .08 of section 330, *Performing Audit Procedures in Response to Assessed Risks and Evaluating the Audit Evidence Obtained.*

acceptably low level. It is therefore a function of the effectiveness of an audit procedure and of its application by the auditor. The following matters assist to enhance the effectiveness of an audit procedure and of its application and reduce the possibility that an auditor might select an inappropriate audit procedure, misapply an appropriate audit procedure, or misinterpret the audit results:

- Adequate planning
- Proper assignment of personnel to the engagement team
- The application of professional skepticism
- Supervision and review of the audit work performed

.A48 Section 300, *Planning an Audit*, and section 330, *Performing Audit Procedures in Response to Assessed Risks and Evaluating the Audit Evidence Obtained*, establish requirements and provide guidance on planning an audit of financial statements and the auditor's responses to assessed risks. Detection risk, however, can only be reduced, not eliminated, because of the inherent limitations of an audit. Accordingly, some detection risk will always exist.

Inherent Limitations of an Audit

.A49 The auditor is not expected to, and cannot, reduce audit risk to zero and cannot, therefore, obtain absolute assurance that the financial statements are free from material misstatement due to fraud or error. This is because inherent limitations of an audit exist, which result in most of the audit evidence on which the auditor draws conclusions and bases the auditor's opinion being persuasive rather than conclusive. The principal inherent limitations of an audit arise from

- the nature of financial reporting;
- the nature of audit procedures; and
- the need for the audit to be conducted within a reasonable period of time and so as to achieve a balance between benefit and cost.

The Nature of Financial Reporting

.A50 The preparation and fair presentation of financial statements involves judgment by management in applying the requirements of the entity's applicable financial reporting framework to the facts and circumstances of the entity. In addition, many financial statement items involve subjective decisions or assessments or a degree of uncertainty, and a range exists of acceptable interpretations or judgments that may be made. Consequently, some financial statement items are subject to an inherent level of variability that cannot be eliminated by the application of additional auditing procedures. For example, this is often the case with respect to certain accounting estimates that are dependent on predictions of future events. Nevertheless, GAAS require the auditor to give specific consideration to whether accounting estimates are reasonable in the context of the applicable financial reporting framework and to related disclosures, and to the qualitative aspects of the entity's accounting practices, including indicators of possible bias in management's judgments.[15]

The Nature of Audit Procedures

.A51 There are practical and legal limitations on the auditor's ability to obtain audit evidence. For example:

---

[15] See section 540, *Auditing Accounting Estimates, Including Fair Value Accounting Estimates, and Related Disclosures*, and section 700, *Forming an Opinion and Reporting on Financial Statements*.

- There is the possibility that management or others may not provide, intentionally or unintentionally, the complete information that is relevant to the preparation and fair presentation of the financial statements or that has been requested by the auditor. Accordingly, the auditor cannot be certain of the completeness of information, even though the auditor has performed audit procedures to obtain assurance that all relevant information has been obtained.
- Fraud may involve sophisticated and carefully organized schemes designed to conceal it. Therefore, audit procedures used to gather audit evidence may be ineffective for detecting an intentional misstatement that involves, for example, collusion to falsify documentation that may cause the auditor to believe that audit evidence is valid when it is not. The auditor is neither trained as nor expected to be an expert in the authentication of documents.
- An audit is not an official investigation into alleged wrongdoing. Accordingly, the auditor is not given specific legal powers, such as the power of search, which may be necessary for such an investigation.

Timeliness of Financial Reporting and the Balance Between Benefit and Cost

.A52 The matter of difficulty, time, or cost involved is not in itself a valid basis for the auditor to omit an audit procedure for which there is no alternative or to be satisfied with audit evidence that is less than persuasive. Appropriate planning assists in making sufficient time and resources available for the conduct of the audit. Notwithstanding this, the relevance of information, and thereby its value, tends to diminish over time, and there is a balance to be struck between the reliability of information and its cost. This is recognized in certain financial reporting frameworks (see, for example, FASB's Statements of Financial Accounting Concepts). Therefore, there is an expectation by users of financial statements that the auditor will form an opinion on the financial statements within a reasonable period of time and so as to achieve a balance between benefit and cost, recognizing that it is impracticable to address all information that may exist or to pursue every matter exhaustively on the assumption that information is fraudulent or erroneous until proved otherwise.

.A53 Consequently, it is necessary for the auditor to

- plan the audit so that it will be performed in an effective manner;
- direct audit effort to areas most expected to contain risks of material misstatement, whether due to fraud or error, with correspondingly less effort directed at other areas; and
- use testing and other means of examining populations for misstatements.

.A54 In light of the approaches described in paragraph .A53, GAAS contain requirements for the planning and performance of the audit and requires the auditor, among other things, to

- have a basis for the identification and assessment of risks of material misstatement at the financial statement and assertion levels by performing risk assessment procedures and related activities;[16] and

---

[16] See section 315.

- use testing and other means of examining populations in a manner that provides a reasonable basis for the auditor to draw conclusions about the population.[17]

Other Matters That Affect the Inherent Limitations of an Audit

.A55 In the case of certain assertions or subject matters, the potential effects of the inherent limitations on the auditor's ability to detect material misstatements are particularly significant. Such assertions or subject matters include the following:

- Fraud, particularly fraud involving senior management or collusion. See section 240, *Consideration of Fraud in a Financial Statement Audit*, for further discussion.
- The existence and completeness of related party relationships and transactions. See section 550, *Related Parties*, for further discussion.
- The occurrence of noncompliance with laws and regulations. See section 250, *Consideration of Laws and Regulations in an Audit of Financial Statements*, for further discussion.
- Future events or conditions that may cause an entity to cease to continue as a going concern. See section 570, *The Auditor's Consideration of an Entity's Ability to Continue as a Going Concern*.

Relevant AU-C sections identify specific audit procedures to assist in lessening the effect of the inherent limitations. [Revised, August 2012, to reflect conforming changes necessary due to the issuance of SAS No. 126.]

.A56 Because of the inherent limitations of an audit, there is an unavoidable risk that some material misstatements of the financial statements may not be detected, even though the audit is properly planned and performed in accordance with GAAS. Accordingly, the subsequent discovery of a material misstatement of the financial statements resulting from fraud or error does not by itself indicate a failure to conduct an audit in accordance with GAAS. However, the inherent limitations of an audit are not a justification for the auditor to be satisfied with less than persuasive audit evidence. Whether the auditor has performed an audit in accordance with GAAS is determined by the audit procedures performed in the circumstances, the sufficiency and appropriateness of the audit evidence obtained as a result thereof, and the suitability of the auditor's report based on an evaluation of that evidence in light of the overall objectives of the auditor.

Conduct of an Audit in Accordance With GAAS

Nature of GAAS (Ref: par. .20)

.A57 Rule 202, *Compliance With Standards* (ET sec. 202 par. .01), of the AICPA Code of Professional Conduct requires an AICPA member who performs an audit to comply with standards promulgated by the Auditing Standards Board (ASB). The ASB develops and issues standards in the form of SASs through a process that includes deliberation in meetings open to the public,

[17] See section 330, section 500, section 520, *Analytical Procedures*, and section 530, *Audit Sampling*.

public exposure of proposed SASs, and a formal vote. The SASs are codified in AU-C sections.

.A58 GAAS provide the standards for the auditor's work in fulfilling the overall objectives of the auditor. GAAS address the general responsibilities of the auditor, as well as the auditor's further considerations relevant to the application of those responsibilities to specific topics.

.A59 The scope, effective date, and any specific limitation of the applicability of a specific AU-C section are made clear in the AU-C section. Unless otherwise stated in the AU-C section, the auditor is permitted to apply an AU-C section before the effective date specified therein.

.A60 In certain audit engagements, the auditor also may be required to comply with other auditing requirements in addition to GAAS. GAAS do not override law or regulation that governs an audit of financial statements. In the event that such law or regulation differs from GAAS, an audit conducted only in accordance with law or regulation will not necessarily comply with GAAS.

.A61 The auditor may also conduct the audit in accordance with both GAAS and

- auditing standards promulgated by the Public Company Accounting Oversight Board,
- International Standards on Auditing,
- *Government Auditing Standards*, or
- auditing standards of a specific jurisdiction or country.

In such cases, in addition to complying with each of the AU-C sections relevant to the audit, it may be necessary for the auditor to perform additional audit procedures in order to comply with the other auditing standards.

Considerations Specific to Audits of Governmental Entities

.A62 GAAS are relevant to financial statement audits of governmental entities. The auditor's responsibilities, however, may be affected by law, regulation, or other authority (such as government policy requirements or resolutions of the legislature), which may encompass a broader scope than an audit of financial statements in accordance with GAAS. These additional responsibilities are not addressed in GAAS. *Government Auditing Standards* are relevant for engagements to audit U.S. government entities, and when required by law, regulation, contract, or grant agreement. The appendix to *Government Auditing Standards* includes a listing of some of the laws, regulations, and guidelines that require use of *Government Auditing Standards*.

Contents of GAAS (Ref: par. .21)

.A63 In addition to objectives and requirements, an AU-C section contains related guidance in the form of application and other explanatory material. It may also contain introductory material that provides context relevant to a proper understanding of the AU-C section and definitions. The entire text of an AU-C section, therefore, is relevant to an understanding of the objectives stated in an AU-C section and the proper application of the requirements of an AU-C section.

.A64 When necessary, the application and other explanatory material provides further explanation of the requirements of an AU-C section and guidance for carrying them out. In particular, it may

- explain more precisely what a requirement means or is intended to cover.
- include examples of procedures that may be appropriate in the circumstances.

Although such guidance does not in itself impose a requirement, it is relevant to the proper application of the requirements of an AU-C section. The auditor is required by paragraph .21 to understand the application and other explanatory material; how the auditor applies the guidance in the engagement depends on the exercise of professional judgment in the circumstances consistent with the objective of the AU-C section. The words "may," "might," and "could" are used to describe these actions and procedures. The application and other explanatory material may also provide background information on matters addressed in an AU-C section.

.A65 Appendixes form part of the application and other explanatory material. The purpose and intended use of an appendix are explained in the body of the related AU-C section or within the title and introduction of the appendix itself.

.A66 Introductory material may include, as needed, such matters as explanation of the following:

- The purpose and scope of the AU-C section, including how the AU-C section relates to other AU-C sections.
- The subject matter of the AU-C section.
- The respective responsibilities of the auditor and others regarding the subject matter of the AU-C section.
- The context in which the AU-C section is set.

.A67 An AU-C section may include, in a separate section under the heading "Definitions," a description of the meanings attributed to certain terms for purposes of GAAS. These are provided to assist in the consistent application and interpretation of GAAS, and are not intended to override definitions that may be established for other purposes, whether in law, regulation, or otherwise. Unless otherwise indicated, those terms will carry the same meanings throughout GAAS.

.A68 When appropriate, additional considerations specific to audits of smaller, less complex entities and governmental entities are included within the application and other explanatory material of an AU-C section. These additional considerations assist in the application of the requirements of GAAS in the audit of such entities. They do not, however, limit or reduce the responsibility of the auditor to apply and comply with the requirements of GAAS.

Considerations Specific to Audits of Smaller, Less Complex Entities

.A69 For purposes of specifying additional considerations to audits of smaller, less complex entities, a *smaller, less complex entity* refers to an entity that typically possesses qualitative characteristics, such as the following:

a. Concentration of ownership and management in a small number of individuals; and

b. One or more of the following:

   i. Straightforward or uncomplicated transactions

   ii. Simple record keeping

   iii. Few lines of business and few products within business lines

iv. Few internal controls

v. Few levels of management with responsibility for a broad range of controls

vi. Few personnel, many having a wide range of duties

These qualitative characteristics are not exhaustive, they are not exclusive to smaller, less complex entities, and smaller, less complex entities do not necessarily display all of these characteristics.

.A70 GAAS refer to the proprietor of a smaller entity who is involved in running the entity on a day-to-day basis as the *owner-manager*.

Considerations Specific to Governmental Entities

.A71 Considerations specific to governmental entities may also be applicable to nongovernmental entities that receive government awards. In audits of governmental entities, the considerations specific to audits of smaller, less complex entities may not apply, even if the governmental entity has few employees, simple operations, or a relatively small budget, because small governmental entities (1) may have complex transactions with federal and state governments, (2) are required to comply with laws, regulations, policies, and systems determined by a higher level of government, and (3) are subject to additional public expectations of accountability and transparency.

Objectives Stated in Individual AU-C Sections (Ref: par. .23)

.A72 Each AU-C section contains one or more objectives that provide a link between the requirements and the overall objectives of the auditor. The objectives in individual AU-C sections serve to focus the auditor on the desired outcome of the AU-C section, while being specific enough to assist the auditor in

- understanding what needs to be accomplished and, when necessary, the appropriate means of doing so; and
- deciding whether more needs to be done to achieve the objectives in the particular circumstances of the audit.

.A73 Objectives are to be understood in the context of the overall objectives of the auditor stated in paragraph .12. As with the overall objectives of the auditor, the ability to achieve an individual objective is equally subject to the inherent limitations of an audit.

.A74 In using the objectives, the auditor is required to consider the interrelationships among the AU-C sections. This is because, as indicated in paragraph .A58, the AU-C sections in some cases address general responsibilities and in others address the application of those responsibilities to specific topics. For example, this section requires the auditor to adopt an attitude of professional skepticism; this is necessary in all aspects of planning and performing an audit but is not repeated as a requirement of each AU-C section. At a more detailed level, section 315 and section 330 contain, among other things, objectives and requirements that address the auditor's responsibilities to identify and assess the risks of material misstatement and to design and perform further audit procedures to respond to those assessed risks, respectively; these objectives and requirements apply throughout the audit. An AU-C section addressing specific aspects of the audit may expand on how the objectives and requirements of other AU-C sections are to be applied regarding the subject of that AU-C section, but does not repeat those objectives and requirements. For example, section 540, *Auditing Accounting Estimates, Including Fair Value Accounting Estimates and Related Disclosures*, expands on how the objectives and requirements of section 315 and section 330 are to be applied regarding the subject of section 540, but section 540 does not repeat those objectives and requirements. Thus, in achieving the objective stated in section 540, the auditor considers the objectives and requirements of other relevant AU-C sections.

Use of Objectives to Determine Need for Additional Audit Procedures (Ref: par. .23a)

.A75 The requirements of GAAS are designed to enable the auditor to achieve the objectives specified in GAAS, and thereby the overall objectives of the auditor. The proper application of the requirements of GAAS by the auditor is therefore expected to provide a sufficient basis for the auditor's achievement of the objectives. However, because the circumstances of audit engagements vary widely and all such circumstances cannot be anticipated in GAAS, the auditor is responsible for determining the audit procedures necessary to fulfill the requirements of GAAS and to achieve the objectives. In the circumstances of an engagement, there may be particular matters that require the auditor to perform audit procedures in addition to those required by GAAS to meet the objectives specified in GAAS.

Use of Objectives to Evaluate Whether Sufficient Appropriate Audit Evidence Has Been Obtained (Ref: par. .23b)

.A76 The auditor is required by paragraph .23*b* to use the objectives stated in the relevant AU-C sections to evaluate whether sufficient appropriate audit evidence has been obtained in the context of the overall objectives of the auditor. If, as a result, the auditor concludes that the audit evidence is not sufficient and appropriate, then the auditor may follow one or more of the following approaches to meeting the requirement of paragraph .23*b*:

- Evaluate whether further relevant audit evidence has been, or will be, obtained as a result of complying with other AU-C sections
- Extend the work performed in applying one or more requirements
- Perform other procedures judged by the auditor to be necessary in the circumstances

When none of the preceding is expected to be practical or possible in the circumstances, the auditor will not be able to obtain sufficient appropriate audit evidence and is required by GAAS to determine the effect on the auditor's report or on the auditor's ability to complete the engagement.

Complying With Relevant Requirements

Relevant Requirements (Ref: par. .24)

.A77 In some cases, an AU-C section (and therefore all of its requirements) may not be relevant in the circumstances. For example, if an entity does not have an internal audit function, nothing in section 610, *The Auditor's Consideration of the Internal Audit Function in an Audit of Financial Statements*,[‡] is relevant.

.A78 Within a relevant AU-C section, there may be conditional requirements. Such a requirement is relevant when the circumstances envisioned in

[‡] SAS No. 65, *The Auditor's Consideration of the Internal Audit Function in an Audit of Financial Statements*, is currently effective and codified as AU section 322. SAS No. 65 has been included in section 610, as designated by SAS No. 122, *Statements on Auditing Standards: Clarification and Recodification*, and will be superseded when it is redrafted for clarity and convergence with International Standard on Auditing 610 (Revised), *Using the Work of Internal Auditors*, as part of the Clarification and Convergence project of the Auditing Standards Board. Until such time, section 610 has been conformed to reflect updated section and paragraph cross references but has not otherwise been subjected to a comprehensive review or revision.

the requirement apply and the condition exists. In general, the conditionality of a requirement will either be explicit or implicit, for example:

- The requirement to modify the auditor's opinion if there is a limitation of scope[18] represents an explicit conditional requirement.
- The requirement to communicate significant deficiencies and material weaknesses in internal control identified during the audit to management and those charged with governance,[19] which depends on the existence and identification of such deficiencies, represents an implicit conditional requirement.

In some cases, a requirement may be expressed as being conditional on applicable law or regulation. For example, the auditor may be required to withdraw from the audit engagement, when withdrawal is possible under applicable law or regulation, or the auditor may be required to perform a certain action, unless prohibited by law or regulation. Depending on the jurisdiction, the legal or regulatory permission or prohibition may be explicit or implicit.

Presumptively Mandatory Requirements (Ref: par. .25)

.A79 If an AU-C section provides that a procedure or action is one that the auditor *should consider*, consideration of the procedure or action is presumptively required. Whether the auditor performs the procedure or action is based upon the outcome of the auditor's consideration and the auditor's professional judgment.

Departure From a Requirement (Ref: par. .26)

.A80 Section 230 establishes documentation requirements in those exceptional circumstances when the auditor departs from a relevant requirement.[20] GAAS do not call for compliance with a requirement that is not relevant in the circumstances of the audit.

Interpretive Publications (Ref: par. .27)

.A81 Interpretive publications are not auditing standards. *Interpretive publications* are recommendations on the application of GAAS in specific circumstances, including engagements for entities in specialized industries. An interpretive publication is issued under the authority of the ASB after all ASB members have been provided an opportunity to consider and comment on whether the proposed interpretive publication is consistent with GAAS. Auditing interpretations of GAAS are included in AU-C sections. AICPA Audit and Accounting Guides and auditing SOPs are listed in AU-C appendix D, *AICPA Audit and Accounting Guides and Statements of Position*.

Other Auditing Publications (Ref: par. .28)

.A82 Other auditing publications have no authoritative status; however, they may help the auditor understand and apply GAAS. The auditor is not expected to be aware of the full body of other auditing publications.

.A83 Although the auditor determines the relevance of these publications in accordance with paragraph .28, the auditor may presume that other auditing publications published by the AICPA that have been reviewed by the AICPA Audit and Attest Standards staff are appropriate. These other auditing publications are listed in AU-C appendix F, *Other Auditing Publications*.

---

[18] See section 705, *Modifications to the Opinion in the Independent Auditor's Report*.

[19] Paragraph .11 of section 265.

[20] Paragraph .13 of section 230.

.A84 In determining whether an other auditing publication that has not been reviewed by the AICPA Audit and Attest Standards staff is appropriate to the circumstances of the audit, the auditor may consider the degree to which the publication is recognized as being helpful in understanding and applying GAAS and the degree to which the issuer or author is recognized as an authority in auditing matters.

Failure to Achieve an Objective (Ref: par. .29)

.A85 Whether an objective has been achieved is a matter for the auditor's professional judgment. That judgment takes account of the results of audit procedures performed in complying with the requirements of GAAS, and the auditor's evaluation of whether sufficient appropriate audit evidence has been obtained and whether more needs to be done in the particular circumstances of the audit to achieve the objectives stated in GAAS. Accordingly, circumstances that may give rise to a failure to achieve an objective include those that

- prevent the auditor from complying with the relevant requirements of an AU-C section.
- result in it not being practicable or possible for the auditor to carry out the additional audit procedures or obtain further audit evidence as determined necessary from the use of the objectives in accordance with paragraph .23; for example, due to a limitation in the available audit evidence.

.A86 Audit documentation that meets the requirements of section 230 and the specific documentation requirements of other relevant AU-C sections provides evidence of the auditor's basis for a conclusion about the achievement of the overall objectives of the auditor. Although it is unnecessary for the auditor to document separately (as in a checklist, for example) that individual objectives have been achieved, the documentation of a failure to achieve an objective assists the auditor's evaluation of whether such a failure has prevented the auditor from achieving the overall objectives of the auditor.

AU-C Section 210 *

Terms of Engagement

Source: SAS No. 122.

Effective for audits of financial statements for periods ending on or after December 15, 2012.

Introduction

Scope of This Section

.01 This section addresses the auditor's responsibilities in agreeing upon the terms of the audit engagement with management and, when appropriate, those charged with governance. This includes establishing that certain preconditions for an audit, for which management and, when appropriate, those charged with governance are responsible, are present. Section 220, *Quality Control for an Engagement Conducted in Accordance With Generally Accepted Auditing Standards*, addresses those aspects of engagement acceptance that are within the control of the auditor. (Ref: par. .A1)

Effective Date

.02 This section is effective for audits of financial statements for periods ending on or after December 15, 2012.

Objective

.03 The objective of the auditor is to accept an audit engagement for a new or existing audit client only when the basis upon which it is to be performed has been agreed upon through

a. establishing whether the preconditions for an audit are present and

b. confirming that a common understanding of the terms of the audit engagement exists between the auditor and management and, when appropriate, those charged with governance.

Definitions

.04 For purposes of generally accepted auditing standards (GAAS), the following terms have the meanings attributed as follows:

Preconditions for an audit. The use by management of an acceptable financial reporting framework in the preparation and fair presentation of the financial statements and the agreement of

---

* This section has been codified using an "AU-C" identifier instead of an "AU" identifier. "AU-C" is a temporary identifier to avoid confusion with references to existing "AU" sections, which will remain in AICPA *Professional Standards* through 2013. The "AU-C" identifier will revert to "AU" in 2014, by which time substantially all engagements for which the "AU" sections were still effective are expected to be completed.

management and, when appropriate, those charged with governance, to the premise[1] on which an audit is conducted.

Recurring audit. An audit engagement for an existing audit client for whom the auditor performed the preceding audit.

.05 For purposes of this section, references to *management* are to be read hereafter as "management and, when appropriate, those charged with governance" unless the context suggests otherwise.

Requirements

Preconditions for an Audit

.06 In order to establish whether the preconditions for an audit are present, the auditor should

a. determine whether the financial reporting framework to be applied in the preparation of the financial statements is acceptable and (Ref: par. .A2–.A8)

b. obtain the agreement of management that it acknowledges and understands its responsibility (Ref: par. .A9–.A12 and .A17)

i. for the preparation and fair presentation of the financial statements in accordance with the applicable financial reporting framework; (Ref: par. .A13)

ii. for the design, implementation, and maintenance of internal control relevant to the preparation and fair presentation of financial statements that are free from material misstatement, whether due to fraud or error; and (Ref: par. .A14–.A16)

iii. to provide the auditor with

(1) access to all information of which management is aware that is relevant to the preparation and fair presentation of the financial statements, such as records, documentation, and other matters;

(2) additional information that the auditor may request from management for the purpose of the audit; and

(3) unrestricted access to persons within the entity from whom the auditor determines it necessary to obtain audit evidence.

Management-Imposed Limitation on Scope Prior to Audit Engagement Acceptance That Would Result in a Disclaimer of Opinion

.07 If management or those charged with governance of an entity that is not required by law or regulation to have an audit impose a limitation on the scope of the auditor's work in the terms of a proposed audit engagement, such that the auditor believes the limitation will result in the auditor disclaiming an opinion on the financial statements as a whole, the auditor should not accept such a limited engagement as an audit engagement. If management or those charged with governance of an entity that is required by law or regulation to

---

[1] Paragraphs .05 and .A2 of section 200, *Overall Objectives of the Independent Auditor and the Conduct of an Audit in Accordance With Generally Accepted Auditing Standards.*

have an audit imposes such a scope limitation and a disclaimer of opinion is acceptable under the applicable law or to the regulator, the auditor is permitted, but not required, to accept the engagement. (Ref: par. .A18–.A19)

Other Factors Affecting Audit Engagement Acceptance

.08 If the preconditions for an audit are not present, the auditor should discuss the matter with management. Unless the auditor is required by law or regulation to do so, the auditor should not accept the proposed audit engagement

a. if the auditor has determined that the financial reporting framework to be applied in the preparation of the financial statements is unacceptable or

b. if the agreement referred to in paragraph .06*b* has not been obtained.

Agreement on Audit Engagement Terms

.09 The auditor should agree upon the terms of the audit engagement with management or those charged with governance, as appropriate. (Ref: par. .A20–.A21)

.10 The agreed-upon terms of the audit engagement should be documented in an audit engagement letter or other suitable form of written agreement and should include the following: (Ref: par. .A22–.A26)

a. The objective and scope of the audit of the financial statements

b. The responsibilities of the auditor

c. The responsibilities of management

d. A statement that because of the inherent limitations of an audit, together with the inherent limitations of internal control, an unavoidable risk exists that some material misstatements may not be detected, even though the audit is properly planned and performed in accordance with GAAS

e. Identification of the applicable financial reporting framework for the preparation of the financial statements

f. Reference to the expected form and content of any reports to be issued by the auditor and a statement that circumstances may arise in which a report may differ from its expected form and content

Initial Audits, Including Reaudit Engagements

.11 Before accepting an engagement for an initial audit, including a reaudit engagement, the auditor should request management to authorize the predecessor auditor to respond fully to the auditor's inquiries regarding matters that will assist the auditor in determining whether to accept the engagement. If management refuses to authorize the predecessor auditor to respond, or limits the response, the auditor should inquire about the reasons and consider the implications of that refusal in deciding whether to accept the engagement.

.12 The auditor should evaluate the predecessor auditor's response, or consider the implications if the predecessor auditor provides no response or a limited response, in determining whether to accept the engagement. (Ref: par. .A27–.A32)

Recurring Audits

.13 On recurring audits, the auditor should assess whether circumstances require the terms of the audit engagement to be revised. If the auditor concludes that the terms of the preceding engagement need not be revised for the current engagement, the auditor should remind management of the terms of the engagement, and the reminder should be documented. (Ref: par. .A33–.A34)

Acceptance of a Change in the Terms of the Audit Engagement

.14 The auditor should not agree to a change in the terms of the audit engagement when no reasonable justification for doing so exists. (Ref: par. .A35–.A37)

.15 If, prior to completing the audit engagement, the auditor is requested to change the audit engagement to an engagement for which the auditor obtains a lower level of assurance, the auditor should determine whether reasonable justification for doing so exists. (Ref: par. .A38–.A39)

.16 If the terms of the audit engagement are changed, the auditor and management should agree on and document the new terms of the engagement in an engagement letter or other suitable form of written agreement.

.17 If the auditor concludes that no reasonable justification for a change of the terms of the audit engagement exists and is not permitted by management to continue the original audit engagement, the auditor should

a. withdraw from the audit engagement when possible under applicable law or regulation,

b. communicate the circumstances to those charged with governance, and

c. determine whether any obligation, either legal, contractual, or otherwise, exists to report the circumstances to other parties, such as owners, or regulators.

Additional Considerations in Engagement Acceptance

Auditor's Report Prescribed by Law or Regulation

.18 If law or regulation prescribes a specific layout, form, or wording of the auditor's report that significantly differs from the requirements of GAAS, the auditor should evaluate

a. whether users might misunderstand the auditor's report and, if so,

b. whether the auditor would be permitted to reword the prescribed form to be in accordance with the requirements of GAAS or attach a separate report.[2]

If the auditor determines that rewording the prescribed form or attaching a separate report would not be permitted or would not mitigate the risk of users misunderstanding the auditor's report, the auditor should not accept the audit engagement unless the auditor is required by law or regulation to do so. An audit performed in accordance with such law or regulation does not comply with GAAS. Accordingly, for such an audit, the auditor should not include any

---

[2] Paragraphs .22–.23 of section 800, *Special Considerations—Audits of Financial Statements Prepared in Accordance With Special Purpose Frameworks.*

reference to the audit having been performed in accordance with GAAS within the auditor's report.[3] (Ref: par. .A40–.A41)

Application and Other Explanatory Material

Scope of This Section (Ref: par. .01)

.A1 The auditor's responsibilities regarding relevant ethical requirements in the context of the acceptance of an audit engagement, insofar as they are within the control of the auditor, are addressed in section 220. This section addresses those matters (or preconditions) that are within the control of the entity and upon which it is necessary for the auditor and the entity's management to agree.

Preconditions for an Audit

The Financial Reporting Framework (Ref: par. .06a)

.A2 An applicable financial reporting framework provides the criteria for management to present the financial statements of an entity, including the fair presentation of those financial statements. The criteria used by the auditor to evaluate or measure the subject matter, including, when relevant, a basis for presentation and disclosure, are also provided by the financial reporting framework. These criteria enable reasonably consistent evaluation or measurement of a subject matter within the context of professional judgment.

.A3 Without an acceptable financial reporting framework, management does not have an appropriate basis for the preparation of the financial statements, and the auditor does not have suitable criteria for auditing the financial statements. In many cases, the auditor may presume that the applicable financial reporting framework is acceptable, as described in paragraphs .A6–.A8.

Determining the Acceptability of the Financial Reporting Framework

.A4 Factors that are relevant to the auditor's determination of the acceptability of the financial reporting framework to be applied in the preparation of the financial statements include the following:

- The nature of the entity (for example, whether it is a business enterprise, a governmental entity, or a not-for-profit organization)
- The purpose of the financial statements (for example, whether they are prepared to meet the common financial information needs of a wide range of users)
- The nature of the financial statements (for example, whether the financial statements are a complete set of financial statements or a single financial statement)
- Whether law or regulation prescribes the applicable financial reporting framework

.A5 Many users of financial statements are not in a position to demand financial statements tailored to meet their specific information needs. Although all the information needs of specific users cannot be met, financial information needs that are common to a wide range of users exist. Financial statements prepared in accordance with a financial reporting framework designed to meet

---

[3] Paragraph .22 of section 800.

the common financial information needs of a wide range of users are referred to as *general purpose financial statements*.

.A6 *General purpose frameworks.* The sources of established accounting principles that are generally accepted are accounting principles promulgated by a body designated by the Council of the AICPA to establish such principles, pursuant to Rule 203, *Accounting Principles* (ET sec. 203 par. .01), of the AICPA Code of Professional Conduct. Such financial reporting standards often are identified as the applicable financial reporting framework in law or regulation governing the preparation of general purpose financial statements.

.A7 *Special purpose frameworks.* In some cases, the financial statements will be prepared in accordance with a special purpose framework. For example, law or regulation may prescribe the financial reporting framework to be used in the preparation of financial statements for certain types of entities. Such financial statements are referred to as *special purpose financial statements*. Section 800, *Special Considerations—Audits of Financial Statements Prepared in Accordance With Special Purpose Frameworks*, addresses the acceptability of special purpose frameworks.[4]

.A8 After the audit engagement has been accepted, the auditor may encounter deficiencies in the applicable financial reporting framework that indicate that the framework is not acceptable. When use of that framework is not prescribed by law or regulation, management may decide to adopt another framework that is acceptable. When management does so, the previously agreed-upon terms will have changed, and the auditor is required by paragraph .16 to agree upon new terms of the audit engagement that reflect the change in the framework.

Agreement of the Responsibilities of Management (Ref: par. .06b)

.A9 An audit in accordance with GAAS is conducted on the premise that management has acknowledged and understands that it has the responsibilities set out in paragraph .06*b*.[5] The auditor may assist in drafting the financial statements, in whole or in part, based on information provided to the auditor by management during the performance of the audit. However, the concept of an independent audit requires that the auditor's role does not involve assuming management's responsibility for the preparation and fair presentation of the financial statements or assuming responsibility for the entity's related internal control and that the auditor has a reasonable expectation of obtaining the information necessary for the audit insofar as management is able to provide or procure it. Accordingly, the premise is fundamental to the conduct of an independent audit. To avoid misunderstanding, agreement is reached with management that it acknowledges and understands that it has such responsibilities as part of agreeing and documenting the terms of the audit engagement as required by paragraphs .09–.10.

.A10 The way in which the responsibilities for financial reporting are divided between management and those charged with governance will vary according to the resources and structure of the entity and any relevant law or regulation and the respective roles of management and those charged with governance within the entity. In most cases, management is responsible for execution and those charged with governance have oversight of management. In some cases, those charged with governance will have, or will assume, responsibility for approving the financial statements or monitoring the entity's

---

[4] Paragraph .10 of section 800.

[5] Paragraphs .05 and .A2 of section 200.

internal control related to financial reporting. In larger entities, a subgroup of those charged with governance, such as an audit committee, may be charged with certain oversight responsibilities.

.A11 Section 580, *Written Representations*, requires the auditor to request management to provide written representations that it has fulfilled certain of its responsibilities.[6] It may therefore be appropriate to make management aware that receipt of such written representations will be expected, together with written representations required by other AU-C sections and, when necessary, written representations to support other audit evidence relevant to the financial statements or one or more specific assertions in the financial statements.

.A12 If management will not acknowledge its responsibilities or indicates that it will not provide written representations as requested, the auditor will be unable to obtain sufficient appropriate audit evidence.[7] In such circumstances, it would not be appropriate for the auditor to accept the audit engagement unless law or regulation requires the auditor to do so. In cases when the auditor is required to accept the audit engagement, the auditor may need to explain to management the importance of these matters and the implications for the auditor's report.

Preparation and Fair Presentation of the Financial Statements (Ref: par. .06b(i))

.A13 In an audit of special purpose financial statements, the auditor is required by section 800 to obtain the agreement of management that it acknowledges and understands its responsibility to include all informative disclosures that are appropriate for the special purpose framework used to prepare the entity's financial statements.[8] This agreement is a precondition of the audit included in the terms of the engagement.

Internal Control (Ref: par. .06b(ii))

.A14 Management maintains such internal control as it determines is necessary to enable the preparation and fair presentation of financial statements that are free from material misstatement, whether due to fraud or error. Internal control, no matter how effective, can provide an entity with only reasonable assurance about achieving the entity's financial reporting objectives, due to the inherent limitations of internal control.

.A15 An independent audit conducted in accordance with GAAS does not act as a substitute for the maintenance of internal control necessary for the preparation and fair presentation of financial statements by management. Accordingly, the auditor is required to obtain the agreement of management that it acknowledges and understands that it has responsibility for the design, implementation, and maintenance of internal control necessary for this purpose. However, the agreement required by paragraph .06*b*(ii) does not imply that the auditor will find that internal control maintained by management has achieved its purpose or will be free from deficiencies.

.A16 Management has the responsibility to determine what internal control is necessary to enable the preparation and fair presentation of the financial statements. The term *internal control* encompasses a wide range of activities within components that may be described as the control environment; the entity's risk assessment process; the information system, including the related business processes relevant to financial reporting, and communication; control

---

[6] Paragraphs .10–.11 of section 580, *Written Representations*.

[7] Paragraph .A34 of section 580.

[8] Paragraph .11 of section 800.

activities; and monitoring of controls. This division, however, does not necessarily reflect how a particular entity may design, implement, and maintain its internal control or how it may classify any particular component.[9] An entity's internal control will reflect the needs of management, the complexity of the business, the nature of the risks to which the entity is subject, and relevant laws or regulations.

Considerations Relevant to Smaller Entities (Ref: par. .06b)

.A17 One of the purposes of agreeing upon the terms of the audit engagement is to avoid misunderstanding about the respective responsibilities of management and the auditor. For example, when the auditor or a third party has assisted with drafting the financial statements, it may be useful to remind management that the preparation and fair presentation of the financial statements in accordance with the applicable financial reporting framework remains its responsibility.

Management-Imposed Limitation on Scope Prior to Audit Engagement Acceptance That Would Result in a Disclaimer of Opinion (Ref: par. .07)

.A18 Scope limitations may be imposed by management or by circumstances. Examples of scope limitations that would not preclude the auditor from accepting the engagement include the following:

- A restriction imposed by management that the auditor believes will result in a qualified opinion
- A restriction imposed by circumstances beyond the control of management

.A19 Employee benefit plans are an example of entities that are required to have an audit by law or regulation and a disclaimer of opinion is acceptable under the applicable law or to the regulator. For such entities, the auditor is neither precluded from accepting, nor required to accept, the engagement, regardless of whether management imposes a scope limitation that is expected to result in the auditor disclaiming an opinion on the financial statements as a whole.

Agreement on Audit Engagement Terms

Agreeing Upon the Terms of the Audit Engagement (Ref: par. .09)

.A20 The roles of management and those charged with governance in agreeing upon the terms of the audit engagement for the entity depend on the governance structure of the entity and relevant law or regulation. Depending on the entity's structure, the agreement may be with management, those charged with governance, or both. When the agreement on the terms of engagement is only with those charged with governance, nonetheless in accordance with paragraph .06, the auditor is required to obtain management's agreement that it acknowledges and understands its responsibilities.

.A21 When a third party has contracted for the audit of the entity's financial statements, agreeing the terms of the audit with management of the entity is necessary in order to establish that the preconditions for an audit are present.

---

[9] Paragraph .A51 and appendix B, "Internal Control Components," of section 315, *Understanding the Entity and Its Environment and Assessing the Risks of Material Misstatement.*

Audit Engagement Letter or Other Form of Written Agreement[10] *(Ref: par. .10)*

.A22 Both management and the auditor have an interest in documenting the agreed-upon terms of the audit engagement before the commencement of the audit to help avoid misunderstandings with respect to the audit. For example, it reduces the risk that management may inappropriately rely on the auditor to protect management against certain risks or to perform certain functions that are management's responsibility.

Form and Content of the Audit Engagement Letter

.A23 The form and content of the audit engagement letter may vary for each entity. Information included in the audit engagement letter on the auditor's responsibilities may be based on section 200, *Overall Objectives of the Independent Auditor and the Conduct of an Audit in Accordance With Generally Accepted Auditing Standards*.[11] Paragraph .06*b* of this section addresses the description of the responsibilities of management. In addition to including the matters required by paragraph .10, an audit engagement letter may make reference to, for example, the following:

- Elaboration of the scope of the audit, including reference to applicable legislation, regulations, GAAS, and ethical and other pronouncements of professional bodies to which the auditor adheres
- The form of any other communication of results of the audit engagement
- Arrangements regarding the planning and performance of the audit, including the composition of the audit team
- The expectation that management will provide written representations (see also paragraph .A11)
- The agreement of management to make available to the auditor draft financial statements and any accompanying other information in time to allow the auditor to complete the audit in accordance with the proposed timetable
- The agreement of management to inform the auditor of events occurring or facts discovered subsequent to the date of the financial statements, of which management may become aware, that may affect the financial statements
- The basis on which fees are computed and any billing arrangements
- A request for management to acknowledge receipt of the audit engagement letter and to agree to the terms of the engagement outlined therein, as may be evidenced by their signature on the engagement letter

.A24 When relevant, the following points also could be made in the audit engagement letter:

- Arrangements concerning the involvement of other auditors and specialists in some aspects of the audit

---

[10] In the paragraphs that follow, any reference to an audit engagement letter is to be taken as a reference to an audit engagement letter or other suitable form of written agreement.

[11] Paragraphs .04–.10 of section 200.

- Arrangements concerning the involvement of internal auditors and other staff of the entity
- Arrangements to be made with the predecessor auditor, if any, in the case of an initial audit
- Any restriction of the auditor's liability when not prohibited
- Any obligations of the auditor to provide audit documentation to other parties
- Additional services to be provided, such as those relating to regulatory requirements
- A reference to any further agreements between the auditor and the entity

.A25 Reference to the expected form and content of any reports to be issued by the auditor may include a description of the types of reports to be issued. The auditor need not describe the type of opinion expected to be expressed. An example of an audit engagement letter is set out in the exhibit "Example of an Audit Engagement Letter."

.A26 *Audits of components.* When the auditor of a parent entity is also the auditor of a component, the factors that may influence the decision whether to obtain a separate audit engagement letter from the component include the following:

- Who engages the component auditor
- Whether a separate auditor's report is to be issued on the component
- Legal requirements regarding the appointment of the auditor
- Degree of ownership by parent
- Degree of independence of the component management from the parent entity

Initial Audits, Including Reaudit Engagements (Ref: par. .11–.12)

.A27 An auditor may make a proposal for an audit engagement before being granted permission to make inquiries of a predecessor auditor. The auditor may advise management in the proposal or otherwise that the auditor's acceptance of the engagement cannot be final until the inquiries have been made and the responses of the predecessor auditor have been evaluated.

.A28 When more than one auditor is considering accepting an engagement, the predecessor auditor is not expected to be available to respond to inquiries until an auditor has been selected by the entity and has accepted the engagement, subject to the evaluation of the communications with the predecessor auditor as provided in paragraph .12.

.A29 Relevant ethical and professional requirements guide the auditor's communications with the predecessor auditor and management, as well as the predecessor auditor's response. Such requirements provide that, except as permitted by the rules of the AICPA Code of Professional Conduct, an auditor is precluded from disclosing confidential information obtained in the course of an engagement unless management specifically consents. Such requirements also provide that both the auditor and the predecessor auditor hold in confidence information obtained from each other. This obligation applies regardless of whether the auditor accepts the engagement.

.A30 In accordance with the AICPA Code of Professional Conduct, which states that members have a responsibility to cooperate with each other, the predecessor auditor is expected to respond to the auditor's inquiries promptly and, in the absence of unusual circumstances, fully, on the basis of known facts. If, due to unusual circumstances, such as pending, threatened, or potential litigation; disciplinary proceedings; or other unusual circumstances, the predecessor auditor decides not to respond fully to the inquiries, the predecessor auditor is expected to clearly state that the response is limited.

.A31 The communication with the predecessor auditor may be either written or oral. Matters subject to the auditor's inquiry of the predecessor auditor may include the following:

- Information that might bear on the integrity of management
- Disagreements with management about accounting policies, auditing procedures, or other similarly significant matters
- Communications to those charged with governance regarding fraud and noncompliance with laws or regulations by the entity
- Communications to management and those charged with governance regarding significant deficiencies and material weaknesses in internal control
- The predecessor auditor's understanding about the reasons for the change of auditors

Considerations Specific to Governmental Entities

.A32 When the auditor is required by law or regulation to audit a governmental entity, inquiries of the predecessor auditor for the purpose of obtaining information about whether to accept the engagement may not be relevant. However, inquiries of the predecessor auditor may still be relevant for the purpose of obtaining information that is used by the auditor in planning and performing the audit.[12]

Recurring Audits (Ref: par. .13)

.A33 The following factors may make it appropriate to revise the terms of the audit engagement:

- Any indication that management misunderstands the objective and scope of the audit
- Any revised or special terms of the audit engagement
- A change of senior management
- A significant change in ownership
- A significant change in the nature or size of the entity's business
- A change in legal or regulatory requirements
- A change in the financial reporting framework adopted in the preparation of the financial statements
- A change in other reporting requirements

---

[12] Section 510, *Opening Balances—Initial Audit Engagements, Including Reaudit Engagements*, addresses the auditor's responsibilities relating to opening balances when conducting an initial audit engagement.

.A34 The auditor may remind management of the terms of the engagement in writing or orally. A written reminder might be a letter confirming that the terms of the preceding engagement will govern the current engagement. If the reminder is oral, audit documentation may include with whom the discussion took place, when, and the significant points discussed.

Acceptance of a Change in the Terms of the Audit Engagement

Request to Change the Terms of the Audit Engagement (Ref: par. .14)

.A35 A request from management for the auditor to change the terms of the audit engagement may result from a change in circumstances affecting the need for the service, a misunderstanding about the nature of an audit as originally requested, or a restriction on the scope of the audit engagement, whether imposed by management or caused by other circumstances. The auditor, as required by paragraph .14, considers the justification given for the request, particularly the implications of a restriction on the scope of the audit engagement.

.A36 A change in circumstances that affects management's requirements or a misunderstanding concerning the nature of the service originally requested may be considered a reasonable basis for requesting a change in the audit engagement.

.A37 In contrast, a change may not be considered reasonable if the change appears to relate to information that is incorrect, incomplete, or otherwise unsatisfactory. An example might be when the auditor is unable to obtain sufficient appropriate audit evidence regarding receivables and management asks for the audit engagement to be changed to a review engagement to avoid a qualified opinion or a disclaimer of opinion.

Request to Change to a Review or Other Service (Ref: par. .15)

.A38 Before agreeing to change an audit engagement to a review or other service, an auditor who was engaged to perform an audit in accordance with GAAS may need to assess, in addition to the matters referred to in paragraphs .A35–.A37, any legal or contractual implications of the change.

.A39 If the auditor concludes that reasonable justification to change the audit engagement to a review or other service exists, the audit work performed to the date of change may be relevant to the changed engagement; however, the work required to be performed and the report to be issued would be those appropriate to the revised engagement. In order to avoid confusing the reader, the report on the other service would not include reference to the following:

a. The original audit engagement

b. Any procedures that may have been performed in the original audit engagement, except when the audit engagement is changed to an engagement to undertake agreed-upon procedures and, thus, reference to the procedures performed is a normal part of the report

Additional Considerations in Engagement Acceptance

Auditor's Report Prescribed by Law or Regulation (Ref: par. .18)

.A40 GAAS require that the auditor not represent compliance with GAAS unless the auditor has complied with all of the AU-C sections relevant to the audit.[13] If the auditor is required by law or regulation to use a specific layout, form, or wording of the auditor's report, section 800 requires that the auditor's report refer to GAAS only if the auditor's report includes the minimum reporting elements.[14] In accordance with section 800, if the specific layout, form, or wording of the auditor's report is not acceptable or would cause an auditor to make a statement that the auditor has no basis to make, the auditor is required to reword the prescribed form of report or attach an appropriately worded separate report.[15] When the auditor concludes that rewording the prescribed form to be in accordance with the requirements of GAAS or attaching a separate report would not be permitted, the auditor may consider including a statement in the auditor's report that the audit is not conducted in accordance with GAAS. The auditor is, however, encouraged to apply GAAS, including the AU-C sections that address the auditor's report, to the extent practicable, notwithstanding that the auditor is not permitted to refer to the audit being conducted in accordance with GAAS.

Considerations Specific to Governmental Entities

.A41 For governmental entities, specific legal or regulatory requirements may exist; for example, the auditor may be required to report directly to the legislature or the public if management attempts to limit the scope of the audit.

---

[13] Paragraph .22 of section 200.

[14] Paragraph .22 of section 800.

[15] Paragraph .23 of section 800.

.A42

Exhibit—Example of an Audit Engagement Letter (Ref: par. .A25)

The following is an example of an audit engagement letter for an audit of general purpose financial statements prepared in accordance with accounting principles generally accepted in the United States of America, as promulgated by the Financial Accounting Standards Board. This letter is not authoritative but is intended only to be a guide that may be used in conjunction with the considerations outlined in this Statement on Auditing Standards. The letter will vary according to individual requirements and circumstances and is drafted to refer to the audit of financial statements for a single reporting period. The auditor may seek legal advice about whether a proposed letter is suitable.

To the appropriate representative of those charged with governance of ABC Company:[1]

[*The objective and scope of the audit*]

You[2] have requested that we audit the financial statements of ABC Company, which comprise the balance sheet as of December 31, 20XX, and the related statements of income, changes in stockholders' equity, and cash flows for the year then ended, and the related notes to the financial statements. We are pleased to confirm our acceptance and our understanding of this audit engagement by means of this letter. Our audit will be conducted with the objective of our expressing an opinion on the financial statements.

[*The responsibilities of the auditor*]

We will conduct our audit in accordance with auditing standards generally accepted in the United States of America (GAAS). Those standards require that we plan and perform the audit to obtain reasonable assurance about whether the financial statements are free from material misstatement. An audit involves performing procedures to obtain audit evidence about the amounts and disclosures in the financial statements. The procedures selected depend on the auditor's judgment, including the assessment of the risks of material misstatement of the financial statements, whether due to fraud or error. An audit also includes evaluating the appropriateness of accounting policies used and the reasonableness of significant accounting estimates made by management, as well as evaluating the overall presentation of the financial statements.

Because of the inherent limitations of an audit, together with the inherent limitations of internal control, an unavoidable risk that some material misstatements may not be detected exists, even though the audit is properly planned and performed in accordance with GAAS.

In making our risk assessments, we consider internal control relevant to the entity's preparation and fair presentation of the financial statements in order to design audit procedures that are appropriate in the circumstances but not for the purpose of expressing an opinion on the effectiveness of the entity's internal control. However, we will communicate to you in writing concerning any significant deficiencies or material weaknesses in internal control relevant to the audit of the financial statements that we have identified during the audit.

---

[1] The addressees and references in the letter would be those that are appropriate in the circumstances of the engagement, including the relevant jurisdiction. It is important to refer to the appropriate persons. See paragraph .A20.

[2] Throughout this letter, references to *you, we, us, management, those charged with governance,* and *auditor* would be used or amended as appropriate in the circumstances.

[*The responsibilities of management and identification of the applicable financial reporting framework*]

Our audit will be conducted on the basis that [*management and, when appropriate, those charged with governance*][3] acknowledge and understand that they have responsibility

a. for the preparation and fair presentation of the financial statements in accordance with accounting principles generally accepted in the United States of America;

b. for the design, implementation, and maintenance of internal control relevant to the preparation and fair presentation of financial statements that are free from material misstatement, whether due to fraud or error; and

c. to provide us with

  i. access to all information of which [*management*] is aware that is relevant to the preparation and fair presentation of the financial statements such as records, documentation, and other matters;

  ii. additional information that we may request from [*management*] for the purpose of the audit; and

  iii. unrestricted access to persons within the entity from whom we determine it necessary to obtain audit evidence.

As part of our audit process, we will request from [*management and, when appropriate, those charged with governance*], written confirmation concerning representations made to us in connection with the audit.

[*Other relevant information*]

[*Insert other information, such as fee arrangements, billings, and other specific terms, as appropriate.*]

[Reporting]

[*Insert appropriate reference to the expected form and content of the auditor's report. Example follows:*]

We will issue a written report upon completion of our audit of ABC Company's financial statements. Our report will be addressed to the board of directors of ABC Company. We cannot provide assurance that an unmodified opinion will be expressed. Circumstances may arise in which it is necessary for us to modify our opinion, add an emphasis-of-matter or other-matter paragraph(s), or withdraw from the engagement.

We also will issue a written report on [*Insert appropriate reference to other auditor's reports expected to be issued.*] upon completion of our audit.

Please sign and return the attached copy of this letter to indicate your acknowledgment of, and agreement with, the arrangements for our audit of the financial statements including our respective responsibilities.

XYZ & Co.

Acknowledged and agreed on behalf of ABC Company by

____

[*Signed*]

[*Name and Title*]

[*Date*] ____________________

---

[3] Use terminology as appropriate in the circumstances.

[illegible] and identification of the [illegible] framework [illegible]

The audit will be conducted on the basis that management [illegible] acknowledge and understand that they have responsibility:

a. for the preparation and fair presentation of the financial statements in accordance with accounting principles generally accepted in the United States of America;

b. for the design, implementation, and maintenance of internal control relevant to the preparation and fair presentation of financial statements that are free from material misstatement, whether due to fraud or error; and

c. to provide us with

   i. access to all information of which management is aware that is relevant to the preparation and fair presentation of the financial statements such as records, documentation, and other matters;

   ii. additional information that we may request from management for the purpose of the audit; and

   iii. unrestricted access to persons within the entity from whom we determine it necessary to obtain audit evidence.

As part of our audit process, we will request from management [illegible] written confirmation concerning representations made to us in connection with the audit.

Other Relevant Information

[Insert other information, such as fee arrangements, billings, and other specific terms, as appropriate.]

Reporting

[Insert appropriate reference to the expected form and content of the auditor's report.]

We will issue a written report upon completion of our audit of ABC Company's financial statements. Our report will be addressed to the board of directors of ABC Company. We cannot provide assurance that an unmodified opinion will be expressed. Circumstances may arise in which it is necessary for us to modify our opinion, add an emphasis-of-matter or other-matter paragraph(s), or withdraw from the engagement.

We also will issue a written report on [Insert appropriate reference to other auditor's reports expected to be issued] upon completion of our audit.

Please sign and return the attached copy of this letter to indicate your acknowledgment of, and agreement with, the arrangements for our audit of the financial statements including our respective responsibilities.

XYZ & Co.

Acknowledged and agreed on behalf of ABC Company by:

____

Signed:

Name and Title:

Date:

[illegible]

AU-C Section 220 *

Quality Control for an Engagement Conducted in Accordance With Generally Accepted Auditing Standards

Source: SAS No. 122.

Effective for engagements conducted in accordance with generally accepted auditing standards for periods ending on or after December 15, 2012.

Introduction

Scope of This Section

.01 This section addresses the specific responsibilities of the auditor regarding quality control procedures for an audit of financial statements. It also addresses, when applicable, the responsibilities of the engagement quality control reviewer. This section also applies, adapted as necessary, to other engagements conducted in accordance with generally accepted auditing standards (GAAS) (for example, a review of interim financial information conducted in accordance with section 930, *Interim Financial Information*). This section is to be read in conjunction with the AICPA Code of Professional Conduct and other relevant ethical requirements.

.02 Although Statements on Quality Control Standards are not applicable to auditors in government audit organizations, this section is applicable to auditors in government audit organizations who perform financial audits in accordance with GAAS.[1]

System of Quality Control and the Role of the Engagement Teams

.03 Quality control systems, policies, and procedures are the responsibility of the audit firm. Under QC section 10, *A Firm's System of Quality Control*, the firm has an obligation to establish and maintain a system of quality control to provide it with reasonable assurance that[2]

a. the firm and its personnel comply with professional standards and applicable legal and regulatory requirements and

b. reports issued by the firm are appropriate in the circumstances. (Ref: par. .A1)

.04 Within the context of the firm's system of quality control, engagement teams have a responsibility to implement quality control procedures that are

---

* This section has been codified using an "AU-C" identifier instead of an "AU" identifier. "AU-C" is a temporary identifier to avoid confusion with references to existing "AU" sections, which will remain in AICPA *Professional Standards* through 2013. The "AU-C" identifier will revert to "AU" in 2014, by which time substantially all engagements for which the "AU" sections were still effective are expected to be completed.

[1] Paragraph .02 of QC section 10, *A Firm's System of Quality Control*.

[2] Paragraph .12 of QC section 10.

applicable to the audit engagement and provide the firm with relevant information to enable the functioning of that part of the firm's system of quality control relating to independence.

.05 Engagement teams are entitled to rely on the firm's system of quality control, unless the engagement partner determines that it is inappropriate to do so based on information provided by the firm or other parties. (Ref: par. .A2)

.06 The engagement partner may use the assistance of other members of the engagement team or other personnel within the firm in meeting the requirements of this section. The requirements imposed by this section on engagement partners do not relieve other members of the engagement team of any of their professional responsibilities.

Effective Date

.07 This section is effective for engagements conducted in accordance with GAAS for periods ending on or after December 15, 2012.

Objective

.08 The objective of the auditor[3] is to implement quality control procedures at the engagement level that provide the auditor with reasonable assurance that

a. the audit complies with professional standards and applicable legal and regulatory requirements and

b. the auditor's report issued is appropriate in the circumstances.

Definitions

.09 For purposes of GAAS, the following terms have the meanings attributed as follows:

Engagement partner.[4] The partner or other person in the firm who is responsible for the audit engagement and its performance and for the auditor's report that is issued on behalf of the firm and who, when required, has the appropriate authority from a professional, legal, or regulatory body.

Engagement quality control review. A process designed to provide an objective evaluation, before the report is released, of the significant judgments the engagement team made and the conclusions it reached in formulating the auditor's report. The engagement quality control review process is only for those audit engagements, if any, for which the firm has determined that an engagement quality control review is required, in accordance with its policies and procedures.

Engagement quality control reviewer. A partner, other person in the firm, suitably qualified external person, or team made up of such individuals, none of whom is part of the engagement team, with sufficient and appropriate experience and authority to objectively evaluate the significant judgments that the engagement

---

[3] See paragraph .14 of section 200, *Overall Objectives of the Independent Auditor and the Conduct of an Audit in Accordance With Generally Accepted Auditing Standards*, for the definition of *auditor*.

[4] *Engagement partner, partner*, and *firm* refer to their governmental equivalents, when relevant.

team made and the conclusions it reached in formulating the auditor's report.

Engagement team. All partners and staff performing the engagement and any individuals engaged by the firm or a network firm who perform audit procedures on the engagement. This excludes an auditor's external specialist engaged by the firm or a network firm.[5]

Firm. A form of organization permitted by law or regulation whose characteristics conform to resolutions of the Council of the AICPA and that is engaged in the practice of public accounting.

Monitoring. A process comprising an ongoing consideration and evaluation of the firm's system of quality control, including inspection or a periodic review of engagement documentation, reports, and clients' financial statements for a selection of completed engagements, designed to provide the firm with reasonable assurance that its system of quality control is designed appropriately and operating effectively.

Network. An association of entities, as defined in ET section 92, *Definitions*.

Network firm. A firm or other entity that belongs to a network, as defined in ET section 92.

Partner. Any individual with authority to bind the firm with respect to the performance of a professional services engagement. For purposes of this definition, *partner* may include an employee with this authority who has not assumed the risks and benefits of ownership. Firms may use different titles to refer to individuals with this authority.

Personnel. Partners and staff.

Professional standards. Standards promulgated by the AICPA Auditing Standards Board or the AICPA Accounting and Review Services Committee under Rule 201, *General Standards* (ET sec. 201 par. .01), or Rule 202, *Compliance With Standards* (ET sec. 202 par. .01), of the AICPA Code of Professional Conduct, or other standards-setting bodies that set auditing and attest standards applicable to the engagement being performed and relevant ethical requirements.

Relevant ethical requirements. Ethical requirements to which the engagement team and engagement quality control reviewer are subject, which consist of the AICPA Code of Professional Conduct together with rules of applicable state boards of accountancy and applicable regulatory agencies that are more restrictive.

Staff. Professionals, other than partners, including any specialists that the firm employs.

Suitably qualified external person. An individual outside the firm with the competence and capabilities to act as an engagement partner (for example, a partner of another firm).

---

[5] Paragraph .06 of section 620, *Using the Work of an Auditor's Specialist*, defines the term *auditor's specialist*.

Requirements

Leadership Responsibilities for Quality on Audits

.10 The engagement partner should take responsibility for the overall quality on each audit engagement to which that partner is assigned. In fulfilling this responsibility, the engagement partner may delegate the performance of certain procedures to, and use the work of, other members of the engagement team and may rely upon the firm's system of quality control. (Ref: par. .A3)

Relevant Ethical Requirements

.11 Throughout the audit engagement, the engagement partner and other members of the engagement team should remain alert for evidence of noncompliance with relevant ethical requirements by members of the engagement team. (Ref: par. .A4)

.12 If matters come to the engagement partner's attention, through the firm's system of quality control or otherwise, that indicate that members of the engagement team have not complied with relevant ethical requirements, the engagement partner, in consultation with others in the firm as appropriate, should determine that appropriate action has been taken.

Independence

.13 The engagement partner should form a conclusion on compliance with independence requirements that apply to the audit engagement. In doing so, the engagement partner should

a. obtain relevant information from the firm and, when applicable, network firms to identify and evaluate circumstances and relationships that create threats to independence;

b. evaluate information on identified breaches, if any, of the firm's independence policies and procedures to determine whether they create a threat to independence for the audit engagement; and

c. take appropriate action to eliminate such threats or reduce them to an acceptable level by applying safeguards or, if considered appropriate, to withdraw from the audit engagement when withdrawal is possible under applicable law or regulation. The engagement partner should promptly report to the firm any inability to resolve the matter so that the firm may take appropriate action. (Ref: par. .A5–.A6)

Acceptance and Continuance of Client Relationships and Audit Engagements

.14 The engagement partner should be satisfied that appropriate procedures regarding the acceptance and continuance of client relationships and audit engagements have been followed and should determine that conclusions reached in this regard are appropriate. (Ref: par. .A7–.A8)

.15 If the engagement partner obtains information that would have caused the firm to decline the audit engagement had that information been available earlier, the engagement partner should communicate that information promptly to the firm so that the firm and the engagement partner can take the necessary action. (Ref: par. .A8)

Assignment of Engagement Teams

.16 The engagement partner should be satisfied that the engagement team and any auditor's external specialists, collectively, have the appropriate competence and capabilities to

a. perform the audit engagement in accordance with professional standards and applicable legal and regulatory requirements and

b. enable an auditor's report that is appropriate in the circumstances to be issued. (Ref: par. .A9–.A11)

Engagement Performance

Direction, Supervision, and Performance

.17 The engagement partner should take responsibility for the following:

a. The direction, supervision, and performance of the audit engagement in compliance with professional standards, applicable legal and regulatory requirements, and the firm's policies and procedures (Ref: par. .A12–.A14 and .A19)

b. The auditor's report being appropriate in the circumstances

Review

.18 The engagement partner should take responsibility for reviews being performed in accordance with the firm's review policies and procedures. (Ref: par. .A15–.A16 and .A19)

.19 On or before the date of the auditor's report, the engagement partner should, through a review of the audit documentation and discussion with the engagement team, be satisfied that sufficient appropriate audit evidence has been obtained to support the conclusions reached and for the auditor's report to be issued. (Ref: par. .A17–.A19)

Consultation

.20 The engagement partner should

a. take responsibility for the engagement team undertaking appropriate consultation on difficult or contentious matters;

b. be satisfied that members of the engagement team have undertaken appropriate consultation during the course of the engagement, both within the engagement team and between the engagement team and others at the appropriate level within or outside the firm;

c. be satisfied that the nature and scope of such consultations are agreed with, and conclusions resulting from such consultations are understood by, the party consulted; and

d. determine that conclusions resulting from such consultations have been implemented. (Ref: par. .A20–.A22)

Engagement Quality Control Review

.21 For those audit engagements, if any, for which the firm has determined that an engagement quality control review is required, the engagement partner should

a. determine that an engagement quality control reviewer has been appointed;

b. discuss significant findings or issues arising during the audit engagement, including those identified during the engagement quality control review, with the engagement quality control reviewer; and

c. not release the auditor's report until the completion of the engagement quality control review. (Ref: par. .A23–.A25)

.22 The engagement quality control reviewer should perform an objective evaluation of the significant judgments made by the engagement team and the conclusions reached in formulating the auditor's report. This evaluation should involve

a. discussion of significant findings or issues with the engagement partner;

b. reading the financial statements and the proposed auditor's report;

c. review of selected audit documentation relating to the significant judgments the engagement team made and the related conclusions it reached; and

d. evaluation of the conclusions reached in formulating the auditor's report and consideration of whether the proposed auditor's report is appropriate. (Ref: par. .A26–.A31)

Differences of Opinion

.23 If differences of opinion arise within the engagement team; with those consulted; or, when applicable, between the engagement partner and the engagement quality control reviewer, the engagement team should follow the firm's policies and procedures for resolving differences of opinion.

Monitoring

.24 An effective system of quality control includes a monitoring process designed to provide the firm with reasonable assurance that its policies and procedures relating to the system of quality control are relevant, adequate, and operating effectively. The engagement partner should consider

a. the results of the firm's monitoring process as evidenced in the latest information circulated to the engagement partner by the firm and, if applicable, other network firms and

b. whether deficiencies noted in that information may affect the audit engagement. (Ref: par. .A32–.A34)

Documentation

.25 The auditor should include in the audit documentation the following:[6] (Ref: par. .A35)

a. Issues identified with respect to compliance with relevant ethical requirements and how they were resolved

b. Conclusions on compliance with independence requirements that apply to the audit engagement and any relevant discussions with the firm that support these conclusions

c. Conclusions reached regarding the acceptance and continuance of client relationships and audit engagements

---

[6] Paragraphs .08–.12 and .A8 of section 230, *Audit Documentation*.

d. The nature and scope of, and conclusions resulting from, consultations undertaken during the course of the audit engagement (Ref: par. .A36)

.26 The engagement quality control reviewer should document, for the audit engagement reviewed

a. that the procedures required by the firm's policies on engagement quality control review have been performed;

b. the date that the engagement quality control review was completed; and

c. that the reviewer is not aware of any unresolved matters that would cause the reviewer to believe that the significant judgments that the engagement team made and the conclusions it reached were not appropriate.

Application and Other Explanatory Material

System of Quality Control and the Role of the Engagement Teams (Ref: par. .02)

.A1 QC section 10 addresses the firm's responsibilities to establish and maintain its system of quality control for audit engagements. The system of quality control includes policies and procedures that address each of the following elements:

- Leadership responsibilities for quality within the firm
- Relevant ethical requirements
- Acceptance and continuance of client relationships and specific engagements
- Human resources
- Engagement performance
- Monitoring

Reliance on the Firm's System of Quality Control (Ref: par. .05)

.A2 Unless information provided by the firm or other parties suggests otherwise, the engagement team may rely on the firm's system of quality control regarding, for example

- competence of personnel through their recruitment and formal training.
- independence through the accumulation and communication of relevant independence information.
- maintenance of client relationships through acceptance and continuance systems.
- adherence to applicable legal and regulatory requirements through the monitoring process.

Leadership Responsibilities for Quality on Audits (Ref: par. .10)

.A3 The engagement partner's actions and communications with the other members of the engagement team demonstrate responsibility for the overall quality on each audit engagement when they emphasize *a.* the importance to audit quality of

i. performing work that complies with professional standards and applicable legal and regulatory requirements;

ii. complying with the firm's applicable quality control policies and procedures;

iii. issuing auditor's reports that are appropriate in the circumstances; and

iv. the engagement team's ability to raise concerns without fear of reprisals and

b. the fact that quality is essential in performing audit engagements.

Relevant Ethical Requirements

Compliance With Relevant Ethical Requirements (Ref: par. .11)

.A4 The AICPA Code of Professional Conduct establishes the fundamental principles of professional ethics, which include the following:

- Responsibilities
- The public interest
- Integrity
- Objectivity and independence
- Due care

Threats to Independence (Ref: par. .13)

.A5 The engagement team may identify a threat to independence regarding the audit engagement that safeguards may not be able to eliminate or reduce to an acceptable level. In that case, as required by paragraph .13*c*, the engagement partner reports to the relevant person(s) within the firm to determine appropriate action, which may include eliminating the activity or interest that creates the threat or withdrawing from the audit engagement when withdrawal is possible under applicable law or regulation.

Considerations Specific to Governmental Entities

.A6 Law or regulation may provide safeguards for the independence of governmental audit organizations and the auditors employed by them. However, in the absence of law or regulation, governmental audit organizations may establish supplemental safeguards to assist the auditor or audit organization in maintaining independence. Additionally, when law or regulation does not permit withdrawal from the engagement, the auditor may disclose in the auditor's report the circumstances affecting the auditor's independence.

Acceptance and Continuance of Client Relationships and Audit Engagements (Ref: par. .14)

.A7 QC section 10 requires the firm to obtain information considered necessary in the circumstances before accepting an engagement with a new client, when deciding whether to continue an existing engagement, and when considering acceptance of a new engagement with an existing client.[7] Information such as the following assists the engagement partner in determining whether

[7] Paragraph .27 of QC section 10.

the conclusions reached regarding the acceptance and continuance of client relationships and audit engagements are appropriate:

- The integrity of the principal owners, key management, and those charged with governance of the entity
- Whether the engagement team is competent to perform the audit engagement and has the necessary capabilities, including time and resources
- Whether the firm and the engagement team can comply with relevant ethical requirements
- Significant findings or issues that have arisen during the current or previous audit engagement and their implications for continuing the relationship

Considerations Specific to Governmental Entities (Ref: par. .14–.15)

.A8 For some governmental entities, auditors may be appointed in accordance with law or regulation, and the auditor may not be permitted to decline or withdraw from the engagement. Accordingly, certain of the requirements and considerations regarding the acceptance and continuance of client relationships and audit engagements as set out in paragraphs .14–.15 and .A7 may not be relevant. Nonetheless, information gathered as a result of the process described may be valuable in planning the audit, performing risk assessments, and carrying out reporting responsibilities.

Assignment of Engagement Teams (Ref: par. .16)

.A9 A person with expertise in a specialized area of accounting or auditing is a member of the engagement team if that person performs audit procedures on the engagement. This applies whether that person is an employee of the firm or a nonemployee engaged by the firm. However, a person with such expertise is not a member of the engagement team if that person's involvement with the engagement is only consultation. Consultations are addressed in paragraphs .20 and .A20–.A22.

.A10 When considering the appropriate competence and capabilities expected of the engagement team as a whole, the engagement partner may take into consideration such matters as the team's

- understanding of, and practical experience with, audit engagements of a similar nature and complexity through appropriate training and participation.
- understanding of professional standards and applicable legal and regulatory requirements.
- technical expertise, including expertise with relevant IT and specialized areas of accounting or auditing.
- knowledge of relevant industries in which the entity operates.
- ability to apply professional judgment.
- understanding of the firm's quality control policies and procedures.

Considerations Specific to Governmental Entities (Ref: par. .16)

.A11 For audits of governmental entities, competence may include skills that are necessary to comply with applicable law or regulation. Such competence may include knowledge of *Government Auditing Standards* and an understanding of the applicable reporting requirements, including reporting to the legislature or other governing body or in the public interest. The scope of a governmental audit may include, for example, additional requirements with respect to detecting misstatements that result from violations of provisions of contracts or grant agreements that could have a direct and material effect on the determination of financial statement amounts or the need to examine and report on internal control over financial reporting or compliance.

Engagement Performance

Direction, Supervision, and Performance (Ref: par. .17a)

.A12 Direction of the engagement team involves informing the members of the engagement team of matters such as the following:

- Their responsibilities, including the need to comply with relevant ethical requirements and to plan and perform an audit with professional skepticism as required by section 200, *Overall Objectives of the Independent Auditor and the Conduct of an Audit in Accordance With Generally Accepted Auditing Standards*[8]
- Responsibilities of respective partners when more than one partner is involved in the conduct of an audit engagement
- The objectives of the work to be performed
- The nature of the entity's business
- Risk-related issues
- Problems that may arise
- The detailed approach to the performance of the engagement

Discussion among members of the engagement team allows team members to raise questions so that appropriate communication can occur within the engagement team.

.A13 Appropriate teamwork and training assist members of the engagement team to clearly understand the objectives of the assigned work.

.A14 Supervision includes matters such as the following:

- Tracking the progress of the audit engagement
- Considering the competence and capabilities of individual members of the engagement team, including whether they have sufficient time to carry out their work, they understand their instructions, and the work is being carried out in accordance with the planned approach to the audit engagement
- Addressing significant findings or issues arising during the audit engagement, considering their significance, and modifying the planned approach appropriately
- Identifying matters for consultation or consideration by qualified engagement team members during the audit engagement

---

[8] Paragraphs .16–.17 of section 200.

Review

Review Responsibilities (Ref: par. .18)

.A15 Under QC section 10, the firm's review responsibility policies and procedures are determined on the basis that suitably experienced team members review the work of other team members.[9] The engagement partner may delegate part of the review responsibility to other members of the engagement team, in accordance with the firm's system of quality control.

.A16 A review consists of consideration of whether, for example

- the work has been performed in accordance with professional standards and applicable legal and regulatory requirements;
- significant findings or issues have been raised for further consideration;
- appropriate consultations have taken place and the resulting conclusions have been documented and implemented;
- the nature, timing, and extent of the work performed is appropriate and without need for revision;
- the work performed supports the conclusions reached and is appropriately documented;
- the evidence obtained is sufficient and appropriate to support the auditor's report; and
- the objectives of the engagement procedures have been achieved.

The Engagement Partner's Review of the Work Performed (Ref: par. .19)

.A17 Timely reviews of the following by the engagement partner at appropriate stages during the engagement allow significant findings or issues to be resolved on a timely basis to the engagement partner's satisfaction on or before the date of the auditor's report:

- Critical areas of judgment, especially those relating to difficult or contentious matters identified during the course of the engagement
- Significant risks
- Other areas that the engagement partner considers important

The engagement partner need not review all audit documentation but may do so. However, as required by section 230, *Audit Documentation*, the partner documents the extent and timing of the reviews.[10]

.A18 An engagement partner taking over an audit during the engagement may apply the review procedures as described in paragraph .A17 to review the work performed to the date of the change in order to assume the responsibilities of an engagement partner.

Considerations Relevant When a Member of the Engagement Team With Expertise in a Specialized Area of Accounting or Auditing Is Used (Ref: par. .17–.19)

.A19 When the engagement team includes a member with expertise in a specialized area of accounting or auditing, direction, supervision, and review of

---

[9] Paragraph .36 of QC section 10.

[10] Paragraph .09*c* of section 230.

that engagement team member's work is the same as for any other engagement team member and may include matters such as the following:

- Agreeing with that member upon the nature, scope, and objectives of that member's work and the respective roles of, and the nature, timing, and extent of communication between, that member and other members of the engagement team
- Evaluating the adequacy of that member's work, including the relevance and reasonableness of that member's findings or conclusions and the consistency of those findings or conclusions with other audit evidence

Consultation (Ref: par. .20)

.A20 Members of the engagement team have a professional responsibility to bring to the attention of appropriate personnel matters that, in their professional judgment, are difficult or contentious and may require consultation.

.A21 Effective consultation on significant technical, ethical, and other matters within the firm or, when applicable, outside the firm can be achieved when those consulted

- are given all the relevant facts that will enable them to provide informed advice and
- have appropriate knowledge, authority, and experience.

.A22 The engagement team may consult outside the firm (for example, when the firm lacks appropriate internal resources). The engagement team may take advantage of advisory services provided by other firms, professional and regulatory bodies, or commercial organizations that provide relevant quality control services.

Engagement Quality Control Review

Completion of the Engagement Quality Control Review Before Releasing the Auditor's Report (Ref: par. .21c)

.A23 Conducting the engagement quality control review in a timely manner at appropriate stages during the engagement allows significant findings or issues to be promptly resolved to the engagement quality control reviewer's satisfaction.

.A24 *Completion of the engagement quality control review* means the completion by the engagement quality control reviewer of the requirements in paragraph .22 and, when applicable, compliance with paragraph .23. Documentation of the engagement quality control review may be completed after the report release date as part of the assembly of the final audit file. Section 230 establishes requirements and provides guidance in this regard.[11]

.A25 When the engagement quality control review is completed after the auditor's report is dated and identifies instances where additional procedures or additional evidence is necessary, the date of the report is changed to the date when the additional procedures have been satisfactorily completed or the additional evidence has been obtained, in accordance with section 700, *Forming an Opinion and Reporting on Financial Statements*.

---

[11] Paragraphs .15–.18 and .A24–.A29 of section 230.

Nature, Timing, and Extent of Engagement Quality Control Review (Ref: par. .22)

.A26 By remaining alert for changes in circumstances, the engagement partner is able to identify situations in which an engagement quality control review is necessary, even though at the start of the engagement such a review was not required.

.A27 The extent of the engagement quality control review may depend, among other things, on the complexity of the audit engagement and the risk that the auditor's report might not be appropriate in the circumstances. The performance of an engagement quality control review does not reduce the responsibilities of the engagement partner for the audit engagement and its performance.

.A28 Matters relevant to evaluating the significant judgments made by the engagement team that may be considered in an engagement quality control review include the following:

- Significant risks identified during the engagement in accordance with section 315, *Understanding the Entity and Its Environment and Assessing the Risks of Material Misstatement*, and the responses to those risks in accordance with section 330, *Performing Audit Procedures in Response to Assessed Risks and Evaluating the Audit Evidence Obtained*, including the engagement team's assessment of, and response to, the risk of fraud in accordance with section 240, *Consideration of Fraud in a Financial Statement Audit*
- Judgments made, particularly with respect to materiality and significant risks
- The significance and disposition of corrected and uncorrected misstatements identified during the audit
- The matters to be communicated to management and those charged with governance and, when applicable, other parties, such as regulatory bodies

.A29 The engagement quality control reviewer may also consider the following:

- The evaluation of the firm's independence with regard to the audit engagement
- Whether appropriate consultation has taken place on matters involving differences of opinion or other difficult or contentious matters and the related conclusions arising from those consultations
- Whether audit documentation selected for review reflects the work performed regarding the significant judgments and supports the conclusions reached

Considerations Specific to Smaller, Less Complex Entities (Ref: par. .21–.22)

.A30 An engagement quality control review is required for audit engagements that meet the criteria established by the firm that subjects engagements to an engagement quality control review. In some cases, none of the firm's audit engagements may meet the criteria that would subject them to such a review.

Considerations Specific to Governmental Entities (Ref: par. .22)

.A31 A statutorily appointed auditor (for example, an auditor general or other suitably qualified person within the audit organization acting on behalf of the auditor general) may act in a role equivalent to that of engagement partner with overall responsibility for the governmental audit. In such circumstances, when applicable, the selection of the engagement quality control reviewer includes consideration of the need for independence from the audited entity and the ability of the engagement quality control reviewer to provide an objective evaluation.

Monitoring (Ref: par. .24)

.A32 QC section 10 requires the firm to establish a monitoring process designed to provide it with reasonable assurance that the policies and procedures relating to the system of quality control are relevant, adequate, and operating effectively.[12]

.A33 In considering deficiencies that may affect the audit engagement, the engagement partner may consider measures the firm took to rectify the situation that the engagement partner considers sufficient in the context of that audit.

.A34 A deficiency in the firm's system of quality control does not necessarily indicate that a particular audit engagement was not performed in accordance with professional standards and applicable legal and regulatory requirements or that the auditor's report was not appropriate.

Documentation (Ref: par. .25)

.A35 Section 230 addresses the auditor's responsibility to prepare audit documentation for an audit of financial statements. Section 230 also states that it is neither necessary nor practicable for the auditor to document every matter considered, or professional judgment made, in an audit.[13]

.A36 Documentation of consultations with other professionals involving difficult or contentious matters that is sufficiently complete and detailed contributes to an understanding of

- the issue on which consultation was sought and
- the results of the consultation, including any decisions made, the basis for those decisions, and how they were implemented.

---

[12] Paragraph .52 of QC section 10.

[13] Paragraph .A9 of section 230.

AU-C Section 230 *

Audit Documentation

Source: SAS No. 122; SAS No. 123.

Effective for audits of financial statements for periods ending on or after December 15, 2012.

Introduction

Scope of This Section

.01 This section addresses the auditor's responsibility to prepare audit documentation for an audit of financial statements. The exhibit, "Audit Documentation Requirements in Other AU-C Sections," lists other AU-C sections that contain specific documentation requirements and guidance. The specific documentation requirements of other AU-C sections do not limit the application of this section. Law, regulation, or other standards may establish additional documentation requirements.

Nature and Purposes of Audit Documentation

.02 Audit documentation that meets the requirements of this section and the specific documentation requirements of other relevant AU-C sections provides

a. evidence of the auditor's basis for a conclusion about the achievement of the overall objectives of the auditor;[1] and

b. evidence that the audit was planned and performed in accordance with generally accepted auditing standards (GAAS) and applicable legal and regulatory requirements.

.03 Audit documentation serves a number of additional purposes, including the following:

- Assisting the engagement team to plan and perform the audit
- Assisting members of the engagement team responsible for supervision to direct and supervise the audit work and to discharge their review responsibilities in accordance with section 220, *Quality Control for an Engagement Conducted in Accordance With Generally Accepted Auditing Standards*[2]
- Enabling the engagement team to demonstrate that it is accountable for its work by documenting the procedures performed, the audit evidence examined, and the conclusions reached

---

* This section has been codified using an "AU-C" identifier instead of an "AU" identifier. "AU-C" is a temporary identifier to avoid confusion with references to existing "AU" sections, which will remain in AICPA *Professional Standards* through 2013. The "AU-C" identifier will revert to "AU" in 2014, by which time substantially all engagements for which the "AU" sections were still effective are expected to be completed.

[1] Paragraph .12 of section 200, *Overall Objectives of the Independent Auditor and the Conduct of an Audit in Accordance With Generally Accepted Auditing Standards.*

[2] Paragraphs .17–.19 of section 220, *Quality Control for an Engagement Conducted in Accordance With Generally Accepted Auditing Standards.*

- Retaining a record of matters of continuing significance to future audits of the same entity
- Enabling the conduct of quality control reviews and inspections in accordance with QC section 10, *A Firm's System of Quality Control*
- Enabling the conduct of external inspections or peer reviews in accordance with applicable legal, regulatory, or other requirements
- Assisting an auditor who reviews a predecessor auditor's audit documentation
- Assisting auditors to understand the work performed in the prior year as an aid in planning and performing the current engagement

Effective Date

.04 This section is effective for audits of financial statements for periods ending on or after December 15, 2012.

Objective

.05 The objective of the auditor is to prepare documentation that provides

a. a sufficient and appropriate record of the basis for the auditor's report; and

b. evidence that the audit was planned and performed in accordance with GAAS and applicable legal and regulatory requirements.

Definitions

.06 For purposes of GAAS, the following terms have the meanings attributed as follows:

Audit documentation. The record of audit procedures performed, relevant audit evidence obtained, and conclusions the auditor reached (terms such as *working papers* or *workpapers* are also sometimes used).

Audit file. One or more folders or other storage media, in physical or electronic form, containing the records that constitute the audit documentation for a specific engagement.

Documentation completion date. The date, no later than 60 days following the report release date, on which the auditor has assembled for retention a complete and final set of documentation in an audit file.

Experienced auditor. An individual (whether internal or external to the firm) who has practical audit experience, and a reasonable understanding of (Ref: par. .A1)

a. audit processes;

b. GAAS and applicable legal and regulatory requirements;

c. the business environment in which the entity operates; and

d. auditing and financial reporting issues relevant to the entity's industry.

Report release date. The date the auditor grants the entity permission to use the auditor's report in connection with the financial statements. (Ref: par. .A2)

Requirements

Timely Preparation of Audit Documentation

.07 The auditor should prepare audit documentation on a timely basis. (Ref: par. .A3)

Documentation of the Audit Procedures Performed and Audit Evidence Obtained

Form, Content, and Extent of Audit Documentation

.08 The auditor should prepare audit documentation that is sufficient to enable an experienced auditor, having no previous connection with the audit, to understand (Ref: par. .A4–.A7 and .A19–.A20)

a. the nature, timing, and extent of the audit procedures performed to comply with GAAS and applicable legal and regulatory requirements; (Ref: par. .A8–.A9)

b. the results of the audit procedures performed, and the audit evidence obtained; and

c. significant findings or issues arising during the audit, the conclusions reached thereon, and significant professional judgments made in reaching those conclusions. (Ref: par. .A10–.A13)

.09 In documenting the nature, timing, and extent of audit procedures performed, the auditor should record

a. the identifying characteristics of the specific items or matters tested; (Ref: par. .A14)

b. who performed the audit work and the date such work was completed; and

c. who reviewed the audit work performed and the date and extent of such review. (Ref: par. .A15)

.10 For audit procedures related to the inspection of significant contracts or agreements, the auditor should include abstracts or copies of those contracts or agreements in the audit documentation.

.11 The auditor should document discussions of significant findings or issues with management, those charged with governance, and others, including the nature of the significant findings or issues discussed, and when and with whom the discussions took place. (Ref: par. .A16)

.12 If the auditor identified information that is inconsistent with the auditor's final conclusion regarding a significant finding or issue, the auditor should document how the auditor addressed the inconsistency. (Ref: par. .A17–.A18)

Departure From a Relevant Requirement

.13 If, in rare circumstances, the auditor judges it necessary to depart from a relevant presumptively mandatory requirement,[3] the auditor must document the justification for the departure and how the alternative audit procedures performed in the circumstances were sufficient to achieve the intent of that requirement. (Ref: par. .A21–.A22)

---

[3] Paragraph .26 of section 200.

Matters Arising After the Date of the Auditor's Report

.14 If, in rare circumstances, the auditor performs new or additional audit procedures or draws new conclusions after the date of the auditor's report, the auditor should document (Ref: par. .A23)

a. the circumstances encountered;

b. the new or additional audit procedures performed, audit evidence obtained, and conclusions reached, and their effect on the auditor's report; and

c. when and by whom the resulting changes to audit documentation were made and reviewed.

Assembly and Retention of the Final Audit File

.15 The auditor should document the report release date in the audit documentation.

.16 The auditor should assemble the audit documentation in an audit file and complete the administrative process of assembling the final audit file on a timely basis, no later than 60 days following the report release date. (Ref: par. .A24–.A26)

.17 After the documentation completion date, the auditor should not delete or discard audit documentation of any nature before the end of the specified retention period. Such retention period, however, should not be shorter than five years from the report release date. (Ref: par. .A27–.A29)

.18 In circumstances other than those addressed in paragraph .14 in which the auditor finds it necessary to modify existing audit documentation or add new audit documentation after the documentation completion date, the auditor should, regardless of the nature of the modifications or additions, document (Ref: par. .A28)

a. the specific reasons for making the changes; and

b. when and by whom they were made and reviewed.

.19 The auditor should adopt reasonable procedures to maintain the confidentiality of client information.

Application and Other Explanatory Material

Definitions (Ref: par. .06)

Experienced Auditor

.A1 Having practical audit experience means possessing the competencies and skills that would have enabled the auditor to perform the audit but does not mean that the auditor is required to have performed comparable audits.

Report Release Date

.A2 In many cases, the report release date will be the date the auditor delivers the audit report to the entity. When there are delays in releasing the report, a fact may become known to the auditor that, had it been known to the auditor at the date of the auditor's report, may have caused the auditor to revise the auditor's report. Section 560, *Subsequent Events and Subsequently Discovered Facts*, addresses the auditor's responsibilities in such circumstances, and paragraph .14 addresses the documentation requirements in the rare circumstances in which the auditor performs new or additional audit procedures or draws new conclusions after the date of the auditor's report.

Timely Preparation of Audit Documentation (Ref: par. .07)

.A3 Preparing sufficient and appropriate audit documentation on a timely basis throughout the audit helps to enhance the quality of the audit and facilitates the effective review and evaluation of the audit evidence obtained and conclusions reached before the auditor's report is finalized. Documentation prepared at the time such work is performed or shortly thereafter is likely to be more accurate than documentation prepared at a much later time.

Documentation of the Audit Procedures Performed and Audit Evidence Obtained

Form, Content, and Extent of Audit Documentation (Ref: par. .08)

.A4 The form, content, and extent of audit documentation depend on factors such as

- the size and complexity of the entity.
- the nature of the audit procedures to be performed.
- the identified risks of material misstatement.
- the significance of the audit evidence obtained.
- the nature and extent of exceptions identified.
- the need to document a conclusion or the basis for a conclusion not readily determinable from the documentation of the work performed or audit evidence obtained.
- the audit methodology and tools used.
- the extent of judgment involved in performing the work and evaluating the results.

.A5 Audit documentation may be recorded on paper or on electronic or other media. QC section 10 addresses a firm's responsibility to establish procedures designed to maintain the integrity, accessibility, and retrievability of documentation; for example, when original paper documentation is electronically scanned or otherwise copied to another media for inclusion in the audit file.[4] Examples of audit documentation include the following:

- Audit plans[5]
- Analyses
- Issues memorandums
- Summaries of significant findings or issues
- Letters of confirmation and representation
- Checklists
- Correspondence (including e-mail) concerning significant findings or issues

---

[4] Paragraph .A58 of QC section 10 No. 8, *A Firm's System of Quality Control*.

[5] Paragraphs .07–.11 of section 300, *Planning an Audit*.

.A6 The auditor need not include in audit documentation superseded drafts of working papers and financial statements, notes that reflect incomplete or preliminary thinking, previous copies of documents corrected for typographical or other errors, and duplicates of documents.

.A7 On their own, oral explanations by the auditor do not represent adequate support for the work the auditor performed or conclusions the auditor reached, but may be used to explain or clarify information contained in the audit documentation.

Documentation of Compliance With GAAS (Ref: par. .08a)

.A8 In principle, compliance with the requirements of this section will result in the audit documentation being sufficient and appropriate in the circumstances. Other AU-C sections contain specific documentation requirements that are intended to clarify the application of this section in the particular circumstances of those other AU-C sections. The specific documentation requirements of other AU-C sections do not limit the application of this section. Furthermore, the absence of a documentation requirement in any particular AU-C section is not intended to suggest that there is no documentation that will be prepared as a result of complying with that AU-C section.

.A9 Audit documentation provides evidence that the audit complies with GAAS. However, it is neither necessary nor practicable for the auditor to document every matter considered, or professional judgment made, in an audit. Further, it is unnecessary for the auditor to document separately (as in a checklist, for example) compliance with matters for which compliance is demonstrated by documents included within the audit file. For example:

- The existence of an adequately documented audit plan demonstrates that the auditor has planned the audit.
- The existence of a signed engagement letter in the audit file demonstrates that the auditor has agreed to the terms of the audit engagement with management or, when appropriate, those charged with governance.
- An auditor's report containing an appropriately qualified opinion on the financial statements demonstrates that the auditor has complied with the requirement to express a qualified opinion under the circumstances in accordance with GAAS.
- Regarding requirements that apply generally throughout the audit, there may be a number of ways in which compliance with them may be demonstrated within the audit file:
  - — For example, there may be no single way in which the auditor's professional skepticism is documented. But the audit documentation may nevertheless provide evidence of the auditor's exercise of professional skepticism in accordance with GAAS. Such evidence may include specific procedures performed to corroborate management's responses to the auditor's inquiries.
  - — Similarly, that the engagement partner has taken responsibility for the direction, supervision, and performance of the audit in compliance with GAAS may be evidenced in a number of ways within the audit documentation. This may include documentation of the engagement partner's timely involvement in aspects of the audit, such as participation

in the team discussions required by section 315, *Understanding the Entity and Its Environment and Assessing the Risks of Material Misstatement.*[6]

Documentation of Significant Findings or Issues and Related Significant Professional Judgments (Ref: par. .08c)

.A10 Judging the significance of a finding or issue requires an objective analysis of the facts and circumstances. Examples of significant findings or issues include

- matters involving the selection, application, and consistency of significant accounting practices, including related disclosures. Such matters include, but are not limited to (*a*) accounting for complex or unusual transactions or (*b*) accounting estimates and uncertainties and, if applicable, the related management assumptions.
- matters that give rise to significant risks (as defined in section 315).[7]
- results of audit procedures (including identification of corrected and uncorrected misstatements)[8] indicating (*a*) that the financial statements could be materially misstated or (*b*) a need to revise the auditor's previous assessment of the risks of material misstatement and the auditor's responses to those risks.
- circumstances that cause the auditor significant difficulty in applying necessary audit procedures.
- findings that could result in a modification to the audit opinion or the inclusion of an emphasis-of-matter paragraph in the auditor's report.

.A11 An important factor in determining the form, content, and extent of audit documentation of significant findings or issues is the extent of professional judgment exercised in performing the work and evaluating the results. Documentation of the professional judgments made, when significant, serves to explain the auditor's conclusions and to reinforce the quality of the judgment. Such findings or issues are of particular interest to those responsible for reviewing audit documentation, including those carrying out subsequent audits when reviewing items of continuing significance (for example, when performing a retrospective review of accounting estimates).

.A12 Some examples of circumstances in which, in accordance with paragraph .08, it is appropriate to prepare audit documentation relating to the exercise of professional judgment include, when the findings, issues, and judgments are significant,

- the rationale for the auditor's conclusion when a requirement provides that the auditor *should consider* certain information or factors, and that consideration is significant in the context of the particular engagement.
- the basis for the auditor's conclusion on the reasonableness of areas of subjective judgments (for example, the reasonableness of significant accounting estimates).

---

[6] Paragraph .33 of section 315, *Understanding the Entity and Its Environment and Assessing the Risks of Material Misstatement.*

[7] Paragraphs .28–.30 of section 315.

[8] See section 450, *Evaluation of Misstatements Identified During the Audit.*

- the basis for the auditor's conclusions about the authenticity of a document when further investigation (such as making appropriate use of a specialist or of confirmation procedures) is undertaken in response to conditions identified during the audit that caused the auditor to believe that the document may not be authentic.

.A13 The auditor may consider it helpful to prepare and retain as part of the audit documentation a summary (sometimes known as a completion memorandum) that describes the significant findings or issues identified during the audit and how they were addressed, or that includes cross-references to other relevant supporting audit documentation that provides such information. Such a summary may facilitate effective and efficient reviews and inspections of the audit documentation, particularly for large and complex audits. Further, the preparation of such a summary may assist the auditor's consideration of the significant findings or issues. It may also help the auditor to consider whether, in light of the audit procedures performed and conclusions reached, there is any individual relevant AU-C section objective that the auditor cannot achieve that would prevent the auditor from achieving the overall objectives of the auditor.

Identification of Specific Items or Matters Tested and of the Preparer and the Reviewer (Ref: par. .09)

.A14 Recording the identifying characteristics serves a number of purposes. For example, it improves the ability of the auditor to supervise and review the work performed and thus demonstrates the accountability of the engagement team for its work and facilitates the investigation of exceptions or inconsistencies. Identifying characteristics will vary with the nature of the audit procedure and the item or matter tested. For example:

- For a detailed test of entity-generated purchase orders, the auditor may identify the documents selected for testing by their dates and unique purchase order numbers.
- For a procedure requiring selection or review of all items over a specific amount from a given population, the auditor may record the scope of the procedure and identify the population (for example, all journal entries over a specified amount from the journal register for the period being audited).
- For a procedure requiring systematic sampling from a population of documents, the auditor may identify the documents selected by recording their source, the starting point, and the sampling interval (for example, a systematic sample of shipping reports selected from the shipping log for the period from April 1 to September 30, starting with report number 12345 and selecting every 125th report).
- For a procedure requiring inquiries of specific entity personnel, the auditor may record the inquiries made, the dates of the inquiries, and the names and job designations of the entity personnel.
- For an observation procedure, the auditor may record the process or matter being observed, the relevant individuals, their respective responsibilities, and where and when the observation was carried out.

.A15 Section 220 requires the auditor to review the audit work performed through review of the audit documentation.[9] The requirement to document who

---

[9] Paragraph .19 of section 220.

reviewed the audit work performed and the extent of the review, in accordance with the firm's policies and procedures addressing review responsibilities, does not imply a need for each specific working paper to include evidence of review. The requirement, however, means documenting what audit work was reviewed, who reviewed such work, and when it was reviewed.

Documentation of Discussions of Significant Findings or Issues With Management, Those Charged With Governance, and Others (Ref: par. .11)

.A16 The audit documentation is not limited to documents prepared by the auditor but may include other appropriate documents such as minutes of meetings prepared by the entity's personnel and recognized by the auditor as an appropriate summary of the meeting. Others with whom the auditor may discuss significant findings or issues may include other personnel within the entity, and external parties, such as persons providing professional advice to the entity.

Documentation of How Inconsistencies Have Been Addressed (Ref: par. .12)

.A17 The requirement to document how the auditor addressed inconsistencies in information does not imply that the auditor needs to retain documentation that is incorrect or superseded.

.A18 The documentation of the inconsistency may include, but is not limited to, procedures performed in response to the information, and documentation of consultations on, or resolutions of, differences in professional judgment among members of the engagement team or between the engagement team and others consulted.

Considerations Specific to Smaller, Less Complex Entities (Ref: par. .08)

.A19 The audit documentation for the audit of a smaller, less complex entity is generally less extensive than that for the audit of a larger, more complex entity. Further, in the case of an audit in which the engagement partner performs all the audit work, the documentation will not include matters that might have to be documented solely to inform or instruct members of an engagement team, or to provide evidence of review by other members of the team (for example, there will be no matters to document relating to team discussions or supervision). Nevertheless, the engagement partner complies with the overriding requirement in paragraph .08 to prepare audit documentation that can be understood by an experienced auditor, as the audit documentation may be subject to review by external parties for regulatory or other purposes.

.A20 When preparing audit documentation, the auditor of a smaller, less complex entity may also find it helpful and efficient to record various aspects of the audit together in a single document, with cross-references to supporting working papers as appropriate. Examples of matters that may be documented together in the audit of a smaller, less complex entity include the understanding of the entity and its internal control; the overall audit strategy and audit plan; materiality; assessed risks, significant findings or issues noted during the audit; and conclusions reached.

Departure From a Relevant Requirement (Ref: par. .13)

.A21 The requirements of GAAS are designed to enable the auditor to achieve the objectives specified in GAAS, and thereby the overall objectives of the auditor. Accordingly, other than in rare circumstances, GAAS call for compliance with each requirement that is relevant in the circumstances of the audit.

.A22 The documentation requirement applies only to requirements that are relevant in the circumstances. A requirement is not relevant[10] only in the cases in which

a. the AU-C section is not relevant (for example, if an entity does not have an internal audit function, nothing in section 610, *The Auditor's Consideration of the Internal Audit Function in an Audit of Financial Statements,*[†] is relevant); or

b. the requirement is conditional and the condition does not exist (for example, the requirement to modify the auditor's opinion when there is an inability to obtain sufficient appropriate audit evidence, and there is no such inability).

Matters Arising After the Date of the Auditor's Report (Ref: par. .14)

.A23 Examples of rare circumstances in which the auditor performs new or additional audit procedures or draws new conclusions after the date of the auditor's report include

- when, after the date of the auditor's report, the auditor becomes aware of facts that existed at that date and which, if known at that date, might have caused the financial statements to be revised or the auditor to modify the opinion in the auditor's report.[11]
- when the auditor concludes that procedures necessary at the time of the audit, in the circumstances then existing, were omitted from the audit of the financial information.[12]

The resulting changes to the audit documentation are reviewed in accordance with the firm's quality control procedures as required by QC section 10.

Assembly and Retention of the Final Audit File (Ref: par. .16–.18)

.A24 Statutes, regulations, or the audit firm's quality control policies may specify a period of time shorter than 60 days following the report release date in which this assembly process is to be completed.

.A25 Certain matters, such as auditor independence and staff training, which are not engagement specific, may be documented either centrally within a firm or in the audit documentation for an audit engagement.

.A26 The completion of the assembly of the final audit file after the date of the auditor's report is an administrative process that does not involve the performance of new audit procedures or the drawing of new conclusions. Changes may, however, be made to the audit documentation during the final assembly process if they are administrative in nature. Examples of such changes include

- deleting or discarding superseded documentation.

---

[10] Paragraph .24 of section 200.

[†] Statement on Auditing Standards (SAS) No. 65, *The Auditor's Consideration of the Internal Audit Function in an Audit of Financial Statements*, is currently effective and codified as AU section 322. SAS No. 65 has been included in section 610, as designated by SAS No. 122, *Statements on Auditing Standards: Clarification and Recodification*, and will be superseded when it is redrafted for clarity and convergence with International Standard on Auditing 610 (Revised), *Using the Work of Internal Auditors*, as part of the Clarification and Convergence project of the Auditing Standards Board. Until such time, section 610 has been conformed to reflect updated section and paragraph cross references but has not otherwise been subjected to a comprehensive review or revision.

[11] Paragraphs .12 and .15 of section 560, *Subsequent Events and Subsequently Discovered Facts.*

[12] Paragraph .07 of section 585, *Consideration of Omitted Procedures After the Report Release Date.*

- sorting, collating, and cross-referencing working papers.
- signing off on completion checklists relating to the file assembly process.
- documenting audit evidence that the auditor has obtained, discussed, and agreed with the relevant members of the engagement team before the date of the auditor's report.
- adding information received after the date of the auditor's report; for example, an original confirmation that was previously faxed.

.A27 Firms are required to establish policies and procedures for the retention of engagement documentation.[13] Statutes, regulations, or the audit firm's quality control policies may specify a retention period longer than five years.

.A28 An example of a circumstance in which the auditor may find it necessary to modify existing audit documentation or add new audit documentation after the documentation completion date is the need to clarify existing audit documentation arising from comments received during monitoring inspections performed by internal or external parties.

.A29 Audit documentation is the property of the auditor, and some states recognize this right of ownership in their statutes. The auditor may make available to the entity at the auditor's discretion copies of the audit documentation, provided such disclosure does not undermine the effectiveness and integrity of the audit process.

---

[13] Paragraph .50 of QC section 10.

.A30

Exhibit—Audit Documentation Requirements in Other AU-C Sections

The following lists the main paragraphs in other AU-C sections that contain specific documentation requirements. This list is not a substitute for knowledge of the AU-C sections:

a. Paragraphs .10, .13, and .16 of section 210, *Terms of Engagement*

b. Paragraphs .25–.26 of section 220, *Quality Control for an Engagement Conducted in Accordance With Generally Accepted Auditing Standards*

c. Paragraphs .43–.46 of section 240, *Consideration of Fraud in a Financial Statement Audit*

d. Paragraph .28 of section 250, *Consideration of Laws and Regulations in an Audit of Financial Statements*

e. Paragraph .20 of section 260, *The Auditor's Communication With Those Charged With Governance*

f. Paragraph .12 of section 265, *Communicating Internal Control Related Matters Identified in an Audit*

g. Paragraph .14 of section 300, *Planning an Audit*

h. Paragraph .33 of section 315, *Understanding the Entity and Its Environment and Assessing the Risks of Material Misstatement*

i. Paragraph .14 of section 320, *Materiality in Planning and Performing an Audit*

j. Paragraphs .30–.33 of section 330, *Performing Audit Procedures in Response to Assessed Risks and Evaluating the Audit Evidence Obtained*

k. Paragraph .12 of section 450, *Evaluation of Misstatements Identified During the Audit*

l. Paragraph .20 of section 501, *Audit Evidence—Specific Considerations for Selected Items*

m. Paragraph .08 of section 520, *Analytical Procedures*

n. Paragraph .22 of section 540, *Auditing Accounting Estimates, Including Fair Value Accounting Estimates, and Related Disclosures*

o. Paragraph .28 of section 550, *Related Parties*

p. Paragraph .22 of section 570, *The Auditor's Consideration of an Entity's Ability to Continue as a Going Concern*

q. Paragraphs .49 and .64 of section 600, *Special Considerations—Audits of Group Financial Statements (Including the Work of Component Auditors)*

r. Paragraph .13 of section 915, *Reports on Application of Requirements of an Applicable Financial Reporting Framework*

s. Paragraphs .42–.43 of section 930, *Interim Financial Information*

t. Paragraphs .39–.42 of section 935, *Compliance Audits*

[Revised, August 2012, to reflect conforming changes necessary due to the issuance of SAS No. 126.]

AU-C Section 9230 *

Audit Documentation: Auditing Interpretations of Section 230

1. Providing Access to or Copies of Audit Documentation to a Regulator [1,2]

.01 *Question*—Paragraph .19 of section 230, *Audit Documentation*, states that "the auditor should adopt reasonable procedures to maintain the confidentiality of client information." However, auditors are sometimes required by law, regulation, or audit contract[3] to provide a regulator, or a duly appointed representative, access to audit documentation. For example, a regulator may request access to the audit documentation to fulfill a quality review requirement or to assist in establishing the scope of a regulatory examination. Furthermore, as part of the regulator's review of the audit documentation, the regulator may request copies of all or selected portions of the audit documentation during or after the review. The regulator may intend, or decide, to make copies (or information derived from the audit documentation) available to others, including other governmental agencies, for their particular purposes, with or without the knowledge of the auditor or the client. When a regulator requests the auditor to provide access to (and possibly copies of) audit documentation pursuant to law, regulation, or audit contract, what steps may the auditor take?

.02 *Interpretation*—When a regulator requests access to audit documentation pursuant to law, regulation, or audit contract, the auditor may take the following steps:

a. Consider advising the client that the regulator has requested access to (and possibly copies of) the audit documentation and that the auditor intends to comply with such request.[4]

---

* This section has been codified using an "AU-C" identifier instead of an "AU" identifier. "AU-C" is a temporary identifier to avoid confusion with references to existing "AU" sections, which will remain in AICPA *Professional Standards* through 2013. The "AU-C" identifier will revert to "AU" in 2014, by which time substantially all engagements for which the "AU" sections were still effective are expected to be completed.

[1] The term *regulator(s)* includes federal, state, and local government officials with legal oversight authority over the entity. Examples of regulators who may request access to audit documentation include, but are not limited to, state insurance and utility regulators, various health care authorities, and federal agencies such as the Federal Deposit Insurance Corporation, the Department of Housing and Urban Development, the Department of Labor, and the Rural Electrification Administration.

[2] The guidance in this interpretation does not apply to requests from the IRS, firm practice-monitoring programs to comply with AICPA or state professional requirements such as peer or quality reviews, proceedings relating to alleged ethics violations, or subpoenas.

[3] Paragraphs .11–.15 of this interpretation address situations in which the auditor is not required by law, regulation, or audit contract to provide a regulator access to the audit documentation.

[4] The auditor may wish (and in some cases may be required by law, regulation, or audit contract) to confirm in writing with the client that the auditor may be required to provide a regulator access to the audit documentation. Sample language that may be used follows:

> The audit documentation for this engagement is the property of [*name of auditor*] and constitutes confidential information. However, we may be requested to make certain audit documentation

(continued)

b. Make appropriate arrangements with the regulator for the review.

c. Maintain control over the audit documentation, and

d. Consider submitting the letter described in paragraph .05 of this interpretation to the regulator.

.03 Making appropriate arrangements with the regulator may include establishing the specific details such as the date, time, and location of the review. The audit documentation may be made available to a regulator at the offices of the client, the auditor, or a mutually agreed-upon location. However, maintaining control of audit documentation is necessary in order for the auditor to maintain the integrity of the audit documentation and the confidentiality of client information. For example, the auditor (or the auditor's representative) may be present when the audit documentation is reviewed by the regulator.

.04 Ordinarily, the auditor may not agree to transfer ownership of the audit documentation to a regulator. Furthermore, the auditor may not agree, without client authorization, that the information contained therein about the client may be communicated to or made available to any other party. In this regard, the action of an auditor providing access to, or copies of, the audit documentation shall not constitute transfer of ownership or authorization to make them available to any other party.

.05 An audit performed in accordance with generally accepted auditing standards is not intended to, and does not, satisfy a regulator's oversight responsibilities. To avoid any misunderstanding, prior to allowing a regulator access to the audit documentation, the auditor may submit a letter to the regulator that

a. sets forth the auditor's understanding of the purpose for which access is being requested;

b. describes the audit process and the limitations inherent in a financial statement audit;

c. explains the purpose for which the audit documentation was prepared, and that any individual conclusions must be read in the context of the auditor's report on the financial statements;

d. states, except when not applicable, that the audit was not planned or conducted in contemplation of the purpose for which access is being granted or to assess the entity's compliance with laws and regulations;

e. states that the audit and the audit documentation should not supplant other inquiries and procedures that should be undertaken by the regulator for its purposes;

f. requests confidential treatment under the Freedom of Information Act or similar laws and regulations,[5] when a request for the audit documentation is made, and that written notice be given to the auditor before transmitting any information contained in

---

(footnote continued)

available to [*name of regulator*] pursuant to authority given to it by law or regulation. If requested, access to such audit documentation will be provided under the supervision of [*name of auditor*] personnel. Furthermore, upon request, we may provide copies of selected audit documentation to [*name of regulator*]. The [*name of regulator*] may intend, or decide, to distribute the copies or information contained therein to others, including other governmental agencies.

[5] The auditor may need to consult the regulations of individual agencies and, if necessary, consult with legal counsel regarding the specific procedures and requirements necessary to gain confidential treatment.

the audit documentation to others, including other governmental agencies, except when such transfer is required by law or regulation; and

g. states that if any copies are to be provided, they will be identified as "Confidential Treatment Requested by [*name of auditor, address, telephone number*]."

The auditor may obtain a signed acknowledgment copy of the letter as evidence of the regulator's receipt of the letter.

.06 An example of a letter containing the elements described in paragraph .05 of this interpretation is presented as follows:

Illustrative Letter to Regulator[6]

[*Date*]

[*Name and Address of Regulatory Agency*]

Your representatives have requested access to our audit documentation in connection with our audit of the December 31, 20XX, financial statements of [*name of client*]. It is our understanding that the purpose of your request is [*state purpose: for example, "to facilitate your regulatory examination"*].[7]

Our audit of [*name of client*] December 31, 20XX, financial statements was conducted in accordance with auditing standards generally accepted in the United States of America,[8] the objective[9] of which is to form an opinion as to whether the financial statements, which are the responsibility and representations of management, present fairly, in all material respects, the financial position, results of operations, and cash flows in conformity with generally accepted accounting principles.[10] Under generally accepted auditing standards, we have the responsibility, within the inherent limitations of the auditing process, to design our audit to provide reasonable assurance that errors and fraud that have a material effect on the financial statements will be detected, and to exercise due care in the conduct of our audit. The concept of selective testing of the data being audited, which involves judgment both as to the number of transactions to be audited and as to the areas to be tested, has been generally accepted as a valid and sufficient basis for an auditor to express an opinion on financial statements. Thus, our audit, based on the concept of selective testing, is subject to the inherent risk that material errors or fraud, if they exist, would not be detected. In addition, an audit does not address the possibility that material errors or fraud may occur in the future. Also, our use of professional judgment and

---

[6] This letter may be modified appropriately when the audit has been performed in accordance with generally accepted auditing standards and also in accordance with additional auditing requirements specified by a regulatory agency (for example, the requirements specified in *Government Auditing Standards* issued by the Comptroller General of the United States).

[7] If the auditor is not required by law, regulation, or audit contract to provide a regulator access to the audit documentation but otherwise intends to provide such access (see paragraphs .11–.15 of this interpretation), the letter may include a statement that "Management of [*name of client*] has authorized us to provide you access to our audit documentation for [*state purpose*]."

[8] See footnote 6.

[9] In an audit performed in accordance with the Single Audit Act of 1984, the Single Audit Act Amendments of 1996, and certain other federal audit requirements, an additional objective of the audit is to assess compliance with laws and regulations applicable to federal financial assistance. Accordingly, in these situations, the illustrative letter provided in this interpretation may be modified to include the additional objective.

[10] If the financial statements have been prepared in conformity with regulatory accounting practices, the phrase "financial position, results of operations, and cash flows in conformity with generally accepted accounting principles" may be replaced with appropriate wording such as, in the case of an insurance company, the "admitted assets, liabilities . . . of the XYZ Insurance Company in conformity with accounting practices prescribed or permitted by the state of . . . insurance department."

the assessment of materiality for the purpose of our audit means that matters may have existed that would have been assessed differently by you.

The audit documentation was prepared for the purpose of providing a sufficient and appropriate record of the basis for our report on [*name of client*] December 31, 20XX, financial statements and to aid in the conduct and supervision of our audit. The audit documentation is the principal record of auditing procedures performed, evidence obtained, and conclusions reached in the engagement. The auditing procedures that we performed were limited to those we considered necessary under generally accepted auditing standards[11] to enable us to formulate and express an opinion on the financial statements[12] taken as a whole. Accordingly, we make no representation as to the sufficiency or appropriateness, for your purposes, of either the information contained in our audit documentation or our auditing procedures. In addition, any notations, comments, and individual conclusions appearing on any of the audit documents do not stand alone, and should not be read as an opinion on any individual amounts, accounts, balances or transactions.

Our audit of [*name of client*] December 31, 20XX, financial statements was performed for the purpose stated above and has not been planned or conducted in contemplation of your [*state purpose: for example, "regulatory examination"*] or for the purpose of assessing [*name of client*] compliance with laws and regulations.[13] Therefore, items of possible interest to you may not have been specifically addressed. Accordingly, our audit and the audit documentation prepared in connection therewith, should not supplant other inquiries and procedures that should be undertaken by the [*name of regulatory agency*] for the purpose of monitoring and regulating the financial affairs of the [*name of client*]. In addition, we have not audited any financial statements of [*name of client*] since [*date of audited balance sheet referred to in the first paragraph above*] nor have we performed any auditing procedures since [*date*], the date of our auditor's report, and significant events or circumstances may have occurred since that date.

The audit documentation constitutes and reflects work performed or evidence obtained by [*name of auditor*] in its capacity as independent auditor for [*name of client*]. The documents contain trade secrets and confidential commercial and financial information of our firm and [*name of client*] that is privileged and confidential, and we expressly reserve all rights with respect to disclosures to third parties. Accordingly, we request confidential treatment under the Freedom of Information Act or similar laws and regulations[14] when requests are made for the audit documentation or information contained therein or any documents created by the [*name of regulatory agency*] containing information derived therefrom. We further request that written notice be given to our firm before distribution of the information in the audit documentation (or copies thereof) to others, including other governmental agencies, except when such distribution is required by law or regulation.

---

[11] See footnote 6

[12] See footnote 9.

[13] See footnote 9.

[14] This illustrative paragraph may not in and of itself be sufficient to gain confidential treatment under the rules and regulations of certain regulatory agencies. The auditor may tailor this paragraph to the circumstances after consulting the regulations of each applicable regulatory agency and, if necessary, may consult with legal counsel regarding the specific procedures and requirements to gain confidential treatment.

[*If it is expected that copies will be requested, add:*

Any copies of our audit documentation we agree to provide you will be identified as "Confidential Treatment Requested by [*name of auditor, address, telephone number*]."]

[*Firm signature*]

.07 *Question*—A regulator may request access to the audit documentation before the audit has been completed and the report released. May the auditor allow access in such circumstances?

.08 *Interpretation*—When the audit has not been completed, the audit documentation is necessarily incomplete because (*a*) additional information may be added as a result of further tests and review by supervisory personnel and (*b*) any audit results and conclusions reflected in the incomplete audit documentation may change. Accordingly, it is preferable that access be delayed until all auditing procedures have been completed and all internal reviews have been performed. If access is provided prior to completion of the audit, the auditor may issue the letter referred to in paragraph .05 of this interpretation, appropriately modified, and including additional language along the following lines:

> We have been engaged to audit in accordance with auditing standards generally accepted in the United States of America the December 31, 20XX, financial statements of XYZ Company, but have not as yet completed our audit. Accordingly, at this time we do not express any opinion on the Company's financial statements. Furthermore, the contents of the audit documentation may change as a result of additional auditing procedures and review of the audit documentation by supervisory personnel of our firm. Accordingly, our audit documentation is incomplete.

Because the audit documentation may change prior to completion of the audit, it is preferable that the auditor not provide copies of the audit documentation until the audit has been completed.

.09 *Question*—Some regulators may engage an independent party, such as another independent public accountant, to perform the audit documentation review on behalf of the regulatory agency. Are there any special precautions the auditor may observe in these circumstances?

.10 *Interpretation*—The auditor may obtain acknowledgment, preferably in writing, from the regulator stating that the third party is acting on behalf of the regulator and agreement from the third party that he or she is subject to the same restrictions on disclosure and use of audit documentation and the information contained therein as the regulator.

.11 *Question*—When a regulator requests the auditor to provide access to (and possibly copies of) audit documentation and the auditor is not otherwise required by law, regulation, or audit contract to provide such access, what steps may the auditor take?

.12 *Interpretation*—The auditor may obtain an understanding of the reasons for the regulator's request for access to the audit documentation and may consider consulting with legal counsel regarding the request. If the auditor decides to provide such access, reasonable procedures to maintain the confidentiality of client information include obtaining the client's consent, preferably in writing, to provide the regulator access to the audit documentation.

.13 Following is an example of language that may be used in the written communication to the client:

> The audit documentation for this engagement is the property of [*name of auditor*] and constitutes confidential information. However, we have been requested

to make certain audit documentation available to [*name of regulator*] for [*describe the regulator's basis for its request*]. Access to such audit documentation will be provided under the supervision of [*name of auditor*] personnel. Furthermore, upon request, we may provide copies of selected audit documentation to [*name of regulator*].

You have authorized [*name of auditor*] to allow [*name of regulator*] access to the audit documentation in the manner discussed above. Please confirm your agreement to the above by signing below and returning to [*name of auditor, address*].

[*Firm signature*]

Agreed and acknowledged:

[*Name and title*]

[*Date*]

.14 If the client requests to review the audit documentation before allowing the regulator access, the auditor may provide the client with the opportunity to obtain an understanding of the nature of the information about its financial statements contained in the audit documentation that is being made available to the regulator. When a client reviews the audit documentation, the need to maintain control of the audit documentation is as discussed in paragraph .03 of this interpretation.

.15 The guidance in paragraphs .03–.10 of this interpretation, which provide guidance on making arrangements with the regulator for access to the audit documentation, maintaining control over the audit documentation, and submitting a letter describing various matters to the regulator, is also applicable.

[Issue Date: July, 1994; Revised: June, 1996; Revised: October, 2000; Revised: January, 2002; Revised: December, 2005; Revised: October, 2011, effective for audits of financial statements for periods ending on or after December 15, 2012.]

AU-C Section 240 *

Consideration of Fraud in a Financial Statement Audit

Source: SAS No. 122.

Effective for audits of financial statements for periods ending on or after December 15, 2012.

Introduction

Scope of This Section

.01 This section addresses the auditor's responsibilities relating to fraud in an audit of financial statements. Specifically, it expands on how section 315, *Understanding the Entity and Its Environment and Assessing the Risks of Material Misstatement*, and section 330, *Performing Audit Procedures in Response to Assessed Risks and Evaluating the Audit Evidence Obtained*, are to be applied regarding risks of material misstatement due to fraud.

Characteristics of Fraud

.02 Misstatements in the financial statements can arise from either fraud or error. The distinguishing factor between fraud and error is whether the underlying action that results in the misstatement of the financial statements is intentional or unintentional.

.03 Although fraud is a broad legal concept, for the purposes of generally accepted auditing standards (GAAS), the auditor is primarily concerned with fraud that causes a material misstatement in the financial statements. Two types of intentional misstatements are relevant to the auditor—misstatements resulting from fraudulent financial reporting and misstatements resulting from misappropriation of assets. Although the auditor may suspect or, in rare cases, identify the occurrence of fraud, the auditor does not make legal determinations of whether fraud has actually occurred. (Ref: par. .A1–.A8)

Responsibility for the Prevention and Detection of Fraud

.04 The primary responsibility for the prevention and detection of fraud rests with both those charged with governance of the entity and management. It is important that management, with the oversight of those charged with governance, places a strong emphasis on fraud prevention, which may reduce opportunities for fraud to take place, and fraud deterrence, which could persuade individuals not to commit fraud because of the likelihood of detection and punishment. This involves a commitment to creating a culture of honesty and ethical behavior, which can be reinforced by active oversight by those

---

* This section has been codified using an "AU-C" identifier instead of an "AU" identifier. "AU-C" is a temporary identifier to avoid confusion with references to existing "AU" sections, which will remain in AICPA *Professional Standards* through 2013. The "AU-C" identifier will revert to "AU" in 2014, by which time substantially all engagements for which the "AU" sections were still effective are expected to be completed.

charged with governance. Oversight by those charged with governance includes considering the potential for override of controls or other inappropriate influence over the financial reporting process, such as efforts by management to manage earnings in order to influence the perceptions of financial statement users regarding the entity's performance and profitability.

Responsibilities of the Auditor

.05 An auditor conducting an audit in accordance with GAAS is responsible for obtaining reasonable assurance that the financial statements as a whole are free from material misstatement, whether caused by fraud or error. Due to the inherent limitations of an audit, an unavoidable risk exists that some material misstatements of the financial statements may not be detected, even though the audit is properly planned and performed in accordance with GAAS.[1]

.06 As described in section 200, *Overall Objectives of the Independent Auditor and the Conduct of an Audit in Accordance With Generally Accepted Auditing Standards*, the potential effects of inherent limitations are particularly significant in the case of misstatement resulting from fraud.[2] The risk of not detecting a material misstatement resulting from fraud is higher than the risk of not detecting one resulting from error. This is because fraud may involve sophisticated and carefully organized schemes designed to conceal it, such as forgery, deliberate failure to record transactions, or intentional misrepresentations being made to the auditor. Such attempts at concealment may be even more difficult to detect when accompanied by collusion. Collusion may cause the auditor to believe that audit evidence is persuasive when it is, in fact, false. The auditor's ability to detect a fraud depends on factors such as the skillfulness of the perpetrator, the frequency and extent of manipulation, the degree of collusion involved, the relative size of individual amounts manipulated, and the seniority of those individuals involved. Although the auditor may be able to identify potential opportunities for fraud to be perpetrated, it is difficult for the auditor to determine whether misstatements in judgment areas, such as accounting estimates, are caused by fraud or error.

.07 Furthermore, the risk of the auditor not detecting a material misstatement resulting from management fraud is greater than for employee fraud because management is frequently in a position to directly or indirectly manipulate accounting records, present fraudulent financial information, or override control procedures designed to prevent similar frauds by other employees.

.08 When obtaining reasonable assurance, the auditor is responsible for maintaining professional skepticism throughout the audit, considering the potential for management override of controls, and recognizing the fact that audit procedures that are effective for detecting error may not be effective in detecting fraud. The requirements in this section are designed to assist the auditor in identifying and assessing the risks of material misstatement due to fraud and in designing procedures to detect such misstatement.

Effective Date

.09 This section is effective for audits of financial statements for periods ending on or after December 15, 2012.

---

[1] Paragraphs .A55–.A56 of section 200, *Overall Objectives of the Independent Auditor and the Conduct of an Audit in Accordance With Generally Accepted Auditing Standards.*

[2] Paragraph .A55 of section 200.

Objectives

.10 The objectives of the auditor are to

a. identify and assess the risks of material misstatement of the financial statements due to fraud;

b. obtain sufficient appropriate audit evidence regarding the assessed risks of material misstatement due to fraud, through designing and implementing appropriate responses; and

c. respond appropriately to fraud or suspected fraud identified during the audit.

Definitions

.11 For purposes of GAAS, the following terms have the meanings attributed as follows:

Fraud. An intentional act by one or more individuals among management, those charged with governance, employees, or third parties, involving the use of deception that results in a misstatement in financial statements that are the subject of an audit.

Fraud risk factors. Events or conditions that indicate an incentive or pressure to perpetrate fraud, provide an opportunity to commit fraud, or indicate attitudes or rationalizations to justify a fraudulent action. (Ref: par. .A11, .A30, and .A56)

Requirements

Professional Skepticism

.12 In accordance with section 200, the auditor should maintain professional skepticism throughout the audit, recognizing the possibility that a material misstatement due to fraud could exist, notwithstanding the auditor's past experience of the honesty and integrity of the entity's management and those charged with governance.[3] (Ref: par. .A9–.A10)

.13 Unless the auditor has reason to believe the contrary, the auditor may accept records and documents as genuine. If conditions identified during the audit cause the auditor to believe that a document may not be authentic or that terms in a document have been modified but not disclosed to the auditor, the auditor should investigate further. (Ref: par. .A11)

.14 When responses to inquiries of management, those charged with governance, or others are inconsistent or otherwise unsatisfactory (for example, vague or implausible), the auditor should further investigate the inconsistencies or unsatisfactory responses.

Discussion Among the Engagement Team

.15 Section 315 requires a discussion among the key engagement team members, including the engagement partner, and a determination by the engagement partner of which matters are to be communicated to those team

---

[3] Paragraph .17 of section 200.

members not involved in the discussion.[4] This discussion should include an exchange of ideas or brainstorming among the engagement team members about how and where the entity's financial statements might be susceptible to material misstatement due to fraud, how management could perpetrate and conceal fraudulent financial reporting, and how assets of the entity could be misappropriated. The discussion should occur setting aside beliefs that the engagement team members may have that management and those charged with governance are honest and have integrity, and should, in particular, also address (Ref: par. .A12–.A13)

a. known external and internal factors affecting the entity that may create an incentive or pressure for management or others to commit fraud, provide the opportunity for fraud to be perpetrated, and indicate a culture or environment that enables management or others to rationalize committing fraud;

b. the risk of management override of controls;

c. consideration of circumstances that might be indicative of earnings management or manipulation of other financial measures and the practices that might be followed by management to manage earnings or other financial measures that could lead to fraudulent financial reporting;

d. the importance of maintaining professional skepticism throughout the audit regarding the potential for material misstatement due to fraud; and

e. how the auditor might respond to the susceptibility of the entity's financial statements to material misstatement due to fraud.

Communication among the engagement team members about the risks of material misstatement due to fraud should continue throughout the audit, particularly upon discovery of new facts during the audit.

Risk Assessment Procedures and Related Activities

.16 When performing risk assessment procedures and related activities to obtain an understanding of the entity and its environment, including the entity's internal control, required by section 315, the auditor should perform the procedures in paragraphs .17–.24 to obtain information for use in identifying the risks of material misstatement due to fraud.[5]

Discussions With Management and Others Within the Entity

.17 The auditor should make inquiries of management regarding

a. management's assessment of the risk that the financial statements may be materially misstated due to fraud, including the nature, extent, and frequency of such assessments; (Ref: par. .A14–.A15)

b. management's process for identifying, responding to, and monitoring the risks of fraud in the entity, including any specific risks of fraud that management has identified or that have been brought to its attention, or classes of transactions, account balances, or disclosures for which a risk of fraud is likely to exist; (Ref: par. .A16)

---

[4] Paragraph .11 of section 315, *Understanding the Entity and Its Environment and Assessing the Risks of Material Misstatement*.

[5] Paragraphs .05–.25 of section 315.

c. management's communication, if any, to those charged with governance regarding its processes for identifying and responding to the risks of fraud in the entity; and

d. management's communication, if any, to employees regarding its views on business practices and ethical behavior.

.18 The auditor should make inquiries of management, and others within the entity as appropriate, to determine whether they have knowledge of any actual, suspected, or alleged fraud affecting the entity. (Ref: par. .A17–.A20)

.19 For those entities that have an internal audit function,[6] the auditor should make inquiries of internal audit to obtain its views about the risks of fraud; determine whether it has knowledge of any actual, suspected, or alleged fraud affecting the entity; whether it has performed any procedures to identify or detect fraud during the year; and whether management has satisfactorily responded to any findings resulting from these procedures.

Those Charged With Governance

.20 Unless all of those charged with governance are involved in managing the entity,[7] the auditor should obtain an understanding of how those charged with governance exercise oversight of management's processes for identifying and responding to the risks of fraud in the entity and the internal control that management has established to mitigate these risks. (Ref: par. .A21–.A23)

.21 Unless all of those charged with governance are involved in managing the entity, the auditor should make inquiries of those charged with governance (or the audit committee or, at least, its chair) to determine their views about the risks of fraud and whether they have knowledge of any actual, suspected, or alleged fraud affecting the entity. These inquiries are made, in part, to corroborate the responses received from the inquiries of management.

Unusual or Unexpected Relationships Identified

.22 Based on analytical procedures performed as part of risk assessment procedures,[8] the auditor should evaluate whether unusual or unexpected relationships that have been identified indicate risks of material misstatement due to fraud. To the extent not already included, the analytical procedures, and evaluation thereof, should include procedures relating to revenue accounts. (Ref: par. .A24–.A26 and .A46)

Other Information

.23 The auditor should consider whether other information obtained by the auditor indicates risks of material misstatement due to fraud. (Ref: par. .A27)

---

[6] Section 610, *The Auditor's Consideration of the Internal Audit Function in an Audit of Financial Statements* , provides guidance in audits of those entities that have an internal audit function. Statement on Auditing Standards (SAS) No. 65, *The Auditor's Consideration of the Internal Audit Function in an Audit of Financial Statements*, is currently effective and codified as AU section 322. SAS No. 65 has been included in section 610, as designated by SAS No. 122, *Statements on Auditing Standards: Clarification and Recodification*, and will be superseded when it is redrafted for clarity and convergence with International Standard on Auditing 610 (Revised), *Using the Work of Internal Auditors*, as part of the Clarification and Convergence project of the Auditing Standards Board. Until such time, section 610 has been conformed to reflect updated section and paragraph cross references but has not otherwise been subjected to a comprehensive review or revision.

[7] Paragraph .09 of section 260, *The Auditor's Communication With Those Charged With Governance*.

[8] Paragraphs .06(*b*) and .A7–.A10 of section 315.

Evaluation of Fraud Risk Factors

.24 The auditor should evaluate whether the information obtained from the risk assessment procedures and related activities performed indicates that one or more fraud risk factors are present. Although fraud risk factors may not necessarily indicate the existence of fraud, they have often been present in circumstances in which frauds have occurred and, therefore, may indicate risks of material misstatement due to fraud. (Ref: par. .A28–.A32)

Identification and Assessment of the Risks of Material Misstatement Due to Fraud

.25 In accordance with section 315, the auditor should identify and assess the risks of material misstatement due to fraud at the financial statement level, and at the assertion level for classes of transactions, account balances, and disclosures.[9] The auditor's risk assessment should be ongoing throughout the audit, following the initial assessment.

.26 When identifying and assessing the risks of material misstatement due to fraud, the auditor should, based on a presumption that risks of fraud exist in revenue recognition, evaluate which types of revenue, revenue transactions, or assertions give rise to such risks. Paragraph .46 specifies the documentation required when the auditor concludes that the presumption is not applicable in the circumstances of the engagement and, accordingly, has not identified revenue recognition as a risk of material misstatement due to fraud. (Ref: par. .A33–.A35)

.27 The auditor should treat those assessed risks of material misstatement due to fraud as significant risks and, accordingly, to the extent not already done so, the auditor should obtain an understanding of the entity's related controls, including control activities, relevant to such risks, including the evaluation of whether such controls have been suitably designed and implemented to mitigate such fraud risks. (Ref: par. .A36–.A37)

Responses to the Assessed Risks of Material Misstatement Due to Fraud

Overall Responses

.28 In accordance with section 330, the auditor should determine overall responses to address the assessed risks of material misstatement due to fraud at the financial statement level.[10] (Ref: par. .A38)

.29 In determining overall responses to address the assessed risks of material misstatement due to fraud at the financial statement level, the auditor should

a. assign and supervise personnel, taking into account the knowledge, skill, and ability of the individuals to be given significant engagement responsibilities and the auditor's assessment of the risks of material misstatement due to fraud for the engagement; (Ref: par. .A39–.A40)

---

[9] Paragraph .26 of section 315.

[10] Paragraph .05 of section 330, *Performing Audit Procedures in Response to Assessed Risks and Evaluating the Audit Evidence Obtained.*

b. evaluate whether the selection and application of accounting policies by the entity, particularly those related to subjective measurements and complex transactions, may be indicative of fraudulent financial reporting resulting from management's effort to manage earnings, or a bias that may create a material misstatement; and (Ref: par. .A41)

c. incorporate an element of unpredictability in the selection of the nature, timing, and extent of audit procedures. (Ref: par. .A42)

Audit Procedures Responsive to Assessed Risks of Material Misstatement Due to Fraud at the Assertion Level

.30 In accordance with section 330, the auditor should design and perform further audit procedures whose nature, timing, and extent are responsive to the assessed risks of material misstatement due to fraud at the assertion level.[11] (Ref: par. .A43–.A46)

Audit Procedures Responsive to Risks Related to Management Override of Controls

.31 Management is in a unique position to perpetrate fraud because of management's ability to manipulate accounting records and prepare fraudulent financial statements by overriding controls that otherwise appear to be operating effectively. Although the level of risk of management override of controls will vary from entity to entity, the risk is, nevertheless, present in all entities. Due to the unpredictable way in which such override could occur, it is a risk of material misstatement due to fraud and, thus, a significant risk.

.32 Even if specific risks of material misstatement due to fraud are not identified by the auditor, a possibility exists that management override of controls could occur. Accordingly, the auditor should address the risk of management override of controls apart from any conclusions regarding the existence of more specifically identifiable risks by designing and performing audit procedures to

a. test the appropriateness of journal entries recorded in the general ledger and other adjustments made in the preparation of the financial statements, including entries posted directly to financial statement drafts. In designing and performing audit procedures for such tests, the auditor should (Ref: par. .A47–.A50 and .A55)

  i. obtain an understanding of the entity's financial reporting process and controls over journal entries and other adjustments,[12] and the suitability of design and implementation of such controls;

  ii. make inquiries of individuals involved in the financial reporting process about inappropriate or unusual activity relating to the processing of journal entries and other adjustments;

  iii. consider fraud risk indicators, the nature and complexity of accounts, and entries processed outside the normal course of business;

  iv. select journal entries and other adjustments made at the end of a reporting period; and

---

[11] Paragraph .06 of section 330.

[12] Paragraph .19 of section 315.

v. consider the need to test journal entries and other adjustments throughout the period.

b. review accounting estimates for biases and evaluate whether the circumstances producing the bias, if any, represent a risk of material misstatement due to fraud. In performing this review, the auditor should

i. evaluate whether the judgments and decisions made by management in making the accounting estimates included in the financial statements, even if they are individually reasonable, indicate a possible bias on the part of the entity's management that may represent a risk of material misstatement due to fraud. If so, the auditor should reevaluate the accounting estimates taken as a whole, and

ii. perform a retrospective review of management judgments and assumptions related to significant accounting estimates reflected in the financial statements of the prior year. Estimates selected for review should include those that are based on highly sensitive assumptions or are otherwise significantly affected by judgments made by management. (Ref: par. .A51–.A53)

c. evaluate, for significant transactions that are outside the normal course of business for the entity or that otherwise appear to be unusual given the auditor's understanding of the entity and its environment and other information obtained during the audit, whether the business rationale (or the lack thereof) of the transactions suggests that they may have been entered into to engage in fraudulent financial reporting or to conceal misappropriation of assets. (Ref: par. .A54)

Other Audit Procedures

.33 The auditor should determine whether, in order to respond to the identified risks of management override of controls, the auditor needs to perform other audit procedures in addition to those specifically referred to previously (that is, when specific additional risks of management override exist that are not covered as part of the procedures performed to address the requirements in paragraph .32). (Ref: par. .A55)

Evaluation of Audit Evidence (Ref: par. .A56)

.34 The auditor should evaluate, at or near the end of the audit, whether the accumulated results of auditing procedures (including analytical procedures that were performed as substantive tests or when forming an overall conclusion) affect the assessment of the risks of material misstatement due to fraud made earlier in the audit or indicate a previously unrecognized risk of material misstatement due to fraud. If not already performed when forming an overall conclusion, the analytical procedures relating to revenue, required by paragraph .22, should be performed through the end of the reporting period. (Ref: par. .A57–.A58)

.35 If the auditor identifies a misstatement, the auditor should evaluate whether such a misstatement is indicative of fraud. If such an indication exists, the auditor should evaluate the implications of the misstatement with regard to other aspects of the audit, particularly the auditor's evaluation of materiality, management and employee integrity, and the reliability of management representations, recognizing that an instance of fraud is unlikely to be an isolated occurrence. (Ref: par. .A59–.A62)

.36 If the auditor identifies a misstatement, whether material or not, and the auditor has reason to believe that it is, or may be, the result of fraud and that management (in particular, senior management) is involved, the auditor should reevaluate the assessment of the risks of material misstatement due to fraud and its resulting effect on the nature, timing, and extent of audit procedures to respond to the assessed risks. The auditor should also consider whether circumstances or conditions indicate possible collusion involving employees, management, or third parties when reconsidering the reliability of evidence previously obtained. (Ref: par. .A60)

.37 If the auditor concludes that, or is unable to conclude whether, the financial statements are materially misstated as a result of fraud, the auditor should evaluate the implications for the audit. (Ref: par. .A61)

Auditor Unable to Continue the Engagement

.38 If, as a result of identified fraud or suspected fraud, the auditor encounters circumstances that bring into question the auditor's ability to continue performing the audit, the auditor should

a. determine the professional and legal responsibilities applicable in the circumstances, including whether a requirement exists for the auditor to report to the person or persons who engaged the auditor or, in some cases, to regulatory authorities;

b. consider whether it is appropriate to withdraw from the engagement, when withdrawal is possible under applicable law or regulation; and

c. if the auditor withdraws

  i. discuss with the appropriate level of management and those charged with governance the auditor's withdrawal from the engagement and the reasons for the withdrawal, and

  ii. determine whether a professional or legal requirement exists to report to the person or persons who engaged the auditor or, in some cases, to regulatory authorities, the auditor's withdrawal from the engagement and the reasons for the withdrawal. (Ref: par. .A63–.A66)

Communications to Management and With Those Charged With Governance

.39 If the auditor has identified a fraud or has obtained information that indicates that a fraud may exist, the auditor should communicate these matters on a timely basis to the appropriate level of management in order to inform those with primary responsibility for the prevention and detection of fraud of matters relevant to their responsibilities. (Ref: par. .A67)

.40 Unless all of those charged with governance are involved in managing the entity, if the auditor has identified or suspects fraud involving

a. management,

b. employees who have significant roles in internal control, or

c. others, when the fraud results in a material misstatement in the financial statements, the auditor should communicate these matters to those charged with governance on a timely basis. If the auditor suspects fraud involving management, the auditor should communicate these suspicions to those charged with governance and discuss with them the nature, timing, and extent of audit procedures necessary to complete the audit. (Ref: par. .A68–.A70)

.41 The auditor should communicate with those charged with governance any other matters related to fraud that are, in the auditor's professional judgment, relevant to their responsibilities. (Ref: par. .A71)

Communications to Regulatory and Enforcement Authorities

.42 If the auditor has identified or suspects a fraud, the auditor should determine whether the auditor has a responsibility to report the occurrence or suspicion to a party outside the entity. Although the auditor's professional duty to maintain the confidentiality of client information may preclude such reporting, the auditor's legal responsibilities may override the duty of confidentiality in some circumstances. (Ref: par. .A72–.A74)

Documentation

.43 The auditor should include in the audit documentation[13] of the auditor's understanding of the entity and its environment and the assessment of the risks of material misstatement required by section 315 the following:[14]

a. The significant decisions reached during the discussion among the engagement team regarding the susceptibility of the entity's financial statements to material misstatement due to fraud, and how and when the discussion occurred and the audit team members who participated

b. The identified and assessed risks of material misstatement due to fraud at the financial statement level and at the assertion level (See paragraphs .16–.27.)

.44 The auditor should include in the audit documentation of the auditor's responses to the assessed risks of material misstatement required by section 330 the following:[15]

a. The overall responses to the assessed risks of material misstatement due to fraud at the financial statement level and the nature, timing, and extent of audit procedures, and the linkage of those procedures with the assessed risks of material misstatement due to fraud at the assertion level

b. The results of the audit procedures, including those designed to address the risk of management override of controls

.45 The auditor should include in the audit documentation communications about fraud made to management, those charged with governance, regulators, and others.

.46 If the auditor has concluded that the presumption that there is a risk of material misstatement due to fraud related to revenue recognition is overcome in the circumstances of the engagement, the auditor should include in the audit documentation the reasons for that conclusion.

---

[13] Paragraphs .08–.12 and .A8 of section 230, *Audit Documentation*.

[14] Paragraph .33 of section 315.

[15] Paragraph .30 of section 330.

Application and Other Explanatory Material

Characteristics of Fraud (Ref: par. .03)

.A1 Fraud, whether fraudulent financial reporting or misappropriation of assets, involves incentive or pressure to commit fraud, a perceived opportunity to do so, and some rationalization of the act, as follows:

- Incentive or pressure to commit fraudulent financial reporting may exist when management is under pressure, from sources outside or inside the entity, to achieve an expected (and perhaps, unrealistic) earnings target or financial outcome—particularly because the consequences to management for failing to meet financial goals can be significant. Similarly, individuals may have an incentive to misappropriate assets (for example, because the individuals are living beyond their means).
- A perceived opportunity to commit fraud may exist when an individual believes internal control can be overridden (for example, because the individual is in a position of trust or has knowledge of specific deficiencies in internal control).
- Individuals may be able to rationalize committing a fraudulent act. Some individuals possess an attitude, character, or set of ethical values that allow them knowingly and intentionally to commit a dishonest act. However, even otherwise honest individuals can commit fraud in an environment that imposes sufficient pressure on them.

.A2 Fraudulent financial reporting involves intentional misstatements, including omissions of amounts or disclosures in financial statements to deceive financial statement users. It can be caused by the efforts of management to manage earnings in order to deceive financial statement users by influencing their perceptions about the entity's performance and profitability. Such earnings management may start out with small actions or inappropriate adjustment of assumptions and changes in judgments by management. Pressures and incentives may lead these actions to increase to the extent that they result in fraudulent financial reporting. Such a situation could occur when, due to pressures to meet expectations or a desire to maximize compensation based on performance, management intentionally takes positions that lead to fraudulent financial reporting by materially misstating the financial statements. In some entities, management may be motivated to reduce earnings by a material amount to minimize tax or to inflate earnings to secure bank financing.

.A3 An auditor conducting an audit in accordance with GAAS is responsible for obtaining reasonable assurance about whether the financial statements as a whole are free from material misstatement, whether caused by fraud or error. Accordingly, the auditor is primarily concerned with fraud that causes a material misstatement of the financial statements. However, in conducting the audit, the auditor may identify misstatements arising from fraud that are not material to the financial statements. Paragraphs .35–.36 and .39–.42 address the auditor's responsibilities in such circumstances in evaluating audit evidence and in communicating audit findings, respectively.

.A4 Intent is often difficult to determine, particularly in matters involving accounting estimates and the application of accounting principles. For example, unreasonable accounting estimates may be unintentional or may be the result of an intentional attempt to misstate the financial statements. Although an audit is not designed to determine intent, the auditor's objective is to obtain reasonable assurance about whether the financial statements as a whole are free from material misstatement, whether due to fraud or error.[16]

.A5 Fraudulent financial reporting may be accomplished by the following:

- Manipulation, falsification (including forgery), or alteration of accounting records or supporting documentation from which the financial statements are prepared
- Misrepresentation in, or intentional omission from, the financial statements of events, transactions, or other significant information
- Intentional misapplication of accounting principles relating to amounts, classification, manner of presentation, or disclosure

.A6 Fraudulent financial reporting often involves management override of controls that otherwise may appear to be operating effectively. Fraud can be committed by management overriding controls using such techniques as the following:

- Recording fictitious journal entries, particularly close to the end of an accounting period, to manipulate operating results or achieve other objectives
- Inappropriately adjusting assumptions and changing judgments used to estimate account balances
- Omitting, advancing, or delaying recognition in the financial statements of events and transactions that have occurred during the reporting period
- Concealing, or not disclosing, facts that could affect the amounts recorded in the financial statements
- Engaging in complex transactions that are structured to misrepresent the financial position or financial performance of the entity
- Altering records and terms related to significant and unusual transactions

.A7 Misappropriation of assets involves the theft of an entity's assets and is often perpetrated by employees in relatively small and immaterial amounts. However, it can also involve management, who is usually better able to disguise or conceal misappropriations in ways that are difficult to detect. Misappropriation of assets can be accomplished in a variety of ways including the following:

- Embezzling receipts (for example, misappropriating collections on accounts receivable or diverting receipts from written-off accounts to personal bank accounts)
- Stealing physical assets or intellectual property (for example, stealing inventory for personal use or for sale, stealing scrap for resale, or colluding with a competitor by disclosing technological data in return for payment)
- Causing an entity to pay for goods and services not received (for example, payments to fictitious vendors, kickbacks paid by vendors to the entity's purchasing agents in return for approving payment at inflated prices, or payments to fictitious employees)

---

[16] Paragraph .12 of section 200.

- Using an entity's assets for personal use (for example, using the entity's assets as collateral for a personal loan or a loan to a related party)

Misappropriation of assets is often accompanied by false or misleading records or documents in order to conceal the fact that the assets are missing or have been pledged without proper authorization.

Considerations Specific to Governmental Entities and Not-for-Profit Organizations

.A8 The auditor of governmental entities and not-for-profit organizations may have additional responsibilities relating to fraud

- as a result of being engaged to conduct an audit in accordance with law or regulation applicable to governmental entities and not-for-profit organizations,
- because of a governmental audit organization's mandate, or
- because of the need to comply with *Government Auditing Standards*.

Consequently, the responsibilities of the auditor of governmental entities and not-for-profit organizations may not be limited to consideration of risks of material misstatement of the financial statements, but may also include a broader responsibility to consider risks of fraud.

Professional Skepticism (Ref: par. .12–.14)

.A9 Maintaining professional skepticism requires an ongoing questioning of whether the information and audit evidence obtained suggests that a material misstatement due to fraud may exist. It includes considering the reliability of the information to be used as audit evidence and the controls over its preparation and maintenance when relevant. Due to the characteristics of fraud, the auditor's professional skepticism is particularly important when considering the risks of material misstatement due to fraud.

.A10 Although the auditor cannot be expected to disregard past experience of the honesty and integrity of the entity's management and those charged with governance, the auditor's professional skepticism is particularly important in considering the risks of material misstatement due to fraud because there may have been changes in circumstances.

.A11 An audit performed in accordance with GAAS rarely involves the authentication of documents, nor is the auditor trained as, or expected to be, an expert in such authentication.[17] However, when the auditor identifies conditions that cause the auditor to believe that a document may not be authentic, that terms in a document have been modified but not disclosed to the auditor, or that undisclosed side agreements may exist, possible procedures to investigate further may include

- confirming directly with the third party.
- using the work of a specialist to assess the document's authenticity.

Appendix C, "Examples of Circumstances That Indicate the Possibility of Fraud," contains examples of circumstances that may indicate the possibility of fraud.

---

[17] Paragraph .A51 of section 200.

Discussion Among the Engagement Team (Ref: par. .15)

.A12 Discussing the susceptibility of the entity's financial statements to material misstatement due to fraud with the engagement team

- provides an opportunity for more experienced engagement team members to share their insights about how and where the financial statements may be susceptible to material misstatement due to fraud.
- enables the auditor to consider an appropriate response to such susceptibility and to determine which members of the engagement team will conduct certain audit procedures.
- permits the auditor to determine how the results of audit procedures will be shared among the engagement team and how to deal with any allegations of fraud that may come to the auditor's attention during the audit.

.A13 The discussion may lead to a thorough probing of the issues, acquiring of additional evidence as necessary, and consulting with other team members and, if appropriate, specialists in or outside the firm. The discussion may include the following matters:

- A consideration of management's involvement in overseeing employees with access to cash or other assets susceptible to misappropriation
- A consideration of any unusual or unexplained changes in behavior or lifestyle of management or employees that have come to the attention of the engagement team
- A consideration of the types of circumstances that, if encountered, might indicate the possibility of fraud
- A consideration of how an element of unpredictability will be incorporated into the nature, timing, and extent of the audit procedures to be performed
- A consideration of the audit procedures that might be selected to respond to the susceptibility of the entity's financial statements to material misstatement due to fraud and whether certain types of audit procedures are more effective than others
- A consideration of any allegations of fraud that have come to the auditor's attention

A number of factors may influence the extent of the discussion and how it may occur. For example, if the audit involves more than one location, there could be multiple discussions with team members in differing locations. Another factor in planning the discussions is whether to include specialists assigned to the audit team.

Risk Assessment Procedures and Related Activities

Inquiries of Management

Management's Assessment of the Risk of Material Misstatement Due to Fraud (Ref: par. .17*a*)

.A14 Management accepts responsibility for the entity's internal control and for the preparation and fair presentation of the entity's financial statements. Accordingly, it is appropriate for the auditor to make inquiries of management regarding management's own assessment of the risk of fraud and the controls in place to prevent and detect it. The nature, extent, and frequency of management's assessment of such risk and controls may vary from entity to entity. In some entities, management may make detailed assessments on an annual basis or as part of continuous monitoring. In other entities, management's assessment may be less structured and less frequent. The nature, extent, and frequency of management's assessment are relevant to the auditor's understanding of the entity's control environment. For example, the fact that management has not made an assessment of the risk of fraud may, in some circumstances, be indicative of the lack of importance that management places on internal control.

.A15 *Considerations specific to smaller, less complex entities.* In some entities, particularly smaller entities, the focus of management's assessment may be on the risks of employee fraud or misappropriation of assets.

Management's Process for Identifying and Responding to the Risks of Fraud (Ref: par. .17*b*)

.A16 In the case of entities with multiple locations, management's processes may include different levels of monitoring of operating locations or business segments. Management may also have identified particular operating locations or business segments for which a risk of fraud may be more likely to exist.

Discussions With Management and Others Within the Entity (Ref: par. .17–.19)

.A17 Inquiries of management and others within the entity are generally most effective when they involve an in-person discussion. The auditor may also determine it useful to provide the interviewee with specific questions and obtain written responses in advance of the discussion.

.A18 The auditor's inquiries of management may provide useful information concerning the risks of material misstatements in the financial statements resulting from employee fraud. However, such inquiries are unlikely to provide useful information regarding the risks of material misstatement in the financial statements resulting from management fraud. Making inquiries of others within the entity, in addition to management, may provide individuals with an opportunity to convey information to the auditor that may not otherwise be communicated. It may be useful in providing the auditor with a perspective that is different from that of individuals in the financial reporting process. The responses to these other inquiries might serve to corroborate responses received from management or, alternatively, might provide information regarding the possibility of management override of controls. The auditor may also obtain information about how effectively management has communicated standards of ethical behavior throughout the organization.

.A19 Examples of others within the entity to whom the auditor may direct inquiries about the existence or suspicion of fraud include the following:

- Operating personnel not directly involved in the financial reporting process
- Employees with different levels of authority
- Employees involved in initiating, processing, or recording complex or unusual transactions and those who supervise or monitor such employees
- In-house legal counsel

- Chief ethics officer or equivalent person
- The person or persons charged with dealing with allegations of fraud

.A20 Management is often in the best position to perpetrate fraud. Accordingly, when evaluating management's responses to inquiries with professional skepticism, the auditor may judge it necessary to corroborate responses to inquiries with other information.

Obtaining an Understanding of Oversight Exercised by Those Charged With Governance (Ref: par. .20)

.A21 Those charged with governance of an entity oversee the entity's systems for monitoring risk, financial control, and compliance with the law. In some circumstances, governance practices are well developed, and those charged with governance play an active role in oversight of the entity's assessment of the risks of fraud and of the relevant internal control. Because the responsibilities of those charged with governance and management may vary by entity, it is important that the auditor understands the respective responsibilities of those charged with governance and management to enable the auditor to obtain an understanding of the oversight exercised by the appropriate individuals.[18]

.A22 An understanding of the oversight exercised by those charged with governance may provide insights regarding the susceptibility of the entity to management fraud, the adequacy of internal control over risks of fraud, and the competency and integrity of management. The auditor may obtain this understanding in a number of ways, such as by attending meetings during which such discussions take place, reading the minutes from such meetings, or making inquiries of those charged with governance.

Considerations Specific to Smaller, Less Complex Entities

.A23 In some cases, all of those charged with governance are involved in managing the entity. This may be the case in a small entity in which a single owner manages the entity, and no one else has a governance role. In these cases, ordinarily, no action exists on the part of the auditor because no oversight exists separate from management.

Unusual or Unexpected Relationships Identified (Ref: par. .22)

.A24 Analytical procedures may include data analysis techniques ranging from a high-level review of data patterns, relationships, and trends to highly sophisticated, computer-assisted investigation of detailed transactions using electronic tools, such as data mining, business intelligence, and file query tools. The degree of reliance that can be placed on such techniques is a function primarily of the source (for example, financial, nonfinancial), completeness and reliability of the data, the level of disaggregation, and the nature of the analysis.

.A25 Analytical procedures relating to revenue that are performed with the objective of identifying unusual or unexpected relationships that may indicate a material misstatement due to fraudulent financial reporting may include

a. a comparison of sales volume, as determined from recorded revenue amounts, with production capacity. An excess of sales volume over production capacity may be indicative of recording fictitious sales.

---

[18] Paragraphs .A6–.A12 of section 260 discuss with whom the auditor communicates when the entity's governance structure is not well defined.

b. a trend analysis of revenues by month and sales returns by month, during and shortly after the reporting period. This may indicate the existence of undisclosed side agreements with customers involving the return of goods, which, if known, would preclude revenue recognition.

c. a trend analysis of sales by month compared with units shipped. This may identify a material misstatement of recorded revenues.

.A26 Analytical procedures performed during planning may be helpful in identifying the risks of material misstatement due to fraud. However, if such analytical procedures use data aggregated at a high level, generally the results of those analytical procedures provide only a broad initial indication about whether a material misstatement of the financial statements may exist. Accordingly, the results of analytical procedures performed during planning may be considered along with other information gathered by the auditor in identifying the risks of material misstatement due to fraud.

Other Information (Ref: par. .23)

.A27 In addition to information obtained from applying analytical procedures, other information obtained about the entity and its environment may be helpful in identifying the risks of material misstatement due to fraud. The discussion among team members may provide information that is helpful in identifying such risks. In addition, information obtained from the auditor's client acceptance and retention processes, and experience gained on other engagements performed for the entity, for example, engagements to review interim financial information, may be relevant in the identification of the risks of material misstatement due to fraud.

Evaluation of Fraud Risk Factors (Ref: par. .24)

.A28 The fact that fraud is usually concealed can make it very difficult to detect. Nevertheless, the auditor may identify events or conditions that indicate an incentive or pressure to commit fraud or provide an opportunity to commit fraud (fraud risk factors), such as the following:

- The need to meet expectations of third parties to obtain additional equity financing may create pressure to commit fraud.
- The granting of significant bonuses if unrealistic profit targets are met may create an incentive to commit fraud.
- A control environment that is not effective may create an opportunity to commit fraud.

.A29 Fraud risk factors cannot easily be ranked in order of importance. The significance of fraud risk factors varies widely. Some of these factors will be present in entities in which the specific conditions do not present risks of material misstatement. Accordingly, the determination of whether a fraud risk factor is present and whether it is to be considered in assessing the risks of material misstatement of the financial statements due to fraud requires the exercise of professional judgment.

.A30 Examples of fraud risk factors related to fraudulent financial reporting and misappropriation of assets are presented in appendix A, "Examples of Fraud Risk Factors." These illustrative risk factors are classified based on the three conditions that are generally present when fraud exists:

- An incentive or pressure to commit fraud

- A perceived opportunity to commit fraud
- An ability to rationalize the fraudulent action

The inability to observe one or more of these conditions does not necessarily mean that no risk of material misstatement due to fraud exists.

Risk factors reflective of an attitude that permits rationalization of the fraudulent action may not be susceptible to observation by the auditor. Nevertheless, the auditor may become aware of the existence of such information. Although the fraud risk factors described in appendix A cover a broad range of situations that may be faced by auditors, they are only examples and other risk factors may exist.

.A31 The size, complexity, and ownership characteristics of the entity have a significant influence on the consideration of relevant fraud risk factors. For example, in the case of a large entity, there may be factors that generally constrain improper conduct by management, such as

- effective oversight by those charged with governance.
- an effective internal audit function.
- the existence and enforcement of a written code of conduct.

Furthermore, fraud risk factors considered at a business segment operating level may provide different insights when compared with those obtained when considered at an entity-wide level.

Considerations Specific to Smaller, Less Complex Entities

.A32 In the case of a small entity, some or all of these considerations may be inapplicable or less relevant. For example, a smaller entity may not have a written code of conduct but, instead, may have developed a culture that emphasizes the importance of integrity and ethical behavior through oral communication and by management example. Domination of management by a single individual in a small entity does not generally, in and of itself, indicate a failure by management to display and communicate an appropriate attitude regarding internal control and the financial reporting process. In some entities, the need for management authorization can compensate for otherwise deficient controls and reduce the risk of employee fraud. However, domination of management by a single individual can be a potential deficiency in internal control because an opportunity exists for management override of controls.

Identification and Assessment of the Risks of Material Misstatement Due to Fraud

Risks of Fraud in Revenue Recognition (Ref: par. .26)

.A33 Material misstatement due to fraudulent financial reporting relating to revenue recognition often results from an overstatement of revenues through, for example, premature revenue recognition or recording fictitious revenues. It may result also from an understatement of revenues through, for example, improperly shifting revenues to a later period.

.A34 The risks of fraud in revenue recognition may be greater in some entities than others. For example, there may be pressures or incentives on management to commit fraudulent financial reporting through inappropriate revenue recognition when, for example, performance is measured in terms of year over year revenue growth or profit. Similarly, for example, there may be greater risks of fraud in revenue recognition in the case of entities that generate a substantial portion of revenues through cash sales.

.A35 The presumption that risks of fraud exist in revenue recognition may be rebutted. For example, the auditor may conclude that no risk of material misstatement due to fraud relating to revenue recognition exists in the case in which a single type of simple revenue transaction exists, for example, leasehold revenue from a single unit rental property.

Identifying and Assessing the Risks of Material Misstatement Due to Fraud and Understanding the Entity's Related Controls (Ref: par. .27)

.A36 Management may make judgments on the nature and extent of the controls it chooses to implement, and the nature and extent of the risks it chooses to assume.[19] In determining which controls to implement to prevent and detect fraud, management considers the risks that the financial statements may be materially misstated as a result of fraud. As part of this consideration, management may conclude that it is not cost effective to implement and maintain a particular control in relation to the reduction in the risks of material misstatement due to fraud to be achieved.

.A37 It is, therefore, important for the auditor to obtain an understanding of the controls that management has designed, implemented, and maintained to prevent and detect fraud. In doing so, the auditor may learn, for example, that management has consciously chosen to accept the risks associated with a lack of segregation of duties. Information from obtaining this understanding may also be useful in identifying fraud risks factors that may affect the auditor's assessment of the risks that the financial statements may contain material misstatement due to fraud.

Responses to the Assessed Risks of Material Misstatement Due to Fraud

Overall Responses (Ref: par. .28)

.A38 Determining overall responses to address the assessed risks of material misstatement due to fraud generally includes the consideration of how the overall conduct of the audit can reflect increased professional skepticism through, for example, increased

- sensitivity in the selection of the nature and extent of documentation to be examined in support of material transactions.
- recognition of the need to corroborate management explanations or representations concerning material matters.

Determining overall responses to address the assessed risks of material misstatement due to fraud also involves more general considerations apart from the specific procedures otherwise planned; these considerations include the matters listed in paragraph .29, which are discussed in the following sections.

Assignment and Supervision of Personnel (Ref: par. .29a)

.A39 The auditor may respond to identified risks of material misstatement due to fraud by, for example, assigning additional individuals with specialized skill and knowledge, such as forensic and IT specialists, or by assigning more experienced individuals to the engagement.

.A40 The extent of supervision reflects the auditor's assessment of risks of material misstatement due to fraud and the competencies of the engagement team members performing the work.

---

[19] Paragraph .A48 of section 315.

Accounting Principles (Ref: par. .29b)

.A41 Management bias in the selection and application of accounting principles may individually or collectively involve matters such as contingencies, fair value measurements, revenue recognition, accounting estimates, related party transactions, or other transactions without a clear business purpose.

Unpredictability in the Selection of Audit Procedures (Ref: par. .29c)

.A42 Incorporating an element of unpredictability in the selection of the nature, timing, and extent of audit procedures to be performed is important because individuals within the entity who are familiar with the audit procedures normally performed on engagements may be better able to conceal fraudulent financial reporting. This can be achieved by, for example,

- performing substantive procedures on selected account balances and assertions not otherwise tested due to their materiality or risk.
- adjusting the timing of audit procedures from that otherwise expected.
- using different sampling methods.
- performing audit procedures at different locations or at locations on an unannounced basis.

Audit Procedures Responsive to Assessed Risks of Material Misstatement Due to Fraud at the Assertion Level (Ref: par. .30)

.A43 The auditor's responses to address the assessed risks of material misstatement due to fraud at the assertion level may include changing the nature, timing, and extent of audit procedures in the following ways:

- The nature of audit procedures to be performed may need to be changed to obtain audit evidence that is more reliable and relevant or to obtain additional corroborative information. This may affect both the type of audit procedures to be performed and their combination. For example:
  - — Physical observation or inspection of certain assets may become more important, or the auditor may choose to use computer-assisted audit techniques to gather more evidence about data contained in significant accounts or electronic transaction files.
  - — The auditor may design procedures to obtain additional corroborative information. For example, if the auditor identifies that management is under pressure to meet earnings expectations, there may be a related risk that management is inflating sales by entering into sales agreements that include terms that preclude revenue recognition or by invoicing sales before delivery. In these circumstances, the auditor may, for example, design external confirmations not only to confirm outstanding amounts, but also to confirm the details of the sales agreements, including date, any rights of return, and delivery terms. In addition, the auditor might find it effective to supplement such external confirmations with inquiries of nonfinancial

personnel in the entity regarding any changes in sales agreements and delivery terms.

- The timing of substantive procedures may need to be modified. The auditor may conclude that performing substantive testing at or near the period end better addresses an assessed risk of material misstatement due to fraud. The auditor may conclude that, given the assessed risks of intentional misstatement or manipulation, audit procedures to extend audit conclusions from an interim date to the period end would not be effective. In contrast, because an intentional misstatement—for example, a misstatement involving improper revenue recognition—may have been initiated in an interim period, the auditor may elect to apply substantive procedures to transactions occurring earlier in or throughout the reporting period.

- The extent of the procedures applied reflects the assessment of the risks of material misstatement due to fraud. For example, increasing sample sizes or performing analytical procedures at a more detailed level may be appropriate. Also, computer-assisted audit techniques may enable more extensive testing of electronic transactions and account files. Such techniques can be used to select sample transactions from key electronic files, to sort transactions with specific characteristics, or to test an entire population instead of a sample.

.A44 If the auditor identifies a risk of material misstatement due to fraud that affects inventory quantities, examining the entity's inventory records may help to identify locations or items that require specific attention during or after the physical inventory count. Such a review may lead to a decision to observe inventory counts at certain locations on an unannounced basis or to conduct inventory counts at all locations on the same date.

.A45 The auditor may identify a risk of material misstatement due to fraud affecting a number of accounts and assertions. These may include asset valuation, estimates relating to specific transactions (such as acquisitions, restructurings, or disposals of segments of the business), and other significant accrued liabilities (such as pension and other postemployment benefit obligations, or environmental remediation liabilities). The risk may also relate to significant changes in assumptions relating to recurring estimates. Information gathered through obtaining an understanding of the entity and its environment may assist the auditor in evaluating the reasonableness of such management estimates and underlying judgments and assumptions. A retrospective review of similar management judgments and assumptions applied in prior periods may also provide insight about the reasonableness of judgments and assumptions supporting management estimates.

.A46 Examples of possible audit procedures to address the assessed risks of material misstatement due to fraud, including those that illustrate the incorporation of an element of unpredictability, are presented in appendix B, "Examples of Possible Audit Procedures to Address the Assessed Risks of Material Misstatement Due to Fraud." The appendix includes examples of responses to the auditor's assessment of the risks of material misstatement resulting from both fraudulent financial reporting, including fraudulent financial reporting resulting from revenue recognition, and misappropriation of assets.

Audit Procedures Responsive to Risks Related to Management Override of Controls

Journal Entries and Other Adjustments (Ref: par. .32a)

.A47 Material misstatements of financial statements due to fraud often involve the manipulation of the financial reporting process by (*a*) recording inappropriate or unauthorized journal entries throughout the year or at period end, or (*b*) making adjustments to amounts reported in the financial statements that are not reflected in formal journal entries, such as through consolidating adjustments, report combinations, and reclassifications.

.A48 The auditor's consideration of the risks of material misstatement associated with inappropriate override of controls over journal entries is important because automated processes and controls may reduce the risk of inadvertent error but do not overcome the risk that individuals may inappropriately override such automated processes, for example, by changing the amounts being automatically passed to the general ledger or to the financial reporting system. Furthermore, when IT is used to transfer information automatically, there may be little or no visible evidence of such intervention in the information systems.

.A49 When identifying and selecting journal entries and other adjustments for testing and determining the appropriate method of examining the underlying support for the items selected, the following matters may be relevant:

- *The assessment of the risks of material misstatement due to fraud.* The presence of fraud risk factors and other information obtained during the auditor's assessment of the risks of material misstatement due to fraud may assist the auditor to identify specific classes of journal entries and other adjustments for testing.
- *Controls that have been implemented over journal entries and other adjustments.* Effective controls over the preparation and posting of journal entries and other adjustments may reduce the extent of substantive testing necessary, provided that the auditor has tested the operating effectiveness of the controls.
- *The entity's financial reporting process and the nature of evidence that can be obtained.* For many entities, routine processing of transactions involves a combination of manual and automated steps and procedures. Similarly, the processing of journal entries and other adjustments may involve both manual and automated procedures and controls. When IT is used in the financial reporting process, journal entries and other adjustments may exist only in electronic form.
- *The characteristics of fraudulent journal entries or other adjustments.* Inappropriate journal entries or other adjustments often have unique identifying characteristics. Such characteristics may include entries (*a*) made to unrelated, unusual, or seldom-used accounts; (*b*) made by individuals who typically do not make journal entries; (*c*) recorded at the end of the period or as postclosing entries that have little or no explanation or description; (*d*) made either before or during the preparation of the financial statements that do not have account numbers; or (*e*) containing round numbers or consistent ending numbers.
- *The nature and complexity of the accounts.* Inappropriate journal entries or adjustments may be applied to accounts that (*a*) contain

transactions that are complex or unusual in nature, (*b*) contain significant estimates and period-end adjustments, (*c*) have been prone to misstatements in the past, (*d*) have not been reconciled on a timely basis or contain unreconciled differences, (*e*) contain intercompany transactions, or (*f*) are otherwise associated with an identified risk of material misstatement due to fraud. In audits of entities that have several locations or components, consideration is given to the need to select journal entries from multiple locations.

- *Journal entries or other adjustments processed outside the normal course of business*. Nonstandard journal entries, and other entries such as consolidating adjustments, may not be subject to the same level of internal control as those journal entries used on a recurring basis to record transactions such as monthly sales, purchases, and cash disbursements.

.A50 The auditor exercises professional judgment in determining the nature, timing, and extent of testing of journal entries and other adjustments. However, because fraudulent journal entries and other adjustments are often made at the end of a reporting period, paragraph .32*a*(iv) requires the auditor to select the journal entries and other adjustments made at that time. Further, because material misstatements in financial statements due to fraud can occur throughout the period and may involve extensive efforts to conceal how the fraud is accomplished, paragraph .32*a*(v) requires the auditor to consider whether a need also exists to test journal entries and other adjustments throughout the period.

Accounting Estimates (Ref: par. .32*b*)

.A51 The preparation and fair presentation of the financial statements requires management to make a number of judgments or assumptions that affect significant accounting estimates and monitor the reasonableness of such estimates on an ongoing basis. Fraudulent financial reporting is often accomplished through intentional misstatement of accounting estimates. This may be achieved by, for example, understating or overstating all provisions or reserves in the same fashion so as to be designed either to smooth earnings over two or more accounting periods, or to achieve a designated earnings level in order to deceive financial statement users by influencing their perceptions about the entity's performance and profitability.

.A52 The purpose of performing a retrospective review of management judgments and assumptions related to significant accounting estimates reflected in the financial statements of the prior year is to determine whether an indication exists of a possible bias on the part of management. This review is not intended to call into question the auditor's professional judgments made in the prior year that were based on information available at the time.

.A53 A retrospective review is also required by section 540, *Auditing Accounting Estimates, Including Fair Value Accounting Estimates, and Related Disclosures*.[20] That review is conducted as a risk assessment procedure to obtain information regarding the effectiveness of management's prior period estimation process, audit evidence about the outcome, or when applicable, the subsequent reestimation of prior period accounting estimates that is pertinent to making current period accounting estimates, and audit evidence of matters,

---

[20] Paragraph .09 of section 540, *Auditing Accounting Estimates, Including Fair Value Accounting Estimates, and Related Disclosures*.

such as estimation uncertainty, that may be required to be disclosed in the financial statements. As a practical matter, the auditor's review of management judgments and assumptions for biases that could represent a risk of material misstatement due to fraud in accordance with this section may be carried out in conjunction with the review required by section 540.

Business Rationale for Significant Transactions (Ref: par. .32c)

.A54 Indicators that may suggest that significant transactions that are outside the normal course of business for the entity, or that otherwise appear to be unusual, may have been entered into to engage in fraudulent financial reporting or to conceal misappropriation of assets include the following:

- The form of such transactions appears overly complex (for example, the transaction involves multiple entities within a consolidated group or multiple unrelated third parties).
- Management has not discussed the nature of and accounting for such transactions with those charged with governance of the entity, and inadequate documentation exists.
- Management is placing more emphasis on the need for a particular accounting treatment than on the underlying economics of the transaction.
- Transactions that involve nonconsolidated related parties, including special purpose entities, have not been properly reviewed or approved by those charged with governance of the entity.
- Transactions that involve previously unidentified related parties or parties that do not have the substance or the financial strength to support the transaction without assistance from the entity under audit.

Other Audit Procedures (Ref: par. .32a and .33)

.A55 Risks of material misstatement, including misstatements due to fraud, cannot be reduced to an appropriately low level by performing only tests of controls.[21]

Evaluation of Audit Evidence (Ref: par. .34–.37)

.A56 Section 330 requires the auditor, based on the audit procedures performed and the audit evidence obtained, to evaluate whether the assessments of the risks of material misstatement at the assertion level remain appropriate.[22] This evaluation is primarily a qualitative matter based on the auditor's professional judgment. Such an evaluation may provide further insight into the risks of material misstatement due to fraud and whether a need exists to perform additional or different audit procedures. Appendix C contains examples of circumstances that may indicate the possibility of fraud.

Analytical Procedures Performed Near the End of the Audit in Forming an Overall Conclusion (Ref: par. .34)

.A57 Determining which particular trends and relationships may indicate a risk of material misstatement due to fraud requires professional judgment. Unusual relationships involving year-end revenue and income are particularly relevant. These might include, for example, uncharacteristically large amounts

---

[21] Paragraph .A9 of section 330.

[22] Paragraph .27 of section 330.

of income being reported in the last few weeks of the reporting period or unusual transactions or income that is inconsistent with trends in cash flow from operations.

.A58 Some unusual or unexpected analytical relationships may have been identified and may indicate a risk of material misstatement due to fraud because management or employees generally are unable to manipulate certain information to create seemingly normal or expected relationships. Some examples are as follows:

- The relationship of net income to cash flows from operations may appear unusual because management recorded fictitious revenues and receivables but was unable to manipulate cash.
- Changes in inventory, accounts payable, sales, or cost of sales from the prior period to the current period may be inconsistent, indicating a possible employee theft of inventory, because the employee was unable to manipulate all of the related accounts.
- A comparison of the entity's profitability to industry trends, which management cannot manipulate, may indicate trends or differences for further consideration when identifying risks of material misstatement due to fraud.
- A comparison of bad debt write-offs to comparable industry data, which employees cannot manipulate, may provide unexplained relationships that could indicate a possible theft of cash receipts.
- An unexpected or unexplained relationship between sales volume, as determined from the accounting records and production statistics maintained by operations personnel, which may be more difficult for management to manipulate, may indicate a possible misstatement of sales.

Consideration of Identified Misstatements (Ref: par. .35–.37)

.A59 Because fraud involves incentive or pressure to commit fraud, a perceived opportunity to do so, or some rationalization of the act, an instance of fraud is unlikely to be an isolated occurrence. Accordingly, misstatements, such as numerous misstatements at a specific location even though the cumulative effect is not material, may be indicative of a risk of material misstatement due to fraud.

.A60 The implications of identified fraud depend on the circumstances. For example, an otherwise insignificant fraud may be significant if it involves senior management. In such circumstances, the reliability of evidence previously obtained may be called into question because there may be doubts about the completeness and truthfulness of representations made and the genuineness of accounting records and documentation. There may also be a possibility of collusion involving employees, management, or third parties.

.A61 Section 450, *Evaluation of Misstatements Identified During the Audit*, and section 700, *Forming an Opinion and Reporting on Financial Statements*, address the evaluation and disposition of misstatements and the effect on the auditor's opinion in the auditor's report.

.A62 Section 580, *Written Representations*, addresses obtaining appropriate representations from management in the audit. In addition to acknowledging its responsibility for the financial statements, it is important that, irrespective of the size of the entity, management acknowledges its responsibility for internal control designed, implemented, and maintained to prevent and detect fraud.

Auditor Unable to Continue the Engagement (Ref: par. .38)

.A63 Examples of circumstances that may arise and bring into question the auditor's ability to continue performing the audit include the following:

a. The entity does not take the appropriate action regarding fraud that the auditor considers necessary in the circumstances, even when the fraud is not material to the financial statements.

b. The auditor's consideration of the risks of material misstatement due to fraud and the results of audit tests indicate a significant risk of material and pervasive fraud.

c. The auditor has significant concern about the competence or integrity of management or those charged with governance.

.A64 Because of the variety of circumstances that may arise, it is not possible to describe definitively when withdrawal from an engagement is appropriate. Factors that affect the auditor's conclusion include the implications of the involvement of a member of management or of those charged with governance (which may affect the reliability of management representations) and the effects on the auditor of a continuing association with the entity.

.A65 The auditor has professional and legal responsibilities in such circumstances, and these responsibilities may vary by engagement. In some circumstances, for example, the auditor may be entitled to, or required to, make a statement or report to the person or persons who engaged the auditor or, in some cases, to regulatory authorities. Given the nature of the circumstances and the need to consider the legal requirements, the auditor may consider it appropriate to seek legal advice when deciding whether to withdraw from an engagement and in determining an appropriate course of action, including the possibility of reporting to regulators or others.[23]

Considerations Specific to Governmental Entities and Not-for-Profit Organizations

.A66 For governmental entities and not-for-profit organizations, the option of withdrawing from the engagement may not be available to the auditor due to the nature of the mandate, public interest considerations, contractual requirements, or law or regulation.

Communications to Management and With Those Charged With Governance

Communication to Management (Ref: par. .39)

.A67 When the auditor has obtained evidence that fraud exists or may exist, it is important that the matter be brought to the attention of the appropriate level of management as soon as practicable. This is true even if the matter might be considered inconsequential (for example, a minor defalcation by an employee at a low level in the entity's organization). The determination of which level of management is the appropriate one is a matter of professional judgment and is affected by such factors as the likelihood of collusion and the nature and magnitude of the suspected fraud. Ordinarily, the appropriate level of management is at least one level above the persons who appear to be involved with the suspected fraud.

---

[23] Section 510, *Opening Balances—Initial Audit Engagements, Including Reaudit Engagements,* provides guidance on communications with an auditor replacing the existing auditor.

Communication With Those Charged With Governance (Ref: par. .40)

.A68 The auditor's communication with those charged with governance may be made orally or in writing. Section 260, *The Auditor's Communication With Those Charged With Governance*, identifies factors the auditor considers in determining whether to communicate orally or in writing.[24] Due to the nature and sensitivity of fraud involving senior management, or fraud that results in a material misstatement in the financial statements, the auditor communicates such matters on a timely basis and may consider it necessary to also communicate such matters in writing.

.A69 In some cases, the auditor may consider it appropriate to communicate with those charged with governance when the auditor becomes aware of fraud involving employees other than management that does not result in a material misstatement. Similarly, those charged with governance may wish to be informed of such circumstances. The communication process is assisted if the auditor and those charged with governance agree at an early stage in the audit about the nature and extent of the auditor's communications in this regard.

.A70 When the auditor has doubts about the integrity or honesty of management or those charged with governance, the auditor may consider it appropriate to obtain legal advice to assist in determining the appropriate course of action.

Other Matters Related to Fraud (Ref: par. .41)

.A71 Other matters related to fraud to be discussed with those charged with governance of the entity may include, for example

- concerns about the nature, extent, and frequency of management's assessments of the controls in place to prevent and detect fraud and of the risk that the financial statements may be misstated.
- a failure by management to appropriately address identified significant deficiencies or material weaknesses in internal control, or to appropriately respond to an identified fraud.
- the auditor's evaluation of the entity's control environment, including questions regarding the competence and integrity of management.
- actions by management that may be indicative of fraudulent financial reporting, such as management's selection and application of accounting policies that may be indicative of management's effort to manage earnings in order to deceive financial statement users by influencing their perceptions concerning the entity's performance and profitability.
- concerns about the adequacy and completeness of the authorization of transactions that appear to be outside the normal course of business.
- the absence of programs or controls to address risks of material misstatement due to fraud that are significant deficiencies or material weaknesses.[25]

---

[24] Paragraph .A40 of section 260.

[25] See section 265, *Communicating Internal Control Related Matters Identified in an Audit*.

Communications to Regulatory and Enforcement Authorities (Ref: par. .42)

.A72 The auditor's professional duty to maintain the confidentiality of client information may preclude reporting fraud to a party outside the client entity. However, in certain circumstances, the duty of confidentiality may be overridden by statute, regulation, courts of law, specific requirements of audits of entities that receive government financial assistance, or waived by agreement. In some circumstances, the auditor has a statutory duty to report the occurrence of fraud to supervisory authorities. Also, in some circumstances, the auditor has a duty to report misstatements to authorities in those cases when management and those charged with governance fail to take corrective action.

.A73 The auditor may consider it appropriate to obtain legal advice to determine the appropriate course of action in the circumstances, the purpose of which is to ascertain the steps necessary in considering the public interest aspects of identified fraud.

Considerations Specific to Governmental Entities and Not-for-Profit Organizations

.A74 For governmental entities and not-for-profit organizations, requirements for reporting fraud, whether or not discovered through the audit process, may be subject to specific provisions of the audit mandate or related law or regulation.

.A75

Appendix A—Examples of Fraud Risk Factors (Ref: par. .11, .24, and .A30)

The fraud risk factors identified in this appendix are examples of such factors that may be faced by auditors in a broad range of situations. Separately presented are examples relating to the two types of fraud relevant to the auditor's consideration—that is, fraudulent financial reporting and misappropriation of assets. For each of these types of fraud, the risk factors are further classified based on the three conditions generally present when material misstatements due to fraud occur: (*a*) incentives and pressures, (*b*) opportunities, and (*c*) attitudes and rationalizations. Although the risk factors cover a broad range of situations, they are only examples and, accordingly, the auditor may identify additional or different risk factors. Not all of these examples are relevant in all circumstances, and some may be of greater or lesser significance in entities of different size or with different ownership characteristics or circumstances. Also, the order of the examples of risk factors provided is not intended to reflect their relative importance or frequency of occurrence.

Risk Factors Relating to Misstatements Arising From Fraudulent Financial Reporting

The following are examples of risk factors relating to misstatements arising from fraudulent financial reporting.

Incentives and Pressures

Financial stability or profitability is threatened by economic, industry, or entity operating conditions, such as (or as indicated by) the following:

- High degree of competition or market saturation, accompanied by declining margins
- High vulnerability to rapid changes, such as changes in technology, product obsolescence, or interest rates
- Significant declines in customer demand and increasing business failures in either the industry or overall economy
- Operating losses making the threat of bankruptcy, foreclosure, or hostile takeover imminent
- Recurring negative cash flows from operations or an inability to generate cash flows from operations while reporting earnings and earnings growth
- Rapid growth or unusual profitability especially compared to that of other companies in the same industry
- New accounting, statutory, or regulatory requirements

Excessive pressure exists for management to meet the requirements or expectations of third parties due to the following:

- Profitability or trend level expectations of investment analysts, institutional investors, significant creditors, or other external parties (particularly expectations that are unduly aggressive or unrealistic), including expectations created by management in, for example, overly optimistic press releases or annual report messages

- Need to obtain additional debt or equity financing to stay competitive—including financing of major research and development or capital expenditures
- Marginal ability to meet exchange listing requirements or debt repayment or other debt covenant requirements
- Perceived or real adverse effects of reporting poor financial results on significant pending transactions, such as business combinations or contract awards
- A need to achieve financial targets required in bond covenants
- Pressure for management to meet the expectations of legislative or oversight bodies or to achieve political outcomes, or both

Information available indicates that the personal financial situation of management or those charged with governance is threatened by the entity's financial performance arising from the following:

- Significant financial interests in the entity
- Significant portions of their compensation (for example, bonuses, stock options, and earn-out arrangements) being contingent upon achieving aggressive targets for stock price, operating results, financial position, or cash flow[1]
- Personal guarantees of debts of the entity

Management or operating personnel are under excessive pressure to meet financial targets established by those charged with governance, including sales or profitability incentive goals.

Opportunities

The nature of the industry or the entity's operations provides opportunities to engage in fraudulent financial reporting that can arise from the following:

- Significant related party transactions not in the ordinary course of business or with related entities not audited or audited by another firm
- A strong financial presence or ability to dominate a certain industry sector that allows the entity to dictate terms or conditions to suppliers or customers that may result in inappropriate or non-arm's-length transactions
- Assets, liabilities, revenues, or expenses based on significant estimates that involve subjective judgments or uncertainties that are difficult to corroborate
- Significant, unusual, or highly complex transactions, especially those close to period end that pose difficult "substance over form" questions
- Significant operations located or conducted across jurisdictional borders where differing business environments and regulations exist

---

[1] Management incentive plans may be contingent upon achieving targets relating only to certain accounts or selected activities of the entity, even though the related accounts or activities may not be material to the entity as a whole.

- Use of business intermediaries for which there appears to be no clear business justification
- Significant bank accounts or subsidiary or branch operations in tax-haven jurisdictions for which there appears to be no clear business justification

The monitoring of management is not effective as a result of the following:

- Domination of management by a single person or small group (in a nonowner-managed business) without compensating controls.
- Oversight by those charged with governance over the financial reporting process and internal control is not effective.

The organizational structure is complex or unstable, as evidenced by the following:

- Difficulty in determining the organization or individuals that have controlling interest in the entity
- Overly complex organizational structure involving unusual legal entities or managerial lines of authority
- High turnover of senior management, legal counsel, or those charged with governance

Internal control components are deficient as a result of the following:

- Inadequate monitoring of controls, including automated controls and controls over interim financial reporting (when external reporting is required)
- High turnover rates or employment of accounting, internal audit, or IT staff who are not effective
- Accounting and information systems that are not effective, including situations involving significant deficiencies or material weaknesses in internal control
- Weak controls over budget preparation and development and compliance with law or regulation.

Attitudes and Rationalizations

- Communication, implementation, support, or enforcement of the entity's values or ethical standards by management, or the communication of inappropriate values or ethical standards that are not effective.
- Nonfinancial management's excessive participation in or preoccupation with the selection of accounting policies or the determination of significant estimates.
- Known history of violations of securities law or other law or regulation, or claims against the entity, its senior management, or those charged with governance alleging fraud or violations of law or regulation.
- Excessive interest by management in maintaining or increasing the entity's stock price or earnings trend.
- The practice by management of committing to analysts, creditors, and other third parties to achieve aggressive or unrealistic forecasts.

- Management failing to remedy known significant deficiencies or material weaknesses in internal control on a timely basis.
- An interest by management in employing inappropriate means to minimize reported earnings for tax-motivated reasons.
- Low morale among senior management.
- The owner-manager makes no distinction between personal and business transactions.
- Dispute between shareholders in a closely held entity.
- Recurring attempts by management to justify marginal or inappropriate accounting on the basis of materiality.
- A strained relationship between management and the current or predecessor auditor, as exhibited by the following:
    - — Frequent disputes with the current or predecessor auditor on accounting, auditing, or reporting matters
    - — Unreasonable demands on the auditor, such as unrealistic time constraints regarding the completion of the audit or the issuance of the auditor's report
    - — Restrictions on the auditor that inappropriately limit access to people or information or the ability to communicate effectively with those charged with governance
    - — Domineering management behavior in dealing with the auditor, especially involving attempts to influence the scope of the auditor's work or the selection or continuance of personnel assigned to or consulted on the audit engagement

Risk Factors Arising From Misstatements Arising From Misappropriation of Assets

Risk factors that relate to misstatements arising from misappropriation of assets are also classified according to the three conditions generally present when fraud exists: incentives and pressures, opportunities, and attitudes and rationalization. Some of the risk factors related to misstatements arising from fraudulent financial reporting also may be present when misstatements arising from misappropriation of assets occur. For example, ineffective monitoring of management and other deficiencies in internal control that are not effective may be present when misstatements due to either fraudulent financial reporting or misappropriation of assets exist. The following are examples of risk factors related to misstatements arising from misappropriation of assets.

Incentives and Pressures

Personal financial obligations may create pressure on management or employees with access to cash or other assets susceptible to theft to misappropriate those assets.

Adverse relationships between the entity and employees with access to cash or other assets susceptible to theft may motivate those employees to misappropriate those assets. For example, adverse relationships may be created by the following:

- Known or anticipated future employee layoffs

- Recent or anticipated changes to employee compensation or benefit plans
- Promotions, compensation, or other rewards inconsistent with expectations

Opportunities

Certain characteristics or circumstances may increase the susceptibility of assets to misappropriation. For example, opportunities to misappropriate assets increase when the following exist:

- Large amounts of cash on hand or processed
- Inventory items that are small in size, of high value, or in high demand
- Easily convertible assets, such as bearer bonds, diamonds, or computer chips
- Fixed assets that are small in size, marketable, or lack observable identification of ownership

Inadequate internal control over assets may increase the susceptibility of misappropriation of those assets. For example, misappropriation of assets may occur because the following exist:

- Inadequate segregation of duties or independent checks
- Inadequate oversight of senior management expenditures, such as travel and other reimbursements
- Inadequate management oversight of employees responsible for assets (for example, inadequate supervision or monitoring of remote locations)
- Inadequate job applicant screening of employees with access to assets
- Inadequate record keeping with respect to assets
- Inadequate system of authorization and approval of transactions (for example, in purchasing)
- Inadequate physical safeguards over cash, investments, inventory, or fixed assets
- Lack of complete and timely reconciliations of assets
- Lack of timely and appropriate documentation of transactions (for example, credits for merchandise returns)
- Lack of mandatory vacations for employees performing key control functions
- Inadequate management understanding of IT, which enables IT employees to perpetrate a misappropriation
- Inadequate access controls over automated records, including controls over and review of computer systems event logs

Attitudes and Rationalizations

- Disregard for the need for monitoring or reducing risks related to misappropriations of assets

- Disregard for internal control over misappropriation of assets by overriding existing controls or by failing to take appropriate remedial action on known deficiencies in internal control
- Behavior indicating displeasure or dissatisfaction with the entity or its treatment of the employee
- Changes in behavior or lifestyle that may indicate assets have been misappropriated
- The belief by some government or other officials that their level of authority justifies a certain level of compensation and personal privileges
- Tolerance of petty theft

.A76

Appendix B—Examples of Possible Audit Procedures to Address the Assessed Risks of Material Misstatement Due to Fraud (Ref: par. .22 and .A46)

The following are examples of possible audit procedures to address the assessed risks of material misstatement due to fraud resulting from both fraudulent financial reporting and misappropriation of assets. Although these procedures cover a broad range of situations, they are only examples and, accordingly, they may not be the most appropriate nor necessary in each circumstance. Also the order of the procedures provided is not intended to reflect their relative importance.

Consideration at the Assertion Level

Specific responses to the auditor's assessment of the risks of material misstatement due to fraud will vary depending upon the types or combinations of fraud risk factors or conditions identified, and the classes of transactions, account balances, disclosures, and assertions they may affect.

The following are specific examples of responses:

- Visiting locations or performing certain tests on a surprise or unannounced basis (for example, observing inventory at locations where auditor attendance has not been previously announced or counting cash at a particular date on a surprise basis)
- Requesting that inventories be counted at the end of the reporting period or on a date closer to period end to minimize the risk of manipulation of balances in the period between the date of completion of the count and the end of the reporting period
- Altering the audit approach in the current year (for example, contacting major customers and suppliers orally in addition to sending written confirmation, sending confirmation requests to a specific party within an organization, or seeking more or different information)
- Performing a detailed review of the entity's quarter-end or year-end adjusting entries and investigating any that appear to have an unusual nature or amount
- For significant and unusual transactions, particularly those occurring at or near year end, investigating the possibility of related parties and the sources of financial resources supporting the transactions
- Performing substantive analytical procedures using disaggregated data (for example, comparing sales and cost of sales by location, line of business, or month to expectations developed by the auditor)
- Conducting interviews of personnel involved in areas in which a risk of material misstatement due to fraud has been identified, to obtain their insights about the risk, and whether, or how, controls address the risk
- When other independent auditors are auditing the financial statements of one or more subsidiaries, divisions, or branches,

discussing with them the extent of work necessary to be performed to address the assessed risk of material misstatement due to fraud resulting from transactions and activities among these components

- If the work of an expert becomes particularly significant with respect to a financial statement item for which the assessed risk of misstatement due to fraud is high, performing additional procedures relating to some or all of the expert's assumptions, methods, or findings to determine that the findings are not unreasonable, or engaging another expert for that purpose
- Performing audit procedures to analyze selected opening balance sheet accounts of previously audited financial statements to assess how certain issues involving accounting estimates and judgments, for example, an allowance for sales returns, were resolved with the benefit of hindsight
- Performing procedures on account or other reconciliations prepared by the entity, including considering reconciliations performed at interim periods
- Performing computer-assisted techniques, such as data mining to test for anomalies in a population
- Testing the integrity of computer-produced records and transactions
- Seeking additional audit evidence from sources outside of the entity being audited

Specific Responses—Misstatement Resulting From Fraudulent Financial Reporting

Examples of responses to the auditor's assessment of the risks of material misstatement due to fraudulent financial reporting are as follows:

Revenue Recognition

- Performing substantive analytical procedures relating to revenue using disaggregated data; for example, comparing revenue reported by month and by product line or business segment during the current reporting period with comparable prior periods or with revenue related to cash collections (computer-assisted audit techniques may be useful in identifying unusual or unexpected revenue relationships or transactions)
- Confirming with customers certain relevant contract terms and the absence of side agreements because the appropriate accounting often is influenced by such terms or agreements and basis for rebates or the period to which they relate are often poorly documented (for example, acceptance criteria, delivery and payment terms, the absence of future or continuing vendor obligations, the right to return the product, guaranteed resale amounts, and cancellation or refund provisions often are relevant in such circumstances)
- Inquiring of the entity's sales and marketing personnel or in-house legal counsel regarding sales or shipments near the end of the period and their knowledge of any unusual terms or conditions associated with these transactions

- Being physically present at one or more locations at period end to observe goods being shipped or being readied for shipment (or returns awaiting processing) and performing other appropriate sales and inventory cutoff procedures
- For those situations for which revenue transactions are electronically initiated, processed, and recorded, testing controls to determine whether they provide assurance that recorded revenue transactions occurred and are properly recorded

Inventory Quantities

- Examining the entity's inventory records to identify locations or items that require specific attention during or after the physical inventory count
- Observing inventory counts at certain locations on an unannounced basis or conducting inventory counts at all locations on the same date
- Conducting inventory counts at or near the end of the reporting period to minimize the risk of inappropriate manipulation during the period between the count and the end of the reporting period
- Performing additional procedures during the observation of the count; for example, more rigorously examining the contents of boxed items, the manner in which the goods are stacked (for example, hollow squares) or labeled, and the quality (that is, purity, grade, or concentration) of liquid substances such as perfumes or specialty chemicals (using the work of an expert may be helpful in this regard)
- Comparing the quantities for the current period with prior periods by class or category of inventory, location or other criteria, or comparison of quantities counted with perpetual records
- Using computer-assisted audit techniques to further test the compilation of the physical inventory counts (for example, sorting by tag number to test tag controls or by item serial number to test the possibility of item omission or duplication)

Management Estimates

- Using an expert to develop an independent estimate for comparison to management's estimate
- Extending inquiries to individuals outside of management and the accounting department to corroborate management's ability and intent to carry out plans that are relevant to developing the estimate

Specific Responses—Misstatements Due to Misappropriation of Assets

Differing circumstances would necessarily dictate different responses. Ordinarily, the audit response to an assessed risk of material misstatement due to fraud relating to misappropriation of assets will be directed toward certain account balances and classes of transactions. Although some of the audit responses noted in the preceding two categories may apply in such circumstances, the scope of the work is to be linked to the specific information about the misappropriation risk that has been identified.

Examples of responses to the auditor's assessment of the risk of material misstatements due to misappropriation of assets are as follows:

- Counting cash or securities at or near year end
- Confirming directly with customers the account activity (including credit memo and sales return activity as well as dates payments were made) for the period under audit
- Analyzing recoveries of written-off accounts
- Analyzing inventory shortages by location or product type
- Comparing key inventory ratios to industry norm
- Reviewing supporting documentation for reductions to the perpetual inventory records
- Performing a computerized match of the vendor list with a list of employees to identify matches of addresses or phone numbers
- Performing a computerized search of payroll records to identify duplicate addresses, employee identification or taxing authority numbers, or bank accounts
- Reviewing personnel files for those that contain little or no evidence of activity; for example, lack of performance evaluations
- Analyzing sales discounts and returns for unusual patterns or trends
- Confirming specific terms of contracts with third parties
- Obtaining evidence that contracts are being carried out in accordance with their terms
- Reviewing the propriety of large and unusual expenses
- Reviewing the authorization and carrying value of senior management and related party loans
- Reviewing the level and propriety of expense reports submitted by senior management

.A77

Appendix C—Examples of Circumstances That Indicate the Possibility of Fraud (Ref: par. .11, .A11, and .A56)

The following are examples of circumstances that may indicate the possibility that the financial statements may contain a material misstatement resulting from fraud.

Discrepancies in the accounting records, including the following:

- Transactions that are not recorded in a complete or timely manner or are improperly recorded by amount, accounting period, classification, or entity policy
- Unsupported or unauthorized balances or transactions
- Last minute adjustments that significantly affect financial results
- Evidence of employees' access to systems and records inconsistent with that necessary to perform their authorized duties
- Tips or complaints to the auditor about alleged fraud

Conflicting or missing evidence, including the following:

- Missing documents
- Documents that appear to have been altered
- Unavailability of other than photocopied or electronically transmitted documents when documents in original form are expected to exist
- Significant unexplained items on reconciliations
- Unusual balance sheet changes, or changes in trends or important financial statement ratios or relationships; for example, receivables growing faster than revenues
- Inconsistent, vague, or implausible responses from management or employees arising from inquiries or analytical procedures
- Unusual discrepancies between the entity's records and confirmation replies
- Large numbers of credit entries and other adjustments made to accounts receivable records
- Unexplained or inadequately explained differences between the accounts receivable subledger and the control account, or between the customer statements and the accounts receivable subledger
- Missing or nonexistent cancelled checks in circumstances in which cancelled checks are ordinarily returned to the entity with the bank statement
- Missing inventory or physical assets of significant magnitude
- Unavailable or missing electronic evidence, inconsistent with the entity's record retention practices or policies
- Fewer responses to confirmations than anticipated or a greater number of responses than anticipated

- Inability to produce evidence of key systems development and program change testing and implementation activities for current-year system changes and deployments

Conditions relating to governmental entities or not-for-profit organizations:

- Significant transfers or transactions between funds or programs, or both, lacking supporting documents
- Abnormal budget conditions, such as
  - — significant budget adjustments
  - — requests for additional funding
  - — budget adjustments made without approval
  - — large amounts of over-or-under spending
  - — programs with an emphasis on spending money quickly
- Procurement conditions, such as
  - — lack of procurement legislation
  - — recent changes to procurement legislation
  - — complex or unclear legislation
  - — involvement of significant monetary amounts (such as in the defense area)
  - — investigation by regulatory authorities
  - — complaints received from potential suppliers about questionable practices related to awarding of contracts
  - — former governmental officials functioning as executives of companies to which contracts have been awarded
- Program conditions, such as
  - — newly implemented programs without existing management and accountability structures
  - — programs established for political purposes
  - — programs established to deal with an immediate emergency or crisis
  - — programs experiencing unusual growth due to conditions beyond the control of management
- Grant and donor funding conditions, such as
  - — noncompliance with grant requirements
  - — unclear grant requirements
  - — grants not reaching the intended recipient
  - — complaints from intended recipients or interest groups, and lack of monitoring of grantee compliance with applicable law or regulation

Problematic or unusual relationships between the auditor and management, including the following:

- Denial of access to records, facilities, certain employees, customers, vendors, or others from whom audit evidence might be sought

- Undue time pressures imposed by management to resolve complex or contentious issues
- Complaints by management about the conduct of the audit or management intimidation of engagement team members, particularly in connection with the auditor's critical assessment of audit evidence or in the resolution of potential disagreements with management
- Unusual delays by the entity in providing requested information
- Unwillingness to facilitate auditor access to key electronic files for testing through the use of computer-assisted audit techniques
- Denial of access to key IT operations staff and facilities, including security, operations, and systems development personnel
- An unwillingness to add or revise disclosures in the financial statements to make them more complete and understandable
- An unwillingness to address identified deficiencies in internal control on a timely basis

Other circumstances, including the following:

- Unwillingness by management to permit the auditor to meet privately with those charged with governance
- Accounting policies that appear to be at variance with industry norms
- Frequent changes in accounting estimates that do not appear to result from changed circumstances
- Tolerance of violations of the entity's code of conduct

AU-C Section 250 *

Consideration of Laws and Regulations in an Audit of Financial Statements

Source: SAS No. 122.

Effective for audits of financial statements for periods ending on or after December 15, 2012.

Introduction

Scope of This Section

.01 This section addresses the auditor's responsibility to consider laws and regulations in an audit of financial statements. This section does not apply to other assurance engagements in which the auditor is specifically engaged to test and report separately on compliance with specific laws or regulations.[1]

Effect of Laws and Regulations

.02 The effect on financial statements of laws and regulations varies considerably. Those laws and regulations to which an entity is subject constitute the legal and regulatory framework. The provisions of some laws or regulations have a direct effect on the financial statements in that they determine the reported amounts and disclosures in an entity's financial statements. Other laws or regulations are to be complied with by management, or set the provisions under which the entity is allowed to conduct its business, but do not have a direct effect on an entity's financial statements. Some entities operate in heavily regulated industries (such as banks and chemical companies). Others are subject only to the many laws and regulations that relate generally to the operating aspects of the business (such as those related to occupational safety and health and equal employment opportunity). Noncompliance with laws and regulations may result in fines, litigation, or other consequences for the entity that may have a material effect on the financial statements.

Responsibility for Compliance With Laws and Regulations (Ref: par. .A1–.A7)

Responsibility of Management

.03 It is the responsibility of management, with the oversight of those charged with governance, to ensure that the entity's operations are conducted in accordance with the provisions of laws and regulations, including compliance with the provisions of laws and regulations that determine the reported amounts and disclosures in an entity's financial statements.

---

* This section has been codified using an "AU-C" identifier instead of an "AU" identifier. "AU-C" is a temporary identifier to avoid confusion with references to existing "AU" sections, which will remain in AICPA *Professional Standards* through 2013. The "AU-C" identifier will revert to "AU" in 2014, by which time substantially all engagements for which the "AU" sections were still effective are expected to be completed.

[1] Section 935, *Compliance Audits*, addresses compliance audits performed in accordance with generally accepted auditing standards, the standards for financial audits under *Government Auditing Standards*, and government audit requirements.

Responsibility of the Auditor

.04 The requirements in this section are designed to assist the auditor in identifying material misstatement of the financial statements due to noncompliance with laws and regulations. However, the auditor is not responsible for preventing noncompliance and cannot be expected to detect noncompliance with all laws and regulations.

.05 The auditor is responsible for obtaining reasonable assurance that the financial statements as a whole are free from material misstatement, whether caused by fraud or error.[2] In conducting an audit of financial statements, the auditor takes into account the applicable legal and regulatory framework. Because of the inherent limitations of an audit, an unavoidable risk exists that some material misstatements in the financial statements may not be detected, even though the audit is properly planned and performed in accordance with generally accepted auditing standards (GAAS).[3] In the context of laws and regulations, the potential effects of inherent limitations on the auditor's ability to detect material misstatements are greater for the following reasons:

- Many laws and regulations relating principally to the operating aspects of an entity typically do not affect the financial statements and are not captured by the entity's information systems relevant to financial reporting.
- Noncompliance may involve conduct designed to conceal it, such as collusion, forgery, deliberate failure to record transactions, management override of controls, or intentional misrepresentations made to the auditor.
- Whether an act constitutes noncompliance is ultimately a matter for legal determination, such as by a court of law.

Ordinarily, the further removed noncompliance is from the events and transactions reflected in the financial statements, the less likely the auditor is to become aware of, or recognize, the noncompliance.

.06 This section distinguishes the auditor's responsibilities regarding compliance with the following two categories of laws and regulations:

a. The provisions of those laws and regulations generally recognized to have a direct effect on the determination of material amounts and disclosures in the financial statements, such as tax and pension laws and regulations (see paragraph .13)

b. The provisions of other laws and regulations that do not have a direct effect on the determination of the amounts and disclosures in the financial statements but compliance with which may be

   i. fundamental to the operating aspects of the business,

   ii. fundamental to an entity's ability to continue its business, or

   iii. necessary for the entity to avoid material penalties

(for example, compliance with the terms of an operating license, regulatory solvency requirements, or environmental regulations); therefore, noncompliance with such laws and regulations may have a material effect on the financial statements (see paragraph .14).

---

[2] Paragraph .12 of section 200, *Overall Objectives of the Independent Auditor and the Conduct of an Audit in Accordance With Generally Accepted Auditing Standards.*

[3] Paragraph .A49 of section 200.

.07 In this section, differing requirements are specified for each of the previously mentioned categories of laws and regulations. For the category referred to in paragraph .06*a*, the auditor's responsibility is to obtain sufficient appropriate audit evidence regarding material amounts and disclosures in the financial statements that are determined by the provisions of those laws and regulations. For the category referred to in paragraph .06*b*, the auditor's responsibility is limited to performing specified audit procedures that may identify noncompliance with those laws and regulations that may have a material effect on the financial statements.

.08 The auditor is required by this section to remain alert to the possibility that other audit procedures applied for the purpose of forming an opinion on financial statements may bring instances of identified or suspected noncompliance with laws and regulations to the auditor's attention. Maintaining professional skepticism throughout the audit, as required by section 200, *Overall Objectives of the Independent Auditor and the Conduct of an Audit in Accordance With Generally Accepted Auditing Standards*, is important in this context, given the extent of laws and regulations that affect the entity.[4]

Effective Date

.09 This section is effective for audits of financial statements for periods ending on or after December 15, 2012.

Objectives

.10 The objectives of the auditor are to

a. obtain sufficient appropriate audit evidence regarding material amounts and disclosures in the financial statements that are determined by the provisions of those laws and regulations generally recognized to have a direct effect on their determination (see paragraph .06*a*),

b. perform specified audit procedures that may identify instances of noncompliance with other laws and regulations that may have a material effect on the financial statements (see paragraph .06*b*), and

c. respond appropriately to noncompliance or suspected noncompliance with laws and regulations identified during the audit.

Definition

.11 For the purposes of this section, the following term has the meaning attributed as follows:

Noncompliance. Acts of omission or commission by the entity, either intentional or unintentional, which are contrary to the prevailing laws or regulations. Such acts include transactions entered into by, or in the name of, the entity or on its behalf by those charged with governance, management, or employees. Noncompliance does not include personal misconduct (unrelated to the business activities of the entity) by those charged with governance, management, or employees of the entity.

---

[4] Paragraph .17 of section 200.

Requirements

The Auditor's Consideration of Compliance With Laws and Regulations

.12 As part of obtaining an understanding of the entity and its environment, in accordance with section 315, *Understanding the Entity and Its Environment and Assessing the Risks of Material Misstatement*, the auditor should obtain a general understanding of the following:[5] (Ref: par. .A8)

a. The legal and regulatory framework applicable to the entity and the industry or sector in which the entity operates

b. How the entity is complying with that framework

.13 The auditor should obtain sufficient appropriate audit evidence regarding material amounts and disclosures in the financial statements that are determined by the provisions of those laws and regulations generally recognized to have a direct effect on their determination (see paragraph .06*a*). (Ref: par. .A9–.A11)

.14 The auditor should perform the following audit procedures that may identify instances of noncompliance with other laws and regulations that may have a material effect on the financial statements (see paragraph .06*b*): (Ref: par. .A12–.A15)

a. Inquiring of management and, when appropriate, those charged with governance about whether the entity is in compliance with such laws and regulations

b. Inspecting correspondence, if any, with the relevant licensing or regulatory authorities (Ref: par. .A16)

.15 During the audit, the auditor should remain alert to the possibility that other audit procedures applied may bring instances of noncompliance or suspected noncompliance with laws and regulations to the auditor's attention. (Ref: par. .A17–.A18)

.16 In the absence of identified or suspected noncompliance, the auditor is not required to perform audit procedures regarding the entity's compliance with laws and regulations, other than those set out in paragraphs .12–.15 of this section and the requirement in section 580, *Written Representations*, related to requesting written representations from management regarding the entity's compliance with laws and regulations.[6]

Audit Procedures When Noncompliance Is Identified or Suspected

.17 If the auditor becomes aware of information concerning an instance of noncompliance or suspected noncompliance with laws and regulations, the auditor should obtain (Ref: par. .A19–.A20)

a. an understanding of the nature of the act and the circumstances in which it has occurred and

b. further information to evaluate the possible effect on the financial statements. (Ref: par. .A21)

---

[5] Paragraph .12 of section 315, *Understanding the Entity and Its Environment and Assessing the Risks of Material Misstatement.*

[6] Paragraph .13 of section 580, *Written Representations.*

.18 If the auditor suspects noncompliance may exist, the auditor should discuss the matter with management (at a level above those involved with the suspected noncompliance, if possible) and, when appropriate, those charged with governance. If management or, as appropriate, those charged with governance do not provide sufficient information that supports that the entity is in compliance with laws and regulations and, in the auditor's professional judgment, the effect of the suspected noncompliance may be material to the financial statements, the auditor should consider the need to obtain legal advice. (Ref: par. .A22–.A23)

.19 If sufficient information about suspected noncompliance cannot be obtained, the auditor should evaluate the effect of the lack of sufficient appropriate audit evidence on the auditor's opinion.

.20 The auditor should evaluate the implications of noncompliance in relation to other aspects of the audit, including the auditor's risk assessment and the reliability of written representations,[7] and take appropriate action. (Ref: par. .A24–.A25)

Reporting of Identified or Suspected Noncompliance

Reporting Noncompliance to Those Charged With Governance

.21 Unless all of those charged with governance are involved in management of the entity and aware of matters involving identified or suspected noncompliance already communicated by the auditor,[8] the auditor should communicate with those charged with governance matters involving noncompliance with laws and regulations that come to the auditor's attention during the course of the audit, other than when the matters are clearly inconsequential. (Ref: par. .A26)

.22 If, in the auditor's professional judgment, the noncompliance referred to in paragraph .21 is believed to be intentional and material, the auditor should communicate the matter to those charged with governance as soon as practicable.

.23 If the auditor suspects that management or those charged with governance are involved in noncompliance, the auditor should communicate the matter to the next higher level of authority at the entity, if it exists. When no higher authority exists, or if the auditor believes that the communication may not be acted upon or is unsure about the person to whom to report, the auditor should consider the need to obtain legal advice.

Reporting Noncompliance in the Auditor's Report on the Financial Statements

.24 If the auditor concludes that the noncompliance has a material effect on the financial statements, and it has not been adequately reflected in the financial statements, the auditor should, in accordance with section 705, *Modifications to the Opinion in the Independent Auditor's Report*, express a qualified or adverse opinion on the financial statements.[9] (Ref: par. .A27)

.25 If the auditor is precluded by management or those charged with governance from obtaining sufficient appropriate audit evidence to evaluate whether

---

[7] Paragraphs .22–.26 of section 580.

[8] Paragraph .09 of section 260, *The Auditor's Communication With Those Charged With Governance*.

[9] Paragraphs .08–.09 of section 705, *Modifications to the Opinion in the Independent Auditor's Report*.

noncompliance that may be material to the financial statements has, or is likely to have, occurred, the auditor should express a qualified opinion or disclaim an opinion on the financial statements on the basis of a limitation on the scope of the audit, in accordance with section 705.[10] (Ref: par. .A27)

.26 If the auditor is unable to determine whether noncompliance has occurred because of limitations imposed by the circumstances rather than by management or those charged with governance, the auditor should evaluate the effect on the auditor's opinion, in accordance with section 705.[11]

Reporting Noncompliance to Regulatory and Enforcement Authorities

.27 If the auditor has identified or suspects noncompliance with laws and regulations, the auditor should determine whether the auditor has a responsibility to report the identified or suspected noncompliance to parties outside the entity. (Ref: par. .A28–.A29)

Documentation

.28 The auditor should include in the audit documentation a description of the identified or suspected noncompliance with laws and regulations and the results of discussion with management and, when applicable, those charged with governance and other parties inside or outside the entity.[12] (Ref: par. .A30)

Application and Other Explanatory Material

Responsibility for Compliance With Laws and Regulations (Ref: par. .03–.08)

Responsibility of Management

.A1 It is the responsibility of management, with the oversight of those charged with governance, to ensure that the entity's operations are conducted in accordance with laws and regulations. Laws and regulations may affect an entity's financial statements in different ways (for example, most directly, they may affect specific disclosures required of the entity in the financial statements, or they may prescribe the applicable financial reporting framework). They also may establish certain legal rights and obligations of the entity, some of which will be recognized in the entity's financial statements. In addition, laws and regulations may provide for the imposition of penalties in cases of noncompliance.

.A2 The following are examples of the types of policies and procedures an entity may implement to assist in the prevention and detection of noncompliance with laws and regulations:

- Monitoring legal requirements and ensuring that operating procedures are designed to meet these requirements
- Instituting and operating appropriate systems of internal control

---

[10] [Footnote deleted, January 2012, to reflect conforming changes necessary due to the issuance of SAS No. 123.]

[11] [Footnote deleted, January 2012, to reflect conforming changes necessary due to the issuance of SAS No. 123.]

[12] Paragraphs .08–.12 and .A8 of section 230, *Audit Documentation*.

- Developing, publicizing, and following a code of ethics or code of conduct
- Ensuring employees are properly trained and understand the code of ethics or code of conduct
- Monitoring compliance with the code of ethics or code of conduct and acting appropriately to discipline employees who fail to comply with it
- Engaging legal advisors to assist in monitoring legal requirements
- Maintaining a register of significant laws and regulations with which the entity has to comply within its particular industry and a record of complaints

In larger entities, these policies and procedures may be supplemented by assigning appropriate responsibilities to the following:

- An internal audit function
- An audit committee
- A legal function
- A compliance function

Responsibility of the Auditor

.A3 Because of the inherent limitations described in paragraph .05, an audit performed in accordance with GAAS provides no assurance that all noncompliance with laws and regulations will be detected or that any contingent liabilities that result will be disclosed.

.A4 Noncompliance by the entity with laws and regulations may result in a material misstatement of the financial statements. Detection of noncompliance, regardless of materiality, may affect other aspects of the audit, including, for example, the auditor's consideration of the integrity of management or employees. Noncompliance can result from fraudulent activity. Section 240, *Consideration of Fraud in a Financial Statement Audit*, addresses the auditor's responsibility if fraud or suspected fraud is detected.

.A5 Whether an act constitutes noncompliance with laws and regulations is a matter for legal determination, which ordinarily is beyond the auditor's professional competence to determine. Nevertheless, the auditor's training, experience, and understanding of the entity and its industry or sector may provide a basis to recognize that some acts coming to the auditor's attention may constitute noncompliance with laws and regulations.

.A6 In accordance with specific statutory requirements, the auditor may be specifically required to report, as part of the audit of the financial statements, on whether the entity complies with certain provisions of laws or regulations. In these circumstances, section 806, *Reporting on Compliance With Aspects of Contractual Agreements or Regulatory Requirements in Connection With Audited Financial Statements*, and section 935, *Compliance Audits*, set forth how these audit responsibilities are addressed in the auditor's report. Furthermore, when specific statutory reporting requirements exist, it may be necessary for the audit plan to include appropriate tests for compliance with these provisions of the laws and regulations.

Considerations Specific to Governmental Entities

.A7 Auditors of governmental entities may have additional responsibilities with respect to the consideration of laws and regulations, which relate to the audit of financial statements or may extend to other aspects of the entity's operations.[13]

The Auditor's Consideration of Compliance With Laws and Regulations

Obtaining an Understanding of the Legal and Regulatory Framework (Ref: par. .12)

.A8 To obtain a general understanding of the legal and regulatory framework and how the entity complies with that framework, the auditor may, for example

- use the auditor's existing understanding of the entity's industry and regulatory and other external factors;
- update the understanding of those laws and regulations that directly determine the reported amounts and disclosures in the financial statements;
- inquire of management about other laws or regulations that may be expected to have a fundamental effect on the operations of the entity;
- inquire of management concerning the entity's policies and procedures regarding compliance with laws and regulations (including the prevention of noncompliance), if appropriate;
- inquire of management regarding the policies or procedures adopted for identifying, evaluating, and accounting for litigation claims;
- inquire of management regarding the use of directives issued by the entity and periodic representations obtained by the entity from management at appropriate levels of authority concerning compliance with laws and regulations; and
- consider the auditor's knowledge of the entity's history of noncompliance with laws and regulations.

Laws and Regulations Generally Recognized to Have a Direct Effect on the Determination of Material Amounts and Disclosures in the Financial Statements (Ref: par. .13)

.A9 Certain laws and regulations are well established, known to the entity and within the entity's industry or sector, and relevant to the entity's financial statements (as described in paragraph .06*a*). These laws and regulations generally are directly relevant to the determination of material amounts and disclosures in the financial statements and readily evident to the auditor. They could include those that relate to, for example

- the form and content of financial statements (for example, statutorily-mandated requirements);
- industry-specific financial reporting issues;
- accounting for transactions under government contracts (for example, laws and regulations that may affect the amount of revenue to be accrued); or

[13] See section 935; *Government Auditing Standards*; and OMB Circular A-133, *Audits of States, Local Governments and Non-Profit Organizations.*

- the accrual or recognition of expenses for income tax or pension costs.

.A10 Some provisions in those laws and regulations may be directly relevant to specific assertions in the financial statements (for example, the completeness of income tax provisions), whereas others may be directly relevant to the financial statements as a whole. The auditor's responsibility regarding misstatements resulting from noncompliance with laws and regulations having a direct effect on the determination of material amounts and disclosures in the financial statements is the same as that for misstatements caused by fraud or error, as described in section 200.

.A11 Noncompliance with other provisions of such laws and regulations, and the laws and regulations described in paragraph .06*b*, may result in fines, litigation, or other consequences for the entity, the costs of which may need to be provided for or disclosed in the financial statements but are not considered to have a direct effect on the financial statements, as described in paragraph .06*a*.

Procedures to Identify Instances of Noncompliance—Other Laws and Regulations (Ref: par. .14)

.A12 Certain other laws and regulations may need particular attention by the auditor because they have a fundamental effect on the operations of the entity (as described in paragraph .06*b*. Noncompliance with laws and regulations that have a fundamental effect on the operations of the entity may cause the entity to cease operations or call into question the entity's continuance as a going concern. For example, noncompliance with the requirements of the entity's license or other entitlement to perform its operations could have such an impact (for example, for a bank, noncompliance with capital or investment requirements).

.A13 Many laws and regulations relating principally to the operating aspects of the entity do not directly affect the financial statements (their financial statement effect is indirect) and are not captured by the entity's information systems relevant to financial reporting. Their indirect effect may result from the need to disclose a contingent liability because of the allegation or determination of identified or suspected noncompliance. Those other laws or regulations may include those related to securities trading, occupational safety and health, food and drug administration, environmental protection, equal employment, and price-fixing or other antitrust violations. An auditor may not have a sufficient basis for recognizing possible noncompliance with such laws and regulations.

.A14 For the category referred to in paragraph .06*b*, the auditor's responsibility is limited to performing specified audit procedures (see paragraph .14) that may identify noncompliance with those laws and regulations that may have a material effect on the financial statements. Even when those procedures are performed, the auditor may not become aware of the existence of noncompliance unless there is evidence of noncompliance in the records, documents, or other information normally inspected in an audit of financial statements.

.A15 Because the financial reporting consequences of other laws and regulations can vary depending on the entity's operations, the audit procedures required by paragraph .14 are intended to bring to the auditor's attention instances of noncompliance with laws and regulations that may have a material effect on the financial statements.

.A16 In some cases, the amount of an entity's correspondence with licensing or regulatory authorities is voluminous. In exercising professional judgment in such circumstances, the auditor may consider the following in determining the extent of inspection that may identify instances of noncompliance:

- The nature of the entity
- The nature and type of correspondence

Noncompliance Brought to the Auditor's Attention by Other Audit Procedures (Ref: par. .15)

.A17 Audit procedures applied to form an opinion on the financial statements may bring instances of noncompliance or suspected noncompliance with laws and regulations to the auditor's attention. For example, such audit procedures may include the following:

- Reading minutes
- Inquiring of the entity's management and in-house or external legal counsel concerning litigation, claims, and assessments
- Performing substantive tests of details of classes of transactions, account balances, or disclosures

.A18 Because the effect of laws and regulations on financial statements can vary considerably, written representations, as required by section 580, provide necessary audit evidence about management's knowledge of identified or suspected noncompliance with laws and regulations, the effects of which may have a material effect on the financial statements. However, written representations do not provide sufficient appropriate audit evidence on their own and, accordingly, do not affect the nature and extent of other audit evidence that is to be obtained by the auditor.[14]

Audit Procedures When Noncompliance Is Identified or Suspected

Indications of Noncompliance With Laws and Regulations (Ref: par. .17)

.A19 If the auditor becomes aware of the existence of, or information about, the following matters, it may be an indication of noncompliance with laws and regulations:

- Investigations by regulatory organizations and government departments or payment of fines or penalties
- Payments for unspecified services or loans to consultants, related parties, employees, or government officials or government employees
- Sales commissions or agent's fees that appear excessive in relation to those ordinarily paid by the entity or in its industry or to the services actually received
- Purchases made at prices significantly above or below market price
- Unusual payments in cash, purchases in the form of cashiers' checks payable to bearer, or transfers to numbered bank accounts

---

[14] Paragraph .04 of section 580.

- Unusual transactions with companies registered in tax havens
- Payments for goods or services made other than to the country from which the goods or services originated
- Existence of an information system that fails, whether by design or accident, to provide an adequate audit trail or sufficient evidence
- Unauthorized transactions or improperly recorded transactions
- Adverse media comment
- Noncompliance with laws or regulations cited in reports of examinations by regulatory agencies that have been made available to the auditor
- Failure to file tax returns or pay government duties or similar fees that are common to the entity's industry or the nature of its business

Obtaining an Understanding of an Act of Identified or Suspected Noncompliance (Ref: par. .17)

.A20 Procedures an auditor may perform to address the requirements of paragraph .17 include the following:

- Examining supporting documents, such as invoices, cancelled checks, and agreements, and comparing with accounting records
- Confirming significant information concerning the matter with the other party to the transaction or intermediaries, such as banks or lawyers
- Determining whether the transaction has been properly authorized
- Considering whether other similar transactions or events may have occurred and applying procedures to identify them

Matters Relevant to the Auditor's Evaluation (Ref: par. .17b)

.A21 Matters relevant to the auditor's evaluation of the possible effect on the financial statements include the following:

- The quantitative effect of noncompliance. The potential financial consequences of noncompliance with laws and regulations on the financial statements may include the imposition of fines, penalties, or damages; the threat of expropriation of assets; enforced discontinuation of operations; and litigation.
- The qualitative materiality of the effect of noncompliance. For example, an illegal payment of an otherwise immaterial amount could be material if a reasonable possibility exists that it could lead to a material contingent liability or a material loss of revenue.
- Whether the potential financial consequences require accrual or disclosure under the applicable financial reporting framework. For example, if material revenue or earnings are derived from transactions involving noncompliance, or if noncompliance creates significant risks associated with material revenue or earnings, such as loss of a significant business relationship, that information may require disclosure. Loss contingencies resulting from noncompliance that may require disclosure may be evaluated in the same

manner as other loss contingencies under the applicable financial reporting framework.

- Whether the potential financial consequences are so serious as to call into question the fair presentation of the financial statements or otherwise make the financial statements misleading.

Audit Procedures (Ref: par. .18)

.A22 The auditor may discuss the findings with those charged with governance, in which case they may be able to provide additional audit evidence. For example, the auditor may confirm that those charged with governance have the same understanding of the facts and circumstances relevant to transactions or events that have led to the possibility of noncompliance with laws and regulations.

.A23 If management or, as appropriate, those charged with governance do not provide sufficient information to the auditor that the entity is in fact in compliance with laws and regulations, the auditor may consider it appropriate to consult with the entity's in-house legal counsel or external legal counsel about the application of the laws and regulations to the circumstances, including the possibility of fraud, and the possible effects on the financial statements. The auditor may request management to arrange for such consultation with the entity's legal counsel. If it is not considered appropriate to consult with the entity's legal counsel or if the auditor is not satisfied with the legal counsel's opinion, the auditor may consider it appropriate to consult the auditor's own legal counsel about whether a violation of a law or regulation is involved; the possible legal consequences, including the possibility of fraud; and what further action, if any, the auditor may take.

Evaluating the Implications of Noncompliance (Ref: par. .20)

.A24 As required by paragraph .20, the auditor evaluates the implications of noncompliance with regard to other aspects of the audit, including the auditor's risk assessment and the reliability of written representations. The implications of particular instances of noncompliance identified by the auditor will depend on the relationship of the perpetration and concealment, if any, of the act to specific control activities and the level of management or employees involved, especially implications arising from the involvement of the highest authority within the entity.

.A25 The auditor may consider whether withdrawal from the engagement, when withdrawal is possible under applicable law or regulation, is necessary when management or those charged with governance do not take the remedial action that the auditor considers appropriate in the circumstances, even when the noncompliance is not material to the financial statements. Factors that may affect the auditor's decision may include the implications of the failure to take remedial action, which may affect the auditor's ability to rely on management representations, and the effects of continuing association with the entity. When deciding whether withdrawal from the engagement is necessary, the auditor may consider seeking legal advice. If withdrawal from the engagement is not possible under applicable law or regulation, the auditor may consider alternative actions, including describing the noncompliance in an other-matter(s) paragraph in the auditor's report.[15]

---

[15] Paragraph .08 of section 706, *Emphasis-of-Matter Paragraphs and Other-Matter Paragraphs in the Independent Auditor's Report.*

Reporting of Identified or Suspected Noncompliance

Reporting Noncompliance to Those Charged With Governance (Ref: par. .21)

.A26 The communication of matters involving identified or suspected noncompliance may describe the act of identified or suspected noncompliance, the circumstances of its occurrence, and the effect on the financial statements. The auditor may reach agreement in advance with those charged with governance on the nature of matters that would be considered clearly inconsequential and, thus, need not be communicated.

Issuance of a Modified Opinion on the Financial Statements (Ref: par. .24–.25)

.A27 If management or those charged with governance refuse to accept a modified opinion on the financial statements for the circumstances described in paragraphs .24–.25, the auditor may withdraw from the engagement, when withdrawal is possible under applicable law or regulation, and indicate the reasons for withdrawal in writing to those charged with governance.

Reporting Noncompliance to Regulatory and Enforcement Authorities (Ref: par. .27)

.A28 The auditor's professional duty to maintain the confidentiality of client information may preclude reporting identified or suspected noncompliance with laws and regulations to a party outside the entity. However, the auditor's legal responsibilities vary by jurisdiction, and in certain circumstances, the duty of confidentiality may be overridden by statute, the law, or courts of law. In the following circumstances, a duty to notify parties outside the entity may exist:

- In response to inquiries from an auditor to a predecessor auditor, in accordance with the requirements of section 210, *Terms of Engagement*[16]
- In response to a court order
- In compliance with requirements for the audits of entities that receive financial assistance from a government agency

Because potential conflicts with the auditor's ethical and legal obligations for confidentiality may be complex, the auditor may consult with legal counsel before discussing noncompliance with parties outside the entity.

Considerations Specific to Governmental Entities

.A29 The auditor of a governmental entity may be required to report on compliance with laws, regulations, and provisions of contracts or grant agreements as part of the audit of the governmental entity's financial statements (for example, in an audit conducted in accordance with *Government Auditing Standards*). The auditor also may be required to communicate instances of noncompliance to appropriate oversight bodies and funding agencies.

---

[16] Paragraphs .11–.12 of section 210, *Terms of Engagement*.

Documentation (Ref: par. .28)

.A30 The auditor's documentation of findings regarding identified or suspected noncompliance with laws and regulations may include, for example

- copies of records or documents.
- minutes of discussions held with management, those charged with governance, or other parties inside or outside the entity.

AU-C Section 260 *

The Auditor's Communication With Those Charged With Governance

Source: SAS No. 122; SAS No. 123; SAS No. 125.

Effective for audits of financial statements for periods ending on or after December 15, 2012.

Introduction

Scope of This Section

.01 This section addresses the auditor's responsibility to communicate with those charged with governance in an audit of financial statements. Although this section applies regardless of an entity's governance structure or size, particular considerations apply when all of those charged with governance are involved in managing an entity. This section does not establish requirements regarding the auditor's communication with an entity's management or owners unless they are also charged with a governance role.

.02 This section is written in the context of an audit of financial statements but may also be applied, adapted as necessary in the circumstances, to audits of other historical financial information when those charged with governance have a responsibility to oversee the preparation and fair presentation of the other historical financial information.

.03 Recognizing the importance of effective two-way communication in an audit of financial statements, this section provides an overarching framework for the auditor's communication with those charged with governance and identifies some specific matters to be communicated. Additional matters to be communicated are identified in other AU-C sections (see the exhibit, "Requirements to Communicate With Those Charged With Governance in Other AU-C Sections"). In addition, section 265, *Communicating Internal Control Related Matters Identified in an Audit*, establishes specific requirements regarding the communication of significant deficiencies and material weaknesses in internal control the auditor has identified during the audit to those charged with governance. Further matters not required by generally accepted auditing standards (GAAS) may be required to be communicated by agreement with those charged with governance or management or in accordance with external requirements. Nothing in this section precludes the auditor from communicating any other matters to those charged with governance.

Effective Date

.04 This section is effective for audits of financial statements for periods ending on or after December 15, 2012.

---

* This section has been codified using an "AU-C" identifier instead of an "AU" identifier. "AU-C" is a temporary identifier to avoid confusion with references to existing "AU" sections, which will remain in AICPA *Professional Standards* through 2013. The "AU-C" identifier will revert to "AU" in 2014, by which time substantially all engagements for which the "AU" sections were still effective are expected to be completed.

Objectives

.05 The objectives of the auditor are to

a. communicate clearly with those charged with governance the responsibilities of the auditor regarding the financial statement audit and an overview of the planned scope and timing of the audit.

b. obtain from those charged with governance information relevant to the audit.

c. provide those charged with governance with timely observations arising from the audit that are significant and relevant to their responsibility to oversee the financial reporting process.

d. promote effective two-way communication between the auditor and those charged with governance. (Ref: par. .A1–.A5)

Definitions

.06 For purposes of GAAS, the following terms have the meanings attributed as follows:

Management. The person(s) with executive responsibility for the conduct of the entity's operations. For some entities, management includes some or all of those charged with governance; for example, executive members of a governance board or an owner-manager.

Those charged with governance. The person(s) or organization(s) (for example, a corporate trustee) with responsibility for overseeing the strategic direction of the entity and the obligations related to the accountability of the entity. This includes overseeing the financial reporting process. Those charged with governance may include management personnel; for example, executive members of a governance board or an owner-manager.

Requirements

Those Charged With Governance

.07 The auditor should determine the appropriate person(s) within the entity's governance structure with whom to communicate. (Ref: par. .A6–.A9)

Communication With the Audit Committee or Other Subgroup of Those Charged With Governance

.08 If the auditor communicates with a subgroup of those charged with governance, such as the audit committee or an individual, the auditor should determine whether the auditor also needs to communicate with the governing body. (Ref: par. .A10–.A12)

When All of Those Charged With Governance Are Involved in Managing the Entity

.09 In some cases, all of those charged with governance are involved in managing the entity; for example, a small business in which a single owner manages the entity and no one else has a governance role. In these cases, if matters required by this section are communicated with a person(s) with management responsibilities and that person(s) also has governance responsibilities, the matters need not be communicated again with the same person(s) in that person's governance role. These matters are noted in paragraph .14. The auditor should, nonetheless, be satisfied that communication with person(s) with management responsibilities adequately informs all of those with whom the auditor would otherwise communicate in their governance capacity.

Matters to Be Communicated

The Auditor's Responsibilities With Regard to the Financial Statement Audit

.10 The auditor should communicate with those charged with governance the auditor's responsibilities with regard to the financial statement audit, including that (Ref: par. .A13–.A17)

- *a.* the auditor is responsible for forming and expressing an opinion about whether the financial statements that have been prepared by management, with the oversight of those charged with governance, are prepared, in all material respects, in accordance with the applicable financial reporting framework.
- *b.* the audit of the financial statements does not relieve management or those charged with governance of their responsibilities.

Planned Scope and Timing of the Audit

.11 The auditor should communicate with those charged with governance an overview of the planned scope and timing of the audit. (Ref: par. .A18–.A22)

Significant Findings or Issues From the Audit

.12 The auditor should communicate with those charged with governance (Ref: par. .A23)

- *a.* the auditor's views about qualitative aspects of the entity's significant accounting practices, including accounting policies, accounting estimates, and financial statement disclosures. When applicable, the auditor should (Ref: par. .A24–.A25)
  - i. explain to those charged with governance why the auditor considers a significant accounting practice that is acceptable under the applicable financial reporting framework not to be most appropriate to the particular circumstances of the entity and
  - ii. determine that those charged with governance are informed about the process used by management in formulating particularly sensitive accounting estimates, including fair value estimates, and about the basis for the auditor's conclusions regarding the reasonableness of those estimates.
- *b.* significant difficulties, if any, encountered during the audit. (Ref: par. .A26)
- *c.* disagreements with management, if any. (Ref: par. .A28)
- *d.* other findings or issues, if any, arising from the audit that are, in the auditor's professional judgment, significant and relevant to those charged with governance regarding their responsibility to oversee the financial reporting process. (Ref: par. .A27)

Uncorrected Misstatements

.13 The auditor should communicate with those charged with governance (Ref: par. .A29–.A30) *a.* uncorrected misstatements accumulated by the auditor and the effect that they, individually or in the aggregate, may have on the opinion in the auditor's report. The auditor's communication should identify material uncorrected misstatements individually. The auditor should request that uncorrected misstatements be corrected.

b. the effect of uncorrected misstatements related to prior periods on the relevant classes of transactions, account balances or disclosures, and the financial statements as a whole.

When Not All of Those Charged With Governance Are Involved in Management

.14 Unless all of those charged with governance are involved in managing the entity, the auditor also should communicate

a. material, corrected misstatements that were brought to the attention of management as a result of audit procedures. (Ref: par. .A31)

b. significant findings or issues, if any, arising from the audit that were discussed, or the subject of correspondence, with management. (Ref: par. .A32)

c. the auditor's views about significant matters that were the subject of management's consultations with other accountants on accounting or auditing matters when the auditor is aware that such consultation has occurred.

d. written representations the auditor is requesting. (Ref: par. .A33)

The Communication Process

Establishing the Communication Process

.15 The auditor should communicate with those charged with governance the form, timing, and expected general content of communications. (Ref: par. .A34–.A38)

Forms of Communication

.16 The auditor should communicate in writing with those charged with governance significant findings or issues from the audit (see paragraphs .12–.14) if, in the auditor's professional judgment, oral communication would not be adequate. This communication need not include matters that arose during the course of the audit that were communicated with those charged with governance and satisfactorily resolved. (Ref: par. .A39–.A41)

Restricted Use

.17 When the auditor communicates matters in accordance with this section in writing, the communication is considered a by-product report.[1] Accordingly, the auditor should indicate in the communication that it is intended solely for the information and use of those charged with governance and, if appropriate, management, and is not intended to be, and should not be, used by anyone other than these specified parties.

---

[1] Paragraphs .06c and .07 of section 905, *Alert That Restricts the Use of the Auditor's Written Communication*. [Footnote amended, effective for the auditor's written communications related to audits of financial statements for periods ending on or after December 15, 2012, by SAS No. 125.]

Timing of Communications

.18 The auditor should communicate with those charged with governance on a timely basis. (Ref: par. .A42–.A43)

Adequacy of the Communication Process

.19 The auditor should evaluate whether the two-way communication between the auditor and those charged with governance has been adequate for the purpose of the audit. If it has not, the auditor should evaluate the effect, if any, on the auditor's assessment of the risks of material misstatement and ability to obtain sufficient appropriate audit evidence and should take appropriate action. (Ref: par. .A44–.A46)

Documentation

.20 When matters required to be communicated by this section have been communicated orally, the auditor should include them in the audit documentation, including when and to whom they were communicated.[2] When matters have been communicated in writing, the auditor should retain a copy of the communication as part of the audit documentation. (Ref: par. .A47)

Application and Other Explanatory Material

Objectives

The Role of Communication (Ref: par. .05)

.A1 This section focuses primarily on communications from the auditor to those charged with governance. Nevertheless, effective two-way communication is important in assisting

- the auditor and those charged with governance in understanding matters related to the audit in context and in developing a constructive working relationship. This relationship is developed while maintaining the auditor's independence and objectivity.
- the auditor in obtaining from those charged with governance information relevant to the audit. For example, those charged with governance may assist the auditor in understanding the entity and its environment, in identifying appropriate sources of audit evidence, and in providing information about specific transactions or events.
- those charged with governance in fulfilling their responsibility to oversee the financial reporting process, thereby reducing the risks of material misstatement of the financial statements.

.A2 Although the auditor is responsible for communicating specific matters in accordance with this section, management also has a responsibility to communicate matters of governance interest to those charged with governance. Communication by the auditor does not relieve management of this responsibility. Similarly, management's communication of these matters to those charged with governance does not relieve the auditor of the responsibility to also communicate them. However, communication of these matters by management may affect the form or timing of the auditor's communication.

---

[2] Paragraphs .08–.12 and .A8 of section 230, *Audit Documentation*.

.A3 Clear communication of specific matters required to be communicated by GAAS is an integral part of every audit. However, GAAS do not require the auditor to perform procedures specifically to identify other significant matters to communicate with those charged with governance.

Legal or Regulatory Restrictions on Communicating With Those Charged With Governance (Ref: par. .05)

.A4 Law or regulation may restrict the auditor's communication of certain matters with those charged with governance. For example, law or regulation may specifically prohibit a communication or other action that might prejudice an investigation by an appropriate authority into an actual, or suspected, illegal act. In some circumstances, potential conflicts between the auditor's obligations of confidentiality and obligations to communicate may be complex. In such cases, the auditor may consider obtaining legal advice.

.A5 In certain circumstances, the auditor may be required to report to a regulatory or enforcement body certain matters that have been communicated with those charged with governance. For example, *Government Auditing Standards* requires auditors to report fraud, illegal acts, violations of provisions of contracts or grant agreements, and abuse directly to such parties in certain circumstances.

Those Charged With Governance (Ref: par. .07)

.A6 Governance structures vary by entity, reflecting influences such as size and ownership characteristics. For example:

- In some entities, those charged with governance hold positions (for example, company directors) that are integral parts of the entity's legal structure. For other entities, a body that is not part of the entity is charged with governance, as with some government agencies.
- In some cases, some or all of those charged with governance also have management responsibilities. In others, those charged with governance and management are different people.
- Parties charged with governance of governmental entities may include members or staff of a legislative oversight committee, oversight bodies, or other parties contracting for the audit.

.A7 In most entities, governance is the collective responsibility of a governing body, such as a board of directors; a supervisory board; partners; proprietors; a committee of management; trustees; or equivalent persons. In some smaller entities, however, one person may be charged with governance, such as the owner-manager, when there are no other owners, or a sole trustee. When governance is a collective responsibility, a subgroup, such as an audit committee or even an individual, may be charged with specific tasks to assist the governing body in meeting its responsibilities.

.A8 Such diversity means that it is not possible for this section to specify for all audits the person(s) with whom the auditor is to communicate particular matters. Also, in some cases, the appropriate person(s) with whom to communicate may not be clearly identifiable from the engagement circumstances. An example of this is entities in which the governance structures are not formally defined, such as some family-owned entities, some not-for-profit organizations, and some government entities. When the appropriate person(s) with whom to communicate is not clearly identifiable, the auditor and the engaging party may need to discuss and agree on the relevant person(s) within the entity's governance structure with whom the auditor will communicate. In deciding with whom to communicate, the auditor's understanding of an entity's governance structure and processes obtained in accordance with section 315, *Understanding the Entity and Its Environment and Assessing the Risks of Material Misstatement*, is relevant. The appropriate person(s) with whom to communicate may vary depending on the matter to be communicated.

.A9 Section 600, *Special Considerations—Audits of Group Financial Statements (Including the Work of Component Auditors)*, includes specific matters to be communicated by group auditors with those charged with governance.[3] When the entity being audited is a component of a group, the appropriate person(s) with whom to communicate is dependent on the nature of the matter to be communicated and the terms of the engagement.

Communication With the Audit Committee or Other Subgroup of Those Charged With Governance (Ref: par. .08)

.A10 When considering communicating with a subgroup of those charged with governance, the auditor may take into account matters such as

- the respective responsibilities of the subgroup and the governing body.
- the nature of the matter to be communicated.
- relevant legal or regulatory requirements.
- whether the subgroup (*a*) has the authority to take action regarding the information communicated and (*b*) can provide further information and explanations the auditor may need.
- whether the auditor is aware of potential conflicts of interest between the subgroup and other members of the governing body.

.A11 When deciding whether there is also a need to communicate information, in full or in summary form, with the governing body, the auditor may be influenced by the auditor's assessment of how effectively and appropriately the subgroup communicates relevant information with the governing body. The auditor may make explicit in the terms of the engagement that the auditor retains the right to communicate directly with the governing body.

.A12 Audit committees (or similar subgroups with different names) exist in many entities. Although the specific authority and functions of audit committees may differ, communication with the audit committee, when one exists, is a key element in the auditor's communication with those charged with governance. Good governance principles suggest that

- the auditor has access to the audit committee as necessary.
- the chair of the audit committee and, when relevant, the other members of the audit committee meet with the auditor periodically.
- the audit committee meets with the auditor without management present at least annually, unless prohibited by law or regulation.

---

[3] Paragraphs .45–.48 of section 600, *Special Considerations—Audits of Group Financial Statements (Including the Work of Component Auditors)*.

Matters to Be Communicated

The Auditor's Responsibilities With Regard to the Financial Statement Audit (Ref: par. .10)

.A13 The auditor's responsibilities with regard to the financial statement audit are often included in the engagement letter or other suitable form of written agreement that documents the terms of the engagement. Providing those charged with governance with a copy of that engagement letter or other suitable form of written agreement may be an appropriate way to communicate with them that

- the auditor is responsible for performing the audit in accordance with GAAS and that the audit is designed to obtain reasonable, rather than absolute, assurance about whether the financial statements as a whole are free from material misstatement.
- an audit of financial statements includes consideration of internal control over financial reporting as a basis for designing audit procedures that are appropriate in the circumstances, but not for the purpose of expressing an opinion on the effectiveness of the entity's internal control over financial reporting.
- the auditor is responsible for communicating significant matters related to the financial statement audit that are, in the auditor's professional judgment, relevant to the responsibilities of those charged with governance in overseeing the financial reporting process. GAAS do not require the auditor to design procedures for the purpose of identifying other matters to communicate with those charged with governance.
- when applicable, the auditor is also responsible for communicating particular matters required by law or regulation, by agreement with the entity, or by additional requirements applicable to the engagement.

Independence (Ref: par. .10)

.A14 GAAS require independence for all audits. Relevant matters to consider in reaching a conclusion about independence include circumstances or relationships that create threats to auditor independence and the related safeguards that have been applied to eliminate those threats or reduce them to an acceptable level. Comprehensive material on threats to independence and safeguards, including application to specific situations, is set forth in the AICPA's *Conceptual Framework for AICPA Independence Standards* (ET sec. 100-1).

.A15 Although the auditor's report affirms the auditor's independence, in certain situations, the auditor may determine that it is appropriate to communicate with those charged with governance circumstances or relationships (for example, financial interests, business or family relationships, or nonaudit services provided or expected to be provided) that, in the auditor's professional judgment, may reasonably be thought to bear on independence, and to which the auditor gave significant consideration, in reaching the conclusion that independence has not been impaired.

.A16 It may be particularly appropriate to communicate with those charged with governance those circumstances or relationships discussed in paragraph .A15 in audits of public interest entities. In addition to entities subject to Securities and Exchange Commission reporting requirements, the AICPA's *Conceptual Framework for AICPA Independence Standards* considers the following entities to be *public interest entities*: (1) employee benefit and health and welfare plans subject to Employee Retirement Income Security Act audit requirements; (2) governmental retirement plans; (3) entities or programs (including for-profit entities) subject to Single Audit Act OMB Circular A-133 audit requirements and entities or programs subject to similar program oversight; and (4) financial institutions, credit unions, and insurance companies. These entities are public interest entities because their audited financial statements are (1) directly relied upon by significant numbers of stakeholders to make investment, credit, or similar decisions or (2) indirectly relied upon through regulatory oversight (for example, in the case of pension plans, banks, and insurance companies) and, therefore, the potential extent of harm to the public from an audit failure involving one of these entities would generally be significant.

.A17 The form and timing of communications regarding independence may be affected by the entity's governance structure and whether a formal subgroup, such as an audit committee, exists. In situations in which all of those charged with governance are involved in managing the entity, the auditor may determine that those charged with governance have been informed of relevant facts regarding the auditor's independence through their management activities or through other means, such as the engagement letter. This is particularly likely when the entity is owner-managed and the auditor's firm has little involvement with the entity beyond a financial statement audit.

Planned Scope and Timing of the Audit (Ref: par. .11)

.A18 Care is required when communicating with those charged with governance about the planned scope and timing of the audit so as not to compromise the effectiveness of the audit, particularly when some or all of those charged with governance are involved in managing the entity. For example, communicating the nature and timing of detailed audit procedures may reduce the effectiveness of those procedures by making them too predictable. Certain factors described in paragraph .A39 may be relevant in determining the nature and extent of this communication.

.A19 Communication regarding the planned scope and timing of the audit may assist

- those charged with governance to discuss issues of risk and materiality with the auditor;
- those charged with governance to understand better the consequences of the auditor's work and to identify any areas in which they may request the auditor to undertake additional procedures; and
- the auditor to understand better the entity and its environment.

.A20 Matters communicated may include the following:

- How the auditor proposes to address the significant risks of material misstatement, whether due to fraud or error
- The auditor's approach to internal control relevant to the audit including, when applicable, whether the auditor will express an opinion on the effectiveness of internal control over financial reporting
- The application of materiality in the context of an audit, as discussed in section 320, *Materiality in Planning and Performing an Audit*

- If the entity has an internal audit function, the extent to which the auditor will use the work of internal audit and how the external and internal auditors can best work together

.A21 Other planning matters that may be appropriate to discuss with those charged with governance include

- the views of those charged with governance about the following matters:
  - — The appropriate person(s) in the entity's governance structure with whom to communicate
  - — The allocation of responsibilities between those charged with governance and management
  - — The entity's objectives and strategies and the related business risks that may result in material misstatements
  - — Matters those charged with governance consider as warranting particular attention during the audit and any areas for which they request additional procedures to be undertaken
  - — Significant communications with regulators
  - — Other matters those charged with governance believe are relevant to the audit of the financial statements
- the attitudes, awareness, and actions of those charged with governance concerning (*a*) the entity's internal control and its importance in the entity, including how those charged with governance oversee the effectiveness of internal control, and (*b*) the detection or the possibility of fraud.
- the actions of those charged with governance in response to developments in law, accounting standards, corporate governance practices, and other related matters.
- the actions of those charged with governance in response to previous communications with the auditor.

.A22 Although communication with those charged with governance may assist the auditor to plan the scope and timing of the audit, it does not change the auditor's sole responsibility to establish the overall audit strategy and the audit plan, including the nature, timing, and extent of procedures necessary to obtain sufficient appropriate audit evidence.

Significant Findings From the Audit (Ref: par. .12)

.A23 The communication of significant findings from the audit may include requesting further information from those charged with governance in order to complete the audit evidence obtained. For example, the auditor may confirm that those charged with governance have the same understanding of the facts and circumstances relevant to specific transactions or events.

Qualitative Aspects of the Entity's Significant Accounting Practices (Ref: par. .12a)

.A24 Financial reporting frameworks ordinarily allow for the entity to make accounting estimates and judgments about accounting policies and financial statement disclosures. Open and constructive communication about qualitative aspects of the entity's significant accounting practices may include comment on the acceptability of significant accounting practices. The appendix,

"Qualitative Aspects of Accounting Practices," identifies matters that may be included in this communication.

.A25 Certain accounting estimates are particularly sensitive because of their significance to the financial statements and because of the possibility that future events affecting them may differ markedly from management's current judgments. In communicating with those charged with governance about the process used by management in formulating particularly sensitive accounting estimates, including fair value estimates, and about the basis for the auditor's conclusions regarding the reasonableness of those estimates, the auditor may consider communicating

- the nature of significant assumptions,
- the degree of subjectivity involved in the development of the assumptions, and
- the relative materiality of the items being measured to the financial statements as a whole.

Significant Difficulties Encountered During the Audit (Ref: par. .12b)

.A26 Significant difficulties encountered during the audit may include matters such as

- significant delays in management providing required information.
- an unnecessarily brief time within which to complete the audit.
- extensive unexpected effort required to obtain sufficient appropriate audit evidence.
- the unavailability of expected information.
- restrictions imposed on the auditor by management.
- management's unwillingness to provide information about management's plans for dealing with the adverse effects of the conditions or events that lead the auditor to believe there is substantial doubt about the entity's ability to continue as a going concern.

In some circumstances, such difficulties may constitute a scope limitation that leads to a modification of the auditor's opinion.

Other Findings or Issues

.A27 The auditor may become aware that the entity is subject to an audit requirement that is not encompassed in the terms of the engagement. The communication to those charged with governance that an audit conducted in accordance with GAAS may not satisfy the relevant legal, regulatory, or contractual requirements may be necessary if, for example, an entity engages an auditor to perform an audit of its financial statements in accordance with GAAS and the auditor becomes aware that by law, regulation, or contractual agreement the entity also is required to have an audit performed in accordance with one or more of the following:

a. *Government Auditing Standards*

b. OMB Circular A-133, *Audits of States, Local Governments, and Non-Profit Organizations*

c. Other compliance audit requirements, such as state or local laws or program-specific audits under federal audit guides

Disagreements With Management (Ref: par. .12c)

.A28 Discussions with those charged with governance include any disagreements with management that arose during the audit, regardless of whether they were satisfactorily resolved, about matters that, individually or in the aggregate, could be significant to the entity's financial statements or the auditor's report. Disagreements with management may occasionally arise over, among other things, the application of accounting principles to the entity's specific transactions and events and the basis for management's judgments about accounting estimates. Disagreements may also arise regarding the scope of the audit, disclosures to be included in the entity's financial statements, and the wording of the auditor's report. For purposes of this section, disagreements do not include differences of opinion based on incomplete facts or preliminary information that are later resolved.

Uncorrected Misstatements (Ref: par. .13)

.A29 The auditor is not required to accumulate misstatements that the auditor believes are trivial.[4] When there are a large number of individually immaterial uncorrected misstatements, the auditor may communicate the number and overall monetary effect of the uncorrected misstatements, rather than the details of each individual uncorrected misstatement.

.A30 The auditor may discuss with those charged with governance the reasons for, and the implications of, a failure to correct misstatements, taking into account the size and nature of the misstatement judged in the surrounding circumstances, and possible implications with regard to future financial statements.

Corrected Misstatements (Ref: par. .14a)

.A31 The auditor also may communicate corrected immaterial misstatements, such as frequently recurring immaterial misstatements that may indicate a particular bias in the preparation of the financial statements.

Significant Findings or Issues Discussed or Subject to Correspondence With Management (Ref: par. .14b)

.A32 Significant findings or issues discussed, or the subject of correspondence, with management may include matters such as

- business conditions affecting the entity and business plans and strategies that may affect the risks of material misstatement.
- discussions or correspondence in connection with the initial or recurring engagement of the auditor including, among other matters, any discussions or correspondence regarding accounting practices or the application of auditing standards.

Written Representations (Ref: par. .14d)

.A33 The auditor may provide those charged with governance with a copy of management's written representations.

The Communication Process

Establishing the Communication Process (Ref: par. .15)

.A34 Clear communication of the following helps establish the basis for effective two-way communication:

- The auditor's responsibilities (paragraphs .10 and .A12–.A15)
- An overview of the planned scope and timing of the audit (paragraphs .11 and .A16–.A20)

[4] Paragraph .05 of section 450, *Evaluation of Misstatements Identified During the Audit.*

- The expected general content of communications

.A35 Matters that may also contribute to effective two-way communication include discussion of

- the purpose of communications. When the purpose is clear, the auditor and those charged with governance are in a better position to have a mutual understanding of relevant issues and the expected actions arising from the communication process.
- the form in which communications will be made.
- the person(s) on the audit team and among those charged with governance who will communicate regarding particular matters.
- the auditor's expectation that communication will be two-way and that those charged with governance will communicate with the auditor matters they consider relevant to the audit. Such matters might include (*a*) strategic decisions that may significantly affect the nature, timing, and extent of audit procedures; (*b*) the suspicion or the detection of fraud; or (*c*) concerns with the integrity or competence of senior management.
- the process for taking action and reporting back on matters communicated by the auditor.
- the process for taking action and reporting back on matters communicated by those charged with governance.

.A36 The communication process will vary with the circumstances, including the size and governance structure of the entity, how those charged with governance operate, and the auditor's view of the significance of matters to be communicated. Difficulty in establishing effective two-way communication may indicate that the communication between the auditor and those charged with governance is not adequate for the purpose of the audit (see paragraph .A44).

Communication With Management

.A37 Many matters may be discussed with management in the ordinary course of an audit, including matters to be communicated with those charged with governance in accordance with this section. Such discussions recognize management's executive responsibility for the conduct of the entity's operations and, in particular, management's responsibility for the preparation and fair presentation of the financial statements.

.A38 Before communicating matters with those charged with governance, the auditor may discuss them with management unless that is inappropriate. For example, it may not be appropriate to discuss with management questions of management's competence or integrity. In addition to recognizing management's responsibility, these initial discussions may clarify facts and issues and give management an opportunity to provide further information and explanations. Similarly, when the entity has an internal audit function, the auditor may discuss matters with the internal auditor before communicating with those charged with governance.

Forms of Communication (Ref: par. .16)

.A39 Effective communication may involve formal presentations and written reports as well as less formal communications, including discussions. The auditor may communicate matters other than those identified in paragraph .16 either orally or in writing. Written communications may include an engagement letter that is provided to those charged with governance.

.A40 In addition to the significance of a particular matter, the form of communication (for example, whether to communicate orally or in writing, the extent of detail or summarization in the communication, and whether to communicate in a formal or informal manner) may be affected by factors such as

- whether the matter has been satisfactorily resolved.
- whether management has previously communicated the matter.
- the size, operating structure, control environment, and legal structure of the entity being audited.
- legal or regulatory requirements that may require a written communication with those charged with governance.
- the expectations of those charged with governance, including arrangements made for periodic meetings or communications with the auditor.
- the amount of ongoing contact and dialogue the auditor has with those charged with governance.
- whether there have been significant changes in the membership of a governing body.
- in the case of an audit of special purpose financial statements, whether the auditor also audits the entity's general purpose financial statements.

.A41 When a significant matter is discussed with an individual member of those charged with governance, such as the chair of an audit committee, it may be appropriate for the auditor to summarize the matter in later communications so that all of those charged with governance have full and balanced information.

Timing of Communications (Ref: par. .18)

.A42 The appropriate timing for communications will vary with the circumstances of the engagement. Considerations include the significance and nature of the matter and the action expected to be taken by those charged with governance. The auditor may consider communicating

- planning matters early in the audit engagement and, for an initial engagement, as part of the terms of the engagement.
- significant difficulties encountered during the audit as soon as practicable if those charged with governance are able to assist the auditor in overcoming the difficulties or if the difficulties are likely to lead to a modified opinion.

.A43 Other factors that may be relevant to the timing of communications include

- the size, operating structure, control environment, and legal structure of the entity being audited.
- any legal obligation to communicate certain matters within a specified timeframe.
- the expectations of those charged with governance, including arrangements made for periodic meetings or communications with the auditor.
- the time at which the auditor identifies certain matters (for example, timely communication of a material weakness to enable appropriate remedial action to be taken).

- whether the auditor is auditing both general purpose and special purpose financial statements.

Adequacy of the Communication Process (Ref: par. .19)

.A44 The auditor need not design specific procedures to support the evaluation of the two-way communication between the auditor and those charged with governance. Rather, that evaluation may be based on observations resulting from audit procedures performed for other purposes. Such observations may include

- the appropriateness and timeliness of actions taken by those charged with governance in response to matters communicated by the auditor. When significant findings or issues raised in previous communications have not been dealt with effectively, it may be appropriate for the auditor to inquire about why appropriate action has not been taken and to consider raising the point again. This avoids the risk of giving an impression that the auditor is satisfied that the matter has been adequately addressed or is no longer significant.
- the apparent openness of those charged with governance in their communications with the auditor.
- the willingness and capacity of those charged with governance to meet with the auditor without management present.
- the apparent ability of those charged with governance to fully comprehend matters raised by the auditor, such as the extent to which those charged with governance probe issues and question recommendations made to them.
- difficulty in establishing with those charged with governance a mutual understanding of the form, timing, and expected general content of communications.
- when all or some of those charged with governance are involved in managing the entity, their apparent awareness of how matters discussed with the auditor affect their broader governance responsibilities as well as their management responsibilities.

.A45 As discussed in paragraph .A1, effective two-way communication assists both the auditor and those charged with governance. Further, section 315 identifies participation by those charged with governance, including their interaction with internal auditors (if any) and external auditors, as an element of the entity's control environment. Inadequate two-way communication may indicate an unsatisfactory control environment, which will influence the auditor's assessment of the risks of material misstatements. There is also a risk that the auditor may not have obtained sufficient appropriate audit evidence to form an opinion on the financial statements.

.A46 If the two-way communication between the auditor and those charged with governance is not adequate and the situation cannot be resolved, the auditor may take actions such as the following:

- Modifying the auditor's opinion on the basis of a scope limitation
- Obtaining legal advice about the consequences of different courses of action
- Communicating with third parties (for example, a regulator) or a higher authority in the governance structure that is outside the entity, such as the owners of a business (for example, shareholders

in a general meeting), or the responsible government agency for certain governmental entities

- Withdrawing from the engagement when withdrawal is possible under applicable law or regulation

Documentation (Ref: par. .20)

.A47 Documentation of oral communication may include a copy of minutes prepared by the entity as part of the audit documentation if those minutes are an appropriate record of the communication.

.A48

Appendix—Qualitative Aspects of Accounting Practices

The communication required by paragraph .12*a* and discussed in paragraphs .A24–.A25 may include such matters as the following:

Accounting Policies

- The appropriateness of the accounting policies to the particular circumstances of the entity, considering the need to balance the cost of providing information with the likely benefit to users of the entity's financial statements (when acceptable alternative accounting policies exist, the communication may include identification of the financial statement items that are affected by the choice of significant policies as well as information on accounting policies used by similar entities)
- The initial selection of, and changes in, significant accounting policies, including the application of new accounting pronouncements (the communication may include the effect of the timing and method of adoption of a change in accounting policy on the current and future earnings of the entity, and the timing of a change in accounting policies with regard to expected new accounting pronouncements)
- The effect of significant accounting policies in controversial or emerging areas (or those unique to an industry, particularly when there is a lack of authoritative material or consensus)
- The effect of the timing of transactions in relation to the period in which they are recorded

Accounting Estimates

- For items for which estimates are significant, issues discussed in section 540, *Auditing Accounting Estimates, Including Fair Value Accounting Estimates, and Related Disclosures*, including the following examples:
  - — Management's identification of accounting estimates
  - — Management's process for making accounting estimates
  - — Risks of material misstatement
  - — Indicators of possible management bias
  - — Disclosure of estimation uncertainty in the financial statements

Financial Statement Disclosures

- The issues involved, and related judgments made, in formulating particularly sensitive financial statement disclosures (for example, disclosures related to revenue recognition, going concern, subsequent events, and contingency issues)
- The overall neutrality, consistency, and clarity of the disclosures in the financial statements

Related Matters

- The potential effect on the financial statements of significant risks and exposures and uncertainties, such as pending litigation, that are disclosed in the financial statements
- The extent to which the financial statements are affected by unusual transactions, including nonrecurring amounts recognized during the period, and the extent to which such transactions are separately disclosed in the financial statements
- The factors affecting asset and liability carrying values, including the entity's bases for determining useful lives assigned to tangible and intangible assets (the communication may explain how factors affecting carrying values were selected and how alternative selections would have affected the financial statements
- The selective correction of misstatements (for example, correcting misstatements with the effect of increasing reported earnings, but not those that have the effect of decreasing reported earnings)

.A49

Exhibit—Requirements to Communicate With Those Charged With Governance in Other AU-C Sections

Requirements for the auditor to communicate with those charged with governance are included in other AU-C sections. This section does not change the requirements in

a. paragraph .17 of section 210, *Terms of Engagement*

b. paragraphs .21, .38*c*(i), and .39–.41 of section 240, *Consideration of Fraud in a Financial Statement Audit*

c. paragraphs .14, .18, and .21–.23 of section 250, *Consideration of Laws and Regulations in an Audit of Financial Statements*

d. paragraph .11 of section 265, *Communicating Internal Control Related Matters Identified in an Audit*

e. paragraph .27 of section 550, *Related Parties*

f. paragraphs .10*b*–*c*, .12*a*, .15*a*, .17*a*, and .18 of section 560, *Subsequent Events and Subsequently Discovered Facts*

g. paragraph .19 of section 570, *The Auditor's Consideration of an Entity's Ability to Continue as a Going Concern*

h. paragraphs .45–.48 of section 600, *Special Considerations—Audits of Group Financial Statements (Including the Work of Component Auditors)*

i. paragraphs .12, .14, .20, and .29 of section 705, *Modifications to the Opinion in the Independent Auditor's Report*

j. paragraph .09 of section 706, *Emphasis-of-Matter Paragraphs and Other-Matter Paragraphs in the Independent Auditor's Report*

k. paragraphs .08, .12, .15, and .18 of section 720, *Other Information in Documents Containing Audited Financial Statements*

l. paragraph .06 of section 730, *Required Supplementary Information*

m. paragraphs .23–.28 of section 930, *Interim Financial Information*

n. paragraphs .36–.37 of section 935, *Compliance Audits*

[Revised: September 2012, to reflect conforming changes necessary due to the issuance of SAS No. 126.]

AU-C Section 265 *

Communicating Internal Control Related Matters Identified in an Audit

Source: SAS No. 122; SAS No. 125.

Effective for audits of financial statements for periods ending on or after December 15, 2012.

Introduction

Scope of This Section

.01 This section addresses the auditor's responsibility to appropriately communicate to those charged with governance and management deficiencies in internal control that the auditor has identified in an audit of financial statements. This section does not impose additional responsibilities on the auditor regarding obtaining an understanding of internal control or designing and performing tests of controls over and above the requirements of section 315, *Understanding the Entity and Its Environment and Assessing the Risks of Material Misstatement*, and section 330, *Performing Audit Procedures in Response to Assessed Risks and Evaluating the Audit Evidence Obtained*. Section 260, *The Auditor's Communication With Those Charged With Governance*, establishes further requirements and provides guidance regarding the auditor's responsibility to communicate with those charged with governance regarding the audit.

.02 The auditor is required to obtain an understanding of internal control relevant to the audit when identifying and assessing the risks of material misstatement.[1] In making those risk assessments, the auditor considers internal control in order to design audit procedures that are appropriate in the circumstances but not for the purpose of expressing an opinion on the effectiveness of internal control. The auditor may identify deficiencies in internal control not only during this risk assessment process but also at any other stage of the audit. This section specifies which identified deficiencies the auditor is required to communicate to those charged with governance and management.

.03 Nothing in this section precludes the auditor from communicating to those charged with governance or management other internal control matters that the auditor has identified during the audit.

.04 This section is not applicable if the auditor is engaged to report on the effectiveness of an entity's internal control over financial reporting under AT section 501, *An Examination of an Entity's Internal Control Over Financial Reporting That Is Integrated With an Audit of Its Financial Statements*.

---

* This section has been codified using an "AU-C" identifier instead of an "AU" identifier. "AU-C" is a temporary identifier to avoid confusion with references to existing "AU" sections, which will remain in AICPA *Professional Standards* through 2013. The "AU-C" identifier will revert to "AU" in 2014, by which time substantially all engagements for which the "AU" sections were still effective are expected to be completed.

[1] Paragraph .13 of section 315, *Understanding the Entity and Its Environment and Assessing the Risks of Material Misstatement*. Paragraphs .A61–.A67 of section 315 provide guidance on obtaining an understanding of internal control relevant to the audit.

Effective Date

.05 This section is effective for audits of financial statements for periods ending on or after December 15, 2012.

Objective

.06 The objective of the auditor is to appropriately communicate to those charged with governance and management deficiencies in internal control that the auditor has identified during the audit and that, in the auditor's professional judgment, are of sufficient importance to merit their respective attentions.

Definitions

.07 For purposes of generally accepted auditing standards, the following terms have the meanings attributed as follows:

Deficiency in internal control. A deficiency in internal control exists when the design or operation of a control does not allow management or employees, in the normal course of performing their assigned functions, to prevent, or detect and correct, misstatements on a timely basis. A deficiency in *design* exists when (*a*) a control necessary to meet the control objective is missing, or (*b*) an existing control is not properly designed so that, even if the control operates as designed, the control objective would not be met. A deficiency in *operation* exists when a properly designed control does not operate as designed or when the person performing the control does not possess the necessary authority or competence to perform the control effectively.

Material weakness. A deficiency, or a combination of deficiencies, in internal control, such that there is a reasonable possibility that a material misstatement of the entity's financial statements will not be prevented, or detected and corrected, on a timely basis.

Significant deficiency. A deficiency, or a combination of deficiencies, in internal control that is less severe than a material weakness yet important enough to merit attention by those charged with governance.

Requirements

Determination of Whether Deficiencies in Internal Control Have Been Identified

.08 The auditor should determine whether, on the basis of the audit work performed, the auditor has identified one or more deficiencies in internal control. (Ref: par. .A1–.A4)

Evaluating Identified Deficiencies in Internal Control (Ref: par. .A5–.A14)

.09 If the auditor has identified one or more deficiencies in internal control, the auditor should evaluate each deficiency to determine, on the basis of the audit work performed, whether, individually or in combination, they constitute significant deficiencies or material weaknesses.

.10 If the auditor determines that a deficiency, or a combination of deficiencies, in internal control is not a material weakness, the auditor should consider whether prudent officials, having knowledge of the same facts and circumstances, would likely reach the same conclusion.

Communication of Deficiencies in Internal Control

.11 The auditor should communicate in writing to those charged with governance on a timely basis significant deficiencies and material weaknesses identified during the audit, including those that were remediated during the audit. (Ref: par. .A15–.A20 and .A28)

.12 The auditor also should communicate to management at an appropriate level of responsibility, on a timely basis (Ref: par. .A21 and .A28)

a. in writing, significant deficiencies and material weaknesses that the auditor has communicated or intends to communicate to those charged with governance, unless it would be inappropriate to communicate directly to management in the circumstances. (Ref: par. .A16 and .A22–.A23)

b. in writing or orally, other deficiencies in internal control identified during the audit that have not been communicated to management by other parties and that, in the auditor's professional judgment, are of sufficient importance to merit management's attention. If other deficiencies in internal control are communicated orally, the auditor should document the communication. (Ref: par. .A24–.A27)

.13 The communications referred to in paragraphs .11–.12 should be made no later than 60 days following the report release date. (Ref: par. .A16–.A17)

.14 The auditor should include in the auditor's written communication of significant deficiencies and material weaknesses (Ref: par. .A29–.A33)

a. the definition of the term *material weakness* and, when relevant, the definition of the term *significant deficiency*.

b. a description of the significant deficiencies and material weaknesses and an explanation of their potential effects. (Ref: par. .A29)

c. sufficient information to enable those charged with governance and management to understand the context of the communication. In particular, the auditor should include in the communication the following elements that explain that (Ref: par. .A30–.A31)

  i. the purpose of the audit was for the auditor to express an opinion on the financial statements.

  ii. the audit included consideration of internal control over financial reporting in order to design audit procedures that are appropriate in the circumstances but not for the purpose of expressing an opinion on the effectiveness of internal control.

  iii. the auditor is not expressing an opinion on the effectiveness of internal control.

  iv. the auditor's consideration of internal control was not designed to identify all deficiencies in internal control that might be material weaknesses or significant deficiencies, and therefore, material weaknesses or significant deficiencies may exist that were not identified.

d. an appropriate alert, in accordance with section 905, *Alert That Restricts the Use of the Auditor's Written Communication.*[2] (Ref: par. .A32)

[As amended, effective for the auditor's written communications related to audits of financial statements for periods ending on or after December 15, 2012, by SAS No. 125.]

.15 When the auditor issues a written communication stating that no material weaknesses were identified during the audit, the communication should include the matters in paragraph .14*a* and *c*–*d*. (Ref: par. .A34–.A36)

.16 The auditor should not issue a written communication stating that no significant deficiencies were identified during the audit. (Ref: par. .A34)

Application and Other Explanatory Material

Determination of Whether Deficiencies in Internal Control Have Been Identified (Ref: par. .08)

.A1 In determining whether the auditor has identified one or more deficiencies in internal control, the auditor may discuss the relevant facts and circumstances of the auditor's findings with the appropriate level of management. This discussion provides an opportunity for the auditor to alert management on a timely basis to the existence of deficiencies of which management may not have been previously aware. The level of management with whom it is appropriate to discuss the findings is one that is familiar with the internal control area concerned and that has the authority to take remedial action on any identified deficiencies in internal control. In some circumstances, it may not be appropriate for the auditor to discuss the auditor's findings directly with management (for example, if the findings appear to call management's integrity or competence into question [see paragraph .A22]).

.A2 In discussing the facts and circumstances of the auditor's findings with management, the auditor may obtain other relevant information for further consideration, such as

- management's understanding of the actual or suspected causes of the deficiencies.
- exceptions arising from the deficiencies that management may have noted (for example, misstatements that were not prevented by the relevant IT controls).
- a preliminary indication from management of its response to the findings.

Considerations Specific to Smaller, Less Complex Entities

.A3 Although the concepts underlying control activities in smaller entities are likely to be similar to those in larger entities, the formality with which controls operate will vary. Further, smaller entities may find that certain types of control activities are not necessary because of controls applied by management. For example, management's sole authority for granting credit to customers and approving significant purchases can provide effective control over important account balances and transactions, lessening or removing the need for more detailed control activities.

---

[2] Paragraphs .06*c*, .07, and .11 of section 905, *Alert That Restricts the Use of the Auditor's Written Communication.* [Footnote added, effective for the auditor's written communications related to audits of financial statements for periods ending on or after December 15, 2012, by SAS No. 125.]

.A4 Also, smaller entities often have fewer employees, which may limit the extent to which segregation of duties is practicable. However, in a small owner-managed entity, the owner-manager may be able to exercise more effective oversight than in a larger entity. On the other hand, such increased management oversight also may increase the risk of management override of controls.

Evaluating Identified Deficiencies in Internal Control (Ref: par. .09–.10)

.A5 The severity of a deficiency, or a combination of deficiencies, in internal control depends not only on whether a misstatement has actually occurred but also on

- the magnitude of the potential misstatement resulting from the deficiency or deficiencies and
- whether there is a reasonable possibility that the entity's controls will fail to prevent, or detect and correct, a misstatement of an account balance or disclosure. A reasonable possibility exists when the chance of the future event or events occurring is more than remote.

Significant deficiencies and material weaknesses may exist even though the auditor has not identified misstatements during the audit.

.A6 Factors that affect the magnitude of a misstatement that might result from a deficiency, or deficiencies, in internal control include, but are not limited to, the following:

- The financial statement amounts or total of transactions exposed to the deficiency
- The volume of activity (in the current period or expected in future periods) in the account or class of transactions exposed to the deficiency

.A7 In evaluating the magnitude of the potential misstatement, the maximum amount by which an account balance or total of transactions can be overstated generally is the recorded amount, whereas understatements could be larger.

.A8 Risk factors affect whether there is a reasonable possibility that a deficiency, or a combination of deficiencies, in internal control will result in a misstatement of an account balance or disclosure. The factors include, but are not limited to, the following:

- The nature of the financial statement accounts, classes of transactions, disclosures, and assertions involved
- The cause and frequency of the exceptions detected as a result of the deficiency, or deficiencies, in internal control
- The susceptibility of the related asset or liability to loss or fraud
- The subjectivity, complexity, or extent of judgment required to determine the amount involved
- The interaction or relationship of the control(s) with other controls
- The interaction with other deficiencies in internal control
- The possible future consequences of the deficiency, or deficiencies, in internal control

- The importance of the controls to the financial reporting process—for example
  - — general monitoring controls (such as oversight of management)
  - — controls over the prevention and detection of fraud
  - — controls over the selection and application of significant accounting policies
  - — controls over significant transactions with related parties
  - — controls over significant transactions outside the entity's normal course of business
  - — controls over the period-end financial reporting process (such as controls over nonrecurring journal entries)

.A9 The evaluation of whether a deficiency in internal control presents a reasonable possibility of misstatement may be made without quantifying the probability of occurrence as a specific percentage or range. Also, in many cases, the probability of a small misstatement will be greater than the probability of a large misstatement.

.A10 Controls may be designed to operate individually, or in combination, to effectively prevent, or detect and correct, misstatements.[3] For example, controls over accounts receivable may consist of both automated and manual controls designed to operate together to prevent, or detect and correct, misstatements in the account balance. A deficiency in internal control on its own may not be sufficiently important to constitute a significant deficiency or a material weakness. However, a combination of deficiencies affecting the same significant account or disclosure, relevant assertion, or component of internal control may increase the risks of misstatement to such an extent to give rise to a significant deficiency or material weakness.

.A11 Indicators of material weaknesses in internal control include

- identification of fraud, whether or not material, on the part of senior management;
- restatement of previously issued financial statements to reflect the correction of a material misstatement due to fraud or error;
- identification by the auditor of a material misstatement of the financial statements under audit in circumstances that indicate that the misstatement would not have been detected by the entity's internal control; and
- ineffective oversight of the entity's financial reporting and internal control by those charged with governance.

Considerations Specific to Governmental Entities

.A12 Law or regulation may require the auditor to communicate to those charged with governance or other relevant parties (such as regulators) deficiencies in internal control that the auditor has identified during the audit using specific terms and definitions that differ from those in this section. In such circumstances, the auditor uses such terms and definitions when communicating deficiencies in internal control in accordance with the requirements of the law or regulation and in accordance with this section.

---

[3] Paragraph .A68 of section 315. [Footnote renumbered, effective for the auditor's written communications related to audits of financial statements for periods ending on or after December 15, 2012, by SAS No. 125.]

.A13 When law or regulation requires the auditor to communicate deficiencies in internal control that the auditor has identified during the audit using specific terms, but such terms have not been defined, the auditor may use the definitions, requirements, and guidance in this section to comply with the law or regulation.

.A14 The requirements of this section remain applicable, notwithstanding that law or regulation may require the auditor to use specific terms or definitions.

Communication of Deficiencies in Internal Control (Ref: par. .11–.16)

Communication of Significant Deficiencies and Material Weaknesses to Those Charged With Governance (Ref: par. .11)

.A15 Communicating significant deficiencies and material weaknesses in writing to those charged with governance reflects the importance of these matters and assists those charged with governance in fulfilling their oversight responsibilities. Section 260 establishes relevant considerations regarding communication with those charged with governance when all of them are involved in managing the entity.[4]

.A16 Although the auditor is required by paragraph .13 to make the communications referred to in paragraphs .11–.12 no later than 60 days following the report release date, the communication is best made by the report release date because receipt of such communication may be an important factor in enabling those charged with governance to discharge their oversight responsibilities. Nevertheless, because the auditor's written communication of significant deficiencies and material weaknesses forms part of the final audit file, the written communication is subject to the overriding requirement for the auditor to complete the assembly of the final audit file on a timely basis, no later than 60 days following the report release date.[5]

.A17 Early communication to those charged with governance or management may be important for some matters because of their relative significance and the urgency for corrective follow-up action. Regardless of the timing of the written communication of significant deficiencies and material weaknesses, the auditor may communicate these orally in the first instance to management and, when appropriate, those charged with governance to assist them in taking timely remedial action to minimize the risks of material misstatement. However, oral communication does not relieve the auditor of the responsibility to communicate the significant deficiencies and material weaknesses in writing, as this section requires.

.A18 The level of detail at which to communicate significant deficiencies and material weaknesses is a matter of the auditor's professional judgment in the circumstances. Factors that the auditor may consider in determining an appropriate level of detail for the communication include, for example, the following:

---

[4] Paragraph .09 of section 260, *The Auditor's Communication With Those Charged With Governance*. [Footnote renumbered, effective for the auditor's written communications related to audits of financial statements for periods ending on or after December 15, 2012, by SAS No. 125.]

[5] Paragraph .16 of section 230, *Audit Documentation*. [Footnote renumbered, effective for the auditor's written communications related to audits of financial statements for periods ending on or after December 15, 2012, by SAS No. 125.]

- The nature of the entity. For example, the communication required for a governmental entity may be different from that for a nongovernmental entity.
- The size and complexity of the entity. For example, the communication required for a complex entity may be different from that for an entity operating a simple business.
- The nature of significant deficiencies and material weaknesses that the auditor has identified.
- The entity's governance composition. For example, more detail may be needed if those charged with governance include members who do not have significant experience in the entity's industry or in the affected areas.
- Legal or regulatory requirements regarding the communication of specific types of deficiencies in internal control.

.A19 Management and those charged with governance may already be aware of significant deficiencies and material weaknesses that the auditor has identified during the audit and may have chosen not to remedy them because of cost or other considerations. The responsibility for evaluating the costs and benefits of implementing remedial action rests with management and those charged with governance. Accordingly, the requirements to communicate significant deficiencies and material weaknesses in paragraphs .11–.12 apply, regardless of cost or other considerations that management and those charged with governance may consider relevant in determining whether to remedy such deficiencies.

.A20 The fact that the auditor communicated a significant deficiency or material weakness to those charged with governance and management in a previous audit does not eliminate the need for the auditor to repeat the communication if remedial action has not yet been taken. If a previously communicated significant deficiency or material weakness remains, the current year's communication may repeat the description from the previous communication or simply reference the previous communication and the date of that communication. The auditor may ask management or, when appropriate, those charged with governance why the significant deficiency or material weakness has not yet been remedied. A failure to act, in the absence of a rational explanation, may in itself represent a significant deficiency or material weakness.

Communication of Deficiencies in Internal Control to Management (Ref: par. .12)

.A21 Ordinarily, the appropriate level of management is the one that has responsibility and authority to evaluate the deficiencies in internal control and to take the necessary remedial action. For significant deficiencies and material weaknesses, the appropriate level is likely to be the CEO or CFO (or equivalent) because these matters also are required to be communicated to those charged with governance. For other deficiencies in internal control, the appropriate level may be operational management with more direct involvement in the control areas affected and with the authority to take appropriate remedial action.

Communication of Significant Deficiencies and Material Weaknesses in Internal Control to Management (Ref: par. .12a)

.A22 Certain identified significant deficiencies or material weaknesses in internal control may call into question the integrity or competence of management. For example, there may be evidence of fraud or intentional noncompliance with laws and regulations by management or management may exhibit an inability to oversee the preparation of adequate financial statements, which may raise doubt about management's competence. Accordingly, it may not be appropriate to communicate such deficiencies directly to management.

.A23 Section 250, *Consideration of Laws and Regulations in an Audit of Financial Statements*, establishes requirements and provides guidance on the reporting of identified or suspected noncompliance with laws and regulations, including when those charged with governance are themselves involved in such noncompliance.[6] Section 240, *Consideration of Fraud in a Financial Statement Audit*, establishes requirements and provides guidance regarding communication to those charged with governance when the auditor has identified fraud or suspected fraud involving management.[7]

Communication of Other Deficiencies in Internal Control to Management (Ref: par. .12b)

.A24 During the audit, the auditor may identify other deficiencies in internal control that are not significant deficiencies or material weaknesses but that may be of sufficient importance to merit management's attention. The determination regarding which other deficiencies in internal control merit management's attention is a matter of the auditor's professional judgment in the circumstances, taking into account the likelihood and potential magnitude of misstatements that may arise in the financial statements as a result of those deficiencies.

.A25 The communication of other deficiencies in internal control that merit management's attention need not be in writing. When the auditor has discussed the facts and circumstances of the auditor's findings with management, the auditor may consider an oral communication of the other deficiencies to have been made to management at the time of these discussions. Accordingly, a formal communication need not be made subsequently.

.A26 If the auditor has communicated deficiencies in internal control, other than significant deficiencies or material weaknesses, to management in a prior period and management has chosen not to remedy them for cost or other reasons, the auditor need not repeat the communication in the current period. The auditor also is not required to repeat information about such deficiencies if the information has been previously communicated to management by other parties, such as internal auditors or regulators. However, the auditor may consider it appropriate to recommunicate these other deficiencies if there has been a change of management or if new information has come to the auditor's attention that alters the prior understanding of the auditor and management regarding the deficiencies. Nevertheless, the failure of management to remedy other deficiencies in internal control that were previously communicated may become a significant deficiency requiring communication with those charged with governance. Whether this is the case depends on the auditor's professional judgment in the circumstances.

.A27 In some circumstances, those charged with governance may wish to be made aware of the details of other deficiencies in internal control that the auditor has communicated to management or be briefly informed of the nature of the other deficiencies. Alternatively, the auditor may inform those charged

---

[6] Paragraphs .21–.27 of section 250, *Consideration of Laws and Regulations in an Audit of Financial Statements*. [Footnote renumbered, effective for the auditor's written communications related to audits of financial statements for periods ending on or after December 15, 2012, by SAS No. 125.]

[7] Paragraph .40 of section 240, *Consideration of Fraud in a Financial Statement Audit*. [Footnote renumbered, effective for the auditor's written communications related to audits of financial statements for periods ending on or after December 15, 2012, by SAS No. 125.]

with governance when a communication of other deficiencies has been made to management. In either case, the auditor may communicate orally or in writing to those charged with governance, as appropriate.

Considerations Specific to Governmental Entities (Ref: par. .11–.12)

.A28 Auditors performing audits of governmental entities may have additional responsibilities to communicate deficiencies in internal control that the auditor identified during the audit, in a different format, at a level of detail or to parties not envisioned in this section. For example, significant deficiencies and material weaknesses may have to be communicated to a governmental authority, and such communications may be required to be made publicly available. Law or regulation also may require auditors to report deficiencies in internal control, irrespective of their severity. Further, law or regulation may require auditors to report on broader internal control-related matters (for example, controls related to compliance with law, regulation, or provisions of contracts or grant agreements).[8]

Content of Written Communication of Significant Deficiencies and Material Weaknesses in Internal Control (Ref: par. .14–.16)

.A29 In explaining the potential effects of the significant deficiencies and material weaknesses, the auditor need not quantify those effects. The potential effects may be described in terms of the control objectives and types of errors the control was designed to prevent, or detect and correct, or in terms of the risk(s) of misstatement that the control was designed to address. The potential effects may be evident from the description of the significant deficiencies or material weaknesses.

.A30 The significant deficiencies or material weaknesses may be grouped together for reporting purposes when it is appropriate to do so. The auditor also may include in the written communication suggestions for remedial action on the deficiencies, management's actual or proposed responses, and a statement about whether the auditor has undertaken any steps to verify whether management's responses have been implemented (see paragraph .A33).

.A31 The auditor may consider it appropriate to include the following information as additional context for the communication:

- The general inherent limitations of internal control, including the possibility of management override of controls
- The specific nature and extent of the auditor's consideration of internal control during the audit

Restriction on Use (Ref: par. .14d)

.A32 In certain cases not involving *Government Auditing Standards*, law or regulation may require the auditor or management to furnish a copy of the auditor's written communication on significant deficiencies and material weaknesses to governmental authorities. When this is the case, the auditor's written communication may identify such governmental authorities in the paragraph containing the alert that restricts the use of the auditor's written communication. Section 905 does not permit the auditor to add parties, other than those

---

[8] See section 935, *Compliance Audits*. [Footnote renumbered, effective for the auditor's written communications related to audits of financial statements for periods ending on or after December 15, 2012, by SAS No. 125.]

identified in paragraph .07*b* of that section.[9] [As amended, effective for the auditor's written communications related to audits of financial statements for periods ending on or after December 15, 2012, by SAS No. 125.]

Management's Written Response

.A33 Management may wish to or may be required by a regulator to prepare a written response to the auditor's communication regarding significant deficiencies or material weaknesses identified during the audit. Such management communications may include a description of corrective actions taken by the entity, the entity's plans to implement new controls, or a statement indicating that management believes the cost of correcting a significant deficiency or material weakness would exceed the benefits to be derived from doing so. If such a written response is included in a document containing the auditor's written communication to management and those charged with governance concerning identified significant deficiencies or material weaknesses, the auditor may add a paragraph to the written communication disclaiming an opinion on such information. The following is an example of such a paragraph:

> ABC Company's written response to the significant deficiencies [*and material weaknesses*] identified in our audit was not subjected to the auditing procedures applied in the audit of the financial statements and, accordingly, we express no opinion on it.

No Material Weakness Communications (Ref: par. .15–.16)

.A34 Management or those charged with governance may request a written communication indicating that no material weaknesses were identified during the audit. A written communication indicating that no material weaknesses were identified during the audit does not provide any assurance about the effectiveness of an entity's internal control over financial reporting. However, an auditor is not precluded from issuing such a communication, provided that the communication includes the matters required by paragraph .15. However, a written communication indicating that no significant deficiencies were identified during the audit is precluded by paragraph .16 because such a communication has the potential to be misunderstood or misused.

.A35 Exhibit B, "Illustrative No Material Weakness Communication," includes an illustrative communication indicating that no material weaknesses were identified during the audit.

Considerations Specific to Governmental Entities

.A36 A written communication indicating that no material weaknesses were identified during the audit may be required to be furnished to governmental authorities. As described in paragraph .A32, the auditor's written communication may identify the governmental authority as a specified party in the restricted use paragraph. The auditor is not permitted to add other parties as specified parties.

---

[9] Paragraph .08 of section 905. [Footnote added, effective for the auditor's written communications related to audits of financial statements for periods ending on or after December 15, 2012, by SAS No. 125.]

.A37

Appendix—Examples of Circumstances That May Be Deficiencies, Significant Deficiencies, or Material Weaknesses

Paragraph .A11 identifies indicators of material weaknesses in internal control. The following are examples of circumstances that may be deficiencies, significant deficiencies, or material weaknesses.

Deficiencies in the Design of Controls

The following are examples of circumstances that may be deficiencies, significant deficiencies, or material weaknesses related to the design of controls:

- Inadequate design of controls over the preparation of the financial statements being audited.
- Inadequate design of controls over a significant account or process.
- Inadequate documentation of the components of internal control.
- Insufficient control consciousness within the organization (for example, the tone at the top and the control environment).
- Evidence of ineffective aspects of the control environment, such as indications that significant transactions in which management is financially interested are not being appropriately scrutinized by those charged with governance.
- Evidence of an ineffective entity risk assessment process, such as management's failure to identify a risk of material misstatement that the auditor would expect the entity's risk assessment process to have identified.
- Evidence of an ineffective response to identified significant risks (for example, absence of controls over such a risk).
- Absent or inadequate segregation of duties within a significant account or process.
- Absent or inadequate controls over the safeguarding of assets (this applies to controls that the auditor determines would be necessary for effective internal control over financial reporting).
- Inadequate design of IT general and application controls that prevents the information system from providing complete and accurate information consistent with financial reporting objectives and current needs.
- Employees or management who lack the qualifications and training to fulfill their assigned functions. For example, in an entity that prepares financial statements in accordance with generally accepted accounting principles (GAAP), the person responsible for the accounting and reporting function lacks the skills and knowledge to apply GAAP in recording the entity's financial transactions or preparing its financial statements.
- Inadequate design of monitoring controls used to assess the design and operating effectiveness of the entity's internal control over time.

- Absence of an internal process to report deficiencies in internal control to management on a timely basis.
- Absence of a risk assessment process within the entity when such a process would ordinarily be expected to have been established.

Failures in the Operation of Controls

The following are examples of circumstances that may be deficiencies, significant deficiencies, or material weaknesses related to the operation of controls:

- Failure in the operation of effectively designed controls over a significant account or process (for example, the failure of a control such as dual authorization for significant disbursements within the purchasing process).
- Failure of the information and communication component of internal control to provide complete and accurate output because of deficiencies in timeliness, completeness, or accuracy (for example, the failure to obtain timely and accurate consolidating information from remote locations that is needed to prepare the financial statements).
- Failure of controls designed to safeguard assets from loss, damage, or misappropriation. This circumstance may need careful consideration before it is evaluated as a significant deficiency or material weakness. For example, assume that a company uses security devices to safeguard its inventory (preventive controls) and also performs timely periodic physical inventory counts (detective control) with regard to its financial reporting. Although the physical inventory count does not safeguard the inventory from theft or loss, it prevents a material misstatement of the financial statements if performed effectively and timely. Therefore, given that the definitions of *material weakness* and *significant deficiency* relate to the likelihood of misstatement of the financial statements, the failure of a preventive control, such as inventory tags, will not result in a significant deficiency or material weakness if the detective control (physical inventory counts) prevents a misstatement of the financial statements. Material weaknesses relating to controls over the safeguarding of assets would only exist if the company does not have effective controls (considering both safeguarding and other controls) to prevent, or detect and correct, a material misstatement of the financial statements.
- Failure to perform reconciliations of significant accounts. For example, accounts receivable subsidiary ledgers are not reconciled to the general ledger account in a timely or accurate manner.
- Undue bias or lack of objectivity by those responsible for accounting decisions (for example, consistent understatement of expenses or overstatement of allowances at the direction of management).
- Misrepresentation by entity personnel to the auditor (an indicator of fraud).
- Management override of controls.
- Failure of an application control caused by a deficiency in the design or operation of an IT general control.
- An observed deviation rate that exceeds the number of deviations expected by the auditor in a test of the operating effectiveness of

a control. For example, if the auditor designs a test in which he or she selects a sample and expects no deviations, the finding of one deviation is a nonnegligible deviation rate because based on the results of the auditor's test of the sample, the desired level of confidence was not obtained.

.A38

Exhibit A—Illustrative Auditor's Written Communication

The following is an illustrative auditor's written communication encompassing the requirements in paragraph .14.

To Management and [*identify the body or individuals charged with governance, such as the entity's Board of Directors*] of ABC Company.

In planning and performing our audit of the financial statements of ABC Company (the "Company") as of and for the year ended December 31, 20XX, in accordance with auditing standards generally accepted in the United States of America, we considered the Company's internal control over financial reporting (internal control) as a basis for designing audit procedures that are appropriate in the circumstances for the purpose of expressing our opinion on the financial statements, but not for the purpose of expressing an opinion on the effectiveness of the Company's internal control. Accordingly, we do not express an opinion on the effectiveness of the Company's internal control.

Our consideration of internal control was for the limited purpose described in the preceding paragraph and was not designed to identify all deficiencies in internal control that might be [*material weaknesses* or *material weaknesses or significant deficiencies*] and therefore, [*material weaknesses* or *material weaknesses or significant deficiencies*] may exist that were not identified. However, as discussed below, we identified certain deficiencies in internal control that we consider to be [*material weaknesses* or *significant deficiencies* or *material weaknesses and significant deficiencies*].

A deficiency in internal control exists when the design or operation of a control does not allow management or employees, in the normal course of performing their assigned functions, to prevent, or detect and correct, misstatements on a timely basis. A material weakness is a deficiency, or a combination of deficiencies, in internal control, such that there is a reasonable possibility that a material misstatement of the entity's financial statements will not be prevented, or detected and corrected, on a timely basis. [*We consider the following deficiencies in the Company's internal control to be material weaknesses:*]

[*Describe the material weaknesses that were identified and an explanation of their potential effects.*]

[*A significant deficiency is a deficiency, or a combination of deficiencies, in internal control that is less severe than a material weakness, yet important enough to merit attention by those charged with governance. We consider the following deficiencies in the Company's internal control to be significant deficiencies:*]

[*Describe the significant deficiencies that were identified and an explanation of their potential effects.*]

[*If the auditor is communicating significant deficiencies and did not identify any material weaknesses, the auditor may state that none of the identified significant deficiencies are considered to be material weaknesses.*]

This communication is intended solely for the information and use of management, [*identify the body or individuals charged with governance*], others within the organization, and [*identify any governmental authorities to which the auditor is required to report*] and is not intended to be, and should not be, used by anyone other than these specified parties.[1]

[*Auditor's signature*]

[*Auditor's city and state*]

[*Date*]

[As amended, effective for the auditor's written communications related to audits of financial statements for periods ending on or after December 15, 2012, by SAS No. 125.]

---

[1] When the engagement is also performed in accordance with *Government Auditing Standards*, the alert required by paragraph .14*d* may read as follows: "The purpose of this communication is solely to describe the scope of our testing of internal control over financial reporting and the results of that testing. This communication is an integral part of an audit performed in accordance with *Government Auditing Standards* in considering the Company's internal control over financial reporting. Accordingly, this communication is not suitable for any other purpose." The AICPA Audit Guide Government Auditing Standards *and Circular A-133 Audits* provides additional interpretative guidance, including illustrative reports. [Footnote added, effective for the auditor's written communications related to audits of financial statements for periods ending on or after December 15, 2012, by SAS No. 125.]

.A39

Exhibit B—Illustrative No Material Weakness Communication

The following is an illustrative auditor's written communication indicating that no material weaknesses were identified during the audit of a not-for-profit organization.

To Management and [*identify the body or individuals charged with governance, such as the entity's Board of Directors*] of NPO Organization.

In planning and performing our audit of the financial statements of NPO Organization (the "Organization") as of and for the year ended December 31, 20XX, in accordance with auditing standards generally accepted in the United States of America, we considered the Organization's internal control over financial reporting (internal control) as a basis for designing audit procedures that are appropriate in the circumstances for the purpose of expressing our opinion on the financial statements, but not for the purpose of expressing an opinion on the effectiveness of the Organization's internal control. Accordingly, we do not express an opinion on the effectiveness of the Organization's internal control.

A deficiency in internal control exists when the design or operation of a control does not allow management or employees, in the normal course of performing their assigned functions, to prevent, or detect and correct, misstatements on a timely basis. A material weakness is a deficiency, or a combination of deficiencies, in internal control, such that there is a reasonable possibility that a material misstatement of the entity's financial statements will not be prevented, or detected and corrected, on a timely basis.

Our consideration of internal control was for the limited purpose described in the first paragraph and was not designed to identify all deficiencies in internal control that might be material weaknesses. Given these limitations, during our audit we did not identify any deficiencies in internal control that we consider to be material weaknesses. However, material weaknesses may exist that have not been identified.

[*If one or more significant deficiencies have been identified, the auditor may add the following: Our audit was also not designed to identify deficiencies in internal control that might be significant deficiencies. A significant deficiency is a deficiency, or a combination of deficiencies, in internal control that is less severe than a material weakness, yet important enough to merit attention by those charged with governance. We communicated the significant deficiencies identified during our audit in a separate communication dated [date].*]

This communication is intended solely for the information and use of management, [*identify the body or individuals charged with governance*], others within the organization, and [*identify any governmental authorities to which the auditor is required to report*] and is not intended to be, and should not be, used by anyone other than these specified parties.[1]

---

[1] When the engagement is also performed in accordance with *Government Auditing Standards*, the alert required by paragraph .14*d* may read as follows: "The purpose of this communication is solely to describe the scope of our testing of internal control over financial reporting and the results of that testing. This communication is an integral part of an audit performed in accordance with *Government Auditing Standards* in considering the Company's internal control over financial reporting. Accordingly, this communication is not suitable for any other purpose." The AICPA Audit Guide Government Auditing Standards *and Circular A-133 Audits* provides additional interpretative guidance, including illustrative reports. [Footnote added, effective for the auditor's written communications related to audits of financial statements for periods ending on or after December 15, 2012, by SAS No. 125.]

[*Auditor's signature*]

[*Auditor's city and state*]

[*Date*]

[As amended, effective for the auditor's written communications related to audits of financial statements for periods ending on or after December 15, 2012, by SAS No. 125.]

AU-C Section 9265 *

Communicating Internal Control Related Matters Identified in an Audit: Auditing Interpretations of Section 265

1. Communication of Significant Deficiencies and Material Weaknesses Prior to the Completion of the Compliance Audit for Participants in Office of Management and Budget Single Audit Pilot Project

.01 *Question*—On October 7, 2009, the Office of Management and Budget (OMB) published the parameters of a pilot project, which is a collaborative effort between volunteer nonfederal entities expending American Recovery and Reinvestment Act of 2009 (ARRA) awards (auditees), the auditors performing compliance audits of auditees with ARRA expenditures under OMB Circular A-133, *Audits of States, Local Governments, and Non-Profit Organizations*, and the federal government. For auditees that volunteer, the pilot project requires their auditors to issue to management an early written communication of significant deficiencies and material weaknesses in internal control over compliance at an interim date, prior to the completion of the compliance audit. Such communication would be based on internal control work performed on specified compliance requirements for two major programs with ARRA expenditures chosen from a list of approved ARRA pilot project programs. This communication also would be required to be submitted by management to the cognizant agency for audit. May an auditor issue such an interim communication in accordance with section 265, *Communicating Internal Control Related Matters Identified in an Audit*?

.02 *Interpretation*—Yes. Section 265 permits an auditor to communicate to management identified significant deficiencies and material weaknesses before the completion of a financial statement audit. It would be equally appropriate for a compliance audit. Regardless of how the early communication is delivered, the auditor should communicate all significant deficiencies and material weaknesses in writing to management and those charged with governance in accordance with section 265.[1]

.03 The following is an illustrative communication that an auditor may use to comply with the pilot project communication requirement to inform management and those charged with governance of deficiencies in internal control over compliance related to ARRA funding that have been identified at an interim date prior to the completion of the compliance audit and are, or likely to be,

---

* This section has been codified using an "AU-C" identifier instead of an "AU" identifier. "AU-C" is a temporary identifier to avoid confusion with references to existing "AU" sections, which will remain in AICPA *Professional Standards* through 2013. The "AU-C" identifier will revert to "AU" in 2014, by which time substantially all engagements for which the "AU" sections were still effective are expected to be completed.

[1] Paragraphs .11–.13 of section 265, *Communicating Internal Control Related Matters Identified in an Audit*.

in the auditor's judgment, significant deficiencies or material weaknesses in internal control over compliance:

> This communication is provided pursuant to the parameters of the 2009 Office of Management and Budget (OMB) pilot project. Such project requires auditors of entities that volunteer for the project to issue, in writing, an early communication of significant deficiencies and material weaknesses in internal control over compliance for certain federal programs having expenditures of American Recovery and Reinvestment Act of 2009 (ARRA) funding at an interim date, prior to the completion of the compliance audit. Accordingly, this communication is based on our audit procedures performed through [insert "as of date"], an interim period. Because we have not completed our compliance audit, additional significant deficiencies and material weaknesses may be identified and communicated in our final report on compliance and internal control over compliance issued to meet the reporting requirements of OMB Circular A-133, *Audits of States, Local Governments, and Non-Profit Organizations*.
>
> In planning and performing our audit through [insert "as of date"] of [identify the federal programs selected to be tested as a major program from the federal list of approved ARRA pilot project programs], we are considering [Example Entity's] compliance with [list the applicable types of compliance requirements subject to the communication requirement in the pilot project (for example, activities allowed or unallowed, allowable costs and cost principles, cash management, eligibility, reporting, and special tests and provisions)] as described in the *OMB Circular A-133 Compliance Supplement* for the year ended June 30, 2009. We are also considering [Example Entity's] internal control over compliance with the requirements previously described that could have a direct and material effect on [identify the federal programs selected to be tested as a major program from the federal list of approved ARRA pilot project programs] in order to determine our auditing procedures for the purpose of expressing our opinion on compliance and to test and report on internal control over compliance in accordance with OMB Circular A-133, but not for the purpose of expressing an opinion on the effectiveness of internal control over compliance. Accordingly, we do not express an opinion on the effectiveness of the [Example Entity's] internal control over compliance.
>
> Our consideration of internal control over compliance is for the limited purpose described in the preceding paragraph and would not necessarily identify all deficiencies in the entity's internal control that might be significant deficiencies or material weaknesses as defined in the following paragraph. However, as discussed subsequently, based on the audit procedures performed through [insert "as of date"], we identified certain deficiencies in internal control over compliance that we consider to be significant deficiencies and other deficiencies that we consider to be material weaknesses.
>
> A *deficiency in internal control* over compliance exists when the design or operation of a control over compliance does not allow management or employees, in the normal course of performing their assigned functions, to prevent, or detect and correct, noncompliance with a type of compliance requirement[2] of a federal

[2] Under Section 510(a)(1) of Office of Management and Budget (OMB) Circular A-133, *Audits of States, Local Governments, and Non-Profit Organizations*, the auditor's determination of whether a deficiency in internal control over compliance is a material weakness or significant deficiency for the purpose of reporting an audit finding is in relation to a type of compliance requirement for a major program or an audit objective identified in the *OMB Circular A-133 Compliance Supplement* (the *Compliance Supplement*). This reference to "type of compliance requirement" refers to the 14 types of compliance requirements (identified as A-N) described in part 3 of the *Compliance Supplement*. For purposes of reporting audit findings, auditors are alerted that certain of the types of compliance requirements may include multiple compliance requirements with multiple audit objectives (for

(continued)

program on a timely basis. A *material weakness* in internal control over compliance is a deficiency, or a combination of deficiencies, in internal control over compliance, such that there is a reasonable possibility that material noncompliance with a type of compliance requirement of a federal program will not be prevented, or detected and corrected, on a timely basis. We consider the following deficiencies in internal control over compliance to be material weaknesses:

[Describe the material weaknesses that were identified either here or by reference to a separate schedule.] [3]

A *significant deficiency* in internal control over compliance is a deficiency, or a combination of deficiencies, in internal control over compliance with a type of compliance requirement of a federal program that is less severe than a material weakness in internal control over compliance, yet important enough to merit attention by those charged with governance. We consider the following deficiencies in internal control over compliance to be significant deficiencies:

[Describe the significant deficiencies that were identified either here or by reference to a separate schedule.] [4]

[Example Entity's] responses to our findings are described [insert either "in the preceding paragraph" or "in the accompanying schedule"]. We did not audit [Example Entity's] responses and, accordingly, we express no opinion on the responses. [5]

This interim communication is intended solely for the information and use of management, [identify the body or individuals charged with governance], others within the entity, [identify the legislative or regulatory body], federal awarding agencies, and pass-through entities and is not intended to be and should not be used by anyone other than these specified parties.

[Issue Date: November 1994; Revised: March 2010; Revised: January 2012, effective for audits of financial statements for periods ending on or after December 15, 2012.]

2. Communication of Significant Deficiencies and Material Weaknesses Prior to the Completion of the Compliance Audit for Auditors That Are Not Participants in Office of Management and Budget Pilot Project

.04 *Question*—Part 6, "Internal Control," of the *OMB Circular A-133 Compliance Supplement* (the *Compliance Supplement*) stresses the importance of internal control testwork over major programs with ARRA expenditures and

---

(footnote continued)

example, compliance requirement "G" covers 3 separate requirements—matching, level of effort, and earmarking; and "N" covers separate requirements specific to each individual special test and provision).

[3] The OMB pilot project requires the auditee, upon receipt of the interim communication from the auditor, to provide it to the federal cognizant agency for audit. Federal agencies are required to follow-up with the auditee concerning actions taken or needed to correct the finding. Therefore, to assist the federal agencies with this responsibility, significant deficiency and material weakness finding descriptions should include the level of detail required by both *Government Auditing Standards* and Section 510(b) of OMB Circular A-133. This would require the inclusion of, among other things, the views of responsible officials (see footnote 5).

[4] See footnote 3.

[5] The OMB pilot project requires the auditor to obtain management responses to the internal control matters identified and to include them in the interim communication.

encourages early communication to management and those charged with governance of any significant deficiencies or material weaknesses in internal control:

> Early communication by auditors to management, and those charged with governance, of identified control deficiencies related to ARRA funding that are, or likely to be, significant deficiencies or material weaknesses in internal control will allow management to expedite corrective action and mitigate the risk of improper expenditure of ARRA awards. Therefore, auditors are encouraged to promptly inform auditee management and those charged with governance during the audit engagement about control deficiencies related to ARRA funding that are, or likely to be, significant deficiencies or material weaknesses in internal control. The auditor should use professional judgment regarding the form of such interim communications.

.05 Although not required, if an auditor decides to make such a communication in writing at an interim date, may the auditor issue the interim communication in accordance with section 265?

.06 *Interpretation*—Yes. As noted in the previous question, section 265 permits an auditor to communicate to management and those charged with governance identified significant deficiencies and material weaknesses before the completion of a financial statement audit. It would be equally appropriate for a compliance audit. The auditor is reminded that, regardless of how the early communication is delivered, the auditor should communicate all significant deficiencies and material weaknesses in writing to management and those charged with governance in accordance with section 265.[6]

.07 If the auditor decides to make the interim communication encouraged in part 6 of the *Compliance Supplement* in writing, the following is an illustrative communication that an auditor may use to inform management and those charged with governance of deficiencies in internal control over compliance related to ARRA funding that have been identified at an interim date prior to the completion of the compliance audit and that are, or likely to be, in the auditor's judgment, significant deficiencies or material weaknesses in internal control:

> This communication is provided pursuant to the *Office of Management and Budget (OMB) Circular A-133 Compliance Supplement*, which encourages auditors to communicate, at an interim date, control deficiencies related to federal programs with expenditures of American Recovery and Reinvestment Act of 2009 (ARRA) funding that are, or likely to be, significant deficiencies or material weaknesses in internal control over compliance. Accordingly, this communication is based on our audit procedures performed through [insert "as of date"], an interim period. Because we have not completed our compliance audit, additional significant deficiencies and material weaknesses may be identified and communicated in our final report on compliance and internal control over compliance issued to meet the reporting requirements of OMB Circular A-133, *Audits of States, Local Governments, and Non-Profit Organizations*.
>
> In planning and performing our audit through [insert "as of date"] of [identify the federal programs with ARRA expenditures selected by the auditor to be tested as a major program], we are considering [Example Entity's] compliance with the applicable types of compliance requirements as described in the *OMB Circular A-133 Compliance Supplement* for the year ended June 30, 20XX. We are also considering [Example Entity's] internal control over compliance with the requirements previously described that could have a direct and material effect on [identify the federal programs with ARRA expenditures selected by the auditor to be tested as a major program] in order to determine our auditing

[6] See footnote 1.

procedures for the purpose of expressing our opinion on compliance and to test and report on internal control over compliance in accordance with OMB Circular A-133, but not for the purpose of expressing an opinion on the effectiveness of internal control over compliance. Accordingly, we do not express an opinion on the effectiveness of the [Example Entity's] internal control over compliance.

Our consideration of internal control over compliance is for the limited purpose described in the preceding paragraph and would not necessarily identify all deficiencies in the entity's internal control that might be significant deficiencies or material weaknesses as defined in the following paragraph. However, as discussed subsequently, based on the audit procedures performed through [insert "as of date"], we identified certain deficiencies in internal control over compliance that we consider to be significant deficiencies and other deficiencies that we consider to be material weaknesses.

A *deficiency in internal control* over compliance exists when the design or operation of a control over compliance does not allow management or employees, in the normal course of performing their assigned functions, to prevent, or detect and correct, noncompliance with a type of compliance requirement[7] of a federal program on a timely basis. A *material weakness* in internal control over compliance is a deficiency, or combination of deficiencies, in internal control over compliance, such that there is a reasonable possibility that material noncompliance with a type of compliance requirement of a federal program will not be prevented, or detected and corrected, on a timely basis. We consider the following deficiencies in internal control over compliance to be material weaknesses:

[Describe the material weaknesses that were identified either here or by reference to a separate schedule.]

A *significant deficiency* in internal control over compliance is a deficiency, or a combination of deficiencies, in internal control over compliance with a type of compliance requirement of a federal program that is less severe than a material weakness in internal control over compliance, yet important enough to merit attention by those charged with governance. We consider the following deficiencies in internal control over compliance to be significant deficiencies:

[Describe the significant deficiencies that were identified either here or by reference to a separate schedule.]

This interim communication is intended solely for the information and use of management, [identify the body or individuals charged with governance], others within the entity, [identify the legislative or regulatory body], federal awarding agencies, and pass-through entities and is not intended to be and should not be used by anyone other than these specified parties.

[Issue Date: November 2009; Revised: March 2010; Revised: January 2012, effective for audits of financial statements for periods ending on or after December 15, 2012.]

3. Appropriateness of Identifying No Significant Deficiencies or No Material Weaknesses in an Interim Communication

.08 *Question*—In either of the previously described scenarios, may the auditor issue an interim communication in accordance with section 265 stating that as of the interim communication date, no significant deficiencies or material weaknesses have been noted?

---

[7] See footnote 2.

.09 *Interpretation*—No. Section 265 states that the auditor should not issue a written communication stating that no significant deficiencies were identified during the audit.[8] Such guidance would also apply to the interim communication contemplated in the previous two questions. Therefore, it would not be appropriate for an auditor to issue an interim communication stating that no significant deficiencies were identified.

.10 Although section 265 would permit the auditor to issue a communication at the end of an audit stating that no material weaknesses were identified by the auditor, it would not be appropriate for an auditor to do so at an interim date.[9] Making such a communication at an interim date could lead to misinterpretation by management and those charged with governance, that there are no identified material weaknesses when, in fact, material weaknesses could be identified before completion of the compliance audit.

[Issue Date: November 2009; Revised: March 2010; Revised: January 2012, effective for audits of financial statements for periods ending on or after December 15, 2012.]

---

[8] Paragraph .16 of section 265.

[9] Paragraph .15 of section 265.

AU-C Sections 300–499

RISK ASSESSMENT AND RESPONSE TO ASSESSED RISKS

TABLE OF CONTENTS

AU-C Section 300 *

Planning an Audit

Source: SAS No. 122.

Effective for audits of financial statements for periods ending on or after December 15, 2012.

Introduction

Scope of This Section

.01 This section addresses the auditor's responsibility to plan an audit of financial statements. This section is written in the context of recurring audits. Additional considerations in an initial audit engagement are separately identified in this section. Matters related to planning audits of group financial statements are addressed in section 600, *Special Considerations—Audits of Group Financial Statements (Including the Work of Component Auditors).* (Ref: par. .A1–.A3)

The Role and Timing of Planning

.02 Planning an audit involves establishing the overall audit strategy for the engagement and developing an audit plan. Adequate planning benefits the audit of financial statements in several ways, including the following:

- Helping the auditor identify and devote appropriate attention to important areas of the audit
- Helping the auditor identify and resolve potential problems on a timely basis
- Helping the auditor properly organize and manage the audit engagement so that it is performed in an effective and efficient manner
- Assisting in the selection of engagement team members with appropriate levels of capabilities and competence to respond to anticipated risks and allocating team member responsibilities
- Facilitating the direction and supervision of engagement team members and the review of their work
- Assisting, when applicable, in coordination of work done by auditors of components and specialists

Effective Date

.03 This section is effective for audits of financial statements for periods ending on or after December 15, 2012.

---

* This section has been codified using an "AU-C" identifier instead of an "AU" identifier. "AU-C" is a temporary identifier to avoid confusion with references to existing "AU" sections, which will remain in AICPA *Professional Standards* through 2013. The "AU-C" identifier will revert to "AU" in 2014, by which time substantially all engagements for which the "AU" sections were still effective are expected to be completed.

Objective

.04 The objective of the auditor is to plan the audit so that it will be performed in an effective manner.

Requirements

Involvement of Key Engagement Team Members

.05 The engagement partner and other key members of the engagement team should be involved in planning the audit, including planning and participating in the discussion among engagement team members. (Ref: par. .A4–.A5)

Preliminary Engagement Activities

.06 The auditor should undertake the following activities at the beginning of the current audit engagement:

a. Performing procedures required by section 220, *Quality Control for an Engagement Conducted in Accordance With Generally Accepted Auditing Standards*, regarding the continuance of the client relationship and the specific audit engagement

b. Evaluating compliance with relevant ethical requirements in accordance with section 220

c. Establishing an understanding of the terms of the engagement as required by section 210, *Terms of Engagement* (Ref: par. .A6–.A8)

Planning Activities

.07 The auditor should establish an overall audit strategy that sets the scope, timing, and direction of the audit and that guides the development of the audit plan.

.08 In establishing the overall audit strategy, the auditor should

a. identify the characteristics of the engagement that define its scope;

b. ascertain the reporting objectives of the engagement in order to plan the timing of the audit and the nature of the communications required;

c. consider the factors that, in the auditor's professional judgment, are significant in directing the engagement team's efforts;

d. consider the results of preliminary engagement activities and, when applicable, whether knowledge gained on other engagements performed by the engagement partner for the entity is relevant; and

e. ascertain the nature, timing, and extent of resources necessary to perform the engagement. (Ref: par. .A9–.A13)

.09 The auditor should develop an audit plan that includes a description of the following:

a. The nature and extent of planned risk assessment procedures, as determined under section 315, *Understanding the Entity and Its Environment and Assessing the Risks of Material Misstatement b.* The nature, timing, and extent of planned further audit procedures at the relevant assertion level, as determined under section 330, *Performing Audit Procedures in Response to Assessed Risks and Evaluating the Audit Evidence Obtained*

c. Other planned audit procedures that are required to be carried out so that the engagement complies with generally accepted auditing standards (Ref: par. .A14)

.10 The auditor should update and change the overall audit strategy and audit plan, as necessary, during the course of the audit. (Ref: par. ,A15)

.11 The auditor should plan the nature, timing, and extent of direction and supervision of engagement team members and the review of their work. (Ref: par. .A16–.A17)

Determining the Extent of Involvement of Professionals Possessing Specialized Skills

.12 The auditor should consider whether specialized skills are needed in performing the audit. If specialized skills are needed, the auditor should seek the assistance of a professional possessing such skills, who either may be on the auditor's staff or an outside professional.[1] In such circumstances, the auditor should have sufficient knowledge to communicate the objectives of the other professional's work; evaluate whether the specified audit procedures will meet the auditor's objectives; and evaluate the results of the audit procedures applied as they relate to the nature, timing, and extent of further planned audit procedures. Section 620, *Using the Work of an Auditor's Specialist*, addresses the auditor's use of the work of specialists in an audit. (Ref: par. .A18–.A19)

Additional Considerations in Initial Audit Engagements

.13 The auditor should undertake the following activities prior to starting an initial audit:

a. Performing procedures required by section 220

b. Communicating with the predecessor auditor when there has been a change of auditors, in accordance with section 210[2] (Ref: par. .A20)

Documentation

.14 The auditor should include in the audit documentation the following:[3]

a. The overall audit strategy

b. The audit plan

c. Any significant changes made during the audit engagement to the overall audit strategy or the audit plan and the reasons for such changes (Ref: par. .A21–.A24)

---

[1] Paragraph .16 of section 220, *Quality Control for an Engagement Conducted in Accordance With Generally Accepted Auditing Standards*.

[2] Paragraph .11 of section 210, *Terms of Engagement*.

[3] Paragraphs .08–.12 and .A8 of section 230, *Audit Documentation*.

Application and Other Explanatory Material

The Role and Timing of Planning (Ref: par. .01)

.A1 The nature and extent of planning activities will vary according to the size and complexity of the entity, the key engagement team members' previous experience with the entity, and changes in circumstances that occur during the audit engagement.

.A2 Planning is not a discrete phase of an audit but rather a continual and iterative process that often begins shortly after (or in connection with) the completion of the previous audit and continues until the completion of the current audit engagement. Planning, however, includes consideration of the timing of certain activities and audit procedures that need to be completed prior to the performance of further audit procedures. For example, planning includes the need to consider, prior to the auditor's identification and assessment of the risks of material misstatement, such matters as the following:

- The analytical procedures to be applied as risk assessment procedures
- A general understanding of the legal and regulatory framework applicable to the entity and how the entity is complying with that framework
- The determination of materiality
- The involvement of specialists
- The performance of other risk assessment procedures

.A3 The auditor may decide to discuss elements of planning with the entity's management to facilitate the conduct and management of the audit engagement (for example, to coordinate some of the planned audit procedures with the work of the entity's personnel). Although these discussions often occur, the overall audit strategy and the audit plan remain the auditor's responsibility. When discussing matters included in the overall audit strategy or audit plan, care is required in order not to compromise the effectiveness of the audit. For example, discussing the nature and timing of detailed audit procedures with management may compromise the effectiveness of the audit by making the audit procedures too predictable.

Involvement of Key Engagement Team Members (Ref: par. .05)

.A4 The involvement of the engagement partner and other key members of the engagement team in planning the audit draws on their experience and insight, thereby enhancing the effectiveness and efficiency of the planning process. The engagement partner may delegate portions of the planning and supervision of the audit to other firm personnel.

.A5 Section 315 requires a discussion among the audit team about the susceptibility of the entity's financial statements to material misstatement.[4] This discussion also may include the discussion regarding the risks of material misstatement due to fraud, as required by section 240, *Consideration of Fraud in a Financial Statement Audit*.[5] The objective of this discussion is for members of the audit team to gain a better understanding of the potential for material

---

[4] Paragraph .11 of section 315, *Understanding the Entity and Its Environment and Assessing the Risks of Material Misstatement*.

[5] Paragraph .15 of section 240, *Consideration of Fraud in a Financial Statement Audit*.

misstatements of the financial statements resulting from fraud or error in the specific areas assigned to them and to understand how the results of the audit procedures that they perform may affect other aspects of the audit, including the decisions about the nature, timing, and extent of further audit procedures.

Preliminary Engagement Activities (Ref: par. .06)

.A6 Performing the preliminary engagement activities, which are specified in paragraph .06, at the beginning of the current audit engagement assists the auditor in identifying and evaluating events or circumstances that may adversely affect the auditor's ability to plan and perform the audit engagement.

.A7 Performing these preliminary engagement activities enables the auditor to plan an audit engagement for which, for example

- the auditor maintains the necessary independence and ability to perform the engagement.
- the auditor has no issues with management integrity that may affect the auditor's willingness to continue the engagement.
- the auditor has no misunderstanding with the entity about the terms of the engagement.

.A8 The auditor's consideration of client continuance and relevant ethical requirements, including independence, occurs throughout the audit engagement as conditions and changes in circumstances occur. Performing initial procedures on both client continuance and evaluation of relevant ethical requirements (including independence) at the beginning of the current audit engagement means that they are completed prior to the performance of other significant activities for the current audit engagement. For continuing audit engagements, such initial procedures often begin shortly after (or in connection with) the completion of the previous audit.

Planning Activities

The Overall Audit Strategy (Ref: par. .07–.08)

.A9 The process of establishing the overall audit strategy assists the auditor to determine, subject to the completion of the auditor's risk assessment procedures, such matters as the following:

- The resources to deploy for specific audit areas, such as the use of appropriately experienced team members for high risk areas or the involvement of specialists on complex matters
- The amount of resources to allocate to specific audit areas, such as the number of team members assigned to observe the inventory count at material locations, the extent of review of component auditors' work in the case of group audits, or the audit budget (in hours) to allocate to high risk areas
- When these resources are to be deployed, such as whether at an interim audit stage or at key cut-off dates
- How such resources are managed, directed, and supervised, such as when team briefing and debriefing meetings are expected to be held, how the engagement partner and manager reviews are expected to take place (for example, on site or off site), and whether to complete engagement quality control reviews

.A10 The appendix, "Considerations in Establishing the Overall Audit Strategy," lists examples of considerations in establishing the overall audit strategy.

.A11 Once the overall audit strategy has been established, an audit plan can be developed to address the various matters identified in the overall audit strategy, taking into account the need to achieve the audit objectives through the efficient use of the auditor's resources. The establishment of the overall audit strategy and the detailed audit plan are not necessarily discrete or sequential processes but are closely interrelated because changes in one may result in consequential changes to the other.

Considerations Specific to Smaller, Less Complex Entities

.A12 In audits of smaller entities, the entire audit may be conducted by a very small audit team. Many audits of smaller entities involve the engagement partner (who may be a sole practitioner) working with one engagement team member (or without any engagement team members). With a smaller team, coordination of, and communication between, team members is easier. Establishing the overall audit strategy for the audit of a smaller entity need not be a complex or time consuming exercise; it varies according to the size and complexity of the entity, the complexity of the audit, and the size of the engagement team. For example, a brief memorandum prepared at the completion of the previous audit, based on a review of the working papers and highlighting issues identified in the audit just completed, updated in the current period, based on discussions with the owner-manager, can serve as the documented audit strategy for the current audit engagement if it covers the matters noted in paragraph .07.

Communications With Those Charged With Governance

.A13 Section 260, *The Auditor's Communication With Those Charged With Governance*, requires the auditor to communicate with those charged with governance an overview of the planned scope and timing of the audit.[6]

The Audit Plan (Ref: par. .09)

.A14 The audit plan is more detailed than the overall audit strategy in that it includes the nature, timing, and extent of audit procedures to be performed by engagement team members. Planning for these audit procedures takes place over the course of the audit as the audit plan for the engagement develops. For example, planning of the auditor's risk assessment procedures occurs early in the audit process. However, planning the nature, timing, and extent of specific further audit procedures depends on the outcome of those risk assessment procedures. In addition, the auditor may begin the execution of further audit procedures for some classes of transactions, account balances, and disclosures before planning all remaining further audit procedures.

Changes to Planning Decisions During the Course of the Audit (Ref: par. .10)

.A15 As a result of unexpected events, changes in conditions, or the audit evidence obtained from the results of audit procedures, the auditor may need to modify the overall audit strategy and audit plan and, thereby, the resulting planned nature, timing, and extent of further audit procedures, based on the revised consideration of assessed risks. This may be the case when information comes to the auditor's attention that differs significantly from the information

---

[6] Paragraph .11 of section 260, *The Auditor's Communication With Those Charged With Governance*.

available when the auditor planned the audit procedures. For example, audit evidence obtained through the performance of substantive procedures may contradict the audit evidence obtained through tests of controls.

Direction, Supervision, and Review (Ref: par. .11)

.A16 The nature, timing, and extent of the direction and supervision of engagement team members and review of their work vary, depending on many factors, including the following:

- The size and complexity of the entity
- The area of the audit
- The assessed risks of material misstatement (for example, an increase in the assessed risk of material misstatement for a given area of the audit ordinarily requires a corresponding increase in the extent and timeliness of direction and supervision of engagement team members and a more detailed review of their work)
- The capabilities and competence of the individual team members performing the audit work

Section 220 contains further guidance on the direction, supervision, and review of audit work.

Considerations Specific to Smaller, Less Complex Entities

.A17 If an audit is carried out entirely by the engagement partner, questions of direction and supervision of engagement team members and review of their work do not arise. In such cases, the engagement partner, having personally conducted all aspects of the work, will be aware of all material issues. Forming an objective view on the appropriateness of the judgments made in the course of the audit can present practical problems when the same individual also performs the entire audit. If particularly complex or unusual issues are involved and the audit is performed by a sole practitioner, it may be desirable to consult with other suitably experienced auditors or the auditor's professional body.

Determining the Extent of Involvement of Professionals Possessing Specialized Skills (Ref: par. .12)

.A18 An auditor may decide to seek the assistance of a professional with specialized skills necessary to complete various aspects of the engagement. These professionals may include valuation experts, appraisers, actuaries, tax specialists, and IT professionals. For example, the use of professionals possessing IT skills to determine the effect of IT on the audit, understand the IT controls, or design and perform tests of IT controls or substantive procedures is a significant aspect of many audit engagements. In determining whether such a professional is needed on the audit team, the auditor may consider such factors as the following:

- The complexity of the entity's systems and IT controls and the manner in which they are used in conducting the entity's business
- The significance of changes made to existing systems or the implementation of new systems
- The extent to which data is shared among systems
- The extent of the entity's participation in electronic commerce
- The entity's use of emerging technologies

- The significance of audit evidence that is available only in electronic form

.A19 Audit procedures that the auditor may assign to a professional possessing IT skills include inquiring of an entity's IT personnel how data and transactions are initiated, authorized, recorded, processed, and reported and how IT controls are designed; inspecting systems documentation; observing the operation of IT controls; and planning and performing tests of IT controls.

Additional Considerations in Initial Audit Engagements (Ref: par. .13)

.A20 The purpose and objective of planning the audit are the same whether the audit is an initial or recurring engagement. However, for an initial audit, the auditor may need to expand the planning activities because the auditor does not ordinarily have the previous experience with the entity that is considered when planning recurring engagements. For an initial audit engagement, additional matters the auditor may consider in establishing the overall audit strategy and audit plan include the following:

- Arrangements to be made with the predecessor auditor (for example, to review the predecessor auditor's working papers [see section 510, *Opening Balances—Initial Audit Engagements, Including Reaudit Engagements*])[7]
- Any major issues (including the application of accounting principles or auditing and reporting standards) discussed with management in connection with the initial selection as auditor, the communication of these matters to those charged with governance, and how these matters affect the overall audit strategy and audit plan
- The audit procedures necessary to obtain sufficient appropriate audit evidence regarding opening balances (see section 510)[8]
- Other procedures required by the firm's system of quality control for initial audit engagements (for example, the firm's system of quality control may require the involvement of another partner or senior individual to review the overall audit strategy prior to commencing significant audit procedures or to review reports prior to their issuance)

Documentation (Ref: par. .14)

.A21 The documentation of the overall audit strategy is a record of the key decisions considered necessary to properly plan the audit and communicate significant issues to the engagement team. For example, the auditor may summarize the overall audit strategy in the form of a memorandum that contains key decisions regarding the overall scope, timing, and conduct of the audit.

.A22 The documentation of the audit plan is a record of the planned nature, timing, and extent of risk assessment procedures and further audit procedures at the relevant assertion level in response to the assessed risks. It also serves as a record of the proper planning of the audit procedures that can be reviewed

---

[7] Paragraphs .07 and .A2–.A11 of section 510, *Opening Balances—Initial Audit Engagements, Including Reaudit Engagements.*

[8] Paragraph .08 of section 510.

and approved prior to their performance. The auditor may use standard audit programs or audit completion checklists, tailored as needed to reflect the particular engagement circumstances.

.A23 A record of the significant changes to the overall audit strategy and the audit plan and resulting changes to the planned nature, timing, and extent of audit procedures explain why the significant changes were made and why the overall strategy and audit plan were finally adopted for the audit. It also reflects the appropriate response to the significant changes occurring during the audit.

Considerations Specific to Smaller, Less Complex Entities

.A24 As discussed in paragraph .A12, a suitable, brief memorandum may serve as the documented strategy for the audit of a smaller entity. For the audit plan, standard audit programs or checklists (see paragraph .A22) drawn up on the assumption of few relevant control activities, which is likely to be the case in a smaller entity, may be used, provided that they are tailored to the circumstances of the engagement, including the auditor's risk assessments.

.A25

Appendix—Considerations in Establishing the Overall Audit Strategy (Ref: par. .07–.08 and .A9–.A12)

This appendix provides examples of matters the auditor may consider in establishing the overall audit strategy. Many of these matters also will influence the auditor's detailed audit plan. The examples provided cover a broad range of matters applicable to many engagements. Although some of the following matters may be required by other AU-C sections, not all matters are relevant to every audit engagement, and the list is not necessarily complete.

Characteristics of the Engagement

The following are some examples of characteristics of the engagement:

- The financial reporting framework on which the financial information to be audited has been prepared, including any need for reconciliations to another financial reporting framework
- Industry specific reporting requirements, such as reports mandated by industry regulators
- The expected audit coverage, including the number and locations of components to be included
- The nature of the control relationships between a parent and its components that determine how the group is to be consolidated
- The extent to which components are audited by other auditors
- The nature of the business divisions to be audited, including the need for specialized knowledge
- The reporting currency to be used, including any need for currency translation for the audited financial information
- The need for statutory or regulatory audit requirements (for example, the Office of Management and Budget Circular A-133, *Audits of States, Local Governments, and Non-Profit Organizations*)
- The availability of the work of internal auditors and the extent of the auditor's potential use of such work
- The entity's use of service organizations and how the auditor may obtain evidence concerning the design or operation of controls performed by them
- The expected use of audit evidence obtained in previous audits (for example, audit evidence related to risk assessment procedures and tests of controls)
- The effect of IT on the audit procedures, including the availability of data and the expected use of computer assisted audit techniques
- The coordination of the expected coverage and timing of the audit work with any reviews of interim financial information and the effect on the audit of the information obtained during such reviews
- The availability of client personnel and data

Reporting Objectives, Timing of the Audit, and Nature of Communications

The following examples illustrate reporting objectives, timing of the audit, and nature of communications:

- The entity's timetable for reporting, including interim periods
- The organization of meetings with management and those charged with governance to discuss the nature, timing, and extent of the audit work
- The discussion with management and those charged with governance regarding the expected type and timing of reports to be issued and other communications, both written and oral, including the auditor's report, management letters, and communications to those charged with governance
- The discussion with management regarding the expected communications on the status of audit work throughout the engagement
- Communication with auditors of components regarding the expected types and timing of reports to be issued and other communications in connection with the audit of components
- The expected nature and timing of communications among engagement team members, including the nature and timing of team meetings and timing of the review of work performed
- Whether there are any other expected communications with third parties, including any statutory or contractual reporting responsibilities arising from the audit

Significant Factors, Preliminary Engagement Activities, and Knowledge Gained on Other Engagements

The following examples illustrate significant factors, preliminary engagement activities, and knowledge gained on other engagements:

- The determination of materiality, in accordance with section 320, *Materiality in Planning and Performing an Audit*, and, when applicable, the following:
  - — The determination of materiality for components and communication thereof to component auditors in accordance with section 600, *Special Considerations—Audits of Group Financial Statements (Including the Work of Component Auditors)*
  - — The preliminary identification of significant components and material classes of transactions, account balances, and disclosures
- Preliminary identification of areas in which there may be a higher risk of material misstatement
- The effect of the assessed risk of material misstatement at the overall financial statement level on direction, supervision, and review
- The manner in which the auditor emphasizes to engagement team members the need to maintain a questioning mind and exercise

professional skepticism in gathering and evaluating audit evidence

- Results of previous audits that involved evaluating the operating effectiveness of internal control, including the nature of identified deficiencies and action taken to address them
- The discussion of matters that may affect the audit with firm personnel responsible for performing other services to the entity
- Evidence of management's commitment to the design, implementation, and maintenance of sound internal control, including evidence of appropriate documentation of such internal control
- Volume of transactions, which may determine whether it is more efficient for the auditor to rely on internal control
- Importance attached to internal control throughout the entity to the successful operation of the business
- Significant business developments affecting the entity, including changes in IT and business processes; changes in key management; and acquisitions, mergers, and divestments
- Significant industry developments, such as changes in industry regulations and new reporting requirements
- Significant changes in the financial reporting framework, such as changes in accounting standards
- Other significant relevant developments, such as changes in the legal environment affecting the entity

Nature, Timing, and Extent of Resources

The following examples illustrate the nature, timing, and extent of resources:

- The selection of the engagement team (including, when necessary, the engagement quality control reviewer [see section 220, *Quality Control for an Engagement Conducted in Accordance With Generally Accepted Auditing Standards*]) and the assignment of audit work to the team members, including the assignment of appropriately experienced team members to areas in which there may be higher risks of material misstatement
- Engagement budgeting, including considering the appropriate amount of time to set aside for areas in which there may be higher risks of material misstatement

AU-C Section 315 *

Understanding the Entity and Its Environment and Assessing the Risks of Material Misstatement

Source: SAS No. 122.

Effective for audits of financial statements for periods ending on or after December 15, 2012.

Introduction

Scope of This Section

.01 This section addresses the auditor's responsibility to identify and assess the risks of material misstatement in the financial statements through understanding the entity and its environment, including the entity's internal control.

Effective Date

.02 This section is effective for audits of financial statements for periods ending on or after December 15, 2012.

Objective

.03 The objective of the auditor is to identify and assess the risks of material misstatement, whether due to fraud or error, at the financial statement and relevant assertion levels through understanding the entity and its environment, including the entity's internal control, thereby providing a basis for designing and implementing responses to the assessed risks of material misstatement.

Definitions

.04 For purposes of generally accepted auditing standards (GAAS), the following terms have the meanings attributed as follows:

Assertions. Representations by management, explicit or otherwise, that are embodied in the financial statements as used by the auditor to consider the different types of potential misstatements that may occur.

Business risk. A risk resulting from significant conditions, events, circumstances, actions, or inactions that could adversely affect an entity's ability to achieve its objectives and execute its strategies or from the setting of inappropriate objectives and strategies.

---

* This section has been codified using an "AU-C" identifier instead of an "AU" identifier. "AU-C" is a temporary identifier to avoid confusion with references to existing "AU" sections, which will remain in AICPA *Professional Standards* through 2013. The "AU-C" identifier will revert to "AU" in 2014, by which time substantially all engagements for which the "AU" sections were still effective are expected to be completed.

Internal control. A process effected by those charged with governance, management, and other personnel that is designed to provide reasonable assurance about the achievement of the entity's objectives with regard to the reliability of financial reporting, effectiveness and efficiency of operations, and compliance with applicable laws and regulations. Internal control over safeguarding of assets against unauthorized acquisition, use, or disposition may include controls relating to financial reporting and operations objectives.[1]

Relevant assertion. A financial statement assertion that has a reasonable possibility of containing a misstatement or misstatements that would cause the financial statements to be materially misstated. The determination of whether an assertion is a relevant assertion is made without regard to the effect of internal controls. (Ref: par. .A117)

Risk assessment procedures. The audit procedures performed to obtain an understanding of the entity and its environment, including the entity's internal control, to identify and assess the risks of material misstatement, whether due to fraud or error, at the financial statement and relevant assertion levels.

Significant risk. An identified and assessed risk of material misstatement that, in the auditor's professional judgment, requires special audit consideration.

Requirements

Risk Assessment Procedures and Related Activities

.05 The auditor should perform risk assessment procedures to provide a basis for the identification and assessment of risks of material misstatement at the financial statement and relevant assertion levels. Risk assessment procedures by themselves, however, do not provide sufficient appropriate audit evidence on which to base the audit opinion. (Ref: par. .A1–.A5)

.06 The risk assessment procedures should include the following:

a. Inquiries of management and others within the entity who, in the auditor's professional judgment, may have information that is likely to assist in identifying risks of material misstatement due to fraud or error (Ref: par. .A6)

b. Analytical procedures (Ref: par. .A7–.A10)

c. Observation and inspection (Ref: par. .A11)

.07 The auditor should consider whether information obtained from the auditor's client acceptance or continuance process is relevant to identifying risks of material misstatement.

.08 If the engagement partner has performed other engagements for the entity, the engagement partner should consider whether information obtained is relevant to identifying risks of material misstatement.

.09 During planning, the auditor should consider the results of the assessment of the risk of material misstatement due to fraud[2] along with other

---

[1] This section recognizes the definition and description of *internal control* contained in *Internal Control—Integrated Framework*, published by the Committee of Sponsoring Organizations of the Treadway Commission.

[2] See section 240, *Consideration of Fraud in a Financial Statement Audit*.

information gathered in the process of identifying the risks of material misstatements.

.10 When the auditor intends to use information obtained from the auditor's previous experience with the entity and from audit procedures performed in previous audits, the auditor should determine whether changes have occurred since the previous audit that may affect its relevance to the current audit. (Ref: par. .A12–.A13)

.11 The engagement partner and other key engagement team members should discuss the susceptibility of the entity's financial statements to material misstatement and the application of the applicable financial reporting framework to the entity's facts and circumstances. The engagement partner should determine which matters are to be communicated to engagement team members not involved in the discussion. (Ref: par. .A14–.A16)

Understanding the Entity and Its Environment, Including the Entity's Internal Control

The Entity and Its Environment (Ref: par. .A17)

.12 The auditor should obtain an understanding of the following:

a. Relevant industry, regulatory, and other external factors, including the applicable financial reporting framework. (Ref: par. .A18–.A22)

b. The nature of the entity, including

i. its operations;

ii. its ownership and governance structures;

iii. the types of investments that the entity is making and plans to make, including investments in entities formed to accomplish specific objectives; and

iv. the way that the entity is structured and how it is financed,

to enable the auditor to understand the classes of transactions, account balances, and disclosures to be expected in the financial statements. (Ref: par. .A23–.A27)

c. The entity's selection and application of accounting policies, including the reasons for changes thereto. The auditor should evaluate whether the entity's accounting policies are appropriate for its business and consistent with the applicable financial reporting framework and accounting policies used in the relevant industry. (Ref: par. .A28)

d. The entity's objectives and strategies and those related business risks that may result in risks of material misstatement. (Ref: par. .A29–.A35)

e. The measurement and review of the entity's financial performance. (Ref: par. .A36–.A41)

The Entity's Internal Control

.13 The auditor should obtain an understanding of internal control relevant to the audit. Although most controls relevant to the audit are likely to relate to financial reporting, not all controls that relate to financial reporting are relevant to the audit. It is a matter of the auditor's professional judgment whether a control, individually or in combination with others, is relevant to the audit. (Ref: par. .A42–.A67)

Nature and Extent of the Understanding of Relevant Controls

.14 When obtaining an understanding of controls that are relevant to the audit, the auditor should evaluate the design of those controls and determine whether they have been implemented by performing procedures in addition to inquiry of the entity's personnel. (Ref: par. .A68–.A70)

Components of Internal Control

.15 *Control environment.* The auditor should obtain an understanding of the control environment. As part of obtaining this understanding, the auditor should evaluate whether

a. management, with the oversight of those charged with governance, has created and maintained a culture of honesty and ethical behavior and

b. the strengths in the control environment elements collectively provide an appropriate foundation for the other components of internal control and whether those other components are not undermined by deficiencies in the control environment. (Ref: par. .A71–.A80)

.16 *The entity's risk assessment process.* The auditor should obtain an understanding of whether the entity has a process for

a. identifying business risks relevant to financial reporting objectives,

b. estimating the significance of the risks,

c. assessing the likelihood of their occurrence, and

d. deciding about actions to address those risks. (Ref: par. .A81–.A82)

.17 If the entity has established a risk assessment process (referred to hereafter as the *entity's risk assessment process*), the auditor should obtain an understanding of it and the results thereof. If the auditor identifies risks of material misstatement that management failed to identify, the auditor should evaluate whether an underlying risk existed that the auditor expects would have been identified by the entity's risk assessment process. If such a risk exists, the auditor should obtain an understanding of why that process failed to identify it and evaluate whether the process is appropriate to its circumstances or determine if a significant deficiency or material weakness exists in internal control regarding the entity's risk assessment process.

.18 If the entity has not established such a process or has an ad hoc process, the auditor should discuss with management whether business risks relevant to financial reporting objectives have been identified and how they have been addressed. The auditor should evaluate whether the absence of a documented risk assessment process is appropriate in the circumstances or determine whether it represents a significant deficiency or material weakness in the entity's internal control. (Ref: par. .A83)

.19 *The information system, including the related business processes relevant to financial reporting and communication.* The auditor should obtain an understanding of the information system, including the related business processes relevant to financial reporting, including the following areas:

a. The classes of transactions in the entity's operations that are significant to the financial statements.

b. The procedures within both IT and manual systems by which those transactions are initiated, authorized, recorded, processed, corrected as necessary, transferred to the general ledger, and reported in the financial statements.

c. The related accounting records supporting information and specific accounts in the financial statements that are used to initiate, authorize, record, process, and report transactions. This includes the correction of incorrect information and how information is transferred to the general ledger. The records may be in either manual or electronic form.

d. How the information system captures events and conditions, other than transactions, that are significant to the financial statements.

e. The financial reporting process used to prepare the entity's financial statements, including significant accounting estimates and disclosures.

f. Controls surrounding journal entries, including nonstandard journal entries used to record nonrecurring, unusual transactions, or adjustments. (Ref: par. .A84–.A88)

.20 The auditor should obtain an understanding of how the entity communicates financial reporting roles and responsibilities and significant matters relating to financial reporting, including

a. communications between management and those charged with governance and

b. external communications, such as those with regulatory authorities. (Ref: par. .A89–.A90)

.21 *Control activities relevant to the audit.* The auditor should obtain an understanding of control activities relevant to the audit, which are those control activities the auditor judges it necessary to understand in order to assess the risks of material misstatement at the assertion level and design further audit procedures responsive to assessed risks. An audit does not require an understanding of all the control activities related to each significant class of transactions, account balance, and disclosure in the financial statements or to every assertion relevant to them. However, the auditor should obtain an understanding of the process of reconciling detailed records to the general ledger for material account balances. (Ref: par. .A91–.A97)

.22 In understanding the entity's control activities, the auditor should obtain an understanding of how the entity has responded to risks arising from IT. (Ref: par. .A98–.A101)

.23 *Monitoring of controls.* The auditor should obtain an understanding of the major activities that the entity uses to monitor internal control over financial reporting, including those related to those control activities relevant to the audit, and how the entity initiates remedial actions to deficiencies in its controls. (Ref: par. .A102–.A103)

.24 If the entity has an internal audit function, the auditor should obtain an understanding of the following in order to determine whether the internal audit function is likely to be relevant to the audit:

a. The nature of the internal audit function's responsibilities and how the internal audit function fits in the entity's organizational structure

b. The activities performed or to be performed by the internal audit function (Ref: par. .A104–.A106)

.25 The auditor should obtain an understanding of the sources of the information used in the entity's monitoring activities and the basis upon which management considers the information to be sufficiently reliable for the purpose. (Ref: par. .A107)

Identifying and Assessing the Risks of Material Misstatement

.26 To provide a basis for designing and performing further audit procedures, the auditor should identify and assess the risks of material misstatement at

a. the financial statement level and (Ref: par. .A108–.A111)

b. the relevant assertion level for classes of transactions, account balances, and disclosures. (Ref: par. .A112–.A119)

.27 For this purpose, the auditor should

a. identify risks throughout the process of obtaining an understanding of the entity and its environment, including relevant controls that relate to the risks, by considering the classes of transactions, account balances, and disclosures in the financial statements; (Ref: par. .A120–.A121)

b. assess the identified risks and evaluate whether they relate more pervasively to the financial statements as a whole and potentially affect many assertions;

c. relate the identified risks to what can go wrong at the relevant assertion level, taking account of relevant controls that the auditor intends to test; and (Ref: par. .A122–.A124)

d. consider the likelihood of misstatement, including the possibility of multiple misstatements, and whether the potential misstatement is of a magnitude that could result in a material misstatement.

Risks That Require Special Audit Consideration

.28 As part of the risk assessment described in paragraph .26, the auditor should determine whether any of the risks identified are, in the auditor's professional judgment, a significant risk. In exercising this judgment, the auditor should exclude the effects of identified controls related to the risk.

.29 In exercising professional judgment about which risks are significant risks, the auditor should consider at least

a. whether the risk is a risk of fraud;

b. whether the risk is related to recent significant economic, accounting, or other developments and, therefore, requires specific attention;

c. the complexity of transactions;

d. whether the risk involves significant transactions with related parties;

e. the degree of subjectivity in the measurement of financial information related to the risk, especially those measurements involving a wide range of measurement uncertainty; and

f. whether the risk involves significant transactions that are outside the normal course of business for the entity or that otherwise appear to be unusual. (Ref: par. .A125–.A129)

.30 If the auditor has determined that a significant risk exists, the auditor should obtain an understanding of the entity's controls, including control activities, relevant to that risk and, based on that understanding, evaluate whether such controls have been suitably designed and implemented to mitigate such risks. (Ref: par. .A130–.A132)

Risks for Which Substantive Procedures Alone Do Not Provide Sufficient Appropriate Audit Evidence

.31 In respect of some risks, the auditor may judge that it is not possible or practicable to obtain sufficient appropriate audit evidence only from substantive procedures. Such risks may relate to the inaccurate or incomplete recording of routine and significant classes of transactions or account balances, the characteristics of which often permit highly automated processing with little or no manual intervention. In such cases, the entity's controls over such risks are relevant to the audit, and the auditor should obtain an understanding of them. (Ref: par. .A133–.A136)

Revision of Risk Assessment

.32 The auditor's assessment of the risks of material misstatement at the assertion level may change during the course of the audit as additional audit evidence is obtained. In circumstances in which the auditor obtains audit evidence from performing further audit procedures or if new information is obtained, either of which is inconsistent with the audit evidence on which the auditor originally based the assessment, the auditor should revise the assessment and modify the further planned audit procedures accordingly. (Ref: par. .A137)

Documentation

.33 The auditor should include in the audit documentation[3] the

a. discussion among the engagement team required by paragraph .11, the significant decisions reached, how and when the discussion occurred, and the audit team members who participated;

b. key elements of the understanding obtained regarding each of the aspects of the entity and its environment specified in paragraph .12 and each of the internal control components specified in paragraphs .15–.25, the sources of information from which the understanding was obtained, and the risk assessment procedures performed;

c. identified and assessed risks of material misstatement at the financial statement level and at the relevant assertion level, as required by paragraph .26; and

d. risks identified and related controls about which the auditor has obtained an understanding as a result of the requirements in paragraphs .28–.31. (Ref: par. .A138–.A141)

Application and Other Explanatory Material

Risk Assessment Procedures and Related Activities (Ref: par. .05)

.A1 Obtaining an understanding of the entity and its environment, including the entity's internal control (referred to hereafter as an *understanding of the*

---

[3] Paragraphs .08–.12 and .A8 of section 230, *Audit Documentation*.

entity), is a continuous, dynamic process of gathering, updating, and analyzing information throughout the audit. The understanding of the entity establishes a frame of reference within which the auditor plans the audit and exercises professional judgment throughout the audit when, for example

- assessing risks of material misstatement of the financial statements;
- determining materiality in accordance with section 320, *Materiality in Planning and Performing an Audit*;
- considering the appropriateness of the selection and application of accounting policies and the adequacy of financial statement disclosures;
- identifying areas for which special audit consideration may be necessary (for example, related party transactions, the appropriateness of management's use of the going concern assumption, considering the business purpose of transactions, or the existence of complex and unusual transactions);
- developing expectations for use when performing analytical procedures;
- responding to the assessed risks of material misstatement, including designing and performing further audit procedures to obtain sufficient appropriate audit evidence; and
- evaluating the sufficiency and appropriateness of audit evidence obtained, such as the appropriateness of assumptions and management's oral and written representations.

.A2 Information obtained by performing risk assessment procedures and related activities may be used by the auditor as audit evidence to support assessments of the risks of material misstatement. In addition, the auditor may obtain audit evidence about classes of transactions, account balances, or disclosures and relevant assertions and about the operating effectiveness of controls, even though such procedures were not specifically planned as substantive procedures or tests of controls. The auditor also may choose to perform substantive procedures or tests of controls concurrently with risk assessment procedures because it is efficient to do so.

.A3 The auditor is required to exercise professional judgment[4] to determine the extent of the required understanding of the entity. The auditor's primary consideration is whether the understanding of the entity that has been obtained is sufficient to meet the objective stated in this section. The depth of the overall understanding that is required by the auditor is less than that possessed by management in managing the entity.

.A4 The risks to be assessed include both those due to fraud and those due to error, and both are covered by this section. However, the significance of fraud is such that further requirements and guidance are included in section 240, *Consideration of Fraud in a Financial Statement Audit*, regarding risk assessment procedures and related activities to obtain information that is used to identify the risks of material misstatement due to fraud.

.A5 Although the auditor is required to perform all the risk assessment procedures described in paragraph .06 in the course of obtaining the required

[4] Paragraph .18 of section 200, *Overall Objectives of the Independent Auditor and the Conduct of an Audit in Accordance With Generally Accepted Auditing Standards*, requires the auditor to exercise professional judgment in planning and performing an audit.

understanding of the entity (see paragraphs .12–.25), the auditor is not required to perform all of them for each aspect of that understanding. Other procedures may be performed when the information to be obtained therefrom may be helpful in identifying risks of material misstatement. Examples of such procedures include the following:

- Reviewing information obtained from external sources, such as trade and economic journals; reports by analysts, banks, or rating agencies; or regulatory or financial publications
- Making inquiries of the entity's external legal counsel or valuation specialists whom the entity has used

Inquiries of Management and Others Within the Entity (Ref: par. .06a)

.A6 Much of the information obtained by the auditor's inquiries is obtained from management and those responsible for financial reporting. However, the auditor also may obtain information or a different perspective in identifying risks of material misstatement through inquiries of others within the entity and other employees with different levels of authority. For example

- inquiries directed toward those charged with governance may help the auditor understand the environment in which the financial statements are prepared.
- inquiries directed toward internal audit personnel may provide information about internal audit procedures performed during the year relating to the design and effectiveness of the entity's internal control and whether management has satisfactorily responded to findings from those procedures.
- inquiries of employees involved in initiating, authorizing, processing, or recording complex or unusual transactions may help the auditor to evaluate the appropriateness of the selection and application of certain accounting policies.
- inquiries directed toward in-house legal counsel may provide information about such matters as litigation, compliance with laws and regulations, knowledge of fraud or suspected fraud affecting the entity, warranties, postsales obligations, arrangements (such as joint ventures) with business partners, and the meaning of contract terms.
- inquiries directed toward marketing or sales personnel may provide information about changes in the entity's marketing strategies, sales trends, or contractual arrangements with its customers.

Analytical Procedures (Ref: par. .06b)

.A7 Analytical procedures performed as risk assessment procedures may identify aspects of the entity of which the auditor was unaware and may assist in assessing the risks of material misstatement in order to provide a basis for designing and implementing responses to the assessed risks. Analytical procedures performed as risk assessment procedures may include both financial and nonfinancial information (for example, the relationship between sales and square footage of selling space or volume of goods sold).

.A8 Analytical procedures may enhance the auditor's understanding of the client's business and the significant transactions and events that have occurred since the prior audit and also may help to identify the existence of unusual transactions or events and amounts, ratios, and trends that might indicate matters that have audit implications. Unusual or unexpected relationships that are identified may assist the auditor in identifying risks of material misstatement, especially risks of material misstatement due to fraud.

.A9 However, when such analytical procedures use data aggregated at a high level (which may be the situation with analytical procedures performed as risk assessment procedures), the results of those analytical procedures provide only a broad initial indication about whether a material misstatement may exist. Accordingly, in such cases, consideration of other information that has been gathered when identifying the risks of material misstatement together with the results of such analytical procedures may assist the auditor in understanding and evaluating the results of the analytical procedures.

Considerations Specific to Smaller, Less Complex Entities

.A10 Some smaller entities may not have interim or monthly financial information that can be used for purposes of analytical procedures. In these circumstances, although the auditor may be able to perform limited analytical procedures for purposes of planning the audit or obtain some information through inquiry, the auditor may need to plan to perform analytical procedures to identify and assess the risks of material misstatement when an early draft of the entity's financial statements is available.

Observation and Inspection (Ref: par. .06c)

.A11 Observation and inspection may support inquiries of management and others and also may provide information about the entity and its environment. Examples of such audit procedures include observation or inspection of the following:

- The entity's operations
- Documents (such as business plans and strategies), records, and internal control manuals
- Reports prepared by management (such as quarterly management reports and interim financial statements), those charged with governance (such as minutes of board of directors' meetings), and internal audit
- The entity's premises and plant facilities

Information Obtained in Prior Periods (Ref: par. .10)

.A12 The auditor's previous experience with the entity and audit procedures performed in previous audits may provide the auditor with information about such matters as

- past misstatements and whether they were corrected on a timely basis.
- the nature of the entity and its environment and the entity's internal control (including deficiencies in internal control).
- significant changes that the entity or its operations may have undergone since the prior financial period, which may assist the auditor in gaining a sufficient understanding of the entity to identify and assess risks of material misstatement.

.A13 Paragraph .10 requires the auditor to determine whether information obtained in prior periods remains relevant if the auditor intends to use that information for the purposes of the current audit. For example, changes in the control environment may affect the relevance of information obtained in the prior year. To determine whether changes have occurred that may affect the relevance of such information, the auditor may make inquiries and perform other appropriate audit procedures, such as walk-throughs of relevant systems.

Discussion Among the Engagement Team (Ref: par. .11)

.A14 The discussion among the engagement team about the susceptibility of the entity's financial statements to material misstatement

- provides an opportunity for more experienced engagement team members, including the engagement partner, to share their insights based on their knowledge of the entity.
- allows the engagement team members to exchange information about the business risks to which the entity is subject and about how and where the financial statements might be susceptible to material misstatement due to fraud or error.
- assists the engagement team members to gain a better understanding of the potential for material misstatement of the financial statements in the specific areas assigned to them and to understand how the results of the audit procedures that they perform may affect other aspects of the audit, including the decisions about the nature, timing, and extent of further audit procedures.
- provides a basis upon which engagement team members communicate and share new information obtained throughout the audit that may affect the assessment of risks of material misstatement or the audit procedures performed to address these risks.

This discussion may be held concurrently with the discussion among the engagement team that is required by section 240 to discuss the susceptibility of the entity's financial statements to fraud.[5] Section 240 further addresses the discussion among the engagement team about the risks of fraud.

.A15 It is not always necessary or practical for the discussion to include all members in a single discussion (as in group audits), nor is it necessary for all the members of the engagement team to be informed of all the decisions reached in the discussion. The engagement partner may discuss matters with key members of the engagement team, including, if considered appropriate, those with specific skills or knowledge, and those responsible for the audits of components, while delegating discussion with others, taking account of the extent of communication considered necessary throughout the engagement team. A communications plan, agreed by the engagement partner, may be useful.

Considerations Specific to Smaller, Less Complex Entities

.A16 Many small audits are carried out entirely by the engagement partner (who may be a sole practitioner). In such situations, it is the engagement partner who, having personally conducted the planning of the audit, would be responsible for considering the susceptibility of the entity's financial statements to material misstatement due to fraud or error.

Understanding the Entity and Its Environment, Including the Entity's Internal Control

.A17 Appendix A, "Understanding the Entity and Its Environment," contains examples of matters that the auditor may consider in obtaining an understanding of the entity and its environment. Appendix B, "Internal Control

---

[5] Paragraph .15 of section 240.

Components," contains a detailed explanation of the internal control components.

The Entity and Its Environment

Industry, Regulatory, and Other External Factors (Ref: par. .12a)

.A18 *Industry factors.* Relevant industry factors include industry conditions such as the competitive environment, supplier and customer relationships, and technological developments. Examples of matters the auditor may consider include

- the market and competition, including demand, capacity, and price competition.
- cyclical or seasonal activity.
- product technology relating to the entity's products.
- energy supply and cost.

.A19 The industry in which the entity operates may give rise to specific risks of material misstatement arising from the nature of the business or the degree of regulation. For example, long term contracts may involve significant estimates of revenues and expenses that give rise to risks of material misstatement. In such cases, it is important that the engagement team includes members with sufficient, relevant knowledge and experience, as required by section 220, *Quality Control for an Engagement Conducted in Accordance With Generally Accepted Auditing Standards*.

.A20 *Regulatory factors.* Relevant regulatory factors include the regulatory environment. The regulatory environment encompasses, among other matters, the applicable financial reporting framework and the legal and political environment. Examples of matters the auditor may consider include the following:

- Accounting principles and industry-specific practices
- Regulatory framework for a regulated industry
- Laws and regulations that significantly affect the entity's operations, including direct supervisory activities
- Taxation (corporate and other)
- Government policies currently affecting the conduct of the entity's business, such as monetary (including foreign exchange controls), fiscal, financial incentives (for example, government aid programs), and tariffs or trade restrictions policies
- Environmental requirements affecting the industry and the entity's business

.A21 Section 250, *Consideration of Laws and Regulations in an Audit of Financial Statements*, includes some specific requirements related to the legal and regulatory framework applicable to the entity and the industry or sector in which the entity operates.

.A22 *Other external factors.* Examples of other external factors affecting the entity that the auditor may consider include the general economic conditions, interest rates and availability of financing, and inflation or currency revaluation.

Nature of the Entity (Ref: par. .12b)

.A23 An understanding of the nature of an entity enables the auditor to understand such matters as

- whether the entity has a complex structure (for example, with subsidiaries or other components in multiple locations). Complex structures often introduce issues that may give rise to risks of material misstatement. Such issues may include whether goodwill, joint ventures, investments, or investments in entities formed to accomplish specific objectives are accounted for appropriately.
- the ownership and relations between owners and other people or entities. This understanding assists in determining whether related party transactions and balances have been identified and accounted for appropriately. Section 550, *Related Parties*, addresses the auditor's considerations relevant to related parties.

.A24 Examples of matters that the auditor may consider when obtaining an understanding of the nature of the entity include

- business operations such as
  - — the nature of revenue sources, products or services, and markets, including involvement in electronic commerce, such as Internet sales and marketing activities.
  - — the conduct of operations (for example, stages and methods of production or activities exposed to environmental risks).
  - — alliances, joint ventures, and outsourcing activities.
  - — geographic dispersion and industry segmentation.
  - — the location of production facilities, warehouses, and offices and the location and quantities of inventories.
  - — key customers and important suppliers of goods and services.
  - — employment arrangements (including the existence of union contracts, pension and other postemployment benefits, stock option or incentive bonus arrangements, and government regulation related to employment matters).
  - — research and development activities and expenditures.
  - — transactions with related parties.
- investments and investment activities such as
  - — planned or recently executed acquisitions or divestitures.
  - — investments and dispositions of securities and loans.
  - — capital investment activities.
  - — investments in nonconsolidated entities, including partnerships, joint ventures, and investments in entities formed to accomplish specific objectives.
- financing and financing activities such as
  - — major subsidiaries and associated entities, including consolidated and nonconsolidated structures.
  - — debt structure and related terms, including off balance sheet financing arrangements and leasing arrangements.
  - — beneficial owners (local and foreign and their business reputation and experience) and related parties.
  - — the use of derivative financial instruments.

- financial reporting such as
  - — accounting principles and industry-specific practices, including industry-specific significant categories (for example, loans and investments for banks or research and development for pharmaceuticals).
  - — revenue recognition practices.
  - — accounting for fair values.
  - — foreign currency assets, liabilities, and transactions.
  - — accounting for unusual or complex transactions, including those in controversial or emerging areas (for example, accounting for stock-based compensation).

.A25 Significant changes in the entity from prior periods may give rise to, or change risks of, material misstatement.

.A26 *Entities formed to accomplish specific purposes*. An entity may form an entity that is intended to accomplish a narrow and well-defined purpose (for example, a variable interest entity), such as to effect a lease or a securitization of financial assets or to carry out research and development activities. It may take the form of a corporation, trust, partnership, or unincorporated entity. The entity on behalf of which an entity has been created may often transfer assets to the latter (for example, as part of a derecognition transaction involving financial assets), obtain the right to use the latter's assets, or perform services for the latter, and other parties may provide the funding to the latter.

.A27 Financial reporting frameworks often specify detailed conditions that are deemed to amount to control or circumstances under which an entity should be considered for consolidation. The financial reporting frameworks also may specify different bases for recognition of income related to transactions with these entities. The interpretation of the requirements of such frameworks often involves a detailed knowledge of the relevant agreements involving an entity formed for a specific purpose.

The Entity's Selection and Application of Accounting Policies (Ref: par. .12c)

.A28 An understanding of the entity's selection and application of accounting policies may encompass such matters as

- the methods the entity uses to account for significant and unusual transactions.
- the effect of significant accounting policies in controversial or emerging areas for which a lack of authoritative guidance or consensus exists.
- significant changes in the entity's accounting policies and disclosures and the reasons for such changes.
- financial reporting standards, and laws and regulations that are new to the entity and when and how the entity will adopt such requirements.
- the financial reporting competencies of personnel involved in selecting and applying significant new or complex accounting standards.

Objectives and Strategies and Related Business Risks (Ref: par. .12d)

.A29 The entity conducts its business in the context of industry, regulatory, and other internal and external factors. To respond to these factors, the entity's management or those charged with governance define objectives, which are the overall plans for the entity. Strategies are the approaches by which management intends to achieve its objectives. The entity's objectives and strategies may change over time.

.A30 Business risk is broader than the risk of material misstatement of the financial statements, though it includes the latter. Business risk may arise from change or complexity. A failure to recognize the need for change also may give rise to business risk. Business risk may arise, for example, from

- the development of new products or services that may fail;
- a market that, even if successfully developed, is inadequate to support a product or service; or
- flaws in a product or service that may result in liabilities and reputational risk.

.A31 An understanding of the business risks facing the entity increases the likelihood of identifying risks of material misstatement. This is because most business risks will eventually have financial consequences and, therefore, an effect on the financial statements. However, the auditor does not have a responsibility to identify or assess all business risks because not all business risks give rise to risks of material misstatement.

.A32 Examples of matters that the auditor may consider when obtaining an understanding of the entity's objectives, strategies, and related business risks that may result in a risk of material misstatement of the financial statements include

- industry developments (a potential related business risk might be, for example, that the entity does not have the personnel or expertise to deal with the changes in the industry).
- new products and services (a potential related business risk might be, for example, product liability is increased).
- expansion of the business (a potential related business risk might be, for example, that the demand has not been accurately estimated).
- new accounting requirements (a potential related business risk might be, for example, incomplete or improper implementation or a cost increase).
- regulatory requirements (a potential related business risk might be, for example, that legal exposure is increased).
- current and prospective financing requirements (a potential related business risk might be, for example, financing is lost due to the entity's inability to meet requirements).
- use of IT (a potential related business risk might be, for example, systems and processes are incompatible).
- the effects of implementing a strategy, particularly any effects that will lead to new accounting requirements (a potential related business risk might be, for example, incomplete or improper implementation).

.A33 A business risk may have an immediate consequence for the risk of material misstatement for classes of transactions, account balances, and disclosures at the assertion level or the financial statement level. For example, the business risk arising from a contracting customer base may increase the risk of material misstatement associated with the valuation of receivables. However, the same risk, particularly in combination with a contracting economy, also may have a longer term consequence, which may lead the auditor to consider whether those conditions, in the aggregate, indicate that substantial doubt could exist about the entity's ability to continue as a going concern.[6] Whether a business risk may result in a risk of material misstatement is, therefore, considered in light of the entity's circumstances. Examples of conditions and events that may indicate risks of material misstatement are provided in appendix C, "Conditions and Events That May Indicate Risks of Material Misstatement."

.A34 Usually, management identifies business risks and develops approaches to address them. Such a risk assessment process is part of internal control and is discussed in paragraphs .16 and .A81–.A83.

.A35 *Considerations specific to governmental entities.* For the audits of governmental entities, management objectives may be influenced by concerns regarding public accountability and may include objectives that have their source in law or regulation.

Measurement and Review of the Entity's Financial Performance (Ref: par. .12e)

.A36 Management and others will measure and review those things they regard as important. Performance measures, whether external or internal, create pressures on the entity. These pressures, in turn, may motivate management or others to take action to improve the business performance or to misstate the financial statements. Accordingly, an understanding of the entity's performance measures assists the auditor in considering whether pressures to achieve performance targets may result in management actions that increase the risks of material misstatement, including those due to fraud. Section 240 addresses the risks of fraud.

.A37 The measurement and review of financial performance are not the same as the monitoring of controls (discussed as a component of internal control in paragraphs .23–.25 and .A102–.A107), though their purposes may overlap as follows:

- The measurement and review of performance is directed at whether business performance is meeting the objectives set by management (or third parties).
- Monitoring of controls is specifically concerned with the effective operation of internal control.

In some cases, however, performance indicators also provide information that enables management to identify deficiencies in internal control.

.A38 Examples of internally generated information used by management for measuring and reviewing financial performance, and which the auditor may consider, include

- key performance indicators (financial and nonfinancial) and key ratios, trends, and operating statistics.
- period-on-period financial performance analyses.
- budgets; forecasts; variance analyses; segment information; and divisional, departmental, or other-level performance reports.

---

[6] See section 570, *The Auditor's Consideration of an Entity's Ability to Continue as a Going Concern.* [Footnote revised, August 2012, to reflect conforming changes necessary due to the issuance of SAS No. 126.]

- employee performance measures and incentive compensation policies.
- comparisons of an entity's performance with that of competitors.

.A39 External parties also may measure and review the entity's financial performance. For example, external information, such as analysts' reports and credit rating agency reports, may represent useful information for the auditor. Such reports often can be obtained from the entity being audited.

.A40 Internal measures may highlight unexpected results or trends requiring management to determine their cause and take corrective action (including, in some cases, the detection and correction of misstatements on a timely basis). Performance measures also may indicate to the auditor that risks of misstatement of related financial statement information do exist. For example, performance measures may indicate that the entity has unusually rapid growth or profitability when compared with that of other entities in the same industry. Such information, particularly if combined with other factors, such as performance-based bonus or incentive remuneration, may indicate the potential risk of management bias in the preparation of the financial statements.

.A41 Considerations specific to smaller, less complex entities. Smaller entities often do not have processes to measure and review financial performance. Inquiry of management may reveal that management relies on certain key indicators for evaluating financial performance and taking appropriate action. If such inquiry indicates an absence of performance measurement or review, an increased risk of misstatements not being detected and corrected may exist.

The Entity's Internal Control

.A42 An understanding of internal control assists the auditor in identifying types of potential misstatements and factors that affect the risks of material misstatement and in designing the nature, timing, and extent of further audit procedures.

.A43 The following application material on internal control is presented in four sections:

- "General Nature and Characteristics of Internal Control"
- "Controls Relevant to the Audit"
- "Nature and Extent of the Understanding of Relevant Controls"
- "Components of Internal Control—Control Environment"

General Nature and Characteristics of Internal Control (Ref: par. .13)

.A44 *Purpose of internal control.* Internal control is designed, implemented, and maintained to address identified business risks that threaten the achievement of any of the entity's objectives that concern

- the reliability of the entity's financial reporting,
- the effectiveness and efficiency of its operations, and
- its compliance with applicable laws and regulations.

The way in which internal control is designed, implemented, and maintained varies with an entity's size and complexity.

.A45 *Considerations specific to smaller, less complex entities.* Smaller entities may use less structured means and simpler processes and procedures to achieve their objectives. For example, smaller entities with active management involvement in the financial reporting process may not have extensive descriptions of accounting procedures or detailed written policies. For some entities, in particular very small entities, the owner-manager (the proprietor of an entity who is involved in running the entity on a day-to-day basis) may perform functions that in a larger entity would be regarded as belonging to several of the components of internal control. Therefore, the components of internal control may not be clearly distinguished within smaller entities, but their underlying purposes are equally valid.

.A46 *Limitations of internal control.* Internal control, no matter how effective, can provide an entity with only reasonable assurance about achieving the entity's financial reporting objectives. The likelihood of their achievement is affected by the inherent limitations of internal control. These include the realities that human judgment in decision making can be faulty and that breakdowns in internal control can occur because of human error. For example, an error in the design of, or in the change to, a control may exist. Equally, the operation of a control may not be effective, such as when information produced for the purposes of internal control (for example, an exception report) is not effectively used because the individual responsible for reviewing the information does not understand its purpose or fails to take appropriate action.

.A47 Additionally, controls can be circumvented by the collusion of two or more people or inappropriate management override of internal control. For example, management may enter into undisclosed agreements with customers that alter the terms and conditions of the entity's standard sales contracts, which may result in improper revenue recognition. Also, edit checks in a software program that are designed to identify and report transactions that exceed specified credit limits may be overridden or disabled.

.A48 Further, in designing and implementing controls, management may make judgments on the nature and extent of the controls it chooses to implement and the nature and extent of the risks it chooses to assume.

.A49 *Considerations specific to smaller, less complex entities.* Smaller entities often have fewer employees, which may limit the extent to which segregation of duties is practicable. However, in a small owner-managed entity, the owner-manager may be able to exercise more effective oversight than in a larger entity. This oversight may compensate for the generally more limited opportunities for segregation of duties.

.A50 *Division of internal control into components.* The division of internal control into the following five components, for purposes of GAAS, provides a useful framework for auditors when considering how different aspects of an entity's internal control may affect the audit:

a. The control environment

b. The entity's risk assessment process

c. The information system, including the related business processes relevant to financial reporting and communication

d. Control activities

e. Monitoring of controls

.A51 The division does not necessarily reflect how an entity designs, implements, and maintains internal control or how it may classify any particular component. Auditors may use different terminology or frameworks to describe the various aspects of internal control and their effect on the audit other than those used in this section, provided that all the components described in this section are addressed.

.A52 Application material relating to the five components of internal control as they relate to a financial statement audit is set out in paragraphs .A71–.A107.

.A53 *Characteristics of manual and automated elements of internal control relevant to the auditor's risk assessment.* An entity's system of internal control contains manual elements and often contains automated elements. The characteristics of manual or automated elements are relevant to the auditor's risk assessment and further audit procedures based thereon.

.A54 An entity's use of IT may affect any of the five components of internal control relevant to the achievement of the entity's financial reporting, operations, or compliance objectives and its operating units or business functions. For example, an entity may use IT as part of discrete systems that support only particular business units, functions, or activities, such as a unique accounts receivable system for a particular business unit or a system that controls the operation of factory equipment. Alternatively, an entity may have complex, highly integrated systems that share data and that are used to support all aspects of the entity's financial reporting, operations, and compliance objectives.

.A55 The following use of manual or automated elements in internal control also affects the manner in which transactions are initiated, authorized, recorded, processed, and reported:

- Controls in a manual system may include such procedures as approvals and reviews of transactions and reconciliations and follow-up of reconciling items. Alternatively, an entity may use automated procedures to initiate, authorize, record, process, and report transactions, in which case records in electronic format replace paper documents.
- Controls in IT systems consist of a combination of automated controls (for example, controls embedded in computer programs) and manual controls. Further, manual controls may be independent of IT or may use information produced by IT. They also may be limited to monitoring the effective functioning of IT and automated controls and to handling exceptions. When IT is used to initiate, authorize, record, process, or report transactions or other financial data for inclusion in financial statements, the systems and programs may include controls related to the corresponding assertions for material accounts or may be critical to the effective functioning of manual controls that depend on IT.

An entity's mix of manual and automated elements in internal control varies with the nature and complexity of the entity's use of IT.

.A56 Generally, IT benefits an entity's internal control by enabling an entity to

- consistently apply predefined business rules and perform complex calculations in processing large volumes of transactions or data;
- enhance the timeliness, availability, and accuracy of information;
- facilitate the additional analysis of information;
- enhance the ability to monitor the performance of the entity's activities and its policies and procedures;
- reduce the risk that controls will be circumvented; and

- enhance the ability to achieve effective segregation of duties by implementing security controls in applications, databases, and operating systems.

.A57 IT also poses specific risks to an entity's internal control, including, for example

- reliance on systems or programs that are inaccurately processing data, processing inaccurate data, or both.
- unauthorized access to data that may result in destruction of data or improper changes to data, including the recording of unauthorized or nonexistent transactions or inaccurate recording of transactions. Particular risks may arise when multiple users access a common database.
- the possibility of IT personnel gaining access privileges beyond those necessary to perform their assigned duties, thereby breaking down segregation of duties.
- unauthorized changes to data in master files.
- unauthorized changes to systems or programs.
- failure to make necessary changes to systems or programs.
- inappropriate manual intervention.
- potential loss of data or inability to access data as required.

.A58 Manual elements in internal control may be more suitable when judgment and discretion are required, such as for the following circumstances:

- Large, unusual, or nonrecurring transactions
- Circumstances in which errors are difficult to define, anticipate, or predict
- Changing circumstances that require a control response outside the scope of an existing automated control
- Monitoring of the effectiveness of automated controls

.A59 Manual elements in internal control may be less reliable than automated elements because they can be more easily bypassed, ignored, or overridden, and they also are more prone to simple errors and mistakes. Consistency of application of a manual control element cannot, therefore, be assumed. Manual control elements may be less suitable for the following circumstances:

- High volume or recurring transactions or in situations in which errors that can be anticipated or predicted can be prevented, or detected and corrected, by control parameters that are automated
- Control activities in which the specific ways to perform the control can be adequately designed and automated

.A60 The extent and nature of the risks to internal control vary depending on the nature and characteristics of the entity's information system. For example, multiple users, either external or internal, may access a common database of information that affects financial reporting. In such circumstances, a lack of control at a single user entry point might compromise the security of the entire database, potentially resulting in improper changes to, or destruction of, data. When IT personnel or users are given, or can gain, access privileges beyond those necessary to perform their assigned duties, a breakdown in segregation of duties can occur. This could result in unauthorized transactions or changes to programs or data that affect the financial statements. The entity responds to the risks arising from the use of IT or the use of manual elements in internal control by establishing effective controls in light of the characteristics of the entity's information system.

Controls Relevant to the Audit

.A61 A direct relationship exists between an entity's objectives and the controls it implements to provide reasonable assurance about their achievement. The entity's objectives and, therefore, controls relate to financial reporting, operations, and compliance; however, not all of these objectives and controls are relevant to the auditor's risk assessment. This relationship is depicted as follows:

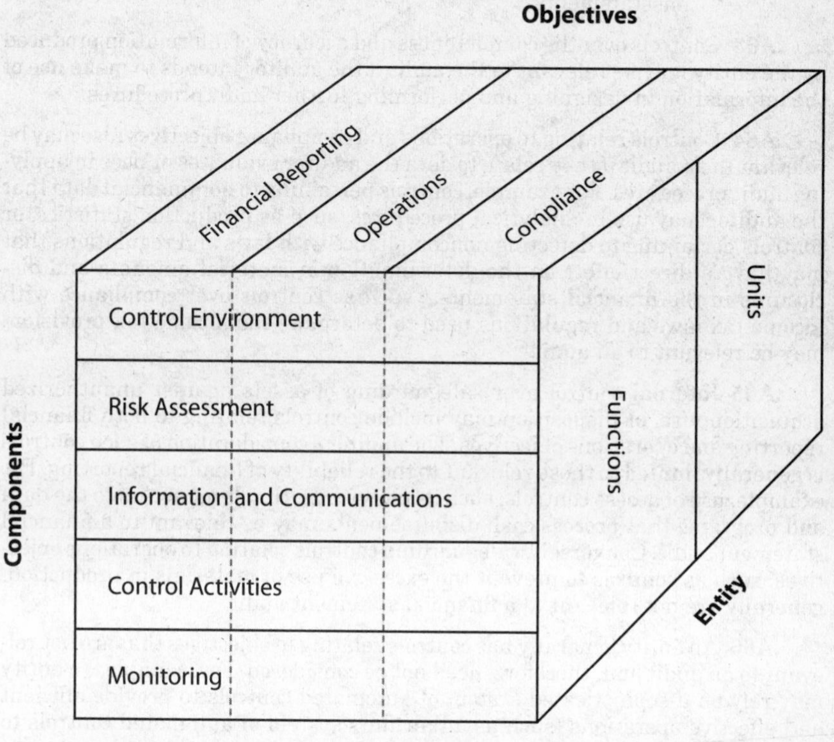

Although internal control applies to the entire entity or any of its operating units or business functions, an understanding of internal control relating to each of the entity's operating units and business functions may not be necessary to the performance of the audit.

.A62 Factors relevant to the auditor's professional judgment about whether a control, individually or in combination with others, is relevant to the audit may include such matters as the following:

- Materiality
- The significance of the related risk
- The size of the entity

- The nature of the entity's business, including its organization and ownership characteristics
- The diversity and complexity of the entity's operations
- Applicable legal and regulatory requirements
- The circumstances and the applicable component of internal control
- The nature and complexity of the systems that are part of the entity's internal control, including the use of service organizations
- Whether and how a specific control, individually or in combination with other controls, prevents, or detects and corrects, material misstatements

.A63 Controls over the completeness and accuracy of information produced by the entity may be relevant to the audit if the auditor intends to make use of the information in designing and performing further audit procedures.

.A64 Controls relating to operations and compliance objectives also may be relevant to an audit if they relate to data the auditor evaluates or uses in applying audit procedures. For example, controls pertaining to nonfinancial data that the auditor may use in analytical procedures, such as production statistics, or controls pertaining to detecting noncompliance with laws and regulations that may have a direct effect on the determination of material amounts and disclosures in the financial statements,[7] such as controls over compliance with income tax laws and regulations used to determine the income tax provision, may be relevant to an audit.

.A65 Internal control over safeguarding of assets against unauthorized acquisition, use, or disposition may include controls relating to both financial reporting and operations objectives. The auditor's consideration of such controls is generally limited to those relevant to the reliability of financial reporting. For example, use of access controls, such as passwords, that limit access to the data and programs that process cash disbursements may be relevant to a financial statement audit. Conversely, safeguarding controls relating to operations objectives, such as controls to prevent the excessive use of materials in production, generally are not relevant to a financial statement audit.

.A66 An entity generally has controls relating to objectives that are not relevant to an audit and, therefore, need not be considered. For example, an entity may rely on a sophisticated system of automated controls to provide efficient and effective operations (such as an airline's system of automated controls to maintain flight schedules), but these controls ordinarily would not be relevant to the audit.

.A67 *Considerations specific to governmental entities*. Governmental entity auditors often have additional responsibilities with respect to internal control (for example, to report on internal control over financial reporting and on internal control over compliance with law, regulation, and provisions of contracts or grant agreements, violations of which could have a direct effect on the determination of material amounts and disclosures in the financial statements). Governmental entity auditors also may have responsibilities to report on the compliance with law or regulation. As a result, their review of internal control may be broader and more detailed.

---

[7] See section 250, *Consideration of Laws and Regulations in an Audit of Financial Statements.*

Nature and Extent of the Understanding of Relevant Controls (Ref: par. .14)

.A68 Evaluating the design of a control involves considering whether the control, individually or in combination with other controls, is capable of effectively preventing, or detecting and correcting, material misstatements. Implementation of a control means that the control exists and that the entity is using it. Assessing the implementation of a control that is not effectively designed is of little use, and so the design of a control is considered first. An improperly designed control may represent a significant deficiency or material weakness in the entity's internal control.

.A69 Risk assessment procedures to obtain audit evidence about the design and implementation of relevant controls may include

- inquiring of entity personnel.
- observing the application of specific controls.
- inspecting documents and reports.
- tracing transactions through the information system relevant to financial reporting.

Inquiry alone, however, is not sufficient for such purposes.

.A70 Obtaining an understanding of an entity's controls is not sufficient to test their operating effectiveness, unless some automation provides for the consistent operation of the controls. For example, obtaining audit evidence about the implementation of a manual control at a point in time does not provide audit evidence about the operating effectiveness of the control at other times during the period under audit. However, because of the inherent consistency of IT processing (see paragraph .A56), performing audit procedures to determine whether an automated control has been implemented may serve as a test of that control's operating effectiveness, depending on the auditor's assessment and testing of controls, such as those over program changes. Tests of the operating effectiveness of controls are further described in section 330, *Performing Audit Procedures in Response to Assessed Risks and Evaluating the Audit Evidence Obtained.*[8]

Components of Internal Control—Control Environment (Ref: par. .15)

.A71 The control environment includes the governance and management functions and the attitudes, awareness, and actions of those charged with governance and management concerning the entity's internal control and its importance in the entity. The control environment sets the tone of an organization, influencing the control consciousness of its people. It is the foundation for all other components of internal control, providing discipline and structure.

.A72 Elements of the control environment that may be relevant when obtaining an understanding of the control environment include the following:

a. *Communication and enforcement of integrity and ethical values.* Essential elements that influence the effectiveness of the design, administration, and monitoring of controls.

b. *Commitment to competence.* Matters such as management's consideration of the competence levels for particular jobs and how those levels translate into requisite skills and knowledge.

c. *Participation by those charged with governance.* Attributes of those charged with governance, such as

---

[8] Paragraphs .08–.17 of section 330, *Performing Audit Procedures in Response to Assessed Risks and Evaluating the Audit Evidence Obtained.*

i. their independence from management.

ii. their experience and stature.

iii. the extent of their involvement and the information they receive and the scrutiny of activities.

iv. the appropriateness of their actions, including the degree to which difficult questions are raised and pursued with management.

v. their interaction with internal and external auditors.

d. *Management's philosophy and operating style.* Characteristics such as management's

i. approach to taking and managing business risks.

ii. attitudes and actions toward financial reporting.

iii. attitudes toward information processing and accounting functions and personnel.

e. *Organizational structure.* The framework within which an entity's activities for achieving its objectives are planned, executed, controlled, and reviewed.

f. *Assignment of authority and responsibility.* Matters such as how authority and responsibility for operating activities are assigned and how reporting relationships and authorization hierarchies are established.

g. *Human resource policies and practices.* Policies and practices that relate to, for example, recruitment, orientation, training, evaluation, counseling, promotion, compensation, and remedial actions.

.A73 *Audit evidence for elements of the control environment.* Relevant audit evidence may be obtained through a combination of inquiries and other risk assessment procedures, such as corroborating inquiries through observation or inspection of documents. For example, through inquiries of management and employees, the auditor may obtain an understanding of how management communicates to employees management's views on business practices and ethical behavior. The auditor may then determine whether relevant controls have been implemented by considering, for example, whether management has a written code of conduct and whether it acts in a manner that supports the code.

.A74 *Effect of the control environment on the assessment of the risks of material misstatement.* Some elements of an entity's control environment have a pervasive effect on assessing the risks of material misstatement. For example, an entity's control consciousness is influenced significantly by those charged with governance because one of their roles is to counterbalance pressures on management regarding financial reporting that may arise from market demands or remuneration schemes. The effectiveness of the design of the control environment with regard to participation by those charged with governance is therefore influenced by such matters as

- their independence from management and their ability to evaluate the actions of management.
- whether they understand the entity's business transactions.
- the extent to which they evaluate whether the financial statements are prepared in accordance with the applicable financial reporting framework.

.A75 An active and independent board of directors may influence the philosophy and operating style of senior management. However, other elements may be more limited in their effect. For example, although human resource policies and practices directed toward hiring competent financial, accounting, and IT personnel may reduce the risk of errors in processing financial information, they may not mitigate a strong bias by top management to overstate earnings.

.A76 The existence of a satisfactory control environment can be a positive factor when the auditor assesses the risks of material misstatement. However, although it may help reduce the risk of fraud, a satisfactory control environment is not an absolute deterrent to fraud. Conversely, deficiencies in the control environment may undermine the effectiveness of controls, particularly with regard to fraud. For example, management's failure to commit sufficient resources to address IT security risks may adversely affect internal control by allowing improper changes to be made to computer programs or data or unauthorized transactions to be processed. As explained in section 330, the control environment also influences the nature, timing, and extent of the auditor's further procedures.[9]

.A77 The control environment in itself does not prevent, or detect and correct, a material misstatement. It may, however, influence the auditor's evaluation of the effectiveness of other controls (for example, the monitoring of controls and the operation of specific control activities) and, thereby, the auditor's assessment of the risks of material misstatement.

.A78 *Considerations specific to smaller, less complex entities.* The control environment within smaller entities is likely to differ from larger entities. For example, those charged with governance in smaller entities may not include an independent or outside member, and the role of governance may be undertaken directly by the owner-manager when no other owners exist. The nature of the control environment also may influence the significance of other controls or their absence. For example, the active involvement of an owner-manager may mitigate certain risks arising from a lack of segregation of duties in a small entity; however, it may increase other risks (for example, the risk of override of controls).

.A79 In addition, audit evidence for elements of the control environment in smaller entities may not be available in documentary form, in particular when communication between management and other personnel may be informal, yet effective. For example, smaller entities might not have a written code of conduct but, instead, develop a culture that emphasizes the importance of integrity and ethical behavior through oral communication and by management example.

.A80 Consequently, the attitudes, awareness, and actions of management or the owner-manager are of particular importance to the auditor's understanding of a smaller entity's control environment.

Components of Internal Control—The Entity's Risk Assessment Process (Ref: par. .16)

.A81 An entity's risk assessment process for financial reporting purposes is its identification, analysis, and management of risks relevant to the preparation and fair presentation of financial statements. If that process is appropriate to the circumstances, including the nature, size, and complexity of the entity, it assists the auditor in identifying risks of material misstatement. For example,

---

[9] Paragraph .A2 of section 330.

risk assessment may address how the entity considers the possibility of unrecorded transactions or identifies and analyzes significant estimates recorded in the financial statements. Risks relevant to reliable financial reporting also relate to specific events or transactions. Whether the entity's risk assessment process is appropriate to the circumstances is a matter of professional judgment.

.A82 Risks relevant to financial reporting include external and internal events and circumstances that may occur and adversely affect an entity's ability to initiate, authorize, record, process, and report financial data consistent with the assertions of management in the financial statements. Risks can arise or change due to circumstances such as the following:

- Changes in operating environment
- New personnel
- New or revamped information systems
- Rapid growth
- New technology
- New business models, products, or activities
- Corporate restructurings
- Expanded foreign operations
- New accounting pronouncements
- Changes in economic conditions

.A83 *Considerations specific to smaller, less complex entities (Ref: par. 18).* A smaller entity is unlikely to have an established risk assessment process in place. In such cases, it is likely that management will identify risks through direct personal involvement in the business. Irrespective of the circumstances, however, inquiry about identified risks and how they are addressed by management is still necessary.

Components of Internal Control—The Information System, Including the Related Business Processes Relevant to Financial Reporting and Communication

.A84 *The information system, including related business processes relevant to financial reporting (Ref: par. .19).* The information system relevant to financial reporting objectives, which includes the accounting system, consists of the procedures and records designed and established to

- initiate, authorize, record, process, and report entity transactions (as well as events and conditions) and maintain accountability for the related assets, liabilities, and equity;
- resolve incorrect processing of transactions (for example, automated suspense files and procedures followed to clear suspense items out on a timely basis);
- process and account for system overrides or bypasses to controls;
- transfer information from transaction processing systems to the general ledger;
- capture information relevant to financial reporting for events and conditions other than transactions, such as the depreciation and amortization of assets and changes in the recoverability of accounts receivables; and

- ensure information required to be disclosed by the applicable financial reporting framework is accumulated, recorded, processed, summarized, and appropriately reported in the financial statements.

.A85 *Journal entries.* An entity's information system typically includes the use of standard journal entries that are required on a recurring basis to record transactions. Examples might be journal entries to record sales, purchases, and cash disbursements in the general ledger or to record accounting estimates that are periodically made by management, such as changes in the estimate of uncollectible accounts receivable.

.A86 An entity's financial reporting process also includes the use of nonstandard journal entries to record nonrecurring, unusual transactions or adjustments. Examples of such entries include consolidating adjustments and entries for a business combination or disposal or nonrecurring estimates, such as the impairment of an asset. In manual general ledger systems, nonstandard journal entries may be identified through inspection of ledgers, journals, and supporting documentation. When automated procedures are used to maintain the general ledger and prepare financial statements, such entries may exist only in electronic form and may, therefore, be more easily identified through the use of computer assisted audit techniques.

.A87 *Related business processes.* An entity's business processes are the activities designed to

- develop, purchase, produce, sell, and distribute an entity's products and services;
- ensure compliance with laws and regulations; and
- record information, including accounting and financial reporting information.

Business processes result in the transactions that are recorded, processed, and reported by the information system. Obtaining an understanding of the entity's business processes, which includes how transactions are originated, assists the auditor to obtain an understanding of the entity's information system relevant to financial reporting in a manner that is appropriate to the entity's circumstances.

.A88 *Considerations specific to smaller, less complex entities.* Information systems and related business processes relevant to financial reporting in smaller entities are likely to be less sophisticated than in larger entities, but their role is just as significant. Smaller entities with active management involvement may not need extensive descriptions of accounting procedures, sophisticated accounting records, or written policies. Understanding the entity's systems and processes may, therefore, be easier in an audit of smaller entities, and it may be more dependent on inquiry than on review of documentation. The need to obtain an understanding, however, remains important.

.A89 *Communication (Ref: par. .20).* Communication by the entity of the financial reporting roles and responsibilities and significant matters relating to financial reporting involves providing an understanding of individual roles and responsibilities pertaining to internal control over financial reporting. It includes such matters as the extent to which personnel understand how their activities in the financial reporting information system relate to the work of others and the means of reporting exceptions to an appropriate higher level within the entity. Communication may take such forms as policy manuals and financial reporting manuals. Open communication channels help ensure that exceptions are reported and acted on.

.A90 *Considerations specific to smaller, less complex entities.* Communication may be less structured and easier to achieve in a smaller entity than in a larger entity due to fewer levels of responsibility and management's greater visibility and availability.

Components of Internal Control—Control Activities (Ref: par. .21)

.A91 Control activities are the policies and procedures that help ensure that management directives are carried out. Control activities, whether within IT or manual systems, have various objectives and are applied at various organizational and functional levels. Examples of specific control activities include those relating to the following:

- Authorization
- Performance reviews
- Information processing
- Physical controls
- Segregation of duties

.A92 Control activities that are relevant to the audit are those that are

- required to be treated as such, being control activities that relate to significant risks and those that relate to risks for which substantive procedures alone do not provide sufficient appropriate audit evidence, as required by paragraphs .30–.31, respectively, or
- considered to be relevant in the professional judgment of the auditor.

.A93 The auditor's professional judgment about whether a control activity is relevant to the audit is influenced by the risk that the auditor has identified that may give rise to a material misstatement and whether the auditor thinks it is likely to be appropriate to test the operating effectiveness of the control in determining the extent of substantive testing.

.A94 The auditor's emphasis may be on identifying and obtaining an understanding of control activities that address the areas in which the auditor considers that risks of material misstatement are likely to be higher. When multiple control activities each achieve the same objective, it is unnecessary to obtain an understanding of each of the control activities related to such objective.

.A95 The auditor's knowledge about the presence or absence of control activities obtained from the understanding of the other components of internal control assists the auditor in determining whether it is necessary to devote additional attention to obtaining an understanding of control activities.

.A96 *Considerations specific to smaller, less complex entities.* The concepts underlying control activities in smaller entities are likely to be similar to those in larger entities, but the formality with which they operate may vary. Further, smaller entities may find that certain types of control activities are not relevant because of controls applied by management. For example, management's sole authority for granting credit to customers and approving significant purchases can provide strong control over important account balances and transactions, lessening or removing the need for more detailed control activities.

.A97 Control activities relevant to the audit of a smaller entity are likely to relate to the main transaction cycles, such as revenues, purchases, and employment expenses.

.A98 *Risks arising from IT (Ref: par. .22).* The use of IT affects the way that control activities are implemented. From the auditor's perspective, controls over IT systems are effective when they maintain the integrity of information and the security of the data such systems process and when they include effective general IT controls and application controls.

.A99 *General IT controls* are policies and procedures that relate to many applications and support the effective functioning of application controls. They apply to mainframe, miniframe, and end-user environments. General IT controls that maintain the integrity of information and security of data commonly include controls over the following:

- Data center and network operations
- System software acquisition, change, and maintenance
- Program change
- Access security
- Application system acquisition, development, and maintenance

They are generally implemented to deal with the risks referred to in paragraph .A57.

.A100 Although ineffective general IT controls do not by themselves cause misstatements, they may permit application controls to operate improperly and allow misstatements to occur and not be detected. For example, if deficiencies in the general IT controls over access security exist and applications are relying on these general controls to prevent unauthorized transactions from being processed, such general IT control deficiencies may have a more severe effect on the effective design and operation of the application control. General IT controls are assessed with regard to their effect on applications and data that become part of the financial statements. For example, if no new systems are implemented during the period of the financial statements, deficiencies in the general IT controls over application system acquisition and development may not be relevant to the financial statements being audited.

.A101 *Application controls* are manual or automated procedures that typically operate at a business process level and apply to the processing of transactions by individual applications. Application controls can be preventive or detective and are designed to ensure the integrity of the accounting records. Accordingly, application controls relate to procedures used to initiate, authorize, record, process, and report transactions or other financial data. These controls help ensure that transactions occurred, are authorized, and are completely and accurately recorded and processed. Examples include edit checks of input data and numerical sequence checks with manual follow-up of exception reports or correction at the point of data entry.

Components of Internal Control—Monitoring of Controls (Ref: par. .23)

.A102 Monitoring of controls is a process to assess the effectiveness of internal control performance over time. It involves assessing the effectiveness of controls on a timely basis and taking necessary remedial actions. Management accomplishes monitoring of controls through ongoing activities, separate evaluations, or a combination of the two. Ongoing monitoring activities often are built into the normal recurring activities of an entity and include regular management and supervisory activities.

.A103 *Considerations specific to smaller, less complex entities.* Management's monitoring of controls often is accomplished by management's or the owner-manager's close involvement in operations. This involvement often will identify significant variances from expectations and inaccuracies in financial data leading to remedial action to the control.

.A104 *Internal audit function (Ref: par. .24).* The entity's internal audit function is likely to be relevant to the audit if the nature of the internal audit function's responsibilities and activities are related to the entity's financial reporting, and the auditor expects to use the work of the internal auditors to modify the nature or timing or reduce the extent of audit procedures to be performed. If the auditor determines that the internal audit function is likely to be relevant to the audit, section 610, *The Auditor's Consideration of the Internal Audit Function in an Audit of Financial Statements,*[†] applies.

.A105 The objectives of an internal audit function and, therefore, the nature of its responsibilities and its status within the organization, vary widely and depend on the size and structure of the entity and the requirements of management and, when applicable, those charged with governance. The responsibilities of an internal audit function may include, for example, monitoring of internal control, risk management, and review of compliance with laws and regulations. On the other hand, the responsibilities of the internal audit function may be limited to the review of the economy, efficiency, and effectiveness of operations, for example, and, accordingly, may not relate to the entity's financial reporting.

.A106 If the nature of the internal audit function's responsibilities is related to the entity's financial reporting, the external auditor's consideration of the activities performed or to be performed by the internal audit function may include review of the internal audit function's audit plan for the period, if any, and discussion of that plan with the internal auditors.

.A107 *Sources of information (Ref: par. .25).* Much of the information used in monitoring may be produced by the entity's information system. If management assumes that data used for monitoring are accurate without having a basis for that assumption, errors that may exist in the information could potentially lead management to incorrect conclusions from its monitoring activities. Accordingly, an understanding of the following is required as part of the auditor's understanding of the entity's monitoring activities component of internal control:

- The sources of the information related to the entity's monitoring activities
- The basis upon which management considers the information to be sufficiently reliable for the purpose

Identifying and Assessing the Risks of Material Misstatement

Assessment of Risks of Material Misstatement at the Financial Statement Level (Ref: par. .26a)

.A108 Risks of material misstatement at the financial statement level refer to risks that relate pervasively to the financial statements as a whole and

---

[†] SAS No. 65, *The Auditor's Consideration of the Internal Audit Function in an Audit of Financial Statements*, is currently effective and codified as AU section 322. SAS No. 65 has been included in section 610, as designated by SAS No. 122, *Statements on Auditing Standards: Clarification and Recodification*, and will be superseded when it is redrafted for clarity and convergence with International Standard on Auditing 610 (Revised), *Using the Work of Internal Auditors*, as part of the Clarification and Convergence project of the Auditing Standards Board. Until such time, section 610 has been conformed to reflect updated section and paragraph cross references but has not otherwise been subjected to a comprehensive review or revision.

potentially affect many assertions. Risks of this nature are not necessarily risks identifiable with specific assertions at the class of transactions, account balance, or disclosure level. Rather, they represent circumstances that may increase the risks of material misstatement at the assertion level (for example, through management override of internal control). Financial statement level risks may be especially relevant to the auditor's consideration of the risks of material misstatement arising from fraud.

.A109 Risks at the financial statement level may derive, in particular, from a deficient control environment (although these risks also may relate to factors such as declining economic conditions). For example, deficiencies such as management's lack of competence may have a more pervasive effect on the financial statements and may require an overall response by the auditor.

.A110 The auditor's understanding of internal control may raise doubts about the auditability of an entity's financial statements. For example

- concerns about the integrity of the entity's management may be so serious to cause the auditor to conclude that the risk of management misrepresentation in the financial statements is such that an audit cannot be conducted.
- concerns about the condition and reliability of an entity's records may cause the auditor to conclude that it is unlikely that sufficient appropriate audit evidence will be available to support an unmodified opinion on the financial statements.

.A111 Section 705, *Modifications to the Opinion in the Independent Auditor's Report*, addresses the determination of whether a need exists for the auditor to express a qualified or adverse opinion or disclaim an opinion or, as may be required in some cases, to withdraw from the engagement when withdrawal is possible under applicable law or regulation.

Assessment of Risks of Material Misstatement at the Relevant Assertion Level (Ref: par. .26b)

.A112 Risks of material misstatement at the relevant assertion level for classes of transactions, account balances, and disclosures need to be considered because such consideration directly assists in determining the nature, timing, and extent of further audit procedures at the assertion level necessary to obtain sufficient appropriate audit evidence. In identifying and assessing risks of material misstatement at the relevant assertion level, the auditor may conclude that the identified risks relate more pervasively to the financial statements as a whole and potentially affect many relevant assertions.

The Use of Assertions

.A113 In representing that the financial statements are in accordance with the applicable financial reporting framework, management implicitly or explicitly makes assertions regarding the recognition, measurement, presentation, and disclosure of the various elements of financial statements and related disclosures.

.A114 Assertions used by the auditor to consider the different types of potential misstatements that may occur fall into the following three categories and may take the following forms:

a. Assertions about classes of transactions and events for the period under audit, such as the following:

   i. *Occurrence*. Transactions and events that have been recorded have occurred and pertain to the entity.

ii. *Completeness*. All transactions and events that should have been recorded have been recorded.

iii. *Accuracy*. Amounts and other data relating to recorded transactions and events have been recorded appropriately.

iv. *Cutoff*. Transactions and events have been recorded in the correct accounting period.

v. *Classification*. Transactions and events have been recorded in the proper accounts.

b. Assertions about account balances at the period-end, such as the following:

i. *Existence*. Assets, liabilities, and equity interests exist.

ii. *Rights and obligations*. The entity holds or controls the rights to assets, and liabilities are the obligations of the entity.

iii. *Completeness*. All assets, liabilities, and equity interests that should have been recorded have been recorded.

iv. *Valuation and allocation*. Assets, liabilities, and equity interests are included in the financial statements at appropriate amounts, and any resulting valuation or allocation adjustments are appropriately recorded.

c. Assertions about presentation and disclosure, such as the following:

i. *Occurrence and rights and obligations*. Disclosed events, transactions, and other matters have occurred and pertain to the entity.

ii. *Completeness*. All disclosures that should have been included in the financial statements have been included.

iii. *Classification and understandability*. Financial information is appropriately presented and described, and disclosures are clearly expressed.

iv. *Accuracy and valuation*. Financial and other information is disclosed fairly and in appropriate amounts.

.A115 The auditor may use the assertions as described previously or may express them differently, provided that all aspects described previously have been covered. For example, the auditor may choose to combine the assertions about transactions and events with the assertions about account balances. As another example, there may not be a separate assertion related to cutoff of transactions and events when the occurrence and completeness assertions include appropriate consideration of recording transactions in the correct accounting period.

Relevant Assertions

.A116 The auditor is required by paragraph .26*b* to use relevant assertions for classes of transactions, account balances, and disclosures in sufficient detail to form a basis for the assessment of risks of material misstatement and the design and performance of further audit procedures. The auditor also is required to use relevant assertions in assessing risks by relating the identified risks to what can go wrong at the relevant assertion, taking account of relevant controls that the auditor intends to test, and designing further audit procedures that are responsive to the assessed risks.

.A117 *Relevant assertions* are assertions that have a reasonable possibility of containing a misstatement or misstatements that would cause the financial statements to be materially misstated and, as such, are assertions that have a meaningful bearing on whether the account is fairly stated. Not all assertions pertaining to a particular account balance will always be relevant. For example, valuation may not be relevant to the cash account unless currency translation is involved; however, existence and completeness are always relevant. Similarly, valuation may not be relevant to the gross amount of the accounts receivable balance but is relevant to the related allowance accounts. Additionally, the auditor might, in some circumstances, focus on the presentation and disclosure assertions separately in connection with the period-end financial reporting process.

.A118 For each significant class of transactions, account balance, and disclosure, the auditor is required to determine the relevance of each of the financial statement assertions. Identifying relevant assertions includes determining the source of likely potential misstatements in each significant class of transactions, account balance, and disclosure. Attributes indicating the potential relevance of an assertion include the

a. nature of the assertion;

b. volume of transactions or data related to the assertion; and

c. nature and complexity of the systems, including the use of IT, by which the entity processes and controls information supporting the assertion.

Considerations Specific to Governmental Entities

.A119 When making assertions about the financial statements of governmental entities, in addition to those assertions set out in paragraph .A114, management asserts that transactions and events have been carried out in accordance with law or regulation. Such assertions may fall within the scope of the financial statement audit.

Process of Identifying Risks of Material Misstatement (Ref: par. .27a)

.A120 Information gathered by performing risk assessment procedures, including the audit evidence obtained in evaluating the design of controls and determining whether they have been implemented, is used as audit evidence to support the risk assessment. The risk assessment determines the nature, timing, and extent of further audit procedures to be performed.

.A121 Appendix C provides examples of conditions and events that may indicate the existence of risks of material misstatement.

Relating Controls to Assertions (Ref: par. .27c)

.A122 In making risk assessments, the auditor may identify the controls that are likely to prevent, or detect and correct, material misstatement in specific assertions. Generally, it is useful to obtain an understanding of controls and relate them to assertions in the context of processes and systems in which they exist because individual control activities often do not in themselves address a risk. Often, only multiple control activities, together with other components of internal control, will be sufficient to address a risk.

.A123 Conversely, some control activities may have a specific effect on an individual assertion embodied in a particular class of transactions or account balance. For example, the control activities that an entity established to ensure that its personnel are properly counting and recording the annual physical inventory relate directly to the existence and completeness assertions for the inventory account balance.

.A124 Controls can be either directly or indirectly related to an assertion. The more indirect the relationship, the less effective that control may be in preventing, or detecting and correcting, misstatements in that assertion. For example, a sales manager's review of a summary of sales activity for specific stores by region ordinarily is only indirectly related to the completeness assertion for sales revenue. Accordingly, it may be less effective in reducing risk for that assertion than controls more directly related to that assertion, such as matching shipping documents with billing documents.

Significant Risks

Identifying Significant Risks (Ref: par. .28–.29)

.A125 Significant risks often relate to significant nonroutine transactions and matters that require significant judgment. *Nonroutine transactions* are transactions that are unusual, either due to size or nature, and that, therefore, occur infrequently. Matters that require significant judgment may include the development of accounting estimates for which a significant measurement uncertainty exists. Routine, noncomplex transactions that are subject to systematic processing are less likely to give rise to significant risks.

.A126 Risks of material misstatement may be greater for significant nonroutine transactions arising from matters such as the following:

- Greater management intervention to specify the accounting treatment
- Greater manual intervention for data collection and processing
- Complex calculations or accounting principles
- The nature of nonroutine transactions, which may make it difficult for the entity to implement effective controls over the risks
- Related party transactions

.A127 Risks of material misstatement may be greater for matters that require significant judgment, such as the development of accounting estimates, arising from matters such as the following:

- Accounting principles for accounting estimates or revenue recognition may be subject to differing interpretation.
- Required judgment may be subjective or complex or it may require assumptions about the effects of future events (for example, judgment about fair value).

.A128 Section 330 describes the consequences for further audit procedures of identifying a risk as significant.[10]

Significant Risks Relating to the Risks of Material Misstatement Due to Fraud

.A129 Section 240 further addresses the identification and assessment of the risks of material misstatement due to fraud.

Understanding Controls Related to Significant Risks (Ref: par. .30)

.A130 Although risks relating to significant nonroutine transactions or matters that require significant judgment are often less likely to be subject to routine controls, management may have other responses intended to deal with such risks. Accordingly, the auditor's understanding of whether the entity has designed and implemented controls for significant risks arising from nonroutine

---

[10] Paragraphs .15 and .22 of section 330.

transactions or matters that require significant judgment includes whether and how management responds to the risks. Such responses might include

- control activities, such as a review of assumptions by senior management or specialists.
- documented processes for estimations.
- approval by those charged with governance.

.A131 For example, when nonrecurring events occur, such as the receipt of notice of a significant lawsuit, consideration of the entity's response may include such matters as whether it has been referred to appropriate specialists (for example, internal or external legal counsel), whether an assessment has been made of the potential effect, and how it is proposed that the circumstances are to be disclosed in the financial statements.

.A132 In some cases, management may not have appropriately responded to significant risks of material misstatement by implementing controls over these significant risks. Failure by management to implement such controls may be a significant deficiency or a material weakness. In these circumstances, the auditor also may consider the implications for the auditor's risk assessment.

Risks for Which Substantive Procedures Alone Do Not Provide Sufficient Appropriate Audit Evidence (Ref: par. .31)

.A133 Risks of material misstatement may relate directly to the recording of routine classes of transactions or account balances and the preparation of reliable financial statements. Such risks may include risks of inaccurate or incomplete processing for routine and significant classes of transactions, such as an entity's revenue; purchases; and cash receipts or cash payments.

.A134 When such routine business transactions are subject to highly automated processing with little or no manual intervention, it may not be possible to perform only substantive procedures regarding the risk. For example, the auditor may consider this to be the case when a significant amount of an entity's information is initiated, authorized, recorded, processed, or reported only in electronic form, such as in an integrated system. In such cases

- audit evidence may be available only in electronic form, and its sufficiency and appropriateness usually depend on the effectiveness of controls over its accuracy and completeness.
- the potential for improper initiation or alteration of information to occur and not be detected may be greater if appropriate controls are not operating effectively.

.A135 Examples of situations in which the auditor may find it impossible to design effective substantive procedures that, by themselves, provide sufficient appropriate audit evidence that certain relevant assertions are not materially misstated include the following:

- An entity that conducts its business using IT to initiate orders for the purchase and delivery of goods based on predetermined rules of what to order and in what quantities and to pay the related accounts payable based on system-generated decisions initiated upon the confirmed receipt of goods and terms of payment. No other documentation of orders placed or goods received is produced or maintained, other than through the IT system.
- An entity that provides services to customers via electronic media (for example, an Internet service provider or a telecommunications company) and uses IT to create a log of the services provided

to its customers, initiate and process its billings for the services, and automatically record such amounts in electronic accounting records that are part of the system used to produce the entity's financial statements.

.A136 The consequences for further audit procedures of identifying such risks are described in section 330.[11]

Revision of Risk Assessment (Ref: par. .32)

.A137 During the audit, information may come to the auditor's attention that differs significantly from the information on which the risk assessment was based. For example, the risk assessment may be based on an expectation that controls are operating effectively. In performing tests of controls, the auditor may obtain audit evidence that they were not operating effectively at relevant times during the audit. Similarly, in performing substantive procedures, the auditor may detect misstatements in amounts or frequency greater than is consistent with the auditor's risk assessment. In such circumstances, the risk assessment may not appropriately reflect the true circumstances of the entity, and the further planned audit procedures may not be effective in detecting material misstatements. See section 330 for further guidance.

Documentation (Ref: par. .33)

.A138 The manner in which the requirements of paragraph .33 are documented is for the auditor to determine exercising professional judgment. For example, in audits of smaller entities, the documentation may be incorporated in the auditor's documentation of the overall strategy and audit plan.[12] Similarly, the results of the risk assessment may be documented separately, or they may be documented as part of the auditor's documentation of further audit procedures.[13] The form and extent of the documentation is influenced by the nature, size, and complexity of the entity and its internal control; availability of information from the entity; and the audit methodology and technology used in the course of the audit.

.A139 For entities that have uncomplicated businesses and processes relevant to financial reporting, the documentation may be simple and relatively brief. It is not necessary to document the entirety of the auditor's understanding of the entity and matters related to it. Key elements of the understanding documented by the auditor include those on which the auditor based the assessment of the risks of material misstatement.

.A140 The extent of documentation also may reflect the experience and capabilities of the members of the audit engagement team. Provided that the requirements of section 230, *Audit Documentation*, are met, an audit undertaken by an engagement team comprising less experienced individuals may contain more detailed documentation to assist them to obtain an appropriate understanding of the entity than one that includes experienced individuals.

.A141 For recurring audits, certain documentation may be carried forward and updated as necessary to reflect changes in the entity's business or processes.

---

[11] Paragraph .08 of section 330.

[12] Paragraphs .07–.09 of section 300, *Planning an Audit*.

[13] Paragraph .30 of section 330.

.A142

Appendix A—Understanding the Entity and Its Environment (Ref: par. .A17)

This appendix provides additional guidance on matters the auditor may consider when obtaining an understanding of the industry and regulatory and other external factors that affect the entity, the nature of the entity, objectives and strategies and related business risks, and the measurement and review of the entity's financial performance. The examples provided cover a broad range of matters applicable to many engagements; however, not all matters are relevant to every engagement, and the list of examples is not necessarily complete. Additional guidance on internal control is contained in appendix B, "Internal Control Components."

Industry, Regulatory, and Other External Factors

Examples of matters an auditor may consider include the following:

- Industry conditions, such as the following:
  - — The market and competition, including demand, capacity, and price competition
  - — Cyclical or seasonal activity
  - — Product technology relating to the entity's products
  - — Supply availability and cost
- Regulatory environment, such as the following:
  - — Accounting principles and industry-specific practices
  - — Regulatory framework for a regulated industry
  - — Legislation and regulation that significantly affect the entity's operations, such as the following:
    - Regulatory requirements
    - Direct supervisory activities
  - — Taxation (corporate and other)
  - — Government policies currently affecting the conduct of the entity's business, such as the following:
    - Monetary, including foreign exchange controls
    - Fiscal
    - Financial incentives (for example, government aid programs)
    - Tariffs and trade restrictions
  - — Environmental requirements affecting the industry and the entity's business
- Other external factors currently affecting the entity's business, such as the following:
  - — General level of economic activity (for example, recession, growth, and so on)
  - — Interest rates and availability of financing
  - — Inflation and currency revaluation

Nature of the Entity

Examples of matters an auditor may consider include the following:

- Business operations, such as the following:
  - — Nature of revenue sources (for example, manufacturer; wholesaler; banking, insurance, or other financial services; import-export trading; utility; transportation; and technology products and services)
  - — Products or services and markets (for example, major customers and contracts, terms of payment, profit margins, market share, competitors, exports, pricing policies, reputation of products, warranties, backlog, trends, marketing strategy and objectives, and manufacturing processes)
  - — Conduct of operations (for example, stages and methods of production, subsidiaries or divisions, delivery of products and services, and details of declining or expanding operations)
  - — Alliances, joint ventures, and outsourcing activities
  - — Involvement in e-commerce, including Internet sales and marketing activities
  - — Geographic dispersion and industry segmentation
  - — Location of production facilities, warehouses, and offices
  - — Key customers
  - — Important suppliers of goods and services (for example, long term contracts, stability of supply, terms of payment, imports, and methods of delivery, such as "just-in-time")
  - — Employment (for example, by location, supply, wage levels, union contracts, pension and other postemployment benefits, stock option or incentive bonus arrangements, and government regulation related to employment matters)
  - — Research and development activities and expenditures
  - — Transactions with related parties
- Investments, such as the following:
  - — Acquisitions, mergers, or disposals of business activities (planned or recently executed)
  - — Investments and dispositions of securities and loans
  - — Capital investment activities, including investments in plant and equipment and technology and any recent or planned changes
  - — Investments in nonconsolidated entities, including partnerships, joint ventures, and investments in entities formed to accomplish specific objectives
  - — Life cycle stage of enterprise (start-up, growing, mature, declining)

- Financing, such as the following:
  - — Group structure of major subsidiaries and associated entities, including consolidated and nonconsolidated structures
  - — Debt structure, including covenants, restrictions, guarantees, and off balance sheet financing arrangements
  - — Leasing of property, plant, or equipment for use in the business
  - — Beneficial owners (local and foreign business reputation and experience)
  - — Related parties
  - — Use of derivative financial instruments
- Financial reporting, such as the following:
  - — Accounting principles and industry-specific practices
  - — Revenue recognition practices
  - — Accounting for fair values
  - — Inventories (for example, locations and quantities)
  - — Foreign currency assets, liabilities, and transactions
  - — Industry-specific significant categories (for example, loans and investments for banks, accounts receivable and inventory for manufacturers, research and development for pharmaceuticals)
  - — Accounting for unusual or complex transactions, including those in controversial or emerging areas (for example, accounting for stock-based compensation)
  - — Financial statement presentation and disclosure

Objectives and Strategies and Related Business Risks

Examples of matters an auditor may consider include the following:

- Existence of objectives (that is, how the entity addresses industry, regulatory, and other external factors) relating to, for example, the following matters:
  - — Industry developments (a potential related business risk might be, for example, the entity does not have the personnel or expertise to deal with the changes in the industry)
  - — New products and services (a potential related business risk might be, for example, product liability has increased)
  - — Expansion of the business (a potential related business risk might be, for example, the demand has not been accurately estimated)
  - — New accounting requirements (a potential related business risk might be, for example, incomplete or improper implementation or increased costs)
  - — Regulatory requirements (a potential related business risk might be, for example, legal exposure has increased)

  - Current and prospective financing requirements (a potential related business risk might be, for example, the entity's inability to meet requirements results in the loss of financing)
  - IT (a potential related business risk might be, for example, systems and processes are not compatible)
  - Risk appetite of managers and stakeholders
- Effects of implementing a strategy, particularly any effects that will lead to new accounting requirements (a potential related business risk might be, for example, implementation is incomplete or improper)

Measurement and Review of the Entity's Financial Performance

Examples of matters an auditor may consider include the following:

- Key ratios and operating statistics
- Key performance indicators
- Employee performance measures and incentive compensation policies
- Trends
- Use of forecasts, budgets, and variance analysis
- Analyst reports and credit rating reports
- Competitor analysis
- Period-on-period financial performance (revenue growth, profitability, and leverage)

.A143

Appendix B—Internal Control Components (Ref: par. .04, .15–.25, and .A71–.A107)

This appendix further explains the components of internal control, as set out in paragraphs .04, .15–.25, and .A71–.A107, as they relate to a financial statement audit.

Control Environment

The control environment encompasses the following elements:

a. *Communication and enforcement of integrity and ethical values.* The effectiveness of controls cannot rise above the integrity and ethical values of the people who create, administer, and monitor them. Integrity and ethical behavior are the products of the entity's ethical and behavioral standards, how they are communicated, and how they are reinforced in practice. The enforcement of integrity and ethical values includes, for example, management actions to eliminate or mitigate incentives or temptations that might prompt personnel to engage in dishonest, illegal, or unethical acts. The communication of entity policies on integrity and ethical values may include the communication of behavioral standards to personnel through policy statements and codes of conduct and by example.

b. *Commitment to competence. Competence* is the knowledge and skills necessary to accomplish tasks that define the individual's job.

c. *Participation by those charged with governance.* An entity's control consciousness is influenced significantly by those charged with governance. The importance of the responsibilities of those charged with governance is recognized in codes of practice and other laws and regulations or guidance produced for the benefit of those charged with governance. Other responsibilities of those charged with governance include oversight of the design and effective operation of whistle-blower procedures and the process for reviewing the effectiveness of the entity's internal control.

d. *Management's philosophy and operating style.* Management's philosophy and operating style encompass a broad range of characteristics. For example, management's attitudes and actions toward financial reporting may manifest themselves through conservative or aggressive selection from available alternative accounting principles or conscientiousness and conservatism with which accounting estimates are developed.

e. *Organizational structure.* Establishing a relevant organizational structure includes considering key areas of authority and responsibility and appropriate lines of reporting. The appropriateness of an entity's organizational structure depends, in part, on its size and the nature of its activities.

f. *Assignment of authority and responsibility.* The assignment of authority and responsibility may include policies relating to appropriate business practices, knowledge and experience of key personnel, and resources provided for carrying out duties. In addition, it may include policies and communications directed at ensuring that all personnel understand the entity's objectives, know how their individual actions interrelate and contribute to those objectives, and recognize how and for what they will be held accountable.

g. *Human resource policies and practices.* Human resource policies and practices often demonstrate important matters regarding the control consciousness of an entity. For example, standards for recruiting the most qualified individuals, with an emphasis on educational background, prior work experience, past accomplishments, and evidence of integrity and ethical behavior, demonstrate an entity's commitment to competent and trustworthy people. Training policies that communicate prospective roles and responsibilities and include practices such as training schools and seminars illustrate expected levels of performance and behavior. Promotions driven by periodic performance appraisals demonstrate the entity's commitment to the advancement of qualified personnel to higher levels of responsibility.

The Entity's Risk Assessment Process

For financial reporting purposes, the entity's risk assessment process includes how management identifies business risks relevant to the preparation and fair presentation of financial statements in accordance with the entity's applicable financial reporting framework, estimates their significance, assesses the likelihood of their occurrence, and decides upon actions to respond to and manage them and the results thereof. For example, the entity's risk assessment process may address how the entity considers the possibility of unrecorded transactions or identifies and analyzes significant estimates recorded in the financial statements.

Risks relevant to reliable financial reporting include external and internal events, as well as transactions or circumstances that may occur and adversely affect an entity's ability to initiate, authorize, record, process, and report financial data consistent with the assertions of management in the financial statements. Management may initiate plans, programs, or actions to address specific risks or it may decide to accept a risk because of cost or other considerations. Risks can arise or change due to circumstances such as the following:

- *Changes in operating environment.* Changes in the regulatory or operating environment can result in changes in competitive pressures and significantly different risks.
- *New personnel.* New personnel may have a different focus on, or understanding of, internal control.
- *New or revamped information systems.* Significant and rapid changes in information systems can change the risk relating to internal control.
- *Rapid growth.* Significant and rapid expansion of operations can strain controls and increase the risk of a breakdown in controls.
- *New technology.* Incorporating new technologies into production processes or information systems may change the risk associated with internal control.
- *New business models, products, or activities.* Entering into business areas or transactions with which an entity has little experience may introduce new risks associated with internal control.

- *Corporate restructurings*. Restructurings may be accompanied by staff reductions and changes in supervision and segregation of duties that may change the risk associated with internal control.
- *Expanded foreign operations*. The expansion or acquisition of foreign operations carries new and often unique risks that may affect internal control (for example, additional or changed risks from foreign currency transactions).
- *New accounting pronouncements*. Adoption of new accounting principles or changing accounting principles may affect risks in preparing financial statements.

The Information System, Including the Related Business Processes Relevant to Financial Reporting and Communication

An information system consists of infrastructure (physical and hardware components), software, people, procedures, and data. Many information systems make extensive use of IT.

The information system relevant to financial reporting objectives, which includes the financial reporting system, encompasses methods and records that

- identify and record all valid transactions.
- describe on a timely basis the transactions in sufficient detail to permit proper classification of transactions for financial reporting.
- measure the value of transactions in a manner that permits recording their proper monetary value in the financial statements.
- determine the time period in which transactions occurred to permit recording of transactions in the proper accounting period.
- present properly the transactions and related disclosures in the financial statements.

The quality of system-generated information affects management's ability to make appropriate decisions in managing and controlling the entity's activities and to prepare reliable financial reports.

Communication, which involves providing an understanding of individual roles and responsibilities pertaining to internal control over financial reporting, may take such forms as policy manuals, accounting and financial reporting manuals, and memoranda. Communication also can be made electronically, orally, and through the actions of management.

Control Activities

Generally, control activities that may be relevant to an audit may be categorized as policies and procedures that pertain to the following:

- *Performance reviews*. These control activities include reviews and analyses of actual performance versus budgets, forecasts, and prior-period performance; relating different sets of data (operating or financial) to one another, together with analyses of the relationships and investigative and corrective actions; comparing internal data with external sources of information; and review of functional or activity performance.

- *Information processing*. The two broad groupings of information systems control activities are application controls, which apply to the processing of individual applications, and general IT controls, which are policies and procedures that relate to many applications and support the effective functioning of application controls by helping to ensure the continued proper operation of information systems. Examples of application controls include checking the arithmetical accuracy of records; maintaining and reviewing accounts and trial balances; automated controls, such as edit checks of input data and numerical sequence checks; and manual follow-up of exception reports. Examples of general IT controls are program change controls; controls that restrict access to programs or data; controls over the implementation of new releases of packaged software applications; and controls over system software that restrict access to, or monitor the use of, system utilities that could change financial data or records without leaving an audit trail.
- *Physical controls*. This includes controls that encompass the
  - — physical security of assets, including adequate safeguards, such as secured facilities over access to assets and records.
  - — authorization for access to computer programs and data files.
  - — periodic counting and comparison with amounts shown on control records (for example comparing the results of cash, security, and inventory counts with accounting records).

  The extent to which physical controls intended to prevent theft of assets are relevant to the reliability of financial statement preparation and, therefore, the audit, depends on circumstances such as when assets are highly susceptible to misappropriation.
- *Segregation of duties*. Assigning different people the responsibilities of authorizing transactions, recording transactions, and maintaining custody of assets. Segregation of duties is intended to reduce the opportunities to allow any person to be in a position to both perpetrate and conceal errors or fraud in the normal course of the person's duties.

Certain control activities may depend on the existence of appropriate higher level policies established by management or those charged with governance. For example, authorization controls may be delegated under established guidelines, such as investment criteria set by those charged with governance; alternatively, nonroutine transactions, such as major acquisitions or divestments, may require specific high level approval, including, in some cases, that of shareholders.

Monitoring of Controls

An important management responsibility is to establish and maintain internal control on an ongoing basis. Management's monitoring of controls includes considering whether they are operating as intended and that they are modified as appropriate for changes in conditions. Monitoring of controls may include activities such as management's review of whether bank reconciliations are being prepared on a timely basis, internal auditors' evaluation of sales personnel's compliance with the entity's policies on terms of sales contracts, and a legal department's oversight of compliance with the entity's ethical or business practice policies. Monitoring also is done to ensure that controls continue to operate effectively over time. For example, if the timeliness and accuracy of bank reconciliations are not monitored, personnel are likely to stop preparing them.

Internal auditors or personnel performing similar functions may contribute to the monitoring of an entity's controls through separate evaluations. Ordinarily, they regularly provide information about the functioning of internal control, focusing considerable attention on evaluating the effectiveness of internal control; communicate information about strengths and deficiencies in internal control; and provide recommendations for improving internal control.

Monitoring activities may include using information from communications from external parties that may indicate problems or highlight areas in need of improvement. Customers implicitly corroborate billing data by paying their invoices or complaining about their charges. In addition, regulators may communicate with the entity concerning matters that affect the functioning of internal control (for example, communications concerning examinations by bank regulatory agencies). Also, management may consider communications relating to internal control from external auditors in performing monitoring activities.

.A144

Appendix C—Conditions and Events That May Indicate Risks of Material Misstatement (Ref: par. .A33 and .A121)

The following are examples of conditions and events that may indicate the existence of risks of material misstatement. The examples provided cover a broad range of conditions and events; however, not all conditions and events are relevant to every audit engagement, and the list of examples is not necessarily complete.

- Operations in regions that are economically unstable (for example, countries with significant currency devaluation or highly inflationary economies)
- Operations exposed to volatile markets (for example, futures trading)
- Operations that are subject to a high degree of complex regulation
- Going concern and liquidity issues, including loss of significant customers
- Constraints on the availability of capital and credit
- Changes in the industry in which the entity operates
- Changes in the supply chain
- Developing or offering new products or services or moving into new lines of business
- Expanding into new locations
- Changes in the entity, such as large acquisitions or reorganizations or other unusual events
- Entities or business segments likely to be sold
- The existence of complex alliances and joint ventures
- Use of off balance sheet finance, investments in entities formed to accomplish specific objectives, and other complex financing arrangements
- Significant transactions with related parties
- Lack of personnel with appropriate accounting and financial reporting skills
- Changes in key personnel, including departure of key executives
- Deficiencies in internal control, especially those not addressed by management
- Inconsistencies between the entity's IT strategy and its business strategies
- Changes in the IT environment
- Installation of significant new IT systems related to financial reporting
- Inquiries into the entity's operations or financial results by regulatory or government bodies

- Past misstatements, history of errors, or a significant amount of adjustments at period-end
- Significant amount of nonroutine or nonsystematic transactions, including intercompany transactions and large revenue transactions at period-end
- Transactions that are recorded based on management's intent (for example, debt refinancing, assets to be sold, and classification of marketable securities)
- Application of new accounting pronouncements
- Accounting measurements that involve complex processes
- Events or transactions that involve significant measurement uncertainty, including accounting estimates
- Pending litigation and contingent liabilities (for example, sales warranties, financial guarantees, and environmental remediation)

AU-C Section 320 *

Materiality in Planning and Performing an Audit

Source: SAS No. 122.

Effective for audits of financial statements for periods ending on or after December 15, 2012.

Introduction

Scope of This Section

.01 This section addresses the auditor's responsibility to apply the concept of materiality in planning and performing an audit of financial statements. Section 450, *Evaluation of Misstatements Identified During the Audit*, explains how materiality is applied in evaluating the effect of identified misstatements on the audit and the effect of uncorrected misstatements, if any, on the financial statements.

Materiality in the Context of an Audit

.02 Financial reporting frameworks often discuss the concept of materiality in the context of the preparation and fair presentation of financial statements. Although financial reporting frameworks may discuss materiality in different terms, they generally explain that

- misstatements, including omissions, are considered to be material if they, individually or in the aggregate, could reasonably be expected to influence the economic decisions of users made on the basis of the financial statements.
- judgments about materiality are made in light of surrounding circumstances and are affected by the size or nature of a misstatement, or a combination of both.
- judgments about matters that are material to users of the financial statements are based on a consideration of the common financial information needs of users as a group. The possible effect of misstatements on specific individual users, whose needs may vary widely, is not considered.

.03 Such a discussion about materiality provides a frame of reference to the auditor in determining materiality for the audit. If the applicable financial reporting framework does not include a discussion of the concept of materiality, the characteristics referred to in paragraph .02 provide the auditor with such a frame of reference.

.04 The auditor's determination of materiality is a matter of professional judgment and is affected by the auditor's perception of the financial information

---

* This section has been codified using an "AU-C" identifier instead of an "AU" identifier. "AU-C" is a temporary identifier to avoid confusion with references to existing "AU" sections, which will remain in AICPA *Professional Standards* through 2013. The "AU-C" identifier will revert to "AU" in 2014, by which time substantially all engagements for which the "AU" sections were still effective are expected to be completed.

needs of users of the financial statements. In this context, it is reasonable for the auditor to assume that users

a. have a reasonable knowledge of business and economic activities and accounting and a willingness to study the information in the financial statements with reasonable diligence;

b. understand that financial statements are prepared, presented, and audited to levels of materiality;

c. recognize the uncertainties inherent in the measurement of amounts based on the use of estimates, judgment, and the consideration of future events; and

d. make reasonable economic decisions on the basis of the information in the financial statements.

.05 The concept of materiality is applied by the auditor both in planning and performing the audit; evaluating the effect of identified misstatements on the audit and the effect of uncorrected misstatements, if any, on the financial statements; and in forming the opinion in the auditor's report. (Ref: par. .A1)

.06 In planning the audit, the auditor makes judgments about the size of misstatements that will be considered material. These judgments provide a basis for

a. determining the nature and extent of risk assessment procedures;

b. identifying and assessing the risks of material misstatement; and

c. determining the nature, timing, and extent of further audit procedures.

The materiality determined when planning the audit does not necessarily establish an amount below which uncorrected misstatements, individually or in the aggregate, will always be evaluated as immaterial. The circumstances related to some misstatements may cause the auditor to evaluate them as material even if they are below materiality. Although it is not practicable to design audit procedures to detect misstatements that could be material solely because of their nature (that is, qualitative considerations), the auditor considers not only the size but also the nature of uncorrected misstatements, and the particular circumstances of their occurrence, when evaluating their effect on the financial statements.[1]

Effective Date

.07 This section is effective for audits of financial statements for periods ending on or after December 15, 2012.

Objective

.08 The objective of the auditor is to apply the concept of materiality appropriately in planning and performing the audit.

Definition

.09 For purposes of generally accepted auditing standards (GAAS), the following term has the meaning attributed as follows:

Performance materiality. The amount or amounts set by the auditor at less than materiality for the financial statements as a whole to reduce to an appropriately low level the probability that the aggregate of uncorrected and undetected misstatements exceeds

[1] Paragraph .A23 of section 450, *Evaluation of Misstatements Identified During the Audit.*

materiality for the financial statements as a whole. If applicable, *performance materiality* also refers to the amount or amounts set by the auditor at less than the materiality level or levels for particular classes of transactions, account balances, or disclosures. Performance materiality is to be distinguished from tolerable misstatement. (Ref: par. .A2)

Requirements

Determining Materiality and Performance Materiality When Planning the Audit

.10 When establishing the overall audit strategy, the auditor should determine materiality for the financial statements as a whole. If, in the specific circumstances of the entity, one or more particular classes of transactions, account balances, or disclosures exist for which misstatements of lesser amounts than materiality for the financial statements as a whole could reasonably be expected to influence the economic decisions of users, then, taken on the basis of the financial statements, the auditor also should determine the materiality level or levels to be applied to those particular classes of transactions, account balances, or disclosures. (Ref: par. .A3–.A13)

.11 The auditor should determine performance materiality for purposes of assessing the risks of material misstatement and determining the nature, timing, and extent of further audit procedures. (Ref: par. .A14)

Revision as the Audit Progresses

.12 The auditor should revise materiality for the financial statements as a whole (and, if applicable, the materiality level or levels for particular classes of transactions, account balances, or disclosures) in the event of becoming aware of information during the audit that would have caused the auditor to have determined a different amount (or amounts) initially. (Ref: par. .A15–.A16)

.13 If the auditor concludes that a lower materiality than that initially determined for the financial statements as a whole (and, if applicable, materiality level or levels for particular classes of transactions, account balances, or disclosures) is appropriate, the auditor should determine whether it is necessary to revise performance materiality and whether the nature, timing, and extent of the further audit procedures remain appropriate.

Documentation

.14 The auditor should include in the audit documentation the following amounts and the factors considered in their determination:[2]

a. Materiality for the financial statements as a whole (see paragraph .10)

b. If applicable, the materiality level or levels for particular classes of transactions, account balances, or disclosures (see paragraph .10)

c. Performance materiality (see paragraph .11)

d. Any revision of (*a*)–(*c*) as the audit progressed (see paragraphs .12–.13)

---

[2] Paragraphs .08–.12 and .A8 of section 230, *Audit Documentation*.

Application and Other Explanatory Material

Materiality in the Context of an Audit

Materiality and Audit Risk (Ref: par. .05)

.A1 In conducting an audit of financial statements, the overall objectives of the auditor are to obtain reasonable assurance about whether the financial statements as a whole are free from material misstatement, whether due to fraud or error, thereby enabling the auditor to express an opinion on whether the financial statements are prepared, in all material respects, in accordance with an applicable financial reporting framework and to report on the financial statements and communicate, as required by GAAS, in accordance with the auditor's findings.[3] The auditor obtains reasonable assurance by obtaining sufficient appropriate audit evidence to reduce audit risk to an acceptably low level.[4] *Audit risk* is the risk that the auditor expresses an inappropriate audit opinion when the financial statements are materially misstated. Audit risk is a function of the risks of material misstatement and detection risk.[5] Materiality and audit risk are considered throughout the audit, in particular, when

a. determining the nature and extent of risk assessment procedures to be performed;

b. identifying and assessing the risks of material misstatement;[6]

c. determining the nature, timing, and extent of further audit procedures;[7] and

d. evaluating the effect of uncorrected misstatements, if any, on the financial statements[8] and in forming the opinion in the auditor's report.

Definition (Ref: par. .09)

.A2 *Tolerable misstatement* is the application of performance materiality to a particular sampling procedure. Section 530, *Audit Sampling*, defines *tolerable misstatement* and provides further application guidance about the concept.[9]

Determining Materiality and Performance Materiality When Planning the Audit

Considerations Specific to Governmental Entities (Ref: par. .10)

.A3 In the case of a governmental entity, legislators and regulators are often the primary users of its financial statements. Furthermore, the financial statements may be used to make decisions other than economic decisions. The determination of materiality for the financial statements as a whole (and,

---

[3] Paragraph .12 of section 200, *Overall Objectives of the Independent Auditor and the Conduct of an Audit in Accordance With Generally Accepted Auditing Standards*.

[4] Paragraph .19 of section 200.

[5] Paragraph .14 of section 200.

[6] See section 315, *Understanding the Entity and Its Environment and Assessing the Risks of Material Misstatement*.

[7] See section 330, *Performing Audit Procedures in Response to Assessed Risks and Evaluating the Audit Evidence Obtained*.

[8] Paragraph .11 of section 450.

[9] Paragraph .A6 of section 530, *Audit Sampling*.

if applicable, materiality level or levels for particular classes of transactions, account balances, or disclosures) in an audit of the financial statements of a governmental entity, therefore, may be influenced by law or regulation.

.A4 For most state or local governments, a governmental entity's applicable financial reporting framework is based on multiple reporting units, and generally, the auditor expresses or disclaims an opinion on a government's financial statements as a whole by providing opinions or disclaimers of opinion on each opinion unit. That is, a state or local governmental entity's applicable financial reporting framework requires the presentation of financial statements for its varied activities in various reporting units. Consequently, a reporting unit, or aggregation of reporting units, of the governmental entity represents an opinion unit to the auditor. Accordingly, in these cases, materiality is established for each opinion unit.

Use of Benchmarks in Determining Materiality for the Financial Statements as a Whole (Ref: par. .10)

.A5 Determining materiality involves the exercise of professional judgment. A percentage is often applied to a chosen benchmark as a starting point in determining materiality for the financial statements as a whole. Factors that may affect the identification of an appropriate benchmark include the following:

- The elements of the financial statements (for example, assets, liabilities, equity, revenue, or expenses)
- Whether items exist on which the attention of the users of the particular entity's financial statements tends to be focused (for example, for the purpose of evaluating financial performance, users may tend to focus on profit, revenue, or net assets)
- The nature of the entity, where the entity is in its life cycle, and the industry and economic environment in which the entity operates
- The entity's ownership structure and the way it is financed (for example, if an entity is financed solely by debt rather than equity, users may put more emphasis on assets, and claims on them, than on the entity's earnings)
- The relative volatility of the benchmark

.A6 Examples of benchmarks that may be appropriate, depending on the circumstances of the entity, include categories of reported income, such as profit before tax, total revenue, gross profit, and total expenses; total equity; or net asset value. Profit before tax from continuing operations is often used for profit-oriented entities. When profit before tax from continuing operations is volatile, other benchmarks may be more appropriate, such as gross profit or total revenues.

.A7 With regard to the chosen benchmark, relevant financial data ordinarily includes prior periods' financial results and financial positions; the period-to-date financial results and financial position, budgets, or forecasts for the current period, adjusted for significant changes in the circumstances of the entity (for example, a significant business acquisition); and relevant changes of conditions in the industry or economic environment in which the entity operates. For example, when, as a starting point, materiality for the financial statements as a whole is determined for a particular entity based on a percentage of profit before tax from continuing operations, circumstances that give rise to an exceptional decrease or increase in such profit may lead the auditor to conclude that materiality for the financial statements as a whole is more appropriately determined using a normalized profit before tax from continuing operations figure based on past results.

.A8 Materiality relates to the financial statements that are being audited. When the financial statements are prepared for a financial reporting period of more or less than 12 months, such as may be the case for a new entity or a change in the financial reporting period, materiality relates to the financial statements prepared for that financial reporting period.

.A9 Determining a percentage to be applied to a chosen benchmark involves the exercise of professional judgment. A relationship exists between the percentage and the chosen benchmark, such that a percentage applied to profit before tax from continuing operations will normally be higher than a percentage applied to total revenue. For example, the auditor may consider a percentage of profit before tax from continuing operations to be appropriate for a profit-oriented entity in a manufacturing industry. Chapter 3 of the AICPA Audit Guide *Assessing and Responding to Audit Risk in a Financial Statement Audit* provides further guidance about the use of benchmarks in determining materiality.

Considerations Specific to Smaller, Less Complex Entities

.A10 When an entity's profit before tax from continuing operations is consistently nominal, which might be the case for an owner-managed business in which the owner takes much of the profit before tax in the form of remuneration, a benchmark such as profit before remuneration and tax may be more relevant.

Considerations Specific to Governmental Entities

.A11 In an audit of a governmental entity, total cost or net cost (expenses less revenues or expenditures less receipts) may be appropriate benchmarks for program activities. When a governmental entity has custody of public assets, assets may be an appropriate benchmark.

Materiality Level or Levels for Particular Classes of Transactions, Account Balances, or Disclosures (Ref: par. .10)

.A12 Factors that may indicate the existence of one or more particular classes of transactions, account balances, or disclosures for which misstatements of lesser amounts than materiality for the financial statements as a whole could reasonably be expected to influence the economic decisions of users taken on the basis of the financial statements include the following:

- Whether law, regulation, or the applicable financial reporting framework affect users' expectations regarding the measurement or disclosure of certain items (for example, related party transactions and the remuneration of management and those charged with governance)
- The key disclosures with regard to the industry in which the entity operates (for example, research and development costs for a pharmaceutical company)
- Whether attention is focused on a particular aspect of the entity's business that is separately disclosed in the financial statements (for example, a newly acquired business)

.A13 In considering whether, in the specific circumstances of the entity, such classes of transactions, account balances, or disclosures exist, the auditor may find it useful to obtain an understanding of the views and expectations of those charged with governance and management.

Performance Materiality (Ref: par. .11)

.A14 Planning the audit solely to detect individual material misstatements overlooks the fact that the aggregate of individually immaterial misstatements may cause the financial statements to be materially misstated and leaves no margin for possible undetected misstatements. *Performance materiality* (which, as defined, is one or more amounts) is set to reduce to an appropriately low level the probability that the aggregate of uncorrected and undetected misstatements in the financial statements exceeds materiality for the financial statements as a whole. Similarly, performance materiality relating to a materiality level determined for a particular class of transactions, account balance, or disclosure is set to reduce to an appropriately low level the probability that the aggregate of uncorrected and undetected misstatements in that particular class of transactions, account balance, or disclosure exceeds the materiality level for that particular class of transactions, account balance, or disclosure. The determination of performance materiality is not a simple mechanical calculation and involves the exercise of professional judgment. It is affected by the auditor's understanding of the entity, updated during the performance of the risk assessment procedures, and the nature and extent of misstatements identified in previous audits and, thereby, the auditor's expectations regarding misstatements in the current period.

Revision as the Audit Progresses (Ref: par. .12)

.A15 In some situations, the auditor may determine materiality for planning purposes before the financial statements to be audited are prepared. In those situations, the auditor's professional judgment about materiality might be based on the entity's annualized interim financial statements or financial statements of one or more prior annual periods. If it appears as though the actual financial results are likely to be substantially different from the anticipated results, such as when there are major changes in the entity's circumstances (for example, a significant merger) or relevant changes in the economy as a whole or the industry in which the entity operates, the auditor may be required, in accordance with paragraph .12, to revise materiality.

.A16 Materiality for the financial statements as a whole (and, if applicable, the materiality level or levels for particular classes of transactions, account balances, or disclosures) may need to be revised as a result of a change in circumstances that occurred during the audit (for example, a decision to dispose of a major part of the entity's business), new information, or a change in the auditor's understanding of the entity and its operations as a result of performing further audit procedures. For example, if, during the audit, it appears as though actual financial results are likely to be substantially different from the anticipated period-end financial results that were used initially to determine materiality for the financial statements as a whole, the auditor may be required, in accordance with paragraph .12, to revise materiality.

AU-C Section 330*

Performing Audit Procedures in Response to Assessed Risks and Evaluating the Audit Evidence Obtained

Source: SAS No. 122.

Effective for audits of financial statements for periods ending on or after December 15, 2012.

Introduction

Scope of This Section

.01 This section addresses the auditor's responsibility to design and implement responses to the risks of material misstatement identified and assessed by the auditor in accordance with section 315, *Understanding the Entity and Its Environment and Assessing the Risks of Material Misstatement*, and to evaluate the audit evidence obtained in an audit of financial statements. Section 700, *Forming an Opinion and Reporting on Financial Statements*, addresses the auditor's responsibility to form an opinion on the financial statements based on the evaluation of the audit evidence obtained.

Effective Date

.02 This section is effective for audits of financial statements for periods ending on or after December 15, 2012.

Objective

.03 The objective of the auditor is to obtain sufficient appropriate audit evidence regarding the assessed risks of material misstatement through designing and implementing appropriate responses to those risks.

Definitions

.04 For purposes of generally accepted auditing standards, the following terms have the meanings attributed as follows:

Substantive procedure. An audit procedure designed to detect material misstatements at the assertion level. Substantive procedures comprise

a. tests of details (classes of transactions, account balances, and disclosures) and

b. substantive analytical procedures.

---

* This section has been codified using an "AU-C" identifier instead of an "AU" identifier. "AU-C" is a temporary identifier to avoid confusion with references to existing "AU" sections, which will remain in AICPA *Professional Standards* through 2013. The "AU-C" identifier will revert to "AU" in 2014, by which time substantially all engagements for which the "AU" sections were still effective are expected to be completed.

Test of controls. An audit procedure designed to evaluate the operating effectiveness of controls in preventing, or detecting and correcting, material misstatements at the assertion level.

Requirements

Overall Responses

.05 The auditor should design and implement overall responses to address the assessed risks of material misstatement at the financial statement level. (Ref: par. .A1–.A3)

Audit Procedures Responsive to the Assessed Risks of Material Misstatement at the Relevant Assertion Level

.06 The auditor should design and perform further audit procedures whose nature, timing, and extent are based on, and are responsive to, the assessed risks of material misstatement at the relevant assertion level. (Ref: par. .A4–.A9)

.07 In designing the further audit procedures to be performed, the auditor should

a. consider the reasons for the assessed risk of material misstatement at the relevant assertion level for each class of transactions, account balance, and disclosure, including

i. the likelihood of material misstatement due to the particular characteristics of the relevant class of transactions, account balance, or disclosure (the inherent risk) and

ii. whether the risk assessment takes account of relevant controls (the control risk), thereby requiring the auditor to obtain audit evidence to determine whether the controls are operating effectively (that is, the auditor intends to rely on the operating effectiveness of controls in determining the nature, timing, and extent of substantive procedures), and (Ref: par. .A10–.A19)

b. obtain more persuasive audit evidence the higher the auditor's assessment of risk. (Ref: par. .A20)

Tests of Controls

.08 The auditor should design and perform tests of controls to obtain sufficient appropriate audit evidence about the operating effectiveness of relevant controls if

a. the auditor's assessment of risks of material misstatement at the relevant assertion level includes an expectation that the controls are operating effectively (that is, the auditor intends to rely on the operating effectiveness of controls in determining the nature, timing, and extent of substantive procedures) or

b. substantive procedures alone cannot provide sufficient appropriate audit evidence at the relevant assertion level. (Ref: par. .A21–.A26)

.09 In designing and performing tests of controls, the auditor should obtain more persuasive audit evidence the greater the reliance the auditor places on the effectiveness of a control. (Ref: par. .A27)

Nature and Extent of Tests of Controls

.10 In designing and performing tests of controls, the auditor should

a. perform other audit procedures in combination with inquiry to obtain audit evidence about the operating effectiveness of the controls, including

  i. how the controls were applied at relevant times during the period under audit;

  ii. the consistency with which they were applied; and

  iii. by whom or by what means they were applied, including, when applicable, whether the person performing the control possesses the necessary authority and competence to perform the control effectively, and (Ref: par. .A28–.A32)

b. determine whether the controls to be tested depend upon other controls (indirect controls) and, if so, whether it is necessary to obtain audit evidence supporting the operating effectiveness of those indirect controls. (Ref: par. .A33–.A34)

Timing of Tests of Controls

.11 The auditor should test controls for the particular time or throughout the period for which the auditor intends to rely on those controls, subject to paragraphs .12 and .15 that follow, in order to provide an appropriate basis for the auditor's intended reliance. (Ref: par. .A35)

Using Audit Evidence Obtained During an Interim Period

.12 If the auditor obtains audit evidence about the operating effectiveness of controls during an interim period, the auditor should

a. obtain audit evidence about significant changes to those controls subsequent to the interim period and

b. determine the additional audit evidence to be obtained for the remaining period. (Ref: par. .A36–.A37)

Using Audit Evidence Obtained in Previous Audits

.13 In determining whether it is appropriate to use audit evidence about the operating effectiveness of controls obtained in previous audits and, if so, the length of the time period that may elapse before retesting a control, the auditor should consider

a. the effectiveness of other elements of internal control, including the control environment, the entity's monitoring of controls, and the entity's risk assessment process;

b. the risks arising from the characteristics of the control, including whether the control is manual or automated;

c. the effectiveness of general IT controls;

d. the effectiveness of the control and its application by the entity, including the nature and extent of deviations in the application of the control noted in previous audits and whether there have been personnel changes that significantly affect the application of the control;

e. whether the lack of a change in a particular control poses a risk due to changing circumstances; and

f. the risks of material misstatement and the extent of reliance on the control. (Ref: par. .A38)

.14 If the auditor plans to use audit evidence from a previous audit about the operating effectiveness of specific controls, the auditor should perform audit procedures to establish the continuing relevance of that information to the current audit. The auditor should obtain this evidence by performing inquiry, combined with observation or inspection, to confirm the understanding of those specific controls, and

a. if there have been changes that affect the continuing relevance of the audit evidence from the previous audit, the auditor should test the controls in the current audit. (Ref: par. .A39)

b. if there have not been such changes, the auditor should test the controls at least once in every third audit and should test some controls during each audit to avoid the possibility of testing all the controls on which the auditor intends to rely in a single audit period with no testing of controls in the subsequent two audit periods. (Ref: par. .A40–.A42)

Controls Over Significant Risks

.15 If the auditor plans to rely on controls over a risk the auditor has determined to be a significant risk,[1] the auditor should test the operating effectiveness of those controls in the current period.

Evaluating the Operating Effectiveness of Controls

.16 When evaluating the operating effectiveness of relevant controls, the auditor should evaluate whether misstatements that have been detected by substantive procedures indicate that controls are not operating effectively. The absence of misstatements detected by substantive procedures, however, does not provide audit evidence that controls related to the relevant assertion being tested are effective. (Ref: par. .A43)

.17 If deviations from controls upon which the auditor intends to rely are detected, the auditor should make specific inquiries to understand these matters and their potential consequences and should determine whether

a. the tests of controls that have been performed provide an appropriate basis for reliance on the controls,

b. additional tests of controls are necessary, or

c. the potential risks of misstatement need to be addressed using substantive procedures. (Ref: par. .A44)

Substantive Procedures

.18 Irrespective of the assessed risks of material misstatement, the auditor should design and perform substantive procedures for all relevant assertions related to each material class of transactions, account balance, and disclosure. (Ref: par. .A45–.A50)

.19 The auditor should consider whether external confirmation procedures are to be performed as substantive audit procedures. (Ref: par. .A51–.A56)

.20 The auditor should use external confirmation procedures for accounts receivable, except when one or more of the following is applicable: (Ref: par. .A55)

a. The overall account balance is immaterial.

---

[1] Paragraphs .28–.30 of section 315, *Understanding the Entity and Its Environment and Assessing the Risks of Material Misstatement.*

b. External confirmation procedures for accounts receivable would be ineffective. (Ref: par. .A54 and .A56)

c. The auditor's assessed level of risk of material misstatement at the relevant assertion level is low, and the other planned substantive procedures address the assessed risk. In many situations, the use of external confirmation procedures for accounts receivable and the performance of other substantive procedures are necessary to reduce the assessed risk of material misstatement to an acceptably low level.

Substantive Procedures Related to the Financial Statement Closing Process

.21 The auditor's substantive procedures should include audit procedures related to the financial statement closing process, such as

a. agreeing or reconciling the financial statements with the underlying accounting records and

b. examining material journal entries and other adjustments made during the course of preparing the financial statements. (Ref: par. .A57)

Substantive Procedures Responsive to Significant Risks

.22 If the auditor has determined that an assessed risk of material misstatement at the relevant assertion level is a significant risk, the auditor should perform substantive procedures that are specifically responsive to that risk. When the approach to a significant risk consists only of substantive procedures, those procedures should include tests of details. (Ref: par. .A58)

Timing of Substantive Procedures

.23 If substantive procedures are performed at an interim date, the auditor should cover the remaining period by performing

a. substantive procedures, combined with tests of controls for the intervening period, or

b. if the auditor determines that it is sufficient, further substantive procedures only,

that provide a reasonable basis for extending the audit conclusions from the interim date to the period-end. (Ref: par. .A59–.A63)

.24 If misstatements that the auditor did not expect when assessing the risks of material misstatement are detected at an interim date, the auditor should evaluate whether the related assessment of risk and the planned nature, timing, or extent of substantive procedures covering the remaining period need to be modified. See section 240, *Consideration of Fraud in a Financial Statement Audit*.[2] (Ref: par. .A64)

Selecting Items for Testing to Obtain Audit Evidence

.25 When designing tests of controls and tests of details, the auditor should determine the means of selecting items for testing that are effective in meeting the purpose of the audit procedure. (Ref: par. .A65–.A71)

---

[2] Paragraphs .35–.36 of section 240, *Consideration of Fraud in a Financial Statement Audit*.

Adequacy of Presentation and Disclosure

.26 The auditor should perform audit procedures to evaluate whether the overall presentation of the financial statements, including the related disclosures, is in accordance with the applicable financial reporting framework. (Ref: par. .A72)

Evaluating the Sufficiency and Appropriateness of Audit Evidence[3]

.27 Based on the audit procedures performed and the audit evidence obtained, the auditor should evaluate, before the conclusion of the audit, whether the assessments of the risks of material misstatement at the relevant assertion level remain appropriate. (Ref: par. .A73–.A74)

.28 The auditor should conclude whether sufficient appropriate audit evidence has been obtained. In forming a conclusion, the auditor should consider all relevant audit evidence, regardless of whether it appears to corroborate or contradict the assertions in the financial statements. (Ref: par. .A75)

.29 If the auditor has not obtained sufficient appropriate audit evidence about a relevant assertion, the auditor should attempt to obtain further audit evidence. If the auditor is unable to obtain sufficient appropriate audit evidence, the auditor should express a qualified opinion or disclaim an opinion on the financial statements.[4]

Documentation

.30 The auditor should include in the audit documentation[5]

a. the overall responses to address the assessed risks of material misstatement at the financial statement level and the nature, timing, and extent of the further audit procedures performed;

b. the linkage of those procedures with the assessed risks at the relevant assertion level; and

c. the results of the audit procedures, including the conclusions when such conclusions are not otherwise clear. (Ref: par. .A76)

.31 If the auditor plans to use audit evidence about the operating effectiveness of controls obtained in previous audits, the auditor should include in the audit documentation the conclusions reached about relying on such controls that were tested in a previous audit.

.32 The auditor should include in the audit documentation the basis for any determination not to use external confirmation procedures for accounts receivable when the account balance is material.

.33 The auditor's documentation should demonstrate that the financial statements agree or reconcile with the underlying accounting records.

---

[3] See section 700, *Forming an Opinion and Reporting on Financial Statements.*

[4] Paragraphs .08–.10 of section 705, *Modifications to the Opinion in the Independent Auditor's Report*, address qualified, adverse, and disclaimer of opinions.

[5] Paragraphs .08–.12 and .A8 of section 230, *Audit Documentation.*

Application and Other Explanatory Material

Overall Responses (Ref: par. .05)

.A1 Overall responses to address the assessed risks of material misstatement at the financial statement level may include[6]

- emphasizing to the audit team the need to maintain professional skepticism.
- assigning more experienced staff or those with specialized skills or using specialists.
- providing more supervision.
- incorporating additional elements of unpredictability in the selection of further audit procedures to be performed.
- making general changes to the nature, timing, or extent of audit procedures (for example, performing substantive procedures at period-end instead of at an interim date or modifying the nature of audit procedures to obtain more persuasive audit evidence).

.A2 The assessment of the risks of material misstatement at the financial statement level and, thereby, the auditor's overall responses are affected by the auditor's understanding of the control environment. An effective control environment may allow the auditor to have more confidence in internal control and the reliability of audit evidence generated internally within the entity and, thus, for example, allow the auditor to conduct some audit procedures at an interim date rather than at the period-end. Deficiencies in the control environment, however, have the opposite effect (for example, the auditor may respond to an ineffective control environment by

- conducting more audit procedures as of the period-end rather than at an interim date,
- obtaining more extensive audit evidence from substantive procedures, and
- increasing the number of locations to be included in the audit scope).

.A3 Such considerations, therefore, have a significant bearing on the auditor's general approach (for example, an emphasis on substantive procedures [substantive approach] or an approach that uses tests of controls as well as substantive procedures [combined approach]).

Audit Procedures Responsive to the Assessed Risks of Material Misstatement at the Relevant Assertion Level

The Nature, Timing, and Extent of Further Audit Procedures (Ref: par. .06)

.A4 The auditor's assessment of the identified risks at the relevant assertion level provides a basis for considering the appropriate audit approach for designing and performing further audit procedures. For example, the auditor may determine that

---

[6] Paragraphs .07–.08 of section 300, *Planning an Audit*, address the auditor's overall audit strategy.

a. in addition to the substantive procedures that are required for all relevant assertions, in accordance with paragraph .18, an effective response to the assessed risk of material misstatement for a particular assertion can be achieved only by also performing tests of controls.

b. performing only substantive procedures is appropriate for particular assertions, and therefore, the auditor excludes the effect of controls from the relevant risk assessment. This may be because the auditor's risk assessment procedures have not identified any effective controls relevant to the assertion or because testing controls would be inefficient, and therefore, the auditor does not intend to rely on the operating effectiveness of controls in determining the nature, timing, and extent of substantive procedures.

c. a combined approach using both tests of controls and substantive procedures is an effective approach.

.A5 The nature of an audit procedure refers to its purpose (test of controls or substantive procedure) and its type (inspection, observation, inquiry, confirmation, recalculation, reperformance, or analytical procedure). See section 500, *Audit Evidence*, which provides further application guidance about audit procedures.[7] The nature of the audit procedures is most important in responding to the assessed risks.

.A6 Timing of an audit procedure refers to when it is performed or the period or date to which the audit evidence applies.

.A7 Extent of an audit procedure refers to the quantity to be performed (for example, a sample size or the number of observations of a control activity).

.A8 Designing and performing further audit procedures whose nature, timing, and extent are based on, and are responsive to, the assessed risks of material misstatement at the relevant assertion level provides a clear linkage between the auditor's further audit procedures and the risk assessment.

.A9 Because effective internal controls generally reduce but do not eliminate the risk of material misstatement, tests of controls reduce but do not eliminate the need for substantive procedures. In addition, analytical procedures alone may not be sufficient in some cases. For example, when auditing certain estimation processes, such as the allowance for doubtful accounts, the auditor may perform substantive procedures beyond analytical procedures (for example, examining cash collections subsequent to the period-end) due to the risk of management override of controls[8] or the subjectivity of the account balance.

Responding to the Assessed Risks at the Assertion Level (Ref: par. .07a)

.A10 *Nature*. The auditor's assessed risks may affect both the types of audit procedures to be performed and their combination. For example, when an assessed risk is high, the auditor may confirm the completeness of the terms of a contract with the counterparty, in addition to inspecting the document. Further, certain audit procedures may be more appropriate for some assertions than others. For example, regarding revenue, tests of controls may be most responsive to the assessed risk of misstatement of the completeness assertion, whereas substantive procedures may be most responsive to the assessed risk of misstatement of the occurrence assertion.

---

[7] Paragraphs .A10–.A26 of section 500, *Audit Evidence*.

[8] The auditor is required by paragraphs .31–.33 of section 240 to perform audit procedures responsive to risks related to management override of controls.

.A11 The reasons for the assessment given to a risk are relevant in determining the nature of audit procedures. For example, if an assessed risk is lower because of the particular characteristics of a class of transactions without consideration of the related controls, then the auditor may determine that substantive analytical procedures alone provide sufficient appropriate audit evidence. On the other hand, if the assessed risk is lower because of internal controls and the auditor intends to base the substantive procedures on that low assessment, then the auditor performs tests of those controls, as required by paragraph .08*a*. This may be the case, for example, for a class of transactions of reasonably uniform, noncomplex characteristics that are routinely processed and controlled by the entity's information system.

.A12 *Timing*. The auditor may perform tests of controls or substantive procedures at an interim date or at the period-end. The higher the risk of material misstatement, the more likely it is that the auditor may decide it is more effective to perform substantive procedures nearer to or at the period-end rather than at an earlier date or to perform audit procedures unannounced or at unpredictable times (for example, performing audit procedures at selected locations on an unannounced basis). This is particularly relevant when considering the response to the risks of fraud. For example, the auditor may conclude that, when the risks of intentional misstatement or manipulation have been identified, audit procedures to extend audit conclusions from the interim date to the period-end would not be effective.

.A13 On the other hand, performing audit procedures before the period-end may assist the auditor in identifying significant issues at an early stage of the audit and consequently resolving them with the assistance of management or developing an effective audit approach to address such issues.

.A14 In addition, certain audit procedures can be performed only at or after the period-end. For example

- agreeing the financial statements to the accounting records,
- examining adjustments made during the course of preparing the financial statements, and
- procedures to respond to a risk that at the period-end the entity may have entered into improper sales contracts or transactions may not have been finalized.

.A15 Further relevant factors that influence the auditor's consideration of when to perform audit procedures include

- the effectiveness of the control environment.
- when relevant information is available (for example, electronic files may subsequently be overwritten, or procedures to be observed may occur only at certain times).
- the nature of the risk (for example, if there is a risk of inflated revenues to meet earnings expectations by subsequent creation of false sales agreements, the auditor may examine contracts available on the date of the period-end).
- the period or date to which the audit evidence relates.

.A16 *Extent*. The extent of an audit procedure judged necessary is determined after considering the materiality, assessed risk, and degree of assurance the auditor plans to obtain. When a single purpose is met by a combination of procedures, the extent of each procedure may be considered separately. In general, the extent of audit procedures increases as the risks of material misstatement increase. For example, in response to the assessed risks of material misstatement due to fraud, increasing sample sizes or performing substantive analytical procedures at a more detailed level may be appropriate. However, increasing the extent of an audit procedure is effective only if the audit procedure itself is relevant to the specific risk.

.A17 The use of computer assisted audit techniques (CAATs) may enable more extensive testing of electronic transactions and account files, which may be useful when the auditor decides to modify the extent of testing (for example, in responding to the risks of material misstatement due to fraud). Such techniques can be used to select sample transactions from key electronic files, sort transactions with specific characteristics, or test an entire population instead of a sample.

.A18 *Considerations specific to governmental entities*. For the audits of governmental entities, the audit mandate and any other special auditing requirements may affect the auditor's consideration of the nature, timing, and extent of further audit procedures. For example, under some governmental audit requirements, the auditor is required to perform tests of controls, even if reliance is not planned.

.A19 *Considerations specific to smaller, less complex entities*. In the case of smaller entities, the auditor may not identify control activities, or the extent to which their existence or operation have been documented by the entity may be limited. In such cases, it may be more efficient for the auditor to perform further audit procedures that are primarily substantive procedures. In some rare cases, however, the absence of control activities or other components of control may make it impossible to obtain sufficient appropriate audit evidence.

Higher Assessments of Risk (Ref: par. .07b)

.A20 When obtaining more persuasive audit evidence because of a higher assessment of risk, the auditor may increase the quantity of the evidence or obtain evidence that is more relevant or reliable (for example by placing more emphasis on obtaining third party evidence or by obtaining corroborating evidence from a number of independent sources).

Tests of Controls

Designing and Performing Tests of Controls (Ref: par. .08)

.A21 Tests of controls are performed only on those controls that the auditor has determined are suitably designed to prevent, or detect and correct, a material misstatement in a relevant assertion. If substantially different controls were used at different times during the period under audit, each is considered separately.

.A22 Testing the operating effectiveness of controls is different from obtaining an understanding of and evaluating the design and implementation of controls. However, the same types of audit procedures are used. The auditor may, therefore, decide it is efficient to test the operating effectiveness of controls at the same time the auditor is evaluating their design and determining that they have been implemented.

.A23 Further, although some risk assessment procedures may not have been specifically designed as tests of controls, they may nevertheless provide audit evidence about the operating effectiveness of the controls and, consequently, serve as tests of controls. For example, the auditor's risk assessment procedures may have included the following:

- Inquiring about management's use of budgets

- Observing management's comparison of monthly budgeted and actual expenses
- Inspecting reports pertaining to the investigation of variances between budgeted and actual amounts

These audit procedures provide knowledge about the design of the entity's budgeting policies and whether they have been implemented but also may provide audit evidence about the effectiveness of the operation of budgeting policies in preventing, or detecting and correcting, material misstatements in the classification of expenses.

.A24 In addition, the auditor may design a test of controls to be performed concurrently with a test of details on the same transaction. Although the purpose of a test of controls is different from the purpose of a test of details, both may be accomplished concurrently by performing a test of controls and a test of details on the same transaction, which also is known as a *dual purpose test*. For example, the auditor may design and evaluate the results of a test to examine an invoice to determine whether it has been approved and to provide substantive audit evidence of a transaction. A dual purpose test is designed and evaluated by considering each purpose of the test separately.

.A25 In some cases, the auditor may find it impossible to design effective substantive procedures that, by themselves, provide sufficient appropriate audit evidence at the relevant assertion level.[9] This may occur when an entity conducts its business using IT and no documentation of transactions is produced or maintained, other than through the IT system. In such cases, paragraph .08*b* requires the auditor to perform tests of relevant controls.

.A26 The auditor may consider testing the operating effectiveness of controls, if any, over the entity's preparation of information used by the auditor in performing substantive analytical procedures in response to assessed risks. See section 520, *Analytical Procedures*, for further guidance.[10]

Audit Evidence and Intended Reliance (Ref: par. .09)

.A27 A higher level of assurance may be sought about the operating effectiveness of controls when the approach adopted consists primarily of tests of controls, in particular when it is not possible or practicable to obtain sufficient appropriate audit evidence only from substantive procedures.

Nature and Extent of Tests of Controls

.A28 *Other audit procedures in combination with inquiry (Ref: par. .10a).* Inquiry alone is not sufficient to test the operating effectiveness of controls. Accordingly, other audit procedures are performed in combination with inquiry. In this regard, inquiry combined with inspection, recalculation, or reperformance may provide more assurance than inquiry and observation because an observation is pertinent only at the point in time at which it is made.

.A29 The nature of the particular control influences the type of audit procedure necessary to obtain audit evidence about whether the control was operating effectively. For example, if operating effectiveness is evidenced by documentation, the auditor may decide to inspect such documentation to obtain audit evidence about operating effectiveness. For other controls, however, documentation may not be available or relevant. For example, documentation of operation may not exist for some factors in the control environment, such as

---

[9] Paragraph .31 of section 315.

[10] Paragraph .A19 of section 520, *Analytical Procedures*.

assignment of authority and responsibility, or for some types of control activities, such as control activities performed by a computer. In such circumstances, audit evidence about operating effectiveness may be obtained through inquiry in combination with other audit procedures, such as observation or the use of CAATs.

.A30 In some situations, particularly in smaller, less complex entities, an entity might use a third party to provide assistance with certain financial reporting functions. When assessing the competence of personnel responsible for an entity's financial reporting and associated controls, the auditor may take into account the combined competence of entity personnel and other parties that assist with functions related to financial reporting.

.A31 *Extent of tests of controls.* When more persuasive audit evidence is needed regarding the effectiveness of a control, it may be appropriate to increase the extent of testing of the control. In addition to the degree of reliance on controls, matters the auditor may consider in determining the extent of tests of controls include the following:

- The frequency of the performance of the control by the entity during the period
- The length of time during the audit period that the auditor is relying on the operating effectiveness of the control
- The expected rate of deviation from a control
- The relevance and reliability of the audit evidence to be obtained regarding the operating effectiveness of the control at the relevant assertion level
- The extent to which audit evidence is obtained from tests of other controls related to the relevant assertion

However, the rate of expected deviation may indicate that obtaining audit evidence from the performance of tests of controls will not be sufficient to reduce the control risk at the relevant assertion level. If the rate of expected deviation is expected to be high, tests of controls for a particular assertion may not provide sufficient appropriate audit evidence. Section 530, *Audit Sampling*, contains further guidance on the extent of testing.

.A32 Because of the inherent consistency of IT processing, it may not be necessary to increase the extent of testing of an automated control. An automated control can be expected to function consistently unless the program (including the tables, files, or other permanent data used by the program) is changed. Once the auditor determines that an automated control is functioning as intended (which could be done at the time the control is initially implemented or at some other date), the auditor may consider performing tests to determine that the control continues to function effectively. Such tests might include determining that

- changes to the program are not made without being subject to the appropriate program change controls,
- the authorized version of the program is used for processing transactions, and
- other relevant general controls are effective.

Such tests also might include determining that changes to the programs have not been made, which may be the case when the entity uses packaged software applications without modifying or maintaining them. For example, the auditor may inspect the record of the administration of IT security to obtain audit evidence that unauthorized access has not occurred during the period.

.A33 *Testing of indirect controls (Ref: par. .10b).* In some circumstances, it may be necessary to obtain audit evidence supporting the effective operation of indirect controls. For example, when the auditor decides to test the effectiveness of a user review of exception reports detailing sales in excess of authorized credit limits, the user review and related follow up is the control that is of direct relevance to the auditor. Controls over the accuracy of the information in the reports (for example, the general IT controls) are described as indirect controls.

.A34 Because of the inherent consistency of IT processing, audit evidence about the implementation of an automated application control, when considered in combination with audit evidence about the operating effectiveness of the entity's general IT controls (in particular, change controls), also may provide substantial audit evidence about its operating effectiveness.

Timing of Tests of Controls

.A35 *Intended period of reliance (Ref: par. .11).* Audit evidence pertaining only to a point in time may be sufficient for the auditor's purpose (for example, when testing controls over the entity's physical inventory counting at the period-end). If, on the other hand, the auditor intends to rely on a control over a period, tests that are capable of providing audit evidence that the control operated effectively at relevant times during that period are appropriate. Such tests may include tests of the entity's monitoring of controls.

.A36 *Using audit evidence obtained during an interim period (Ref: par. .12).* Relevant factors in determining what additional audit evidence to obtain about controls that were operating during the period remaining after an interim period, include the following:

- The significance of the assessed risks of material misstatement at the relevant assertion level
- The specific controls that were tested during the interim period and the results of those tests
- Significant changes to the controls since they were tested, including changes in the information system, processes, and personnel
- The degree to which audit evidence about the operating effectiveness of those controls was obtained
- The length of the remaining period
- The extent to which the auditor intends to reduce further substantive procedures based on the reliance of controls
- The effectiveness of the control environment

.A37 Additional audit evidence may be obtained, for example, by extending the testing of the operating effectiveness of controls over the remaining period or testing the entity's monitoring of controls.

.A38 *Using audit evidence obtained in previous audits (Ref: par. .13).* In certain circumstances, audit evidence obtained from previous audits may provide audit evidence, provided that the auditor has determined whether changes have occurred since the previous audit that may affect its relevance to the current audit. For example, in performing a previous audit, the auditor may have determined that an automated control was functioning as intended. The auditor may obtain audit evidence to determine whether changes to the automated control have been made that affect its continued effective functioning through, for example, inquiries of management and the inspection of logs to indicate what controls have been changed. Consideration of audit evidence about these changes may support either increasing or decreasing the expected audit evidence to be obtained in the current period about the operating effectiveness of the controls.

.A39 *Controls that have changed from previous audits (Ref: par. .14a).* Changes may affect the relevance of the audit evidence obtained in previous audits such that there may no longer be a basis for continued reliance. For example, changes in a system that enable an entity to receive a new report from the system probably do not affect the relevance of audit evidence from a previous audit; however, a change that causes data to be accumulated or calculated differently does affect it.

.A40 *Controls that have not changed from previous audits (Ref: par. .14b).* The auditor's decision on whether to rely on audit evidence obtained in previous audits for controls that

- have not changed since they were last tested and
- are not controls that mitigate a significant risk

is a matter of professional judgment. In addition, the length of time between retesting such controls is also a matter of professional judgment but is required by paragraph .14*b* to be at least once in every third audit. (This guidance may not be appropriate for audits not performed at least on an annual basis.)

.A41 In general, the higher the risk of material misstatement or the greater the reliance on controls, the shorter the time period elapsed, if any, is likely to be. Factors that may decrease the period for retesting a control or result in not relying on audit evidence obtained in previous audits at all include the following:

- A deficient control environment
- Deficient monitoring of controls
- A significant manual element to the relevant controls
- Personnel changes that significantly affect the application of the control
- Changing circumstances that indicate the need for changes in the control
- Deficient general IT controls

.A42 When there are a number of controls for which the auditor intends to rely on audit evidence obtained in previous audits, testing some of those controls in each audit provides corroborating information about the continuing effectiveness of the control environment. This contributes to the auditor's decision about whether it is appropriate to rely on audit evidence obtained in previous audits.

Evaluating the Operating Effectiveness of Controls (Ref: par. .16–.17)

.A43 In accordance with section 265, *Communicating Internal Control Related Matters Identified in an Audit*, the identification by the auditor of a material misstatement of the financial statements under audit in circumstances that indicate that the misstatement would not have been detected by the entity's internal control is an indicator of a material weakness.[11]

---

[11] Paragraph .A11 of section 265, *Communicating Internal Control Related Matters Identified in an Audit.*

.A44 The concept of effectiveness of the operation of controls recognizes that some deviations in the way controls are applied by the entity may occur. Deviations from prescribed controls may be caused by such factors as changes in key personnel, significant seasonal fluctuations in volume of transactions, and human error. The detected rate of deviation, in particular, in comparison with the expected rate, may indicate that the control cannot be relied on to reduce risk at the relevant assertion level to that assessed by the auditor.

Substantive Procedures (Ref: par. .18)

.A45 Paragraph .18 requires the auditor to design and perform substantive procedures for all relevant assertions related to each material class of transactions, account balance, and disclosure, irrespective of the assessed risks of material misstatement. This requirement reflects the facts that (i) the auditor's assessment of risk is judgmental and may not identify all risks of material misstatement and (ii) inherent limitations to internal control exist, including management override.

Nature and Extent of Substantive Procedures

.A46 Depending on the circumstances, the auditor may determine the following:

- Performing only substantive analytical procedures will be sufficient to reduce audit risk to an acceptably low level, such as, for example, when the auditor's assessment of risk is supported by audit evidence from tests of controls.
- Only tests of details are appropriate.
- A combination of substantive analytical procedures and tests of details are most responsive to the assessed risks.

.A47 Substantive analytical procedures are generally more applicable to large volumes of transactions that tend to be predictable over time. Section 520 addresses the application of analytical procedures during an audit.

.A48 The nature of the risk and assertion is relevant to the design of tests of details. For example, tests of details related to the existence or occurrence assertion may involve selecting from items contained in a financial statement amount and obtaining the relevant audit evidence. On the other hand, tests of details related to the completeness assertion may involve selecting from items that are expected to be included in the relevant financial statement amount and investigating whether they are included. For example, the auditor might inspect subsequent cash disbursements and compare them with the recorded accounts payable to determine whether any purchases had been omitted from accounts payable.

.A49 Because the assessment of the risks of material misstatement takes account of internal control, the extent of substantive procedures may need to be increased when the results from tests of controls are unsatisfactory. However, increasing the extent of an audit procedure is appropriate only if the audit procedure itself is relevant to the specific risk.

.A50 In designing tests of details, the extent of testing is ordinarily thought of in terms of the sample size. However, other matters also are relevant, including whether it is more effective to use other selective means of testing. See paragraphs .A65–.A71.

Considering Whether External Confirmation Procedures Are to Be Performed (Ref: par. .19–.20)

.A51 External confirmation procedures frequently may be relevant when addressing assertions associated with account balances and their elements but need not be restricted to these items. For example, the auditor may request external confirmation of the terms of agreements, contracts, or transactions between an entity and other parties. External confirmation procedures also may be performed to obtain audit evidence about the absence of certain conditions. For example, a request may specifically seek confirmation that no "side agreement" exists that may be relevant to an entity's revenue cut-off assertion. Other situations in which external confirmation procedures may provide relevant audit evidence in responding to assessed risks of material misstatement include the following:

- Bank balances and other information relevant to banking relationships
- Inventories held by third parties at bonded warehouses for processing or on consignment
- Property title deeds held by lawyers or financiers for safe custody or as security
- Investments held for safekeeping by third parties or purchased from stockbrokers but not delivered at the balance sheet date
- Amounts due to lenders, including relevant terms of repayment and restrictive covenants
- Accounts payable balances and terms

.A52 Although external confirmations may provide relevant audit evidence relating to certain assertions, some assertions exist for which external confirmations provide less relevant audit evidence. For example, external confirmations provide less relevant audit evidence relating to the recoverability of accounts receivable balances than they do of their existence.

.A53 The auditor may determine that external confirmation procedures performed for one purpose provide an opportunity to obtain audit evidence about other matters. For example, confirmation requests for bank balances often include requests for information relevant to other financial statement assertions. Such considerations may influence the auditor's decision about whether to perform external confirmation procedures.

.A54 Factors that may assist the auditor in determining whether external confirmation procedures are to be performed as substantive audit procedures include the following:

- The confirming party's knowledge of the subject matter. Responses may be more reliable if provided by a person at the confirming party who has the requisite knowledge about the information being confirmed.
- The ability or willingness of the intended confirming party to respond. For example, the confirming party
  - — may not accept responsibility for responding to a confirmation request,
  - — may consider responding too costly or time consuming,
  - — may have concerns about the potential legal liability resulting from responding,

— may account for transactions in different currencies, or

— may operate in an environment in which responding to confirmation requests is not a significant aspect of day-to-day operations.

In such situations, confirming parties may not respond, may respond in a casual manner, or may attempt to restrict the reliance placed on the response.

- The objectivity of the intended confirming party. If the confirming party is a related party of the entity, responses to confirmation requests may be less reliable.

.A55 For purposes of this section, *accounts receivable* means

a. the entity's claims against customers that have arisen from the sale of goods or services in the normal course of business; and

b. a financial institution's loans.

.A56 External confirmation procedures may be ineffective when, based on prior years' audit experience or experience with similar entities

- response rates to properly designed confirmation requests will be inadequate; or
- responses are known or expected to be unreliable.

If the auditor has experienced poor response rates to properly designed confirmation requests in prior audits, the auditor may instead consider changing the manner in which the confirmation process is performed, with the objective of increasing the response rates, or may consider obtaining audit evidence from other sources.

Substantive Procedures Related to the Financial Statement Closing Process (Ref: par. .21b)

.A57 The nature and also the extent of the auditor's examination of journal entries and other adjustments depends on the nature and complexity of the entity's financial reporting process and the related risks of material misstatement.

Substantive Procedures Responsive to Significant Risks (Ref: par. .22)

.A58 Paragraph .22 requires the auditor to perform substantive procedures that are specifically responsive to risks the auditor has determined to be significant risks. Audit evidence in the form of external confirmations received directly by the auditor from appropriate confirming parties may assist the auditor in obtaining audit evidence with the high level of reliability that the auditor requires to respond to significant risks of material misstatement, whether due to fraud or error. For example, if the auditor identifies that management is under pressure to meet earnings expectations, a risk may exist that management is inflating sales by improperly recognizing revenue related to sales agreements with terms that preclude revenue recognition or by invoicing sales before shipment. In these circumstances, the auditor may, for example, design external confirmation procedures not only to confirm outstanding amounts but also to confirm the details of the sales agreements, including date, any rights of return, and delivery terms. In addition, the auditor may find it effective to supplement such external confirmation procedures with inquiries of nonfinancial personnel in the entity regarding any changes in sales agreements and delivery terms.

Timing of Substantive Procedures (Ref: par. .23–.24)

.A59 In most cases, audit evidence from a previous audit's substantive procedures provides little or no audit evidence for the current period. However, exceptions exist (for example, a legal opinion obtained in a previous audit related to the structure of a securitization to which no changes have occurred may be relevant in the current period). In such cases, it may be appropriate to use audit evidence from a previous audit's substantive procedures if that evidence and the related subject matter have not fundamentally changed and audit procedures have been performed during the current period to establish its continuing relevance.

.A60 *Using audit evidence obtained during an interim period (Ref: par. .23).* In some circumstances, the auditor may determine that it is effective to perform substantive procedures at an interim date and compare and reconcile information concerning the balance at the period-end with the comparable information at the interim date to

a. identify amounts that appear unusual,

b. investigate any such amounts, and

c. perform substantive analytical procedures or tests of details to test the intervening period.

.A61 Performing substantive procedures at an interim date without undertaking additional procedures at a later date increases the risk that the auditor will not detect misstatements that may exist at the period-end. This risk increases as the remaining period is lengthened. Factors such as the following may influence whether to perform substantive procedures at an interim date:

- The effectiveness of the control environment and other relevant controls
- The availability at a later date of information necessary for the auditor's procedures
- The purpose of the substantive procedure
- The assessed risk of material misstatement
- The nature of the class of transactions or account balance and relevant assertions
- The ability of the auditor to perform appropriate substantive procedures or substantive procedures combined with tests of controls to cover the remaining period in order to reduce the risk that misstatements that may exist at the period-end will not be detected

.A62 In circumstances in which the auditor has identified risks of material misstatement due to fraud, the auditor's responses to address those risks may include changing the timing of audit procedures. For example, the auditor might conclude that, given the risks of intentional misstatement or manipulation, audit procedures to extend audit conclusions from an interim date to the period-end reporting date would not be effective. In such circumstances, the auditor might conclude that substantive procedures performed at or near the end of the reporting period best address an identified risk of material misstatement due to fraud.

.A63 Factors such as the following may influence whether to perform substantive analytical procedures with respect to the period between the interim date and the period-end:

- Whether the period-end balances of the particular classes of transactions or account balances are reasonably predictable with respect to amount, relative significance, and composition

- Whether the entity's procedures for analyzing and adjusting such classes of transactions or account balances at interim dates and establishing proper accounting cutoffs are appropriate
- Whether the information system relevant to financial reporting will provide information concerning the balances at the period-end and the transactions in the remaining period that is sufficient to permit investigation of the following:
  - — Significant unusual transactions or entries (including those at or near the period-end)
  - — Other causes of significant fluctuations or expected fluctuations that did not occur
  - — Changes in the composition of the classes of transactions or account balances

.A64 *Misstatements detected at an interim date (Ref: par. .24).* When the auditor concludes that the planned nature, timing, or extent of substantive procedures covering the remaining period need to be modified as a result of unexpected misstatements detected at an interim date, such modification may include extending or repeating, at the period-end, the procedures performed at the interim date.

Selecting Items for Testing to Obtain Audit Evidence (Ref: par. .25)

.A65 An effective test provides appropriate audit evidence to the extent that it will be sufficient for the auditor's purpose when taken with other audit evidence obtained or to be obtained. In selecting items for testing, the auditor is required by section 500 to determine the relevance and reliability of information to be used as audit evidence;[12] the other aspect of effectiveness (sufficiency) is an important consideration in selecting items to test. The means available to the auditor for selecting items for testing are

a. selecting all items (100 percent examination),

b. selecting specific items, and

c. audit sampling.

.A66 The application of any one or combination of these means may be appropriate depending on the particular circumstances (for example, the risks of material misstatement related to the assertion being tested and the practicality and efficiency of the different means).

Selecting All Items

.A67 The auditor may decide that it will be most appropriate to examine the entire population of items that make up a class of transactions or account balance (or a stratum within that population). A 100 percent examination is unlikely in the case of tests of controls; however, it may be more common for tests of details. A 100 percent examination may be appropriate when, for example

- the population constitutes a small number of large value items,
- a significant risk exists and other means do not provide sufficient appropriate audit evidence, or

---

[12] Paragraph .07 of section 500.

- the repetitive nature of a calculation or other process performed automatically by an information system makes a 100 percent examination cost effective.

Selecting Specific Items

.A68 The auditor may decide to select specific items from a population. In making this decision, factors that may be relevant include the auditor's understanding of the entity, the assessed risks of material misstatement, and the characteristics of the population being tested. The judgmental selection of specific items is subject to nonsampling risk. Specific items selected may include

- high value or key items. The auditor may decide to select specific items within a population because they are of high value or exhibit some other characteristic (for example, items that are suspicious, unusual, particularly risk prone, or have a history of error).
- all items over a certain amount. The auditor may decide to examine items whose recorded values exceed a certain amount in order to verify a large proportion of the total amount of a class of transactions or account balance.
- items to obtain information. The auditor may examine items to obtain information about matters such as the nature of the entity or the nature of transactions.

.A69 Although selective examination of specific items from a class of transactions or account balance often will be an efficient means of obtaining audit evidence, it does not constitute audit sampling. Consequently, the results of audit procedures applied to items selected in this way cannot be projected to the entire population; furthermore, selective examination of specific items does not, by itself, provide sufficient appropriate audit evidence concerning the remainder of the population.

Audit Sampling

.A70 Audit sampling is designed to enable conclusions to be drawn about an entire population on the basis of testing a sample drawn from the population. Audit sampling is discussed in section 530.

.A71 Valid conclusions ordinarily may be drawn using sampling approaches. However, if the sample size is too small, the sampling approach or the method of selection is not appropriate to achieve the specific audit objective or exceptions are not appropriately followed up, an unacceptable risk will exist that the auditor's conclusion based on a sample may be different from the conclusion reached if the entire population was subjected to the same audit procedure. Section 530 addresses planning, performing, and evaluating audit samples.

Adequacy of Presentation and Disclosure (Ref: par. .26)

.A72 Evaluating the overall presentation of the financial statements, including the related disclosures, relates to whether the individual financial statements are presented in a manner that reflects the appropriate classification and description of financial information and the form, arrangement, and content of the financial statements, including the related notes. This includes, for example, the terminology used, the amount of detail given, the classification of items in the financial statements, and the basis of amounts set forth.

Evaluating the Sufficiency and Appropriateness of Audit Evidence (Ref: par. .27–.29)

.A73 An audit of financial statements is a cumulative and iterative process. As the auditor performs planned audit procedures, the audit evidence obtained may cause the auditor to modify the nature, timing, or extent of other planned audit procedures. Information may come to the auditor's attention that differs significantly from the information on which the risk assessments were based. For example

- the extent of misstatements that the auditor detects by performing substantive procedures may alter the auditor's professional judgment about the risk assessments and indicate a significant deficiency or material weakness in internal control.
- the auditor may become aware of discrepancies in accounting records or conflicting or missing evidence.
- analytical procedures performed at the overall review stage of the audit may indicate a previously unrecognized risk of material misstatement.

In such circumstances, the auditor may need to reevaluate the planned audit procedures, based on the revised consideration of assessed risks for all or some of the classes of transactions, account balances, or disclosures and related assertions. Section 315 contains further guidance on revising the auditor's risk assessment.[13]

.A74 The auditor cannot assume that an instance of fraud or error is an isolated occurrence. Therefore, the consideration of how the detection of a misstatement affects the assessed risks of material misstatement is important in determining whether the assessment remains appropriate.

.A75 The auditor's professional judgment about what constitutes sufficient appropriate audit evidence is influenced by such factors as the

- significance of the potential misstatement in the relevant assertion and the likelihood of its having a material effect, individually or aggregated with other potential misstatements, on the financial statements (see section 450, *Evaluation of Misstatements Identified During the Audit*).
- effectiveness of management's responses and controls to address the risks.
- experience gained during previous audits with respect to similar potential misstatements.
- results of audit procedures performed, including whether such audit procedures identified specific instances of fraud or error.
- source and reliability of the available information.
- persuasiveness of the audit evidence.
- understanding of the entity and its environment, including its internal control.

---

[13] Paragraph .32 of section 315.

Documentation (Ref: par. .30)

.A76 The form and extent of audit documentation is a matter of professional judgment and is influenced by the nature, size, and complexity of the entity; internal control of the entity; availability of information from the entity; and the audit methodology and technology used in the audit.

AU-C Section 402 *

Audit Considerations Relating to an Entity Using a Service Organization

Source: SAS No. 122.

Effective for audits of financial statements for periods ending on or after December 15, 2012.

Introduction

Scope of This Section

.01 This section addresses the user auditor's responsibility for obtaining sufficient appropriate audit evidence in an audit of the financial statements of a user entity that uses one or more service organizations. Specifically, it expands on how the user auditor applies section 315, *Understanding the Entity and Its Environment and Assessing the Risks of Material Misstatement*, and section 330, *Performing Audit Procedures in Response to Assessed Risks and Evaluating the Audit Evidence Obtained*, in obtaining an understanding of the user entity, including internal control relevant to the audit, sufficient to identify and assess the risks of material misstatement and in designing and performing further audit procedures responsive to those risks.

.02 Many entities outsource aspects of their business activities to organizations that provide services ranging from performing a specific task under the direction of the entity to replacing entire business units or functions of the entity. Many of the services provided by such organizations are integral to the entity's business operations; however, not all of those services are relevant to the audit.

.03 Services provided by a service organization are relevant to the audit of a user entity's financial statements when those services and the controls over them affect the user entity's information system, including related business processes, relevant to financial reporting. Although most controls at the service organization are likely to relate to financial reporting, other controls also may be relevant to the audit, such as controls over the safeguarding of assets. A service organization's services are part of a user entity's information system, including related business processes, relevant to financial reporting if these services affect any of the following:

a. The classes of transactions in the user entity's operations that are significant to the user entity's financial statements;

b. The procedures within both IT and manual systems by which the user entity's transactions are initiated, authorized, recorded, processed, corrected as necessary, transferred to the general ledger, and reported in the financial statements;

---

* This section has been codified using an "AU-C" identifier instead of an "AU" identifier. "AU-C" is a temporary identifier to avoid confusion with references to existing "AU" sections, which will remain in AICPA *Professional Standards* through 2013. The "AU-C" identifier will revert to "AU" in 2014, by which time substantially all engagements for which the "AU" sections were still effective are expected to be completed.

c. The related accounting records, supporting information, and specific accounts in the user entity's financial statements that are used to initiate, authorize, record, process, and report the user entity's transactions. This includes the correction of incorrect information and how information is transferred to the general ledger; the records may be in either manual or electronic form;

d. How the user entity's information system captures events and conditions, other than transactions, that are significant to the financial statements;

e. The financial reporting process used to prepare the user entity's financial statements, including significant accounting estimates and disclosures; and

f. Controls surrounding journal entries, including nonstandard journal entries used to record nonrecurring, unusual transactions, or adjustments.

.04 The nature and extent of work to be performed by the user auditor regarding the services provided by a service organization depend on the nature and significance of those services to the user entity and the relevance of those services to the audit.

.05 This section does not apply to services that are limited to processing an entity's transactions that are specifically authorized by the entity, such as the processing of checking account transactions by a bank or the processing of securities transactions by a broker (that is, when the user entity retains responsibility for authorizing the transactions and maintaining the related accountability). In addition, this section does not apply to the audit of transactions arising from an entity that holds a proprietary financial interest in another entity, such as a partnership, corporation, or joint venture, when the partnership, corporation, or joint venture performs no processing on behalf of the entity.

Effective Date

.06 This section is effective for audits of financial statements for periods ending on or after December 15, 2012.

Objectives

.07 The objectives of the user auditor, when the user entity uses the services of a service organization, are to

a. obtain an understanding of the nature and significance of the services provided by the service organization and their effect on the user entity's internal control relevant to the audit, sufficient to identify and assess the risks of material misstatement.

b. design and perform audit procedures responsive to those risks.

Definitions

.08 For purposes of generally accepted auditing standards, the following terms have the meanings attributed as follows:

Complementary user entity controls. Controls that management of the service organization assumes, in the design of its service, will be implemented by user entities, and which, if necessary to achieve the control objectives stated in management's description of the service organization's system, are identified as such in that description.

Report on management's description of a service organization's system and the suitability of the design of controls (referred to in this section as a *type 1 report*). A report that comprises the following:

a. Management's description of the service organization's system

b. A written assertion by management of the service organization about whether, in all material respects, and based on suitable criteria

i. management's description of the service organization's system fairly presents the service organization's system that was designed and implemented as of a specified date

ii. the controls related to the control objectives stated in management's description of the service organization's system were suitably designed to achieve those control objectives as of the specified date

c. A service auditor's report that expresses an opinion on the matters in *b*(i–ii)

Report on management's description of a service organization's system and the suitability of the design and operating effectiveness of controls (referred to in this section as a *type 2 report*). A report that comprises the following:

a. Management's description of the service organization's system

b. A written assertion by management of the service organization about whether in all material respects and, based on suitable criteria

i. management's description of the service organization's system fairly presents the service organization's system that was designed and implemented throughout the specified period

ii. the controls related to the control objectives stated in management's description of the service organization's system were suitably designed throughout the specified period to achieve those control objectives

iii. the controls related to the control objectives stated in management's description of the service organization's system operated effectively throughout the specified period to achieve those control objectives

c. A service auditor's report that

i. expresses an opinion on the matters in *b*(i–iii)

ii. includes a description of the service auditor's tests of controls and the results thereof

Service auditor. A practitioner who reports on controls at a service organization.

Service organization. An organization or segment of an organization that provides services to user entities that are relevant to those user entities' internal control over financial reporting.

Service organization's system. The policies and procedures designed, implemented, and documented by management of the service organization to provide user entities with the services covered by the service auditor's report. Management's description of the service organization's system identifies the services covered, the period to which the description relates (or in the case of a type 1 report, the date to which the description relates), the control objectives specified by management or an outside party, the party specifying the control objectives (if not specified by management), and the related controls.

Subservice organization. A service organization used by another service organization to perform some of the services provided to user entities that are relevant to those user entities' internal control over financial reporting. (Ref: par. .A20)

User auditor. An auditor who audits and reports on the financial statements of a user entity.

User entity. An entity that uses a service organization and whose financial statements are being audited.

Requirements

Obtaining an Understanding of the Services Provided by a Service Organization, Including Internal Control

.09 When obtaining an understanding of the user entity in accordance with section 315, the user auditor should obtain an understanding of how the user entity uses the services of a service organization in the user entity's operations, including the following:[1] (Ref: par. .A1–.A2)

a. The nature of the services provided by the service organization and the significance of those services to the user entity, including their effect on the user entity's internal control (Ref: par. .A3–.A5)

b. The nature and materiality of the transactions processed or accounts or financial reporting processes affected by the service organization (Ref: par. .A6)

c. The degree of interaction between the activities of the service organization and those of the user entity (Ref: par. .A7)

d. The nature of the relationship between the user entity and the service organization, including the relevant contractual terms for the activities undertaken by the service organization (Ref: par. .A8–.A11)

.10 When obtaining an understanding of internal control relevant to the audit in accordance with section 315, the user auditor should evaluate the design and implementation of relevant controls at the user entity that relate to the services provided by the service organization, including those that are applied to the transactions processed by the service organization.[2] (Ref: par. .A12–.A14)

.11 The user auditor should determine whether a sufficient understanding of the nature and significance of the services provided by the service organization and their effect on the user entity's internal control relevant to the audit

---

[1] Paragraph .12 of section 315, *Understanding the Entity and Its Environment and Assessing the Risks of Material Misstatement*.

[2] Paragraph .13 of section 315.

has been obtained to provide a basis for the identification and assessment of risks of material misstatement.

.12 If the user auditor is unable to obtain a sufficient understanding from the user entity, the user auditor should obtain that understanding from one or more of the following procedures:

a. Obtaining and reading a type 1 or type 2 report, if available

b. Contacting the service organization, through the user entity, to obtain specific information

c. Visiting the service organization and performing procedures that will provide the necessary information about the relevant controls at the service organization

d. Using another auditor to perform procedures that will provide the necessary information about the relevant controls at the service organization (Ref: par. .A15–.A20)

Using a Type 1 or Type 2 Report to Support the User Auditor's Understanding of the Service Organization

.13 In determining the sufficiency and appropriateness of the audit evidence provided by a type 1 or type 2 report, the user auditor should be satisfied regarding the following:

a. The service auditor's professional competence and independence from the service organization

b. The adequacy of the standards under which the type 1 or type 2 report was issued (Ref: par. .A21–.A22)

.14 If the user auditor plans to use a type 1 or type 2 report as audit evidence to support the user auditor's understanding about the design and implementation of controls at the service organization, the user auditor should

a. evaluate whether the type 1 report is as of a date, or in the case of a type 2 report, is for a period that is appropriate for the user auditor's purposes;

b. evaluate the sufficiency and appropriateness of the evidence provided by the report for the understanding of the user entity's internal control relevant to the audit; and

c. determine whether complementary user entity controls identified by the service organization are relevant in addressing the risks of material misstatement relating to the relevant assertions in the user entity's financial statements and, if so, obtain an understanding of whether the user entity has designed and implemented such controls. (Ref: par. .A23–.A24)

Responding to the Assessed Risks of Material Misstatement

.15 In responding to assessed risks in accordance with section 330, the user auditor should

a. determine whether sufficient appropriate audit evidence concerning the relevant financial statement assertions is available from records held at the user entity and, if not,

b. perform further audit procedures to obtain sufficient appropriate audit evidence or use another auditor to perform those procedures at the service organization on the user auditor's behalf. (Ref: par. .A25–.A29)

Tests of Controls

.16 When the user auditor's risk assessment includes an expectation that controls at the service organization are operating effectively, the user auditor should obtain audit evidence about the operating effectiveness of those controls from one or more of the following procedures:

a. Obtaining and reading a type 2 report, if available

b. Performing appropriate tests of controls at the service organization

c. Using another auditor to perform tests of controls at the service organization on behalf of the user auditor (Ref: par. .A30–.A31)

Using a Type 2 Report as Audit Evidence That Controls at the Service Organization Are Operating Effectively

.17 If, in accordance with paragraph .16*a*, the user auditor plans to use a type 2 report as audit evidence that controls at the service organization are operating effectively, the user auditor should determine whether the service auditor's report provides sufficient appropriate audit evidence about the effectiveness of the controls to support the user auditor's risk assessment by

a. evaluating whether the type 2 report is for a period that is appropriate for the user auditor's purposes;

b. determining whether complementary user entity controls identified by the service organization are relevant in addressing the risks of material misstatement relating to the relevant assertions in the user entity's financial statements and, if so, obtaining an understanding of whether the user entity has designed and implemented such controls and, if so, testing their operating effectiveness;

c. evaluating the adequacy of the time period covered by the tests of controls and the time elapsed since the performance of the tests of controls; and

d. evaluating whether the tests of controls performed by the service auditor and the results thereof, as described in the service auditor's report, are relevant to the assertions in the user entity's financial statements and provide sufficient appropriate audit evidence to support the user auditor's risk assessment. (Ref: par. .A32–.A40)

Type 1 and Type 2 Reports That Exclude the Services of a Subservice Organization

.18 If the user auditor plans to use a type 1 or a type 2 report that excludes the services provided by a subservice organization and those services are relevant to the audit of the user entity's financial statements, the user auditor should apply the requirements of this section with respect to the services provided by the subservice organization. (Ref: par. .A41)

Fraud, Noncompliance With Laws and Regulations, and Uncorrected Misstatements Related to Activities at the Service Organization

.19 The user auditor should inquire of management of the user entity about whether the service organization has reported to the user entity, or whether the user entity is otherwise aware of, any fraud, noncompliance with laws and regulations, or uncorrected misstatements affecting the financial statements of the user entity. The user auditor should evaluate how such matters, if any, affect the nature, timing, and extent of the user auditor's further audit procedures, including the effect on the user auditor's conclusions and user auditor's report. (Ref: par. .A42)

Reporting by the User Auditor

.20 The user auditor should modify the opinion in the user auditor's report in accordance with section 705, *Modifications to the Opinion in the Independent Auditor's Report*, if the user auditor is unable to obtain sufficient appropriate audit evidence regarding the services provided by the service organization relevant to the audit of the user entity's financial statements. (Ref: par. .A43)

.21 The user auditor should not refer to the work of a service auditor in the user auditor's report containing an unmodified opinion. (Ref: par. .A44)

.22 If reference to the work of a service auditor is relevant to an understanding of a modification of the user auditor's opinion, the user auditor's report should indicate that such reference does not diminish the user auditor's responsibility for that opinion. (Ref: par. .A44)

Application and Other Explanatory Material

Obtaining an Understanding of the Services Provided by a Service Organization, Including Internal Control

Sources of Information (Ref: par. .09)

.A1 Information about the nature of the services provided by a service organization may be available from a wide variety of sources, such as the following:

- User manuals
- System overviews
- Technical manuals
- The contract or service level agreement between the user entity and the service organization
- Reports by service organizations, internal auditors, or regulatory authorities on controls at the service organization
- Reports by the service auditor, if available

.A2 Knowledge obtained through the user auditor's experience with the service organization—for example, through experience with other audit engagements—may also be helpful in obtaining an understanding of the nature of the services provided by the service organization. This may be particularly helpful if the services and controls at the service organization over those services are highly standardized.

Nature of the Services Provided by the Service Organization (Ref: par. .09a)

.A3 A user entity may use a service organization, such as one that processes transactions and maintains the related accountability for the user entity or records transactions and processes related data. Service organizations that provide such services include, for example, bank trust departments that invest and service assets for employee benefit plans or for others, mortgage servicers that service mortgages for others, and application service providers that provide packaged software applications and a technology environment that enables customers to process financial and operational transactions.

.A4 Examples of services provided by service organizations that may be relevant to the audit include the following:

- Maintenance of the user entity's accounting records
- Management of the user entity's assets
- Initiating, authorizing, recording, or processing transactions as an agent of the user entity

Considerations Specific to Smaller Entities

.A5 Smaller entities may use external bookkeeping services ranging from the processing of certain transactions (for example, payment of payroll taxes) and maintenance of their accounting records to the preparation of their financial statements. The use of such a service organization for the preparation of its financial statements does not relieve management of the smaller entity and, when appropriate, those charged with governance of their responsibilities for the financial statements.[3]

Nature and Materiality of Transactions Processed by the Service Organization (Ref: par. .09b)

.A6 A service organization may establish policies and procedures (controls) that affect the user entity's internal control. These controls are at least in part physically and operationally separate from the user entity. The significance of the controls at the service organization to the user entity's internal control depends on the nature of the services provided by the service organization, including the nature and materiality of the transactions it processes for the user entity. In certain situations, the transactions processed and the accounts affected by the service organization may not appear to be material to the user entity's financial statements, but the nature of the transactions processed may be significant and the user auditor may determine that an understanding of controls over the processing of those transactions is necessary in the circumstances.

The Degree of Interaction Between the Activities of the Service Organization and the User Entity (Ref: par. .09c)

.A7 The significance of the controls at the service organization to the user entity's internal control also depends on the degree of interaction between the service organization's activities and those of the user entity. The degree of interaction refers to the extent to which a user entity is able to and elects to implement effective controls over the processing performed by the service organization. For example, a high degree of interaction exists between the activities of the user entity and those at the service organization when the user entity authorizes transactions and the service organization processes and accounts for those transactions. In these circumstances, it may be practicable for the user entity to implement effective controls over those transactions. On the other hand, when the service organization initiates or initially records, processes, and accounts for the user entity's transactions, a lower degree of interaction exists between the two organizations. In these circumstances, the user entity may be unable to, or may elect not to, implement effective controls over these

---

[3] Paragraph .05 of section 200, *Overall Objectives of the Independent Auditor and the Conduct of an Audit in Accordance With Generally Accepted Auditing Standards.*

transactions at the user entity and may rely on controls at the service organization.

Nature of the Relationship Between the User Entity and the Service Organization (Ref: par. .09d)

.A8 The contract or service level agreement between the user entity and the service organization may provide for matters such as the following:

- The information to be provided to the user entity and the responsibilities for initiating transactions relating to the activities undertaken by the service organization
- Complying with the requirements of regulatory bodies concerning the form of records to be maintained or access to them
- The indemnification, if any, to be provided to the user entity in the event of a performance failure
- Whether the service organization will provide a report on its controls and, if so, whether such a report will be a type 1 or type 2 report
- Whether the user auditor has rights of access to the accounting records of the user entity maintained by the service organization and other information necessary for the conduct of the audit
- Whether the agreement allows for direct communication between the user auditor and the service auditor

.A9 A direct relationship exists between the service organization and the user entity when the user entity enters into an agreement with the service organization, and between the service organization and the service auditor when the service organization engages the service auditor. These relationships do not create a direct relationship between the user auditor and the service auditor.

.A10 Communications between the user auditor and the service auditor usually are conducted through the user entity and the service organization. A user auditor may request through the user entity that a service auditor perform procedures for the benefit of the user auditor. For example, a service auditor may be engaged by the service organization to perform an agreed-upon procedures engagement related to testing controls at a service organization or performing procedures related to a user entity's transactions or balances maintained by the service organization. AT section 201, *Agreed-Upon Procedures Engagements*, establishes standards and provides guidance for agreed-upon procedures engagements.

Considerations Specific to Governmental Entities

.A11 For governmental entities, the auditor may be required to perform audit procedures with respect to the entity's compliance with laws and regulations. Such required procedures may include obtaining an understanding of internal control over compliance, performing tests of controls over compliance, and performing tests of compliance. Consequently, auditors of governmental entities that use a service organization may determine that it is appropriate to request, through the governmental entity, that the service auditor perform specified compliance-related audit procedures with respect to services provided by the service organization.[4]

---

[4] Section 935, *Compliance Audits*, addresses audits of an entity's compliance.

Understanding the Controls Relating to Services Provided by the Service Organization (Ref: par. .10)

.A12 The user entity may establish controls over the service organization's services that may be tested by the user auditor and that may enable the user auditor to conclude that the user entity's controls are operating effectively for some or all of the related assertions, regardless of the controls in place at the service organization. If a user entity, for example, uses a service organization to process its payroll transactions, the user entity may establish controls over the submission and receipt of payroll information that could prevent, or detect and correct, material misstatements. These controls may include the following:

- Comparing the data submitted to the service organization with reports of information received from the service organization after the data has been processed
- Recomputing a sample of the payroll amounts for clerical accuracy and reviewing the total amount of the payroll for reasonableness

.A13 In this situation, the user auditor may perform tests of the user entity's controls over payroll processing that would provide a basis for the user auditor to conclude that the user entity's controls are operating effectively for the assertions related to payroll transactions.

.A14 As noted in section 315, for some risks the auditor may judge that it is not possible or practicable to obtain sufficient appropriate audit evidence only from substantive procedures.[5] Such risks may relate to the inaccurate or incomplete recording of routine and significant classes of transactions and account balances that may involve highly automated processing with little or no manual intervention. Risks related to such automated processing may be particularly present when the user entity uses a service organization. In such cases, the user entity's controls over such risks are relevant to the audit and the user auditor is required to obtain an understanding of and to evaluate such controls in accordance with paragraphs .09–.10 of this section.

Further Procedures When a Sufficient Understanding Cannot Be Obtained From the User Entity (Ref: par. .12)

.A15 The user auditor's decision regarding which procedure, individually or in combination, in paragraph .12 to undertake in order to obtain the information necessary to provide a basis for the identification and assessment of the risks of material misstatement regarding the user entity's use of the service organization, may be influenced by such matters as the following:

- The size of both the user entity and the service organization
- The complexity of the transactions at the user entity and the complexity of the services provided by the service organization
- The location of the service organization (for example, the user auditor may decide to use another auditor to perform procedures at the service organization on the user auditor's behalf if the service organization is in a remote location)
- Whether the procedure(s) is expected to effectively provide the user auditor with sufficient appropriate audit evidence
- The nature of the relationship between the user entity and the service organization

---

[5] Paragraph .31 of section 315.

.A16 A service organization may engage a service auditor to report on the description and design of its controls (type 1 report) or on the description and design of its controls and their operating effectiveness (type 2 report). Type 1 or type 2 reports may be issued under Statement on Standards for Attestation Engagements No. 16, *Reporting on Controls at a Service Organization* (AT sec. 801), or under standards promulgated by an authorized or recognized standards-setting organization (for example, the International Auditing and Assurance Standards Board).

.A17 The availability of a type 1 or type 2 report generally will depend on whether the contract between the service organization and the user entity includes the provision of such a report by the service organization. A service organization may also elect, for practical reasons, to make a type 1 or type 2 report available to the user entities. However, in some cases, a type 1 or type 2 report may not be available to user entities.

.A18 In some circumstances, a user entity may outsource one or more significant business units or functions, such as its entire tax planning and compliance functions, finance and accounting functions, or the controllership function to one or more service organizations. As a report on controls at the service organization may not be available in these circumstances, visiting the service organization may be the most effective procedure for the user auditor to gain an understanding of controls at the service organization because there is likely to be direct interaction of management of the user entity with management of the service organization.

.A19 Another auditor may be used to perform procedures that will provide the necessary information about the relevant controls at the service organization. If a type 1 or type 2 report has been issued, the user auditor may use the service auditor to perform these procedures as the service auditor has an existing relationship with the service organization. The user auditor using the work of another auditor may find the guidance in section 600, *Special Considerations—Audits of Group Financial Statements (Including the Work of Component Auditors)*, useful as it relates to understanding another auditor (including that auditor's independence and professional competence); involvement in the work of another auditor in planning the nature, extent, and timing of such work; and in evaluating the sufficiency and appropriateness of the audit evidence obtained.[6]

.A20 A user entity may use a service organization that in turn uses a subservice organization to provide some of the services provided to a user entity that are relevant to those user entities' internal control over financial reporting. The subservice organization may be a separate entity from the service organization or may be related to the service organization. A user auditor may need to consider controls at the subservice organization. In situations in which one or more subservice organizations are used, the interaction between the activities of the user entity and those of the service organization is expanded to include the interaction between the user entity, the service organization, and the subservice organizations. The degree of this interaction as well as the nature and materiality of the transactions processed by the service organization and the subservice organizations are the most important factors for the user auditor to consider in determining the significance of the service organization's and subservice organization's controls to the user entity's controls. (Ref: par. .08)

---

[6] Paragraphs .02 and .22 of section 600, *Special Considerations—Audits of Group Financial Statements (Including the Work of Component Auditors)*.

Using a Type 1 or Type 2 Report to Support the User Auditor's Understanding of the Service Organization (Ref: par. .13–.14)

.A21 The user auditor may make inquiries about the service auditor to the service auditor's professional organization or other practitioners and inquire whether the service auditor is subject to regulatory oversight. The service auditor may be practicing in a jurisdiction in which different standards are followed with respect to reports on controls at a service organization. In such a situation, the user auditor may obtain information about the standards used by the service auditor from the standards-setting organization in that jurisdiction.

.A22 Unless evidence to the contrary comes to the user auditor's attention, a service auditor's report implies that the service auditor is independent of the service organization. However, a service auditor need not be independent of the user entities.

.A23 A type 1 or type 2 report, along with information about the user entity, may assist the user auditor in obtaining an understanding of the following:

- *a.* The controls at the service organization that may affect the processing of the user entity's transactions, including the use of subservice organizations
- *b.* The flow of significant transactions through the service organization's system to determine the points in the transaction flow where material misstatements in the user entity's financial statements could occur
- *c.* The control objectives stated in the description of the service organization's system that are relevant to the user entity's financial statement assertions
- *d.* Whether controls at the service organization are suitably designed and implemented to prevent, or detect and correct, processing errors that could result in material misstatements in the user entity's financial statements

A type 1 or type 2 report may assist the user auditor in obtaining a sufficient understanding to identify and assess the risks of material misstatement of the user entity's financial statements. A type 1 report, however, does not provide any evidence of the operating effectiveness of the relevant controls.

.A24 A type 1 report that is as of a date, or a type 2 report that is for a period outside of the reporting period of a user entity, may assist the user auditor in obtaining a preliminary understanding of the controls implemented at the service organization if the report is supplemented by additional current information from other sources. If the description of the service organization's system is as of a date or for a period that precedes the beginning of the period under audit, the user auditor may perform procedures to update the information in a type 1 or type 2 report, such as the following:

- Discussing changes at the service organization with user entity personnel who would be in a position to know of such changes
- Reviewing current documentation and correspondence issued by the service organization
- Discussing the changes with service organization personnel

Responding to the Assessed Risks of Material Misstatement (Ref: par. .15)

.A25 Whether the use of a service organization increases a user entity's risk of material misstatement depends on the nature of the services provided and the controls over these services; in some cases, the use of a service organization may decrease a user entity's risk of material misstatement, particularly if the user entity itself does not possess the expertise necessary to undertake particular activities, such as initiating, processing, and recording transactions, or does not have adequate resources (for example, an IT system).

.A26 When the service organization maintains material elements of the accounting records of the user entity, direct access to those records may be necessary for the user auditor to obtain sufficient appropriate audit evidence relating to the operations of controls over those records, to substantiate transactions and balances recorded in them, or both. Such access may involve physical inspection of records at the service organization's premises or electronic interrogation of records, or both. When direct access is achieved electronically, the user auditor may also obtain evidence concerning the adequacy of the service organization's controls over the completeness and integrity of the user entity's data for which the service organization is responsible.

.A27 In determining the nature and extent of audit evidence to be obtained for financial statement balances representing assets held or transactions processed by a service organization for a user entity, the following procedures may be considered by the user auditor:

a. *Inspecting records and documents held by the user entity.* The reliability of this source of evidence is determined by the nature and extent of the accounting records and supporting documentation retained by the user entity. In some cases, the user entity may not maintain independent detailed records or documentation of specific transactions undertaken on its behalf.

b. *Inspecting records and documents held by the service organization.* The user auditor's access to the records of the service organization may be established as part of the contractual arrangements between the user entity and the service organization. The user auditor may also use another auditor, on its behalf, to gain access to the user entity's records maintained by the service organization, or ask the service organization through the user entity for access to the user entity's records maintained by the service organization.

c. *Obtaining confirmations of balances and transactions from the service organization.* When the user entity maintains independent records of balances and transactions, confirmation from the service organization corroborating those records usually constitutes reliable audit evidence concerning the existence of the transactions and assets concerned. For example, when multiple service organizations are used, such as an investment manager and a custodian, and these service organizations maintain independent records, the user auditor may confirm balances with these organizations in order to compare this information with the independent records of the user entity. If the user entity does not maintain independent records, information obtained in confirmations from the service organization is merely a statement of what is reflected in the records maintained by the service organization. Therefore, such confirmations do not, taken alone, constitute reliable audit evidence. In these circumstances, the user auditor may consider whether an alternative source of independent evidence can be identified.

d. *Performing analytical procedures on the records maintained by the user entity or on the reports received from the service organization.* The effectiveness of analytical procedures is likely to vary by assertion and will be affected by the extent and detail of information available.

.A28 As noted in paragraph .A10, a service auditor may perform procedures under AT section 201 that are substantive in nature for the benefit of user auditors. Such an engagement may involve the performance by the service auditor of procedures agreed upon by the user entity and its user auditor and by the service organization and its service auditor. The findings resulting from the procedures performed by the service auditor are reviewed by the user auditor to determine whether they constitute sufficient appropriate audit evidence. In addition, requirements may be imposed by governmental authorities or through contractual arrangements whereby a service auditor performs designated procedures that are substantive in nature. The results of the application of the required procedures to balances and transactions processed by the service organization may be used by the user auditor as part of the evidence necessary to support the user auditor's audit opinion. In these circumstances, it may be useful for the user auditor and the service auditor to establish an understanding prior to the performance of the procedures concerning the audit documentation or means of accessing the audit documentation that will be provided to the user auditor.

.A29 In certain circumstances, in particular when a user entity outsources some or all of its finance function to a service organization, the user auditor may face a situation in which a significant portion of the audit evidence resides at the service organization. Substantive procedures may need to be performed at the service organization by the user auditor or the service auditor on behalf of the user auditor. A service auditor may provide a type 2 report and, in addition, may perform substantive procedures on behalf of the user auditor. As noted in paragraph .A44, the involvement of a service auditor does not alter the user auditor's responsibility to obtain sufficient appropriate audit evidence to afford a reasonable basis to support the user auditor's opinion. Accordingly, relevant information for the user auditor to consider when determining whether sufficient appropriate audit evidence has been obtained and whether the user auditor needs to perform further substantive procedures includes the user auditor's involvement with, or evidence of, the direction, supervision, and performance of the substantive procedures performed by the service auditor.

Tests of Controls (Ref: par. .16)

.A30 The user auditor is required by section 330 to design and perform tests of controls to obtain sufficient appropriate audit evidence concerning the operating effectiveness of relevant controls in certain circumstances.[7] In the context of a service organization, this requirement applies when

a. the user auditor's assessment of risks of material misstatement includes an expectation that the controls at the service organization are operating effectively (that is, the user auditor intends to

[7] Paragraph .08 of section 330, *Performing Audit Procedures in Response to Assessed Risks and Evaluating the Audit Evidence Obtained.*

rely on the operating effectiveness of controls at the service organization in determining the nature, timing and extent of substantive procedures); or

b. substantive procedures alone, or in combination with tests of the operating effectiveness of controls at the user entity, cannot provide sufficient appropriate audit evidence at the assertion level.

.A31 If a type 2 report is not available, a user auditor may contact the service organization through the user entity to request that a service auditor be engaged to perform a type 2 engagement that includes tests of the operating effectiveness of the relevant controls or the user auditor may use another auditor to perform agreed-upon procedures at the service organization that test the operating effectiveness of those controls. A user auditor may also visit the service organization and perform tests of relevant controls if the service organization agrees to it. The user auditor's risk assessments are based on the combined evidence provided by the service auditor's report and the user auditor's own procedures.

Using a Type 2 Report as Audit Evidence That Controls at the Service Organization Are Operating Effectively (Ref: par. .17)

.A32 A type 2 report may be intended to satisfy the needs of several different user auditors; therefore, specific tests of controls and results described in a type 2 report may not be relevant to assertions that are significant in the user entity's financial statements. The relevant tests of controls and results of the tests are evaluated to determine whether the type 2 report provides sufficient appropriate audit evidence about the effectiveness of the controls to support the user auditor's risk assessment. In doing so, the user auditor may consider the following factors:

a. The time period covered by the tests of controls and the time elapsed since the performance of the tests of controls

b. The scope of the service auditor's work and the services and processes covered, the controls tested and the tests that were performed, and the way in which tested controls relate to the user entity's controls

c. The results of those tests of controls and the service auditor's opinion on the operating effectiveness of the controls

.A33 For certain assertions, the shorter the period covered by a specific test and the longer the time elapsed since the performance of the test, the less audit evidence the test may provide. In comparing the period covered by the type 2 report to the user entity's financial reporting period, the user auditor may conclude that the type 2 report offers less audit evidence if little overlap exists between the period covered by the type 2 report and the period for which the user auditor intends to rely on the report. When this is the case, an additional type 2 report covering a preceding or subsequent period may provide additional audit evidence. In other cases, the user auditor may determine it is necessary to perform, or use another auditor to perform, tests of controls at the service organization in order to obtain sufficient appropriate audit evidence about the operating effectiveness of those controls.

.A34 It may also be necessary for the user auditor to obtain additional evidence about significant changes in the relevant controls at the service organization during a period outside the period covered by the type 2 report, or to determine what additional audit procedures need to be performed (for example, when little or no overlap exists between the period covered by the type 2 report and the period covered by the user entity's financial statements). Relevant factors in determining what additional audit evidence to obtain about controls at the service organization that were operating outside the period covered by the service auditor's report may include the following:

- The significance of the assessed risks of material misstatement at the assertion level
- The specific controls that were tested during the interim period and significant changes to them since they were tested including changes in the information systems, processes, and personnel
- The degree to which audit evidence about the operating effectiveness of those controls was obtained
- The length of the remaining period
- The extent to which the user auditor intends to reduce further substantive procedures based on the reliance on controls
- The effectiveness of the control environment and monitoring controls at the user entity

.A35 Additional audit evidence may be obtained, for example, by performing tests of controls that operated during the remaining period or testing the user entity's monitoring controls.

.A36 If the service auditor's testing period is completely outside the user entity's financial reporting period, the user auditor will be unable to rely on such tests to conclude that the user entity's controls are operating effectively because the tests do not provide current audit period evidence of the effectiveness of the controls, unless other procedures are performed.

.A37 In certain circumstances, a service provided by the service organization may be designed with the assumption that certain controls will be implemented by the user entity. For example, the service may be designed with the assumption that the user entity will have controls in place for authorizing transactions before they are sent to the service organization for processing. In such a situation, the description of the service organization's system may include a description of those complementary user entity controls. The user auditor considers whether those complementary user entity controls are relevant to the service provided to the user entity.

.A38 If the user auditor believes that the service auditor's report may not provide sufficient appropriate audit evidence (for example, if a service auditor's report does not contain a description of the service auditor's tests of controls and results thereof), the user auditor may supplement his or her understanding of the service auditor's procedures and conclusions by contacting the service organization through the user entity to request a discussion with the service auditor about the scope and results of the service auditor's work. Also, if the user auditor believes it is necessary, the user auditor may contact the service organization through the user entity to request that the service auditor perform procedures at the service organization, or the user auditor may perform such procedures.

.A39 The service auditor's type 2 report identifies results of tests, including deviations, and other information that could affect the user auditor's conclusions. Deviations noted by the service auditor or a modified opinion in the service auditor's report do not automatically mean that the service auditor's report will not be useful for the audit of the user entity's financial statements in assessing the risks of material misstatement. Rather, the deviations and the matter giving rise to a modified opinion in the service auditor's type 2 report are considered in the user auditor's assessment of the tests of controls performed by the service auditor. In considering the deviations and matters giving rise to a modified opinion, the user auditor may discuss such matters with the service auditor. Such communication is dependent upon the user entity contacting the service organization, and obtaining the service organization's approval for the communication to take place.

.A40 *Communication of significant deficiencies and material weaknesses in internal control identified during the audit.* The user auditor is required by section 265, *Communicating Internal Control Related Matters Identified in an Audit*, to communicate in writing to management and those charged with governance significant deficiencies and material weaknesses identified during the audit.[8] Matters related to the use of a service organization that the user auditor may identify during the audit and may communicate to management and those charged with governance of the user entity include the following:

- Any needed monitoring controls that could be implemented by the user entity, including those identified as a result of obtaining a type 1 or type 2 report
- Instances when complementary user entity controls identified in the type 1 or type 2 report are not implemented at the user entity
- Controls that may be needed at the service organization that do not appear to have been implemented or that were implemented, but are not operating effectively

The auditor also may communicate other control related matters, including deficiencies that are not significant deficiencies or material weaknesses.

Type 1 and Type 2 Reports That Exclude the Services of a Subservice Organization (Ref: par. .18)

.A41 If a service organization uses a subservice organization, the service auditor's report may either include or exclude the subservice organization's relevant control objectives and related controls in the service organization's description of its system and in the scope of the service auditor's engagement. These two methods of reporting are known as the *inclusive method* and the *carve-out method*, respectively. If the type 1 or type 2 report excludes the controls at a subservice organization and the services provided by the subservice organization are relevant to the audit of the user entity's financial statements, the user auditor is required to apply the requirements of this section with respect to the subservice organization. The nature and extent of work to be performed by the user auditor regarding the services provided by a subservice organization depend on the nature and significance of those services to the user entity and the relevance of those services to the audit. The application of the requirement in paragraph .09 assists the user auditor in determining the effect of the subservice organization and the nature and extent of work to be performed.

Fraud, Noncompliance With Laws and Regulations, and Uncorrected Misstatements Related to Activities at the Service Organization (Ref: par. .19)

.A42 A service organization may be required under the terms of the contract with user entities to disclose to affected user entities any fraud, noncompliance with laws and regulations, or uncorrected misstatements attributable

---

[8] Paragraphs .11–.12 of section 265, *Communicating Internal Control Related Matters Identified in an Audit*.

to the service organization's management or employees. As required by paragraph .19, the user auditor makes inquiries of the user entity management regarding whether the service organization has reported any such matters and evaluates whether any matters reported by the service organization affect the nature, timing, and extent of the user auditor's further audit procedures. In certain circumstances, the user auditor may require additional information to perform this evaluation and may request that the user entity contact the service organization to obtain the necessary information.

Reporting by the User Auditor (Ref: par. .20)

.A43 When a user auditor is unable to obtain sufficient appropriate audit evidence regarding the services provided by the service organization relevant to the audit of the user entity's financial statements, a limitation on the scope of the audit exists. This may be the case when

- the user auditor is unable to obtain a sufficient understanding of the services provided by the service organization and does not have a basis for the identification and assessment of the risks of material misstatement;
- a user auditor's risk assessment includes an expectation that controls at the service organization are operating effectively and the user auditor is unable to obtain sufficient appropriate audit evidence about the operating effectiveness of these controls; or
- sufficient appropriate audit evidence is only available from records held at the service organization, and the user auditor is unable to obtain direct access to these records.

Whether the user auditor expresses a qualified opinion or disclaims an opinion depends on the user auditor's conclusion regarding whether the possible effects on the financial statements are material, pervasive, or both.[9]

Reference to the Work of the Service Auditor (Ref: par. .21–.22)

.A44 The fact that a user entity uses a service organization does not alter the user auditor's responsibility to obtain sufficient appropriate audit evidence to afford a reasonable basis to support the user auditor's opinion. Therefore, the user auditor does not make reference to the service auditor's report as a basis, in part, for the user auditor's opinion on the user entity's financial statements. However, when the user auditor expresses a modified opinion because of a modified opinion in a service auditor's report, the user auditor is not precluded from referring to the service auditor's report if such reference assists in explaining the reason for the user auditor's modified opinion. In such circumstances, the user auditor need not identify the service auditor by name and may need the consent of the service auditor before making such a reference.

---

[9] Paragraphs .07–.10 of section 705, *Modifications to the Opinion in the Independent Auditor's Report*.

AU-C Section 450*

Evaluation of Misstatements Identified During the Audit

Source: SAS No. 122.

Effective for audits of financial statements for periods ending on or after December 15, 2012.

Introduction

Scope of This Section

.01 This section addresses the auditor's responsibility to evaluate the effect of identified misstatements on the audit and the effect of uncorrected misstatements, if any, on the financial statements. Section 700, *Forming an Opinion and Reporting on Financial Statements*, addresses the auditor's responsibility in forming an opinion on the financial statements based on the evaluation of the audit evidence obtained. The auditor's conclusion, required by section 700, takes into account the auditor's evaluation of uncorrected misstatements, if any, on the financial statements, in accordance with this section. Section 320, *Materiality in Planning and Performing an Audit*, addresses the auditor's responsibility to appropriately apply the concept of materiality in planning and performing an audit of financial statements.

Effective Date

.02 This section is effective for audits of financial statements for periods ending on or after December 15, 2012.

Objective

.03 The objective of the auditor is to evaluate the effect of

a. identified misstatements on the audit and

b. uncorrected misstatements, if any, on the financial statements.

Definitions

.04 For purposes of generally accepted auditing standards, the following terms have the meanings attributed as follows:

Misstatement. A difference between the amount, classification, presentation, or disclosure of a reported financial statement item and the amount, classification, presentation, or disclosure that is required for the item to be presented fairly in accordance with

---

* This section has been codified using an "AU-C" identifier instead of an "AU" identifier. "AU-C" is a temporary identifier to avoid confusion with references to existing "AU" sections, which will remain in AICPA *Professional Standards* through 2013. The "AU-C" identifier will revert to "AU" in 2014, by which time substantially all engagements for which the "AU" sections were still effective are expected to be completed.

the applicable financial reporting framework. Misstatements can arise from fraud or error. (Ref: par. .A1)

Misstatements also include those adjustments of amounts, classifications, presentations, or disclosures that, in the auditor's professional judgment, are necessary for the financial statements to be presented fairly, in all material respects.

Uncorrected misstatements. Misstatements that the auditor has accumulated during the audit and that have not been corrected.

Requirements

Accumulation of Identified Misstatements

.05 The auditor should accumulate misstatements identified during the audit, other than those that are clearly trivial. (Ref: par. .A2–.A3)

Consideration of Identified Misstatements as the Audit Progresses

.06 The auditor should determine whether the overall audit strategy and audit plan need to be revised if

a. the nature of identified misstatements and the circumstances of their occurrence indicate that other misstatements may exist that, when aggregated with misstatements accumulated during the audit, could be material or (Ref: par. .A4)

b. the aggregate of misstatements accumulated during the audit approaches materiality determined in accordance with section 320.[1] (Ref: par. .A5)

Communication and Correction of Misstatements

.07 The auditor should communicate on a timely basis with the appropriate level of management all misstatements accumulated during the audit. The auditor should request management to correct those misstatements. (Ref: par. .A6–.A8)

.08 If, at the auditor's request, management has examined a class of transactions, account balance, or disclosure and corrected misstatements that were detected, the auditor should perform additional audit procedures to determine whether misstatements remain. (Ref: par. .A9–.A11)

.09 If management refuses to correct some or all of the misstatements communicated by the auditor, the auditor should obtain an understanding of management's reasons for not making the corrections and should take that understanding into account when evaluating whether the financial statements as a whole are free from material misstatement.[2] (Ref: par. .A12–.A15)

---

[1] Paragraph .10 of section 320, *Materiality in Planning and Performing an Audit*.

[2] Paragraph .14 of section 700, *Forming an Opinion and Reporting on Financial Statements*.

Evaluating the Effect of Uncorrected Misstatements

.10 Prior to evaluating the effect of uncorrected misstatements, the auditor should reassess materiality[3] to confirm whether it remains appropriate in the context of the entity's actual financial results. (Ref: par. .A16–.A18)

.11 The auditor should determine whether uncorrected misstatements are material, individually or in the aggregate. In making this determination, the auditor should consider

a. the size and nature of the misstatements, both in relation to particular classes of transactions, account balances, or disclosures and the financial statements as a whole, and the particular circumstances of their occurrence and (Ref: par. .A19–.A24 and .A26–.A27)

b. the effect of uncorrected misstatements related to prior periods on the relevant classes of transactions, account balances, or disclosures and the financial statements as a whole. (Ref: par. .A25)

Documentation

.12 The auditor should include in the audit documentation[4] (Ref: par. .A28)

a. the amount below which misstatements would be regarded as clearly trivial; (See paragraph .05)

b. all misstatements accumulated during the audit and whether they have been corrected; and (See paragraphs .05–.07)

c. the auditor's conclusion about whether uncorrected misstatements are material, individually or in the aggregate, and the basis for that conclusion. (See paragraph .11)

Application and Other Explanatory Material

Definitions

Misstatement (Ref: par. .04)

.A1 Misstatements may result from fraud or error, such as

a. an inaccuracy in gathering or processing data from which the financial statements are prepared,

b. an omission of an amount or disclosure,

c. a financial statement disclosure that is not presented in accordance with the applicable financial reporting framework,

d. an incorrect accounting estimate arising from overlooking or clear misinterpretation of facts, and

e. judgments of management concerning accounting estimates that the auditor considers unreasonable or the selection or application of accounting policies that the auditor considers inappropriate.

Other examples of misstatements arising from fraud are provided in section 240, *Consideration of Fraud in a Financial Statement Audit*.[5]

---

[3] Paragraph .12 of section 320.

[4] Paragraphs .08–.12 and .A8 of section 230, *Audit Documentation*.

[5] Paragraphs .A1–.A8 of section 240, *Consideration of Fraud in a Financial Statement Audit*.

Accumulation of Identified Misstatements (Ref: par. .05)

.A2 The auditor may designate an amount below which misstatements would be clearly trivial and would not need to be accumulated because the auditor expects that the accumulation of such amounts clearly would not have a material effect on the financial statements. "Clearly trivial" is not another expression for "not material." Matters that are clearly trivial will be of a wholly different (smaller) order of magnitude than materiality determined in accordance with section 320 and will be matters that are clearly inconsequential, whether taken individually or in the aggregate and whether judged by any criteria of size, nature, or circumstances. When there is any uncertainty about whether one or more items are clearly trivial, the matter is considered not to be clearly trivial.

.A3 To assist the auditor in evaluating the effect of misstatements accumulated during the audit and in communicating misstatements to management and those charged with governance, the auditor may find it useful to distinguish between factual misstatements, judgmental misstatements, and projected misstatements, described as follows:

- *Factual misstatements* are misstatements about which there is no doubt.
- *Judgmental misstatements* are differences arising from the judgments of management concerning accounting estimates that the auditor considers unreasonable or the selection or application of accounting policies that the auditor considers inappropriate.
- *Projected misstatements* are the auditor's best estimate of misstatements in populations, involving the projection of misstatements identified in audit samples to the entire population from which the samples were drawn. Guidance on the determination of projected misstatements and evaluation of the results is set out in section 530, *Audit Sampling*.[6]

Consideration of Identified Misstatements as the Audit Progresses (Ref: par. .06)

.A4 A misstatement may not be an isolated occurrence. Evidence that other misstatements may exist include, for example, when the auditor identifies that a misstatement arose from a breakdown in internal control or from inappropriate assumptions or valuation methods that have been widely applied by the entity.

.A5 If the aggregate of misstatements accumulated during the audit approaches materiality,[7] a greater than acceptably low level of risk may exist that possible undetected misstatements, when taken with the aggregate of uncorrected misstatements accumulated during the audit, could exceed materiality. Undetected misstatements could exist because of the presence of sampling risk and nonsampling risk.[8]

---

[6] Paragraphs .13–.14 of section 530, *Audit Sampling*.

[7] Paragraph .12 of section 320.

[8] Paragraph .05 of section 530.

Communication and Correction of Misstatements (Ref: par. .07–.09)

.A6 Timely communication of misstatements to the appropriate level of management is important because it enables management to evaluate whether the items are misstatements, inform the auditor if it disagrees, and take action as necessary. Ordinarily, the appropriate level of management is the one that has responsibility and authority to evaluate the misstatements and take the necessary action.

.A7 Law or regulation may restrict the auditor's communication of certain misstatements to management or others within the entity. For example, laws or regulations may specifically prohibit a communication or other action that might prejudice an investigation by an appropriate authority into an instance of noncompliance or suspected noncompliance with laws or regulations. In some circumstances, potential conflicts between the auditor's obligations of confidentiality and obligations to communicate may be complex. In such cases, the auditor may consider seeking legal advice.

.A8 The correction by management of all misstatements, including those communicated by the auditor, enables management to maintain accurate accounting books and records and reduces the risks of material misstatement of future financial statements because of the cumulative effect of immaterial uncorrected misstatements related to prior periods.

.A9 The auditor may request management to examine a class of transactions, account balance, or disclosure in order for management to understand the cause of a misstatement identified by the auditor; perform procedures to determine the amount of the actual misstatement in the class of transactions, account balance, or disclosure; and make appropriate adjustments to the financial statements. Such a request may be made, for example, based on the auditor's projection of misstatements identified in an audit sample to the entire population from which it was drawn.

.A10 The auditor may request management to record an adjustment needed to correct all factual misstatements, including the effect of prior period misstatements (see paragraph .08), other than those that the auditor believes are clearly trivial.

.A11 When the auditor has identified a judgmental misstatement involving differences in estimates, such as a difference in a fair value estimate, the auditor may request management to review the assumptions and methods used in developing management's estimate.

.A12 Section 700 requires the auditor to evaluate whether the financial statements are presented fairly, in all material respects, in accordance with the requirements of the applicable financial reporting framework.[9] This evaluation includes consideration of the qualitative aspects of the entity's accounting practices, including indicators of possible bias in management's judgments, which may be affected by the auditor's understanding of management's reasons for not making the corrections (see section 700).[10]

.A13 Section 580, *Written Representations*, addresses management representations, including representations with respect to uncorrected misstatements.[11]

---

[9] Paragraph .13 of section 700.

[10] Paragraph .15 of section 700.

[11] Paragraph .14 of section 580, *Written Representations*.

.A14 In accordance with section 265, *Communicating Internal Control Related Matters Identified in an Audit*, identification by the auditor of a material misstatement of the financial statements under audit in circumstances that indicate that the misstatement would not have been detected by the entity's internal control is an indicator of a material weakness.[12]

.A15 Section 260, *The Auditor's Communication With Those Charged With Governance*, addresses matters to be communicated by the auditor to those charged with governance, including uncorrected misstatements.

Evaluating the Effect of Uncorrected Misstatements (Ref: par. .10–.11)

.A16 The auditor's determination of materiality in accordance with section 320 often is based on estimates of the entity's financial results because the actual financial results may not yet be known.[13] Therefore, prior to the auditor's evaluation of the effect of uncorrected misstatements, it may be necessary to revise materiality determined in accordance with section 320 based on the actual financial results.

.A17 Section 320 explains that, as the audit progresses, materiality for the financial statements as a whole (and, if applicable, the materiality level or levels for particular classes of transactions, account balances, or disclosures) is revised in the event of the auditor becoming aware of information during the audit that would have caused the auditor to have determined a different amount (or amounts) initially.[14] Thus, any significant revision is likely to have been made before the auditor evaluates the effect of uncorrected misstatements. However, if the auditor's reassessment of materiality determined in accordance with section 320 (see paragraph .10 of this section) gives rise to a lower amount (or amounts), then performance materiality and the appropriateness of the nature, timing, and extent of the further audit procedures are reconsidered in order to obtain sufficient appropriate audit evidence on which to base the audit opinion.

.A18 Materiality is determined based on the auditor's understanding of the user needs and expectations (see section 320).[15] Although user expectations may differ based on inherent uncertainty associated with the measurement of particular items in the financial statements, these expectations have already been considered in the auditor's determination of materiality. For example, the fact that the financial statements include very large provisions with a high degree of estimation uncertainty (for example, provisions for insurance claims in the case of an insurance company; oil rig decommissioning costs in the case of an oil company; or, more generally, legal claims against an entity) may influence the auditor's assessment of what users might consider material. However, after materiality is reassessed, this section requires the auditor to evaluate any misstatements in accordance with that level of materiality, regardless of the degree of inherent uncertainty associated with the measurement of particular items in the financial statements.

.A19 Each individual misstatement is considered to evaluate its effect on the relevant classes of transactions, account balances, or disclosures, including

---

[12] Paragraph .A11 of section 265, *Communicating Internal Control Related Matters Identified in an Audit*.

[13] Paragraph .10 of section 320.

[14] Paragraph .12 of section 320.

[15] Paragraph .10 of section 320.

whether the materiality level for that particular class of transactions, account balance, or disclosure, if any, has been exceeded.

.A20 The auditor is required by section 600, *Special Considerations—Audits of Group Financial Statements (Including the Work of Component Auditors)*, to evaluate the effect on the group audit opinion of any uncorrected misstatement identified by the group engagement team or communicated by the component auditors.[16]

.A21 If an individual misstatement is judged to be material, it is unlikely that it can be offset by other misstatements. For example, if revenue has been materially overstated, the financial statements as a whole will be materially misstated, even if the effect of the misstatement on earnings is completely offset by an equivalent overstatement of expenses. It may be appropriate to offset misstatements within the same account balance or class of transactions; however, the risk that further undetected misstatements may exist is considered before concluding that offsetting even immaterial misstatements is appropriate. The auditor may need to reassess the risks of material misstatement for a specific account balance or class of transactions upon identification of a number of immaterial misstatements within that account balance or class of transactions.

.A22 Determining whether a classification misstatement is material involves the evaluation of qualitative considerations, such as the effect of the classification misstatement on debt or other contractual covenants, the effect on individual line items or subtotals, or the effect on key ratios. Circumstances may exist in which the auditor concludes that a classification misstatement is not material in the context of the financial statements as a whole, even though it may exceed the materiality level or levels applied in evaluating other misstatements. For example, a misclassification between balance sheet line items may not be considered material in the context of the financial statements as a whole when the amount of the misclassification is small in relation to the size of the related balance sheet line items and the misclassification does not affect the income statement or any key ratios.

.A23 The circumstances related to some misstatements may cause the auditor to evaluate them as material, individually or when considered together with other misstatements accumulated during the audit, even if they are lower than materiality for the financial statements as a whole. Circumstances that may affect the evaluation include the extent to which the misstatement

- affects compliance with regulatory requirements.
- affects compliance with debt covenants or other contractual requirements.
- relates to the incorrect selection or application of an accounting policy that has an immaterial effect on the current period's financial statements but is likely to have a material effect on future periods' financial statements.
- masks a change in earnings or other trends, especially in the context of general economic and industry conditions.
- affects ratios used to evaluate the entity's financial position, results of operations, or cash flows.

---

[16] Paragraph .44 of section 600, *Special Considerations—Audits of Group Financial Statements (Including the Work of Component Auditors)*.

- affects segment information presented in the financial statements (for example, the significance of the matter to a segment or other portion of the entity's business that has been identified as playing a significant role in the entity's operations or profitability).
- has the effect of increasing management compensation (for example, by ensuring that the requirements for the award of bonuses or other incentives are satisfied).
- is significant with regard to the auditor's understanding of known previous communications to users (for example, regarding forecast earnings).
- relates to items involving particular parties (for example, whether external parties to the transaction are related to members of the entity's management).
- is an omission of information not specifically required by the applicable financial reporting framework but that, in the professional judgment of the auditor, is important to the users' understanding of the financial position, financial performance, or cash flows of the entity.
- affects other information that will be communicated in documents containing the audited financial statements (for example, information to be included in a "Management Discussion and Analysis" or an "Operating and Financial Review") that may reasonably be expected to influence the economic decisions of the users of the financial statements. Section 720, *Other Information in Documents Containing Audited Financial Statements*, addresses the auditor's consideration of other information, on which the auditor has no obligation to report, in documents containing audited financial statements.
- is a misclassification between certain account balances affecting items disclosed separately in the financial statements (for example, misclassification between operating and nonoperating income or recurring and nonrecurring income items or a misclassification between restricted and unrestricted resources in a not-for-profit entity).
- offsets effects of individually significant but different misstatements.
- is currently immaterial and likely to have a material effect in future periods because of a cumulative effect, for example, that builds over several periods.
- is too costly to correct. It may not be cost beneficial for the client to develop a system to calculate a basis to record the effect of an immaterial misstatement. On the other hand, if management appears to have developed a system to calculate an amount that represents an immaterial misstatement, it may reflect a motivation of management.
- represents a risk that possible additional undetected misstatements would affect the auditor's evaluation.
- changes a loss into income or vice versa.
- heightens the sensitivity of the circumstances surrounding the misstatement (for example, the implications of misstatements involving fraud and possible instances of noncompliance with laws

or regulations, violations of contractual provisions, and conflicts of interest).

- has a significant effect relative to reasonable user needs (for example,
  - — earnings to investors and the equity amounts to creditors,
  - — the magnifying effects of a misstatement on the calculation of purchase price in a transfer of interests [buy-sell agreement], and
  - — the effect of misstatements of earnings when contrasted with expectations).
- relates to the definitive character of the misstatement (for example, the precision of an error that is objectively determinable as contrasted with a misstatement that unavoidably involves a degree of subjectivity through estimation, allocation, or uncertainty).
- indicates the motivation of management (for example, [i] an indication of a possible pattern of bias by management when developing and accumulating accounting estimates, [ii] a misstatement precipitated by management's continued unwillingness to correct weaknesses in the financial reporting process, or [iii] an intentional decision not to follow the applicable financial reporting framework).

These circumstances are only examples—not all are likely to be present in all audits nor is the list necessarily complete. The existence of any circumstances such as these does not necessarily lead to a conclusion that the misstatement is material.

.A24 Section 240 explains how the implications of a misstatement that is, or may be, the result of fraud are required to be considered with regard to other aspects of the audit, even if the size of the misstatement is not material in relation to the financial statements.[17]

.A25 The cumulative effect of immaterial uncorrected misstatements related to prior periods may have a material effect on the current period's financial statements. Different acceptable approaches to the auditor's evaluation of such uncorrected misstatements on the current period's financial statements are available. Using the same evaluation approach provides consistency from period to period.

Considerations Specific to Governmental Entities

.A26 In the case of an audit of a governmental entity, the evaluation of whether a misstatement is material also may be affected by the auditor's responsibilities established by law or regulation to report specific matters, including, for example, fraud.

.A27 Furthermore, issues such as public interest, accountability, integrity, and ensuring effective legislative oversight, in particular, may affect the assessment of whether an item is material by virtue of its nature. This is particularly so for items that relate to compliance with law or regulation.

---

[17] Paragraph .35 of section 240.

Documentation (Ref: par. .12)

.A28 The auditor's documentation of uncorrected misstatements may take into account the following:

a. The consideration of the aggregate effect of uncorrected misstatements

b. The evaluation of whether the materiality level or levels for particular classes of transactions, account balances, or disclosures, if any, have been exceeded

c. The evaluation of the effect of uncorrected misstatements on key ratios or trends and compliance with legal, regulatory, and contractual requirements (for example, debt covenants)

AU-C Sections 500–599
AUDIT EVIDENCE

TABLE OF CONTENTS

AU-C Section 500 *

Audit Evidence

Source: SAS No. 122.

Effective for audits of financial statements for periods ending on or after December 15, 2012.

Introduction

Scope of This Section

.01 This section explains what constitutes audit evidence in an audit of financial statements and addresses the auditor's responsibility to design and perform audit procedures to obtain sufficient appropriate audit evidence to be able to draw reasonable conclusions on which to base the auditor's opinion.

.02 This section is applicable to all the audit evidence obtained during the course of the audit. Other AU-C sections address

- specific aspects of the audit (for example, section 315, *Understanding the Entity and Its Environment and Assessing the Risks of Material Misstatement*);
- the audit evidence to be obtained regarding a particular topic (for example, section 570, *The Auditor's Consideration of an Entity's Ability to Continue as a Going Concern*);
- specific procedures to obtain audit evidence (for example, section 520, *Analytical Procedures*); and
- the evaluation of whether sufficient appropriate audit evidence has been obtained (for example, section 200, *Overall Objectives of the Independent Auditor and the Conduct of an Audit in Accordance With Generally Accepted Auditing Standards*, and section 330, *Performing Audit Procedures in Response to Assessed Risks and Evaluating the Audit Evidence Obtained*).

[Revised, August 2012, to reflect conforming changes necessary due to the issuance of SAS No. 126.]

Effective Date

.03 This section is effective for audits of financial statements for periods ending on or after December 15, 2012.

---

* This section has been codified using an "AU-C" identifier instead of an "AU" identifier. "AU-C" is a temporary identifier to avoid confusion with references to existing "AU" sections, which will remain in AICPA *Professional Standards* through 2013. The "AU-C" identifier will revert to "AU" in 2014, by which time substantially all engagements for which the "AU" sections were still effective are expected to be completed.

Objective

.04 The objective of the auditor is to design and perform audit procedures that enable the auditor to obtain sufficient appropriate audit evidence to be able to draw reasonable conclusions on which to base the auditor's opinion.

Definitions

.05 For purposes of generally accepted auditing standards, the following terms have the meanings attributed as follows:

Accounting records. The records of initial accounting entries and supporting records, such as checks and records of electronic fund transfers; invoices; contracts; the general and subsidiary ledgers; journal entries and other adjustments to the financial statements that are not reflected in journal entries; and records, such as work sheets and spreadsheets, supporting cost allocations, computations, reconciliations, and disclosures.

Appropriateness (of audit evidence). The measure of the quality of audit evidence (that is, its relevance and reliability in providing support for the conclusions on which the auditor's opinion is based).

Audit evidence. Information used by the auditor in arriving at the conclusions on which the auditor's opinion is based. Audit evidence includes both information contained in the accounting records underlying the financial statements and other information.

Management's specialist. An individual or organization possessing expertise in a field other than accounting or auditing, whose work in that field is used by the entity to assist the entity in preparing the financial statements.

Sufficiency (of audit evidence). The measure of the quantity of audit evidence. The quantity of the audit evidence needed is affected by the auditor's assessment of the risks of material misstatement and also by the quality of such audit evidence.

Requirements

Sufficient Appropriate Audit Evidence

.06 The auditor should design and perform audit procedures that are appropriate in the circumstances for the purpose of obtaining sufficient appropriate audit evidence. (Ref: par. .A1–.A26)

Information to Be Used as Audit Evidence

.07 When designing and performing audit procedures, the auditor should consider the relevance and reliability of the information to be used as audit evidence. (Ref: par. .A27–.A34)

.08 If information to be used as audit evidence has been prepared using the work of a management's specialist, the auditor should, to the extent necessary, taking into account the significance of that specialist's work for the auditor's purposes, (Ref: par. .A35–.A37) *a.* evaluate the competence, capabilities, and objectivity of that specialist; (Ref: par. .A38–.A44)

b. obtain an understanding of the work of that specialist; and (Ref: par. .A45–.A48)

c. evaluate the appropriateness of that specialist's work as audit evidence for the relevant assertion. (Ref: par. .A49)

.09 When using information produced by the entity, the auditor should evaluate whether the information is sufficiently reliable for the auditor's purposes, including, as necessary, in the following circumstances:

a. Obtaining audit evidence about the accuracy and completeness of the information (Ref: par. .A50–.A51)

b. Evaluating whether the information is sufficiently precise and detailed for the auditor's purposes (Ref: par. .A52)

Inconsistency in, or Doubts Over Reliability of, Audit Evidence

.10 If

a. audit evidence obtained from one source is inconsistent with that obtained from another or

b. the auditor has doubts about the reliability of information to be used as audit evidence,

the auditor should determine what modifications or additions to audit procedures are necessary to resolve the matter and should consider the effect of the matter, if any, on other aspects of the audit. (Ref: par. .A53)

Application and Other Explanatory Material

Sufficient Appropriate Audit Evidence (Ref: par. .06)

.A1 Audit evidence is necessary to support the auditor's opinion and report. It is cumulative in nature and is primarily obtained from audit procedures performed during the course of the audit. It may, however, also include information obtained from other sources, such as previous audits (provided that the auditor has determined whether changes have occurred since the previous audits that may affect its relevance to the current audit[1]), or a firm's quality control procedures for client acceptance and continuance. In addition to other sources inside and outside the entity, the entity's accounting records are an important source of audit evidence. Also, information that may be used as audit evidence may have been prepared using the work of management's specialist. Audit evidence comprises both information that supports and corroborates management's assertions and any information that contradicts such assertions. In addition, in some cases, the absence of information (for example, management's refusal to provide a requested representation) is used by the auditor and, therefore, also constitutes audit evidence.[2]

.A2 Most of the auditor's work in forming the auditor's opinion consists of obtaining and evaluating audit evidence. Audit procedures to obtain audit

---

[1] Paragraph .10 of section 315, *Understanding the Entity and Its Environment and Assessing the Risks of Material Misstatement*.

[2] Paragraph .A32 of section 200, *Overall Objectives of the Independent Auditor and the Conduct of an Audit in Accordance With Generally Accepted Auditing Standards*.

evidence can include inspection, observation, confirmation, recalculation, reperformance, and analytical procedures, often in some combination, in addition to inquiry. Although inquiry may provide important audit evidence and may even produce evidence of a misstatement, inquiry alone ordinarily does not provide sufficient audit evidence of the absence of a material misstatement at the assertion level, nor is inquiry alone sufficient to test the operating effectiveness of controls.

.A3 As explained in section 200, reasonable assurance is obtained when the auditor has obtained sufficient appropriate audit evidence to reduce audit risk (that is, the risk that the auditor expresses an inappropriate opinion when the financial statements are materially misstated) to an acceptably low level.[3]

.A4 The sufficiency and appropriateness of audit evidence are interrelated. *Sufficiency* is the measure of the quantity of audit evidence. The quantity of audit evidence needed is affected by the auditor's assessment of the risks of misstatement (the higher the assessed risks, the more audit evidence is likely to be required) and also by the quality of such audit evidence (the higher the quality, the less may be required). However, obtaining more audit evidence may not compensate for its poor quality.

.A5 *Appropriateness* is the measure of the quality of audit evidence (that is, its relevance and reliability in providing support for the conclusions on which the auditor's opinion is based). The reliability of evidence is influenced by its source and nature and is dependent on the individual circumstances under which it is obtained.

.A6 Section 330 requires the auditor to conclude whether sufficient appropriate audit evidence has been obtained.[4] Whether sufficient appropriate audit evidence has been obtained to reduce audit risk to an acceptably low level and, thereby, enable the auditor to draw reasonable conclusions on which to base the auditor's opinion, is a matter of professional judgment. Section 200 contains discussion of relevant factors when the auditor exercises professional judgment regarding whether sufficient appropriate audit evidence has been obtained.[5]

Sources of Audit Evidence

.A7 Some audit evidence is obtained by performing audit procedures to test the accounting records (for example, through analysis and review, by reperforming procedures followed in the financial reporting process, and by reconciling related types and applications of the same information). Through the performance of such audit procedures, the auditor may determine that the accounting records are internally consistent and agree to the financial statements. However, accounting records alone do not provide sufficient appropriate audit evidence on which to base an audit opinion on the financial statements.

.A8 More assurance is ordinarily obtained from consistent audit evidence obtained from different sources or of a different nature than from items of audit evidence considered individually. For example, corroborating information obtained from a source independent of the entity may increase the assurance that the auditor obtains from audit evidence that is generated internally, such as evidence existing within the accounting records, minutes of meetings, or a management representation.

---

[3] Paragraph .06 of section 200.

[4] Paragraph .28 of section 330, *Performing Audit Procedures in Response to Assessed Risks and Evaluating the Audit Evidence Obtained.*

[5] Paragraphs .A49–.A54 of section 200.

.A9 Information from sources independent of the entity that the auditor may use as audit evidence include confirmations from third parties, analysts' reports, and comparable data about competitors (benchmarking data).

Audit Procedures for Obtaining Audit Evidence

.A10 As required by and explained further in section 315 and section 330, audit evidence to draw reasonable conclusions on which to base the auditor's opinion is obtained by performing the following:[6, 7]

a. Risk assessment procedures

b. Further audit procedures, which comprise

i. tests of controls, when required by the AU-C sections or when the auditor has chosen to do so, and

ii. substantive procedures, which include tests of details and substantive analytical procedures.

.A11 The audit procedures described in paragraphs .A14–.A26 that follow may be used as risk assessment procedures, tests of controls, or substantive procedures, depending on the context in which they are applied by the auditor. As explained in section 330, audit evidence obtained from previous audits may, in certain circumstances, provide appropriate audit evidence, provided that the auditor has determined whether changes have occurred since the previous audit that may affect its relevance to the current audit.[8]

.A12 The nature and timing of the audit procedures to be used may be affected by the fact that some of the accounting data and other information may be available only in electronic form or only at certain points or periods in time. For example, source documents, such as purchase orders and invoices, may exist only in electronic form when an entity uses electronic commerce or may be discarded after scanning when an entity uses image processing systems to facilitate storage and reference.

.A13 Certain electronic information may not be retrievable after a specified period of time (for example, if files are changed and if backup files do not exist). Accordingly, the auditor may find it necessary, as a result of an entity's data retention policies, to request retention of some information for the performance of audit procedures at a later point in time or to perform audit procedures at a time when the information is available.

Inspection

.A14 Inspection involves examining records or documents, whether internal or external, in paper form, electronic form, or other media or a physical examination of an asset. Inspection of records and documents provides audit evidence of varying degrees of reliability, depending on their nature and source and, in the case of internal records and documents, the effectiveness of the controls over their production. An example of inspection used as a test of controls is inspection of records for evidence of authorization.

.A15 Some documents represent direct audit evidence of the existence of an asset (for example, a document constituting a financial instrument such as a stock or bond). Inspection of such documents may not necessarily provide audit evidence about ownership or value. In addition, inspecting an executed contract

---

[6] Paragraphs .05–.06 of section 315.

[7] Paragraphs .06–.07 of section 330.

[8] Paragraph .A38 of section 330.

may provide audit evidence relevant to the entity's application of accounting policies, such as revenue recognition.

.A16 Inspection of tangible assets may provide reliable audit evidence with respect to their existence but not necessarily about the entity's rights and obligations or the valuation of the assets. Inspection of individual inventory items may accompany the observation of inventory counting. For example, when observing an inventory count, the auditor may inspect individual inventory items (such as opening containers included in the inventory count to determine whether they are full or empty) to verify their existence.

Observation

.A17 Observation consists of looking at a process or procedure being performed by others (for example, the auditor's observation of inventory counting by the entity's personnel or the performance of control activities). Observation provides audit evidence about the performance of a process or procedure but is limited to the point in time at which the observation takes place and by the fact that the act of being observed may affect how the process or procedure is performed. Section 501, *Audit Evidence—Specific Considerations for Selected Items*, addresses the observation of the counting of inventory.[9]

External Confirmation

.A18 An external confirmation represents audit evidence obtained by the auditor as a direct written response to the auditor from a third party (the confirming party) in paper form or by electronic or other medium. External confirmation procedures frequently are relevant when addressing assertions associated with certain account balances and their elements. However, external confirmations need not be restricted to account balances only. For example, the auditor may request confirmation of the terms of agreements or transactions an entity has with third parties; the confirmation request may be designed to ask if any modifications have been made to the agreement and, if so, their relevant details. External confirmation procedures also are used to obtain audit evidence about the absence of certain conditions (for example, the absence of a side agreement that may influence revenue recognition). See section 505, *External Confirmations*, for further guidance.

Recalculation

.A19 Recalculation consists of checking the mathematical accuracy of documents or records. Recalculation may be performed manually or electronically.

Reperformance

.A20 Reperformance involves the independent execution of procedures or controls that were originally performed as part of the entity's internal control.

Analytical Procedures

.A21 Analytical procedures consist of evaluations of financial information through analysis of plausible relationships among both financial and nonfinancial data. Analytical procedures also encompass such investigation as is necessary of identified fluctuations and relationships that are inconsistent with other relevant information or that differ from expected values by a significant amount. See section 520 for further guidance.

.A22 *Scanning* is a type of analytical procedure involving the auditor's exercise of professional judgment to review accounting data to identify significant

---

[9] Paragraphs .11–.15 of section 501, *Audit Evidence—Specific Considerations for Selected Items*.

or unusual items to test. This may include the identification of unusual individual items within account balances or other data through the reading or analysis of, for example, entries in transaction listings, subsidiary ledgers, general ledger control accounts, adjusting entries, suspense accounts, reconciliations, and other detailed reports. Scanning may include searching for large or unusual items in the accounting records (for example, nonstandard journal entries), as well as in transaction data (for example, suspense accounts and adjusting journal entries) for indications of misstatements that have occurred. Electronic audit procedures may assist the auditor in identifying unusual items. When the auditor selects items for testing by scanning and those items are tested, the auditor obtains audit evidence about those items. The auditor's scanning also may provide some audit evidence about the items not selected for testing because the auditor has exercised professional judgment to determine that the items not selected are less likely to be misstated.

Inquiry

.A23 Inquiry consists of seeking information of knowledgeable persons, both financial and nonfinancial, within the entity or outside the entity. Inquiry is used extensively throughout the audit, in addition to other audit procedures. Inquiries may range from formal written inquiries to informal oral inquiries. Evaluating responses to inquiries is an integral part of the inquiry process.

.A24 Responses to inquiries may provide the auditor with information not previously possessed or with corroborative audit evidence. Alternatively, responses might provide information that differs significantly from other information that the auditor has obtained (for example, information regarding the possibility of management override of controls). In some cases, responses to inquiries provide a basis for the auditor to modify or perform additional audit procedures.

.A25 Although corroboration of evidence obtained through inquiry is often of particular importance, in the case of inquiries about management intent, the information available to support management's intent may be limited. In these cases, understanding management's past history of carrying out its stated intentions, management's stated reasons for choosing a particular course of action, and management's ability to pursue a specific course of action may provide relevant information to corroborate the evidence obtained through inquiry.

.A26 Regarding some matters, the auditor may consider it necessary to obtain written representations from management and, when appropriate, those charged with governance to confirm responses to oral inquiries. See section 580, *Written Representations*, for further guidance.

Information to Be Used as Audit Evidence

Relevance and Reliability (Ref: par. .07)

.A27 As noted in paragraph .A1, although audit evidence is primarily obtained from audit procedures performed during the course of the audit, it also may include information obtained from other sources (for example, previous audits, in certain circumstances, and a firm's quality control procedures for client acceptance and continuance). The quality of all audit evidence is affected by the relevance and reliability of the information upon which it is based.

Relevance

.A28 Relevance relates to the logical connection with, or bearing upon, the purpose of the audit procedure and, when appropriate, the assertion under consideration. The relevance of information to be used as audit evidence may be affected by the direction of testing. For example, if the purpose of an audit procedure is to test for overstatement in the existence or valuation of accounts payable, testing the recorded accounts payable may be a relevant audit procedure. On the other hand, when testing for understatement in the existence or valuation of accounts payable, testing the recorded accounts payable would not be relevant, but testing such information as subsequent disbursements, unpaid invoices, suppliers' statements, and unmatched receiving reports may be relevant.

.A29 A given set of audit procedures may provide audit evidence that is relevant to certain assertions but not others. For example, inspection of documents related to the collection of receivables after the period-end may provide audit evidence regarding existence and valuation but not necessarily cutoff. Similarly, obtaining audit evidence regarding a particular assertion (for example, the existence of inventory) is not a substitute for obtaining audit evidence regarding another assertion (for example, the valuation of that inventory). On the other hand, audit evidence from different sources or of a different nature may often be relevant to the same assertion.

.A30 Tests of controls are designed to evaluate the operating effectiveness of controls in preventing, or detecting and correcting, material misstatements at the assertion level. Designing tests of controls to obtain relevant audit evidence includes identifying conditions (characteristics or attributes) that indicate performance of a control and identifying deviation conditions that indicate departures from adequate performance. The presence or absence of those conditions can then be tested by the auditor.

.A31 Substantive procedures are designed to detect material misstatements at the assertion level. They comprise tests of details and substantive analytical procedures. Designing substantive procedures includes identifying conditions relevant to the purpose of the test that constitute a misstatement in the relevant assertion.

Reliability

.A32 The reliability of information to be used as audit evidence and, therefore, of the audit evidence itself is influenced by its source and nature and the circumstances under which it is obtained, including the controls over its preparation and maintenance, when relevant. Therefore, generalizations about the reliability of various kinds of audit evidence are subject to important exceptions. Even when information to be used as audit evidence is obtained from sources external to the entity, circumstances may exist that could affect its reliability. Information obtained from an independent external source may not be reliable, for example, if the source is not knowledgeable or a management specialist lacks objectivity. While recognizing that exceptions may exist, the following generalizations about the reliability of audit evidence may be useful:

- The reliability of audit evidence is increased when it is obtained from independent sources outside the entity.
- The reliability of audit evidence that is generated internally is increased when the related controls, including those over its preparation and maintenance, imposed by the entity are effective.
- Audit evidence obtained directly by the auditor (for example, observation of the application of a control) is more reliable than audit evidence obtained indirectly or by inference (for example, inquiry about the application of a control).
- Audit evidence in documentary form, whether paper, electronic, or other medium, is more reliable than evidence obtained orally

(for example, a contemporaneously written record of a meeting is more reliable than a subsequent oral representation of the matters discussed).

- Audit evidence provided by original documents is more reliable than audit evidence provided by photocopies, facsimiles, or documents that have been filmed, digitized, or otherwise transformed into electronic form, the reliability of which may depend on the controls over their preparation and maintenance.

.A33 Section 520 provides further guidance regarding the reliability of data used for purposes of designing analytical procedures as substantive procedures.[10]

.A34 Section 240, *Consideration of Fraud in a Financial Statement Audit*, addresses circumstances in which the auditor has reason to believe that a document may not be authentic or may have been modified without that modification having been disclosed to the auditor.[11]

Reliability of Information Produced by a Management's Specialist (Ref: par. .08)

.A35 The preparation of an entity's financial statements may require expertise in a field other than accounting or auditing, such as actuarial calculations, valuations, or engineering data. The entity uses a management's specialist in these fields to obtain the needed expertise to prepare the financial statements. Failure to do so when such expertise is necessary increases the risks of material misstatement and may be a significant deficiency or material weakness.[12]

.A36 When information to be used as audit evidence has been prepared using the work of a management's specialist, the requirement in paragraph .08 applies. For example, an individual or organization may possess expertise in the application of models to estimate the fair value of securities for which no observable market exists. If the individual or organization applies that expertise in making an estimate which the entity uses in preparing its financial statements, the individual or organization is a management's specialist and paragraph .08 applies. If, on the other hand, that individual or organization merely provides price data regarding private transactions not otherwise available to the entity which the entity uses in its own estimation methods, such information, if used as audit evidence, is subject to paragraph .07, but it is not the use of a management's specialist by the entity.

.A37 The nature, timing, and extent of audit procedures with regard to the requirement in paragraph .08 may be affected by such matters as the following:

- The nature and complexity of the matter to which the management's specialist relates
- The risks of material misstatement of the matter
- The availability of alternative sources of audit evidence
- The nature, scope, and objectives of the work of the management's specialist

---

[10] Paragraph .05 of section 520, *Analytical Procedures*.

[11] Paragraph .A11 of section 240, *Consideration of Fraud in a Financial Statement Audit*.

[12] See section 265, *Communicating Internal Control Related Matters Identified in an Audit*, for further guidance.

- Whether the management's specialist is employed by the entity or is a party engaged by it to provide relevant services
- The extent to which management can exercise control or influence over the work of the management's specialist
- Whether the management's specialist is subject to technical performance standards or other professional or industry requirements
- The nature and extent of any controls within the entity over the work of the management's specialist
- The auditor's knowledge and experience of the field of expertise management's specialist
- The auditor's previous experience of the work of that specialist

The Competence, Capabilities, and Objectivity of a Management's Specialist (Ref: par. .08a)

.A38 Competence relates to the nature and level of expertise of the management's specialist. Capability relates to the ability of the management's specialist to exercise that competence in the circumstances. Factors that influence capability may include, for example, geographic location and the availability of time and resources. Objectivity relates to the possible effects that bias, conflict of interest, or the influence of others may have on the professional or business judgment of the management's specialist. The competence, capabilities, and objectivity of a management's specialist, and any controls within the entity over that specialist's work, are important factors with regard to the reliability of any information produced by a management's specialist.

.A39 Information regarding the competence, capabilities, and objectivity of a management's specialist may come from a variety of sources, such as the following:

- Personal experience with previous work of that specialist
- Discussions with that specialist
- Discussions with others who are familiar with that specialist's work
- Knowledge of that specialist's qualifications, membership in a professional body or industry association, license to practice, or other forms of external recognition
- Published papers or books written by that specialist
- An auditor's specialist, if any, that assists the auditor in obtaining sufficient appropriate audit evidence with respect to information produced by the management's specialist

.A40 Matters relevant to evaluating the competence, capabilities, and objectivity of a management's specialist include whether that specialist's work is subject to technical performance standards or other professional or industry requirements, for example, ethical standards and other membership requirements of a professional body or industry association, accreditation standards of a licensing body, or requirements imposed by law or regulation.

.A41 Other matters that may be relevant include

- the relevance of the capabilities and competence of the management's specialist to the matter for which that specialist's work will be used, including any areas of specialty within that specialist's field. For example, a particular actuary may specialize in property and casualty insurance but have limited expertise regarding pension calculations.

- the competence of the management's specialist with respect to relevant accounting requirements, for example, knowledge of assumptions and methods, including models, when applicable, that are consistent with the applicable financial reporting framework.
- whether unexpected events, changes in conditions, or the audit evidence obtained from the results of audit procedures indicate that it may be necessary to reconsider the initial evaluation of the competence, capabilities, and objectivity of the management's specialist as the audit progresses.

.A42 A broad range of circumstances may threaten objectivity, for example, self-interest threats, advocacy threats, familiarity threats, self-review threats, and intimidation threats. Safeguards may reduce such threats and may be created either by external structures (for example, the profession, legislation, or regulation of the management's specialist) or by the work of the management's specialist environment (for example, quality control policies and procedures).

.A43 Although safeguards cannot eliminate all threats to the objectivity of a management's specialist, threats such as intimidation threats may be of less significance to a specialist engaged by the entity than to a specialist employed by the entity, and the effectiveness of safeguards such as quality control policies and procedures may be greater. Because the threat to objectivity created by being an employee of the entity will always be present, a specialist employed by the entity cannot ordinarily be regarded as being more likely to be objective than other employees of the entity.

.A44 When evaluating the objectivity of a specialist engaged by the entity, it may be relevant to discuss with management and that specialist any interests and relationships that may create threats to the specialist's objectivity and any applicable safeguards, including any professional requirements that apply to the specialist, and to evaluate whether the safeguards are adequate. Interests and relationships creating threats may include the following:

- Financial interests
- Business and personal relationships
- Provision of other services

Obtaining an Understanding of the Work of the Management's Specialist (Ref: par. .08b)

.A45 An understanding of the work of the management's specialist includes an understanding of the relevant field of expertise. An understanding of the relevant field of expertise may be obtained in conjunction with the auditor's determination of whether the auditor has the expertise to evaluate the work of the management's specialist, or whether the auditor needs an auditor's specialist for this purpose.[13]

.A46 Aspects of the field of the management's specialist relevant to the auditor's understanding may include

- whether that specialist's field has areas of specialty within it that are relevant to the audit.

---

[13] Paragraph .07 of section 620, *Using the Work of an Auditor's Specialist*.

- whether any professional or other standards and regulatory or legal requirements apply.
- what assumptions and methods are used by the management's specialist and whether they are generally accepted within that specialist's field and appropriate for financial reporting purposes.
- the nature of internal and external data or information the management's specialist uses.

.A47 In the case of a management's specialist engaged by the entity, there will ordinarily be an engagement letter or other written form of agreement between the entity and that specialist. Evaluating that agreement when obtaining an understanding of the work of the management's specialist may assist the auditor in determining for the auditor's purposes the appropriateness of

- the nature, scope, and objectives of that specialist's work;
- the respective roles and responsibilities of management and that specialist; and
- the nature, timing, and extent of communication between management and that specialist, including the form of any report to be provided by that specialist.

.A48 In the case of a management's specialist employed by the entity, it is less likely that there will be a written agreement of this kind. Inquiry of the specialist and other members of management may be the most appropriate way for the auditor to obtain the necessary understanding.

Evaluating the Appropriateness of the Work of the Management's Specialist (Ref: par. .08c)

.A49 Considerations when evaluating the appropriateness of the work of the management's specialist as audit evidence for the relevant assertion may include

- the relevance and reasonableness of that specialist's findings or conclusions, their consistency with other audit evidence, and whether they have been appropriately reflected in the financial statements;
- if that specialist's work involves use of significant assumptions and methods, the relevance and reasonableness of those assumptions and methods; and
- if that specialist's work involves significant use of source data, the relevance, completeness, and accuracy of that source data.

Information Produced by the Entity and Used for the Auditor's Purposes (Ref: par. .09a–b)

.A50 In order for the auditor to obtain reliable audit evidence, information produced by the entity, including any management's specialist, that is used for performing audit procedures needs to be sufficiently complete and accurate. For example, the effectiveness of an audit procedure, such as applying standard prices to records of sales volume to develop an expectation of sales revenue, is affected by the accuracy of the price information and the completeness and accuracy of the sales volume data. Similarly, if the auditor intends to test a population (for example, payments) for a certain characteristic (for example, authorization), the results of the test will be less reliable if the population from which items are selected for testing is not complete.

.A51 Obtaining audit evidence about the accuracy and completeness of such information may be accomplished concurrently with the actual audit procedure applied to the information when obtaining such audit evidence is an integral part of the audit procedure itself. In other situations, the auditor may have obtained audit evidence of the accuracy and completeness of such information by testing controls over the preparation and maintenance of the information. In some situations, however, the auditor may determine that additional audit procedures are needed.

.A52 In some cases, the auditor may intend to use information produced by the entity for other audit purposes. For example, the auditor may intend to use the entity's performance measures for the purpose of analytical procedures or use the entity's information produced for monitoring activities such as internal auditor's reports. In such cases, the appropriateness of the audit evidence obtained is affected by whether the information is sufficiently precise or detailed for the auditor's purposes. For example, performance measures used by management may not be precise enough to detect material misstatements.

Inconsistency in, or Doubts Over Reliability of, Audit Evidence (Ref: par. .10)

.A53 Obtaining audit evidence from different sources or of a different nature may indicate that an individual item of audit evidence is not reliable, such as when audit evidence obtained from one source is inconsistent with that obtained from another. This may be the case when, for example, responses to inquiries of management, internal audit, and others are inconsistent or when responses to inquiries of those charged with governance made to corroborate the responses to inquiries of management are inconsistent with the response by management. Section 230, *Audit Documentation*, includes a specific documentation requirement if the auditor identified information that is inconsistent with the auditor's final conclusion regarding a significant finding or issue.[14]

---

[14] Paragraph .12 of section 230, *Audit Documentation*.

AU-C Section 9500 *

Audit Evidence: Auditing Interpretations of Section 500

1. The Effect of an Inability to Obtain Audit Evidence Relating to Income Tax Accruals

.01 *Question*—The IRS's audit manual instructs its examiners on how to secure from corporate officials "tax accrual workpapers" or the "tax liability contingency analysis," including "a memorandum discussing items reflected in the financial statements as income or expense where the ultimate tax treatment is unclear." The audit manual states that the examiner may question or summons a corporate officer or manager concerning the "knowledge of the items that make up the corporation's contingent reserve accounts." It also states that "in unusual circumstances, access may be had to the audit or tax workpapers" of an independent accountant or an accounting firm after attempting to obtain the information from the taxpayer. IRS policy also includes specific procedures to be followed in circumstances involving "listed transactions," to help address what the IRS considers to be abusive tax avoidance transactions (Internal Revenue Manual, section 4024.2-.5, 5/14/81, and Internal Revenue Service Announcement 2002-63, 6/17/02).

.02 Concern over IRS access to tax accrual working papers might cause some entities to not prepare or maintain appropriate documentation of the calculation or contents of the accrual for income taxes included in the financial statements or to deny the independent auditor access to such information.

.03 What effect does this situation have on the auditor's opinion on the financial statements?

.04 *Interpretation*—The entity is responsible for its tax accrual, the underlying support for the accrual, and the related disclosures. Limitations on the auditor's access to information considered necessary to audit the tax accrual will affect the auditor's ability to issue an unmodified opinion on the financial statements.

.05 The auditor is required to design and perform audit procedures that are appropriate in the circumstances for the purpose of obtaining sufficient appropriate audit evidence.[1]

.06 If the entity does not have appropriate documentation of the calculation or contents of the accrual for income taxes and denies the auditor access to entity personnel responsible for making the judgments and estimates relating to the accrual, the auditor is required to conclude whether sufficient appropriate audit evidence has been obtained. If the auditor has not obtained sufficient

---

* This section has been codified using an "AU-C" identifier instead of an "AU" identifier. "AU-C" is a temporary identifier to avoid confusion with references to existing "AU" sections, which will remain in AICPA *Professional Standards* through 2013. The "AU-C" identifier will revert to "AU" in 2014, by which time substantially all engagements for which the "AU" sections were still effective are expected to be completed.

[1] Paragraph .06 of section 500, *Audit Evidence*.

appropriate audit evidence about a relevant assertion, the auditor is required to attempt to obtain further audit evidence.[2]

.07 If the auditor is unable to obtain sufficient appropriate audit evidence, the auditor is required to express a qualified opinion or disclaim an opinion on the financial statements.[3]

.08 If the entity has appropriate documentation but denies the auditor access to it and to entity personnel who possess the information, the auditor is required to perform procedures to evaluate the consequence of an inability to obtain sufficient appropriate audit evidence due to a management-imposed limitation.[4]

.09 The auditor is required to request management to provide a written representation that it has provided the auditor with all relevant information and access, as agreed upon in the terms of the audit engagement.[5] If management does not provide the written representations required by section 580, *Written Representations*, the auditor is required to disclaim an opinion on the financial statements in accordance section 705, *Modifications to the Opinion in the Independent Auditor's Report*, or withdraw from the engagement.[6]

.10 *Question*—An entity may allow the auditor to inspect its tax accrual workpapers but request that copies not be retained for audit documentation, particularly copies of the tax liability contingency analysis. The entity also may suggest that the auditor not prepare and maintain similar documentation of his or her own. What are the auditor's requirements in deciding a response to such a request?

.11 *Interpretation*—Section 230, *Audit Documentation*, defines *audit documentation* as the record of audit procedures performed, relevant audit evidence obtained, and conclusions the auditor reached.[7] The auditor is required to prepare audit documentation that is sufficient to enable an experienced auditor, having no previous connection with the audit, to understand

a. the nature, timing, and extent of the audit procedures performed to comply with generally accepted auditing standards and applicable legal and regulatory requirements;

b. the results of the audit procedures performed and the audit evidence obtained; and

c. significant findings or issues arising during the audit, the conclusions reached thereon, and significant judgments made in reaching those conclusions.[8]

Section 500, *Audit Evidence*, states that other information includes information obtained by the auditor from inquiry, observation, inspection, and physical examination. The quantity, type, and content of audit documentation are matters of the auditor's judgment.

.12 The audit documentation of the results of auditing procedures directed at the tax accounts and related disclosures also includes sufficient appropriate

---

[2] Paragraphs .28–.29 of section 330, *Performing Audit Procedures in Response to Assessed Risks and Evaluating the Audit Evidence Obtained*.

[3] Paragraphs .08 and .10 of section 705, *Modifications to the Opinion in the Independent Auditor's Report*.

[4] Paragraphs .11–.14 of section 705.

[5] Paragraph .11*a* of section 580, *Written Representations*.

[6] Paragraph .25 of section 580.

[7] Paragraph .06 of section 230, *Audit Documentation*.

[8] Paragraph .08 of section 230.

audit evidence about the significant elements of the entity's tax liability contingency analysis. This audit documentation includes copies of the entity's documents, schedules, or analyses (or auditor-prepared summaries thereof) to enable the auditor to support his or her conclusions regarding the appropriateness of the entity's accounting and disclosure of significant tax-related contingency matters. The audit documentation reflects the procedures performed and conclusions reached by the auditor and, for significant matters, include the entity's documentary support for its financial statement amounts and disclosures.

.13 The audit documentation includes the significant elements of the entity's analysis of tax contingencies or reserves, including roll-forward of material changes to such reserves. In addition, the audit documentation provides the entity's position and support for income tax related disclosures, such as its effective tax rate reconciliation, and support for its intraperiod allocation of income tax expense or benefit to continuing operations and to items other than continuing operations. When applicable, the audit documentation also includes the entity's basis for assessing deferred tax assets and related valuation allowances and its support for applying the "indefinite reversal criteria" discussed in FASB ASC 740-30-25-17, including its specific plans for reinvestment of undistributed foreign earnings.

.14 *Question*—In some situations, an entity may furnish its external legal counsel or in-house legal or tax counsel with information concerning the tax contingencies covered by the accrual for income taxes included in the financial statements and ask counsel to provide the auditor an opinion on the adequacy of the accrual for those contingencies.

.15 In such circumstances, rather than inspecting and obtaining documentary evidence of the entity's tax liability contingency analysis and making inquiries of the entity, may the auditor consider the counsel as a management's specialist within the meaning of section 500 and rely solely on counsel's opinion as an appropriate procedure for obtaining audit evidence to support his or her opinion on the financial statements?

.16 *Interpretation*—No. The opinion of legal counsel in this situation does not provide sufficient appropriate audit evidence to afford a reasonable basis for an opinion on the financial statements. The opinion of legal counsel on specific tax issues that he or she is asked to address and to which he or she has devoted substantive attention, as contemplated by the legal counsel's response to an auditor's letter of inquiry, can be useful to the auditor in forming his or her own opinion.

.17 An opinion from an entity's legal or tax counsel, similar to other work products obtained from a management's specialist, is useful in situations in which the auditor does not have adequate technical training and proficiency. In this case, however, the auditor's education, training, and experience, on the other hand, do enable him or her to be knowledgeable concerning income tax matters and competent to assess their presentation in the financial statements.

.18 Therefore, while the opinion of legal counsel on specific tax issues can be useful to the auditor in forming his or her own opinion, the audit of income tax accounts requires a combination of tax expertise and knowledge about the entity's business that is accumulated during all aspects of an audit. Therefore, as previously stated, it is not appropriate for the auditor to rely solely on such legal opinion.

.19 *Question*—A entity may have obtained the advice or opinion of an outside tax adviser related to the tax accrual or matters affecting it, including tax contingencies, and further may attempt to limit the auditor's access to such advice or opinion, or limit the auditor's documentation of such advice or opinion. This limitation on the auditor's access may be proposed on the basis that such information is privileged. Can the auditor rely solely on the conclusions of third-party tax advisers? What audit evidence should the auditor obtain and include in the audit documentation?

.20 *Interpretation*—As discussed in paragraphs .16–.18 of this interpretation, the auditor cannot accept an entity's or a third party's analysis or opinion with respect to tax matters without careful consideration and application of the auditor's tax expertise and knowledge about the entity's business. As a result of applying such knowledge to the facts, the auditor may encounter situations in which the auditor either disagrees with the position taken by the entity, or its advisers, or does not have sufficient appropriate audit evidence to support his or her opinion.

.21 If the entity's support for the tax accrual or matters affecting it, including tax contingencies, is based upon an opinion issued by an outside adviser with respect to a potentially material matter, the auditor is required to obtain access to the opinion,[9] notwithstanding potential concerns regarding attorney-client or other forms of privilege. The audit documentation includes either the actual advice or opinions rendered by an outside adviser or other sufficient documentation or abstracts supporting both the transactions or facts addressed as well as the analysis and conclusions reached by the entity and adviser. Alternatives such as redacted or modified opinions may be considered but must, nonetheless, include sufficient content to articulate and document the entity's position so that the auditor can formulate his or her conclusion. Similarly, it may be possible to accept an entity's analysis summarizing an outside adviser's opinion, but the entity's analysis must provide sufficient appropriate audit evidence for the auditor to formulate his or her conclusion. In addition, written representations may be obtained stating that the entity has not received any advice or opinions that are contradictory to the entity's support for the tax accrual.

.22 If the auditor is unable to accumulate sufficient appropriate audit evidence about whether there is a supported and reasonable basis for the entity's position, the auditor is required to consider the effect of this scope limitation on his or her opinion.[10]

[Issue Date: March 1981; Amended: April 9, 2003; Revised: December 2005; Revised: March 2006; Revised: March 2008; Revised: June 2009; Revised: October 2011, effective for audits of financial statements for periods ending on or after December 15, 2012.]

---

[9] Paragraph .11 of this interpretation.

[10] Paragraphs .11–.14 of section 705.

AU-C Section 501 *

Audit Evidence—Specific Considerations for Selected Items

Source: SAS No. 122.

Effective for audits of financial statements for periods ending on or after December 15, 2012.

Introduction

Scope of This Section

.01 This section addresses specific considerations by the auditor in obtaining sufficient appropriate audit evidence, in accordance with section 330, *Performing Audit Procedures in Response to Assessed Risks and Evaluating the Audit Evidence Obtained*; section 500, *Audit Evidence*; and other relevant AU-C sections, regarding certain aspects of (*a*) investments in securities and derivative instruments; (*b*) inventory; (*c*) litigation, claims, and assessments involving the entity; and (*d*) segment information in an audit of financial statements.

Effective Date

.02 This section is effective for audits of financial statements for periods ending on or after December 15, 2012.

Objective

.03 The objective of the auditor is to obtain sufficient appropriate audit evidence regarding the

a. valuation of investments in securities and derivative instruments;

b. existence and condition of inventory;

c. completeness of litigation, claims, and assessments involving the entity; and

d. presentation and disclosure of segment information, in accordance with the applicable financial reporting framework.

---

* This section has been codified using an "AU-C" identifier instead of an "AU" identifier. "AU-C" is a temporary identifier to avoid confusion with references to existing "AU" sections, which will remain in AICPA *Professional Standards* through 2013. The "AU-C" identifier will revert to "AU" in 2014, by which time substantially all engagements for which the "AU" sections were still effective are expected to be completed.

Requirements

Investments in Securities and Derivative Instruments (Ref: par. .A1–.A3)

Investments in Securities When Valuations Are Based on the Investee's Financial Results (Excluding Investments Accounted for Using the Equity Method of Accounting)

.04 When investments in securities are valued based on an investee's financial results, excluding investments accounted for using the equity method of accounting, the auditor should obtain sufficient appropriate audit evidence in support of the investee's financial results, as follows: (Ref: par. .A4–.A8)

a. Obtain and read available financial statements of the investee and the accompanying audit report, if any, including determining whether the report of the other auditor is satisfactory for this purpose.

b. If the investee's financial statements are not audited, or if the audit report on such financial statements is not satisfactory to the auditor, apply, or request that the investor entity arrange with the investee to have another auditor apply, appropriate auditing procedures to such financial statements, considering the materiality of the investment in relation to the financial statements of the investor entity.

c. If the carrying amount of the investment reflects factors that are not recognized in the investee's financial statements or fair values of assets that are materially different from the investee's carrying amounts, obtain sufficient appropriate audit evidence in support of such amounts.

d. If the difference between the financial statement period of the entity and the investee has or could have a material effect on the entity's financial statements, determine whether the entity's management has properly considered the lack of comparability and determine the effect, if any, on the auditor's report. (Ref: par. .A9)

If the auditor is not able to obtain sufficient appropriate audit evidence because of an inability to perform one or more of these procedures, the auditor should determine the effect on the auditor's opinion, in accordance with section 705, *Modifications to the Opinion in the Independent Auditor's Report*.

.05 With respect to subsequent events and transactions of the investee occurring after the date of the investee's financial statements but before the date of the auditor's report, the auditor should obtain and read available interim financial statements of the investee and make appropriate inquiries of management of the investor to identify such events and transactions that may be material to the investor's financial statements and that may need to be recognized or disclosed in the investor's financial statements. (Ref: par. .A10)

Investments in Derivative Instruments and Securities Measured or Disclosed at Fair Value

.06 With respect to investments in derivative instruments and securities measured or disclosed at fair value, the auditor should

a. determine whether the applicable financial reporting framework specifies the method to be used to determine the fair value of the entity's derivative instruments and investments in securities and *b.* evaluate whether the determination of fair value is consistent with the specified valuation method. (Ref: par. .A11–.A13)

.07 If estimates of fair value of derivative instruments or securities are obtained from broker-dealers or other third-party sources based on valuation models, the auditor should understand the method used by the broker-dealer or other third-party source in developing the estimate and consider the applicability of section 500.[1] (Ref: par. .A14–.A15)

.08 If derivative instruments or securities are valued by the entity using a valuation model, the auditor should obtain sufficient appropriate audit evidence supporting management's assertions about fair value determined using the model. (Ref: par. .A16)

Impairment Losses

.09 The auditor should

a. evaluate management's conclusion (including the relevance of the information considered) about the need to recognize an impairment loss for a decline in a security's fair value below its cost or carrying amount and

b. obtain sufficient appropriate audit evidence supporting the amount of any impairment adjustment recorded, including evaluating whether the requirements of the applicable financial reporting framework have been complied with. (Ref: par. .A17–.A18)

Unrealized Appreciation or Depreciation

.10 The auditor should obtain sufficient appropriate audit evidence about the amount of unrealized appreciation or depreciation in the fair value of a derivative that is recognized or that is disclosed because of the ineffectiveness of a hedge, including evaluating whether the requirements of the applicable financial reporting framework have been complied with. (Ref: par. .A19)

Inventory

.11 If inventory is material to the financial statements, the auditor should obtain sufficient appropriate audit evidence regarding the existence and condition of inventory[2] by

a. attending physical inventory counting, unless impracticable, to (Ref: par. .A20–.A22)

i. evaluate management's instructions and procedures for recording and controlling the results of the entity's physical inventory counting, (Ref: par. .A23)

ii. observe the performance of management's count procedures, (Ref: par. .A24)

iii. inspect the inventory, and (Ref: par. .A25)

iv. perform test counts and (Ref: par. .A26)

b. performing audit procedures over the entity's final inventory records to determine whether they accurately reflect actual inventory count results. (Ref: par. .A27–.A30)

---

[1] Paragraph .08 of section 500, *Audit Evidence*, addresses management's specialists.

[2] Section 330, *Performing Audit Procedures in Response to Assessed Risks and Evaluating the Audit Evidence Obtained*, addresses the auditor's procedures to respond to the assessed risks of material misstatements at the relevant assertion level.

.12 If physical inventory counting is conducted at a date other than the date of the financial statements, the auditor should, in addition to the procedures required by paragraph .11, perform audit procedures to obtain audit evidence about whether changes in inventory between the count date and the date of the financial statements are recorded properly. (Ref: par. .A31–.A33)

.13 If the auditor is unable to attend physical inventory counting due to unforeseen circumstances, the auditor should make or observe some physical counts on an alternative date and perform audit procedures on intervening transactions.

.14 If attendance at physical inventory counting is impracticable, the auditor should perform alternative audit procedures to obtain sufficient appropriate audit evidence regarding the existence and condition of inventory. If it is not possible to do so, the auditor should modify the opinion in the auditor's report, in accordance with section 705. (Ref: par. .A34–.A36)

.15 If inventory under the custody and control of a third party is material to the financial statements, the auditor should obtain sufficient appropriate audit evidence regarding the existence and condition of that inventory by performing one or both of the following:

a. Request confirmation from the third party regarding the quantities and condition of inventory held on behalf of the entity (Ref: par. .A37)

b. Perform inspection or other audit procedures appropriate in the circumstances (Ref: par. .A38)

Litigation, Claims, and Assessments

.16 The auditor should design and perform audit procedures to identify litigation, claims, and assessments involving the entity that may give rise to a risk of material misstatement, including (Ref: par. .A39–.A45)

a. inquiring of management and, when applicable, others within the entity, including in-house legal counsel;

b. obtaining from management a description and evaluation of litigation, claims, and assessments that existed at the date of the financial statements being reported on and during the period from the date of the financial statements to the date the information is furnished, including an identification of those matters referred to legal counsel;[3]

c. reviewing minutes of meetings of those charged with governance; documents obtained from management concerning litigation, claims, and assessments; and correspondence between the entity and its external legal counsel; and

d. reviewing legal expense accounts and invoices from external legal counsel.

.17 For actual or potential litigation, claims, and assessments identified based on the audit procedures required in paragraph .16, the auditor should obtain audit evidence relevant to the following factors:

a. The period in which the underlying cause for legal action occurred

---

[3] For purposes of this section, the term *legal counsel* refers to the entity's in-house legal counsel and external legal counsel.

b. The degree of probability of an unfavorable outcome

c. The amount or range of potential loss

Communication With the Entity's Legal Counsel

.18 Unless the audit procedures required by paragraph .16 indicate that no actual or potential litigation, claims, or assessments that may give rise to a risk of material misstatement exist, the auditor should, in addition to the procedures required by other AU-C sections, seek direct communication with the entity's external legal counsel. The auditor should do so through a letter of inquiry prepared by management and sent by the auditor requesting the entity's external legal counsel to communicate directly with the auditor. (Ref: par. .A40 and .A46–.A63)

.19 In addition to the direct communications with the entity's external legal counsel referred to in paragraph .18, the auditor should, in cases when the entity's in-house legal counsel has the responsibility for the entity's litigation, claims, and assessments, seek direct communication with the entity's in-house legal counsel through a letter of inquiry similar to the letter referred to in paragraph .18. Audit evidence obtained from in-house legal counsel in this manner is not, however, a substitute for the auditor seeking direct communication with the entity's external legal counsel, as described in paragraph .18. (Ref: par. .A64)

.20 The auditor should document the basis for any determination not to seek direct communication with the entity's legal counsel, as required by paragraphs .18–.19.

.21 The auditor should request management to authorize the entity's legal counsel to discuss applicable matters with the auditor.

.22 As described in paragraphs .18–.19, the auditor should request, through letter(s) of inquiry, the entity's legal counsel to inform the auditor of any litigation, claims, assessments, and unasserted claims that the counsel is aware of, together with an assessment of the outcome of the litigation, claims, and assessments, and an estimate of the financial implications, including costs involved. Each letter of inquiry should include, but not be limited to, the following matters: (Ref: par. .A69)

a. Identification of the entity, including subsidiaries, and the date of the audit

b. A list prepared by management (or a request by management that the legal counsel prepare a list) that describes and evaluates pending or threatened litigation, claims, and assessments with respect to which the legal counsel has been engaged and to which the legal counsel has devoted substantive attention on behalf of the company in the form of legal consultation or representation

c. A list prepared by management that describes and evaluates unasserted claims and assessments that management considers to be probable of assertion and that, if asserted, would have at least a reasonable possibility of an unfavorable outcome with respect to which the legal counsel has been engaged and to which the legal counsel has devoted substantive attention on behalf of the entity in the form of legal consultation or representation

d. Regarding each matter listed in item *b*, a request that the legal counsel either provide the following information or comment on those matters on which the legal counsel's views may differ from those stated by management, as appropriate:

i. A description of the nature of the matter, the progress of the case to date, and the action that the entity intends to take (for example, to contest the matter vigorously or to seek an out-of-court settlement)

ii. An evaluation of the likelihood of an unfavorable outcome and an estimate, if one can be made, of the amount or range of potential loss (Ref: par. .A65)

iii. With respect to a list prepared by management (or by the legal counsel at management's request), an identification of the omission of any pending or threatened litigation, claims, and assessments or a statement that the list of such matters is complete

e. Regarding each matter listed in item *c*, a request that the legal counsel comment on those matters on which the legal counsel's views concerning the description or evaluation of the matter may differ from those stated by management

f. A statement that management understands that whenever, in the course of performing legal services for the entity with respect to a matter recognized to involve an unasserted possible claim or assessment that may call for financial statement disclosure, the legal counsel has formed a professional conclusion that the entity should disclose or consider disclosure concerning such possible claim or assessment, the legal counsel, as a matter of professional responsibility to the entity, will so advise the entity and will consult with the entity concerning the question of such disclosure and the requirements of the applicable financial reporting framework (for example, the requirements of Financial Accounting Standards Board [FASB] *Accounting Standards Codification* [ASC] 450, *Contingencies*)

g. A request that the legal counsel confirm whether the understanding described in item *f* is correct

h. A request that the legal counsel specifically identify the nature of, and reasons for, any limitation on the response

i. A request that the legal counsel specify the effective date of the response

.23 When the auditor is aware that an entity has changed legal counsel or that the legal counsel previously engaged by the entity has resigned, the auditor should consider making inquiries of management or others about the reasons such legal counsel is no longer associated with the entity. (Ref: par. .A55)

.24 The auditor should modify the opinion in the auditor's report, in accordance with section 705, if (Ref: par. .A56–.A65)

a. the entity's legal counsel refuses to respond appropriately to the letter of inquiry and the auditor is unable to obtain sufficient appropriate audit evidence by performing alternative audit procedures or

b. management refuses to give the auditor permission to communicate or meet with the entity's external legal counsel.

Segment Information

.25 The auditor should obtain sufficient appropriate audit evidence regarding the presentation and disclosure of segment information, in accordance with the applicable financial reporting framework, by (Ref: par. .A66–.A67)

a. obtaining an understanding of the methods used by management in determining segment information and (Ref: par. .A68)

   i. evaluating whether such methods are likely to result in disclosure in accordance with the applicable financial reporting framework and

   ii. when appropriate, testing the application of such methods and

b. performing analytical procedures or other audit procedures appropriate in the circumstances.

Application and Other Explanatory Material

Investments in Securities and Derivative Instruments (Ref: par. .04–.10)

.A1 Evaluating audit evidence for assertions about investments in securities and derivative instruments may involve professional judgment because the assertions, especially those about valuation, are based on highly subjective assumptions or are particularly sensitive to changes in the underlying circumstances. Valuation assertions may be based on assumptions about the occurrence of future events for which expectations are difficult to develop or on assumptions about conditions expected to exist over a long period (for example, default rates or prepayment rates). Accordingly, competent persons could reach different conclusions about estimates of fair values or estimates of ranges of fair values. Professional judgment also may be necessary when evaluating audit evidence for assertions based on features of the security or derivative and the requirements of the applicable financial reporting framework, including underlying criteria for hedge accounting, which are extremely complex. For example, determining the fair value of a structured note may require consideration of a variety of features of the note that react differently to changes in economic conditions. In addition, one or more other derivatives may be designated to hedge changes in cash flows under the note. Evaluating audit evidence about the fair value of the note, the determination of whether the hedge is highly effective, and the allocation of changes in fair value to earnings and other comprehensive income requires professional judgment.

.A2 This section addresses only certain specific aspects relating to auditing valuation of investments in securities and derivative instruments. Section 540, *Auditing Accounting Estimates, Including Fair Value Accounting Estimates, and Related Disclosures*, addresses the auditor's responsibilities relating to accounting estimates, including fair value accounting estimates and related disclosures in an audit of financial statements. The Audit Guide *Auditing Derivative Instruments, Hedging Activities, and Investments in Securities* provides additional and more detailed guidance to auditors related to planning and performing auditing procedures for assertions about derivative instruments, hedging activities, and investments in securities.

Investments in Securities When Valuations Are Based on Cost

.A3 Procedures to obtain evidence about the valuation of securities that are recorded at cost may include inspection of documentation of the purchase price, confirmation with the issuer or holder, and testing discount or premium amortization either by recomputation or through the use of analytical procedures.

Investments in Securities When Valuations Are Based on the Investee's Financial Results (Excluding Investments Accounted for Using the Equity Method of Accounting) (Ref: par. .04–.05)

.A4 Section 600, *Special Considerations—Audits of Group Financial Statements (Including the Work of Component Auditors)*, addresses auditing investments accounted for using the equity method of accounting.

.A5 For valuations based on an investee's financial results (excluding investments accounted for using the equity method of accounting), obtaining and reading the financial statements of the investee that have been audited by an auditor whose report is satisfactory may be sufficient for the purpose of obtaining sufficient appropriate audit evidence. In determining whether the report of another auditor is satisfactory, the auditor may perform procedures such as making inquiries regarding the professional reputation and standing of the other auditor, visiting the other auditor, discussing the audit procedures followed and the results thereof, and reviewing the audit plan and audit documentation of the other auditor.

.A6 After obtaining and reading the audited financial statements of an investee, the auditor may conclude that additional audit procedures are necessary to obtain sufficient appropriate audit evidence. For example, the auditor may conclude that additional audit evidence is needed because of significant differences in fiscal year-ends, significant differences in accounting principles, changes in ownership, or the significance of the investment to the investor's financial position or results of operations. Examples of procedures that the auditor may perform are reviewing information in the investor's files that relates to the investee, such as investee minutes and budgets, and investee cash flow information and making inquiries of investor management about the investee's financial results.

.A7 The auditor may need to obtain evidence relating to transactions between the entity and investee to evaluate

a. the propriety of the elimination of unrealized profits and losses on transactions between the entity and investee, if applicable, and

b. the adequacy of disclosures about material related party transactions or relationships.

.A8 Section 540 and paragraphs .06–.08 of this section address auditing fair value accounting estimates. The Audit Guide *Auditing Derivative Instruments, Hedging Activities, and Investments in Securities* also provides guidance on audit evidence that may be relevant to the fair value of derivative instruments and securities and on procedures that may be performed by the auditor to evaluate management's consideration of the need to recognize impairment losses.

.A9 The date of the investor's financial statements and those of the investee may be different. If the difference between the date of the entity's financial statements and those of the investee has or could have a material effect on the entity's financial statements, the auditor is required, in accordance with paragraph .04*d*, to determine whether the entity's management has properly considered the lack of comparability. The effect may be material, for example, because the difference between the financial statement period ends of the entity and investee is not consistent with the prior period in comparative statements or because a significant transaction occurred during the time period between the financial statement period end of the entity and investee. If a change in the difference between the financial statement period end of the entity and investee has a material effect on the investor's financial statements, the auditor may be required, in accordance with section 708, *Consistency of Financial Statements*, to add an emphasis-of-matter paragraph to the auditor's report because the comparability of financial statements between periods has been materially affected by a change in reporting period.

.A10 Section 560, *Subsequent Events and Subsequently Discovered Facts*, addresses the auditor's responsibilities relating to subsequent events and subsequently discovered facts in an audit of financial statements.

Investments in Derivative Instruments and Securities Measured or Disclosed at Fair Value (Ref: par. .06–.08)

.A11 The method for determining fair value may be specified by the applicable financial reporting framework and may vary depending on the industry in which the entity operates or the nature of the entity. Such differences may relate to the consideration of price quotations from inactive markets and significant liquidity discounts, control premiums, and commissions and other costs that would be incurred to dispose of the derivative instrument or security.

.A12 If the determination of fair value requires the use of accounting estimates, see section 540, which addresses auditing fair value accounting estimates, including requirements and guidance relating to the auditor's understanding of the applicable financial reporting framework relevant to accounting estimates and the method used in making the estimate[4] and the auditor's determination of whether management has appropriately applied the requirements of the applicable financial reporting framework relevant to the accounting estimate.[5] The Audit Guide *Auditing Derivative Instruments, Hedging Activities, and Investments in Securities* also provides guidance on audit evidence that may be relevant to the fair value of derivative instruments and investments in securities.

.A13 Quoted market prices for derivative instruments and securities listed on national exchanges or over-the-counter markets are available from sources such as financial publications, the exchanges, NASDAQ, or pricing services based on sources such as those. Quoted market prices obtained from those sources generally provide sufficient evidence of the fair value of the derivative instruments and securities.

.A14 For certain other derivative instruments and securities, quoted market prices may be obtained from broker-dealers who are market makers in them or through the National Quotation Bureau. However, using such a price quote to test valuation assertions may require special knowledge to understand the circumstances in which the quote was developed. For example, quotations published by the National Quotation Bureau may not be based on recent trades and may be only an indication of interest and not an actual price for which a counterparty will purchase or sell the underlying derivative instrument or security.

.A15 If quoted market prices are not available for the derivative instrument or security, estimates of fair value frequently may be obtained from broker-dealers or other third-party sources, based on proprietary valuation models, or

---

[4] Paragraphs .08*a*, .08*c*, .A12–.A14, and .A23–.A25 of section 540, *Auditing Accounting Estimates, Including Fair Value Accounting Estimates, and Related Disclosures*.

[5] Paragraphs .12*a* and .A53–.A57 of section 540.

from the entity, based on internally or externally developed valuation models (for example, the Black-Scholes option pricing model). Understanding the method used by the broker-dealer or other third-party source in developing the estimate may include, for example, understanding whether a pricing model or cash flow projection was used. The auditor also may determine that it is necessary to obtain estimates from more than one pricing source. For example, this may be appropriate if either of the following occurs:

- The pricing source has a relationship with an entity that might impair its objectivity, such as an affiliate or a counterparty involved in selling or structuring the product.
- The valuation is based on assumptions that are highly subjective or particularly sensitive to changes in the underlying circumstances.

See also section 540.[6]

.A16 Examples of valuation models include the present value of expected future cash flows, option-pricing models, matrix pricing, option-adjusted spread models, and fundamental analysis. Refer to section 540 for the auditor's procedures to obtain evidence supporting management's assertions about fair value that are determined using a valuation model.

Impairment Losses (Ref: par. .09)

.A17 Regardless of the valuation method used, the applicable financial reporting framework might require recognizing, in earnings or other comprehensive income, an impairment loss for a decline in fair value that is other than temporary. Determinations of whether losses are other than temporary may involve estimating the outcome of future events and making judgments in determining whether factors exist that indicate that an impairment loss has been incurred at the end of the reporting period. These judgments are based on subjective as well as objective factors, including knowledge and experience about past and current events and assumptions about future events. The following are examples of such factors:

- Fair value is significantly below cost or carrying value and
  - — the decline is attributable to adverse conditions specifically related to the security or specific conditions in an industry or a geographic area.
  - — the decline has existed for an extended period of time.
  - — for an equity security, management has the intent to sell the security or it is more likely than not that it will be required to sell the security before recovery.
  - — for a debt security, management has the intent to sell the security or it is more likely than not it will be required to sell the security before the security's anticipated recovery of its amortized cost basis (for example, if the entity's cash or working capital requirements or contractual or regulatory obligations indicate that the debt security will be required to be sold before the forecasted recovery occurs).
- The security has been downgraded by a rating agency.
- The financial condition of the issuer has deteriorated.

---

[6] Paragraphs .A68–.A89 of section 540.

- Dividends have been reduced or eliminated or scheduled interest payments have not been made.
- The entity recorded losses from the security subsequent to the end of the reporting period.

.A18 Evaluating the relevance of the information considered may include obtaining evidence about factors such as those referred to in paragraph .A17 that tend to corroborate or conflict with management's conclusions.

Unrealized Appreciation or Depreciation (Ref: par. .10)

.A19 Obtaining audit evidence about the amount of unrealized appreciation or depreciation in the fair value of a derivative that is recognized or that is disclosed because of the ineffectiveness of a hedge may include understanding the methods used to determine whether the hedge is highly effective and to determine the ineffective portion of the hedge.

Inventory

Attendance at Physical Inventory Counting (Ref: par. .11a)

.A20 Management ordinarily establishes procedures under which inventory is physically counted at least once per year to serve as a basis for the preparation of the financial statements and, if applicable, to ascertain the reliability of the entity's perpetual inventory system.

.A21 Attendance at physical inventory counting involves

- inspecting the inventory to ascertain its existence and evaluate its condition and performing test counts,
- observing compliance with management's instructions and the performance of procedures for recording and controlling the results of the physical inventory count, and
- obtaining audit evidence about the reliability of management's count procedures.

These procedures may serve as tests of controls or substantive procedures, or both, depending on the auditor's risk assessment, planned approach, and the specific procedures carried out.

.A22 Matters relevant in planning attendance at physical inventory counting (or in designing and performing audit procedures pursuant to paragraphs .11–.15) include, for example, the following:

- The risks of material misstatement related to inventory.
- The control risk related to inventory.
- Whether adequate procedures are expected to be established and proper instructions issued for physical inventory counting.
- The timing of physical inventory counting.
- Whether the entity maintains a perpetual inventory system.
- The locations at which inventory is held, including the materiality of the inventory and the risks of material misstatement at different locations, in deciding at which locations attendance is appropriate. Section 600 addresses the involvement of component auditors and, accordingly, may be relevant if such involvement is with regard to attendance of physical inventory counting at a remote location.

- Whether the assistance of an auditor's specialist is needed. Section 620, *Using the Work of an Auditor's Specialist*, addresses the use of an auditor's specialist to assist the auditor in obtaining sufficient appropriate audit evidence.

Evaluate Management's Instructions and Procedures (Ref: par. .11a(i))

.A23 Matters relevant in evaluating management's instructions and procedures for recording and controlling the physical inventory counting include whether they address, for example, the following:

- The application of appropriate control activities (for example, the collection of used physical inventory count records, accounting for unused physical inventory count records, and count and recount procedures)
- The accurate identification of the stage of completion of work in progress; slow moving, obsolete, or damaged items; and inventory owned by a third party (for example, on consignment)
- The procedures used to estimate physical quantities, when applicable, such as may be needed in estimating the physical quantity of a coal pile
- Control over the movement of inventory between areas and the shipping and receipt of inventory before and after the cutoff date

Observe the Performance of Management's Count Procedures (Ref: par. .11a(ii))

.A24 Observing the performance of management's count procedures (for example, those relating to control over the movement of inventory before, during, and after the count) assists the auditor in obtaining audit evidence that management's instructions and count procedures are designed and implemented adequately. In addition, the auditor may obtain copies of cutoff information, such as details of the movement of inventory, to assist the auditor in performing audit procedures over the accounting for such movements at a later date.

Inspect the Inventory (Ref: par. .11a(iii))

.A25 Inspecting inventory when attending physical inventory counting assists the auditor in ascertaining the existence of the inventory (though not necessarily its ownership) and in identifying obsolete, damaged, or aging inventory.

Perform Test Counts (Ref: par. .11a(iv))

.A26 Performing test counts (for example, by tracing items selected from management's count records to the physical inventory and tracing items selected from the physical inventory to management's count records) provides audit evidence about the completeness and accuracy of those records.

.A27 In addition to recording the auditor's test counts, obtaining copies of management's completed physical inventory count records assists the auditor in performing subsequent audit procedures to determine whether the entity's final inventory records accurately reflect actual inventory count results.

Use of Management's Specialists

.A28 Management may engage specialists who have expertise in the taking of physical inventories to count, list, price, and subsequently compute the total dollar amount of inventory on hand at the date of the physical count. For example, entities such as retail stores, hospitals, and automobile dealers may use specialists in this manner.

.A29 An inventory count performed by an external inventory firm engaged as a management specialist does not, by itself, provide the auditor with sufficient appropriate audit evidence. The auditor is required by section 500 to perform certain procedures if information to be used as audit evidence has been prepared using the work of a management's specialist.[7] The auditor may, for example, examine the specialist's program, observe its procedures and controls, make or observe some physical counts of the inventory, recompute calculations of the submitted inventory on a test basis, and apply appropriate tests to the intervening transactions.

.A30 Although the auditor may adjust the extent of the work on the physical count of inventory because of the work of management's specialist, any restriction imposed on the auditor such that the auditor is unable to perform the procedures that the auditor considers necessary is a scope limitation. In such cases, section 705 requires the auditor to modify the opinion in the auditor's report as a result of the scope limitation.

Physical Inventory Counting Conducted Other Than at the Date of the Financial Statements (Ref: par. .12)

.A31 For practical reasons, the physical inventory counting may be conducted at a date, or dates, other than the date of the financial statements. This may be done irrespective of whether management determines inventory quantities by an annual physical inventory counting or maintains a perpetual inventory system. In either case, the effectiveness of the design, implementation, and maintenance of controls over changes in inventory determines whether the conduct of physical inventory counting at a date (or dates) other than the date of the financial statements is appropriate for audit purposes. Section 330 addresses substantive procedures performed at an interim date.[8]

.A32 When a perpetual inventory system is maintained, management may perform physical counts or other tests to ascertain the reliability of inventory quantity information included in the entity's perpetual inventory records. In some cases, management or the auditor may identify differences between the perpetual inventory records and actual physical inventory quantities on hand; this may indicate that the controls over changes in inventory are not operating effectively.

.A33 Relevant matters for consideration when designing audit procedures to obtain audit evidence about whether changes in inventory amounts between the count date, or dates, and the final inventory records are recorded properly include the following:

- Whether the perpetual inventory records are properly adjusted
- Reliability of the entity's perpetual inventory records
- Reasons for significant differences between the information obtained during the physical count and the perpetual inventory records

Attendance at Physical Inventory Counting Is Impracticable (Ref: par. .14)

.A34 In some cases, attendance at physical inventory counting may be impracticable. This may be due to factors such as the nature and location of the inventory (for example, when inventory is held in a location that may pose threats to the safety of the auditor). The matter of general inconvenience to

---

[7] Paragraph .08 of section 500 addresses management's specialists.

[8] Paragraphs .23–.24 of section 330.

the auditor, however, is not sufficient to support a decision by the auditor that attendance is impracticable. Further, as explained in section 200, *Overall Objectives of the Independent Auditor and the Conduct of an Audit in Accordance With Generally Accepted Auditing Standards*, the matter of difficulty, time, or cost involved is not, in itself, a valid basis for the auditor to omit an audit procedure for which no alternative exists or to be satisfied with audit evidence that is less than persuasive.

.A35 In some cases, when attendance is impracticable, alternative audit procedures (for example, observing a current physical inventory count and reconciling it to the opening inventory quantities or inspection of documentation of the subsequent sale of specific inventory items acquired or purchased prior to the physical inventory counting) may provide sufficient appropriate audit evidence about the existence and condition of inventory. If the audit covers the current period and one or more periods for which the auditor had not observed or made some physical counts of prior inventories, alternative audit procedures, such as tests of prior transactions or reviews of the records of prior counts, may provide sufficient appropriate audit evidence about the prior inventories. The effectiveness of the alternative procedures that an auditor may perform is affected by the length of the period that the alternative procedures cover.

.A36 In other cases, however, it may not be possible to obtain sufficient appropriate audit evidence regarding the existence and condition of inventory by performing alternative audit procedures. In such cases, section 705 requires the auditor to modify the opinion in the auditor's report as a result of the scope limitation. In addition, section 510, *Opening Balances—Initial Audit Engagements, Including Reaudit Engagements*, addresses the auditor's procedures regarding inventory opening balances in initial audit engagements.[9]

Inventory Under the Custody and Control of a Third Party

Confirmation (Ref: par. .15a)

.A37 Section 505, *External Confirmations*, addresses external confirmation procedures.

Other Audit Procedures (Ref: par. .15*b*)

.A38 Depending on the circumstances (for example, when information is obtained that raises doubt about the integrity and objectivity of the third party), the auditor may consider it appropriate to perform other audit procedures instead of, or in addition to, confirmation with the third party. Examples of other audit procedures include the following:

- Attending, or arranging for another auditor to attend, the third party's physical counting of inventory, if practicable
- Obtaining another auditor's report on the adequacy of the third party's internal control for ensuring that inventory is properly counted and adequately safeguarded
- Inspecting documentation regarding inventory held by third parties (for example, warehouse receipts)
- Requesting confirmation from other parties when inventory has been pledged as collateral

---

[9] Paragraph .A13 of section 510, *Opening Balances—Initial Audit Engagements, Including Reaudit Engagements*.

Litigation, Claims, and Assessments

Completeness of Litigation, Claims, and Assessments (Ref: par. .16)

.A39 Litigation, claims, and assessments involving the entity may have a material effect on the financial statements and, thus, may be required to be recognized, measured, or disclosed in the financial statements.

.A40 Other legal matters involving the entity may not have a material effect on the entity's financial statements and, accordingly, would not give rise to risks of material misstatement. Examples of such other legal matters may be

- matters unrelated to actual or potential litigation, claims, or assessments, such as consulting services related to real estate or potential merger and acquisition transactions;
- matters in which the entity records indicate that management or the legal counsel has not devoted substantive attention to the matter;
- matters in which the entity's insurance coverage exceeds the amount of the actual or potential litigation, claim, or assessment sought against the entity; or
- matters that are clearly trivial to the financial statements.

.A41 Management is responsible for adopting policies and procedures to identify, evaluate, and account for litigation, claims, and assessments as a basis for the preparation of financial statements, in accordance with the requirements of the applicable financial reporting framework.

.A42 Management is the primary source of information about events or conditions considered in the financial accounting for, and reporting of, litigation, claims, and assessments because these matters are within the direct knowledge and, often, control of management. Accordingly, the auditor's procedures with respect to litigation, claims, and assessments include the following:

- Making inquiries of management as required by paragraph .16*a*, which may include a discussion about the policies and procedures adopted for identifying, evaluating, and accounting for litigation, claims, and assessments involving the entity that may give rise to a risk of material misstatement
- Obtaining written representations from management, in accordance with section 580, *Written Representations*, that all known actual or possible litigation, claims, and assessments whose effects should be considered when preparing the financial statements have been disclosed to the auditor and accounted for and disclosed in accordance with the applicable financial reporting framework[10]

.A43 In addition to the procedures identified in paragraph .16, other relevant procedures include, for example, using information obtained through risk assessment procedures carried out as part of obtaining an understanding of the entity and its environment to assist the auditor to become aware of litigation, claims, and assessments involving the entity. Examples of such procedures are as follows:

---

[10] Paragraph .15 of section 580, *Written Representations*.

- Reading minutes of meetings of stockholders; directors; governing bodies of governmental entities; and appropriate committees held during, and subsequent to, the period being audited
- Reading contracts, loan agreements, leases, correspondence from taxing or other governmental agencies, and similar documents
- Obtaining information concerning guarantees from bank confirmation forms
- Inspecting other documents for possible guarantees by the entity

Section 315, *Understanding the Entity and Its Environment and Assessing the Risks of Material Misstatement*, requires the auditor to obtain an understanding of the entity and its environment.[11] In addition, section 250, *Consideration of Laws and Regulations in an Audit of Financial Statements*, requires the auditor to obtain an understanding of the entity's legal and regulatory framework applicable to the entity and industry or sector in which the entity operates and how the entity is complying with that framework.

.A44 Audit evidence obtained for purposes of identifying litigation, claims, and assessments that may give rise to a risk of material misstatement also may provide audit evidence regarding other relevant considerations, such as valuation or measurement, regarding litigation, claims, and assessments. Section 540 establishes requirements and provides guidance relevant to the auditor's consideration of litigation, claims, and assessments requiring accounting estimates or related disclosures in the financial statements.

.A45 This section addresses inquiries of the entity's legal counsel with whom management has consulted. If management has not consulted legal counsel, the auditor would rely on the procedures required by paragraph .16 to identify litigation, claims, and assessments involving the entity, which may give rise to a risk of material misstatement, and the written representation of management regarding litigation, claims, and assessments, as required by section 580.

Communication With the Entity's Legal Counsel (Ref: par. .18–.24)

.A46 An auditor ordinarily does not possess legal skills and, therefore, cannot make legal judgments concerning information coming to the auditor's attention.

.A47 Direct communication with the entity's legal counsel assists the auditor in obtaining sufficient appropriate audit evidence about whether potentially material litigation, claims, and assessments are known and management's estimates of the financial implications, including costs, are reasonable.

.A48 The American Bar Association (ABA) has approved *Statement of Policy Regarding Lawyers' Responses to Auditors' Requests for Information* (the ABA statement), which explains the concerns of the legal counsel and the nature of the limitations that an auditor is likely to encounter in connection with seeking direct communication with the entity's legal counsel about litigation, claims, assessments, and unasserted claims.[12]

---

[11] Paragraph .12 of section 315, *Understanding the Entity and Its Environment and Assessing the Risks of Material Misstatement*.

[12] The *Statement of Policy Regarding Lawyers' Responses to Auditors' Requests for Information* is reprinted as exhibit A, "American Bar Association Statement of Policy Regarding Lawyers' Responses to Auditors' Requests for Information," for the convenience of readers but is not an integral part of this section.

.A49 A letter of inquiry to the entity's legal counsel is the auditor's primary means of obtaining corroboration of the information provided by management concerning material litigation, claims, and assessments. Audit evidence obtained from the entity's in-house general counsel or legal department may provide the auditor with the necessary corroboration.

.A50 In certain circumstances, the auditor also may judge it necessary to meet with the entity's legal counsel to discuss the likely outcome of the litigation or claims. This may be the case, for example, when

- the auditor determines that the matter is a significant risk.
- the matter is complex.
- a disagreement exists between management and the entity's external legal counsel.

Ordinarily, such meetings require management's permission and are held with a representative of management in attendance.

.A51 An external legal counsel's response to a letter of inquiry and the procedures set forth in paragraphs .16–.17 provide the auditor with sufficient appropriate audit evidence concerning the accounting for, and reporting of, pending and threatened litigation, claims, and assessments.

.A52 Audit evidence about the status of litigation, claims, and assessments up to the date of the auditor's report may be obtained by inquiry of management, including in-house legal counsel responsible for dealing with the relevant matters. The auditor may need to obtain updated information from the entity's legal counsel.

.A53 In accordance with section 700, *Forming an Opinion and Reporting on Financial Statements*, the auditor is required to date the auditor's report no earlier than the date on which the auditor has obtained sufficient appropriate audit evidence on which to base the auditor's opinion on the financial statements.[13] Accordingly, it is preferable that the entity's legal counsel's response be as close to the date of the auditor's report as is practicable in the circumstances. Specifying the effective date of the entity's legal counsel's response to reasonably approximate the expected date of the auditor's report may obviate the need to obtain updated information from the entity's legal counsel.

.A54 Clearly specifying the earliest acceptable effective date of the response and the latest date by which it is to be sent to the auditor and informing the entity's legal counsel of these dates timely facilitates the entity's legal counsel's ability to respond timely and adequately. A two-week period between the specified effective date of the entity's legal counsel's response and the latest date by which the response is to be sent to the auditor is generally sufficient.

.A55 In some circumstances, the legal counsel may be required by relevant ethical requirements to resign the engagement if the legal counsel's advice concerning financial accounting and reporting for litigation, claims, and assessments is disregarded by the entity.

.A56 The legal counsel appropriately may limit the response to matters to which the legal counsel has given substantive attention in the form of legal consultation or representation. Also, the legal counsel's response may be limited to matters that are considered individually or collectively material to the financial statements, such as when the entity and auditor have reached an understanding on the limits of materiality for this purpose and management

---

[13] Paragraph .41 of section 700, *Forming an Opinion and Reporting on Financial Statements.*

has communicated such understanding to the legal counsel. Such limitations are not limitations on the scope of the audit.

.A57 The legal counsel may be unable to respond concerning the likelihood of an unfavorable outcome of litigation, claims, and assessments or the amount or range of potential loss because of inherent uncertainties. Factors influencing the likelihood of an unfavorable outcome sometimes may not be within the legal counsel's competence to judge; historical experience of the entity in similar litigation or the experience of other entities may not be relevant or available, and the amount of the possible loss frequently may vary widely at different stages of litigation. Consequently, the legal counsel may not be able to form a conclusion with respect to such matters. In such circumstances, the auditor may conclude that the financial statements are affected by an uncertainty concerning the outcome of a future event that cannot be reasonably estimated. If the auditor is unable to obtain sufficient appropriate audit evidence to conclude that the financial statements as a whole are free from material misstatement, section 705 requires the auditor to modify the opinion in addressing the effect, if any, of the legal counsel's response on the auditor's report as a result of the scope limitation.[14]

.A58 An external legal counsel's refusal to furnish the information requested in an inquiry letter either in writing or orally may cause a scope limitation of the audit sufficient to preclude an unmodified opinion.

.A59 Although the auditor would consider the inability to review information that could have a significant bearing on the audit as a scope limitation, in recognition of the public interest in protecting the confidentiality of lawyer-client communications, such inability is not intended to require an auditor to examine documents that the client identifies as subject to the lawyer-client privilege. In the event of questions concerning the applicability of this privilege, the auditor may request confirmation from the entity's legal counsel that the information is subject to that privilege and that the information was considered by the legal counsel in responding to the letter of inquiry or, if the matters are being handled by another legal counsel, an identification of such legal counsel for the purpose of sending a letter of inquiry.

.A60 If management imposes a limitation on the scope of the audit and the auditor is unable to obtain sufficient appropriate audit evidence by performing alternative audit procedures, the auditor is required by section 705 to either disclaim an opinion on the financial statements or, when practicable, withdraw from the audit.[15]

.A61 In some cases, in order to emphasize the preservation of the attorney-client privilege or the attorney work-product privilege, some entities may include the following or substantially similar language in the audit inquiry letter to legal counsel:

> We do not intend that either our request to you to provide information to our auditor or your response to our auditor should be construed in any way to constitute a waiver of the attorney-client privilege or the attorney work-product privilege.

For the same reason, some legal counsel may include the following or substantially similar language in their response letters to auditors:

> The Company [*or other defined term*] has advised us that, by making the request set forth in its letter to us, the Company [*or other defined term*] does not intend

---

[14] Paragraph .07 of section 705, *Modifications to the Opinion in the Independent Auditor's Report*.

[15] Paragraph .13 of section 705.

> to waive the attorney-client privilege with respect to any information which the Company [*or other defined term*] has furnished to us. Moreover, please be advised that our response to you should not be construed in any way to constitute a waiver of the protection of the attorney work-product privilege with respect to any of our files involving the Company [*or other defined term*].

Explanatory language similar to the foregoing in the letters of the entity or legal counsel is not a limitation on the scope of the legal counsel's response. See exhibit B, "Report of the Subcommittee on Audit Inquiry Responses."

.A62 In order to emphasize the preservation of the attorney-client privilege with respect to unasserted possible claims or assessments, some legal counsel may include the following or substantially similar language in their responses to audit inquiry letters:

> Please be advised that pursuant to clauses (b) and (c) of Paragraph 5 of the ABA Statement of Policy [*American Bar Association's Statement of Policy Regarding Lawyers' Responses to Auditors' Requests for Information*] and related Commentary referred to in the last paragraph of this letter, it would be inappropriate for this firm to respond to a general inquiry relating to the existence of unasserted possible claims or assessments involving the Company. We can only furnish information concerning those unasserted possible claims or assessments upon which the Company has specifically requested in writing that we comment. We also cannot comment upon the adequacy of the Company's listing, if any, of unasserted possible claims or assessments or its assertions concerning the advice, if any, about the need to disclose same.

Additional language similar to the foregoing in a letter from legal counsel is not a limitation on the scope of the audit. However, the ABA statement and the understanding between the legal and accounting professions assumes that the legal counsel, under certain circumstances, will advise and consult with the entity concerning the entity's obligation to make financial statement disclosure with respect to unasserted possible claims or assessments. Confirmation of this understanding is included in the legal counsel's response.

.A63 If the auditor believes that there may be actual or potential material litigation, claims, or assessments and the entity has not engaged external legal counsel relating to such matters, the auditor may discuss with the client the possible need to consult legal counsel to assist the client in determining the appropriate measurement, recognition, or disclosure of related liabilities or loss contingencies in the financial statements, in accordance with the applicable financial reporting framework. Depending on the significance of the matter(s), refusal by management to consult legal counsel in these circumstances may result in a scope limitation of the audit sufficient to preclude an unmodified opinion.

Direct Communication With the Entity's In-House Legal Counsel

.A64 In-house legal counsel can range from one lawyer to a large staff, with responsibilities ranging from specific internal matters to a comprehensive coverage of all of the entity's legal needs, including litigation with outside parties. Because both in-house and external legal counsel are bound by an applicable code of ethics, there should be no significant difference in their professional obligations and responsibilities. In some circumstances, external legal counsel, if used at all, may be used only for limited purposes, such as data accumulation or account collection activity. In such circumstances, in-house legal counsel may have the primary responsibility for corporate legal matters and may be in the best position to know and precisely describe the status of all litigation, claims, and assessments or to corroborate information provided by management.

Evaluation of the Outcome of Litigation, Claims, or Assessment (Ref: par. .22d(ii))

.A65 Although paragraph 5 of the ABA statement states that the legal counsel "may in appropriate circumstances communicate to the auditor his view that an unfavorable outcome is probable' or remote,'" the legal counsel is not required to use those terms in communicating the evaluation to the auditor. The auditor may find other wording sufficiently clear, as long as the terms can be used to classify the outcome of the uncertainty under one of the three probability classifications established in FASB ASC 450. Some examples of evaluations concerning litigation that may be considered to provide sufficient clarity that the likelihood of an unfavorable outcome is remote, even though they do not use that term, are the following:

- "We are of the opinion that this action will not result in any liability to the company."
- "It is our opinion that the possible liability to the company in this proceeding is nominal in amount."
- "We believe the company will be able to defend this action successfully."
- "We believe that the plaintiff's case against the company is without merit."
- "Based on the facts known to us, after a full investigation, it is our opinion that no liability will be established against the company in these suits."

Absent any contradictory information obtained by the auditor either in other parts of the legal counsel's letter or otherwise, the auditor need not obtain further clarification of evaluations such as the foregoing. Because of inherent uncertainties described in paragraph .A57 and the ABA statement, an evaluation furnished by the legal counsel may indicate significant uncertainties or stipulations about whether the client will prevail. The following are examples of the legal counsel's evaluations that are unclear about the likelihood of an unfavorable outcome:

- "This action involves unique characteristics wherein authoritative legal precedents do not seem to exist. We believe that the plaintiff will have serious problems establishing the company's liability under the act; nevertheless, if the plaintiff is successful, the award may be substantial."
- "It is our opinion that the company will be able to assert meritorious defenses to this action." (The term *meritorious defenses* indicates that the entity's defenses will not be summarily dismissed by the court; it does not necessarily indicate the legal counsel's opinion that the entity will prevail.)
- "We believe the action can be settled for less than the damages claimed."
- "We are unable to express an opinion as to the merits of the litigation at this time. The company believes there is absolutely no merit to the litigation." (If the entity's legal counsel, with the benefit of all relevant information, is unable to conclude that the likelihood of an unfavorable outcome is remote, it is unlikely that management would be able to form a judgment to that effect.)
- "In our opinion, the company has a substantial chance of prevailing in this action." (A *substantial chance*, a *reasonable opportunity*,

and similar terms indicate more uncertainty than an opinion that the company will prevail.)

If the auditor is uncertain about the meaning of the legal counsel's evaluation, clarification either in a follow-up letter or conference with the legal counsel and entity, appropriately documented, may be appropriate. If the legal counsel is still unable to give an unequivocal evaluation of the likelihood of an unfavorable outcome in writing or orally, the auditor is required by section 700 to determine the effect, if any, of the legal counsel's response on the auditor's report.

Segment Information (Ref: par. .25)

.A66 Depending on the applicable financial reporting framework, the entity may be required or permitted to disclose segment information in the financial statements. The auditor's responsibility regarding the presentation and disclosure of segment information is in relation to the financial statements as a whole. Accordingly, the auditor is not required to perform audit procedures that would be necessary to express an opinion on the segment information presented on a stand-alone basis.

Considerations Specific to Governmental Entities

.A67 For governmental entities required by the applicable financial reporting framework to disclose segment information, the auditor's responsibility regarding the presentation and disclosure of segment information is in relation to the financial statements of the opinion unit(s) on which the segment information is based.[16]

Understanding of the Methods Used by Management (Ref: par. .25a)

.A68 Depending on the circumstances, examples of matters that may be relevant when obtaining an understanding of the methods used by management in determining segment information and evaluating whether such methods are likely to result in disclosure in accordance with the applicable financial reporting framework include the following:

- Sales, transfers, and charges between segments and elimination of intersegment amounts
- Comparisons with budgets and other expected results (for example, operating profits as a percentage of sales)
- The allocation of assets and costs among segments
- Consistency with prior periods and the adequacy of the disclosures with respect to inconsistencies
- Management's process for identifying those segments that require disclosure in accordance with the entity's financial reporting framework

---

[16] Paragraph .A14 of section 200, *Overall Objectives of the Independent Auditor and the Conduct of an Audit in Accordance With Generally Accepted Auditing Standards.*

.A69

Appendix—Illustrative Audit Inquiry Letter to Legal Counsel (Ref: par. .22)

In connection with an audit of our financial statements at (balance sheet date) and for the (period) then ended, management of the Company has prepared, and furnished to our auditors (name and address of auditors), a description and evaluation of certain contingencies, including those set forth below involving matters with respect to which you have been engaged and to which you have devoted substantive attention on behalf of the Company in the form of legal consultation or representation. These contingencies are regarded by management of the Company as material for this purpose (management may indicate a materiality limit if an understanding has been reached with the auditor). Your response should include matters that existed at (balance sheet date) and during the period from that date to the date of your response.

[*Alternative wording when management requests the lawyer to prepare the list that describes and evaluates pending or threatened litigation, claims, and assessments is as follows:*]

> In connection with an audit of our financial statements as of (balance-sheet date) and for the (period) then ended, please furnish our auditors, (name and address of auditors), with the information requested below concerning certain contingencies involving matters with respect to which you have devoted substantive attention on behalf of the Company in the form of legal consultation or representation. [*When a materiality limit has been established based on an understanding between management and the auditor, the following sentence should be added: This request is limited to contingencies amounting to (amount) individually or items involving lesser amounts that exceed (amount) in the aggregate.*]

Pending or Threatened Litigation (Excluding Unasserted Claims)

[*Ordinarily the information would include the following: (1) the nature of the litigation, (2) the progress of the case to date, (3) how management is responding or intends to respond to the litigation (for example, to contest the case vigorously or to seek an out-of-court settlement), and (4) an evaluation of the likelihood of an unfavorable outcome and an estimate, if one can be made, of the amount or range of potential loss.*] This letter will serve as our consent for you to furnish to our auditor all the information requested herein. Accordingly, please furnish to our auditors such explanation, if any, that you consider necessary to supplement the foregoing information, including an explanation of those matters for which your views may differ from those stated and an identification of the omission of any pending or threatened litigation, claims, and assessments or a statement that the list of such matters is complete.

[*Alternative wording when management requests the lawyer to prepare the list that describes and evaluates pending or threatened litigation, claims, and assessments is as follows:*]

> Regarding pending or threatened litigation, claims, and assessments, please include in your response: (1) the nature of each matter, (2) the progress of each matter to date, (3) how the Company is responding or intends to respond (for example, to contest the case vigorously or seek an out-of-court settlement), and (4) an evaluation of the likelihood of an unfavorable outcome and an estimate, if one can be made, of the amount or range of potential loss.

Unasserted Claims and Assessments (Considered by Management to be Probable of Assertion and That, if Asserted, Would Have at Least a Reasonable Possibility of an Unfavorable Outcome)

[*Ordinarily management's information would include the following: (1) the nature of the matter, (2) how management intends to respond if the claim is asserted, and (3) an evaluation of the likelihood of an unfavorable outcome and an estimate, if one can be made, of the amount or range of potential loss.*] Please furnish to our auditors such explanation, if any, that you consider necessary to supplement the foregoing information, including an explanation of those matters for which your views may differ from those stated.

We understand that whenever, in the course of performing legal services for us with respect to a matter recognized to involve an unasserted possible claim or assessment that may call for financial statement disclosure, if you have formed a professional conclusion that we should disclose or consider disclosure concerning such possible claim or assessment, as a matter of professional responsibility to us, you will so advise us and will consult with us concerning the question of such disclosure and the applicable requirements of Financial Accounting Standards Board (FASB) *Accounting Standards Codification* (ASC) 450, *Contingencies*. Please specifically confirm to our auditors that our understanding is correct.

[*Alternative wording when management requests the lawyer to prepare the list that describes and evaluates pending or threatened litigation, claims, and assessments is as follows:*]

> We have represented to our auditors that there are no unasserted possible claims or assessments that you have advised us are probable of assertion and must be disclosed in accordance with FASB ASC 450. We understand that whenever, in the course of performing legal services for us with respect to a matter recognized to involve an unasserted possible claim or assessment that may call for financial statement disclosure, you have formed a professional conclusion that we should disclose or consider disclosure concerning such possible claim or assessment, as a matter of professional responsibility to us, you will so advise us and will consult with us concerning the question of such disclosure and the applicable requirements of FASB ASC 450. Please specifically confirm to our auditors that our understanding is correct.

Please specifically identify the nature of and reasons for any limitation on your response.

[*The auditor may request the client to inquire about additional matters, for example, unpaid or unbilled charges or specified information on certain contractually assumed obligations of the Company, such as guarantees of indebtedness of others.*]

[*Alternative wording when management requests the lawyer to prepare the list that describes and evaluates pending or threatened litigation, claims, and assessments is as follows:*]

> Your response should include matters that existed as of (balance-sheet date) and during the period from that date to the effective date of your response. Please specifically identify the nature of and reasons for any limitations on your response. Our auditors expect to have the audit completed about (expected completion date). They would appreciate receiving your reply by that date with a specified effective date no earlier than (ordinarily two weeks before expected completion date).

[*Wording that could be used in an audit inquiry letter, instead of the heading and first paragraph, when the client believes that there are no unasserted claims or assessments (to be specified to the lawyer for comment) that are probable of assertion and that, if asserted, would have a reasonable possibility of an unfavorable outcome as specified by Financial Accounting Standards Board* Accounting Standards Codification *450,* Contingencies, *is as follows:*]

Unasserted claims and assessments—We have represented to our auditors that there are no unasserted possible claims that you have advised us are probable of assertion and must be disclosed, in accordance with Financial Accounting Standards Board *Accounting Standards Codification* 450, *Contingencies*. (The second paragraph in the section relating to unasserted claims and assessments would not be altered.)

.A70

Exhibit A—American Bar Association Statement of Policy Regarding Lawyers' Responses to Auditors' Requests for Information (Ref: par. .A48)

> *Note:* This document, in the form herein set forth, was approved by the Board of Governors of the American Bar Association (ABA) in December 1975, which official action permitted its release to lawyers and accountants as the standard recommended by the ABA for the lawyer's response to letters of audit inquiry.

Source: Statement on Auditing Standards No. 12 section 337C, *Exhibit II—American Bar Association Statement of Policy Regarding Lawyers' Responses to Auditors' Requests for Information**

Preamble

The public interest in protecting the confidentiality of lawyer-client communications is fundamental. The American legal, political and economic systems depend heavily upon voluntary compliance with the law and upon ready access to a respected body of professionals able to interpret and advise on the law. The expanding complexity of our laws and governmental regulations increases the need for prompt, specific and unhampered lawyer-client communication. The benefits of such communication and early consultation underlie the strict statutory and ethical obligations of the lawyer to preserve the confidences and secrets of the client, as well as the long-recognized testimonial privilege for lawyer-client communication.

Both the Code of Professional Responsibility and the cases applying the evidentiary privilege recognize that the privilege against disclosure can be knowingly and voluntarily waived by the client. It is equally clear that disclosure to a third party may result in loss of the "confidentiality" essential to maintain the privilege. Disclosure to a third party of the lawyer-client communication on a particular subject may also destroy the privilege as to other communications on that subject. Thus, the mere disclosure by the lawyer to the outside auditor, with due client consent, of the substance of communications between the lawyer and client may significantly impair the client's ability in other contexts to maintain the confidentiality of such communications.

Under the circumstances a policy of audit procedure which requires clients to give consent and authorize lawyers to respond to general inquiries and disclose information to auditors concerning matters which have been communicated in confidence is essentially destructive of free and open communication and early consultation between lawyer and client. The institution of such a policy would inevitably discourage management from discussing potential legal problems

* Statement on Auditing Standards No. 12 section 337C, *Exhibit II—American Bar Association Statement of Policy Regarding Lawyers' Responses to Auditors' Requests for Information*, has been superseded by this section.

with counsel for fear that such discussion might become public and precipitate a loss to or possible liability of the business enterprise and its stockholders that might otherwise never materialize.

It is also recognized that our legal, political and economic systems depend to an important extent on public confidence in published financial statements. To meet this need the accounting profession must adopt and adhere to standards and procedures that will command confidence in the auditing process. It is not, however, believed necessary, or sound public policy, to intrude upon the confidentiality of the lawyer-client relationship in order to command such confidence. On the contrary, the objective of fair disclosure in financial statements is more likely to be better served by maintaining the integrity of the confidential relationship between lawyer and client, thereby strengthening corporate management's confidence in counsel and encouraging its readiness to seek advice of counsel and to act in accordance with counsel's advice.

Consistent with the foregoing public policy considerations, it is believed appropriate to distinguish between, on the one hand, litigation which is pending or which a third party has manifested to the client a present intention to commence and, on the other hand, other contingencies of a legal nature or having legal aspects. As regards the former category, unquestionably the lawyer representing the client in a litigation matter may be the best source for a description of the claim or claims asserted, the client's position (e.g., denial, contest, etc.), and the client's possible exposure in the litigation (to the extent the lawyer is in a position to do so). As to the latter category, it is submitted that, for the reasons set forth above, it is not in the public interest for the lawyer to be required to respond to general inquiries from auditors concerning possible claims.

It is recognized that the disclosure requirements for enterprises subject to the reporting requirements of the Federal securities laws are a major concern of managements and counsel, as well as auditors. It is submitted that compliance therewith is best assured when clients are afforded maximum encouragement, by protecting lawyer-client confidentiality, freely to consult counsel. Likewise, lawyers must be keenly conscious of the importance of their clients being competently advised in these matters.

Statement of Policy

NOW, THEREFORE, BE IT RESOLVED that it is desirable and in the public interest that this Association adopt the following Statement of Policy regarding the appropriate scope of the lawyer's response to the auditor's request, made by the client at the request of the auditor, for information concerning matters referred to the lawyer during the course of his representation of the client:

1. *Client Consent to Response.* The lawyer may properly respond to the auditor's requests for information concerning loss contingencies (the term and concept established by Statement of Financial Accounting Standards No. 5,[†] promulgated by the Financial Accounting Standards Board in March 1975 and discussed in Paragraph 5.1 of the accompanying Commentary), to the extent hereinafter set forth, subject to the following:

[†] In July 2009, the Financial Accounting Standards Board (FASB) issued FASB *Accounting Standards Codification*™ (ASC) as authoritative. FASB ASC is now the source of authoritative U.S. accounting and reporting standards for nongovernmental entities, in addition to guidance promulgated by the Securities and Exchange Commission (SEC). As of July 1, 2009, all other nongrandfathered, non-SEC accounting literature not included in FASB ASC became nonauthoritative. FASB Statement No. 5, *Accounting for Contingencies*, has been codified as FASB ASC 450, *Contingencies*.

a. Assuming that the client's initial letter requesting the lawyer to provide information to the auditor is signed by an agent of the client having apparent authority to make such a request, the lawyer may provide to the auditor information requested, without further consent, unless such information discloses a confidence or a secret or requires an evaluation of a claim.

b. In the normal case, the initial request letter does not provide the necessary consent to the disclosure of a confidence or secret or to the evaluation of a claim since that consent may only be given after full disclosure to the client of the legal consequences of such action.

c. Lawyers should bear in mind, in evaluating claims, that an adverse party may assert that any evaluation of potential liability is an admission.

d. In securing the client's consent to the disclosure of confidences or secrets, or the evaluation of claims, the lawyer may wish to have a draft of his letter reviewed and approved by the client before releasing it to the auditor; in such cases, additional explanation would in all probability be necessary so that the legal consequences of the consent are fully disclosed to the client.

2. *Limitation on Scope of Response.* It is appropriate for the lawyer to set forth in his response, by way of limitation, the scope of his engagement by the client. It is also appropriate for the lawyer to indicate the date as of which information is furnished and to disclaim any undertaking to advise the auditor of changes which may thereafter be brought to the lawyer's attention. *Unless the lawyer's response indicates otherwise, (a) it is properly limited to matters which have been given substantive attention by the lawyer in the form of legal consultation and, where appropriate, legal representation since the beginning of the period or periods being reported upon, and (b) if a law firm or a law department, the auditor may assume that the firm or department has endeavored, to the extent believed necessary by the firm or department, to determine from lawyers currently in the firm or department who have performed services for the client since the beginning of the fiscal period under audit whether such services involved substantive attention in the form of legal consultation concerning those loss contingencies referred to in Paragraph 5(a) below but, beyond that, no review has been made of any of the client's transactions or other matters for the purpose of identifying loss contingencies to be described in the response.*‡

3. *Response may be Limited to Material Items.* In response to an auditor's request for disclosure of loss contingencies of a client, it is appropriate for the lawyer's response to indicate that the response is limited to items which are considered individually or collectively material to the presentation of the client's financial statements.

4. *Limited Responses.* Where the lawyer is limiting his response in accordance with the Statement of Policy, his response should so

---

‡ As contemplated by Paragraph 8 of this Statement of Policy, this sentence is intended to be the subject of incorporation by reference as therein provided.

indicate (see Paragraph 8). If in any other respect the lawyer is not undertaking to respond to or comment on particular aspects of the inquiry when responding to the auditor, he should consider advising the auditor that his response is limited, in order to avoid any inference that the lawyer has responded to all aspects; otherwise, he may be assuming a responsibility which he does not intend.

5. *Loss Contingencies*. When properly requested by the client, it is appropriate for the lawyer to furnish to the auditor information concerning the following matters if the lawyer has been engaged by the client to represent or advise the client professionally with respect thereto and he has devoted substantive attention to them in the form of legal representation or consultation:

   a. *overtly threatened or pending litigation*, whether or not specified by the client;

   b. *a contractually assumed obligation* which the client has specifically identified and upon which the client has specifically requested, in the inquiry letter or a supplement thereto, comment to the auditor;

   c. *an unasserted possible claim or assessment* which the client has specifically identified and upon which the client has specifically requested, in the inquiry letter or a supplement thereto, comment to the auditor.

   With respect to clause (a), overtly threatened litigation means that a potential claimant has manifested to the client an awareness of and present intention to assert a possible claim or assessment unless the likelihood of litigation (or of settlement when litigation would normally be avoided) is considered remote. With respect to clause (c), where there has been no manifestation by a potential claimant of an awareness of and present intention to assert a possible claim or assessment, consistent with the considerations and concerns outlined in the Preamble and Paragraph 1 hereof, the client should request the lawyer to furnish information to the auditor only if the client has determined that it is probable that a possible claim will be asserted, that there is a reasonable possibility that the outcome (assuming such assertion) will be unfavorable, and that the resulting liability would be material to the financial condition of the client. Examples of such situations might (depending in each case upon the particular circumstances) include the following: (i) a catastrophe, accident or other similar physical occurrence in which the client's involvement is open and notorious, or (ii) an investigation by a government agency where enforcement proceedings have been instituted or where the likelihood that they will not be instituted is remote, under circumstances where assertion of one or more private claims for redress would normally be expected, or (iii) a public disclosure by the client acknowledging (and thus focusing attention upon) the existence of one or more probable claims arising out of an event or circumstance. In assessing whether or not the assertion of a possible claim is probable, it is expected that the client would normally employ, by reason of the inherent uncertainties involved and insufficiency of available data, concepts parallel to those used by the lawyer (discussed below) in assessing whether or not an unfavorable outcome is probable; thus, assertion of a possible claim would be considered probable only when the prospects of its being asserted seem reasonably certain (i.e., supported by extrinsic evidence strong enough to establish a presumption that it will happen) and the prospects of nonassertion seem slight.

It would not be appropriate, however, for the lawyer to be requested to furnish information in response to an inquiry letter or supplement thereto if it appears that (a) the client has been required to specify unasserted possible claims without regard to the standard suggested in the preceding paragraph, or (b) the client has been required to specify all or substantially all unasserted possible claims as to which legal advice may have been obtained, since, in either case, such a request would be in substance a general inquiry and would be inconsistent with the intent of this Statement of Policy.

The information that lawyers may properly give to the auditor concerning the foregoing matters would include (to the extent appropriate) an identification of the proceedings or matter, the stage of proceedings, the claim(s) asserted, and the position taken by the client.

In view of the inherent uncertainties, the lawyer should normally refrain from expressing judgments as to outcome except in those relatively few clear cases where it appears to the lawyer that an unfavorable outcome is either "probable" or "remote"; for purposes of any such judgment it is appropriate to use the following meanings:

i. *probable*—an unfavorable outcome for the client is probable if the prospects of the claimant not succeeding are judged to be extremely doubtful and the prospects for success by the client in its defense are judged to be slight.

ii. *remote*—an unfavorable outcome is remote if the prospects for the client not succeeding in its defense are judged to be extremely doubtful and the prospects of success by the claimant are judged to be slight.

If, in the opinion of the lawyer, considerations within the province of his professional judgment bear on a particular loss contingency to the degree necessary to make an informed judgment, he may in appropriate circumstances communicate to the auditor his view that an unfavorable outcome is "probable" or "remote," applying the above meanings. No inference should be drawn, from the absence of such a judgment, that the client will not prevail.

The lawyer also may be asked to estimate, in dollar terms, the potential amount of loss or range of loss in the event that an unfavorable outcome is not viewed to be "remote." In such a case, the amount or range of potential loss will normally be as inherently impossible to ascertain, with any degree of certainty, as the outcome of the litigation. Therefore, it is appropriate for the lawyer to provide an estimate of the amount or range of potential loss (if the outcome should be unfavorable) only if he believes that the probability of inaccuracy of the estimate of the amount or range of potential loss is slight.

The considerations bearing upon the difficulty in estimating loss (or range of loss) where pending litigation is concerned are obviously even more compelling in the case of unasserted possible claims. In most cases, the lawyer will not be able to provide any such estimate to the auditor.

As indicated in Paragraph 4 hereof, the auditor may assume that all loss contingencies specified by the client in the manner specified in clauses (b) and (c) above have received comment in the response, unless otherwise therein indicated. The lawyer should not be asked, nor need the lawyer undertake, to furnish information to the auditor concerning loss contingencies except as contemplated by this Paragraph 5.

6. *Lawyer's Professional Responsibility*. Independent of the scope of his response to the auditor's request for information, the lawyer, depending upon the nature of the matters as to which he is engaged, may have as part of his professional responsibility to his client an obligation to advise the client concerning the need for or advisability of public disclosure of a wide range of events and circumstances. The lawyer has an obligation not knowingly to participate in any violation by the client of the disclosure requirements of the securities laws. In appropriate circumstances, the lawyer also may be required under the Code of Professional Responsibility to resign his engagement if his advice concerning disclosures is disregarded by the client. The auditor may properly assume that whenever, in the course of performing legal services for the client with respect to a matter recognized to involve an unasserted possible claim or assessment which may call for financial statement disclosure, the lawyer has formed a professional conclusion that the client must disclose or consider disclosure concerning such possible claim or assessment, the lawyer, as a matter of professional responsibility to the client, will so advise the client and will consult with the client concerning the question of such disclosure and the applicable requirements [||] of FAS 5.

7. *Limitation on Use of Response. Unless otherwise stated in the lawyer's response, it shall be solely for the auditor's information in connection with his audit of the financial condition of the client and is not to be quoted in whole or in part or otherwise referred to in any financial statements of the client or related documents, nor is it to be filed with any governmental agency or other person, without the lawyer's prior written consent.*[‡] *Notwithstanding such limitation, the response can properly be furnished to others in compliance with court process or when necessary in order to defend the auditor against a challenge of the audit by the client or a regulatory agency, provided that the lawyer is given written notice of the circumstances at least twenty days before the response is so to be furnished to others, or as long in advance as possible if the situation does not permit such period of notice.*[‡]

8. *General*. This Statement of Policy, together with the accompanying Commentary (which is an integral part hereof), has been developed for the general guidance of the legal profession. In a

---

|| Under FAS 5, when there has been no manifestation by a potential claimant of an awareness of a possible claim or assessment, disclosure of an unasserted possible claim is required only if the enterprise concludes that (i) it is probable that a claim will be asserted, (ii) there is a reasonable possibility, if the claim is in fact asserted, that the outcome will be unfavorable, and (iii) the liability resulting from such unfavorable outcome would be material to its financial condition.

‡ As contemplated by Paragraph 8 of this Statement of Policy, this sentence is intended to be the subject of incorporation by reference as therein provided.

particular case, the lawyer may elect to supplement or modify the approach hereby set forth. If desired, this Statement of Policy may be incorporated by reference in the lawyer's response by the following statement: "This response is limited by, and in accordance with, the ABA Statement of Policy Regarding Lawyers' Responses to Auditors' Requests for Information (December 1975); without limiting the generality of the foregoing, the limitations set forth in such Statement on the scope and use of this response (Paragraphs 2 and 7) are specifically incorporated herein by reference, and any description herein of any loss contingencies' is qualified in its entirety by Paragraph 5 of the Statement and the accompanying Commentary (which is an integral part of the Statement)."

The accompanying Commentary is an integral part of this Statement of Policy.

Commentary

Paragraph 1 (Client Consent to Response)

In responding to any aspect of an auditor's inquiry letter, the lawyer must be guided by his ethical obligations as set forth in the Code of Professional Responsibility. Under Canon 4 of the Code of Professional Responsibility a lawyer is enjoined to preserve the client's confidences (defined as information protected by the attorney-client privilege under applicable law) and the client's secrets (defined as other information gained in the professional relationship that the client has requested be held inviolate or the disclosure of which would be embarrassing or would be likely to be detrimental to the client). The observance of this ethical obligation, in the context of public policy, ". . . not only facilitates the full development of facts essential to proper representation of the client but also encourages laymen to seek early legal assistance." (Ethical Consideration 4-1).

The lawyer's ethical obligation therefore includes a much broader range of information than that protected by the attorney-client privilege. As stated in Ethical Consideration 4-4: "The attorney-client privilege is more limited than the ethical obligation of a lawyer to guard the confidences and secrets of his client. This ethical precept, unlike the evidentiary privilege, exists without regard to the nature or source of information or the fact that others share the knowledge."

In recognition of this ethical obligation, the lawyer should be careful to disclose fully to his client any confidence, secret or evaluation that is to be revealed to another, including the client's auditor, and to satisfy himself that the officer or agent of a corporate client consenting to the disclosure understands the legal consequences thereof and has authority to provide the required consent.

The law in the area of attorney-client privilege and the impact of statements made in letters to auditors upon that privilege has not yet been developed. Based upon cases treating the attorney-client privilege in other contexts, however, certain generalizations can be made with respect to the possible impact of statements in letters to auditors.

It is now generally accepted that a corporation may claim the attorney-client privilege. Whether the privilege extends beyond the control group of the corporation (a concept found in the existing decisional authority), and if so, how far, is yet unresolved.

If a client discloses to a third party a part of any privileged communication he has made to his attorney, there may have been a waiver as to the whole communication; further, it has been suggested that giving accountants access to privileged statements made to attorneys may waive any privilege as to those statements. Any disclosure of privileged communications relating to a particular subject matter may have the effect of waiving the privilege on other communications with respect to the same subject matter.

To the extent that the lawyer's knowledge of unasserted possible claims is obtained by means of confidential communications from the client, any disclosure thereof might constitute a waiver as fully as if the communication related to pending claims.

A further difficulty arises with respect to requests for evaluation of either pending or unasserted possible claims. It might be argued that any evaluation of a claim, to the extent based upon a confidential communication with the client, waives any privilege with respect to that claim.

Another danger inherent in a lawyer's placing a value on a claim, or estimating the likely result, is that such a statement might be treated as an admission or might be otherwise prejudicial to the client.

The Statement of Policy has been prepared in the expectation that judicial development of the law in the foregoing areas will be such that useful communication between lawyers and auditors in the manner envisaged in the Statement will not prove prejudicial to clients engaged in or threatened with adversary proceedings. If developments occur contrary to this expectation, appropriate review and revision of the Statement of Policy may be necessary.

Paragraph 2 (Limitation on Scope of Response)

In furnishing information to an auditor, the lawyer can properly limit himself to loss contingencies which he is handling on a substantive basis for the client in the form of legal consultation (advice and other attention to matters not in litigation by the lawyer in his professional capacity) or legal representation (counsel of record or other direct professional responsibility for a matter in litigation). Some auditors' inquiries go further and ask for information on matters of which the lawyer "has knowledge." Lawyers are concerned that such a broad request may be deemed to include information coming from a variety of sources including social contact and third party contacts as well as professional engagement and that the lawyer might be criticized or subjected to liability if some of this information is forgotten at the time of the auditor's request.

It is also believed appropriate to recognize that the lawyer will not necessarily have been authorized to investigate, or have investigated, all legal problems of the client, even when on notice of some facts which might conceivably constitute a legal problem upon exploration and development. Thus, consideration in the form of preliminary or passing advice, or regarding an incomplete or hypothetical state of facts, or where the lawyer has not been requested to give studied attention to the matter in question, would not come within the concept of "substantive attention" and would therefore be excluded. Similarly excluded are matters which may have been mentioned by the client but which are not actually being handled by the lawyer. Paragraph 2 undertakes to deal with these concerns.

Paragraph 2 is also intended to recognize the principle that the appropriate lawyer to respond as to a particular loss contingency is the lawyer having charge of the matter for the client (e.g., the lawyer representing the client in a litigation matter and/or the lawyer having overall charge and supervision of the matter), and that the lawyer not having that kind of role with respect to the matter should not be expected to respond merely because of having become aware of its existence in a general or incidental way.

The internal procedures to be followed by a law firm or law department may vary based on factors such as the scope of the lawyer's engagement and the complexity and magnitude of the client's affairs. Such procedures could, but need not, include use of a docket system to record litigation, consultation with lawyers in the firm or department having principal responsibility for the client's affairs or other procedures which, in light of the cost to the client, are not disproportionate to the anticipated benefit to be derived. Although these procedures may not necessarily identify all matters relevant to the response, the evolution and application of the lawyer's customary procedures should constitute a reasonable basis for the lawyer's response.

As the lawyer's response is limited to matters involving his professional engagement as counsel, such response should not include information concerning the client which the lawyer receives in another role. In particular, a lawyer who is also a director or officer of the client would not include information which he received as a director or officer unless the information was also received (or, absent the dual role, would in the normal course be received) in his capacity as legal counsel in the context of his professional engagement. Where the auditor's request for information is addressed to a law firm as a firm, the law firm may properly assume that its response is not expected to include any information which may have been communicated to the particular individual by reason of his serving in the capacity of director or officer of the client. The question of the individual's duty, in his role as a director or officer, is not here addressed.

Paragraph 3 (Response May Cover only Material Items in Certain Cases)

Paragraph 3 makes it clear that the lawyer may optionally limit his responses to those items which are individually or collectively material to the auditor's inquiry. If the lawyer takes responsibility for making a determination that a matter is not material for the purposes of his response to the audit inquiry, he should make it clear that his response is so limited. The auditor, in such circumstance, should properly be entitled to rely upon the lawyer's response as providing him with the necessary corroboration. It should be emphasized that the employment of inside general counsel by the client should not detract from the acceptability of his response since inside general counsel is as fully bound by the professional obligations and responsibilities contained in the Code of Professional Responsibility as outside counsel. If the audit inquiry sets forth a definition of materiality but the lawyer utilizes a different test of materiality, he should specifically so state. The lawyer may wish to reach an understanding with the auditor concerning the test of materiality to be used in his response, but he need not do so if he assumes responsibility for the criteria used in making materiality determinations. Any such understanding with the auditor should be referred to or set forth in the lawyer's response. In this connection, it is assumed that the test of materiality so agreed upon would not be so low in amount as to result in a disservice to the client and an unreasonable burden on counsel.

Paragraph 4 (Limited Responses)

The Statement of Policy is designed to recognize the obligation of the auditor to complete the procedures considered necessary to satisfy himself as to the fair presentation of the company's financial condition and results, in order to render a report which includes an opinion not qualified because of a limitation on the scope of the audit. In this connection, reference is made to SEC Accounting Series Release No. 90 [*Financial Reporting Release No. 1, section 607.01(b)*], in which it is stated:

"A 'subject to' or 'except for' opinion paragraph in which these phrases refer to the scope of the audit, indicating that the accountant has not been able to satisfy himself on some significant element in the financial statements, is not acceptable in certificates filed with the Commission in connection with the public offering of securities. The 'subject to' qualification is appropriate when the reference is to a middle paragraph or to footnotes explaining the status of matters which cannot be resolved at statement date."

Paragraph 5 (Loss Contingencies)

Paragraph 5 of the Statement of Policy summarizes the categories of "loss contingencies" about which the lawyer may furnish information to the auditor. The term loss contingencies and the categories relate to concepts of accounting accrual and disclosure specified for the accounting profession in Statement of Financial Accounting Standards No. 5[†] ("FAS 5") issued by the Financial Accounting Standards Board in March, 1975.

5.1 Accounting Requirements

To understand the significance of the auditor's inquiry and the implications of any response the lawyer may give, the lawyer should be aware of the following accounting concepts and requirements set out in FAS 5:[#]

a. A "loss contingency" is an existing condition, situation or set of circumstances involving uncertainty as to possible loss to an enterprise that will ultimately be resolved when one or more events occur or fail to occur. Resolutions of the uncertainty may confirm the loss or impairment of an asset or the incurrence of a liability. (Para. 1)

b. When a "loss contingency" exists, the likelihood that a future event or events will confirm the loss or impairment of an asset or the incurrence of a liability can range from probable to remote. There are three areas within that range, defined as follows:

  i. Probable—"The future event or events are likely to occur."

  ii. Reasonably possible—"The chance of the future event or events occurring is more than remote but less than likely."

  iii. Remote—"The chance of the future event or events occurring is slight." (Para. 3)

c. *Accrual* in a client's financial statements by a charge to income of the period will be required if both the following conditions are met:

  i. "Information available prior to issuance of the financial statements indicates that it is *probable* that an asset had been impaired or a liability had been incurred at the date of the financial statements. It is implicit in this condition that it must be *probable* that one or more future events will occur confirming the fact of the loss." (emphasis added; footnote omitted)

  ii. "The amount of loss can be reasonably estimated." (Para. 8)

d. If there is no *accrual* of the loss contingency in the client's financial statements because one of the two conditions outlined in (c)

---

† In July 2009, the Financial Accounting Standards Board (FASB) issued FASB *Accounting Standards Codification*™ (ASC) as authoritative. FASB ASC is now the source of authoritative U.S. accounting and reporting standards for nongovernmental entities, in addition to guidance promulgated by the Securities and Exchange Commission (SEC). As of July 1, 2009, all other nongrandfathered, non-SEC accounting literature not included in FASB ASC became nonauthoritative. FASB Statement No. 5, *Accounting for Contingencies*, has been codified as FASB ASC 450, *Contingencies*.

\# Citations are to paragraph numbers of FAS 5.

above are not met, disclosure may be required as provided in the following:

> "If no accrual is made for a loss contingency because one or both of the conditions in paragraph 8 are not met, or if an exposure to loss exists in excess of the amount accrued pursuant to the provisions of paragraph 8, *disclosure* of the contingency *shall be made when there is at least a reasonable possibility* that a loss or an additional loss may have been incurred. *The disclosure shall indicate the nature of the contingency and shall give an estimate of the possible loss or range of loss or state that such an estimate cannot be made. Disclosure is not required of a loss contingency involving an unasserted claim* or assessment *when there has been no manifestation by potential claimant of an awareness of a possible claim or assessment unless it is considered probable that a claim will be asserted and there is a reasonable possibility that the outcome will be unfavorable*." (emphasis added; footnote omitted) (Para. 10)

e. The accounting requirements recognize or specify that (i) the opinions or views of counsel are not the sole source of audit evidence in making determinations about the accounting recognition or treatment to be given to litigation, and (ii) the fact that the lawyer is notable to express an opinion that the outcome will be favorable does not necessarily require an accrual of a loss. Paragraphs 36 and 37 of FAS 5 state as follows:

> "If the underlying cause of the litigation, claim, or assessment is an event occurring before the date of an enterprise's financial statements, the probability of an outcome unfavorable to the enterprise must be assessed to determine whether the condition in paragraph 8(a) is met. Among the factors that should be considered are the nature of the litigation, claim, or assessment, the progress of the case (including progress after the date of the financial statements but before those statements are issued), the opinions or views of legal counsel and other advisers, the experience of the enterprise in similar cases, the experience of other enterprises, and any decision of the enterprise's management as to how the enterprise intends to respond to the lawsuit, claim, or assessment (for example, a decision to contest the case vigorously or a decision to seek an out-of-court settlement). The fact that legal counsel is unable to express an opinion that the outcome will be favorable to the enterprise should not necessarily be interpreted to mean that the condition for accrual of a loss in paragraph 8(a) is met.
>
> "The filing of a suit or formal assertion of a claim or assessment does not automatically indicate that accrual of a loss may be appropriate. The degree of probability of an unfavorable outcome must be assessed. The condition for accrual in paragraph 8(a) would be met if an unfavorable outcome is determined to be probable. If an unfavorable outcome is determined to be reasonably possible but not probable, or if the amount of loss cannot be reasonably estimated, accrual would be inappropriate, but disclosure would be required by paragraph 10 of this Statement."

f. Paragraph 38 of FAS 5 focuses on certain examples concerning the determination by the enterprise whether an assertion of an *unasserted possible claim* may be considered probable:

"With respect to unasserted claims and assessments, an enterprise must determine the degree of probability that a suit may be filed or a claim or assessment may be asserted and the possibility of an unfavorable outcome. For example, a catastrophe, accident, or other similar physical occurrence predictably engenders claims for redress, and in such circumstances their assertion may be probable; similarly, an investigation of an enterprise by a governmental agency, if enforcement proceedings have been or are likely to be instituted, is often followed by private claims for redress, and the probability of their assertion and the possibility of loss should be considered in each case. By way of further example, an enterprise may believe there is a possibility that it has infringed on another enterprise's patent rights, but the enterprise owning the patent rights has not indicated an intention to take any action and has not even indicated an awareness of the possible infringement. In that case, a judgment must first be made as to whether the assertion of a claim is probable. If the judgment is that assertion is not probable, no accrual or disclosure would be required. On the other hand, if the judgment is that assertion is probable, then a second judgment must be made as to the degree of probability of an unfavorable outcome. If an unfavorable outcome is probable and the amount of loss can be reasonably estimated, accrual of a loss is required by paragraph 8. If an unfavorable outcome is probable but the amount of loss cannot be reasonably estimated, accrual would not be appropriate, but disclosure would be required by paragraph 10. If an unfavorable outcome is reasonably possible but not probable, disclosure would be required by paragraph 10."

For a more complete presentation of FAS 5, reference is made to AU section 337B, *Exhibit I—Excerpts From Financial Accounting Standards Board* Accounting Standards Codification *450,* Contingencies,[**] in which are set forth excerpts selected by the AICPA as relevant to a Statement on Auditing Standards, issued by its Auditing Standards Executive Committee, captioned "Inquiry of a Client's Lawyer Concerning Litigation, Claims, and Assessments."

5.2 Lawyer's Response

Concepts of probability inherent in the usage of terms like "probable" or "reasonably possible" or "remote" mean different things in different contexts. Generally, the outcome of, or the loss which may result from, litigation cannot be assessed in any way that is comparable to a statistically or empirically determined concept of "probability" that may be applicable when determining such matters as reserves for warranty obligations or accounts receivable or loan losses when there is a large number of transactions and a substantial body of known historical experience for the enterprise or comparable enterprises. While lawyers are accustomed to counseling clients during the progress of litigation as to the possible amount required for settlement purposes, the estimated risks of the proceedings at particular times and the possible application or establishment

[**] Statement on Auditing Standards No. 12 section 337B, *Exhibit I—Excerpts From Financial Accounting Standards Board* Accounting Standards Codification *450*, Contingencies, has been withdrawn by this section.

of points of law that may be relevant, such advice to the client is not possible at many stages of the litigation and may change dramatically depending upon the development of the proceedings. Lawyers do not generally quantify for clients the "odds" in numerical terms; if they do, the quantification is generally only undertaken in an effort to make meaningful, for limited purposes, a whole host of judgmental factors applicable at a particular time, without any intention to depict "probability" in any statistical, scientific or empirically-grounded sense. Thus, for example, statements that litigation is being defended vigorously and that the client has meritorious defenses do not, and do not purport to, make a statement about the probability of outcome in any measurable sense.

Likewise, the "amount" of loss—that is, the total of costs and damages that ultimately might be assessed against a client—will, in most litigation, be a subject of wide possible variance at most stages; it is the rare case where the amount is precise and where the question is whether the client against which claim is made is liable either for all of it or none of it.

In light of the foregoing considerations, it must be concluded that, as a general rule, it should not be anticipated that meaningful quantifications of "probability" of outcome or amount of damages can be given by lawyers in assessing litigation. To provide content to the definitions set forth in Paragraph 5 of the Statement of Policy, this Commentary amplifies the meanings of the terms under discussion, as follows:

> "*probable*"—An unfavorable outcome is normally "probable" if, but only if, investigation, preparation (including development of the factual data and legal research) and progress of the matter have reached a stage where a judgment can be made, taking all relevant factors into account which may affect the outcome, that it is extremely doubtful that the client will prevail.

> "*remote*"—The prospect for an unfavorable outcome appears, at the time, to be slight; i.e., it is extremely doubtful that the client will not prevail. Normally, this would entail the ability to make an unqualified judgment, taking into account all relevant factors which may affect the outcome, that the client may confidently expect to prevail on a motion for summary judgment on all issues due to the clarity of the facts and the law.

In other words, for purposes of the lawyer's response to the request to advise auditors about litigation, an unfavorable outcome will be "probable" only if the chances of the client prevailing appear slight and of the claimant losing appear extremely doubtful; it will be "remote" when the client's chances of losing appear slight and of not winning appear extremely doubtful. It is, therefore, to be anticipated that, in most situations, an unfavorable outcome will be neither "probable" nor "remote" as defined in the Statement of Policy.

The discussion above about the very limited basis for furnishing judgments about the outcome of litigation applies with even more force to a judgment concerning whether or not the assertion of a claim not yet asserted is "probable." That judgment will infrequently be one within the professional competence of lawyers and therefore the lawyer should not undertake such assessment except where such judgment may become meaningful because of the presence of special circumstances, such as catastrophes, investigations and previous public disclosure as cited in Paragraph 5 of the Statement of Policy, or similar extrinsic evidence relevant to such assessment. Moreover, it is unlikely, absent relevant extrinsic evidence, that the client or anyone else will be in a position to make an informed judgment that assertion of a possible claim is "probable" as opposed to "reasonably possible" (in which event disclosure is not required). In light of the legitimate concern that the public interest would not be well served by resolving uncertainties in a way that invites the assertion of claims or otherwise causes unnecessary harm to the client and its stockholders, a decision to treat an unasserted claim as "probable" of assertion should be based only upon compelling judgment.

Consistent with these limitations believed appropriate for the lawyer, he should not represent to the auditor, nor should any inference from his response be drawn, that the unasserted possible claims identified by the client (as contemplated by Paragraph 5(c) of the Statement of Policy) represent all such claims of which the lawyer may be aware or that he necessarily concurs in his client's determination of which unasserted possible claims warrant specification by the client; within proper limits, this determination is one which the client is entitled to make—and should make—and it would be inconsistent with his professional obligations for the lawyer to volunteer information arising from his confidential relationship with his client.

As indicated in Paragraph 5, the lawyer also may be asked to estimate the potential loss (or range) in the event that an unfavorable outcome is not viewed to be "remote." In such a case, the lawyer would provide an estimate only if he believes that the probability of inaccuracy of the estimate of the range or amount is slight. What is meant here is that the estimate of amount of loss presents the same difficulty as assessment of outcome and that the same formulation of "probability" should be used with respect to the determination of estimated loss amounts as should be used with respect to estimating the outcome of the matter.

In special circumstances, with the proper consent of the client, the lawyer may be better able to provide the auditor with information concerning loss contingencies through conferences where there is opportunity for more detailed discussion and interchange. However, the principles set forth in the Statement of Policy and this Commentary are fully applicable to such conferences.

Subsumed throughout this discussion is the ongoing responsibility of the lawyer to assist his client, at the client's request, in complying with the requirements of FAS 5 to the extent such assistance falls within his professional competence. This will continue to involve, to the extent appropriate, privileged discussions with the client to provide a better basis on which the client can make accrual and disclosure determinations in respect of its financial statements.

In addition to the considerations discussed above with respect to the making of any judgment or estimate by the lawyer in his response to the auditor, including with respect to a matter specifically identified by the client, the lawyer should also bear in mind the risk that the furnishing of such a judgment or estimate to any one other than the client might constitute an admission or be otherwise prejudicial to the client's position in its defense against such litigation or claim (see Paragraph 1 of the Statement of Policy and of this Commentary).

Paragraph 6 (Lawyer's Professional Responsibility)

The client must satisfy whatever duties it has relative to timely disclosure, including appropriate disclosure concerning material loss contingencies, and, to the extent such matters are given substantive attention in the form of legal consultation, the lawyer, when his engagement is to advise his client concerning a disclosure obligation, has a responsibility to advise his client concerning its obligations in this regard. Although lawyers who normally confine themselves to a legal specialty such as tax, antitrust, patent or admiralty law, unlike lawyers consulted about SEC or general corporate matters, would not be expected to advise generally concerning the client's disclosure obligations in respect of a matter on which the lawyer is working, the legal specialist should counsel his client with respect to the client's obligations under FAS 5 to the extent contemplated herein. Without regard to legal specialty, the lawyer should be mindful of his professional responsibility to the client described in Paragraph 6 of the Statement of Policy concerning disclosure.

The lawyer's responsibilities with respect to his client's disclosure obligations have been a subject of considerable discussion and there may be, in due course, clarification and further guidance in this regard. In any event, where in the lawyer's view it is clear that (i) the matter is of material importance and seriousness, and (ii) there can be no reasonable doubt that its non-disclosure in the client's financial statements would be a violation of law giving rise to material claims, rejection by the client of his advice to call the matter to the attention of the auditor would almost certainly require the lawyer's withdrawal from employment in accordance with the Code of Professional Responsibility. (See, e.g., Disciplinary Rule 7-102 (A)(3) and (7), and Disciplinary Rule 2-110 (B)(2).) Withdrawal under such circumstances is obviously undesirable and might present serious problems for the client. Accordingly, in the context of financial accounting and reporting for loss contingencies arising from unasserted claims, the standards for which are contained in FAS 5, clients should be urged to disclose to the auditor information concerning an unasserted possible claim or assessment (not otherwise specifically identified by the client) where in the course of the services performed for the client it has become clear to the lawyer that (i) the client has no reasonable basis to conclude that assertion of the claim is not probable (employing the concepts hereby enunciated) and (ii) given the probability of assertion, disclosure of the loss contingency in the client's financial statements is beyond reasonable dispute required.

Paragraph 7 (Limitation on Use of Response)

Some inquiry letters make specific reference to, and one might infer from others, an intention to quote verbatim or include the substance of the lawyer's reply in footnotes to the client's financial statements. Because the client's prospects in pending litigation may shift as a result of interim developments, and because the lawyer should have an opportunity, if quotation is to be made, to review the footnote in full, it would seem prudent to limit the use of the lawyer's reply letter. Paragraph 7 sets out such a limitation.

Paragraph 7 also recognizes that it may be in the client's interest to protect information contained in the lawyer's response to the auditor, if and to the extent possible, against unnecessary further disclosure or use beyond its intended purpose of informing the auditor. For example, the response may contain information which could prejudice efforts to negotiate a favorable settlement of a pending litigation described in the response. The requirement of consent to further disclosure, or of reasonable advance notice where disclosure may be required by court process or necessary in defense of the audit, is designed to give the lawyer an opportunity to consult with the client as to whether consent should be refused or limited or, in the case of legal process or the auditor's defense of the audit, as to whether steps can and should be taken to challenge the necessity of further disclosure or to seek protective measures in connection therewith. It is believed that the suggested standard of twenty days advance notice would normally be a minimum reasonable time for this purpose.

Paragraph 8 (General)

It is reasonable to assume that the Statement of Policy will receive wide distribution and will be readily available to the accounting profession. Specifically, the Statement of Policy has been reprinted as Exhibit II to the Statement on Auditing Standards, "Inquiry of a Client's Lawyer Concerning Litigation, Claims, and Assessments," issued by the Auditing Standards Executive Committee of the American Institute of Certified Public Accountants. Accordingly, the mechanic for its incorporation by reference will facilitate lawyer-auditor communication. The incorporation is intended to include not only limitations, such as those provided by Paragraphs 2 and 7 of the Statement of Policy, but also the explanatory material set forth in this Commentary.

Annex A

[*Illustrative forms of letters for full response by outside practitioner or law firm and inside general counsel to the auditor's inquiry letter. These illustrative forms, which are not part of the Statement of Policy, have been prepared by the Committee on Audit Inquiry Responses solely in order to assist those who may wish to have, for reference purposes, a form of response which incorporates the principles of the Statement of Policy and accompanying Commentary. Other forms of response letters will be appropriate depending on the circumstances.*]

Illustrative Form of Letter for Use by Outside Practitioner or Law Firm:

[*Name and Address of Accounting Firm*]

Re: [*Name of Client*] [*and Subsidiaries*]

Dear Sirs:

By letter date [*insert date of request*] Mr. [*insert name and title of officer signing request*] of [*insert name of client*] [*(the "Company") or (together with its subsidiaries, the "Company")*] has requested us to furnish you with certain information in connection with your examination of the accounts of the Company as at [*insert fiscal year-end*].

[*Insert description of the scope of the lawyer's engagement; the following are sample descriptions:*]

While this firm represents the Company on a regular basis, our engagement has been limited to specific matters as to which we were consulted by the Company.

[*or*]

We call your attention to the fact that this firm has during the past year represented the Company only in connection with certain [*Federal income tax matters*] [*litigation*] [*real estate transactions*] [*describe other specific matters, as appropriate*] and has not been engaged for any other purpose.

Subject to the foregoing and to the last paragraph of this letter, we advise you that since [*insert date of beginning of fiscal period under audit*] we have not been engaged to give substantive attention to, or represent the Company in connection with, [*material*][††] loss contingencies coming within the scope of clause (a) of Paragraph 5 of the Statement of Policy referred to in the last paragraph of this letter, except as follows:

[*Describe litigation and claims which fit the foregoing criteria.*]

[*If the inquiry letter requests information concerning specified unasserted possible claims or assessments and / or contractually assumed obligations:*]

With respect to the matters specifically identified in the Company's letter and upon which comment has been specifically requested, as contemplated by clauses (b) or (c) of Paragraph 5 of the ABA Statement of Policy, we advise you, subject to the last paragraph of this letter, as follows:

[*Insert information as appropriate*]

[††] ***Note:*** See Paragraph 3 of the Statement of Policy and the accompanying Commentary for guidance where the response is limited to material items.

The information set forth herein is [*as of the date of this letter*] [*as of (insert date), the date on which we commenced our internal review procedures for purposes of preparing this response*], except as otherwise noted, and we disclaim any undertaking to advise you of changes which thereafter may be brought to our attention.

[*Insert information with respect to outstanding bills for services and disbursements.*]

This response is limited by, and in accordance with, the ABA Statement of Policy Regarding Lawyers' Responses to Auditors' Requests for Information (December 1975); without limiting the generality of the foregoing, the limitations set forth in such Statement on the scope and use of this response (Paragraphs 2 and 7) are specifically incorporated herein by reference, and any description herein of any "loss contingencies" is qualified in its entirety by Paragraph 5 of the Statement and the accompanying Commentary (which is an integral part of the Statement). Consistent with the last sentence of Paragraph 6 of the ABA Statement of Policy and pursuant to the Company's request, this will confirm as correct the Company's understanding as set forth in its audit inquiry letter to us that whenever, in the course of performing legal services for the Company with respect to a matter recognized to involve an unasserted possible claim or assessment that may call for financial statement disclosure, we have formed a professional conclusion that the Company must disclose or consider disclosure concerning such possible claim or assessment, we, as a matter of professional responsibility to the Company, will so advise the Company and will consult with the Company concerning the question of such disclosure and the applicable requirements of Statement of Financial Accounting Standards No. 5.† [*Describe any other or additional limitation as indicated by Paragraph 4 of the Statement*]

Very truly yours,

Illustrative Form of Letter for Use by Inside General Counsel:

[*Name and Address of Accounting Firm*]

Re: [*Name of Company*] [*and Subsidiaries*]

Dear Sirs:

As General Counsel‡‡ of [*insert name of client*] [*(the "Company")*] [*(together with its subsidiaries, the "Company")*], I advise you as follows in connection with your examination of the accounts of the Company as at [*insert fiscal year-end*].

I call your attention to the fact that as General Counsel‡‡ for the Company I have general supervision of the Company's legal affairs. [*If the general legal supervisory responsibilities of the person signing the letter are limited, set forth here a clear description of those legal matters over which such person exercises general supervision, indicating exceptions to such supervision and situations where primary reliance should be placed on other sources.*] In such capacity, I have reviewed litigation and claims threatened or asserted

---

† In July 2009, the Financial Accounting Standards Board (FASB) issued FASB *Accounting Standards Codification*™ (ASC) as authoritative. FASB ASC is now the source of authoritative U.S. accounting and reporting standards for nongovernmental entities, in addition to guidance promulgated by the Securities and Exchange Commission (SEC). As of July 1, 2009, all other nongrandfathered, non-SEC accounting literature not included in FASB ASC became nonauthoritative. FASB Statement No. 5, *Accounting for Contingencies*, has been codified as FASB ASC 450, *Contingencies*.

‡‡ It may be appropriate in some cases for the response to be given by inside counsel other than inside general counsel, in which event this letter should be appropriately modified.

involving the Company and have consulted with outside legal counsel with respect thereto where I have deemed appropriate.

Subject to the foregoing and to the last paragraph of this letter, I advise you that since [*insert date of beginning of fiscal period under audit*] neither I, nor any of the lawyers over whom I exercise general legal supervision, have given substantive attention to, or represented the Company in connection with, [*material*][††] loss contingencies coming within the scope of clause (a) of Paragraph 5 of the Statement of Policy referred to in the last paragraph of this letter, except as follows:

[*Describe litigation and claims which fit the foregoing criteria.*]

[*If information concerning specified unasserted possible claims or assessments and / or contractually assumed obligations is to be supplied:*]

With respect to matters which have been specifically identified as contemplated by clauses (b) or (c) of Paragraph 5 of the ABA Statement of Policy, I advise you, subject to the last paragraph of this letter, as follows:

[*Insert information as appropriate*]

The information set forth herein is [*as of the date of this letter*] as of [*insert date*], the date on which we commenced our internal review procedures for purposes of preparing this response, except as otherwise noted, and I disclaim any undertaking to advise you of changes which thereafter may be brought to my attention or to the attention of the lawyers over whom I exercise general legal supervision.

This response is limited by, and in accordance with, the ABA Statement of Policy Regarding Lawyers' Responses to Auditors' Requests for Information (December 1975); without limiting the generality of the foregoing, the limitations set forth in such Statement on the scope and use of this response (Paragraphs 2 and 7) are specifically incorporated herein by reference, and any description herein of any "loss contingencies" is qualified in its entirety by Paragraph 5 of the Statement and the accompanying Commentary (which is an integral part of the Statement). Consistent with the last sentence of Paragraph 6 of the ABA Statement of Policy, this will confirm as correct the Company's understanding that whenever, in the course of performing legal services for the Company with respect to a matter recognized to involve an unasserted possible claim or assessment that may call for financial statement disclosure, I have formed a professional conclusion that the Company must disclose or consider disclosure concerning such possible claim or assessment, I, as a matter of professional responsibility to the Company, will so advise the Company and will consult with the Company concerning the question of such disclosure and the applicable requirements of Statement of Financial Accounting Standards No. 5.[†] [*Describe any other or additional limitation as indicated by Paragraph 4 of the Statement.*]

Very truly yours,

[††] ***Note:*** See Paragraph 3 of the Statement of Policy and the accompanying Commentary for guidance where the response is limited to material items.

[†] In July 2009, the Financial Accounting Standards Board (FASB) issued FASB *Accounting Standards Codification*™ (ASC) as authoritative. FASB ASC is now the source of authoritative U.S. accounting and reporting standards for nongovernmental entities, in addition to guidance promulgated by the Securities and Exchange Commission (SEC). As of July 1, 2009, all other nongrandfathered, non-SEC accounting literature not included in FASB ASC became nonauthoritative. FASB Statement No. 5, *Accounting for Contingencies*, has been codified as FASB ASC 450, *Contingencies*.

.A71

Exhibit B—Report of the Subcommittee on Audit Inquiry Responses[1]

Because of a recent court case and other judicial decisions involving lawyers' responses to auditors' requests for information, an area of uncertainty or concern has been brought to the Subcommittee's attention and is the subject of the following comment:

This Committee's report does not modify the ABA Statement of Policy, nor does it constitute an interpretation thereof. The Preamble to the ABA Statement of Policy states as follows:

Both the Code of Professional Responsibility and the cases applying the evidentiary privilege recognize that the privilege against disclosure can be knowingly and voluntarily waived by the client. It is equally clear that disclosure to a third party may result in loss of the "confidentiality" essential to maintain the privilege. Disclosure to a third party of the lawyer-client communication on a particular subject may also destroy the privilege as to other communications on that subject. Thus, the mere disclosure by the lawyer to the outside auditor, with due client consent, of the substance of communications between the lawyer and client may significantly impair the client's ability in other contexts to maintain the confidentiality of such communications.

Under the circumstances a policy of audit procedure which requires clients to give consent and authorize lawyers to respond to general inquiries and disclose information to auditors concerning matters which have been communicated in confidence is essentially destructive of free and open communication and early consultation between lawyer and client. The institution of such a policy would inevitably discourage management from discussing potential legal problems with counsel for fear that such discussion might become public and precipitate a loss to or possible liability of the business enterprise and its stockholders that might otherwise never materialize.

It is also recognized that our legal, political, and economic systems depend to an important extent on public confidence in published financial statements. To meet this need the accounting profession must adopt and adhere to standards and procedures that will command confidence in the auditing process. It is not, however, believed necessary, or sound public policy, to intrude upon the confidentiality of the lawyer-client relationship in order to command such confidence. On the contrary, the objective of fair disclosure in financial statements is more likely to be better served by maintaining the integrity of the confidential relationship between lawyer and client, thereby strengthening corporate management's confidence in counsel and to act in accordance with counsel's advice.

Paragraph 1 of the ABA Statement of Policy provides as follows:

> 1. *Client Consent to Response.* The lawyer may properly respond to the auditor's requests for information concerning loss contingencies (the term and concept established by Statement of Financial Accounting Standards No. 5, promulgated by the Financial Accounting Standards Board in March 1975 and discussed in

---

[1] Excerpted from "Statement of Policy Regarding Lawyers' Responses to Auditors' Requests for Information," *The Business Lawyer* 31, no. 3 (1976). Reprinted by permission of the American Bar Association.

Paragraph 5.1 of the accompanying commentary), to the extent hereinafter set forth, subject to the following:

a. Assuming that the client's initial letter requesting the lawyer to provide information to the auditor is signed by an agent of the client having apparent authority to make such a request, the lawyer may provide to the auditor information requested, without further consent, unless such information discloses a confidence or a secret or requires an evaluation of a claim.

b. In the normal case, the initial request letter does not provide the necessary consent to the disclosure of a confidence or secret or to the evaluation of a claim since that consent may only be given after full disclosure to the client of the legal consequences of such action.

c. Lawyers should bear in mind, in evaluating claims, that an adverse party may assert that any evaluation of potential liability is an admission.

d. In securing the client's consent to the disclosure of confidences or secrets, or the evaluation of claims, the lawyer may wish to have a draft of his letter reviewed and approved by the client before releasing it to the auditor; in such cases, additional explanation would in all probability be necessary so that the legal consequences of the consent are fully disclosed to the client.

In order to preserve explicitly the evidentiary privileges, some lawyers have suggested that clients include language in the following or substantially similar form:

> We do not intend that either our request to you to provide information to our auditor or your response to our auditor should be construed in any way to constitute a waiver of the attorney-client privilege or the attorney work-product privilege.

If client's request letter does not contain language similar to that in the preceding paragraph, the lawyer's statement that the client has so advised him or her may be based upon the fact that the client has in fact so advised the lawyer, in writing or orally, in other communications or in discussions.

For the same reason, the response letter from some lawyers also includes language in the following or substantially similar form:

> The Company [*or other defined term*] has advised us that, by making the request set forth in its letter to us, the Company [*or other defined term*] does not intend to waive the attorney-client privilege with respect to any information which the Company [*or other defined term*] has furnished to us. Moreover, please be advised that our response to you should not be construed in any way to constitute a waiver of the protection of the attorney work-product privilege with respect to any of our files involving the Company [*or other defined term*].

We believe that language similar to the foregoing in letters of the client or the lawyer simply makes explicit what has always been implicit, namely, it expressly states clearly that neither the client nor the lawyer intended a waiver. It follows that non-inclusion of either or both of the foregoing statements by the client or the lawyer in their respective letters at any time in the past or the future would not constitute an expression of intent to waive the privileges.

On the other hand, the inclusion of such language does not necessarily assure the client that, depending on the facts and circumstances, a waiver may not be found by a court of law to have occurred.

We do not believe that the foregoing types of inclusions cause a negative impact upon the public policy considerations described in the Preamble to the ABA Statement of Policy nor do they intrude upon the arrangements between the legal profession and the accounting profession contemplated by the ABA Statement of Policy. Moreover, we do not believe that such language interferes in any way with the standards and procedures of the accounting profession in the auditing process nor should it be construed as a limitation upon the lawyer's reply to the auditors. We have been informed that the Auditing Standards Board of the AICPA has adopted an interpretation of SAS 12 recognizing the propriety of these statements.

Lawyers, in any case, should be encouraged to have their draft letters to auditors reviewed and approved by the client before releasing them to the auditors and may wish to explain to the client the legal consequences of the client's consent to lawyer's response as contemplated by subparagraph 1(d) of the Statement of Policy.

AU-C Section 505 *

External Confirmations

Source: SAS No. 122.

Effective for audits of financial statements for periods ending on or after December 15, 2012.

Introduction

Scope of This Section

.01 This section addresses the auditor's use of external confirmation procedures to obtain audit evidence, in accordance with the requirements of section 330, *Performing Audit Procedures in Response to Assessed Risks and Evaluating the Audit Evidence Obtained*, and section 500, *Audit Evidence*. It does not address inquiries regarding litigation, claims, and assessments, which are addressed in section 501, *Audit Evidence—Specific Considerations for Selected Items*.

External Confirmation Procedures to Obtain Audit Evidence

.02 Section 500 indicates that the reliability of audit evidence is influenced by its source and nature and is dependent on the individual circumstances under which it is obtained.[1] Section 500 also includes the following generalizations applicable to audit evidence:[2]

- Audit evidence is more reliable when it is obtained from independent sources outside the entity.
- Audit evidence obtained directly by the auditor is more reliable than audit evidence obtained indirectly or by inference.
- Audit evidence is more reliable when it exists in documentary form, whether paper, electronic, or other medium.

Accordingly, depending on the circumstances of the audit, audit evidence in the form of external confirmations received directly by the auditor from confirming parties may be more reliable than evidence generated internally by the entity. This section is intended to assist the auditor in designing and performing external confirmation procedures to obtain relevant and reliable audit evidence.

.03 Other AU-C sections recognize the importance of external confirmations as audit evidence; for example

- section 330 discusses the auditor's responsibility (*a*) to design and implement overall responses to address the assessed risks of material misstatement at the financial statement level and (*b*) to

---

* This section has been codified using an "AU-C" identifier instead of an "AU" identifier. "AU-C" is a temporary identifier to avoid confusion with references to existing "AU" sections, which will remain in AICPA *Professional Standards* through 2013. The "AU-C" identifier will revert to "AU" in 2014, by which time substantially all engagements for which the "AU" sections were still effective are expected to be completed.

[1] Paragraph .A5 of section 500, *Audit Evidence*.

[2] Paragraph .A32 of section 500.

design and perform further audit procedures whose nature, timing, and extent are based on, and are responsive to, the assessed risks of material misstatement at the relevant assertion level.[3] In addition, section 330 requires that, irrespective of the assessed risks of material misstatement, the auditor design and perform substantive procedures for all relevant assertions related to each material class of transactions, account balance, and disclosure.[4] The auditor is required to consider whether external confirmation procedures are to be performed as substantive audit procedures and is required to use external confirmation procedures for accounts receivable unless

- — the overall account balance is immaterial,
- — external confirmation procedures would be ineffective, or
- — the auditor's assessed level of risk of material misstatement at the relevant assertion level is low, and the other planned substantive procedures address the assessed risk.[5]

- section 330 requires that the auditor obtain more persuasive audit evidence the higher the auditor's assessment of risk.[6] To do this, the auditor may increase the quantity of the evidence or obtain evidence that is more relevant or reliable, or both. For example, the auditor may place more emphasis on obtaining evidence directly from third parties or obtaining corroborating evidence from a number of independent sources. Section 330 also indicates that external confirmation procedures may assist the auditor in obtaining audit evidence with the high level of reliability that the auditor requires to respond to significant risks of material misstatement, whether due to fraud or error.[7]
- section 240, *Consideration of Fraud in a Financial Statement Audit*, indicates that the auditor may design confirmation requests to obtain additional corroborative information as a response to address the assessed risks of material misstatement due to fraud at the assertion level.[8]
- section 500 indicates that corroborating information obtained from a source independent of the entity (such as external confirmations) may increase the assurance the auditor obtains from evidence existing within the accounting records or representations made by management.[9]

Effective Date

.04 This section is effective for audits of financial statements for periods ending on or after December 15, 2012.

---

[3] Paragraphs .05–.06 of section 330, *Performing Audit Procedures in Response to Assessed Risks and Evaluating the Audit Evidence Obtained.*

[4] Paragraph .18 of section 330.

[5] Paragraphs .19–.20 of section 330.

[6] Paragraph .07*b* of section 330.

[7] Paragraph .A58 of section 330.

[8] Paragraph .A43 of section 240, *Consideration of Fraud in a Financial Statement Audit.*

[9] Paragraph .A8 of section 500.

Objective

.05 The objective of the auditor, when using external confirmation procedures, is to design and perform such procedures to obtain relevant and reliable audit evidence.

Definitions

.06 For purposes of generally accepted auditing standards, the following terms have the meanings attributed as follows:

Exception. A response that indicates a difference between information requested to be confirmed, or contained in the entity's records, and information provided by the confirming party.

External confirmation. Audit evidence obtained as a direct written response to the auditor from a third party (the confirming party), either in paper form or by electronic or other medium (for example, through the auditor's direct access to information held by a third party). (Ref: par. .A1)

Negative confirmation request. A request that the confirming party respond directly to the auditor only if the confirming party disagrees with the information provided in the request.

Nonresponse. A failure of the confirming party to respond, or fully respond, to a positive confirmation request or a confirmation request returned undelivered.

Positive confirmation request. A request that the confirming party respond directly to the auditor by providing the requested information or indicating whether the confirming party agrees or disagrees with the information in the request.

Requirements

External Confirmation Procedures

.07 When using external confirmation procedures, the auditor should maintain control over external confirmation requests, including

a. determining the information to be confirmed or requested; (Ref: par. .A2)

b. selecting the appropriate confirming party; (Ref: par. .A3)

c. designing the confirmation requests, including determining that requests are properly directed to the appropriate confirming party and provide for being responded to directly to the auditor; and (Ref: par. .A4–.A7)

d. sending the requests, including follow-up requests, when applicable, to the confirming party. (Ref: par. .A8)

Management's Refusal to Allow the Auditor to Perform External Confirmation Procedures

.08 If management refuses to allow the auditor to perform external confirmation procedures, the auditor should *a.* inquire about management's reasons for the refusal and seek audit evidence about their validity and reasonableness; (Ref: par. .A9)

b. evaluate the implications of management's refusal on the auditor's assessment of the relevant risks of material misstatement, including the risk of fraud, and on the nature, timing, and extent of other audit procedures; and (Ref: par. .A10)

c. perform alternative audit procedures designed to obtain relevant and reliable audit evidence. (Ref: par. .A11)

.09 If the auditor concludes that management's refusal to allow the auditor to perform external confirmation procedures is unreasonable or the auditor is unable to obtain relevant and reliable audit evidence from alternative audit procedures, the auditor should communicate with those charged with governance, in accordance with section 260, *The Auditor's Communication With Those Charged With Governance.*[10] The auditor also should determine the implications for the audit and the auditor's opinion, in accordance with section 705, *Modifications to the Opinion in the Independent Auditor's Report*.

Results of the External Confirmation Procedures

Reliability of Responses to Confirmation Requests

.10 If the auditor identifies factors that give rise to doubts about the reliability of the response to a confirmation request, the auditor should obtain further audit evidence to resolve those doubts. (Ref: par. .A12–.A22)

.11 If the auditor determines that a response to a confirmation request is not reliable, the auditor should evaluate the implications on the assessment of the relevant risks of material misstatement, including the risk of fraud, and on the related nature, timing, and extent of other audit procedures. (Ref: par. .A23)

Nonresponses and Oral Responses

.12 In the case of each nonresponse, the auditor should perform alternative audit procedures to obtain relevant and reliable audit evidence. (Ref: par. .A24–.A27)

When a Written Response to a Positive Confirmation Request Is Necessary to Obtain Sufficient Appropriate Audit Evidence

.13 If the auditor has determined that a written response to a positive confirmation request is necessary to obtain sufficient appropriate audit evidence, alternative audit procedures will not provide the audit evidence the auditor requires. If the auditor does not obtain such confirmation, the auditor should determine the implications for the audit and the auditor's opinion, in accordance with section 705. (Ref: par. .A28–.A29)

Exceptions

.14 The auditor should investigate exceptions to determine whether they are indicative of misstatements. (Ref: par. .A30–.A31)

---

[10] Paragraph .12 of section 260, *The Auditor's Communication With Those Charged With Governance*.

Negative Confirmations

.15 Negative confirmations provide less persuasive audit evidence than positive confirmations. Accordingly, the auditor should not use negative confirmation requests as the sole substantive audit procedure to address an assessed risk of material misstatement at the assertion level, unless all of the following are present:

a. The auditor has assessed the risk of material misstatement as low and has obtained sufficient appropriate audit evidence regarding the operating effectiveness of controls relevant to the assertion.

b. The population of items subject to negative confirmation procedures comprises a large number of small, homogeneous account balances, transactions, or conditions.

c. A very low exception rate is expected.

d. The auditor is not aware of circumstances or conditions that would cause recipients of negative confirmation requests to disregard such requests. (Ref: par. .A32)

Evaluating the Evidence Obtained

.16 The auditor should evaluate whether the results of the external confirmation procedures provide relevant and reliable audit evidence or whether further audit evidence is necessary. (Ref: par. .A33–.A34)

Application and Other Explanatory Material

Definitions

External Confirmation (Ref: par. .06)

.A1 The auditor's direct access to information held by a third party (the confirming party) may meet the definition of an *external confirmation* when, for example, the auditor is provided by the confirming party with the electronic access codes or information necessary to access a secure website where data that addresses the subject matter of the confirmation is held. The auditor's access to information held by the confirming party may also be facilitated by a third-party service provider. When access codes or information necessary to access the confirming party's data is provided to the auditor by management, evidence obtained by the auditor from access to such information does not meet the definition of an *external confirmation*.

External Confirmation Procedures

Determining the Information to Be Confirmed or Requested (Ref: par. .07a)

.A2 External confirmation procedures frequently are performed to confirm or request information regarding account balances, elements thereof, and disclosures. They also may be used to confirm the terms of agreements, contracts, or transactions between an entity and other parties or to confirm the absence of certain conditions, such as a "side agreement."

Selecting the Appropriate Confirming Party (Ref: par. .07b)

.A3 Responses to confirmation requests provide more relevant and reliable audit evidence when confirmation requests are sent to a confirming party who the auditor believes is knowledgeable about the information to be confirmed. For example, a financial institution official who is knowledgeable about the transactions or arrangements for which confirmation is requested may be the most appropriate person at the financial institution from whom to request confirmation.

Designing Confirmation Requests (Ref: par. .07c)

.A4 The design of a confirmation request may directly affect the confirmation response rate and the reliability and nature of the audit evidence obtained from responses.

.A5 Factors to consider when designing confirmation requests include the following:

- The assertions being addressed.
- Specific identified risks of material misstatement, including fraud risks.
- The layout and presentation of the confirmation request.
- Prior experience on the audit or similar engagements.
- The method of communication (for example, in paper form or by electronic or other medium).
- Management's authorization or encouragement to the confirming parties to respond to the auditor. Confirming parties may only be willing to respond to a confirmation request containing management's authorization.
- The ability of the intended confirming party to confirm or provide the requested information (for example, individual invoice amount versus total balance).

.A6 A positive external confirmation request asks the confirming party to reply to the auditor in all cases, either by indicating the confirming party's agreement with the given information or asking the confirming party to provide information. A response to a properly designed positive confirmation request ordinarily is expected to provide reliable audit evidence. A risk exists, however, that a confirming party may reply to the confirmation request without verifying that the information is correct. The auditor may reduce this risk by using positive confirmation requests that do not state the amount (or other information) on the confirmation request and that ask the confirming party to fill in the amount or furnish other information. On the other hand, use of this type of "blank" confirmation request may result in lower response rates because additional effort is required from the confirming parties to provide the requested information.

.A7 Determining that requests are properly addressed includes verifying the accuracy of the addresses, including testing the validity of some or all of the addresses on the confirmation requests before they are sent out, regardless of the confirmation method used. When a confirmation request is sent by e-mail, the auditor's determination that the request is being properly directed to the appropriate confirming party may include performing procedures to test the validity of some or all of the e-mail addresses supplied by management. The nature and extent of the necessary procedures is dependent on the risks associated with the particular type of confirmation or address. For example, a confirmation addressing a higher risk assertion or a confirmation address that appears to be potentially less reliable (for example, an electronic confirmation addressed in a manner that appears easier to falsify) may necessitate different or more extensive procedures to determine that the request is directed to the intended recipient. See further guidance in paragraphs .A14–.A15.

Follow-Up on Confirmation Requests (Ref: par. .07d)

.A8 The auditor may send an additional confirmation request when a reply to a previous request has not been received within a reasonable time. For example, the auditor may, having reverified the accuracy of the original address, send an additional or follow-up request.

Management's Refusal to Allow the Auditor to Perform External Confirmation Procedures

Reasonableness of Management's Refusal (Ref: par. .08a)

.A9 A refusal by management to allow the auditor to perform external confirmation procedures is a limitation on the audit evidence the auditor seeks to obtain; therefore, the auditor is required to inquire about the reasons for the limitation. A common reason offered by management is the existence of a legal dispute or ongoing negotiation with the intended confirming party, the resolution of which may be affected by an untimely confirmation request. The auditor is required to seek audit evidence about the validity and reasonableness of the reasons for management's refusal because of the risk that management may be attempting to deny the auditor access to audit evidence that may reveal fraud or error.

Implications for the Assessment of Risks of Material Misstatement (Ref: par. .08b)

.A10 The auditor may conclude from the evaluation in paragraph .08*b* that it would be appropriate to revise the assessment of the risks of material misstatement at the assertion level and modify planned audit procedures, in accordance with section 315, *Understanding the Entity and Its Environment and Assessing the Risks of Material Misstatement.*[11] For example, if management's request to not confirm is unreasonable, this may indicate a fraud risk factor that requires evaluation, in accordance with section 240.[12]

Alternative Audit Procedures (Ref: par. .08c)

.A11 The alternative audit procedures performed may be similar to those appropriate for a nonresponse, as set out in paragraphs .A24–.A27. Such procedures also would take into account the results of the auditor's evaluation in paragraph .08*b*.

Results of the External Confirmation Procedures

Reliability of Responses to Confirmation Requests (Ref: par. .10)

.A12 Section 500 indicates that even when audit evidence is obtained from sources external to the entity, circumstances may exist that affect its reliability.[13] All responses carry some risk of interception, alteration, or fraud. Such risk exists regardless of whether a response is obtained in paper form

---

[11] Paragraph .32 of section 315, *Understanding the Entity and Its Environment and Assessing the Risks of Material Misstatement.*

[12] Paragraph .24 of section 240.

[13] Paragraph .A32 of section 500.

or by electronic or other medium. Factors that may indicate doubts about the reliability of a response include whether it

- was received by the auditor indirectly or
- appeared not to come from the originally intended confirming party.

.A13 The auditor's consideration of the reliability of the information obtained through the confirmation process to be used as audit evidence includes consideration of the risks that

a. the information obtained may not be from an authentic source,

b. a respondent may not be knowledgeable about the information to be confirmed, and

c. the integrity of the information may have been compromised.

When an electronic confirmation process or system is used, the auditor's consideration of the risks described in *a–c* includes the consideration of risks that the electronic confirmation process is not secure or is improperly controlled.

.A14 Responses received electronically (for example, by fax or e-mail) involve risks relating to reliability because proof of origin or identity of the confirming party may be difficult to establish, and alterations may be difficult to detect. The auditor may determine that it is appropriate to address such risks by utilizing a system or process that validates the respondent or by directly contacting the purported sender (for example, by telephone) to validate the identity of the sender of the response and to validate that the information received by the auditor corresponds to what was transmitted by the sender.

.A15 An electronic confirmation system or process that creates a secure confirmation environment may mitigate the risks of interception or alteration. Creating a secure confirmation environment depends on the process or mechanism used by the auditor and the respondent to minimize the possibility that the results will be compromised because of interception or alteration of the confirmation. If the auditor is satisfied that such a system or process is secure and properly controlled, evidence provided by responses received using the system or process may be considered reliable. Various means might be used to validate the source of the electronic information. For example, the use of encryption, electronic digital signatures, and procedures to verify website authenticity may improve the security of the electronic confirmation system or process. If a system or process that facilitates electronic confirmation between the auditor and the respondent is in place and the auditor plans to rely on the controls over such a system or process, an assurance trust services report (for example, Systrust) or another assurance report on that system or process may assist the auditor in assessing the design and operating effectiveness of the electronic and manual controls with respect to that system or process. Such an assurance report may address the risks described in paragraph .A13. If these risks are not adequately addressed in such a report, the auditor may perform additional procedures to address those risks.

.A16 The auditor is required by section 500 to determine whether to modify or add procedures to resolve doubts over the reliability of information to be used as audit evidence.[14] The auditor may choose to verify the source and contents of a response to a confirmation request by contacting the confirming party (for example, as described in paragraph .A14). When a response has been returned to the auditor indirectly (for example, because the confirming party incorrectly

[14] Paragraph .10 of section 500.

addressed it to the entity rather than the auditor), the auditor may request the confirming party to respond in writing directly to the auditor.

Disclaimers and Other Restrictions in Confirmation Responses

.A17 A response to a confirmation request may contain restrictive language regarding its use. Such restrictions do not necessarily invalidate the reliability of the response as audit evidence. Whether the auditor may rely on the information confirmed and the degree of such reliance will depend on the nature and substance of the restrictive language.

.A18 Restrictions that appear to be boilerplate disclaimers of liability may not affect the reliability of the information being confirmed. Examples of such disclaimers may include the following:

- Information is furnished as a matter of courtesy without a duty to do so and without responsibility, liability, or warranty, express or implied.
- The reply is given solely for the purpose of the audit without any responsibility on the part of the respondent, its employees, or its agents, and it does not relieve the auditor from any other inquiry or the performance of any other duty.

.A19 Other restrictive language also may not affect the reliability of a response if it does not relate to the assertion being tested. For example, in a confirmation of investments, a disclaimer regarding the valuation of the investments may not affect the reliability of the response if the auditor's objective in using the confirmation request is to obtain audit evidence regarding whether the investments exist.

.A20 Certain restrictive language may, however, cast doubt about the completeness or accuracy of the information contained in the response or on the auditor's ability to rely on such information. Examples of such restrictions may include the following:

- Information is obtained from electronic data sources, which may not contain all information in the respondent's possession.
- Information is not guaranteed to be accurate nor current and may be a matter of opinion.
- The recipient may not rely upon the information in the confirmation.

.A21 When the auditor has doubts about the reliability of the response as a result of restrictive language, then, in accordance with paragraph .10, the auditor is required to obtain further audit evidence to resolve those doubts. When the practical effect of the restrictive language is difficult to ascertain in the particular circumstances, the auditor may consider it appropriate to seek clarification from the respondent or seek legal advice.

.A22 If the auditor is unable to resolve the doubts about the reliability of a response as a result of restrictive language, then, in accordance with paragraph .11, the auditor is required to evaluate the implications on the assessment of the relevant risks of misstatement, including the risk of fraud, and on the related nature, timing, and extent of other audit procedures. The nature, timing, and extent of such procedures will depend on factors such as the nature of the financial statement item, the assertion being tested, the nature and substance of the restrictive language, and relevant information obtained through other audit procedures.

Unreliable Responses (Ref: par. .11)

.A23 When the auditor concludes that a response is unreliable, the auditor may need to revise the assessment of the risks of material misstatement at the assertion level and modify planned audit procedures accordingly, in accordance with section 315.[15] For example, an unreliable response may indicate a fraud risk factor that requires evaluation, in accordance with section 240.[16]

Nonresponses and Oral Responses (Ref: par. .12)

.A24 The nature and extent of alternative procedures are affected by the account and assertion in question. Examples of alternative audit procedures the auditor may perform include the following:

- For accounts receivable balances, examining specific subsequent cash receipts (including matching such receipts with the actual items being paid), shipping documentation, or other client documentation providing evidence for the existence assertion
- For accounts payable balances, examining subsequent cash disbursements or correspondence from third parties and other records, such as receiving reports and statements that the client receives from vendors providing evidence for the completeness assertion

.A25 A nonresponse to a confirmation request may indicate a previously unidentified risk of material misstatement. In such situations, the auditor may need to revise the assessed risk of material misstatement at the assertion level and modify planned audit procedures, in accordance with section 315.[17] For example, a fewer or greater number of responses to confirmation requests than anticipated may indicate a previously unidentified fraud risk factor that requires evaluation, in accordance with section 240.[18]

.A26 The auditor may determine that it is not necessary to perform additional alternative audit procedures beyond the evaluation of the confirmation results if such evaluation indicates that relevant and reliable audit evidence has already been obtained. This may be the case when testing for overstatement of amounts and (*a*) the nonresponses in the aggregate, projected as 100 percent misstatements to the population and added to the sum of all other unadjusted differences, would not affect the auditor's decision about whether the financial statements are materially misstated and (*b*) the auditor has not identified unusual qualitative factors or systematic characteristics related to the nonresponses, such as that all nonresponses pertain to year-end transactions.

.A27 An oral response to a confirmation request does not meet the definition of an *external confirmation* because it is not a direct written response to the auditor. Provided that the auditor has not concluded that a direct written response to a positive confirmation is necessary to obtain sufficient appropriate audit evidence, the auditor may take the receipt of an oral response to a confirmation request into consideration when determining the nature and extent of alternative audit procedures required to be performed for nonresponses, in accordance with paragraph .12. The auditor may perform additional procedures to address the reliability of the evidence provided by the oral response, such as initiating a call to the respondent using a telephone number that the auditor

---

[15] Paragraph .32 of section 315.

[16] Paragraph .24 of section 240.

[17] Paragraph .32 of section 315.

[18] Paragraph .24 of section 240.

has independently verified as being associated with the entity. For example, the auditor might call the main telephone number obtained from a reliable source and ask to be directed to the named respondent instead of calling a direct extension provided by the client or included in the statement or other correspondence received by the entity. The auditor may determine that the additional evidence provided by contacting the respondent directly, together with the evidence upon which the original confirmation request is based (for example, a statement or other correspondence received by the entity), is sufficient appropriate audit evidence. In appropriately documenting the oral response, the auditor may include specific details, such as the identity of the person from whom the response was received, his or her position, and the date and time of the conversation.

When a Written Response to a Positive Confirmation Request Is Necessary to Obtain Sufficient Appropriate Audit Evidence (Ref: par. .13)

.A28 In certain circumstances, the auditor may identify an assessed risk of material misstatement at the assertion level for which a response to a positive confirmation request is necessary to obtain sufficient appropriate audit evidence. Such circumstances may include the following:

- The information available to corroborate management's assertion(s) is only available outside the entity.
- Specific fraud risk factors, such as the risk of management override of controls or the risk of collusion, which can involve employee(s) or management, or both, prevent the auditor from relying on evidence from the entity.

.A29 When the auditor has determined that a written response is necessary to obtain sufficient appropriate audit evidence and the auditor has obtained only an oral response to a confirmation request, the auditor may request the confirming party to respond in writing directly to the auditor. If no such response is received, in accordance with paragraph .13, alternative audit procedures will not provide the audit evidence the auditor requires, and the auditor is required to determine the implications for the audit and the auditor's opinion, in accordance with section 705.

Exceptions (Ref: par. .14)

.A30 Exceptions noted in responses to confirmation requests may indicate misstatements or potential misstatements in the financial statements. When a misstatement is identified, the auditor is required by section 240 to evaluate whether such misstatement is indicative of fraud.[19] Exceptions may provide a guide to the quality of responses from similar confirming parties or for similar accounts. Exceptions also may indicate a deficiency, or deficiencies, in the entity's internal control over financial reporting.

.A31 Some exceptions do not represent misstatements. For example, the auditor may conclude that differences in responses to confirmation requests are due to timing, measurement, or clerical errors in the external confirmation procedures.

Negative Confirmations (Ref: par. .15)

.A32 The failure to receive a response to a negative confirmation request does not indicate receipt by the intended confirming party of the confirmation request or verification of the accuracy of the information contained in the

---

[19] Paragraph .35 of section 240.

request. Accordingly, a failure of a confirming party to respond to a negative confirmation request provides significantly less persuasive audit evidence than does a response to a positive confirmation request. Confirming parties also may be more likely to respond indicating their disagreement with a confirmation request when the information in the request is not in their favor but less likely to respond otherwise. For example, holders of bank deposit accounts may be more likely to respond if they believe that the balance in their account is understated in the confirmation request but less likely to respond when they believe the balance is overstated. Therefore, sending negative confirmation requests to holders of bank deposit accounts may be a useful procedure in considering whether such balances may be understated but is unlikely to be effective if the auditor is seeking evidence regarding overstatement.

Evaluating the Evidence Obtained (Ref: par. .16)

.A33 When evaluating the results of individual external confirmation requests, the auditor may categorize such results as follows:

a. A response by the appropriate confirming party indicating agreement with the information provided in the confirmation request or providing requested information without exception

b. A response deemed unreliable

c. A nonresponse

d. A response indicating an exception

.A34 The auditor's evaluation, when taken into account with other audit procedures the auditor may have performed, may assist the auditor in concluding whether sufficient appropriate audit evidence has been obtained or whether further audit evidence is necessary, as required by section 330.[20]

---

[20] Paragraphs .28–.29 of section 330.

AU-C Section 510 *

Opening Balances—Initial Audit Engagements, Including Reaudit Engagements

Source: SAS No. 122.

Effective for audits of financial statements for periods ending on or after December 15, 2012.

Introduction

Scope of This Section

.01 This section addresses the auditor's responsibilities relating to opening balances in an initial audit engagement, including a reaudit engagement. In addition to financial statement amounts, opening balances include matters requiring disclosure that existed at the beginning of the period, such as contingencies and commitments. When comparative financial statements are presented, the relevant requirements and guidance for comparative financial statements in section 700, *Forming an Opinion and Reporting on Financial Statements*, also apply. Section 300, *Planning an Audit*, includes additional requirements and guidance regarding activities prior to starting an initial audit. Section 708, *Consistency of Financial Statements*, also applies with respect to the auditor's evaluation of the consistency of accounting principles between the periods presented and covered by the auditor's opinion. Section 210, *Terms of Engagement*, includes requirements and guidance with respect to communications with a predecessor auditor before accepting an initial audit engagement, including a reaudit engagement.

.02 This section, with respect to predecessor auditors, does not apply if the most recent audited financial statements are more than one year prior to the beginning of the earliest period to be audited.

Effective Date

.03 This section is effective for audits of financial statements for periods ending on or after December 15, 2012.

Objective

.04 The objective of the auditor, in conducting an initial audit engagement, including a reaudit engagement, is to obtain sufficient appropriate audit evidence regarding opening balances about whether (Ref: par. .A1)

---

* This section has been codified using an "AU-C" identifier instead of an "AU" identifier. "AU-C" is a temporary identifier to avoid confusion with references to existing "AU" sections, which will remain in AICPA *Professional Standards* through 2013. The "AU-C" identifier will revert to "AU" in 2014, by which time substantially all engagements for which the "AU" sections were still effective are expected to be completed.

a. opening balances contain misstatements that materially affect the current period's financial statements and

b. appropriate accounting policies reflected in the opening balances have been consistently applied in the current period's financial statements or changes thereto are appropriately accounted for and adequately presented and disclosed in accordance with the applicable financial reporting framework.

Definitions

.05 For the purposes of generally accepted auditing standards, the following terms have the meanings attributed as follows:

Initial audit engagement. An engagement in which either (*a*) the financial statements for the prior period were not audited, or (*b*) the financial statements for the prior period were audited by a predecessor auditor.

Opening balances. Those account balances that exist at the beginning of the period. Opening balances are based upon the closing balances of the prior period and reflect the effects of transactions and events of prior periods and accounting policies applied in the prior period. Opening balances also include matters requiring disclosure that existed at the beginning of the period, such as contingencies and commitments.

Predecessor auditor. The auditor from a different audit firm who has reported on the most recent audited financial statements or was engaged to perform but did not complete an audit of the financial statements. (Ref: par. .A2)

Reaudit. An initial audit engagement to audit financial statements that have been previously audited by a predecessor auditor.

Requirements

Audit Procedures

.06 The auditor should read the most recent financial statements, if any, and the predecessor auditor's report thereon, if any, for information relevant to opening balances, including disclosures, and consistency in the application of accounting policies.

.07 In instances in which the prior period financial statements were audited by a predecessor auditor, the auditor should request management to authorize the predecessor auditor to allow a review of the predecessor auditor's audit documentation and for the predecessor auditor to respond fully to inquiries by the auditor, thereby providing the auditor with information to assist in planning and performing the engagement. (Ref: par. .A3–.A11)

Opening Balances

.08 The auditor should obtain sufficient appropriate audit evidence about whether the opening balances contain misstatements that materially affect the current period's financial statements by

a. determining whether the prior period's closing balances have been correctly brought forward to the current period or, when appropriate, have been restated;

b. determining whether the opening balances reflect the application of appropriate accounting policies; and

c. evaluating whether audit procedures performed in the current period provide evidence relevant to the opening balances and performing one or both of the following: (Ref: par. .A7–.A9 and .A12–.A14)

i. When the prior year financial statements were audited, reviewing the predecessor auditor's audit documentation to obtain evidence regarding the opening balances

ii. Performing specific audit procedures to obtain evidence regarding the opening balances

.09 If the auditor obtains audit evidence that the opening balances contain misstatements that could materially affect the current period's financial statements, the auditor should perform such additional audit procedures as are appropriate in the circumstances to determine the effect on the current period's financial statements. If the auditor concludes that such misstatements exist in the current period's financial statements, the auditor should communicate the misstatements to the appropriate level of management and those charged with governance, in accordance with section 260, *The Auditor's Communication With Those Charged With Governance*. If the prior period financial statements were audited by a predecessor auditor, the auditor should also refer to paragraphs .12–.13.

Consistency of Accounting Policies

.10 The auditor should obtain sufficient appropriate audit evidence about whether the accounting policies reflected in the opening balances have been consistently applied in the current period's financial statements and whether changes in the accounting policies have been appropriately accounted for and adequately presented and disclosed in accordance with the applicable financial reporting framework.

Relevant Information in the Predecessor Auditor's Report

.11 If the prior period's financial statements were audited by a predecessor auditor, and a modification was made to the opinion, the auditor should evaluate the effect of the matter giving rise to the modification in assessing the risks of material misstatement in the current period's financial statements, in accordance with section 315, *Understanding the Entity and Its Environment and Assessing the Risks of Material Misstatement*.

Discovery of Possible Material Misstatements in Financial Statements Reported on by a Predecessor Auditor

.12 If the auditor becomes aware of information during the audit that leads the auditor to believe that financial statements reported on by the predecessor auditor may require revision, the auditor should request management to inform the predecessor auditor of the situation and arrange for the three parties to discuss this information and attempt to resolve the matter. The auditor should communicate to the predecessor auditor information that the auditor believes the predecessor auditor may need to consider, in accordance with section 560, *Subsequent Events and Subsequently Discovered Facts*, which addresses the auditor's responsibilities when facts become known to the auditor after the date of the auditor's report that, had they been known to the auditor at that date, may have caused the auditor to amend the auditor's report. (Ref: par. .A15)

.13 If management refuses to inform the predecessor auditor that the prior period financial statements may need revision or if the auditor is not satisfied with the resolution of the matter, the auditor should evaluate (*a*) the implications on the current engagement and (*b*) whether to withdraw from the engagement or, when withdrawal is not possible under applicable law or regulation, disclaim an opinion on the financial statements. (Ref: par. .A16)

Audit Conclusions and Reporting

.14 The auditor should not make reference to the report or work of the predecessor auditor as the basis, in part, for the auditor's own opinion.

Opening Balances

.15 If the auditor is unable to obtain sufficient appropriate audit evidence regarding the opening balances, the auditor should express a qualified opinion or disclaim an opinion on the financial statements, as appropriate, in accordance with section 705, *Modifications to the Opinion in the Independent Auditor's Report*. (Ref: par. .A17)

.16 If the auditor concludes that the opening balances contain a misstatement that materially affects the current period's financial statements, and the effect of the misstatement is not appropriately accounted for or adequately presented or disclosed, the auditor should express a qualified opinion or an adverse opinion, as appropriate, in accordance with section 705.

Consistency of Accounting Policies

.17 If the auditor concludes that

a. the current period's accounting policies are not consistently applied regarding opening balances, in accordance with the applicable financial reporting framework, or

b. a change in accounting policies is not appropriately accounted for or adequately presented or disclosed, in accordance with the applicable financial reporting framework,

the auditor should express a qualified opinion or an adverse opinion, as appropriate, in accordance with section 705.

Modification to the Opinion in the Predecessor Auditor's Report

.18 If the predecessor auditor's opinion regarding the prior period's financial statements included a modification to the auditor's opinion that remains relevant and material to the current period's financial statements, the auditor should modify the auditor's opinion on the current period's financial statements, in accordance with section 705. (Ref: par. .A18)

Application and Other Explanatory Material

Objective (Ref: par. .04)

.A1 Audit evidence regarding opening balances and the consistency of accounting principles may include the most recent audited financial statements, the predecessor auditor's report thereon, the results of inquiry of the predecessor auditor, the results of the auditor's review of the predecessor auditor's audit documentation relating to the most recently completed audit, and audit procedures performed on the current period's transactions that may provide evidence about the opening balances or consistency.

Definitions

Predecessor Auditor (Ref: par. .05)

.A2 Two predecessor auditors may exist: the auditor who reported on the most recent audited financial statements and the auditor who was engaged to perform, but did not complete, an audit of any subsequent financial statements.

Audit Procedures (Ref: par. .07)

.A3 The auditor may initiate communications with management to authorize review of the predecessor auditor's audit documentation and for the predecessor auditor to respond fully to inquiries by the auditor, either before or after accepting the engagement. Relevant ethical and professional requirements guide the auditor's communications with the predecessor auditor.

.A4 The predecessor auditor may request a consent and acknowledgment letter from the entity to document this authorization in an effort to reduce misunderstandings about the scope of the communications being authorized. Exhibit B, "Illustrative Entity Consent and Acknowledgment Letter," contains an illustrative entity consent and acknowledgment letter.

.A5 It is customary for the predecessor auditor to make himself or herself available to the auditor and to make available for review certain audit documentation. The predecessor auditor determines which audit documentation is to be made available for review and which may be copied. The predecessor auditor ordinarily permits the auditor to review audit documentation, including documentation of planning; risk assessment procedures; further audit procedures; audit results; and other matters of continuing accounting and auditing significance, such as the schedule of uncorrected misstatements, working paper analysis of balance sheet accounts, and those relating to contingencies.

.A6 Before permitting access to the audit documentation, the predecessor auditor may request written confirmation of the auditor's agreement regarding the use of the audit documentation. Exhibit C, "Illustrative Successor Auditor Acknowledgment Letter," contains an illustrative successor auditor acknowledgment letter.

.A7 The extent, if any, to which a predecessor auditor permits access to the audit documentation or responds to inquiries from the auditor is a matter of the predecessor auditor's professional judgment. The predecessor auditor's denial or limitation of access may affect the auditor's assessment of risk regarding the opening balances or the nature, timing, and extent of the auditor's procedures with respect to the opening balances and consistency of accounting principles. (Ref: par. .07 and .08*c*)

.A8 If the predecessor auditor permits access to the audit documentation, the auditor may review the predecessor auditor's audit documentation for information relevant to planning and performing the audit. The auditor's determination whether to use information resulting from such review as part of the auditor's risk assessment procedures or as evidence regarding the opening balances is influenced by the auditor's assessment of the professional competence and independence of the predecessor auditor. Although the predecessor auditor is not a component auditor, as defined in section 600, *Special Considerations—Audits of Group Financial Statements (Including the Work of Component Auditors)*, the auditor may make inquiries similar to those listed in section 600 concerning the professional competence and independence of the predecessor auditor.[1] (Ref: par. .07 and .08*c*)

.A9 The auditor's review of the predecessor auditor's audit documentation may provide audit evidence about the opening balances and consistency of accounting principles. However, the nature, timing, and extent of audit work performed and the conclusions reached are solely the responsibility of the auditor, as required by section 200, *Overall Objectives of the Independent Auditor and the Conduct of an Audit in Accordance With Generally Accepted Auditing Standards*. (Ref: par. .07 and .08*c*)

Considerations Specific to Governmental Entities (Ref: par. .07)

.A10 In audits of governmental entities, law or regulation may limit the information that the auditor can obtain from a predecessor auditor. Certain information may be identified as classified or otherwise prohibited from disclosure by federal, state, or local laws or public safety or security concerns. For example, if a governmental entity that has previously been audited by a government audit organization (for example, the U.S. Government Accountability Office, a federal inspector general, an elected or statutorily appointed state auditor general, or other suitably qualified audit organization) engages a public accounting firm, the amount of access to audit documentation or other information that the government audit organization can provide an incoming auditor may be constrained by privacy or confidentiality laws or regulations. In situations when communications with a predecessor auditor are restricted, audit evidence may need to be obtained through other means and, if sufficient appropriate audit evidence cannot be obtained, consideration given to the effect on the auditor's opinion, in accordance with the requirement in paragraph .15.

.A11 If a government audit organization engages a public accounting firm in an agency capacity to perform an audit of a governmental entity and such firm did not audit the financial statements of the governmental entity in the prior period, this is usually regarded as a change in auditors; therefore, this section applies.

Opening Balances (Ref: par. .08c)

.A12 The nature and extent of audit procedures necessary to obtain sufficient appropriate audit evidence regarding opening balances depend on such matters as the following:

- The accounting policies followed by the entity
- The nature of the account balances, classes of transactions and disclosures, and the risks of material misstatement in the current period's financial statements
- The significance of the opening balances relative to the current period's financial statements
- Whether the prior period's financial statements were audited and, if so, whether the predecessor auditor's opinion was modified

.A13 For current assets and liabilities, some audit evidence about opening balances may be obtained as part of the current period's audit procedures. For example, the collection (payment) of opening accounts receivable (accounts payable) during the current period will provide some audit evidence of their existence, rights and obligations, completeness, and valuation at the beginning

---

[1] Paragraph .22 of section 600, *Special Considerations—Audits of Group Financial Statements (Including the Work of Component Auditors)*.

of the period. In the case of inventories, however, the current period's audit procedures on the closing inventory balance provide little audit evidence regarding inventory on hand at the beginning of the period. Therefore, additional audit procedures, such as one or more of the following, may be necessary to obtain sufficient appropriate audit evidence:

- Observing a current physical inventory count and reconciling it to the opening inventory quantities
- Performing audit procedures on the valuation of the opening inventory items
- Performing audit procedures on gross profit and cutoff

.A14 For noncurrent assets and liabilities, such as property, plant, and equipment; investments; and long-term debt, some audit evidence may be obtained by examining the accounting records and other information underlying the opening balances. In certain cases, the auditor may be able to obtain some audit evidence regarding opening balances through confirmation with third parties (for example, for long-term debt and investments). In other cases, the auditor may need to carry out additional audit procedures.

Discovery of Possible Material Misstatements in Financial Statements Reported on by a Predecessor Auditor

.A15 Section 560 provides reporting guidance to the predecessor auditor who is requested to reissue a previously issued report on financial statements of a prior period when those financial statements are to be presented on a comparative basis with audited financial statements of a subsequent period.[2] Section 700 provides reporting guidance to the auditor reporting on comparative financial statements when the predecessor auditor is unable or unwilling to reissue the auditor's report on prior period financial statements that have been restated.[3] (Ref: par. .12)

.A16 If management refuses to inform the predecessor auditor that the prior period financial statements may need revision, or if the auditor is not satisfied with the resolution of the matter, the auditor may seek legal advice in determining an appropriate course of action, including evaluating whether to withdraw from the engagement when withdrawal is possible under applicable law or regulation. (Ref: par. .13)

Audit Conclusions and Reporting

Opening Balances (Ref: par. .15)

.A17 Section 705 addresses circumstances that may result in a modification to the auditor's opinion on the financial statements, the type of opinion appropriate in the circumstances, and the content of the auditor's report when the auditor's opinion is modified. The inability of the auditor to obtain sufficient appropriate audit evidence regarding opening balances may result in one of the following modifications to the opinion in the auditor's report:

a. A qualified opinion or a disclaimer of opinion, as is appropriate in the circumstances.

b. An opinion that is qualified or disclaimed, as appropriate, regarding the results of operations and cash flows, when relevant, and

---

[2] Paragraphs .19–.20 of section 560, *Subsequent Events and Subsequently Discovered Facts.*

[3] Paragraph .A52 of section 700, *Forming an Opinion and Reporting on Financial Statements.*

unmodified regarding financial position. Exhibit A, "Illustration of Report With Disclaimer of Opinion on Results of Operations and Cash Flows and Unmodified Opinion on Financial Position," includes such an illustrative report.

Modification to the Opinion in the Predecessor Auditor's Report (Ref: par. .18)

.A18 In some situations, a modification to the predecessor auditor's opinion may not be relevant and material to the opinion on the current period's financial statements. This may be the case when, for example, there was a scope limitation in the prior period but the matter giving rise to the scope limitation has been resolved in the current period.

.A19

Exhibit A—Illustration of Report With Disclaimer of Opinion on Results of Operations and Cash Flows and Unmodified Opinion on Financial Position

Circumstances include the following:

- The auditor did not observe the counting of the physical inventory at the beginning of the current period and was unable to obtain sufficient appropriate audit evidence regarding the opening balances of inventory.
- The possible effects of the inability to obtain sufficient appropriate audit evidence regarding opening balances of inventory are deemed to be material and pervasive to the entity's results of operations and cash flows.[1]
- The financial position at year-end is fairly presented.
- A disclaimer of opinion regarding the results of operations and cash flows and an unmodified opinion regarding financial position is considered appropriate in the circumstances.

Independent Auditor's Report

[*Appropriate Addressee*]

Report on the Financial Statements[2]

We have audited the accompanying balance sheet of ABC Company as of December 31, 20X1, and were engaged to audit the related statements of income, changes in stockholders' equity, and cash flows for the year then ended, and the related notes to the financial statements.

Management's Responsibility for the Financial Statements

Management is responsible for the preparation and fair presentation of these financial statements in accordance with accounting principles generally accepted in the United States of America; this includes the design, implementation, and maintenance of internal control relevant to the preparation and fair presentation of financial statements that are free from material misstatement, whether due to fraud or error.

Auditor's Responsibility

Our responsibility is to express an opinion on these financial statements based on conducting the audit in accordance with auditing standards generally accepted in the United States of America. Because of the matters described in the Basis for Disclaimer of Opinion paragraph, however, we were not able to obtain sufficient appropriate audit evidence to provide a basis for an audit opinion on the income statement and the cash flow statement.

We conducted our audit of the balance sheet in accordance with auditing standards generally accepted in the United States of America. Those standards require that we plan and perform the audit to obtain reasonable assurance about whether the balance sheet is free from material misstatement.

---

[1] If the possible effects, in the auditor's professional judgment, are considered to be material but not pervasive to the entity's results of operations and cash flows, the auditor would express a qualified opinion on the results of operations and cash flows.

[2] The subtitle "Report on the Financial Statements" is unnecessary in circumstances when the second subtitle, "Report on Other Legal and Regulatory Requirements," is not applicable.

An audit involves performing procedures to obtain audit evidence about the amounts and disclosures in the financial statements. The procedures selected depend on the auditor's judgment, including the assessment of the risks of material misstatement of the financial statements, whether due to fraud or error. In making those risk assessments, the auditor considers internal control relevant to the entity's preparation and fair presentation of the financial statements in order to design audit procedures that are appropriate in the circumstances, but not for the purpose of expressing an opinion on the effectiveness of the entity's internal control.[3] Accordingly, we express no such opinion. An audit also includes evaluating the appropriateness of accounting policies used and the reasonableness of significant accounting estimates made by management, as well as evaluating the overall presentation of the financial statements.

We believe that the audit evidence we have obtained is sufficient and appropriate to provide a basis for our unmodified opinion on the financial position.

Basis for Disclaimer of Opinion on the Results of Operations and Cash Flows

We were not engaged as auditors of the Company until after December 31, 20X0, and, therefore, did not observe the counting of physical inventories at the beginning of the year. We were unable to satisfy ourselves by performing other auditing procedures concerning the inventory held at December 31, 20X0. Since opening inventories enter into the determination of net income and cash flows, we were unable to determine whether any adjustments might have been necessary in respect of the profit for the year reported in the income statement and the net cash flows from operating activities reported in the cash flow statement.

Disclaimer of Opinion on the Results of Operations and Cash Flows

Because of the significance of the matter described in the Basis for Disclaimer of Opinion paragraph, we have not been able to obtain sufficient appropriate audit evidence to provide a basis for an audit opinion on the results of operations and cash flows for the year ended December 31, 20X1. Accordingly, we do not express an opinion on the results of operations and cash flows for the year ended December 31, 20X1.

Opinion on the Financial Position

In our opinion, the balance sheet presents fairly, in all material respects, the financial position of ABC Company as of December 31, 20X1, in accordance with accounting principles generally accepted in the United States of America.

Report on Other Legal and Regulatory Requirements

[*Form and content of this section of the auditor's report will vary depending on the nature of the auditor's other reporting responsibilities.*]

[*Auditor's signature*]

[*Auditor's city and state*]

[*Date of the auditor's report*]

---

[3] In circumstances when the auditor also has responsibility to express an opinion on the effectiveness of internal control in conjunction with the audit of the financial statements, this sentence would be worded as follows: "In making those risk assessments, the auditor considers internal control relevant to the entity's preparation and fair presentation of the financial statements in order to design audit procedures that are appropriate in the circumstances." In addition, the next sentence, "Accordingly, we express no such opinion." would not be included.

.A20

Exhibit B—Illustrative Entity Consent and Acknowledgment Letter (Ref: par. .07 and .A4)

Paragraph .07 requires that the auditor request management to authorize the predecessor auditor to allow a review of the predecessor auditor's audit documentation and for the predecessor auditor to respond fully to inquiries by the auditor, thereby providing the auditor with information to assist in planning and performing the engagement. Paragraph .A4 states that the predecessor auditor may request a consent and acknowledgment letter from the entity to document this authorization in an effort to reduce misunderstandings about the scope of the communications being authorized. The following letter is presented for illustrative purposes only and is not required by professional standards.

[*Date*]

ABC Enterprises

[*Address*]

You have given your consent to allow [*name of successor CPA firm*], as independent auditors for ABC Enterprises (ABC), access to our audit documentation for our audit of the December 31, 20X1, financial statements of ABC. You also have given your consent to us to respond fully to [*name of successor CPA firm*] inquiries. You understand and agree that the review of our audit documentation is undertaken solely for the purpose of obtaining an understanding about ABC and certain information about our audit to assist [*name of successor CPA firm*] in planning and performing the audit of the December 31, 20X2, financial statements of ABC.

Please confirm your agreement with the foregoing by signing and dating a copy of this letter and returning it to us.

Attached is the form of the letter we will furnish [*name of successor CPA firm*] regarding the use of the audit documentation.

Very truly yours,

[*Predecessor Auditor*]

By: ________________

Accepted:

ABC Enterprises

By: ________________

Date: ____________

.A21

Exhibit C—Illustrative Successor Auditor Acknowledgment Letter (Ref: par. .A6)

Paragraph .A6 states that the predecessor auditor may request that the auditor confirm in writing his or her agreement regarding the use of the predecessor auditor's audit documentation before permitting access to it. The following letter is presented for illustrative purposes only and is not required by professional standards.

[*Date*]

[*Successor Auditor*]

[*Address*]

We have previously audited, in accordance with auditing standards generally accepted in the United States of America, the December 31, 20X1, financial statements of ABC Enterprises (ABC). We rendered a report on those financial statements and have not performed any audit procedures subsequent to the audit report date. In connection with your audit of ABC's 20X2 financial statements, you have requested access to our audit documentation prepared in connection with that audit. ABC has authorized our firm to allow you to review that audit documentation.

Our audit, and the audit documentation prepared in connection therewith, of ABC's financial statements were not planned or conducted in contemplation of your review. Therefore, items of possible interest to you may not have been specifically addressed. Our use of professional judgment and the assessment of audit risk and materiality for the purpose of our audit mean that matters may have existed that would have been assessed differently by you. We make no representation about the sufficiency or appropriateness of the information in our audit documentation for your purposes.

We understand that the purpose of your review is to obtain information about ABC and our 20X1 audit results to assist you in planning and performing your 20X2 audit of ABC. For that purpose only, we will provide you access to our audit documentation that relates to that objective.

Upon request, we will provide copies of audit documentation that provides factual information about ABC. You agree to subject any such copies or information otherwise derived from our audit documentation to your normal policy for retention of audit documentation and protection of confidential entity information. Furthermore, in the event of a third-party request for access to your audit documentation prepared in connection with your audits of ABC, you agree to obtain our permission before voluntarily allowing any such access to our audit documentation or information otherwise derived from our audit documentation, and to obtain on our behalf any releases that you obtain from such third party. You agree to advise us promptly and provide us a copy of any subpoena, summons, or other court order for access to your audit documentation that include copies of our audit documentation or information otherwise derived therefrom.

Please confirm your agreement with the foregoing by signing and dating a copy of this letter and returning it to us.

Very truly yours,

[*Predecessor Auditor*]

By: ____________________

Accepted:

[*Successor Auditor*]

By: ________________

Date: ___________

Even with management's consent, access to the predecessor auditor's audit documentation may still be limited. Experience has shown that the predecessor auditor may be willing to grant broader access if given additional assurance concerning the use of the audit documentation. Accordingly, the auditor might consider agreeing to the following additional limitations on the review of the predecessor auditor's audit documentation in order to obtain broader access:

- The auditor will not comment, orally or in writing, to anyone as a result of the review about whether the predecessor auditor's engagement was performed in accordance with generally accepted auditing standards.
- The auditor will not provide expert testimony or litigation support services or otherwise accept an engagement to comment on issues relating to the quality of the predecessor auditor's audit.
- The auditor accepts sole responsibility for the nature, timing, and extent of audit work performed and the conclusions reached in expressing an opinion on the 20X2 financial statements of ABC.

The following paragraph illustrates the previous text:

> Because your review of our audit documentation is undertaken solely for the purpose described previously and may not entail a review of all our audit documentation, you agree that (1) the information obtained from the review will not be used by you for any other purpose, (2) you will not comment, orally or in writing, to anyone as a result of that review about whether our audit was performed in accordance with generally accepted auditing standards, (3) you will not provide expert testimony or litigation support services or otherwise accept an engagement to comment on issues relating to the quality of our audit, and (4) you accept sole responsibility for the nature, timing and extent of audit work performed and the conclusions reached in expressing your opinion on the 20X2 financial statements of ABC.

AU-C Section 520 *

Analytical Procedures

Source: SAS No. 122.

Effective for audits of financial statements for periods ending on or after December 15, 2012.

Introduction

Scope of This Section

.01 This section addresses the auditor's use of analytical procedures as substantive procedures (substantive analytical procedures). It also addresses the auditor's responsibility to perform analytical procedures near the end of the audit that assist the auditor when forming an overall conclusion on the financial statements. Section 315, *Understanding the Entity and Its Environment and Assessing the Risks of Material Misstatement*, addresses the use of analytical procedures as risk assessment procedures (which may be referred to as analytical procedures used to plan the audit).[1] Section 330, *Performing Audit Procedures in Response to Assessed Risks and Evaluating the Audit Evidence Obtained*, addresses the nature, timing, and extent of audit procedures in response to assessed risks; these audit procedures may include substantive analytical procedures.[2]

Effective Date

.02 This section is effective for audits of financial statements for periods ending on or after December 15, 2012.

Objectives

.03 The objectives of the auditor are to

a. obtain relevant and reliable audit evidence when using substantive analytical procedures and

b. design and perform analytical procedures near the end of the audit that assist the auditor when forming an overall conclusion about whether the financial statements are consistent with the auditor's understanding of the entity. (Ref: par. .A1)

Definition

.04 For the purposes of generally accepted auditing standards, the following term has the meaning attributed as follows:

---

* This section has been codified using an "AU-C" identifier instead of an "AU" identifier. "AU-C" is a temporary identifier to avoid confusion with references to existing "AU" sections, which will remain in AICPA *Professional Standards* through 2013. The "AU-C" identifier will revert to "AU" in 2014, by which time substantially all engagements for which the "AU" sections were still effective are expected to be completed.

[1] Paragraph .06*b* of section 315, *Understanding the Entity and Its Environment and Assessing the Risks of Material Misstatement*.

[2] Paragraphs .06 and .18 of section 330, *Performing Audit Procedures in Response to Assessed Risks and Evaluating the Audit Evidence Obtained*.

Analytical procedures. Evaluations of financial information through analysis of plausible relationships among both financial and nonfinancial data. Analytical procedures also encompass such investigation, as is necessary, of identified fluctuations or relationships that are inconsistent with other relevant information or that differ from expected values by a significant amount. (Ref: par. .A2–.A6)

Requirements

Substantive Analytical Procedures

.05 When designing and performing analytical procedures, either alone or in combination with tests of details, as substantive procedures in accordance with section 330, the auditor should[3] (Ref: par. .A7–.A9)

a. determine the suitability of particular substantive analytical procedures for given assertions, taking into account the assessed risks of material misstatement and tests of details, if any, for these assertions; (Ref: par. .A10–.A16)

b. evaluate the reliability of data from which the auditor's expectation of recorded amounts or ratios is developed, taking into account the source, comparability, and nature and relevance of information available and controls over preparation; (Ref: par. .A17–.A20)

c. develop an expectation of recorded amounts or ratios and evaluate whether the expectation is sufficiently precise (taking into account whether substantive analytical procedures are to be performed alone or in combination with tests of details) to identify a misstatement that, individually or when aggregated with other misstatements, may cause the financial statements to be materially misstated; and (Ref: par. .A21–.A23)

d. determine the amount of any difference of recorded amounts from expected values that is acceptable without further investigation as required by paragraph .07 and compare the recorded amounts, or ratios developed from recorded amounts, with the expectations. (Ref: par. .A24)

Analytical Procedures That Assist When Forming an Overall Conclusion

.06 The auditor should design and perform analytical procedures near the end of the audit that assist the auditor when forming an overall conclusion about whether the financial statements are consistent with the auditor's understanding of the entity. (Ref: par. .A25–.A27)

Investigating Results of Analytical Procedures

.07 If analytical procedures performed in accordance with this section identify fluctuations or relationships that are inconsistent with other relevant information or that differ from expected values by a significant amount, the auditor should investigate such differences by

---

[3] Paragraph .18 of section 330.

a. inquiring of management and obtaining appropriate audit evidence relevant to management's responses and

b. performing other audit procedures as necessary in the circumstances. (Ref: par. .A28–.A29)

Documentation (Ref: par. .A30)

.08 When substantive analytical procedures have been performed, the auditor should include in the audit documentation the following:[4]

a. The expectation referred to in paragraph .05*c* and the factors considered in its development when that expectation or those factors are not otherwise readily determinable from the audit documentation

b. Results of the comparison referred to in paragraph .05*d* of the recorded amounts, or ratios developed from recorded amounts, with the expectations

c. Any additional auditing procedures performed in accordance with paragraph .07 relating to the investigation of fluctuations or relationships that are inconsistent with other relevant information or that differ from expected values by a significant amount and the results of such additional procedures

Application and Other Explanatory Material

Objectives (Ref: par. .03b)

.A1 Analytical procedures performed near the end of the audit are intended to corroborate audit evidence obtained during the audit of the financial statements to assist the auditor in drawing reasonable conclusions on which to base the auditor's opinion.

Definition (Ref: par. .04)

.A2 Analytical procedures include the consideration of comparisons of the entity's financial information with, for example

- comparable information for prior periods.
- anticipated results of the entity, such as budgets or forecasts, or expectations of the auditor, such as an estimation of depreciation.
- similar industry information, such as a comparison of the entity's ratio of sales to accounts receivable and gross margin percentages with industry averages or other entities of comparable size in the same industry.

.A3 Analytical procedures also include consideration of relationships, for example

- among elements of financial information, such as gross margin percentages, that would be expected to conform to a predictable pattern based on recent history of the entity and industry.
- between financial information and relevant nonfinancial information, such as payroll costs to number of employees.

[4] Paragraphs .08–.12 and .A8 of section 230, *Audit Documentation*.

.A4 Various methods may be used to perform analytical procedures. These methods range from performing simple comparisons to performing complex analyses using advanced statistical techniques. Analytical procedures may be applied to consolidated financial statements, components, and individual elements of information.

.A5 *Scanning* is a type of analytical procedure involving the auditor's exercise of professional judgment to review accounting data to identify significant or unusual items to test. This type of analytical procedure is described further in section 500, *Audit Evidence*.[5]

.A6 A basic premise underlying the application of analytical procedures is that plausible relationships among data may reasonably be expected to exist and continue in the absence of known conditions to the contrary. The reasons that make relationships plausible are an important consideration because data sometimes appears to be related when it is not, which may lead the auditor to erroneous conclusions. In addition, the presence of an unexpected relationship may provide important evidence when appropriately scrutinized.

Substantive Analytical Procedures (Ref: par. .05)

.A7 The auditor's substantive procedures to address the assessed risk of material misstatement for relevant assertions may be tests of details, substantive analytical procedures, or a combination of both. The decision about which audit procedures to perform, including whether to use substantive analytical procedures, is based on the auditor's professional judgment about the expected effectiveness and efficiency of the available audit procedures to reduce the assessed risk of material misstatement to an acceptably low level.

.A8 The expected effectiveness and efficiency of a substantive analytical procedure in addressing risks of material misstatement depends on, among other things, (*a*) the nature of the assertion, (*b*) the plausibility and predictability of the relationship, (*c*) the availability and reliability of the data used to develop the expectation, and (*d*) the precision of the expectation.

.A9 The auditor may inquire of management about the availability and reliability of information needed to apply substantive analytical procedures and the results of any such analytical procedures performed by the entity. It may be effective to use analytical data prepared by management, provided that the auditor is satisfied that such data is properly prepared.

Suitability of Particular Substantive Analytical Procedures for Given Assertions (Ref: par. .05a)

.A10 When more persuasive audit evidence is desired from substantive analytical procedures, more predictable relationships are necessary to develop the expectation. Relationships in a stable environment are usually more predictable than relationships in a dynamic or unstable environment. Relationships involving income statement accounts tend to be more predictable than relationships involving only balance sheet accounts because income statement accounts represent transactions over a period of time, whereas balance sheet accounts represent amounts as of a point in time. Relationships involving transactions subject to management discretion may be less predictable. For example, management may elect to incur maintenance expense rather than replace plant and equipment, or they may delay advertising expenditures.

---

[5] Paragraph .A22 of section 500, *Audit Evidence*.

.A11 Substantive analytical procedures are generally more effective for large volumes of transactions that tend to be predictable over time. The application of planned analytical procedures is based on the expectation that relationships among data exist and continue in the absence of known conditions to the contrary. Particular conditions that can cause variations in these relationships include, for example, specific unusual transactions or events, accounting changes, business changes, random fluctuations, or misstatements. The suitability of a particular analytical procedure will depend upon the auditor's assessment of how effective it will be in detecting a misstatement that, individually or when aggregated with other misstatements, may cause the financial statements to be materially misstated.

.A12 In some cases, even an unsophisticated predictive model may be effective as an analytical procedure. For example, when an entity has a known number of employees at fixed rates of pay throughout the period, it may be possible for the auditor to use this data to estimate the total payroll costs for the period with a high degree of accuracy, thereby providing audit evidence for a significant item in the financial statements and reducing the need to perform tests of details on the payroll. The use of widely recognized trade ratios (such as profit margins for different types of retail entities) can often be used effectively in substantive analytical procedures to provide evidence to support the reasonableness of recorded amounts.

.A13 Different types of analytical procedures provide different levels of assurance. Analytical procedures involving, for example, the prediction of total rental income on a building divided into apartments, taking the rental rates, the number of apartments, and vacancy rates into consideration, can provide persuasive evidence and may eliminate the need for further verification by means of tests of details, provided that the elements are appropriately verified. In contrast, calculation and comparison of gross margin percentages as a means of confirming a revenue figure may provide less persuasive evidence but may provide useful corroboration if used in combination with other audit procedures.

.A14 The determination of the suitability of particular substantive analytical procedures is influenced by the nature of the assertion and the auditor's assessment of the risk of material misstatement. For example, if controls over payroll processing are deficient, the auditor may need to perform more extensive tests of details for assertions related to compensation.

.A15 Particular substantive analytical procedures may also be considered suitable when tests of details are performed on the same assertion. For example, when obtaining audit evidence regarding the valuation assertion for accounts receivable balances, the auditor may apply analytical procedures to an aging of customers' accounts, in addition to performing tests of details on subsequent cash receipts, to determine the collectability of the receivables.

Considerations Specific to Governmental Entities

.A16 The relationships between individual financial statement items traditionally considered in the audit of for-profit businesses may not always be relevant in the audit of governmental entities. For example, relationships describing profitability or return on investment may have limited or no applicability. In addition, the nature of balances reported by a governmental entity may result in different expected relationships than those traditionally assumed for businesses. For example, relationships between revenue, receivables, and inventory may be different when revenue and receivables arise from nonexchange transactions and inventory does not represent products held for sale. Also, governmental entities' budgets are a source of data that may be used as a benchmark for evaluating individual financial statements.

The Reliability of the Data (Ref: par. .05b)

.A17 The reliability of data is influenced by its source and nature and is dependent on the circumstances under which it is obtained. Accordingly, the following are relevant when determining whether data is reliable for purposes of designing substantive analytical procedures:

a. The source of the information available. For example, information may be more reliable when it is obtained from independent sources outside the entity.[6]

b. The comparability of the information available. For example, broad industry data may need to be supplemented to be comparable to that of an entity that produces and sells specialized products.

c. The nature and relevance of the information available. For example, whether budgets have been established as results to be expected rather than as goals to be achieved.

d. Controls over the preparation of the information that are designed to ensure its completeness, accuracy, and validity. For example, controls over the preparation, review, and maintenance of budgets.

.A18 Data may be readily available to develop expectations for some assertions. For example, the auditor may consider whether financial information, such as budgets or forecasts, and nonfinancial information, such as the number of units produced or sold, is available to design substantive analytical procedures.

.A19 The auditor may consider testing the operating effectiveness of controls, if any, over the entity's preparation of information used by the auditor in performing substantive analytical procedures in response to assessed risks. When such controls are effective, the auditor may have greater confidence in the reliability of the information and, therefore, in the results of analytical procedures. The operating effectiveness of controls over nonfinancial information may often be tested in conjunction with other tests of controls. For example, in establishing controls over the processing of sales invoices, an entity may include controls over the recording of unit sales. In these circumstances, the auditor may test the operating effectiveness of controls over the recording of unit sales in conjunction with tests of the operating effectiveness of controls over the processing of sales invoices. Alternatively, the auditor may consider whether the information was subjected to audit testing. Section 330 addresses determining the audit procedures to be performed on the information to be used for substantive analytical procedures.[7]

.A20 The matters discussed in paragraph .A17*a–d* are relevant irrespective of whether the auditor performs substantive analytical procedures on the entity's period-end financial statements or at an interim date and plans to perform substantive analytical procedures for the remaining period. Section 330 addresses performing substantive procedures at an interim date.[8]

Evaluation of Whether the Expectation Is Sufficiently Precise (Ref: par. .05c)

.A21 In evaluating whether the expectation is sufficiently precise when performing a substantive analytical procedure, it is appropriate for the auditor

---

[6] Paragraph .A32 of section 500.

[7] Paragraph .25 of section 330.

[8] Paragraphs .23–.24 of section 330.

to take into account whether substantive analytical procedures are the only substantive procedures planned to address a particular risk of misstatement at the relevant assertion level or whether the risk will be addressed through a combination of substantive analytical procedures and tests of details. A less precise expectation may be appropriate when evidence obtained from performing the substantive analytical procedure will be combined with audit evidence from performing tests of details. A more precise expectation, however, is necessary when the substantive analytical procedure is the only procedure planned to address a particular risk of misstatement for a relevant assertion.

.A22 As expectations become more precise, the range of expected differences becomes narrower, and accordingly, the likelihood increases that significant differences from the expectations are due to misstatements. Matters relevant to the auditor's evaluation of whether the expectation can be developed with sufficient precision to identify a misstatement that, when aggregated with other misstatements, may cause the financial statements to be materially misstated, include the following:

- The accuracy with which the expected results of substantive analytical procedures can be predicted. For example, the auditor may expect greater consistency in comparing gross profit margins from one period to another than in comparing discretionary expenses, such as research or advertising.
- The degree to which information can be disaggregated. For example, substantive analytical procedures may be more effective when applied to financial information on individual sections of an operation or to financial statements of components of a diversified entity than when applied to the financial statements of the entity as a whole.

.A23 When expectations are developed at a more detailed level, it is more likely that the analytical procedure will more effectively address the assessed risk of misstatement to which it is directed. Monthly amounts may be more effective than annual amounts, and comparisons by location or line of business usually are more effective than companywide comparisons. The appropriate level of detail may be influenced by the nature of the entity, its size, and its complexity. The risk that material misstatements may be obscured by offsetting factors increases as an entity's operations become more complex and diversified. Disaggregation of the information helps reduce this risk.

Amount of Acceptable Difference of Recorded Amounts From Expected Values (Ref: par. .05d)

.A24 The auditor's determination of the amount of difference from the expectation that can be accepted without further investigation is influenced by materiality[9] and the desired level of assurance, while taking into account the possibility that a misstatement, individually or when aggregated with other misstatements, may cause the financial statements to be materially misstated. Section 330 requires the auditor to obtain more persuasive audit evidence the higher the auditor's assessment of risk.[10] Accordingly, as the assessed risk increases, the amount of difference considered acceptable without further investigation decreases in order to achieve the desired level of persuasive evidence.[11]

---

[9] Paragraph .A16 of section 320, *Materiality in Planning and Performing an Audit.*

[10] Paragraph .07*b* of section 330.

[11] Paragraph .A20 of section 330.

Analytical Procedures That Assist When Forming an Overall Conclusion (Ref: par. .06)

.A25 A wide variety of analytical procedures may be used when forming an overall conclusion. These procedures may include reading the financial statements and considering (*a*) the adequacy of the evidence gathered in response to unusual or unexpected balances identified during the course of the audit and (*b*) unusual or unexpected balances or relationships that were not previously identified. Results of these analytical procedures may indicate that additional evidence is needed.

.A26 The results of analytical procedures designed and performed in accordance with paragraph .06 may identify a previously unrecognized risk of material misstatement. In such circumstances, section 315 requires the auditor to revise the auditor's assessment of the risks of material misstatement and modify the further planned audit procedures accordingly.[12]

.A27 The analytical procedures performed in accordance with paragraph .06 may be similar to those that would be used as risk assessment procedures.

Investigating Results of Analytical Procedures (Ref: par. .07)

.A28 Audit evidence relevant to management's responses may be obtained by evaluating those responses, taking into account the auditor's understanding of the entity and its environment and other audit evidence obtained during the course of the audit.

.A29 The need to perform other audit procedures may arise when, for example, management is unable to provide an explanation, or the explanation, together with the audit evidence obtained relevant to management's response, is not considered adequate.

Documentation (Ref: par. .08)

.A30 Section 230, *Audit Documentation*, addresses the auditor's responsibilities for preparing audit documentation and applies to substantive analytical procedures and analytical procedures performed near the end of the audit. Paragraph .08 of this section addresses specific requirements that apply to substantive analytical procedures but is not intended to provide a complete list of items that are required to be documented by section 230.

---

[12] Paragraph .32 of section 315.

AU-C Section 530 *
Audit Sampling

Source: SAS No. 122.

Effective for audits of financial statements for periods ending on or after December 15, 2012.

Introduction

Scope of This Section

.01 This section applies when the auditor has decided to use audit sampling in performing audit procedures. It addresses the auditor's use of statistical and nonstatistical sampling when designing and selecting the audit sample, performing tests of controls and tests of details, and evaluating the results from the sample. (Ref: par. .A1–.A2)

.02 This section complements section 500, *Audit Evidence*, which addresses the auditor's responsibility to design and perform audit procedures to obtain sufficient appropriate audit evidence to be able to draw reasonable conclusions as a basis for forming the auditor's opinion. Section 330, *Performing Audit Procedures in Response to Assessed Risks and Evaluating the Audit Evidence Obtained*, provides guidance on the means available to the auditor for selecting items for testing, one of which is audit sampling.[1]

Effective Date

.03 This section is effective for audits of financial statements for periods ending on or after December 15, 2012.

Objective

.04 The objective of the auditor, when using audit sampling, is to provide a reasonable basis for the auditor to draw conclusions about the population from which the sample is selected.

Definitions

.05 For purposes of generally accepted auditing standards, the following terms have the meanings attributed as follows:

Audit sampling (sampling). The selection and evaluation of less than 100 percent of the population of audit relevance such that the auditor expects the items selected (the sample) to be representative of the population and, thus, likely to provide a reasonable

---

* This section has been codified using an "AU-C" identifier instead of an "AU" identifier. "AU-C" is a temporary identifier to avoid confusion with references to existing "AU" sections, which will remain in AICPA *Professional Standards* through 2013. The "AU-C" identifier will revert to "AU" in 2014, by which time substantially all engagements for which the "AU" sections were still effective are expected to be completed.

[1] Paragraphs .A65–.A71 of section 330, *Performing Audit Procedures in Response to Assessed Risks and Evaluating the Audit Evidence Obtained.*

basis for conclusions about the population. In this context, *representative* means that evaluation of the sample will result in conclusions that, subject to the limitations of sampling risk, are similar to those that would be drawn if the same procedures were applied to the entire population. (Ref: par. .A3)

Nonsampling risk. The risk that the auditor reaches an erroneous conclusion for any reason not related to sampling risk. (Ref: par. .A4)

Population. The entire set of data from which a sample is selected and about which the auditor wishes to draw conclusions.

Sampling risk. The risk that the auditor's conclusion based on a sample may be different from the conclusion if the entire population were subjected to the same audit procedure. Sampling risk can lead to two types of erroneous conclusions:

a. In the case of a test of controls, that controls are more effective than they actually are, or in the case of a test of details, that a material misstatement does not exist when, in fact, it does. The auditor is primarily concerned with this type of erroneous conclusion because it affects audit effectiveness and is more likely to lead to an inappropriate audit opinion.

b. In the case of a test of controls, that controls are less effective than they actually are, or in the case of a test of details, that a material misstatement exists when, in fact, it does not. This type of erroneous conclusion affects audit efficiency because it would usually lead to additional work to establish that initial conclusions were incorrect.

Sampling unit. The individual items constituting a population. (Ref: par. .A5)

Statistical sampling. An approach to sampling that has the following characteristics:

a. Random selection of the sample items (Ref: par. .A16)

b. The use of an appropriate statistical technique to evaluate sample results, including measurement of sampling risk

A sampling approach that does not have characteristics *a* and *b* is considered nonstatistical sampling.

Stratification. The process of dividing a population into subpopulations, each of which is a group of sampling units that have similar characteristics.

Tolerable misstatement. A monetary amount set by the auditor in respect of which the auditor seeks to obtain an appropriate level of assurance that the monetary amount set by the auditor is not exceeded by the actual misstatement in the population. (Ref: par. .A6)

Tolerable rate of deviation. A rate of deviation set by the auditor in respect of which the auditor seeks to obtain an appropriate level of assurance that the rate of deviation set by the auditor is not exceeded by the actual rate of deviation in the population.

Requirements

Sample Design, Size, and Selection of Items for Testing

.06 When designing an audit sample, the auditor should consider the purpose of the audit procedure and the characteristics of the population from which the sample will be drawn. (Ref: par. .A7–.A11)

.07 The auditor should determine a sample size sufficient to reduce sampling risk to an acceptably low level. (Ref: par. .A12–.A14)

.08 The auditor should select items for the sample in such a way that the auditor can reasonably expect the sample to be representative of the relevant population and likely to provide the auditor with a reasonable basis for conclusions about the population. (Ref: par. .A15–.A17)

Performing Audit Procedures

.09 The auditor should perform audit procedures, appropriate to the purpose, on each item selected.

.10 If the audit procedure is not applicable to the selected item, the auditor should perform the procedure on a replacement item. (Ref: par. .A18)

.11 If the auditor is unable to apply the designed audit procedures, or suitable alternative procedures, to a selected item, the auditor should treat that item as a deviation from the prescribed control (in the case of tests of controls) or a misstatement (in the case of tests of details). (Ref: par. .A19–.A20)

Nature and Cause of Deviations and Misstatements

.12 The auditor should investigate the nature and cause of any deviations or misstatements identified and evaluate their possible effect on the purpose of the audit procedure and on other areas of the audit. (Ref: par. .A21–.A23)

Projecting the Results of Audit Sampling

.13 The auditor should project the results of audit sampling to the population. (Ref: par. .A24–.A25)

Evaluating the Results of Audit Sampling

.14 The auditor should evaluate

a. the results of the sample, including sampling risk, and (Ref: par. .A26–.A27)

b. whether the use of audit sampling has provided a reasonable basis for conclusions about the population that has been tested. (Ref: par. .A28)

Application and Other Explanatory Material

Scope of This Section (Ref: par. .01)

.A1 The AICPA Audit Guide *Audit Sampling* provides interpretative guidance to apply the concepts in this section, including its definitions.

Considerations Specific to Governmental Entities

.A2 Chapter 11 of the AICPA Audit Guide Government Auditing Standards *and Circular A-133 Audits* provides interpretative guidance in designing an audit approach that includes audit sampling to achieve audit objectives related to both compliance and internal control over compliance in a Circular A-133 compliance audit or program-specific audit performed in accordance with Office of Management and Budget Circular A-133, *Audits of States, Local Governments and Non-Profit Organizations*.

Definitions

Audit Sampling (Ref: par. .05)

.A3 There may be audit procedures that are not considered audit sampling but that involve examination of fewer than 100 percent of the items comprising an account balance or class of transactions. For example, an auditor may examine only a few transactions from an account balance or class of transactions to (*a*) gain an understanding of the nature of an entity's operations or (*b*) clarify the auditor's understanding of the entity's internal control. In such cases, the guidance in this section is not applicable.

Nonsampling Risk (Ref: par. .05)

.A4 Examples of nonsampling risk include the use of inappropriate audit procedures or misinterpretation of audit evidence and failure to recognize a misstatement or deviation. Nonsampling risk may be reduced to an acceptable level through such factors as adequate planning (see section 300, *Planning an Audit*) and proper conduct of a firm's audit practice (see section 220, *Quality Control for an Engagement Conducted in Accordance With Generally Accepted Auditing Standards*).

Sampling Unit (Ref: par. .05)

.A5 The sampling units might be physical items (for example, checks listed on deposit slips, credit entries on bank statements, sales invoices, or accounts receivable) or monetary units.

Tolerable Misstatement (Ref: par. .05)

.A6 The auditor is required by section 320, *Materiality in Planning and Performing an Audit*, to determine performance materiality.[2] Performance materiality is determined to reduce to an appropriately low level the probability that the aggregate of uncorrected and undetected misstatements in the financial statements exceeds materiality for the financial statements as a whole. *Tolerable misstatement* is the application of performance materiality to a particular sampling procedure. Tolerable misstatement may be the same amount or an amount smaller than performance materiality (for example, when the population from which the sample is selected is smaller than the account balance).

Sample Design, Size, and Selection of Items for Testing

Sample Design (Ref: par. .06)

.A7 Audit sampling enables the auditor to obtain and evaluate audit evidence about some characteristic of the items selected in order to form or assist in forming a conclusion concerning the population from which the sample is

---

[2] Paragraph .11 of section 320, *Materiality in Planning and Performing an Audit*.

drawn. Audit sampling can be applied using either statistical or nonstatistical sampling approaches.

.A8 When designing an audit sample, the auditor's consideration includes the specific purpose to be achieved and the combination of audit procedures that is likely to achieve that purpose. Consideration of the nature of the audit evidence sought and possible deviation or misstatement conditions or other characteristics relating to that audit evidence will assist the auditor in defining what constitutes a deviation or misstatement and what population to use for sampling. In fulfilling the requirement in section 500 when performing audit sampling, the auditor is required to perform audit procedures to obtain evidence that the population from which the audit sample is drawn is complete.[3]

.A9 The auditor's consideration of the purpose of the audit procedure, as required by paragraph .06, includes a clear understanding of what constitutes a deviation or misstatement so that all, and only, those conditions that are relevant to the assertions are included in the evaluation of deviations or projection of misstatements. For example, in a test of details relating to the existence of accounts receivable, such as confirmation, payments made by the customer before the confirmation date but received shortly after that date by the client are not considered a misstatement. Also, an incorrect posting between customer accounts does not affect the total accounts receivable balance. Therefore, it may not be appropriate to consider this a misstatement in relation to the relevant assertion even though it may have an important effect on other areas of the audit, such as the assessment of the risk of fraud or the adequacy of the allowance for doubtful accounts.

.A10 In considering the test objective and characteristics of a population for tests of controls, the auditor makes an assessment of the expected rate of deviation based on the auditor's understanding of the relevant controls. This assessment is made in order to design an audit sample and determine sample size. For example, if the expected rate of deviation is unacceptably high, the auditor will normally decide not to perform tests of controls. Similarly, for tests of details, the auditor makes an assessment of the expected misstatement in the population. If the expected misstatement is high, 100 percent examination or increasing the sample size may be appropriate when performing tests of details.

.A11 In considering the characteristics of the population from which the sample will be drawn, the auditor may determine that stratification or value-weighted selection is appropriate.

Sample Size (Ref: par. .07)

.A12 The level of sampling risk that the auditor is willing to accept affects the sample size required. The lower the risk the auditor is willing to accept, the greater the sample size necessary.

.A13 The sample size can be determined by the application of a statistically based formula or through the exercise of professional judgment. Various factors typically influence determination of sample size, as follows:

- For tests of controls:
  - — The tolerable rate of deviation of the population to be tested
  - — The expected rate of deviation of the population to be tested

---

[3] Paragraph .09 of section 500, *Audit Evidence*.

— The desired level of assurance (complement of risk of overreliance) that the tolerable rate of deviation is not exceeded by the actual rate of deviation in the population; the auditor may decide the desired level of assurance based on the extent to which the auditor's risk assessment takes into account relevant controls

— The number of sampling units in the population if the population is very small

- For substantive tests of details:

  — The auditor's desired level of assurance (complement of risk of incorrect acceptance) that tolerable misstatement is not exceeded by actual misstatement in the population; the auditor may decide the desired level of assurance based on the following:

    - The auditor's assessment of the risk of material misstatement
    - The assurance obtained from other substantive procedures directed at the same assertion
    - Tolerable misstatement
    - Expected misstatement for the population
    - Stratification of the population when performed
    - For some sampling methods, the number of sampling units in each stratum

.A14 The decision whether to use a statistical or nonstatistical sampling approach is a matter for the auditor's professional judgment; however, sample size is not a valid criterion to use in deciding between statistical and nonstatistical approaches. An auditor who applies statistical sampling may use tables or formulas to compute sample size based on the factors in paragraph .A13. An auditor who applies nonstatistical sampling exercises professional judgment to relate the same factors used in statistical sampling in determining the appropriate sample size. Ordinarily, this would result in a sample size comparable with the sample size resulting from an efficient and effectively designed statistical sample, considering the same sampling parameters. This guidance does not suggest that the auditor using nonstatistical sampling also compute a corresponding sample size using an appropriate statistical technique.

Selection of Items for Testing (Ref: par. .08)

.A15 Audit sampling involves selection techniques that are probabilistic in nature. For example, through the assessment of the risk of material misstatement, an auditor might identify areas in which misstatement is relatively likely. The auditor might first separately examine those items deemed to be of relatively high risk and then use audit sampling (which will involve some form of probabilistic selection) to form an estimate of some characteristic of the remaining population.

.A16 Random selection techniques include the following:

a. Simple random

b. Systematic random

c. Probability weighted, including monetary unit

A detailed discussion of selection techniques is included in the AICPA Audit Guide *Audit Sampling*.

.A17 With statistical sampling, sample items are selected using random selection techniques. The principal techniques of selecting a nonstatistical sample are the use of random selection and haphazard selection to select sample items.

Performing Audit Procedures (Ref: par. .10–.11)

.A18 An example of when it is necessary to perform the procedure on a replacement item is when a voided check is selected while testing for evidence of payment authorization. If the auditor is satisfied that the check has been properly voided such that it does not constitute a deviation, an appropriately chosen replacement is examined.

.A19 In some circumstances, the auditor may not be able to apply the planned audit procedures to selected sample items because, for example, the entity might not be able to locate supporting documentation. The auditor's treatment of unexamined items will depend on their effect on the auditor's evaluation of the sample. If the auditor's evaluation of the sample results would not be altered by considering those unexamined items to be misstated, it may not be necessary to examine the items, for example, if the aggregate amount of the unexamined items, if treated as misstatements or deviations, would not cause the auditor's assessment of the amount of the misstatement or deviation in the population to exceed tolerable misstatement or tolerable deviation, respectively. However, when this is not the case, the auditor is required by paragraph .11 to perform alternative procedures that provide sufficient appropriate audit evidence to form a conclusion about the sample item and use the results of these procedures in assessing the sample results. If alternative procedures cannot be satisfactorily performed in these cases, the auditor is required to treat the items as misstatements or deviations, as appropriate, in evaluating the results of the sample. Section 240, *Consideration of Fraud in a Financial Statement Audit*, also requires the auditor to consider whether the reasons for the auditor's inability to examine the items have implications with regard to assessing risks of material misstatement due to fraud, the assessed level of control risk that the auditor expects to be supported, or the degree of reliance on management representations.

.A20 An example of a suitable alternative procedure for an accounts receivable positive confirmation request for which no reply has been received might be the examination of subsequent cash receipts, together with evidence of their source and the items they are intended to settle.

Nature and Cause of Deviations and Misstatements (Ref: par. .12)

.A21 Section 450, *Evaluation of Misstatements Identified During the Audit*, explains that the auditor may request management to examine a class of transactions, account balance, or disclosure in order for management to understand the cause of a misstatement identified by the auditor; perform procedures to determine the amount of the actual misstatement in the class of transactions, account balance, or disclosure; and make appropriate adjustments to the financial statements.[4]

---

[4] Paragraph .A9 of section 450, *Evaluation of Misstatements Identified During the Audit*.

.A22 In analyzing the deviations and misstatements identified, the auditor may observe that many have a common feature (for example, type of transaction, location, product line, or period of time). In such circumstances, the auditor may decide to identify all items in the population that possess the common feature and extend audit procedures to those items. In addition, such deviations or misstatements may be intentional and may indicate the possibility of fraud.

.A23 In addition to the evaluation of the frequency and amounts of monetary misstatements, section 450 requires the auditor to consider the qualitative aspects of the misstatements.[5] These include (*a*) the nature and cause of misstatements, such as whether they are differences in principle or application, are errors, or are caused by fraud or are due to misunderstanding of instructions or carelessness, and (*b*) the possible relationship of the misstatements to other phases of the audit. The discovery of fraud requires a broader consideration of possible implications than does the discovery of an error.

Projecting the Results of Audit Sampling (Ref: par. .13)

.A24 For tests of details, the auditor is required by paragraph .13 to project misstatements observed in an audit sample to the population in order to obtain a likely misstatement. Due to sampling risk, this projection may not be sufficient to determine an amount to be recorded.

.A25 For tests of controls, the sample deviation rate is also the projected deviation rate for the population as a whole. Section 330 addresses the auditor's response when deviations from controls upon which the auditor intends to rely are detected.[6]

Evaluating the Results of Audit Sampling (Ref: par. .14)

.A26 For tests of controls, an unexpectedly high sample deviation rate may lead to an increase in the assessed risks of material misstatement, unless further audit evidence substantiating the initial assessment is obtained. For tests of details, an unexpectedly high misstatement amount in a sample may cause the auditor to believe that a class of transactions or account balance is materially misstated, in the absence of further audit evidence that no material misstatement exists.

.A27 Considering the results of other audit procedures helps the auditor assess the risk that actual misstatement in the population exceeds tolerable misstatement; such risk may be reduced if additional audit evidence is obtained. In the case of tests of details, the *projected misstatement* is the auditor's best estimate of misstatement in the population. As the projected misstatement approaches or exceeds tolerable misstatement, the more likely that actual misstatement in the population exceeds tolerable misstatement. Also, if the projected misstatement is greater than the auditor's expectations of misstatement used to determine the sample size, the auditor may conclude that there is an unacceptable sampling risk that the actual misstatement in the population exceeds the tolerable misstatement. The AICPA Audit Guide *Audit Sampling* contains further guidance regarding the concept of sampling risk.

.A28 If the auditor concludes that audit sampling has not provided a reasonable basis for conclusions about the population that has been tested, the auditor may

---

[5] Paragraph .11 of section 450.

[6] Paragraph .17 of section 330.

- request management to investigate misstatements that have been identified and the potential for further misstatements and to make any necessary adjustments or
- tailor the nature, timing, and extent of those further audit procedures to best achieve the required assurance. For example, in the case of tests of controls, the auditor might extend the sample size, test an alternative control, or modify related substantive procedures.

Section 450 addresses misstatements identified by the auditor during the audit.

AU-C Section 540 *

Auditing Accounting Estimates, Including Fair Value Accounting Estimates, and Related Disclosures

Source: SAS No. 122.

Effective for audits of financial statements for periods ending on or after December 15, 2012.

Introduction

Scope of This Section

.01 This section addresses the auditor's responsibilities relating to accounting estimates, including fair value accounting estimates and related disclosures, in an audit of financial statements. Specifically, it expands on how section 315, *Understanding the Entity and Its Environment and Assessing the Risks of Material Misstatement*; section 330, *Performing Audit Procedures in Response to Assessed Risks and Evaluating the Audit Evidence Obtained*; and other relevant AU-C sections are to be applied with regard to accounting estimates. It also includes requirements and guidance related to misstatements of individual accounting estimates and indicators of possible management bias.

Nature of Accounting Estimates

.02 Some financial statement items cannot be measured precisely but can only be estimated. For purposes of this section, such financial statement items are referred to as *accounting estimates*. The nature and reliability of information available to management to support the making of an accounting estimate varies widely, which thereby affects the degree of estimation uncertainty associated with accounting estimates. The degree of estimation uncertainty affects, in turn, the risks of material misstatement of accounting estimates, including their susceptibility to unintentional or intentional management bias. (Ref: par. .A1–.A10 and .A136)

.03 The measurement objective of accounting estimates can vary, depending on the applicable financial reporting framework and the financial item being reported.[1] The measurement objective for some accounting estimates is to forecast the outcome of one or more transactions, events, or conditions giving rise to the need for the accounting estimate. For other accounting estimates, including many fair value accounting estimates, the measurement objective is different and is expressed in terms of the value of a current transaction or

---

* This section has been codified using an "AU-C" identifier instead of an "AU" identifier. "AU-C" is a temporary identifier to avoid confusion with references to existing "AU" sections, which will remain in AICPA *Professional Standards* through 2013. The "AU-C" identifier will revert to "AU" in 2014, by which time substantially all engagements for which the "AU" sections were still effective are expected to be completed.

[1] Paragraph .14 of section 200, *Overall Objectives of the Independent Auditor and the Conduct of an Audit in Accordance With Generally Accepted Auditing Standards*, defines *financial report framework* and the term *fair presentation framework*.

financial statement item based on conditions prevalent at the measurement date, such as estimated market price for a particular type of asset or liability. For example, the applicable financial reporting framework may require fair value measurement based on an assumed hypothetical current transaction between knowledgeable, willing parties (sometimes referred to as *market participants* or equivalent) in an arm's length transaction, rather than the settlement of a transaction at some past or future date.[2]

.04 A difference between the outcome of an accounting estimate and the amount originally recognized or disclosed in the financial statements does not necessarily represent a misstatement of the financial statements; rather, it could be an outcome of estimation uncertainty (see paragraph .02). This is particularly the case for fair value accounting estimates because any observed outcome may be affected by events or conditions subsequent to the date at which the measurement is estimated for purposes of the financial statements.

Effective Date

.05 This section is effective for audits of financial statements for periods ending on or after December 15, 2012.

Objective

.06 The objective of the auditor is to obtain sufficient appropriate audit evidence about whether, in the context of the applicable financial reporting framework

a. accounting estimates, including fair value accounting estimates, in the financial statements, whether recognized or disclosed, are reasonable and

b. related disclosures in the financial statements are adequate.

Definitions

.07 For purposes of generally accepted auditing standards, the following terms have the meanings attributed as follows:

Accounting estimate. An approximation of a monetary amount in the absence of a precise means of measurement. This term is used for an amount measured at fair value when there is estimation uncertainty, as well as for other amounts that require estimation. When this section addresses only accounting estimates involving measurement at fair value, the term *fair value accounting estimates* is used.

Auditor's point estimate or auditor's range. The amount or range of amounts, respectively, derived from audit evidence for use in evaluating the recorded or disclosed amount(s).

Estimation uncertainty. The susceptibility of an accounting estimate and related disclosures to an inherent lack of precision in its measurement.

Management bias. A lack of neutrality by management in the preparation and fair presentation of information.

Management's point estimate. The amount selected by management for recognition or disclosure in the financial statements as an accounting estimate.

---

[2] Different definitions of *fair value* may exist among financial reporting frameworks.

Outcome of an accounting estimate. The actual monetary amount that results from the resolution of the underlying transaction(s), event(s), or condition(s) addressed by the accounting estimate.

Requirements

Risk Assessment Procedures and Related Activities

.08 When performing risk assessment procedures and related activities to obtain an understanding of the entity and its environment, including the entity's internal control, as required by section 315, the auditor should obtain an understanding of the following in order to provide a basis for the identification and assessment of the risks of material misstatement for accounting estimates:[3] (Ref: par. .A11)

a. The requirements of the applicable financial reporting framework relevant to accounting estimates, including related disclosures. (Ref: par. .A12–.A14)

b. How management identifies those transactions, events, and conditions that may give rise to the need for accounting estimates to be recognized or disclosed in the financial statements. In obtaining this understanding, the auditor should make inquiries of management about changes in circumstances that may give rise to new, or the need to revise existing, accounting estimates. (Ref: par. .A15–.A20)

c. How management makes the accounting estimates and the data on which they are based, including (Ref: par. .A21–.A22)

   i. the method(s), including, when applicable, the model, used in making the accounting estimate; (Ref: par. .A23–.A25)

   ii. relevant controls; (Ref: par. .A26–.A27)

   iii. whether management has used a specialist; (Ref: par. .A28–.A29)

   iv. the assumptions underlying the accounting estimates; (Ref: par. .A30–.A35)

   v. whether there has been or ought to have been a change from the prior period in the method(s) or assumption(s) for making the accounting estimates and, if so, why; and (Ref: par. .A36)

   vi. whether and, if so, how management has assessed the effect of estimation uncertainty. (Ref: par. .A37)

.09 The auditor should review the outcome of accounting estimates included in the prior period financial statements or, when applicable, their subsequent reestimation for the purpose of the current period. The nature and extent of the auditor's review takes account of the nature of the accounting estimates and whether the information obtained from the review would be relevant to identifying and assessing risks of material misstatement of accounting estimates made in the current period financial statements. However, the review is not intended to call into question the auditor's professional judgments made

---

[3] Paragraphs .05–.06 and .12–.13 of section 315, *Understanding the Entity and Its Environment and Assessing the Risks of Material Misstatement.*

in the prior periods that were based on information available at the time. (Ref: par. .A38–.A44)

Identifying and Assessing the Risks of Material Misstatement

.10 In identifying and assessing the risks of material misstatement, as required by section 315, the auditor should evaluate the degree of estimation uncertainty associated with an accounting estimate.[4] (Ref: par. .A45–.A46)

.11 The auditor should determine whether, in the auditor's professional judgment, any of those accounting estimates that have been identified as having high estimation uncertainty give rise to significant risks. (Ref: par. .A47–.A51)

Responding to the Assessed Risks of Material Misstatement

.12 Based on the assessed risks of material misstatement, the auditor should determine (Ref: par. .A52)

a. whether management has appropriately applied the requirements of the applicable financial reporting framework relevant to the accounting estimate and (Ref: par. .A53–.A57)

b. whether the methods for making the accounting estimates are appropriate and have been applied consistently and whether changes from the prior period, if any, in accounting estimates or the method for making them are appropriate in the circumstances. (Ref: par. .A58–.A59)

.13 In responding to the assessed risks of material misstatement, as required by section 330, the auditor should undertake one or more of the following, taking into account the nature of the accounting estimate:[5] (Ref: par. .A60–.A62)

a. Determine whether events occurring up to the date of the auditor's report provide audit evidence regarding the accounting estimate. (Ref: par. .A63–.A67)

b. Test how management made the accounting estimate and the data on which it is based. In doing so, the auditor should evaluate whether (Ref: par. .A68–.A71)

  i. the method of measurement used is appropriate in the circumstances, (Ref: par. .A72–.A77)

  ii. the assumptions used by management are reasonable in light of the measurement objectives of the applicable financial reporting framework, and (Ref: par. .A78–.A89)

  iii. the data on which the estimate is based is sufficiently reliable for the auditor's purposes. (Ref: par. .A70)

c. Test the operating effectiveness of the controls over how management made the accounting estimate, together with appropriate substantive procedures. (Ref: par. .A90–.A92)

d. Develop a point estimate or range to evaluate management's point estimate. For this purpose (Ref: par. .A93–.A97)

---

[4] Paragraph .26 of section 315.

[5] Paragraphs .05–.06 of section 330, *Performing Audit Procedures in Response to Assessed Risks and Evaluating the Audit Evidence Obtained.*

i. if the auditor uses assumptions or methods that differ from management's, the auditor should obtain an understanding of management's assumptions or methods sufficient to establish that the auditor's point estimate or range takes into account relevant variables and to evaluate any significant differences from management's point estimate. (Ref: par. .A98)

ii. if the auditor concludes that it is appropriate to use a range, the auditor should narrow the range, based on audit evidence available, until all outcomes within the range are considered reasonable. (Ref: par. .A99–.A101)

.14 In determining the matters identified in paragraph .12 or in responding to the assessed risks of material misstatement in accordance with paragraph .13, the auditor should consider whether specialized skills or knowledge with regard to one or more aspects of the accounting estimates is required in order to obtain sufficient appropriate audit evidence. (Ref: par. .A102–.A107)

Further Substantive Procedures to Respond to Significant Risks (Ref: par. .A108)

Estimation Uncertainty

.15 For accounting estimates that give rise to significant risks, in addition to other substantive procedures performed to meet the requirements of section 330, the auditor should evaluate the following:[6]

a. How management has considered alternative assumptions or outcomes and why it has rejected them or how management has otherwise addressed estimation uncertainty in making the accounting estimate (Ref: par. .A109–.A112)

b. Whether the significant assumptions used by management are reasonable (Ref: par. .A113–.A115)

c. When relevant to the reasonableness of the significant assumptions used by management or the appropriate application of the applicable financial reporting framework, management's intent to carry out specific courses of action and its ability to do so (Ref: par. .A116)

.16 If, in the auditor's professional judgment, management has not addressed adequately the effects of estimation uncertainty on the accounting estimates that give rise to significant risks, the auditor should, if considered necessary, develop a range with which to evaluate the reasonableness of the accounting estimate. (Ref: par. .A117–.A118)

Recognition and Measurement Criteria

.17 For accounting estimates that give rise to significant risks, the auditor should obtain sufficient appropriate audit evidence about whether

a. management's decision to recognize or not recognize the accounting estimates in the financial statements and (Ref: par. .A119–.A120)

b. the selected measurement basis for the accounting estimates (Ref: par. .A121)

---

[6] Paragraph .18 of section 330.

are in accordance with the requirements of the applicable financial reporting framework.

Evaluating the Reasonableness of the Accounting Estimates and Determining Misstatements

.18 The auditor should evaluate, based on the audit evidence, whether the accounting estimates in the financial statements are either reasonable in the context of the applicable financial reporting framework or are misstated. (Ref: par. .A122–.A127)

Disclosures Related to Accounting Estimates

.19 The auditor should obtain sufficient appropriate audit evidence about whether the disclosures in the financial statements related to accounting estimates are in accordance with the requirements of the applicable financial reporting framework. (Ref: par. .A128–.A129)

.20 For accounting estimates that give rise to significant risks, the auditor also should evaluate the adequacy of the disclosure of estimation uncertainty in the financial statements in the context of the applicable financial reporting framework. (Ref: par. .A108 and .A130–.A132)

Indicators of Possible Management Bias

.21 The auditor should review the judgments and decisions made by management in the making of accounting estimates to identify whether indicators of possible management bias exist. Indicators of possible management bias do not, themselves, constitute misstatements for the purposes of drawing conclusions on the reasonableness of individual accounting estimates. (Ref: par. .A133–.A134)

Documentation

.22 The auditor should include in the audit documentation[7]

a. for those accounting estimates that give rise to significant risks, the basis for the auditor's conclusions about the reasonableness of accounting estimates and their disclosure and

b. indicators of possible management bias, if any. (Ref: par. .A135)

Application and Other Explanatory Material

Nature of Accounting Estimates (Ref: par. .02)

.A1 Because of the uncertainties inherent in business activities, some financial statement items can only be estimated. Further, the specific characteristics of an asset, a liability, or a component of equity or the basis or method of measurement prescribed by the financial reporting framework may give rise to the need to estimate a financial statement item. Some financial reporting frameworks prescribe specific methods of measurement and the disclosures that are required to be made in the financial statements whereas other financial reporting frameworks are less specific.

---

[7] Paragraphs .08–.12 and .A8 of section 230, *Audit Documentation*.

.A2 Some accounting estimates involve relatively low estimation uncertainty and may give rise to lower risks of material misstatements. For example

- accounting estimates arising in entities that engage in business activities that are not complex.
- accounting estimates that are frequently made and updated because they relate to routine transactions.
- accounting estimates derived from data that is readily available, such as published interest rate data or exchange-traded prices of securities. Such data may be referred to as *observable* in the context of a fair value accounting estimate.
- fair value accounting estimates in which the method of measurement prescribed by the applicable financial reporting framework is simple and applied easily to the asset or liability requiring measurement at fair value.
- fair value accounting estimates in which the model used to measure the accounting estimate is well-known or generally accepted, provided that the assumptions or inputs to the model are observable.

.A3 However, for some accounting estimates, relatively high estimation uncertainty may exist, particularly when they are based on significant assumptions. For example

- accounting estimates relating to the outcome of litigation.
- fair value accounting estimates for derivative financial instruments not publicly traded.
- fair value accounting estimates for which a highly specialized entity-developed model is used or for which there are assumptions or inputs that cannot be observed in the marketplace.

.A4 The degree of estimation uncertainty varies based on the nature of the accounting estimate, the extent to which there is a generally accepted method or model used to make the accounting estimate, and the subjectivity of the assumptions used to make the accounting estimate. In some cases, estimation uncertainty associated with an accounting estimate may be so great that the recognition criteria in the applicable financial reporting framework are not met, and the accounting estimate cannot be made.

.A5 Not all financial statement items requiring measurement at fair value involve estimation uncertainty. For example, this may be the case for some financial statement items when an active and open market exists that provides readily available and reliable information on the prices at which actual exchanges occur, in which case the existence of published price quotations ordinarily is the best audit evidence of fair value. However, estimation uncertainty may exist even when the valuation technique and data are well-defined. For example, valuation of securities quoted on an active and open market at the listed market price may require adjustment if the holding is significant in relation to the market or is subject to restrictions in marketability. In addition, general economic circumstances prevailing at the time (for example, illiquidity in a particular market) may affect estimation uncertainty.

.A6 Additional examples of situations when accounting estimates, other than fair value accounting estimates, may be required include the following:

- Allowance for doubtful accounts
- Inventory obsolescence

- Warranty obligations
- Depreciation method or asset useful life
- Provision against the carrying amount of an investment when uncertainty regarding its recoverability exists
- Outcome of long-term contracts
- Costs arising from litigation settlements and judgments

.A7 Additional examples of situations when fair value accounting estimates may be required include the following:

- Complex financial instruments, which are not traded in an active and open market
- Share-based payments
- Property or equipment held for disposal
- Certain assets or liabilities acquired in a business combination, including goodwill and intangible assets
- Transactions involving the exchange of assets or liabilities between independent parties without monetary consideration (for example, a nonmonetary exchange of plant facilities in different lines of business)

.A8 Estimation involves judgments based on information available when the financial statements are prepared. For many accounting estimates, these include making assumptions about matters that are uncertain at the time of estimation. The auditor is not responsible for predicting future conditions, transactions, or events that, if known at the time of the audit, might have significantly affected management's actions or the assumptions used by management.

Management Bias

.A9 Financial reporting frameworks often call for neutrality (that is, freedom from bias). However, accounting estimates are imprecise and can be influenced by management judgment. Such judgment may involve unintentional or intentional management bias (for example, as a result of motivation to achieve a desired result). The susceptibility of an accounting estimate to management bias increases with the subjectivity involved in making it. Unintentional management bias and the potential for intentional management bias are inherent in subjective decisions that are often required in making an accounting estimate. For continuing audits, indicators of possible management bias identified during the audit of the preceding periods influence the planning and risk identification and assessment activities of the auditor in the current period.

.A10 Management bias can be difficult to detect at an account level. It may only be identified when considered in the aggregate of groups of accounting estimates or all accounting estimates or when observed over a number of accounting periods. Although some form of management bias is inherent in subjective decisions, in making such judgments, there may be no intention by management to mislead the users of financial statements. However, when intention to mislead exists, management bias is fraudulent in nature.

Risk Assessment Procedures and Related Activities (Ref: par. .08)

.A11 The risk assessment procedures and related activities required by paragraphs .08–.09 assist the auditor in developing an expectation of the nature and type of accounting estimates that an entity may have. The nature and extent of the risk assessment procedures and activities are matters of professional judgment. The auditor's primary consideration is whether the understanding that has been obtained is sufficient to identify and assess the risks of material misstatement related to accounting estimates and to plan the nature, timing, and extent of further audit procedures. When the risk of material misstatement related to an accounting estimate has been significantly reduced by audit evidence relating to events occurring after management has made the estimate (for example, if litigation has been settled, the entity has sold an impaired asset, or receivables have been collected), the nature and extent of the procedures and activities required by paragraphs .08*c* and .09 may be significantly reduced or may not be necessary at all.

Obtaining an Understanding of the Requirements of the Applicable Financial Reporting Framework (Ref: par. .08a)

.A12 Obtaining an understanding of the requirements of the applicable financial reporting framework assists the auditor in determining, for example, whether it

- prescribes certain conditions for the recognition,[8] or methods for the measurement, of accounting estimates.
- specifies certain conditions that permit or require measurement at a fair value.
- specifies required or permitted disclosures.

Obtaining this understanding also provides the auditor with a basis for discussion with management about how management has applied those requirements relevant to the accounting estimate and the auditor's determination of whether they have been appropriately applied.

.A13 Financial reporting frameworks may provide guidance for management on determining point estimates when alternatives exist. For example, some financial reporting frameworks require that the point estimate selected be the alternative that reflects management's judgment of the most likely outcome;[9] others may require the use of a discounted probability-weighted expected value. In some cases, management may be able to make a point estimate directly. In other cases, management may be able to make a reliable point estimate only after considering alternative assumptions or outcomes from which it is able to determine a point estimate.

.A14 Financial reporting frameworks may require the disclosure of information concerning the significant assumptions to which the accounting estimate is particularly sensitive. Furthermore, when a high degree of estimation uncertainty exists, some financial reporting frameworks do not permit an accounting estimate to be recognized in the financial statements, but certain disclosures may be required in the notes to the financial statements.

Obtaining an Understanding of How Management Identifies the Need for Accounting Estimates (Ref: par. .08b)

.A15 The preparation and fair presentation of the financial statements requires management to determine whether a transaction, an event, or a condition gives rise to the need to make an accounting estimate and that all

---

[8] Most financial reporting frameworks require incorporation in the balance sheet or income statement of items that satisfy their criteria for recognition. Disclosure of accounting policies or adding notes to the financial statements does not rectify a failure to recognize such items, including accounting estimates.

[9] Different financial reporting frameworks may use different terminology to describe point estimates determined in this way.

necessary accounting estimates have been recognized, measured, and disclosed in the financial statements in accordance with the applicable financial reporting framework.

.A16 Management's identification of transactions, events, and conditions that give rise to the need for accounting estimates is likely to be based on

- management's knowledge of the entity's business and the industry in which it operates.
- management's knowledge of the implementation of business strategies in the current period.
- when applicable, management's cumulative experience of preparing the entity's financial statements in prior periods.

In such cases, the auditor may obtain an understanding of how management identifies the need for accounting estimates primarily through inquiry of management. In other cases, when management's process is more structured (for example, when management has a formal risk management function), the auditor may perform risk assessment procedures directed at the methods and practices followed by management for periodically reviewing the circumstances that give rise to the accounting estimates and reestimating the accounting estimates as necessary. The completeness of accounting estimates is often an important consideration of the auditor, particularly accounting estimates relating to liabilities.

.A17 The auditor's understanding of the entity and its environment obtained during the performance of risk assessment procedures, together with other audit evidence obtained during the course of the audit, assist the auditor in identifying circumstances or changes in circumstances that may give rise to the need for an accounting estimate.

.A18 Inquiries of management about changes in circumstances may include, for example, inquiries about whether

- the entity has engaged in new types of transactions that may give rise to accounting estimates.
- terms of transactions that gave rise to accounting estimates have changed.
- accounting policies relating to accounting estimates have changed as a result of changes to the requirements of the applicable financial reporting framework or otherwise.
- regulatory or other changes outside the control of management have occurred that may require management to revise, or make new, accounting estimates.
- new conditions or events have occurred that may give rise to the need for new or revised accounting estimates.

.A19 During the audit, the auditor may identify transactions, events, and conditions that give rise to the need for accounting estimates that management failed to identify. Section 315 addresses circumstances in which the auditor identifies risks of material misstatement that management failed to identify, including determining whether a significant deficiency or material weakness in internal control exists with regard to the entity's risk assessment processes.[10]

---

[10] Paragraph .17 of section 315.

Considerations Specific to Smaller, Less Complex Entities

.A20 Obtaining this understanding for smaller entities is often less complex because their business activities are often limited, and transactions are less complex. Further, often, a single person (for example, the owner-manager) identifies the need to make an accounting estimate, and the auditor may focus inquiries accordingly.

Obtaining an Understanding of How Management Makes the Accounting Estimates (Ref: par. .08c)

.A21 The preparation and fair presentation of the financial statements also requires management to establish financial reporting processes for making accounting estimates, including adequate internal control. Such processes include the following:

- Selecting appropriate accounting policies and prescribing estimation processes, including appropriate estimation or valuation techniques, including, when applicable, the appropriate models
- Developing or identifying relevant data and assumptions that affect accounting estimates
- Periodically reviewing the circumstances that give rise to the accounting estimates and reestimating the accounting estimates as necessary

.A22 Matters that the auditor may consider in obtaining an understanding of how management makes the accounting estimates include, for example

- the types of accounts or transactions to which the accounting estimates relate (for example, whether the accounting estimates arise from the recording of routine and recurring transactions or whether they arise from nonrecurring or unusual transactions).
- whether and, if so, how management has used recognized measurement techniques for making particular accounting estimates.
- whether the accounting estimates were made based on data available at an interim date and, if so, whether and how management has taken into account the effect of events, transactions, and changes in circumstances occurring between that date and the period end.

Method of Measurement, Including the Use of Models (Ref: par. .08c(i))

.A23 In some cases, the applicable financial reporting framework may prescribe the method of measurement for an accounting estimate (for example, a particular model that is to be used in measuring a fair value estimate). In many cases, however, the applicable financial reporting framework does not prescribe the method of measurement or may specify alternative methods for measurement.

.A24 When the applicable financial reporting framework does not prescribe a particular method to be used in the circumstances, matters that the auditor may consider in obtaining an understanding of the method or, when applicable, the model used to make accounting estimates include, for example

- how management considered the nature of the asset or liability being estimated when selecting a particular method.
- whether the entity operates in a particular business, industry, or environment in which methods commonly used to make the particular type of accounting estimate exist.

.A25 There may be greater risks of material misstatement, for example, in cases when management has internally developed a model to be used to make the accounting estimate or is departing from a method commonly used in a particular business, industry, or environment.

Relevant Controls (Ref: par. .08c(ii))

.A26 Matters that the auditor may consider in obtaining an understanding of relevant controls include, for example, the experience and competence of those who make the accounting estimates and controls related to

- how management determines the completeness, relevance, and accuracy of the data used to develop accounting estimates.
- the review and approval of accounting estimates, including the assumptions or inputs used in their development, by appropriate levels of management and, when appropriate, those charged with governance.
- the segregation of duties between those committing the entity to the underlying transactions and those responsible for making the accounting estimates, including whether the assignment of responsibilities appropriately takes account of the nature of the entity and its products or services (for example, in the case of a large financial institution, relevant segregation of duties may include an independent function responsible for estimation and validation of fair value pricing of the entity's proprietary financial products staffed by individuals whose remuneration is not tied to such products).
- services provided by a service organization, if any, to provide fair value or other accounting estimates measurements or the data that supports the measurement. When an entity uses a service organization, section 402, *Audit Considerations Relating to an Entity Using a Service Organization*, applies.

.A27 Other controls may be relevant to making the accounting estimates, depending on the circumstances. For example, if the entity uses specific models for making accounting estimates, management may put into place specific policies and procedures around such models. These may include, for example, those established over

- the design and development or selection of a particular model for a particular purpose.
- the use of the model.
- the maintenance and periodic validation of the integrity of the model.
- security, such as controls that prevent changes to the model or data without authorization.

Management's Use of Specialists[11] (Ref: par. .08c(iii))

.A28 Management may have, or the entity may employ individuals with, the experience and competence necessary to make estimates. In some cases, however, management may need to engage a specialist to make estimates or assist in making them. This need may arise because of, for example

---

[11] See paragraph .08 of section 500, *Audit Evidence*, which addresses management's specialists.

- the specialized nature of the matter requiring estimation (for example, the measurement of mineral or hydrocarbon reserves in extractive industries).
- the technical nature of the models required to meet the relevant requirements of the applicable financial reporting framework, as may be the case in certain measurements at fair value.
- the unusual or infrequent nature of the condition, transaction, or event requiring an accounting estimate.

.A29 *Considerations specific to smaller, less complex entities.* Discussion with the owner-manager early in the audit process about the nature of any accounting estimates, the completeness of the required accounting estimates, and the adequacy of the estimating process may assist the owner-manager in determining the need to use a specialist.

Assumptions (Ref: par. .08c(iv))

.A30 Assumptions may be characterized by predictions of future conditions, transactions, or events used in making an estimate and are integral components of accounting estimates. Matters that the auditor may consider in obtaining an understanding of the assumptions underlying the accounting estimates include, for example

- the nature of the assumptions, including which of the assumptions are likely to be significant assumptions.
- how management assesses whether the assumptions are relevant and complete (that is, that all relevant variables have been taken into account).
- when applicable, how management determines that the assumptions used are internally consistent.
- whether the assumptions relate to matters within the control of management (for example, assumptions about the maintenance programs that may affect the estimation of an asset's useful life) and how they conform to the entity's business plans and the external environment or to matters that are outside its control (for example, assumptions about interest rates, mortality rates, potential judicial or regulatory actions, or the variability and timing of future cash flows).
- the nature and extent of documentation, if any, supporting the assumptions.

Assumptions may be made or identified by a specialist to assist management in making the accounting estimates. Such assumptions, when used by management, become management's assumptions.

.A31 In some cases, assumptions may be referred to as *inputs* (for example, when management uses a model to make an accounting estimate), though the term *inputs* may also be used to refer to the underlying data to which specific assumptions are applied.

.A32 Management may support assumptions with different types of information drawn from internal and external sources, the relevance and reliability of which will vary. In some cases, an assumption may be reliably based on applicable information from either external sources (for example, published interest rate or other statistical data) or internal sources (for example, historical information or previous conditions experienced by the entity). In other cases, an assumption may be more subjective (for example, when the entity has no experience or external sources from which to draw).

.A33 In the case of fair value accounting estimates, assumptions reflect, or are consistent with, what knowledgeable, willing arm's length parties (sometimes referred to as *market participants* or equivalent) would use in determining fair value when exchanging an asset or settling a liability. Specific assumptions also will vary with the characteristics of the asset or liability being valued; the valuation technique used (for example, a market approach or an income approach); and the requirements of the applicable financial reporting framework.

.A34 With respect to fair value accounting estimates, assumptions or inputs vary in terms of their source and bases, as follows:

a. Those that reflect what market participants would use in pricing an asset or a liability, developed based on market data obtained from sources independent of the reporting entity (sometimes referred to as *observable inputs* or equivalent)

b. Those that reflect the entity's own judgments about what assumptions market participants would use in pricing the asset or liability, developed based on the best information available in the circumstances (sometimes referred to as *unobservable inputs* or equivalent)

In practice, however, the distinction between *a* and *b* is not always apparent. Further, it may be necessary for management to select from a number of different assumptions used by different market participants.

.A35 The extent of subjectivity, such as whether an assumption or input is observable, influences the degree of estimation uncertainty and, thereby, the auditor's assessment of the risks of material misstatement for a particular accounting estimate.

Changes in Methods or Assumptions for Making Accounting Estimates (Ref: par. .08c(v))

.A36 In obtaining an understanding of how management makes the accounting estimates, the auditor is required to obtain an understanding about whether there has been or ought to have been a change from the prior period in the methods or assumptions for making the accounting estimates. A specific estimation method or assumption may need to be changed in response to changes in the environment or circumstances affecting the entity or in the requirements of the applicable financial reporting framework. If management has changed the method or assumption for making an accounting estimate, it is important that management can demonstrate that the new method or assumption is more appropriate or is responsive to such changes. For example, if management changes the basis of making an accounting estimate from a liquid market approach to an illiquid market approach, the auditor challenges whether management's assumptions about the marketplace are reasonable in light of economic circumstances.

Estimation Uncertainty (Ref: par. .08c(vi))

.A37 Matters that the auditor may consider in obtaining an understanding of whether and, if so, how management has assessed the effect of estimation uncertainty include, for example,

- whether and, if so, how management has considered alternative assumptions or outcomes by, for example, performing a sensitivity analysis to determine the effect of changes in the assumptions on an accounting estimate.

- how management determines the accounting estimate when analysis indicates a number of outcome scenarios.
- whether management monitors the outcome of accounting estimates made in the prior period and whether management has appropriately responded to the outcome of that monitoring procedure.

Reviewing Prior Period Accounting Estimates (Ref: par. .09)

.A38 The nature and extent of the review of the outcome of accounting estimates included in the prior period financial statements is a matter of professional judgment. In performing the procedures required in paragraph .09, it may not be necessary to review the outcome of every accounting estimate included in the prior period.

.A39 The outcome of an accounting estimate will often differ from the accounting estimate recognized in the prior period financial statements. By performing risk assessment procedures to identify and understand the reasons for such differences, the auditor may obtain

- information regarding the effectiveness of management's prior period estimation process, from which the auditor can judge the likely effectiveness of management's current process;
- audit evidence that is pertinent to the reestimation, in the current period, of prior period accounting estimates; or
- audit evidence of matters that may be required to be disclosed in the financial statements, such as estimation uncertainty.

.A40 The review of prior period accounting estimates may also assist the auditor, in the current period, in identifying circumstances or conditions that increase the susceptibility of accounting estimates to, or indicate the presence of, possible management bias. The auditor's professional skepticism assists in identifying such circumstances or conditions and in determining the nature, timing, and extent of further audit procedures.

.A41 A retrospective review of management judgments and assumptions related to significant accounting estimates is also required by section 240, *Consideration of Fraud in a Financial Statement Audit*.[12] That review is conducted as part of the requirement for the auditor to design and perform procedures to review accounting estimates for biases that could represent a risk of material misstatement due to fraud, in response to the risks of management override of controls. As a practical matter, the auditor's review of prior period accounting estimates as a risk assessment procedure in accordance with this section may be carried out in conjunction with the review required by section 240.

.A42 The auditor may judge that a more detailed review is required for those accounting estimates that were identified during the prior period audit as having high estimation uncertainty or for those accounting estimates that have changed significantly from the prior period. On the other hand, for example, for accounting estimates that arise from the recording of routine and recurring transactions, the auditor may judge that the application of analytical procedures as risk assessment procedures is sufficient for purposes of the review.

---

[12] Paragraph .32 of section 240, *Consideration of Fraud in a Financial Statement Audit*.

.A43 For fair value accounting estimates and other accounting estimates based on current conditions at the measurement date, more variation may exist between the fair value amount recognized in the prior period financial statements and the outcome (or the amount reestimated for the purpose of the current period). This is because the measurement objective for such accounting estimates deals with perceptions about value at a point in time, which may change significantly and rapidly as the environment in which the entity operates changes. Therefore, the auditor may focus the review on obtaining information that would be relevant to identifying and assessing risks of material misstatement. For example, in some cases, obtaining an understanding of changes in market participant assumptions that affected the outcome of a prior period fair value accounting estimate may be unlikely to provide relevant information for audit purposes. If so, then the auditor's consideration of the outcome of prior period fair value accounting estimates may be more appropriately directed toward understanding the effectiveness of management's prior estimation process (that is, management's track record) from which the auditor can judge the likely effectiveness of management's current process.

.A44 A difference between the outcome of an accounting estimate and the amount recognized in the prior period financial statements does not necessarily represent a misstatement of the prior period financial statements. However, it may do so if, for example, the difference arises from information that was available to management when the prior period's financial statements were finalized or that could reasonably be expected to have been obtained and taken into account in the preparation of those financial statements. Section 560, *Subsequent Events and Subsequently Discovered Facts*, addresses situations when facts become known to the auditor after the date of the auditor's report that, had they been known to the auditor at the date of the auditor's report, may have caused the auditor to revise the auditor's report. The applicable financial reporting framework may contain guidance on distinguishing between changes in accounting estimates that constitute misstatements and changes that do not and the accounting treatment required to be followed.

Identifying and Assessing the Risks of Material Misstatement

Estimation Uncertainty (Ref: par. .10)

.A45 The degree of estimation uncertainty associated with an accounting estimate may be influenced by factors such as

- the extent to which the accounting estimate depends on judgment.
- the sensitivity of the accounting estimate to changes in assumptions.
- the existence of recognized measurement techniques that may mitigate the estimation uncertainty (though the subjectivity of the assumptions used as inputs may, nevertheless, give rise to estimation uncertainty).
- the length of the forecast period and the relevance of data drawn from past events to forecast future events.
- the availability of reliable data from external sources.
- the extent to which the accounting estimate is based on observable or unobservable inputs.

The degree of estimation uncertainty associated with an accounting estimate may influence the estimate's susceptibility to bias.

.A46 Matters that the auditor considers in assessing the risks of material misstatement may also include the following:

- The actual or expected magnitude of an accounting estimate
- The recorded amount of the accounting estimate (that is, management's point estimate) in relation to the amount expected by the auditor to be recorded
- Whether management has used a specialist in making the accounting estimate
- The outcome of the review of prior period accounting estimates

High Estimation Uncertainty and Significant Risks (Ref: par. .11)

.A47 Examples of accounting estimates that may have high estimation uncertainty include the following:

- Accounting estimates that are highly dependent upon judgment (for example, judgments about the outcome of pending litigation or the amount and timing of future cash flows dependent on uncertain events many years in the future)
- Accounting estimates that are not calculated using recognized measurement techniques
- Accounting estimates in which the results of the auditor's review of similar accounting estimates made in the prior period financial statements indicate a substantial difference between the original accounting estimate and the actual outcome
- Fair value accounting estimates for which a highly specialized, entity-developed model is used or for which there are no observable inputs

.A48 A seemingly immaterial accounting estimate may have the potential to result in a material misstatement due to the estimation uncertainty associated with the estimation (that is, the size of the amount recognized or disclosed in the financial statements for an accounting estimate may not be an indicator of its estimation uncertainty).

.A49 In some circumstances, the estimation uncertainty is so high that a reasonable accounting estimate cannot be made. The applicable financial reporting framework may, therefore, preclude recognition of the item in the financial statements or its measurement at fair value. In such cases, the significant risks relate not only to whether an accounting estimate should be recognized or whether it should be measured at fair value but also to the adequacy of the disclosures. With respect to such accounting estimates, the applicable financial reporting framework may require disclosure of the accounting estimates and the high estimation uncertainty associated with them (see paragraphs .A128–.A131).

.A50 If the auditor determines that an accounting estimate gives rise to a significant risk, the auditor is required by section 315 to obtain an understanding of the entity's controls, including control activities.[13]

.A51 In some cases, the estimation uncertainty of an accounting estimate may lead the auditor to consider whether such estimation uncertainty indicates that substantial doubt could exist about the entity's ability to continue as a going concern. Section 570, *The Auditor's Consideration of an Entity's Ability to*

---

[13] Paragraph .30 of section 315.

Continue as a Going Concern, addresses such circumstances. [Revised, August 2012, to reflect conforming changes necessary due to the issuance of SAS No. 126.]

Responding to the Assessed Risks of Material Misstatement (Ref: par. .12)

.A52 Section 330 requires the auditor to design and perform audit procedures whose nature, timing, and extent are responsive to the assessed risks of material misstatement related to accounting estimates at both the financial statement and relevant assertion levels.[14] Paragraphs .A53–.A121 focus on specific responses at the relevant assertion level only. Based on the assessed risks of material misstatement, the auditor is required to exercise professional judgment[15] in determining the nature, timing, and extent of the procedures necessary to conclude whether management appropriately applied the requirements of the financial reporting framework, including that the methods used for making the estimates are appropriate.

Application of the Requirements of the Applicable Financial Reporting Framework (Ref: par. .12a)

.A53 Many financial reporting frameworks prescribe certain conditions for the recognition of accounting estimates and specify the methods for making them and required disclosures. Such requirements may be complex and require the application of judgment. Based on the understanding obtained in performing risk assessment procedures, the requirements of the applicable financial reporting framework that may be susceptible to misapplication or differing interpretations become the focus of the auditor's attention.

.A54 Determining whether management has appropriately applied the requirements of the applicable financial reporting framework is based, in part, on the auditor's understanding of the entity and its environment. For example, the measurement of the fair value of some items, such as intangible assets acquired in a business combination, may involve special considerations that are affected by the nature of the entity and its operations.

.A55 In some situations, additional audit procedures, such as the inspection by the auditor of the current physical condition of an asset, may be necessary to determine whether management has appropriately applied the requirements of the applicable financial reporting framework.

.A56 Collateral often is assigned for certain types of investments in debt instruments that either are required to be measured at fair value or are evaluated for possible impairment. If the collateral is an important factor in measuring the fair value of the investment or evaluating its carrying amount, it may be necessary for the auditor—in determining whether management has appropriately applied the requirements of the applicable financial reporting framework—to obtain sufficient appropriate audit evidence regarding the existence; value; rights; and access to, or transferability of, such collateral (including consideration of whether all appropriate liens have been filed and appropriate disclosures have been made).

.A57 The application of the requirements of the applicable financial reporting framework requires management to consider changes in the environment or circumstances that affect the entity. For example, the introduction of an

---

[14] Paragraph .18 of section 330.

[15] Paragraph .18 of section 200.

active market for a particular class of asset or liability may indicate that the use of discounted cash flows to estimate the fair value of such asset or liability is no longer appropriate.

Consistency in Methods and Basis for Changes (Ref: par. .12b)

.A58 The auditor's consideration of a change in an accounting estimate or in the method for making it from the prior period is important because a change that is not based on a change in circumstances or new information is considered arbitrary. Arbitrary changes in an accounting estimate result in inconsistent financial statements over time and may give rise to a financial statement misstatement or be an indicator of possible management bias.

.A59 Management often is able to demonstrate good reason for a change in an accounting estimate or the method for making an accounting estimate from one period to another based on a change in circumstances. What constitutes a good reason and the adequacy of support for management's contention that there has been a change in circumstances that warrants a change in an accounting estimate or the method for making an accounting estimate are matters of judgment.

Responses to the Assessed Risks of Material Misstatements (Ref: par. .13)

.A60 The auditor's decision about which response, individually or in combination, in paragraph .13 to undertake to respond to the risks of material misstatement may be influenced by such matters as the following:

- The nature of the accounting estimate, including whether it arises from routine or nonroutine transactions
- Whether the procedure(s) is expected to effectively provide the auditor with sufficient appropriate audit evidence
- The assessed risk of material misstatement, including whether the assessed risk is a significant risk

.A61 For example, when evaluating the reasonableness of the allowance for doubtful accounts, an effective procedure for the auditor may be to review subsequent cash collections in combination with other procedures. When the estimation uncertainty associated with an accounting estimate is high (for example, an accounting estimate based on a proprietary model for which unobservable inputs exist), it may be that a combination of the responses to assessed risks in paragraph .13 is necessary in order to obtain sufficient appropriate audit evidence.

.A62 Additional guidance explaining the circumstances in which each of the responses may be appropriate is provided in paragraphs .A63–.A101.

Events Occurring Up to the Date of the Auditor's Report (Ref: par. .13a)

.A63 Determining whether events occurring up to the date of the auditor's report provide audit evidence regarding the accounting estimate may be an appropriate response when such events are expected to

- occur and
- provide audit evidence that confirms or contradicts the accounting estimate.

.A64 Events occurring up to the date of the auditor's report may sometimes provide sufficient appropriate audit evidence about an accounting estimate. For example, sale of the complete inventory of a superseded product shortly after the period-end may provide audit evidence relating to the estimate of its net realizable value. In such cases, there may be no need to perform additional audit procedures on the accounting estimate, provided that sufficient appropriate evidence about the events is obtained.

.A65 For some accounting estimates, events occurring up to the date of the auditor's report are unlikely to provide audit evidence regarding the accounting estimate. For example, the conditions or events relating to some accounting estimates develop only over an extended period. Also, because of the measurement objective of fair value accounting estimates, information after the period-end may not reflect the events or conditions existing at the balance sheet date and, therefore, may not be relevant to the measurement of the fair value accounting estimate. Paragraph .13 identifies other responses to the risks of material misstatement that the auditor may undertake.

.A66 In some cases, events that contradict the accounting estimate may indicate that the amount recorded is misstated, that management has ineffective processes for making accounting estimates, or that management bias exists in the making of accounting estimates.

.A67 Even though the auditor may decide not to undertake the approach referred to in paragraph .13*a* with respect to specific accounting estimates, the auditor is required to comply with section 560. The auditor is required to perform audit procedures designed to obtain sufficient appropriate audit evidence that all subsequent events that require adjustment of, or disclosure in, the financial statements have been identified.[16] Because the measurement of many accounting estimates, other than fair value accounting estimates, usually depends on the outcome of future conditions, transactions, or events, the auditor's work under section 560 is particularly relevant.

Testing How Management Made the Accounting Estimate (Ref: par. .13b)

.A68 Testing how management made the accounting estimate and the data on which it is based may be an appropriate response when the accounting estimate is a fair value accounting estimate developed on a model that uses observable and unobservable inputs. It may also be appropriate when, for example

- the accounting estimate is derived from the routine processing of data by the entity's accounting system.
- the auditor's review of similar accounting estimates made in the prior period financial statements suggests that management's current period process is likely to be effective.
- the accounting estimate is based on a large population of items of a similar nature that individually are not significant.

.A69 Testing how management made the accounting estimate and the data on which it is based may involve, for example, the following:

- Testing the extent to which data on which the accounting estimate is based is accurate, complete, and relevant and whether the accounting estimate has been properly determined using such data and management assumptions

---

[16] Paragraphs .09 and .11 of section 560, *Subsequent Events and Subsequently Discovered Facts.*

- Considering the source, relevance, and reliability of external data or information, including that received from management's specialists,[17] to assist in making an accounting estimate
- Determining how management has taken into account the effect of events, transactions, and changes in circumstances occurring between the date that the estimate or inputs to the estimate were determined and the reporting date, if the estimate was not made as of a date that coincides with the reporting date (for example, a valuation by an independent appraiser may be as of a different date)
- Recalculating the accounting estimate and reviewing, for internal consistency, information used to determine the estimate
- Considering management's review and approval processes

.A70 In accordance with section 500, *Audit Evidence*, the auditor is required to evaluate whether the data on which the estimate is based is sufficiently reliable for the auditor's purposes, including, as necessary[18]

a. obtaining audit evidence about the accuracy and completeness of the data.

b. evaluating whether the data is sufficiently precise and detailed for the auditor's purposes.

.A71 *Considerations specific to smaller, less complex entities.* In smaller entities, the process for making accounting estimates is likely to be less structured than in larger entities. Smaller entities with active management involvement may have limited descriptions of accounting procedures, unsophisticated accounting records, or few written policies. Even if the entity has no formal established process, management may still be able to provide a basis upon which the auditor can test the accounting estimate.

.A72 *Evaluating the method of measurement (Ref: par. .13b(i)).* When the applicable financial reporting framework does not prescribe the method of measurement, evaluating whether the method used (including any applicable model) is appropriate in the circumstances is a matter of professional judgment.

.A73 For this purpose, matters that the auditor may consider include, for example, whether

- management's rationale for the method selected is reasonable.
- management sufficiently and appropriately has evaluated and applied the criteria, if any, provided in the applicable financial reporting framework to support the selected method.
- the method is appropriate and sufficient data is available in the circumstances, given the nature of the asset or liability being estimated and the requirements of the applicable financial reporting framework relevant to accounting estimates.

---

[17] Paragraph .05 of section 500 defines a *management's specialist* as "[a]n individual or organization possessing expertise in a field other than accounting or auditing, whose work in that field is used by the entity to assist the entity in preparing the financial statements."

[18] Paragraph .09 of section 500.

- the method is appropriate with regard to the business, industry, and environment in which the entity operates.

.A74 In some cases, management may have determined that different methods result in a range of significantly different estimates. In such cases, obtaining an understanding of how the entity has investigated the reasons for these differences may assist the auditor in evaluating the appropriateness of the method selected.

.A75 *Evaluating the use of models.* In some cases, particularly when making fair value accounting estimates, management may use a model. Whether the model used is appropriate in the circumstances may depend on a number of factors, such as the nature of the entity and its environment, including the industry in which it operates and the specific asset or liability being measured.

.A76 The extent to which the considerations in paragraph .A77 are relevant depends on the circumstances, including whether the model is one that is commercially available for use in a particular sector or industry, or a proprietary model. In some cases, an entity may use a management specialist[19] to develop and test a model.

.A77 Depending on the circumstances, matters that the auditor may also consider in testing the model include, for example, whether

- the model is validated prior to usage, with periodic reviews to ensure it is still suitable for its intended use. The entity's validation process may include evaluation of
  - — the model's theoretical soundness and mathematical integrity, including the appropriateness of model parameters.
  - — the consistency and completeness of the model's inputs with market practices.
  - — the model's output compared with actual transactions.
- appropriate change control policies and procedures exist.
- the model is periodically calibrated and tested for validity, particularly when inputs are subjective.
- adjustments are made to the output of the model, including in the case of fair value accounting estimates whether such adjustments reflect the assumptions that market participants would use in similar circumstances.
- the model is adequately documented, including the model's intended applications and limitations and its key parameters, required inputs, and results of any validation analysis performed.

.A78 *Assumptions used by management (Ref: par. .13b(ii)).* The auditor's evaluation of the assumptions used by management is based only on information available to the auditor at the time of the audit. Audit procedures dealing with management assumptions, including those used as inputs to valuation models, are performed in the context of the audit of the entity's financial statements and not for the purpose of providing an opinion on the assumptions themselves.

---

[19] Paragraph .08 of section 500.

.A79 Matters that the auditor may consider in evaluating the reasonableness of the assumptions used by management include, for example

- whether individual assumptions appear reasonable.
- whether the assumptions are interdependent and internally consistent.
- whether the assumptions appear reasonable when considered collectively or in conjunction with other assumptions, either for that accounting estimate or for other accounting estimates.
- in the case of fair value accounting estimates, whether the assumptions appropriately reflect observable market assumptions.

.A80 In evaluating the reasonableness of the assumptions supporting an accounting estimate, the auditor may identify one or more significant assumptions. If so, the existence of one or more significant assumptions may be an indicator that the accounting estimate has high estimation uncertainty and may, therefore, give rise to a significant risk related to recognition, measurement, or disclosure. Additional responses to significant risks are described in paragraphs .A108–.A121.

.A81 The assumptions on which accounting estimates are based may reflect what management expects will be the outcome of specific objectives and strategies. In such cases, the auditor may perform audit procedures to evaluate the reasonableness of such assumptions by considering, for example, whether the assumptions are consistent with

- the general economic environment and the entity's economic circumstances.
- the plans of the entity.
- assumptions made in prior periods, if relevant.
- the experience of, or previous conditions experienced by, the entity to the extent this historical information may be considered representative of future conditions or events.
- other assumptions used by management relating to the financial statements.

.A82 The reasonableness of the assumptions used may depend on management's intent and ability to carry out certain courses of action. Management often documents plans and intentions relevant to specific assets or liabilities, and the financial reporting framework may require it to do so. Although the extent of audit evidence to be obtained about management's intent and ability is a matter of professional judgment, the auditor's procedures may include the following:

- Review of management's history of carrying out its stated intentions
- Review of written plans and other documentation, including, when applicable, formally approved budgets, authorizations, or minutes
- Inquiry of management about its reasons for a particular course of action
- Review of events occurring subsequent to the date of the financial statements and up to the date of the auditor's report
- Evaluation of the entity's ability to carry out a particular course of action given the entity's economic circumstances, including the implications of its existing commitments

Certain financial reporting frameworks, however, may not permit management's intentions or plans to be taken into account when making an accounting estimate. This is often the case for fair value accounting estimates because their measurement objective requires that assumptions reflect those used by market participants.

.A83 Matters that the auditor may consider in evaluating the reasonableness of assumptions used by management underlying fair value accounting estimates, in addition to those discussed previously, when applicable, may include, for example

- when relevant, whether and, if so, how management has incorporated market-specific inputs into the development of assumptions.
- whether the assumptions are consistent with observable market conditions and the characteristics of the asset or liability being measured at fair value.
- whether the sources of market-participant assumptions are relevant and reliable and how management has selected the assumptions to use when a number of different market participant assumptions exist.
- when appropriate, whether and, if so, how management considered assumptions used in, or information about, comparable transactions, assets, or liabilities.

.A84 Further, fair value accounting estimates may comprise observable inputs, as well as unobservable inputs. When fair value accounting estimates are based on unobservable inputs, matters that the auditor may consider include, for example, how management supports

- the identification of the characteristics of market participants relevant to the accounting estimate.
- modifications it has made to its own assumptions to reflect its view of assumptions market participants would use.
- whether it has incorporated appropriate information.
- when applicable, how its assumptions take account of comparable transactions, assets, or liabilities.

If there are unobservable inputs, it is more likely that the auditor's evaluation of the assumptions will need to be combined with other responses to assessed risks in paragraph .13 in order to obtain sufficient appropriate audit evidence. In such cases, it may be necessary for the auditor to perform other audit procedures (for example, examining documentation supporting the review and approval of the accounting estimate by appropriate levels of management and, when appropriate, those charged with governance).

.A85 Challenges may exist for management when fair value accounting estimates have unobservable inputs, in particular, as a result of illiquid markets. Management may not have the expertise internally to value illiquid or complex financial instruments, and there may be limited sources of information available to establish their values. It may be necessary for management to make assumptions, including assumptions utilized by management based upon the work of a specialist, to develop fair value measurements for illiquid assets.

.A86 The reliability of audit evidence is influenced by its source and nature. For example, management may use a broker quote to support a fair value measurement; however, when the quote is obtained from the institution that initially sold the instrument, this evidence may be less objective and may need to be supplemented with evidence from one or more other brokers or information from a pricing service. Pricing services and brokers may use methods of valuation that are not known to management or the auditor. In accordance with paragraph .08*c*(i), the auditor is required to obtain an understanding of how such information was developed. For example, the auditor might inquire whether the value is based on private trades, trades of similar instruments, a cash flow model, or some combination of inputs. Inquiry into the nature of a broker quote is directed at its reliability and consistency with the objective of fair value measurement.

.A87 Changes in market conditions may require changes in valuation techniques. Consistency is generally a desirable quality in financial information but may be inappropriate if circumstances change. Paragraph .A57 gives the example of the introduction of an active market as an illustration of changed circumstances leading to a move from valuation by model to valuation by market price. In a period of market instability, the changes could be in the opposite direction because markets could become inactive. Even when models have been consistently used, a need for management to examine the continuing appropriateness of the assumptions exists. Further, models may have been calibrated in times when reasonable market information was available but may not provide reasonable valuations in times of unanticipated stress. Consequently, the degree of consistency of valuation techniques and the appropriateness of changes in technique or assumptions require the auditor's attention.

.A88 A change in valuation technique does not, however, justify a change in the underlying measurement objective (that is, fair value as defined in the financial reporting framework) to a different standard of value, such as an individual opinion of value. Section 500 addresses what constitutes audit evidence, the quantity and quality of audit evidence to be obtained, and the audit procedures that the auditor uses for obtaining that audit evidence. Unless management is able to support its valuations, it will be difficult for the auditor to obtain sufficient appropriate audit evidence. However, as evidence about assumptions and the validity of models is necessarily less reliable than evidence of a market price taken from an active market, it may be necessary to look at more sources of evidence to accumulate sufficient appropriate evidence because the audit evidence needed is affected by the risk of misstatement (the greater the risk, the more audit evidence is likely to be required). For example, an auditor or auditor's specialist may use an independent model to compare its results with those of the model used by management in order to evaluate whether the values determined by management's model are reasonable.

.A89 In addition, the auditor may consider whether external sources provide audit evidence to which the auditor could benchmark an entity's practices. For example, sources that track losses recorded by institutions may provide the auditor with audit evidence about whether the entity's valuations are reasonable if it has invested in similar instruments as those institutions.

Testing the Operating Effectiveness of Controls (Ref: par. .13c)

.A90 Testing the operating effectiveness of the controls over how management made the accounting estimate may be an appropriate response when management's process has been well-designed, implemented, and maintained. For example

- when controls exist for the review and approval of the accounting estimates by appropriate levels of management and, when appropriate, those charged with governance.
- when the accounting estimate is derived from the routine processing of data by the entity's accounting system.

.A91 Testing the operating effectiveness of the controls is required by section 330 when[20]

a. the auditor's assessment of risks of material misstatement at the relevant assertion level includes an expectation that controls over the process are operating effectively or

b. substantive procedures alone do not provide sufficient appropriate audit evidence at the relevant assertion level.

.A92 *Considerations specific to smaller, less complex entities.* Controls over the process to make an accounting estimate may exist in smaller entities, but the formality with which they operate varies. Further, smaller entities may determine that certain types of controls are not necessary because of active management involvement in the financial reporting process. In the case of very small entities, however, there may not be many controls that the auditor can identify. For this reason, the auditor's response to the assessed risks is likely to be substantive in nature, with the auditor performing one or more of the other responses in paragraph .13.

Developing a Point Estimate or Range (Ref: par. .13d)

.A93 Developing a point estimate or range to evaluate management's point estimate may be an appropriate response when, for example

- an accounting estimate is not derived from the routine processing of data by the accounting system.
- the auditor's review of similar accounting estimates made in the prior period financial statements suggests that management's current period process is unlikely to be effective.
- the entity's controls within and over management's processes for determining accounting estimates are not well-designed or properly implemented.
- events or transactions between the period-end and the date of the auditor's report contradict management's point estimate.
- there are alternative sources of relevant data available to the auditor that can be used in developing a point estimate or range.

.A94 Even when the entity's controls are well-designed and properly implemented, developing a point estimate or range may be an effective and efficient response to the assessed risks. In other situations, the auditor may consider this approach as part of determining whether further procedures are necessary and, if so, their nature and extent.

.A95 The approach taken by the auditor in developing either a point estimate or range may vary based on what is considered most effective in the circumstances. For example, the auditor may initially develop a preliminary point estimate and then assess its sensitivity to changes in assumptions to ascertain a range with which to evaluate management's point estimate. Alternatively, the auditor may begin by developing a range for purposes of determining, when possible, a point estimate.

.A96 The ability of the auditor to develop a point estimate, as opposed to a range, depends on several factors, including the model used, the nature and extent of data available, and the estimation uncertainty involved with the accounting estimate. Further, the decision to develop a point estimate or range may be influenced by the applicable financial reporting framework, which may

---

[20] Paragraph .08 of section 330.

prescribe the point estimate that is to be used after consideration of the alternative outcomes and assumptions or prescribe a specific measurement method (for example, the use of a discounted probability-weighted expected value).

.A97 The auditor may develop a point estimate or range in a number of ways. For example, by

- using a model (for example, one that is commercially available for use in a particular sector or industry or a proprietary or an auditor-developed model).
- further developing management's consideration of alternative assumptions or outcomes (for example, by introducing a different set of assumptions).
- employing or engaging a person with specialized expertise to develop or execute the model or provide relevant assumptions.
- making reference to other comparable conditions, transactions, or events or, when relevant, markets for comparable assets or liabilities.

Understanding Management's Assumptions or Method (Ref: par. .13d(i))

.A98 When the auditor develops a point estimate or range and uses assumptions or a method different from those used by management, paragraph .13*d*(i) requires the auditor to obtain a sufficient understanding of the assumptions or method used by management in making the accounting estimate. This understanding provides the auditor with information that may be relevant to the auditor's development of an appropriate point estimate or range. Further, it assists the auditor to understand and evaluate any significant differences from management's point estimate. For example, a difference may arise because the auditor used different, but equally valid, assumptions, compared with those used by management. This may reveal that the accounting estimate is highly sensitive to certain assumptions and, therefore, subject to high estimation uncertainty, indicating that the accounting estimate may be a significant risk. Alternatively, a difference may arise as a result of a factual error made by management. Depending on the circumstances, the auditor may find it helpful in drawing conclusions to discuss with management the basis for the assumptions used and their validity and the difference, if any, in the approach taken to making the accounting estimate.

Narrowing a Range (Ref: par. .13d(ii))

.A99 When the auditor concludes that it is appropriate to use a range to evaluate the reasonableness of management's point estimate (the auditor's range), paragraph .13*d*(ii) requires that range to encompass all reasonable outcomes, rather than all possible outcomes. The range cannot be one that comprises all possible outcomes if it is to be useful because such a range would be too wide to be effective for purposes of the audit. The auditor's range is useful and effective when it is sufficiently narrow to enable the auditor to conclude whether the accounting estimate is materially misstated.

.A100 Ordinarily, a range that has been narrowed to be equal to or less than performance materiality (see section 320, *Materiality in Planning and Performing an Audit*) is adequate for the purposes of evaluating the reasonableness of management's point estimate.[21] However, particularly in certain industries, it may not be possible to narrow the range to below such an amount. This does not necessarily preclude recognition of the accounting estimate. It

---

[21] Paragraph .11 of section 320, *Materiality in Planning and Performing an Audit.*

may indicate, however, that the estimation uncertainty associated with the accounting estimate is such that it gives rise to a significant risk. Additional responses to significant risks are described in paragraphs .A108–.A121.

.A101 Narrowing the range to a position at which all outcomes within the range are considered reasonable may be achieved by

a. eliminating from the range those outcomes at the extremities of the range judged by the auditor to be unlikely to occur and

b. continuing to narrow the range, based on audit evidence available, until the auditor concludes that all outcomes within the range are considered reasonable. In some rare cases, the auditor may be able to narrow the range until the audit evidence indicates a point estimate.

Considering Whether Specialized Skills or Knowledge Are Required (Ref: par. .14)

.A102 In planning the audit, the auditor is required by section 300, *Planning an Audit*, to ascertain the nature, timing, and extent of resources necessary to perform the audit engagement.[22] This may include, as necessary, the involvement of those with specialized skills or knowledge. In addition, section 220, *Quality Control for an Engagement Conducted in Accordance With Generally Accepted Auditing Standards*, requires the engagement partner to be satisfied that the engagement team and any auditor's specialists who are not part of the engagement team collectively have the appropriate competence and capabilities to perform the audit engagement.[23] During the course of the audit of accounting estimates, the auditor may identify, in light of the experience of the auditor and the circumstances of the engagement, the need for specialized skills or knowledge to be applied regarding one or more aspects of the accounting estimates.

.A103 Matters that may affect the auditor's consideration of whether specialized skills or knowledge is required include, for example, the following:

- The nature of the underlying asset, liability, or component of equity in a particular business or industry (for example, mineral deposits, agricultural assets, or complex financial instruments)
- A high degree of estimation uncertainty
- Complex calculations or specialized models are involved (for example, when estimating fair values when no observable market exists)
- The complexity of the requirements of the applicable financial reporting framework relevant to accounting estimates, including whether there are areas known to be subject to differing interpretation or practice is inconsistent or developing
- The procedures that the auditor intends to undertake in responding to assessed risks

.A104 For the majority of accounting estimates, even when estimation uncertainty exists, it is unlikely that specialized skills or knowledge will be required. For example, it is unlikely that specialized skills or knowledge would be necessary for an auditor to evaluate an allowance for doubtful accounts.

[22] Paragraph .08 of section 300, *Planning an Audit*.

[23] Paragraph .16 of section 220, *Quality Control for an Engagement Conducted in Accordance With Generally Accepted Auditing Standards*.

.A105 However, the auditor may not possess the specialized skills or knowledge required when the matter involved is in a field other than accounting or auditing and may need to obtain it from an auditor's specialist. Section 620, *Using the Work of an Auditor's Specialist*, addresses determining the need to employ or engage an auditor's specialist and the auditor's responsibilities when using the work of an auditor's specialist.

.A106 Further, in some cases, the auditor may conclude that it is necessary to obtain specialized skills or knowledge related to specific areas of accounting or auditing. Individuals with such skills or knowledge may be employed by the auditor's firm or engaged from an external organization outside of the auditor's firm. When such individuals perform audit procedures on the engagement, they are part of the engagement team, and accordingly, they are subject to the requirements in section 220.

.A107 Depending on the auditor's understanding of, and experience working with, the auditor's specialist or those other individuals with specialized skills or knowledge, the auditor may consider it appropriate to discuss matters such as the requirements of the applicable financial reporting framework with the individuals involved to establish that their work is relevant for audit purposes.

Further Substantive Procedures to Respond to Significant Risks (Ref: par. .15–.17 and .20)

.A108 In auditing accounting estimates that give rise to significant risks, the auditor's further substantive procedures are focused on the evaluation of

a. how management has assessed the effect of estimation uncertainty on the accounting estimate and the effect that such uncertainty may have on the appropriateness of the recognition of the accounting estimate in the financial statements and

b. the adequacy of related disclosures.

For estimates that give rise to significant risks, the procedures that the auditor is required to perform to address the requirements in paragraphs .12–.13 may be performed in conjunction with the procedures performed to address the requirements in paragraphs .15–.17.

Estimation Uncertainty

Management's Consideration of Estimation Uncertainty (Ref: par. .15a)

.A109 Management may evaluate alternative assumptions or outcomes of the accounting estimates through a number of methods, depending on the circumstances. One possible method used by management is to undertake a sensitivity analysis. This might involve determining how the monetary amount of an accounting estimate varies with different assumptions. Even for accounting estimates measured at fair value, there can be variation because different market participants will use different assumptions. A sensitivity analysis could lead to the development of a number of outcome scenarios, sometimes characterized as a range of outcomes by management, such as "pessimistic" and "optimistic" scenarios.

.A110 A sensitivity analysis may demonstrate that an accounting estimate is not sensitive to changes in particular assumptions. Alternatively, it may demonstrate that the accounting estimate is sensitive to one or more assumptions that then become the focus of the auditor's attention.

.A111 This is not intended to suggest that one particular method of addressing estimation uncertainty (such as sensitivity analysis) is more suitable than another or that management's consideration of alternative assumptions or outcomes needs to be conducted through a detailed process supported by extensive documentation. Rather, it is whether management has assessed how estimation uncertainty may affect the accounting estimate that is important, not the specific manner in which it is done. Accordingly, when management has not considered alternative assumptions or outcomes, it may be necessary for the auditor to discuss with management, and request support for how it has addressed, the effects of estimation uncertainty on the accounting estimate.

.A112 *Considerations specific to smaller, less complex entities.* Smaller entities may use simple means to assess the estimation uncertainty. In addition to the auditor's review of available documentation, the auditor may obtain other audit evidence of management consideration of alternative assumptions or outcomes by inquiry of management. In addition, management may not have the expertise to consider alternative outcomes or otherwise address the estimation uncertainty of the accounting estimate. In such cases, the auditor may explain to management the process or the different methods available for doing so and the documentation thereof. This would not, however, change the responsibilities of management for the preparation and fair presentation of the financial statements.

Significant Assumptions (Ref: par. .15b)

.A113 An assumption used in making an accounting estimate may be deemed to be significant if a reasonable variation in the assumption would materially affect the measurement of the accounting estimate.

.A114 Support for significant assumptions derived from management's knowledge may be obtained from management's continuing processes of strategic analysis and risk management. Even without formal established processes, such as may be the case in smaller entities, the auditor may be able to evaluate the assumptions through inquiries of, and discussions with, management, along with other audit procedures, in order to obtain sufficient appropriate audit evidence.

.A115 The auditor's considerations in evaluating assumptions made by management are described in paragraphs .A78–.A89.

Management Intent and Ability (Ref: par. .15c)

.A116 The auditor's considerations regarding assumptions made by management and management's intent and ability are described in paragraphs .A12 and .A82.

Development of a Range (Ref: par. .16)

.A117 In preparing the financial statements, management may be satisfied that it has adequately addressed the effects of estimation uncertainty on the accounting estimates that give rise to significant risks. In some circumstances, however, the auditor may view the efforts of management as inadequate. This may be the case, for example, when, in the auditor's professional judgment

- sufficient appropriate audit evidence could not be obtained through the auditor's evaluation of how management has addressed the effects of estimation uncertainty.
- it is necessary to explore further the degree of estimation uncertainty associated with an accounting estimate (for example, when the auditor is aware of wide variation in outcomes for similar accounting estimates in similar circumstances).

- it is unlikely that other audit evidence can be obtained (for example, through the review of events occurring up to the date of the auditor's report).
- indicators of management bias in the making of accounting estimates may exist.

.A118 The auditor's considerations in determining a range for this purpose are described in paragraphs .A93–.A101.

Recognition and Measurement Criteria

Recognition of the Accounting Estimates in the Financial Statements (Ref: par. .17a)

.A119 When management has recognized an accounting estimate in the financial statements, the focus of the auditor's evaluation is on whether the measurement of the accounting estimate is sufficiently reliable to meet the recognition criteria of the applicable financial reporting framework.

.A120 With respect to accounting estimates that have not been recognized, the focus of the auditor's evaluation is on whether the recognition criteria of the applicable financial reporting framework have, in fact, been met. Even when an accounting estimate has not been recognized and the auditor concludes that this treatment is appropriate, there may be a need for disclosure of the circumstances in the notes to the financial statements. The auditor may also determine that there is a need to draw the reader's attention to a significant uncertainty by adding an emphasis-of-matter paragraph to the auditor's report. Section 706, *Emphasis-of-Matter Paragraphs and Other-Matter Paragraphs in the Independent Auditor's Report*, addresses the use of such paragraphs.

Measurement Basis for the Accounting Estimates (Ref: par. .17b)

.A121 With respect to fair value accounting estimates, some financial reporting frameworks presume that fair value can be measured reliably as a prerequisite to either requiring or permitting fair value measurements and disclosures. In some cases, this presumption may be overcome when, for example, no appropriate method or basis for measurement exists. In such cases, the focus of the auditor's evaluation is on whether management's basis for overcoming the presumption relating to the use of fair value set forth under the applicable financial reporting framework is appropriate.

Evaluating the Reasonableness of the Accounting Estimates and Determining Misstatements (Ref: par. .18)

.A122 Based on the audit evidence obtained, the auditor may conclude that the evidence points to an accounting estimate that differs from management's point estimate. When the audit evidence supports a point estimate, the difference between the auditor's point estimate and management's point estimate constitutes a misstatement. When the auditor has concluded that using the auditor's range provides sufficient appropriate audit evidence, a management point estimate that lies outside the auditor's range would not be supported by audit evidence. In such cases, the misstatement is no less than the difference between management's point estimate and the nearest point of the auditor's range.

.A123 When management has changed an accounting estimate, or the method in making it, from the prior period based on a subjective assessment that there has been a change in circumstances, the auditor may conclude, based on the audit evidence, that the accounting estimate is misstated as a result of an arbitrary change by management or may regard it as an indicator of possible management bias (see paragraphs .A133–.A134).

.A124 Section 450, *Evaluation of Misstatements Identified During the Audit*, provides guidance on distinguishing misstatements for purposes of the auditor's evaluation of the effect of uncorrected misstatements on the financial statements.[24] With regard to accounting estimates, a misstatement, whether caused by fraud or error, may arise as a result of

- misstatements about which no doubt exists (factual misstatements).
- differences arising from management's judgments concerning accounting estimates that the auditor considers unreasonable or the selection or application of accounting policies that the auditor considers inappropriate (judgmental misstatements).
- the auditor's best estimate of misstatements in populations involving the projection of misstatements identified in audit samples to the entire population from which the samples were drawn (projected misstatements).

In some cases involving accounting estimates, a misstatement could arise as a result of a combination of these circumstances, making separate identification difficult or impossible.

.A125 Evaluating the reasonableness of accounting estimates and related disclosures included in the notes to the financial statements, whether required by the applicable financial reporting framework or disclosed voluntarily, involves essentially the same types of considerations applied when auditing an accounting estimate recognized in the financial statements.

Written Representations

.A126 Part of the auditor's audit evidence includes obtaining representations from management about whether management believes significant assumptions used in making accounting estimates are reasonable. See section 580, *Written Representations*.[25]

Communication With Those Charged With Governance

.A127 Section 260, *The Auditor's Communication With Those Charged With Governance*, addresses the auditor's communications of certain matters related to the conduct of an audit to those charged with governance. The auditor is required by section 260 to communicate the auditor's views about the qualitative aspects of the entity's significant accounting practices, including accounting estimates, and, when applicable, is required to determine that those charged with governance are informed about the process used by management in formulating particularly sensitive accounting estimates and about the basis for the auditor's conclusions regarding the reasonableness of those estimates.[26]

---

[24] Paragraph .A3 of section 450, *Evaluation of Misstatements Identified During the Audit*.

[25] Paragraph .16 of section 580, *Written Representations*.

[26] Paragraph .12 of section 260, *The Auditor's Communication With Those Charged With Governance*.

Disclosures Related to Accounting Estimates

Disclosures in Accordance With the Applicable Financial Reporting Framework (Ref: par. .19)

.A128 The presentation of financial statements in accordance with the applicable financial reporting framework includes adequate disclosure of material matters. The applicable financial reporting framework may permit or prescribe disclosures related to accounting estimates, and some entities may disclose voluntarily additional information in the notes to the financial statements. These disclosures may include, for example

- the assumptions used.
- the method of estimation used, including any applicable model(s).
- the basis for the selection of the method of estimation.
- the effect of any changes to the method of estimation from the prior period.
- the sources and implications of estimation uncertainty.

Such disclosures are relevant to users in understanding the accounting estimates recognized or disclosed in the financial statements, and sufficient appropriate audit evidence needs to be obtained about whether the disclosures are in accordance with the requirements of the applicable financial reporting framework.

.A129 In some cases, the applicable financial reporting framework may require specific disclosures regarding uncertainties. For example, some financial reporting frameworks prescribe the following:

- The disclosure of key assumptions and other sources of estimation uncertainty that have a significant risk of causing a material adjustment to the carrying amounts of assets and liabilities. Such requirements may be described using terms such as *key sources of estimation uncertainty* or *critical accounting estimates*.
- The disclosure of the range of possible outcomes and the assumptions used in determining the range.
- The disclosure of information regarding the significance of fair value accounting estimates to the entity's financial position and performance.
- Qualitative disclosures, such as the exposures to risk and how they arise; the entity's objectives, policies, and procedures for managing the risk; and the methods used to measure the risk, and any changes from the previous period of these qualitative concepts.
- Quantitative disclosures, such as the extent to which the entity is exposed to risk, based on information provided internally to the entity's key management personnel, including credit risk, liquidity risk, and market risk.

Disclosures of Estimation Uncertainty for Accounting Estimates That Give Rise to Significant Risks (Ref: par. .20)

.A130 Regarding accounting estimates having significant risk, even when the disclosures are in accordance with the applicable financial reporting framework, the auditor may conclude that the disclosure of estimation uncertainty is inadequate in light of the circumstances and facts involved. The auditor's evaluation of the adequacy of disclosure of estimation uncertainty increases in importance the greater the range of possible outcomes of the accounting estimate in relation to materiality (see the related discussion in paragraphs .A98–.A101).

.A131 In some cases, the auditor may consider it appropriate to encourage management to describe the circumstances relating to the estimation uncertainty in the notes to the financial statements.

.A132 Section 705, *Modifications to the Opinion in the Independent Auditor's Report*, addresses the implications for the auditor's opinion when the auditor believes that management's disclosure of estimation uncertainty in the financial statements is inadequate or misleading.

Indicators of Possible Management Bias (Ref: par. .21)

.A133 During the audit, the auditor may become aware of judgments and decisions made by management that give rise to indicators of possible management bias (see paragraph .A9). Such indicators may affect the auditor's conclusion about whether the auditor's risk assessment and related responses remain appropriate, and the auditor may need to consider the implications for the rest of the audit. Further, they may affect the auditor's evaluation of whether the financial statements as a whole are free from material misstatement, as discussed in section 700, *Forming an Opinion and Reporting on Financial Statements*.

.A134 Examples of indicators of possible management bias with respect to accounting estimates include the following:

- Changes in an accounting estimate, or the method for making it, when management has made a subjective assessment that there has been a change in circumstances
- The use of an entity's own assumptions for fair value accounting estimates when they are inconsistent with observable market assumptions
- The selection or construction of significant assumptions that yield a point estimate favorable for management objectives
- The selection of a point estimate that may indicate a pattern of optimism or pessimism

Documentation (Ref: par. .22)

.A135 Documentation of indicators of possible management bias identified during the audit assists the auditor in concluding whether the auditor's risk assessment and related responses remain appropriate and in evaluating whether the financial statements as a whole are free from material misstatement. See paragraph .A134 for examples of indicators of possible management bias.

.A136

Exhibit—Examples of Accounting Estimates (Ref: par. .02)

The following are examples of accounting estimates that are included in financial statements. The list is presented for information only. It is not considered to be all-inclusive.

- **Receivables**
  - Uncollectible receivables
  - Allowance for loan losses
  - Valuation of long-term unconditional promises to give
- **Inventories**
  - Obsolete inventory
  - Net realizable value of inventories when future selling prices and future costs are involved
  - Losses on purchase commitments
- **Financial instruments**
  - Valuation of securities
  - Probability of high correlation of a hedge
  - Sales of securities with puts and calls
- **Productive facilities, natural resources, and intangibles**
  - Useful lives and residual values
  - Depreciation and amortization methods
  - Impairment analysis
  - Recoverability of costs
  - Recoverable reserves
- **Accruals**
  - Property and casualty insurance company loss reserves
  - Compensation in stock option plans and deferred plans
  - Warranty claims
  - Taxes on real and personal property
  - Renegotiation refunds
  - Actuarial assumptions in benefit costs
- **Revenues**
  - Airline passenger revenue
  - Subscription income
  - Freight and cargo revenue
  - Dues income
  - Losses on sales contracts

- **Contracts**
    - — Revenue to be earned
    - — Costs to be incurred
    - — Percent of completion
- **Leases**
    - — Initial direct costs
    - — Executory costs
- **Litigation**
    - — Probability of loss
    - — Amount of loss
- **Rates**
    - — Annual effective tax rate in interim reporting
    - — Imputed interest rates on receivables and payables
    - — Gross profit rates under program method of accounting
- **Other**
    - — Losses and net realizable value on disposal of segment or restructuring of a business
    - — Fair values in nonmonetary exchanges
    - — Interim period costs in interim reporting
    - — Current values in personal financial statements

AU-C Section 550*

Related Parties

Source: SAS No. 122.

Effective for audits of financial statements for periods ending on or after December 15, 2012.

Introduction

Scope of This Section

.01 This section addresses the auditor's responsibilities relating to related party relationships and transactions in an audit of financial statements. Specifically, it expands on how section 315, *Understanding the Entity and Its Environment and Assessing the Risks of Material Misstatement*; section 330, *Performing Audit Procedures in Response to Assessed Risks and Evaluating the Audit Evidence Obtained*; and section 240, *Consideration of Fraud in a Financial Statement Audit*, are to be applied regarding risks of material misstatement associated with related party relationships and transactions.

.02 Section 700, *Forming an Opinion and Reporting on Financial Statements*, requires the auditor to evaluate whether the financial statements achieve fair presentation.[1] Section 800, *Special Considerations—Audits of Financial Statements Prepared in Accordance With Special Purpose Frameworks*, requires that, in audits of special purpose financial statements that contain related party transactions, the auditor evaluate whether the financial statements include informative disclosures similar to those required by generally accepted accounting principles (GAAP).[2] Section 800 also requires the auditor to evaluate whether additional disclosures beyond those specifically required by the framework and related to matters that are not specifically identified on the face of the financial statements or other disclosures may be necessary for the financial statements to achieve fair presentation.[3] Thus, this section applies to all audits of financial statements. (Ref: par. .A1–.A3)

Nature of Related Party Relationships and Transactions (Ref: par. .A1–.A6)

.03 Many related party transactions are in the normal course of business. In such circumstances, they may carry no higher risk of material misstatement of the financial statements than similar transactions with unrelated parties. However, the nature of related party relationships and transactions may, in

---

* This section has been codified using an "AU-C" identifier instead of an "AU" identifier. "AU-C" is a temporary identifier to avoid confusion with references to existing "AU" sections, which will remain in AICPA *Professional Standards* through 2013. The "AU-C" identifier will revert to "AU" in 2014, by which time substantially all engagements for which the "AU" sections were still effective are expected to be completed.

[1] Paragraph .17 of section 700, *Forming an Opinion and Reporting on Financial Statements*.

[2] Paragraph .17 of section 800, *Special Considerations—Audits of Financial Statements Prepared in Accordance With Special Purpose Frameworks*.

[3] Paragraph .17 of section 800.

some circumstances, give rise to higher risks of material misstatement of the financial statements than transactions with unrelated parties. For example

- related parties may operate through an extensive and complex range of relationships and structures, with a corresponding increase in the complexity of related party transactions.
- information systems may be ineffective at identifying or summarizing transactions and outstanding balances between an entity and its related parties.
- related party transactions may not be conducted under normal market terms and conditions (for example, some related party transactions may be conducted with no exchange of consideration).
- related party transactions may be motivated solely or in large measure to engage in fraudulent financial reporting or conceal misappropriation of assets.

Responsibilities of the Auditor

.04 Because related parties are not independent of each other, financial reporting frameworks establish specific accounting and disclosure requirements for related party relationships, transactions, and balances to enable users of the financial statements to understand their nature and actual or potential effects on the financial statements. Therefore, the auditor has a responsibility to perform audit procedures to identify, assess, and respond to the risks of material misstatement arising from the entity's failure to appropriately account for or disclose related party relationships, transactions, or balances. (Ref: par. .A3)

.05 In addition, an understanding of the entity's related party relationships and transactions is relevant to the auditor's evaluation of whether one or more fraud risk factors are present, as required by section 240, because fraud may be more easily committed through related parties.[4]

.06 Owing to the inherent limitations of an audit, an unavoidable risk exists that some material misstatements of the financial statements may not be detected, even though the audit is properly planned and performed in accordance with generally accepted auditing standards (GAAS).[5] In the context of related parties, the potential effects of inherent limitations on the auditor's ability to detect material misstatements are greater because of reasons such as the following:

- Management may be unaware of the existence of all related party relationships and transactions.
- Related party relationships may present a greater opportunity for collusion, concealment, or manipulation by management.

.07 Planning and performing the audit with professional skepticism as required by section 200, *Overall Objectives of the Independent Auditor and the Conduct of an Audit in Accordance With Generally Accepted Auditing Standards*, is, therefore, particularly important in this context, given the potential for undisclosed related party relationships and transactions.[6] The requirements in this section are designed to assist the auditor in identifying and

---

[4] Paragraph .24 of section 240, *Consideration of Fraud in a Financial Statement Audit*.

[5] Paragraph .A56 of section 200, *Overall Objectives of the Independent Auditor and the Conduct of an Audit in Accordance With Generally Accepted Auditing Standards*.

[6] Paragraph .17 of section 200.

assessing the risks of material misstatement associated with related party relationships and transactions and in designing audit procedures to respond to the assessed risks.

Effective Date

.08 This section is effective for audits of financial statements for periods ending on or after December 15, 2012.

Objectives

.09 The objectives of the auditor are to

a. obtain an understanding of related party relationships and transactions sufficient to be able to

  i. recognize fraud risk factors, if any, arising from related party relationships and transactions that are relevant to the identification and assessment of the risks of material misstatement due to fraud.

  ii. conclude, based on the audit evidence obtained, whether the financial statements, insofar as they are affected by those relationships and transactions, achieve fair presentation.

b. obtain sufficient appropriate audit evidence about whether related party relationships and transactions have been appropriately identified, accounted for, and disclosed in the financial statements.

Definitions

.10 For purposes of GAAS, the following terms have the meanings attributed as follows:

Arm's length transaction. A transaction conducted on such terms and conditions between a willing buyer and a willing seller who are unrelated and are acting independently of each other and pursuing their own best interests.

Related party. A party defined as a related party in GAAP. (Ref: par. .A1)

.11 Reference to GAAP in GAAS means generally accepted accounting principles promulgated by bodies designated by the Council of the AICPA pursuant to Rule 202, *Compliance With Standards* (ET sec. 202 par. .01), and Rule 203, *Accounting Principles* (ET sec. 203 par. .01), of the AICPA Code of Professional Conduct.

Requirements

Risk Assessment Procedures and Related Activities

.12 As part of the risk assessment procedures and related activities that section 240 and section 315 require the auditor to perform during the audit, the auditor should perform the audit procedures and related activities set out in paragraphs .13–.18 to obtain information relevant to identifying the risks of material misstatement associated with related party relationships and transactions.[7,8]

Understanding the Entity's Related Party Relationships and Transactions

.13 In connection with the engagement team discussion(s) that section 240 and section 315 require, the auditor should include specific consideration of the susceptibility of the financial statements to material misstatement due to fraud or error that could result from the entity's related party relationships and transactions.[9,10] (Ref: par. .A7–.A8)

.14 The auditor should inquire of management regarding the following:

a. The identity of the entity's related parties, including changes from the prior period (Ref: par. .A9–.A14)

b. The nature of the relationships between the entity and these related parties

c. Whether the entity entered into any transactions with these related parties during the period and, if so, the type and purpose of the transactions

.15 The auditor should inquire of management and others within the entity and perform other risk assessment procedures[11] considered appropriate to obtain an understanding of the controls, if any, that management has established to (Ref: par. .A15–.A20)

a. identify, account for, and disclose related party relationships and transactions.

b. authorize and approve significant transactions and arrangements with related parties. (Ref: par. .A21)

c. authorize and approve significant transactions and arrangements outside the normal course of business.

Maintaining Alertness for Related Party Information When Reviewing Records or Documents

.16 During the audit, the auditor should remain alert when inspecting records or documents for arrangements or other information that may indicate the existence of related party relationships or transactions that management has not previously identified or disclosed to the auditor. In particular, the auditor should inspect the following for indications of the existence of related party relationships or transactions that management has not previously identified or disclosed to the auditor: (Ref: par. .A22–.A24)

a. Bank and legal confirmations obtained as part of the auditor's procedures

b. Minutes of meetings of shareholders and of those charged with governance

c. Such other records or documents as the auditor considers necessary in the circumstances of the entity

---

7 Paragraph .16 of section 240.

8 Paragraph .05 of section 315, *Understanding the Entity and Its Environment and Assessing the Risks of Material Misstatement*.

9 Paragraph .15 of section 240.

10 Paragraph .11 of section 315.

11 Paragraph .06 of section 315.

.17 If the auditor identifies significant transactions outside the entity's normal course of business when performing the audit procedures required by paragraph .16 or through other audit procedures, the auditor should inquire of management about the following: (Ref: par. .A25–.A26)

a. The nature of these transactions (Ref: par. .A27)

b. Whether related parties could be involved (Ref: par. .A28)

Sharing Related Party Information With the Engagement Team

.18 The auditor should share with the other members of the engagement team the identity of the entity's related parties and other relevant information obtained about the related parties. (Ref: par. .A29–.A30)

Identification and Assessment of the Risks of Material Misstatement Associated With Related Party Relationships and Transactions

.19 In meeting the requirement of section 315 to identify and assess the risks of material misstatement, the auditor should identify and assess the risks of material misstatement associated with related party relationships and transactions and determine whether any of those risks are significant risks.[12] In making this determination, the auditor should treat identified significant related party transactions outside the entity's normal course of business as giving rise to significant risks.

.20 If the auditor identifies fraud risk factors (including circumstances relating to the existence of a related party with dominant influence) when performing the risk assessment procedures and related activities in connection with related parties, the auditor should consider such information when identifying and assessing the risks of material misstatement due to fraud, in accordance with section 240.[13] (Ref: par. .A31–.A33)

Responses to the Risks of Material Misstatement Associated With Related Party Relationships and Transactions

.21 As part of the requirement in section 330 that the auditor respond to assessed risks, that the auditor respond to assessed risks, the auditor should design and perform further audit procedures to obtain sufficient appropriate audit evidence about the assessed risks of material misstatement associated with related party relationships and transactions.[14] (Ref: par. .A34–.A37)

Identification of Previously Unidentified or Undisclosed Related Parties or Significant Related Party Transactions

.22 If the auditor identifies arrangements or information that suggests the existence of related party relationships or transactions that management has not previously identified or disclosed to the auditor, the auditor should determine whether the underlying circumstances confirm the existence of those relationships or transactions.

---

[12] Paragraph .26 of section 315.

[13] Paragraph .24 of section 240.

[14] Paragraphs .05–.06 of section 330, *Performing Audit Procedures in Response to Assessed Risks and Evaluating the Audit Evidence Obtained.*

.23 If the auditor identifies related parties or significant related party transactions that management has not previously identified or disclosed to the auditor, the auditor should

a. promptly communicate the relevant information to the other members of the engagement team. (Ref: par. .A29 and .A38)

b. request management to identify all transactions with the newly identified related parties for the auditor's further evaluation.

c. inquire why the entity's controls over related party relationships and transactions failed to enable the identification or disclosure of the related party relationships or transactions.

d. perform appropriate substantive audit procedures relating to such newly identified related parties or significant related party transactions. (Ref: par. .A39)

e. reconsider the risk that other related parties or significant related party transactions may exist that management has not previously identified or disclosed to the auditor and perform additional audit procedures as necessary.

f. evaluate the implications for the audit if the nondisclosure by management appears intentional (and, therefore, indicative of a risk of material misstatement due to fraud). (Ref: par. .A40)

Identified Significant Related Party Transactions Outside the Entity's Normal Course of Business

.24 For identified significant related party transactions outside the entity's normal course of business, the auditor should

a. inspect the underlying contracts or agreements, if any, and evaluate whether

  i. the business rationale (or lack thereof) of the transactions suggests that they may have been entered into to engage in fraudulent financial reporting or to conceal misappropriation of assets.[15] (Ref: par. .A41–.A42)

  ii. the terms of the transactions are consistent with management's explanations.

  iii. the transactions have been appropriately accounted for and disclosed.

b. obtain audit evidence that the transactions have been appropriately authorized and approved. (Ref: par. .A43–.A44)

Assertions That Related Party Transactions Were Conducted on Terms Equivalent to Those Prevailing in an Arm's Length Transaction

.25 If management has made an assertion in the financial statements to the effect that a related party transaction was conducted on terms equivalent to those prevailing in an arm's length transaction, the auditor should obtain sufficient appropriate audit evidence about the assertion. (Ref: par. .A45–.A49)

[15] Paragraph .32*c* of section 240.

Evaluation of the Accounting for, and Disclosure of, Identified Related Party Relationships and Transactions

.26 In forming an opinion on the financial statements, in accordance with section 700, the auditor should evaluate the following:[16] (Ref: par. .A50)

a. Whether the identified related party relationships and transactions have been appropriately accounted for and disclosed (Ref: par. .A51)

b. Whether the effects of the related party relationships and transactions prevent the financial statements from achieving fair presentation (Ref: par. .A3)

Communication With Those Charged With Governance

.27 Unless all of those charged with governance are involved in managing the entity, the auditor should communicate with those charged with governance significant findings and issues arising during the audit in connection with the entity's related parties.[17] (Ref: par. .A52)

Documentation

.28 The auditor should include in the audit documentation the names of the identified related parties and the nature of the related party relationships.[18]

Application and Other Explanatory Material

Nature of Related Party Relationships and Transactions (Ref: par. .02–.04, .10, and .26b)

.A1 GAAP frameworks include or refer to specific disclosure requirements for related party relationships and transactions. If the applicable financial reporting framework does not have specific disclosure requirements, the auditor, nonetheless, evaluates whether related party information is disclosed in a manner comparable to GAAP in order for the financial statements to achieve fair presentation.[19]

.A2 Certain accounting pronouncements prescribe the accounting treatment when related parties are involved; however, established accounting principles ordinarily do not require transactions with related parties to be accounted for on a basis different from that which would be appropriate if the parties were not related. In addition, the substance of a particular transaction may be significantly different from its form. Accordingly, financial statements prepared in accordance with GAAP generally recognize the substance of particular transactions rather than merely their legal form.

.A3 Related party relationships and transactions may cause the financial statements to fail to achieve fair presentation if, for example, the economic reality of such relationships and transactions is not appropriately reflected in the financial statements. For instance, fair presentation may not be achieved if the sale of a property by the entity to a controlling shareholder at a price above

---

[16] Paragraphs .13–.18 of section 700.

[17] Paragraph .09 of section 260, *The Auditor's Communication With Those Charged With Governance*.

[18] Paragraphs .08–.12 and .A8 of section 230, *Audit Documentation*.

[19] Paragraph .17 of section 800.

or below fair market value has been accounted for as a transaction involving a profit or loss for the entity when it may constitute a contribution or return of capital or the payment of a dividend.

.A4 Transactions that because of their nature may be indicative of the existence of related parties include the following:

a. Borrowing or lending on an interest free basis or at a rate of interest significantly above or below market rates prevailing at the time of the transaction

b. Selling real estate at a price that differs significantly from its appraised value

c. Exchanging property for similar property in a nonmonetary transaction

d. Making loans with no scheduled terms for when or how the funds will be repaid

.A5 Although many related party transactions are in the normal course of business, a possibility exists that transactions with related parties may have been motivated solely or in large measure by conditions similar to the following:

a. Lack of sufficient working capital or credit to continue the business

b. An overly optimistic earnings forecast

c. Dependence on a single or relatively few products, customers, or transactions for the continued success of the venture

d. A declining industry characterized by a large number of business failures

e. Excess capacity

f. Significant litigation, especially litigation between stockholders and management

g. Significant obsolescence dangers because the company is in a high technology industry

For these reasons, related party transactions may indicate an increased risk of material misstatement of the financial statements.

Considerations Specific to Governmental Entities

.A6 For state and local governmental entities, related party relationships and transactions can result from interactions with other governments, not-for-profit entities, for-profit entities, and individuals. The applicable financial reporting framework used by most state and local governmental entities addresses related party relationships and transactions using terms that include *related parties*, *related organizations*, and *component units*, and can result in the inclusion of the related parties' financial statements as a reporting unit, inclusion within a reporting unit, disclosure of the related party transactions, or disclosure about why the related party or its transactions are not included. In all such cases, the objectives described in paragraph .09 are relevant to the auditor.

Risk Assessment Procedures and Related Activities

Understanding the Entity's Related Party Relationships and Transactions

Discussion Among the Engagement Team (Ref: par. .13)

.A7 Matters that may be addressed in the discussion among the engagement team include the following:

- The nature and extent of the entity's relationships and transactions with related parties (using, for example, the auditor's record of identified related parties updated after each audit)
- An emphasis on the importance of maintaining professional skepticism throughout the audit regarding the potential for material misstatement associated with related party relationships and transactions
- The circumstances or conditions of the entity that may indicate the existence of related party relationships or transactions that management has not identified or disclosed to the auditor (for example, a complex organizational structure, use of entities formed to accomplish specific purposes,[20] or an inadequate information system)
- The records or documents that may indicate the existence of related party relationships or transactions
- The importance that management and those charged with governance attach to the identification of, appropriate accounting for, and disclosure of related party relationships and transactions and the related risk of management override of relevant controls

.A8 In addition, the discussion in the context of fraud may include specific consideration of how related parties may be involved in fraud. For example:

- Entities formed to accomplish specific purposes and that are controlled by management might be used to facilitate earnings management.
- Transactions between the entity and a known business partner of a key member of management could be arranged to facilitate misappropriation of the entity's assets.
- As indicated in paragraph .A2, the form of a related party transaction may mask its substance. For example, equity distributions or capital contributions may be structured as loans.
- Related party transactions may be subject to period-end window dressing. For example, a stockholder may pay a loan shortly before period-end, but the entity loans the same amount to the stockholder shortly after period-end.
- Certain entities, such as governmental entities or entities operating in regulated industries, may circumvent laws or regulations that limit or restrict their ability to engage in transactions with related parties.

The Identity of the Entity's Related Parties (Ref: par. .14a)

.A9 Information regarding the identity of the entity's related parties is likely to be readily available to management if the entity's information systems record, process, and summarize related party relationships and transactions to enable the entity to meet applicable disclosure requirements. Therefore, management may have a comprehensive list of related parties and changes from the prior period. For recurring engagements, making the inquiries specified by paragraph .14 provides a basis for comparing the information supplied by management with the auditor's record of related parties noted in previous audits.

---

[20] Entities formed to accomplish specific purposes are discussed in paragraphs .A26–.A27 of section 315.

.A10 However, if the entity does not have such information systems in place, management may not be aware of the existence of all related parties. Nevertheless, the requirement to make the inquiries specified by paragraph .14 still applies because management may be aware of parties that meet the related party definition set out in GAAP. In such a case, however, the auditor's inquiries regarding the identity of the entity's related parties are likely to form part of the auditor's risk assessment procedures and related activities performed in accordance with section 315 to obtain information regarding the following:[21]

- The entity's ownership and governance structures
- The types of investments that the entity is making and plans to make
- The way the entity is structured and how it is financed

In the particular case of common control relationships, because management is more likely to be aware of such relationships if they have economic significance to the entity, the auditor's inquiries are likely to be more effective if they are focused on whether parties with which the entity engages in significant transactions or shares resources to a significant degree are related parties.

.A11 In the context of a group audit, section 600, *Special Considerations—Audits of Group Financial Statements (Including the Work of Component Auditors)*, requires the group engagement team to provide each component auditor with a list of related parties prepared by group management and any other related parties of which the group engagement team is aware.[22] When the entity is a component within a group, this information provides a useful basis for the auditor's inquiries of management regarding the identity of the entity's related parties.

.A12 The auditor also may obtain some information regarding the identity of the entity's related parties through inquiries of management during the engagement acceptance or continuance process.

.A13 Section 580, *Written Representations*, addresses requirements to obtain management representations, including representations that management and, when appropriate, those charged with governance have[23]

a. disclosed to the auditor the identity of the entity's related parties and all the related party relationships of which they are aware.

b. appropriately accounted for and disclosed such relationships and transactions.

.A14 *Considerations specific to governmental entities.* Because of the variety of the types of relationships and transactions among governmental and other entities, some of which are highly complex, identifying the nature of the related party relationship and its appropriate treatment in the financial statements relies heavily on a governmental entity's application of its financial reporting framework. Further, in some circumstances, the governmental entity may have no legal jurisdiction over the related party even when the application of the financial reporting framework concludes that the related party's financial statements are to be included in the governmental entity's financial statements. In such cases, the auditor's inquiries regarding the identity of the entity's related parties are likely to include the concepts and guidance from

---

[21] Paragraph .12 of section 315.

[22] Paragraph .40c of section 600, *Special Considerations—Audits of Group Financial Statements (Including the Work of Component Auditors)*.

[23] Paragraph .17 of section 580, *Written Representations*.

the applicable financial reporting framework to assist in making appropriate assessments about the existence and nature of related party relationships.

The Entity's Controls Over Related Party Relationships and Transactions (Ref: par. .15)

.A15 Others within the entity are those considered likely to have knowledge of the entity's related party relationships and transactions and the entity's controls over such relationships and transactions. These may include, to the extent that they do not form part of management, the following:

- Those charged with governance
- Personnel in a position to initiate, authorize, process, or record transactions that are both significant and outside the entity's normal course of business and those who supervise or monitor such personnel
- Internal auditors
- In-house legal counsel
- The chief ethics officer or equivalent person
- Chief compliance officer

.A16 The audit is conducted on the premise that management and, when appropriate, those charged with governance have acknowledged and understand that they have responsibility for the preparation and fair presentation of the financial statements in accordance with the applicable financial reporting framework and for the design, implementation, and maintenance of internal control relevant to the preparation and fair presentation of financial statements that are free from material misstatement, whether due to fraud or error.[24] Accordingly, the preparation of the financial statements requires management, with oversight from those charged with governance, to design, implement, and maintain adequate controls over related party relationships and transactions so that these are identified and appropriately accounted for and disclosed. In their oversight role, those charged with governance monitor how management is discharging its responsibility for such controls. Those charged with governance may, in their oversight role, obtain information from management to enable them to understand the nature and business rationale of the entity's related party relationships and transactions.

.A17 In meeting the requirement of section 315 to obtain an understanding of internal control, the auditor may consider features or elements relevant to mitigating the risks of material misstatement associated with related party relationships and transactions, such as the following:[25]

- Internal ethical codes, appropriately communicated to the entity's personnel and enforced, governing the circumstances in which the entity may enter into specific types of related party transactions
- Policies and procedures for open and timely disclosure of the interests that management and those charged with governance have in related party transactions
- The assignment of responsibilities within the entity for identifying, recording, summarizing, and disclosing related party transactions

---

[24] Paragraphs .05 and .A2 of section 200.

[25] Paragraph .13 of section 315.

- Timely disclosure and discussion between management and those charged with governance of significant related party transactions outside the entity's normal course of business, including whether those charged with governance have appropriately challenged the business rationale of such transactions (for example, by seeking advice from external professional advisors)
- Clear guidelines for the approval of related party transactions involving actual or perceived conflicts of interest, such as approval by a subcommittee of those charged with governance comprising individuals independent of management
- Periodic reviews by internal auditors, when applicable
- Proactive action taken by management to resolve related party disclosure issues, such as by seeking advice from the auditor or external legal counsel
- The existence of whistle-blowing policies and procedures, when applicable

.A18 Controls over related party relationships and transactions within some entities may be deficient or nonexistent for a number of reasons, such as the following:

- The low importance attached by management to identifying and disclosing related party relationships and transactions
- The lack of appropriate oversight by those charged with governance
- An intentional disregard for such controls because related party disclosures may reveal information that management considers sensitive (for example, the existence of transactions involving family members of management)
- An insufficient understanding by management of the applicable related party disclosure requirements

When such controls are ineffective or nonexistent, the auditor may be unable to obtain sufficient appropriate audit evidence about related party relationships and transactions. If this were the case, the auditor would, in accordance with section 705, *Modifications to the Opinion in the Independent Auditor's Report*, consider the implications for the audit, including the opinion in the auditor's report.

.A19 Fraudulent financial reporting often involves management override of controls that otherwise may appear to be operating effectively.[26] The risk of management override of controls is higher if management has relationships that involve control or significant influence with parties with which the entity does business because these relationships may present management with greater incentives and opportunities to perpetrate fraud. For example, management's financial interests in certain related parties may provide incentives for management to override controls by (*a*) directing the entity, against its interests, to conclude transactions for the benefit of these parties, or (*b*) colluding with such parties or controlling their actions. Examples of possible fraud include the following:

- Creating fictitious terms of transactions with related parties designed to misrepresent the business rationale of these transactions

[26] Paragraph .31 of section 240.

- Fraudulently organizing the transfer of assets from or to management or others at amounts significantly above or below market value
- Engaging in complex transactions with related parties, such as entities formed to accomplish specific purposes, that are structured to misrepresent the financial position or financial performance of the entity

.A20 *Considerations specific to smaller entities.* Control activities in smaller entities are likely to be less formal, and smaller entities may have no documented processes for dealing with related party relationships and transactions. An owner-manager may mitigate some of the risks arising from related party transactions or potentially increase those risks through active involvement in all the main aspects of the transactions. For such entities, the auditor may obtain an understanding of the related party relationships and transactions, and any controls that may exist over these, through inquiry of management combined with other procedures, such as observation of management's oversight and review activities and inspection of available relevant documentation.

.A21 *Authorization and approval of significant transactions and arrangements (Ref: par. .15b).* Authorization involves the granting of permission by a party or parties with the appropriate authority (whether management, those charged with governance, or the entity's shareholders) for the entity to enter into specific transactions in accordance with predetermined criteria, whether or not judgmental. Approval involves those parties' acceptance of the transactions the entity has entered into as having satisfied the criteria on which authorization was granted. Examples of controls the entity may have established to authorize and approve significant transactions and arrangements with related parties or significant transactions and arrangements outside the normal course of business include the following:

- Monitoring controls to identify such transactions and arrangements for authorization and approval
- Approval of the terms and conditions of the transactions and arrangements by management, those charged with governance, or, when applicable, shareholders

Maintaining Alertness for Related Party Information When Reviewing Records or Documents

Records or Documents That the Auditor May Inspect (Ref: par. .16)

.A22 During the audit, the auditor may inspect records or documents that indicate the existence of related party relationships or transactions that management has not previously identified or disclosed to the auditor. Examples of those records or documents include the following:

- Third party confirmations obtained by the auditor (in addition to bank and legal confirmations)
- Entity income tax returns
- Information supplied by the entity to regulatory authorities
- Shareholder registers to identify the entity's principal shareholders
- Statements of conflicts of interest from management and those charged with governance

- Records of the entity's investments and those of its benefit plans
- Contracts and agreements with key management or those charged with governance
- Significant contracts and agreements not in the entity's ordinary course of business
- Specific invoices and correspondence from the entity's professional advisors
- Life insurance policies acquired by the entity
- Significant contracts renegotiated by the entity during the period
- Internal auditors' reports
- Capital financing arrangements with entities other than financial institutions (for example, construction of a governmental entity facility associated with the issuance of debt by a related not-for-profit entity)
- Economic development arrangements for capital additions (for example, a governmental entity's use and eventual ownership of properties and facilities financed and operated by a company or another governmental entity)

.A23 Additionally, the auditor may review the prior years' audit documentation for information about related party relationships and transactions. If applicable, the auditor may inquire of a predecessor auditor about the predecessor's knowledge of existing relationships and the extent of management involvement in material transactions.

.A24 *Arrangements that may indicate the existence of previously unidentified or undisclosed related party relationships or transactions.* An arrangement involves a formal or informal agreement between the entity and one or more other parties for such purposes as the following:

- The establishment of a business relationship through appropriate vehicles or structures
- The conduct of certain types of transactions under specific terms and conditions
- The provision of designated services or financial support

Examples of arrangements that may indicate the existence of related party relationships or transactions that management has not previously identified or disclosed to the auditor include the following:

- Participation in unincorporated partnerships with other parties
- Agreements for the provision of services to certain parties under terms and conditions that are outside the entity's normal course of business
- Guarantees and guarantor relationships

Identification of Significant Transactions Outside the Normal Course of Business (Ref: par. .17)

.A25 Obtaining further information on significant transactions outside the entity's normal course of business enables the auditor to evaluate whether fraud risk factors, if any, are present and to identify the risks of material misstatement due to fraud.

.A26 Examples of transactions outside the entity's normal course of business may include the following:

- Complex equity transactions, such as corporate restructurings or acquisitions
- Transactions with offshore entities in jurisdictions with less rigorous corporate governance structures, laws, or regulations
- The leasing of premises or the rendering of management services by the entity to another party if no consideration is exchanged
- Sales transactions with unusually large discounts or returns
- Transactions with circular arrangements (for example, sales with a commitment to repurchase)
- Transactions under contracts whose terms are changed before expiration

.A27 *Understanding the nature of significant transactions outside the normal course of business (Ref: par. .17a).* Inquiring into the nature of the significant transactions outside the entity's normal course of business involves obtaining an understanding of the business rationale of the transactions and the terms and conditions under which these have been entered into.[27]

.A28 *Inquiring into whether related parties could be involved (Ref: par. .17b).* A related party could be involved in a significant transaction outside the entity's normal course of business not only by directly influencing the transaction by being a party to the transaction but also by indirectly influencing it through an intermediary. Such influence may indicate the presence of a fraud risk factor.

Sharing Related Party Information With the Engagement Team (Ref: par. .18 and .23a)

.A29 Relevant related party information shared with the engagement team members may include the following:

- The nature of the related party relationships and transactions
- Significant or complex related party relationships or transactions that may require special audit consideration, particularly transactions in which management or those charged with governance are financially involved

The exchange of information is most useful if made at an early stage of the audit.

.A30 Section 600 addresses the communications that apply to group audits, particularly those that involve component auditors.

Identification and Assessment of the Risks of Material Misstatement Associated With Related Party Relationships and Transactions

Fraud Risk Factors Associated With a Related Party With Dominant Influence (Ref: par. .20)

.A31 Related parties with the ability to exert control or significant influence may be in a position to exert dominant influence over the entity or its management. Consideration of such behavior is relevant when identifying and

[27] Paragraph .32*c* of section 240.

assessing the risks of material misstatement due to fraud, as further explained in paragraphs .A32–.A33.

.A32 Domination of management by a single person or small group of persons without compensating controls is a fraud risk factor.[28] Indicators of dominant influence exerted by a related party include the following:

- The related party has vetoed significant business decisions taken by management or those charged with governance.
- Significant transactions are referred to the related party for final approval.
- Little or no debate occurs among management and those charged with governance regarding business proposals initiated by the related party.
- Transactions involving the related party (or a close family member of the related party) are rarely independently reviewed and approved.

Dominant influence also may exist, in some cases, if the related party has played a leading role in founding the entity and continues to play a leading role in managing the entity.

.A33 In the presence of other risk factors, the existence of a related party with dominant influence may indicate significant risks of material misstatement due to fraud. For example

- an unusually high turnover of senior management or professional advisors may suggest unethical or fraudulent business practices that serve the related party's purposes.
- the use of business intermediaries for significant transactions for which there appears to be no clear business justification may suggest that the related party could have an interest in such transactions through control of such intermediaries for fraudulent purposes.

Evidence of the related party's excessive participation in, or preoccupation with, the selection of accounting policies or the determination of significant estimates may suggest the possibility of fraudulent financial reporting.

Responses to the Risks of Material Misstatement Associated With Related Party Relationships and Transactions (Ref: par. .21)

.A34 The nature, timing, and extent of the further audit procedures that the auditor may select to respond to the assessed risks of material misstatement associated with related party relationships and transactions depend upon the nature of those risks and the circumstances of the entity.

.A35 Examples of substantive audit procedures that the auditor may perform when the auditor has assessed a significant risk that management has not appropriately accounted for or disclosed specific related party transactions (whether due to fraud or error) include the following:

- Confirming the purposes, specific terms, or amounts of the transactions with the related parties (this audit procedure may be less effective when the auditor judges that the entity is likely to influence the related parties in their responses to the auditor).

---

[28] Paragraph .A75 of section 240.

- Inspecting evidence in possession of the other party or parties to the transaction.
- Confirming or discussing significant information with intermediaries, such as banks, guarantors, agents, or attorneys, to obtain a better understanding of the transaction.
- Referring to financial publications, trade journals, credit agencies, and other information sources when there is reason to believe that unfamiliar customers, suppliers, or other business enterprises with which material amounts of business have been transacted may lack substance.
- With respect to material uncollected balances, guarantees, and other obligations, obtaining information about the financial capability of the other party or parties to the transaction. Such information may be obtained from audited financial statements, unaudited financial statements, income tax returns, and reports issued by regulatory agencies, taxing authorities, financial publications, or credit agencies.

.A36 If the auditor has assessed a significant risk of material misstatement due to fraud as a result of the presence of a related party with dominant influence, the auditor may, in addition to the general requirements of section 240, perform audit procedures such as the following to obtain an understanding of the business relationships that such a related party may have established directly or indirectly with the entity and to determine the need for further appropriate substantive audit procedures:

- Inquiries of, and discussion with, management and those charged with governance
- Inquiries of the related party
- Inspection of significant contracts with the related party
- Appropriate background research, such as through the Internet or specific external business information databases
- Review of employee whistle-blowing reports when these are retained

.A37 Depending upon the results of the auditor's risk assessment procedures, the auditor may consider it appropriate to obtain audit evidence without testing the entity's controls over related party relationships and transactions. In some circumstances, however, it may not be possible to obtain sufficient appropriate audit evidence from substantive audit procedures alone, regarding the risks of material misstatement associated with related party relationships and transactions. For example, when intragroup transactions between the entity and its components are numerous and a significant amount of information regarding these transactions is initiated, authorized, recorded, processed, or reported electronically in an integrated system, the auditor may determine that it is not possible to design effective substantive audit procedures that by themselves would reduce the risks of material misstatement associated with these transactions to an acceptably low level. In such a case, in meeting the requirement of section 330 to obtain sufficient appropriate audit evidence about the operating effectiveness of relevant controls, the auditor is required to test the entity's controls over the completeness and accuracy of the recording of the related party relationships and transactions.[29]

---

[29] Paragraph .08*b* of section 330.

Identification of Previously Unidentified or Undisclosed Related Parties or Significant Related Party Transactions

Communicating Newly Identified Related Party Information to the Engagement Team (Ref: par. .23a)

.A38 Promptly communicating any newly identified related parties to the other members of the engagement team assists them in determining whether this information affects the results of, and conclusions drawn from, risk assessment procedures already performed, including whether the risks of material misstatement need to be reassessed.

Substantive Procedures Relating to Newly Identified Related Parties or Significant Related Party Transactions (Ref: par. .23d)

.A39 Examples of substantive audit procedures that the auditor may perform relating to newly identified related parties or significant related party transactions include the following:

- Making inquiries regarding the nature of the entity's relationships with the newly identified related parties, including inquiring of parties outside the entity who are presumed to have significant knowledge of the entity and its business, such as legal counsel, principal agents, major representatives, consultants, guarantors, or other close business partners.
- Conducting an analysis of accounting records for transactions with the newly identified related parties. Such an analysis may be facilitated using computer assisted audit techniques.
- Verifying the terms and conditions of the newly identified related party transactions and evaluating whether the transactions have been appropriately accounted for and disclosed.

Intentional Nondisclosure by Management (Ref: par. .23f)

.A40 The requirements and guidance in section 240 regarding the auditor's responsibilities relating to fraud in an audit of financial statements are relevant when management appears to have intentionally failed to disclose related parties or significant related party transactions to the auditor. The auditor also may consider whether it is necessary to reevaluate the reliability of management's responses to the auditor's inquiries and management's representations to the auditor.[30]

Identified Significant Related Party Transactions Outside the Entity's Normal Course of Business

Evaluating the Business Rationale of Significant Related Party Transactions (Ref: par. .24a(i))

.A41 In evaluating the business rationale of a significant related party transaction outside the entity's normal course of business, the auditor may consider the following:

- Whether the transaction
  - — is overly complex (for example, it may involve multiple related parties within a consolidated group)
  - — has unusual terms of trade, such as unusual prices, interest rates, guarantees, and repayment terms

[30] Paragraphs .22–.24 and .26 of section 580.

— lacks an apparent logical business reason for its occurrence
— involves previously unidentified related parties
— is processed in an unusual manner

- Whether management has discussed the nature of, and accounting for, such a transaction with those charged with governance
- Whether management is placing more emphasis on a particular accounting treatment rather than giving due regard to the underlying economics of the transaction

If management's explanations are materially inconsistent with the terms of the related party transaction, the auditor is required to consider the reliability of management's explanations and representations on other significant matters.[31]

.A42 The auditor also may seek to understand the business rationale of such a transaction from the related party's perspective because this may help the auditor to better understand the economic reality of the transaction and why it was carried out. A business rationale from the related party's perspective that appears inconsistent with the nature of its business may represent a fraud risk factor.

Authorization and Approval of Significant Related Party Transactions (Ref: par. .24b)

.A43 Authorization and approval by management, those charged with governance, or, when applicable, the shareholders of significant related party transactions outside the entity's normal course of business may provide audit evidence that these have been duly considered at the appropriate levels within the entity, and that their terms and conditions have been appropriately reflected in the financial statements. The existence of transactions of this nature that were not subject to such authorization and approval, in the absence of rational explanations based on discussion with management or those charged with governance, may indicate risks of material misstatement due to fraud or error. In these circumstances, the auditor may need to be alert for other transactions of a similar nature. Authorization and approval alone, however, may not be sufficient in concluding whether risks of material misstatement due to fraud are absent because authorization and approval may be ineffective if there has been collusion between the related parties or if the entity is subject to the dominant influence of a related party.

.A44 *Considerations specific to smaller entities.* A smaller entity may not have the same controls provided by different levels of authority and approval that may exist in a larger entity. Accordingly, when auditing a smaller entity, the auditor may rely to a lesser degree on authorization and approval for audit evidence regarding the validity of significant related party transactions outside the entity's normal course of business. Instead, the auditor may consider performing other audit procedures, such as inspecting relevant documents, confirming specific aspects of the transactions with relevant parties, or observing the owner-manager's involvement with the transactions. The discussion of management domination in paragraph .A32 and the fraud considerations discussed in paragraph .A8 provide further relevant guidance.

Assertions That Related Party Transactions Were Conducted on Terms Equivalent to Those Prevailing in an Arm's Length Transaction (Ref: par. .25)

.A45 It will generally not be possible to determine whether a particular transaction would have taken place if the parties had not been related or,

---

[31] Paragraph .10 of section 500, *Audit Evidence*.

assuming it would have taken place, what the terms and manner of settlement would have been. Accordingly, it is difficult to substantiate representations that a transaction was consummated on terms equivalent to those that prevail in arm's length transactions.

.A46 Although audit evidence may be readily available regarding how the price of a related party transaction compares to that of a similar arm's length transaction, practical difficulties ordinarily limit the auditor's ability to obtain audit evidence that all other aspects of the transaction are equivalent to those of the arm's length transaction. For example, although the auditor may be able to confirm that a related party transaction has been conducted at a market price, it may be impracticable to confirm whether other terms and conditions of the transaction (such as credit terms, contingencies, and specific charges) are equivalent to those that would ordinarily be agreed between independent parties. Accordingly, there may be a risk that management's assertion that a related party transaction was conducted on terms equivalent to those prevailing in an arm's length transaction may be materially misstated.

.A47 The preparation and fair presentation of the financial statements requires management to substantiate an assertion included in financial statements that a related party transaction was conducted on terms equivalent to those prevailing in an arm's length transaction, giving appropriate consideration to the difficulties described in paragraphs .A45–.A46. Management's support for the assertion may include the following:

- Comparing the terms of the related party transaction to those of an identical or similar transaction with one or more unrelated parties
- Engaging an external specialist to determine a market value and confirm market terms and conditions for the transaction
- Comparing the terms of the transaction to known market terms for broadly similar transactions on an open market

.A48 Evaluating management's support for this assertion may involve one or more of the following:

- Considering the appropriateness of management's process for supporting the assertion
- Verifying the source of the internal or external data supporting the assertion and testing the data to determine their accuracy, completeness, and relevance

.A49 If the auditor believes that management's assertion is unsubstantiated or the auditor cannot obtain sufficient appropriate audit evidence to support the assertion, the auditor, in accordance with section 705, considers the implications for the audit, including the opinion in the auditor's report.

Evaluation of the Accounting for, and Disclosure of, Identified Related Party Relationships and Transactions

Materiality Considerations in Evaluating Misstatements (Ref: par. .26)

.A50 Section 450, *Evaluation of Misstatements Identified During the Audit*, requires the auditor to consider both the size and nature of a misstatement and the particular circumstances of its occurrence when evaluating whether the misstatement is material.[32] The significance of the transaction to the

[32] Paragraph .11*a* of section 450, *Evaluation of Misstatements Identified During the Audit.*

financial statement users may not depend solely on the recorded amount of the transaction but also on other specific relevant factors, such as the nature of the related party relationship.

Evaluation of Related Party Disclosures (Ref: par. .26a)

.A51 Evaluating the related party disclosures means considering whether the facts and circumstances of the entity's related party relationships and transactions have been appropriately summarized and presented so that the disclosures are understandable. Disclosures of related party transactions may not be understandable if

a. the business rationale and the effects of the transactions on the financial statements are unclear or misstated.

b. key terms, conditions, or other important elements of the transactions necessary for understanding them are not appropriately disclosed.

Communication With Those Charged With Governance (Ref: par. .27)

.A52 Communicating significant findings and issues arising during the audit in connection with the entity's related parties helps the auditor establish a common understanding with those charged with governance of the nature and resolution of these matters.[33] Examples of significant related party findings and issues include the following:

- Nondisclosure (whether or not intentional) by management to the auditor of related parties or significant related party transactions, which may alert those charged with governance to significant related party relationships and transactions of which they may not have been previously aware
- The identification of significant related party transactions that have not been appropriately authorized and approved, which may give rise to suspected fraud
- Disagreement with management regarding the accounting for, and disclosure of, significant related party transactions
- Noncompliance with applicable laws or regulations prohibiting or restricting specific types of related party transactions
- Difficulties in identifying the party that ultimately controls the entity

---

[33] Paragraph .A10 of section 230 provides further guidance on the nature of significant findings or issues arising during the audit.

- [illegible] of the transactions [illegible] the [illegible] or [illegible]

- [illegible] the ultimate controlling party of the entity

[illegible] significant findings [illegible] the [illegible] of significant [illegible] during the audit.

AU-C Section 560 *

Subsequent Events and Subsequently Discovered Facts

Source: SAS No. 122.

Effective for audits of financial statements for periods ending on or after December 15, 2012.

Introduction

Scope of This Section

.01 This section addresses the auditor's responsibilities relating to subsequent events and subsequently discovered facts in an audit of financial statements. It also addresses a predecessor auditor's responsibilities for subsequent events and subsequently discovered facts when reissuing the auditor's report on previously issued financial statements that are to be presented on a comparative basis with audited financial statements of a subsequent period. (Ref: par. .A1)

Subsequent Events and Subsequently Discovered Facts

.02 Financial statements may be affected by certain events that occur after the date of the financial statements. Many financial reporting frameworks specifically refer to such events. Such financial reporting frameworks ordinarily identify two types of events:

a. Those that provide evidence of conditions that existed at the date of the financial statements

b. Those that provide evidence of conditions that arose after the date of the financial statements

.03 Section 700, *Forming an Opinion and Reporting on Financial Statements*, explains that the date of the auditor's report informs the user of the auditor's report that the auditor has considered the effect of events and transactions of which the auditor becomes aware and that occurred up to that date.[1] Accordingly, this section addresses the auditor's responsibilities relating to subsequent events occurring between the date of the financial statements and the date of the auditor's report that require adjustment of, or disclosure in, the financial statements. It also addresses the auditor's responsibilities relating to subsequently discovered facts that become known to the auditor after the date of the auditor's report.

---

* This section has been codified using an "AU-C" identifier instead of an "AU" identifier. "AU-C" is a temporary identifier to avoid confusion with references to existing "AU" sections, which will remain in AICPA *Professional Standards* through 2013. The "AU-C" identifier will revert to "AU" in 2014, by which time substantially all engagements for which the "AU" sections were still effective are expected to be completed.

[1] Paragraph .A38 of section 700, *Forming an Opinion and Reporting on Financial Statements.*

Effective Date

.04 This section is effective for audits of financial statements for periods ending on or after December 15, 2012.

Objectives

.05 The objectives of the auditor are to

a. obtain sufficient appropriate audit evidence about whether events occurring between the date of the financial statements and the date of the auditor's report that require adjustment of, or disclosure in, the financial statements are appropriately reflected in those financial statements in accordance with the applicable financial reporting framework and

b. respond appropriately to facts that become known to the auditor after the date of the auditor's report that, had they been known to the auditor at that date, may have caused the auditor to revise the auditor's report.

.06 The objective of a predecessor auditor who is requested to reissue a previously issued auditor's report on financial statements that are to be presented on a comparative basis with audited financial statements of a subsequent period is to perform specified procedures to determine whether the previously issued auditor's report is still appropriate before such report is reissued.

Definitions

.07 For purposes of generally accepted auditing standards, the following terms have the meanings attributed as follows:

Date of the auditor's report. The date that the auditor dates the report on the financial statements, in accordance with section 700.[2] (Ref: par. .A14)

Date of the financial statements. The date of the end of the latest period covered by the financial statements.

Subsequent events. Events occurring between the date of the financial statements and the date of the auditor's report.

Subsequently discovered facts. Facts that become known to the auditor after the date of the auditor's report that, had they been known to the auditor at that date, may have caused the auditor to revise the auditor's report.

.08 Reference to *audited financial statements* in this section means *the financial statements, together with the auditor's report thereon*.

Requirements

Subsequent Events

.09 The auditor should perform audit procedures designed to obtain sufficient appropriate audit evidence that all subsequent events that require adjustment of, or disclosure in, the financial statements have been identified. The auditor is not, however, expected to perform additional audit procedures on

---

[2] Paragraph .41 of section 700.

matters to which previously applied audit procedures have provided satisfactory conclusions. (Ref: par. .A2–.A3)

.10 The auditor should perform the procedures required by paragraph .09 so that they cover the period from the date of the financial statements to the date of the auditor's report or as near as practicable thereto. The auditor should take into account the auditor's risk assessment in determining the nature and extent of such audit procedures, which should include the following: (Ref: par. .A4–.A5 and .A8–.A10)

a. Obtaining an understanding of any procedures that management has established to ensure that subsequent events are identified

b. Inquiring of management and, when appropriate, those charged with governance about whether any subsequent events have occurred that might affect the financial statements (Ref: par. .A6)

c. Reading minutes, if any, of the meetings of the entity's owners, management, and those charged with governance that have been held after the date of the financial statements and inquiring about matters discussed at any such meetings for which minutes are not yet available (Ref: par. .A4 and .A7)

d. Reading the entity's latest subsequent interim financial statements, if any

.11 If, as a result of the procedures performed as required by paragraphs .09–.10, the auditor identifies subsequent events that require adjustment of, or disclosure in, the financial statements, the auditor should determine whether each such event is appropriately reflected in the financial statements in accordance with the applicable financial reporting framework.

Subsequently Discovered Facts That Become Known to the Auditor Before the Report Release Date

.12 The auditor is not required to perform any audit procedures regarding the financial statements after the date of the auditor's report. However, if a subsequently discovered fact becomes known to the auditor before the report release date,[3] the auditor should

a. discuss the matter with management and, when appropriate, those charged with governance.

b. determine whether the financial statements need revision and, if so, inquire how management intends to address the matter in the financial statements.

.13 If management revises the financial statements, the auditor should perform the audit procedures necessary in the circumstances on the revision. The auditor also should either (Ref: par. .A11–.A16)

a. date the auditor's report as of a later date; extend the audit procedures referred to in paragraphs .09–.10 to the new date of the auditor's report on the revised financial statements; and request written representations from management as of the new date of the auditor's report, in accordance with the requirements of section 580, *Written Representations*, or

---

[3] The term *report release date* is defined in paragraph .06 of section 230, *Audit Documentation*.

b. include an additional date in the auditor's report on the revised financial statements that is limited to the revision (that is, dual-date the auditor's report for that revision), thereby indicating that the auditor's procedures subsequent to the original date of the auditor's report are limited solely to the revision of the financial statements described in the relevant note to the financial statements. In this circumstance, the auditor should request written representations from management as of the additional date in the auditor's report about whether

  i. any information has come to management's attention that would cause management to believe that any of the previous representations should be modified.

  ii. any other events have occurred subsequent to the date of the financial statements that would require adjustment to, or disclosure in, those financial statements.

.14 If management does not revise the financial statements in circumstances when the auditor believes they need to be revised, the auditor should modify the opinion (express a qualified opinion or an adverse opinion), as required by section 705, *Modifications to the Opinion in the Independent Auditor's Report*. (Ref: par. .A17)

Subsequently Discovered Facts That Become Known to the Auditor After the Report Release Date

.15 If a subsequently discovered fact becomes known to the auditor after the report release date, the auditor should (Ref: par. .A18–.A20)

a. discuss the matter with management and, when appropriate, those charged with governance.

b. determine whether the financial statements need revision and, if so, inquire how management intends to address the matter in the financial statements.

.16 If management revises the financial statements, the auditor should

a. apply the requirements of paragraph .13.

b. if the audited financial statements (before revision) have been made available to third parties, assess whether the steps taken by management are timely and appropriate to ensure that anyone in receipt of those financial statements is informed of the situation, including that the audited financial statements are not to be relied upon. If management does not take the necessary steps, the auditor should apply the requirements of paragraph .18. (Ref: par. .A21–.A22)

c. if the auditor's opinion on the revised financial statements differs from the opinion the auditor previously expressed, disclose the following matters in an emphasis-of-matter or other-matter paragraph, in accordance with section 706, *Emphasis-of-Matter Paragraphs and Other-Matter Paragraphs in the Independent Auditor's Report*:

  i. The date of the auditor's previous report

  ii. The type of opinion previously expressed

  iii. The substantive reasons for the different opinion

  iv. That the auditor's opinion on the revised financial statements is different from the auditor's previous opinion

.17 If management does not revise the financial statements in circumstances when the auditor believes they need to be revised, then

a. if the audited financial statements have not been made available to third parties, the auditor should notify management and those charged with governance—unless all of those charged with governance are involved in managing the entity[4]—not to make the audited financial statements available to third parties before the necessary revisions have been made and a new auditor's report on the revised financial statements has been provided. If the audited financial statements are, nevertheless, subsequently made available to third parties without the necessary revisions, the auditor should apply the requirements of paragraph .17*b*.

b. if the audited financial statements have been made available to third parties, the auditor should assess whether the steps taken by management are timely and appropriate to ensure that anyone in receipt of the audited financial statements is informed of the situation, including that the audited financial statements are not to be relied upon. If management does not take the necessary steps, the auditor should apply the requirements of paragraph .18. (Ref: par. .A21–.A22)

.18 If management does not take the necessary steps to ensure that anyone in receipt of the audited financial statements is informed of the situation, as provided by paragraphs .16*b* or .17*b*, the auditor should notify management and those charged with governance—unless all of those charged with governance are involved in managing the entity[5]—that the auditor will seek to prevent future reliance on the auditor's report. If, despite such notification, management or those charged with governance do not take the necessary steps, the auditor should take appropriate action to seek to prevent reliance on the auditor's report. (Ref: par. .A23–.A26)

Predecessor Auditor's Reissuance of the Auditor's Report in Comparative Financial Statements (Ref: par. .A27–.A28)

Predecessor Auditor's Report Reissued (Ref: par. .A29–.A30)

.19 Before reissuing a previously issued auditor's report on financial statements that are to be presented on a comparative basis with audited financial statements of a subsequent period, the predecessor auditor should perform the following procedures to determine whether the previously issued auditor's report is still appropriate:

a. Read the financial statements of the subsequent period to be presented on a comparative basis

b. Compare the prior period financial statements that the predecessor auditor reported on with the financial statements of the subsequent period to be presented on a comparative basis

c. Inquire of, and request written representations from, management of the former client, at or near the date of reissuance, about whether

---

[4] Paragraph .14 of section 260, *The Auditor's Communication With Those Charged With Governance*.

[5] Paragraph .14 of section 260.

i. any information has come to management's attention that would cause management to believe that any of the previous representations should be modified

ii. any events have occurred subsequent to the date of the latest prior period financial statements reported on by the predecessor auditor that would require adjustment to, or disclosure in, those financial statements

d. Obtain a representation letter from the successor auditor stating whether the successor auditor's audit revealed any matters that, in the successor auditor's opinion, might have a material effect on, or require disclosure in, the financial statements reported on by the predecessor auditor

.20 If, in performing the procedures in paragraph .19, a subsequently discovered fact becomes known to the predecessor auditor, then

a. the predecessor auditor should apply the requirements of paragraph .15.

b. if management revises the financial statements and the predecessor auditor plans to issue a new auditor's report on the revised financial statements, the predecessor auditor should apply the requirements of paragraph .16.

c. if management revises the financial statements and the predecessor auditor does not plan to issue a new auditor's report on the revised financial statements, or if management does not revise the financial statements in circumstances when the predecessor auditor believes they need to be revised, the predecessor auditor should assess the steps taken by management, as required by paragraph .17*b*.

Application and Other Explanatory Material

Scope of This Section (Ref: par. .01)

.A1 When audited financial statements are included in other documents subsequent to their issuance, the auditor may have additional responsibilities to consider, such as legal or regulatory requirements involving private placement offerings, exempt public offerings (including offerings pursuant to Securities and Exchange Commission [SEC] Rule 144A), or other offerings of securities to the public in jurisdictions outside the United States. Section 720, *Other Information in Documents Containing Audited Financial Statements*, may be applied, adapted as necessary in the circumstances, to such other documents. Section 925, *Filings With the U.S. Securities and Exchange Commission Under the Securities Act of 1933*, addresses the auditor's responsibilities in connection with financial statements of a nonissuer included in a registration statement filed with the SEC under the Securities Act of 1933, as amended.

Subsequent Events (Ref: par. .09–.11)

.A2 The period between the date of the financial statements and the date of the auditor's report may vary from a relatively short period to one or more months. Some phases of the audit will be performed during this period, whereas other phases will be substantially completed on or before the date of the financial statements. As an audit approaches completion, the auditor is not expected to perform additional audit procedures on matters to which previously applied audit procedures have provided satisfactory conclusions. New information, however, may be inconsistent with the audit evidence obtained, in which case the auditor is required to determine what modifications or additions to audit procedures are necessary to resolve the matter and consider the effect of the matter, if any, on other aspects of the audit.[6]

.A3 Depending on the auditor's risk assessment, the audit procedures required by paragraphs .09–.10 may include procedures necessary to obtain sufficient appropriate audit evidence involving the review or testing of accounting records or transactions occurring between the date of the financial statements and the date of the auditor's report. The audit procedures required by paragraphs .09–.10 are in addition to procedures that the auditor may perform for other purposes that, nevertheless, may provide evidence about subsequent events (for example, to obtain audit evidence for account balances as of the date of the financial statements, such as cut-off procedures or procedures regarding subsequent receipts of accounts receivable).

.A4 Paragraph .10 stipulates certain audit procedures that the auditor is required to perform pursuant to paragraph .09. However, the subsequent events procedures that the auditor performs may depend on the information that is available and, in particular, the manner in which the accounting records have been maintained and the extent to which information has been prepared since the date of the financial statements. When interim financial statements (whether for internal or external purposes) or minutes of meetings of management or those charged with governance have not been prepared, relevant audit procedures may take the form of inspection of available books and records.

.A5 In addition to the audit procedures required by paragraphs .09–.10, the auditor may consider it necessary and appropriate to read the entity's latest available budgets, cash flow forecasts, and other related management reports for periods after the date of the financial statements. Paragraphs .A6–.A10 provide guidance on additional matters that the auditor may consider in the course of performing subsequent events procedures.

Inquiry (Ref: par. .10b)

.A6 In inquiring of management and, when appropriate, those charged with governance about whether any subsequent events have occurred that might affect the financial statements, the auditor may inquire about the current status of items that were accounted for on the basis of preliminary or inconclusive data and may make specific inquiries about the following matters:

- Whether new commitments, borrowings, or guarantees have been entered into
- Whether sales or acquisitions of assets have occurred or are planned
- Whether there have been increases in capital or issuance of debt instruments, such as the issue of new shares or debentures, or an agreement to merge or liquidate has been made or is planned
- Whether any assets have been appropriated by the government or destroyed (for example, by fire or flood)
- Whether there have been any developments regarding contingencies

---

[6] Paragraph .10 of section 500, *Audit Evidence*.

- Whether any unusual accounting adjustments have been made or are contemplated
- Whether any events have occurred or are likely to occur that will bring into question the appropriateness of accounting policies used in the financial statements, as would be the case, for example, if such events call into question the validity of the going concern assumption
- Whether any events have occurred that are relevant to the measurement of estimates or provisions made in the financial statements
- Whether any events have occurred that are relevant to the recoverability of assets

Reading Minutes (Ref: par. .10c)

Considerations Specific to Governmental Entities

.A7 In audits of governmental entities, the auditor may, in performing the requirement in paragraph .10*c*, read the official records of relevant proceedings of the legislative or governing body, or other relevant regulatory or oversight body, and inquire about matters addressed in proceedings for which official records are not yet available.

Inquiries of Legal Counsel

.A8 Section 501, *Audit Evidence—Specific Considerations for Selected Items*, addresses the auditor's responsibility to seek direct communication with the entity's legal counsel concerning litigation, claims, and assessments through the date of the auditor's report.

Written Representations

.A9 Section 580 requires the auditor to request that management and, when appropriate, those charged with governance provide written representations as of the date of the auditor's report that all events occurring subsequent to the date of the financial statements, and for which the applicable financial reporting framework requires adjustment or disclosure, have been adjusted or disclosed.[7] The auditor may consider whether written representations covering particular subsequent events or significant matters disclosed to the auditor in the performance of the audit procedures required by paragraphs .09–.10 may be necessary to support other audit evidence to obtain sufficient appropriate audit evidence.

.A10 The applicable financial reporting framework may require management to evaluate subsequent events through the date the financial statements are issued or available to be issued and to disclose the date through which subsequent events were evaluated in the financial statements. In most cases, this will result in the date that management discloses as the date through which management has evaluated subsequent events being the same date as the auditor's report. This is because section 700 requires the auditor's report to be dated no earlier than the date on which the auditor has obtained sufficient appropriate audit evidence on which to base the auditor's opinion on the financial statements, including evidence that the audit documentation has been reviewed; that all the statements that comprise the financial statements, including related notes, have been prepared; and that management has asserted

---

[7] Paragraph .18 of section 580, *Written Representations*.

that they have taken responsibility for those financial statements.[8] Also, the auditor is concerned with subsequent events that require adjustment of, or disclosure in, the financial statements through the date of the auditor's report or as near as practicable thereto. Therefore, management's representations concerning events occurring subsequent to the date of the financial statements and for which the applicable financial reporting framework requires adjustment or disclosure are required to be made as of the date of the auditor's report on the financial statements.[9] To align the date disclosed by management in the financial statements, the representation letter date, and the auditor's report date, the auditor may discuss the dating requirements with management and may also include, in the terms of the audit engagement,[10] that management will not date the subsequent event disclosure earlier than the date of the representation letter (also the date of the auditor's report).

Subsequently Discovered Facts That Become Known to the Auditor Before the Report Release Date (Ref: par. .12–.14)

Dating the Auditor's Report on the Revised Financial Statements (Ref: par. .13)

.A11 The auditor has two methods available for dating the auditor's report when the financial statements are revised after the original date of the auditor's report. The auditor may include an additional date limited to the revision (that is, dual-date the auditor's report for that revision) or date the auditor's report as of a later date. In the former instance, the auditor's responsibility for events occurring subsequent to the original date of the auditor's report is limited to the specific event described in the relevant note to the financial statements. In the latter instance, the auditor's responsibility for subsequent events extends to the new date of the auditor's report on the revised financial statements.

.A12 Generally, when the revision of the financial statements is specifically limited to the effects of the specific event described in the relevant note to the financial statements, the auditor may decide to limit the audit procedures to that revision, as provided by paragraph .13*b*. Even when the financial statements are revised and disclosure of the revision is made, the auditor is not precluded from extending the audit procedures referred to in paragraphs .09–.10 to the new date of the auditor's report on the revised financial statements, as provided by paragraph .13*a*.

.A13 When, in the circumstances described in paragraph .13*b*, the auditor includes an additional date limited to the revision (a dual date), the original date of the auditor's report on the financial statements prior to their subsequent revision by management remains unchanged because this date informs the reader about when the auditor obtained sufficient appropriate audit evidence with respect to those financial statements prior to their subsequent revision. However, an additional date is included in the auditor's report to inform users that the auditor's procedures subsequent to the original date of the auditor's report were limited to the subsequent revision of the financial statements. The following is an illustration of such wording:

> (Date of auditor's report), except as to note Y, which is as of (date of completion of audit procedures limited to revision described in note Y).

---

[8] Paragraph .41 of section 700.

[9] Paragraph .20 of section 580.

[10] Paragraph .A23 of section 210, *Terms of Engagement*.

.A14 As discussed in paragraph .A10, section 700 requires the auditor's report to be dated no earlier than the date on which the auditor has obtained sufficient appropriate audit evidence on which to base the auditor's opinion on the financial statements.[11] When management revises the financial statements and the auditor reports on the revised financial statements, the new date (or the dual date) included in the auditor's report cannot be earlier than the date on which the auditor carried out the audit procedures necessary in the circumstances on the revision, including that the documentation has been reviewed and management has prepared and asserted that they have taken responsibility for the revised financial statements.

Updated Written Representations

.A15 Section 580 requires the date of the written representations to be as of the date of the auditor's report on the financial statements.[12] If management revises the financial statements and, in accordance with paragraph .13*a*, the auditor dates the auditor's report on the revised financial statements as of a later date, written representations from management are required as of the later date to comply with section 580. The auditor may request management to provide a new representation letter or may agree with management on a form of written representations that update the written representations previously provided by addressing whether there are any changes to such written representations and, if so, what they are. An updated written representation letter may be in the form of the representations required by paragraph .13*b* when the auditor dual-dates the auditor's report for the revision.

Unaudited Events

.A16 To prevent the financial statements from being misleading, management may revise the financial statements by disclosing an event that arose after the original date of the auditor's report. When such event is included in a separate financial statement note that is labeled as unaudited (for example, when the event is captioned "Event (Unaudited) Subsequent to the Date of the Independent Auditor's Report"), the auditor is not required to perform any procedures on the revision, and the auditor's report carries the original date of the auditor's report.

Considerations Specific to Governmental Entities (Ref: par. .14)

.A17 In audits of governmental entities in which management does not revise the financial statements, the actions taken in accordance with paragraph .14 may also include reporting separately to the legislative or governing body, or other relevant regulatory or oversight body, on the implications of the subsequent event for the financial statements and the auditor's report and, if applicable, for the entity's internal control over financial reporting and compliance with law or regulation.

Subsequently Discovered Facts That Become Known to the Auditor After the Report Release Date (Ref: par. .15–.18)

Auditor's Responsibility After the Report Release Date (Ref: par. .15)

.A18 New information may come to the auditor's attention that, had such information been known to the auditor at the date of the auditor's report, may have caused the auditor to revise the auditor's report. When such information

---

[11] Paragraph .41 of section 700.

[12] Paragraph .20 of section 580.

becomes known to the auditor after the report release date, the requirements in paragraphs .15–.18 apply, even if the auditor has withdrawn or been discharged.

.A19 Because of the variety of conditions that might be encountered, the specific procedures or actions to be taken in a particular case may vary somewhat in light of the circumstances. For example, in determining whether the financial statements need revision, as required by paragraph .15*b*, the auditor may consider, in addition to the requirements of the applicable financial reporting framework, whether the auditor believes there are persons currently relying or likely to rely on the financial statements who would attach importance to the subsequently discovered facts. Consideration may be given, among other things, to the issuance of audited financial statements for a subsequent period, the time elapsed since the financial statements were issued and the auditor's report released, and any legal implications.

.A20 Section 708, *Consistency of Financial Statements*, addresses the auditor's evaluation of the consistency of the financial statements, including changes to previously issued financial statements, and the effect of that evaluation on the auditor's report.

Revision of Financial Statements by Management (Ref: par. .16b and .17b)

.A21 The steps taken by management to ensure that anyone in receipt of the audited financial statements is informed of the situation, including that the audited financial statements are not to be relied upon, depend on the circumstances. Management's steps may include the following:

- Notification to anyone who is known to be relying or who is likely to rely on the financial statements and the auditor's report that they are not to be relied upon and that revised financial statements, together with a new auditor's report, will be issued. This may be necessary when the issuance of revised financial statements and a new auditor's report is not imminent.
- Issuing, as soon as practicable, revised financial statements with appropriate disclosure of the matter.
- Issuing the subsequent period's financial statements with appropriate disclosure of the matter. This may be appropriate when issuance of the subsequent period's audited financial statements is imminent.

Considerations Specific to Governmental Entities

.A22 For audits performed under *Government Auditing Standards*, additional requirements exist, such as those pertaining to the evaluation of the timeliness and appropriateness of management's disclosure and actions to determine and correct misstatements in previously issued financial statements, reporting on the revised financial statements, and reporting directly to appropriate officials when management does not take the necessary steps.

Auditor Action to Seek to Prevent Reliance on the Auditor's Report (Ref: par. .18)

.A23 If management made the audited financial statements available to third parties despite the auditor's notification not to do so, or if the auditor believes that management or those charged with governance have failed to take the necessary steps to prevent reliance on the auditor's report on the previously issued audited financial statements despite the auditor's prior notification that the auditor will take action to seek to prevent such reliance, the auditor's course of action depends upon the auditor's legal rights and obligations. Consequently, the auditor may consider it appropriate to seek legal advice.

.A24 The actions that the auditor may take to seek to prevent reliance on the auditor's report may depend upon the degree of certainty of the auditor's knowledge that persons or entities exist who are currently relying or who will rely on the audited financial statements, and who would attach importance to the information, and the auditor's ability as a practical matter to communicate with them. In addition to seeking legal advice, the auditor may consider taking the following steps to the extent applicable:

- Notify management and those charged with governance that the auditor's report is not to be relied upon.
- Notify regulatory agencies having jurisdiction over the entity that the auditor's report is not to be relied upon, including a request that the agency take whatever steps it may deem appropriate to accomplish the necessary disclosure.
- Notify anyone known to the auditor to be relying on the financial statements that the auditor's report is not to be relied upon. In some instances, it will not be practicable for the auditor to give appropriate individual notification to stockholders or investors at large whose identities are unknown to the auditor; notification to a regulatory agency having jurisdiction over the entity will usually be the only practical means for the auditor to provide appropriate disclosure, together with a request that the agency take whatever steps it may deem appropriate to accomplish the necessary disclosure.

.A25 Depending on the circumstances, if the auditor is able to determine that the financial statements need revision, the auditor's notification to anyone in receipt of the audited financial statements may, if permitted by law, regulation, and relevant ethical requirements,

- include a description of the nature of the matter and of its effect on the financial statements, avoiding comments concerning the conduct or motives of any person.
- describe the effect that the matter would have had on the auditor's report if it had been known to the auditor at the date of the report and had not been reflected in the financial statements.

.A26 If the auditor was not able to determine whether the financial statements need revision, the notification to anyone in receipt of the audited financial statements may indicate that information became known to the auditor and that, if the information is true, the auditor believes that the auditor's report is not to be relied upon. The specific matter need not be detailed in the notification.

Predecessor Auditor's Reissuance of the Auditor's Report in Comparative Financial Statements (Ref: par. .19–.20)

.A27 An auditor may be requested by management or those charged with governance to furnish additional copies of the auditor's report after the report release date. Providing additional copies of the auditor's report is not a report reissuance. In such cases, the auditor has no responsibility to make further investigation or inquiry about events that may have occurred during the period between the date of the auditor's report and the date of the release of the additional copies.

.A28 Additional responsibilities relating to the reissuance of a previously issued auditor's report in connection with financial statements of a nonissuer included in a registration statement filed with the SEC under the Securities Act of 1933, as discussed in paragraph .A1, are addressed in section 925.

Predecessor Auditor's Report Reissued

.A29 A predecessor auditor may be requested to reissue the auditor's report by a former client when prior period financial statements audited by the predecessor auditor are to be presented on a comparative basis with audited financial statements of a subsequent period. A predecessor auditor's knowledge of the current affairs of the former client is limited in the absence of a continuing relationship. Accordingly, a predecessor auditor may be in a position to reissue the report if the predecessor auditor is able to make satisfactory arrangements with the former client to perform this service and if the predecessor auditor complies with paragraph .19 to determine whether the previous auditor's report is still appropriate. A predecessor auditor is not required to reissue the auditor's report. Either the current form or manner of presentation of the financial statements of the prior period or one or more events might make a predecessor auditor's previous report inappropriate.

.A30 Section 700 addresses the auditor's responsibilities when the auditor is engaged to audit and report on a revision to prior period financial statements audited by the predecessor auditor.[13] It also addresses the auditor's responsibilities when the predecessor auditor's report will not be presented.[14]

---

[13] Paragraph .A52 of section 700.

[14] Paragraph .54 of section 700.

AU-C Section 570 *

The Auditor's Consideration of an Entity's Ability to Continue as a Going Concern

Source: SAS No. 126.

Effective for audits of financial statements for periods ending on or after December 15, 2012.

Introduction

Scope of This Statement on Auditing Standards

.01 This section addresses the auditor's responsibilities in an audit of financial statements with respect to evaluating whether there is substantial doubt about the entity's ability to continue as a going concern. This section applies to all audits of financial statements, regardless of whether the financial statements are prepared in accordance with a general purpose or a special purpose framework.[1] This section does not apply to an audit of financial statements based on the assumption of liquidation (for example, when [*a*] an entity is in the process of liquidation, [*b*] the owners have decided to commence dissolution or liquidation, or [*c*] legal proceedings, including bankruptcy, have reached a point at which dissolution or liquidation is probable).[2]

.02 Continuation of an entity as a going concern is assumed in financial reporting in the absence of significant information to the contrary. Ordinarily, information that significantly contradicts the going concern assumption relates to the entity's inability to continue to meet its obligations as they become due without substantial disposition of assets outside the ordinary course of business, restructuring of debt, externally forced revisions of its operations, or similar actions.

The Auditor's Responsibility

.03 The auditor's responsibility is to evaluate whether there is substantial doubt about the entity's ability to continue as a going concern for a reasonable period of time. The auditor's evaluation is based on the auditor's knowledge of relevant conditions or events that exist at, or have occurred prior to, the date of the auditor's report. Information about such conditions or events is obtained from the application of audit procedures planned and performed to achieve audit objectives that are related to management's assertions embodied in the

---

* This section contains has been codified using an "AU-C" identifier instead of an "AU" identifier. "AU-C" is a temporary identifier to avoid confusion with references to existing "AU" sections, which remain effective will remain in AICPA *Professional Standards* through 2013. The "AU-C" identifier will revert to "AU" in 2014, by which time this section becomes fully effective for all engagements substantially all engagements for which the "AU" sections were still effective are expected to be completed.

[1] *General purpose* and *special purpose frameworks* are defined in section 700, *Forming an Opinion and Reporting on Financial Statements*, and section 800, *Special Considerations—Audits of Financial Statements Prepared in Accordance With Special Purpose Frameworks*, respectively.

[2] See Interpretation No. 1, "Reporting on Financial Statements Prepared on a Liquidation Basis of Accounting," of section 700, (sec. 9700 par. .01–.05).

financial statements being audited, as described in section 315, *Understanding the Entity and Its Environment and Assessing the Risks of Material Misstatement*.

.04 As described in section 200, *Overall Objectives of the Independent Auditor and the Conduct of an Audit in Accordance With Generally Accepted Auditing Standards*, the potential effects of inherent limitations on the auditor's ability to detect material misstatements are particularly significant for future conditions or events that may cause an entity to cease to continue as a going concern. The auditor cannot predict such future conditions or events. The fact that the entity may cease to exist as a going concern subsequent to receiving a report from the auditor that does not refer to the auditor having substantial doubt, even within one year following the date of the financial statements, does not, in itself, indicate inadequate performance by the auditor. Accordingly, the absence of any reference to substantial doubt in an auditor's report cannot be viewed as a guarantee as to the entity's ability to continue as a going concern.

Effective Date

.05 This section is effective for audits of financial statements for periods ending on or after December 15, 2012.

Objectives

.06 The objectives of the auditor are to

a. evaluate and conclude, based on the audit evidence obtained, whether there is substantial doubt about the entity's ability to continue as a going concern for a reasonable period of time;

b. assess the possible financial statement effects, including the adequacy of disclosure regarding uncertainties about the entity's ability to continue as a going concern for a reasonable period of time; and

c. determine the implications for the auditor's report.

Definition

.07 For purposes of this section, the following term has the meaning attributed as follows:

Reasonable period of time. A period of time not to exceed one year beyond the date of the financial statements being audited.

Requirements

Evaluating Whether Substantial Doubt Exists

.08 The auditor should evaluate whether there is substantial doubt about the entity's ability to continue as a going concern for a reasonable period of time based on the results of the audit procedures performed pursuant to paragraphs .09–.11 and .14 of this section.

Identifying Conditions or Events That Indicate Substantial Doubt Could Exist (Ref: par. .A1–.A2)

.09 The auditor should consider whether the results of the procedures performed during the course of the audit identify conditions or events that, when considered in the aggregate, indicate there could be substantial doubt about the entity's ability to continue as a going concern for a reasonable period of time. The auditor should consider the need to obtain additional information about such conditions or events, as well as the appropriate audit evidence to support information that mitigates the auditor's doubt.

Consideration of Management's Plans When the Auditor Believes There Is Substantial Doubt

.10 If, after considering the identified conditions or events in the aggregate, the auditor believes there is substantial doubt about the entity's ability to continue as a going concern for a reasonable period of time, the auditor should obtain information about management's plans that are intended to mitigate the adverse effects of such conditions or events. The auditor should

a. assess whether it is likely that the adverse effects would be mitigated by management's plans for a reasonable period of time;

b. identify those elements of management's plans that are particularly significant to overcoming the adverse effects of the conditions or events and plan and perform procedures to obtain audit evidence about them, including, when applicable, considering the adequacy of support regarding the ability to obtain additional financing or the planned disposal of assets; and

c. assess whether it is likely that such plans can be effectively implemented. (Ref: par. .A3)

.11 When prospective financial information is particularly significant to management's plans, the auditor should request management to provide that information and should consider the adequacy of support for significant assumptions underlying that information. The auditor should give particular attention to assumptions that are

- material to the prospective financial information.
- especially sensitive or susceptible to change.
- inconsistent with historical trends.

The auditor's consideration should be based on knowledge of the entity, its business, and its management and should include (*a*) reading the prospective financial information and the underlying assumptions and (*b*) comparing prospective financial information from prior periods with actual results and comparing prospective information for the current period with results achieved to date. If the auditor becomes aware of factors, the effects of which are not reflected in such prospective financial information, the auditor should discuss those factors with management and, if necessary, request revision of the prospective financial information.

Consideration of Financial Statement Effects (Ref: par. .A4)

.12 When, after considering management's plans, the auditor concludes there is substantial doubt about the entity's ability to continue as a going concern for a reasonable period of time, the auditor should consider the possible effects on the financial statements and the adequacy of the related disclosure.

.13 When the auditor concludes, primarily because of the auditor's consideration of management's plans, that substantial doubt about the entity's ability to continue as a going concern for a reasonable period of time has been alleviated, the auditor should consider the need for, and evaluate the adequacy of, disclosure of the principal conditions or events that initially caused the auditor to believe there was substantial doubt. The auditor's consideration of disclosure should include the possible effects of such conditions or events, and any mitigating factors, including management's plans.

Written Representations (Ref: par. .A5)

.14 If the auditor believes, before consideration of management's plans pursuant to paragraph .10 of this section, there is substantial doubt about the entity's ability to continue as a going concern for a reasonable period of time, the auditor should obtain written representations from management

a. regarding its plans that are intended to mitigate the adverse effects of conditions or events that indicate there is substantial doubt about the entity's ability to continue as a going concern for a reasonable period of time and the likelihood that those plans can be effectively implemented, and

b. that the financial statements disclose all the matters of which management is aware that are relevant to the entity's ability to continue as a going concern, including principal conditions or events and management's plans.

Consideration of the Effects on the Auditor's Report (Ref: par. .A6–.A8)

.15 If, after considering identified conditions or events and management's plans, the auditor concludes that substantial doubt about the entity's ability to continue as a going concern for a reasonable period of time remains, the auditor should include an emphasis-of-matter paragraph[3] in the auditor's report to reflect that conclusion.

.16 The auditor's conclusion about the entity's ability to continue as a going concern should be expressed through the use of the phrase "substantial doubt about its (the entity's) ability to continue as a going concern" or similar wording that includes the terms *substantial doubt* and *going concern*. In a going-concern emphasis-of-matter paragraph, the auditor should not use conditional language in expressing a conclusion concerning the existence of substantial doubt about the entity's ability to continue as a going concern.

.17 If the auditor concludes that the entity's disclosures with respect to the entity's ability to continue as a going concern for a reasonable period of time are inadequate, the auditor should modify the opinion in accordance with section 705, *Modifications to the Opinion in the Independent Auditor's Report*.

.18 Nothing in this section precludes an auditor from disclaiming an opinion in cases involving uncertainties. When the auditor disclaims an opinion, the report should not include the going-concern emphasis-of-matter paragraph described in paragraph .15 of this section but, rather, describe the substantive reasons for the auditor's disclaimer of opinion in the auditor's report as required by section 705.[4] The auditor should consider the adequacy of disclosure of the uncertainties and their possible effects on the financial statements as described in paragraph .12 of this section even when disclaiming an opinion.

---

[3] Paragraphs .06–.07 of section 706, *Emphasis-of-Matter Paragraphs and Other-Matter Paragraphs in the Independent Auditor's Report*, address requirements concerning emphasis-of-matter paragraphs.

[4] Paragraph .17 of section 705, *Modifications to the Opinion in the Independent Auditor's Report*.

Communication With Those Charged With Governance

.19 If, after considering identified conditions or events in the aggregate and after considering management's plans, the auditor concludes that substantial doubt about the entity's ability to continue as a going concern for a reasonable period of time remains, the auditor should communicate the following to those charged with governance:

a. The nature of the conditions or events identified

b. The possible effect on the financial statements and the adequacy of related disclosures in the financial statements

c. The effects on the auditor's report

Comparative Presentations

.20 If substantial doubt about the entity's ability to continue as a going concern for a reasonable period of time existed at the date of prior period financial statements that are presented on a comparative basis, and that doubt has been removed in the current period, the going-concern emphasis-of-matter paragraph included in the auditor's report on the financial statements of the prior period should not be repeated. (Ref: par. .A9)

Eliminating a Going-Concern Emphasis-of-Matter Paragraph From a Reissued Report (Ref: par. .A10–.A11)

.21 The auditor may be requested to reissue an auditor's report and eliminate a going-concern emphasis-of-matter paragraph contained therein. Although an auditor has no obligation to reissue the report, if the auditor decides to reissue the report, the auditor should reassess the going-concern status of the entity by

a. performing audit procedures related to the event or transaction that prompted the request to reissue the report without the going-concern emphasis-of-matter paragraph.

b. performing the procedures listed in section 560, *Subsequent Events and Subsequently Discovered Facts*, at or near the date of reissuance.[5]

c. considering the matters described in paragraphs .09–.11 and .14 of this section based on the conditions or circumstances at the date of reissuance.

d. considering the implications for the auditor's report in accordance with section 560.[6]

Documentation

.22 If the auditor believes, before consideration of management's plans pursuant to paragraph .10 of this section, there is substantial doubt about the ability of the entity to continue as a going concern for a reasonable period of time, the auditor should document the following:

a. The conditions or events that led the auditor to believe that there is substantial doubt about the entity's ability to continue as a going concern for a reasonable period of time.

---

[5] Paragraphs .09–.10 of section 560, *Subsequent Events and Subsequently Discovered Facts*.

[6] Paragraph .13 of section 560.

b. The elements of management's plans that the auditor considered to be particularly significant to overcoming the adverse effects of the conditions or events.

c. The audit procedures performed to evaluate the significant elements of management's plans and evidence obtained.

d. The auditor's conclusion as to whether substantial doubt about the entity's ability to continue as a going concern for a reasonable period of time remains or is alleviated. If substantial doubt remains, the auditor also should document the possible effects of the conditions or events on the financial statements and the adequacy of the related disclosures. If substantial doubt is alleviated, the auditor also should document the auditor's conclusion as to the need for, and, if applicable, the adequacy of, disclosure of the principal conditions or events that initially caused the auditor to believe there was substantial doubt.

e. The auditor's conclusion with respect to the effects on the auditor's report.

Application and Other Explanatory Material

Evaluating Whether Substantial Doubt Exists

Identifying Conditions or Events That Indicate Substantial Doubt Could Exist (Ref: par. .09)

.A1 It is not necessary to design audit procedures solely to identify conditions or events that, when considered in the aggregate, indicate there could be substantial doubt about the entity's ability to continue as a going concern for a reasonable period of time. The results of audit procedures designed and performed to identify and assess risk in accordance with section 315, gather audit evidence in response to assessed risks in accordance with section 330, *Performing Audit Procedures in Response to Assessed Risks and Evaluating the Audit Evidence Obtained*, and complete the audit are expected to be sufficient for that purpose. The following are examples of procedures that may identify such conditions or events:

- Analytical procedures
- Review of subsequent events
- Review of compliance with the terms of debt and loan agreements
- Reading of minutes of meetings of stockholders, board of directors, and important committees of the board
- Inquiry of an entity's legal counsel about litigation, claims, and assessments
- Confirmation with related and third parties of the details of arrangements to provide or maintain financial support

.A2 In performing audit procedures such as those described in paragraph .A1 of this section, the auditor may identify information about certain conditions or events that, when considered in the aggregate, indicate there could be substantial doubt about the entity's ability to continue as a going concern for a reasonable period of time. The significance of such conditions or events will depend on the circumstances, and some conditions or events may have significance only when viewed in conjunction with others. The following are examples of such conditions or events:

- *Negative trends*—for example, recurring operating losses, working capital deficiencies, negative cash flows from operating activities, adverse key financial ratios
- *Other indications of possible financial difficulties*—for example, default on loan or similar agreements, arrearages in dividends, denial of usual trade credit from suppliers, restructuring of debt, noncompliance with statutory capital requirements, need to seek new sources or methods of financing or to dispose of substantial assets
- *Internal matters*—for example, work stoppages or other labor difficulties, substantial dependence on the success of a particular project, uneconomic long-term commitments, need to significantly revise operations
- *External matters that have occurred*—for example, legal proceedings, legislation, or similar matters that might jeopardize an entity's ability to operate; loss of a key franchise, license, or patent; loss of a principal customer or supplier; uninsured or underinsured catastrophe such as a drought, earthquake, or flood

Consideration of Management's Plans When the Auditor Believes There Is Substantial Doubt (Ref: par. .10)

.A3 The auditor's considerations relating to management's plans may include the following:

- Plans to dispose of assets
  - — Restrictions on disposal of assets, such as covenants limiting such transactions in loan or similar agreements or encumbrances against assets
  - — Apparent marketability of assets that management plans to sell
  - — Possible direct or indirect effects of disposal of assets
- Plans to borrow money or restructure debt
  - — Availability of debt financing, including existing or committed credit arrangements, such as lines of credit or arrangements for factoring receivables or sale-leaseback of assets
  - — Existing or committed arrangements to restructure or subordinate debt or to guarantee loans to the entity
  - — Possible effects on management's borrowing plans of existing restrictions on additional borrowing or the sufficiency of available collateral
- Plans to reduce or delay expenditures
  - — Apparent feasibility of plans to reduce overhead or administrative expenditures, to postpone maintenance or research and development projects, or to lease rather than purchase assets

— Possible direct or indirect effects of reduced or delayed expenditures

- Plans to increase ownership equity

— Apparent feasibility of plans to increase ownership equity, including existing or committed arrangements to raise additional capital

— Existing or committed arrangements to reduce current dividend requirements or to accelerate cash distributions from affiliates or other investors

Consideration of Financial Statement Effects (Ref: par. .12–.13)

.A4 In considering the adequacy of disclosure, some of the information that might be disclosed includes the following:

- Principal conditions or events giving rise to the assessment of substantial doubt about the entity's ability to continue as a going concern for a reasonable period of time
- The possible effects of such conditions or events
- Management's evaluation of the significance of those conditions or events and any mitigating factors
- Possible discontinuance of operations
- Management's plans (including relevant prospective financial information)
- Information about the recoverability or classification of recorded asset amounts or the amounts or classification of liabilities

Written Representations (Ref: par. .14)

.A5 If the auditor determines that it is necessary to obtain one or more representations with respect to identified conditions or events that indicate there could be substantial doubt about the entity's ability to continue as a going concern for a reasonable period of time pursuant to paragraph .09 of this section, section 580, *Written Representations*, applies.[7]

Consideration of the Effects on the Auditor's Report (Ref: par. .15–.18)

.A6 The inclusion of a going-concern emphasis-of-matter paragraph in the auditor's report is sufficient to inform the users of the financial statements that substantial doubt exists about the entity's ability to continue as a going concern for a reasonable period of time. The following is an illustration of a going-concern emphasis-of-matter paragraph when the auditor concludes that there is substantial doubt about the entity's ability to continue as a going concern for a reasonable period of time:

> Emphasis of Matter Regarding Going Concern
>
> The accompanying financial statements have been prepared assuming that the Company will continue as a going concern. As discussed in Note X to the financial statements, the Company has suffered recurring losses from operations

---

[7] Paragraph .19 of AU-C section 580, *Written Representations*.

and has a net capital deficiency that raise substantial doubt about its ability to continue as a going concern. Management's plans in regard to these matters are also described in Note X. The financial statements do not include any adjustments that might result from the outcome of this uncertainty. Our opinion is not modified with respect to this matter.

.A7 Examples of conditional language that is inappropriate to use in the emphasis-of-matter paragraph include the following:

- "If the Company continues to suffer recurring losses from operations and continues to have a net capital deficiency, there may be substantial doubt about its ability to continue as a going concern."
- "The Company has been unable to renegotiate its expiring credit agreements. Unless the Company is able to obtain financial support, there is substantial doubt about its ability to continue as a going concern."

.A8 Disclaiming an opinion, rather than expressing an opinion and including a going-concern emphasis-of-matter paragraph in the auditor's report, does not obviate the need for disclosure in the auditor's report of the matter giving rise to the disclaimer.

Comparative Presentations (Ref: par. .20)

.A9 Substantial doubt about the entity's ability to continue as a going concern for a reasonable period of time that arose in the current period does not imply that a basis for such doubt existed in the prior period and, therefore, does not affect the auditor's report on the financial statements of the prior period that are presented on a comparative basis. section 700, *Forming an Opinion and Reporting on Financial Statements*, provides guidance on reporting when financial statements of one or more prior periods are presented on a comparative basis with financial statements of the current period.

Eliminating a Going-Concern Emphasis-of-Matter Paragraph From a Reissued Report (Ref: par. .21)

.A10 After the auditor has issued the auditor's report containing a going-concern emphasis-of-matter paragraph, the auditor may be asked to reissue the auditor's report on the financial statements and eliminate the going-concern emphasis-of-matter paragraph that appeared in the original report. Such requests ordinarily occur after the conditions or events that gave rise to substantial doubt about the entity's ability to continue as a going concern for a reasonable period of time have been resolved. For example, subsequent to the date of the auditor's original report, an entity might obtain needed financing.

.A11 The auditor may perform procedures in addition to those required by paragraph .21 of this section that the auditor deems necessary in the circumstances when reassessing the entity's ability to continue as a going concern for a reasonable period of time.

AU-C Section 580 *

Written Representations

Source: SAS No. 122.

Effective for audits of financial statements for periods ending on or after December 15, 2012.

Introduction

Scope of This Section

.01 This section addresses the auditor's responsibility to obtain written representations from management and, when appropriate, those charged with governance in an audit of financial statements.

.02 Exhibit D, "List of AU-C Sections Containing Requirements for Written Representations," lists other AU-C sections containing subject matter-specific requirements for written representations. The specific requirements for written representations of other AU-C sections do not limit the application of this section.

Written Representations as Audit Evidence

.03 *Audit evidence* is the information used by the auditor in arriving at the conclusions on which the auditor's opinion is based.[1] Written representations are necessary information that the auditor requires in connection with the audit of the entity's financial statements. Accordingly, similar to responses to inquiries, written representations are audit evidence. (Ref: par. .A1)

.04 Although written representations provide necessary audit evidence, they complement other auditing procedures and do not provide sufficient appropriate audit evidence on their own about any of the matters with which they deal. Furthermore, obtaining reliable written representations does not affect the nature or extent of other audit procedures that the auditor applies to obtain audit evidence about the fulfillment of management's responsibilities or about specific assertions.

Effective Date

.05 This section is effective for audits of financial statements for periods ending on or after December 15, 2012.

---

* This section has been codified using an "AU-C" identifier instead of an "AU" identifier. "AU-C" is a temporary identifier to avoid confusion with references to existing "AU" sections, which will remain in AICPA *Professional Standards* through 2013. The "AU-C" identifier will revert to "AU" in 2014, by which time substantially all engagements for which the "AU" sections were still effective are expected to be completed.

[1] Paragraph .05 of section 500, *Audit Evidence*.

Objectives

.06 The objectives of the auditor are to

a. obtain written representations from management and, when appropriate, those charged with governance that they believe that they have fulfilled their responsibility for the preparation and fair presentation of the financial statements and for the completeness of the information provided to the auditor;

b. support other audit evidence relevant to the financial statements or specific assertions in the financial statements by means of written representations if determined necessary by the auditor or required by other AU-C sections; and

c. respond appropriately to written representations provided by management and, when appropriate, those charged with governance or if management or, when appropriate, those charged with governance do not provide the written representations requested by the auditor.

Definition

.07 For purposes of generally accepted auditing standards, the following term has the meaning attributed as follows:

Written representation. A written statement by management provided to the auditor to confirm certain matters or to support other audit evidence. Written representations in this context do not include financial statements, the assertions therein, or supporting books and records.

.08 For purposes of this section, references to *management* are to be read as "management and, when appropriate, those charged with governance" unless the context suggests otherwise.

Requirements

Management From Whom Written Representations Are Requested

.09 The auditor should request written representations from management with appropriate responsibilities for the financial statements and knowledge of the matters concerned. (Ref: par. .A2–.A6)

Written Representations About Management's Responsibilities

Preparation and Fair Presentation of the Financial Statements

.10 The auditor should request management to provide a written representation that it has fulfilled its responsibility, as set out in the terms of the audit engagement,

a. for the preparation and fair presentation of the financial statements in accordance with the applicable financial reporting framework; and

b. for the design, implementation, and maintenance of internal control relevant to the preparation and fair presentation of financial statements that are free from material misstatement, whether due to fraud or error.[2] (Ref: par. .A7–.A10, .A22, and .A29)

Information Provided and Completeness of Transactions

.11 The auditor should request management to provide written representations that

a. it has provided the auditor with all relevant information and access, as agreed upon in the terms of the audit engagement, and

b. all transactions have been recorded and are reflected in the financial statements. (Ref: par. .A7–.A10, .A22, and .A29)

Other Written Representations

Fraud

.12 The auditor should request management to provide written representations that it

a. acknowledges its responsibility for the design, implementation, and maintenance of internal controls to prevent and detect fraud;

b. has disclosed to the auditor the results of its assessment of the risk that the financial statements may be materially misstated as a result of fraud;

c. has disclosed to the auditor its knowledge of fraud or suspected fraud affecting the entity involving

   i. management,

   ii. employees who have significant roles in internal control, or

   iii. others when the fraud could have a material effect on the financial statements; and

d. has disclosed to the auditor its knowledge of any allegations of fraud or suspected fraud affecting the entity's financial statements communicated by employees, former employees, regulators, or others. (Ref: par. .A11)

Laws and Regulations

.13 The auditor should request management to provide written representations that all instances of identified or suspected noncompliance with laws and regulations whose effects should be considered by management when preparing financial statements have been disclosed to the auditor.[3]

Uncorrected Misstatements

.14 The auditor should request management to provide written representations about whether it believes the effects of uncorrected misstatements are immaterial, individually and in the aggregate, to the financial statements as a whole. A summary of such items should be included in, or attached to, the written representation. (Ref: par. .A12)

---

[2] Paragraph .06*b*(i–ii) of section 210, *Terms of Engagement*.

[3] Paragraph .A18 of section 250, *Consideration of Laws and Regulations in an Audit of Financial Statements*.

Litigation and Claims

.15 The auditor should request management to provide written representations that all known actual or possible litigation and claims whose effects should be considered by management when preparing the financial statements have been disclosed to the auditor and accounted for and disclosed in accordance with the applicable financial reporting framework.

Estimates

.16 The auditor should request management to provide written representations about whether it believes significant assumptions used by it in making accounting estimates are reasonable. (Ref: par. .A13–.A14)

Related Party Transactions

.17 The auditor should request management to provide written representations that (Ref: par. .A15–.A16)

a. it has disclosed to the auditor the identity of the entity's related parties and all the related party relationships and transactions of which it is aware and

b. it has appropriately accounted for and disclosed such relationships and transactions.

Subsequent Events

.18 The auditor should request management to provide written representations that all events occurring subsequent to the date of the financial statements and for which the applicable financial reporting framework requires adjustment or disclosure have been adjusted or disclosed. (Ref: par. .A17)

Additional Written Representations About the Financial Statements

.19 Other AU-C sections require the auditor to request written representations. If, in addition to such required representations, the auditor determines that it is necessary to obtain one or more written representations to support other audit evidence relevant to the financial statements or one or more specific assertions in the financial statements, the auditor should request such other written representations. (Ref: par. .A18–.A22 and .A29)

Date of, and Period(s) Covered by, Written Representations

.20 The date of the written representations should be as of the date of the auditor's report on the financial statements. The written representations should be for all financial statements and period(s) referred to in the auditor's report. (Ref: par. .A23–.A26)

Form of Written Representations

.21 The written representations should be in the form of a representation letter addressed to the auditor. (Ref: par. .A27–.A28)

Doubt About the Reliability of Written Representations and Requested Written Representations Not Provided

Doubt About the Reliability of Written Representations

.22 If the auditor has concerns about the competence, integrity, ethical values, or diligence of management or about management's commitment to, or enforcement of, these, the auditor should determine the effect that such concerns may have on the reliability of representations (oral or written) and audit evidence in general. (Ref: par. .A30)

.23 In particular, if written representations are inconsistent with other audit evidence, the auditor should perform audit procedures to attempt to resolve the matter. If the matter remains unresolved, the auditor should reconsider the assessment of the competence, integrity, ethical values, or diligence of management or of management's commitment to, or enforcement of, these and should determine the effect that this may have on the reliability of representations (oral or written) and audit evidence in general. (Ref: par. .A31)

.24 If the auditor concludes that the written representations are not reliable, the auditor should take appropriate action, including determining the possible effect on the opinion in the auditor's report in accordance with section 705, *Modifications to the Opinion in the Independent Auditor's Report*, considering the requirement in paragraph .25 of this section.

Written Representations About Management's Responsibilities

.25 The auditor should disclaim an opinion on the financial statements in accordance with section 705 or withdraw from the engagement if (Ref: par. .A32–.A33)

a. the auditor concludes that sufficient doubt exists about the integrity of management such that the written representations required by paragraphs .10–.11 are not reliable or

b. management does not provide the written representations required by paragraphs .10–.11.

Requested Written Representations Not Provided

.26 If management does not provide one or more of the requested written representations, the auditor should

a. discuss the matter with management;

b. reevaluate the integrity of management and evaluate the effect that this may have on the reliability of representations (oral or written) and audit evidence in general; and

c. take appropriate actions, including determining the possible effect on the opinion in the auditor's report in accordance with section 705, considering the requirement in paragraph .25 of this section. (Ref: par. .A34)

Application and Other Explanatory Material

Written Representations as Audit Evidence (Ref: par. .03)

.A1 Written representations are an important source of audit evidence. If management modifies or does not provide the requested written representations, it may alert the auditor to the possibility that one or more significant issues may exist. Further, a request for written rather than oral representations, in many cases, may prompt management to consider such matters more rigorously, thereby enhancing the quality of the representations.

Management From Whom Written Representations Are Requested (Ref: par. .09)

.A2 Written representations are requested from those with overall responsibility for financial and operating matters whom the auditor believes are responsible for, and knowledgeable about, directly or through others in the organization, the matters covered by the representations, including the preparation and fair presentation of the financial statements. Those individuals may vary depending on the governance structure of the entity; however, management (rather than those charged with governance) is often the responsible party. Written representations may therefore be requested from the entity's chief executive officer and chief financial officer or other equivalent persons in entities that do not use such titles. In some circumstances, however, other parties, such as those charged with governance, also are responsible for the preparation and fair presentation of the financial statements.

.A3 Due to its responsibility for the preparation and fair presentation of the financial statements and its responsibility for the conduct of the entity's business, management would be expected to have sufficient knowledge of the process followed by the entity in preparing the financial statements and the assertions therein on which to base the written representations.

.A4 In some cases, however, management may decide to make inquiries of others who participate in preparing the financial statements and assertions therein, including individuals who have specialized knowledge relating to the matters about which written representations are requested. Such individuals may include the following:

- An actuary responsible for actuarially determined accounting measurements
- Staff engineers who may have responsibility for environmental liability measurements
- Internal counsel who may provide information essential to provisions for legal claims

.A5 To reinforce the need for management to make informed representations, the auditor may request that management include in the written representations confirmation that it has made such inquiries as it considered appropriate to place it in the position to be able to make the requested written representations. It is not expected that such inquiries would usually require a formal internal process beyond those already established by the entity.

.A6 In some cases, management may include in the written representations qualifying language to the effect that representations are made to the best of its knowledge and belief. It is reasonable for the auditor to accept such wording if, in the auditor's professional judgment, the representations are being made by those with appropriate responsibilities and knowledge of the matters included in the representations.

Written Representations About Management's Responsibilities (Ref: par. .10–.11)

.A7 Audit evidence obtained during the audit that management has fulfilled the responsibilities referred to in paragraphs .10–.11 is not sufficient without obtaining confirmation from management that it believes that it has fulfilled those responsibilities. This is because the auditor is not able to judge solely on other audit evidence whether management has prepared and fairly presented the financial statements and provided information to the auditor on the basis of the agreed acknowledgment and understanding of its responsibilities. For example, the auditor could not conclude that management has provided the auditor with all relevant information agreed upon in the terms of the audit engagement without asking management whether, and receiving confirmation that, such information has been provided.

.A8 The written representations required by paragraphs .10–.11 draw on the agreed acknowledgment and understanding of management of its responsibilities in the terms of the audit engagement by requesting confirmation that it has fulfilled them. In addition to requesting management to confirm that it has fulfilled its responsibilities, the auditor also may ask management to reconfirm its acknowledgment and understanding of those responsibilities in written representations. This is common but, in any event, may be particularly appropriate when

- those who signed the terms of the audit engagement on behalf of the entity no longer have the relevant responsibilities,
- the terms of the audit engagement were prepared in a previous year,
- any indication exists that management misunderstands those responsibilities, or
- changes in circumstances make it appropriate to do so.

Consistent with the requirement of section 210, *Terms of Engagement*, such reconfirmation of management's acknowledgment and understanding of its responsibilities is unconditional and is not made subject to the best of management's knowledge and belief (as discussed in paragraph .A6 of this section).

.A9 Relevant information may include such matters as the following:

- Completeness and availability of all minutes of meetings of stockholders, directors, and committees of directors or summaries of actions of recent meetings for which minutes have not yet been prepared
- Communications from regulatory agencies concerning noncompliance with, or deficiencies in, financial reporting practices

Considerations Specific to Governmental Entities

.A10 The legal or regulatory requirements for audits of the financial statements of governmental entities may be broader than those of other entities. As a result, the premise, relating to management's responsibilities, on which an audit of the financial statements of a governmental entity is conducted may give rise to additional written representations. These may include written representations confirming that transactions and events have been carried out in accordance with applicable law or regulation.

Other Written Representations

Fraud (Ref: par. .12)

.A11 The written representations relating to fraud required by paragraph .12 are important for the auditor to obtain, regardless of the size of the entity, because of the nature of fraud and the difficulties encountered by auditors in detecting material misstatements in the financial statements resulting from fraud.

Uncorrected Misstatements (Ref: par. .14)

.A12 Because the preparation of the financial statements requires management to adjust the financial statements to correct material misstatements, the auditor is required to request management to provide a written representation about uncorrected misstatements. In some circumstances, management may not believe that certain uncorrected misstatements are misstatements. For that reason, management may want to add to their written representation words such as "We do not agree that items . . . and . . . constitute misstatements because [*description of reasons*]." Obtaining this representation does not, however, relieve the auditor of the need to form a conclusion on the effect of uncorrected misstatements in accordance with section 450, *Evaluation of Misstatements Identified During the Audit*.

Estimates (Ref: par. .16)

.A13 Depending on the nature, materiality, and extent of estimation uncertainty, written representations about accounting estimates recognized or disclosed in the financial statements may include representations

- about the appropriateness of the measurement processes, including related assumptions and models, used by management in determining accounting estimates in the context of the applicable financial reporting framework and the consistency in the application of the processes.
- that the assumptions appropriately reflect management's intent and ability to carry out specific courses of action on behalf of the entity when relevant to the accounting estimates and disclosures.
- that disclosures related to accounting estimates are complete and appropriate under the applicable financial reporting framework.
- that no subsequent event has occurred that would require adjustment to the accounting estimates and disclosures included in the financial statements.

.A14 For those accounting estimates not recognized or disclosed in the financial statements, written representations also may include representations about the following:

- The appropriateness of the basis used by management for determining that the criteria of the applicable financial reporting framework for recognition or disclosure have not been met[4]
- The appropriateness of the basis used by management to overcome a presumption relating to the use of fair value set forth under the entity's applicable financial reporting framework for those accounting estimates not measured or disclosed at fair value

Related Parties (Ref: par. .17)

.A15 Circumstances in which it may be appropriate to obtain written representations about related parties from those charged with governance in addition to management include the following:

- When they have approved specific related party transactions that (*a*) materially affect the financial statements or (*b*) involve management

---

[4] Paragraph .A121 of section 540, *Auditing Accounting Estimates, Including Fair Value Accounting Estimates, and Related Disclosures.*

- When they have made specific oral representations to the auditor on details of certain related party transactions
- When they have financial or other interests in the related parties or the related party transactions

.A16 The auditor also may decide to obtain written representations regarding specific assertions that management may have made, such as a representation that specific related party transactions do not involve undisclosed side agreements.

Subsequent Events (Ref: par. .18)

.A17 Section 560, *Subsequent Events and Subsequently Discovered Facts*, addresses circumstances when the auditor includes an additional date on the auditor's report (that is, dual-dates the auditor's report for a revision relating to a subsequent event).[5] In such circumstances, the auditor may determine that obtaining additional representations relating to the subsequent event is appropriate.

Additional Written Representations About the Financial Statements (Ref: par. .19)

.A18 In addition to the written representations required by paragraphs .10–.18, the auditor may consider it necessary to request other written representations about the financial statements. Such written representations may supplement, but do not form part of, the written representations required by paragraphs .10–.18. They may include representations about the following:

- Whether the selection and application of accounting policies are appropriate
- Whether matters such as the following, when relevant under the applicable financial reporting framework, have been recognized, measured, presented, or disclosed in accordance with that framework:
  - Plans or intentions that may affect the carrying value or classification of assets and liabilities
  - Liabilities, both actual and contingent
  - Title to, or control over, assets and the liens or encumbrances on assets and assets pledged as collateral
- Aspects of laws, regulations, and contractual agreements that may affect the financial statements, including noncompliance

Exhibit B, "Illustrative Specific Written Representations," contains illustrations of additional representations that may be appropriate in certain situations.

Additional Written Representations About Information Provided to the Auditor

.A19 In addition to the written representation required by paragraph .11, the auditor may consider it necessary to request management to provide a written representation that it has communicated to the auditor all deficiencies in internal control of which management is aware.

---

[5] Paragraph .13 of section 560, *Subsequent Events and Subsequently Discovered Facts*.

Written Representations About Specific Assertions

.A20 When obtaining evidence about or evaluating judgments and intentions, the auditor may consider one or more of the following:

- The entity's past history in carrying out its stated intentions
- The entity's reasons for choosing a particular course of action
- The entity's ability to pursue a specific course of action
- The existence, or lack thereof, of any other information obtained during the course of the audit that may be inconsistent with management's judgment or intent

.A21 In addition, the auditor may consider it necessary to request management to provide written representations about specific assertions in the financial statements; in particular, to support an understanding that the auditor has obtained from other audit evidence of management's judgment or intent regarding, or the completeness of, a specific assertion. For example, if the intent of management is important to the valuation basis for investments, it may not be possible to obtain sufficient appropriate audit evidence without a written representation from management about its intentions. Although such written representations provide necessary audit evidence, they do not provide sufficient appropriate audit evidence on their own for that assertion.

Communicating a Threshold Amount (Ref: par. .10–.11 and .19)

.A22 Management's representations may be limited to matters that are considered either individually or collectively material to the financial statements, provided management and the auditor have reached an understanding on materiality for this purpose. Materiality may be different for different representations. A discussion of materiality may be included explicitly in the representation letter in either qualitative or quantitative terms. Materiality considerations do not apply to those representations that are not directly related to amounts included in the financial statements (for example, management's representations about the premise underlying the audit). In addition, because of the possible effects of fraud on other aspects of the audit, materiality would not apply to management's acknowledgment regarding its responsibility for the design, implementation, and maintenance of internal control to prevent and detect fraud.

Date of, and Period(s) Covered by, Written Representations (Ref: par. .20)

.A23 Because written representations are necessary audit evidence, the auditor's opinion cannot be expressed, and the auditor's report cannot be dated, before the date of the written representations. Furthermore, because the auditor is concerned with events occurring up to the date of the auditor's report that may require adjustment to, or disclosure in, the financial statements, the written representations are dated as of the date of the auditor's report on the financial statements.

.A24 In some circumstances, it may be appropriate for the auditor to obtain a written representation about a specific assertion in the financial statements during the course of the audit. When this is the case, it may be necessary to request an updated written representation.

.A25 The written representations cover all periods referred to in the auditor's report because management needs to reaffirm that the written representations it previously made with respect to the prior periods remain appropriate.

The auditor and management may agree to a form of written representation that updates written representations relating to the prior periods by addressing whether there are any changes to such written representations and, if so, what they are.

.A26 Situations may arise in which current management was not present during all periods referred to in the auditor's report. Such persons may assert that they are not in a position to provide some or all of the written representations because they were not in place during the period. This fact, however, does not diminish such persons' responsibilities for the financial statements as a whole. Accordingly, the requirement for the auditor to request from them written representations that cover the whole of the relevant period(s) still applies.

Form of Written Representations (Ref: par. .21)

.A27 Occasionally, circumstances may prevent management from signing the representation letter and returning it to the auditor on the date of the auditor's report. In those circumstances, the auditor may accept management's oral confirmation, on or before the date of the auditor's report, that management has reviewed the final representation letter and will sign the representation letter without exception as of the date of the auditor's report thereby providing sufficient appropriate audit evidence for the auditor to date the report. However, possession of the signed management representation letter prior to releasing the auditor's report is necessary because paragraph .21 requires that the representations be in the form of a written letter from management. Furthermore, when there are delays in releasing the report, a fact may become known to the auditor that, had it been known to the auditor at the date of the auditor's report, might affect the auditor's report and result in the need for updated representations. Section 560 addresses the auditor's responsibilities in such circumstances.

.A28 Exhibit A, "Illustrative Representation Letter," provides an illustrative example of a representation letter.

Communication With Those Charged With Governance (Ref: par. .10–.11 and .19)

.A29 Section 260, *The Auditor's Communication With Those Charged With Governance*, requires the auditor to communicate with those charged with governance the written representations that the auditor has requested from management.[6]

Doubt About the Reliability of Written Representations and Requested Written Representations Not Provided

Doubt About the Reliability of Written Representations (Ref: par. .22–.23)

.A30 Concerns about the competence, integrity, ethical values, or diligence of management or about its commitment to, or enforcement of, these may cause the auditor to conclude that the risk of management misrepresentation in the financial statements is such that an audit cannot be conducted. In such a case, the auditor may consider withdrawing from the engagement, when withdrawal

---

[6] Paragraph .14*d* of section 260, *The Auditor's Communication With Those Charged With Governance*.

is possible under applicable law or regulation, unless those charged with governance put in place appropriate corrective measures. Such measures, however, may not be sufficient to enable the auditor to issue an unmodified audit opinion.

.A31 In the case of identified inconsistencies between one or more written representations and audit evidence obtained from another source, the auditor may consider whether the risk assessment remains appropriate and, if not, may revise the risk assessment and determine the nature, timing, and extent of further audit procedures to respond to the assessed risks.

Written Representations About Management's Responsibilities (Ref: par. .25)

.A32 As explained in paragraph .A7, the auditor is not able to judge solely on other audit evidence whether management has fulfilled the responsibilities referred to in paragraphs .10–.11. Therefore, if, as described in paragraph .25*a*, the auditor concludes that the written representations about these matters are unreliable or if management does not provide those written representations, the auditor is unable to obtain sufficient appropriate audit evidence. The possible effects on the financial statements of such inability are not confined to specific elements, accounts, or items of the financial statements and are hence pervasive. Section 705 requires the auditor to disclaim an opinion on the financial statements in such circumstances.[7]

.A33 A written representation that has been modified from that requested by the auditor does not necessarily mean that management did not provide the written representation. However, the underlying reason for such modification may affect the opinion in the auditor's report. For example

- the written representation about management's fulfillment of its responsibility for the preparation and fair presentation of the financial statements may state that management believes that, except for material noncompliance with a particular requirement of the applicable financial reporting framework, the financial statements are prepared and fairly presented in accordance with that framework. The requirement in paragraph .25 does not apply because the auditor concluded that management has provided reliable written representations. However, the auditor is required to consider the effect of the noncompliance on the opinion in the auditor's report in accordance with section 705.
- the written representation about the responsibility of management to provide the auditor with all relevant information agreed upon in the terms of the audit engagement may state that management believes that, except for information destroyed in a fire, it has provided the auditor with such information. The requirement in paragraph .25 does not apply because the auditor concluded that management has provided reliable written representations. However, the auditor is required to consider the effects of the pervasiveness of the information destroyed in the fire on the financial statements and the effect thereof on the opinion in the auditor's report in accordance with section 705.

Requested Written Representations Not Provided (Ref: par. .26)

.A34 Management's refusal to furnish written representations constitutes a limitation on the scope of the audit. Such refusal is often sufficient to preclude

---

[7] Paragraph .10 of section 705, *Modifications to the Opinion in the Independent Auditor's Report*.

an unmodified opinion and, in particular with respect to the representations in paragraphs .12–.18, may cause an auditor to disclaim an opinion or withdraw from the engagement when withdrawal is possible under applicable law or regulation. However, based on the nature of the representations not obtained or the circumstances of the refusal, the auditor may conclude that a qualified opinion is appropriate.

.A35

Exhibit A—Illustrative Representation Letter

The following illustrative letter includes written representations that are required by this and other AU-C sections in effect for audits of financial statements for periods ending on or after December 15, 2012. It is assumed in this illustration that the applicable financial reporting framework is accounting principles generally accepted in the United States, that the requirement in section 570, *The Auditor's Consideration of an Entity's Ability to Continue as a Going Concern*, to obtain a written representation is not relevant, and that no exceptions exist to the requested written representations. If there were exceptions, the representations would need to be modified to reflect the exceptions.

(Entity Letterhead)

(To Auditor)

(Date)

This representation letter is provided in connection with your audit of the financial statements of ABC Company, which comprise the balance sheet as of December 31, 20XX, and the related statements of income, changes in stockholders' equity, and cash flows for the year then ended, and the related notes to the financial statements, for the purpose of expressing an opinion on whether the financial statements are presented fairly, in all material respects, in accordance with accounting principles generally accepted in the United States (U.S. GAAP).

Certain representations in this letter are described as being limited to matters that are material. Items are considered material, regardless of size, if they involve an omission or misstatement of accounting information that, in the light of surrounding circumstances, makes it probable that the judgment of a reasonable person relying on the information would be changed or influenced by the omission or misstatement.

Except where otherwise stated below, immaterial matters less than $[*insert amount*] collectively are not considered to be exceptions that require disclosure for the purpose of the following representations. This amount is not necessarily indicative of amounts that would require adjustment to or disclosure in the financial statements.

We confirm that [, *to the best of our knowledge and belief, having made such inquiries as we considered necessary for the purpose of appropriately informing ourselves*] [*as of (date of auditor's report),*]:

Financial Statements

- We have fulfilled our responsibilities, as set out in the terms of the audit engagement dated [*insert date*], for the preparation and fair presentation of the financial statements in accordance with U.S. GAAP. (par. .10*a*)
- We acknowledge our responsibility for the design, implementation, and maintenance of internal control relevant to the preparation and fair presentation of financial statements that are free from material misstatement, whether due to fraud or error. (par. .10*b*)
- We acknowledge our responsibility for the design, implementation, and maintenance of internal control to prevent and detect fraud. (par. .12*a*)

- Significant assumptions used by us in making accounting estimates, including those measured at fair value, are reasonable. (par. .16)
- Related party relationships and transactions have been appropriately accounted for and disclosed in accordance with the requirements of U.S. GAAP. (par. .17*b*)
- All events subsequent to the date of the financial statements and for which U.S. GAAP requires adjustment or disclosure have been adjusted or disclosed. (par. .18)
- The effects of uncorrected misstatements are immaterial, both individually and in the aggregate, to the financial statements as a whole. A list of the uncorrected misstatements is attached to the representation letter. (par. .14)
- The effects of all known actual or possible litigation and claims have been accounted for and disclosed in accordance with U.S. GAAP. (par. .15)

[*Any other matters that the auditor may consider appropriate (see paragraph .A21).*]

Information Provided

- We have provided you with:
  - — Access to all information, of which we are aware that is relevant to the preparation and fair presentation of the financial statements such as records, documentation and other matters; (par. .11*a*)
  - — Additional information that you have requested from us for the purpose of the audit; (par. .11*a*) and
  - — Unrestricted access to persons within the entity from whom you determined it necessary to obtain audit evidence. (par. .11*a*)
- All transactions have been recorded in the accounting records and are reflected in the financial statements. (par. .11*b*)
- We have disclosed to you the results of our assessment of the risk that the financial statements may be materially misstated as a result of fraud. (par. .12*b*)
- We have [*no knowledge of any*] [*disclosed to you all information that we are aware of regarding*] fraud or suspected fraud that affects the entity and involves:
  - — Management;
  - — Employees who have significant roles in internal control; or
  - — Others when the fraud could have a material effect on the financial statements (par. .12*c*)
- We have [*no knowledge of any*] [*disclosed to you all information that we are aware of regarding*] allegations of fraud, or suspected fraud, affecting the entity's financial statements communicated by employees, former employees, analysts, regulators or others. (par. .12*d*)

- We have disclosed to you all known instances of non-compliance or suspected non-compliance with laws and regulations whose effects should be considered when preparing financial statements. (par. .13)
- We [*have disclosed to you all known actual or possible*] [*are not aware of any pending or threatened*] litigation, claims, and assessments whose effects should be considered when preparing the financial statements [and we have not consulted legal counsel concerning litigation, claims, or assessments] (par. .15)
- We have disclosed to you the identity of the entity's related parties and all the related party relationships and transactions of which we are aware. (par. .17*a*)

[*Any other matters that the auditor may consider necessary (see paragraph .A21).*]

____

[*Name of Chief Executive Officer and Title*]

____

[*Name of Chief Financial Officer and Title*]

[Revised, March 2012, to reflect conforming changes necessary due to the issuance of SAS No. 122. Revised, August 2012, to reflect conforming changes necessary due to the issuance of SAS No. 126.]

.A36

Exhibit B—Illustrative Specific Written Representations

As discussed in paragraph .19, the auditor may determine that a specific written representation is necessary to corroborate other audit evidence. Certain AICPA Audit and Accounting Guides recommend that the auditor obtain written representations concerning matters that are unique to a particular industry. The following is a list of additional representations that may be appropriate in certain situations. This list is not intended to be all-inclusive. The existence of a condition listed subsequently does not mean that the representation is required; professional judgment is necessary to determine whether corroborative audit evidence in the form of a specific written representation is necessary.

Condition	*Illustrative Specific Written Representation*
General	
Unaudited interim information accompanies the financial statements.	The unaudited interim financial information accompanying [*presented in Note X to*] the financial statements for the [*identify all related periods*] has been prepared and fairly presented in conformity with generally accepted accounting principles applicable to interim financial information. The accounting principles used to prepare the unaudited interim financial information are consistent with those used to prepare the audited financial statements.
The effect of a new accounting principle is not known.	We have not completed the process of evaluating the effect that will result from adopting the guidance in Financial Accounting Standards Board (FASB) Accounting Standards Update 20YY-XX, as discussed in Note [*X*]. The company is therefore unable to disclose the effect that adopting the guidance in FASB Accounting Standards Update 20YY-XX will have on its financial position and the results of operations when such guidance is adopted.
Financial circumstances are strained, with disclosure of management's intentions and the entity's ability to continue as a going concern.	Note [*X*] to the financial statements discloses all of the matters of which we are aware that are relevant to the company's ability to continue as a going concern, including significant conditions and events, and management's plans.
The possibility exists that the value of specific significant long-lived assets or certain identifiable intangibles may be impaired.	We have reviewed long-lived assets and certain identifiable intangibles to be held and used for impairment whenever events or changes in circumstances have indicated that the carrying amount of the assets might not be recoverable and have appropriately recorded the adjustment.

(continued)

Condition	*Illustrative Specific Written Representation*
General	
The entity has a variable interest in another entity.	Variable interest entities (VIEs) and potential VIEs and transactions with VIEs and potential VIEs have been properly recorded and disclosed in the financial statements in accordance with generally accepted accounting principles. We have considered both implicit and explicit variable interests in (*a*) determining whether potential VIEs should be considered VIEs, (*b*) calculating expected losses and residual returns, and (*c*) determining which party, if any, is the primary beneficiary. We have provided you with lists of all identified variable interests in (i) VIEs, (ii) potential VIEs that we considered but judged not to be VIEs, and (iii) entities that were afforded the scope exceptions of Financial Accounting Standards Board (FASB) *Accounting Standards Codification*™ (ASC) 810, *Consolidation*. We have advised you of all transactions with identified VIEs, potential VIEs, or entities afforded the scope exceptions of FASB ASC 810. We have made available all relevant information about financial interests and contractual arrangements with related parties, de facto agents and other entities, including but not limited to, their governing documents, equity and debt instruments, contracts, leases, guarantee arrangements, and other financial contracts and arrangements. The information we provided about financial interests and contractual arrangements with related parties, de facto agents and other entities includes information about all transactions, unwritten understandings, agreement modifications, and written and oral side agreements. Our computations of expected losses and expected residual returns of entities that are VIEs and potential VIEs are based on the best information available and include all reasonably possible outcomes. Regarding entities in which the company has variable interests (implicit and explicit), we have provided all information

Condition	*Illustrative Specific Written Representation*
General	
	about events and changes in circumstances that could potentially cause reconsideration about whether the entities are VIEs or whether the company is the primary beneficiary or has a significant variable interest in the entity. We have made and continue to make exhaustive efforts to obtain information about entities in which the company has an implicit or explicit interest but that were excluded from complete analysis under FASB ASC 810 due to lack of essential information to determine one or more of the following: whether the entity is a VIE, whether the company is the primary beneficiary, or the accounting required to consolidate the entity.
The work of a specialist has been used by the entity.	We agree with the findings of specialists in evaluating the [*describe assertion*] and have adequately considered the qualifications of the specialist in determining the amounts and disclosures used in the financial statements and underlying accounting records. We did not give or cause any instructions to be given to specialists with respect to the values or amounts derived in an attempt to bias their work, and we are not otherwise aware of any matters that have had an effect on the independence or objectivity of the specialists.
Assets	
Cash Disclosure is required of compensating balances or other arrangements involving restrictions on cash balances, lines of credit, or similar arrangements.	Arrangements with financial institutions involving compensating balances or other arrangements involving restrictions on cash balances, line of credit, or similar arrangements have been properly disclosed.
Financial Instruments Management intends to and has the ability to hold to maturity debt securities classified as held-to-maturity.	Debt securities that have been classified as held-to-maturity have been so classified due to the company's intent to hold such securities, to maturity and the company's ability to do so. All other debt securities have been classified as available-for-sale or trading.
Management considers the decline in value of debt or equity securities to be temporary.	We consider the decline in value of debt or equity securities classified as either available-for-sale or held-to-maturity to be temporary.

(continued)

Condition	*Illustrative Specific Written Representation*
Assets	
Management has determined the fair value of significant financial instruments that do not have readily determinable market values.	The methods and significant assumptions used to determine fair values of financial instruments are as follows: [*describe methods and significant assumptions used to determine fair values of financial instruments*]. The methods and significant assumptions used result in a measure of fair value appropriate for financial statement measurement and disclosure purposes.
Financial instruments with off-balance-sheet risk and financial instruments with concentrations of credit risk exist.	The following information about financial instruments with off-balance-sheet risk and financial instruments with concentrations of credit risk has been properly disclosed in the financial statements: 1. The extent, nature, and terms of financial instruments with off-balance-sheet risk 2. The amount of credit risk of financial instruments with off-balance-sheet risk and information about the collateral supporting such financial instruments 3. Significant concentrations of credit risk arising from all financial instruments and information about the collateral supporting such financial instruments
Investments Unusual considerations are involved in determining the application of equity accounting.	[*For investments in common stock that are either nonmarketable or of which the entity has a 20 percent or greater ownership interest, select the appropriate representation from the following:*] • The equity method is used to account for the company's investment in the common stock of [*investee*] because the company has the ability to exercise significant influence over the investee's operating and financial policies. • The cost method is used to account for the company's investment in the common stock of [*investee*] because the company does not have the ability to exercise significant influence over the investee's operating and financial policies.

Condition	Illustrative Specific Written Representation
Assets	
The entity had loans to executive officers, nonaccrued loans or zero interest rate loans.	Loans to executive officers have been properly accounted for and disclosed.
Liabilities	
Debt Short-term debt could be refinanced on a long-term basis and management intends to do so.	The company has excluded short-term obligations totaling $[*amount*] from current liabilities because it intends to refinance the obligations on a long-term basis. [*Complete with appropriate wording detailing how amounts will be refinanced as follows:*] • The company has issued a long-term obligation [*debt security*] after the date of the balance sheet but prior to the issuance of the financial statements for the purpose of refinancing the short-term obligations on a long-term basis. • The company has the ability to consummate the refinancing, by using the financing agreement referred to in Note [*X*] to the financial statements.
Tax-exempt bonds have been issued.	Tax-exempt bonds issued have retained their tax-exempt status.
Taxes Management intends to reinvest undistributed earnings of a foreign subsidiary.	We intend to reinvest the undistributed earnings of [*name of foreign subsidiary*].
Pension and Postretirement Benefits An actuary has been used to measure pension liabilities and costs.	We believe that the actuarial assumptions and methods used to measure pension liabilities and costs for financial accounting purposes are appropriate in the circumstances.
Involvement with a multiemployer plan exists.	We are unable to determine the possibility of a withdrawal liability in a multiemployer benefit plan. or We have determined that there is the possibility of a withdrawal liability in a multiemployer plan in the amount of $[*XX*].

(continued)

Condition	Illustrative Specific Written Representation
Liabilities	
Postretirement benefits have been eliminated.	We do not intend to compensate for the elimination of postretirement benefits by granting an increase in pension benefits. or We plan to compensate for the elimination of postretirement benefits by granting an increase in pension benefits in the amount of $[*XX*].
Employee layoffs that would otherwise lead to a curtailment of a benefit plan are intended to be temporary.	Current employee layoffs are intended to be temporary.
Management intends to either continue to make or not make frequent amendments to its pension or other postretirement benefit plans, which may affect the amortization period of prior service cost, or has expressed a substantive commitment to increase benefit obligations.	We plan to continue to make frequent amendments to the pension or other postretirement benefit plans, which may affect the amortization period of prior service cost. or We do not plan to make frequent amendments to the pension or other postretirement benefit plans.
Equity	
Capital stock repurchase options or agreements or capital stock reserved for options, warrants, conversions, or other requirements exist.	Capital stock repurchase options or agreements or capital stock reserved for options, warrants, conversions, or other requirements have been properly disclosed.

.A37

Exhibit C—Illustrative Updating Management Representation Letter

The following letter is presented for illustrative purposes only. It may be used in the circumstances described in paragraph .A17 of this section. Management need not repeat all of the representations made in the previous representation letter.

If matters to be disclosed to the auditor exist, they may be listed following the representation. For example, if an event subsequent to the date of the balance sheet has been disclosed in the financial statements, the final paragraph could be modified as follows: "To the best of our knowledge and belief, except as discussed in Note X to the financial statements, no events have occurred. . . ."

[*Date*]

To [*Auditor*]

In connection with your audit(s) of the [*identification of financial statements*] of [*name of entity*] as of [*dates*] and for the [*periods*] for the purpose of expressing an opinion as to whether the [*consolidated*] financial statements present fairly, in all material respects, the financial position, results of operations, and cash flows of [*name of entity*] in accordance with accounting principles generally accepted in the United States of America, you were previously provided with a representation letter under date of [*date of previous representation letter*]. No information has come to our attention that would cause us to believe that any of those previous representations should be modified.

To the best of our knowledge and belief, no events have occurred subsequent to [*date of latest balance sheet reported on by the auditor*] and through the date of this letter that would require adjustment to or disclosure in the aforementioned financial statements.

____

[*Name of Chief Executive Officer and Title*]

____

[*Name of Chief Financial Officer and Title*]

[Paragraph added, March 2012, to reflect conforming changes necessary due to the issuance of SAS No. 122.]

.A38

Exhibit D—List of AU-C Sections Containing Requirements for Written Representations

This exhibit identifies paragraphs in other AU-C sections that require specific written representations that may not be required for every audit. The list is not a substitute for considering the requirements and related application and other explanatory material in AU-C sections:

- Paragraph .19 of section 560, *Subsequent Events and Subsequently Discovered Facts*
- Paragraph .52 of section 700, *Forming an Opinion and Reporting on Financial Statements*
- Paragraph .07*g* of section 725, *Supplementary Information in Relation to the Financial Statements as a Whole*
- Paragraph .23 of section 935, *Compliance Audits*

In addition, certain AICPA Audit and Accounting Guides suggest written representations concerning matters that are unique to a particular industry.

[Paragraph renumbered, March 2012, to reflect conforming changes necessary due to the issuance of SAS No. 122.]

AU-C Section 585 *

Consideration of Omitted Procedures After the Report Release Date

Source: SAS No. 122.

Effective for audits of financial statements for periods ending on or after December 15, 2012.

Introduction

Scope of This Section

.01 This section addresses the auditor's responsibilities when, subsequent to the report release date, the auditor becomes aware that one or more auditing procedures that the auditor considered necessary in the circumstances existing at the time of the audit were omitted from the audit of the financial statements. Section 560, *Subsequent Events and Subsequently Discovered Facts*, is applicable when a fact becomes known to the auditor after the report release date that, had it been known to the auditor at that date, may have caused the auditor to revise the auditor's report.

.02 The provisions of this section do not apply to an engagement in which an auditor's work is at issue in a threatened or pending legal proceeding or regulatory investigation. A *threatened legal proceeding* means that a potential claimant has manifested to the auditor an awareness of, and a present intention to assert, a possible claim.

Effective Date

.03 This section is effective for audits of financial statements for periods ending on or after December 15, 2012.

Objectives

.04 The objectives of the auditor are to

a. assess the effect of omitted procedures of which the auditor becomes aware on the auditor's present ability to support the previously expressed opinion on the financial statements, and

b. respond appropriately.

Definition

.05 For purposes of generally accepted auditing standards, the following term has the meaning attributed as follows:

Omitted procedure. An auditing procedure that the auditor considered necessary in the circumstances existing at the time of the audit of the financial statements but which was not performed.

---

* This section has been codified using an "AU-C" identifier instead of an "AU" identifier. "AU-C" is a temporary identifier to avoid confusion with references to existing "AU" sections, which will remain in AICPA *Professional Standards* through 2013. The "AU-C" identifier will revert to "AU" in 2014, by which time substantially all engagements for which the "AU" sections were still effective are expected to be completed.

Requirements

.06 If, subsequent to the report release date, the auditor becomes aware of an omitted procedure, the auditor should assess the effect of the omitted procedure on the auditor's present ability to support the previously expressed opinion on the financial statements. (Ref: par. .A1–.A4)

.07 If the auditor concludes that an omitted procedure of which the auditor has become aware impairs the auditor's present ability to support a previously expressed opinion on the financial statements and the auditor believes that there are users currently relying, or likely to rely, on the previously released report, the auditor should promptly perform the omitted procedure, or alternative procedures, to determine whether there is a satisfactory basis for the auditor's previously expressed opinion. The auditor should include in the audit documentation the procedures performed, in accordance with the provisions of section 230, *Audit Documentation*.[1] (Ref: par. .A3–.A5)

.08 When, as a result of the subsequent performance of an omitted procedure or alternative procedures, the auditor becomes aware of facts regarding the financial statements that existed at the report release date that, had they been known to the auditor at that date, may have caused the auditor to revise the auditor's report, the auditor should apply the provisions of section 560.[2]

Application and Other Explanatory Material

.A1 The auditor's present ability to support the previously expressed opinion on the financial statements is dependent on whether the omitted procedure affects the auditor's conclusion that sufficient appropriate audit evidence was obtained. In accordance with section 200, *Overall Objectives of the Independent Auditor and the Conduct of an Audit in Accordance With Generally Accepted Auditing Standards*, the auditor is required to obtain sufficient appropriate audit evidence to reduce audit risk to an acceptably low level and thereby enable the auditor to draw reasonable conclusions on which to base the auditor's opinion.[3] (Ref: par. .06)

.A2 After the report release date, the auditor has no responsibility to carry out any retrospective review of the audit work performed. However, situations may arise in which the auditor becomes aware that an auditing procedure considered necessary by the auditor in the circumstances existing at the time of the audit was omitted. For example, after the report release date, reports and supporting audit documentation for particular engagements may be subjected to review in connection with a firm's inspection or monitoring process,[4] or otherwise, and the omission of a necessary audit procedure may be identified. (Ref: par. .06)

.A3 Procedures that the auditor may perform in connection with assessing the effect of an omitted procedure on the auditor's present ability to support a previously expressed opinion on financial statements include the following:

- Review of the audit documentation

---

[1] Paragraph .14 of section 230, *Audit Documentation*.

[2] Paragraphs .15–.18 of section 560, *Subsequent Events and Subsequently Discovered Facts*.

[3] Paragraph .19 of section 200, *Overall Objectives of the Independent Auditor and the Conduct of an Audit in Accordance With Generally Accepted Auditing Standards*.

[4] See QC section 10, *A Firm's System of Quality Control*, regarding inspection in the context of the monitoring element of quality control.

- Discussion of the circumstances with engagement personnel and others within the firm
- Reevaluation of the overall scope of the audit

The results of other audit procedures that were performed may tend to compensate for the omitted procedure or make the effect of its omission less significant. Additionally, subsequent audits may provide audit evidence in support of the previously expressed opinion. (Ref: par. .06–.07)

.A4 The period of time during which the auditor considers whether this section applies to the circumstances of a particular engagement and then takes the actions, if any, that are required hereunder may be important. Because of the legal implications that may be involved in taking the actions contemplated herein, the auditor may decide to seek legal advice in determining an appropriate course of action. (Ref: par. .06–.07)

.A5 If, in the circumstances addressed in paragraph .07, the auditor is unable to perform a previously omitted procedure, or alternative procedures, to determine that there is a satisfactory basis for the auditor's previously expressed opinion, the auditor may decide to seek legal advice to determine an appropriate course of action concerning the auditor's responsibilities to the entity; regulatory authorities, if any, having jurisdiction over the entity; and users relying, or likely to rely, on the auditor's report. (Ref: par. .07)

AU-C Sections 600–699

USING THE WORK OF OTHERS

TABLE OF CONTENTS

AU-C Section 600 *

Special Considerations—Audits of Group Financial Statements (Including the Work of Component Auditors)

Source: SAS No. 122; SAS No. 127.

Effective for audits of group financial statements for periods ending on or after December 15, 2012.

Introduction

Scope of This Section

.01 Generally accepted auditing standards (GAAS) apply to group audits. This section addresses special considerations that apply to group audits, in particular those that involve component auditors.

.02 An auditor may find this section, adapted as necessary in the circumstances, useful when that auditor involves other auditors in the audit of financial statements that are not group financial statements. For example, an auditor may involve another auditor to observe the inventory count or inspect physical fixed assets at a remote location.

.03 A component auditor may be required by law or regulation or may have been engaged by component management for another reason to express an audit opinion on the financial statements of a component. The requirements of this section apply, nonetheless, regardless of whether the group engagement partner decides to make reference to the component auditor in the auditor's report on the group financial statements or to assume responsibility for the work of component auditors.

.04 Governmental entities frequently prepare group financial statements. The AICPA Audit and Accounting Guide *State and Local Governments* provides guidance to assist auditors in auditing and reporting on those financial statements in accordance with GAAS, including the requirements of this section.

.05 In accordance with section 220, *Quality Control for an Engagement Conducted in Accordance With Generally Accepted Auditing Standards*, the group engagement partner is required to be satisfied that those performing the group audit engagement, including component auditors, collectively possess the appropriate competence and capabilities.[1] The group engagement partner also is responsible for the direction, supervision, and performance of the group audit engagement. In this section, requirements to be undertaken by the group engagement partner are addressed to the group engagement partner. When the

---

* This section has been codified using an "AU-C" identifier instead of an "AU" identifier. "AU-C" is a temporary identifier to avoid confusion with references to existing "AU" sections, which will remain in AICPA *Professional Standards* through 2013. The "AU-C" identifier will revert to "AU" in 2014, by which time substantially all engagements for which the "AU" sections were still effective are expected to be completed.

[1] Paragraph .16 of section 220, *Quality Control for an Engagement Conducted in Accordance With Generally Accepted Auditing Standards*.

group engagement team may assist the group engagement partner in fulfilling a requirement, the requirement is addressed to the group engagement team. When it may be appropriate in the circumstances for the firm to fulfill a requirement, the requirement is addressed to the auditor of the group financial statements.

.06 The requirements of section 220 apply regardless of whether the group engagement team or a component auditor performs the work on the financial information of a component. This section assists the group engagement partner to meet the requirements of section 220 when component auditors perform work on the financial information of components.

.07 Audit risk is a function of the risk of material misstatement of the financial statements and the risk that the auditor will not detect such misstatements.[2] In a group audit, detection risk includes the risk that a component auditor may not detect a misstatement in the financial information of a component that could cause a material misstatement of the group financial statements and the risk that the group engagement team may not detect this misstatement. This section explains the matters that the group engagement team considers when determining the nature, timing, and extent of its involvement in the risk assessment procedures and further audit procedures performed by the component auditors on the financial information of the components. The purpose of this involvement is to obtain sufficient appropriate audit evidence on which to base the audit opinion on the group financial statements.

.08 The group engagement partner is responsible for deciding, individually for each component, to either

- assume responsibility for, and thus be required to be involved in, the work of a component auditor, insofar as that work relates to the expression of an opinion on the group financial statements, or
- not assume responsibility for, and accordingly make reference to, the audit of a component auditor in the auditor's report on the group financial statements.

The requirements in paragraphs .51–.65 are applicable only when the auditor of the group financial statements is assuming responsibility for the work of component auditors. All other requirements in this section apply to all audits of group financial statements.

Effective Date

.09 This section is effective for audits of group financial statements for periods ending on or after December 15, 2012.

Objectives

.10 The objectives of the auditor are to determine whether to act as the auditor of the group financial statements and, if so, to

a. determine whether to make reference to the audit of a component auditor in the auditor's report on the group financial statements;

b. communicate clearly with component auditors; and

---

[2] Paragraph .A36 of section 200, *Overall Objectives of the Independent Auditor and the Conduct of an Audit in Accordance With Generally Accepted Auditing Standards.*

c. obtain sufficient appropriate audit evidence regarding the financial information of the components and the consolidation process to express an opinion about whether the group financial statements are prepared, in all material respects, in accordance with the applicable financial reporting framework.

Definitions

.11 For purposes of GAAS, the following terms have the meanings attributed as follows:

Component. An entity or business activity for which group or component management prepares financial information that is required by the applicable financial reporting framework to be included in the group financial statements. (Ref: par. .A1–.A5)

Component auditor. An auditor who performs work on the financial information of a component that will be used as audit evidence for the group audit. A component auditor may be part of the group engagement partner's firm, a network firm of the group engagement partner's firm, or another firm. (Ref: par. .A9–.A11)

Component management. Management responsible for preparing the financial information of a component.

Component materiality. The materiality for a component determined by the group engagement team for the purposes of the group audit.

Group. All the components whose financial information is included in the group financial statements. A group always has more than one component.

Group audit. The audit of group financial statements.

Group audit opinion. The audit opinion on the group financial statements.

Group engagement partner. The partner or other person in the firm[3] who is responsible for the group audit engagement and its performance and for the auditor's report on the group financial statements that is issued on behalf of the firm. When joint auditors conduct the group audit, the joint engagement partners and their engagement teams collectively constitute the group engagement partner and the group engagement team. This section does not, however, address the relationship between joint auditors or the work that one joint auditor performs in relation to the work of the other joint auditor.

Group engagement team. Partners, including the group engagement partner, and staff who establish the overall group audit strategy, communicate with component auditors, perform work on the consolidation process, and evaluate the conclusions drawn from the audit evidence as the basis for forming an opinion on the group financial statements.

Group financial statements. Financial statements that include the financial information of more than one component. The term *group financial statements* also refers to combined financial statements aggregating the financial information prepared by components that are under common control.

---

[3] *Group engagement partner* and *firm* refer to their governmental equivalents when relevant.

Group management. Management responsible for the preparation and fair presentation of the group financial statements.

Group-wide controls. Controls designed, implemented, and maintained by group management over group financial reporting.

Significant component. A component identified by the group engagement team (i) that is of individual financial significance to the group, or (ii) that, due to its specific nature or circumstances, is likely to include significant risks of material misstatement of the group financial statements. (Ref: par. .A6–.A8)

.12 Reference to *the applicable financial reporting framework* means the financial reporting framework that applies to the group financial statements. Reference to *the consolidation process* includes the following:

a. The recognition, measurement, presentation, and disclosure of the financial information of the components in the group financial statements by way of inclusion, consolidation, proportionate consolidation, or the equity or cost methods of accounting (Ref: par. .A12)

b. The aggregation in combined financial statements of the financial information of components that are under common control

Requirements

Responsibility

.13 In accordance with section 220, the group engagement partner is responsible for (1) the direction, supervision, and performance of the group audit engagement in compliance with professional standards, applicable regulatory and legal requirements, and the firm's policies and procedures; and (2) determining whether the auditor's report that is issued is appropriate in the circumstances.[4] (Ref: par. .A13–.A14)

Acceptance and Continuance

.14 The group engagement partner should determine whether sufficient appropriate audit evidence can reasonably be expected to be obtained regarding the consolidation process and the financial information of the components on which to base the group audit opinion. For this purpose, the group engagement team should obtain an understanding of the group, its components, and their environments that is sufficient to identify components that are likely to be significant components. (Ref: par. .A15–.A17)

.15 The group engagement partner should evaluate whether the group engagement team will be able to obtain sufficient appropriate audit evidence through the group engagement team's work or use of the work of component auditors (that is, through assuming responsibility for the work of component auditors or through making reference to the audit of a component auditor in the auditor's report), to act as the auditor of the group financial statements and report as such on the group financial statements. (Ref: par. .A18–.A21)

.16 In some circumstances, the group engagement partner may conclude that it will not be possible, due to restrictions imposed by group management, for the group engagement team to obtain sufficient appropriate audit evidence

---

[4] Paragraph .17 of section 220.

through the group engagement team's work or use of the work of component auditors, and the possible effect of this inability, will result in a disclaimer of opinion on the group financial statements.[5] In such circumstances, the auditor of the group financial statements should

- in the case of a new engagement, not accept the engagement, or, in the case of a continuing engagement, withdraw from the engagement when withdrawal is possible under applicable law or regulation, or
- when the entity is required by law or regulation to have an audit, having performed the audit of the group financial statements to the extent possible, disclaim an opinion on the group financial statements. (Ref: par. .A22–.A27)

Terms of Engagement

.17 The auditor of the group financial statements is required, in accordance with section 210, *Terms of Engagement*, to agree upon the terms of the group audit engagement.[6] (Ref: par. .A28–.A29)

Overall Audit Strategy and Audit Plan

.18 The group engagement team should establish an overall group audit strategy and should develop a group audit plan. In developing the group audit plan, the group engagement team should assess the extent to which the group engagement team will use the work of component auditors and whether the auditor's report on the group financial statements will make reference to the audit of a component auditor, as discussed in paragraphs .24–.30.

.19 The group engagement partner should review and approve the overall group audit strategy and group audit plan. (Ref: par. .A30)

Understanding the Group, Its Components, and Their Environments

.20 The auditor is required to identify and assess the risks of material misstatement through obtaining an understanding of the entity and its environment.[7] The group engagement team should

a. enhance its understanding of the group, its components, and their environments, including group-wide controls, obtained during the acceptance or continuance stage.

b. obtain an understanding of the consolidation process, including the instructions issued by group management to components. (Ref: par. .A31–.A37)

.21 The group engagement team should obtain an understanding that is sufficient to

a. confirm or revise its initial identification of components that are likely to be significant.

---

[5] Paragraphs .11–.14 of section 705, *Modifications to the Opinion in the Independent Auditor's Report*.

[6] Paragraph .09 of section 210, *Terms of Engagement*.

[7] See section 315, *Understanding the Entity and Its Environment and Assessing the Risks of Material Misstatement*.

b. assess the risks of material misstatement of the group financial statements, whether due to fraud or error.[8] (Ref: par. .A38–.A39)

Understanding a Component Auditor

.22 Regardless of whether reference will be made in the auditor's report on the group financial statements to the audit of a component auditor, the group engagement team should obtain an understanding of the following: (Ref: par. .A40–.A44)

a. Whether a component auditor understands and will comply with the ethical requirements that are relevant to the group audit and, in particular, is independent (Ref: par. .A46)

b. A component auditor's professional competence (Ref: par. .A47–.A48)

c. The extent, if any, to which the group engagement team will be able to be involved in the work of the component auditor

d. Whether the group engagement team will be able to obtain information affecting the consolidation process from a component auditor

e. Whether a component auditor operates in a regulatory environment that actively oversees auditors (Ref: par. .A45)

.23 When a component auditor does not meet the independence requirements that are relevant to the group audit or the group engagement team has serious concerns about the other matters listed in paragraph .22*a–b*, the group engagement team should obtain sufficient appropriate audit evidence relating to the financial information of the component without making reference to the audit of that component auditor in the auditor's report on the group financial statements or otherwise using the work of that component auditor. (Ref: par. .A49–.A51)

Determining Whether to Make Reference to a Component Auditor in the Auditor's Report on the Group Financial Statements

.24 Having gained an understanding of each component auditor, the group engagement partner should decide whether to make reference to a component auditor in the auditor's report on the group financial statements. (Ref: par. .A52)

.25 Reference to the audit of a component auditor in the auditor's report on the group financial statements should not be made unless

a. the group engagement partner has determined that the component auditor has performed an audit of the financial statements of the component in accordance with the relevant requirements of GAAS (Ref: par. .A53), and

b. the component auditor has issued an auditor's report that is not restricted as to use.[9]

[As amended, effective for audits of financial statements for periods ending on or after December 15, 2012, by SAS No. 127.]

---

[8] See section 315.

[9] See section 905, *Alert That Restricts the Use of the Auditor's Written Communication*. [Footnote revised, August 2012, to reflect conforming changes necessary due to the issuance of SAS No. 125.]

.26 If the component's financial statements are prepared using a different financial reporting framework from that used for the group financial statements, reference to the audit of a component auditor in the auditor's report on the group financial statements should not be made unless

a. the measurement, recognition, presentation, and disclosure criteria that are applicable to all material items in the component's financial statements under the financial reporting framework used by the component are similar to the criteria that are applicable to all material items in the group's financial statements under the financial reporting framework used by the group, and

b. the group engagement team has obtained sufficient appropriate audit evidence for purposes of evaluating the appropriateness of the adjustments to convert the component's financial statements to the financial reporting framework used by the group without the need to assume responsibility for, and, thus, be involved in, the work of the component auditor. (Ref: par. .A54–.A57)

[Paragraph added, effective for audits of financial statements for periods ending on or after December 15, 2012, by SAS No. 127.]

.27 When the group engagement partner decides to make reference in the auditor's report on the group financial statements to the audit of a component auditor, the group engagement team should obtain sufficient appropriate audit evidence with regard to such components by performing the following procedures:

a. The procedures required by this section, except for those required by paragraphs .51–.65

b. Reading the component's financial statements and the component auditor's report thereon to identify significant findings and issues and, when considered necessary, communicating with the component auditor in this regard

[Paragraph renumbered, effective for audits of financial statements for periods ending on or after December 15, 2012, by SAS No. 127.]

Making Reference in the Auditor's Report

.28 When the group engagement partner decides to make reference to the audit of a component auditor in the auditor's report on the group financial statements, the report on the group financial statements should clearly indicate

a. that the component was not audited by the auditor of the group financial statements but was audited by the component auditor.

b. the magnitude of the portion of the financial statements audited by the component auditor.

c. when the component's financial statements are prepared using a different financial reporting framework from that used for the group financial statements

   i. the financial reporting framework used by the component and

   ii. that the auditor of the group financial statements is taking responsibility for evaluating the appropriateness of the adjustments to convert the component's financial statements to the financial reporting framework used by the group.

d. when

i. the component auditor's report on the component's financial statements does not state that the audit of the component's financial statements was performed in accordance with GAAS or the standards promulgated by the PCAOB, and

ii. the group engagement partner has determined that the component auditor performed additional audit procedures in order to meet the relevant requirements of GAAS

(1) the set of auditing standards used by the component auditor and

(2) that additional audit procedures were performed by the component auditor to meet the relevant requirements of GAAS. (Ref: par. .A58–.A60)

[Paragraph renumbered and amended, effective for audits of financial statements for periods ending on or after December 15, 2012, by SAS No. 127.]

.29 If the group engagement partner decides to name a component auditor in the auditor's report on the group financial statements

a. the component auditor's express permission should be obtained.

b. the component auditor's report should be presented together with that of the auditor's report on the group financial statements.

[Paragraph renumbered, effective for audits of financial statements for periods ending on or after December 15, 2012, by SAS No. 127.]

.30 If the opinion of a component auditor is modified or that report includes an emphasis-of-matter or other-matter paragraph, the auditor of the group financial statements should determine the effect that this may have on the auditor's report on the group financial statements. When deemed appropriate, the auditor of the group financial statements should modify the opinion on the group financial statements or include an emphasis-of-matter paragraph or an other-matter paragraph in the auditor's report on the group financial statements. (Ref: par. .A61) [Paragraph renumbered, effective for audits of financial statements for periods ending on or after December 15, 2012, by SAS No. 127.]

.31 If the group engagement partner decides to assume responsibility for work of a component auditor, no reference should be made to the component auditor in the auditor's report on the group financial statements. (Ref: par. .A62) [Paragraph renumbered, effective for audits of financial statements for periods ending on or after December 15, 2012, by SAS No. 127.]

Materiality

.32 The group engagement team should determine the following: (Ref: par. .A63)

a. Materiality, including performance materiality, for the group financial statements as a whole when establishing the overall group audit strategy.[10]

b. Whether, in the specific circumstances of the group, particular classes of transactions, account balances, or disclosures in the group financial statements exist for which misstatements of lesser amounts than materiality for the group financial statements as

---

[10] See section 320, *Materiality in Planning and Performing an Audit.*

a whole could reasonably be expected to influence the economic decisions of users taken on the basis of the group financial statements. In such circumstances, the group engagement team should determine materiality to be applied to those particular classes of transactions, account balances, or disclosures.

c. Component materiality for those components on which the group engagement team will perform, or for which the auditor of the group financial statements will assume responsibility for the work of a component auditor who performs, an audit or a review. Component materiality should be determined taking into account all components, regardless of whether reference is made in the auditor's report on the group financial statements to the audit of a component auditor. To reduce the risk that the aggregate of uncorrected and undetected misstatements in the group financial statements exceeds the materiality for the group financial statements as a whole, component materiality should be lower than the materiality for the group financial statements as a whole, and component performance materiality should be lower than performance materiality for the group financial statements as a whole. (Ref: par. .A64–.A66)

d. The threshold above which misstatements cannot be regarded as clearly trivial to the group financial statements. (Ref: par. .A67)

See paragraph .51 for additional requirements that apply when the auditor of the group financial statements is assuming responsibility for the work of a component auditor. [Paragraph renumbered and amended, effective for audits of financial statements for periods ending on or after December 15, 2012, by SAS No. 127.]

Responding to Assessed Risks

.33 The auditor is required to design and implement appropriate responses to address the assessed risks of material misstatement of the financial statements.[11] If the nature, timing, and extent of the work to be performed on the consolidation process or the financial information of the components is based on an expectation that group-wide controls are operating effectively or when substantive procedures alone cannot provide sufficient appropriate audit evidence at the assertion level, the group engagement team should test, or have a component auditor test on the group engagement team's behalf, the operating effectiveness of those controls. See paragraphs .52–.58 for additional requirements that apply when the auditor of the group financial statements is assuming responsibility for the work of a component auditor. (Ref: par. .A68) [Paragraph renumbered, effective for audits of financial statements for periods ending on or after December 15, 2012, by SAS No. 127.]

Consolidation Process

.34 In accordance with paragraph .20, the group engagement team obtains an understanding of group-wide controls and the consolidation process, including the instructions issued by group management to components. In accordance with paragraph .33, the group engagement team, or component auditor at the request of the group engagement team, tests the operating effectiveness of group-wide controls if the nature, timing, and extent of the work

---

[11] See section 330, *Performing Audit Procedures in Response to Assessed Risks and Evaluating the Audit Evidence Obtained.*

to be performed on the consolidation process are based on an expectation that group-wide controls are operating effectively or when substantive procedures alone cannot provide sufficient appropriate audit evidence at the assertion level. [Paragraph renumbered, effective for audits of financial statements for periods ending on or after December 15, 2012, by SAS No. 127.]

.35 The group engagement team should design and perform further audit procedures on the consolidation process to respond to the assessed risks of material misstatement of the group financial statements arising from the consolidation process. This should include evaluating whether all components have been included in the group financial statements. [Paragraph renumbered, effective for audits of financial statements for periods ending on or after December 15, 2012, by SAS No. 127.]

.36 The group engagement team should evaluate the appropriateness, completeness, and accuracy of consolidation adjustments and reclassifications and should evaluate whether any fraud risk factors or indicators of possible management bias exist. (Ref: par. .A69) [Paragraph renumbered, effective for audits of financial statements for periods ending on or after December 15, 2012, by SAS No. 127.]

.37 If the financial information of a component has not been prepared in accordance with the same accounting policies applied to the group financial statements, the group engagement team should evaluate whether the financial information of that component has been appropriately adjusted for purposes of the preparation and fair presentation of the group financial statements in accordance with the applicable financial reporting framework. (Ref: par. .A57) [Paragraph renumbered, effective for audits of financial statements for periods ending on or after December 15, 2012, by SAS No. 127.]

.38 The group engagement team should determine whether the financial information identified in a component auditor's communication (see paragraph .42*b*) is the financial information that is incorporated in the group financial statements. [Paragraph renumbered, effective for audits of financial statements for periods ending on or after December 15, 2012, by SAS No. 127.]

.39 If the group financial statements include the financial statements of a component with a financial reporting period-end that differs from that of the group, the group engagement team should evaluate whether appropriate adjustments have been made to those financial statements in accordance with the applicable financial reporting framework. [Paragraph renumbered, effective for audits of financial statements for periods ending on or after December 15, 2012, by SAS No. 127.]

Subsequent Events

.40 When the group engagement team or component auditors perform audits on the financial information of components, the group engagement team or the component auditors should perform procedures designed to identify events at those components that occur between the dates of the financial information of the components and the date of the auditor's report on the group financial statements and that may require adjustment to, or disclosure in, the group financial statements. See paragraph .59 for additional requirements that apply when the auditor of the group financial statements is assuming responsibility for the work of a component auditor. (Ref: par. .A70) [Paragraph renumbered, effective for audits of financial statements for periods ending on or after December 15, 2012, by SAS No. 127.]

Communication With a Component Auditor

.41 The group engagement team should communicate its requirements to a component auditor on a timely basis. This communication should include the following:

a. A request that the component auditor, knowing the context in which the group engagement team will use the work of the component auditor, confirm that the component auditor will cooperate with the group engagement team.

b. The ethical requirements that are relevant to the group audit and, in particular, the independence requirements.

c. A list of related parties prepared by group management and any other related parties of which the group engagement team is aware. The group engagement team should request the component auditor to communicate on a timely basis related parties not previously identified by group management or the group engagement team. The group engagement team should identify such additional related parties to other component auditors.

d. Identified significant risks of material misstatement of the group financial statements, due to fraud or error, that are relevant to the work of the component auditor.

[Paragraph renumbered, effective for audits of financial statements for periods ending on or after December 15, 2012, by SAS No. 127.]

.42 The group engagement team should request a component auditor to communicate matters relevant to the group engagement team's conclusion, with regard to the group audit. Such communication should include the following:

a. Whether the component auditor has complied with ethical requirements relevant to the group audit, including independence and professional competence

b. Identification of the financial information of the component on which the component auditor is reporting

c. The component auditor's overall findings, conclusions, or opinion

See paragraphs .60–.61 for additional requirements that apply when the auditor of the group financial statements is assuming responsibility for the work of a component auditor. [Paragraph renumbered, effective for audits of financial statements for periods ending on or after December 15, 2012, by SAS No. 127.]

Evaluating the Sufficiency and Appropriateness of Audit Evidence Obtained

Evaluating a Component Auditor's Communication and Adequacy of Their Work

.43 The group engagement team should evaluate a component auditor's communication (see paragraph .42). The group engagement team should discuss significant findings and issues arising from that evaluation with the component auditor, component management, or group management, as appropriate. See paragraphs .60–.63 for additional requirements that apply when the auditor of the group financial statements is assuming responsibility for the work of a component auditor. [Paragraph renumbered, effective for audits of financial statements for periods ending on or after December 15, 2012, by SAS No. 127.]

Sufficiency and Appropriateness of Audit Evidence

.44 The auditor is required to obtain sufficient appropriate audit evidence on which to base the audit opinion.[12] The group engagement team should evaluate whether sufficient appropriate audit evidence on which to base the group audit opinion has been obtained from the audit procedures performed on the consolidation process and the work performed by the group engagement team and the component auditors on the financial information of the components. (Ref: par. .A71) [Paragraph renumbered, effective for audits of financial statements for periods ending on or after December 15, 2012, by SAS No. 127.]

.45 The group engagement partner should evaluate the effect on the group audit opinion of any uncorrected misstatements (either identified by the group engagement team or communicated by component auditors) and any instances in which there has been an inability to obtain sufficient appropriate audit evidence. (Ref: par. .A72) [Paragraph renumbered, effective for audits of financial statements for periods ending on or after December 15, 2012, by SAS No. 127.]

Communication With Group Management and Those Charged With Governance of the Group

Communication With Group Management and Those Charged With Governance

.46 The group engagement team should communicate to group management and those charged with governance of the group material weaknesses and significant deficiencies in internal control that are relevant to the group (either identified by the group engagement team or brought to its attention by a component auditor during the audit), in accordance with section 265, *Communicating Internal Control Related Matters Identified in an Audit*. [Paragraph renumbered, effective for audits of financial statements for periods ending on or after December 15, 2012, by SAS No. 127.]

.47 If fraud has been identified by the group engagement team or brought to its attention by a component auditor or information indicates that a fraud may exist, the group engagement team should communicate this on a timely basis to the appropriate level of group management in order to inform those with primary responsibility for the prevention and detection of fraud of matters relevant to their responsibilities. (Ref: par. .A73) [Paragraph renumbered, effective for audits of financial statements for periods ending on or after December 15, 2012, by SAS No. 127.]

.48 When a component auditor has been engaged to express an audit opinion on the financial statements of a component, the group engagement team should request group management to inform component management of any matter of which the group engagement team becomes aware that may be significant to the financial statements of the component, but of which component management may be unaware. If group management refuses to communicate the matter to component management, the group engagement team should discuss the matter with those charged with governance of the group. If the matter remains unresolved, the group engagement team, subject to legal and professional confidentiality considerations, should consider whether to advise the component auditor not to issue the auditor's report on the financial statements of the component until the matter is resolved and whether to withdraw from the engagement. (Ref: par. .A74) [Paragraph renumbered, effective for audits of

[12] Paragraph .19 of section 200.

financial statements for periods ending on or after December 15, 2012, by SAS No. 127.]

Communication With Those Charged With Governance of the Group

.49 The group engagement team should communicate the following matters with those charged with governance of the group, in addition to those required by section 260, *The Auditor's Communication With Those Charged With Governance*, and other AU-C sections: (Ref: par. .A75)

a. An overview of the type of work to be performed on the financial information of the components, including the basis for the decision to make reference to the audit of a component auditor in the auditor's report on the group financial statements

b. An overview of the nature of the group engagement team's planned involvement in the work to be performed by the component auditors on the financial information of significant components

c. Instances in which the group engagement team's evaluation of the work of a component auditor gave rise to a concern about the quality of that auditor's work

d. Any limitations on the group audit (for example, when the group engagement team's access to information may have been restricted)

e. Fraud or suspected fraud involving group management, component management, employees who have significant roles in group-wide controls, or others in which a material misstatement of the group financial statements has or may have resulted from fraud

[Paragraph renumbered, effective for audits of financial statements for periods ending on or after December 15, 2012, by SAS No. 127.]

Documentation

.50 The group engagement team should include in the audit documentation the following:[13]

a. An analysis of components indicating those that are significant and the type of work performed on the financial information of the components

b. Those components for which reference to the reports of component auditors is made in the auditor's report on the group financial statements

c. Written communications between the group engagement team and the component auditors about the group engagement team's requirements

d. For those components for which reference is made in the auditor's report on the group financial statements to the audit of a component auditor

i. the financial statements of the component and the report of the component auditor thereon

---

[13] Paragraphs .08–.12 and .A8 of section 230, *Audit Documentation*.

ii. when the component auditor's report on the component's financial statements does not state that the audit of the component's financial statements was performed in accordance with GAAS or the standards promulgated by the PCAOB, the basis for the group engagement partner's determination that the audit performed by the component auditor met the relevant requirements of GAAS

See paragraph .65 for additional requirements that apply when the auditor of the group financial statements is assuming responsibility for the work of a component auditor. [Paragraph renumbered and amended, effective for audits of financial statements for periods ending on or after December 15, 2012, by SAS No. 127.]

Additional Requirements Applicable When Assuming Responsibility for the Work of a Component Auditor

Materiality (See paragraph .32)

.51 In the case of an audit of the financial information of a component in which the auditor of the group financial statements is assuming responsibility for the component auditor's work, the group engagement team should evaluate the appropriateness of performance materiality at the component level. (Ref: par. .A76–.A77) [Paragraph renumbered, effective for audits of financial statements for periods ending on or after December 15, 2012, by SAS No. 127.]

Determining the Type of Work to Be Performed on the Financial Information of Components (See paragraph .33)

.52 For components for which the auditor of the group financial statements is assuming responsibility for the work of component auditors, the group engagement team should determine the type of work to be performed by the group engagement team or by component auditors on its behalf on the financial information of the components (see paragraphs .53–.56). The group engagement team also should determine the nature, timing, and extent of its involvement in the work of component auditors. [Paragraph renumbered, effective for audits of financial statements for periods ending on or after December 15, 2012, by SAS No. 127.]

Significant Components

.53 For a component that is significant due to its individual financial significance to the group, the group engagement team, or a component auditor on its behalf, should perform an audit of the financial information of the component, adapted as necessary to meet the needs of the group engagement team, using component materiality. (Ref: par. .A78) [Paragraph renumbered, effective for audits of financial statements for periods ending on or after December 15, 2012, by SAS No. 127.]

.54 For a component that is significant not due to its individual financial significance but because it is likely to include significant risks of material misstatement of the group financial statements due to its specific nature or circumstances, the group engagement team, or a component auditor on its behalf, should perform one or more of the following: (Ref: par. .A79)

a. An audit, adapted as necessary to meet the needs of the group engagement team, of the financial information of the component, using component materiality

b. An audit, adapted as necessary to meet the needs of the group engagement team, of one or more account balances, classes of transactions, or disclosures relating to the likely significant risks of material misstatement of the group financial statements (Ref: par. .A80)

c. Specified audit procedures relating to the likely significant risks of material misstatement of the group financial statements (Ref: par. .A81)

[Paragraph renumbered, effective for audits of financial statements for periods ending on or after December 15, 2012, by SAS No. 127.]

Components That Are Not Significant Components

.55 For components that are not significant components, the group engagement team should perform analytical procedures at the group level. (Ref: par. .A82) [Paragraph renumbered, effective for audits of financial statements for periods ending on or after December 15, 2012, by SAS No. 127.]

.56 In some circumstances, the group engagement team may determine that sufficient appropriate audit evidence on which to base the group audit opinion will not be obtained from the following:

a. The work performed on the financial information of significant components

b. The work performed on group-wide controls and the consolidation process

c. The analytical procedures performed at group level

In such circumstances, the group engagement team should select additional components that are not significant components and should perform or request a component auditor to perform one or more of the following on the financial information of the individual components selected: (Ref: par. .A83–.A86)

- An audit, adapted as necessary to meet the needs of the group engagement team, of the financial information of the component, using component materiality
- An audit, adapted as necessary to meet the needs of the group engagement team, of one or more account balances, classes of transactions, or disclosures
- A review of the financial information of the component, adapted as necessary to meet the needs of the group engagement team, using component materiality
- Specified audit procedures

The group engagement team should vary the selection of such individual components over a period of time. [Paragraph renumbered, effective for audits of financial statements for periods ending on or after December 15, 2012, by SAS No. 127.]

Involvement in the Work Performed by Component Auditors (Ref: par. .A87–.A88)

Significant Components—Risk Assessment

.57 When a component auditor performs an audit or other specified audit procedures of the financial information of a significant component for which the auditor of the group financial statements is assuming responsibility for the component auditor's work, the group engagement team should be involved in the risk assessment of the component to identify significant risks of material misstatement of the group financial statements. The nature, timing, and extent of this involvement are affected by the group engagement team's understanding of the component auditor but, at a minimum, should include the following:

a. Discussing with the component auditor or component management the component's business activities of significance to the group.

b. Discussing with the component auditor the susceptibility of the component to material misstatement of the financial information due to fraud or error.

c. Reviewing the component auditor's documentation of identified significant risks of material misstatement of the group financial statements. Such documentation may take the form of a memorandum that reflects the component auditor's conclusion with regard to the identified significant risks.

[Paragraph renumbered, effective for audits of financial statements for periods ending on or after December 15, 2012, by SAS No. 127.]

Identified Significant Risks of Material Misstatement of the Group Financial Statements—Further Audit Procedures

.58 When significant risks of material misstatement of the group financial statements have been identified in a component for which the auditor of the group financial statements is assuming responsibility for the work of a component auditor, the group engagement team should evaluate the appropriateness of the further audit procedures to be performed to respond to the identified significant risks of material misstatement of the group financial statements. Based on its understanding of the component auditor, the group engagement team should determine whether it is necessary to be involved in the further audit procedures. [Paragraph renumbered, effective for audits of financial statements for periods ending on or after December 15, 2012, by SAS No. 127.]

Subsequent Events (See paragraph .40)

.59 When component auditors perform work other than audits of the financial information of components at the request of the group engagement team, the group engagement team should request the component auditors to notify the group engagement team if they become aware of events at those components that occur between the dates of the financial information of the components and the date of the auditor's report on the group financial statements that may require an adjustment to, or disclosure in, the group financial statements. [Paragraph renumbered, effective for audits of financial statements for periods ending on or after December 15, 2012, by SAS No. 127.]

Communication With a Component Auditor (See paragraph .42)

.60 When the auditor of the group financial statements is assuming responsibility for the work of a component auditor, the communication required in paragraph .41 should set out the work to be performed and the form and content of the component auditor's communication with the group engagement team. It also should include, in the case of an audit or review of the financial information of the component, component materiality (and the amount or amounts lower than the materiality for particular classes of transactions, account balances, or disclosures, if applicable) and the threshold above which misstatements cannot be regarded as clearly trivial to the group financial statements. (Ref: par. .A89–.A92) [Paragraph renumbered, effective for audits of financial statements for periods ending on or after December 15, 2012, by SAS No. 127.]

.61 When the auditor of the group financial statements is assuming responsibility for the work of a component auditor, the communication requested from the component auditor, as required in paragraph .42, also should include the following:

a. Whether the component auditor has complied with the group engagement team's requirements.

b. Information on instances of noncompliance with laws or regulations at the component or group level that could give rise to a material misstatement of the group financial statements.

c. Significant risks of material misstatement of the group financial statements, due to fraud or error, identified by the component auditor in the component and the component auditor's responses to such risks. The group engagement team should request the component auditor to communicate such significant risks on a timely basis.

d. A list of corrected and uncorrected misstatements of the financial information of the component (the list need not include misstatements that are below the threshold for clearly trivial misstatements communicated by the group engagement team).

e. Indicators of possible management bias regarding accounting estimates and the application of accounting principles.

f. Description of any identified material weaknesses and significant deficiencies in internal control at the component level.

g. Other significant findings and issues that the component auditor communicated or expects to communicate to those charged with governance of the component, including fraud or suspected fraud involving component management, employees who have significant roles in internal control at the component level, or others that resulted in a material misstatement of the financial information of the component.

h. Any other matters that may be relevant to the group audit or that the component auditor wishes to draw to the attention of the group engagement team, including exceptions noted in the written representations that the component auditor requested from component management.

[Paragraph renumbered, effective for audits of financial statements for periods ending on or after December 15, 2012, by SAS No. 127.]

Evaluating a Component Auditor's Communication and Adequacy of Their Work (See paragraph .43)

.62 The group engagement team should determine, based on the evaluation required in paragraph .43, whether it is necessary to review other relevant parts of a component auditor's audit documentation. (Ref: par. .A93) [Paragraph renumbered, effective for audits of financial statements for periods ending on or after December 15, 2012, by SAS No. 127.]

.63 If the group engagement team concludes that the work of a component auditor is insufficient, the group engagement team should determine additional procedures to be performed and whether they are to be performed by the component auditor or by the group engagement team. [Paragraph renumbered, effective for audits of financial statements for periods ending on or after December 15, 2012, by SAS No. 127.]

Communication With Group Management and Those Charged With Governance of the Group (See paragraphs .46–.49)

.64 The group engagement team should determine which material weaknesses and significant deficiencies in internal control that component auditors have brought to the attention of the group engagement team should be communicated to group management and those charged with governance of the group. [Paragraph renumbered, effective for audits of financial statements for periods ending on or after December 15, 2012, by SAS No. 127.]

Documentation (See paragraph .50)

.65 The group engagement team should include in the audit documentation the nature, timing, and extent of the group engagement team's involvement in the work performed by the component auditors on significant components, including, when applicable, the group engagement team's review of relevant parts of the component auditors' audit documentation and conclusions thereon. [Paragraph renumbered, effective for audits of financial statements for periods ending on or after December 15, 2012, by SAS No. 127.]

Application and Other Explanatory Material

Definitions

Component (Ref: par. .11)

.A1 The structure of a group affects how components are identified. For example, the group financial reporting system may be based on an organizational structure that provides for financial information to be prepared by a parent and one or more subsidiaries, joint ventures, or investees accounted for by the equity or cost methods of accounting; by a head office and one or more divisions or branches; or by a combination of both. Some groups, however, may organize their financial reporting system by function, process, product or service (or by groups of products or services), or geographical locations. In these cases, the entity or business activity for which group or component management prepares financial information that is included in the group financial statements may be a function, process, product or service (or group of products or services), or geographical location.

.A2 An investment accounted for under the equity method constitutes a component for purposes of this section. Investments accounted for under the cost method may be analogous to a component for purposes of this section when the work and reports of other auditors constitute a major element of evidence for such investments.

.A3 Various levels of components may exist within the group financial reporting system, in which case it may be more appropriate to identify components at certain levels of aggregation rather than individually.

.A4 Components aggregated at a certain level may constitute a component for purposes of the group audit; however, such a component also may prepare group financial statements that incorporate the financial information of the components it encompasses (that is, a subgroup). This section may, therefore, be applied by different group engagement partners and teams for different subgroups within a larger group.

Considerations Specific to Audits of Governmental Entities

.A5 In audits of state and local governments, a component may be a separate legal entity reported as a component unit or part of the governmental entity, such as a business activity, department, or program.

Significant Component (Ref: par. .11)

.A6 As the individual financial significance of a component increases, the risks of material misstatement of the group financial statements ordinarily increase. The group engagement team may apply a percentage to a chosen benchmark as an aid to identify components that are of individual financial significance. Identifying a benchmark and determining a percentage to be applied to it involve the exercise of professional judgment. Depending on the nature and circumstances of the group, appropriate benchmarks might include group assets, liabilities, cash flows, revenues, expenditures, or net income. For example, the group engagement team may consider that components exceeding a specified percentage of the chosen benchmark are significant components.

.A7 The group engagement team also may identify a component as likely to include significant risks of material misstatement of the group financial statements due to its specific nature or circumstances (that is, risks that require special audit consideration[14]). For example, a component could be responsible for foreign exchange trading and, thus, expose the group to a significant risk of material misstatement, even though the component is not otherwise of individual financial significance to the group.

Considerations Specific to Governmental Entities

.A8 In audits of governmental entities, appropriate quantitative benchmarks for identifying significant components might include net costs or total budget. Qualitative considerations in audits of governmental entities may involve matters of heightened public sensitivity, such as national security issues, donor funded projects, or reporting of tax revenue.

Component Auditor (Ref: par. .11)

.A9 For purposes of this section, auditors who do not meet the definition of a member of the group engagement team are considered to be component auditors. However, an auditor who performs work on a component when the group engagement team will not use that work to provide audit evidence for the group audit is not considered a component auditor.

.A10 When two or more component auditors exist, the provisions of this section are applicable to each component auditor.

.A11 A member of the group engagement team may perform work on the financial information of a component for the group audit at the request of the group engagement team. When this is the case, such a member of the group engagement team also is a component auditor.

Consolidation Process (Ref: par. .12)

Considerations Specific to Governmental Entities

.A12 In audits of state and local governments, the applicable financial reporting framework may be based on multiple reporting units. Therefore, the consolidation process may involve the inclusion, but separate presentation, of the financial statements of each reporting unit in the governmental entity.

---

[14] Paragraphs .28–.30 of section 315.

Responsibility (Ref: par. .13)

.A13 Component auditors may perform work on the financial information of the components for the group audit and, as such, are responsible for their overall findings, conclusions, or opinions. However, regardless of whether reference is made in the auditor's report on the group financial statements to the report of a component auditor, the auditor of the group financial statements is responsible for the group audit opinion.

Considerations Specific to Governmental Entities

.A14 When the auditor of the group financial statements is engaged to express opinions on both the group financial statements and the separate financial statements of the components presented in the group financial statements, the auditor's reporting responsibilities with respect to the separate financial statements are the same as the auditor's responsibilities with respect to the group financial statements.

Acceptance and Continuance

Obtaining an Understanding at the Acceptance or Continuance Stage (Ref: par. .14)

.A15 In the case of a new engagement, the group engagement team's understanding of the group, its components, and their environments may be obtained from the following:

- Information provided by group management
- Communication with group management
- When applicable, communication with the previous group engagement team, component management, or component auditors

.A16 The group engagement team's understanding may include matters such as the following:

- The group structure, including both the legal and organizational structure (that is, how the group financial reporting system is organized)
- Components' business activities that are significant to the group, including the industry and regulatory, economic, and political environments in which those activities take place
- The use of service organizations, including shared service centers
- A description of group-wide controls
- The complexity of the consolidation process
- Whether component auditors that are not from the group engagement partner's firm or network will perform work on the financial information of any of the components and group management's rationale for engaging more than one auditor, if applicable
- Whether the group engagement team
    - — will have unrestricted access to those charged with governance of the group, group management, those charged with governance of the component, component management, component information, and the component auditors (including relevant audit documentation sought by the group engagement team)

— will be able to perform necessary work on the financial information of the components

.A17 In the case of a continuing engagement, the group engagement team's ability to obtain sufficient appropriate audit evidence may be affected by significant changes, such as the following:

- Changes in the group structure (for example, acquisitions, disposals, reorganizations, or changes in how the group financial reporting system is organized)
- Changes in components' business activities that are significant to the group
- Changes in the composition of those charged with governance of the group, group management, or key management of significant components
- Concerns the group engagement team has with regard to the integrity and competence of group or component management
- Changes in group-wide controls
- Changes in the applicable financial reporting framework

Expectation to Obtain Sufficient Appropriate Audit Evidence (Ref: par. .15)

.A18 Relevant factors in determining whether to act as the auditor of the group financial statements include, among other things, the following:

- The individual financial significance of the components, as determined in accordance with the guidance in paragraph .A6, for which the auditor of the group financial statements will be assuming responsibility
- The extent to which significant risks of material misstatement of the group financial statements are included in the components for which the auditor of the group financial statements will be assuming responsibility
- The extent of the group engagement team's knowledge of the overall financial statements

.A19 A group may consist only of components not considered significant components. In these circumstances, the group engagement partner can reasonably expect to obtain sufficient appropriate audit evidence on which to base the group audit opinion if the group engagement team will be able to

a. perform the work on the financial information of some of these components.

b. use the work performed by component auditors on the financial information of other components to the extent necessary to obtain sufficient appropriate audit evidence.

.A20 When the auditor of the group financial statements is assuming responsibility for the work performed by a component auditor, the group engagement team is required by the provisions of this section to be involved in the work of the component auditor. Paragraph .27 describes the procedures to be followed to obtain sufficient appropriate audit evidence when the group engagement partner decides to make reference in the auditor's report on the group financial statements to the audit of a component auditor.

Considerations Specific to Governmental Entities

.A21 Additional factors in determining whether to act as the auditor of the group financial statements in audits of state and local governments include, the following:

- Engagement by the primary government as the auditor of the financial reporting entity
- Responsibility for auditing the primary government's general fund (or other primary operating fund)

Access to Information (Ref: par. .16)

.A22 The group engagement team's access to information may be restricted by group management, or it may be restricted by circumstances that cannot be overcome by group management (for example, laws relating to confidentiality and data privacy or denial by a component auditor of access to relevant audit documentation sought by the group engagement team).

.A23 When access to information is restricted by circumstances, the group engagement team may still be able to obtain sufficient appropriate audit evidence; however, this is less likely as the significance of the component increases. For example, the group engagement team may not have access to those charged with governance, management, or the auditor (including relevant audit documentation sought by the group engagement team) of a component that is accounted for by the equity method of accounting. If the component is not a significant component and the group engagement team has a complete set of financial statements of the component, including the auditor's report thereon, and has access to information kept by group management regarding that component, the group engagement team may conclude that this information constitutes sufficient appropriate audit evidence regarding that component. If the component is a significant component, however, and the auditor of the group financial statements is not making reference to the audit of a component auditor in the auditor's report on the group financial statements, then the group engagement team will not be able to comply with the requirements of this section that are relevant in the circumstances of the group audit. For example, the group engagement team will not be able to comply with the requirement in paragraphs .57–.58 to be involved in the work of a component auditor. Therefore, the group engagement team will not be able to obtain sufficient appropriate audit evidence regarding that component. The effect on the auditor's report of the group engagement team's inability to obtain sufficient appropriate audit evidence is considered in terms of section 705, *Modifications to the Opinion in the Independent Auditor's Report*.

.A24 The group engagement team will not be able to obtain sufficient appropriate audit evidence if group management restricts the access of the group engagement team or a component auditor to the information of a significant component.

.A25 Although the group engagement team may be able to obtain sufficient appropriate audit evidence if such restriction relates to a component considered not a significant component, the reason for the restriction may affect the group audit opinion. For example, it may affect the reliability of group management's responses to the group engagement team's inquiries and group management's representations to the group engagement team.

.A26 Section 210 addresses circumstances when an entity is required by law or regulation to have an audit.[15] In these circumstances, this section still applies to the group audit, and the effect of the group engagement team's inability to obtain sufficient appropriate audit evidence is considered in terms of section 705.

.A27 Exhibit A, "Illustrations of Auditor's Reports on Group Financial Statements," contains an example of an auditor's report containing a qualified opinion based on the group engagement team's inability to obtain sufficient appropriate audit evidence regarding a significant component accounted for by the equity method of accounting when, in the group engagement team's professional judgment, the effect is material but not pervasive.

Terms of Engagement (Ref: par. .17)

.A28 The terms of engagement identify the applicable financial reporting framework.[16] Additional matters that may be included in the terms of a group audit engagement include whether reference will be made to the audit of a component auditor in the auditor's report on the group financial statements, when relevant, or arrangements to facilitate the following:

- Unrestricted communication between the group engagement team and component auditors to the extent permitted by law or regulation
- Communication to the group engagement team of important communications between
  — the component auditors, those charged with governance of the component, and component management, including communications on significant deficiencies and material weaknesses in internal control
  — regulatory authorities and components related to financial reporting matters
- To the extent the group engagement team considers necessary
  — access to component information, those charged with governance of components, component management, and the component auditors (including relevant audit documentation sought by the group engagement team)
  — permission to perform work, or request a component auditor to perform work, on the financial information of the components

.A29 Certain restrictions imposed after acceptance of the group audit engagement result in an inability to obtain sufficient appropriate audit evidence that may affect the group audit opinion including, specifically, restrictions imposed on the following:

- The group engagement team's access to component information, those charged with governance of components, component management, or the component auditors (including relevant audit documentation sought by the group engagement team)

---

[15] Paragraphs .07 and .A19 of section 210.

[16] Paragraph .10 of section 210.

- The work to be performed on the financial information of the components

These restrictions may even lead to withdrawal from the engagement unless that is not possible under law or regulation. Section 705 addresses the auditor's responsibilities when management has imposed a limitation on the scope of the audit after the auditor has accepted the engagement.[17]

Overall Audit Strategy and Audit Plan (Ref: par. .19)

.A30 The group engagement partner's review of the overall group audit strategy and group audit plan is an important part of fulfilling the group engagement partner's responsibility for the direction of the group audit engagement.

Understanding the Group, Its Components, and Their Environments

Matters About Which the Group Engagement Team Obtains an Understanding (Ref: par. .20)

.A31 Section 315, *Understanding the Entity and Its Environment and Assessing the Risks of Material Misstatement*, contains guidance on matters the auditor may consider when obtaining an understanding of the industry, regulatory, and other external factors that affect the entity, including the applicable financial reporting framework; the nature of the entity; objectives and strategies and related business risks; and measurement and review of the entity's financial performance.[18] Appendix A, "Understanding the Group, Its Components, and Their Environments—Examples of Matters About Which the Group Engagement Team Obtains an Understanding," of this section contains guidance on matters specific to a group, including the consolidation process.

Instructions Issued by Group Management to Components (Ref: par. .20)

.A32 To achieve uniformity and comparability of financial information, group management ordinarily issues instructions to components. Such instructions specify the requirements for financial information of the components to be included in the group financial statements and often include financial reporting procedures manuals and a reporting package. A reporting package ordinarily consists of standard formats for providing financial information for incorporation in the group financial statements. Reporting packages generally do not, however, take the form of complete financial statements prepared and presented in accordance with the applicable financial reporting framework.

.A33 The instructions ordinarily cover the following:

- The accounting policies to be applied
- Statutory and other disclosure requirements applicable to the group financial statements, including the following:
  - — The identification and reporting of segments
  - — Related party relationships and transactions

---

[17] Paragraphs .11–.14 and .A15–.A16 of section 705.

[18] Paragraphs .A17–.A41 of section 315.

- — Intragroup transactions and unrealized profits or losses
- — Intragroup account balances
- A reporting timetable

.A34 The group engagement team's understanding of the instructions may include the following:

- The clarity and practicality of the instructions for completing the reporting package
- Whether the instructions
  - — adequately describe the characteristics of the applicable financial reporting framework
  - — provide for disclosures that are sufficient to comply with the requirements of the applicable financial reporting framework (for example, disclosure of related party relationships, related party transactions, and segment information)
  - — provide for the identification of consolidation adjustments (for example, intragroup account balances, transactions, and unrealized profits or losses)
  - — provide for the approval of the financial information by component management

Fraud (Ref: par. .20)

.A35 The auditor is required to identify and assess the risks of material misstatement of the financial statements due to fraud and to design and implement appropriate responses to the assessed risks.[19] Information used to identify the risks of material misstatement of the group financial statements due to fraud may include the following:

- Group management's assessment of the risks that the group financial statements may be materially misstated as a result of fraud
- Group management's process for identifying and responding to the risks of fraud in the group, including any specific fraud risks identified by group management or account balances, classes of transactions, or disclosures for which a risk of fraud is likely
- Whether particular components exist for which a risk of fraud is likely
- How those charged with governance of the group monitor group management's processes for identifying and responding to the risks of fraud in the group and the controls group management has established to mitigate these risks
- Responses of those charged with governance of the group, group management, and internal audit (and, if considered appropriate, component management, the component auditors, and others) to the group engagement team's inquiry whether they have knowledge of any actual, suspected, or alleged fraud affecting a component or the group

---

[19] See section 240, *Consideration of Fraud in a Financial Statement Audit*.

Discussion Among Group Engagement Team Members and Component Auditors Regarding the Risks of Material Misstatement of the Group Financial Statements, Including Risks of Fraud (Ref: par. .20)

.A36 The key members of the engagement team are required to discuss the susceptibility of an entity to material misstatement of the financial statements due to fraud or error, specifically emphasizing the risks due to fraud. In a group audit, these discussions also may include the component auditors.[20,21] The group engagement partner's determination of who to include in the discussions, how and when they occur, and their extent is affected by factors, such as prior experience with the group.

.A37 The discussions provide an opportunity to

- share knowledge of the components and their environments, including group-wide controls.
- exchange information about the business risks of the components or the group.
- exchange ideas about how and where the group financial statements may be susceptible to material misstatement due to fraud or error; how group management and component management could perpetrate and conceal fraudulent financial reporting; and how assets of the components could be misappropriated.
- identify practices followed by group or component management that may be biased or designed to manage earnings that could lead to fraudulent financial reporting (for example, revenue recognition practices that do not comply with the applicable financial reporting framework).
- consider known external and internal factors affecting the group that may create an incentive or pressure for group management, component management, or others to commit fraud; provide the opportunity for fraud to be perpetrated; or indicate a culture or environment that enables group management, component management, or others to rationalize committing fraud.
- consider the risk that group or component management may override controls.
- consider whether uniform accounting policies are used to prepare the financial information of the components for the group financial statements and, if not, how differences in accounting policies are identified and adjusted (when required by the applicable financial reporting framework).
- discuss fraud that has been identified in components or information that indicates the existence of a fraud in a component.
- share information that may indicate noncompliance with laws or regulations (for example, payments of bribes and improper transfer pricing practices).

Risk Factors (Ref: par. .21)

.A38 Appendix B, "Examples of Conditions or Events That May Indicate Risks of Material Misstatement of the Group Financial Statements," sets out

---

[20] Paragraph .15 of section 240.

[21] Paragraph .11 of section 315.

examples of conditions or events that, individually or together, may indicate risks of material misstatement of the group financial statements, including risks due to fraud.

Risk Assessment (Ref: par. .21)

.A39 The group engagement team's assessment at group level of the risks of material misstatement of the group financial statements is based on information, such as the following:

- Information obtained from the understanding of the group, its components, and their environments and of the consolidation process, including audit evidence obtained in evaluating the design and implementation of group-wide controls and controls that are relevant to the consolidation
- Information obtained from the component auditors

Understanding a Component Auditor (Ref: par. .22)

Group Engagement Team's Procedures to Obtain an Understanding of a Component Auditor and Sources of Audit Evidence (Ref: par. .22)

.A40 Factors that may affect the group engagement partner's decisions whether to use the work of a component auditor to provide audit evidence for the group audit and whether to make reference to the audit of a component auditor in the auditor's report on the group financial statements include the following:

- Differences in the financial reporting framework applied in preparing the financial statements of the component and that applied in preparing the group financial statements
- Whether the audit of the financial statements of the component will be completed in time to meet the group reporting timetable
- Differences in the auditing and other standards applied by the component auditor and those applied in the audit of the group financial statements
- Whether it is impracticable for the group engagement team to be involved in the work of a component auditor

.A41 It will not be necessary to obtain an understanding of the auditors of those components for which the group engagement team plans to perform analytical procedures at group level only.

.A42 The nature, timing, and extent of the group engagement team's procedures to obtain an understanding of a component auditor are affected by factors, such as previous experience with, or knowledge of, the component auditor and the degree to which the group engagement team and the component auditor are subject to common policies and procedures, such as the following:

- Whether the group engagement team and a component auditor share the following:
  - — Common policies and procedures for performing the work (for example, audit methodologies)
  - — Common quality control policies and procedures
  - — Common monitoring policies and procedures
- The consistency or similarity of the following:

— Laws and regulations or legal system

— Professional oversight, discipline, and external quality assurance

— Education and training

— Professional organizations and standards

— Language and culture

.A43 These factors interact and are not mutually exclusive. For example, the extent of the group engagement team's procedures to obtain an understanding of component auditor A, who consistently applies common quality control and monitoring policies and procedures and a common audit methodology or operates in the same jurisdiction as the auditor of the group financial statements, may be less than the extent of the group engagement team's procedures to obtain an understanding of component auditor B, who does not consistently apply common quality control and monitoring policies and procedures and a common audit methodology or operates in a different jurisdiction. The nature of the procedures performed regarding component auditors A and B also may be different.

.A44 The group engagement team may obtain an understanding of a component auditor in a number of ways. In the first year of involving a component auditor, the group engagement team may, for example

- determine through communication with a component auditor that
  - — the component auditor is aware that
    - the financial statements of the component are to be included in the group financial statements on which the auditor of the group financial statements will report.
    - the component auditor's report thereon will be relied upon by the auditor of the group financial statements.
    - either the auditor of the group financial statements will make reference to the component auditor's report in the opinion on the group financial statements or the group engagement team will be involved in the work of the component auditor.
- a review will be made of matters affecting elimination of intercompany transactions and accounts and, if appropriate in the circumstances, the uniformity of accounting practices among the components included in the financial statements.
- evaluate the results of the quality control monitoring system when the group engagement team and component auditor are from a firm or network that operates under, and complies with, common monitoring policies and procedures.[22]
- visit a component auditor to discuss the matters in paragraph .22*a–d*.
- request a component auditor to confirm the matters referred to in paragraph .22*a–d* in writing. Exhibit B, "Illustrative Component

[22] Paragraph 57 of QC section 10, *A Firm's System of Quality Control*.

Auditor's Confirmation Letter," contains an example of written confirmations by a component auditor.

- request a component auditor to complete questionnaires about the matters in paragraph .22*a–d*.
- discuss a component auditor with colleagues in the group engagement partner's firm or with a reputable third party that has knowledge of the component auditor, such as other practitioners or bankers and other credit grantors.

In subsequent years, the understanding of a component auditor may be based on the group engagement team's previous experience with that component auditor. The group engagement team may request the component auditor to confirm whether anything regarding the matters listed in paragraph .22*a–d* has changed since the previous year.

.A45 Where independent oversight bodies have been established to oversee the auditing profession and monitor the quality of audits, awareness of the regulatory environment may assist the group engagement team in evaluating the independence and competence of a component auditor. Information about the regulatory environment and the public results of any inspections performed by oversight bodies may be obtained from the component auditor or information provided by the independent oversight bodies.

Ethical Requirements That Are Relevant to the Group Audit (Ref: par. .22a)

.A46 When performing work on the financial information of a component for a group audit, the component auditor is subject to ethical requirements that are relevant to the group audit. Such requirements may be different or in addition to those applying to the component auditor when performing an audit in the component auditor's jurisdiction. The group engagement team, therefore, obtains an understanding about the component auditor's understanding of, and compliance with, the ethical requirements that are relevant to the group audit and whether that is sufficient to fulfill the component auditor's responsibilities in the group audit. When the component auditor is not subject to the AICPA Code of Professional Conduct, compliance by the component auditor with the ethics and independence requirements set forth in the International Federation of Accountants *Code of Ethics for Professional Accountants* is sufficient to fulfill the component auditor's ethical responsibilities in the group audit.[23]

A Component Auditor's Professional Competence (Ref: par. .22b)

.A47 Inquiries about the professional reputation and standing of a component auditor may be made of the AICPA, the state board of accountancy by which the component auditor is licensed, the applicable state society of CPAs, or the local chapter, or, in the case of an auditor from a foreign jurisdiction, the corresponding professional organization, and if applicable, the PCAOB. The group engagement team may obtain the peer review report, if available, on the component auditor's firm. Exhibit C, "Sources of Information," provides information about specific inquires that may be directed to the AICPA.

---

[23] At its May 25–26, 2010, meeting, the AICPA Professional Ethics Executive Committee (PEEC) agreed that an AICPA member who is the group engagement partner of a U.S. consolidated entity should be considered to have performed an audit in accordance with generally accepted auditing standards, and in compliance with the AICPA Code of Professional Conduct, provided that component auditors that are not subject to the AICPA Code are in compliance with the ethics and independence requirements set forth in the International Federation of Accountants Code of Ethics. PEEC adopted a nonenforcement policy to this effect and agreed to pursue a revision to ET section 91, *Applicability*, of the code to make it authoritative.

.A48 The group engagement team's understanding of a component auditor's professional competence may include whether the component auditor

- possesses an understanding of the auditing and other standards applicable to the group audit, such as U.S. GAAS, that is sufficient to fulfill the component auditor's responsibilities.
- possesses the special skills (for example, industry-specific knowledge or knowledge of relevant financial reporting requirements for statements and schedules to be filed with regulatory agencies) necessary to perform the work on the financial information of the particular component.
- when relevant, possesses an understanding of the applicable financial reporting framework that is sufficient to fulfill the component auditor's responsibilities in the group audit (instructions issued by group management to components often describe the characteristics of the applicable financial reporting framework).

Application of the Group Engagement Team's Understanding of a Component Auditor (Ref: par. .23)

.A49 The group engagement team cannot overcome the fact that a component auditor is not independent by being involved in the work of the component auditor or by performing additional risk assessment or further audit procedures on the financial information of the component or by making reference in the auditor's report on the group financial statements to the audit of the component auditor.

.A50 However, the group engagement team may be able to overcome less than serious concerns about a component auditor's professional competency (for example, lack of industry-specific knowledge) or the fact that a component auditor does not operate in an environment that actively oversees auditors by being involved in the work of that component auditor or by performing additional risk assessment or further audit procedures on the financial information of the component.

.A51 When law or regulation prohibits access to relevant parts of the audit documentation of a component auditor, the group engagement team may request the component auditor to overcome this by preparing a memorandum that covers the relevant information.

Determining Whether to Make Reference to a Component Auditor in the Auditor's Report on the Group Financial Statements (Ref: par. .24)

.A52 In group audits involving two or more component auditors, the decision to make reference to the audit of a component auditor is made individually for each component auditor, regardless of the decision whether to refer to any other component auditor. The auditor of the group financial statements may make reference to any, all, or none of the component auditors. For example, if significant components are audited by a component auditor from a network firm and one component is audited by another firm, the group engagement partner may decide to assume responsibility for the work of the component auditor from the network firm and to make reference to the work of the component auditor from the other firm.

Determining Whether the Audit Was Conducted in Accordance With GAAS (Ref: par. .25a)

.A53 A component auditor's report stating that the audit was conducted in accordance with GAAS or, if applicable, the auditing standards promulgated by the PCAOB is sufficient to make the determination required by paragraph .25*a*. When the component auditor has performed an audit of the component financial statements in accordance with auditing standards other than GAAS or, if applicable, the auditing standards promulgated by the PCAOB, the group engagement partner may evaluate, exercising professional judgment, whether the audit performed by the component auditor meets the relevant requirements of GAAS. For the purposes of complying with paragraph .25*a*, relevant requirements of GAAS are those that pertain to planning and performing the audit of the component financial statements and do not include those related to the form of the auditor's report. Audits performed in accordance with International Standards on Auditing (ISAs) promulgated by the International Auditing and Assurance Standards Board (IAASB) are more likely to meet the relevant requirements of GAAS than audits performed in accordance with auditing standards promulgated by bodies other than the IAASB. The group engagement team may provide the component auditor with appendix B, *Substantive Differences Between the International Standards on Auditing and Generally Accepted Auditing Standards*, that identifies substantive requirements of GAAS that are not requirements in the ISAs. The component auditor may perform additional procedures in order to meet the relevant requirements of GAAS. The communication requested of the component auditor required by paragraph .42 may address whether the audit of the component auditor met the relevant requirements of GAAS. The group engagement partner, having determined that all relevant requirements of GAAS have been met by the component auditor, may decide to make reference to the audit of that component auditor in the auditor's report on the group financial statements. [Paragraph renumbered and amended, effective for audits of financial statements for periods ending on or after December 15, 2012, by SAS No. 127.]

Determining Whether to Make Reference When the Financial Reporting Framework Is Not the Same (Ref: par. .26)

.A54 When the component's financial statements are prepared using a financial reporting framework that differs from the financial reporting framework used to prepare the group financial statements, the group engagement team is required by paragraph .37 to evaluate whether the financial information of the component has been appropriately adjusted for purposes of the preparation and fair presentation of the group financial statements in accordance with the applicable financial reporting framework. Evaluating whether the financial statements of the component have been appropriately adjusted to conform with the financial reporting framework used by the group is based on a depth of understanding of the component's financial statements that ordinarily is not obtained unless the auditor of the group financial statements assumes responsibility for, and, thus, is involved in, the work of the component auditor. In rare circumstances, however, the group engagement partner may conclude that the group engagement team can reasonably expect to obtain sufficient appropriate audit evidence for purposes of evaluating the appropriateness of the adjustments to convert the component's financial statements to the financial reporting framework used by the group without the need to assume responsibility for, and, thus, be involved in, the work of the component auditor. [Paragraph added, effective for audits of financial statements for periods ending on or after December 15, 2012, by SAS No. 127.]

.A55 The greater the number of differences or the greater the significance of the differences between the criteria used for measurement, recognition, presentation, and disclosure of all material items in the component's financial statements under the financial reporting framework used by the component and the financial reporting framework used by the group, the less similar they are. Financial statements prepared and presented in accordance with International Financial Reporting Standards (IFRSs) and *International Financial Reporting Standard for Small and Medium-sized Entities*, as issued by the International Accounting Standards Board, are generally viewed as more similar to financial statements prepared and presented in accordance with accounting principles generally accepted in the United States of America (GAAP) than financial statements prepared and presented in accordance with jurisdiction-specific reporting frameworks or adaptations of IFRSs. In most cases, special purpose frameworks set forth in section 800, *Special Considerations—Audits of Financial Statements Prepared in Accordance With Special Purpose Frameworks*, are not similar to GAAP. [Paragraph added, effective for audits of financial statements for periods ending on or after December 15, 2012, by SAS No. 127.]

.A56 Additional considerations in determining whether it may be appropriate to make reference to the audit of a component auditor in the auditor's report on the group financial statements when the component prepares financial statements using a different financial reporting framework than that used by the group include the

- effectiveness of groupwide controls and the adequacy of the consolidation process specifically related to the adjustments to convert the component's financial statements to the financial reporting framework used by the group, including the financial reporting competencies of personnel involved in the adjustments.
- depth of the group engagement team's understanding of the component and its environment, including the complexity of the events and transactions subject to the differing financial reporting requirements and the assessed risk of material misstatement related to the adjustments.
- extent of the group engagement team's knowledge of the financial reporting framework used to prepare the component financial statements.
- group engagement team's ability to obtain information from group or component management that is relevant to the adjustments.
- need and ability to seek, as necessary, the assistance of professionals possessing specialized skills or knowledge related to the adjustments.

[Paragraph added, effective for audits of financial statements for periods ending on or after December 15, 2012, by SAS No. 127.]

Considerations for Governmental Entities

.A57 When the applicable financial reporting framework used by the group provides for the inclusion of component financial statements that are prepared in accordance with a different financial reporting framework, the component financial statements are deemed to be in accordance with the applicable financial reporting framework used for the group financial statements. For example, both the financial reporting framework established by the Governmental Accounting Standards Board and the financial reporting framework established by the Federal Accounting Standards Advisory Board have such provisions. Accordingly, when the provisions established by the applicable financial reporting framework for inclusion of those component financial statements have been followed, the requirements in paragraphs .26 and .28*c* are not relevant. [Paragraph renumbered and amended, effective for audits of financial statements for periods ending on or after December 15, 2012, by SAS No. 127.]

Making Reference in the Auditor's Report (Ref: par. .28–.31)

.A58 The disclosure of the magnitude of the portion of the financial statements audited by a component auditor may be achieved by stating the dollar amounts or percentages of one or more of the following: total assets, total revenues, or other appropriate criteria, whichever most clearly describes the portion of the financial statements audited by a component auditor. When two or more component auditors participate in the audit, the dollar amounts or the percentages covered by the component auditors may be stated in the aggregate. [Paragraph renumbered, effective for audits of financial statements for periods ending on or after December 15, 2012, by SAS No. 127.]

.A59 Reference in the auditor's report on the group financial statements to the fact that part of the audit was conducted by a component auditor is not to be construed as a qualification of the opinion, but rather is intended to communicate (1) that the auditor of the group financial statements is not assuming responsibility for the work of the component auditor, and (2) the source of the audit evidence with respect to those components for which reference to the audit of component auditors is made. [Paragraph renumbered, effective for audits of financial statements for periods ending on or after December 15, 2012, by SAS No. 127.]

.A60 Exhibit A contains examples of appropriate reporting in the auditor's report on the group financial statements when reference is made to the audit of a component auditor. [Paragraph renumbered and amended, effective for audits of financial statements for periods ending on or after December 15, 2012, by SAS No. 127.]

.A61 If the modified opinion, emphasis-of-matter paragraph, or other-matter paragraph in the component auditor's report does not affect the report on the group financial statements and the component auditor's report is not presented, the auditor of the group financial statements need not make reference to those paragraphs in the auditor's report on the group financial statements. If the component auditor's report is presented, the auditor of the group financial statements may make reference to those paragraphs and their disposition. [Paragraph renumbered, effective for audits of financial statements for periods ending on or after December 15, 2012, by SAS No. 127.]

.A62 When the auditor of the group financial statements is assuming responsibility for the work of a component auditor, no reference is made to the component auditor in the report on the group audit because to do so may cause a reader to misinterpret the degree of responsibility being assumed. [Paragraph renumbered, effective for audits of financial statements for periods ending on or after December 15, 2012, by SAS No. 127.]

Materiality (Ref: par. .32)

.A63 The auditor is required[24]

a. when establishing the overall audit strategy

---

[24] Paragraphs .10–.11 of section 320.

i. to determine materiality for the financial statements as a whole.

ii. to consider whether, in the specific circumstances of the entity, particular classes of transactions, account balances, or disclosures exist for which misstatements of lesser amounts than materiality for the financial statements as a whole could reasonably be expected to influence the economic decisions of users taken on the basis of the financial statements. In such circumstances, the auditor determines materiality to be applied to those particular classes of transactions, account balances, or disclosures.

b. to determine performance materiality for purposes of assessing the risks of material misstatement and designing further audit procedures to respond to assessed risks.

In the context of a group audit, materiality is established for both the group financial statements as a whole and the financial information of those components on which the group engagement team will perform, or request a component auditor to perform, an audit or review. Materiality for the group financial statements as a whole is used when establishing the overall group audit strategy. [Paragraph renumbered, effective for audits of financial statements for periods ending on or after December 15, 2012, by SAS No. 127.]

.A64 Different materiality may be established for different components. The aggregate of component materiality may exceed group materiality. [Paragraph renumbered, effective for audits of financial statements for periods ending on or after December 15, 2012, by SAS No. 127.]

.A65 Consideration of all components, regardless of whether reference is made in the auditor's report on the group financial statements to the audit of a component auditor, is necessary when determining component materiality to reduce the risk that the aggregate of detected and undetected misstatements in the group financial statements exceeds materiality for the group financial statements as a whole. Determining component materiality is necessary for the group engagement team to determine the overall group audit plan for the components for which the auditor of the group financial statements is not making reference to the component auditor. [Paragraph renumbered, effective for audits of financial statements for periods ending on or after December 15, 2012, by SAS No. 127.]

.A66 When the component is subject to an audit required by law or regulation or performed for another reason, the materiality used by the component auditor for purposes of such audit ordinarily can be expected to be less than the group materiality and, accordingly, be acceptable for purposes of the group audit. In the case of an equity method investment, the investee may be larger than the investor, and the auditor's evidence to support the investor's share of earnings from the investment may consist largely of the audited financial statements of the investee. In such cases, the materiality used by the investee's auditor may be larger than the materiality used by the investor's auditor. When such circumstances exist, the group engagement team may take into consideration matters such as the group's ownership percentage and its share of the investee's profits and losses when determining whether the component materiality used by the investee's auditor is appropriate for purposes of the audit of the group financial statements. [Paragraph renumbered, effective for audits of financial statements for periods ending on or after December 15, 2012, by SAS No. 127.]

.A67 A threshold for misstatements is determined in addition to component materiality. Misstatements identified in the financial information of the component that are above the threshold for misstatements of the group are communicated to the group engagement team. [Paragraph renumbered, effective for audits of financial statements for periods ending on or after December 15, 2012, by SAS No. 127.]

Responding to Assessed Risks (Ref: par. .33)

.A68 In an audit of group financial statements, appropriate responses to assessed risks of material misstatement for some or all accounts or classes of transactions may be implemented at the group level, without the involvement of component auditors. [Paragraph renumbered, effective for audits of financial statements for periods ending on or after December 15, 2012, by SAS No. 127.]

Consolidation Process

Consolidation Adjustments and Reclassifications (Ref: par. .36)

.A69 The consolidation process may require adjustments to amounts reported in the group financial statements that do not pass through the usual transaction processing systems and may not be subject to the same internal controls to which other financial information is subject. The group engagement team's evaluation of the appropriateness, completeness, and accuracy of the adjustments may include the following:

- Evaluating whether significant adjustments appropriately reflect the events and transactions underlying them
- Determining whether significant adjustments have been correctly calculated, processed, and authorized by group management and, when applicable, by component management
- Determining whether significant adjustments are properly supported and sufficiently documented
- Checking the reconciliation and elimination of intragroup account balances, transactions, and unrealized profits or losses
- Communicating with the component auditor, regardless of whether reference is made in the auditor's report on the group financial statements to the audit of the component auditor.

[Paragraph renumbered, effective for audits of financial statements for periods ending on or after December 15, 2012, by SAS No. 127.]

Subsequent Events (Ref: par. .40)

.A70 When the auditor's report on the group financial statements will make reference to the audit of a component auditor, procedures designed to identify subsequent events between the date of the component auditor's report and the date of the auditor's report on the group financial statements may include

- obtaining an understanding of any procedures that group management has established to ensure that such subsequent events are identified.
- requesting the component auditor to update subsequent events procedures to the date of the auditor's report on the group financial statements.

- requesting written representation from component management regarding subsequent events.
- reading available interim financial information of the component and making inquiries of group management.
- reading minutes of meetings of the governing board, or any other administrative board with management oversight, held since the financial statement date.
- reading the subsequent year's capital and operating budgets.
- inquiring of group management regarding currently known facts, decisions, or conditions that are expected to have a significant effect on financial position or results of operations for items that represent subsequent events.
- considering the implications for the auditor's report on the group financial statements if the group engagement team has been unable to obtain sufficient appropriate audit evidence regarding subsequent events.

[Paragraph renumbered, effective for audits of financial statements for periods ending on or after December 15, 2012, by SAS No. 127.]

Evaluating the Sufficiency and Appropriateness of Audit Evidence Obtained

Sufficiency and Appropriateness of Audit Evidence (Ref: par. .44–.45)

.A71 If the group engagement team concludes that sufficient appropriate audit evidence on which to base the group audit opinion has not been obtained, the group engagement team may request a component auditor to perform additional procedures. Alternatively, the group engagement team may perform its own procedures on the financial information of the component. [Paragraph renumbered, effective for audits of financial statements for periods ending on or after December 15, 2012, by SAS No. 127.]

.A72 The group engagement partner's evaluation of the aggregate effect of any misstatements (either identified by the group engagement team or communicated by component auditors) allows the group engagement partner to determine whether the group financial statements as a whole are materially misstated. [Paragraph renumbered, effective for audits of financial statements for periods ending on or after December 15, 2012, by SAS No. 127.]

Communication With Group Management and Those Charged With Governance of the Group

Communication With Group Management (Ref: par. .46–.48)

.A73 Section 240, *Consideration of Fraud in a Financial Statement Audit*, contains requirements and guidance on communication of fraud to management and, when management may be involved in the fraud, those charged with governance.[25] [Paragraph renumbered, effective for audits of financial statements for periods ending on or after December 15, 2012, by SAS No. 127.]

---

[25] Paragraphs .39–.41 of section 240.

.A74 Group management may need to keep certain material sensitive information confidential. Examples of matters that may be significant to the financial statements of the component of which component management may be unaware include the following:

- Potential litigation
- Plans for abandonment of material operating assets
- Subsequent events
- Significant legal agreements

[Paragraph renumbered, effective for audits of financial statements for periods ending on or after December 15, 2012, by SAS No. 127.]

Communication With Those Charged With Governance of the Group (Ref: par. .49)

.A75 The matters the group engagement team communicates to those charged with governance of the group may include those brought to the attention of the group engagement team by component auditors that the group engagement team judges to be significant to the responsibilities of those charged with governance of the group. Communication with those charged with governance of the group takes place at various times during the group audit. For example, the matters referred to in paragraph .49*a–b* may be communicated after the group engagement team has determined the work to be performed on the financial information of the components. On the other hand, the matter referred to in paragraph .49*c* may be communicated at the end of the audit, and the matters referred to in paragraph .49*d–e* may be communicated when they occur. [Paragraph renumbered, effective for audits of financial statements for periods ending on or after December 15, 2012, by SAS No. 127.]

Additional Requirements Applicable When Assuming Responsibility for the Work of a Component Auditor

Materiality (Ref: par. .51)

.A76 Component materiality for those components whose financial information will be audited or reviewed as part of the group audit in accordance with paragraphs .53, .54*a*, and .56, is communicated to the component auditor and is used by the component auditor to evaluate whether uncorrected detected misstatements are material, individually or in the aggregate. [Paragraph renumbered, effective for audits of financial statements for periods ending on or after December 15, 2012, by SAS No. 127.]

.A77 In the case of an audit of the financial information of a component, section 320, *Materiality in Planning and Performing an Audit*, requires the component auditor (or group engagement team) to determine performance materiality for purposes of assessing the risks of material misstatement of the financial information of the component and to design further audit procedures in response to assessed risks.[26] This is necessary to reduce the risk that the aggregate of detected and undetected misstatements in the financial information of the component exceeds component materiality. In practice, the group engagement team may set component materiality at the level of performance materiality for the component. When this is the case, the component auditor uses component materiality for purposes of assessing the risks of material

[26] Paragraph .11 of section 320.

misstatement of the financial information of the component and to design further audit procedures in response to assessed risks, as well as for evaluating whether detected misstatements are material individually or in the aggregate. [Paragraph renumbered, effective for audits of financial statements for periods ending on or after December 15, 2012, by SAS No. 127.]

Determining the Type of Work to Be Performed on the Financial Information of Components

Significant Components (Ref: par. .53–.54)

.A78 Adapting an audit of the financial information of a significant component to meet the specific needs of the group engagement team may include requesting the component auditor to

- perform an audit, using component materiality, in accordance with GAAS, with the exception of performing audit procedures on, for example, tax accounts or litigation, claims, and assessments because those procedures are performed at the group level.
- communicate the results of the audit in a form that is responsive to the needs of the group engagement team.

[Paragraph renumbered, effective for audits of financial statements for periods ending on or after December 15, 2012, by SAS No. 127.]

.A79 The group engagement team's determination of the type of work to be performed on the financial information of a component and its involvement in the work of the component auditor is affected by the following:

a. The significance of the component

b. The identified significant risks of material misstatement of the group financial statements

c. The group engagement team's evaluation of the design of group-wide controls and the determination of whether they have been implemented

d. The group engagement team's understanding of the component auditor

The following diagram shows how the significance of the component affects the group engagement team's determination of the type of work to be performed on the financial information of the component.

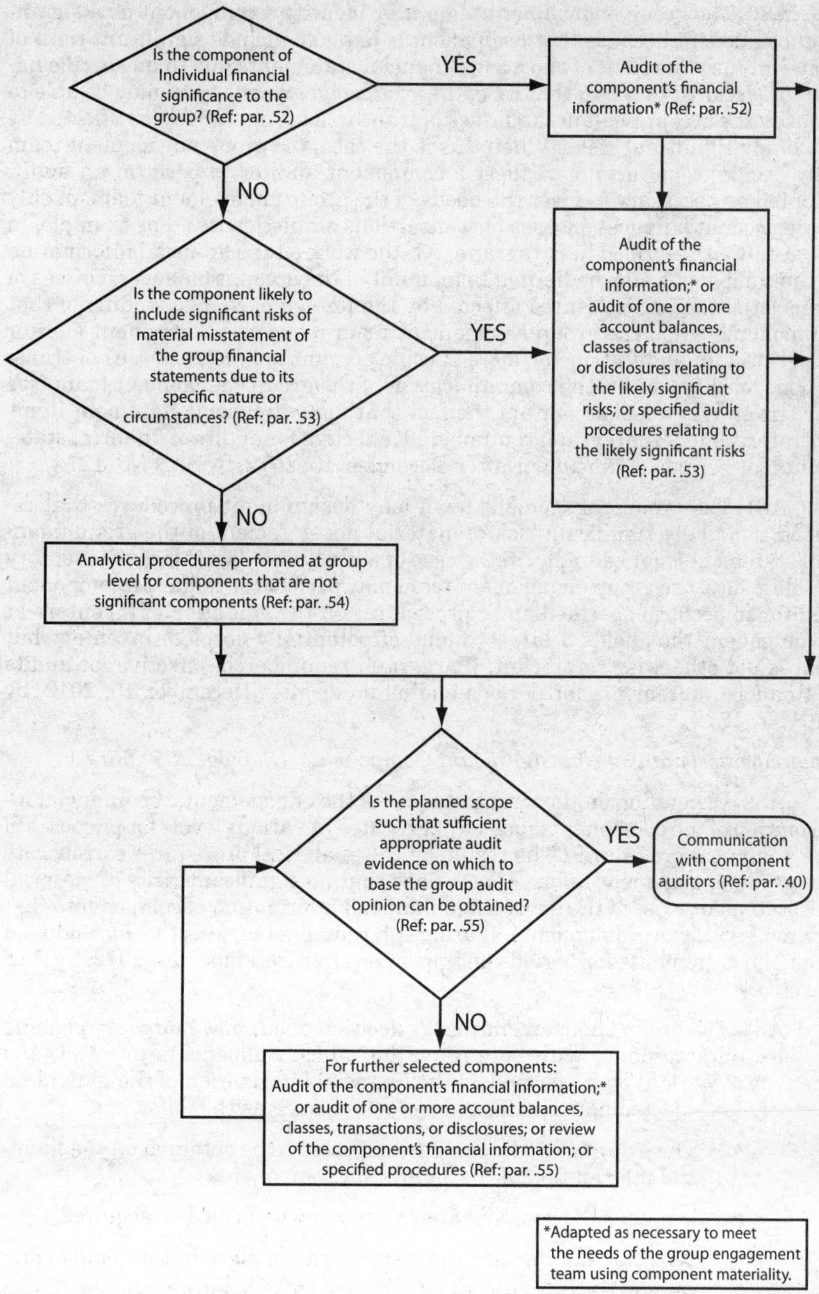

[Paragraph renumbered, effective for audits of financial statements for periods ending on or after December 15, 2012, by SAS No. 127.]

.A80 The group engagement team may identify a component as a significant component because that component is likely to include significant risks of material misstatement of the group financial statements due to its specific nature or circumstances. In that case, the group engagement team may be able to identify the account balances, classes of transactions, or disclosures affected by the likely significant risks. When this is the case, the group engagement team may decide to perform or request a component auditor to perform an audit, adapted as necessary to meet the needs of the group engagement team, of only those account balances, classes of transactions, or disclosures. For example, in the situation described in paragraph .A7, the work on the financial information of the component may be limited to an audit of the account balances, classes of transactions, and disclosures affected by the foreign exchange trading of that component. When the group engagement team requests a component auditor to perform an audit of one or more specific account balances, classes of transactions, or disclosures, the communication of the group engagement team (see paragraph .41) takes account of the fact that many financial statement items are interrelated. [Paragraph renumbered, effective for audits of financial statements for periods ending on or after December 15, 2012, by SAS No. 127.]

.A81 The group engagement team may design audit procedures that respond to a likely significant risk of material misstatement of the group financial statements. For example, in the case of a likely significant risk of inventory obsolescence, the group engagement team may perform or request a component auditor to perform specified audit procedures on the valuation of inventory at a component that holds a large volume of potentially obsolete inventory but that is not otherwise significant. [Paragraph renumbered, effective for audits of financial statements for periods ending on or after December 15, 2012, by SAS No. 127.]

Components That Are Not Significant Components (Ref: par. .55–.56)

.A82 Depending on the circumstances of the engagement, the financial information of the components may be aggregated at various levels for purposes of the analytical procedures. The results of the analytical procedures corroborate the group engagement team's conclusions that no significant risks of material misstatement exist of the aggregated financial information of components that are not significant components. [Paragraph renumbered, effective for audits of financial statements for periods ending on or after December 15, 2012, by SAS No. 127.]

.A83 The group engagement team's decision about how many components to select in accordance with paragraph .56, which components to select, and the type of work to be performed on the financial information of the individual components selected may be affected by factors, such as the following:

- The extent of audit evidence expected to be obtained on the financial information of the significant components
- Whether the component has been newly formed or acquired
- Whether significant changes have taken place in the component
- Whether internal audit has performed work at the component and any effect of that work on the group audit
- Whether the components apply common systems and processes
- The operating effectiveness of group-wide controls
- Abnormal fluctuations identified by analytical procedures performed at group level

- The individual financial significance of, or the risk posed by, the component in comparison with other components within this category
- Whether the component is subject to an audit required by law or regulation or performed for another reason

Including an element of unpredictability in selecting components in this category may increase the likelihood of identifying material misstatement of the components' financial information. The selection of components is often varied on a cyclical basis. [Paragraph renumbered, effective for audits of financial statements for periods ending on or after December 15, 2012, by SAS No. 127.]

.A84 An audit of a component that is not a significant component may have already been performed. Once the group engagement team decides to use that work to provide audit evidence for the group audit, the provisions of this section apply. [Paragraph renumbered, effective for audits of financial statements for periods ending on or after December 15, 2012, by SAS No. 127.]

.A85 A review of the financial information of a component may be performed in accordance with Statements on Standards for Accounting and Review Services, adapted as necessary in the circumstances. A review is designed to obtain only limited assurance that there are no material modifications that should be made to the financial statements in order for the statements to be in conformity with the applicable financial reporting framework. The group engagement team also may specify additional procedures to supplement this work. [Paragraph renumbered, effective for audits of financial statements for periods ending on or after December 15, 2012, by SAS No. 127.]

.A86 As explained in paragraph .A19, a group may consist only of components that are not significant components. In these circumstances, the group engagement team can obtain sufficient appropriate audit evidence on which to base the group audit opinion by determining the type of work to be performed on the financial information of the components, in accordance with paragraph .56. It is unlikely that the group engagement team will obtain sufficient appropriate audit evidence on which to base the group audit opinion if the group engagement team or a component auditor only tests group-wide controls and performs analytical procedures on the financial information of the components. [Paragraph renumbered, effective for audits of financial statements for periods ending on or after December 15, 2012, by SAS No. 127.]

Involvement in the Work Performed by Component Auditors (Ref: par. .57–.58)

.A87 Factors that may affect the group engagement team's involvement in the work of a component auditor include the following:

a. The significance of the component

b. The identified significant risks of material misstatement of the group financial statements

c. The group engagement team's understanding of the component auditor

In the case of a significant component or identified significant risks, the group engagement team performs the procedures described in paragraphs .57–.58. In the case of a component that is not a significant component, the nature, timing, and extent of the group engagement team's involvement in the work of the component auditor will vary based on the group engagement team's understanding of that component auditor. The fact that the component is not a significant component becomes secondary. For example, even though a component is not considered a significant component, the group engagement team, nevertheless, may decide to be involved in the component auditor's risk assessment because it has concerns (although less than serious concerns) about the component auditor's professional competency (for example, lack of industry-specific knowledge), or the component auditor does not operate in an environment that actively oversees auditors. [Paragraph renumbered, effective for audits of financial statements for periods ending on or after December 15, 2012, by SAS No. 127.]

.A88 Forms of involvement in the work of a component auditor other than those described in paragraphs .43 and .57–.58 may, based on the group engagement team's understanding of the component auditor, include one or more of the following:

- Meeting with component management or the component auditor to obtain an understanding of the component and its environment.
- Reviewing the component auditor's overall audit strategy and audit plan.
- Performing risk assessment procedures to identify and assess the risks of material misstatement at the component level. These may be performed with the component auditor or by the group engagement team.
- Designing and performing further audit procedures. These may be designed and performed with the component auditor or by the group engagement team.
- Participating in the closing and other key meetings between the component auditor and component management.
- Reviewing other relevant parts of the component auditor's audit documentation.

[Paragraph renumbered, effective for audits of financial statements for periods ending on or after December 15, 2012, by SAS No. 127.]

Communication With a Component Auditor (Ref: par. .60)

.A89 If effective two-way communication does not exist between the group engagement team and component auditors, whose work the auditor of the group financial statements is assuming responsibility for, a risk exists that the group engagement team may not obtain sufficient appropriate audit evidence on which to base the group audit opinion. Clear and timely communication of the group engagement team's requirements forms the basis of effective two-way communication between the group engagement team and a component auditor. This two-way communication also may be initiated by the component auditor regarding matters that may be significant to the component audit such as

- transactions, adjustments, or other matters that have come to the group engagement team's attention that it believes require adjustment to or disclosure in the financial statements of the component being audited by the component auditor.
- any relevant limitation on the scope of the audit performed by the group engagement team.

[Paragraph renumbered, effective for audits of financial statements for periods ending on or after December 15, 2012, by SAS No. 127.]

.A90 The group engagement team's requirements often are communicated in a letter of instruction. Appendix C, "Required and Additional Matters Included in the Group Engagement Team's Letter of Instruction," contains guidance on required and additional matters that may be included in such a letter of instruction. A component auditor's communication with the group engagement team often takes the form of a memorandum or report of work performed. Communication between the group engagement team and a component auditor, however, may not necessarily be in writing. For example, the group engagement team may visit the component auditor to discuss identified significant risks or review relevant parts of the component auditor's audit documentation. Nevertheless, the documentation requirements of this section and other AU-C sections apply. [Paragraph renumbered, effective for audits of financial statements for periods ending on or after December 15, 2012, by SAS No. 127.]

.A91 In cooperating with the group engagement team, a component auditor, for example, would provide the group engagement team with access to relevant audit documentation, if not prohibited by law or regulation. [Paragraph renumbered, effective for audits of financial statements for periods ending on or after December 15, 2012, by SAS No. 127.]

.A92 When a member of the group engagement team is also a component auditor, the objective for the group engagement team to communicate clearly with the component auditor often can be achieved by means other than specific written communication. For example

- access by the component auditor to the overall audit strategy and audit plan may be sufficient to communicate the group engagement team's requirements set out in paragraph .41.
- a review of the component auditor's audit documentation by the group engagement team may be sufficient to communicate matters relevant to the group engagement team's conclusion set out in paragraph .42.

[Paragraph renumbered, effective for audits of financial statements for periods ending on or after December 15, 2012, by SAS No. 127.]

Evaluating the Sufficiency and Appropriateness of Audit Evidence Obtained

Reviewing a Component Auditor's Audit Documentation (Ref: par. .62)

.A93 The parts of the audit documentation of a component auditor that will be relevant to the group audit may vary depending on the circumstances. Often, the focus is on audit documentation that is relevant to the significant risks of material misstatement of the group financial statements. The extent of the review may be affected by the fact that a component auditor's audit documentation has been subjected to the review procedures of the component auditor's firm. [Paragraph renumbered, effective for audits of financial statements for periods ending on or after December 15, 2012, by SAS No. 127.]

.A94

Appendix A—Understanding the Group, Its Components, and Their Environments—Examples of Matters About Which the Group Engagement Team Obtains an Understanding (Ref: par. .A31)

The examples provided cover a broad range of matters; however, not all matters are relevant to every group audit engagement, and the list of examples is not necessarily complete.

Group-Wide Controls

Group-wide controls may include a combination of the following:

- Regular meetings between group and component management to discuss business developments and review performance
- Monitoring of components' operations and their financial results, including regular reporting routines, which enables group management to monitor components' performance against budgets and take appropriate action
- Group management's risk assessment process (that is, the process for identifying, analyzing, and managing business risks, including the risk of fraud, that may result in material misstatement of the group financial statements)
- Monitoring, controlling, reconciling, and eliminating intragroup account balances, transactions, and unrealized profits or losses at group level
- A process for monitoring the timeliness and assessing the accuracy and completeness of financial information received from components
- A central IT system controlled by the same general IT controls for all or part of the group
- Control activities within an IT system that are common for all or some components
- Monitoring of controls, including activities of internal audit and self-assessment programs
- Consistent policies and procedures, including a group financial reporting procedures manual
- Group-wide programs, such as codes of conduct and fraud prevention programs
- Arrangements for assigning authority and responsibility to component management

Internal audit may be regarded as part of group-wide controls, for example, when the internal audit function is centralized. Section 610, *The Auditor's Consideration of the Internal Audit Function in an Audit of Financial Statements*, addresses the group engagement team's evaluation of the competence and objectivity of the internal auditors when it plans to use their work.[1]

Consolidation Process

The group engagement team's understanding of the consolidation process may include matters such as the following:

- Matters relating to the applicable financial reporting framework, such as the following:
  - — The extent to which component management has an understanding of the applicable financial reporting framework
  - — The process for identifying and accounting for components, in accordance with the applicable financial reporting framework
  - — The process for identifying reportable segments for segment reporting, in accordance with the applicable financial reporting framework
  - — The process for identifying related party relationships and related party transactions for reporting, in accordance with the applicable financial reporting framework
  - — The accounting policies applied to the group financial statements, changes from those of the previous financial year, and changes resulting from new or revised standards under the applicable financial reporting framework
  - — The procedures for dealing with components with financial year-ends different from the group's year-end
- Matters relating to the consolidation process, such as the following:
  - — Group management's process for obtaining an understanding of the accounting policies used by components and, when applicable, ensuring that uniform accounting policies are used to prepare the financial information of the components for the group financial statements and that differences in accounting policies are identified and adjusted, when required, in terms of the applicable financial reporting framework. Uniform accounting policies are the specific principles, bases, conventions, rules, and practices adopted by the group, based on the applicable financial reporting framework, that the components use to report similar transactions consistently. These policies are ordinarily described in the financial reporting procedures manual and reporting package issued by group management.

---

[1] Paragraphs .10–.11 of section 610, *The Auditor's Consideration of the Internal Audit Function in an Audit of Financial Statements*. SAS No. 65, *The Auditor's Consideration of the Internal Audit Function in an Audit of Financial Statements*, is currently effective and codified as AU section 322. SAS No. 65 has been included in section 610, as designated by SAS No. 122, *Statements on Auditing Standards: Clarification and Recodification*, and will be superseded when it is redrafted for clarity and convergence with International Standard on Auditing 610 (Revised), *Using the Work of Internal Auditors*, as part of the Clarification and Convergence project of the Auditing Standards Board. Until such time, section 610 has been conformed to reflect updated section and paragraph cross references but has not otherwise been subjected to a comprehensive review or revision.

  - — Group management's process for ensuring complete, accurate, and timely financial reporting by the components for the consolidation.
  - — The process for translating the financial information of foreign components into the currency of the group financial statements.
  - — How IT is organized for the consolidation, including the manual and automated stages of the process and the manual and programmed controls in place at various stages of the consolidation process.
  - — Group management's process for obtaining information on subsequent events.

- Matters relating to consolidation adjustments, such as the following:
  - — The process for recording consolidation adjustments, including the preparation, authorization, and processing of related journal entries and the experience of personnel responsible for the consolidation
  - — The consolidation adjustments required by the applicable financial reporting framework
  - — Business rationale for the events and transactions that gave rise to the consolidation adjustments
  - — Frequency, nature, and size of transactions between components
  - — Procedures for monitoring, controlling, reconciling, and eliminating intragroup account balances, transactions, and unrealized profits or losses
  - — Steps taken to arrive at the fair value of acquired assets and liabilities, procedures for amortizing goodwill (when applicable), and impairment testing of goodwill, in accordance with the applicable financial reporting framework
  - — Arrangements with a controlling interest or noncontrolling interest regarding losses incurred by a component (for example, an obligation of the noncontrolling interest to compensate such losses)

[Paragraph renumbered, effective for audits of financial statements for periods ending on or after December 15, 2012, by SAS No. 127.]

.A95

Appendix B—Examples of Conditions or Events That May Indicate Risks of Material Misstatement of the Group Financial Statements (Ref: par. .A38)

The examples provided cover a broad range of conditions or events; however, not all conditions or events are relevant to every group audit engagement, and the following list of examples is not necessarily complete:

- A complex group structure, especially when there are frequent acquisitions, disposals, or reorganizations
- Poor corporate governance structures, including decision-making processes, that are not transparent
- Nonexistent or ineffective group-wide controls, including inadequate group management information on monitoring of components' operations and their results
- Components operating in foreign jurisdictions that may be exposed to factors, such as unusual government intervention in areas such as trade and fiscal policy, restrictions on currency and dividend movements, and fluctuations in exchange rates
- Business activities of components that involve high risk, such as long-term contracts or trading in innovative or complex financial instruments
- Uncertainties regarding which components' financial information requires incorporation in the group financial statements, in accordance with the applicable financial reporting framework (for example, whether any special purpose entities or nontrading entities exist and require incorporation)
- Unusual related party relationships and transactions
- Prior occurrences of intragroup account balances that did not balance or reconcile on consolidation
- The existence of complex transactions that are accounted for in more than one component
- Components' application of accounting policies that differ from those applied to the group financial statements
- Components with different financial year-ends, which may be utilized to manipulate the timing of transactions
- Prior occurrences of unauthorized or incomplete consolidation adjustments
- Aggressive tax planning within the group or large cash transactions with entities in tax havens
- Frequent changes of auditors engaged to audit the financial statements of components

[Paragraph renumbered, effective for audits of financial statements for periods ending on or after December 15, 2012, by SAS No. 127.]

.A96

Appendix C—Required and Additional Matters Included in the Group Engagement Team's Letter of Instruction (Ref: par. .A87)

The following matters are relevant to the planning of the work of a component auditor:

[*Required matters are italicized.*]

- *A request for the component auditor, knowing the context in which the group engagement team will use the work of the component auditor, to confirm that the component auditor will cooperate with the group engagement team*
- The timetable for completing the audit
- Dates of planned visits by group management and the group engagement team and dates of planned meetings with component management and the component auditor
- A list of key contacts
- *The work to be performed by the component auditor, the use to be made of that work,* and arrangements for coordinating efforts at the initial stage of and during the audit, including the group engagement team's planned involvement in the work of the component auditor
- *The ethical requirements that are relevant to the group audit and, in particular, the independence requirements*
- *In the case of an audit or review of the financial information of the component, component materiality*
- *In the case of an audit or review of, or specified audit procedures performed on, the financial information of the component, the threshold above which misstatements cannot be regarded as clearly trivial to the group financial statements*
- *A list of related parties prepared by group management and any other related parties of which the group engagement team is aware and a request that the component auditor communicates on a timely basis to the group engagement team related parties not previously identified by group management or the group engagement team*
- Work to be performed on intragroup account balances, transactions, and unrealized profits or losses
- Guidance on other statutory reporting responsibilities (for example, reporting on group management's assertion on the effectiveness of internal control)
- When a time lag between completion of the work on the financial information of the components and the group engagement team's conclusion on the group financial statements is likely, specific instructions for a subsequent events review

The following matters are relevant to the conduct of the work of the component auditor:

- The findings of the group engagement team's tests of control activities of a processing system that is common for all or some components and tests of controls to be performed by the component auditor
- *Identified significant risks of material misstatement of the group financial statements, due to fraud or error, that are relevant to the work of the component auditor and a request that the component auditor communicates on a timely basis any other significant risks of material misstatement of the group financial statements, due to fraud or error, identified in the component and the component auditor's response to such risks*
- The findings of internal audit, based on work performed on controls at or relevant to components
- A request for timely communication of audit evidence obtained from performing work on the financial information of the components that contradicts the audit evidence on which the group engagement team originally based the risk assessment performed at group level
- A request for a written representation on component management's compliance with the applicable financial reporting framework or a statement that differences between the accounting policies applied to the financial information of the component and those applied to the group financial statements have been disclosed
- Matters to be documented by the component auditor

Other information, such as the following:

- A request that the following be reported to the group engagement team on a timely basis:
  - — Significant accounting, financial reporting, and auditing matters, including accounting estimates and related judgments
  - — Matters relating to the going concern status of the component
  - — Matters relating to litigation and claims
  - — Material weaknesses in controls that have come to the attention of the component auditor during the performance of the work on the financial information of the component and information that indicates the existence of fraud
- A request that the group engagement team be notified of any significant or unusual events as early as possible
- A request that the matters listed in paragraph .49 be communicated to the group engagement team when the work on the financial information of the component is completed

[Paragraph renumbered, effective for audits of financial statements for periods ending on or after December 15, 2012, by SAS No. 127.]

.A97

Exhibit A—Illustrations of Auditor's Reports on Group Financial Statements

Illustration 1—A Report With a Qualified Opinion When the Group Engagement Team Is Not Able to Obtain Sufficient Appropriate Audit Evidence on Which to Base the Group Audit Opinion

In this example, the group engagement team is unable to obtain sufficient appropriate audit evidence relating to a significant component accounted for by the equity method because the group engagement team was unable to obtain the audited financial statements of the component as of December 31, 20X1 and 20X0, including the auditor's report thereon. In this example, the auditor of the group financial statements is not making reference to the report of a component auditor.

In the auditor's professional judgment, the effect on the group financial statements of this inability to obtain sufficient appropriate audit evidence is material but not pervasive.

If, in the auditor's professional judgment, the effect on the group financial statements of the inability to obtain sufficient appropriate audit evidence is material and pervasive, the auditor would disclaim an opinion, in accordance with section 705, *Modifications to the Opinion in the Independent Auditor's Report.*

Independent Auditor's Report

[*Appropriate Addressee*]

Report on the Consolidated Financial Statements[1]

We have audited the accompanying consolidated financial statements of ABC Company and its subsidiaries, which comprise the consolidated balance sheets as of December 31, 20X1 and 20X0, and the related consolidated statements of income, changes in stockholders' equity, and cash flows for the years then ended, and the related notes to the financial statements.

Management's Responsibility for the Financial Statements

Management is responsible for the preparation and fair presentation of these consolidated financial statements in accordance with accounting principles generally accepted in the United States of America; this includes the design, implementation, and maintenance of internal control relevant to the preparation and fair presentation of consolidated financial statements that are free from material misstatement, whether due to fraud or error.

Auditor's Responsibility

Our responsibility is to express an opinion on these consolidated financial statements based on our audits. We conducted our audits in accordance with auditing standards generally accepted in the United States of America. Those standards require that we plan and perform the audit to obtain reasonable assurance whether the consolidated financial statements are free from material misstatement.

An audit involves performing procedures to obtain audit evidence about the amounts and disclosures in the consolidated financial statements. The procedures selected depend on the auditor's judgment, including the assessment of the risks of material misstatement of the consolidated financial statements, whether due to fraud or error. In making those risk assessments, the auditor

---

[1] The subtitle "Report on the Consolidated Financial Statements" is unnecessary in circumstances when the second subtitle, "Report on Other Legal and Regulatory Requirements," is not applicable.

considers internal control relevant to the entity's preparation and fair presentation of the consolidated financial statements in order to design audit procedures that are appropriate in the circumstances, but not for the purpose of expressing an opinion on the effectiveness of the entity's internal control.[2] Accordingly, we express no such opinion. An audit also includes evaluating the appropriateness of accounting policies used and the reasonableness of significant accounting estimates made by management, as well as evaluating the overall presentation of the consolidated financial statements.

We believe that the audit evidence we have obtained is sufficient and appropriate to provide a basis for our qualified audit opinion.

Basis for Qualified Opinion

We were unable to obtain audited financial statements supporting the Company's investment in a foreign affiliate stated at $_____ and $_____ at December 31, 20X1 and 20X0, respectively, or its equity in earnings of that affiliate of $_____ and $_____, which is included in net income for the years then ended as described in Note X to the consolidated financial statements; nor were we able to satisfy ourselves as to the carrying value of the investment in the foreign affiliate or the equity in its earnings by other auditing procedures.

Qualified Opinion

In our opinion, except for the possible effects of the matter described in the Basis for Qualified Opinion paragraph, the consolidated financial statements referred to above present fairly, in all material respects, the financial position of ABC Company and its subsidiaries as of December 31, 20X1 and 20X0, and the results of their operations and their cash flows for the years then ended in accordance with accounting principles generally accepted in the United States of America.

Report on Other Legal and Regulatory Requirements

[*Form and content of this section of the auditor's report will vary depending on the nature of the auditor's other reporting responsibilities.*]

[*Auditor's signature*]

[*Auditor's city and state*]

[*Date of the auditor's report*]

---

[2] In circumstances when the auditor also has responsibility to express an opinion on the effectiveness of internal control in conjunction with the audit of the consolidated financial statements, this sentence would be worded as follows: "In making those risk assessments, the auditor considers internal control relevant to the entity's preparation and fair presentation of the consolidated financial statements in order to design audit procedures that are appropriate in the circumstances." In addition, the next sentence, "Accordingly, we express no such opinion." would not be included.

Illustration 2—A Report in Which the Auditor of the Group Financial Statements Is Making Reference to the Audit of the Financial Statements of a Component Prepared Using the Same Financial Reporting Framework as That Used for the Group Financial Statements and Performed by a Component Auditor in Accordance With Generally Accepted Auditing Standards

In this example, the auditor of the group financial statements is making reference to the audit of the financial statements of a component prepared using the same financial reporting framework as that used for the group financial statements and performed by a component auditor in accordance with generally accepted auditing standards (GAAS).

Independent Auditor's Report

[*Appropriate Addressee*]

Report on the Consolidated Financial Statements[1]

We have audited the accompanying consolidated financial statements of ABC Company and its subsidiaries, which comprise the consolidated balance sheets as of December 31, 20X1 and 20X0, and the related consolidated statements of income, changes in stockholders' equity, and cash flows for the years then ended, and the related notes to the financial statements.

Management's Responsibility for the Financial Statements

Management is responsible for the preparation and fair presentation of these consolidated financial statements in accordance with accounting principles generally accepted in the United States of America; this includes the design, implementation, and maintenance of internal control relevant to the preparation and fair presentation of consolidated financial statements that are free from material misstatement, whether due to fraud or error.

Auditor's Responsibility

Our responsibility is to express an opinion on these consolidated financial statements based on our audits. We did not audit the financial statements of B Company, a wholly-owned subsidiary, which statements reflect total assets constituting 20 percent and 22 percent, respectively, of consolidated total assets at December 31, 20X1 and 20X0, and total revenues constituting 18 percent and 20 percent, respectively, of consolidated total revenues for the years then ended. Those statements were audited by other auditors, whose report has been furnished to us, and our opinion, insofar as it relates to the amounts included for B Company, is based solely on the report of the other auditors. We conducted our audits in accordance with auditing standards generally accepted in the United States of America. Those standards require that we plan and perform the audit to obtain reasonable assurance about whether the consolidated financial statements are free from material misstatement.

An audit involves performing procedures to obtain audit evidence about the amounts and disclosures in the consolidated financial statements. The procedures selected depend on the auditor's judgment, including the assessment of the risks of material misstatement of the consolidated financial statements,

---

[1] The subtitle "Report on the Consolidated Financial Statements" is unnecessary in circumstances when the second subtitle, "Report on Other Legal and Regulatory Requirements," is not applicable.

whether due to fraud or error. In making those risk assessments, the auditor considers internal control relevant to the entity's preparation and fair presentation of the consolidated financial statements in order to design audit procedures that are appropriate in the circumstances, but not for the purpose of expressing an opinion on the effectiveness of the entity's internal control.[2] Accordingly, we express no such opinion. An audit also includes evaluating the appropriateness of accounting policies used and the reasonableness of significant accounting estimates made by management, as well as evaluating the overall presentation of the consolidated financial statements.

We believe that the audit evidence we have obtained is sufficient and appropriate to provide a basis for our audit opinion.

Opinion

In our opinion, based on our audits and the report of the other auditors, the consolidated financial statements referred to above present fairly, in all material respects, the financial position of ABC Company and its subsidiaries as of December 31, 20X1 and 20X0, and the results of their operations and their cash flows for the years then ended in accordance with accounting principles generally accepted in the United States of America.

Report on Other Legal and Regulatory Requirements

[*Form and content of this section of the auditor's report will vary depending on the nature of the auditor's other reporting responsibilities.*]

[*Auditor's signature*]

[*Auditor's city and state*]

[*Date of the auditor's report*]

[2] In circumstances when the auditor also has responsibility to express an opinion on the effectiveness of internal control in conjunction with the audit of the consolidated financial statements, this sentence would be worded as follows: "In making those risk assessments, the auditor considers internal control relevant to the entity's preparation and fair presentation of the consolidated financial statements in order to design audit procedures that are appropriate in the circumstances." In addition, the next sentence, "Accordingly, we express no such opinion." would not be included.

Illustration 3—A Report in Which the Auditor of the Group Financial Statements Is Making Reference to the Audit of the Financial Statements of a Component Prepared Using a Different Financial Reporting Framework From That Used for the Group Financial Statements and Performed by a Component Auditor in Accordance With GAAS

In this example, the auditor of the group financial statements is making reference to the audit of the financial statements of a component prepared using a different financial reporting framework than that used for the group financial statements and performed by a component auditor in accordance with GAAS.

Independent Auditor's Report

[*Appropriate Addressee*]

Report on the Consolidated Financial Statements[1]

We have audited the accompanying consolidated financial statements of ABC Company and its subsidiaries, which comprise the consolidated balance sheets as of December 31, 20X1 and 20X0, and the related consolidated statements of income, changes in stockholders' equity, and cash flows for the years then ended, and the related notes to the financial statements.

Management's Responsibility for the Financial Statements

Management is responsible for the preparation and fair presentation of these consolidated financial statements in accordance with accounting principles generally accepted in the United States of America; this includes the design, implementation, and maintenance of internal control relevant to the preparation and fair presentation of consolidated financial statements that are free from material misstatement, whether due to fraud or error.

Auditor's Responsibility

Our responsibility is to express an opinion on these consolidated financial statements based on our audits. We did not audit the financial statements of B Company, a wholly-owned subsidiary, which statements reflect total assets constituting 20 percent and 22 percent, respectively, of consolidated total assets at December 31, 20X1 and 20X0, and total revenues constituting 18 percent and 20 percent, respectively, of consolidated total revenues for the years then ended. Those statements, which were prepared in accordance with International Financial Reporting Standards as issued by the International Accounting Standards Board, were audited by other auditors, whose report has been furnished to us. We have applied audit procedures on the conversion adjustments to the financial statements of B Company, which conform those financial statements to accounting principles generally accepted in the United States of America. Our opinion, insofar as it relates to the amounts included for B Company, prior to these conversion adjustments, is based solely on the report of the other auditors. We conducted our audits in accordance with auditing standards generally accepted in the United States of America. Those standards require that we plan and perform the audit to obtain reasonable assurance about whether the consolidated financial statements are free from material misstatement.

---

[1] The subtitle "Report on the Consolidated Financial Statements" is unnecessary in circumstances when the second subtitle, "Report on Other Legal and Regulatory Requirements," is not applicable.

An audit involves performing procedures to obtain audit evidence about the amounts and disclosures in the consolidated financial statements. The procedures selected depend on the auditor's judgment, including the assessment of the risks of material misstatement of the consolidated financial statements, whether due to fraud or error. In making those risk assessments, the auditor considers internal control relevant to the entity's preparation and fair presentation of the consolidated financial statements in order to design audit procedures that are appropriate in the circumstances, but not for the purpose of expressing an opinion on the effectiveness of the entity's internal control.[2] Accordingly, we express no such opinion. An audit also includes evaluating the appropriateness of accounting policies used and the reasonableness of significant accounting estimates made by management, as well as evaluating the overall presentation of the consolidated financial statements.

We believe that the audit evidence we have obtained is sufficient and appropriate to provide a basis for our audit opinion.

Opinion

In our opinion, based on our audits and the report of the other auditors, the consolidated financial statements referred to above present fairly, in all material respects, the financial position of ABC Company and its subsidiaries as of December 31, 20X1 and 20X0, and the results of their operations and their cash flows for the years then ended in accordance with accounting principles generally accepted in the United States of America.

Report on Other Legal and Regulatory Requirements

[*Form and content of this section of the auditor's report will vary depending on the nature of the auditor's other reporting responsibilities.*]

[*Auditor's signature*]

[*Auditor's city and state*]

[*Date of the auditor's report*]

---

[2] In circumstances when the auditor also has responsibility to express an opinion on the effectiveness of internal control in conjunction with the audit of the consolidated financial statements, this sentence would be worded as follows: "In making those risk assessments, the auditor considers internal control relevant to the entity's preparation and fair presentation of the consolidated financial statements in order to design audit procedures that are appropriate in the circumstances." In addition, the next sentence, "Accordingly, we express no such opinion." would not be included.

Illustration 4—A Report in Which the Auditor of the Group Financial Statements Is Making Reference to the Audit of the Financial Statements of a Component Prepared Using the Same Financial Reporting Framework as That Used for the Group Financial Statements and Performed by a Component Auditor in Accordance With Auditing Standards Other Than GAAS

In this example, the auditor of the group financial statements is making reference to the audit of the financial statements of a component prepared using the same financial reporting framework as that used for the group financial statements and performed by a component auditor in accordance with auditing standards other than GAAS or standards promulgated by the Public Company Accounting Oversight Board. The group engagement partner has determined that the component auditor performed additional audit procedures to meet the relevant requirements of GAAS. If additional procedures were not necessary for the audit of the component auditor to meet the relevant requirements of GAAS, illustration 2 is applicable.

Independent Auditor's Report

[*Appropriate Addressee*]

Report on the Consolidated Financial Statements[1]

We have audited the accompanying consolidated financial statements of ABC Company and its subsidiaries, which comprise the consolidated balance sheets as of December 31, 20X1 and 20X0, and the related consolidated statements of income, changes in stockholders' equity, and cash flows for the years then ended, and the related notes to the financial statements.

Management's Responsibility for the Financial Statements

Management is responsible for the preparation and fair presentation of these consolidated financial statements in accordance with accounting principles generally accepted in the United States of America; this includes the design, implementation, and maintenance of internal control relevant to the preparation and fair presentation of consolidated financial statements that are free from material misstatement, whether due to fraud or error.

Auditor's Responsibility

Our responsibility is to express an opinion on these consolidated financial statements based on our audits. We did not audit the financial statements of B Company, a wholly-owned subsidiary, which statements reflect total assets constituting 20 percent and 22 percent, respectively, of consolidated total assets at December 31, 20X1 and 20X0, and total revenues constituting 18 percent and 20 percent, respectively, of consolidated total revenues for the years then ended. Those statements were audited by other auditors in accordance with [*describe the set of auditing standards*], whose report has been furnished to us, and our opinion, insofar as it relates to the amounts included for B Company, is based solely on the report of, and additional audit procedures to meet the relevant requirements of auditing standards generally accepted in the United States

---

[1] The subtitle "Report on the Consolidated Financial Statements" is unnecessary in circumstances when the second subtitle, "Report on Other Legal and Regulatory Requirements," is not applicable.

of America performed by, the other auditors. We conducted our audits in accordance with auditing standards generally accepted in the United States of America. Those standards require that we plan and perform the audit to obtain reasonable assurance about whether the consolidated financial statements are free of material misstatement.

An audit involves performing procedures to obtain audit evidence about the amounts and disclosures in the consolidated financial statements. The procedures selected depend on the auditor's judgment, including the assessment of the risks of material misstatement of the consolidated financial statements, whether due to fraud or error. In making those risk assessments, the auditor considers internal control relevant to the entity's preparation and fair presentation of the consolidated financial statements in order to design audit procedures that are appropriate in the circumstances, but not for the purpose of expressing an opinion on the effectiveness of the entity's internal control.[2] Accordingly, we express no such opinion. An audit also includes evaluating the appropriateness of accounting policies used and the reasonableness of significant accounting estimates made by management, as well as evaluating the overall presentation of the consolidated financial statements.

We believe that the audit evidence we have obtained is sufficient and appropriate to provide a basis for our audit opinion.

Opinion

In our opinion, based on our audits and the report of, and additional audit procedures performed by, the other auditors, the consolidated financial statements referred to above present fairly, in all material respects, the financial position of ABC Company and its subsidiaries as of December 31, 20X1 and 20X0, and the results of their operations and their cash flows for the years then ended in accordance with accounting principles generally accepted in the United States of America.

Report on Other Legal and Regulatory Requirements

[*Form and content of this section of the auditor's report will vary depending on the nature of the auditor's other reporting responsibilities.*]

[*Auditor's signature*]

[*Auditor's city and state*]

[*Date of the auditor's report*]

[Paragraph renumbered and amended, effective for audits of financial statements for periods ending on or after December 15, 2012, by SAS No. 127.]

---

[2] In circumstances when the auditor also has responsibility to express an opinion on the effectiveness of internal control in conjunction with the audit of the consolidated financial statements, this sentence would be worded as follows: "In making those risk assessments, the auditor considers internal control relevant to the entity's preparation and fair presentation of the consolidated financial statements in order to design audit procedures that are appropriate in the circumstances." In addition, the next sentence, "Accordingly, we express no such opinion." would not be included.

.A98

Exhibit B—Illustrative Component Auditor's Confirmation Letter (Ref: par. .A44)

The following is not intended to be a standard letter. Confirmations may vary from one component auditor to another and from one period to the next. In this example, confirmations expected only when the auditor of the group financial statements is assuming responsibility have been italicized.

Confirmations often are obtained before work on the financial information of the component commences.

[*Component Auditor Letterhead*]

[*Date*]

[*To Audit Firm*]

This letter is provided in connection with your audit of the group financial statements of [*name of parent*] as of and for the year ended [*date*] for the purpose of expressing an opinion on whether the group financial statements present fairly, in all material respects, the financial position of the group as of [*date*] and of the results of its operations and its cash flows for the year then ended in accordance with [*indicate applicable financial reporting framework*].

We acknowledge receipt of your instructions dated [*date*], requesting us to perform the specified work on the financial information of [*name of component*] as of and for the year ended [*date*].

We confirm that:

1. *We will be able to comply with the instructions. / We advise you that we will not be able to comply with the following instructions [*specify instructions*] for the following reasons [*specify reasons*].*
2. *The instructions are clear, and we understand them. / We would appreciate it if you could clarify the following instructions [*specify instructions*].*
3. *We will cooperate with you and provide you with access to relevant audit documentation.*

We acknowledge that:

1. The financial information of [*name of component*] will be included in the group financial statements of [*name of parent*].
2. *You may consider it necessary to be further involved in the work you have requested us to perform on the financial information of [*name of component*] as of and for the year ended [*date*].*
3. *You intend to evaluate and, if considered appropriate, use our work for the audit of the group financial statements of [*name of parent*].*

In connection with the work that we will perform on the financial information of [*name of component*], a [*describe component, e.g., wholly-owned subsidiary, subsidiary, joint venture, investee accounted for by the equity or cost methods of accounting*] of [*name of parent*], we confirm the following:

1. We have an understanding of [*indicate relevant ethical requirements*] that is sufficient to fulfill our responsibilities in the audit of the group financial statements and will comply therewith. In particular, and with respect to [*name of parent*] and the other components in the group, we are independent within the meaning of

[*indicate relevant ethical requirements*] and comply with the applicable requirements of [*refer to rules*] promulgated by [*name of regulatory agency*].

2. We have an understanding of auditing standards generally accepted in the United States of America and [*indicate other auditing standards applicable to the audit of the group financial statements, such as* Government Auditing Standards] that is sufficient to fulfill our responsibilities in the audit of the group financial statements and will conduct our work on the financial information of [*name of component*] as of and for the year ended [*date*] in accordance with those standards.
3. We possess the special skills (e.g., industry specific knowledge) necessary to perform the work on the financial information of the particular component.
4. We have an understanding of [*indicate applicable financial reporting framework or group financial reporting procedures manual*] that is sufficient to fulfill our responsibilities in the audit of the group financial statements.

We will inform you of any changes in the above representations during the course of our work on the financial information of [*name of component*].

[*Auditor's signature*]

Illustration of Potential Component Auditor Representations in Governmental Entities and Not-for-Profit Organizations

5. We have an understanding of relevant laws and regulations that may have a direct and material effect on the financial statements of [*name of component*]. In particular, we have an understanding of [*indicate relevant laws and regulations*].

[Paragraph renumbered, effective for audits of financial statements for periods ending on or after December 15, 2012, by SAS No. 127.]

.A99

Exhibit C—Sources of Information (Ref: par. .A47)

The AICPA Professional Ethics Team can respond to inquiries about whether individuals are members of the AICPA and whether complaints against members have been adjudicated by the Joint Trial Board. The team cannot respond to inquiries about public accounting firms or provide information about letters of required corrective action issued by the team or pending disciplinary proceedings or investigations. The AICPA Peer Review Program staff or the applicable state CPA society administering entity can respond to inquiries about whether specific public accounting firms are enrolled in the AICPA Peer Review Program and the date of acceptance and the period covered by the firm's most recently accepted peer review. [Paragraph renumbered, effective for audits of financial statements for periods ending on or after December 15, 2012, by SAS No. 127.]

AU-C Section 610 *

The Auditor's Consideration of the Internal Audit Function in an Audit of Financial Statements

(Supersedes SAS No. 9.)

Source: SAS No. 65; SAS No. 122.

Effective for audits of financial statements for periods ending after December 15, 1991, unless otherwise indicated.

NOTE

Statement on Auditing Standards (SAS) No. 65, *The Auditor's Consideration of the Internal Audit Function in an Audit of Financial Statements*, is currently effective and codified as AU section 322.

SAS No. 122, *Statements on Auditing Standards: Clarification and Recodification*, redesignates AU section 322 as section 610, which will be superseded when it is redrafted for clarity and convergence with International Standard on Auditing 610 (Revised), *Using the Work of Internal Auditors*, as part of the Clarification and Convergence Project of the Auditing Standards Board. Until such time, this section has been conformed to reflect updated section and paragraph cross references, but has not otherwise been subjected to a comprehensive review or revision.

.01 The auditor considers many factors in determining the nature, timing, and extent of auditing procedures to be performed in an audit of an entity's financial statements. One of the factors is the existence of an internal audit function.[1] This section provides the auditor with guidance on considering the work of internal auditors and on using internal auditors to provide direct assistance to the auditor in an audit performed in accordance with generally accepted auditing standards (GAAS).

Roles of the Auditor and the Internal Auditors

.02 One of the auditor's responsibilities in an audit conducted in accordance with GAAS is to obtain sufficient appropriate audit evidence to provide a reasonable basis for the opinion on the entity's financial statements. In fulfilling

---

* This section has been codified using an "AU-C" identifier instead of an "AU" identifier. "AU-C" is a temporary identifier to avoid confusion with references to existing "AU" sections, which will remain in AICPA *Professional Standards* through 2013. The "AU-C" identifier will revert to "AU" in 2014, by which time substantially all engagements for which the "AU" sections were still effective are expected to be completed. [Footnote added, October 2011, to reflect conforming changes necessary due to the issuance of SAS No. 122.]

[1] An *internal audit function* may consist of one or more individuals who perform internal auditing activities within an entity. This section is not applicable to personnel who have the title *internal auditor* but who do not perform internal auditing activities as described herein.

this responsibility, the auditor maintains independence from the entity.[2] [Revised, March 2006, to reflect conforming changes necessary due to the issuance of SAS No. 105.]

.03 Internal auditors are responsible for providing analyses, evaluations, assurances, recommendations, and other information to the entity's management and those charged with governance. To fulfill this responsibility, internal auditors maintain objectivity with respect to the activity being audited. [Revised, April 2007, to reflect conforming changes necessary due to the issuance of SAS No. 114.]

Obtaining an Understanding of the Internal Audit Function

.04 An important responsibility of the internal audit function is to monitor the performance of an entity's controls. When obtaining an understanding of internal control,[3] the auditor should obtain an understanding of the internal audit function sufficient to identify those internal audit activities that are relevant to planning the audit. The extent of the procedures necessary to obtain this understanding will vary, depending on the nature of those activities.

.05 The auditor ordinarily should make inquiries of appropriate management and internal audit personnel about the internal auditors'

a. organizational status within the entity.

b. application of professional standards (see paragraph .11).

c. audit plan, including the nature, timing, and extent of audit work.

d. access to records and whether there are limitations on the scope of their activities.

In addition, the auditor might inquire about the internal audit function's charter, mission statement, or similar directive from management or those charged with governance. This inquiry will normally provide information about the goals and objectives established for the internal audit function. [Revised, April 2007, to reflect conforming changes necessary due to the issuance of SAS No. 114.]

.06 Certain internal audit activities may not be relevant to an audit of the entity's financial statements. For example, the internal auditors' procedures to evaluate the efficiency of certain management decision-making processes are ordinarily not relevant to a financial statement audit.

.07 Relevant activities are those that provide evidence about the design and effectiveness of controls that pertain to the entity's ability to initiate, authorize, record, process, and report financial data consistent with the assertions embodied in the financial statements or that provide direct evidence about potential misstatements of such data. The auditor may find the results of the

---

[2] Although internal auditors are not independent from the entity, The Institute of Internal Auditors' *Standards for the Professional Practice of Internal Auditing* defines internal auditing as an independent appraisal function and requires internal auditors to be independent of the activities they audit. This concept of independence is different from the independence the auditor maintains under the AICPA Code of Professional Conduct.

[3] Section 315, *Understanding the Entity and Its Environment and Assessing the Risks of Material Misstatement*, describes the procedures the auditor follows to obtain an understanding of internal control and indicates that the internal audit function is part of the entity's monitoring component. [Footnote revised, March 2006, to reflect conforming changes necessary due to the issuance of SAS No. 109. Footnote revised, October 2011, to reflect conforming changes necessary due to the issuance of SAS No. 122.]

following procedures helpful in assessing the relevancy of internal audit activities:

a. Considering knowledge from prior-year audits

b. Reviewing how the internal auditors allocate their audit resources to financial or operating areas in response to their risk-assessment process

c. Reading internal audit reports to obtain detailed information about the scope of internal audit activities

[Revised, April 2002, to reflect conforming changes necessary due to the issuance of SAS No. 94. Revised, March 2006, to reflect conforming changes necessary due to the issuance of SAS No. 106.]

.08 If, after obtaining an understanding of the internal audit function, the auditor concludes that the internal auditors' activities are not relevant to the financial statement audit, the auditor does not have to give further consideration to the internal audit function unless the auditor requests direct assistance from the internal auditors as described in paragraph .27. Even if some of the internal auditors' activities are relevant to the audit, the auditor may conclude that it would not be efficient to consider further the work of the internal auditors. If the auditor decides that it would be efficient to consider how the internal auditors' work might affect the nature, timing, and extent of audit procedures, the auditor should assess the competence and objectivity of the internal audit function in light of the intended effect of the internal auditors' work on the audit.

Assessing the Competence and Objectivity of the Internal Auditors

Competence of the Internal Auditors

.09 When assessing the internal auditors' competence, the auditor should obtain or update information from prior years about such factors as

- educational level and professional experience of internal auditors.
- professional certification and continuing education.
- audit policies, programs, and procedures.
- practices regarding assignment of internal auditors.
- supervision and review of internal auditors' activities.
- quality of working-paper documentation, reports, and recommendations.
- evaluation of internal auditors' performance.

Objectivity of the Internal Auditors

.10 When assessing the internal auditors' objectivity, the auditor should obtain or update information from prior years about such factors as

- the organizational status of the internal auditor responsible for the internal audit function, including
  - — whether the internal auditor reports to an officer of sufficient status to ensure broad audit coverage and adequate

- consideration of, and action on, the findings and recommendations of the internal auditors.
- whether the internal auditor has direct access and reports regularly to those charged with governance.
- whether those charged with governance oversee employment decisions related to the internal auditor.

- policies to maintain internal auditors' objectivity about the areas audited, including
  - policies prohibiting internal auditors from auditing areas where relatives are employed in important or audit-sensitive positions.
  - policies prohibiting internal auditors from auditing areas where they were recently assigned or are scheduled to be assigned on completion of responsibilities in the internal audit function.

[Revised, April 2007, to reflect conforming changes necessary due to the issuance of SAS No. 114.]

Assessing Competence and Objectivity

.11 In assessing competence and objectivity, the auditor usually considers information obtained from previous experience with the internal audit function, from discussions with management personnel, and from a recent external quality review, if performed, of the internal audit function's activities. The auditor may also use professional internal auditing standards[4] as criteria in making the assessment. The auditor also considers the need to test the effectiveness of the factors described in paragraphs .09–.10. The extent of such testing will vary in light of the intended effect of the internal auditors' work on the audit. If the auditor determines that the internal auditors are sufficiently competent and objective, the auditor should then consider how the internal auditors' work may affect the audit.

Effect of the Internal Auditors' Work on the Audit

.12 The internal auditors' work may affect the nature, timing, and extent of the audit, including

- procedures the auditor performs when obtaining an understanding of the entity's internal control (paragraph .13).
- procedures the auditor performs when assessing risk (paragraphs .14–.16).
- substantive procedures the auditor performs (paragraph .17).

When the work of the internal auditors is expected to affect the audit, the guidance in paragraphs .18–.26 should be followed for considering the extent of the effect, coordinating audit work with internal auditors, and evaluating and testing the effectiveness of internal auditors' work.

---

[4] Standards have been developed for the professional practice of internal auditing by The Institute of Internal Auditors and the General Accounting Office. These standards are meant to (*a*) impart an understanding of the role and responsibilities of internal auditing to all levels of management, boards of directors, public bodies, external auditors, and related professional organizations; (*b*) permit measurement of internal auditing performance; and (*c*) improve the practice of internal auditing.

Understanding of Internal Control

.13 The auditor obtains a sufficient understanding of the design of controls relevant to the audit of financial statements to plan the audit and to determine whether they have been placed in operation. Since a primary objective of many internal audit functions is to review, assess, and monitor controls, the procedures performed by the internal auditors in this area may provide useful information to the auditor. For example, internal auditors may develop a flowchart of a new computerized sales and receivables system. The auditor may review the flowchart to obtain information about the design of the related controls. In addition, the auditor may consider the results of procedures performed by the internal auditors on related controls to obtain information about whether the controls have been placed in operation. [Revised, February 1997, to reflect conforming changes necessary due to the issuance of SAS No. 78.]

Risk Assessment

.14 The auditor assesses the risk of material misstatement at both the financial-statement level and the account-balance or class-of-transaction level.

Financial-Statement Level

.15 At the financial-statement level, the auditor makes an overall assessment of the risk of material misstatement. When making this assessment, the auditor should recognize that certain controls may have a pervasive effect on many financial statement assertions. The control environment and accounting system often have a pervasive effect on a number of account balances and transaction classes and therefore can affect many assertions. The auditor's assessment of risk at the financial-statement level often affects the overall audit strategy. The entity's internal audit function may influence this overall assessment of risk as well as the auditor's resulting decisions concerning the nature, timing, and extent of auditing procedures to be performed. For example, if the internal auditors' plan includes relevant audit work at various locations, the auditor may coordinate work with the internal auditors (see paragraph .23) and reduce the number of the entity's locations at which the auditor would otherwise need to perform auditing procedures.

Account-Balance or Class-of-Transaction Level

.16 At the account-balance or class-of-transaction level, the auditor performs procedures to obtain and evaluate audit evidence concerning management's assertions. The auditor assesses control risk for each of the significant assertions and performs tests of controls to support assessments below the maximum. When planning and performing tests of controls, the auditor may consider the results of procedures planned or performed by the internal auditors. For example, the internal auditors' scope may include tests of controls for the completeness of accounts payable. The results of internal auditors' tests may provide appropriate information about the effectiveness of controls and change the nature, timing, and extent of testing the auditor would otherwise need to perform. [Revised, March 2006, to reflect conforming changes necessary due to the issuance of SAS No. 105.]

Substantive Procedures

.17 Some procedures performed by the internal auditors may provide direct evidence about material misstatements in assertions about specific account balances or classes of transactions. For example, the internal auditors, as part of their work, may confirm certain accounts receivable and observe certain physical inventories. The results of these procedures can provide evidence the auditor may consider in restricting detection risk for the related assertions. Consequently, the auditor may be able to change the timing of the confirmation procedures, the number of accounts receivable to be confirmed, or the number of locations of physical inventories to be observed.

Extent of the Effect of the Internal Auditors' Work

.18 Even though the internal auditors' work may affect the auditor's procedures, the auditor should perform procedures to obtain sufficient appropriate audit evidence to support the auditor's report. Evidence obtained through the auditor's direct personal knowledge, including physical examination, observation, computation, and inspection, is generally more persuasive than information obtained indirectly.[5] [Revised, March 2006, to reflect conforming changes necessary due to the issuance of SAS No. 105.]

.19 The responsibility to report on the financial statements rests solely with the auditor. Unlike the situation in which the auditor uses the work of other independent auditors,[6] this responsibility cannot be shared with the internal auditors. Because the auditor has the ultimate responsibility to express an opinion on the financial statements, judgments about assessments of inherent and control risks, the materiality of misstatements, the sufficiency of tests performed, the evaluation of significant accounting estimates, and other matters affecting the auditor's report should always be those of the auditor.

.20 In making judgments about the extent of the effect of the internal auditors' work on the auditor's procedures, the auditor considers

a. the materiality of financial statement amounts—that is, account balances or classes of transactions.

b. the risk (consisting of inherent risk and control risk) of material misstatement of the assertions related to these financial statement amounts.

c. the degree of subjectivity involved in the evaluation of the audit evidence gathered in support of the assertions.[7]

As the materiality of the financial statement amounts increases and either the risk of material misstatement or the degree of subjectivity increases, the need for the auditor to perform his or her own tests of the assertions increases. As these factors decrease, the need for the auditor to perform his or her own tests of the assertions decreases.

.21 For assertions related to material financial statement amounts where the risk of material misstatement or the degree of subjectivity involved in the evaluation of the audit evidence is high, the auditor should perform sufficient procedures to fulfill the responsibilities described in paragraphs .18–.19. In determining these procedures, the auditor gives consideration to the results of work (either tests of controls or substantive tests) performed by internal

---

[5] See paragraph .A32 of section 500, *Audit Evidence*. [Footnote revised, March 2006, to reflect conforming changes necessary due to the issuance of SAS No. 106. Footnote revised, October 2011, to reflect conforming changes necessary due to the issuance of SAS No. 122.]

[6] See section 600, *Special Considerations—Audits of Group Financial Statements (Including the Work of Component Auditors)*. [Footnote revised, October 2011, to reflect conforming changes necessary due to the issuance of SAS No. 122.]

[7] For some assertions, such as existence and occurrence, the evaluation of audit evidence is generally objective. More subjective evaluation of the audit evidence is often required for other assertions, such as the valuation and disclosure assertions.

auditors on those particular assertions. However, for such assertions, the consideration of internal auditors' work cannot alone reduce audit risk to an acceptable level to eliminate the necessity to perform tests of those assertions directly by the auditor. Assertions about the valuation of assets and liabilities involving significant accounting estimates, and about the existence and disclosure of related-party transactions, contingencies, uncertainties, and subsequent events, are examples of assertions that might have a high risk of material misstatement or involve a high degree of subjectivity in the evaluation of audit evidence.

.22 On the other hand, for certain assertions related to less material financial statement amounts where the risk of material misstatement or the degree of subjectivity involved in the evaluation of the audit evidence is low, the auditor may decide, after considering the circumstances and the results of work (either tests of controls or substantive tests) performed by internal auditors on those particular assertions, that audit risk has been reduced to an acceptable level and that testing of the assertions directly by the auditor may not be necessary. Assertions about the existence of cash, prepaid assets, and fixed-asset additions are examples of assertions that might have a low risk of material misstatement or involve a low degree of subjectivity in the evaluation of audit evidence.

Coordination of the Audit Work With Internal Auditors

.23 If the work of the internal auditors is expected to have an effect on the auditor's procedures, it may be efficient for the auditor and the internal auditors to coordinate their work by

- holding periodic meetings.
- scheduling audit work.
- providing access to internal auditors' working papers.
- reviewing audit reports.
- discussing possible accounting and auditing issues.

Evaluating and Testing the Effectiveness of Internal Auditors' Work

.24 The auditor should perform procedures to evaluate the quality and effectiveness of the internal auditors' work, as described in paragraphs .12–.17, that significantly affects the nature, timing, and extent of the auditor's procedures. The nature and extent of the procedures the auditor should perform when making this evaluation are a matter of judgment depending on the extent of the effect of the internal auditors' work on the auditor's procedures for significant account balances or classes of transactions.

.25 In developing the evaluation procedures, the auditor should consider such factors as whether the internal auditors'

- scope of work is appropriate to meet the objectives.
- audit programs are adequate.
- working papers adequately document work performed, including evidence of supervision and review.
- conclusions are appropriate in the circumstances.
- reports are consistent with the results of the work performed.

.26 In making the evaluation, the auditor should test some of the internal auditors' work related to the significant financial statement assertions. These tests may be accomplished by either (*a*) examining some of the controls, transactions, or balances that the internal auditors examined or (*b*) examining similar controls, transactions, or balances not actually examined by the internal auditors. In reaching conclusions about the internal auditors' work, the auditor should compare the results of his or her tests with the results of the internal auditors' work. The extent of this testing will depend on the circumstances and should be sufficient to enable the auditor to make an evaluation of the overall quality and effectiveness of the internal audit work being considered by the auditor.

Using Internal Auditors to Provide Direct Assistance to the Auditor

.27 In performing the audit, the auditor may request direct assistance from the internal auditors. This direct assistance relates to work the auditor specifically requests the internal auditors to perform to complete some aspect of the auditor's work. For example, internal auditors may assist the auditor in obtaining an understanding of internal control or in performing tests of controls or substantive tests, consistent with the guidance about the auditor's responsibility in paragraphs .18–.22. When direct assistance is provided, the auditor should assess the internal auditors' competence and objectivity (see paragraphs .09–.11) and supervise,[8] review, evaluate, and test the work performed by internal auditors to the extent appropriate in the circumstances. The auditor should inform the internal auditors of their responsibilities, the objectives of the procedures they are to perform, and matters that may affect the nature, timing, and extent of audit procedures, such as possible accounting and auditing issues. The auditor should also inform the internal auditors that all significant accounting and auditing issues identified during the audit should be brought to the auditor's attention.

Effective Date

.28 This section is effective for audits of financial statements for periods ending after December 15, 1991. Early application of the provisions of this section is permissible.

---

[8] See paragraphs .17–.19 of section 220, *Quality Control for an Engagement Conducted in Accordance With Generally Accepted Auditing Standards*, for the type of supervisory procedures to apply. [Footnote revised, March 2006, to reflect conforming changes necessary due to the issuance of SAS No. 108. Footnote revised, October 2011, to reflect conforming changes necessary due to the issuance of SAS No. 122.]

.29

Appendix—The Auditor's Consideration of the Internal Audit Function in an Audit of Financial Statements

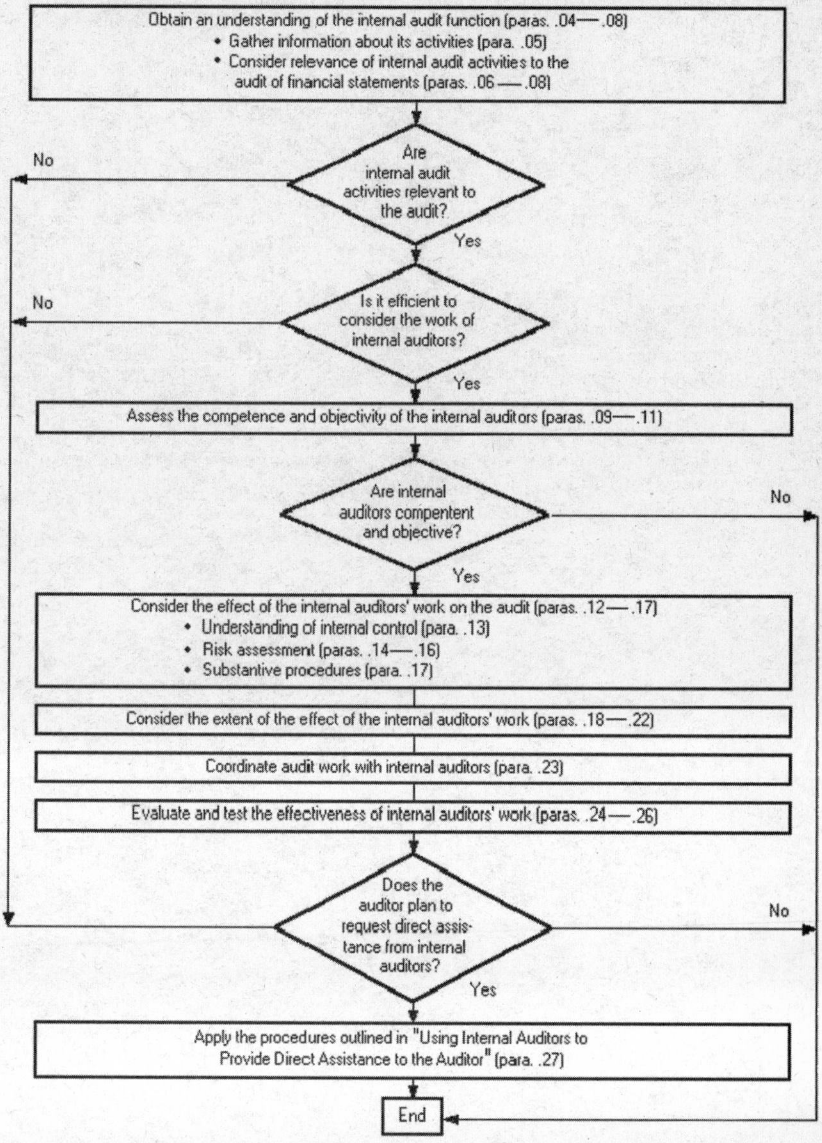

AU-C Section 620 *

Using the Work of an Auditor's Specialist

Source: SAS No. 122.

Effective for audits of financial statements for periods ending on or after December 15, 2012.

Introduction

Scope of This Section

.01 This section addresses the auditor's responsibilities relating to the work of an individual or organization possessing expertise in a field other than accounting or auditing when that work is used to assist the auditor in obtaining sufficient appropriate audit evidence.

.02 This section does not address

a. situations in which the engagement team includes a member or consults an individual or organization with expertise in a specialized area of accounting or auditing, which are addressed in section 220, *Quality Control for an Engagement Conducted in Accordance With Generally Accepted Auditing Standards*, and section 300, *Planning an Audit*,[1,2] or

b. the auditor's use of the work of an individual or organization possessing expertise in a field other than accounting or auditing, whose work in that field is used by the entity to assist the entity in preparing the financial statements (a management's specialist), which is addressed in section 500, *Audit Evidence*.[3]

The Auditor's Responsibility for the Audit Opinion

.03 The auditor has sole responsibility for the audit opinion expressed, and that responsibility is not reduced by the auditor's use of the work of an auditor's specialist. Nonetheless, if the auditor using the work of an auditor's specialist, having followed this section, concludes that the work of that specialist is adequate for the auditor's purposes, the auditor may accept that specialist's findings or conclusions in the specialist's field as appropriate audit evidence.

Effective Date

.04 This section is effective for audits of financial statements for periods ending on or after December 15, 2012.

---

* This section has been codified using an "AU-C" identifier instead of an "AU" identifier. "AU-C" is a temporary identifier to avoid confusion with references to existing "AU" sections, which will remain in AICPA *Professional Standards* through 2013. The "AU-C" identifier will revert to "AU" in 2014, by which time substantially all engagements for which the "AU" sections were still effective are expected to be completed.

[1] Paragraphs .A10 and .A20–.A22 of section 220, *Quality Control for an Engagement Conducted in Accordance With Generally Accepted Auditing Standards.*

[2] Paragraph .12 of section 300, *Planning an Audit.*

[3] Paragraphs .A35–.A49 of section 500, *Audit Evidence.*

Objectives

.05 The objectives of the auditor are

a. to determine whether to use the work of an auditor's specialist and

b. if using the work of an auditor's specialist, to determine whether that work is adequate for the auditor's purposes.

Definitions

.06 For purposes of generally accepted auditing standards, the following terms have the meanings attributed as follows:

Auditor's specialist. An individual or organization possessing expertise in a field other than accounting or auditing, whose work in that field is used by the auditor to assist the auditor in obtaining sufficient appropriate audit evidence. An auditor's specialist may be either an auditor's internal specialist (who is a partner[4] or staff, including temporary staff, of the auditor's firm or a network firm) or an auditor's external specialist. (Ref: par. .A1–.A4)

Expertise. Skills, knowledge, and experience in a particular field.

Management's specialist. An individual or organization possessing expertise in a field other than accounting or auditing, whose work in that field is used by the entity to assist the entity in preparing the financial statements.

Requirements

Determining the Need for an Auditor's Specialist

.07 If expertise in a field other than accounting or auditing is necessary to obtain sufficient appropriate audit evidence, the auditor should determine whether to use the work of an auditor's specialist. (Ref: par. .A5–.A10)

Nature, Timing, and Extent of Audit Procedures

.08 The nature, timing, and extent of the auditor's procedures with respect to the requirements in paragraphs .09–.13 will vary depending on the circumstances. In determining the nature, timing, and extent of those procedures, the auditor should consider matters including (Ref: par. .A11)

a. the nature of the matter to which the work of the auditor's specialist relates;

b. the risks of material misstatement in the matter to which the work of the auditor's specialist relates;

c. the significance of the work of the auditor's specialist in the context of the audit;

d. the auditor's knowledge of, and experience with, previous work performed by the auditor's specialist; and

e. whether the auditor's specialist is subject to the auditor's firm's quality control policies and procedures. (Ref: par. .A12–.A14)

---

[4] *Partner* and *firm* should be read as referring to their governmental equivalents when relevant.

The Competence, Capabilities, and Objectivity of the Auditor's Specialist

.09 The auditor should evaluate whether the auditor's specialist has the necessary competence, capabilities, and objectivity for the auditor's purposes. In the case of an auditor's external specialist, the evaluation of objectivity should include inquiry regarding interests and relationships that may create a threat to the objectivity of the auditor's specialist. (Ref: par. .A15–.A22)

Obtaining an Understanding of the Field of Expertise of the Auditor's Specialist

.10 The auditor should obtain a sufficient understanding of the field of expertise of the auditor's specialist to enable the auditor to (Ref: par. .A23–.A24)

a. determine the nature, scope, and objectives of the work of the auditor's specialist for the auditor's purposes and

b. evaluate the adequacy of that work for the auditor's purposes.

Agreement With the Auditor's Specialist

.11 The auditor should agree, in writing when appropriate, with the auditor's specialist regarding (Ref: par. .A25–.A29)

a. the nature, scope, and objectives of the work of the auditor's specialist; (Ref: par. .A30)

b. the respective roles and responsibilities of the auditor and the auditor's specialist; (Ref: par. .A31–.A32)

c. the nature, timing, and extent of communication between the auditor and the auditor's specialist, including the form of any report to be provided by the auditor's specialist; and (Ref: par. .A33)

d. the need for the auditor's specialist to observe confidentiality requirements. (Ref: par. .A34)

Evaluating the Adequacy of the Work of the Auditor's Specialist

.12 The auditor should evaluate the adequacy of the work of the auditor's specialist for the auditor's purposes, including

a. the relevance and reasonableness of the findings and conclusions of the auditor's specialist and their consistency with other audit evidence. (Ref: par. .A35–.A37)

b. If the work of the auditor's specialist involves the use of significant assumptions and methods,

   i. obtaining an understanding of those assumptions and methods and

   ii. evaluating the relevance and reasonableness of those assumptions and methods in the circumstances, giving consideration to the rationale and support provided by the specialist, and in relation to the auditor's other findings and conclusions. (Ref: par. .A38–.A40)

c. If the work of the auditor's specialist involves the use of source data that is significant to the work of the auditor's specialist, the relevance, completeness, and accuracy of that source data. (Ref: par. .A41–.A42)

.13 If the auditor determines that the work of the auditor's specialist is not adequate for the auditor's purposes, the auditor should (Ref: par. .A43)

a. agree with the auditor's specialist on the nature and extent of further work to be performed by the auditor's specialist or

b. perform additional audit procedures appropriate to the circumstances.

Reference to the Auditor's Specialist in the Auditor's Report

.14 The auditor should not refer to the work of an auditor's specialist in an auditor's report containing an unmodified opinion.

.15 If the auditor makes reference to the work of an auditor's external specialist in the auditor's report because such reference is relevant to an understanding of a modification to the auditor's opinion, the auditor should indicate in the auditor's report that such reference does not reduce the auditor's responsibility for that opinion. (Ref: par. .A44)

Application and Other Explanatory Material

Definitions

Auditor's Specialist (Ref: par. .06)

.A1 Expertise in a field other than accounting or auditing may include expertise regarding such matters as the following:

- The valuation of complex financial instruments and nonfinancial assets and liabilities measured at fair value such as land and buildings, plant and machinery, jewelry, works of art, antiques, intangible assets, assets acquired and liabilities assumed in business combinations, and assets that may have been impaired
- The actuarial calculation of liabilities associated with insurance contracts or employee benefit plans
- The estimation of oil and other mineral reserves
- The valuation of environmental liabilities and site cleanup costs
- The interpretation of contracts, laws, and regulations
- The analysis of complex or unusual tax compliance issues
- The determination of physical characteristics relating to quantity on hand or condition (for example, quantity or condition of minerals, or materials stored in stockpiles)

.A2 In many cases, distinguishing between expertise in accounting or auditing and expertise in another field will be straightforward, even when this involves a specialized area of accounting or auditing.[5] For example, an individual with expertise in applying methods of accounting for deferred income tax can often be easily distinguished from a specialist in taxation law. The former is not a specialist for the purposes of this section because this constitutes

---

[5] Paragraphs .A18–.A19 of section 300 address the auditor's determination of the extent of involvement of professionals possessing specialized skills.

accounting expertise; the latter is a specialist for the purposes of this section because this constitutes legal expertise. Similar distinctions also may be able to be made in other areas (for example, between expertise in methods of accounting for financial instruments and expertise in complex modeling for the purpose of valuing financial instruments). However, in some cases, particularly those involving an emerging area of accounting or auditing expertise, distinguishing between specialized areas of accounting or auditing and expertise in another field will be a matter of professional judgment. Applicable professional rules and standards regarding education and competency requirements for accountants and auditors may assist the auditor in exercising that judgment.

.A3 An individual may possess expertise in accounting or auditing, as well as expertise in a field other than accounting or auditing (for example, an actuary also may be an accountant). In that circumstance, the determination of whether that individual is an auditor or an auditor's specialist depends on the nature of the work performed by that individual that the auditor is using for purposes of the audit.

.A4 It is necessary to apply professional judgment when considering how the requirements of this section are affected by the fact that an auditor's specialist may be either an individual or an organization. For example, when evaluating the competence, capabilities, and objectivity of an auditor's specialist, it may be that the specialist is an organization the auditor has previously used, but the auditor has no prior experience with the individual specialist assigned by the organization for the particular engagement, or it may be the reverse (that is, the auditor may be familiar with the work of an individual specialist but not with the organization that specialist has joined). In either case, both the personal attributes of the individual and the managerial attributes of the organization (such as systems of quality control the organization implements) may be relevant to the auditor's evaluation.

Determining the Need for an Auditor's Specialist (Ref: par. .07)

.A5 An auditor's specialist may be needed to assist the auditor in one or more of the following:

- Obtaining an understanding of the entity and its environment, including its internal control
- Identifying and assessing the risks of material misstatement
- Determining and implementing overall responses to assessed risks at the financial statement level
- Designing and performing additional audit procedures to respond to assessed risks at the relevant assertion level, which may comprise tests of controls or substantive procedures
- Evaluating the sufficiency and appropriateness of audit evidence obtained in forming an opinion on the financial statements

.A6 The risks of material misstatement may increase when expertise in a field other than accounting is needed for management to prepare the financial statements, for example, because this may indicate some complexity or because management may not possess knowledge of the field of expertise. If, in preparing the financial statements, management does not possess the necessary expertise, a management's specialist may be used in addressing those risks. Relevant controls, including controls that relate to the work of a management's specialist, if any, also may reduce the risks of material misstatement.

.A7 If the preparation of the financial statements involves the use of expertise in a field other than accounting, the auditor, who is skilled in accounting and auditing, may not possess the necessary expertise to audit those financial statements. The engagement partner is required by section 220 to be satisfied that the engagement team and any external auditor's specialists who are not part of the engagement team, collectively, have the appropriate competence and capabilities to perform the audit engagement.[6] Further, the auditor is required by section 300 to ascertain the nature, timing, and extent of resources necessary to perform the engagement.[7] The auditor's determination of whether to use the work of an auditor's specialist, and, if so, when and to what extent, assists the auditor in meeting these requirements. As the audit progresses or as circumstances change, the auditor may need to revise earlier decisions about using the work of an auditor's specialist.

.A8 An auditor who is not a specialist in a relevant field other than accounting or auditing may nevertheless be able to obtain a sufficient understanding of that field to perform the audit without an auditor's specialist. This understanding may be obtained through, for example

- experience in auditing entities that require such expertise in the preparation of their financial statements.
- education or professional development in the particular field. This may include formal courses or discussion with individuals possessing expertise in the relevant field for the purpose of enhancing the auditor's own capacity to deal with matters in that field. Such discussion differs from consultation with an auditor's specialist regarding a specific set of circumstances encountered on the engagement in which that specialist is given all the relevant facts that will enable the specialist to provide informed advice about the particular matter (see section 220).[8]

.A9 In other cases, however, the auditor may determine that it is necessary, or may choose, to use an auditor's specialist to assist in obtaining sufficient appropriate audit evidence. Considerations when deciding whether to use an auditor's specialist may include the following:

- Whether management has used a specialist in preparing the financial statements (see paragraph .A10)
- The nature and significance of the matter, including its complexity
- The risks of material misstatement of the matter
- The expected nature of procedures to respond to identified risks, including the auditor's knowledge of, and experience with, the work of specialists regarding such matters and the availability of alternative sources of audit evidence

.A10 When management uses a management specialist in preparing the financial statements, the auditor's decision on whether to use an auditor's specialist also may be influenced by such factors as the following:

- The nature, scope, and objectives of the work of the management's specialist
- Whether the management's specialist is employed by the entity or is a party engaged by it to provide relevant services

---

[6] Paragraph .16 of section 220.

[7] Paragraph .08*e* of section 300.

[8] Paragraph .A21 of section 220.

- The extent to which management can exercise control or influence over the work of the management's specialist
- The competence and capabilities of the management's specialist
- Whether the management's specialist is subject to technical performance standards or other professional or industry requirements
- Any controls within the entity over the work of the management's specialist
- The auditor's ability to evaluate the work and findings of the management's specialist without the assistance of an auditor's specialist.

Section 500 addresses the effect of the competence, capabilities, and objectivity of management's specialists on the reliability of audit evidence.[9]

Nature, Timing, and Extent of Audit Procedures (Ref: par. .08)

.A11 The following factors may suggest the need for different or more extensive procedures than would otherwise be the case:

- The work of the auditor's specialist relates to a significant finding or issue that involves subjective and complex judgments.
- The auditor has not previously used the work of the auditor's specialist and has no prior knowledge of that specialist's competence, capabilities, and objectivity.
- The auditor's specialist is performing procedures that are integral to the audit rather than being consulted to provide advice on an individual matter.
- The specialist is an auditor's external specialist and is not, therefore, subject to the firm's quality control policies and procedures.

The Auditor's Firm's Quality Control Policies and Procedures (Ref: par. .08e)

.A12 An auditor's internal specialist may be a partner or staff, including temporary staff, of the auditor's firm and, therefore, subject to the quality control policies and procedures of that firm in accordance with QC section 10, *A Firm's System of Quality Control*.[10] An auditor's internal specialist also may be a partner or staff, including temporary staff, of a network firm, which may share common quality control policies and procedures with the auditor's firm.

.A13 In accordance with section 220, engagement teams are entitled to rely on the firm's system of quality control unless the engagement partner determines that it is inappropriate to do so based on information provided by the firm or other parties.[11] The extent of that reliance will vary with the circumstances and may affect the nature, timing, and extent of the auditor's procedures with respect to such matters as the following:

- Competence and capabilities through recruitment and training programs.

---

[9] Paragraphs .A38–.A44 of section 500.

[10] Paragraph .13 of QC section 10, *A Firm's System of Quality Control*.

[11] Paragraph .05 of section 220.

- Objectivity. The auditor's internal specialists are subject to relevant ethical requirements, including those pertaining to independence.
- Agreement with the auditor's specialist.
- The auditor's evaluation of the adequacy of the work of the auditor's specialist. For example, the firm's training programs may provide the auditor's internal specialists with an appropriate understanding of the interrelationship of their expertise with the audit process. Reliance on such training and other firm processes, such as protocols for scoping the work of the auditor's internal specialists, may affect the nature, timing, and extent of the auditor's procedures to evaluate the adequacy of the work of the auditor's specialist.
- Adherence to regulatory and legal requirements through monitoring processes.

Such reliance does not reduce the auditor's responsibility to meet the requirements of this section.

.A14 An auditor's external specialist is not a member of the engagement team and is not subject to quality control policies and procedures in accordance with QC section 10.[12]

The Competence, Capabilities, and Objectivity of the Auditor's Specialist (Ref: par. .09)

.A15 The competence, capabilities, and objectivity of an auditor's specialist are factors that significantly affect whether the work of the auditor's specialist will be adequate for the auditor's purposes. Competence relates to the nature and level of expertise of the auditor's specialist. Capability relates to the ability of the auditor's specialist to exercise that competence in the circumstances of the engagement. Factors that influence capability may include, for example, geographic location and the availability of time and resources. Objectivity relates to the possible effects that bias, conflict of interest, or the influence of others may have on the professional or business judgment of the auditor's specialist.

.A16 Information regarding the competence, capabilities, and objectivity of an auditor's specialist may come from a variety of sources, such as the following:

- Personal experience with previous work of that specialist
- Discussions with that specialist
- Discussions with other auditors or others who are familiar with that specialist's work
- Knowledge of that specialist's qualifications, membership in a professional body or industry association, license to practice, or other forms of external recognition
- Published papers or books written by that specialist
- The quality control policies and procedures of the auditor's firm and such other procedures the auditor considers necessary in the circumstances (see paragraphs .A12–.A13).

---

[12] Paragraph .13 of QC section 10.

.A17 Matters relevant to evaluating the competence, capabilities, and objectivity of the auditor's specialist include whether that specialist's work is subject to technical performance standards or other professional or industry requirements (for example, ethical standards and other membership requirements of a professional body or industry association, accreditation standards of a licensing body, or requirements imposed by law or regulation).

.A18 Other matters that may be relevant include the following:

- The relevance of the competence of the auditor's specialist to the matter for which that specialist's work will be used, including any areas of specialty within that specialist's field. For example, a particular actuary may specialize in property and casualty insurance but have limited expertise regarding pension calculations.
- The competence of the auditor's specialist with respect to relevant accounting and auditing requirements (for example, knowledge of assumptions and methods, including models, when applicable, that are consistent with the applicable financial reporting framework).
- Whether unexpected events, changes in conditions, or the audit evidence obtained from the results of audit procedures indicate that it may be necessary to reconsider the initial evaluation of the competence, capabilities, and objectivity of the auditor's specialist as the audit progresses.

.A19 A broad range of circumstances may threaten objectivity (for example, self-interest threats, advocacy threats, familiarity threats, self-review threats, and intimidation threats). Safeguards may eliminate or reduce such threats and may be created by external structures (for example, the profession, legislation, or regulation of the auditor's specialist) or by the work environment of the auditor's specialist (for example, quality control policies and procedures). There also may be safeguards specific to the audit engagement.

.A20 The evaluation of the significance of threats to objectivity and of whether a need exists for safeguards may depend upon the role of the auditor's specialist and the significance of the specialist's work in the context of the audit. There may be some circumstances in which safeguards cannot reduce threats to an acceptable level (for example, if a proposed auditor's specialist is an individual who has played a significant role in preparing the information that is being audited [that is, if the proposed auditor's specialist is a management's specialist]).

.A21 When evaluating the objectivity of an auditor's external specialist, the auditor may

a. inquire of the entity and the auditor's specialist about any known interests or relationships that the entity has with the auditor's external specialist that may affect that specialist's objectivity or

b. discuss with that specialist any applicable safeguards, including any professional requirements that apply to that specialist, and evaluate whether the safeguards are adequate to reduce threats to an acceptable level. Interests and relationships that may be relevant to discuss with the auditor's specialist include the following:

  i. Financial interests

  ii. Business and personal relationships

iii. Provision of other services by the specialist, including by the organization in the case of an external specialist that is an organization

In some cases, the auditor may obtain a written representation from the auditor's external specialist about any interests or relationships with the entity of which that specialist is aware.

.A22 If the auditor believes a relationship between the entity and the auditor's specialist might impair the objectivity of the auditor's specialist, the auditor may perform additional procedures with respect to some or all of the assumptions, methods, or findings of the auditor's specialist to determine that the findings are reasonable or may engage another auditor's specialist for that purpose.

Obtaining an Understanding of the Field of Expertise of the Auditor's Specialist (Ref: par. .10)

.A23 The auditor may obtain an understanding of the field of expertise of the auditor's specialist through the means described in paragraph .A8 or through discussion with the auditor's specialist.

.A24 Aspects of the field of the auditor's specialist relevant to the auditor's understanding may include the following:

- Whether that field of the auditor's specialist has areas of specialty within it that are relevant to the audit (see paragraph .A18)
- Whether any professional or other standards and regulatory or legal requirements apply
- What assumptions and methods, including models, when applicable, are used by the auditor's specialist, and whether they are generally accepted within that field of the auditor's specialist and appropriate for financial reporting purposes
- The nature of internal and external data or information the auditor's specialist uses

Agreement With the Auditor's Specialist (Ref: par. .11)

.A25 The following matters may vary considerably with the circumstances:

a. The nature, scope, and objectives of the work of the auditor's specialist

b. The respective roles and responsibilities of the auditor and the auditor's specialist

c. The nature, timing, and extent of communication between the auditor and the auditor's specialist.

Therefore, it is required that these matters are agreed between the auditor and the auditor's specialist regardless of whether the specialist is an auditor's external specialist or internal specialist.

.A26 The matters noted in paragraph .08 may affect the level of detail and formality of the agreement between the auditor and the auditor's specialist, including whether it is appropriate that the agreement be in writing. For example, the following factors may suggest the need for a more detailed agreement than would otherwise be the case or for the agreement to be in writing:

- The auditor's specialist will have access to sensitive or confidential entity information.

- The respective roles or responsibilities of the auditor and the auditor's specialist are different from those normally expected.
- Multijurisdictional legal or regulatory requirements apply.
- The matter to which the work of the auditor's specialist relates is highly complex.
- The auditor has not previously used work performed by the auditor's specialist.
- The auditor's use of the work of the auditor's specialist and its significance in the context of the audit is extensive.

.A27 In establishing the agreement with the auditor's specialist, an important consideration is whether the work of the auditor's specialist is subject to any reservation, limitation, or restriction and whether this has implications for the auditor.

.A28 The agreement between the auditor and an auditor's external specialist is generally in the form of an engagement letter. The appendix "Considerations for Agreement Between the Auditor and an Auditor's External Specialist" lists matters that the auditor may consider for inclusion in such an engagement letter or in any other form of agreement with an auditor's external specialist.

.A29 When no written agreement exists between the auditor and the auditor's specialist, evidence of the agreement may be included in, for example

- planning memoranda or related working papers, such as the audit program.
- the policies and procedures of the auditor's firm. In the case of an auditor's internal specialist, the established policies and procedures to which the auditor's specialist is subject may include particular policies and procedures regarding the work of the auditor's specialist. The extent of documentation in the auditor's working papers depends on the nature of such policies and procedures. For example, no documentation may be required in the auditor's working papers if the auditor's firm has detailed protocols covering the circumstances in which the work of such an auditor's specialist is used.

Nature, Scope, and Objectives of Work (Ref: par. .11a)

.A30 It often may be relevant when agreeing on the nature, scope, and objectives of the work of the auditor's specialist to include discussion of any relevant technical performance standards or other professional or industry requirements that the auditor's specialist will follow.

Respective Roles and Responsibilities (Ref: par. .11b)

.A31 Agreement on the respective roles and responsibilities of the auditor and the auditor's specialist may include the following:

- Whether the auditor or the auditor's specialist will perform detailed testing of source data
- Consent for the auditor to discuss the findings or conclusions of the auditor's specialist with the entity and others and to include details of the findings or conclusions of the auditor's specialist in the basis for a modified opinion in the auditor's report, if necessary (see paragraph .A44)

- Any agreement to inform the auditor's specialist of the auditor's conclusions concerning the work of the auditor's specialist

Working Papers

.A32 Agreement on the respective roles and responsibilities of the auditor and the auditor's specialist also may include agreement about access to, and retention of, each other's working papers. When the auditor uses the work of an internal specialist, the working papers of the auditor's specialist form part of the audit documentation. Subject to any agreement to the contrary, the auditor's external specialist's working papers are its own and do not form part of the audit documentation.

Communication (Ref: par. .11c)

.A33 Effective two way communication facilitates the proper integration of the nature, timing, and extent of the procedures of the auditor's specialist with other work on the audit and appropriate modification of the objectives of the auditor's specialist during the course of the audit. For example, when the work of the auditor's specialist relates to the auditor's conclusions regarding a significant risk, both a formal written report at the conclusion of the work of the auditor's specialist and oral reports as the work progresses may be appropriate. Identification of specific partners or staff who will interact with the auditor's specialist and procedures for communication between the auditor's specialist and the entity assist timely and effective communication, particularly on larger engagements.

Confidentiality (Ref: par. .11d)

.A34 It is necessary for the confidentiality provisions of relevant ethical requirements that apply to the auditor also to apply to the auditor's specialist.[13] Additional requirements may be imposed by law or regulation. The entity also may have requested that specific confidentiality provisions be agreed with the auditor's external specialists.

Evaluating the Adequacy of the Work of the Auditor's Specialist (Ref: par. .12)

.A35 The auditor's evaluation of the competence, capabilities, and objectivity of the auditor's specialist; the auditor's familiarity with the field of expertise of the auditor's specialist; and the nature of the work performed by the auditor's specialist affect the nature, timing, and extent of audit procedures to evaluate the adequacy of the work of the auditor's specialist for the auditor's purposes.

The Findings and Conclusions of the Auditor's Specialist (Ref: par. .12a)

.A36 Specific procedures to evaluate the adequacy of the work of the auditor's specialist for the auditor's purposes may include the following:

- Making inquiries of the auditor's specialist
- Reviewing the working papers and reports of the auditor's specialist
- Performing corroborative procedures, such as
    — observing the work of the auditor's specialist;

---

[13] See also paragraph .001 of ET section 391, *Ethics Rulings on Responsibilities to Clients.*

— examining published data, such as statistical reports from reputable, authoritative sources;

— confirming relevant matters with third parties;

— performing detailed analytical procedures; and

— reperforming calculations

- Engaging in discussion with another specialist with relevant expertise when, for example, the findings or conclusions of the auditor's specialist are not consistent with other audit evidence
- Discussing the report of the auditor's specialist with management

.A37 Relevant factors when evaluating the relevance and reasonableness of the findings or conclusions of the auditor's specialist, whether in a report or other form, may include whether they are

- presented in a manner that is consistent with any standards of the profession or industry of the auditor's specialist;
- clearly expressed, including reference to the objectives agreed with the auditor, the scope of the work performed, and standards applied;
- based on an appropriate period and take into account subsequent events, when relevant; and
- based on appropriate consideration of errors or deviations encountered by the auditor's specialist.

Assumptions, Methods, and Source Data

Assumptions and Methods (Ref: par. .12b)

.A38 When the purpose of the work of the auditor's specialist is to evaluate underlying assumptions and methods, including models, when applicable, used by management in developing an accounting estimate, the auditor's procedures are likely to be primarily directed to evaluating whether the auditor's specialist has adequately reviewed those assumptions and methods. When the purpose of the work of the auditor's specialist is to develop an auditor's point estimate or an auditor's range for comparison with management's point estimate, the auditor's procedures may be primarily directed to evaluating the assumptions and methods, including models, when appropriate, used by the auditor's specialist.

.A39 Section 540, *Auditing Accounting Estimates, Including Fair Value Accounting Estimates, and Related Disclosures*, discusses the assumptions and methods used by management in making accounting estimates, including the use, in some cases, of highly specialized, entity-developed models.[14] Although that discussion is written in the context of the auditor obtaining sufficient appropriate audit evidence regarding management's assumptions and methods, it also may assist the auditor when evaluating the assumptions and methods of an auditor's specialist.

.A40 When the work of an auditor's specialist involves the use of significant assumptions and methods, the appropriateness and reasonableness of those assumptions and methods used and their application are the responsibility of the auditor's specialist. Factors relevant to the auditor's evaluation of those assumptions and methods include whether they are

---

[14] Paragraphs .08, .13, and .15 of section 540, *Auditing Accounting Estimates, Including Fair Value Accounting Estimates, and Related Disclosures.*

- generally accepted within the field of the auditor's specialist;
- consistent with the requirements of the applicable financial reporting framework;
- dependent on the use of specialized models;[15] and
- consistent with those of management and, if not, the reason for, and effects of, the differences.

Source Data Used by the Auditor's Specialist (Ref: par. .12c)

.A41 When the work of an auditor's specialist involves the use of source data that is significant to the work of the auditor's specialist, procedures such as the following may be used to test that data:

- Verifying the origin of the data, including obtaining an understanding of and, when applicable, testing the internal controls over the data and, when relevant, its transmission to the auditor's specialist
- Reviewing the data for completeness and internal consistency

.A42 In many cases, the auditor may test source data. However, in other cases, when the nature of the source data used by an auditor's specialist is highly technical in relation to the field of the auditor's specialist, that specialist may test the source data. If the auditor's specialist has tested the source data, inquiry of the auditor's specialist by the auditor or supervision or review of the test of the auditor's specialist may be an appropriate way for the auditor to evaluate that data's relevance, completeness, and accuracy.

Inadequate Work (Ref: par. .13)

.A43 If the auditor concludes that the work of the auditor's specialist is not adequate for the auditor's purposes and the auditor cannot resolve the matter through the additional audit procedures required by paragraph .13, which may involve additional work being performed by both the auditor's specialist and the auditor or include employing or engaging another specialist, it may be necessary to express a modified opinion in the auditor's report in accordance with section 705, *Modifications to the Opinion in the Independent Auditor's Report*.

Reference to the Auditor's Specialist in the Auditor's Report (Ref: par. .14–.15)

.A44 It may be appropriate to refer to the auditor's external specialist in an auditor's report containing a modified opinion to explain the nature of the modification. In such circumstances, the auditor may need the permission of the auditor's specialist before making such a reference.

---

[15] Paragraph .14 of section 540 addresses the auditor's consideration of whether specialized skills or knowledge with regard to one or more aspects of the accounting estimates is required in order to obtain sufficient appropriate audit evidence.

.A45

Appendix—Considerations for Agreement Between the Auditor and an Auditor's External Specialist (Ref: par. .A28)

This appendix lists matters that the auditor may consider for inclusion in any agreement with an auditor's external specialist. The following list is illustrative and is not exhaustive; it is intended only to be a guide that may be used in conjunction with the considerations outlined in this section. Whether to include particular matters in the agreement depends on the circumstances of the engagement. The list also may be of assistance in considering the matters to be included in an agreement with an auditor's internal specialist.

Nature, Scope, and Objectives of the Auditor's External Specialist's Work

The following matters are examples of the nature, scope, and objectives of the auditor's external specialist's work:

- The nature and scope of the procedures to be performed by the auditor's external specialist
- The objectives of the auditor's external specialist's work in the context of materiality and risk considerations concerning the matter to which the auditor's external specialist's work relates and, when relevant, the applicable financial reporting framework
- Any relevant technical performance standards or other professional or industry requirements the auditor's external specialist will follow
- The assumptions and methods, including models, when applicable, the auditor's external specialist will use and their authority
- The effective date of, or, when applicable, the testing period for, the subject matter of the auditor's external specialist's work and requirements regarding subsequent events

The Respective Roles and Responsibilities of the Auditor and the Auditor's External Specialist

The following matters are examples of the respective roles and responsibilities of the auditor and the auditor's external specialist:

- Relevant auditing and accounting standards and relevant regulatory or legal requirements
- The consent of the auditor's external specialist to the auditor's intended use of the report of the auditor's specialist, including any reference to it or disclosure of it to others (for example, reference to it in the basis for a modified opinion in the auditor's report, if necessary, or disclosure of it to management or an audit committee)
- The nature and extent of the auditor's review of the auditor's external specialist's work

- Whether the auditor or the auditor's external specialist will test source data
- The auditor's external specialist's access to the entity's records, files, personnel, and specialists engaged by the entity
- Procedures for communication between the auditor's external specialist and the entity
- The auditor's and the auditor's external specialist's access to each other's working papers
- Ownership and control of working papers during and after the engagement, including any file retention requirements
- The auditor's external specialist's responsibility to perform work with due skill and care
- The auditor's external specialist's competence and capability to perform the work
- The expectation that the auditor's external specialist will use all knowledge that the specialist has that is relevant to the audit or, if not, will inform the auditor
- Any restriction on the auditor's external specialist's association with the auditor's report
- Any agreement to inform the auditor's external specialist of the auditor's conclusions concerning the work of the auditor's external specialist

Communications and Reporting

The following matters are examples of communications and reporting:

- Methods and frequency of communications, including the following:
    - — How the auditor's external specialist's findings or conclusions will be reported (for example, written report, oral report, ongoing input to the engagement team)
    - — Identification of specific persons within the engagement team who will liaise with the auditor's external specialist
- When the auditor's external specialist will complete the work and report findings or conclusions to the auditor
- The auditor's external specialist's responsibility to communicate promptly any potential delay in completing the work and any potential reservation or limitation on the findings and conclusions of the auditor's specialist
- The auditor's external specialist's responsibility to communicate promptly instances in which the entity restricts the access to records, files, personnel of the auditor's external specialist, or management's specialists engaged by the entity
- The auditor's external specialist's responsibility to communicate to the auditor all information that the auditor's external specialist believes may be relevant to the audit, including any changes in circumstances previously communicated

- The auditor's external specialist's responsibility to communicate circumstances that may create threats to the objectivity of the auditor's external specialist and any relevant safeguards that may eliminate or reduce such threats to an acceptable level

Confidentiality

The following matters are examples of confidentiality:

- The need for the auditor's specialist to observe confidentiality requirements, including the following:
  - — The confidentiality provisions of relevant ethical requirements that apply to the auditor
  - — Additional requirements that may be imposed by law or regulation, if any (for example, specific confidentiality provisions requested by the entity)

AU-C Section 9620 *

Using the Work of an Auditor's Specialist: Auditing Interpretations of Section 620

Interpretation No. 1, "The Use of Legal Interpretations as Audit Evidence to Support Management's Assertion That a Transfer of Financial Assets Has Met the Isolation Criterion in Paragraphs 7–14 of Financial Accounting Standards Board *Accounting Standards Codification* 860-10-40," has not been updated to reflect the issuance of Financial Accounting Standards Board (FASB) Statement No. 166, *Accounting for Transfers of Financial Assets*. FASB Statement No. 166 was incorporated into FASB *Accounting Standards Codification*™ (ASC) by FASB Accounting Standards Update No. 2009-16, *Transfers and Servicing (Topic 860): Accounting for Transfers of Financial Assets*, and is discussed in FASB ASC 860, *Transfers and Servicing*.

In addition, this interpretation has not been updated for changes to the Federal Deposit Insurance Corporation's (FDIC's) safe harbor for financial assets transferred in connection with securitizations and participations. The FDIC's final amendments to the safe harbor, *Treatment by the Federal Deposit Insurance Corporation as Conservator or Receiver of Financial Assets Transferred by an Insured Depository Institution in Connection With a Securitization or Participation After September 30, 2010* (www.fdic.gov/news/news/press/2010/pr10216.html), were issued in September 2010. The safe harbor provides important protections for securitizations and participations by confirming that in the event of a bank failure, the FDIC would not try to reclaim loans transferred into such transactions.

In light of the issuance of FASB Statement No. 166 and the FDIC's changes to the safe harbor, the AICPA's Auditing Standards Board is currently in the process of revising this interpretation. Auditors should be alert for such revisions; however, the guidance in this interpretation continues to be relevant.

* This section contains an "AU-C" identifier instead of an "AU" identifier. "AU-C" is a temporary identifier to avoid confusion with references to existing "AU" sections, which remain effective through 2013. The "AU-C" identifier will revert to "AU" in 2014, by which time this section becomes fully effective for all engagements.

1. The Use of Legal Interpretations as Audit Evidence to Support Management's Assertion That a Transfer of Financial Assets Has Met the Isolation Criterion in Paragraphs 7–14 of Financial Accounting Standards Board *Accounting Standards Codification* 860-10-40

.01 *Introduction*—Financial Accounting Standards Board (FASB) *Accounting Standards Codification* (ASC) 860,[1] *Transfers and Servicing*, requires that a transferor of financial assets must surrender control over the financial assets to account for the transfer as a sale. According to FASB ASC 860-10-40-5(a), one of several conditions that must be met to provide evidence of surrender of control is that the transferred assets have been isolated from the transferor—put presumptively beyond the reach of the transferor and its creditors, even in bankruptcy or other receivership.

Paragraphs 8–10 of FASB ASC 860-10-40 describe in greater detail the evidence required to support management's assertion that transferred financial assets have been isolated:

> Derecognition of transferred assets is appropriate only if the available evidence provides reasonable assurance that the transferred assets would be beyond the reach of the powers of a bankruptcy trustee or other receiver for the transferor or any *consolidated affiliate of the transferor*[2] that is not a special-purpose corporation or other entity designed to make remote the possibility that it would enter bankruptcy or other receivership (see FASB ASC 860-10-55-23[c]).The nature and extent of supporting evidence required for an assertion in financial statements that transferred financial assets have been isolated—put presumptively beyond the reach of the transferor and its creditors, either by a single transaction or a series of transactions taken as a whole—depend on the facts and circumstances. FASB ASC 860 does not provide guidance as to the type and amount of evidence that must be obtained to conclude that transferred financial assets have been isolated from the transferor. All available evidence that either supports or questions an assertion shall be considered. That consideration includes making judgments about whether the contract or circumstances permit the transferor to revoke the transfer. It also may include making judgments about the kind of bankruptcy or other receivership into which a transferor or SPE might be placed, whether a transfer of financial assets would likely be deemed a true sale at law, whether the transferor is affiliated with the transferee, and other factors pertinent under applicable law.

A determination about whether the isolation criterion has been met to support a conclusion regarding surrender of control is largely a matter of law. This aspect of surrender of control, therefore, is assessed primarily from a legal perspective.

.02 *Effective Date and Applicability*—This interpretation is effective for auditing procedures related to transfers of financial assets that are required to be accounted for under FASB ASC 860.[3]

---

[1] [Footnote deleted, June 2009, to reflect conforming changes necessary due to the issuance of FASB ASC.]

[2] The Financial Accounting Standards Board (FASB) *Accounting Standards Codification* (ASC) glossary defines *consolidated affiliate of the transferor* as "an entity whose assets and liabilities are included with those of the transferor in the consolidated, combined, or other financial statements being presented." [Footnote added, June 2009, to reflect conforming changes necessary due to the issuance of FASB ASC.]

[3] [Footnote renumbered and deleted, June 2009, to reflect conforming changes necessary due to the issuance of FASB ASC.]

.03 *Question*—What are the auditor's responsibilities in determining whether to use the work of a legal specialist[4] to obtain persuasive evidence to support management's assertion that a transfer of financial assets meets the isolation criterion of FASB ASC 860-10-40-5(a)?

.04 *Interpretation*—Section 500, *Audit Evidence*, states that the "preparation of an entity's financial statements may require expertise in a field other than accounting or auditing, such as actuarial calculations, valuations, or engineering data. The entity uses a management's specialist in these fields to obtain the needed expertise to prepare the financial statements."[5]

.05 Use of a management's specialist may not be necessary to obtain appropriate audit evidence to support management's assertion that the isolation criterion is met in certain situations, such as when there is a routine transfer of financial assets that does not result in any continuing involvement by the transferor.[6]

.06 Many transfers of financial assets involve complex legal structures, continuing involvement by the transferor, or other legal issues that, in the auditor's judgment, make it difficult to determine whether the isolation criterion is met. In these situations, use of a legal specialist usually is necessary. A legal specialist formulating an opinion about whether a transfer isolates the transferred assets beyond the reach of the transferor and its creditors may consider, among other things, the structure of the transaction taken as a whole, the nature of any continuing involvement, the type of insolvency or other receivership proceedings to which the transferor might become subject, and other factors pertinent under applicable law.

.07 If a legal opinion is used as evidence to support the accounting conclusion related to multiple transfers under a single structure, and such transfers occur over an extended period of time under that structure, the auditor is required to evaluate the appropriateness of the legal opinion,[7] which includes evaluating the need for management to obtain periodic updates of that opinion to confirm that there have been no subsequent changes in relevant law or applicable regulations that may change the applicability of the previous opinion to such transfers. The auditor also is required to evaluate the need for management to obtain periodic updates of an opinion to confirm that there have been no subsequent changes in relevant law or applicable regulations that may affect the conclusions reached in the previous opinion in the case of other transfers (see FASB ASC 860-10-40-41 and FASB ASC 860-20-25).

.08 If management's assertion with respect to a new transaction is that the transaction structure is the same as a prior structure for which a legal opinion that complies with this interpretation was used as evidence to support

---

[4] Client's internal or external attorney who is knowledgeable about relevant sections of the U.S. Bankruptcy Code and other federal, state, or foreign laws, as applicable. [Footnote renumbered, June 2009, to reflect conforming changes necessary due to the issuance of FASB ASC.]

[5] Paragraph .A35 of section 500, *Audit Evidence.*

[6] FASB ASC 860-10-55-28 characterizes no continuing involvement with the transferred assets as "no servicing responsibilities, no participation in future cash flows, no recourse obligations other than standard representations and warranties that the financial assets transferred met the delivery requirements under the arrangement, no further involvement of any kind. The transferee is significantly limited in its ability to pledge or exchange the transferred assets."

If a contractual provision (such as a call or removal of accounts provision) gives the transferor the unilateral ability to require the return of specific financial assets, the auditor should consider the effect of FASB ASC 860-10-40-5(c). [Footnote renumbered and revised, June 2009, to reflect conforming changes necessary due to the issuance of FASB ASC.]

[7] Paragraph .08*c* of section 500.

an assertion that the transfer of assets met the isolation criterion, the auditor is required[8] to determine whether management needs to obtain an update of that opinion to confirm that there have been no changes in relevant law, applicable regulations, or in the pertinent facts of the transaction that may affect the applicability of the previous opinion to the new transaction.

.09 *Question*—If the auditor determines that the use of a management's legal specialist is required, what should he or she consider in assessing the adequacy of the legal opinion?

.10 *Interpretation*—In assessing the adequacy of the legal opinion, the auditor is required to evaluate the competence and capabilities[9] of the legal specialist to determine whether the legal specialist has experience with relevant matters, including knowledge of the U.S. Bankruptcy Code, and other federal, state, or foreign law, as applicable, as well as knowledge of the transaction upon which management's assertion is based. For transactions that may be affected by provisions of the Federal Deposit Insurance Act (FDIA), it is important to consider whether the legal specialist has experience with the rights and powers of receivers, conservators, and liquidating agents under that act. The auditor is required to obtain an understanding of the work of the specialist,[10] which includes obtaining an understanding of the assumptions that are used by the legal specialist, and make appropriate tests of any information that management provides to the legal specialist and upon which the specialist indicates it relied. For example, testing management's information underlying a legal specialist's assumption regarding the adequacy of consideration received may depend on the nature of the transaction and the relationship of the parties. When the legal specialist's opinion has assumed the adequacy of consideration for transfers from a particular legal entity to its wholly owned subsidiary, changes in the subsidiary's capital accounts plus other consideration generally would be sufficient audit evidence about the adequacy of consideration. In the case of other transfers, such as those that are not to a wholly owned subsidiary of a particular legal entity that is the transferor, obtaining additional audit evidence may be necessary to evaluate management's assertion with regard to the adequacy of consideration upon which the legal specialist relied, because changes in the transferee's capital accounts do not solely benefit the transferring entity.

.11 The auditor also is required to evaluate the appropriateness of that specialist work as audit evidence for the relevant assertion,[11] which includes considering the form and content of the documentation that the legal specialist provides and evaluating whether the legal specialist's findings support management's assertions with respect to the isolation criterion. The requirement in FASB ASC 860 regarding reasonable assurance that the transferred assets would be isolated provides the basis for what the auditor is required to consider in evaluating the work of a legal specialist.

.12 Findings of a legal specialist that relate to the isolation of transferred financial assets are often in the form of a reasoned legal opinion that is restricted to particular facts and circumstances relevant to the specific transaction. The reasoning of such opinion may rely upon analogy to legal precedents that may not involve facts and circumstances that are comparable to that specific

---

[8] Paragraph .10 of section 315, *Understanding the Entity and Its Environment and Assessing the Risks of Material Misstatement.*

[9] Paragraph .08*a* of section 500.

[10] Paragraph .08*b* of section 500.

[11] Paragraph .08*c* of section 500.

transaction. It is important to consider the effect of any limitations or disclaimers of opinion in assessing the adequacy of any legal opinion.

.13 An example of the conclusions in a legal opinion for an entity that is subject to the U.S. Bankruptcy Code that provides persuasive evidence, in the absence of contradictory evidence, to support management's assertion that the transferred financial assets have been put presumptively beyond the reach of the entity and its creditors, even in bankruptcy or other receivership, follows:

> *We believe (or it is our opinion) that* in a properly presented and argued case, as a legal matter, in the event the Seller were to become a Debtor, the transfer of the Financial Assets from the Seller to the Purchaser *would be considered to be a sale* (or a true sale) of the Financial Assets from the Seller to the Purchaser and not a loan and, accordingly, the Financial Assets and the proceeds thereof transferred to the Purchaser by the Seller in accordance with the Purchase Agreement would not be deemed to be property of the Seller's estate for purposes of [the relevant sections] of the U.S. Bankruptcy Code.

The following additional paragraph addressing substantive consolidation applies when the entity to which the assets are sold (as described in the opinion) is an affiliate of the selling entity and may also apply in other situations as noted by the legal specialist. For example, if a so-called two-step structure has been used to achieve isolation, this paragraph usually will be required with respect to the transferee in the first step of such structure (see paragraph .15 [and related footnotes] of this interpretation for additional guidance on the second step of a two-step structure as described in paragraphs 22–23 of FASB ASC 860-10-55). When the transferor has entered into transactions with an affiliate that could affect the issue of substantive consolidation, the opinion should address the effect of that involvement on the opinion.

> Based upon the assumptions of fact and the discussion set forth previously, and on a reasoned analysis of analogous case law, *we are of the opinion that* in a properly presented and argued case, as a legal matter, in a proceeding under the U.S. Bankruptcy Code,[12] in which the Seller is a Debtor, a court *would not* grant an order consolidating the assets and liabilities of the Purchaser with those of the Seller in a case involving the insolvency of the Seller under the doctrine of substantive consolidation.

In the case of a transferor that is not entitled to become a debtor under the U.S. Bankruptcy Code, a legal opinion regarding whether the isolation criterion is met would consider whether isolation is satisfactorily achieved under the insolvency or receivership laws that apply to the transferor.

.14 Following are two examples of the conclusions in a legal opinion for an entity that is subject to receivership or conservatorship under provisions of the Federal Deposit Insurance Corporation (FDIC). The conclusions in these two examples provide persuasive evidence, in the absence of contradictory evidence, to support management's assertion that the transferred financial assets have been put presumptively beyond the reach of the entity and its creditors, even in conservatorship or receivership. Insolvency and receivership laws applicable to depository institutions, and how those laws affect the legal isolation criterion, differ depending upon the nature of the depository institution and its chartering

---

[12] For an entity subject to additional regulation (for example, a broker-dealer subject to the Securities Investor Protection Act), the legal opinion also generally should address the effect of such regulation and the policies of the regulators implementing such regulations (for example, the Securities Investor Protection Corporation). [Footnote renumbered, June 2009, to reflect conforming changes necessary due to the issuance of FASB ASC.]

authority. Accordingly, legal opinions addressing the legal isolation criterion may be formulated in different ways to accommodate those differences.[13]

Example 1. *We believe (or it is our opinion) that* in a properly presented and argued case, as a legal matter, in the event the Seller were to become subject to receivership or conservatorship, the transfer of the Financial Assets from the Seller to the Purchaser *would be considered to be a sale* (or a true sale) of the Financial Assets from the Seller to the Purchaser and not a loan and, accordingly, the Financial Assets and the proceeds thereof transferred to the Purchaser by the Seller in accordance with the Purchase Agreement would not be deemed to be property of, or subject to repudiation, reclamation, recovery, or recharacterization by, the receiver or conservator appointed with respect to the Seller.[14]

Example 2. The Federal Deposit Insurance Corporation (FDIC) has issued a regulation, 'Treatment by the Federal Deposit Insurance Corporation as Conservator or Receiver of Financial Assets Transferred by an Insured Depository Institution in Connection with a Securitization or Participation,' 12 CFR section 360.6 (the Rule). Based on and subject to the discussion, assumptions, and qualifications herein, it is our opinion that:

A. Following the appointment of the FDIC as the conservator or receiver for the Bank:

(i) The Rule will apply to the Transfers,

(ii) Under the Rule, the FDIC acting as conservator or receiver for the Bank could not, by exercise of its authority to disaffirm or repudiate contracts under 12 U.S.C. §821(e), reclaim or recover the Transferred Assets from the Issuer or recharacterize the Transferred Assets as property of the Bank or of the conservatorship or receivership for the Bank,

(iii) Neither the FDIC (acting for itself as a creditor or as representative of the Bank or its shareholders or creditors) nor any creditor of the Bank would have the right, under any bankruptcy or insolvency law applicable in the conservatorship or receivership of the Bank, to avoid the Transfers, to recover the Transferred Assets, or to require the Transferred Assets to be turned over to the FDIC or such creditor, and

(iv) There is no other power exercisable by the FDIC as conservator or receiver for the Bank that would permit the FDIC as such conservator or receiver to reclaim or recover the Transferred Assets from the Issuer, or to recharacterize the Transferred

---

[13] For an entity subject to conservatorship or liquidation under the National Credit Union Act, the examples and discussion in this paragraph would be modified to make appropriate references to "liquidation" and "liquidating agent" and additional information relating to rights and regulations of the National Credit Union Administration. [Footnote renumbered, June 2009, to reflect conforming changes necessary due to the issuance of FASB ASC.]

[14] When the opinion indicates that isolation is achieved without reference to a true sale, the opinion also should provide reasonable assurance that the transferred assets are beyond the reach of the transferor and its creditors other than the transferee to the same extent that is provided in paragraph B of example 2. [Footnote renumbered, June 2009, to reflect conforming changes necessary due to the issuance of FASB ASC.]

Assets as property of the Bank or of the conservatorship or receivership for the Bank; provided, however, that we offer no opinion as to whether, in receivership, the FDIC or any creditor of the Bank may take any such actions if the Holders [*holders of beneficial interests in the transferred assets*] receive payment of the principal amount of the Interests and the interest earned thereon (at the contractual yield) through the date the Holders are so paid; and

B. Prior to the appointment of the FDIC as conservator or receiver for the Bank, the Bank and its other creditors would not have the right to reclaim or recover the Transferred Assets from the Issuer, except by the exercise of a contractual provision [insert appropriate citation] to require the transfer, or return, of the Transferred Assets that exists solely as a result of the contract between the Bank and the Issuer.[15]

The following additional paragraph addressing substantive consolidation applies when the entity to which the assets are sold or transferred (as described in the opinion) is an affiliate of the selling entity and may also apply in other situations as noted by the legal specialist.[16] For example, if a so-called two-step structure has been used to achieve isolation, the following paragraph usually will be required with respect to the transferee in the first step of the structure (see paragraph .15 [and related footnotes] of this interpretation for additional guidance on the second step of a two-step structure as described in paragraphs 22–23 of FASB ASC 860-10-55). When the transferor has entered into transactions with an affiliate that could affect the issue of substantive consolidation, the opinion should address the effect of that involvement on the opinion:

> Based upon the assumptions of fact and the discussion set forth previously, and on a reasoned analysis of analogous case law, *we are of the opinion that* in a properly presented and argued case, as a legal matter, in a receivership, conservatorship, or liquidation proceeding in respect of the Seller, a court *would not* grant an order consolidating the assets and liabilities of the Purchaser with those of the Seller.

Certain powers to repudiate contracts, recover, reclaim, or recharacterize transferred assets as property of a transferor that are exercisable by the FDIC under the FDIA may, as of the date of the transfer, be limited by a regulation that may be repealed or amended only in respect of transfers occurring on or after the effective date of such repeal or amendment.[17] With respect to the powers of a receiver or conservator that may not be exercised under that regulation, it

---

[15] See the second paragraph of footnote 6.

Paragraph B is not required if the opinion includes both a conclusion, as set forth in example 1, that the transfer constitutes a "true sale" and the conclusions set forth in paragraph A of example 2. It is not necessary to include any provision of example 2 if the opinion is as set forth in example 1. [Footnote renumbered and revised, June 2009, to reflect conforming changes necessary due to the issuance of FASB ASC.]

[16] An additional substantive consolidation opinion is not required if the opinion states that its conclusion includes the inability to recover the transferred financial assets or recharacterize the transfer by application of the doctrine of "substantive consolidation." [Footnote renumbered, June 2009, to reflect conforming changes necessary due to the issuance of FASB ASC.]

[17] The applicable regulation is 12 U.S. *Code of Federal Regulations* 360.6, effective September 11, 2000. [Footnote renumbered, June 2009, to reflect conforming changes necessary due to the issuance of FASB ASC.]

is acceptable for attorneys to rely upon the effectiveness of the limitation on such powers set forth in the applicable regulation, provided that the attorney states, based on reasonable assumptions, that (*a*) the affected transfer of financial assets meets all qualification requirements of the regulation, and (*b*) the regulation had not, as of the date of the opinion, been amended, repealed, or held inapplicable by a court with jurisdiction with respect to such transfer. The opinion should separately address any powers of repudiation, recovery, reclamation, or recharacterization exercisable by a receiver or conservator notwithstanding that regulation (for example, rights, powers, or remedies regarding transfers specifically excluded from the regulation) in a manner that provides the same level of assurance as would be provided in the case of opinions that conform with requirements of paragraph .13 of this interpretation, except that such opinion shall address powers arising under the FDIA. The considerations in the immediately preceding three sentences are adequately addressed either by the example 1 opinion or the example 2 opinion described in this paragraph or by the variations described in the second paragraph of footnote 15 and in footnote 16 of this interpretation.

.15 A legal letter that includes an inadequate opinion, inappropriate limitations, or a disclaimer of opinion, or that effectively limits the scope of the opinion to facts and circumstances that are not applicable to the transaction, does not provide persuasive evidence to support the entity's assertion that the transferred assets have been put presumptively beyond the reach of the transferor and its creditors, even in bankruptcy or other receivership. Likewise, a legal letter that includes conclusions that are expressed using some of the following language would not provide persuasive evidence that a transfer of financial assets has met the isolation criterion of FASB ASC 860-10-40-5(a) (see paragraphs .20–.21 of this interpretation):

- "We are unable to express an opinion . . ."
- "It is our opinion, based upon limited facts . . ."
- "We are of the view . . ." or "it appears . . ."
- "There is a reasonable basis to conclude that . . ."
- "In our opinion, the transfer would *either* be a sale *or* a grant of a perfected security interest . . ."[18]
- "In our opinion, there is a reasonable possibility . . ."
- "In our opinion, the transfer *should* be considered a sale . . ."
- "It is our opinion that the company will be able to assert meritorious arguments . . ."
- "In our opinion, it is more likely than not . . ."
- "In our opinion, the transfer would *presumptively* be . . ."
- "In our opinion, it is probable that . . ."

---

[18] Certain transferors are subject only to receivership (and not to proceedings under the U.S. Bankruptcy Code or the Federal Deposit Insurance Act) under laws that do not allow a receiver to reach assets in which a security interest has been granted. In such circumstances, an opinion that concludes that the transfer would either be a sale or a grant of a security interest that puts the transferred assets beyond the reach of such receiver and other creditors would provide persuasive evidence that the isolation criterion is met.

In certain circumstances, a legal specialist may provide an opinion on both steps of a two-step structure. Such language would be acceptable in an opinion for a transfer of assets in the second step of a two-step structure as described in paragraphs 22–23 of FASB ASC 860-10-55 provided that the opinion on the transfer in the first step is consistent with paragraphs .13 or .14 of this interpretation. [Footnote renumbered and revised, June 2009, to reflect conforming changes necessary due to the issuance of FASB ASC.]

Furthermore, conclusions about hypothetical transactions may not be relevant to the transaction that is the subject of management's assertions. Section 500 states that the "auditor should design and perform audit procedures that are appropriate in the circumstances for the purpose of obtaining sufficient appropriate audit evidence."[19] Additionally, conclusions about hypothetical transactions may not contemplate all of the facts and circumstances or the provisions in the agreements of the transaction that is the subject of management's assertions, and generally would not provide persuasive evidence.[20]

.16 *Question*—Are legal opinions that restrict the use of the opinion to the client, or to third parties other than the auditor, acceptable audit evidence?

.17 *Interpretation*—No. In some cases, the auditor may decide it is necessary to contact the specialist to determine that the specialist is aware that his or her work will be used for evaluating the assertions in the financial statements.[21] Given the importance of the legal opinion to the assertion in this case, and the precision that legal specialists use in drafting such opinions, an auditor should not use as evidence a legal opinion that he or she deems otherwise adequate if the letter restricts use of the findings expressed therein to the client or to third parties other than the auditor. In that event, the auditor requests that the client obtain the legal specialist's written permission for the auditor to use the opinion for the purpose of evaluating management's assertion that a transfer of financial assets meets the isolation criterion of FASB ASC 860-10-40-5(a).

.18 An example of a letter from a legal specialist to a client that adequately communicates permission for the auditor to use the legal specialist's opinion for the purpose of evaluating management's assertion that a transfer of financial assets meets the isolation criterion of FASB ASC 860-10-40-5(a) is as follows:

> Notwithstanding any language to the contrary in our opinions of even date with respect to certain bankruptcy issues relating to the previously referenced transaction, you are authorized to make available to your auditors such opinions solely as audit evidence in support of their evaluation of management's assertion that the transfer of the receivables meets the isolation criterion of Financial Accounting Standards Board *Accounting Standards Codification* 860-10-40-5(a), provided a copy of this letter is furnished to them in connection therewith. In authorizing you to make copies of such opinions available to your auditors for such purpose, we are not undertaking or assuming any duty or obligation to your auditors or establishing any lawyer-client relationship with them. Further, we do not undertake or assume any responsibility with respect to financial statements of you or your affiliates.[22]

.19 A letter from a legal specialist to a client might authorize the client to make copies of the legal opinion available to the auditor to use in his or her evaluation of management's assertion that a transfer of financial assets meets the isolation criterion of FASB ASC 860-10-40-5(a) but then state that the auditor is not authorized to rely thereon. Such "use but not rely on" language, or other language that similarly restricts the auditor's use of the legal specialist's

---

[19] Paragraph .06 of section 500.

[20] For example, a memorandum of law from a legal specialist usually analyzes (and may make conclusions about) a transaction that may be completed subsequently. Such memorandum generally would not provide persuasive evidence unless the conclusions conform with this interpretation and a legal specialist opines that such conclusions apply to a completed transaction that is the subject of management's assertion. [Footnote renumbered, June 2009, to reflect conforming changes necessary due to the issuance of FASB ASC.]

[21] Paragraph .A39 of section 500.

[22] This language may appear in the legal specialist's opinion rather than in a separate letter. In that case, the wording would be modified slightly to indicate the context. [Footnote renumbered, June 2009, to reflect conforming changes necessary due to the issuance of FASB ASC.]

opinion, does not adequately communicate permission for the auditor to use the legal specialist's opinion as audit evidence. The auditor may consider consulting with his or her legal counsel in circumstances in which it is not clear that the auditor may use the legal specialist's opinion.

.20 *Question*—If the auditor determines that it is appropriate to use the work of a legal specialist, and either the resulting legal response does not provide persuasive evidence that a transfer of assets has met the isolation criterion or the legal specialist does not grant permission for the auditor to use a legal opinion that is restricted to the client or to third parties other than the auditor, what other steps might an auditor consider?

.21 *Interpretation*—When other relevant audit evidence exists, the auditor should consider it before reaching a conclusion about the appropriateness of management's accounting for a transfer.[23] However, because the isolation aspect of surrender of control is assessed primarily from a legal perspective, the auditor usually will not be able to obtain persuasive evidence in a form other than a legal opinion. In the absence of persuasive evidence that a transfer has met the isolation criterion, derecognition of the transferred assets is not in conformity with generally accepted accounting principles and the auditor may need to express a qualified or adverse opinion in accordance with section 705, *Modifications to the Opinion in the Independent Auditor's Report*.[24] However, if permission for the auditor to use a legal opinion that he or she deems otherwise adequate is not granted, this would be a scope limitation and the auditor should consider the need to express a qualified opinion or to disclaim an opinion in accordance with section 705.[25]

[Issue Date: December 2001; Revised: March 2006; Revised: June 2009; Revised: October 2011, effective for audits of financial statements for periods ending on or after December 15, 2012.]

---

[23] See paragraph .13 of section 620, *Using the Work of an Auditor's Specialist*, regarding additional procedures that may be applied. [Footnote renumbered, June 2009, to reflect conforming changes necessary due to the issuance of FASB ASC.]

[24] Paragraphs .07–.09 of section 705, *Modifications to the Opinion in the Independent Auditor's Report*.

[25] Paragraphs .11–.14 of section 705.

AU-C Sections 700–799

AUDIT CONCLUSIONS AND REPORTING

TABLE OF CONTENTS

AU-C Section 700 *

Forming an Opinion and Reporting on Financial Statements

Source: SAS No. 122.

Effective for audits of financial statements for periods ending on or after December 15, 2012.

Introduction

Scope of This Section

.01 This section addresses the auditor's responsibility to form an opinion on the financial statements. It also addresses the form and content of the auditor's report issued as a result of an audit of financial statements.

.02 This section is written in the context of a complete set of general purpose financial statements.

.03 Section 705, *Modifications to the Opinion in the Independent Auditor's Report*, and section 706, *Emphasis-of-Matter Paragraphs and Other-Matter Paragraphs in the Independent Auditor's Report*, address how the form and content of the auditor's report are affected when the auditor expresses a modified opinion (a qualified opinion, an adverse opinion, or a disclaimer of opinion) or includes an emphasis-of-matter paragraph or other-matter paragraph in the auditor's report.

.04 Section 800, *Special Considerations—Audits of Financial Statements Prepared in Accordance With Special Purpose Frameworks*, addresses special considerations when financial statements are prepared in accordance with a special purpose framework.[1] Section 805, *Special Considerations—Audits of Single Financial Statements and Specific Elements, Accounts, or Items of a Financial Statement*, addresses special considerations relevant to an audit of a single financial statement or of a specific element, account, or item of a financial statement. (Ref: par. .A1)

.05 Section 810, *Engagements to Report on Summary Financial Statements*, applies when an auditor is engaged to report separately on summary financial statements[2] derived from financial statements audited in accordance with generally accepted auditing standards (GAAS) by the same auditor. Section 730, *Required Supplementary Information*, addresses the auditor's responsibilities relating to information supplementary to the basic financial

---

* This section has been codified using an "AU-C" identifier instead of an "AU" identifier. "AU-C" is a temporary identifier to avoid confusion with references to existing "AU" sections, which will remain in AICPA *Professional Standards* through 2013. The "AU-C" identifier will revert to "AU" in 2014, by which time substantially all engagements for which the "AU" sections were still effective are expected to be completed.

[1] See section 800, *Special Considerations—Audits of Financial Statements Prepared in Accordance With Special Purpose Frameworks*, for a definition of *special purpose framework*.

[2] Paragraph .06 of section 810, *Engagements to Report on Summary Financial Statements*, defines the term *summary financial statements*.

statements that is required by a designated accounting standards setter to accompany such financial statements.

.06 Section 910, *Financial Statements Prepared in Accordance With a Financial Reporting Framework Generally Accepted in Another Country*, applies when an auditor practicing in the United States is engaged to report on financial statements that have been prepared in accordance with a financial reporting framework generally accepted in another country not adopted by a body designated by the Council of the AICPA (Council) to establish generally accepted accounting principles that are intended for use outside the United States.

.07 Section 510, *Opening Balances—Initial Audit Engagements, Including Reaudit Engagements*, applies when the financial statements of the prior period have been audited by a predecessor auditor or were not audited.

.08 This section promotes consistency in the auditor's report. Consistency in the auditor's report, when the audit has been conducted in accordance with GAAS, promotes credibility in the marketplace by making more readily identifiable those audits that have been conducted in accordance with recognized standards. Consistency also helps promote users' understanding and identification of unusual circumstances when they occur.

Effective Date

.09 This section is effective for audits of financial statements for periods ending on or after December 15, 2012.

Objectives

.10 The objectives of the auditor are to

a. form an opinion on the financial statements based on an evaluation of the audit evidence obtained, including evidence obtained about comparative financial statements or comparative financial information, and

b. express clearly that opinion on the financial statements through a written report that also describes the basis for that opinion. (Ref: par. .A2)

Definitions

.11 For purposes of GAAS, the following terms have the meanings attributed as follows:

Comparative financial statements. A complete set of financial statements[3] for one or more prior periods included for comparison with the financial statements of the current period.

Comparative information. Prior period information presented for purposes of comparison with current period amounts or disclosures that is not in the form of a complete set of financial statements. Comparative information includes prior period information presented as condensed financial statements or summarized financial information.

---

[3] See section 200, *Overall Objectives of the Independent Auditor and the Conduct of an Audit in Accordance With Generally Accepted Auditing Standards*, for a definition of *financial statements*.

Condensed financial statements. Historical financial information[4] that is presented in less detail than a complete set of financial statements, in accordance with an appropriate financial reporting framework. Condensed financial statements may be separately presented as unaudited financial information or may be presented as comparative information.

General purpose financial statements. Financial statements prepared in accordance with a general purpose framework. (Ref: par. .A3)

General purpose framework. A financial reporting framework designed to meet the common financial information needs of a wide range of users.

Unmodified opinion. The opinion expressed by the auditor when the auditor concludes that the financial statements are presented fairly, in all material respects, in accordance with the applicable financial reporting framework.[5]

.12 Reference to *financial statements* in this section means a complete set of general purpose financial statements, including the related notes. The related notes ordinarily comprise a summary of significant accounting policies and other explanatory information. The requirements of the applicable financial reporting framework determine the form and content of the financial statements and what constitutes a complete set of financial statements.

Requirements

Forming an Opinion on the Financial Statements

.13 The auditor should form an opinion on whether the financial statements are presented fairly, in all material respects, in accordance with the applicable financial reporting framework.

.14 In order to form that opinion, the auditor should conclude whether the auditor has obtained reasonable assurance about whether the financial statements as a whole are free from material misstatement, whether due to fraud or error. That conclusion should take into account the following: (Ref: par. .A4)

a. The auditor's conclusion, in accordance with section 330, *Performing Audit Procedures in Response to Assessed Risks and Evaluating the Audit Evidence Obtained*, about whether sufficient appropriate audit evidence has been obtained[6]

b. The auditor's conclusion, in accordance with section 450, *Evaluation of Misstatements Identified During the Audit*, about whether uncorrected misstatements are material, individually or in aggregate[7]

c. The evaluations required by paragraphs .15–.18

---

[4] Paragraph .14 of section 200 defines the term *historical financial information*.

[5] See section 200 for a definition of *applicable financial reporting framework*.

[6] Paragraph .28 of section 330, *Performing Audit Procedures in Response to Assessed Risks and Evaluating the Audit Evidence Obtained*.

[7] Paragraph .11 of section 450, *Evaluation of Misstatements Identified During the Audit*.

.15 The auditor should evaluate whether the financial statements are prepared, in all material respects, in accordance with the requirements of the applicable financial reporting framework. This evaluation should include consideration of the qualitative aspects of the entity's accounting practices, including indicators of possible bias in management's judgments. (Ref: par. .A5–.A7)

.16 In particular, the auditor should evaluate whether, in view of the requirements of the applicable financial reporting framework

- *a.* the financial statements adequately disclose the significant accounting policies selected and applied;
- *b.* the accounting policies selected and applied are consistent with the applicable financial reporting framework and are appropriate;
- *c.* the accounting estimates made by management are reasonable;
- *d.* the information presented in the financial statements is relevant, reliable, comparable, and understandable;
- *e.* the financial statements provide adequate disclosures to enable the intended users to understand the effect of material transactions and events on the information conveyed in the financial statements; and (Ref: par. .A8)
- *f.* the terminology used in the financial statements, including the title of each financial statement, is appropriate.

.17 The auditor's evaluation about whether the financial statements achieve fair presentation should also include consideration of the following:

- *a.* The overall presentation, structure, and content of the financial statements
- *b.* Whether the financial statements, including the related notes, represent the underlying transactions and events in a manner that achieves fair presentation (Ref: par. .A9)

.18 The auditor should evaluate whether the financial statements adequately refer to or describe the applicable financial reporting framework. (Ref: par. .A10–.A13)

Form of Opinion

.19 The auditor should express an unmodified opinion when the auditor concludes that the financial statements are presented fairly, in all material respects, in accordance with the applicable financial reporting framework.

.20 The auditor should modify the opinion in the auditor's report, in accordance with section 705, if the auditor

- *a.* concludes that, based on the audit evidence obtained, the financial statements as a whole are materially misstated or
- *b.* is unable to obtain sufficient appropriate audit evidence to conclude that the financial statements as a whole are free from material misstatement.

.21 If the auditor concludes that the financial statements do not achieve fair presentation, the auditor should discuss the matter with management and, depending on how the matter is resolved, should determine whether it is necessary to modify the opinion in the auditor's report in accordance with section 705. (Ref: par. .A14–.A15)

Auditor's Report

.22 The auditor's report should be in writing. (Ref: par. .A16–.A17)

Auditor's Report for Audits Conducted in Accordance With GAAS

Title

.23 The auditor's report should have a title that includes the word *independent* to clearly indicate that it is the report of an independent auditor. (Ref: par. .A18)

Addressee

.24 The auditor's report should be addressed as required by the circumstances of the engagement. (Ref: par. .A19)

Introductory Paragraph

.25 The introductory paragraph in the auditor's report should (Ref: par. .A20–.A23)

a. identify the entity whose financial statements have been audited,

b. state that the financial statements have been audited,

c. identify the title of each statement that the financial statements comprise, and

d. specify the date or period covered by each financial statement that the financial statements comprise.

Management's Responsibility for the Financial Statements

.26 The auditor's report should include a section with the heading "Management's Responsibility for the Financial Statements."

.27 The auditor's report should describe management's responsibility for the preparation and fair presentation of the financial statements. The description should include an explanation that management is responsible for the preparation and fair presentation of the financial statements in accordance with the applicable financial reporting framework; this responsibility includes the design, implementation, and maintenance of internal control relevant to the preparation and fair presentation of financial statements that are free from material misstatement, whether due to fraud or error. (Ref: par. .A24)

.28 The description about management's responsibility for the financial statements in the auditor's report should not be referenced to a separate statement by management about such responsibilities if such a statement is included in a document containing the auditor's report. (Ref: par. .A25)

Auditor's Responsibility

.29 The auditor's report should include a section with the heading "Auditor's Responsibility."

.30 The auditor's report should state that the responsibility of the auditor is to express an opinion on the financial statements based on the audit. (Ref: par. .A26)

.31 The auditor's report should state that the audit was conducted in accordance with generally accepted auditing standards and should identify the United States of America as the country of origin of those standards. The auditor's report should also explain that those standards require that the auditor plan and perform the audit to obtain reasonable assurance about whether the financial statements are free from material misstatement. (Ref: par. .A27–.A28)

.32 The auditor's report should describe an audit by stating that

a. an audit involves performing procedures to obtain audit evidence about the amounts and disclosures in the financial statements.

b. the procedures selected depend on the auditor's judgment, including the assessment of the risks of material misstatement of the financial statements, whether due to fraud or error. In making those risk assessments, the auditor considers internal control relevant to the entity's preparation and fair presentation of the financial statements in order to design audit procedures that are appropriate in the circumstances but not for the purpose of expressing an opinion on the effectiveness of the entity's internal control, and accordingly, no such opinion is expressed.

c. an audit also includes evaluating the appropriateness of the accounting policies used and the reasonableness of significant accounting estimates made by management, as well as the overall presentation of the financial statements.

In circumstances when the auditor also has a responsibility to express an opinion on the effectiveness of internal control in conjunction with the audit of the financial statements, the auditor should omit the phrase required in paragraph .32*b* that the auditor's consideration of internal control is not for the purpose of expressing an opinion on the effectiveness of internal control, and accordingly, no such opinion is expressed.

.33 The auditor's report should state whether the auditor believes that the audit evidence the auditor has obtained is sufficient and appropriate to provide a basis for the auditor's opinion.

Auditor's Opinion

.34 The auditor's report should include a section with the heading "Opinion."

.35 When expressing an unmodified opinion on financial statements, the auditor's opinion should state that the financial statements present fairly, in all material respects, the financial position of the entity as of the balance sheet date and the results of its operations and its cash flows for the period then ended, in accordance with the applicable financial reporting framework. (Ref: par. .A9 and .A29–.A30)

.36 The auditor's opinion should identify the applicable financial reporting framework and its origin. (Ref: par. .A31)

Other Reporting Responsibilities

.37 If the auditor addresses other reporting responsibilities in the auditor's report on the financial statements that are in addition to the auditor's responsibility under GAAS to report on the financial statements, these other reporting responsibilities should be addressed in a separate section in the auditor's report that should be subtitled "Report on Other Legal and Regulatory Requirements" or otherwise, as appropriate to the content of the section. (Ref: par. .A32–.A33)

.38 If the auditor's report contains a separate section on other reporting responsibilities, the headings, statements, and explanations referred to in paragraphs .25–.36 should be under the subtitle "Report on the Financial Statements." The "Report on Other Legal and Regulatory Requirements" should follow the "Report on the Financial Statements." (Ref: par. .A34)

Signature of the Auditor

.39 The auditor's report should include the manual or printed signature of the auditor's firm. (Ref: par. .A35–.A36)

Auditor's Address

.40 The auditor's report should name the city and state where the auditor practices. (Ref: par. .A37)

Date of the Auditor's Report

.41 The auditor's report should be dated no earlier than the date on which the auditor has obtained sufficient appropriate audit evidence on which to base the auditor's opinion on the financial statements, including evidence that

a. the audit documentation has been reviewed;

b. all the statements that the financial statements comprise, including the related notes, have been prepared; and

c. management has asserted that they have taken responsibility for those financial statements. (Ref: par. .A38–.A41)

Auditor's Report for Audits Conducted in Accordance With Both GAAS and Another Set of Auditing Standards

.42 Paragraph .31 requires that the auditor's report state that the audit was conducted in accordance with GAAS and identify the United States of America as the country of origin of those standards. However, an auditor may indicate that the audit was also conducted in accordance with another set of auditing standards (for example, International Standards on Auditing (ISAs), the standards of the Public Company Accounting Oversight Board, or *Government Auditing Standards*). The auditor should not refer to having conducted an audit in accordance with another set of auditing standards in addition to GAAS, unless the audit was conducted in accordance with both sets of standards in their entirety. (Ref: par. .A42)

.43 When the auditor's report refers to both GAAS and another set of auditing standards, the auditor's report should identify the other set of auditing standards, as well as their origin.

Comparative Financial Statements and Comparative Information

.44 Comparative financial statements may be required by the applicable financial reporting framework, or management may elect to provide such information. When comparative financial statements are presented, the auditor's report should refer to each period for which financial statements are presented and on which an audit opinion is expressed. (Ref: par. .A43–.A44)

.45 When expressing an opinion on all periods presented, a continuing auditor should update the report on the financial statements of one or more prior periods presented on a comparative basis with those of the current period. The auditor's report on comparative financial statements should not be dated earlier than the date on which the auditor has obtained sufficient appropriate audit evidence on which to support the opinion for the most recent audit. (Ref: par. .A45–.A46)

.46 If comparative information is presented but not covered by the auditor's opinion, the auditor should clearly indicate in the auditor's report the character of the auditor's work, if any, and the degree of responsibility the auditor is taking. (Ref: par. .A47–.A48)

.47 If comparative information is presented and the entity requests the auditor to express an opinion on all periods presented, the auditor should consider whether the information included for the prior period(s) contains sufficient detail to constitute a fair presentation in accordance with the applicable financial reporting framework. (Ref: par. .A49)

Audit Procedures

.48 The auditor should perform the procedures required by paragraphs .49–.51 if comparative financial statements or comparative information is presented for the prior period(s).

.49 The auditor should determine whether the comparative financial statements or comparative information has been presented in accordance with the relevant requirements, if any, of the applicable financial reporting framework.

.50 The auditor should evaluate whether

a. the comparative financial statements or comparative information agree with the amounts and other disclosures presented in the prior period or, when appropriate, has been restated for the correction of a material misstatement or adjusted for the retrospective application of an accounting principle, and

b. the accounting policies reflected in the comparative financial statements or comparative information are consistent with those applied in the current period or if there have been changes in accounting policies, whether those changes have been properly accounted for and adequately presented and disclosed.[8]

.51 If the auditor becomes aware of a possible material misstatement in the comparative financial statements or comparative information while performing the current period audit, the auditor should perform such additional audit procedures as are necessary in the circumstances to obtain sufficient appropriate audit evidence to determine whether a material misstatement exists. If the auditor audited the prior period's financial statements and becomes aware of a material misstatement in those financial statements, the auditor should also follow the relevant requirements of section 560, *Subsequent Events and Subsequently Discovered Facts*. If the prior period financial statements are restated, the auditor should determine that the comparative financial statements or comparative information agree with the restated financial statements.

.52 As required by section 580, *Written Representations*, the auditor should request written representations for all periods referred to in the auditor's opinion. The auditor also should obtain a specific written representation regarding any restatement made to correct a material misstatement in a prior period that affects the comparative financial statements. (Ref: par. .A50)

.53 When reporting on prior period financial statements in connection with the current period's audit, if the auditor's opinion on such prior period financial statements differs from the opinion the auditor previously expressed, the auditor should disclose the following matters in an emphasis-of-matter or other-matter paragraph, in accordance with section 706:

a. The date of the auditor's previous report

b. The type of opinion previously expressed

c. The substantive reasons for the different opinion

d. That the auditor's opinion on the amended financial statements is different from the auditor's previous opinion (Ref: par. .A51)

---

[8] See section 708, *Consistency of Financial Statements*.

Prior Period Financial Statements Audited by a Predecessor Auditor

.54 If the financial statements of the prior period were audited by a predecessor auditor, and the predecessor auditor's report on the prior period's financial statements is not reissued,[9] in addition to expressing an opinion on the current period's financial statements, the auditor should state the following in an other-matter paragraph:[10]

a. That the financial statements of the prior period were audited by a predecessor auditor

b. The type of opinion expressed by the predecessor auditor and, if the opinion was modified, the reasons therefore

c. The nature of an emphasis-of-matter paragraph or other-matter paragraph included in the predecessor auditor's report, if any

d. The date of that report

.55 If the auditor concludes that a material misstatement exists that affects the prior period financial statements on which the predecessor auditor had previously reported without modification, the auditor should follow the communication requirements in section 510.[11] If the prior period financial statements are restated, and the predecessor auditor agrees to issue a new auditor's report on the restated financial statements of the prior period, the auditor should express an opinion only on the current period. (Ref: par. .A52)

Prior Period Financial Statements Not Audited

.56 When current period financial statements are audited and presented in comparative form with compiled or reviewed financial statements for the prior period, and the report on the prior period is not reissued, the auditor should include an other-matter paragraph[12] in the current period auditor's report that includes the following:

a. The service performed in the prior period

b. The date of the report on that service

c. A description of any material modifications noted in that report

d. A statement that the service was less in scope than an audit and does not provide the basis for the expression of an opinion on the financial statements (Ref: par. .A53–.A54)

.57 If the prior period financial statements were not audited, reviewed, or compiled, the financial statements should be clearly marked to indicate their status, and the auditor's report should include an other-matter paragraph to indicate that the auditor has not audited, reviewed, or compiled the prior period financial statements and that the auditor assumes no responsibility for them. (Ref: par. .A55)

---

[9] Paragraphs .19–.20 of section 560, *Subsequent Events and Subsequently Discovered Facts.*

[10] See section 706, *Emphasis-of-Matter Paragraphs and Other-Matter Paragraphs in the Independent Auditor's Report.*

[11] Paragraphs .12–.13 of section 510, *Opening Balances—Initial Audit Engagements, Including Reaudit Engagements.*

[12] See section 706.

Information Presented in the Financial Statements (Ref: par. .A56–.A57)

.58 Information that is not required by the applicable financial reporting framework but is nevertheless presented as part of the basic financial statements should be covered by the auditor's opinion if it cannot be clearly differentiated.

Application and Other Explanatory Material

Scope of This Section (Ref: par. .04)

.A1 Section 800 also addresses the auditor's responsibilities when the auditor is reporting on financial statements prepared in accordance with a special purpose framework and is required by law or regulation to use a specific layout, form, or wording of the auditor's report. When reporting on financial statements prepared in accordance with a general purpose framework, and law or regulation requires a specific layout, form, or wording of the auditor's report, the auditor may adapt and apply the requirements in section 800.

Objectives

Considerations Specific to Governmental Entities (Ref: par. .10)

.A2 For audits of governmental entities, the objectives of a financial statement audit are often broader than forming and expressing an opinion on the financial statements. Law, regulation, and *Government Auditing Standards* require that the auditor satisfy additional objectives. These additional objectives include audit and reporting responsibilities, for example, relating to reporting instances of noncompliance with applicable laws and regulations or reporting material weaknesses and significant deficiencies in internal control noted during the audit. Such reporting on compliance and internal control is an integral part of a *Government Auditing Standards* audit.

Definitions

General Purpose Financial Statements

Considerations Specific to Governmental Entities (Ref: par. .11)

.A3 For audits of governmental entities, the term *general purpose financial statements*, in the context of this section, would be considered or referred to as basic financial statements using the terms in the governmental entity's applicable financial reporting framework.

Forming an Opinion on the Financial Statements (Ref: par. .14)

Considerations Specific to Governmental Entities

.A4 For most state or local governmental entities, the applicable financial reporting framework is based on multiple reporting units and, therefore, requires the presentation of financial statements for its activities in various reporting units. Consequently, a reporting unit, or aggregation of reporting units, of the governmental entity represents an opinion unit to the auditor. In the context of this section, the auditor is responsible for forming an opinion on the financial statements for each opinion unit within a governmental entity.

Qualitative Aspects of the Entity's Accounting Practices (Ref: par. .15)

.A5 Management makes a number of judgments about the amounts and disclosures in the financial statements.

.A6 Section 260, *The Auditor's Communication With Those Charged With Governance*, contains a discussion of the qualitative aspects of accounting practices.[13] In considering the qualitative aspects of the entity's accounting practices, the auditor may become aware of possible bias in management's judgments. The auditor may conclude that the cumulative effect of a lack of neutrality, together with the effect of uncorrected misstatements, causes the financial statements as a whole to be materially misstated. Indicators of a lack of neutrality that may affect the auditor's evaluation of whether the financial statements as a whole are materially misstated include the following:

- The selective correction of misstatements brought to management's attention during the audit (for example, correcting misstatements with the effect of increasing reported earnings but not correcting misstatements that have the effect of decreasing reported earnings)
- Possible management bias in the making of accounting estimates

.A7 Section 540, *Auditing Accounting Estimates, Including Fair Value Accounting Estimates, and Related Disclosures*, addresses possible management bias in making accounting estimates. Indicators of possible management bias, themselves, do not constitute misstatements for purposes of drawing conclusions on the reasonableness of individual accounting estimates. They may, however, affect the auditor's evaluation of whether the financial statements as a whole are free from material misstatement.

Disclosure of the Effect of Material Transactions and Events on the Information Conveyed in the Financial Statements (Ref: par. .16e)

.A8 It is common for financial statements prepared in accordance with a general purpose framework to present an entity's financial position, results of operations, and cash flows. In such circumstances, paragraph .16*e* requires the auditor to evaluate whether the financial statements provide adequate disclosures to enable the intended users to understand the effect of material transactions and events on the entity's financial position, results of operations, and cash flows.

Evaluation of Whether the Financial Statements Achieve Fair Presentation (Ref: par. .17b)

.A9 As described in section 200, *Overall Objectives of the Independent Auditor and the Conduct of an Audit in Accordance With Generally Accepted Auditing Standards*, a *financial reporting framework* is a set of criteria used to determine measurement, recognition, presentation, and disclosure of all material items appearing in the financial statements. The auditor's professional judgment concerning the fairness of the presentation of the financial statements is applied within the context of the financial reporting framework. Without that framework, the auditor would have no consistent standard for evaluating the presentation of financial position, results of operations, and cash flows in financial statements.

---

[13] The appendix, "Qualitative Aspects of Accounting Practices," of section 260, *The Auditor's Communication With Those Charged With Governance*.

Description of the Applicable Financial Reporting Framework (Ref: par. .18)

.A10 As explained in section 200, the preparation and fair presentation of the financial statements by management and, when appropriate, those charged with governance requires the inclusion of an adequate description of the applicable financial reporting framework in the financial statements.[14] That description is important because it advises users of the financial statements of the framework on which the financial statements are based.

.A11 A description that the financial statements are prepared in accordance with a particular applicable financial reporting framework is appropriate only if the financial statements comply with all the requirements of that framework that are effective during the period covered by the financial statements.

.A12 A description of the applicable financial reporting framework that contains imprecise qualifying or limiting language (for example, "the financial statements are in substantial compliance with International Financial Reporting Standards") is not an adequate description of that framework because it may mislead users of the financial statements.

.A13 Financial statements that are prepared in accordance with one financial reporting framework and that contain a note or supplementary statement reconciling the results to those that would be shown under another framework are not prepared in accordance with that other framework. This is because the financial statements do not include all the information in the manner required by that other framework. The financial statements may, however, be prepared in accordance with one applicable financial reporting framework and, in addition, describe in the notes to the financial statements the extent to which the financial statements comply with another framework. Such information may not be required by the applicable financial reporting framework but may be presented as part of the basic financial statements. As discussed in paragraph .58, such information is considered an integral part of the financial statements if it cannot be clearly differentiated and, accordingly, is covered by the auditor's opinion.

Form of Opinion (Ref: par. .21)

.A14 There may be cases when the financial statements, although prepared in accordance with the requirements of a fair presentation framework, do not achieve fair presentation. When this is the case, it may be possible for management to include additional disclosures in the financial statements beyond those specifically required by the framework or, in unusual circumstances, to depart from a requirement in the framework in order to achieve fair presentation of the financial statements, which would be extremely rare.

.A15 Rule 203, *Accounting Principles*, of the AICPA Code of Professional Conduct states the following:

> A member shall not (1) express an opinion or state affirmatively that the financial statements or other financial data of any entity are presented in conformity with generally accepted accounting principles or (2) state that he or she is not aware of any material modifications that should be made to such statements or data in order for them to be in conformity with generally accepted accounting principles, if such statements or data contain any departure from an accounting principle promulgated by bodies designated by Council to establish such principles that has a material effect on the statements or data taken as a whole.

---

[14] Paragraphs .A2–.A3 of section 200.

If, however, the statements or data contain such a departure and the member can demonstrate that due to unusual circumstances the financial statements or data would otherwise have been misleading, the member can comply with the rule by describing the departure, its approximate effects, if practicable, and the reasons why compliance with the principle would result in a misleading statement.

Auditor's Report (Ref: par. .22)

.A16 A written report encompasses reports issued in hard copy format and those using an electronic medium.

.A17 The exhibit "Illustrations of Auditor's Reports on Financial Statements" contains illustrations of auditor's reports on financial statements incorporating the elements required by paragraphs .23–.41.

Auditor's Report for Audits Conducted in Accordance With GAAS

Title (Ref: par. .23)

.A18 A title indicating the report is the report of an independent auditor (for example, "Independent Auditor's Report") affirms that the auditor has met all of the relevant ethical requirements regarding independence and, therefore, distinguishes the independent auditor's report from reports issued by others. Section 200 provides guidance on reporting when the auditor is not independent.

Addressee (Ref: par. .24)

.A19 The auditor's report is normally addressed to those for whom the report is prepared. The report may be addressed to the entity whose financial statements are being audited or to those charged with governance. A report on the financial statements of an unincorporated entity may be addressed as circumstances dictate (for example, to the partners, general partner, or proprietor). Occasionally, an auditor may be retained to audit the financial statements of an entity that is not a client; in such a case, the report may be addressed to the client and not to those charged with governance of the entity whose financial statements are being audited.

Introductory Paragraph (Ref: par. .25)

.A20 The introductory paragraph states, for example, that the auditor has "audited the accompanying financial statements of ABC Company, which comprise the balance sheet as of December 31, 20X1, and the related statements of income, changes in stockholders' equity, and cash flows for the year then ended, and the related notes to the financial statements." If the financial statements include a separate statement of changes in stockholders' equity accounts or a separate statement of comprehensive income, paragraph .25c requires such statements to be identified in the introductory paragraph of the report as a statement to which the financial statements are comprised, but they need not be reported on separately in the opinion paragraph because changes in stockholders' equity accounts and comprehensive income are considered part of the presentation of financial position, results of operations, and cash flows.

.A21 When the auditor is aware that the audited financial statements will be included in a document that contains other information, such as an annual report, the auditor may consider, if the form of presentation allows, identifying the page numbers on which the audited financial statements are presented. This helps users identify the financial statements to which the auditor's report relates.

.A22 The auditor's opinion covers the complete set of financial statements, as defined by the applicable financial reporting framework. For example, in the case of many general purpose frameworks, the financial statements include a balance sheet; an income statement; a statement of changes in equity; and a cash flow statement, including related notes. In some circumstances, additional or different statements, schedules, or information also might be considered to be an integral part of the financial statements.

.A23 The identification of the title for each statement that the financial statements comprise may be achieved by referencing the table of contents.

Management's Responsibility for the Financial Statements (Ref: par. .27–.28)

.A24 Section 200 explains the premise relating to the responsibilities of management and, when appropriate, those charged with governance on which an audit in accordance with GAAS is conducted.[15] Management and, when appropriate, those charged with governance accept responsibility for the preparation of the financial statements in accordance with the applicable financial reporting framework, including their fair presentation. Management also accepts responsibility for the design, implementation, and maintenance of internal control relevant to the preparation and fair presentation of financial statements that are free from material misstatement, whether due to fraud or error. The description of management's responsibilities in the auditor's report includes reference to both responsibilities because it helps explain to users the premise on which an audit is conducted.

.A25 In some instances, a document containing the auditor's report may include a separate statement by management regarding its responsibility for the preparation of the financial statements. Any elaboration in the auditor's report about management's responsibilities regarding the preparation of the financial statements, or reference to a separate statement by management about such responsibilities if one is included in a document containing the auditor's report, may lead users to erroneously believe that the auditor is providing assurances about representations made by management about their responsibility for financial reporting, internal control, and other matters that might be discussed in the management report.

Auditor's Responsibility (Ref: par. .30–.31)

.A26 The auditor's report states that the auditor's responsibility is to express an opinion on the financial statements based on the audit in order to contrast it to management's responsibility for the preparation of the financial statements.

.A27 The reference to the standards used conveys to the users of the auditor's report that the audit has been conducted in accordance with established standards. For example, the auditor's report may refer to auditing standards generally accepted in the United States of America or U.S. generally accepted auditing standards.

.A28 In accordance with section 200, the auditor does not represent compliance with GAAS in the auditor's report, unless the auditor has complied with the requirements of section 200 and all other AU-C sections relevant to the audit.[16]

---

[15] Paragraphs .05 and .A2 of section 200.

[16] Paragraph .22 of section 200.

Auditor's Opinion (Ref: par. .35)

.A29 *Description of information that the financial statements present.* The auditor's opinion states that the financial statements present fairly, in all material respects, the information that the financial statements are designed to present.

.A30 The title of the financial statements identified in the introductory paragraph of the auditor's report (see paragraph .25) describes the information that is the subject of the auditor's opinion.

.A31 *Description of the applicable financial reporting framework and how it may affect the auditor's opinion (Ref: par. .36).* The identification of the applicable financial reporting framework in the auditor's opinion is intended to advise users of the auditor's report of the context in which the auditor's opinion is expressed; it is not intended to limit the evaluation required in paragraph .17. For example, the applicable financial reporting framework may be identified as accounting principles generally accepted in the United States of America or U.S. generally accepted accounting principles or International Financial Reporting Standards promulgated by the International Accounting Standards Board (IASB) or *International Financial Reporting Standard for Small and Medium-Sized Entities* promulgated by the IASB.

Other Reporting Responsibilities (Ref: par. .37–.38)

.A32 In some circumstances, the auditor may have additional responsibilities to report on other matters that are supplementary to the auditor's responsibility under GAAS to report on the financial statements. The form and content of the "Other Reporting Responsibilities" section of the auditor's report described in paragraph .37 will vary depending on the nature of the auditor's other reporting responsibilities. For example, for audits conducted under *Government Auditing Standards*, the auditor may be required to report on internal control over financial reporting and compliance with laws, regulations, and provisions of contracts or grant agreements, which may be included in the "Other Reporting Responsibilities" section of the auditor's report.[17] However, when the auditor is engaged or required by law or regulation to perform a compliance audit in accordance with GAAS, *Government Auditing Standards*, and a governmental audit requirement, reporting requirements in section 935, *Compliance Audits*, apply.

.A33 In some cases, the relevant law or regulation may require or permit the auditor to report on these other responsibilities within the auditor's report on the financial statements. In other cases, the auditor may be required or permitted to report on them in a separate report.

.A34 These other reporting responsibilities are addressed in a separate section of the auditor's report in order to clearly distinguish them from the auditor's responsibility under GAAS to report on the financial statements. When relevant, this section may contain subheading(s) that describe(s) the content of the other reporting responsibility paragraph(s).

Signature of the Auditor (Ref: par. .39)

.A35 In certain situations, the auditor's report may be required by law or regulation to include the personal name and signature of the auditor, in addition to the auditor's firm. In addition to the auditor's signature, in certain circumstances, the auditor may be required to declare in the auditor's report the

---

[17] See the AICPA Audit and Accounting Guide *State and Local Governments* for illustrative auditor reports.

auditor's professional accountancy designation or the fact that the auditor or firm, as appropriate, has been recognized by the appropriate licensing authority.

.A36 *Considerations specific to governmental entities.* This section would not preclude a governmental auditor from including the personal name and signature of the auditor in the auditor's report when, in certain situations, the governmental auditor is required by law or regulation or chooses to do so.

Auditor's Address (Ref: par. .40)

.A37 In the United States, the location of the issuing office is the city and state. In another country, it may be the city and country.

Date of the Auditor's Report (Ref: par. .41)

.A38 The date of the auditor's report informs the user of the auditor's report that the auditor has considered the effect of events and transactions of which the auditor became aware and that occurred up to that date. The auditor's responsibility for events and transactions after the date of the auditor's report is addressed in section 560.

.A39 Section 220, *Quality Control for an Engagement Conducted in Accordance With Generally Accepted Auditing Standards*, requires that on or before the date of the auditor's report, the engagement partner, through a review of the audit documentation and discussion with the engagement team, be satisfied that sufficient appropriate audit evidence has been obtained to support the conclusions reached and for the auditor's report to be issued.[18] Section 220 also requires that the auditor's report not be released prior to the completion of the engagement quality control review.[19]

.A40 Because the auditor's opinion is provided on the financial statements, and the financial statements are the responsibility of management, the auditor is not in a position to conclude that sufficient appropriate audit evidence has been obtained until evidence is obtained that all the statements that the financial statements comprise, including the related notes, have been prepared, and management has accepted responsibility for them.

.A41 *Considerations specific to governmental entities.* In some circumstances, final approval of the financial statements by governmental legislative bodies (or subsets of such legislative bodies) is required before the financial statements are issued. In these circumstances, final approval by such legislative bodies (or subsets of such legislative bodies) is not necessary for the auditor to conclude that sufficient appropriate audit evidence has been obtained. The date of approval of the financial statements, for purposes of GAAS, is the earlier date on which those with the recognized authority determine that all the statements that the financial statements comprise, including the related notes, have been prepared and that those with the recognized authority have asserted that they have taken responsibility for them.

Auditor's Report for Audits Conducted in Accordance With Both GAAS and Another Set of Auditing Standards (Ref: par. .42)

.A42 If the audit is performed in accordance with both GAAS and ISAs, the auditor may find it helpful to refer to AU-C appendix B, "Substantive Differences Between the International Standards on Auditing and Generally Accepted Auditing Standards." This appendix summarizes substantive differences

---

[18] See paragraphs .19 and .A17 of section 220, *Quality Control for an Engagement Conducted in Accordance With Generally Accepted Auditing Standards*, for further discussion.

[19] Paragraph .21 of section 220.

between the ISAs and GAAS to assist the auditor in planning and performing an engagement in accordance with ISAs.

Comparative Financial Statements and Comparative Information

Comparative Financial Statements (Ref: par. .44–.45)

.A43 The level of information included for the prior periods in comparative financial statements is comparable with that of the financial statements of the current period.

.A44 Because the auditor's report on comparative financial statements applies to the financial statements for each of the periods presented, the auditor may express a qualified opinion or an adverse opinion, disclaim an opinion, or include an emphasis-of-matter paragraph with respect to one or more financial statements for one or more periods while expressing a different auditor's opinion on one or more financial statements of another period presented.

Updating the Report

.A45 An updated report on prior period financial statements is distinguished from a reissuance of a previous report.[20] When issuing an updated report, the information considered by the continuing auditor is that which the auditor has become aware of during the audit of the current period financial statements. In addition, an updated report is issued in conjunction with the auditor's report on the current period financial statements.

Other Considerations Relating to Comparative Financial Statements

.A46 If one firm of independent auditors merges with another firm, and the new firm becomes the auditor of a former client of one of the two former firms, the new firm may accept responsibility and express an opinion on the financial statements for the prior period(s), as well as for those of the current period. In such circumstances, paragraphs .44–.57 apply. The new firm may indicate in the auditor's report or as part of the signature that a merger took place and may name the firm of independent auditors that was merged with it. If the new firm decides not to express an opinion on the prior period financial statements, the guidance for the reissuance of reports in section 560 would apply.

Comparative Information (Ref: par. .46–.47)

.A47 Comparative information, which may be condensed financial statements or prior period summarized financial information, is not considered comparative financial statements because it is not a complete set of financial statements. For example, entities such as state and local governmental units frequently present total-all-funds information for the prior periods rather than information by individual funds because of space limitations or to avoid cumbersome or confusing formats. Also, not-for-profit organizations frequently present certain summarized financial information for the prior period(s) in total rather than by net asset class. Accordingly, the auditor need not opine on comparative information in accordance with this section.

.A48 Paragraph .46 requires the auditor to clearly indicate the character of the auditor's work, if any, and the degree of responsibility the auditor is taking in the auditor's report when comparative information is presented but not covered by the auditor's opinion on the financial statements of the current

---

[20] See section 560.

period. The requirements and guidance in section 930, *Interim Financial Information*, may be adapted to report on condensed financial statements or prior period summarized financial information that is derived from audited financial statements and is presented comparatively with the complete set of financial statements of the current period.[21,22] The exhibit provides examples of auditor's reports when comparative summarized financial information for the prior period is presented.[23]

.A49 If an entity requests the auditor to express an opinion on all periods presented, and comparative information is presented for one or more prior periods, in most cases, this will necessitate including additional columns or separate detail by fund or net asset class, or the auditor may need to modify the auditor's opinion, as required by section 705.

Written Representations (Ref: par. .52)

.A50 In the case of comparative financial statements, the written representations are requested for all periods referred to in the auditor's opinion because management needs to reaffirm that the written representations it previously made with respect to the prior period remain appropriate.

Opinion on Prior Period Financial Statements Different From Previous Opinion (Ref: par. .53)

.A51 When reporting on the prior period financial statements in connection with the current period's audit, the opinion expressed on the prior period financial statements may be different from the opinion previously expressed if the auditor becomes aware of circumstances or events that materially affect the financial statements of a prior period during the course of the audit of the current period. In some circumstances, the auditor may have additional reporting responsibilities designed to prevent future reliance on the auditor's previously issued report on the prior period financial statements.[24]

Prior Period Financial Statements Audited by a Predecessor Auditor (Ref: par. .55)

.A52 The predecessor auditor may be unable or unwilling to reissue the auditor's report on the prior period financial statements that have been restated. In this situation, provided that the auditor has audited the adjustments to the prior period financial statements, the auditor may include an other-matter paragraph[25] in the auditor's report indicating that the predecessor auditor reported on the financial statements of the prior period before restatement. In addition, if the auditor is engaged to audit and obtains sufficient appropriate audit evidence to be satisfied about the appropriateness of the restatement, the auditor's report may also include the following paragraph within the other-matter paragraph section:

> As part of our audit of the 20X2 financial statements, we also audited the adjustments described in Note X that were applied to restate the 20X1 financial

---

[21] Paragraph .33 of section 930, *Interim Financial Information.*

[22] See the AICPA Audit and Accounting Guides *State and Local Governments* and *Not-for-Profit Entities* for further guidance on reporting on summarized comparative financial information.

[23] Illustration 4, "An Auditor's Report on a Single Year Prepared in Accordance with Accounting Principles Generally Accepted in the United States of America When Comparative Summarized Financial Information for the Prior Year is Presented," of the exhibit, "Illustrations of Auditor's Reports on Financial Statements."

[24] See section 560.

[25] See section 706.

statements. In our opinion, such adjustments are appropriate and have been properly applied. We were not engaged to audit, review, or apply any procedures to the 20X1 financial statements of the Company other than with respect to the adjustments and, accordingly, we do not express an opinion or any other form of assurance on the 20X1 financial statements as a whole.

Prior Period Financial Statements Not Audited (Ref: par. .56–.57)

.A53 If the prior period financial statements were reviewed, the following is an example of an other-matter paragraph:

Other Matter

The 20X1 financial statements were reviewed by us (other accountants) and our (their) report thereon, dated March 1, 20X2, stated we (they) were not aware of any material modifications that should be made to those statements for them to be in conformity with accounting principles generally accepted in the United States of America. However, a review is substantially less in scope than an audit and does not provide a basis for the expression of an opinion on the financial statements.

.A54 If the prior period financial statements were compiled, the following is an example of an other-matter paragraph:

Other Matter

The 20X1 financial statements were compiled by us (other accountants) and our (their) report thereon, dated March 1, 20X2, stated we (they) did not audit or review those financial statements and, accordingly, express no opinion or other form of assurance on them.

.A55 If the prior period financial statements were not audited, reviewed, or compiled, the following is an example of an other-matter paragraph:

Other Matter

The accompanying balance sheet of X Company as of December 31, 20X1, and the related statements of income and cash flows for the year then ended were not audited, reviewed, or compiled by us and, accordingly, we do not express an opinion or any other form of assurance on them.

Information Presented in the Financial Statements (Ref: par. .58)

.A56 In some circumstances, the entity may be required by law, regulation, or standards, or may voluntarily choose, to include in the basic financial statements information that is not required by the applicable financial reporting framework. The auditor's opinion covers information that cannot be clearly differentiated from the financial statements because of its nature and how it is presented.

.A57 If the information included in the basic financial statements is not required by the applicable financial reporting framework and is not necessary for fair presentation but is clearly differentiated, then such information may be identified as *unaudited* or as *not covered by the auditor's report*.

.A58

Exhibit—Illustrations of Auditor's Reports on Financial Statements (Ref: par. .A17)

Illustration 1—An Auditor's Report on Consolidated Comparative Financial Statements Prepared in Accordance With Accounting Principles Generally Accepted in the United States of America

Circumstances include the following:

- Audit of a complete set of general purpose consolidated financial statements (comparative).
- The financial statements are prepared in accordance with accounting principles generally accepted in the United States of America.

Independent Auditor's Report

[*Appropriate Addressee*]

Report on the Financial Statements[1]

We have audited the accompanying consolidated financial statements of ABC Company and its subsidiaries, which comprise the consolidated balance sheets as of December 31, 20X1 and 20X0, and the related consolidated statements of income, changes in stockholders' equity, and cash flows for the years then ended, and the related notes to the financial statements.

Management's Responsibility for the Financial Statements

Management is responsible for the preparation and fair presentation of these consolidated financial statements in accordance with accounting principles generally accepted in the United States of America; this includes the design, implementation, and maintenance of internal control relevant to the preparation and fair presentation of consolidated financial statements that are free from material misstatement, whether due to fraud or error.

Auditor's Responsibility

Our responsibility is to express an opinion on these consolidated financial statements based on our audits. We conducted our audits in accordance with auditing standards generally accepted in the United States of America. Those standards require that we plan and perform the audit to obtain reasonable assurance about whether the consolidated financial statements are free from material misstatement.

An audit involves performing procedures to obtain audit evidence about the amounts and disclosures in the consolidated financial statements. The procedures selected depend on the auditor's judgment, including the assessment of the risks of material misstatement of the consolidated financial statements, whether due to fraud or error. In making those risk assessments, the auditor considers internal control relevant to the entity's preparation and fair presentation of the consolidated financial statements in order to design audit procedures that are appropriate in the circumstances, but not for the purpose of expressing an opinion on the effectiveness of the entity's internal control.[2] Accordingly, we express no such opinion. An audit also includes evaluating the appropriateness

---

[1] The subtitle "Report on the Financial Statements" is unnecessary in circumstances when the second subtitle, "Report on Other Legal and Regulatory Requirements," is not applicable.

[2] In circumstances when the auditor also has responsibility to express an opinion on the effectiveness of internal control in conjunction with the audit of the consolidated financial statements, this sentence would be worded as follows: "In making those risk assessments, the auditor considers internal control relevant to the entity's preparation and fair presentation of the consolidated financial statements in order to design audit procedures that are appropriate in the circumstances." In addition, the next sentence, "Accordingly, we express no such opinion." would not be included.

of accounting policies used and the reasonableness of significant accounting estimates made by management, as well as evaluating the overall presentation of the consolidated financial statements.

We believe that the audit evidence we have obtained is sufficient and appropriate to provide a basis for our audit opinion.

Opinion

In our opinion, the consolidated financial statements referred to above present fairly, in all material respects, the financial position of ABC Company and its subsidiaries as of December 31, 20X1 and 20X0, and the results of their operations and their cash flows for the years then ended in accordance with accounting principles generally accepted in the United States of America.

Report on Other Legal and Regulatory Requirements

[*Form and content of this section of the auditor's report will vary depending on the nature of the auditor's other reporting responsibilities.*]

[*Auditor's signature*]

[*Auditor's city and state*]

[*Date of the auditor's report*]

Illustration 2—An Auditor's Report on a Single Year Prepared in Accordance With Accounting Principles Generally Accepted in the United States of America

Circumstances include the following:

- Audit of a complete set of general purpose financial statements (single year).
- The financial statements are prepared in accordance with accounting principles generally accepted in the United States of America.

Independent Auditor's Report

[Appropriate Addressee]

Report on the Financial Statements[1]

We have audited the accompanying financial statements of ABC Company, which comprise the balance sheet as of December 31, 20X1, and the related statements of income, changes in stockholders' equity, and cash flows for the year then ended, and the related notes to the financial statements.

Management's Responsibility for the Financial Statements

Management is responsible for the preparation and fair presentation of these financial statements in accordance with accounting principles generally accepted in the United States of America; this includes the design, implementation, and maintenance of internal control relevant to the preparation and fair presentation of financial statements that are free from material misstatement, whether due to fraud or error.

Auditor's Responsibility

Our responsibility is to express an opinion on these financial statements based on our audit. We conducted our audit in accordance with auditing standards generally accepted in the United States of America. Those standards require that we plan and perform the audit to obtain reasonable assurance about whether the financial statements are free from material misstatement.

An audit involves performing procedures to obtain audit evidence about the amounts and disclosures in the financial statements. The procedures selected depend on the auditor's judgment, including the assessment of the risks of material misstatement of the financial statements, whether due to fraud or error. In making those risk assessments, the auditor considers internal control relevant to the entity's preparation and fair presentation of the financial statements in order to design audit procedures that are appropriate in the circumstances, but not for the purpose of expressing an opinion on the effectiveness of the entity's internal control.[2] Accordingly, we express no such opinion. An audit also includes evaluating the appropriateness of accounting policies used and the reasonableness of significant accounting estimates made by management, as well as evaluating the overall presentation of the financial statements.

We believe that the audit evidence we have obtained is sufficient and appropriate to provide a basis for our audit opinion.

---

[1] The subtitle "Report on the Financial Statements" is unnecessary in circumstances when the second subtitle, "Report on Other Legal and Regulatory Requirements," is not applicable.

[2] In circumstances when the auditor also has responsibility to express an opinion on the effectiveness of internal control in conjunction with the audit of the financial statements, this sentence would be worded as follows: "In making those risk assessments, the auditor considers internal control relevant to the entity's preparation and fair presentation of the financial statements in order to design audit procedures that are appropriate in the circumstances." In addition, the next sentence, "Accordingly, we express no such opinion." would not be included.

Opinion

In our opinion, the financial statements referred to above present fairly, in all material respects, the financial position of ABC Company as of December 31, 20X1, and the results of its operations and its cash flows for the year then ended in accordance with accounting principles generally accepted in the United States of America.

Report on Other Legal and Regulatory Requirements

[*Form and content of this section of the auditor's report will vary depending on the nature of the auditor's other reporting responsibilities.*]

[*Auditor's signature*]

[*Auditor's city and state*]

[*Date of the auditor's report*]

Illustration 3—An Auditor's Report on Consolidated Comparative Financial Statements Prepared in Accordance With Accounting Principles Generally Accepted in the United States of America When the Audit Has Been Conducted in Accordance With Both Auditing Standards Generally Accepted in the United States of America and International Standards on Auditing

Circumstances include the following:

- Audit of a complete set of general purpose financial statements (comparative).
- The financial statements are prepared in accordance with accounting principles generally accepted in the United States of America.
- The financial statements are audited in accordance with auditing standards generally accepted in the United States of America and International Standards on Auditing.

Independent Auditor's Report

[*Appropriate Addressee*]

Report on the Financial Statements[1]

We have audited the accompanying financial statements of ABC Company, which comprise the balance sheets as of December 31, 20X1 and 20X0, and the related statements of income, changes in stockholders' equity, and cash flows for the years then ended, and the related notes to the financial statements.

Management's Responsibility for the Financial Statements

Management is responsible for the preparation and fair presentation of these financial statements in accordance with accounting principles generally accepted in the United States of America; this includes the design, implementation, and maintenance of internal control relevant to the preparation and fair presentation of financial statements that are free from material misstatement, whether due to fraud or error.

Auditor's Responsibility

Our responsibility is to express an opinion on these financial statements based on our audits. We conducted our audits in accordance with auditing standards generally accepted in the United States of America and in accordance with International Standards on Auditing. Those standards require that we plan and perform the audit to obtain reasonable assurance about whether the financial statements are free from material misstatement.

An audit involves performing procedures to obtain audit evidence about the amounts and disclosures in the financial statements. The procedures selected depend on the auditor's judgment, including the assessment of the risks of material misstatement of the financial statements, whether due to fraud or error. In making those risk assessments, the auditor considers internal control relevant to the entity's preparation and fair presentation of the financial statements in order to design audit procedures that are appropriate in the circumstances, but not for the purpose of expressing an opinion on the effectiveness of the

---

[1] The subtitle "Report on the Financial Statements" is unnecessary in circumstances when the second subtitle, "Report on Other Legal and Regulatory Requirements," is not applicable.

entity's internal control.[2] Accordingly, we express no such opinion. An audit also includes evaluating the appropriateness of accounting policies used and the reasonableness of significant accounting estimates made by management, as well as evaluating the overall presentation of the financial statements.

We believe that the audit evidence we have obtained is sufficient and appropriate to provide a basis for our audit opinion.

Opinion

In our opinion, the financial statements referred to above present fairly, in all material respects, the financial position of ABC Company as of December 31, 20X1 and 20X0, and the results of its operations and its cash flows for the years then ended in accordance with accounting principles generally accepted in the United States of America.

Report on Other Legal and Regulatory Requirements

[*Form and content of this section of the auditor's report will vary depending on the nature of the auditor's other reporting responsibilities.*]

[*Auditor's signature*]

[*Auditor's city and state*]

[*Date of the auditor's report*]

[2] In circumstances when the auditor also has responsibility to express an opinion on the effectiveness of internal control in conjunction with the audit of the financial statements, this sentence would be worded as follows: "In making those risk assessments, the auditor considers internal control relevant to the entity's preparation and fair presentation of the financial statements in order to design audit procedures that are appropriate in the circumstances." In addition, the next sentence, "Accordingly, we express no such opinion." would not be included.

Illustration 4—An Auditor's Report on a Single Year Prepared in Accordance With Accounting Principles Generally Accepted in the United States of America When Comparative Summarized Financial Information Derived From Audited Financial Statements for the Prior Year Is Presented

Circumstances include the following:

- Audit of a complete set of general purpose financial statements (single year).
- Prior year summarized comparative financial information derived from audited financial statements is presented.
- The financial statements are prepared in accordance with accounting principles generally accepted in the United States of America.

Independent Auditor's Report

[*Appropriate Addressee*]

Report on the Financial Statements[1]

We have audited the accompanying financial statements of XYZ Not-for-Profit Organization, which comprise the statement of financial position as of September 30, 20X1, and the related statements of activities and cash flows for the year then ended, and the related notes to the financial statements.

Management's Responsibility for the Financial Statements

Management is responsible for the preparation and fair presentation of these financial statements in accordance with accounting principles generally accepted in the United States of America; this includes the design, implementation, and maintenance of internal control relevant to the preparation and fair presentation of financial statements that are free from material misstatement, whether due to fraud or error.

Auditor's Responsibility

Our responsibility is to express an opinion on these financial statements based on our audit. We conducted our audit in accordance with auditing standards generally accepted in the United States of America. Those standards require that we plan and perform the audit to obtain reasonable assurance about whether the financial statements are free from material misstatement.

An audit involves performing procedures to obtain audit evidence about the amounts and disclosures in the financial statements. The procedures selected depend on the auditor's judgment, including the assessment of the risks of material misstatement of the financial statements, whether due to fraud or error. In making those risk assessments, the auditor considers internal control relevant to the organization's preparation and fair presentation of the financial statements in order to design audit procedures that are appropriate in the circumstances, but not for the purpose of expressing an opinion on the effectiveness of the organization's internal control.[2] Accordingly, we express no such opinion. An audit also includes evaluating the appropriateness of accounting

---

[1] The subtitle "Report on the Financial Statements" is unnecessary in circumstances when the second subtitle, "Report on Other Legal and Regulatory Requirements," is not applicable.

[2] In circumstances when the auditor also has responsibility to express an opinion on the effectiveness of internal control in conjunction with the audit of the financial statements, this sentence would be worded as follows: "In making those risk assessments, the auditor considers internal control

(continued)

policies used and the reasonableness of significant accounting estimates made by management, as well as evaluating the overall presentation of the financial statements.

We believe that the audit evidence we have obtained is sufficient and appropriate to provide a basis for our audit opinion.

Opinion

In our opinion, the financial statements referred to above present fairly, in all material respects, the financial position of XYZ Not-for-Profit Organization as of September 30, 20X1, and the changes in its net assets and its cash flows for the year then ended in accordance with accounting principles generally accepted in the United States of America.

Report on Summarized Comparative Information

We have previously audited the XYZ Not-for-Profit Organization's 20X0 financial statements, and we expressed an unmodified audit opinion on those audited financial statements in our report dated December 15, 20X0. In our opinion, the summarized comparative information presented herein as of and for the year ended September 30, 20X0 is consistent, in all material respects, with the audited financial statements from which it has been derived.

Report on Other Legal and Regulatory Requirements

[*Form and content of this section of the auditor's report will vary depending on the nature of the auditor's other reporting responsibilities.*]

[*Auditor's signature*]

[*Auditor's city and state*]

[*Date of the auditor's report*]

(footnote continued)

relevant to the organization's preparation and fair presentation of the financial statements in order to design audit procedures that are appropriate in the circumstances." In addition, the next sentence, "Accordingly, we express no such opinion." would not be included.

Illustration 5—An Auditor's Report on a Single Year Prepared in Accordance With Accounting Principles Generally Accepted in the United States of America When Comparative Summarized Financial Information Derived From Unaudited Financial Statements for the Prior Year Is Presented

Circumstances include the following:

- Audit of a complete set of general purpose financial statements (single year).
- Prior year summarized comparative financial information derived from unaudited financial statements is presented.
- The financial statements are prepared in accordance with accounting principles generally accepted in the United States of America.

Independent Auditor's Report

[*Appropriate Addressee*]

Report on the Financial Statements[1]

We have audited the accompanying financial statements of XYZ Not-for-Profit Organization, which comprise the statement of financial position as of September 30, 20X1, and the related statements of activities and cash flows for the year then ended, and the related notes to the financial statements.

Management's Responsibility for the Financial Statements

Management is responsible for the preparation and fair presentation of these financial statements in accordance with accounting principles generally accepted in the United States of America; this includes the design, implementation, and maintenance of internal control relevant to the preparation and fair presentation of financial statements that are free from material misstatement, whether due to fraud or error.

Auditor's Responsibility

Our responsibility is to express an opinion on these financial statements based on our audit. We conducted our audit in accordance with auditing standards generally accepted in the United States of America. Those standards require that we plan and perform the audit to obtain reasonable assurance about whether the financial statements are free from material misstatement.

An audit involves performing procedures to obtain audit evidence about the amounts and disclosures in the financial statements. The procedures selected depend on the auditor's judgment, including the assessment of the risks of material misstatement of the financial statements, whether due to fraud or error. In making those risk assessments, the auditor considers internal control relevant to the organization's preparation and fair presentation of the financial statements in order to design audit procedures that are appropriate in the circumstances, but not for the purpose of expressing an opinion on the effectiveness of the organization's internal control.[2] Accordingly, we express no such opinion. An audit also includes evaluating the appropriateness of accounting

---

[1] The subtitle "Report on the Financial Statements" is unnecessary in circumstances when the second subtitle, "Report on Other Legal and Regulatory Requirements," is not applicable.

[2] In circumstances when the auditor also has responsibility to express an opinion on the effectiveness of internal control in conjunction with the audit of the financial statements, this sentence would be worded as follows: "In making those risk assessments, the auditor considers internal control

(continued)

policies used and the reasonableness of significant accounting estimates made by management, as well as evaluating the overall presentation of the financial statements.

We believe that the audit evidence we have obtained is sufficient and appropriate to provide a basis for our audit opinion.

Opinion

In our opinion, the financial statements referred to above present fairly, in all material respects, the financial position of XYZ Not-for-Profit Organization as of September 30, 20X1, and the changes in its net assets and its cash flows for the year then ended in accordance with accounting principles generally accepted in the United States of America.

Report on Summarized Comparative Information

The summarized comparative information presented herein as of and for the year ended September 30, 20X0, derived from those unaudited financial statements, has not been audited, reviewed, or compiled and, accordingly, we express no opinion on it.

Report on Other Legal and Regulatory Requirements

[*Form and content of this section of the auditor's report will vary depending on the nature of the auditor's other reporting responsibilities.*]

[*Auditor's signature*]

[*Auditor's city and state*]

[*Date of the auditor's report*]

(footnote continued)

relevant to the organization's preparation and fair presentation of the financial statements in order to design audit procedures that are appropriate in the circumstances." In addition, the next sentence, "Accordingly, we express no such opinion." would not be included.

AU-C Section 9700 *

Forming an Opinion and Reporting on Financial Statements: Auditing Interpretations of Section 700

1. Reporting on Financial Statements Prepared on a Liquidation Basis of Accounting

.01 *Question*—An entity prepares its financial statements on a liquidation basis of accounting because the entity is either in liquidation or liquidation appears imminent. Is the auditor permitted to issue an unmodified opinion on such financial statements?

.02 *Answer*—Yes. A liquidation basis of accounting may be considered generally accepted accounting principles (GAAP) for entities in liquidation or for which liquidation appears imminent. Therefore, the auditor is permitted to issue an unmodified opinion on such financial statements, provided that the liquidation basis of accounting has been properly applied and that adequate disclosures are made in the financial statements.

.03 Typically, the financial statements of entities that adopt a liquidation basis of accounting are presented along with financial statements of a period prior to adoption of a liquidation basis that were prepared on the basis of GAAP for going concerns. Section 706, *Emphasis-of Matter Paragraphs and Other-Matter Paragraphs in the Independent Auditor's Report*, requires the auditor to include an emphasis-of-matter paragraph when a matter that is appropriately presented or disclosed in the financial statements is of such importance, in the auditor's professional judgment, that it is fundamental to users' understanding of the financial statements. In such circumstances, the emphasis-of-matter paragraph would state that the entity has changed the basis of accounting used to determine the amounts at which assets and liabilities are carried from the going concern basis to a liquidation basis.

.04 Examples of auditor's reports with such an emphasis-of-matter paragraph follow:

Report on Single-Year Financial Statements in Year of Adoption of Liquidation Basis

We have audited the accompanying financial statements of XYZ Company, which comprise the statement of net assets in liquidation as of December 31, 20X2, the related statement of changes in net assets in liquidation for the period from April 26, 20X2 to December 31, 20X2, and the statements of income, changes in stockholders' equity, and cash flows for the period from January 1, 20X2 to April 25, 20X2, and the related notes to the financial statements.

---

* This section has been codified using an "AU-C" identifier instead of an "AU" identifier. "AU-C" is a temporary identifier to avoid confusion with references to existing "AU" sections, which will remain in AICPA *Professional Standards* through 2013. The "AU-C" identifier will revert to "AU" in 2014, by which time substantially all engagements for which the "AU" sections were still effective are expected to be completed.

Management's Responsibility for the Financial Statements

Management is responsible for the preparation and fair presentation of these financial statements in accordance with accounting principles generally accepted in the United States of America; this includes the design, implementation, and maintenance of internal control relevant to the preparation and fair presentation of financial statements that are free from material misstatement, whether due to fraud or error.

Auditor's Responsibility

Our responsibility is to express an opinion on these financial statements based on our audit. We conducted our audit in accordance with auditing standards generally accepted in the United States of America. Those standards require that we plan and perform the audit to obtain reasonable assurance about whether the financial statements are free from material misstatement.

An audit involves performing procedures to obtain audit evidence about the amounts and disclosures in the financial statements. The procedures selected depend on the auditor's judgment, including the assessment of the risks of material misstatement of the financial statements, whether due to fraud or error. In making those risk assessments, the auditor considers internal control relevant to the entity's preparation and fair presentation of the financial statements in order to design audit procedures that are appropriate in the circumstances, but not for the purpose of expressing an opinion on the effectiveness of the entity's internal control.[1] Accordingly, we express no such opinion. An audit also includes evaluating the appropriateness of accounting policies used and the reasonableness of significant accounting estimates made by management, as well as evaluating the overall presentation of the financial statements.

We believe that the audit evidence we have obtained is sufficient and appropriate to provide a basis for our audit opinion.

Opinion

In our opinion, the financial statements referred to above present fairly, in all material respects, the net assets in liquidation of XYZ Company as of December 31, 20X2, the changes in its net assets in liquidation for the period from April 26, 20X2 to December 31, 20X2, and the results of its operations and its cash flows for the period from January 1, 20X2 to April 25, 20X2, in accordance with accounting principles generally accepted in the United States of America applied on the bases described in Note X to the financial statements.

Emphasis of Matter

As discussed in Note X to the financial statements, the stockholders of XYZ Company approved a plan of liquidation on April 25, 20X2, and the Company commenced liquidation shortly thereafter. As a result, the Company has changed its basis of accounting for periods subsequent to April 25, 20X2 from the going-concern basis to a liquidation basis.

Report on Comparative Financial Statements in Year of Adoption of Liquidation Basis

We have audited the accompanying financial statements of XYZ Company, which comprise the balance sheet as of December 31, 20X1, the related statements of income, changes in stockholders' equity, and cash flows for the year

---

[1] In circumstances when the auditor also has responsibility to express an opinion on the effectiveness of internal control in conjunction with the audit of the financial statements, this sentence would be worded as follows: "In making those risk assessments, the auditor considers internal control relevant to the entity's preparation and fair presentation of the financial statements in order to design audit procedures that are appropriate in the circumstances." In addition, the next sentence, "Accordingly, we express no such opinion." would not be included.

then ended, the statements of income, changes in stockholders' equity, and cash flows for the period from January 1, 20X2 to April 25, 20X2, the statement of net assets in liquidation as of December 31, 20X2, the related statement of changes in net assets in liquidation for the period from April 26, 20X2 to December 31, 20X2, and the related notes to the financial statements.

Management's Responsibility for the Financial Statements

Management is responsible for the preparation and fair presentation of these financial statements in accordance with accounting principles generally accepted in the United States of America; this includes the design, implementation, and maintenance of internal control relevant to the preparation and fair presentation of financial statements that are free from material misstatement, whether due to fraud or error.

Auditor's Responsibility

Our responsibility is to express an opinion on these financial statements based on our audit. We conducted our audit in accordance with auditing standards generally accepted in the United States of America. Those standards require that we plan and perform the audit to obtain reasonable assurance about whether the financial statements are free from material misstatement.

An audit involves performing procedures to obtain audit evidence about the amounts and disclosures in the financial statements. The procedures selected depend on the auditor's judgment, including the assessment of the risks of material misstatement of the financial statements, whether due to fraud or error. In making those risk assessments, the auditor considers internal control relevant to the entity's preparation and fair presentation of the financial statements in order to design audit procedures that are appropriate in the circumstances, but not for the purpose of expressing an opinion on the effectiveness of the entity's internal control.[2] Accordingly, we express no such opinion. An audit also includes evaluating the appropriateness of accounting policies used and the reasonableness of significant accounting estimates made by management, as well as evaluating the overall presentation of the financial statements.

We believe that the audit evidence we have obtained is sufficient and appropriate to provide a basis for our audit opinion.

Opinion

In our opinion, the financial statements referred to above present fairly, in all material respects, the financial position of XYZ Company as of December 31, 20X1, the results of its operations and its cash flows for the year then ended and for the period from January 1, 20X2 to April 25, 20X2, its net assets in liquidation as of December 31, 20X2, and the changes in its net assets in liquidation for the period from April 26, 20X2 to December 31, 20X2, in accordance with accounting principles generally accepted in the United States of America applied on the bases described in Note X to the financial statements.

Emphasis of Matter

As discussed in Note X to the financial statements, the stockholders of XYZ Company approved a plan of liquidation on April 25, 20X2, and the Company commenced liquidation shortly thereafter. As a result, the Company has changed

---

[2] In circumstances when the auditor also has responsibility to express an opinion on the effectiveness of internal control in conjunction with the audit of the financial statements, this sentence would be worded as follows: "In making those risk assessments, the auditor considers internal control relevant to the entity's preparation and fair presentation of the financial statements in order to design audit procedures that are appropriate in the circumstances." In addition, the next sentence, "Accordingly, we express no such opinion." would not be included.

its basis of accounting for periods subsequent to April 25, 20X2 from the going-concern basis to a liquidation basis.

.05 The auditor may, in subsequent years, continue to include an emphasis-of-matter paragraph in the auditor's report to emphasize that the financial statements are presented on a liquidation basis of accounting.

[Issue Date: December 1984; Revised: June 1993; Revised: February 1997; Revised: October 2000; Revised: June 2009; Revised: October 2011, effective for audits of financial statements for periods ending on or after December 15, 2012.]

AU-C Section 705 *

Modifications to the Opinion in the Independent Auditor's Report

Source: SAS No. 122; SAS No. 123.

Effective for audits of financial statements for periods ending on or after December 15, 2012.

Introduction

Scope of This Section

.01 This section addresses the auditor's responsibility to issue an appropriate report in circumstances when, in forming an opinion in accordance with section 700, *Forming an Opinion and Reporting on Financial Statements*, the auditor concludes that a modification to the auditor's opinion on the financial statements is necessary.

Types of Modified Opinions

.02 This section establishes three types of modified opinions: namely, a qualified opinion, an adverse opinion, and a disclaimer of opinion. The decision regarding which type of modified opinion is appropriate depends upon the following: (Ref: par. .A1)

a. The nature of the matter giving rise to the modification (that is, whether the financial statements are materially misstated or, in the case of an inability to obtain sufficient appropriate audit evidence, may be materially misstated)

b. The auditor's professional judgment about the pervasiveness of the effects or possible effects of the matter on the financial statements

.03 Section 706, *Emphasis-of-Matter Paragraphs and Other-Matter Paragraphs in the Independent Auditor's Report*, addresses situations when the auditor considers it necessary, or is required, to include additional communications in the auditor's report that are not modifications to the auditor's opinion.

Effective Date

.04 This section is effective for audits of financial statements for periods ending on or after December 15, 2012.

---

* This section has been codified using an "AU-C" identifier instead of an "AU" identifier. "AU-C" is a temporary identifier to avoid confusion with references to existing "AU" sections, which will remain in AICPA *Professional Standards* through 2013. The "AU-C" identifier will revert to "AU" in 2014, by which time substantially all engagements for which the "AU" sections were still effective are expected to be completed.

Objective

.05 The objective of the auditor is to express clearly an appropriately modified opinion on the financial statements that is necessary when

a. the auditor concludes, based on the audit evidence obtained, that the financial statements as a whole are materially misstated or

b. the auditor is unable to obtain sufficient appropriate audit evidence to conclude that the financial statements as a whole are free from material misstatement.

Definitions

.06 For purposes of generally accepted auditing standards, the following terms have the meanings attributed as follows:

Modified opinion. A qualified opinion, an adverse opinion, or a disclaimer of opinion.

Pervasive. A term used in the context of misstatements to describe the effects on the financial statements of misstatements or the possible effects on the financial statements of misstatements, if any, that are undetected due to an inability to obtain sufficient appropriate audit evidence. Pervasive effects on the financial statements are those that, in the auditor's professional judgment

- are not confined to specific elements, accounts, or items of the financial statements;
- if so confined, represent or could represent a substantial proportion of the financial statements; or
- with regard to disclosures, are fundamental to users' understanding of the financial statements.

Requirements

Circumstances When a Modification to the Auditor's Opinion Is Required

.07 The auditor should modify the opinion in the auditor's report when

a. the auditor concludes that, based on the audit evidence obtained, the financial statements as a whole are materially misstated or (Ref: par. .A2–.A7)

b. the auditor is unable to obtain sufficient appropriate audit evidence to conclude that the financial statements as a whole are free from material misstatement. (Ref: par. .A8–.A12)

Determining the Type of Modification to the Auditor's Opinion

Qualified Opinion

.08 The auditor should express a qualified opinion when

a. the auditor, having obtained sufficient appropriate audit evidence, concludes that misstatements, individually or in the aggregate, are material but not pervasive to the financial statements or

b. the auditor is unable to obtain sufficient appropriate audit evidence on which to base the opinion, but the auditor concludes that the possible effects on the financial statements of undetected misstatements, if any, could be material but not pervasive.

Adverse Opinion

.09 The auditor should express an adverse opinion when the auditor, having obtained sufficient appropriate audit evidence, concludes that misstatements, individually or in the aggregate, are both material and pervasive to the financial statements.

Disclaimer of Opinion

.10 The auditor should disclaim an opinion when the auditor is unable to obtain sufficient appropriate audit evidence on which to base the opinion, and the auditor concludes that the possible effects on the financial statements of undetected misstatements, if any, could be both material and pervasive. (Ref: par. .A13–.A14)

Consequence of an Inability to Obtain Sufficient Appropriate Audit Evidence Due to a Management-Imposed Limitation After the Auditor Has Accepted the Engagement

.11 If, after accepting the engagement, the auditor becomes aware that management has imposed a limitation on the scope of the audit that the auditor considers likely to result in the need to express a qualified opinion or to disclaim an opinion on the financial statements, the auditor should request that management remove the limitation.

.12 If management refuses to remove the limitation referred to in paragraph .11, the auditor should communicate the matter to those charged with governance, unless all of those charged with governance are involved in managing the entity,[1] and determine whether it is possible to perform alternative procedures to obtain sufficient appropriate audit evidence.

.13 If the auditor is unable to obtain sufficient appropriate audit evidence due to a management-imposed limitation, and the auditor concludes that the possible effects on the financial statements of undetected misstatements, if any, could be both material and pervasive, the auditor should either disclaim an opinion on the financial statements or, when practicable, withdraw from the audit.

.14 If the auditor withdraws, as contemplated by paragraph .13, before withdrawing, the auditor should communicate to those charged with governance any matters regarding misstatements identified during the audit that would have given rise to a modification of the opinion. (Ref: par. .A15–.A16)

Other Considerations Relating to an Adverse Opinion or Disclaimer of Opinion

.15 When the auditor considers it necessary to express an adverse opinion or disclaim an opinion on the financial statements as a whole, the auditor's report should not also include an unmodified opinion with respect to the same financial reporting framework on a single financial statement or one or more specific elements, accounts, or items of a financial statement.[2] To include such

---

[1] Paragraph .09 of section 260, *The Auditor's Communication With Those Charged With Governance*.

[2] Paragraph .21 of section 805, *Special Considerations—Audits of Single Financial Statements and Specific Elements, Accounts, or Items of a Financial Statement*.

an unmodified opinion in the same report in these circumstances would contradict the auditor's adverse opinion or disclaimer of opinion on the financial statements as a whole. (Ref: par. .A17–.A18)

Auditor Is Not Independent but Is Required by Law or Regulation to Report on the Financial Statements

.16 When the auditor is not independent but is required by law or regulation to report on the financial statements, the auditor should disclaim an opinion and should specifically state that the auditor is not independent. The auditor is neither required to provide, nor precluded from providing, the reasons for the lack of independence; however, if the auditor chooses to provide the reasons for the lack of independence, the auditor should include all the reasons therefor. (Ref: par. .A20)

Form and Content of the Auditor's Report When the Opinion Is Modified

Basis for Modification Paragraph

.17 When the auditor modifies the opinion on the financial statements, the auditor should, in addition to the specific elements required by section 700, include a paragraph in the auditor's report that provides a description of the matter giving rise to the modification. The auditor should place this paragraph immediately before the opinion paragraph in the auditor's report and use a heading that includes "Basis for Qualified Opinion," "Basis for Adverse Opinion," or "Basis for Disclaimer of Opinion," as appropriate. (Ref: par. .A20)

.18 If there is a material misstatement of the financial statements that relates to specific amounts in the financial statements (including quantitative disclosures), the auditor should include in the basis for modification paragraph a description and quantification of the financial effects of the misstatement, unless impracticable. If it is not practicable to quantify the financial effects, the auditor should so state in the basis for modification paragraph. (Ref: par. .A21–.A23)

.19 If there is a material misstatement of the financial statements that relates to narrative disclosures, the auditor should include in the basis for modification paragraph an explanation of how the disclosures are misstated.

.20 If there is a material misstatement of the financial statements that relates to the omission of information required to be presented or disclosed, the auditor should

a. discuss the omission of such information with those charged with governance;

b. describe in the basis for modification paragraph the nature of the omitted information; and

c. include the omitted information, provided that it is practicable to do so and the auditor has obtained sufficient appropriate audit evidence about the omitted information. (Ref: par. .A24–.A25)

.21 If the modification results from an inability to obtain sufficient appropriate audit evidence, the auditor should include in the basis for modification paragraph the reasons for that inability. (Ref: par. .A26)

.22 Even if the auditor has expressed an adverse opinion or disclaimed an opinion on the financial statements, the auditor should *a.* describe in the basis for modification paragraph any other matters of which the auditor is aware that would have required a modification to the opinion and the effects thereof and (Ref: par. .A27)

b. consider the need to describe in an emphasis-of-matter or other-matter paragraph(s)[3] any other matters of which the auditor is aware that would have resulted in additional communications in the auditor's report on the financial statements that are not modifications of the auditor's opinion.

Opinion Paragraph

.23 When the auditor modifies the audit opinion, the auditor should use a heading that includes "Qualified Opinion," "Adverse Opinion," or "Disclaimer of Opinion," as appropriate, for the opinion paragraph. (Ref: par. .A28)

.24 When the auditor expresses a qualified opinion due to a material misstatement in the financial statements, the auditor should state in the opinion paragraph that, in the auditor's opinion, except for the effects of the matter(s) described in the basis for qualified opinion paragraph, the financial statements are presented fairly, in all material respects, in accordance with the applicable financial reporting framework. When the modification arises from an inability to obtain sufficient appropriate audit evidence, the auditor should use the corresponding phrase "except for the possible effects of the matter(s) . . ." for the modified opinion. (Ref: par. .A29–.A30)

.25 When the auditor expresses an adverse opinion, the auditor should state in the opinion paragraph that, in the auditor's opinion, because of the significance of the matter(s) described in the basis for adverse opinion paragraph, the financial statements are not presented fairly in accordance with the applicable financial reporting framework.

.26 When the auditor disclaims an opinion due to an inability to obtain sufficient appropriate audit evidence, the auditor should state in the opinion paragraph that

a. because of the significance of the matter(s) described in the basis for disclaimer of opinion paragraph, the auditor has not been able to obtain sufficient appropriate audit evidence to provide a basis for an audit opinion and

b. accordingly, the auditor does not express an opinion on the financial statements.

Description of the Auditor's Responsibility When the Auditor Expresses a Qualified or an Adverse Opinion

.27 When the auditor expresses a qualified or an adverse opinion, the auditor should amend the description of the auditor's responsibility to state that the auditor believes that the audit evidence the auditor has obtained is sufficient and appropriate to provide a basis for the auditor's modified audit opinion.

---

[3] See section 706, *Emphasis-of-Matter Paragraphs and Other-Matter Paragraphs in the Independent Auditor's Report.*

Description of the Auditor's Responsibility When the Auditor Disclaims an Opinion

.28 When the auditor disclaims an opinion due to an inability to obtain sufficient appropriate audit evidence, the auditor should amend the introductory paragraph of the auditor's report to state that the auditor was engaged to audit the financial statements. The auditor should also amend the description of the auditor's responsibility and the description of the scope of the audit to state only the following: "Our responsibility is to express an opinion on the financial statements based on conducting the audit in accordance with auditing standards generally accepted in the United States of America. Because of the matter(s) described in the basis for disclaimer of opinion paragraph, however, we were not able to obtain sufficient appropriate audit evidence to provide a basis for an audit opinion."

Communication With Those Charged With Governance

.29 When the auditor expects to modify the opinion in the auditor's report, the auditor should communicate with those charged with governance the circumstances that led to the expected modification and the proposed wording of the modification. (Ref: par. .A31)

Application and Other Explanatory Material

Types of Modified Opinions (Ref: par. .02)

.A1 The following table illustrates how the auditor's professional judgment about the nature of the matter giving rise to the modification and the pervasiveness of its effects or possible effects on the financial statements affects the type of opinion to be expressed:

Nature of Matter Giving Rise to the Modification	*Auditor's Professional Judgment About the Pervasiveness of the Effects or Possible Effects on the Financial Statements*	
	Material but Not Pervasive	*Material and Pervasive*
Financial statements are materially misstated	Qualified opinion	Adverse opinion
Inability to obtain sufficient appropriate audit evidence	Qualified opinion	Disclaimer of opinion

Circumstances When a Modification to the Auditor's Opinion Is Required

Nature of Material Misstatements (Ref: par. .07a)

.A2 Section 700 requires the auditor, in order to form an opinion on the financial statements, to conclude whether reasonable assurance has been obtained about whether the financial statements as a whole are free from material misstatement.[4] This conclusion takes into account the auditor's evaluation of uncorrected misstatements, if any, on the financial statements, in accordance with section 450, *Evaluation of Misstatements Identified During the Audit*.

---

[4] Paragraph .14 of section 700, *Forming an Opinion and Reporting on Financial Statements*.

.A3 Section 450 defines a *misstatement* as a difference between the amount, classification, presentation, or disclosure of a reported financial statement item and the amount, classification, presentation, or disclosure that is required for the item to be presented fairly in accordance with the applicable financial reporting framework. Accordingly, a material misstatement of the financial statements may arise in relation to the following:

a. The appropriateness of the selected accounting policies

b. The application of the selected accounting policies

c. The appropriateness of the financial statement presentation or the appropriateness or adequacy of disclosures in the financial statements

Appropriateness of the Selected Accounting Policies

.A4 With regard to the appropriateness of the accounting policies management has selected, material misstatements of the financial statements may arise when

a. the selected accounting policies are not in accordance with the applicable financial reporting framework or

b. the financial statements, including the related notes, do not represent the underlying transactions and events in a manner that achieves fair presentation.

.A5 Financial reporting frameworks often contain requirements for the accounting for, and disclosure of, changes in accounting policies. When the entity has changed its selection of significant accounting policies, a material misstatement of the financial statements may arise when the entity has not complied with these requirements. If a change in accounting policy does not meet the conditions described in section 708, *Consistency of Financial Statements*, then a material misstatement of the financial statements may arise.

Application of the Selected Accounting Policies

.A6 With regard to the application of the selected accounting policies, material misstatements of the financial statements may arise

a. when management has not applied the selected accounting policies in accordance with the financial reporting framework, including when management has not applied the selected accounting policies consistently between periods or to similar transactions and events (consistency in application), or

b. due to the method of application of the selected accounting policies (such as an unintentional error in application).

Appropriateness of the Financial Statement Presentation or Appropriateness or Adequacy of Disclosures in the Financial Statements

.A7 With regard to the appropriateness of the financial statement presentation or the appropriateness or adequacy of disclosures in the financial statements, material misstatements of the financial statements may arise when

a. the financial statements do not include all of the disclosures required by the applicable financial reporting framework;

b. the disclosures in the financial statements are not presented in accordance with the applicable financial reporting framework;

c. the financial statements do not provide the disclosures necessary to achieve fair presentation; or *d.* information required to be presented in accordance with the applicable financial reporting framework is omitted either because a required statement (for example, a statement of cash flows) has not been included or the information has not otherwise been disclosed in the financial statements.

Nature of an Inability to Obtain Sufficient Appropriate Audit Evidence (Ref: par. .07b)

.A8 The auditor's inability to obtain sufficient appropriate audit evidence (also referred to as a limitation on the scope of the audit) may arise from the following:

a. Circumstances beyond the control of the entity

b. Circumstances relating to the nature or timing of the auditor's work

c. Limitations imposed by management

.A9 An inability to perform a specific procedure does not constitute a limitation on the scope of the audit if the auditor is able to obtain sufficient appropriate audit evidence by performing alternative procedures. If this is not possible, the requirement in paragraph .08*b* applies. Limitations imposed by management may have other implications for the audit, such as for the auditor's assessment of risks of material misstatement due to fraud and consideration of engagement continuance.

.A10 Examples of circumstances beyond the control of the entity include the following:

- The entity's accounting records have been destroyed.
- The accounting records of a significant component have been seized indefinitely by governmental authorities.

.A11 Examples of circumstances relating to the nature or timing of the auditor's work include the following:

- The entity is required to use the equity method of accounting for an associated entity, and the auditor is unable to obtain sufficient appropriate audit evidence about the latter's financial information to evaluate whether the equity method has been appropriately applied.
- The timing of the auditor's engagement is such that the auditor is unable to observe the counting of the physical inventories, and the auditor is unable to perform a rollback of the inventory or other appropriate procedures.
- The auditor determines that performing substantive procedures alone is not sufficient, but the entity's controls are not effective.
- When accounting for long-term investments, the auditor is unable to obtain audited financial statements of an investee.

.A12 Examples of an inability to obtain sufficient appropriate audit evidence arising from a limitation on the scope of the audit imposed by management include the following:

- Management prevents the auditor from observing the counting of the physical inventory.
- Management prevents the auditor from requesting external confirmation of specific account balances.

Determining the Type of Modification to the Auditor's Opinion

Effect of Uncertainties (Ref: par. .10)

.A13 Conclusive audit evidence concerning the ultimate outcome of uncertainties cannot be expected to exist at the time of the audit because the outcome and related audit evidence are prospective. In these circumstances, management is responsible for estimating the effect of future events on the financial statements or determining that a reasonable estimate cannot be made and making the required disclosures, all in accordance with the applicable financial reporting framework, based on management's analysis of existing conditions. An audit includes an assessment of whether the audit evidence is sufficient to support management's analysis. Absence of the existence of information related to the outcome of an uncertainty does not necessarily lead to a conclusion that the audit evidence supporting management's assertion is not sufficient. Rather, the auditor's professional judgment regarding the sufficiency of the audit evidence is based on the audit evidence that is, or should be, available. If, after considering the existing conditions and available evidence, the auditor concludes that sufficient appropriate audit evidence supports management's assertions about the nature of a matter involving an uncertainty and its presentation or disclosure in the financial statements, an unmodified opinion ordinarily is appropriate.

.A14 In cases involving multiple uncertainties, the auditor may conclude that it is not possible to form an opinion on the financial statements as a whole due to the interaction and possible cumulative effects of the uncertainties.

Consequence of an Inability to Obtain Sufficient Appropriate Audit Evidence Due to a Management-Imposed Limitation After the Auditor Has Accepted the Engagement (Ref: par. .14)

.A15 The practicality of withdrawing from the audit may depend on the stage of completion of the engagement at the time that management imposes the scope limitation. If the auditor has substantially completed the audit, the auditor may decide to complete the audit to the extent possible, disclaim an opinion, and explain the scope limitation in the basis for disclaimer of opinion paragraph.

.A16 In certain circumstances, withdrawal from the audit may not be possible if the auditor is required by law or regulation to continue the audit engagement. This may be the case for an auditor who is appointed to audit the financial statements of governmental entities. It may also be the case in circumstances when the auditor is appointed to audit the financial statements covering a specific period, or appointed for a specific period, and is prohibited from withdrawing before the completion of the audit of those financial statements or before the end of that period, respectively. In these circumstances, the auditor may also consider it necessary to include an other-matter paragraph in the auditor's report.[5]

Other Considerations Relating to a Disclaimer of Opinion (Ref: par. .15)

.A17 In an initial audit, it is acceptable for the auditor to express an unmodified opinion regarding the financial position and disclaim an opinion

[5] Paragraph .A6 of section 706.

regarding the results of operations and cash flows, when relevant.[6] In this case, the auditor has not disclaimed an opinion on the financial statements as a whole.

Considerations Specific to Audits of Governmental Entities

.A18 Because the auditor of a state and local government entity expresses an opinion or disclaims an opinion for each opinion unit,[7] an auditor's report in these circumstances may include an unmodified opinion with respect to one or more opinion units and a modified opinion for one or more other opinion units.

Considerations Specific to Governmental Entities

.A19 The nature of a government auditor's lack of independence may have a limited effect because the impairment may result from the government auditor's association with only a component of the overall governmental entity. A government auditor may determine that the lack of independence only affects one or more, but not all, of the governmental entity's opinion units and, in such circumstances, the auditor may disclaim an opinion on the affected opinion units while expressing unmodified, qualified, or adverse opinions on other opinion units. The more significant the affected opinion units are to the overall governmental entity, the more likely that it will be appropriate for the auditor to disclaim an opinion on the financial statements of the overall governmental entity.

Form and Content of the Auditor's Report When the Opinion Is Modified

Basis for Modification Paragraph (Ref: par. .17–.18, .20c, and .21–.22)

.A20 Consistency in the auditor's report helps promote users' understanding and identify unusual circumstances when they occur. Accordingly, although uniformity in the wording of a modified opinion and the description of the basis for the modification may not be possible, consistency in both the form and content of the auditor's report is desirable.

.A21 An example of the financial effects of material misstatements that the auditor may describe in the basis for modification paragraph in the auditor's report is the quantification of the effects on income before taxes, income taxes, net income, and equity if inventory is overstated. If such disclosures are made in a note to the financial statements, the basis for modification paragraph may be shortened by referring to it.

.A22 Adequate disclosures relate to the form, arrangement, and content of the financial statements and their related notes, including, for example, the terminology used, the amount of detail given, the classification of items in the statements, and the bases of amounts set forth. An auditor considers the disclosure of a particular matter in light of the circumstances and facts of which the auditor is aware at the time.

.A23 In considering the adequacy of disclosure, and in other aspects of the audit, the auditor uses information received in confidence from management. Without such confidence, the auditor would find it difficult to obtain information necessary to form an opinion on the financial statements. Rule 301, *Confidential Client Information* (ET sec. 301 par. .01), of the AICPA Code of Professional

---

[6] Paragraph .A17 of section 510, *Opening Balances—Initial Audit Engagements, Including Reaudit Engagements.*

[7] Paragraph .A4 of section 700.

Conduct states that the auditor should not disclose any confidential client information without the specific consent of the client. Accordingly, the auditor may not make available, without management's consent, information that is not required to be disclosed in the financial statements to comply with the applicable financial reporting framework.

.A24 *Practicable*, as used in the context of paragraphs .18 and .20*c*, means that the information is reasonably obtainable from management's accounts and records and that providing the information in the report does not require the auditor to assume the position of a preparer of financial information. For example, the auditor would not be expected to prepare a basic financial statement or segment information and include it in the auditor's report when management omits such information.

.A25 Disclosing the omitted information in the basis for modification paragraph would not be practicable if

a. the information has not been prepared by management or the information is otherwise not readily available to the auditor or

b. in the auditor's professional judgment, the information would be unduly voluminous in relation to the auditor's report.

.A26 When the auditor modifies the opinion due to an inability to obtain sufficient appropriate audit evidence, it is not appropriate for the scope of the audit to be explained in a note to the financial statements because the description of the audit scope is the responsibility of the auditor and not that of management.

.A27 An adverse opinion or a disclaimer of opinion relating to a specific matter described in the basis for qualification paragraph does not justify the omission of a description of other identified matters that would have otherwise required a modification of the auditor's opinion. In such cases, the disclosure of such other matters of which the auditor is aware may be relevant to users of the financial statements.

Opinion Paragraph (Ref: par. .23–.24)

.A28 Inclusion of the paragraph heading required by paragraph .23 makes it clear to the user that the auditor's opinion is modified and indicates the type of modification.

.A29 When the auditor expresses a qualified opinion, it would not be appropriate to use phrases such as *with the foregoing explanation* or *subject to* in the opinion paragraph because these are not sufficiently clear or forceful. Because accompanying notes are part of the financial statements, wording such as "fairly presented, in all material respects, when read in conjunction with note 1" is likely to be misunderstood and would also not be appropriate.

.A30 When the auditor expresses a qualified opinion due to a scope limitation, paragraph .24 requires that the auditor state in the opinion paragraph that the qualification pertains to the possible effects of the matter on the financial statements and not to the scope limitation itself. Wording such as "In our opinion, except for the above-mentioned limitation on the scope of our audit . . ." bases the exception on the restriction itself rather than on the possible effects on the financial statements and, therefore, is unacceptable.

Communication With Those Charged With Governance (Ref: par. .29)

.A31 Communicating with those charged with governance the circumstances that lead to an expected modification to the auditor's opinion and the proposed wording of the modification enables

a. the auditor to give notice to those charged with governance of the intended modification(s) and the reasons (or circumstances) for the modification(s);

b. the auditor to seek the concurrence of those charged with governance regarding the facts of the matter(s) giving rise to the expected modification(s) or to confirm matters of disagreement with management as such; and

c. those charged with governance to have an opportunity, when appropriate, to provide the auditor with further information and explanations in respect of the matter(s) giving rise to the expected modification(s).

.A32

Exhibit—Illustrations of Auditor's Reports With Modifications to the Opinion

Illustration 1—An Auditor's Report Containing a Qualified Opinion Due to a Material Misstatement of the Financial Statements

Circumstances include the following:

- Audit of a complete set of general purpose financial statements (comparative) prepared in accordance with accounting principles generally accepted in the United States of America.
- Inventories are misstated. The misstatement is deemed to be material but not pervasive to the financial statements. Accordingly, the auditor's report contains a qualified opinion.

Independent Auditor's Report

[*Appropriate Addressee*]

Report on the Financial Statements[1]

We have audited the accompanying financial statements of ABC Company, which comprise the balance sheets as of December 31, 20X1 and 20X0, and the related statements of income, changes in stockholders' equity, and cash flows for the years then ended, and the related notes to the financial statements.

Management's Responsibility for the Financial Statements

Management is responsible for the preparation and fair presentation of these financial statements in accordance with accounting principles generally accepted in the United States of America; this includes the design, implementation, and maintenance of internal control relevant to the preparation and fair presentation of financial statements that are free from material misstatement, whether due to fraud or error.

Auditor's Responsibility

Our responsibility is to express an opinion on these financial statements based on our audits. We conducted our audits in accordance with auditing standards generally accepted in the United States of America. Those standards require that we plan and perform the audit to obtain reasonable assurance about whether the financial statements are free from material misstatement.

An audit involves performing procedures to obtain audit evidence about the amounts and disclosures in the financial statements. The procedures selected depend on the auditor's judgment, including the assessment of the risks of material misstatement of the financial statements, whether due to fraud or error. In making those risk assessments, the auditor considers internal control relevant to the entity's preparation and fair presentation of the financial statements in order to design audit procedures that are appropriate in the circumstances, but not for the purpose of expressing an opinion on the effectiveness of the entity's internal control.[2] Accordingly, we express no such opinion. An audit also includes evaluating the appropriateness of accounting policies used and the reasonableness of significant accounting estimates made by management, as well as evaluating the overall presentation of the financial statements.

---

[1] The subtitle "Report on the Financial Statements" is unnecessary in circumstances when the second subtitle, "Report on Other Legal and Regulatory Requirements," is not applicable.

[2] In circumstances when the auditor also has responsibility to express an opinion on the effectiveness of internal control in conjunction with the audit of the financial statements, this sentence would be worded as follows: "In making those risk assessments, the auditor considers internal control relevant to the entity's preparation and fair presentation of the financial statements in order to design audit procedures that are appropriate in the circumstances." In addition, the next sentence, "Accordingly, we express no such opinion." would not be included.

We believe that the audit evidence we have obtained is sufficient and appropriate to provide a basis for our qualified audit opinion.

Basis for Qualified Opinion

The Company has stated inventories at cost in the accompanying balance sheets. Accounting principles generally accepted in the United States of America require inventories to be stated at the lower of cost or market. If the Company stated inventories at the lower of cost or market, a write down of $XXX and $XXX would have been required as of December 31, 20X1 and 20X0, respectively. Accordingly, cost of sales would have been increased by $XXX and $XXX, and net income, income taxes, and stockholders' equity would have been reduced by $XXX, $XXX, and $XXX, and $XXX, $XXX, and $XXX, as of and for the years ended December 31, 20X1 and 20X0, respectively.

Qualified Opinion

In our opinion, except for the effects of the matter described in the Basis for Qualified Opinion paragraph, the financial statements referred to above present fairly, in all material respects, the financial position of ABC Company as of December 31, 20X1 and 20X0, and the results of its operations and its cash flows for the years then ended in accordance with accounting principles generally accepted in the United States of America.

Report on Other Legal and Regulatory Requirements

[*Form and content of this section of the auditor's report will vary depending on the nature of the auditor's other reporting responsibilities.*]

[*Auditor's signature*]

[*Auditor's city and state*]

[*Date of the auditor's report*]

Illustration 2—An Auditor's Report Containing a Qualified Opinion for Inadequate Disclosure

Circumstances include the following:

- Audit of a complete set of general purpose financial statements (comparative) prepared in accordance with accounting principles generally accepted in the United States of America.
- The financial statements have inadequate disclosures. The auditor has concluded that (*a*) it is not practicable to present the required information and (*b*) the effects are such that an adverse opinion is not appropriate. Accordingly, the auditor's report contains a qualified opinion.

Independent Auditor's Report

[*Appropriate Addressee*]

Report on the Financial Statements[1]

We have audited the accompanying financial statements of ABC Company, which comprise the balance sheets as of December 31, 20X1 and 20X0, and the related statements of income, changes in stockholders' equity, and cash flows for the years then ended, and the related notes to the financial statements.

Management's Responsibility for the Financial Statements

Management is responsible for the preparation and fair presentation of these financial statements in accordance with accounting principles generally accepted in the United States of America; this includes the design, implementation, and maintenance of internal control relevant to the preparation and fair presentation of financial statements that are free from material misstatement, whether due to fraud or error.

Auditor's Responsibility

Our responsibility is to express an opinion on these financial statements based on our audits. We conducted our audits in accordance with auditing standards generally accepted in the United States of America. Those standards require that we plan and perform the audit to obtain reasonable assurance about whether the financial statements are free from material misstatement.

An audit involves performing procedures to obtain audit evidence about the amounts and disclosures in the financial statements. The procedures selected depend on the auditor's judgment, including the assessment of the risks of material misstatement of the financial statements, whether due to fraud or error. In making those risk assessments, the auditor considers internal control relevant to the entity's preparation and fair presentation of the financial statements in order to design audit procedures that are appropriate in the circumstances, but not for the purpose of expressing an opinion on the effectiveness of the entity's internal control.[2] Accordingly, we express no such opinion. An audit also includes evaluating the appropriateness of accounting policies used and

---

[1] The subtitle "Report on the Financial Statements" is unnecessary in circumstances when the second subtitle, "Report on Other Legal and Regulatory Requirements," is not applicable.

[2] In circumstances when the auditor also has responsibility to express an opinion on the effectiveness of internal control in conjunction with the audit of the financial statements, this sentence would be worded as follows: "In making those risk assessments, the auditor considers internal control relevant to the entity's preparation and fair presentation of the financial statements in order to design audit procedures that are appropriate in the circumstances." In addition, the next sentence, "Accordingly, we express no such opinion." would not be included.

the reasonableness of significant accounting estimates made by management, as well as evaluating the overall presentation of the financial statements.

We believe that the audit evidence we have obtained is sufficient and appropriate to provide a basis for our qualified audit opinion.

Basis for Qualified Opinion

The Company's financial statements do not disclose [*describe the nature of the omitted information that is not practicable to present in the auditor's report*]. In our opinion, disclosure of this information is required by accounting principles generally accepted in the United States of America.

Qualified Opinion

In our opinion, except for the omission of the information described in the Basis for Qualified Opinion paragraph, the financial statements referred to above present fairly, in all material respects, the financial position of ABC Company as of December 31, 20X1 and 20X0, and the results of its operations and its cash flows for the years then ended in accordance with accounting principles generally accepted in the United States of America.

Report on Other Legal and Regulatory Requirements

[*Form and content of this section of the auditor's report will vary depending on the nature of the auditor's other reporting responsibilities.*]

[*Auditor's signature*]

[*Auditor's city and state*]

[*Date of the auditor's report*]

Illustration 3—An Auditor's Report Containing an Adverse Opinion Due to a Material Misstatement of the Financial Statements

Circumstances include the following:

- Audit of a complete set of consolidated general purpose financial statements (single year) prepared in accordance with accounting principles generally accepted in the United States of America.
- The financial statements are materially misstated due to the nonconsolidation of a subsidiary. The material misstatement is deemed to be pervasive to the financial statements. Accordingly, the auditor's report contains an adverse opinion. The effects of the misstatement on the financial statements have not been determined because it was not practicable to do so.

Independent Auditor's Report

[*Appropriate Addressee*]

Report on the Consolidated Financial Statements[1]

We have audited the accompanying consolidated financial statements of ABC Company and its subsidiaries, which comprise the consolidated balance sheet as of December 31, 20X1, and the related consolidated statements of income, changes in stockholders' equity, and cash flows for the year then ended, and the related notes to the financial statements.

Management's Responsibility for the Financial Statements

Management is responsible for the preparation and fair presentation of these consolidated financial statements in accordance with accounting principles generally accepted in the United States of America; this includes the design, implementation, and maintenance of internal control relevant to the preparation and fair presentation of consolidated financial statements that are free from material misstatement, whether due to fraud or error.

Auditor's Responsibility

Our responsibility is to express an opinion on these consolidated financial statements based on our audit. We conducted our audit in accordance with auditing standards generally accepted in the United States of America. Those standards require that we plan and perform the audit to obtain reasonable assurance about whether the consolidated financial statements are free from material misstatement.

An audit involves performing procedures to obtain audit evidence about the amounts and disclosures in the consolidated financial statements. The procedures selected depend on the auditor's judgment, including the assessment of the risks of material misstatement of the consolidated financial statements, whether due to fraud or error. In making those risk assessments, the auditor considers internal control relevant to the entity's preparation and fair presentation of the consolidated financial statements in order to design audit procedures that are appropriate in the circumstances, but not for the purpose of expressing

---

[1] The subtitle "Report on the Consolidated Financial Statements" is unnecessary in circumstances when the second subtitle, "Report on Other Legal and Regulatory Requirements," is not applicable.

an opinion on the effectiveness of the entity's internal control.[2] Accordingly, we express no such opinion. An audit also includes evaluating the appropriateness of accounting policies used and the reasonableness of significant accounting estimates made by management, as well as evaluating the overall presentation of the consolidated financial statements.

We believe that the audit evidence we have obtained is sufficient and appropriate to provide a basis for our adverse audit opinion.

Basis for Adverse Opinion

As described in Note X, the Company has not consolidated the financial statements of subsidiary XYZ Company that it acquired during 20X1 because it has not yet been able to ascertain the fair values of certain of the subsidiary's material assets and liabilities at the acquisition date. This investment is therefore accounted for on a cost basis by the Company. Under accounting principles generally accepted in the United States of America, the subsidiary should have been consolidated because it is controlled by the Company. Had XYZ Company been consolidated, many elements in the accompanying consolidated financial statements would have been materially affected. The effects on the consolidated financial statements of the failure to consolidate have not been determined.

Adverse Opinion

In our opinion, because of the significance of the matter discussed in the Basis for Adverse Opinion paragraph, the consolidated financial statements referred to above do not present fairly the financial position of ABC Company and its subsidiaries as of December 31, 20X1, or the results of their operations or their cash flows for the year then ended in accordance with accounting principles generally accepted in the United States of America.

Report on Other Legal and Regulatory Requirements

[*Form and content of this section of the auditor's report will vary depending on the nature of the auditor's other reporting responsibilities.*]

[*Auditor's signature*]

[*Auditor's city and state*]

[*Date of the auditor's report*]

---

2 In circumstances when the auditor also has responsibility to express an opinion on the effectiveness of internal control in conjunction with the audit of the consolidated financial statements, this sentence would be worded as follows: "In making those risk assessments, the auditor considers internal control relevant to the entity's preparation and fair presentation of the consolidated financial statements in order to design audit procedures that are appropriate in the circumstances." In addition, the next sentence, "Accordingly, we express no such opinion." would not be included.

Illustration 4—An Auditor's Report Containing a Qualified Opinion Due to the Auditor's Inability to Obtain Sufficient Appropriate Audit Evidence

Circumstances include the following:

- Audit of a complete set of general purpose financial statements (single year) prepared in accordance with accounting principles generally accepted in the United States of America.
- The auditor was unable to obtain sufficient appropriate audit evidence regarding an investment in a foreign affiliate. The possible effects of the inability to obtain sufficient appropriate audit evidence are deemed to be material but not pervasive to the financial statements. Accordingly, the auditor's report contains a qualified opinion.

Independent Auditor's Report

[*Appropriate Addressee*]

Report on the Financial Statements[1]

We have audited the accompanying financial statements of ABC Company, which comprise the balance sheet as of December 31, 20X1, and the related statements of income, changes in stockholders' equity, and cash flows for the year then ended, and the related notes to the financial statements.

Management's Responsibility for the Financial Statements

Management is responsible for the preparation and fair presentation of these financial statements in accordance with accounting principles generally accepted in the United States of America; this includes the design, implementation, and maintenance of internal control relevant to the preparation and fair presentation of financial statements that are free from material misstatement, whether due to fraud or error.

Auditor's Responsibility

Our responsibility is to express an opinion on these financial statements based on our audit. We conducted our audit in accordance with auditing standards generally accepted in the United States of America. Those standards require that we plan and perform the audit to obtain reasonable assurance about whether the financial statements are free from material misstatement.

An audit involves performing procedures to obtain audit evidence about the amounts and disclosures in the financial statements. The procedures selected depend on the auditor's judgment, including the assessment of the risks of material misstatement of the financial statements, whether due to fraud or error. In making those risk assessments, the auditor considers internal control relevant to the entity's preparation and fair presentation of the financial statements in order to design audit procedures that are appropriate in the circumstances, but not for the purpose of expressing an opinion on the effectiveness of the entity's internal control.[2] Accordingly, we express no such opinion. An audit

---

[1] The subtitle "Report on the Financial Statements" is unnecessary in circumstances when the second subtitle, "Report on Other Legal and Regulatory Requirements," is not applicable.

[2] In circumstances when the auditor also has responsibility to express an opinion on the effectiveness of internal control in conjunction with the audit of the financial statements, this sentence would be worded as follows: "In making those risk assessments, the auditor considers internal control relevant to the entity's preparation and fair presentation of the financial statements in order to design audit procedures that are appropriate in the circumstances." In addition, the next sentence, "Accordingly, we express no such opinion." would not be included.

also includes evaluating the appropriateness of accounting policies used and the reasonableness of significant accounting estimates made by management, as well as evaluating the overall presentation of the financial statements.

We believe that the audit evidence we have obtained is sufficient and appropriate to provide a basis for our qualified audit opinion.

Basis for Qualified Opinion

ABC Company's investment in XYZ Company, a foreign affiliate acquired during the year and accounted for under the equity method, is carried at $XXX on the balance sheet at December 31, 20X1, and ABC Company's share of XYZ Company's net income of $XXX is included in ABC Company's net income for the year then ended. We were unable to obtain sufficient appropriate audit evidence about the carrying amount of ABC Company's investment in XYZ Company as of December 31, 20X1 and ABC Company's share of XYZ Company's net income for the year then ended because we were denied access to the financial information, management, and the auditors of XYZ Company. Consequently, we were unable to determine whether any adjustments to these amounts were necessary.

Qualified Opinion

In our opinion, except for the possible effects of the matter described in the Basis for Qualified Opinion paragraph, the financial statements referred to above present fairly, in all material respects, the financial position of ABC Company as of December 31, 20X1, and the results of its operations and its cash flows for the year then ended in accordance with accounting principles generally accepted in the United States of America.

Report on Other Legal and Regulatory Requirements

[*Form and content of this section of the auditor's report will vary depending on the nature of the auditor's other reporting responsibilities.*]

[*Auditor's signature*]

[*Auditor's city and state*]

[*Date of the auditor's report*]

Illustration 5—An Auditor's Report Containing a Disclaimer of Opinion Due to the Auditor's Inability to Obtain Sufficient Appropriate Audit Evidence About a Single Element of the Financial Statements

Circumstances include the following:

- Audit of a complete set of general purpose financial statements (single year) prepared in accordance with accounting principles generally accepted in the United States of America.
- The auditor was unable to obtain sufficient appropriate audit evidence about a single element of the financial statements. That is, the auditor was unable to obtain audit evidence about the financial information of a joint venture investment accounted for under the proportionate consolidation approach. The investment represents over 90 percent of the Company's net assets. The possible effects of this inability to obtain sufficient appropriate audit evidence are deemed to be both material and pervasive to the financial statements. Accordingly, the auditor's report contains a disclaimer of opinion.
- The auditor concluded that it was unnecessary to include in the auditor's report specific amounts for the Company's proportional share of the assets, liabilities, income, and expenses of the joint venture investment because the investment represents over 90 percent of the Company's net assets, and that fact is disclosed in the auditor's report.

Independent Auditor's Report

[*Appropriate Addressee*]

Report on the Financial Statements[1]

We were engaged to audit the accompanying financial statements of ABC Company, which comprise the balance sheet as of December 31, 20X1, and the related statements of income, changes in stockholders' equity, and cash flows for the year then ended, and the related notes to the financial statements.

Management's Responsibility for the Financial Statements

Management is responsible for the preparation and fair presentation of these financial statements in accordance with accounting principles generally accepted in the United States of America; this includes the design, implementation, and maintenance of internal control relevant to the preparation and fair presentation of financial statements that are free from material misstatement, whether due to fraud or error.

Auditor's Responsibility

Our responsibility is to express an opinion on these financial statements based on conducting the audit in accordance with auditing standards generally accepted in the United States of America. Because of the matter described in the Basis for Disclaimer of Opinion paragraph, however, we were not able to obtain sufficient appropriate audit evidence to provide a basis for an audit opinion.

---

[1] The subtitle "Report on the Financial Statements" is unnecessary in circumstances when the second subtitle, "Report on Other Legal and Regulatory Requirements," is not applicable.

Basis for Disclaimer of Opinion

The Company's investment in XYZ Company, a joint venture, is carried at $XXX on the Company's balance sheet, which represents over 90 percent of the Company's net assets as of December 31, 20X1. We were not allowed access to the management and the auditors of XYZ Company. As a result, we were unable to determine whether any adjustments were necessary relating to the Company's proportional share of XYZ Company's assets that it controls jointly, its proportional share of XYZ Company's liabilities for which it is jointly responsible, its proportional share of XYZ Company's income and expenses for the year, and the elements making up the statements of changes in stockholders' equity and cash flows.

Disclaimer of Opinion

Because of the significance of the matter described in the Basis for Disclaimer of Opinion paragraph, we have not been able to obtain sufficient appropriate audit evidence to provide a basis for an audit opinion. Accordingly, we do not express an opinion on these financial statements.

Report on Other Legal and Regulatory Requirements

[*Form and content of this section of the auditor's report will vary depending on the nature of the auditor's other reporting responsibilities.*]

[*Auditor's signature*]

[*Auditor's city and state*]

[*Date of the auditor's report*]

Illustration 6—An Auditor's Report Containing a Disclaimer of Opinion Due to the Auditor's Inability to Obtain Sufficient Appropriate Audit Evidence About Multiple Elements of the Financial Statements

Circumstances include the following:

- Audit of a complete set of general purpose financial statements (single year) prepared in accordance with accounting principles generally accepted in the United States of America.
- The auditor was unable to obtain sufficient appropriate audit evidence about multiple elements of the financial statements. That is, the auditor was unable to obtain audit evidence about the entity's inventories and accounts receivable. The possible effects of this inability to obtain sufficient appropriate audit evidence are deemed to be both material and pervasive to the financial statements. Accordingly, the auditor's opinion contains a disclaimer of opinion.

Independent Auditor's Report

[*Appropriate Addressee*]

Report on the Financial Statements[1]

We were engaged to audit the accompanying financial statements of ABC Company, which comprise the balance sheet as of December 31, 20X1, and the related statements of income, changes in stockholders' equity, and cash flows for the year then ended, and the related notes to the financial statements.

Management's Responsibility for the Financial Statements

Management is responsible for the preparation and fair presentation of these financial statements in accordance with accounting principles generally accepted in the United States of America; this includes the design, implementation, and maintenance of internal control relevant to the preparation and fair presentation of financial statements that are free from material misstatement, whether due to fraud or error.

Auditor's Responsibility

Our responsibility is to express an opinion on these financial statements based on conducting the audit in accordance with auditing standards generally accepted in the United States of America. Because of the matters described in the Basis for Disclaimer of Opinion paragraph, however, we were not able to obtain sufficient appropriate audit evidence to provide a basis for an audit opinion.

Basis for Disclaimer of Opinion

We were not engaged as auditors of the Company until after December 31, 20X1, and, therefore, did not observe the counting of physical inventories at the beginning or end of the year. We were unable to satisfy ourselves by other auditing procedures concerning the inventory held at December 31, 20X1, which is stated in the balance sheet at $XXX. In addition, the introduction of a new computerized accounts receivable system in September 20X1 resulted in numerous misstatements in accounts receivable. As of the date of our audit report, management was still in the process of rectifying the system deficiencies and

---

[1] The subtitle "Report on the Financial Statements" is unnecessary in circumstances when the second subtitle, "Report on Other Legal and Regulatory Requirements," is not applicable.

correcting the misstatements. We were unable to confirm or verify by alternative means accounts receivable included in the balance sheet at a total amount of $XXX at December 31, 20X1. As a result of these matters, we were unable to determine whether any adjustments might have been found necessary in respect of recorded or unrecorded inventories and accounts receivable, and the elements making up the statements of income, changes in stockholders' equity, and cash flows.

Disclaimer of Opinion

Because of the significance of the matters described in the Basis for Disclaimer of Opinion paragraph, we have not been able to obtain sufficient appropriate audit evidence to provide a basis for an audit opinion. Accordingly, we do not express an opinion on these financial statements.

Report on Other Legal and Regulatory Requirements

[*Form and content of this section of the auditor's report will vary depending on the nature of the auditor's other reporting responsibilities.*]

[*Auditor's signature*]

[*Auditor's city and state*]

[*Date of the auditor's report*]

Illustration 7—An Auditor's Report in Which the Auditor Is Expressing an Unmodified Opinion in the Prior Year and a Modified Opinion (Qualified Opinion) in the Current Year

Circumstances include the following:

- Audit of a complete set of general purpose financial statements (comparative) prepared in accordance with accounting principles generally accepted in the United States of America.
- Certain lease obligations have been excluded from the financial statements in the current year. The effect of the exclusion is material but not pervasive. The auditor expressed an unmodified opinion in the prior year and is expressing a modified opinion (qualified opinion) in the current year.

Independent Auditor's Report

[*Appropriate Addressee*]

Report on the Financial Statements[1]

We have audited the accompanying financial statements of ABC Company, which comprise the balance sheets as of December 31, 20X1 and 20X0, and the related statements of income, changes in stockholders' equity, and cash flows for the years then ended, and the related notes to the financial statements.

Management's Responsibility for the Financial Statements

Management is responsible for the preparation and fair presentation of these financial statements in accordance with accounting principles generally accepted in the United States of America; this includes the design, implementation, and maintenance of internal control relevant to the preparation and fair presentation of financial statements that are free from material misstatement, whether due to fraud or error.

Auditor's Responsibility

Our responsibility is to express an opinion on these financial statements based on our audits. We conducted our audits in accordance with auditing standards generally accepted in the United States of America. Those standards require that we plan and perform the audit to obtain reasonable assurance about whether the financial statements are free from material misstatement.

An audit involves performing procedures to obtain audit evidence about the amounts and disclosures in the financial statements. The procedures selected depend on the auditor's judgment, including the assessment of the risks of material misstatement of the financial statements, whether due to fraud or error. In making those risk assessments, the auditor considers internal control relevant to the entity's preparation and fair presentation of the financial statements in order to design audit procedures that are appropriate in the circumstances, but not for the purpose of expressing an opinion on the effectiveness of the entity's internal control.[2] Accordingly, we express no such opinion. An audit

---

[1] The subtitle "Report on the Financial Statements" is unnecessary in circumstances when the second subtitle, "Report on Other Legal and Regulatory Requirements," is not applicable.

[2] In circumstances when the auditor also has responsibility to express an opinion on the effectiveness of internal control in conjunction with the audit of the financial statements, this sentence would be worded as follows: "In making those risk assessments, the auditor considers internal control relevant to the entity's preparation and fair presentation of the financial statements in order to design audit procedures that are appropriate in the circumstances." In addition, the next sentence, "Accordingly, we express no such opinion." would not be included.

also includes evaluating the appropriateness of accounting policies used and the reasonableness of significant accounting estimates made by management, as well as evaluating the overall presentation of the financial statements.

We believe that the audit evidence we have obtained is sufficient and appropriate to provide a basis for our qualified audit opinion.

Basis for Qualified Opinion

The Company has excluded, from property and debt in the accompanying 20X1 balance sheet, certain lease obligations that were entered into in 20X1 which, in our opinion, should be capitalized in accordance with accounting principles generally accepted in the United States of America. If these lease obligations were capitalized, property would be increased by $XXX, long-term debt by $XXX, and retained earnings by $XXX as of December 31, 20X1, and net income and earnings per share would be increased (decreased) by $XXX and $XXX, respectively, for the year then ended.

Qualified Opinion

In our opinion, except for the effects on the 20X1 financial statements of not capitalizing certain lease obligations as described in the Basis for Qualified Opinion paragraph, the financial statements referred to above present fairly, in all material respects, the financial position of ABC Company as of December 31, 20X1 and 20X0, and the results of its operations and its cash flows for the years then ended in accordance with accounting principles generally accepted in the United States of America.

Report on Other Legal and Regulatory Requirements

[*Form and content of this section of the auditor's report will vary depending on the nature of the auditor's other reporting responsibilities.*]

[*Auditor's signature*]

[*Auditor's city and state*]

[*Date of the auditor's report*]

Illustration 8—An Auditor's Report in Which the Auditor Is Expressing an Unmodified Opinion in the Current Year and a Disclaimer of Opinion on the Prior-Year Statements of Income, Changes in Stockholders' Equity, and Cash Flows

Circumstances include the following:

- Audit of a complete set of general purpose financial statements (comparative) prepared in accordance with accounting principles generally accepted in the United States of America.
- The auditor was unable to observe the physical inventory as at December 31, 20X0, as at that time the auditor had not been engaged. Accordingly, the auditor was unable to obtain sufficient appropriate audit evidence regarding the net income and cash flows for the year ended December 31, 20X1. The effects of the inability to obtain sufficient appropriate audit evidence are deemed material and pervasive.
- The auditor expressed an unmodified opinion on December 31, 20X1 and 20X0 balance sheets and a disclaimer of opinion on the 20X0 statements of income, changes in stockholders' equity, and cash flows.

Independent Auditor's Report

[*Appropriate Addressee*]

Report on the Financial Statements[1]

We have audited the accompanying financial statements of ABC Company, which comprise the balance sheets as of December 31, 20X2 and 20X1, and the related statements of income, changes in stockholders' equity, and cash flows for the years then ended, and the related notes to the financial statements.

Management's Responsibility for the Financial Statements

Management is responsible for the preparation and fair presentation of these financial statements in accordance with accounting principles generally accepted in the United States of America; this includes the design, implementation, and maintenance of internal control relevant to the preparation and fair presentation of financial statements that are free from material misstatement, whether due to fraud or error.

Auditor's Responsibility

Our responsibility is to express an opinion on these financial statements based on our audits. Except as explained in the Basis for Disclaimer of Opinion paragraph, we conducted our audits in accordance with auditing standards generally accepted in the United States of America. Those standards require that we plan and perform the audit to obtain reasonable assurance about whether the financial statements are free from material misstatement.

An audit involves performing procedures to obtain audit evidence about the amounts and disclosures in the financial statements. The procedures selected depend on the auditor's judgment, including the assessment of the risks of material misstatement of the financial statements, whether due to fraud or error. In making those risk assessments, the auditor considers internal control relevant to the entity's preparation and fair presentation of the financial statements

---

[1] The subtitle "Report on the Financial Statements" is unnecessary in circumstances when the second subtitle, "Report on Other Legal and Regulatory Requirements," is not applicable.

in order to design audit procedures that are appropriate in the circumstances, but not for the purpose of expressing an opinion on the effectiveness of the entity's internal control.[2] Accordingly, we express no such opinion. An audit also includes evaluating the appropriateness of accounting policies used and the reasonableness of significant accounting estimates made by management, as well as evaluating the overall presentation of the financial statements.

We believe that the audit evidence we have obtained is sufficient and appropriate to provide a basis for our audit opinions on the balance sheets as of December 31, 20X2 and 20X1, and the statements of income, changes in stockholders' equity, and cash flows for the year ended December 31, 20X2.

Basis for Disclaimer of Opinion on 20X1 Operations and Cash Flows

We did not observe the taking of the physical inventory as of December 31, 20X0, since that date was prior to our engagement as auditors for the Company, and we were unable to satisfy ourselves regarding inventory quantities by means of other auditing procedures. Inventory amounts as of December 31, 20X0 enter into the determination of net income and cash flows for the year ended December 31, 20X1.

Disclaimer of Opinion on 20X1 Operations and Cash Flows

Because of the significance of the matter described in the Basis for Disclaimer of Opinion paragraph, we have not been able to obtain sufficient appropriate audit evidence to provide a basis for an audit opinion on the results of operations and cash flows for the year ended December 31, 20X1. Accordingly, we do not express an opinion on the results of operations and cash flows for the year ended December 31, 20X1.

Opinion

In our opinion, the balance sheets of ABC Company as of December 31, 20X2 and 20X1, and the statements of income, changes in stockholders' equity, and cash flows for the year ended December 31, 20X2, present fairly, in all material respects, the financial position of ABC Company as of December 31, 20X2 and 20X1, and the results of its operations and its cash flows for the year ended December 31, 20X2 in accordance with accounting principles generally accepted in the United States of America.

Report on Other Legal and Regulatory Requirements

[*Form and content of this section of the auditor's report will vary depending on the nature of the auditor's other reporting responsibilities.*]

[*Auditor's signature*]

[*Auditor's city and state*]

[*Date of the auditor's report*]

---

[2] In circumstances when the auditor also has responsibility to express an opinion on the effectiveness of internal control in conjunction with the audit of the financial statements, this sentence would be worded as follows: "In making those risk assessments, the auditor considers internal control relevant to the entity's preparation and fair presentation of the financial statements in order to design audit procedures that are appropriate in the circumstances." In addition, the next sentence, "Accordingly, we express no such opinion." would not be included.

AU-C Section 706 *

Emphasis-of-Matter Paragraphs and Other-Matter Paragraphs in the Independent Auditor's Report

Source: SAS No. 122.

Effective for audits of financial statements for periods ending on or after December 15, 2012.

Introduction

Scope of This Section

.01 This section addresses additional communications in the auditor's report when the auditor considers it necessary to

a. draw users' attention to a matter or matters presented or disclosed in the financial statements that are of such importance that they are fundamental to users' understanding of the financial statements (emphasis-of-matter paragraph) or

b. draw users' attention to any matter or matters other than those presented or disclosed in the financial statements that are relevant to users' understanding of the audit, the auditor's responsibilities, or the auditor's report (other-matter paragraph).

.02 Exhibit B, "List of AU-C Sections Containing Requirements for Emphasis-of-Matter Paragraphs," and exhibit C, "List of AU-C Sections Containing Requirements for Other-Matter Paragraphs," identify AU-C sections containing specific requirements for the auditor to include an emphasis-of-matter paragraph or other-matter paragraph, respectively, in the auditor's report. Accordingly, the requirements in this section regarding the form and placement of such paragraphs apply. (Ref: par. .A1)

Effective Date

.03 This section is effective for audits of financial statements for periods ending on or after December 15, 2012.

Objective

.04 The objective of the auditor, having formed an opinion on the financial statements, is to draw users' attention, when in the auditor's judgment it is necessary to do so, by way of clear additional communication in the auditor's report, to

---

* This section has been codified using an "AU-C" identifier instead of an "AU" identifier. "AU-C" is a temporary identifier to avoid confusion with references to existing "AU" sections, which will remain in AICPA *Professional Standards* through 2013. The "AU-C" identifier will revert to "AU" in 2014, by which time substantially all engagements for which the "AU" sections were still effective are expected to be completed.

a. a matter, although appropriately presented or disclosed in the financial statements, that is of such importance that it is fundamental to users' understanding of the financial statements or

b. as appropriate, any other matter that is relevant to users' understanding of the audit, the auditor's responsibilities, or the auditor's report.

Definitions

.05 For the purposes of generally accepted auditing standards (GAAS), the following terms have the meanings attributed as follows:

Emphasis-of-matter paragraph. A paragraph included in the auditor's report that is required by GAAS, or is included at the auditor's discretion, and that refers to a matter appropriately presented or disclosed in the financial statements that, in the auditor's professional judgment, is of such importance that it is fundamental to users' understanding of the financial statements.

Other-matter paragraph. A paragraph included in the auditor's report that is required by GAAS, or is included at the auditor's discretion, and that refers to a matter other than those presented or disclosed in the financial statements that, in the auditor's professional judgment, is relevant to users' understanding of the audit, the auditor's responsibilities, or the auditor's report.

Requirements

Emphasis-of-Matter Paragraphs in the Auditor's Report

.06 If the auditor considers it necessary to draw users' attention to a matter appropriately presented or disclosed in the financial statements that, in the auditor's professional judgment, is of such importance that it is fundamental to users' understanding of the financial statements, the auditor should include an emphasis-of-matter paragraph in the auditor's report, provided that the auditor has obtained sufficient appropriate audit evidence that the matter is not materially misstated in the financial statements. Such a paragraph should refer only to information presented or disclosed in the financial statements. (Ref: par. .A2–.A3)

.07 When the auditor includes an emphasis-of-matter paragraph in the auditor's report, the auditor should

a. include it immediately after the opinion paragraph in the auditor's report,

b. use the heading "Emphasis of Matter" or other appropriate heading, (Ref: par. .A4)

c. include in the paragraph a clear reference to the matter being emphasized and to where relevant disclosures that fully describe the matter can be found in the financial statements, and

d. indicate that the auditor's opinion is not modified with respect to the matter emphasized. (Ref: par. .A5)

Other-Matter Paragraphs in the Auditor's Report

.08 If the auditor considers it necessary to communicate a matter other than those that are presented or disclosed in the financial statements that, in the auditor's professional judgment, is relevant to users' understanding of the audit, the auditor's responsibilities, or the auditor's report, the auditor should do so in a paragraph in the auditor's report with the heading "Other Matter" or other appropriate heading. The auditor should include this paragraph immediately after the opinion paragraph and any emphasis-of-matter paragraph or elsewhere in the auditor's report if the content of the other-matter paragraph is relevant to the "Other Reporting Responsibilities" section. (Ref: par. .A6–.A11)

Communication With Those Charged With Governance

.09 If the auditor expects to include an emphasis-of-matter or other-matter paragraph in the auditor's report, the auditor should communicate with those charged with governance regarding this expectation and the proposed wording of this paragraph. (Ref: par. .A12)

Application and Other Explanatory Material

Scope of This Section (Ref: par. .02)

.A1 The AU-C sections identified in exhibits B and C require the auditor to include an emphasis-of-matter paragraph or other-matter paragraph, respectively, in the auditor's report relating to certain matters. The nature of these matters is such that they are brought to the attention of users of the auditor's report in all instances rather than at the discretion of the auditor. The explanatory language provided by such required paragraphs achieves the same objective as an emphasis-of-matter or other-matter paragraph that is included based on the professional judgment of the auditor (that is, to provide additional communication to the users of the auditor's report). Therefore, the auditor follows the requirements in this section regarding the form and placement of these required paragraphs.

Emphasis-of-Matter Paragraphs in the Auditor's Report

Circumstances in Which an Emphasis-of-Matter Paragraph May Be Necessary (Ref: par. .06)

.A2 In addition to the required emphasis-of-matter paragraphs listed in exhibit B, the following are examples of circumstances when the auditor may consider it necessary to include an emphasis-of-matter paragraph:

- An uncertainty relating to the future outcome of unusually important litigation or regulatory action
- A major catastrophe that has had, or continues to have, a significant effect on the entity's financial position
- Significant transactions with related parties
- Unusually important subsequent events

.A3 Paragraph .06 requires that an emphasis-of-matter paragraph refer only to matters appropriately presented or disclosed in the financial statements. To include information in an emphasis-of-matter paragraph about a matter beyond what is presented or disclosed in the financial statements may raise questions about the appropriateness of such presentation or disclosure.

Including an Emphasis-of-Matter Paragraph in the Auditor's Report (Ref: par. .07)

.A4 If the heading "Emphasis of Matter" is not used, another heading may be considered appropriate if it adequately describes the nature of the matter being disclosed or communicated.

.A5 The inclusion of an emphasis-of-matter paragraph in the auditor's report does not affect the auditor's opinion. An emphasis-of-matter paragraph is not a substitute for either

a. the auditor expressing a qualified opinion or an adverse opinion, or disclaiming an opinion, when required by the circumstances of a specific audit engagement (see section 705, *Modifications to the Opinion in the Independent Auditor's Report*) or

b. disclosures in the financial statements that the applicable financial reporting framework requires management to make.

Other-Matter Paragraphs in the Auditor's Report (Ref: par. .08)

Circumstances in Which an Other-Matter Paragraph May Be Necessary

Relevant to Users' Understanding of the Audit

.A6 In the rare circumstance when the auditor is unable to withdraw from an engagement even though the possible effect of an inability to obtain sufficient appropriate audit evidence due to a limitation on the scope of the audit imposed by management is pervasive,[1] the auditor may consider it necessary to include an other-matter paragraph in the auditor's report to explain why it is not possible for the auditor to withdraw from the engagement.

Relevant to Users' Understanding of the Auditor's Responsibilities or the Auditor's Report

.A7 Law, regulation, or generally accepted practice may require or permit the auditor to elaborate on matters that provide further explanation of the auditor's responsibilities in the audit of the financial statements or the auditor's report thereon. When relevant, one or more subheadings may be used that describe the content of the other-matter paragraph.

.A8 An other-matter paragraph does not address circumstances when the auditor has other reporting responsibilities that are in addition to the auditor's responsibility under GAAS to report on the financial statements (see the "Other Reporting Responsibilities" section in section 700, *Forming an Opinion and Reporting on Financial Statements*) or when the auditor has been asked to perform and report on additional specified procedures or to express an opinion on specific matters.

Reporting on More Than One Set of Financial Statements

.A9 An entity may prepare one set of financial statements in accordance with a general purpose framework (for example, accounting principles generally accepted in the United States of America) and another set of financial statements in accordance with another general purpose framework (for example, International Financial Reporting Standards promulgated by the International Accounting Standards Board) and engage the auditor to report on both sets of financial statements. If the auditor has determined that the frameworks are

---

[1] See paragraph .13 of section 705, *Modifications to the Opinion in the Independent Auditor's Report*, for a discussion of this circumstance.

acceptable in the respective circumstances, the auditor may include an other-matter paragraph in the auditor's report referring to the fact that another set of financial statements has been prepared by the same entity in accordance with another general purpose framework and that the auditor has issued a report on those financial statements.

Including an Other-Matter Paragraph in the Auditor's Report

.A10 The content of an other-matter paragraph reflects clearly that such other matter is not required to be presented and disclosed in the financial statements. An other-matter paragraph does not include information that the auditor is prohibited from providing by law, regulation, or other professional standards (for example, ethical standards relating to the confidentiality of information). An other-matter paragraph also does not include information that is required to be provided by management.

.A11 The placement of an other-matter paragraph depends on the nature of the information to be communicated. When an other-matter paragraph is included to draw users' attention to a matter relevant to their understanding of the audit of the financial statements, the paragraph is included immediately after the opinion paragraph and any emphasis-of-matter paragraph. When an other-matter paragraph is included to draw users' attention to a matter relating to other reporting responsibilities addressed in the auditor's report, the paragraph may be included in the section subtitled "Report on Other Legal and Regulatory Requirements." Alternatively, when relevant to all the auditor's responsibilities or users' understanding of the auditor's report, the other-matter paragraph may be included as a separate section following the "Report on the Financial Statements" and the "Report on Other Legal and Regulatory Requirements."

Communication With Those Charged With Governance (Ref: par. .09)

.A12 The auditor's communication with those charged with governance, as described in paragraph .09, enables those charged with governance to be made aware of the nature of any specific matters that the auditor intends to highlight in the auditor's report and provides them with an opportunity to obtain further clarification from the auditor, when necessary. When the inclusion of an other-matter paragraph on a particular matter in the auditor's report recurs on each successive engagement, the auditor may determine that it is unnecessary to repeat the communication on each engagement.

.A13

Exhibit A—Illustrations of Auditor's Reports With Emphasis-of-Matter or Other-Matter Paragraphs

Illustration 1—An Auditor's Report With an Emphasis-of-Matter Paragraph Because There Is Uncertainty Relating to a Pending Unusually Important Litigation Matter

Circumstances include the following:

- Audit of a complete set of general purpose financial statements (single year) prepared in accordance with accounting principles generally accepted in the United States of America.
- There is uncertainty relating to a pending unusually important litigation matter.
- The auditor's report includes an emphasis-of-matter paragraph.

Independent Auditor's Report

[*Appropriate Addressee*]

Report on the Financial Statements[1]

We have audited the accompanying financial statements of ABC Company, which comprise the balance sheet as of December 31, 20X1, and the related statements of income, changes in stockholders' equity, and cash flows for the year then ended, and the related notes to the financial statements.

Management's Responsibility for the Financial Statements

Management is responsible for the preparation and fair presentation of these financial statements in accordance with accounting principles generally accepted in the United States of America; this includes the design, implementation, and maintenance of internal control relevant to the preparation and fair presentation of financial statements that are free from material misstatement, whether due to fraud or error.

Auditor's Responsibility

Our responsibility is to express an opinion on these financial statements based on our audit. We conducted our audit in accordance with auditing standards generally accepted in the United States of America. Those standards require that we plan and perform the audit to obtain reasonable assurance about whether the financial statements are free from material misstatement.

An audit involves performing procedures to obtain audit evidence about the amounts and disclosures in the financial statements. The procedures selected depend on the auditor's judgment, including the assessment of the risks of material misstatement of the financial statements, whether due to fraud or error. In making those risk assessments, the auditor considers internal control relevant to the entity's preparation and fair presentation of the financial statements in order to design audit procedures that are appropriate in the circumstances, but not for the purpose of expressing an opinion on the effectiveness of the entity's internal control.[2] Accordingly, we express no such opinion. An audit also includes evaluating the appropriateness of accounting policies used and

---

[1] The subtitle "Report on the Financial Statements" is unnecessary in circumstances when the second subtitle, "Report on Other Legal and Regulatory Requirements," is not applicable.

[2] In circumstances when the auditor also has responsibility to express an opinion on the effectiveness of internal control in conjunction with the audit of the financial statements, this sentence would be worded as follows: "In making those risk assessments, the auditor considers internal control relevant to the entity's preparation and fair presentation of the financial statements in order to design audit procedures that are appropriate in the circumstances." In addition, the next sentence, "Accordingly, we express no such opinion." would not be included.

the reasonableness of significant accounting estimates made by management, as well as evaluating the overall presentation of the financial statements.

We believe that the audit evidence that we have obtained is sufficient and appropriate to provide a basis for our audit opinion.

Opinion

In our opinion, the financial statements referred to above present fairly, in all material respects the financial position of ABC Company as of December 31, 20X1, and the results of its operations and its cash flows for the year then ended in accordance with accounting principles generally accepted in the United States of America.

Emphasis of Matter

As discussed in Note X to the financial statements, the Company is a defendant in a lawsuit [*briefly describe the nature of the litigation consistent with the Company's description in the note to the financial statements*]. Our opinion is not modified with respect to this matter.

Report on Other Legal and Regulatory Requirements

[*Form and content of this section of the auditor's report will vary depending on the nature of the auditor's other reporting responsibilities.*]

[*Auditor's signature*]

[*Auditor's city and state*]

[*Date of the auditor's report*]

Illustration 2—An Auditor's Report With an Other-Matter Paragraph That May Be Appropriate When an Auditor Issues an Updated Report on the Financial Statements of a Prior Period That Contains an Opinion Different From the Opinion Previously Expressed

Circumstances include the following:

- Audit of a complete set of general purpose financial statements (comparative) prepared in accordance with accounting principles generally accepted in the United States of America.
- The auditor's report on the prior period financial statements expressed an adverse opinion due to identified departures from accounting principles generally accepted in the United States of America that resulted in the financial statements being materially misstated. The entity has elected to change its method of accounting for the matters that gave rise to the adverse opinion in the prior period, and has restated the prior period financial statements. Therefore, the auditor has expressed an unmodified opinion on the comparative financial statements.
- The auditor's report includes an other-matter paragraph indicating that the updated report on the financial statements of the prior period contains an opinion different from the opinion previously expressed, as required by section 700, *Forming an Opinion and Reporting on Financial Statements*.
- Although the entity changed its method of accounting for the matters that gave rise to the adverse opinion in the prior period, the principal objective of the communication in the other-matter paragraph is to draw users' attention to the change in the auditor's opinion on the prior period financial statements. The other-matter paragraph also refers to the change in accounting principle and the related disclosure in the financial statements. Therefore, the other-matter paragraph also meets the objective of communicating the change in accounting principle as required by section 708, *Consistency of Financial Statements*, and a separate emphasis-of-matter paragraph is not considered necessary.

Independent Auditor's Report

[*Appropriate Addressee*]

Report on the Financial Statements[1]

We have audited the accompanying financial statements of ABC Company, which comprise the balance sheets as of December 31, 20X1 and 20X0, and the related statements of income, changes in stockholders' equity, and cash flows for the years then ended, and the related notes to the financial statements.

Management's Responsibility for the Financial Statements

Management is responsible for the preparation and fair presentation of these financial statements in accordance with accounting principles generally accepted in the United States of America; this includes the design, implementation, and

[1] The subtitle "Report on the Financial Statements" is unnecessary in circumstances when the second subtitle, "Report on Other Legal and Regulatory Requirements," is not applicable.

maintenance of internal control relevant to the preparation and fair presentation of financial statements that are free from material misstatement, whether due to fraud or error.

Auditor's Responsibility

Our responsibility is to express an opinion on these financial statements based on our audits. We conducted our audits in accordance with auditing standards generally accepted in the United States of America. Those standards require that we plan and perform the audit to obtain reasonable assurance about whether the financial statements are free from material misstatement.

An audit involves performing procedures to obtain audit evidence about the amounts and disclosures in the financial statements. The procedures selected depend on the auditor's judgment, including the assessment of the risks of material misstatement of the financial statements, whether due to fraud or error. In making those risk assessments, the auditor considers internal control relevant to the entity's preparation and fair presentation of the financial statements in order to design audit procedures that are appropriate in the circumstances, but not for the purpose of expressing an opinion on the effectiveness of the entity's internal control.[2] Accordingly, we express no such opinion. An audit also includes evaluating the appropriateness of accounting policies used and the reasonableness of significant accounting estimates made by management, as well as evaluating the overall presentation of the financial statements.

We believe that the audit evidence that we have obtained is sufficient and appropriate to provide a basis for our audit opinion.

Opinion

In our opinion, the financial statements referred to above present fairly, in all material respects, the financial position of ABC Company as of December 31, 20X1 and 20X0, and the results of its operations and its cash flows for the years then ended in accordance with accounting principles generally accepted in the United States of America.

Other Matter

In our report dated March 1, 20X1, we expressed an opinion that the 20X0 financial statements did not fairly present the financial position, results of operations, and cash flows of ABC Company in accordance with accounting principles generally accepted in the United States of America because of two departures from such principles: (1) ABC Company carried its property, plant, and equipment at appraisal values, and provided for depreciation on the basis of such values, and (2) ABC Company did not provide for deferred income taxes with respect to differences between income for financial reporting purposes and taxable income. As described in Note X, the Company has changed its method of accounting for these items and restated its 20X0 financial statements to conform with accounting principles generally accepted in the United States of America. Accordingly, our present opinion on the restated 20X0 financial statements, as presented herein, is different from that expressed in our previous report.

---

[2] In circumstances when the auditor also has responsibility to express an opinion on the effectiveness of internal control in conjunction with the audit of the financial statements, this sentence would be worded as follows: "In making those risk assessments, the auditor considers internal control relevant to the entity's preparation and fair presentation of the financial statements in order to design audit procedures that are appropriate in the circumstances." In addition, the next sentence, "Accordingly, we express no such opinion." would not be included.

Report on Other Legal and Regulatory Requirements

[*Form and content of this section of the auditor's report will vary depending on the nature of the auditor's other reporting responsibilities.*]

[*Auditor's signature*]

[*Auditor's city and state*]

[*Date of the auditor's report*]

Illustration 3—An Auditor's Report With a Qualified Opinion Due to a Material Misstatement of the Financial Statements and an Emphasis-of-Matter Paragraph Because There Is Uncertainty Relating to a Pending Unusually Important Litigation Matter

Circumstances include the following:

- Audit of a complete set of general purpose financial statements (single year) prepared in accordance with accounting principles generally accepted in the United States of America.
- Inventories are misstated. The misstatement is deemed to be material but not pervasive to the financial statements.
- There is uncertainty relating to a pending unusually important litigation matter.
- The auditor's report includes a qualified opinion and also includes an emphasis-of-matter paragraph.

Independent Auditor's Report

[*Appropriate Addressee*]

Report on the Financial Statements[1]

We have audited the accompanying financial statements of ABC Company, which comprise the balance sheet as of December 31, 20X1, and related statements of income, changes in stockholders' equity, and cash flows for the year then ended, and the related notes to the financial statements.

Management's Responsibility for the Financial Statements

Management is responsible for the preparation and fair presentation of these financial statements in accordance with accounting principles generally accepted in the United States of America; this includes the design, implementation, and maintenance of internal control relevant to the preparation and fair presentation of financial statements that are free from material misstatement, whether due to fraud or error.

Auditor's Responsibility

Our responsibility is to express an opinion on these financial statements based on our audit. We conducted our audit in accordance with auditing standards generally accepted in the United States of America. Those standards require that we plan and perform the audit to obtain reasonable assurance about whether the financial statements are free from material misstatement.

An audit involves performing procedures to obtain audit evidence about the amounts and disclosures in the financial statements. The procedures selected depend on the auditor's judgment, including the assessment of the risks of material misstatement of the financial statements, whether due to fraud or error. In making those risk assessments, the auditor considers internal control relevant to the entity's preparation and fair presentation of the financial statements in order to design audit procedures that are appropriate in the circumstances, but not for the purpose of expressing an opinion on the effectiveness of the

---

[1] The subtitle "Report on the Financial Statements" is unnecessary in circumstances when the second subtitle, "Report on Other Legal and Regulatory Requirements," is not applicable.

entity's internal control.[2] Accordingly, we express no such opinion. An audit also includes evaluating the appropriateness of accounting policies used and the reasonableness of significant accounting estimates made by management, as well as evaluating the overall presentation of the financial statements.

We believe that the audit evidence we have obtained is sufficient and appropriate to provide a basis for our qualified audit opinion.

Basis for Qualified Opinion

The Company has stated inventories at cost in the accompanying balance sheet. Accounting principles generally accepted in the United States of America require inventories to be stated at the lower of cost or market. If the Company stated inventories at the lower of cost or market, a write down of $XXX would have been required as of December 31, 20X1. Accordingly, cost of sales would have been increased by $XXX and net income, income taxes, and stockholders' equity would have been reduced by $XXX, $XXX, and $XXX, as of and for the year ended December 31, 20X1, respectively.

Qualified Opinion

In our opinion, except for the effects of the matter described in the Basis for Qualified Opinion paragraph, the financial statements referred to above present fairly, in all material respects, the financial position of ABC Company as of December 31, 20X1, and the results of its operations and its cash flows for the year then ended in accordance with accounting principles generally accepted in the United States of America.

Emphasis of Matter

As discussed in Note X to the financial statements, the Company is a defendant in a lawsuit [*briefly describe the nature of the litigation consistent with the Company's description in the note to the financial statements*]. Our opinion is not modified with respect to this matter.

Report on Other Legal and Regulatory Requirements

[*Form and content of this section of the auditor's report will vary depending on the nature of the auditor's other reporting responsibilities.*]

[*Auditor's signature*]

[*Auditor's city and state*]

[*Date of the auditor's report*]

---

[2] In circumstances when the auditor also has responsibility to express an opinion on the effectiveness of internal control in conjunction with the audit of the financial statements, this sentence would be worded as follows: "In making those risk assessments, the auditor considers internal control relevant to the entity's preparation and fair presentation of the financial statements in order to design audit procedures that are appropriate in the circumstances." In addition, the next sentence, "Accordingly, we express no such opinion." would not be included.

.A14

Exhibit B—List of AU-C Sections Containing Requirements for Emphasis-of-Matter Paragraphs (Ref: par. .02)

This exhibit identifies paragraphs in other AU-C sections that require the auditor to include an emphasis-of-matter paragraph in the auditor's report in certain circumstances. The list is not a substitute for considering the requirements and related application and other explanatory material in AU-C sections.

- Paragraph .16*c* of section 560, *Subsequent Events and Subsequently Discovered Facts*
- Paragraphs .15–.16 of section 570, *The Auditor's Consideration of an Entity's Ability to Continue as a Going Concern*
- Paragraphs .08–.09 and .11–.13 of section 708, *Consistency of Financial Statements*
- Paragraphs .19 and .21 of section 800, *Special Considerations—Audits of Financial Statements Prepared in Accordance With Special Purpose Frameworks*

[Revised, August 2012, to reflect conforming changes necessary due to the issuance of SAS No. 126.]

.A15

Exhibit C—List of AU-C Sections Containing Requirements for Other-Matter Paragraphs (Ref: par. .02)

This exhibit identifies paragraphs in other AU-C sections that require the auditor to include an other-matter paragraph in the auditor's report in certain circumstances. The list is not a substitute for considering the requirements and related application and other explanatory material in AU-C sections.

- Paragraph .16*c* of section 560, *Subsequent Events and Subsequently Discovered Facts*
- Paragraphs .53–.54 and .56–.57 of section 700, *Forming an Opinion and Reporting on Financial Statements*
- Paragraph .12 of section 720, *Other Information in Documents Containing Audited Financial Statements*
- Paragraph .09 of section 725, *Supplementary Information in Relation to the Financial Statements as a Whole*
- Paragraph .07 of section 730, *Required Supplementary Information*
- Paragraph .20 of section 800, *Special Considerations—Audits of Financial Statements Prepared in Accordance With Special Purpose Frameworks*
- Paragraph .13 of section 806, *Reporting on Compliance With Aspects of Contractual Agreements or Regulatory Requirements in Connection With Audited Financial Statements*
- Paragraph .07 of section 905, *Alert That Restricts the Use of the Auditor's Written Communication*

[Amended, December 2011, to reflect conforming changes necessary due to the issuance of SAS No. 125.]

AU-C Section 708 *

Consistency of Financial Statements

Source: SAS No. 122.

Effective for audits of financial statements for periods ending on or after December 15, 2012.

Introduction

Scope of This Section

.01 This section addresses the auditor's evaluation of the consistency of the financial statements between periods, including changes to previously issued financial statements and the effect of that evaluation on the auditor's report on the financial statements.

Effective Date

.02 This section is effective for audits of financial statements for periods ending on or after December 15, 2012.

Objectives

.03 The objectives of the auditor are to

a. evaluate the consistency of the financial statements for the periods presented and

b. communicate appropriately in the auditor's report when the comparability of financial statements between periods has been materially affected by a change in accounting principle or by adjustments to correct a material misstatement in previously issued financial statements.

Definition

.04 For purposes of generally accepted auditing standards, the following term has the meaning attributed as follows:

Current period. The most recent period upon which the auditor is reporting.

Requirements

Evaluating Consistency

.05 The auditor should evaluate whether the comparability of the financial statements between periods has been materially affected by a change in accounting principle or by adjustments to correct a material misstatement in previously issued financial statements. (Ref: par. .A1)

---

* This section has been codified using an "AU-C" identifier instead of an "AU" identifier. "AU-C" is a temporary identifier to avoid confusion with references to existing "AU" sections, which will remain in AICPA *Professional Standards* through 2013. The "AU-C" identifier will revert to "AU" in 2014, by which time substantially all engagements for which the "AU" sections were still effective are expected to be completed.

.06 The periods included in the auditor's evaluation of consistency depend on the periods covered by the auditor's opinion on the financial statements. When the auditor's opinion covers only the current period, the auditor should evaluate whether the current-period financial statements are consistent with those of the preceding period, regardless of whether financial statements for the preceding period are presented. When the auditor's opinion covers two or more periods, the auditor should evaluate consistency between such periods and the consistency of the earliest period covered by the auditor's opinion with the period prior thereto, if such prior period is presented with the financial statements being reported upon. The auditor also should evaluate whether the financial statements for the periods being reported upon are consistent with previously issued financial statements for the relevant periods. (Ref: par. .A2–.A3)

Change in Accounting Principle

.07 The auditor should evaluate a change in accounting principle to determine whether (Ref: par. .A4–.A6)

a. the newly adopted accounting principle is in accordance with the applicable financial reporting framework,

b. the method of accounting for the effect of the change is in accordance with the applicable financial reporting framework,

c. the disclosures related to the accounting change are appropriate and adequate, and

d. the entity has justified that the alternative accounting principle is preferable.

.08 If the auditor concludes that the criteria in paragraph .07 have been met, and the change in accounting principle has a material effect on the financial statements, the auditor should include an emphasis-of-matter paragraph[1] in the auditor's report that describes the change in accounting principle and provides a reference to the entity's disclosure. If the criteria in paragraph .07 are not met, the auditor should evaluate whether the accounting change results in a material misstatement and whether the auditor should modify the opinion accordingly.[2] (Ref: par. .A7–.A9)

.09 The auditor should include an emphasis-of-matter paragraph relating to a change in accounting principle in reports on financial statements in the period of the change, and in subsequent periods, until the new accounting principle is applied in all periods presented. If the change in accounting principle is accounted for by retrospective application to the financial statements of all prior periods presented, the emphasis-of-matter paragraph is needed only in the period of such change.

.10 The auditor should evaluate and report on a change in accounting estimate that is inseparable from the effect of a related change in accounting principle like other changes in accounting principle, as required by paragraphs .08–.09. (Ref: par. .A10)

.11 When a change in the reporting entity results in financial statements that, in effect, are those of a different reporting entity, the auditor should include an emphasis-of-matter paragraph in the auditor's report that describes the

---

[1] Paragraphs .06–.07 of section 706, *Emphasis-of-Matter Paragraphs and Other-Matter Paragraphs in the Independent Auditor's Report.*

[2] See section 705, *Modifications to the Opinion in the Independent Auditor's Report.*

change in the reporting entity and provides a reference to the entity's disclosure, unless the change in reporting entity results from a transaction or event. The requirements in paragraph .09 also apply. (Ref: par. .A11)

.12 If an entity's financial statements contain an investment accounted for by the equity method, the auditor's evaluation of consistency should include consideration of the investee. If the investee makes a change in accounting principle that is material to the investing entity's financial statements, the auditor should include an emphasis-of-matter paragraph in the auditor's report to describe the change in accounting principle. The requirements in paragraph .09 also apply.

Correction of a Material Misstatement in Previously Issued Financial Statements

.13 The auditor should include an emphasis-of-matter paragraph in the auditor's report when there are adjustments to correct a material misstatement in previously issued financial statements. The auditor should include this type of emphasis-of-matter paragraph in the auditor's report when the related financial statements are restated to correct the prior material misstatement. The paragraph need not be repeated in subsequent periods. (Ref: par. .A12–.A13)

.14 The emphasis-of-matter paragraph should include

a. a statement that the previously issued financial statements have been restated for the correction of a material misstatement in the respective period and

b. a reference to the entity's disclosure of the correction of the material misstatement. (Ref: par. .A14)

.15 If the financial statement disclosures relating to the restatement to correct a material misstatement in previously issued financial statements are not adequate, the auditor should address the inadequacy of disclosure as described in section 705, *Modifications to the Opinion in the Independent Auditor's Report.*

Change in Classification

.16 The auditor should evaluate a material change in financial statement classification and the related disclosure to determine whether such a change is also either a change in accounting principle or an adjustment to correct a material misstatement in previously issued financial statements. If so, the requirements of paragraphs .07–.15 apply. (Ref: par. .A15–.A16)

Application and Other Explanatory Material

Evaluating Consistency (Ref: par. .05–.06)

.A1 Unless the auditor's report explicitly states otherwise, the auditor's report implies that the auditor is satisfied that the comparability of financial statements between periods has not been materially affected by a change in accounting principle or by adjustments to correct a material misstatement in previously issued financial statements. There may be no effect on comparability between or among periods because either (*a*) no change in an accounting principle has occurred, or (*b*) there has been a change in an accounting principle or in the method of application, but the effect of the change on the comparability of the financial statements is not material. When no material effect on comparability results from a change in accounting principle or an adjustment to previously issued financial statements, the auditor need not refer to consistency in the auditor's report.

.A2 The periods covered in the auditor's evaluation of consistency depend on the periods covered by the auditor's opinion on the financial statements. If an entity presents comparative financial statements and has a change in auditors in the current year, the auditor evaluates consistency between the year covered by the auditor's opinion and the immediately preceding year in accordance with the requirements in paragraph .06.

.A3 When an entity accounts for a change in accounting principle by applying the principle to one or more prior periods that were included in previously issued financial statements, as if that principle had always been used (commonly referred to as *retrospective application*), the financial statements presented generally will be consistent. However, the previous periods' financial statements presented with the current period's financial statements will reflect the change in accounting principle and, therefore, will appear different from those previous periods' financial statements on which the auditor previously reported. The evaluation required by paragraph .06 encompasses previously issued financial statements for the relevant periods.

Change in Accounting Principle (Ref: par. .07)

.A4 A change in accounting principle is a change from one accounting principle in accordance with the applicable financial reporting framework to another accounting principle in accordance with the applicable financial reporting framework when (1) two or more accounting principles apply or (2) the accounting principle formerly used is no longer in accordance with the applicable financial reporting framework. A change in the method of applying an accounting principle also is considered a change in accounting principle.

.A5 The applicable financial reporting framework usually sets forth the method of accounting for the effects of a change in accounting principle and the related disclosures.

.A6 The issuance of an accounting pronouncement that requires use of a new accounting principle, interprets an existing principle, expresses a preference for an accounting principle, or rejects a specific principle is sufficient justification for a change in accounting principle, as long as the change in accounting principle is made in accordance with the applicable financial reporting framework.

Reporting on Changes in Accounting Principles (Ref: par. .08–.11)

.A7 The following is an example of an emphasis-of-matter paragraph for a change in accounting principle resulting from the adoption of a new accounting pronouncement:

> *Emphasis of Matter*
>
> As discussed in Note X to the financial statements, in [*insert year(s) of financial statements that reflect the accounting method change*], the entity adopted new accounting guidance [*insert description of new accounting guidance*]. Our opinion is not modified with respect to this matter.

.A8 The following is an example of an emphasis-of-matter paragraph when the entity has made a voluntary change in accounting principle (that is, other than a change due to the adoption of a new accounting pronouncement).

Emphasis of Matter

As discussed in Note X to the financial statements, the entity has elected to change its method of accounting for [*describe accounting method change*] in [*insert year(s) of financial statements that reflect the accounting method change*]. Our opinion is not modified with respect to this matter.

.A9 If a change in accounting principle does not have a material effect on the financial statements in the current year but the change is expected to have a material effect in later years, the auditor is not required to recognize the change in the auditor's report in the current year. The applicable financial reporting framework may include a requirement for the entity to disclose such situations in the notes to the financial statements. Section 700, *Forming an Opinion and Reporting on Financial Statements*, and section 705 require the auditor to evaluate the appropriateness and adequacy of disclosures in connection with forming an opinion and reporting on the financial statements.[3]

.A10 Paragraph .10 requires the auditor to evaluate and report on a change in accounting estimate that is inseparable from the effect of a related change in accounting principle like other changes in accounting principle. It is sometimes difficult to differentiate between a change in an accounting estimate and a change in an accounting principle because the change in accounting estimate may be inseparable from the effect of a related change in accounting principle. For example, when a change is made to the method of depreciation of an asset to reflect a change in the estimated future benefit of the asset or the pattern of consumption for those benefits, such change in accounting may be inseparable from a change in estimate.

Change in Reporting Entity

.A11 A change in reporting entity that results from a transaction or event, such as the creation, cessation, or complete or partial purchase or disposition of a subsidiary or other business unit, does not require recognition in the auditor's report. Examples of a change in the reporting entity that is not a result of a transaction or event include

- *a.* presenting consolidated or combined financial statements in place of financial statements of individual entities.
- *b.* changing specific subsidiaries that make up the group of entities for which consolidated financial statements are presented.
- *c.* changing the entities included in combined financial statements.

Correction of a Material Misstatement in Previously Issued Financial Statements (Ref: par. .13–.14)

.A12 A change from an accounting principle that is not in accordance with the applicable financial reporting framework to one that is in accordance with the applicable financial reporting framework is a correction of a misstatement.

.A13 Section 560, *Subsequent Events and Subsequently Discovered Facts*, addresses the auditor's responsibilities when adjustments have been made to correct a material misstatement in previously issued financial statements.

---

[3] Paragraph .16 of section 700, *Forming an Opinion and Reporting on Financial Statements*, and paragraphs .07 and .A7 of section 705.

Reporting on a Correction of a Material Misstatement in Previously Issued Financial Statements

.A14 The following is an example of an emphasis-of-matter paragraph when there has been a correction of a material misstatement in previously issued financial statements:

> *Emphasis of Matter*
>
> As discussed in Note X to the financial statements, the 20X2 financial statements have been restated to correct a misstatement. Our opinion is not modified with respect to this matter.

Change in Classification (Ref: par. .16)

.A15 Changes in classification in previously issued financial statements do not require recognition in the auditor's report unless the change represents the correction of a material misstatement or a change in accounting principle. For example, certain reclassifications in previously issued financial statements, such as reclassifications of debt from long-term to short-term or reclassifications of cash flows from the operating activities category to the financing activities category, might occur because those items were classified incorrectly in the previously issued financial statements. In such situations, the reclassification also is the correction of a misstatement.

.A16 In some cases, changes in classification in previously issued financial statements may result from changes in the entity's business or operating structure. The auditor may need to obtain a further understanding of the underlying rationale for such reclassifications to determine whether the requirements of paragraph .16 apply.

AU-C Section 720 *

Other Information in Documents Containing Audited Financial Statements

(Supersedes SAS No. 8 and with SAS No. 119 supersedes SAS No. 29.)

Source: SAS No. 118; SAS No. 122; SAS No. 123.

Effective for audits of financial statements for periods beginning on or after December 15, 2010. Early application is permitted.

> **NOTE**
>
> To address practice issues, Statement on Auditing Standards (SAS) No. 118, *Other Information in Documents Containing Audited Financial Statements*, was issued in February 2010 as a SAS resulting from the Clarification and Convergence Project of the Auditing Standards Board, and is effective for audits of financial statements for periods beginning on or after December 15, 2010.
>
> SAS No. 118 was originally codified as AU section 550. SAS No. 122, *Statement on Auditing Standards: Clarification and Recodification*, redesignates AU section 550 as section 720, but does not supersede SAS No. 118.
>
> This section contains conforming changes necessary in specific paragraphs and footnotes due to the issuance of SAS No. 122.

Introduction

Scope of This Section

.01 This section addresses the auditor's responsibility with respect to other information in documents containing audited financial statements and the auditor's report thereon. In the absence of any separate requirement in the particular circumstances of the engagement, the auditor's opinion on the financial statements does not cover other information, and the auditor has no responsibility for determining whether such information is properly stated. This section establishes the requirement for the auditor to read the other information of which the auditor is aware because the credibility of the audited financial statements may be undermined by material inconsistencies between the audited financial statements and other information. (Ref: par. .A1–.A2) [Revised, October 2011, to reflect conforming changes necessary due to the issuance of SAS No. 122.]

* This section has been codified using an "AU-C" identifier instead of an "AU" identifier. "AU-C" is a temporary identifier to avoid confusion with references to existing "AU" sections, which will remain in AICPA *Professional Standards* through 2013. The "AU-C" identifier will revert to "AU" in 2014, by which time substantially all engagements for which the "AU" sections were still effective are expected to be completed. [Footnote added, October 2011, to reflect conforming changes necessary due to the issuance of SAS No. 122.]

.02 In this section, *documents containing audited financial statements* refers to annual reports (or similar documents) that are issued to owners (or similar stakeholders) and annual reports of governments and organizations for charitable or philanthropic purposes that are available to the public that contain audited financial statements and the auditor's report thereon. This section also may be applied, adapted as necessary in the circumstances, to other documents to which the auditor, at management's request, devotes attention. (Ref: par. .A3–.A5)

Effective Date

.03 This section is effective for audits of financial statements for periods beginning on or after December 15, 2010. Early application is permitted.

Objective

.04 The objective of the auditor is to respond appropriately when the auditor becomes aware that documents containing audited financial statements and the auditor's report thereon include other information that could undermine the credibility of those financial statements and the auditor's report.

Definitions

.05 For purposes of generally accepted auditing standards (GAAS), the following terms have the meanings attributed as follows:

Inconsistency. Other information that conflicts with information contained in the audited financial statements. A material inconsistency may raise doubt about the audit conclusions drawn from audit evidence previously obtained and, possibly, about the basis for the auditor's opinion on the financial statements.

Misstatement of fact. Other information that is unrelated to matters appearing in the audited financial statements that is incorrectly stated or presented. A material misstatement of fact may undermine the credibility of the document containing audited financial statements.

Other information. Financial and nonfinancial information (other than the financial statements and the auditor's report thereon) that is included in a document containing audited financial statements and the auditor's report thereon, excluding required supplementary information.[1]

[Revised, October 2011, to reflect conforming changes necessary due to the issuance of SAS No. 122.]

Requirements

Reading Other Information

.06 The auditor should read the other information of which the auditor is aware in order to identify material inconsistencies, if any, with the audited financial statements.

---

[1] *Required supplementary information* is defined in paragraph .04 of section 730, *Required Supplementary Information*. [Footnote revised, October 2011, to reflect conforming changes necessary due to the issuance of SAS No. 122.]

.07 The auditor should make appropriate arrangements with management or those charged with governance to obtain the other information prior to the report release date.[2] If it is not possible to obtain all of the other information prior to the report release date, the auditor should read such other information as soon as practicable. (Ref: par. .A6)

.08 The auditor should communicate with those charged with governance the auditor's responsibility with respect to the other information, any procedures performed relating to the other information, and the results.

Material Inconsistencies

.09 If, on reading the other information, the auditor identifies a material inconsistency, the auditor should determine whether the audited financial statements or the other information needs to be revised.

Material Inconsistencies Identified Prior to the Date of the Auditor's Report That Require Revision of the Audited Financial Statements

.10 When the auditor identifies a material inconsistency prior to the date of the auditor's report that requires revision of the audited financial statements and management refuses to make the revision, the auditor should modify the auditor's opinion in accordance with section 705, *Modifications to the Opinion in the Independent Auditor's Report*. [Revised, October 2011, to reflect conforming changes necessary due to the issuance of SAS Nos. 122 and 123.]

Material Inconsistencies Identified After the Date of the Auditor's Report But Prior to the Report Release Date That Require Revision of the Audited Financial Statements

.11 When the auditor identifies a material inconsistency after the date of the auditor's report but prior to the report release date that requires revision of the audited financial statements, the auditor should apply the relevant requirements in section 560, *Subsequent Events and Subsequently Discovered Facts*.[3] [Paragraph added, October 2011, to reflect conforming changes necessary due to the issuance of SAS No. 123.]

Material Inconsistencies Identified Prior to the Report Release Date That Require Revision of the Other Information

.12 When the auditor identifies a material inconsistency prior to the report release date that requires revision of the other information and management refuses to make the revision, the auditor should communicate this matter to those charged with governance and (Ref: par. .A7–.A8)

a. include in the auditor's report an other-matter paragraph describing the material inconsistency, in accordance with section 706, *Emphasis-of-Matter Paragraphs and Other-Matter Paragraphs in the Independent Auditor's Report*;[4]

---

[2] See paragraph .06 of section 230, *Audit Documentation*, for the definition of *report release date*. [Footnote revised, October 2011, to reflect conforming changes necessary due to the issuance of SAS No. 122.]

[3] Paragraphs .12–.14 of section 560, *Subsequent Events and Subsequently Discovered Facts*. [Footnote added, October 2011, to reflect conforming changes necessary due to the issuance of SAS No. 123.]

[4] Paragraph .08 of section 706, *Emphasis-of-Matter Paragraphs and Other-Matter Paragraphs in the Independent Auditor's Report*. [Footnote added, October 2011, to reflect conforming changes necessary due to the issuance of SAS No. 122. Footnote renumbered, October 2011, to reflect conforming changes necessary due to the issuance of SAS No. 123.]

b. withhold the auditor's report; or

c. when withdrawal is possible under applicable law or regulation, withdraw from the engagement.

[Revised, October 2011, to reflect conforming changes necessary due to the issuance of SAS No. 122. Paragraph renumbered, October 2011, to reflect conforming changes necessary due to the issuance of SAS No. 123.]

Material Inconsistencies Identified Subsequent to the Report Release Date

.13 When revision of the audited financial statements is necessary as a result of a material inconsistency with other information and the auditor's report on the financial statements has already been released, the auditor should apply the relevant requirements in section 560, *Subsequent Events and Subsequently Discovered Facts*.[5] [Revised, October 2011, to reflect conforming changes necessary due to the issuance of SAS No. 122. Paragraph renumbered, October 2011, to reflect conforming changes necessary due to the issuance of SAS No. 123.]

.14 When revision of the other information is necessary after the report release date and management agrees to make the revision, the auditor should carry out the procedures necessary under the circumstances. (Ref: par. .A9) [Paragraph renumbered, October 2011, to reflect conforming changes necessary due to the issuance of SAS No. 123.]

.15 When revision of the other information is necessary after the report release date but management refuses to make the revision, the auditor should notify those charged with governance of the auditor's concerns regarding the other information and take any further appropriate action. (Ref: par. .A10) [Paragraph renumbered, October 2011, to reflect conforming changes necessary due to the issuance of SAS No. 123.]

Material Misstatements of Fact

.16 If, on reading the other information for the purpose of identifying material inconsistencies, the auditor becomes aware of an apparent material misstatement of fact, the auditor should discuss the matter with management. (Ref: par. .A11) [Paragraph renumbered, October 2011, to reflect conforming changes necessary due to the issuance of SAS No. 123.]

.17 When, following such discussions, the auditor still considers that there is an apparent material misstatement of fact, the auditor should request management to consult with a qualified third party, such as the entity's legal counsel, and the auditor should consider the advice received by the entity in determining whether such matter is a material misstatement of fact. [Paragraph renumbered, October 2011, to reflect conforming changes necessary due to the issuance of SAS No. 123.]

.18 When the auditor concludes that there is a material misstatement of fact in the other information that management refuses to correct, the auditor should notify those charged with governance of the auditor's concerns regarding the other information and take any further appropriate action. (Ref: par. .A12) [Paragraph renumbered, October 2011, to reflect conforming changes necessary due to the issuance of SAS No. 123.]

---

[5] Paragraphs .15–.18 of section 560, *Subsequent Events and Subsequently Discovered Facts*. [Footnote added, October 2011, to reflect conforming changes necessary due to the issuance of SAS No. 122. Footnote renumbered, October 2011, to reflect conforming changes necessary due to the issuance of SAS No. 123.]

Application and Other Explanatory Material

Scope of This Section (Ref: par. .01–.02)

.A1 This section also addresses other information for which a designated accounting standard setter[6] has issued standards or guidance regarding the format to be used and content to be included when such information is voluntarily presented in a document containing the audited financial statements and the auditor's report thereon. The auditor's responsibility for other information presented in a document containing audited financial statements that is required to be included by a designated accounting standards setter is addressed in section 730, *Required Supplementary Information*. [Revised, October 2011, to reflect conforming changes necessary due to the issuance of SAS No. 122.]

.A2 The auditor is not required to make reference to the other information in the auditor's report on the financial statements. However, the auditor may include an other-matter paragraph disclaiming an opinion on the other information. For example, an auditor may choose to include a disclaimer on the other information when the auditor believes that the auditor could be associated with the information and the user may infer a level of assurance that is not intended. Exhibit A, "Example of an Other-Matter Paragraph to Disclaim an Opinion on Other Information," has an example of how an auditor may word such a disclaimer of opinion on other information. [Revised, October 2011, to reflect conforming changes necessary due to the issuance of SAS No. 122.]

.A3 Other information may comprise the following:

- A report by management or those charged with governance on operations
- Financial summaries or highlights
- Employment data
- Planned capital expenditures
- Financial ratios
- Names of officers and directors
- Selected quarterly data

.A4 For purposes of GAAS, other information does not encompass, for example, the following:

- A press release or similar memorandum or cover letter accompanying the document containing audited financial statements and the auditor's report thereon.
- Information contained in analyst briefings.
- Information contained on the entity's website. Websites are a means of distributing information and are not, themselves, documents containing audited financial statements.

[Revised, October 2011, to reflect conforming changes necessary due to the issuance of SAS No. 123.]

---

[6] *Designated accounting standards setter* is defined in paragraph .04 of section 730. [Footnote renumbered and revised, October 2011, to reflect conforming changes necessary due to the issuance of SAS No. 122. Footnote renumbered, October 2011, to reflect conforming changes necessary due to the issuance of SAS No. 123.]

Considerations Specific to Governmental Entities (Ref: par. .02)

.A5 The term *annual reports of governments* is intended to include comprehensive annual reports or other annual financial reports that include the government's financial statements and the auditor's report thereon.

Reading Other Information (Ref: par. .07)

.A6 Obtaining the other information prior to the report release date enables the auditor to resolve possible material inconsistencies and apparent material misstatements of fact with management on a timely basis. An agreement with management regarding when other information will be available may be helpful. The auditor may delay the release of the auditor's report until management provides the other information to the auditor.

Material Inconsistencies

Material Inconsistencies Identified Prior to the Report Release Date (Ref: par. .11)

.A7 When management refuses to revise the other information, the auditor may base any decision on what further action to take on advice from the auditor's legal counsel. [Revised, October 2011, to reflect conforming changes necessary due to the issuance of SAS No. 122.]

Considerations Specific to Governmental Entities (Ref: par. .11)

.A8 In audits of governmental entities, withdrawal from the engagement or withholding the auditor's report may not be possible under law or regulation. In such cases, the auditor may issue a report to those charged with governance and the appropriate statutory body, if applicable, giving details of the inconsistency. [Revised, October 2011, to reflect conforming changes necessary due to the issuance of SAS No. 122.]

Material Inconsistencies Identified Subsequent to the Report Release Date (Ref: par. .13–.14)

.A9 When revision of other information is necessary after the report release date and management agrees to make the revision, the auditor's procedures may include reviewing the steps taken by management to ensure that individuals in receipt of the previously issued financial statements, the auditor's report thereon, and the other information are informed of the need for revision. [Revised, October 2011, to reflect conforming changes necessary due to the issuance of SAS No. 122.]

.A10 When revision of other information is necessary after the report release date but management refuses to make the revision, appropriate further actions by the auditor may include obtaining legal advice. [Revised, October 2011, to reflect conforming changes necessary due to the issuance of SAS No. 122.]

Material Misstatements of Fact (Ref: par. .15–.17)

.A11 When discussing an apparent material misstatement of fact with management, the auditor may not be able to evaluate the validity of some disclosures included within the other information and management's responses to the auditor's inquiries and may conclude that valid differences of judgment or opinion exist.

.A12 When the auditor concludes that there is a material misstatement of fact that management refuses to correct, appropriate further actions by the auditor may include obtaining legal advice, withholding the auditor's report if such report has not been released, or withdrawing from the engagement. [Revised, October 2011, to reflect conforming changes necessary due to the issuance of SAS No. 122.]

.A13

Exhibit A—Example of an Other-Matter Paragraph to Disclaim an Opinion on Other Information

The following is an example of an other-matter paragraph that the auditor may use to disclaim an opinion on other information:

> Our audit was conducted for the purpose of forming an opinion on the basic financial statements as a whole. The [*identify the other information*] is presented for purposes of additional analysis and is not a required part of the basic financial statements. Such information has not been subjected to the auditing procedures applied in the audit of the basic financial statements, and accordingly, we do not express an opinion or provide any assurance on it.

[Revised, October 2011, to reflect conforming changes necessary due to the issuance of SAS No. 122.]

[.A14]

Exhibit B—[Reserved]

[Exhibit deleted, October 2011, to reflect conforming changes necessary due to the issuance of SAS No. 122. See appendix B, *Substantive Differences Between the International Standards on Auditing and Generally Accepted Auditing Standards*.]

AU-C Section 725 *

Supplementary Information in Relation to the Financial Statements as a Whole

(With SAS No. 118 supersedes SAS No. 29.)

Source: SAS No. 119; SAS No. 122; SAS No. 125.

Effective for audits of financial statements for periods beginning on or after December 15, 2010. Early application is permitted.

> **NOTE**
>
> To address practice issues, Statement on Auditing Standards (SAS) No. 119, *Supplementary Information in Relation to the Financial Statements as a Whole*, was issued in February 2010 as a SAS resulting from the Clarification and Convergence Project of the Auditing Standards Board, and is effective for audits of financial statements for periods beginning on or after December 15, 2010.
>
> SAS No. 119 was originally codified as AU section 551. SAS No. 122, *Statement on Auditing Standards: Clarification and Recodification*, redesignates AU section 551 as section 725, but does not supersede SAS No. 119.
>
> This section contains conforming changes necessary in specific paragraphs and footnotes due to the issuance of SAS No. 122.

Introduction

Scope of This Section

.01 This section addresses the auditor's responsibility when engaged to report on whether supplementary information is fairly stated, in all material respects, in relation to the financial statements as a whole. The information covered by this section is presented outside the basic financial statements and is not considered necessary for the financial statements to be fairly presented in accordance with the applicable financial reporting framework. This section also may be applied, with the report wording adapted as necessary, when an auditor has been engaged to report on whether required supplementary information[1]

---

* This section has been codified using an "AU-C" identifier instead of an "AU" identifier. "AU-C" is a temporary identifier to avoid confusion with references to existing "AU" sections, which will remain in AICPA *Professional Standards* through 2013. The "AU-C" identifier will revert to "AU" in 2014, by which time substantially all engagements for which the "AU" sections were still effective are expected to be completed. [Footnote added, October 2011, to reflect conforming changes necessary due to the issuance of SAS No. 122.]

[1] *Required supplementary information* is defined in paragraph .04 of section 730, *Required Supplementary Information*. [Footnote revised, October 2011, to reflect conforming changes necessary due to the issuance of SAS No. 122.]

is fairly stated, in all material respects, in relation to the financial statements as a whole. (Ref: par. .A1–.A6)

Effective Date

.02 This section is effective for audits of financial statements for periods beginning on or after December 15, 2010. Early application is permitted.

Objective

.03 The objective of the auditor, when engaged to report on supplementary information in relation to the financial statements as a whole, is to

a. evaluate the presentation of the supplementary information in relation to the financial statements as a whole and

b. report on whether the supplementary information is fairly stated, in all material respects, in relation to the financial statements as a whole.

Definition

.04 For purposes of generally accepted auditing standards, the following term has the meaning attributed as follows:

Supplementary information. Information presented outside the basic financial statements, excluding required supplementary information that is not considered necessary for the financial statements to be fairly presented in accordance with the applicable financial reporting framework. Such information may be presented in a document containing the audited financial statements or separate from the financial statements. (Ref: par. .A7–.A8)

[Revised, October 2011, to reflect conforming changes necessary due to the issuance of SAS No. 122.]

Requirements

Procedures to Determine Whether Supplementary Information Is Fairly Stated, in All Material Respects, in Relation to the Financial Statements as a Whole (Ref: par. .A9–.A15)

.05 In order to opine on whether supplementary information is fairly stated, in all material respects, in relation to the financial statements as a whole, the auditor should determine that all of the following conditions are met:

a. The supplementary information was derived from, and relates directly to, the underlying accounting and other records used to prepare the financial statements.

b. The supplementary information relates to the same period as the financial statements.

c. The auditor issued an audit report on the financial statements that contained neither an adverse opinion nor a disclaimer of opinion. (Paragraph .11 addresses reporting while not opining on supplementary information when the report on the financial statements contains an adverse opinion or a disclaimer of opinion.)

d. The supplementary information will accompany the entity's audited financial statements, or such audited financial statements will be made readily available by the entity. (Ref: par. .A9)

[Revised, April 2012 and January 2013, to reflect conforming changes necessary due to the issuance of SAS No. 122.]

.06 The auditor should obtain the agreement of management that it acknowledges and understands its responsibility

a. for the preparation of the supplementary information in accordance with the applicable criteria.

b. to provide the auditor with the written representations described in paragraph .07*g*.

c. to include the auditor's report on the supplementary information in any document that contains the supplementary information and that indicates that the auditor has reported on such supplementary information.

d. to present the supplementary information with the audited financial statements or, if the supplementary information will not be presented with the audited financial statements, to make the audited financial statements readily available to the intended users of the supplementary information no later than the date of issuance by the entity of the supplementary information and the auditor's report thereon. (Ref: par. .A9)

.07 In addition to the procedures performed during the audit of the financial statements, in order to opine on whether supplementary information is fairly stated, in all material respects, in relation to the financial statements as a whole, the auditor should perform the following procedures using the same materiality level used in the audit of the financial statements:

a. Inquire of management about the purpose of the supplementary information and the criteria used by management to prepare the supplementary information, such as an applicable financial reporting framework, criteria established by a regulator, a contractual agreement, or other requirements

b. Determine whether the form and content of the supplementary information complies with the applicable criteria

c. Obtain an understanding about the methods of preparing the supplementary information and determine whether the methods of preparing the supplementary information have changed from those used in the prior period and, if the methods have changed, the reasons for such changes

d. Compare and reconcile the supplementary information to the underlying accounting and other records used in preparing the financial statements or to the financial statements themselves

e. Inquire of management about any significant assumptions or interpretations underlying the measurement or presentation of the supplementary information

f. Evaluate the appropriateness and completeness of the supplementary information, considering the results of the procedures performed and other knowledge obtained during the audit of the financial statements (Ref: par. .A13) *g.* Obtain written representations from management

i. that it acknowledges its responsibility for the presentation of the supplementary information in accordance with the applicable criteria;

ii. that it believes the supplementary information, including its form and content, is fairly presented in accordance with the applicable criteria;

iii. that the methods of measurement or presentation have not changed from those used in the prior period or, if the methods of measurement or presentation have changed, the reasons for such changes;

iv. about any significant assumptions or interpretations underlying the measurement or presentation of the supplementary information; and

v. that when the supplementary information is not presented with the audited financial statements, management will make the audited financial statements readily available to the intended users of the supplementary information no later than the date of issuance by the entity of the supplementary information and the auditor's report thereon. (Ref: par. .A9)

.08 The auditor has no responsibility for the consideration of subsequent events with respect to the supplementary information. However, if information comes to the auditor's attention

a. prior to the release of the auditor's report on the financial statements regarding subsequent events that affect the financial statements, or

b. subsequent to the release of the auditor's report on the financial statements regarding facts that, had they been known to the auditor at the date of the auditor's report, may have caused the auditor to revise the auditor's report,

the auditor should apply the relevant requirements in section 560, *Subsequent Events and Subsequently Discovered Facts*. [Revised, October 2011, to reflect conforming changes necessary due to the issuance of SAS No. 122.]

Reporting

.09 When the entity presents the supplementary information with the financial statements, the auditor should report on the supplementary information in either (*a*) an other-matter paragraph in accordance with section 706, *Emphasis-of-Matter Paragraphs and Other-Matter Paragraphs in the Independent Auditor's Report*, or (*b*) in a separate report on the supplementary information.[2] The other-matter paragraph or separate report should include the following elements:

a. A statement that the audit was conducted for the purpose of forming an opinion on the financial statements as a whole

b. A statement that the supplementary information is presented for purposes of additional analysis and is not a required part of the financial statements

---

[2] Paragraph .08 of section 706, *Emphasis-of-Matter Paragraphs and Other-Matter Paragraphs in the Independent Auditor's Report*. [Footnote added, October 2011, to reflect conforming changes necessary due to the issuance of SAS No. 122.]

c. A statement that the supplementary information is the responsibility of management and was derived from, and relates directly to, the underlying accounting and other records used to prepare the financial statements

d. A statement that the supplementary information has been subjected to the auditing procedures applied in the audit of the financial statements and certain additional procedures, including comparing and reconciling such information directly to the underlying accounting and other records used to prepare the financial statements or to the financial statements themselves and other additional procedures, in accordance with auditing standards generally accepted in the United States of America

e. If the auditor issues an unmodified opinion on the financial statements and the auditor has concluded that the supplementary information is fairly stated, in all material respects, in relation to the financial statements as a whole, a statement that, in the auditor's opinion, the supplementary information is fairly stated, in all material respects, in relation to the financial statements as a whole

f. If the auditor issues a qualified opinion on the financial statements and the qualification has an effect on the supplementary information, a statement that, in the auditor's opinion, except for the effects on the supplementary information of (refer to the paragraph in the auditor's report explaining the qualification), such information is fairly stated, in all material respects, in relation to the financial statements as a whole

[Revised, October 2011, to reflect conforming changes necessary due to the issuance of SAS No. 122.]

.10 When the audited financial statements are not presented with the supplementary information, the auditor should report on the supplementary information in a separate report. When reporting separately on the supplementary information, the report should include, in addition to the elements in paragraph .09, a reference to the report on the financial statements, the date of that report, the nature of the opinion expressed on the financial statements, and any report modifications. (Ref: par. .A16)

.11 When the auditor's report on the audited financial statements contains an adverse opinion or a disclaimer of opinion and the auditor has been engaged to report on whether supplementary information is fairly stated, in all material respects, in relation to such financial statements as a whole, the auditor is precluded from expressing an opinion on the supplementary information. When permitted by law or regulation, the auditor may withdraw from the engagement to report on the supplementary information. If the auditor does not withdraw, the auditor's report on the supplementary information should state that because of the significance of the matter disclosed in the auditor's report, it is inappropriate to, and the auditor does not, express an opinion on the supplementary information.

.12 The date of the auditor's report on the supplementary information in relation to the financial statements as a whole should not be earlier than the date on which the auditor completed the procedures required in paragraph .07.

.13 If the auditor concludes, on the basis of the procedures performed, that the supplementary information is materially misstated in relation to the financial statements as a whole, the auditor should discuss the matter with management and propose appropriate revision of the supplementary information.

If management does not revise the supplementary information, the auditor should either

a. modify the auditor's opinion on the supplementary information and describe the misstatement in the auditor's report or

b. if a separate report is being issued on the supplementary information, withhold the auditor's report on the supplementary information.

Application and Other Explanatory Material

Scope of This Section (Ref: par. .01)

.A1 The auditor's responsibility for information that a designated accounting standard setter[3] requires to accompany an entity's basic financial statements is addressed in section 730, *Required Supplementary Information*. [Revised, October 2011, to reflect conforming changes necessary due to the issuance of SAS No. 122.]

.A2 The auditor's responsibility for financial and nonfinancial information (other than the financial statements and the auditor's report thereon) that is included in a document containing audited financial statements and the auditor's report thereon, excluding required supplementary information, is addressed in section 720, *Other Information in Documents Containing Audited Financial Statements*. [Revised, October 2011, to reflect conforming changes necessary due to the issuance of SAS No. 122.]

.A3 The supplementary information need not be presented with the audited financial statements in order for the auditor to express an opinion on whether such supplementary information is fairly stated, in all material respects, in relation to the financial statements as a whole. However, in accordance with paragraph .10, if the supplementary information is not presented with the audited financial statements, the auditor's report on the supplementary information is required to make reference to the auditor's report on the financial statements.

.A4 The auditor may be engaged to audit a specified element, account, or item of a financial statement for the purpose of a separate presentation, in accordance with section 805, *Special Considerations—Audits of Single Financial Statements and Specific Elements, Accounts, or Items of a Financial Statement*. In such an engagement, the auditor's procedures are designed to provide the auditor with reasonable assurance that the supplementary information is not misstated by an amount that would be material to the information itself. An engagement to examine the supplementary information or an assertion related to the supplementary information also may be performed in accordance with AT section 101, *Attest Engagements*. [Revised, October 2011, to reflect conforming changes necessary due to the issuance of SAS No. 122.]

.A5 Although an auditor has no obligation to apply auditing procedures to supplementary information presented outside the basic financial statements, the auditor may choose to modify or redirect certain of the procedures to be applied in the audit of the basic financial statements so that the auditor may express an opinion on the supplementary information in relation to the financial statements as a whole.

---

[3] *Designated accounting standards setter* is defined in paragraph .04 of section 730. [Footnote renumbered and revised, October 2011, to reflect conforming changes necessary due to the issuance of SAS No. 122.]

.A6 Management may include nonaccounting information and accounting information that is not directly related to the basic financial statements in a document containing the basic financial statements. Ordinarily, such information would not have been subjected to the auditing procedures applied in the audit of the basic financial statements, and accordingly, the auditor would be unable to opine on the information in relation to the financial statements as a whole. In some circumstances, however, such information may have been obtained or derived from accounting records that have been tested by the auditor (for example, number of units produced related to royalties under a license agreement or number of employees related to a given payroll period). Accordingly, the auditor may be in a position to express an opinion on such information in relation to the financial statements as a whole.

Definition (Ref: par. .04)

.A7 Supplementary information includes additional details or explanations of items in or related to the basic financial statements, consolidating information, historical summaries of items extracted from the basic financial statements, statistical data, and other material, some of which may be from sources outside the accounting system or outside the entity.

.A8 Supplementary information may be prepared in accordance with an applicable financial reporting framework, by regulatory or contractual requirements, in accordance with management's criteria, or in accordance with other requirements.

Procedures to Determine Whether Supplementary Information Is Fairly Stated, in All Material Respects, in Relation to the Financial Statements as a Whole (Ref: par. .05–.08)

The Meaning of Readily Available (Ref: par. .05e, .06d, and .07f)

.A9 Audited financial statements are deemed to be readily available if a third party user can obtain the audited financial statements without any further action by the entity. For example, financial statements on an entity's website may be considered readily available, but being available upon request is not considered readily available.

Procedures Performed on Supplementary Information (Ref: par. .07)

.A10 When engaged to report on supplementary information in relation to the financial statements as a whole, the auditor need not apply procedures as extensive as would be necessary to express an opinion on the information on a stand-alone basis.

.A11 With respect to the supplementary information, the auditor is not required to obtain a separate understanding of the entity's internal control or to assess fraud risk.

.A12 The auditor may consider materiality in determining which information to compare and reconcile to the underlying accounting and other records used in preparing the financial statements or to the financial statements themselves.

.A13 In evaluating the appropriateness and completeness of the supplementary information as required by paragraph 07*f*, the auditor may consider testing accounting or other records through observation or examination of source documents or other procedures ordinarily performed in an audit of the financial statements.

.A14 The auditor may consider whether it is appropriate to address the supplementary information in procedures that the auditor performs in auditing the financial statements, including, but not limited to, the following:

a. Obtaining an updated representation letter, in accordance with section 580, *Written Representations*[4]

b. Performing subsequent events procedures, in accordance with section 560

c. Sending a letter of audit inquiry to the client's lawyer specifically regarding the information contained in the supplementary information, in accordance with section 501, *Audit Evidence—Specific Considerations for Selected Items*[5]

[Revised, October 2011, to reflect conforming changes necessary due to the issuance of SAS No. 122.]

Considerations Specific to Audits of Governmental Entities

.A15 For most state and local governments, the auditor's report on the financial statements includes multiple opinions to address individual reporting units or aggregation of reporting units of the governmental entity. Accordingly, materiality is considered by the auditor for each opinion unit. However, in the context of this section, the auditor's opinion on the supplementary information is in relation to the financial statements as a whole. Accordingly, in this situation, materiality is considered at a level that represents the entire governmental entity.

Reporting (Ref: par. .09–.13)

.A16 When reporting on supplementary information in a separate report, the auditor may consider including an alert that restricts the use of the separate report solely to the appropriate specified parties, in accordance with section 905, *Alert That Restricts the Use of the Auditor's Written Communication*, to avoid potential misinterpretation or misunderstanding of the supplementary information that is not presented with the financial statements. [Revised, October 2011, to reflect conforming changes necessary due to the issuance of SAS No. 122. As amended, effective for the auditor's written communications related to audits of financial statements for periods ending on or after December 15, 2012, by SAS No. 125.]

---

[4] Paragraph .A24 of section 580, *Written Representations*. [Footnote added, October 2011, to reflect conforming changes necessary due to the issuance of SAS No. 122.]

[5] Paragraphs .18–.24 of section 501, *Audit Evidence—Specific Considerations for Selected Items*. [Footnote added, October 2011, to reflect conforming changes necessary due to the issuance of SAS No. 122.]

.A17

Exhibit—Illustrative Reporting Examples When the Auditor Is Reporting on Supplementary Information in Relation to the Financial Statements as a Whole

Illustration 1—An Other-Matter Paragraph When the Auditor Is Issuing an Unmodified Opinion on the Financial Statements and an Unmodified Opinion on the Supplementary Information

Our audit was conducted for the purpose of forming an opinion on the financial statements as a whole. The [*identify accompanying supplementary information*] is presented for purposes of additional analysis and is not a required part of the financial statements. Such information is the responsibility of management and was derived from and relates directly to the underlying accounting and other records used to prepare the financial statements. The information has been subjected to the auditing procedures applied in the audit of the financial statements and certain additional procedures, including comparing and reconciling such information directly to the underlying accounting and other records used to prepare the financial statements or to the financial statements themselves, and other additional procedures in accordance with auditing standards generally accepted in the United States of America. In our opinion, the information is fairly stated in all material respects in relation to the financial statements as a whole.

Illustration 2—An Other-Matter Paragraph When the Auditor Is Issuing a Qualified Opinion on the Financial Statements and a Qualified Opinion on the Supplementary Information

Our audit was conducted for the purpose of forming an opinion on the financial statements as a whole. The [*identify accompanying supplementary information*] is presented for purposes of additional analysis and is not a required part of the financial statements. Such information is the responsibility of management and was derived from and relates directly to the underlying accounting and other records used to prepare the financial statements. The information has been subjected to the auditing procedures applied in the audit of the financial statements and certain additional procedures, including comparing and reconciling such information directly to the underlying accounting and other records used to prepare the financial statements or to the financial statements themselves, and other additional procedures in accordance with auditing standards generally accepted in the United States of America. In our opinion, except for the effect on the supplementary information of [*describe reason for qualification of the auditor's opinion on the financial statements and reference the other-matter paragraph*], the information is fairly stated in all material respects in relation to the financial statements as a whole.

Illustration 3—An Other-Matter Paragraph When the Auditor Is Disclaiming an Opinion on the Financial Statements

We were engaged for the purpose of forming an opinion on the basic financial statements as a whole. The [*identify accompanying supplementary information*] is presented for the purposes of additional analysis and is not a required part of the financial statements. Because of the significance of the matter described above [*the auditor may describe the basis for the disclaimer of opinion*], it is inappropriate to and we do not express an opinion on the supplementary information referred to above.

Illustration 4—An Other-Matter Paragraph When the Auditor Is Issuing an Adverse Opinion on the Financial Statements

Our audit was conducted for the purpose of forming an opinion on the financial statements as a whole. The [*identify accompanying supplementary information*] is presented for the purposes of additional analysis and is not a required part of the financial statements. Because of the significance of the matter described above [*the auditor may describe the basis for the adverse opinion*], it is inappropriate to and we do not express an opinion on the supplementary information referred to above.

Illustration 5—A Separate Report When the Auditor Is Issuing an Unmodified Opinion on the Financial Statements and an Unmodified Opinion on the Supplementary Information

We have audited the financial statements of XYZ Entity as of and for the year ended June 30, 20X1, and have issued our report thereon dated [*date of the auditor's report on the financial statements*] which contained an unmodified opinion on those financial statements. Our audit was performed for the purpose of forming an opinion on the financial statements as a whole. The [*identify supplementary information*] is presented for the purposes of additional analysis and is not a required part of the financial statements. Such information is the responsibility of management and was derived from and relates directly to the underlying accounting and other records used to prepare the financial statements. The information has been subjected to the auditing procedures applied in the audit of the financial statements and certain additional procedures, including comparing and reconciling such information directly to the underlying accounting and other records used to prepare the financial statements or to the financial statements themselves, and other additional procedures in accordance with auditing standards generally accepted in the United States of America. In our opinion, the information is fairly stated in all material respects in relation to the financial statements as a whole.

Illustration 6—A Separate Report When the Auditor Is Issuing a Qualified Opinion on the Financial Statements and a Qualified Opinion on the Supplementary Information

We have audited the financial statements of XYZ Entity as of and for the year ended June 30, 20X1, and have issued our report thereon dated [*date of the auditor's report on the financial statements, the nature of the opinion expressed on the financial statements, and a description of the report modifications*]. Our audit was performed for the purpose of forming an opinion on the financial statements as a whole. The [*identify supplementary information*] is presented for the purposes of additional analysis and is not a required part of the financial statements. Such information is the responsibility of management and was derived from and relates directly to the underlying accounting and other records used to prepare the financial statements. The information has been subjected to the auditing procedures applied in the audit of the financial statements and certain additional procedures, including comparing and reconciling such information directly to the underlying accounting and other records used to prepare the financial statements or to the financial statements themselves, and other additional procedures in accordance with auditing standards generally accepted in the United States of America. In our opinion, except for the effect on the accompanying information of the qualified opinion on the financial statements as described above, the information is fairly stated in all material respects in relation to the financial statements as a whole.

Illustration 7—A Separate Report When the Auditor Is Disclaiming an Opinion on the Financial Statements

We were engaged to audit the financial statements of XYZ Entity as of and for the year ended June 30, 20X1, and have issued our report thereon dated [*date of the auditor's report on the financial statements*]. However, the scope of our audit of the financial statements was not sufficient to enable us to express an opinion because [*describe reasons*] and accordingly we did not express an opinion on such financial statements. The [*identify the supplementary information*] is presented for purposes of additional analysis and is not a required part of the basic financial statements. Because of the significance of the matter discussed above, it is inappropriate to and we do not express an opinion on the supplementary information referred to above.

Illustration 8—A Separate Report When the Auditor Is Issuing an Adverse Opinion on the Financial Statements

We have audited the financial statements of XYZ Entity as of and for the year ended June 30, 20X1, and have issued our report thereon dated [*date of the auditor's report on the financial statements*] which stated that the financial statements are not presented fairly in accordance with [*identify the applicable financial reporting framework (for example, accounting principles generally accepted in the United States of America [GAAP])*] because [*describe reasons*]. The [*identify the supplementary information*] is presented for purposes of additional analysis and is not a required part of the basic financial statements. Because of the significance of the matter discussed above, it is inappropriate to and we do not express an opinion on the supplementary information referred to above.

[Revised, October 2011, to reflect conforming changes necessary due to the issuance of SAS No. 122.]

AU-C Section 9725 *

Supplementary Information in Relation to the Financial Statements as a Whole: Auditing Interpretations of Section 725

1. Dating the Auditor's Report on Supplementary Information

.01 *Question*—In accordance with section 725, *Supplementary Information in Relation to the Financial Statements as a Whole*,[1] the auditor's report on supplementary information should not be dated earlier than the date on which the auditor completed the procedures required by section 725.[2] When the auditor completes those procedures subsequent to the date of the auditor's report on the audited financial statements, the auditor is not required to obtain additional evidence with respect to the audited financial statements. When reporting on the supplementary information (either in a separate report or in an other-matter paragraph within the auditor's report on the financial statements) after the date of the auditor's report on the financial statements, how may an auditor make it clear that no additional procedures were performed on the audited financial statements subsequent to the date of the auditor's report on those financial statements?

.02 *Interpretation*—Although not required, an auditor may

a. when issuing a separate report on the supplementary information, include in such report a statement that the auditor has not performed any auditing procedures with respect to the audited financial statements subsequent to the date of the auditor's report on those audited financial statements (see paragraph .03 of this interpretation), or

b. when reissuing a report on the audited financial statements to include an other-matter paragraph to report on the supplementary information, include two report dates to indicate that the date of reporting on the supplementary information is as of a later date (see paragraph .04 of this interpretation).

.03 The following illustrative separate report on supplementary information includes additional language intended to make it clear that no procedures were performed subsequent to the date of the auditor's report on the audited financial statements.

---

* This section has been codified using an "AU-C" identifier instead of an "AU" identifier. "AU-C" is a temporary identifier to avoid confusion with references to existing "AU" sections, which will remain in AICPA *Professional Standards* through 2013. The "AU-C" identifier will revert to "AU" in 2014, by which time substantially all engagements for which the "AU" sections were still effective are expected to be completed.

[1] Paragraph .12 of section 725, *Supplementary Information in Relation to the Financial Statements as a Whole*.

[2] Paragraph .07 of section 725.

Independent Auditor's Report on [*Identify Supplementary Information*]

[*Appropriate Addressee*]

We have audited the financial statements of XYZ Entity as of and for the year ended June 30, 20X1, and have issued our report thereon dated [*date of the auditor's report on the financial statements, for example, "September 15, 20X1"*] which contained an unmodified opinion on those financial statements. Our audit was performed for the purpose of forming an opinion on the financial statements as a whole. *We have not performed any procedures with respect to the audited financial statements subsequent to* [*date of the auditor's report on the financial statements, for example, "September 15, 20X1"*].

The [*identify supplementary information*] is presented for the purposes of additional analysis and is not a required part of the financial statements. Such information is the responsibility of management and was derived from and relates directly to the underlying accounting and other records used to prepare the financial statements. The information has been subjected to the auditing procedures applied in the audit of the financial statements and certain additional procedures, including comparing and reconciling such information directly to the underlying accounting and other records used to prepare the financial statements or to the financial statements themselves, and other additional procedures in accordance with auditing standards generally accepted in the United States of America. In our opinion, the information is fairly stated in all material respects in relation to the financial statements as a whole.

[*Auditor's signature*]

[*Auditor's city and state*]

December 1, 20X1 [*Date of the auditor's report on the supplementary information—not to be earlier than the date on which the auditor completed the procedures required by section 725*[3]]

.04 The following illustrative report on the audited financial statements includes an other-matter paragraph to report on supplementary information subsequent to the date of the report on the audited financial statements. For this illustration, March 31, 20X2, is the original date of the report on the audited financial statements.

Independent Auditor's Report

[*Appropriate Addressee*]

Report on the Financial Statements

We have audited the accompanying consolidated financial statements of ABC Company and its subsidiaries, which comprise the consolidated balance sheets as of December 31, 20X1 and 20X0, and the related consolidated statements of income, changes in stockholders' equity and cash flows for the years then ended, and the related notes to the financial statements.

Management's Responsibility for the Financial Statements

Management is responsible for the preparation and fair presentation of these consolidated financial statements in accordance with accounting principles generally accepted in the United States of America; this includes the design, implementation, and maintenance of internal control relevant to the preparation and fair presentation of consolidated financial statements that are free from material misstatement, whether due to fraud or error.

---

[3] Paragraph .07 of section 725.

Auditor's Responsibility

Our responsibility is to express an opinion on these consolidated financial statements based on our audits. We conducted our audits in accordance with auditing standards generally accepted in the United States of America. Those standards require that we plan and perform the audit to obtain reasonable assurance about whether the consolidated financial statements are free from material misstatement.

An audit involves performing procedures to obtain audit evidence about the amounts and disclosures in the consolidated financial statements. The procedures selected depend on the auditor's judgment, including the assessment of the risks of material misstatement of the consolidated financial statements, whether due to fraud or error. In making those risk assessments, the auditor considers internal control relevant to the entity's preparation and fair presentation of the consolidated financial statements in order to design audit procedures that are appropriate in the circumstances, but not for the purpose of expressing an opinion on the effectiveness of the entity's internal control. Accordingly, we express no such opinion. An audit also includes evaluating the appropriateness of accounting policies used and the reasonableness of significant accounting estimates made by management, as well as evaluating the overall presentation of the consolidated financial statements.

We believe that the audit evidence we have obtained is sufficient and appropriate to provide a basis for our audit opinion.

Opinion

In our opinion, the consolidated financial statements referred to above present fairly, in all material respects, the financial position of ABC Company and its subsidiaries as of December 31, 20X1 and 20X0, and the results of their operations and their cash flows for the years then ended in accordance with accounting principles generally accepted in the United States of America.

Report on [*Identify Supplementary Information*]

Our audit was conducted for the purpose of forming an opinion on the financial statements as a whole. The [*identify accompanying supplementary information*] is presented for purposes of additional analysis and is not a required part of the financial statements. Such information is the responsibility of management and was derived from and relates directly to the underlying accounting and other records used to prepare the financial statements. The information has been subjected to the auditing procedures applied in the audit of the financial statements and certain additional procedures, including comparing and reconciling such information directly to the underlying accounting and other records used to prepare the financial statements or to the financial statements themselves, and other additional procedures in accordance with auditing standards generally accepted in the United States of America. In our opinion, the information is fairly stated in all material respects in relation to the financial statements as a whole.

[*Auditor's signature*]

[*Auditor's city and state*]

March 31, 20X2, except for our report on the supplementary information for which the date is June 1, 20X2 [Date of the auditor's report on the audited financial statements, with a later date used for the paragraph labeled "Report on [*identify supplementary information*]," which is as of a date not earlier than the date on which the auditor completed the procedures required by paragraph .07 of section 725.]

[Issue Date: July 2011; Revised: October 2011.]

AU-C Section 730 *

Required Supplementary Information

(Supersedes SAS No. 52 section 558.)

Source: SAS No. 120; SAS No. 122.

Effective for audits of financial statements for periods beginning on or after December 15, 2010. Early application is permitted.

> **NOTE**
>
> To address practice issues, Statement on Auditing Standards (SAS) No. 120, *Required Supplementary Information*, was issued in February 2010 as a SAS resulting from the Clarification and Convergence Project of the Auditing Standards Board, and is effective for audits of financial statements for periods beginning on or after December 15, 2010.
>
> SAS No. 120 was originally codified as AU section 558. SAS No. 122, *Statement on Auditing Standards: Clarification and Recodification*, redesignates AU section 558 as section 730, but does not supersede SAS No. 120.
>
> This section contains conforming changes necessary in specific paragraphs and footnotes due to the issuance of SAS No. 122.

Introduction

Scope of This Section

.01 This section addresses the auditor's responsibility with respect to information that a designated accounting standards setter requires to accompany an entity's basic financial statements (hereinafter referred to as *required supplementary information*). In the absence of any separate requirement in the particular circumstances of the engagement, the auditor's opinion on the basic financial statements does not cover required supplementary information. (Ref: par. .A1) [Revised, October 2011, to reflect conforming changes necessary due to the issuance of SAS No. 122.]

Effective Date

.02 This section is effective for audits of financial statements for periods beginning on or after December 15, 2010. Early application is permitted.

---

* This section has been codified using an "AU-C" identifier instead of an "AU" identifier. "AU-C" is a temporary identifier to avoid confusion with references to existing "AU" sections, which will remain in AICPA *Professional Standards* through 2013. The "AU-C" identifier will revert to "AU" in 2014, by which time substantially all engagements for which the "AU" sections were still effective are expected to be completed. [Footnote added, October 2011, to reflect conforming changes necessary due to the issuance of SAS No. 122.]

Objective

.03 The objectives of the auditor when a designated accounting standards setter requires information to accompany an entity's basic financial statements are to perform specified procedures in order to

a. describe, in the auditor's report, whether required supplementary information is presented and

b. communicate therein when some or all of the required supplementary information has not been presented in accordance with guidelines established by a designated accounting standards setter or when the auditor has identified material modifications that should be made to the required supplementary information for it to be in accordance with guidelines established by the designated accounting standards setter.

[Revised, October 2011, to reflect conforming changes necessary due to the issuance of SAS No. 122.]

Definitions

.04 For purposes of generally accepted auditing standards, the following terms have the meanings attributed as follows:

Applicable financial reporting framework. The financial reporting framework adopted by management and, when appropriate, those charged with governance in the preparation and fair presentation of the financial statements that is acceptable in view of the nature of the entity and the objective of the financial statements, or that is required by law or regulation.

Basic financial statements. Financial statements presented in accordance with an applicable financial reporting framework as established by a designated accounting standards setter, excluding required supplementary information.

Designated accounting standards setter. A body designated by the Council of the AICPA to promulgate GAAP pursuant to Rule 202, *Compliance With Standards* (ET sec. 202 par. .01), and Rule 203, *Accounting Principles* (ET sec. 203 par. .01) of the AICPA Code of Professional Conduct.

Prescribed guidelines. The authoritative guidelines established by the designated accounting standards setter for the methods of measurement and presentation of the required supplementary information.

Required supplementary information. Information that a designated accounting standards setter requires to accompany an entity's basic financial statements. Required supplementary information is not part of the basic financial statements; however, a designated accounting standards setter considers the information to be an essential part of financial reporting for placing the basic financial statements in an appropriate operational, economic, or historical context. In addition, authoritative guidelines for the methods of measurement and presentation of the information have been established.

[Revised, October 2011, to reflect conforming changes necessary due to the issuance of SAS No. 122.]

Requirements

Procedures

.05 The auditor should apply the following procedures to required supplementary information:

a. Inquire of management about the methods of preparing the information, including (i) whether it has been measured and presented in accordance with prescribed guidelines, (ii) whether methods of measurement or presentation have been changed from those used in the prior period and the reasons for any such changes, and (iii) whether there were any significant assumptions or interpretations underlying the measurement or presentation of the information

b. Compare the information for consistency with (i) management's responses to the foregoing inquiries, (ii) the basic financial statements, and (iii) other knowledge obtained during the audit of the basic financial statements

c. Obtain written representations from management (i) that it acknowledges its responsibility for the required supplementary information; (ii) about whether the required supplementary information is measured and presented in accordance with prescribed guidelines; (iii) about whether the methods of measurement or presentation have changed from those used in the prior period and, if so, the reasons for such changes; and (iv) about any significant assumptions or interpretations underlying the measurement or presentation of the required supplementary information[1]

.06 If the auditor is unable to complete the procedures in paragraph .05, the auditor should consider whether management contributed to the auditor's inability to complete the procedures. If the auditor concludes that the inability to complete the procedures was due to significant difficulties encountered in dealing with management, the auditor should inform those charged with governance.[2]

Reporting

.07 The auditor should include an other-matter paragraph in the auditor's report on the financial statements to refer to the required supplementary information in accordance with section 706, *Emphasis-of-Matter Paragraphs and Other-Matter Paragraphs in the Independent Auditor's Report.*[3] The other-matter paragraph should include language to explain the following circumstances, as applicable:

---

[1] See section 580, *Written Representations*, for additional requirements and guidance with respect to obtaining written representations from management as part of an audit of financial statements performed in accordance with generally accepted auditing standards. [Footnote revised, October 2011, to reflect conforming changes necessary due to the issuance of SAS No. 122.]

[2] See paragraph .12 of section 260, *The Auditor's Communication With Those Charged With Governance*, for additional guidance when the auditor encounters significant difficulties in dealing with management during the audit. [Footnote revised, October 2011, to reflect conforming changes necessary due to the issuance of SAS No. 122.]

[3] Paragraph .08 of section 706, *Emphasis-of-Matter Paragraphs and Other-Matter Paragraphs in the Independent Auditor's Report*. [Footnote added, October 2011, to reflect conforming changes necessary due to the issuance of SAS No. 122.]

a. The required supplementary information is included, and the auditor has applied the procedures in paragraph .05 of this section.

b. The required supplementary information is omitted.

c. Some required supplementary information is missing and some is presented in accordance with the prescribed guidelines.

d. The auditor has identified material departures from the prescribed guidelines.

e. The auditor is unable to complete the procedures in paragraph .05 of this section.

f. The auditor has unresolved doubts about whether the required supplementary information is presented in accordance with prescribed guidelines.

[Revised, October 2011, to reflect conforming changes necessary due to the issuance of SAS No. 122.]

.08 If the entity has presented all or some of the required supplementary information, the other-matter paragraph referred to in paragraph .07 should include the following elements: (Ref: par. .A2)

a. A statement that [*identify the applicable financial reporting framework (for example, accounting principles generally accepted in the United States of America)*] require that the [*identify the required supplementary information*] be presented to supplement the basic financial statements

b. A statement that such information, although not a part of the basic financial statements, is required by [*identify designated accounting standards setter*], who considers it to be an essential part of financial reporting for placing the basic financial statements in an appropriate operational, economic, or historical context

c. If the auditor is able to complete the procedures in paragraph .05,

i. a statement that the auditor has applied certain limited procedures to the required supplementary information in accordance with auditing standards generally accepted in the United States of America, which consisted of inquiries of management about the methods of preparing the information and comparing the information for consistency with management's responses to the auditor's inquiries, the basic financial statements, and other knowledge the auditor obtained during the audit of the basic financial statements

ii. a statement that the auditor does not express an opinion or provide any assurance on the information because the limited procedures do not provide the auditor with sufficient evidence to express an opinion or provide any assurance

d. If the auditor is unable to complete the procedures in paragraph .05,

i. a statement that the auditor was unable to apply certain limited procedures to the required supplementary information in accordance with auditing standards generally accepted in the United States because [*state the reasons*]

ii. a statement that the auditor does not express an opinion or provide any assurance on the information

e. If some of the required supplementary information is omitted,

i. a statement that management has omitted [*description of the missing required supplementary information*] that [*identify the applicable financial reporting framework (for example, accounting principles generally accepted in the United States of America)*] require to be presented to supplement the basic financial statements

ii. a statement that such missing information, although not a part of the basic financial statements, is required by [*identify designated accounting standards setter*], who considers it to be an essential part of financial reporting for placing the basic financial statements in an appropriate operational, economic, or historical context

iii. a statement that the auditor's opinion on the basic financial statements is not affected by the missing information

f. If the measurement or presentation of the required supplementary information departs materially from the prescribed guidelines, a statement that although the auditor's opinion on the basic financial statements is not affected, material departures from prescribed guidelines exist [*describe the material departures from the applicable financial reporting framework*]

g. If the auditor has unresolved doubts about whether the required supplementary information is measured or presented in accordance with prescribed guidelines, a statement that although the auditor's opinion on the basic financial statements is not affected, the results of the limited procedures have raised doubts about whether material modifications should be made to the required supplementary information for it to be presented in accordance with guidelines established by [*identify designated accounting standards setter*]

[Revised, October 2011, to reflect conforming changes necessary due to the issuance of SAS No. 122.]

.09 If all of the required supplementary information is omitted, the other-matter paragraph should include the following elements:

a. A statement that management has omitted [*description of the missing required supplementary information*] that [*identify the applicable financial reporting framework (for example, accounting principles generally accepted in the United States of America)*] require to be presented to supplement the basic financial statements

b. A statement that such missing information, although not a part of the basic financial statements, is required by [*identify designated accounting standards setter*], who considers it to be an essential part of financial reporting for placing the basic financial statements in an appropriate operational, economic, or historical context

c. A statement that the auditor's opinion on the basic financial statements is not affected by the missing information

[Revised, October 2011, to reflect conforming changes necessary due to the issuance of SAS No. 122.]

Application and Other Explanatory Material

Scope of This Section (Ref: par. .01)

.A1 The auditor's responsibility for financial and nonfinancial information (other than the financial statements and the auditor's report thereon) that is included in a document containing audited financial statements and the auditor's report thereon but that is not required by a designated accounting standards setter is addressed in section 720, *Other Information in Documents Containing Audited Financial Statements*. [Revised, October 2011, to reflect conforming changes necessary due to the issuance of SAS No. 122.]

Reporting (Ref: par. .07–.09)

.A2 Because the required supplementary information accompanies the basic financial statements, the auditor's report on the financial statements includes a discussion of the responsibility taken by the auditor on that information. However, because the required supplementary information is not part of the basic financial statements, the auditor's opinion on the fairness of presentation of such financial statements in accordance with the applicable financial reporting framework is not affected by the presentation by the entity of the required supplementary information or the failure to present some or all of such required supplementary information. Furthermore, if the required supplementary information is omitted by the entity, the auditor does not have a responsibility to present that information.

.A3

Exhibit—Examples of Other-Matter Paragraphs When Reporting on Required Supplementary Information

Illustration 1—The Required Supplementary Information Is Included, the Auditor Has Applied the Specified Procedures, and No Material Departures From Prescribed Guidelines Have Been Identified

[*Identify the applicable financial reporting framework (for example, accounting principles generally accepted in the United States of America)*] require that the [*identify the required supplementary information*] on page XX be presented to supplement the basic financial statements. Such information, although not a part of the basic financial statements, is required by [*identify designated accounting standards setter*] who considers it to be an essential part of financial reporting for placing the basic financial statements in an appropriate operational, economic, or historical context. We have applied certain limited procedures to the required supplementary information in accordance with auditing standards generally accepted in the United States of America, which consisted of inquiries of management about the methods of preparing the information and comparing the information for consistency with management's responses to our inquiries, the basic financial statements, and other knowledge we obtained during our audit of the basic financial statements. We do not express an opinion or provide any assurance on the information because the limited procedures do not provide us with sufficient evidence to express an opinion or provide any assurance.

Illustration 2—All Required Supplementary Information Omitted

Management has omitted [*describe the missing required supplementary information*] that [*identify the applicable financial reporting framework (for example, accounting principles generally accepted in the United States of America)*] require to be presented to supplement the basic financial statements. Such missing information, although not a part of the basic financial statements, is required by [*identify designated accounting standards setter*] who considers it to be an essential part of financial reporting for placing the basic financial statements in an appropriate operational, economic, or historical context. Our opinion on the basic financial statements is not affected by this missing information.

Illustration 3—Some Required Supplementary Information Is Omitted and Some Is Presented in Accordance With the Prescribed Guidelines

[*Identify the applicable financial reporting framework (for example, accounting principles generally accepted in the United States of America)*] require that [*identify the included supplementary information*] be presented to supplement the basic financial statements. Such information, although not a part of the basic financial statements, is required by [*identify designated accounting standards setter*] who considers it to be an essential part of financial reporting for placing the basic financial statements in an appropriate operational, economic, or historical context. We have applied certain limited procedures to the required supplementary information in accordance with auditing standards generally accepted in the United States of America, which consisted of inquiries of management about the methods of preparing the information and comparing the information for consistency with management's responses to our inquiries, the basic financial statements, and other knowledge we obtained during our audit of the basic financial statements. We do not express an opinion or provide any assurance on the information because the limited procedures do not provide us with evidence sufficient to express an opinion or provide any assurance.

Management has omitted [*describe the missing required supplementary information*] that [*identify the applicable financial reporting framework*] require to be presented to supplement the basic financial statements. Such missing information, although not a part of the basic financial statements, is required by [*identify designated accounting standards setter*] who considers it to be an essential part of financial reporting for placing the basic financial statements in an appropriate operational, economic, or historical context. Our opinion on the basic financial statements is not affected by this missing information.

Illustration 4—Material Departures From Prescribed Guidelines Identified

[*Identify the applicable financial reporting framework (for example, accounting principles generally accepted in the United States of America)*] require that the [*identify the supplementary information*] on page XX be presented to supplement the basic financial statements. Such information, although not a part of the basic financial statements, is required by [*identify designated accounting standards setter*] who considers it to be an essential part of financial reporting for placing the basic financial statements in an appropriate operational, economic, or historical context. We have applied certain limited procedures to the required supplementary information in accordance with auditing standards generally accepted in the United States of America, which consisted of inquiries of management about the methods of preparing the information and comparing the information for consistency with management's responses to our inquiries, the basic financial statements, and other knowledge we obtained during our audit of the basic financial statements. Although our opinion on the basic financial statements is not affected, the following material departures from the prescribed guidelines exist [*identify the required supplementary information and describe the material departures from the prescribed guidelines*]. We do not express an opinion or provide any assurance on the information.

Illustration 5—Specified Procedures Not Completed

[*Identify the applicable financial reporting framework (for example, accounting principles generally accepted in the United States of America)*] require that the [*identify the supplementary information*] on page XX be presented to supplement the basic financial statements. Such information, although not a part of the basic financial statements, is required by [*identify designated accounting standards setter*] who considers it to be an essential part of financial reporting for placing the basic financial statements in an appropriate operational, economic, or historical context. We were unable to apply certain limited procedures to the required supplementary information in accordance with auditing standards generally accepted in the United States of America because [*state the reasons*]. We do not express an opinion or provide any assurance on the information.

Illustration 6—Unresolved Doubts About Whether the Required Supplementary Information Is in Accordance With Prescribed Guidelines

[*Identify the applicable financial reporting framework (for example, accounting principles generally accepted in the United States of America)*] require that the [*identify the supplementary information*] on page XX be presented to supplement the basic financial statements. Such information, although not a part of the basic financial statements, is required by [*identify designated accounting standards setter*] who considers it to be an essential part of financial reporting for placing the basic financial statements in an appropriate operational, economic, or historical context. We have applied certain limited procedures to the required supplementary information in accordance with auditing standards generally accepted in the United States of America, which consisted of inquiries of management about the methods of preparing the information and comparing the information for consistency with management's responses to our inquiries, the basic financial statements, and other knowledge we obtained during our audit of the basic financial statements. We do not express an opinion or provide any assurance on the information because the limited procedures do not provide us with sufficient evidence to express an opinion or provide any assurance. Although our opinion on the basic financial statements is not affected, the results of the limited procedures have raised doubts about whether material modifications should be made to the required supplementary information for it to be presented in accordance with guidelines established by [*identify designated accounting standards setter*]. [*The auditor may consider including in the report the reason(s) he or she was unable to resolve his or her doubts.*]

[Revised, October 2011, to reflect conforming changes necessary due to the issuance of SAS No. 122.]

AU-C Sections 800–899
SPECIAL CONSIDERATIONS

TABLE OF CONTENTS

AU-C Section 800 *

Special Considerations—Audits of Financial Statements Prepared in Accordance With Special Purpose Frameworks

Source: SAS No. 122; SAS No. 125; SAS No. 127.

Effective for audits of financial statements for periods ending on or after December 15, 2012.

Introduction

Scope of This Section

.01 AU-C sections 200–700 apply to an audit of financial statements. This section addresses special considerations in the application of those AU-C sections to an audit of financial statements prepared in accordance with a special purpose framework, which is a cash, a tax, a regulatory, a contractual, or an other basis of accounting. This section does not purport to address all special considerations that may be relevant in the circumstances. [As amended, effective for audits of financial statements for periods ending on or after December 15, 2012, by SAS No. 127.]

.02 This section is written in the context of a complete set of financial statements prepared in accordance with a special purpose framework. Section 805, *Special Considerations—Audits of Single Financial Statements and Specific Elements, Accounts, or Items of a Financial Statement*, addresses special considerations relevant to an audit of a single financial statement or of a specific element, account, or item of a financial statement.

.03 Section 910, *Financial Statements Prepared in Accordance With a Financial Reporting Framework Generally Accepted in Another Country*, addresses circumstances in which an auditor practicing in the United States is engaged to report on financial statements that have been prepared in accordance with a financial reporting framework generally accepted in another country not adopted by a body designated by the Council of the AICPA (Council) to promulgate generally accepted accounting principles (GAAP) when such audited financial statements are intended for use outside the United States.

.04 Section 806, *Reporting on Compliance With Aspects of Contractual Agreements or Regulatory Requirements in Connection With Audited Financial Statements*, addresses the auditor's responsibility and the form and content of the report when the auditor is requested to report on the entity's compliance with aspects of contractual agreements or regulatory requirements in connection with the audit of financial statements.

---

* This section has been codified using an "AU-C" identifier instead of an "AU" identifier. "AU-C" is a temporary identifier to avoid confusion with references to existing "AU" sections, which will remain in AICPA *Professional Standards* through 2013. The "AU-C" identifier will revert to "AU" in 2014, by which time substantially all engagements for which the "AU" sections were still effective are expected to be completed.

Effective Date

.05 This section is effective for audits of financial statements for periods ending on or after December 15, 2012.

Objective

.06 The objective of the auditor, when applying generally accepted auditing standards (GAAS) in an audit of financial statements prepared in accordance with a special purpose framework, is to address appropriately the special considerations that are relevant to

a. the acceptance of the engagement,

b. the planning and performance of that engagement, and

c. forming an opinion and reporting on the financial statements.

Definitions

.07 For purposes of GAAS, the following terms have the meanings attributed as follows:

Special purpose financial statements. Financial statements prepared in accordance with a special purpose framework. (Ref: par. .A1)

Special purpose framework. A financial reporting framework other than GAAP that is one of the following bases of accounting: (Ref: par. .A2–.A5)

a. **Cash basis.** A basis of accounting that the entity uses to record cash receipts and disbursements and modifications of the cash basis having substantial support (for example, recording depreciation on fixed assets).

b. **Tax basis.** A basis of accounting that the entity uses to file its tax return for the period covered by the financial statements.

c. **Regulatory basis.** A basis of accounting that the entity uses to comply with the requirements or financial reporting provisions of a regulatory agency to whose jurisdiction the entity is subject (for example, a basis of accounting that insurance companies use pursuant to the accounting practices prescribed or permitted by a state insurance commission).

d. **Contractual basis.** A basis of accounting that the entity uses to comply with an agreement between the entity and one or more third parties other than the auditor.

e. **Other basis.** A basis of accounting that uses a definite set of logical, reasonable criteria that is applied to all material items appearing in financial statements.

The cash basis, tax basis, regulatory basis, and other basis of accounting are commonly referred to as *other comprehensive bases of accounting*.

[As amended, effective for audits of financial statements for periods ending on or after December 15, 2012, by SAS No. 127.]

.08 Reference to *financial statements* in this section means "a complete set of special purpose financial statements, including the related notes."[1] The related notes ordinarily comprise a summary of significant accounting policies and other explanatory information. The requirements of the applicable financial reporting framework determine the form and content of the financial statements and what constitutes a complete set of financial statements.

.09 Reference to *GAAP* in GAAS means generally accepted accounting principles promulgated by bodies designated by Council pursuant to Rule 202, *Compliance With Standards* (ET sec. 202 par. .01), and Rule 203, *Accounting Principles* (ET sec. 203 par. .01), of the AICPA Code of Professional Conduct.

Requirements

Considerations When Accepting the Engagement

Acceptability of the Financial Reporting Framework (Ref: par. .A6–.A9)

.10 Section 210, *Terms of Engagement*, requires the auditor to determine the acceptability of the financial reporting framework applied in the preparation of the financial statements.[2] In an audit of special purpose financial statements, the auditor should obtain an understanding of

a. the purpose for which the financial statements are prepared,

b. the intended users, and

c. the steps taken by management to determine that the applicable financial reporting framework is acceptable in the circumstances.

Preconditions for an Audit (Ref: par. .A10)

.11 Section 210 requires the auditor to establish whether the preconditions for an audit are present, including determining whether the financial reporting framework to be applied in the preparation of the financial statements is acceptable.[3] In an audit of special purpose financial statements, the auditor should obtain the agreement of management that it acknowledges and understands its responsibility to include all informative disclosures that are appropriate for the special purpose framework used to prepare the entity's financial statements, including

a. a description of the special purpose framework, including a summary of significant accounting policies, and how the framework differs from GAAP, the effects of which need not be quantified.

b. informative disclosures similar to those required by GAAP, in the case of special purpose financial statements that contain items that are the same as, or similar to, those in financial statements prepared in accordance with GAAP.

c. a description of any significant interpretations of the contract on which the special purpose financial statements are based, in the case of special purpose financial statements prepared in accordance with a contractual basis of accounting.

---

[1] Paragraphs .14 and .A9 of section 200, *Overall Objectives of the Independent Auditor and the Conduct of an Audit in Accordance With Generally Accepted Auditing Standards.*

[2] Paragraph .06*a* of section 210, *Terms of Engagement.*

[3] Paragraph .06 of section 210.

d. additional disclosures beyond those specifically required by the framework that may be necessary for the special purpose financial statements to achieve fair presentation. (Ref: par. .A11)

[As amended, effective for audits of financial statements for periods ending on or after December 15, 2012, by SAS No. 127.]

Considerations When Planning and Performing the Audit (Ref: par. .A12–.A15)

.12 Section 200, *Overall Objectives of the Independent Auditor and the Conduct of an Audit in Accordance With Generally Accepted Auditing Standards*, requires the auditor to comply with all AU-C sections relevant to the audit.[4] In planning and performing an audit of special purpose financial statements, the auditor should adapt and apply all AU-C sections relevant to the audit as necessary in the circumstances of the engagement.

.13 Section 315, *Understanding the Entity and Its Environment and Assessing the Risks of Material Misstatement*, requires the auditor to obtain an understanding of the entity's selection and application of accounting policies.[5] In the case of special purpose financial statements prepared in accordance with a contractual basis of accounting, the auditor should obtain an understanding of any significant interpretations of the contract that management made in the preparation of those financial statements. An interpretation is significant when adoption of another reasonable interpretation would have produced a material difference in the information presented in the financial statements.

Forming an Opinion and Reporting Considerations

.14 When forming an opinion and reporting on special purpose financial statements, the auditor should apply the requirements in section 700, *Forming an Opinion and Reporting on Financial Statements*. When, in forming an opinion, the auditor concludes that a modification to the auditor's opinion on the financial statements is necessary, the auditor should apply the requirements in section 705, *Modifications to the Opinion in the Independent Auditor's Report*. (Ref: par. .A16)

Description of the Applicable Financial Reporting Framework (Ref: par. .A17–.A18)

.15 Section 700 requires the auditor to evaluate whether the financial statements adequately refer to or describe the applicable financial reporting framework.[6] In an audit of special purpose financial statements, the auditor should evaluate whether the financial statements are suitably titled, include a summary of significant accounting policies, and adequately describe how the special purpose framework differs from GAAP. The effects of these differences need not be quantified.

.16 In the case of special purpose financial statements prepared in accordance with a contractual basis of accounting, the auditor should also evaluate whether the financial statements adequately describe any significant interpretations of the contract on which the financial statements are based.

---

[4] Paragraph .20 of section 200.

[5] Paragraph .12c of section 315, *Understanding the Entity and Its Environment and Assessing the Risks of Material Misstatement*.

[6] Paragraph .18 of section 700, *Forming an Opinion and Reporting on Financial Statements*.

Fair Presentation (Ref: par. .A19–.A23)

.17 Section 700 requires the auditor to evaluate whether the financial statements achieve fair presentation.[7] In an audit of special purpose financial statements when the special purpose financial statements contain items that are the same as, or similar to, those in financial statements prepared in accordance with GAAP, the auditor should evaluate whether the financial statements include informative disclosures similar to those required by GAAP. The auditor should also evaluate whether additional disclosures, beyond those specifically required by the framework, related to matters that are not specifically identified on the face of the financial statements or other disclosures are necessary for the financial statements to achieve fair presentation.

Auditor's Report

.18 Section 700 addresses the form and content of the auditor's report. In the case of an auditor's report on special purpose financial statements, the

a. explanation of management's responsibility for the financial statements should also make reference to its responsibility for determining that the applicable financial reporting framework is acceptable in the circumstances, when management has a choice of financial reporting frameworks in the preparation of such financial statements.

b. auditor's report should also describe the purpose for which the financial statements are prepared or refer to a note in the special purpose financial statements that contains that information, when the financial statements are prepared in accordance with

i. a regulatory or contractual basis of accounting or

ii. an other basis of accounting, and the auditor is required to restrict use of the auditor's report pursuant to paragraph .06*a–b* of section 905, *Alert That Restricts the Use of the Auditor's Written Communication*. (Ref: par. .A24)

[As amended, effective for audits of financial statements for periods ending on or after December 15, 2012, by SAS No. 127.]

Alerting Readers in an Emphasis-of-Matter Paragraph That the Financial Statements Are Prepared in Accordance With a Special Purpose Framework (Ref: par. .A25)

.19 Except for the circumstances described in paragraph .21, the auditor's report on special purpose financial statements should include an *emphasis-of-matter* paragraph,[8] under an appropriate heading, that

a. indicates that the financial statements are prepared in accordance with the applicable special purpose framework,

b. refers to the note to the financial statements that describes that framework, and

c. states that the special purpose framework is a basis of accounting other than GAAP.

---

[7] Paragraph .17 of section 700.

[8] Paragraphs .06–.07 of section 706, *Emphasis-of-Matter Paragraphs and Other-Matter Paragraphs in the Independent Auditor's Report.*

Restricting the Use of the Auditor's Report in an Other-Matter Paragraph (Ref: par. .A26–.A27)

.20 Except for the circumstances described in paragraph .21, the auditor's report on special purpose financial statements should include an *other-matter* paragraph,[9] under an appropriate heading, that restricts[10] the use of the auditor's report when the special purpose financial statements are prepared in accordance with

a. a contractual basis of accounting,

b. a regulatory basis of accounting, or

c. an other basis of accounting when required pursuant to paragraph .06*a*–*b* of section 905.

[As amended, effective for the auditor's written communications related to audits of financial statements for periods ending on or after December 15, 2012, by SAS No. 125. As amended, effective for audits of financial statements for periods ending on or after December 15, 2012, by SAS No. 127.]

Regulatory Basis Financial Statements Intended for General Use (Ref: par. .A28)

.21 If the special purpose financial statements are prepared in accordance with a regulatory basis of accounting, and the special purpose financial statements together with the auditor's report are intended for general use, the auditor should not include the *emphasis-of-matter* or *other-matter* paragraphs required by paragraphs .19–.20. Instead, the auditor should express an opinion about whether the special purpose financial statements are presented fairly, in all material respects, in accordance with GAAP. The auditor should also, in a separate paragraph, express an opinion about whether the financial statements are prepared in accordance with the special purpose framework.

Auditor's Report Prescribed by Law or Regulation (Ref: par. .A29–.A32)

.22 If the auditor is required by law or regulation to use a specific layout, form, or wording of the auditor's report, the auditor's report should refer to GAAS only if the auditor's report includes, at a minimum, each of the following elements:

a. A title

b. An addressee

c. An introductory paragraph that identifies the special purpose financial statements audited

d. A description of the responsibility of management for the preparation and fair presentation of the special purpose financial statements

e. A reference to management's responsibility for determining that the applicable financial reporting framework is acceptable in the circumstances when required by paragraph .18*a*

f. A description of the purpose for which the financial statements are prepared when required by paragraph .18*b*

---

[9] Paragraph .08 of section 706.

[10] See paragraphs .06*a*–*b* and .07 of section 905, *Alert That Restricts the Use of the Auditor's Written Communication*. [Footnote amended, effective for the auditor's written communications related to audits of financial statements for periods ending on or after December 15, 2012, by SAS No. 125.]

g. A description of the auditor's responsibility to express an opinion on the special purpose financial statements and the scope of the audit, that includes
   i. A reference to GAAS and, if applicable, the law or regulation
   ii. A description of an audit in accordance with those standards

h. An opinion paragraph containing an expression of opinion on the special purpose financial statements and a reference to the special purpose framework used to prepare the financial statements (including identifying the origin of the framework) and, if applicable, an opinion on whether the special purpose financial statements are presented fairly, in all material respects, in accordance with GAAP when required by paragraph .21

i. An *emphasis-of-matter* paragraph that indicates that the financial statements are prepared in accordance with a special purpose framework when required by paragraph .19

j. An *other-matter* paragraph that restricts the use of the auditor's report when required by paragraph .20

k. The auditor's signature

l. The auditor's city and state

m. The date of the auditor's report

.23 If the prescribed specific layout, form, or wording of the auditor's report is not acceptable or would cause an auditor to make a statement that the auditor has no basis to make, the auditor should reword the prescribed form of report or attach an appropriately worded separate report.

Application and Other Explanatory Material

Definitions

Special Purpose Financial Statements and Special Purpose Frameworks (Ref: par. .07)

.A1 Special purpose financial statements may be prepared for use by regulatory bodies, the parties to a contract or agreement, or other specified parties. For example, a loan agreement may require the borrower to prepare consolidated financial statements for the lender presented on a contractual basis of accounting, which is not in accordance with accounting principles generally accepted in the United States of America (U.S. GAAP) or International Financial Reporting Standards promulgated by the International Accounting Standards Board.

.A2 There may be circumstances when a regulatory or contractual basis of accounting is based on a general purpose framework, such as U.S. GAAP, but does not comply with all the requirements of that framework.[11] An example is a contract that requires financial statements to be prepared in accordance with most, but not all, of U.S. GAAP. If the financial statements purport to be prepared in accordance with a general purpose framework and such financial statements are materially misstated due to a departure from that framework, section 705 applies.

---

[11] The term *general purpose framework* is defined in paragraph .11 of section 700.

.A3 When it is acceptable in the circumstances of the engagement to report, in accordance with this section, on special purpose financial statements that purport to be prepared in accordance with a regulatory or contractual basis of accounting that is based on a general purpose framework, it is inappropriate for the description of the applicable financial reporting framework in the special purpose financial statements to imply full compliance with the general purpose framework. In the example of the contract in paragraph .A2, the description of the applicable financial reporting framework would refer to the financial reporting provisions of the contract, rather than make reference to U.S. GAAP. The requirements in paragraphs .19–.21 are designed to avoid misunderstandings about compliance with the general purpose framework.

.A4 Financial statements prepared in accordance with a cash basis, tax basis, or an other basis of accounting may be the only financial statements an entity prepares. Such special purpose financial statements may be used by users other than those for whom the financial reporting framework is designed. Despite the broad distribution of the financial statements, the financial statements are still considered to be special purpose financial statements for purposes of GAAS. The requirement in paragraph .19 is designed to avoid misunderstandings about the framework used to prepare the financial statements. [As amended, effective for audits of financial statements for periods ending on or after December 15, 2012, by SAS No. 127.]

.A5 Certain regulators, including state and local government legislators, regulatory agencies, or departments, require financial statements to be prepared in accordance with a financial reporting framework that is based on U.S. GAAP but does not comply with all of the requirements of U.S. GAAP. Such frameworks are regulatory bases of accounting, as defined in paragraph .07. In some circumstances, however, the cash or tax basis of accounting may be permitted by a regulator. For purposes of this section, the cash and tax bases of accounting are not regulatory bases of accounting. [As amended, effective for audits of financial statements for periods ending on or after December 15, 2012, by SAS No. 127.]

Considerations When Accepting the Engagement

Acceptability of the Financial Reporting Framework (Ref: par. .10)

.A6 In the case of special purpose financial statements, the financial information needs of the intended users are a factor in determining the acceptability of the financial reporting framework applied in the preparation of the financial statements.

.A7 The applicable financial reporting framework may encompass the financial reporting standards established by an organization that is authorized or recognized to promulgate standards for special purpose financial statements. In that case, those standards will be presumed acceptable for that purpose if the organization follows an established and transparent process involving deliberation and consideration of the views of relevant stakeholders. In some circumstances, law or regulation may prescribe the financial reporting framework to be used by management in the preparation of special purpose financial statements for a certain type of entity. For example, a regulator may establish financial reporting provisions to meet the requirements of that regulator. In the absence of indications to the contrary, such a financial reporting framework is presumed acceptable for special purpose financial statements prepared by such an entity.

.A8 The acceptability of the financial reporting framework in the circumstances of the engagement is determined by considering whether the framework exhibits attributes normally exhibited by acceptable financial reporting frameworks. Section 210 discusses the attributes of acceptable financial reporting frameworks, which provide management with an appropriate basis for preparing the financial statements and the auditor with suitable criteria for auditing the financial statements.[12] In the case of a special purpose framework, the relative importance to a particular engagement of each of the attributes normally exhibited by acceptable financial reporting frameworks is a matter of professional judgment. For example, for purposes of establishing the value of net assets of an entity at the date of its sale, the seller and purchaser may have agreed that conservative estimates of allowances for uncollectible accounts receivable are appropriate for their needs, even though such financial information may be biased when compared with financial information prepared in accordance with a general purpose framework. [As amended, effective for audits of financial statements for periods ending on or after December 15, 2012, by SAS No. 127.]

.A9 In the case of financial statements prepared in accordance with a contractual basis of accounting, the parties to the contract or agreement may need to agree on the significant interpretations of the contract on which the special purpose financial statements are based. If agreement cannot be reached, the auditor may determine that the framework is not acceptable.

Preconditions for an Audit (Ref: par. .11)

.A10 Section 210 also requires the agreed-upon terms of the audit engagement to include references to the expected form and content of any reports to be issued by the auditor and a statement that there may be circumstances in which a report may differ from its expected form and content.[13] The auditor may discuss with management and, when appropriate, those charged with governance how an audit report on financial statements prepared in accordance with a special purpose framework differs from an audit report on financial statements prepared in accordance with a general purpose framework. Discussing the expected form and content of the auditor's report may assist management in understanding its responsibilities related to the audit engagement.

Achieving Fair Presentation (Ref: par. .11d)

.A11 In accordance with section 700, the auditor's evaluation of whether the financial statements achieve fair presentation in accordance with the applicable financial reporting framework requires consideration of[14]

a. the overall presentation, structure and content of the financial statements and

b. whether the financial statements, including the related notes, represent the underlying transactions and events in a manner that achieves fair presentation.

Also see paragraphs .A19–.A23 of this section.

---

[12] Paragraphs .A2-.A3 of section 210, *Terms of Engagement*. [Footnote added, effective for audits of financial statements for periods ending on or after December 15, 2012, by SAS No. 127.]

[13] Paragraph .10*f* of section 210. [Footnote renumbered, effective for audits of financial statements for periods ending on or after December 15, 2012, by SAS No. 127.]

[14] Paragraph .17 of section 700. [Footnote renumbered, effective for audits of financial statements for periods ending on or after December 15, 2012, by SAS No. 127.]

Considerations When Planning and Performing the Audit (Ref: par. .12–.13)

.A12 Section 200 requires the auditor to comply with (*a*) relevant ethical requirements relating to financial statement audit engagements and (*b*) all AU-C sections relevant to the audit. It also requires the auditor to comply with each requirement of an AU-C section unless, in the circumstances of the audit, the entire AU-C section is not relevant or the requirement is not relevant because it is conditional and the condition does not exist. In rare circumstances, the auditor may judge it necessary to depart from a relevant presumptively mandatory requirement in an AU-C section by performing alternative audit procedures to achieve the intent of that requirement.[15]

.A13 An AU-C section is relevant to the audit when the AU-C section is in effect and the circumstances addressed by the AU-C section exist.[16] In an audit of special purpose financial statements, some of the requirements within the relevant AU-C sections may need to be adapted by the auditor. For example, in section 320, *Materiality in Planning and Performing an Audit*, judgments about matters that are material to users of the financial statements are based on a consideration of the common financial information needs of users as a group.[17] In an audit of special purpose financial statements, those judgments may be based on a consideration of the financial information needs of the intended users.

.A14 In the case of special purpose financial statements, such as those prepared in accordance with a contractual basis of accounting, management may agree with the intended users on a threshold below which misstatements identified during the audit will not be corrected or otherwise adjusted. The existence of such a threshold does not relieve the auditor from the requirement to determine materiality in accordance with section 320 for purposes of planning and performing the audit of the special purpose financial statements. With respect to interpretations of the contract on which the special purpose financial statements are based, the auditor may determine that an interpretation is significant based on qualitative considerations.

.A15 Communication with those charged with governance in accordance with GAAS is based on the relationship between those charged with governance and the financial statements subject to audit, in particular, whether those charged with governance are responsible for overseeing the preparation of those financial statements. In the case of special purpose financial statements, those charged with governance may not have such a responsibility; for example, when the financial information is prepared solely for management's use. In such cases, the requirements of section 260, *The Auditor's Communication With Those Charged With Governance*, may not be relevant to the audit of the special purpose financial statements, except when the auditor is also responsible for the audit of the entity's general purpose financial statements or, for example, has agreed to communicate with those charged with governance of the entity relevant matters identified during the audit of the special purpose financial statements.

---

[15] Paragraphs .16, .20, and .24–.26 of section 200. [Footnote renumbered, effective for audits of financial statements for periods ending on or after December 15, 2012, by SAS No. 127.]

[16] Paragraph .20 of section 200. [Footnote renumbered, effective for audits of financial statements for periods ending on or after December 15, 2012, by SAS No. 127.]

[17] Paragraph .02 of section 320, *Materiality in Planning and Performing an Audit*. [Footnote renumbered, effective for audits of financial statements for periods ending on or after December 15, 2012, by SAS No. 127.]

Forming an Opinion and Reporting Considerations (Ref: par. .14)

.A16 Appendix A, "Overview of Reporting Requirements," provides an overview of the reporting requirements depending on the special purpose framework. The exhibit, "Illustrations of Auditor's Reports on Special Purpose Financial Statements," contains illustrations of auditor's reports on special purpose financial statements.

Description of the Applicable Financial Reporting Framework (Ref: par. .15–.16)

.A17 Terms such as *balance sheet*, *statement of financial position*, *statement of income*, *statement of operations*, and *statement of cash flows*, or similar unmodified titles, are generally understood to be applicable only to financial statements that are intended to present financial position, results of operations, or cash flows in accordance with GAAP. Accordingly, the auditor is required by paragraph .15 to evaluate whether the financial statements are suitably titled. For example, cash basis financial statements might be titled as a statement of assets and liabilities arising from cash transactions or as a statement of revenue collected and expenses paid; a financial statement prepared on a regulatory basis of accounting might be titled as a statement of income—regulatory basis.

.A18 The description of how the special purpose framework differs from GAAP ordinarily only includes the material differences between GAAP and the special purpose framework. For example, if several items are accounted for differently under the special purpose framework than they would be under U.S. GAAP, but only the differences in how depreciation is calculated are material, a brief description of the depreciation differences is all that would be necessary, and the remaining differences need not be described. The differences need not be quantified.

Fair Presentation (Ref: par. .17)

.A19 Financial statements, including the related notes, that achieve a fair presentation include all informative disclosures that are appropriate for the applicable financial reporting framework, including matters that affect their use, understanding, and interpretation. Also refer to paragraph .A11.

.A20 When the special purpose financial statements contain items that are the same as, or similar to, those in financial statements prepared in accordance with GAAP, informative disclosures similar to those required by GAAP are necessary to achieve fair presentation. For example, financial statements prepared on a tax basis or on a modified cash basis of accounting usually reflect depreciation, long-term debt, and owners' equity. Thus, the informative disclosures for depreciation, long-term debt, and owners' equity in such financial statements would be comparable to those in financial statements prepared in accordance with GAAP.

.A21 Disclosures in special purpose financial statements may substitute qualitative information for some of the quantitative information required by GAAP or may provide information that communicates the substance of those requirements. For example, disclosing estimated percentages of revenues, rather than amounts that GAAP presentations would require, may sufficiently convey the significance of sales or leasing to related parties or major customers.

.A22 The auditor is required by paragraph .17 to evaluate whether additional disclosures, beyond those specifically required by the framework, related to matters that are not specifically identified on the face of the financial statements or other disclosures may be necessary for the special purpose financial statements to achieve fair presentation. For example, these disclosures may include matters about related party transactions, restrictions on assets and owners' equity, subsequent events, and significant uncertainties. In such circumstances, the special purpose financial statements would include the same disclosure required by GAAP or disclosure that communicates the substance of those requirements.

.A23 Appendix B, "Fair Presentation and Adequate Disclosures," provides additional guidance on evaluating the adequacy of disclosures in financial statements prepared in accordance with a special purpose framework, including matters related to the presentation of financial statements.

Auditor's Report (Ref: par. .18b)

.A24 When the special purpose financial statements are prepared in accordance with a regulatory or contractual basis of accounting or an other basis of accounting that requires an alert that restricts the use of the auditor's report pursuant to paragraph .06*a–b* of section 905, the auditor is required by paragraph .18*b* to describe the purpose for which the financial statements are prepared or refer to a note in the financial statements that contains that information. This is necessary to avoid misunderstandings when the special purpose financial statements are used for purposes other than those for which they were intended. The note to the financial statements may also describe any significant interpretations of the contract on which the financial statements are based. [As amended, effective for audits of financial statements for periods ending on or after December 15, 2012, by SAS No. 127.]

Alerting Readers in an Emphasis-of-Matter Paragraph That the Financial Statements Are Prepared in Accordance With a Special Purpose Framework (Ref: par. .19)

.A25 Special purpose financial statements may be used for purposes other than those for which they were intended. To avoid misunderstandings, paragraph .19 requires the auditor to include an *emphasis-of-matter* paragraph in the auditor's report that alerts users of the auditor's report that the financial statements are prepared in accordance with a special purpose framework and that the basis of accounting is a basis of accounting other than GAAP.

Restricting the Use of the Auditor's Report in an Other-Matter Paragraph (Ref: par. .20)

.A26 Special purpose financial statements prepared in accordance with a contractual or regulatory basis of accounting are suitable only for a limited number of users who can be presumed to have an adequate understanding of such bases of accounting. For example, special purpose financial statements prepared in accordance with a contractual basis of accounting are developed for and directed only to the parties to the contract or agreement. Accordingly, the alert that restricts the use of the auditor's report is required due to the nature of the report and the potential for the report to be taken out of the context in which the auditor's report was intended to be used. Section 905, *Alert That Restricts the Use of the Auditor's Written Communication*, addresses adding other parties as specified parties. [As amended, effective for the auditor's written communications related to audits of financial statements for periods ending on or after December 15, 2012, by SAS No. 125.]

.A27 In the case of special purpose financial statements prepared in accordance with a cash or tax basis of accounting, the auditor may consider it necessary in the circumstances of the engagement to include an alert that restricts the use of the auditor's report. [As amended, effective for the auditor's written communications related to audits of financial statements for periods ending on or after December 15, 2012, by SAS No. 125.]

Regulatory Basis Financial Statements Intended for General Use (Ref: par. .21)

.A28 Special purpose financial statements prepared in accordance with a regulatory basis of accounting may be intended for general use. Such special purpose financial statements are intended for general use when the financial statements together with the auditor's report are intended for use by parties other than those within the entity and the regulatory agencies to whose jurisdiction the entity is subject or when the financial statements together with the auditor's report are distributed by the entity to parties other than the regulatory agencies to whose jurisdiction the entity is subject, either voluntarily or upon specific request. In such circumstances, the *emphasis-of-matter* and *other-matter* paragraphs described in paragraphs .19–.20 are not required because the auditor is required, in accordance with paragraph .21, to express an opinion about whether the special purpose financial statements are prepared in accordance with GAAP and an opinion about whether the financial statements are prepared in accordance with the special purpose framework.

Auditor's Report Prescribed by Law or Regulation (Ref: par. .22–.23)

.A29 The auditor may be required to comply with legal or regulatory requirements in addition to GAAS. When this is the case, the auditor may be required to use a layout, form, or wording in the auditor's report that differs from that described in this section, such as when printed forms or schedules designed or adopted by the bodies with which they are to be filed prescribe the wording of the auditor's report.

.A30 When the differences between the legal or regulatory requirements and GAAS relate only to the layout, form, and wording of the auditor's report and, at a minimum, each of the elements identified in paragraph .22 are included in the auditor's report, the auditor's report may refer to GAAS. Accordingly, in such circumstances the auditor is considered to have complied with the requirements of GAAS, even when the layout, form, and wording used in the auditor's report are specified by legal or regulatory reporting requirements. Section 210 addresses circumstances in which law or regulation prescribes the layout, form, or wording of the auditor's report in terms that are significantly different from the requirements of GAAS.[18]

.A31 Some report forms can be made acceptable by inserting additional wording to include the elements identified in paragraph .22. Other report forms can be made acceptable only by complete revision because the prescribed language of the report calls for statements by the auditor that are not consistent with the auditor's function or responsibility; for example, a report form that requests the auditor to certify the financial statements.

.A32 This guidance can be applied to other circumstances, for example, reports on financial statements prepared in accordance with a general purpose framework for which a specific layout, form, or wording of the auditor's report is required.

---

[18] Paragraph .18 of section 210. [Footnote renumbered, effective for audits of financial statements for periods ending on or after December 15, 2012, by SAS No. 127.]

.A33

Appendix A—Overview of Reporting Requirements

The following table provides an overview of the reporting requirements depending on the special purpose framework:

	Cash Basis	*Tax Basis*	*Regulatory Basis*	*Regulatory Basis (General Use)*	*Contractual Basis*	*Other Basis*
Opinion(s)	Single opinion on special purpose frame-work	Single opinion on special purpose frame-work	Single opinion on special purpose frame-work	Dual opinion on special purpose framework and generally accepted accounting principles[19]	Single opinion on special purpose framework	Single opinion on special purpose framework
Description of purpose for which special purpose financial statements are prepared[20]	No	No	Yes	Yes	Yes	As required by paragraph .18*b*(ii)
Emphasis-of-matter paragraph alerting readers regarding the preparation in accordance with a special purpose framework[21]	Yes	Yes	Yes	No	Yes	Yes
Other-matter paragraph including an alert restricting the use of the auditor's report[22]	No	No	Yes	No	Yes	As required by section 905, *Alert That Restricts the Use of the Auditor's Written Communication*[23]
Exhibit A Illustrations	1	2	3	4	5	

[As amended, effective for the auditor's written communications related to audits of financial statements for periods ending on or after December 15, 2012, by SAS No. 125. As amended, effective for audits of financial statements for periods ending on or after December 15, 2012, by SAS No. 127.]

---

[19] Paragraph .21. [Footnote renumbered, effective for audits of financial statements for periods ending on or after December 15, 2012, by SAS No. 127.]

[20] Paragraph .18*b*. [Footnote renumbered, effective for audits of financial statements for periods ending on or after December 15, 2012, by SAS No. 127.]

[21] Paragraphs .19 and .21. [Footnote renumbered, effective for audits of financial statements for periods ending on or after December 15, 2012, by SAS No. 127.]

[22] Paragraphs .20–.21. [Footnote renumbered, effective for audits of financial statements for periods ending on or after December 15, 2012, by SAS No. 127.]

[23] Paragraph .06*a*–*b* of section 905. [Footnote added, effective for audits of financial statements for periods ending on or after December 15, 2012, by SAS No. 127.]

.A34

Appendix B—Fair Presentation and Adequate Disclosures (Ref: par. .A19–.A22)

When special purpose financial statements contain items that are the same as, or similar to, those in financial statements prepared in accordance with generally accepted accounting principles (GAAP), paragraph .17 requires the auditor to evaluate whether, the financial statements include informative disclosures similar to those required by GAAP. The auditor is also required to evaluate whether additional disclosures, beyond those specifically required by the framework, related to matters that are not specifically identified on the face of the financial statements or other disclosures are necessary for the financial statements to achieve fair presentation. This appendix provides guidance, in addition to paragraphs .A19–.A22, on evaluating the adequacy of disclosures in financial statements prepared in accordance with a special purpose framework, including matters related to the presentation of financial statements.

If special purpose financial statements contain items for which GAAP would require disclosure, the financial statements may either provide the relevant disclosure that would be required for those items in a GAAP presentation or provide information that communicates the substance of that disclosure. Likewise, if GAAP sets forth requirements that apply to the presentation of financial statements, special purpose financial statements may either comply with those requirements or provide information that communicates the substance of those requirements, without modifying the format of the special purpose financial statements. This may result in substituting qualitative information for some of the quantitative information required for GAAP presentations. For example:

- Disclosure of the repayment terms of significant long-term borrowings may sufficiently communicate information about future principal reduction without providing the summary of principal reduction during each of the next five years.
- Information about the effects of accounting changes, discontinued operations, and extraordinary items could be disclosed in a note to the financial statements without following the GAAP presentation requirements in the statement of results of operations, using those terms, or disclosing net-of-tax effects.
- Instead of showing expenses by their functional classifications in certain industries, a statement of activities could present expenses according to their natural classifications, and a note to the statement could use estimated percentages to communicate information about expenses incurred by the major program and supporting services.
- Instead of showing the amounts of, and changes in, the unrestricted and temporarily and permanently restricted classes of net assets in certain industries, a statement of assets and liabilities could report total net assets or fund balances, a related statement of activities could report changes in those totals, and a note to the financial statements could provide information, using estimated or actual amounts or percentages, about the restrictions on those amounts and on any deferred restricted amounts, describe the major restrictions, and provide information about significant changes in restricted amounts.

For special purpose financial statements, GAAP disclosure requirements that are not relevant to the measurement of the item need not be considered. To illustrate:

- Fair value disclosures for debt and equity securities would not be relevant when the basis of presentation does not adjust the cost of such securities to their fair value.
- Disclosures related to actuarial calculations for contributions to defined benefit plans would not be relevant in financial statements prepared in accordance with the cash or tax basis of accounting.
- Disclosures related to the use of estimates would not be relevant in a presentation that has no estimates, such as the cash basis of accounting.

Special purpose financial statements may not include a statement of cash flows. If a presentation of cash receipts and disbursements is presented in a format similar to a statement of cash flows or if the entity chooses to present such a statement, the statement would either conform to the requirements for a GAAP presentation or communicate their substance. As an example, the statement of cash flows might disclose noncash acquisitions through captions on its face.

.A35

Exhibit—Illustrations of Auditor's Reports on Special Purpose Financial Statements (Ref: par. .A16)

Illustration 1—An Auditor's Report on a Complete Set of Financial Statements Prepared in Accordance With the Cash Basis of Accounting

Circumstances include the following:

- The financial statements have been prepared by management of the entity in accordance with the cash basis of accounting (that is, a special purpose framework).
- Management has a choice of financial reporting frameworks.[1]

Independent Auditor's Report

[*Appropriate Addressee*]

Report on the Financial Statements[2]

We have audited the accompanying financial statements of ABC Partnership, which comprise the statement of assets and liabilities arising from cash transactions as of December 31, 20X1, and the related statement of revenue collected and expenses paid for the year then ended, and the related notes to the financial statements.

Management's Responsibility for the Financial Statements

Management is responsible for the preparation and fair presentation of these financial statements in accordance with the cash basis of accounting described in Note X; this includes determining that the cash basis of accounting is an acceptable basis for the preparation of the financial statements in the circumstances. Management is also responsible for the design, implementation, and maintenance of internal control relevant to the preparation and fair presentation of financial statements that are free from material misstatement, whether due to fraud or error.

Auditor's Responsibility

Our responsibility is to express an opinion on these financial statements based on our audit. We conducted our audit in accordance with auditing standards generally accepted in the United States of America. Those standards require that we plan and perform the audit to obtain reasonable assurance about whether the financial statements are free from material misstatement.

An audit involves performing procedures to obtain audit evidence about the amounts and disclosures in the financial statements. The procedures selected depend on the auditor's judgment, including the assessment of the risks of material misstatement of the financial statements, whether due to fraud or error. In making those risk assessments, the auditor considers internal control relevant to the partnership's preparation and fair presentation of the financial statements in order to design audit procedures that are appropriate in the circumstances, but not for the purpose of expressing an opinion on the effectiveness of the partnership's internal control.[3] Accordingly, we express no such

---

[1] If management does not have a choice of financial reporting frameworks, the auditor is not required by paragraph .18*a* to make reference to management's responsibility for determining that the applicable financial reporting framework is acceptable in the circumstances.

[2] The subtitle "Report on the Financial Statements" is unnecessary in circumstances when the second subtitle "Report on Other Legal and Regulatory Requirements" is not applicable.

[3] In circumstances when the auditor also has responsibility to express an opinion on the effectiveness of internal control in conjunction with the audit of the financial statements, this sentence would be worded as follows: "In making those risk assessments, the auditor considers internal

(continued)

opinion. An audit also includes evaluating the appropriateness of accounting policies used and the reasonableness of significant accounting estimates made by management, as well as evaluating the overall presentation of the financial statements.

We believe that the audit evidence we have obtained is sufficient and appropriate to provide a basis for our audit opinion.

Opinion

In our opinion, the financial statements referred to above present fairly, in all material respects, the assets and liabilities arising from cash transactions of ABC Partnership as of December 31, 20X1, and its revenue collected and expenses paid during the year then ended in accordance with the cash basis of accounting described in Note X.

Basis of Accounting[4]

We draw attention to Note X of the financial statements, which describes the basis of accounting. The financial statements are prepared on the cash basis of accounting, which is a basis of accounting other than accounting principles generally accepted in the United States of America. Our opinion is not modified with respect to this matter.

Report on Other Legal and Regulatory Requirements

[*Form and content of this section of the auditor's report will vary depending on the nature of the auditor's other reporting responsibilities.*]

[*Auditor's signature*]

[*Auditor's city and state*]

[*Date of the auditor's report*]

(footnote continued)

control relevant to the entity's preparation and fair presentation of the financial statements in order to design audit procedures that are appropriate in the circumstances." In addition, the next sentence, "Accordingly, we express no such opinion." would not be included.

[4] Another appropriate heading may be used.

Illustration 2—An Auditor's Report on a Complete Set of Financial Statements Prepared in Accordance With the Tax Basis of Accounting

Circumstances include the following:

- The financial statements have been prepared by management of a partnership in accordance with the basis of accounting the partnership uses for income tax purposes (that is, a special purpose framework).
- Based on the partnership agreement, management does not have a choice of financial reporting frameworks.[1]

Independent Auditor's Report

[*Appropriate Addressee*]

Report on the Financial Statements[2]

We have audited the accompanying financial statements of ABC Partnership, which comprise the statements of assets, liabilities, and capital-income tax basis as of December 31, 20X1, and the related statements of revenue and expenses—income tax basis and of changes in partners' capital accounts—income tax basis for the year then ended, and the related notes to the financial statements.

Management's Responsibility for the Financial Statements

Management is responsible for the preparation and fair presentation of these financial statements in accordance with the basis of accounting the Partnership uses for income tax purposes; this includes the design, implementation, and maintenance of internal control relevant to the preparation and fair presentation of financial statements that are free from material misstatement, whether due to fraud or error.

Auditor's Responsibility

Our responsibility is to express an opinion on these financial statements based on our audit. We conducted our audit in accordance with auditing standards generally accepted in the United States of America. Those standards require that we plan and perform the audit to obtain reasonable assurance about whether the financial statements are free from material misstatement.

An audit involves performing procedures to obtain audit evidence about the amounts and disclosures in the financial statements. The procedures selected depend on the auditor's judgment, including the assessment of the risks of material misstatement of the financial statements, whether due to fraud or error. In making those risk assessments, the auditor considers internal control relevant to the partnership's preparation and fair presentation of the financial statements in order to design audit procedures that are appropriate in the circumstances, but not for the purpose of expressing an opinion on the

---

[1] If management has a choice of financial reporting frameworks, paragraph .18*a* requires that the explanation of management's responsibility for the financial statements also make reference to its responsibility for determining that the applicable financial reporting framework is acceptable in the circumstances.

[2] The subtitle "Report on the Financial Statements" is unnecessary in circumstances when the second subtitle "Report on Other Legal and Regulatory Requirements" is not applicable.

effectiveness of the partnership's internal control.[3] Accordingly, we express no such opinion. An audit also includes evaluating the appropriateness of accounting policies used and the reasonableness of significant accounting estimates made by management, as well as evaluating the overall presentation of the financial statements.

We believe that the audit evidence we have obtained is sufficient and appropriate to provide a basis for our audit opinion.

Opinion

In our opinion, the financial statements referred to above present fairly, in all material respects, the assets, liabilities, and capital of ABC Partnership as of December 31, 20X1, and its revenue and expenses and changes in partners' capital accounts for the year then ended in accordance with the basis of accounting the Partnership uses for income tax purposes described in Note X.

Basis of Accounting[4]

We draw attention to Note X of the financial statements, which describes the basis of accounting. The financial statements are prepared on the basis of accounting the Partnership uses for income tax purposes, which is a basis of accounting other than accounting principles generally accepted in the United States of America. Our opinion is not modified with respect to this matter.

Report on Other Legal and Regulatory Requirements

[*Form and content of this section of the auditor's report will vary depending on the nature of the auditor's other reporting responsibilities.*]

[*Auditor's signature*]

[*Auditor's city and state*]

[*Date of the auditor's report*]

---

[3] In circumstances when the auditor also has responsibility to express an opinion on the effectiveness of internal control in conjunction with the audit of the financial statements, this sentence would be worded as follows: "In making those risk assessments, the auditor considers internal control relevant to the entity's preparation and fair presentation of the financial statements in order to design audit procedures that are appropriate in the circumstances." In addition, the next sentence, "Accordingly, we express no such opinion." would not be included.

[4] Another appropriate heading may be used.

Illustration 3—An Auditor's Report on a Complete Set of Financial Statements Prepared in Accordance With a Regulatory Basis of Accounting (the Financial Statements Together With the Auditor's Report Are Not Intended for General Use)

Circumstances include the following:

- The financial statements have been prepared by management of the entity in accordance with the financial reporting provisions established by a regulatory agency (that is, a special purpose framework).
- The financial statements together with the auditor's report are not intended for general use.
- Based on the regulatory requirements, management does not have a choice of financial reporting frameworks.[1]

Independent Auditor's Report

[*Appropriate Addressee*]

Report on the Financial Statements[2]

We have audited the accompanying financial statements of ABC City, Any State, which comprise cash and unencumbered cash for each fund as of December 31, 20X1, and the related statements of cash receipts and disbursements and disbursements—budget and actual for the year then ended, and the related notes to the financial statements.

Management's Responsibility for the Financial Statements

Management is responsible for the preparation and fair presentation of these financial statements in accordance with the financial reporting provisions of Section Y of Regulation Z of Any State. Management is also responsible for the design, implementation, and maintenance of internal control relevant to the preparation and fair presentation of financial statements that are free from material misstatement, whether due to fraud or error.

Auditor's Responsibility

Our responsibility is to express an opinion on these financial statements based on our audit. We conducted our audit in accordance with auditing standards generally accepted in the United States of America. Those standards require that we plan and perform the audit to obtain reasonable assurance about whether the financial statements are free from material misstatement.

An audit involves performing procedures to obtain audit evidence about the amounts and disclosures in the financial statements. The procedures selected depend on the auditor's judgment, including the assessment of the risks of material misstatement of the financial statements, whether due to fraud or error. In making those risk assessments, the auditor considers internal control relevant to the entity's preparation and fair presentation of the financial statements in order to design audit procedures that are appropriate in the circumstances, but not for the purpose of expressing an opinion on the effectiveness of the

---

[1] If management has a choice of financial reporting frameworks, paragraph .18*a* requires that the explanation of management's responsibility for the financial statements also make reference to its responsibility for determining that the applicable financial reporting framework is acceptable in the circumstances.

[2] The subtitle "Report on the Financial Statements" is unnecessary in circumstances when the second subtitle "Report on Other Legal and Regulatory Requirements" is not applicable.

entity's internal control.[3] Accordingly, we express no such opinion. An audit also includes evaluating the appropriateness of accounting policies used and the reasonableness of significant accounting estimates made by management, as well as evaluating the overall presentation of the financial statements.

We believe that the audit evidence we have obtained is sufficient and appropriate to provide a basis for our audit opinion.

Opinion

In our opinion, the financial statements referred to above present fairly, in all material respects, the cash and unencumbered cash of each fund of ABC City as of December 31, 20X1, and their respective cash receipts and disbursements, and budgetary results for the year then ended in accordance with the financial reporting provisions of Section Y of Regulation Z of Any State described in Note X.

Basis of Accounting[4]

We draw attention to Note X of the financial statements, which describes the basis of accounting. As described in Note X to the financial statements, the financial statements are prepared by ABC City on the basis of the financial reporting provisions of Section Y of Regulation Z of Any State, which is a basis of accounting other than accounting principles generally accepted in the United States of America, to meet the requirements of Any State. Our opinion is not modified with respect to this matter.

Restriction on Use[5]

Our report is intended solely for the information and use of ABC City and Any State and is not intended to be and should not be used by anyone other than these specified parties.

Report on Other Legal and Regulatory Requirements

[*Form and content of this section of the auditor's report will vary depending on the nature of the auditor's other reporting responsibilities.*]

[*Auditor's signature*]

[*Auditor's city and state*]

[*Date of the auditor's report*]

---

[3] In circumstances when the auditor also has responsibility to express an opinion on the effectiveness of internal control in conjunction with the audit of the financial statements, this sentence would be worded as follows: "In making those risk assessments, the auditor considers internal control relevant to the entity's preparation and fair presentation of the financial statements in order to design audit procedures that are appropriate in the circumstances." In addition, the next sentence, "Accordingly, we express no such opinion." would not be included.

[4] Another appropriate heading may be used.

[5] Another appropriate heading may be used.

Illustration 4—An Auditor's Report on a Complete Set of Financial Statements Prepared in Accordance With a Regulatory Basis of Accounting (the Financial Statements Together With the Auditor's Report Are Intended for General Use)

Circumstances include the following:

- The financial statements have been prepared by management of the entity in accordance with the financial reporting provisions established by a regulatory agency (that is, a special purpose framework).
- The financial statements together with the auditor's report are intended for general use.
- Based on the regulatory requirements, management does not have a choice of financial reporting frameworks.[1]
- The variances between the regulatory basis of accounting and accounting principles generally accepted in the United States of America (U.S. GAAP) are not reasonably determinable and are presumed to be material.

Independent Auditor's Report

[*Appropriate Addressee*]

Report on the Financial Statements[2]

We have audited the accompanying financial statements of XYZ City, Any State, which comprise cash and unencumbered cash for each fund as of December 31, 20X1, and the related statements of cash receipts and disbursements and disbursements—budget and actual for the year then ended, and the related notes to the financial statements.

Management's Responsibility for the Financial Statements

Management is responsible for the preparation and fair presentation of these financial statements in accordance with the financial reporting provisions of Section Y of Regulation Z of Any State. Management is also responsible for the design, implementation, and maintenance of internal control relevant to the preparation and fair presentation of financial statements that are free from material misstatement, whether due to fraud or error.

Auditor's Responsibility

Our responsibility is to express an opinion on these financial statements based on our audit. We conducted our audit in accordance with auditing standards generally accepted in the United States of America. Those standards require that we plan and perform the audit to obtain reasonable assurance about whether the financial statements are free from material misstatement.

An audit involves performing procedures to obtain audit evidence about the amounts and disclosures in the financial statements. The procedures selected depend on the auditor's judgment, including the assessment of the risks of material misstatement of the financial statements, whether due to fraud or error.

---

[1] If management has a choice of financial reporting frameworks, paragraph .18*a* requires that the explanation of management's responsibility for the financial statements also make reference to its responsibility for determining that the applicable financial reporting framework is acceptable in the circumstances.

[2] The subtitle "Report on the Financial Statements" is unnecessary in circumstances when the second subtitle "Report on Other Legal and Regulatory Requirements" is not applicable.

In making those risk assessments, the auditor considers internal control relevant to the entity's preparation and fair presentation of the financial statements in order to design audit procedures that are appropriate in the circumstances, but not for the purpose of expressing an opinion on the effectiveness of the entity's internal control.[3] Accordingly, we express no such opinion. An audit also includes evaluating the appropriateness of accounting policies used and the reasonableness of significant accounting estimates made by management, as well as evaluating the overall presentation of the financial statements.

We believe that the audit evidence we have obtained is sufficient and appropriate to provide a basis for our audit opinions.

Basis for Adverse Opinion on U.S. Generally Accepted Accounting Principles

As described in Note X of the financial statements, the financial statements are prepared by XYZ City on the basis of the financial reporting provisions of Section Y of Regulation Z of Any State, which is a basis of accounting other than accounting principles generally accepted in the United States of America, to meet the requirements of Any State.

The effects on the financial statements of the variances between the regulatory basis of accounting described in Note X and accounting principles generally accepted in the United States of America, although not reasonably determinable, are presumed to be material.

Adverse Opinion on U.S. Generally Accepted Accounting Principles

In our opinion, because of the significance of the matter discussed in the "Basis for Adverse Opinion on U.S. Generally Accepted Accounting Principles" paragraph, the financial statements referred to above do not present fairly, in accordance with accounting principles generally accepted in the United States of America, the financial position of each fund of XYZ City as of December 31, 20X1, or changes in financial position or cash flows thereof for the year then ended.

Opinion on Regulatory Basis of Accounting

In our opinion, the financial statements referred to above present fairly, in all material respects, the cash and unencumbered cash of each fund of XYZ City as of December 31, 20X1, and their respective cash receipts and disbursements, and budgetary results for the year then ended in accordance with the financial reporting provisions of Section Y of Regulation Z of Any State described in Note X.

Report on Other Legal and Regulatory Requirements

[*Form and content of this section of the auditor's report will vary depending on the nature of the auditor's other reporting responsibilities.*]

[*Auditor's signature*]

[*Auditor's city and state*]

[*Date of the auditor's report*]

---

[3] In circumstances when the auditor also has responsibility to express an opinion on the effectiveness of internal control in conjunction with the audit of the financial statements, this sentence would be worded as follows: "In making those risk assessments, the auditor considers internal control relevant to the entity's preparation and fair presentation of the financial statements in order to design audit procedures that are appropriate in the circumstances." In addition, the next sentence, "Accordingly, we express no such opinion." would not be included.

Illustration 5—An Auditor's Report on a Complete Set of Financial Statements Prepared in Accordance With a Contractual Basis of Accounting

Circumstances include the following:

- The financial statements have been prepared by management of the entity in accordance with a contractual basis of accounting (that is, a special purpose framework) to comply with the provisions of that contract.
- Based on the provisions of the contract, management does not have a choice of financial reporting frameworks.[1]

Independent Auditor's Report

[*Appropriate Addressee*]

Report on the Financial Statements[2]

We have audited the accompanying financial statements of ABC Company, which comprise the assets and liabilities-contractual basis as of December 31, 20X1, and the revenues and expenses—contractual basis, changes in equity—contractual basis, and cash flows—contractual basis for the year then ended, and the related notes to the financial statements.

Management's Responsibility for the Financial Statements

Management is responsible for the preparation and fair presentation of these financial statements in accordance with the financial reporting provisions of Section Z of the contract between ABC Company and DEF Company dated January 1, 20X1 (the contract). Management is also responsible for the design, implementation, and maintenance of internal control relevant to the preparation and fair presentation of financial statements that are free from material misstatement, whether due to fraud or error.

Auditor's Responsibility

Our responsibility is to express an opinion on these financial statements based on our audit. We conducted our audit in accordance with auditing standards generally accepted in the United States of America. Those standards require that we plan and perform the audit to obtain reasonable assurance about whether the financial statements are free from material misstatement.

An audit involves performing procedures to obtain audit evidence about the amounts and disclosures in the financial statements. The procedures selected depend on the auditor's judgment, including the assessment of the risks of material misstatement of the financial statements, whether due to fraud or error. In making those risk assessments, the auditor considers internal control relevant to the entity's preparation and fair presentation of the financial statements in order to design audit procedures that are appropriate in the circumstances, but not for the purpose of expressing an opinion on the effectiveness of the

---

[1] If management has a choice of financial reporting frameworks, paragraph .18*a* requires that the explanation of management's responsibility for the financial statements also make reference to its responsibility for determining that the applicable financial reporting framework is acceptable in the circumstances.

[2] The subtitle "Report on the Financial Statements" is unnecessary in circumstances when the second subtitle "Report on Other Legal and Regulatory Requirements" is not applicable.

entity's internal control.[3] Accordingly, we express no such opinion. An audit also includes evaluating the appropriateness of accounting policies used and the reasonableness of significant accounting estimates made by management, as well as evaluating the overall presentation of the financial statements.

We believe that the audit evidence we have obtained is sufficient and appropriate to provide a basis for our audit opinion.

Opinion

In our opinion, the financial statements referred to above present fairly, in all material respects, the assets and liabilities of ABC Company as of December 31, 20X1, and revenues, expenses, changes in equity, and cash flows for the year then ended in accordance with the financial reporting provisions of Section Z of the contract.

Basis of Accounting[4]

We draw attention to Note X of the financial statements, which describes the basis of accounting. The financial statements are prepared by ABC Company on the basis of the financial reporting provisions of Section Z of the contract, which is a basis of accounting other than accounting principles generally accepted in the United States of America, to comply with the financial reporting provisions of the contract referred to above. Our opinion is not modified with respect to this matter.

Restriction on Use[5]

Our report is intended solely for the information and use of ABC Company and DEF Company and is not intended to be and should not be used by anyone other than these specified parties.

Report on Other Legal and Regulatory Requirements

[*Form and content of this section of the auditor's report will vary depending on the nature of the auditor's other reporting responsibilities.*]

[*Auditor's signature*]

[*Auditor's city and state*]

[*Date of the auditor's report*]

---

[3] In circumstances when the auditor also has responsibility to express an opinion on the effectiveness of internal control in conjunction with the audit of the financial statements, this sentence would be worded as follows: "In making those risk assessments, the auditor considers internal control relevant to the entity's preparation and fair presentation of the financial statements in order to design audit procedures that are appropriate in the circumstances." In addition, the next sentence, "Accordingly, we express no such opinion." would not be included.

[4] Another appropriate heading may be used.

[5] Another appropriate heading may be used.

AU-C Section 805 *

Special Considerations—Audits of Single Financial Statements and Specific Elements, Accounts, or Items of a Financial Statement

Source: SAS No. 122.

Effective for audits of single financial statements or specific elements, accounts, or items of a financial statement as of or for periods ending on or after December 15, 2012.

Introduction

Scope of This Section

.01 AU-C sections 200–700 apply to an audit of financial statements and are to be adapted as necessary in the circumstances when applied to audits of other historical financial information. This section addresses special considerations in the application of those AU-C sections to an audit of a single financial statement or of a specific element, account, or item of a financial statement. The single financial statement or the specific element, account, or item of a financial statement may be prepared in accordance with a general or special purpose framework. If prepared in accordance with a special purpose framework, section 800, *Special Considerations—Audits of Financial Statements Prepared in Accordance With Special Purpose Frameworks*, also applies to the audit. (Ref: par. .A1–.A3)

.02 This section does not apply to the report of a component auditor issued as a result of work performed on the financial information of a component at the request of a group engagement team for purposes of an audit of group financial statements (see section 600, *Special Considerations—Audits of Group Financial Statements [Including the Work of Component Auditors]*).

.03 This section does not override the requirements of the other AU-C sections nor does it purport to address all special considerations that may be relevant in the circumstances of the engagement.

Effective Date

.04 This section is effective for audits of single financial statements or specific elements, accounts, or items of a financial statement as of or for periods ending on or after December 15, 2012.

---

* This section has been codified using an "AU-C" identifier instead of an "AU" identifier. "AU-C" is a temporary identifier to avoid confusion with references to existing "AU" sections, which will remain in AICPA *Professional Standards* through 2013. The "AU-C" identifier will revert to "AU" in 2014, by which time substantially all engagements for which the "AU" sections were still effective are expected to be completed.

Objective

.05 The objective of the auditor, when applying generally accepted auditing standards (GAAS) in an audit of a single financial statement or of a specific element, account, or item of a financial statement, is to address appropriately the special considerations that are relevant to

a. the acceptance of the engagement;

b. the planning and performance of that engagement; and

c. forming an opinion and reporting on the single financial statement or the specific element, account, or item of a financial statement.

Definitions

.06 For purposes of this section, reference to

a. an *element of a financial statement* or an *element* means an *element, account, or item of a financial statement*. (Ref: par. .A4)

b. a *single financial statement* or a *specific element of a financial statement* includes the related notes. The related notes ordinarily comprise a summary of significant accounting policies and other explanatory information relevant to the financial statement or the specific element.

.07 Reference to *generally accepted accounting principles* (GAAP) in GAAS means GAAP promulgated by bodies designated by the Council of the AICPA pursuant to Rule 202, *Compliance With Standards* (ET sec. 202 par. .01), and Rule 203, *Accounting Principles* (ET sec. 203 par. .01), of the AICPA Code of Professional Conduct.

Requirements

Considerations When Accepting the Engagement

Application of GAAS (Ref: par. .A5–.A7)

.08 Section 200, *Overall Objectives of the Independent Auditor and the Conduct of an Audit in Accordance With Generally Accepted Auditing Standards*, requires the auditor to comply with all AU-C sections relevant to the audit.[1] In the case of an audit of a single financial statement or a specific element of a financial statement, this requirement applies irrespective of whether the auditor is also engaged to audit the entity's complete set of financial statements.

.09 If the auditor is not also engaged to audit the entity's complete set of financial statements, the auditor should determine whether the audit of a single financial statement or a specific element of those financial statements in accordance with GAAS is practicable. The auditor should also determine whether the auditor will be able to perform procedures on interrelated items, as required by paragraph .13.

---

[1] Paragraph .20 of section 200, *Overall Objectives of the Independent Auditor and the Conduct of an Audit in Accordance With Generally Accepted Auditing Standards.*

Acceptability of the Financial Reporting Framework (Ref: par. .A8–.A11)

.10 Section 210, *Terms of Engagement*, requires the auditor to determine the acceptability of the financial reporting framework applied in the preparation of the financial statements.[2] In the case of an audit of a single financial statement or a specific element of a financial statement, the auditor should obtain an understanding of

a. the purpose for which the single financial statement or specific element of a financial statement is prepared,

b. the intended users, and

c. the steps taken by management to determine that the application of the financial reporting framework is acceptable in the circumstances.

.11 The auditor's determination required by paragraph .10 should include consideration of whether the application of the financial reporting framework will result in a presentation that provides adequate disclosures to enable the intended users to understand the information conveyed in the financial statement or the specific element and the effect of material transactions and events on the information conveyed in the financial statement or the specific element.

Considerations When Planning and Performing the Audit

.12 Section 200 states that GAAS is written in the context of an audit of financial statements; it is to be adapted as necessary in the circumstances when applied to audits of other historical financial information.[3] In planning and performing the audit of a single financial statement or a specific element of a financial statement, the auditor should adapt all AU-C sections relevant to the audit as necessary in the circumstances of the engagement. (Ref: par. .A12–.A14)

.13 In the case of an audit of a single financial statement or a specific element of a financial statement, the auditor should perform procedures on interrelated items as necessary to meet the objective of the audit. In the case of an audit of a specific element of a financial statement (Ref: par. .A15)

a. the auditor should, if the specific element is, or is based upon, the entity's stockholders' equity or the equivalent, perform procedures necessary to obtain sufficient appropriate audit evidence to enable the auditor to express an opinion about financial position, excluding matters related to classification or disclosure that are not relevant to the audit of the specific element.

b. the auditor should, if the specific element is, or is based upon, the entity's net income or the equivalent, perform procedures necessary to obtain sufficient appropriate audit evidence to enable the auditor to express an opinion about financial position and results of operations, excluding matters related to classification or disclosure that are not relevant to the audit of the specific element.

Materiality (Ref: par. .A16)

.14 Section 320, *Materiality in Planning and Performing an Audit*, requires the auditor to determine, when establishing the overall audit strategy,

---

[2] Paragraph .06*a* of section 210, *Terms of Engagement*.

[3] Paragraph .02 of section 200.

materiality for the financial statements as a whole.[4] In the case of an audit of a single financial statement, the auditor should determine materiality for the single financial statement being reported on rather than for the complete set of financial statements. In the case of an audit of one or more specific elements of a financial statement, the auditor should determine materiality for each individual element reported on rather than the aggregate of all elements or the complete set of financial statements.

Forming an Opinion and Reporting Considerations

.15 When forming an opinion and reporting on a single financial statement or a specific element of a financial statement, the auditor should apply the requirements in section 700, *Forming an Opinion and Reporting on Financial Statements*, adapted as necessary in the circumstances of the engagement. (Ref: par. .A17–.A18)

Reporting on the Entity's Complete Set of Financial Statements and a Single Financial Statement or a Specific Element of Those Financial Statements

.16 If, in conjunction with an engagement to audit the entity's complete set of financial statements, the auditor undertakes an engagement to audit a single financial statement or a specific element of a financial statement, the auditor should

a. issue a separate auditor's report and express a separate opinion for each engagement.

b. indicate in the report on a specific element of a financial statement the date of the auditor's report on the complete set of financial statements and the nature of opinion expressed on those financial statements under an appropriate heading.

.17 Except as required by paragraph .21, an audited single financial statement or an audited specific element of a financial statement may be published together with the entity's audited complete set of financial statements, provided that the presentation of the single financial statement or the specific element is sufficiently differentiated from the complete set of financial statements. The auditor should also differentiate the report on the single financial statement or the specific element of a financial statement from the report on the complete set of financial statements.

.18 If the auditor concludes that the presentation of the audited single financial statement or the audited specific element does not differentiate it sufficiently from the complete set of financial statements, as described in paragraph .17, the auditor should ask management to remedy the situation. The auditor should not release the auditor's report containing the opinion on the single financial statement or the specific element of a financial statement until satisfied with the differentiation.

Modified Opinion, Emphasis-of-Matter Paragraph, or Other-Matter Paragraph in the Auditor's Report on the Entity's Complete Set of Financial Statements

.19 If the opinion in the auditor's report on an entity's complete set of financial statements is modified, the auditor should determine the effect that

---

[4] Paragraph .10 of section 320, *Materiality in Planning and Performing an Audit.*

this may have on the auditor's opinion on a single financial statement or a specific element of those financial statements, in accordance with section 705, *Modifications to the Opinion in the Independent Auditor's Report*.

.20 In the case of an audit of a specific element of a financial statement, if the auditor's modified opinion on the entity's complete set of financial statements as a whole is relevant to the audit of the specific element, the auditor should (Ref: par. .A19–.A20)

a. express an adverse opinion on the specific element when the modification of the auditor's opinion on the complete set of financial statements as a whole arises from a material misstatement in such financial statements.

b. disclaim an opinion on the specific element when the modification of the auditor's opinion on the complete set of financial statements as a whole arises from an inability to obtain sufficient appropriate audit evidence.

.21 If the auditor concludes that it is necessary to express an adverse opinion or disclaim an opinion on the entity's complete set of financial statements as a whole, an unmodified opinion on a specific element in the same auditor's report would contradict the adverse opinion or disclaimer of opinion on the entity's complete set of financial statements as a whole and would be tantamount to expressing a piecemeal opinion. In the context of a separate audit of a specific element that is included in those financial statements, when the auditor nevertheless considers it appropriate to express an unmodified opinion on that specific element, the auditor should only do so if

a. that opinion is expressed in an auditor's report that is neither published together with nor otherwise accompanies the auditor's report containing the adverse opinion or disclaimer of opinion and

b. the specific element does not constitute a major portion of the entity's complete set of financial statements or the specific element is not, or is not based upon, the entity's stockholders' equity or net income or the equivalent.

.22 A single financial statement is deemed to constitute a major portion of a complete set of financial statements. Therefore, the auditor should not express an unmodified opinion on a single financial statement of a complete set of financial statements if the auditor has expressed an adverse opinion or disclaimed an opinion on the complete set of financial statements as a whole, even if the auditor's report on the single financial statement is neither published together with nor otherwise accompanies the auditor's report containing the adverse opinion or disclaimer of opinion. (Ref: par. .A21)

.23 If the auditor's report on an entity's complete set of financial statements includes an emphasis-of-matter paragraph or an other-matter paragraph that is relevant to the audit of the single financial statement or the specific element, the auditor should include a similar emphasis-of-matter paragraph or an other-matter paragraph in the auditor's report on the single financial statement or the specific element, in accordance with section 706, *Emphasis-of-Matter Paragraphs and Other-Matter Paragraphs in the Independent Auditor's Report*. (Ref: par. .A20)

Reporting on an Incomplete Presentation but One That Is Otherwise in Accordance With Generally Accepted Accounting Principles (Ref: par. .A22–.A23)

.24 When the auditor reports on an incomplete presentation but one that is otherwise in accordance with GAAP, the auditor should include an emphasis-of-matter paragraph[5] in the auditor's report that

a. states the purpose for which the presentation is prepared and refers to a note in the financial statements that describes the basis of presentation and

b. indicates that the presentation is not intended to be a complete presentation of the entity's assets, liabilities, revenues, or expenses.

Application and Other Explanatory Material

Scope of This Section (Ref: par. .01)

.A1 Section 200 defines the term *historical financial information* as information expressed in financial terms regarding a particular entity, derived primarily from that entity's accounting system, about economic events occurring in past time periods or about economic conditions or circumstances at points in time in the past. It also defines the term *financial statements* as a structured representation of historical financial information, including related notes, intended to communicate an entity's economic resources or obligations at a point in time or the changes therein for a period of time in accordance with a financial reporting framework. The term *financial statements* ordinarily refers to a complete set of financial statements as determined by the requirements of the applicable financial reporting framework, but can also refer to a single financial statement.[6]

.A2 Paragraph .A9 of section 200 provides guidance on what constitutes a complete set of financial statements and also provides the following examples of single financial statements, each of which would include related notes:

- Balance sheet
- Statement of income or statement of operations
- Statement of retained earnings
- Statement of cash flows
- Statement of assets and liabilities
- Statement of changes in owner's equity
- Statement of revenue and expenses
- Statement of operations by product lines

.A3 An attest engagement other than an audit of historical financial information is performed in accordance with Statements on Standards for Attestation Engagements. For example, AT section 201, *Agreed-Upon Procedures Engagements*, applies when reporting on the results of applying agreed-upon procedures to one or more specific elements of a financial statement, and

---

[5] Paragraphs .06–.07 of section 706, *Emphasis-of-Matter Paragraphs and Other-Matter Paragraphs in the Independent Auditor's Report.*

[6] Paragraph .14 of section 200.

AT section 101, *Attest Engagements*, provides guidance when reporting on a review of one or more specific elements of a financial statement.

Definitions

Element of a Financial Statement (Ref: par. .06)

.A4 The appendix, "Examples of Specific Elements, Accounts, or Items of a Financial Statement," lists examples of an element of a financial statement.

Considerations When Accepting the Engagement

Application of GAAS (Ref: par. .08–.09)

.A5 Section 200 requires the auditor to comply with (*a*) relevant ethical requirements relating to financial statement audit engagements and (*b*) all AU-C sections relevant to the audit. It also requires the auditor to comply with each requirement of an AU-C section, unless, in the circumstances of the audit, the entire AU-C section is not relevant or the requirement is not relevant because it is conditional and the condition does not exist. In rare circumstances, the auditor may judge it necessary to depart from a relevant presumptively mandatory requirement in an AU-C section by performing alternative audit procedures to achieve the intent of that requirement.[7]

Complying With Relevant Requirements

.A6 Compliance with the requirements of AU-C sections relevant to the audit of a single financial statement or a specific element of a financial statement may not be practicable when the auditor is not also engaged to audit the entity's complete set of financial statements. In such cases, the auditor often does not have the same understanding of the entity and its environment, including its internal control, as an auditor who also audits the entity's complete set of financial statements. The auditor also does not have the audit evidence about the general quality of the accounting records or other accounting information that would be acquired in an audit of the entity's complete set of financial statements. Accordingly, the auditor may need further evidence to corroborate audit evidence acquired from the accounting records. Also see paragraph .A15.

.A7 In the case of an audit of a specific element of a financial statement, certain AU-C sections require audit work that may be disproportionate to the specific element being audited. For example, although the requirements of section 570, *The Auditor's Consideration of an Entity's Ability to Continue as a Going Concern*, are likely to be relevant in the circumstances of an audit of a schedule of accounts receivable (see paragraph .A12), complying with those requirements may not be practicable because of the audit effort required. If the auditor concludes that an audit of a single financial statement or a specific element of a financial statement in accordance with GAAS may not be practicable, the auditor may discuss with management whether another type of engagement might be more practicable, as described in paragraph .A3. [Revised, August 2012, to reflect conforming changes necessary due to the issuance of SAS No. 126.]

Acceptability of the Financial Reporting Framework (Ref: par. .10–.11)

.A8 In the case of an audit of a single financial statement or a specific element of a financial statement, the financial information needs of the intended

---

[7] Paragraphs .16, .20, and .24–.26 of section 200.

users are relevant in determining the acceptability of the financial reporting framework applied in the preparation of the single financial statement or the specific element.

.A9 A single financial statement or a specific element of a financial statement may be prepared in accordance with relevant requirements of a financial reporting framework established by an authorized or recognized standards-setting organization for the preparation of a complete set of financial statements (for example, accounting principles generally accepted in the United States of America [U.S. GAAP] or International Financial Reporting Standards promulgated by the International Accounting Standards Board). If this is the case, determination of the acceptability of the applicable framework may involve considering whether that framework includes all the requirements of the framework that are relevant to the presentation of a single financial statement or a specific element of a financial statement that provides adequate disclosures. The determination of the acceptability of the applicable framework may also include consideration of the following:

- Whether the applicable financial reporting framework is explicitly or implicitly restricted to the preparation of a complete set of financial statements.
- Whether the single financial statement or the specific element of a financial statement will
  - — comply fully with each of those requirements of the framework relevant to the particular financial statement or the particular element and the presentation of the financial statement or the specific element, including the related notes. For example, when reporting on a schedule of long-term debt prepared in accordance with U.S. GAAP relevant to that schedule, the schedule of long-term debt, including the related notes, would be comparable to such information in financial statements prepared in accordance with U.S. GAAP.
  - — provide, if necessary to achieve fair presentation, disclosures beyond those specifically required by the framework or, in extremely rare circumstances, depart from a requirement of the framework.[8] A single financial statement or a specific element of a financial statement, including the related notes, that achieves a fair presentation includes all informative disclosures that are appropriate for the applicable financial reporting framework, including matters that affect their use, understanding, and interpretation.

.A10 The auditor may be requested to audit an incomplete presentation but one that is otherwise in accordance with GAAP. For example, an entity wishing to sell a division or product line may present certain assets and liabilities, revenues, and expenses relating to the division or product line being sold. Incomplete presentations may also be required by a regulatory agency or a contract or an agreement. For example, a regulatory agency may require a schedule of gross income and certain expenses of an entity's real estate operation in which income and expenses are measured in accordance with GAAP, but *expenses* are defined to exclude certain items, such as interest, depreciation, and income taxes. Also, an acquisition agreement may specify a schedule

[8] See paragraph .14 of section 200 for a definition of *financial reporting framework*.

of gross assets and liabilities of the entity measured in accordance with GAAP but limited to the assets to be sold and liabilities to be transferred pursuant to the agreement. These types of presentations are generally regarded as single financial statements, even though certain items may be excluded only to the extent necessary to meet the purpose for which they were prepared. The requirement in paragraph .24 is designed to avoid misunderstandings about the purpose for which the presentation is prepared.

.A11 As indicated in paragraph .A10, incomplete presentations may be required by a regulatory agency or a contract or an agreement. Paragraphs .A2–.A3 of section 800 provide guidance on the acceptability of the financial reporting framework when the regulatory or contractual basis of accounting is based on a general purpose framework, such as GAAP. The auditor may determine that it is more appropriate for the description of the applicable financial reporting framework to refer to the regulatory or contractual basis of accounting, rather than make reference to GAAP. As indicated in paragraph .01, if the presentation is prepared in accordance with a special purpose framework, which includes the regulatory and contractual bases of accounting, section 800 also applies to the audit.

Considerations When Planning and Performing the Audit (Ref: par. .12–.13)

.A12 An AU-C section is relevant to the audit when the AU-C section is in effect and the circumstances addressed by the AU-C section exist.[9] Even when only a specific element of a financial statement is the subject of the audit, AU-C sections such as section 240, *Consideration of Fraud in a Financial Statement Audit*, section 550, *Related Parties*, and section 570 are, in principle, relevant. This is because the specific element could be misstated as a result of fraud, the effect of related party transactions, or the incorrect application of the going concern assumption under the applicable financial reporting framework. [Revised, August 2012, to reflect conforming changes necessary due to the issuance of SAS No. 126.]

.A13 Furthermore, GAAS is written in the context of an audit of financial statements; it is to be adapted as necessary in the circumstances when applied to the audit of a single financial statement or a specific element of a financial statement.[10] For example, written representations from management about the complete set of financial statements would be replaced by written representations about the presentation of the single financial statement or the specific element, in accordance with the applicable financial reporting framework.

.A14 When auditing a single financial statement or a specific element of a financial statement in conjunction with the audit of the entity's complete set of financial statements, the auditor may use audit evidence obtained as part of the audit of the entity's complete set of financial statements in the audit of the single financial statement or the specific element. GAAS, however, requires the auditor to plan and perform the audit of the single financial statement or specific element to obtain sufficient appropriate audit evidence on which to base the opinion on the single financial statement or the specific element.

---

[9] Paragraph .20 of section 200.

[10] Paragraph .02 of section 200.

.A15 The individual financial statements that comprise a complete set of financial statements, and many of the elements of those financial statements, including their related notes, are interrelated. For example, sales and receivables, inventory and payables, and buildings and equipment and depreciation each are interrelated. Accordingly, when auditing a single financial statement or a specific element of a financial statement, the auditor may not be able to consider the single financial statement or the specific element in isolation. Consequently, paragraph .13 requires the auditor to perform procedures on interrelated items as necessary to meet the objective of the audit. In the case of an audit of a specific element that is, or is based upon, the entity's stockholders' equity or net income (or the equivalents thereto), paragraph .13 requires the auditor to perform procedures necessary to obtain sufficient appropriate audit evidence about financial position, or financial position and results of operations, respectively, because of the interrelationship between the specific element and the balance sheet accounts and the income statement accounts. However, matters related to classification or disclosure may not be relevant to the audit of the specific element; therefore, audit procedures on such matters may not be necessary in an audit of a specific element.

Materiality (Ref: par. .14)

.A16 The materiality determined for a single financial statement or a specific element of a financial statement differs from the materiality determined for the entity's complete set of financial statements; this will affect the nature, timing, and extent of the audit procedures and the evaluation of uncorrected misstatements. In the case of an audit of a single financial statement, paragraph .14 requires the auditor to determine materiality for the single financial statement being reported on rather than for the complete set of financial statements. In the case of an audit of one or more specific elements of a financial statement, the auditor's opinion is on each of the specific elements; therefore, paragraph .14 requires the auditor to determine materiality for each individual element reported on rather than the aggregate of all elements or the complete set of financial statements. Consequently, an audit of one or more specific elements of a financial statement is usually more extensive than if the same information was being considered in conjunction with an audit of the complete set of financial statements.

Forming an Opinion and Reporting Considerations (Ref: par. .15)

.A17 Section 700 requires the auditor, in forming an opinion, to evaluate whether the financial statements provide adequate disclosures to enable the intended users to understand the effect of material transactions and events on the information conveyed in the financial statements.[11] In the case of an audit of a single financial statement or a specific element of a financial statement, it is important, in view of the requirements of the applicable financial reporting framework, that the disclosures enable the intended users to understand

- the information conveyed in the financial statement or the specific element and
- the effect of material transactions and events on the information conveyed in the financial statement or the specific element.

---

[11] Paragraph .16*e* of section 700, *Forming an Opinion and Reporting on Financial Statements.*

.A18 The exhibit, "Illustrations of Auditor's Reports on a Single Financial Statement and a Specific Element of a Financial Statements," contains illustrations of auditor's reports.

Modified Opinion, Emphasis-of-Matter Paragraph, or Other-Matter Paragraph in the Auditor's Report on the Entity's Complete Set of Financial Statements (Ref: par. .19–.23)

.A19 In the case of an audit of a specific element of a financial statement, if the opinion in the auditor's report on an entity's complete set of financial statements is modified and the modification is relevant to the audit of the specific element, the modification is material and pervasive with respect to the specific element. Modifications related to an interrelated item of the specific element may also be relevant to the audit of the specific element. Conversely, modifications related solely to classification or disclosure may not be relevant to the audit of the specific element.

.A20 Even when the modified opinion, emphasis-of-matter paragraph, or other-matter paragraph in the auditor's report on the entity's complete set of financial statements does not relate to the audited single financial statement or the audited element, the auditor may nevertheless deem it appropriate to refer to the modification in an other-matter paragraph in an auditor's report on the single financial statement or the specific element because the auditor judges it to be relevant to the users' understanding of the audited single financial statement or the audited element or the related auditor's report (see section 706).

.A21 In the auditor's report on an entity's complete set of financial statements, the expression of a disclaimer of opinion regarding the results of operations and cash flows, when relevant, and an unmodified opinion regarding the financial position are permitted because the disclaimer of opinion is being issued on the results of operations and cash flows only and not on the financial statements as a whole.[12]

Reporting on an Incomplete Presentation but One That Is Otherwise in Accordance With GAAP (Ref: par. .24)

.A22 As described in paragraph .A10, the auditor may be requested to audit an incomplete presentation but one that is otherwise in accordance with GAAP. When the auditor reports on an incomplete presentation but one that is otherwise in accordance with GAAP, paragraph .24 requires the auditor to include an emphasis-of-matter paragraph in the auditor's report, which alerts users as to the purpose of the presentation and that the presentation is incomplete. The exhibit illustrates such a paragraph.

.A23 If the presentation is prepared in accordance with a regulatory or contractual basis of accounting, the requirement in paragraph .24 does not apply. In such circumstances, refer to section 800. See also paragraph .A11 of this section.

---

[12] Paragraph .A17 of section 510, *Opening Balances—Initial Audit Engagements, Including Reaudit Engagements*, and paragraph .A17 of section 705, *Modifications to the Opinion in the Independent Auditor's Report*.

.A24

Appendix—Examples of Specific Elements, Accounts, or Items of a Financial Statement (Ref: par. .A4)

The following are examples of specific elements, accounts, or items of a financial statement:

- Accounts receivable; allowance for doubtful accounts receivable; inventory; the liability for accrued benefits of a private benefit plan; the recorded value of identified intangible assets; or the liability for incurred but not reported claims in an insurance portfolio, including related notes
- A schedule of externally managed assets and income of a private benefit plan, including related notes
- A schedule of disbursements regarding a lease property, including related notes
- A schedule of profit participation or employee bonuses, including related notes

.A25

Exhibit—Illustrations of Auditor's Reports on a Single Financial Statement and a Specific Element of a Financial Statement (Ref: par. .A18 and .A22)

Illustration 1—An Auditor's Report on a Single Financial Statement Prepared in Accordance With a General Purpose Framework

Circumstances include the following:

- Audit of a balance sheet (that is, a single financial statement).
- The balance sheet has been prepared by management of the entity in accordance with accounting principles generally accepted in the United States of America.

Independent Auditor's Report

[Appropriate Addressee]

Report on the Financial Statement[1]

We have audited the accompanying balance sheet of ABC Company as of December 31, 20X1, and the related notes (the financial statement).[2]

Management's Responsibility for the Financial Statement

Management is responsible for the preparation and fair presentation of this financial statement in accordance with accounting principles generally accepted in the United States of America; this includes the design, implementation, and maintenance of internal control relevant to the preparation and fair presentation of the financial statement that is free from material misstatement, whether due to fraud or error.

Auditor's Responsibility

Our responsibility is to express an opinion on the financial statement based on our audit. We conducted our audit in accordance with auditing standards generally accepted in the United States of America. Those standards require that we plan and perform the audit to obtain reasonable assurance about whether the financial statement is free from material misstatement.

An audit involves performing procedures to obtain audit evidence about the amounts and disclosures in the financial statement. The procedures selected depend on the auditor's judgment, including the assessment of the risks of material misstatement of the financial statement, whether due to fraud or error. In making those risk assessments, the auditor considers internal control relevant to the entity's preparation and fair presentation of the financial statement in order to design audit procedures that are appropriate in the circumstances, but not for the purpose of expressing an opinion on the effectiveness of the entity's internal control. Accordingly, we express no such opinion. An audit also includes evaluating the appropriateness of accounting policies used and the reasonableness of significant accounting estimates made by management, as well as evaluating the overall presentation of the financial statement.

We believe that the audit evidence we have obtained is sufficient and appropriate to provide a basis for our audit opinion.

Opinion

In our opinion, the financial statement referred to above presents fairly, in all material respects, the financial position of ABC Company as of December 31, 20X1, in accordance with accounting principles generally accepted in the United States of America.

---

[1] The subtitle "Report on the Financial Statement" is unnecessary in circumstances when the second subtitle, "Report on Other Legal and Regulatory Requirements," is not applicable.

[2] The auditor may refer to the financial statement as the *balance sheet*.

Report on Other Legal and Regulatory Requirements

[*Form and content of this section of the auditor's report will vary depending on the nature of the auditor's other reporting responsibilities.*]

[*Auditor's signature*]

[*Auditor's city and state*]

[*Date of the auditor's report*]

Illustration 2—An Auditor's Report on a Single Financial Statement Prepared in Accordance With a Special Purpose Framework

Circumstances include the following:

- Audit of a statement of cash receipts and disbursements (that is, a single financial statement).
- The financial statement has been prepared by management of the entity in accordance with the cash basis of accounting (a special purpose framework) to respond to a request for cash flow information received from a creditor.[1]
- Management has a choice of financial reporting frameworks.[2]

Independent Auditor's Report

[*Appropriate Addressee*]

Report on the Financial Statement[3]

We have audited the accompanying statement of cash receipts and disbursements of ABC Company for the year ended December 31, 20X1, and the related notes (the financial statement).[4]

Management's Responsibility for the Financial Statement

Management is responsible for the preparation and fair presentation of this financial statement in accordance with the cash basis of accounting described in Note X; this includes determining that the cash basis of accounting is an acceptable basis for the preparation of the financial statement in the circumstances. Management is also responsible for the design, implementation, and maintenance of internal control relevant to the preparation and fair presentation of the financial statement that is free from material misstatement, whether due to fraud or error.

Auditor's Responsibility

Our responsibility is to express an opinion on the financial statement based on our audit. We conducted our audit in accordance with auditing standards generally accepted in the United States of America. Those standards require that we plan and perform the audit to obtain reasonable assurance about whether the financial statement is free from material misstatement.

An audit involves performing procedures to obtain audit evidence about the amounts and disclosures in the financial statement. The procedures selected depend on the auditor's judgment, including the assessment of the risks of material misstatement of the financial statement, whether due to fraud or error. In making those risk assessments, the auditor considers internal control relevant to the entity's preparation and fair presentation of the financial statement in order to design audit procedures that are appropriate in the circumstances, but not for the purpose of expressing an opinion on the effectiveness of the entity's internal control. Accordingly, we express no such opinion. An audit also

---

[1] Section 800, *Special Considerations—Audits of Financial Statements Prepared in Accordance With Special Purpose Frameworks*, contains requirements and guidance on the form and content of financial statements prepared in accordance with a special purpose framework.

[2] Paragraph .18*a* of section 800.

[3] The subtitle "Report on the Financial Statement" is unnecessary in circumstances when the second subtitle, "Report on Other Legal and Regulatory Requirements," is not applicable.

[4] The auditor may refer to the financial statement as the *statement of cash receipts and disbursements*.

includes evaluating the appropriateness of accounting policies used and the reasonableness of significant accounting estimates made by management, as well as evaluating the overall presentation of the financial statement.

We believe that the audit evidence we have obtained is sufficient and appropriate to provide a basis for our audit opinion.

Opinion

In our opinion, the financial statement referred to above presents fairly, in all material respects, the cash receipts and disbursements of ABC Company for the year ended December 31, 20X1, in accordance with the cash basis of accounting described in Note X.

Basis of Accounting[5]

We draw attention to Note X to the financial statement, which describes the basis of accounting. The financial statement is prepared on the cash basis of accounting, which is a basis of accounting other than accounting principles generally accepted in the United States of America. Our opinion is not modified with respect to this matter.

Report on Other Legal and Regulatory Requirements

[*Form and content of this section of the auditor's report will vary depending on the nature of the auditor's other reporting responsibilities.*]

[*Auditor's signature*]

[*Auditor's city and state*]

[*Date of the auditor's report*]

---

[5] Another appropriate heading may be used.

Illustration 3—An Auditor's Report on a Specific Element, Account, or Item of a Financial Statement Prepared in Accordance With a General Purpose Framework

Circumstances include the following:

- Audit of a schedule of accounts receivable (that is, a specific element, account, or item of a financial statement).
- The schedule of accounts receivable has been prepared by management of the entity in accordance with accounting principles generally accepted in the United States of America.
- The audit of the schedule of accounts receivable was performed in conjunction with an engagement to audit the entity's complete set of financial statements. The opinion on those financial statements was not modified, and the report did not include an emphasis-of-matter paragraph or other-matter paragraph.

Independent Auditor's Report

[*Appropriate Addressee*]

Report on the Schedule[1]

We have audited the accompanying schedule of accounts receivable of ABC Company as of December 31, 20X1, and the related notes (the schedule).[2]

Management's Responsibility for the Schedule

Management is responsible for the preparation and fair presentation of this schedule in accordance with accounting principles generally accepted in the United States of America; this includes the design, implementation, and maintenance of internal control relevant to the preparation and fair presentation of the schedule that is free from material misstatement, whether due to fraud or error.

Auditor's Responsibility

Our responsibility is to express an opinion on the schedule based on our audit. We conducted our audit in accordance with auditing standards generally accepted in the United States of America. Those standards require that we plan and perform the audit to obtain reasonable assurance about whether the schedule is free from material misstatement.

An audit involves performing procedures to obtain audit evidence about the amounts and disclosures in the schedule. The procedures selected depend on the auditor's judgment, including the assessment of the risks of material misstatement of the schedule, whether due to fraud or error. In making those risk assessments, the auditor considers internal control relevant to the entity's preparation and fair presentation of the schedule in order to design audit procedures that are appropriate in the circumstances, but not for the purpose of expressing an opinion on the effectiveness of the entity's internal control. Accordingly, we express no such opinion. An audit also includes evaluating the appropriateness of accounting policies used and the reasonableness of significant accounting estimates made by management, as well as evaluating the overall presentation of the schedule.

---

[1] The subtitle "Report on the Schedule" is unnecessary in circumstances when the second subtitle, "Report on Other Legal and Regulatory Requirements," is not applicable.

[2] The auditor may refer to the schedule as the *schedule of accounts receivable*.

We believe that the audit evidence we have obtained is sufficient and appropriate to provide a basis for our audit opinion.

Opinion

In our opinion, the schedule referred to above presents fairly, in all material respects, the accounts receivable of ABC Company as of December 31, 20X1, in accordance with accounting principles generally accepted in the United States of America.

Other Matter

We have audited, in accordance with auditing standards generally accepted in the United States of America, the financial statements of ABC Company as of and for the year ended December 31, 20X1, and our report thereon, dated March 15, 20X2, expressed an unmodified opinion on those financial statements.

Report on Other Legal and Regulatory Requirements

[*Form and content of this section of the auditor's report will vary depending on the nature of the auditor's other reporting responsibilities.*]

[*Auditor's signature*]

[*Auditor's city and state*]

[*Date of the auditor's report*]

Illustration 4—An Auditor's Report on a Specific Element, Account, or Item of a Financial Statement Prepared in Accordance With a Special Purpose Framework

Circumstances include the following:

- Audit of a schedule of royalties applicable to engine production (that is, a specific element, account, or item of a financial statement)
- The financial information has been prepared by management of the entity in accordance with a contractual basis of accounting (that is, a special purpose framework) to comply with the provisions of that contract.[1]
- Based on the provisions of the contract, management does not have a choice of financial reporting frameworks.[2]
- The audit of the schedule was not performed in conjunction with an engagement to audit the entity's complete set of financial statements.[3]

Independent Auditor's Report

[*Appropriate Addressee*]

Report on the Schedule[4]

We have audited the accompanying schedule of royalties applicable to engine production of the Q Division of ABC Company for the year ended December 31, 20X1, and the related notes (the schedule).[5]

Management's Responsibility for the Schedule

Management is responsible for the preparation and fair presentation of the schedule in accordance with the financial reporting provisions of Section Z of the license agreement between ABC Company and XYZ Corporation dated January 1, 20X1 (the contract). Management is also responsible for the design, implementation, and maintenance of internal control relevant to the preparation and fair presentation of the schedule that is free from material misstatement, whether due to fraud or error.

Auditor's Responsibility

Our responsibility is to express an opinion on the schedule based on our audit. We conducted our audit in accordance with auditing standards generally accepted in the United States of America. Those standards require that we plan and perform the audit to obtain reasonable assurance about whether the schedule is free from material misstatement.

---

[1] Section 800 contains requirements and guidance on the form and content of financial statements prepared in accordance with a special purpose framework.

[2] Paragraph .18*a* of section 800.

[3] If the auditor undertakes an engagement to audit a specific element of a financial statement in conjunction with an engagement to audit the entity's complete set of financial statements, paragraph .16 requires the auditor to indicate in the report on the specific element of a financial statement the date of the auditor's report on the complete set of financial statements and the nature of opinion expressed on those financial statements under an appropriate heading.

[4] The subtitle "Report on the Schedule" is unnecessary in circumstances when the second subtitle, "Report on Other Legal and Regulatory Requirements," is not applicable.

[5] The auditor may refer to the schedule as the *schedule of royalties*.

An audit involves performing procedures to obtain audit evidence about the amounts and disclosures in the schedule. The procedures selected depend on the auditor's judgment, including the assessment of the risks of material misstatement of the schedule, whether due to fraud or error. In making those risk assessments, the auditor considers internal control relevant to the entity's preparation and fair presentation of the schedule in order to design audit procedures that are appropriate in the circumstances, but not for the purpose of expressing an opinion on the effectiveness of the entity's internal control. Accordingly, we express no such opinion. An audit also includes evaluating the appropriateness of accounting policies used and the reasonableness of significant accounting estimates made by management, as well as evaluating the overall presentation of the schedule.

We believe that the audit evidence we have obtained is sufficient and appropriate to provide a basis for our audit opinion.

Opinion

In our opinion, the schedule referred to above, presents fairly, in all material respects, the royalties applicable to engine production of the Q Division of ABC Company for the year ended December 31, 20X1, in accordance with the financial reporting provisions of Section Z of the contract.

Basis of Accounting[6]

We draw attention to Note X to the schedule, which describes the basis of accounting. The schedule was prepared by ABC Company on the basis of the financial reporting provisions of Section Z of the contract, which is a basis of accounting other than accounting principles generally accepted in the United States of America, to comply with the financial reporting provisions of the contract referred to above. Our opinion is not modified with respect to this matter.

Restriction on Use[7]

Our report is intended solely for the information and use of ABC Company and XYZ Corporation and is not intended to be and should not be used by anyone other than these specified parties.

Report on Other Legal and Regulatory Requirements

[*Form and content of this section of the auditor's report will vary depending on the nature of the auditor's other reporting responsibilities.*]

[*Auditor's signature*]

[*Auditor's city and state*]

[*Date of the auditor's report*]

---

[6] Another appropriate heading may be used.

[7] Another appropriate heading may be used.

Illustration 5—An Auditor's Report on an Incomplete Presentation but One That Is Otherwise in Accordance With Generally Accepted Accounting Principles

Circumstances include the following:

- Audit of the historical summaries of gross income and direct operating expenses (that is, a single financial statement).
- The historical summaries have been prepared by management of the entity in accordance with accounting principles generally accepted in the United States of America but are an incomplete presentation of revenues and expenses.

Independent Auditor's Report

[*Appropriate Addressee*]

Report on the Historical Summaries[1]

We have audited the accompanying Historical Summaries of Gross Income and Direct Operating Expenses of ABC Apartments for each of the three years in the period ended December 31, 20X1, and the related notes (the historical summaries).[2]

Management's Responsibility for the Historical Summaries

Management is responsible for the preparation and fair presentation of these historical summaries in accordance with accounting principles generally accepted in the United States of America; this includes the design, implementation, and maintenance of internal control relevant to the preparation and fair presentation of the historical summaries that are free from material misstatement, whether due to fraud or error.

Auditor's Responsibility

Our responsibility is to express an opinion on the historical summaries based on our audit. We conducted our audit in accordance with auditing standards generally accepted in the United States of America. Those standards require that we plan and perform the audit to obtain reasonable assurance about whether the historical summaries are free from material misstatement.

An audit involves performing procedures to obtain audit evidence about the amounts and disclosures in the historical summaries. The procedures selected depend on the auditor's judgment, including the assessment of the risks of material misstatement of the historical summaries, whether due to fraud or error. In making those risk assessments, the auditor considers internal control relevant to the entity's preparation and fair presentation of the historical summaries in order to design audit procedures that are appropriate in the circumstances, but not for the purpose of expressing an opinion on the effectiveness of the entity's internal control. Accordingly, we express no such opinion. An audit also includes evaluating the appropriateness of accounting policies used and the reasonableness of significant accounting estimates made by management, as well as evaluating the overall presentation of the historical summaries.

We believe that the audit evidence we have obtained is sufficient and appropriate to provide a basis for our audit opinion.

---

[1] The subtitle "Report on the Historical Summaries" is unnecessary in circumstances when the second subtitle, "Report on Other Legal and Regulatory Requirements," is not applicable.

[2] The auditor may refer to the historical summaries as the *financial statement*.

Opinion

In our opinion, the historical summaries referred to above present fairly, in all material respects, the gross income and direct operating expenses described in Note X of ABC Apartments for each of the three years in the period ended December 31, 20X1, in accordance with accounting principles generally accepted in the United States of America.

Emphasis of Matter

We draw attention to Note X to the historical summaries, which describes that the accompanying historical summaries were prepared for the purpose of complying with the rules and regulations of Regulator DEF (for inclusion in the filing of Form Z of ABC Company) and are not intended to be a complete presentation of the Company's revenues and expenses. Our opinion is not modified with respect to this matter.

Report on Other Legal and Regulatory Requirements

[*Form and content of this section of the auditor's report will vary depending on the nature of the auditor's other reporting responsibilities.*]

[*Auditor's signature*]

[*Auditor's city and state*]

[*Date of the auditor's report*]

AU-C Section 806 *

Reporting on Compliance With Aspects of Contractual Agreements or Regulatory Requirements in Connection With Audited Financial Statements

Source: SAS No. 122; SAS No. 125.

Effective for reports on compliance issued in connection with audits of financial statements for periods ending on or after December 15, 2012.

Introduction

Scope of This Section

.01 This section addresses the auditor's responsibility when the auditor is requested to report on an entity's compliance with aspects of contractual agreements or regulatory requirements, insofar as they relate to accounting matters, in connection with an audit of financial statements (referred to hereinafter as a report on compliance). Such a report is commonly referred to as a by-product report. (Ref: par. .A1–.A2)

.02 Entities may be required by contractual agreements, such as certain bond indentures and loan agreements, or regulatory agencies to provide an auditor's report on compliance. For example, loan agreements may impose a variety of obligations on borrowers involving matters such as payments into sinking funds, payments of interest, maintenance of current ratios, and restrictions of dividend payments. Loan agreements may also require the borrower to provide annual financial statements that have been audited. In some instances, the lenders or their trustees may request the auditor to report that the borrower has complied with certain covenants of the agreement relating to accounting matters. The auditor may satisfy this request by issuing a report on compliance in accordance with the requirements of this section.

.03 As described in paragraph .01, this section addresses reporting on an entity's compliance with aspects of contractual agreements or regulatory requirements in connection with an audit of financial statements. When the auditor is engaged or required by law or regulation to perform a compliance audit in accordance with generally accepted auditing standards (GAAS), the standards for financial audits under *Government Auditing Standards*, and a governmental audit requirement that requires the auditor to express an opinion on compliance with applicable compliance requirements, section 935, *Compliance Audits*, applies.

---

* This section has been codified using an "AU-C" identifier instead of an "AU" identifier. "AU-C" is a temporary identifier to avoid confusion with references to existing "AU" sections, which will remain in AICPA *Professional Standards* through 2013. The "AU-C" identifier will revert to "AU" in 2014, by which time substantially all engagements for which the "AU" sections were still effective are expected to be completed.

.04 When the auditor is engaged to perform a separate attest engagement on (*a*) an entity's compliance with requirements of specific laws, regulations, rules, contracts, or grants or (*b*) the effectiveness of an entity's internal control over compliance with specified requirements, AT section 601, *Compliance Attestation*, applies.

Effective Date

.05 This section is effective for reports on compliance issued in connection with audits of financial statements for periods ending on or after December 15, 2012.

Objective

.06 The objective of the auditor is to report appropriately on an entity's compliance with aspects of contractual agreements or regulatory requirements, in connection with the audit of financial statements, when the auditor is requested to report on such matters.

Requirements

Reports on Compliance With Aspects of Contractual Agreements or Regulatory Requirements

.07 The auditor's report on compliance should include a statement that nothing came to the auditor's attention that caused the auditor to believe that the entity failed to comply with specified aspects of the contractual agreements or regulatory requirements, insofar as they relate to accounting matters, only when

a. the auditor has not identified any instances of noncompliance,

b. the auditor has expressed an unmodified or qualified opinion on the financial statements to which the applicable covenants of such contractual agreements or regulatory requirements relate, and

c. the applicable covenants or regulatory requirements relate to accounting matters that have been subjected to the audit procedures applied in the audit of financial statements.

.08 When the auditor has identified one or more instances of noncompliance, the report on compliance should describe such noncompliance (see paragraphs .12*f* and .13*b*).

.09 When the auditor has expressed an adverse opinion or disclaimed an opinion on the financial statements, the auditor should issue a report on compliance only when instances of noncompliance are identified. Therefore, the requirement in paragraph .08 also applies in such circumstances. The auditor should modify the wording of the report on compliance, as appropriate to the circumstances. (Ref: par. .A3)

.10 Notwithstanding the requirements in paragraphs .07–.09, the auditor is not precluded from issuing a report on compliance if such report is required by another set of auditing standards (for example, *Government Auditing Standards*), and the auditor has been engaged to audit the financial statements in accordance with both GAAS and those other standards.

.11 The report on compliance should be in writing and should be provided either in a separate report (see paragraph .12) or in one or more paragraphs included in the auditor's report on the financial statements (see paragraph .13).

Separate Report on Compliance With Aspects of Contractual Agreements or Regulatory Requirements

.12 When the auditor reports on compliance in a separate report, the report should include the following:

a. A title that includes the word *independent* to clearly indicate that it is the report of an independent auditor.

b. An appropriate addressee.

c. A paragraph that states that the financial statements were audited in accordance with generally accepted auditing standards and an identification of the United States of America as the country of origin of those standards (for example, auditing standards generally accepted in the United States of America or U.S. generally accepted auditing standards) and the date of the auditor's report on those financial statements.

d. If the auditor expressed a modified opinion[1] on the financial statements, a statement describing the nature of the modification. (Ref: par. .A4)

e. When no instances of noncompliance are identified by the auditor, a reference to the specific covenants or paragraphs of the contractual agreement or regulatory requirement and a statement that nothing came to the auditor's attention that caused the auditor to believe that the entity failed to comply with specified aspects of the contractual agreements or regulatory requirements, insofar as they relate to accounting matters (see paragraphs .07 and .10).

f. When instances of noncompliance are identified by the auditor, a reference to the specific covenants or paragraphs of the contractual agreement or regulatory requirement, insofar as they relate to accounting matters, and a description of the identified instances of noncompliance. (Ref: par. .A5)

g. A statement that the report is being provided in connection with the audit of the financial statements.

h. A statement that the audit was not directed primarily toward obtaining knowledge regarding compliance, and accordingly, had the auditor performed additional procedures, other matters may have come to the auditor's attention regarding noncompliance with the specific covenants or paragraphs of the contractual agreement or regulatory requirement, insofar as they relate to accounting matters.

i. A paragraph that includes a description and the source of significant interpretations, if any, made by the entity's management relating to the provisions of the relevant contractual agreement or regulatory requirement.

j. A paragraph that includes an appropriate alert in accordance with the section 905, *Alert That Restricts the Use of the Auditor's Written Communication*.[2] (Ref: par. .A6–.A7)

k. The manual or printed signature of the auditor's firm and the city and state where the auditor practices.

---

[1] See section 705, *Modifications to the Opinion in the Independent Auditor's Report*.

[2] Paragraphs .06*c*, .07, and .11 of section 905, *Alert That Restricts the Use of the Auditor's Written Communication*. [Footnote amended, effective for the auditor's written communications related to audits of financial statements for periods ending on or after December 15, 2012, by SAS No. 125.]

l. The date of the report, which should be the same date as the auditor's report on the financial statements.[3]

[As amended, effective for the auditor's written communications related to audits of financial statements for periods ending on or after December 15, 2012, by SAS No. 125.]

Report on Compliance With Aspects of Contractual Agreements or Regulatory Requirements Included in the Auditor's Report

.13 When a report on compliance is included in the auditor's report on the financial statements, the auditor's report should include an other-matter paragraph[4] that includes a reference to the specific covenants or paragraphs of the contractual agreement or regulatory requirement, insofar as they relate to accounting matters, and also should include the following:

a. When no instances of noncompliance are identified by the auditor, a statement that nothing came to the auditor's attention that caused the auditor to believe that the entity failed to comply with specified aspects of the contractual agreements or regulatory requirements, insofar as they relate to accounting matters (see paragraphs .07 and .10).

b. When instances of noncompliance are identified by the auditor, a description of the identified instances of noncompliance. (Ref: par. .A5)

c. A statement that the communication is being provided in connection with the audit of the financial statements.

d. A statement that the audit was not directed primarily toward obtaining knowledge regarding compliance, and accordingly, had the auditor performed additional procedures, other matters may have come to the auditor's attention regarding noncompliance with the specific covenants or paragraphs of the contractual agreement or regulatory requirement, insofar as they relate to accounting matters.

e. A paragraph that includes a description and the source of significant interpretations, if any, made by the entity's management relating to the provisions of the relevant contractual agreement or regulatory requirement.

f. A paragraph that includes an appropriate alert in accordance with section 905.[5] (Ref: par. .A6–.A7)

[As amended, effective for the auditor's written communications related to audits of financial statements for periods ending on or after December 15, 2012, by SAS No. 125.]

Application and Other Explanatory Material

Scope of This Section (Ref: par. .01)

.A1 The financial statements being audited and to which the applicable covenants of the contractual agreements or regulatory requirements relate may be either general purpose or special purpose financial statements.

---

[3] Paragraph .41 of section 700, *Forming an Opinion and Reporting on Financial Statements.*

[4] See section 706, *Emphasis-of-Matter Paragraphs and Other-Matter Paragraphs in the Independent Auditor's Report*, for guidance on other-matter paragraphs.

[5] See footnote 2.

Considerations Specific to Governmental Entities

.A2 For most state or local governmental entities, the applicable financial reporting framework is based on multiple reporting units and, therefore, requires the presentation of financial statements for its activities in various reporting units. Consequently, a reporting unit or aggregation of reporting units of the governmental entity represents an opinion unit to the auditor. In the context of this section, the auditor is responsible for reporting on compliance for each opinion unit within a governmental entity, when requested.

Reports on Compliance With Aspects of Contractual Agreements or Regulatory Requirements (Ref: par. .09)

.A3 The exhibit, "Illustrations of Reports on Compliance With Aspects of Contractual Agreements or Regulatory Requirements in Connection With Audited Financial Statements," provides an example of the wording of the report on compliance when the auditor has disclaimed an opinion on the financial statements.[6]

Separate Report on Compliance With Aspects of Contractual Agreements or Regulatory Requirements (Ref: par. .12d)

.A4 The auditor may include certain additional communications in the separate report on compliance when the auditor included such additional communications in the auditor's report on the financial statements[7] that are not modifications to the auditor's opinion. For example, if the auditor included an emphasis-of-matter paragraph in the auditor's report on the financial statements because of an uncertainty about the entity's ability to continue as a going concern for a reasonable period of time,[8] the auditor may also include this in the separate report on compliance.

Reporting When Instances of Noncompliance Are Identified (Ref: par. .12f and .13b)

.A5 When instances of noncompliance are identified, and the entity has obtained a waiver for such noncompliance, the auditor may include a statement in the report on compliance that a waiver has been obtained. The determination of whether to include such a statement is based on the procedures performed by the auditor to evaluate the waiver for the purposes of obtaining sufficient appropriate audit evidence in connection with the audit of the financial statements. All instances of noncompliance are required to be described in the report on compliance, in accordance with paragraph .08, including those for which a waiver has been obtained.

Restrictions on the Use of the Auditor's Report[9] (Ref: par. .12j and .13f)

.A6 An alert, as discussed in paragraphs .12*j* and .13*f*, is necessary because, although compliance matters may be identified by the auditor during the

---

[6] Illustration 4, "A Report on Compliance With Aspects of Contractual Agreements Provided in a Separate Report When Instances of Noncompliance Are Identified, and the Auditor Has Disclaimed an Opinion on the Financial Statements," in the exhibit, "Illustrations of Reports on Compliance With Aspects of Contractual Agreements or Regulatory Requirements in Connection With Audited Financial Statements."

[7] See section 706.

[8] See section 570, *The Auditor's Consideration of an Entity's Ability to Continue as a Going Concern*. [Footnote revised, August 2012, to reflect conforming changes necessary due to the issuance of SAS No. 126.]

[9] See footnote 2.

course of the audit engagement, the identification of such matters is not the primary objective of the audit engagement. In addition, the basis, assumptions, or purpose of the provisions in contractual agreements or regulatory requirements to which the report on compliance relates are developed for, and directed only to, the parties to the contractual agreement or the regulatory agency responsible for the requirements. [As amended, effective for the auditor's written communications related to audits of financial statements for periods ending on or after December 15, 2012, by SAS No. 125.]

.A7 The alert that restricts the use of the report indicates that only the report on compliance with aspects of contractual agreements or regulatory requirements is restricted. Accordingly, the intended use of the auditor's report on the financial statements is not affected by this alert. [As amended, effective for the auditor's written communications related to audits of financial statements for periods ending on or after December 15, 2012, by SAS No. 125.]

.A8

Exhibit—Illustrations of Reports on Compliance With Aspects of Contractual Agreements or Regulatory Requirements in Connection With Audited Financial Statements (Ref: par. .12–.13)

Illustration 1—A Report on Compliance With Aspects of Contractual Agreements Provided in a Separate Report When No Instances of Noncompliance Are Identified

Independent Auditor's Report

[*Appropriate Addressee*]

We have audited, in accordance with auditing standards generally accepted in the United States of America, the financial statements of XYZ Company, which comprise the balance sheet as of December 31, 20X2, and the related statements of income, changes in stockholders' equity, and cash flows for the year then ended, and the related notes to the financial statements, and have issued our report thereon dated February 16, 20X3.

In connection with our audit, nothing came to our attention that caused us to believe that XYZ Company failed to comply with the terms, covenants, provisions, or conditions of sections XX to YY, inclusive, of the Indenture dated July 21, 20X0, with ABC Bank, insofar as they relate to accounting matters. However, our audit was not directed primarily toward obtaining knowledge of such noncompliance. Accordingly, had we performed additional procedures, other matters may have come to our attention regarding the Company's noncompliance with the above-referenced terms, covenants, provisions, or conditions of the Indenture, insofar as they relate to accounting matters.

This report is intended solely for the information and use of the board of directors and management of XYZ Company and ABC Bank and is not intended to be and should not be used by anyone other than these specified parties.

[*Auditor's signature*]

[*Auditor's city and state*]

[*Date of the auditor's report*]

Illustration 2—A Report on Compliance With Aspects of Contractual Agreements Provided in a Separate Report When Instances of Noncompliance Are Identified

Independent Auditor's Report

[*Appropriate Addressee*]

We have audited, in accordance with auditing standards generally accepted in the United States of America, the financial statements of XYZ Company, which comprise the balance sheet as of December 31, 20X2, and the related statements of income, changes in stockholders' equity, and cash flows for the year then ended, and the related notes to the financial statements, and have issued our report thereon dated March 5, 20X3.

In connection with our audit, we noted that XYZ Company failed to comply with the "Working Capital" provision of section XX of the Loan Agreement dated March 1, 20X2, with ABC Bank. Our audit was not directed primarily toward obtaining knowledge as to whether XYZ Company failed to comply with the terms, covenants, provisions, or conditions of sections XX to YY, inclusive, of the Loan Agreement, insofar as they relate to accounting matters. Accordingly, had we performed additional procedures, other matters may have come to our attention regarding noncompliance with the above-referenced terms, covenants, provisions, or conditions of the Loan Agreement, insofar as they relate to accounting matters.

This report is intended solely for the information and use of the board of directors and management of XYZ Company and ABC Bank and is not intended to be and should not be used by anyone other than these specified parties.

[*Auditor's signature*]

[*Auditor's city and state*]

[*Date of the auditor's report*]

Illustration 3—A Report on Compliance With Aspects of Contractual Agreements Provided in a Separate Report When Instances of Noncompliance Are Identified, and a Waiver Has Been Obtained

Independent Auditor's Report

[*Appropriate Addressee*]

We have audited, in accordance with auditing standards generally accepted in the United States of America, the financial statements of XYZ Company, which comprise the balance sheet as of December 31, 20X2, and the related statements of income, changes in stockholders' equity, and cash flows for the year then ended, and the related notes to the financial statements, and have issued our report thereon dated March 5, 20X3.

In connection with our audit, we noted that XYZ Company failed to comply with the "Working Capital" provision of section XX of the Loan Agreement dated March 1, 20X2, with ABC Bank. The Company has received a waiver dated February 5, 20X3, from ABC Bank. Our audit was not directed primarily toward obtaining knowledge as to whether XYZ Company failed to comply with the terms, covenants, provisions, or conditions of sections XX to YY, inclusive, of the Loan Agreement, insofar as they relate to accounting matters. Accordingly, had we performed additional procedures, other matters may have come to our attention regarding noncompliance with the above-referenced terms, covenants, provisions, or conditions of the Loan Agreement, insofar as they relate to accounting matters.

This report is intended solely for the information and use of the board of directors and management of XYZ Company and ABC Bank and is not intended to be and should not be used by anyone other than these specified parties.

[*Auditor's signature*]

[*Auditor's city and state*]

[*Date of the auditor's report*]

Illustration 4—A Report on Compliance With Aspects of Contractual Agreements Provided in a Separate Report When Instances of Noncompliance Are Identified, and the Auditor Has Disclaimed an Opinion on the Financial Statements

Independent Auditor's Report

[*Appropriate Addressee*]

We were engaged to audit, in accordance with auditing standards generally accepted in the United States of America, the financial statements of XYZ Company, which comprise the balance sheet as of December 31, 20X2, and the related statements of income, changes in stockholders' equity, and cash flows for the year then ended, and the related notes to the financial statements, and have issued our report thereon dated March 5, 20X3. Our report disclaims an opinion on such financial statements because of [*describe the scope limitation or matter causing the disclaimer*].

In connection with our engagement, we noted that XYZ Company failed to comply with the "Working Capital" provision of section XX of the Loan Agreement dated March 1, 20X2, with ABC Bank. Our engagement was not directed primarily toward obtaining knowledge as to whether XYZ Company failed to comply with the terms, covenants, provisions, or conditions of sections XX to YY, inclusive, of the Loan Agreement, insofar as they relate to accounting matters. Accordingly, had we been able to complete the audit, other matters may have come to our attention regarding noncompliance with the above-referenced terms, covenants, provisions, or conditions of the Loan Agreement, insofar as they relate to accounting matters.

This report is intended solely for the information and use of the board of directors and management of XYZ Company and ABC Bank and is not intended to be and should not be used by anyone other than these specified parties.

[*Auditor's signature*]

[*Auditor's city and state*]

[*Date of the auditor's report*]

Illustration 5—A Report on Compliance With Aspects of Contractual Agreements Provided in a Separate Report When No Instances of Noncompliance Are Identified

Independent Auditor's Report

[*Appropriate Addressee*]

Report on the Financial Statements[1]

We have audited the accompanying financial statements of ABC Company, which comprise the balance sheet as of December 31, 20X1, and the related statements of income, changes in stockholders' equity, and cash flows for the year then ended, and the related notes to the financial statements.

Management's Responsibility for the Financial Statements

Management is responsible for the preparation and fair presentation of these financial statements in accordance with accounting principles generally accepted in the United States of America; this includes the design, implementation, and maintenance of internal control relevant to the preparation and fair presentation of financial statements that are free from material misstatement, whether due to fraud or error.

Auditor's Responsibility

Our responsibility is to express an opinion on these financial statements based on our audit. We conducted our audit in accordance with auditing standards generally accepted in the United States of America. Those standards require that we plan and perform the audit to obtain reasonable assurance about whether the financial statements are free from material misstatement.

An audit involves performing procedures to obtain audit evidence about the amounts and disclosures in the financial statements. The procedures selected depend on the auditor's judgment, including the assessment of the risks of material misstatement of the financial statements, whether due to fraud or error. In making those risk assessments, the auditor considers internal control relevant to the entity's preparation and fair presentation of the financial statements in order to design audit procedures that are appropriate in the circumstances, but not for the purpose of expressing an opinion on the effectiveness of the entity's internal control.[2] Accordingly, we express no such opinion. An audit also includes evaluating the appropriateness of accounting policies used and the reasonableness of significant accounting estimates made by management, as well as evaluating the overall presentation of the financial statements.

We believe that the audit evidence we have obtained is sufficient and appropriate to provide a basis for our audit opinion.

---

[1] The subtitle "Report on the Financial Statements" is unnecessary in circumstances when the second subtitle "Report on Other Legal and Regulatory Requirements" is not applicable. [Footnote added, effective for the auditor's written communications related to audits of financial statements for periods ending on or after December 15, 2012, by SAS No. 125.]

[2] In circumstances when the auditor also has responsibility to express an opinion on the effectiveness of internal control in conjunction with the audit of the financial statements, this sentence would be worded as follows: "In making those risk assessments, the auditor considers internal control relevant to the entity's preparation and fair presentation of the financial statements in order to design audit procedures that are appropriate in the circumstances." In addition, the next sentence "Accordingly, we express no such opinion," would not be included. [Footnote added, effective for the auditor's written communications related to audits of financial statements for periods ending on or after December 15, 2012, by SAS No. 125.]

Opinion

In our opinion, the financial statements referred to above present fairly, in all material respects, the financial position of ABC Company as of December 31, 20X1, and the results of its operations and its cash flows for the year then ended in accordance with accounting principles generally accepted in the United States of America.

Other Matter

In connection with our audit, nothing came to our attention that caused us to believe that ABC Company failed to comply with the terms, covenants, provisions, or conditions of sections XX to YY, inclusive, of the Indenture dated July 21, 20X0 with XYZ Bank, insofar as they relate to accounting matters. However, our audit was not directed primarily toward obtaining knowledge of such noncompliance. Accordingly, had we performed additional procedures, other matters may have come to our attention regarding the Company's noncompliance with the above-referenced terms, covenants, provisions, or conditions of the Indenture, insofar as they relate to accounting matters.

Restricted Use Relating to the Other Matter

The communication related to compliance with the aforementioned Indenture described in the Other Matter paragraph is intended solely for the information and use of the boards of directors and management of ABC Company and XYZ Bank and is not intended to be and should not be used by anyone other than these specified parties.[3]

Report on Other Legal and Regulatory Requirements

[*Form and content of this section of the auditor's report will vary depending on the nature of the auditor's other reporting responsibilities.*]

[*Auditor's signature*]

[*Auditor's city and state*]

[*Date of the auditor's report*]

[Illustration added, effective for the auditor's written communications related to audits of financial statements for periods ending on or after December 15, 2012, by SAS No. 125.]

---

[3] When the engagement is also performed in accordance with *Government Auditing Standards*, the alert may read as follows: "The purpose of the communication related to compliance with the aforementioned [*compliance requirements*] described in the Other Matter paragraph [*or, Report on Compliance*] is solely to describe the scope of our testing of compliance and the results of that testing. This communication is an integral part of an audit performed in accordance with *Government Auditing Standards* in considering ABC Company's compliance. Accordingly, this communication is not suitable for any other purpose." The AICPA Audit Guide Government Auditing Standards *and Circular A-133 Audits* provides additional interpretative guidance, including illustrative reports. [Footnote added, effective for the auditor's written communications related to audits of financial statements for periods ending on or after December 15, 2012, by SAS No. 125.]

AU-C Section 810 *

Engagements to Report on Summary Financial Statements

Source: SAS No. 122.

Effective for audits of financial statements for periods ending on or after December 15, 2012.

Introduction

Scope of This Section

.01 This section addresses the auditor's responsibilities relating to an engagement to report separately on summary financial statements derived from financial statements audited in accordance with generally accepted auditing standards (GAAS) by the same auditor. In such an engagement, the auditor forms an opinion about whether the summary financial statements are consistent, in all material respects, with the audited financial statements from which they have been derived, in accordance with the applied criteria.

.02 This section does not apply to condensed financial statements or summarized financial information presented as comparative information.[1] Section 700, *Forming an Opinion and Reporting on Financial Statements*, addresses the auditor's responsibility for comparative information.[2] (Ref: par. .A1)

.03 Summary financial statements may be required by a designated accounting standards setter (for example, the Governmental Accounting Standards Board) to accompany the basic financial statements. This section does not apply in such circumstances. Section 730, *Required Supplementary Information*, addresses the auditor's responsibilities relating to information supplementary to the basic financial statements that is required by a designated accounting standards setter to accompany such financial statements.

Effective Date

.04 This section is effective for audits of financial statements for periods ending on or after December 15, 2012.

Objectives

.05 The objectives of the auditor are

a. to determine whether it is appropriate to accept the engagement to report on summary financial statements and,

---

* This section has been codified using an "AU-C" identifier instead of an "AU" identifier. "AU-C" is a temporary identifier to avoid confusion with references to existing "AU" sections, which will remain in AICPA *Professional Standards* through 2013. The "AU-C" identifier will revert to "AU" in 2014, by which time substantially all engagements for which the "AU" sections were still effective are expected to be completed.

[1] Paragraph .11 of section 700, *Forming an Opinion and Reporting on Financial Statements*, defines the terms *condensed financial statements* and *comparative information*.

[2] Paragraphs .44–.51 of section 700.

b. if engaged to report on summary financial statements, to

i. perform the procedures necessary as the basis for the auditor's opinion on the summary financial statements;

ii. form an opinion on whether the summary financial statements are consistent, in all material respects, with the audited financial statements from which they have been derived, in accordance with the applied criteria, based on an evaluation of the conclusions drawn from the evidence obtained; and

iii. express clearly that opinion through a written report that also describes the basis for that opinion.

Definitions

.06 For purposes of this section, the following terms have the meanings attributed as follows:

Applied criteria. The criteria applied by management in the preparation of the summary financial statements.

Summary financial statements. Historical financial information[3] that is derived from financial statements but that contains less detail than the financial statements, while still providing a structured representation consistent with that provided by the financial statements of the entity's economic resources or obligations at a point in time or the changes therein for a period of time. Summary financial statements are separately presented and are not presented as comparative information.

.07 In this section, the term *audited financial statements* refers to those financial statements[4] audited by the auditor in accordance with GAAS and from which the summary financial statements are derived.

Requirements

Engagement Acceptance

.08 The auditor should not accept an engagement to report on summary financial statements in accordance with this section unless the auditor has been engaged to conduct an audit in accordance with GAAS of the financial statements from which the summary financial statements are derived. (Ref: par. .A2)

.09 Before accepting an engagement to report on summary financial statements, the auditor should

a. determine whether the applied criteria are acceptable, including determining that the applied criteria (Ref: par. .A3–.A5)

i. are free from bias so that the summary financial statements are not misleading.

---

[3] Paragraph .14 of section 200, *Overall Objectives of the Independent Auditor and the Conduct of an Audit in Accordance With Generally Accepted Auditing Standards*, defines the term *historical financial information*.

[4] Paragraph .14 of section 200 defines the term *financial statements*.

ii. permit reasonably consistent qualitative or quantitative measurements so that the information in the summary financial statements agrees with or can be recalculated from the related information in the audited financial statements.

iii. are sufficiently complete so that the summary financial statements contain the information necessary and are at an appropriate level of aggregation, so that they are not misleading in the circumstances.

iv. are relevant to the summary financial statements in view of their purpose.

b. obtain the agreement of management, in writing, that it acknowledges and understands its responsibility

i. for the preparation of the summary financial statements in accordance with the applied criteria.

ii. to clearly describe in the summary financial statements where the audited financial statements are available and to make the audited financial statements readily available to the intended users of the summary financial statements when the summary financial statements will not be accompanied by the audited financial statements. (Ref: par. .A6–.A7)

iii. to provide the auditor with written representations, as described in paragraph .12.

iv. to include the auditor's report on the summary financial statements in any document that contains the summary financial statements and indicates the auditor has reported on them.

c. obtain the agreement of management, in writing, about the expected form and content of the report on the summary financial statements, including the agreement that there may be circumstances in which the report may differ from its expected form and content. (Ref: par. .A8)

.10 If the auditor concludes that the applied criteria are unacceptable or is unable to obtain the agreement of management set out in paragraph .09*b–c*, the auditor should not accept the engagement to report on the summary financial statements.

Nature of Procedures

.11 The auditor should perform the following procedures, and any other procedures that the auditor may consider necessary, as the basis for the auditor's opinion on the summary financial statements:

a. Evaluate whether the summary financial statements adequately disclose their summarized nature and identify the audited financial statements. (Ref: par. .A9)

b. When the summary financial statements are not accompanied by the audited financial statements, evaluate

i. whether the summary financial statements clearly describe where the audited financial statements are available and

ii. whether the audited financial statements are readily available to the intended users of the summary financial statements. (Ref: par. .A7)

c. Evaluate whether the summary financial statements adequately disclose the applied criteria.

d. Compare the summary financial statements with the related information in the audited financial statements to determine whether the summary financial statements agree with or can be recalculated from the related information in the audited financial statements.

e. Evaluate whether the summary financial statements are prepared in accordance with the applied criteria.

f. Evaluate, in view of the purpose of the summary financial statements, whether the summary financial statements contain the information necessary, and are at an appropriate level of aggregation, so that they are not misleading in the circumstances.

Written Representations

.12 The auditor should request management to provide written representations, in the form of a representation letter addressed to the auditor, for the following matters:

a. Management has fulfilled its responsibility for the preparation of the summary financial statements in accordance with the applied criteria and believes the applied criteria are acceptable

b. Management has made the audited financial statements readily available to the intended users of the summary financial statements, when the summary financial statements will not be accompanied by the audited financial statements

c. If the date of the auditor's report on the summary financial statements is later than the date of the auditor's report on the audited financial statements,

i. whether any information has come to management's attention that would cause management to believe that any of the previous representations on the audited financial statements need to be modified

ii. whether any events have occurred subsequent to the date of the audited financial statements that may require adjustment of, or disclosure in, the audited financial statements

.13 The date of the written representations should be as of the date of the auditor's report on the summary financial statements. The written representations should be for all summary financial statements and period(s) referred to in the auditor's report on the summary financial statements.

Form of Opinion (Ref: par. .A10–.A11)

.14 When the auditor has concluded that an unmodified opinion on the summary financial statements is appropriate, the auditor's opinion should state that the summary financial statements are consistent, in all material respects, with the audited financial statements from which they have been derived, in accordance with the applied criteria.

.15 If the summary financial statements are not consistent, in all material respects, with the audited financial statements, in accordance with the applied criteria, and management does not agree to make the necessary changes, the auditor should express an adverse opinion on the summary financial statements. The auditor should state in the opinion paragraph that, in the auditor's opinion, because of the significance of the matter(s) described in the basis for adverse opinion paragraph, the summary financial statements are not consistent, in all material respects, with the audited financial statements from which they have been derived, in accordance with the applied criteria.

.16 When the auditor's report on the audited financial statements contains an adverse opinion or a disclaimer of opinion, the auditor should withdraw from the engagement to report on the summary financial statements, when withdrawal is possible under applicable law or regulation. If it is not possible for the auditor to withdraw from the engagement, the auditor's report on the summary financial statements should

a. state that the auditor's report on the audited financial statements contains an adverse opinion or disclaimer of opinion.

b. describe the basis for that adverse opinion or disclaimer of opinion.

c. state that, as a result of the adverse opinion or disclaimer of opinion, it is inappropriate to express, and the auditor does not express, an opinion on the summary financial statements.

d. include the reporting elements in paragraph .17, except for paragraph .17*c*(iv–v) and *e–f*.

Auditor's Report on Summary Financial Statements

Elements of the Auditor's Report (Ref: par. .A12)

.17 The auditor's report on summary financial statements should include the following elements:

a. Title that includes the word *independent* to clearly indicate that it is the report of an independent auditor (Ref: par. .A13)

b. Addressee

c. Introductory paragraph that

i. identifies the summary financial statements on which the auditor is reporting, including the title of each statement included in the summary financial statements (Ref: par. .A14)

ii. identifies the audited financial statements from which the summary financial statements have been derived

iii. refers to the auditor's report on the audited financial statements, the date of that report, and, subject to paragraphs .15–.16, the fact that an unmodified opinion is expressed on the audited financial statements

iv. if the date of the auditor's report on the summary financial statements is later than the date of the auditor's report on the audited financial statements, states that the summary financial statements and the audited financial statements do not reflect the effects of events, if any, that occurred subsequent to the date of the auditor's report on the audited financial statements (see paragraph .19) (Ref: par. .A15)

v. indicates that the summary financial statements do not contain all the disclosures required by the [*financial reporting framework applied in the preparation of the financial statements*] and that reading the summary financial statements is not a substitute for reading the audited financial statements

d. Description of management's responsibility for the summary financial statements, explaining that management is responsible for the preparation of the summary financial statements in accordance with the applied criteria

e. Statement that the auditor is responsible for expressing an opinion about whether the summary financial statements are consistent, in all material respects, with the audited financial statements based on the procedures required by GAAS and an identification of the United States of America as the country of origin of those standards, including the following:

i. The procedures consisted principally of comparing the summary financial statements with the related information in the audited financial statements from which the summary financial statements have been derived and evaluating whether the summary financial statements are prepared in accordance with the applied criteria

ii. If the date of the auditor's report on the summary financial statements is later than the date of the auditor's report on the audited financial statements, the auditor did not perform any audit procedures regarding the audited financial statements after the date of the report on those financial statements.

f. A paragraph that clearly expresses an opinion, as described in paragraphs .14–.15

g. Auditor's signature

h. Auditor's city and state

i. Date of the auditor's report

.18 The auditor should date the auditor's report on the summary financial statements no earlier than

a. the date on which the auditor has obtained sufficient appropriate evidence on which to base the opinion, including evidence that the summary financial statements have been prepared and that management and, when appropriate, those charged with governance, have asserted that they have taken responsibility for them; and

b. the date of the auditor's report on the audited financial statements.

.19 When the auditor's report on the summary financial statements is dated later than the date of the auditor's report on the audited financial statements, the auditor may become aware of *subsequently discovered facts* as defined in section 560, *Subsequent Events and Subsequently Discovered Facts*. In such cases, the auditor should not release the auditor's report on the summary financial statements until the auditor's consideration of subsequently discovered facts in relation to the audited financial statements, in accordance with section 560, has been completed.

Modifications to the Opinion, Emphasis-of-Matter Paragraph, or Other-Matter Paragraph in the Auditor's Report on the Audited Financial Statements (Ref: par. .A16)

.20 If the auditor's report on the audited financial statements contains a qualified opinion, an emphasis-of-matter paragraph, or an other-matter paragraph, and the auditor expresses an unmodified opinion (see paragraph .14) or an adverse opinion (see paragraph .15) on the summary financial statements, in addition to the elements in paragraph .17, the auditor's report on the summary financial statements should

a. state that the auditor's report on the audited financial statements contains a qualified opinion, an emphasis-of-matter paragraph, or an other-matter paragraph and

b. describe

i. the basis for the qualified opinion on the audited financial statements and that qualified opinion; or the emphasis-of-matter or other-matter paragraph in the auditor's report on the audited financial statements and

ii. the effect on the summary financial statements, if any.

Restriction on Use or Alerting Readers to the Basis of Accounting

.21 When use of the auditor's report on the audited financial statements is restricted or the auditor's report on the audited financial statements alerts readers that the audited financial statements are prepared in accordance with a special purpose framework, the auditor should include a similar restriction or alert in the auditor's report on the summary financial statements.

Comparatives

.22 If the audited financial statements contain comparative financial statements but the summary financial statements do not, the auditor should determine whether such omission is reasonable in the circumstances of the engagement. The auditor should determine the effect of an unreasonable omission on the auditor's report on the summary financial statements. (Ref: par. .A17–.A18)

.23 Unless the predecessor auditor's report on the prior period's summary financial statements is reissued with the summary financial statements, if the summary financial statements contain comparatives that were reported on by another auditor, the auditor's report on the summary financial statements should state

a. that the summary financial statements of the prior period were audited by a predecessor auditor.

b. the type of opinion expressed by the predecessor auditor and, if the opinion was modified, the reasons therefore.

c. the date of that report.

.24 If the summary financial statements contain comparatives that were not reported on by the auditor or another auditor, the auditor's report on the summary financial statements should state that the comparative summary financial statements were not reported on by the auditor and, accordingly, the auditor does not express an opinion on the comparative summary financial statements.

Unaudited Information Presented With Summary Financial Statements (Ref: par. .A19)

.25 The auditor should evaluate whether any unaudited information presented with the summary financial statements is clearly differentiated from the summary financial statements. If the auditor concludes that the entity's presentation of the unaudited information is not clearly differentiated from the summary financial statements, the auditor should ask management to change the presentation of the unaudited information. If management refuses to do so, the auditor should explain in the auditor's report on the summary financial statements that such information is not covered by that report and accordingly, the auditor does not express an opinion on the information.

Other Information in Documents Containing Summary Financial Statements (Ref: par. .A20)

.26 The auditor should read other information included in a document containing the summary financial statements and related auditor's report to identify material inconsistencies, if any, with the summary financial statements and the audited financial statements.

.27 If, upon reading the other information, the auditor identifies a material inconsistency or becomes aware of an apparent material misstatement of fact, the auditor should discuss the matter with management and should consider appropriate further action in the circumstances. For an identified material inconsistency, the auditor should also determine whether the summary financial statements or the other information needs to be revised.

Auditor Association (Ref: par. .A21)

.28 If the auditor becomes aware that the entity plans to state that the auditor has reported on summary financial statements in a document containing the summary financial statements, but does not plan to include the related auditor's report, the auditor should request management to include the auditor's report in the document. If management does not do so, the auditor should determine and carry out other appropriate actions designed to prevent management from inappropriately associating the auditor with the summary financial statements in that document.

.29 The auditor may be engaged to report on the financial statements of an entity, while not engaged to report on the summary financial statements. If, in this case, the auditor becomes aware that the entity plans to make a statement in a document that refers to the auditor and the fact that summary financial statements are derived from the financial statements audited by the auditor, the auditor should be satisfied that

a. the reference to the auditor is made in the context of the auditor's report on the audited financial statements, and

b. the statement does not give the impression that the auditor has reported on the summary financial statements.

If either *a* or *b* is not met, the auditor should request management to change the statement to meet both of the criteria in *a* and *b*, or not to refer to the auditor in the document. Alternatively, the entity may engage the auditor to report on the summary financial statements and include the related auditor's report in the document. If management does not change the statement, delete the reference to the auditor, or include an auditor's report on the summary financial statements in the document containing the summary financial statements, the auditor should advise management that the auditor disagrees with the reference to the auditor, and the auditor should determine and carry out other appropriate actions designed to prevent management from inappropriately associating the auditor with the summary financial statements in that document.

Application and Other Explanatory Material

Scope of This Section (Ref: par. .02)

.A1 Financial statements may present comparative information in the form of condensed financial statements or summarized financial information. For example, entities such as state and local governmental units may present prior period financial information in their government-wide financial statements only for the total reporting entity rather than disaggregated by governmental activities, business-type activities, total primary government, and discretely presented component units. Also, not-for-profit organizations frequently present certain information for the prior period in total rather than by net asset class. As described in paragraph .02, this section does not apply to reporting on financial statements containing such comparative information. Summary financial statements differ from comparative information. Summary financial statements may be presented in a document containing financial statements or in a separate document, whereas comparative information is presented within the financial statements. Refer to section 700 for the auditor's responsibilities for reporting on comparative information.[5]

Engagement Acceptance

.A2 The audit of the financial statements from which the summary financial statements are derived provides the auditor with the necessary knowledge to discharge the auditor's responsibilities regarding the summary financial statements, in accordance with this section. Application of this section will not provide sufficient appropriate evidence on which to base the opinion on the summary financial statements if the auditor also has not audited the financial statements from which the summary financial statements are derived. (Ref: par. .08)

Criteria (Ref: par. .09a)

.A3 The preparation of summary financial statements requires management to determine the information that needs to be reflected in the summary financial statements so that they are consistent, in all material respects, with the audited financial statements. Because summary financial statements by their nature contain aggregated information and limited disclosure, there is an increased risk that they may not contain the information necessary so that they are not misleading in the circumstances. This risk increases when established criteria for the preparation of summary financial statements do not exist.

.A4 Factors that may affect the auditor's determination of the acceptability of the applied criteria include the following:

- The nature of the entity
- The purpose of the summary financial statements

---

[5] Paragraphs .44–.51 of section 700.

- The information needs of the intended users of the summary financial statements
- Whether the applied criteria will result in summary financial statements that are not misleading in the circumstances

.A5 The criteria for the preparation of summary financial statements may be established by an authorized or recognized standards-setting organization or by law or regulation. In many such cases, the auditor may presume that such criteria are acceptable. When established criteria for the preparation of summary financial statements do not exist, criteria may be developed by management, for example, based on practice in a particular industry.

Availability of the Audited Financial Statements (Ref: par. .09b(ii) and .11b(ii))

.A6 Summary financial statements are presented in considerably less detail than the complete set of financial statements and do not contain all the disclosures required by the financial reporting framework applied in the preparation of the complete set of financial statements. In addition, reading the summary financial statements is not a substitute for reading the audited financial statements. Accordingly, before accepting an engagement to report on summary financial statements, the auditor is required by paragraph .09*b*(ii) to obtain management's agreement that it acknowledges and understands its responsibility to make the audited financial statements readily available to the intended users of the summary financial statements, when the summary financial statements will not be accompanied by the audited financial statements.

.A7 Audited financial statements are deemed to be readily available if a third-party user can obtain the audited financial statements without any further action by the entity (for example, financial statements on an entity's website may be considered readily available but being available upon request is not considered readily available).

Agreement on the Expected Form and Content of the Report (Ref: par. .09c)

.A8 Agreement with management about the expected form and content of the report on the summary financial statements may include a description of the types of opinions the auditor may express. It is not necessary to describe the type of opinion expected to be issued. The auditor also may indicate that circumstances may arise in which it is necessary for the auditor to withdraw from the engagement.

Nature of Procedures (Ref: par. .11)

.A9 Adequate disclosure of the summarized nature of summary financial statements and the identity of the audited financial statements, as referred to in paragraph .11*a*, may, for example, be provided by a title such as "Summary Financial Statements Prepared From the Audited Financial Statements as of and for the Year Ended December 31, 20X1."

Form of Opinion (Ref: par. .14–.16)

.A10 If the summary financial statements are not consistent, in all material respects, with the audited financial statements in accordance with the applied criteria, and management does not agree to make the necessary changes, the auditor is required by paragraph .15 to express an adverse opinion on the summary financial statements. Due to the summarized nature of the summary financial statements, a qualified opinion would not be appropriate; the summary financial statements either are or are not consistent, in all material respects, with the audited financial statements, in accordance with the applied criteria.

.A11 When the auditor's report on the audited financial statements contains an adverse opinion or a disclaimer of opinion, paragraph .16 requires the auditor to withdraw from the engagement to report on the summary financial statements, when withdrawal is possible under applicable law or regulation. When an entity is required by law or regulation to provide a report on summary financial statements, the auditor is neither precluded from withdrawing, nor required to withdraw, from the engagement.

Auditor's Report on Summary Financial Statements

Elements of the Auditor's Report (Ref: par. .17)

.A12 An auditor who is engaged to report on summary financial statements does not report in the same manner as the auditor reported on the complete set of financial statements from which they are derived. To do so might lead users to assume, erroneously, that the summary financial statements include all the disclosures necessary for the complete set of financial statements. For the same reason, summary financial statements need to adequately disclose their summarized nature, as referred to in paragraphs .11*a* and .A9.

Title (Ref: par. .17a)

.A13 A title that includes the word *independent* to clearly indicate the report is the report of an independent auditor (for example, *Report of the Independent Auditor*) affirms that the auditor has met all of the relevant ethical requirements regarding independence. This distinguishes the report of the independent auditor from reports issued by others.

Introductory Paragraph (Ref: par. .17c(i))

.A14 When the auditor is aware that the summary financial statements will be included in a document that contains other information, the auditor may consider, if the form of presentation allows, identifying the page numbers on which the summary financial statements are presented. This helps readers identify the summary financial statements that relate to the auditor's report.

Date of the Auditor's Report on the Summary Financial Statements and Events Subsequent to the Date of the Auditor's Report on the Audited Financial Statements (Ref: par. .17c(iv))

.A15 The auditor's report on the summary financial statements may be dated as of the same date or later than the date of the auditor's report on the audited financial statements, depending on when the procedures in paragraph .11 are performed and, as required by paragraph .18, when the auditor has obtained sufficient appropriate evidence on which to base the opinion. When the auditor reports on the summary financial statements after the completion of the financial statement audit, the auditor is not required to obtain additional audit evidence on the audited financial statements, or report on the effects of events that occurred subsequent to the date of the auditor's report on the audited financial statements because the summary financial statements are derived from the audited financial statements and do not update them. In such cases, however, paragraph .17*c*(iv) requires the auditor's report to state that the summary financial statements and the audited financial statements do not reflect the effects of events, if any, that occurred subsequent to the date of the auditor's report on the audited financial statements.

Modifications to the Opinion, Emphasis-of-Matter Paragraph, or Other-Matter Paragraph in the Auditor's Report on the Audited Financial Statements (Ref: par. .20)

.A16 If the auditor's report on the audited financial statements contains a qualified opinion, the auditor may determine that, due to the effect on the summary financial statements, it is inappropriate to express an opinion on the summary financial statements. In such circumstances, the auditor may adapt and apply the requirement in paragraph .16.

Comparatives (Ref: par. .22)

.A17 If the audited financial statements contain comparative financial statements, a presumption exists that the summary financial statements also would contain comparatives. Section 700 addresses the auditor's responsibilities regarding comparative financial statements in an audit of financial statements.[6]

.A18 Circumstances that may affect the auditor's determination whether an omission of comparatives is reasonable include:

- The nature and objective of the summary financial statements
- The applied criteria
- The information needs of the intended users of the summary financial statements

Unaudited Information Presented With Summary Financial Statements (Ref: par. .25)

.A19 Section 700 contains a requirement and guidance related to information presented in the financial statements that is not required by the applicable financial reporting framework.[7] Such requirement and guidance, adapted as necessary in the circumstances, may be helpful in applying the requirement in paragraph .25.

Other Information in Documents Containing Summary Financial Statements (Ref: par. .26–.27)

.A20 Section 720, *Other Information in Documents Containing Audited Financial Statements*, contains requirements and guidance relating to reading other information included in a document containing the audited financial statements and related auditor's report and responding to material inconsistencies and material misstatements of fact. Adapted as necessary in the circumstances, these requirements and related guidance may be helpful in applying the requirements in paragraphs .26–.27.

Auditor Association (Ref: par. .28–.29)

.A21 Other appropriate actions the auditor may take when management does not take the requested action may include informing the intended users and other known third-party users of the inappropriate reference to the auditor,

---

[6] Paragraphs .44–.51 of section 700.

[7] Paragraph .58 of section 700.

including that the auditor did not report, and does not express an opinion on, the summary financial statements. The auditor's course of action depends on the auditor's association with misleading information and the auditor's legal rights and obligations. Consequently, the auditor may consider it appropriate to seek legal advice.

.A22

Exhibit—Illustrations of Reports on Summary Financial Statements

Illustration 1—An Unmodified Opinion Is Expressed on the Summary Financial Statements (the Auditor's Report on the Summary Financial Statements Is Dated Later Than the Date of the Auditor's Report on the Financial Statements From Which the Summary Financial Statements Are Derived)

Illustration 2—An Unmodified Opinion Is Expressed on the Summary Financial Statements and a Qualified Opinion Is Expressed on the Audited Financial Statements

Illustration 3—An Adverse Opinion Is Expressed on the Audited Financial Statements (as a Result of the Adverse Opinion on the Audited Financial Statements, It Is Inappropriate to Express, and the Auditor Does Not Express, an Opinion on the Summary Financial Statements)

Illustration 4—An Adverse Opinion Is Expressed on the Summary Financial Statements Because They Are Not Consistent, in All Material Respects, With the Audited Financial Statements, in Accordance With the Applied Criteria

Illustration 1—An Unmodified Opinion Is Expressed on the Summary Financial Statements (the Auditor's Report on the Summary Financial Statements Is Dated Later Than the Date of the Auditor's Report on the Financial Statements From Which the Summary Financial Statements Are Derived)

Circumstances include all of the following:

- An unmodified opinion is expressed on the audited financial statements.
- Criteria are developed by management for the preparation of the summary financial statements and are adequately disclosed in Note X. The auditor has determined that the criteria are acceptable in the circumstances.
- An unmodified opinion is expressed on the summary financial statements.
- The auditor's report on the summary financial statements is dated later than the date of the auditor's report on the financial statements from which the summary financial statements are derived.

Independent Auditor's Report on Summary Financial Statements

[*Appropriate Addressee*]

The accompanying summary financial statements, which comprise the summary balance sheet as of December 31, 20X1, the summary income statement, summary statement of changes in stockholders' equity, and summary cash flow statement for the year then ended, and the related notes, are derived from the audited financial statements of ABC Company as of and for the year ended December 31, 20X1. We expressed an unmodified audit opinion on those audited financial statements in our report dated February 15, 20X2. The audited financial statements, and the summary financial statements derived therefrom, do not reflect the effects of events, if any, that occurred subsequent to the date of our report on the audited financial statements.

The summary financial statements do not contain all the disclosures required by [*describe financial reporting framework applied in the preparation of the financial statements of ABC Company*]. Reading the summary financial statements, therefore, is not a substitute for reading the audited financial statements of ABC Company.

Management's Responsibility for the Summary Financial Statements

Management is responsible for the preparation of the summary financial statements on the basis described in Note X.

Auditor's Responsibility

Our responsibility is to express an opinion about whether the summary financial statements are consistent, in all material respects, with the audited financial statements based on our procedures, which were conducted in accordance with auditing standards generally accepted in the United States of America. The procedures consisted principally of comparing the summary financial statements with the related information in the audited financial statements from which the summary financial statements have been derived, and evaluating whether the summary financial statements are prepared in accordance with the basis described in Note X. We did not perform any audit procedures regarding the audited financial statements after the date of our report on those financial statements.

Opinion

In our opinion, the summary financial statements of ABC Company as of and for the year ended December 31, 20X1 referred to above are consistent, in all material respects, with the audited financial statements from which they have been derived, on the basis described in Note X.

[*Auditor's signature*]

[*Auditor's city and state*]

[*Date of the auditor's report*]

Illustration 2—An Unmodified Opinion Is Expressed on the Summary Financial Statements and a Qualified Opinion Is Expressed on the Audited Financial Statements

Circumstances include all of the following:

- A qualified opinion is expressed on the audited financial statements.
- Criteria are developed by management for the preparation of the summary financial statements and are adequately disclosed in Note X. The auditor has determined that the criteria are acceptable in the circumstances.
- An unmodified opinion is expressed on the summary financial statements.

Independent Auditor's Report on Summary Financial Statements

[*Appropriate Addressee*]

The accompanying summary financial statements, which comprise the summary balance sheet as of December 31, 20X1, the summary income statement, summary statement of changes in stockholders' equity, and summary cash flow statement for the year then ended, and the related notes, are derived from the audited financial statements of ABC Company as of and for the year ended December 31, 20X1. We expressed a qualified audit opinion on those audited financial statements in our report dated February 15, 20X2 (see below).[1]

The summary financial statements do not contain all the disclosures required by [*describe financial reporting framework applied in the preparation of the financial statements of ABC Company*]. Reading the summary financial statements, therefore, is not a substitute for reading the audited financial statements of ABC Company.

Management's Responsibility for the Summary Financial Statements

Management is responsible for the preparation of the summary financial statements on the basis described in Note X.

Auditor's Responsibility

Our responsibility is to express an opinion about whether the summary financial statements are consistent, in all material respects, with the audited financial statements based on our procedures, which were conducted in accordance with auditing standards generally accepted in the United States of America. The procedures consisted principally of comparing the summary financial statements with the related information in the audited financial statements from which the summary financial statements have been derived, and evaluating whether the summary financial statements are prepared in accordance with the basis described in Note X.[2]

---

[1] When the auditor's report on the summary financial statements is dated later than the date of the auditor's report on the audited financial statements, the following sentence is added to this paragraph: "The audited financial statements, and the summary financial statements derived therefrom, do not reflect the effects of events, if any, that occurred subsequent to the date of our report on the audited financial statements."

[2] When the auditor's report on the summary financial statements is dated later than the date of the auditor's report on the audited financial statements, the following sentence is added to this paragraph: "We did not perform any audit procedures regarding the audited financial statements after the date of our report on those financial statements."

Opinion

In our opinion, the summary financial statements of ABC Company as of and for the year ended December 31, 20X1 referred to above are consistent, in all material respects, with the audited financial statements from which they have been derived, on the basis described in Note X.

The summary financial statements are misstated to the equivalent extent as the audited financial statements of ABC Company as of and for the year ended December 31, 20X1. The misstatement of the audited financial statements is described in our qualified audit opinion in our report dated February 15, 20X2. Our qualified audit opinion is based on the fact that the Company's inventories are carried in the balance sheet in those audited financial statements at $XXX. Management has not stated the inventories at the lower of cost or net realizable value but has stated them solely at cost, which constitutes a departure from [*describe financial reporting framework applied in the preparation of the financial statements of ABC Company*]. The Company's records indicate that, had management stated the inventories at the lower of cost or net realizable value, an amount of $XXX would have been required to write the inventories down to their net realizable value. Accordingly, cost of sales would have been increased by $XXX, and income tax, net income, and stockholders' equity would have been reduced by $XXX, $XXX, and $XXX, respectively. Our qualified audit opinion states that, except for the effects of the described matter, those financial statements present fairly, in all material respects, the financial position of ABC Company as of December 31, 20X1, and the results of its operations and its cash flows for the year then ended in accordance with [*describe financial reporting framework applied in the preparation of the financial statements of ABC Company*].

[*Auditor's signature*]

[*Auditor's city and state*]

[*Date of the auditor's report*]

Illustration 3—An Adverse Opinion Is Expressed on the Audited Financial Statements (as a Result of the Adverse Opinion on the Audited Financial Statements, It Is Inappropriate to Express, and the Auditor Does Not Express, an Opinion on the Summary Financial Statements)

Circumstances include both of the following:

- An adverse opinion is expressed on the audited financial statements. As a result of the adverse opinion on the audited financial statements, it is inappropriate to express, and the auditor does not express, an opinion on the summary financial statements, as described in paragraph .16.
- Criteria are developed by management for the preparation of the summary financial statements and are adequately disclosed in Note X. The auditor has determined that the criteria are acceptable in the circumstances.

Independent Auditor's Report on Summary Financial Statements

[*Appropriate Addressee*]

Management derived the accompanying summary financial statements, which comprise the summary balance sheet as of December 31, 20X1, the summary income statement, summary statement of changes in stockholders' equity, and summary cash flow statement for the year then ended, and the related notes, from the audited financial statements of ABC Company as of and for the year ended December 31, 20X1. Management is responsible for the preparation of these summary financial statements on the basis described in Note X.

In our report dated February 15, 20X2, we expressed an adverse audit opinion on the financial statements of ABC Company as of and for the year ended December 31, 20X1. The basis for our adverse audit opinion was [*describe basis for adverse audit opinion*]. Our adverse audit opinion stated that [*describe adverse audit opinion*].

Because of the significance of the matter discussed above, it is inappropriate to express, and we do not express, an opinion on the summary financial statements of ABC Company as of and for the year ended December 31, 20X1.

[*Auditor's signature*]

[*Auditor's city and state*]

[*Date of the auditor's report*]

Illustration 4—An Adverse Opinion Is Expressed on the Summary Financial Statements Because They Are Not Consistent, in All Material Respects, With the Audited Financial Statements, in Accordance With the Applied Criteria

Circumstances include all of the following:

- An unmodified opinion is expressed on the audited financial statements.
- Established criteria for the preparation of summary financial statements exist.
- The auditor expresses an adverse opinion on the summary financial statements because they are not consistent, in all material respects, with the audited financial statements, in accordance with the applied criteria.

Independent Auditor's Report on Summary Financial Statements

[*Appropriate Addressee*]

The accompanying summary financial statements, which comprise the summary balance sheet as of December 31, 20X1, the summary income statement, summary statement of changes in stockholders' equity, and summary cash flow statement for the year then ended, and the related notes, are derived from the audited financial statements of ABC Company as of and for the year ended December 31, 20X1. We expressed an unmodified audit opinion on those audited financial statements in our report dated February 15, 20X2.[1]

The summary financial statements do not contain all the disclosures required by [*describe financial reporting framework applied in the preparation of the financial statements of ABC Company*]. Reading the summary financial statements, therefore, is not a substitute for reading the audited financial statements of ABC Company.

Management's Responsibility for the Summary Financial Statements

Management is responsible for the preparation of the summary financial statements on the basis described in Note X.

Auditor's Responsibility

Our responsibility is to express an opinion about whether the summary financial statements are consistent, in all material respects, with the audited financial statements based on our procedures, which were conducted in accordance with auditing standards generally accepted in the United States of America. The procedures consisted principally of comparing the summary financial statements with the related information in the audited financial statements from which the summary financial statements have been derived, and evaluating whether the summary financial statements are prepared in accordance with the basis described in Note X.[2]

---

[1] When the auditor's report on the summary financial statements is dated later than the date of the auditor's report on the audited financial statements, the following sentence is added to this paragraph: "The audited financial statements, and the summary financial statements derived therefrom, do not reflect the effects of events, if any, that occurred subsequent to the date of our report on the audited financial statements."

[2] When the auditor's report on the summary financial statements is dated later than the date of the auditor's report on the audited financial statements, the following sentence is added to this paragraph: "We did not perform any audit procedures regarding the audited financial statements after the date of our report on those financial statements."

Basis for Adverse Opinion

[*Describe matter that caused the summary financial statements not to be consistent, in all material respects, with the audited financial statements, in accordance with the applied criteria.*]

Adverse Opinion

In our opinion, because of the significance of the matter discussed in the *Basis for Adverse Opinion* paragraph, the summary financial statements of ABC Company as of and for the year ended December 31, 20X1 referred to above are not consistent with the audited financial statements from which they have been derived, on the basis described in Note X.

[*Auditor's signature*]

[*Auditor's city and state*]

[*Date of the auditor's report*]

AU-C Sections 900–999

SPECIAL CONSIDERATIONS IN THE UNITED STATES

TABLE OF CONTENTS

AU-C Section 905 *

Alert That Restricts the Use of the Auditor's Written Communication

Source: SAS No. 125.

Effective for the auditor's written communications related to audits of financial statements for periods ending on or after December 15, 2012. For all other engagements conducted in accordance with GAAS, this section is effective for the auditor's written communications issued on or after December 15, 2012.

Introduction

Scope of This Section

.01 This section addresses the auditor's responsibility, when required or the auditor decides, to include in the auditor's report or other written communication issued by the auditor in connection with an engagement conducted in accordance with generally accepted auditing standards (GAAS) (hereinafter referred to in this section as auditor's written communication) language that restricts the use of the auditor's written communication. This language is referred to in this section as an alert. In an auditor's report, such language is included in an other-matter paragraph. (Ref: par. .A1 and .A3)

.02 Appendix A, "List of AU-C Sections Relating to the Restricted Use of the Auditor's Written Communication," identifies sections that contain specific requirements to include an alert that restricts the use of the auditor's written communication or that otherwise address the inclusion of such alerts. Accordingly, the requirements in this section regarding the form of such alert apply. (Ref: par. .A2)

Effective Date

.03 This section is effective for the auditor's written communications related to audits of financial statements for periods ending on or after December 15, 2012. For all other engagements conducted in accordance with GAAS, this section is effective for the auditor's written communications issued on or after December 15, 2012.

Objective

.04 The objective of the auditor is to restrict the use of the auditor's written communication by including an alert when the potential exists for the auditor's written communication to be misunderstood if taken out of the context in which the auditor's written communication is intended to be used.

---

* This section has been codified using an "AU-C" identifier instead of an "AU" identifier. "AU-C" is a temporary identifier to avoid confusion with references to existing "AU" sections, which will remain in AICPA *Professional Standards* through 2013. The "AU-C" identifier will revert to "AU" in 2014, by which time substantially all engagements for which the "AU" sections were still effective are expected to be completed.

Definition

.05 For purposes of GAAS, the following term has the meaning attributed as follows:

Specified parties. The intended users of the auditor's written communication.

Requirements

Alert That Restricts the Use of the Auditor's Written Communication

.06 The auditor's written communication should include an alert, in a separate paragraph, that restricts its use when the subject matter of the auditor's written communication is based on (Ref: par. .A2–.A3)

a. measurement or disclosure criteria that are determined by the auditor to be suitable only for a limited number of users who can be presumed to have an adequate understanding of the criteria,

b. measurement or disclosure criteria that are available only to the specified parties, or

c. matters identified by the auditor during the course of the audit engagement when the identification of such matters is not the primary objective of the audit engagement (commonly referred to as a by-product report). (Ref: par. .A4–.A7)

.07 Unless specified otherwise by this section or other relevant sections, the alert that restricts the use of the auditor's written communication required by paragraph .06 should

a. state that the auditor's written communication is intended solely for the information and use of the specified parties.

b. identify the specified parties for whom use is intended. In situations covered by paragraph .06*c*, the specified parties should only include management, those charged with governance, others within the entity, the parties to the contract or agreement, or the regulatory agencies to whose jurisdiction the entity is subject, as appropriate in the circumstances.

c. state that the auditor's written communication is not intended to be and should not be used by anyone other than the specified parties. (Ref: par. .A8–.A9)

Adding Other Specified Parties (Ref: par. .A10)

.08 When, in accordance with paragraph .06, the auditor includes an alert that restricts the use of the auditor's written communication to certain specified parties, and the auditor is requested to add other parties as specified parties, the auditor should determine whether to agree to add the other parties as specified parties. In situations covered by paragraph .06*c*, the auditor should not agree to add as specified parties any other parties not described in paragraph .07*b*.

.09 When the auditor agrees to add other parties as specified parties, the auditor should obtain affirmative acknowledgment, in writing, from the other parties of their understanding of

a. the nature of the engagement resulting in the auditor's written communication, *b.* the measurement or disclosure criteria related to the subject matter of the auditor's written communication, and

c. the auditor's written communication.

.10 If the other parties are added after the release of the auditor's written communication, in addition to the requirements of paragraph .09, the auditor should take one of the following actions:

a. Amend the auditor's written communication to add the other parties. In such circumstances, the auditor should not change the original date of the auditor's written communication.

b. Provide a written acknowledgment to management and the other parties that such parties have been added as specified parties. The auditor should state in the acknowledgment that no procedures were performed subsequent to the original date of the auditor's written communication or the date that the engagement was completed, as appropriate.

Alert for Engagements Performed in Accordance With *Government Auditing Standards* (Ref: par. .A11)

.11 The alert language required by paragraph .07 should not be used when

a. the engagement is performed in accordance with *Government Auditing Standards*, and

b. the auditor's written communication pursuant to that engagement is issued in accordance with

i. section 265, *Communicating Internal Control Related Matters Identified in an Audit*;

ii. section 806, *Reporting on Compliance With Aspects of Contractual Agreements or Regulatory Requirements in Connection With Audited Financial Statements* ; or

iii. section 935, *Compliance Audits* .

Instead, the alert required by paragraph .06 should

a. describe the purpose of the auditor's written communication and

b. state that the auditor's written communication is not suitable for any other purpose.

Application and Other Explanatory Material

Alert That Restricts the Use of the Auditor's Written Communication (Ref: par. .01–.02 and .06)

.A1 In addition to auditor's reports, auditor's written communications may include letters or presentation materials (for example, letters communicating internal control related matters or presentations addressing communications with those charged with governance).

.A2 Certain sections, identified in appendix A, contain specific requirements to include an alert that restricts the use of the auditor's written communication or that otherwise address the inclusion of such alerts. The need for an alert that restricts the use of the auditor's written communication arises from the potential for the auditor's written communication to be misunderstood if taken out of the context in which the auditor's written communication is intended to be used. The context in which the auditor's written communication is intended to be used may consist of a number of circumstances, including

- the purpose of the auditor's written communication;
- the nature of the procedures applied in its preparation;
- the basis of, or assumptions used in, its preparation; and
- the extent to which the procedures performed generally are known or understood.

.A3 Auditor's reports on financial statements prepared in accordance with a general purpose framework ordinarily do not include an alert that restricts their use. However, nothing in GAAS precludes an auditor from including such an alert in any auditor's report or other auditor's written communication. For example, financial statements prepared specifically for use in connection with an acquisition may be prepared in accordance with a general purpose framework because the parties involved in the transaction have agreed that such general purpose financial statements are appropriate for their purposes. Nevertheless, when the terms of the engagement to audit those financial statements require the auditor to supply the auditor's report only to specified parties, the auditor may consider it necessary in the circumstances to include an other-matter paragraph in the auditor's report that restricts the use of the auditor's report.[1]

.A4 The subject matter of the auditor's written communication may be based on matters identified by the auditor during the course of the audit engagement when identification of such matters is not the primary objective of the audit engagement (commonly referred to as a by-product report) (for example, communication about internal control or compliance related matters identified in an audit of financial statements, the primary objective of which is to express an opinion on the financial statements). Because such communication can only be understood in relation to the primary objective of the audit engagement, it may be misinterpreted or misunderstood. Accordingly, paragraph .06*c* requires such auditor's written communication to include an alert that restricts its use.

Alert That Restricts the Use of the Auditor's Written Communication Included in General Use Communications

.A5 An auditor's written communication that is required by paragraph .06 to include an alert that restricts its use may be included in a document that also contains an auditor's written communication that is for general use. In such circumstances, the use of the general use communication is not affected.

.A6 An auditor may also issue a single combined auditor's written communication that includes (*a*) communications that are required by paragraph .06 to include an alert that restricts their use and (*b*) communications that are for general use. If these two types of communications are clearly differentiated within the combined communication, such as through the use of appropriate headers, the alert that restricts the use of the auditor's written communication may be limited to the communications required by paragraph .06 to include such an alert. In such circumstances, the use of the general use communication is not affected. An example of a single combined auditor's written communication addressing a matter that was not the primary objective of the audit engagement

---

[1] Paragraph .08 of section 706, *Emphasis-of-Matter Paragraphs and Other-Matter Paragraphs in the Independent Auditor's Report*.

that is included in a general use communication is provided in the exhibit "Illustrations of Reports on Compliance With Aspects of Contractual Agreements or Regulatory Requirements in Connection With Audited Financial Statements," of section 806.[2]

Distribution of the Auditor's Written Communication

.A7 An auditor is not responsible for controlling, and cannot control, distribution of the auditor's written communication after its release. The alert that restricts the use of the auditor's written communication is designed to avoid misunderstandings related to the use of the auditor's written communication, particularly if the auditor's written communication is taken out of the context in which the auditor's written communication is intended to be used. An auditor may consider informing the entity or other specified parties that the auditor's written communication is not intended for distribution to parties other than those specified in the auditor's written communication. The auditor may, in connection with establishing the terms of the engagement, reach an understanding with the entity that the intended use of the auditor's written communication will be restricted and may obtain the entity's agreement that the entity and specified parties will not distribute such auditor's written communication to parties other than those identified therein.

Illustrative Alert Language (Ref: par. .07)

.A8 The alert that restricts the use of the auditor's written communication may list the specified parties or refer to the specified parties listed elsewhere in the auditor's written communication. The following illustrates language that includes the elements required by paragraph .07:

> This [*report, letter, presentation, or communication*] is intended solely for the information and use of [*list or refer to the specified parties*] and is not intended to be and should not be used by anyone other than these specified parties.

.A9 Other sections, such as section 920, *Letters for Underwriters and Certain Other Requesting Parties*, may include specific requirements relating to the matters to be included in the alert that restrict the use of the auditor's written communication, as required by paragraph .06, including identifying the specified parties.

Adding Other Specified Parties (Ref: par. .08–.10)

.A10 When the auditor is requested to add other parties as specified parties, the auditor may agree to add the other parties as specified parties based on the auditor's consideration of factors such as the identity of the other parties and the intended use of the auditor's written communication.

Alert for Engagements Performed in Accordance With *Government Auditing Standards* (Ref: par. .11)

.A11 *Government Auditing Standards* regard the auditor's written communications issued pursuant to the sections, identified in paragraph .11, to be an integral part of the audit engagement for the purpose of assessing the

---

[2] Illustration 5, "Report on Compliance With Aspects of Contractual Agreements Given in a Combined Report, and No Instances of Noncompliance Were Identified," in the exhibit "Illustrations of Reports on Compliance With Aspects of Contractual Agreements or Regulatory Requirements in Connection With Audited Financial Statements," of section 806, *Reporting on Compliance With Aspects of Contractual Agreements or Regulatory Requirements in Connection With Audited Financial Statements* .

results of the engagement. Accordingly, different alert language is used. The following illustrates language that includes the elements of the alert required by paragraph .11:

> The purpose of this [*report, letter, presentation, or communication*] is solely to [*describe the purpose of the auditor's written communication, such as to describe the scope of our testing of internal control over financial reporting and compliance, and the result of that testing, and not to provide an opinion on the effectiveness of the entity's internal control over financial reporting or on compliance*]. This [*report, letter, presentation, or communication*] is an integral part of an audit performed in accordance with *Government Auditing Standards* in considering [*describe the results that are being assessed, such as the entity's internal control over financial reporting and compliance*]. Accordingly, this [*report, letter, presentation, or communication*] is not suitable for any other purpose.

.A12

Appendix A—List of AU-C Sections Relating to the Restricted Use of the Auditor's Written Communication

This appendix identifies paragraphs in other sections that contain specific requirements to include an alert that restricts the use of the auditor's written communication or that otherwise address the inclusion of such alerts. The list is not a substitute for considering the requirements and related application and other explanatory material in the other sections.

- Paragraph .17 of section 260, *The Auditor's Communication With Those Charged With Governance*
- Paragraphs .14*d*, .A32, and .A38–.A39 of section 265, *Communicating Internal Control Related Matters Identified in an Audit*
- Paragraph .A16 of section 725, *Supplementary Information in Relation to the Financial Statements as a Whole*
- Paragraphs .20, .A26–.A27, and .A33 of section 800, *Special Considerations—Audits of Financial Statements Prepared in Accordance With Special Purpose Frameworks*
- Paragraphs .12–.13 and .A6–.A8 of section 806, *Reporting on Compliance With Aspects of Contractual Agreements or Regulatory Requirements in Connection With Audited Financial Statements*
- Paragraphs .14*f* and .A6 of section 915, *Reports on Application of Requirements of an Applicable Financial Reporting Framework*
- Paragraphs .33 and .A34 of section 920, *Letters for Underwriters and Certain Other Requesting Parties*
- Paragraphs .30, .31*i*, and .A33 of section 935, *Compliance Audits*

.A13

Appendix B—Amendments to Other Sections

Boldface italic denotes new language. Deleted text is shown in ~~strikethrough~~. Amended footnote text is found at the end of appendix B.

Section 260, *The Auditor's Communication With Those Charged With Governance*

[No amendments to paragraphs .01–.16.]

Restricted Use

.17

When the auditor communicates matters in accordance with this section in writing, the communication is considered a by-product report.[1] Accordingly, the auditor should indicate in the communication that it is intended solely for the information and use of those charged with governance and, if appropriate, management, and is not intended to be, and should not be, used by anyone other than these specified parties.

[No amendments to paragraphs .18–.20 or .A1–.A48.]

Section 265, *Communicating Internal Control Related Matters Identified in an Audit*

[No amendments to paragraphs .01–.13.]

.14

The auditor should include in the ***auditor's*** written communication of significant deficiencies and material weaknesses (Ref: par. .A29–.A33)

a. the definition of the term *material weakness* and, when relevant, the definition of the term *significant deficiency*.

b. a description of the significant deficiencies and material weaknesses and an explanation of their potential effects. (Ref: par. .A29)

c. sufficient information to enable those charged with governance and management to understand the context of the communication. In particular, the auditor should include in the communication the following elements that explain that (Ref: par. .A30–.A31)

   i. the purpose of the audit was for the auditor to express an opinion on the financial statements.

   ii. the audit included consideration of internal control over financial reporting in order to design audit procedures that are appropriate in the circumstances but not for the purpose of expressing an opinion on the effectiveness of internal control.

   iii. the auditor is not expressing an opinion on the effectiveness of internal control.

   iv. the auditor's consideration of internal control was not designed to identify all deficiencies in internal control that might be material weaknesses or significant deficiencies, and therefore, material weaknesses or significant deficiencies may exist that were not identified.

d. ***an appropriate alert,*** in accordance with section 905, ~~*Restricting the Use of an Auditor's Report,*~~ **Alert That Restricts the Use of the Auditor's Written Communication.**[2,†] ~~a restriction regarding the use of the communication to management, those charged with governance, others within the organization, and any governmental authority to which the auditor is required to report.~~ (Ref: par. A32)

[Footnotes 2–7 will be renumbered as footnotes 3–8. No amendments to paragraphs .15–.16 and .A1–.A31.]

Restriction on Use (Ref: par. .14d)

.A32

In certain cases not involving* Government Auditing Standards,** ~~L~~law*** or regulation may require the auditor or management to furnish a copy of the auditor's written communication on significant deficiencies and material weaknesses to governmental authorities. When this is the case, the auditor's written communication may identify such governmental authorities in the ~~restricted-use~~ paragraph ***containing the alert that restricts the use of the auditor's written communication.*** ~~Because the written communication is a by-product of the audit, s~~*S*ection 905**, Alert That Restricts the Use of the Auditor's Written Communication**[†] does not permit the auditor to add parties, other than those identified in paragraph ~~.14*d*, as specified parties.~~**.07b** ***of that section.***[9] ~~In some instances, the restricted-use communication may be included in a document that also contains a general-use report. The restricted-use communication remains restricted as to use, and the general-use report continues to be for general use.~~

[No amendments to paragraphs .A33–.A37.]

Exhibit A—Illustrative *Auditor's* **Written Communication**

.A38

The following is an illustrative ***auditor's*** written communication encompassing the requirements in paragraph .14.

To Management and [*identify the body or individuals charged with governance, such as the entity's Board of Directors*] of ABC Company

In planning and performing our audit of the financial statements of ABC Company (the "Company") as of and for the year ended December 31, 20XX, in accordance with auditing standards generally accepted in the United States of America, we considered the Company's internal control over financial reporting (internal control) as a basis for designing audit procedures that are appropriate in the circumstances for the purpose of expressing our opinion on the financial statements, but not for the purpose of expressing an opinion on the effectiveness of the Company's internal control. Accordingly, we do not express an opinion on the effectiveness of the Company's internal control.

Our consideration of internal control was for the limited purpose described in the preceding paragraph and was not designed to identify all deficiencies in internal control that might be [*material weaknesses* or *material weaknesses or significant deficiencies*] and therefore, [*material weaknesses* or *material weaknesses or significant deficiencies*] may exist that were not identified. However, as discussed below, we identified certain deficiencies in internal control that we consider to be [*material weaknesses* or *significant deficiencies* or *material weaknesses and significant deficiencies*].

A deficiency in internal control exists when the design or operation of a control does not allow management or employees, in the normal course of performing their assigned functions, to prevent, or detect and correct, misstatements on a timely basis. A material weakness is a deficiency, or a combination of deficiencies, in internal control, such that there is a reasonable possibility that a material misstatement of the entity's financial statements will not be prevented, or detected and corrected, on a timely basis. [*We consider the following deficiencies in the Company's internal control to be material weaknesses:*]

[*Describe the material weaknesses that were identified and an explanation of their potential effects.*]

[*A significant deficiency is a deficiency, or a combination of deficiencies, in internal control that is less severe than a material weakness, yet important enough to merit attention by those charged with governance. We consider the following deficiencies in the Company's internal control to be significant deficiencies:*]

[*Describe the significant deficiencies that were identified and an explanation of their potential effects.*]

[*If the auditor is communicating significant deficiencies and did not identify any material weaknesses, the auditor may state that none of the identified significant deficiencies are considered to be material weaknesses.*]

This communication is intended solely for the information and use of management, [*identify the body or individuals charged with governance*], others within the organization, and [*identify any governmental authorities to which the auditor is required to report*] and is not intended to be, and should not be, used by anyone other than these specified parties.[1]

[*Auditor's Signature*]

[Auditor's City and State]

[*Date*]

Exhibit B—Illustrative No Material Weakness Communication

.A39

The following is an illustrative ***auditor's*** written communication indicating that no material weaknesses were identified during the audit ***of a not-for-profit organization***.

To Management and [*identify the body or individuals charged with governance, such as the entity's Board of Directors*] of ~~ABC Company~~ ***NPO Organization***

In planning and performing our audit of the financial statements of ~~ABC Company (the "Company")~~ ***NPO Organization (the "Organization")*** as of and for the year ended December 31, 20XX, in accordance with auditing standards generally accepted in the United States of America, we considered the ~~Company's~~ ***Organization's*** internal control over financial reporting (internal control) as a basis for designing audit procedures that are appropriate in the circumstances for the purpose of expressing our opinion on the financial statements, but not for the purpose of expressing an opinion on the effectiveness of the ~~Company's~~ ***Organization's*** internal control. Accordingly, we do not express an opinion on the effectiveness of the ~~Company's~~ ***Organization's*** internal control.

A deficiency in internal control exists when the design or operation of a control does not allow management or employees, in the normal course of performing their assigned functions, to prevent, or detect and correct, misstatements on a timely basis. A material weakness is a deficiency, or a combination of deficiencies, in internal control, such that there is a reasonable possibility that a material misstatement of the entity's financial statements will not be prevented, or detected and corrected, on a timely basis.

Our consideration of internal control was for the limited purpose described in the first paragraph and was not designed to identify all deficiencies in internal control that might be material weaknesses. Given these limitations, during our audit we did not identify any deficiencies in internal control that we consider to be material weaknesses. However, material weaknesses may exist that have not been identified.

[*If one or more significant deficiencies have been identified, the auditor may add the following: Our audit was also not designed to identify deficiencies in internal control that might be significant deficiencies. A significant deficiency is a deficiency, or a combination of deficiencies, in internal control that is less severe than a material weakness, yet important enough to merit attention by those charged with governance. We communicated the significant deficiencies identified during our audit in a separate communication dated [date].*]

This communication is intended solely for the information and use of management, [*identify the body or individuals charged with governance*], others within the organization, and [*identify any governmental authorities to which the auditor is required to report*] and is not intended to be, and should not be, used by anyone other than these specified parties.[1]

[*Auditor's Signature*]

[Auditor's City and State]

[*Date*]

[No amendments to paragraph A40.]

Section 725, *Supplementary Information in Relation to the Financial Statements as a Whole*

[No amendments to paragraphs .01–.13 and paragraphs .A1–.A15.]

.A16 ***When reporting on supplementary information in a separate report, t***~~The~~ the auditor may consider ***including an alert that restricts*** ~~restricting~~ the use of ~~a~~ ***the*** separate report ~~on supplementary information~~ to ***solely to*** the appropriate specified parties, in accordance with section 905, ~~*Restricting the Use of an Auditor's Report,*~~[†] **Alert That Restricts the Use of the Auditor's Written Communication**, to avoid potential misinterpretation or misunderstanding of the supplementary information that is not presented with the financial statements.

[No amendments to paragraph .A17.]

Section 800, *Special Considerations—Audits of Financial Statements Prepared in Accordance With Special Purpose Frameworks*

[No amendments to paragraphs .01–.19.]

Restricting the Use of the Auditor's Report in an Other-Matter Paragraph ***(Ref: par. .A26–.A27)***

.20

Except for the circumstances described in paragraph .21, the auditor's report on special purpose financial statements should include an *other-matter* paragraph,[9] under an appropriate heading, that restricts[10] the use of the auditor's report ***solely*** to those within the entity, the parties to the contract or agreement, or the regulatory agencies to whose jurisdiction the entity is subject when the special purpose financial statements are prepared in accordance with either

- *a.* a contractual basis of accounting or
- *b.* a regulatory basis of accounting.

[No amendments to paragraphs .21–.23 or paragraphs .A1–.A25.]

Restricting the Use of the Auditor's Report in an Other-Matter Paragraph ***(Ref: par. .20)***

.A26

~~When use of the auditor's report is restricted, the intended users are the specified parties.~~ ***Special purpose financial statements prepared in accordance with a contractual or regulatory basis of accounting are suitable only for a limited number of users who can be presumed to have an adequate understanding of such bases of accounting.*** ~~The restriction on use of the auditor's report is necessary due to the nature of the report and the potential for the report to be misunderstood when taken out of the context in which it was intended to be used.~~ For example, special purpose financial statements prepared in accordance with a contractual basis of accounting are developed for and directed only to the parties to the contract or agreement. ***Accordingly, the alert that restricts the use of the auditor's report is required due to the nature of the report and the potential for the report to be taken out of the context in which the auditor's report was intended to be used.*** Section 905, ~~*Restricting the Use of an Auditor's Report*~~[‡], **Alert That Restricts the Use of the Auditor's Written Communication,** addresses adding other parties as specified parties.

.A27

In the case of special purpose financial statements prepared in accordance with a cash or tax basis of accounting, the auditor may consider it necessary in the circumstances of the engagement to ~~restrict the~~ ***include an alert that restricts the*** use of the auditor's report.

[No amendments to paragraphs .A28–.A32.]

Appendix A—Overview of Reporting Requirements

.A33

The following table provides an overview of the reporting requirements depending on the special purpose framework.

	Cash Basis	*Tax Basis*	*Regulatory Basis*	*Regulatory Basis (General Use)*	*Contractual Basis*
Opinion(s)	Single opinion on special purpose framework	Single opinion on special purpose framework	Single opinion on special purpose framework	Dual opinion on special purpose framework and generally accepted accounting principles (GAAP)[18]	Single opinion on special purpose framework
Description of purpose for which special purpose financial statements are prepared[19]	No	No	Yes	Yes	Yes
*Emphasis-of-matter paragraph alerting readers ~~about~~ **regarding** the preparation in accordance with a special purpose framework*[20]	Yes	Yes	Yes	No	Yes
*Other-matter paragraph **including an alert** restricting the use of the auditor's report*[21]	No	No	Yes	No	Yes
Exhibit A Illustrations	1	2	3	4	5

Section 806, *Reporting on Compliance With Aspects of Contractual Agreements or Regulatory Requirements in Connection With Audited Financial Statements*

[No amendments to paragraphs .01–.11.]

Separate Report on Compliance With Aspects of Contractual Agreements or Regulatory Requirements

.12

When the auditor reports on compliance in a separate report, the report should include the following:

a. A title that includes the word *independent* to clearly indicate that it is the report of an independent auditor.

b. An appropriate addressee

c. A paragraph that states that the financial statements were audited in accordance with generally accepted auditing standards and an identification of the United States of America as the country of origin of those standards (for example, auditing standards generally accepted in the United States of America or U.S. generally accepted auditing standards) and the date of the auditor's report on those financial statements.

d. If the auditor expressed a modified opinion[1] on the financial statements, a statement describing the nature of the modification. (Ref: par. .A4)

e. When no instances of noncompliance are identified by the auditor, a reference to the specific covenants or paragraphs of the contractual agreement or regulatory requirement and a statement that nothing came to the auditor's attention that caused the auditor to believe that the entity failed to comply with specified aspects of contractual agreements or regulatory requirements, insofar as they relate to accounting matters (see paragraphs .07 and .10).

f. When instances of noncompliance are identified by the auditor, a reference to the specific covenants or paragraphs of the contractual agreement or regulatory requirement, insofar as they relate to accounting matters, and a description of the identified instances of noncompliance. (Ref: par. .A5)

g. A statement that the report is being provided in connection with the audit of the financial statements.

h. A statement that the audit was not directed primarily toward obtaining knowledge regarding compliance, and accordingly, had the auditor performed additional procedures, other matters may have come to the auditor's attention regarding noncompliance with the specific covenants or paragraphs of the contractual agreement or regulatory requirement, insofar as they relate to accounting matters.

i. A paragraph that includes a description and the source of significant interpretations, if any, made by the entity's management relating to the provisions of the relevant contractual agreement or regulatory requirement.

j. A paragraph that ***includes an appropriate alert*** ~~restricts the use[2] of the report to management, those charged with governance, others within the organization, the regulatory agency responsible~~

~~for the provisions, or other parties to the contract or agreement,~~ ***in accordance with the section 905,*** **Alert That Restricts the Use of the Auditor's Written Communication.**[2] (Ref: par. .A6 and .A7)

k. The manual or printed signature of the auditor's firm and the city and state where the auditor practices.

l. The date of the report, which should be the same date as the auditor's report on the financial statements.[3]

Report on Compliance With Aspects of Contractual Agreements or Regulatory Requirements Included in the Auditor's Report

.13

When a report on compliance is included in the auditor's report on the financial statements, the auditor's report should include an other-matter paragraph[fn 4] that includes a reference to the specific covenants or paragraphs of the contractual agreement or regulatory requirement, insofar as they relate to accounting matters, and also should include the following:

a. When no instances of noncompliance are identified by the auditor, a statement that nothing came to the auditor's attention that caused the auditor to believe that the entity failed to comply with specified aspects of the contractual agreements or regulatory requirements, insofar as they relate to accounting matters (see paragraphs .07 and .10).

b. When instances of noncompliance are identified by the auditor, a description of the identified instances of noncompliance. (Ref: par. .A5)

c. A statement that the communication is being provided in connection with the audit of the financial statements.

d. A statement that the audit was not directed primarily toward obtaining knowledge regarding compliance, and accordingly, had the auditor performed additional procedures, other matters may have come to the auditor's attention regarding noncompliance with the specific covenants or paragraphs of the contractual agreement or regulatory requirement, insofar as they relate to accounting matters.

e. A paragraph that includes a description and the source of significant interpretations, if any, made by the entity's management relating to the provisions of the relevant contractual agreement or regulatory requirement.

f. A paragraph that ***includes an appropriate alert*** ~~restricts the use[5] of the report to management, those charged with governance, others within the organization, the regulatory agency responsible for the provisions, or other parties to the contract or agreement,~~ ***in accordance with section 905.***[5] (Ref: par. .A6–.A7)

[No amendments to paragraphs .A1–.A5.]

Restrictions on the Use of the Auditor's Report [9] (Ref: par. .12*j* and .13*f*)

.A6

~~A restriction on~~ ***An alert,*** ~~the use of the report on compliance to the specified parties~~, as discussed in paragraphs .12*j* and .13*f*, is necessary because***, although compliance matters may be identified by the auditor during the course of the audit engagement, the identification of such matters is not***

the primary objective of the audit engagement. In addition, the basis, assumptions, or purpose of the provisions in contractual agreements or regulatory requirements to which the report on compliance relates are developed for, and directed only to, the parties to the contractual agreement or the regulatory agency responsible for the requirements.

.A7

~~If the auditor's report on compliance is included in the auditor's report on the financial statements, the restriction on the use of the report on compliance to specified parties, as required by paragraph .13f, would apply to the entire auditor's report. If a separate report is issued, as described in paragraph .11, then only the report on compliance need be restricted as to use by the specified parties.~~ ***The alert that restricts the use of the report indicates that only the report on compliance with aspects of contractual agreements or regulatory requirements is restricted. Accordingly, the intended use of the auditor's report on the financial statements is not affected by this alert.***

.A8

[No amendments to illustrations 1–4.]

Illustration 5—A Report on Compliance With Aspects of Contractual Agreements Given in a Combined Report, and No Instances of Noncompliance Were Identified

Independent Auditor's Report

[Appropriate Addressee]

Report on the Financial Statements[1]

We have audited the accompanying financial statements of ABC Company, which comprise the balance sheet as of December 31, 20X1, and the related statements of income, changes in stockholders' equity, and cash flows for the year then ended, and the related notes to the financial statements.

Management's Responsibility for the Financial Statements

Management is responsible for the preparation and fair presentation of these financial statements in accordance with accounting principles generally accepted in the United States of America; this includes the design, implementation, and maintenance of internal control relevant to the preparation and fair presentation of financial statements that are free from material misstatement, whether due to fraud or error.

Auditor's Responsibility

Our responsibility is to express an opinion on these financial statements based on our audit. We conducted our audit in accordance with auditing standards generally accepted in the United States of America. Those standards require that we plan and perform the audit to obtain reasonable assurance about whether the financial statements are free from material misstatement.

An audit involves performing procedures to obtain audit evidence about the amounts and disclosures in the financial statements. The procedures selected depend on the auditor's judgment, including the assessment of the risks of material misstatement of the financial statements, whether due to fraud or error. In making those risk assessments, the auditor considers internal control relevant to the entity's preparation and fair presentation of the financial statements in order to design audit procedures that are appropriate in the circumstances, but not

for the purpose of expressing an opinion on the effectiveness of the entity's internal control.[2] *Accordingly, we express no such opinion. An audit also includes evaluating the appropriateness of accounting policies used and the reasonableness of significant accounting estimates made by management, as well as evaluating the overall presentation of the financial statements.*

We believe that the audit evidence we have obtained is sufficient and appropriate to provide a basis for our audit opinion.

Opinion

In our opinion, the financial statements referred to above present fairly, in all material respects, the financial position of ABC Company as of December 31, 20X1, and the results of its operations and its cash flows for the year then ended in accordance with accounting principles generally accepted in the United States of America.

Other Matter

In connection with our audit, nothing came to our attention that caused us to believe that ABC Company failed to comply with the terms, covenants, provisions, or conditions of sections XX to YY, inclusive, of the Indenture dated July 21, 20X0 with XYZ Bank, insofar as they relate to accounting matters. However, our audit was not directed primarily toward obtaining knowledge of such noncompliance. Accordingly, had we performed additional procedures, other matters may have come to our attention regarding the Company's noncompliance with the above-referenced terms, covenants, provisions, or conditions of the Indenture, insofar as they relate to accounting matters.

Restricted Use Relating to the Other Matter

The communication related to compliance with the aforementioned Indenture described in the Other Matter paragraph is intended solely for the information and use of the boards of directors and management of ABC Company and XYZ Bank and is not intended to be and should not be used by anyone other than these specified parties.[3]

Report on Other Legal and Regulatory Requirements

[Form and content of this section of the auditor's report will vary depending on the nature of the auditor's other reporting responsibilities.]

[Auditor's Signature]

[Auditor's City and State]

[Date of the Auditor's Report]

Section 915, *Reports on Application of Requirements of an Applicable Financial Reporting Framework*

[No amendments to paragraphs .01–.13.]

.14

The reporting accountant's written report should be addressed to the requesting party (for example, management or those charged with governance) and should include the following:

a. A brief description of the nature of the engagement and a statement that the engagement was performed in accordance with this section

b. Identification of the specific entity; a description of the specific transaction(s), if applicable; a statement of the relevant facts, circumstances, and assumptions; and a statement about the source of such information

c. A statement describing the appropriate application of the requirements of an applicable financial reporting framework (including the country of origin) to the specific transaction or type of report that may be issued on the entity's financial statements and, if appropriate, a description of the reasons for the reporting accountant's conclusion

d. A statement that the responsibility for the proper accounting treatment rests with the preparers of the financial statements, who should consult with their continuing accountant

e. A statement that any difference in the facts, circumstances, or assumptions presented may change the report

f. ***An alert that restricts the use of the report solely to the specified parties, as required by section 905,* Alert That Restricts the Use of the Auditor's Written Communication**[2] ~~A separate paragraph at the end of the report that includes the following elements:~~

~~i. A statement indicating that the report is intended solely for the information and use of the specified parties~~

~~ii. An identification of the specified parties to whom use is restricted~~

~~iii. A statement that the report is not intended to be and should not be used by anyone other than the specified parties~~

g. If the reporting accountant is not independent of the entity, a statement indicating the reporting accountant's lack of independence. The reporting accountant is neither required to provide, nor precluded from providing, the reasons for the lack of independence; however, if the reporting accountant chooses to provide the reasons for the lack of independence, the reporting accountant should include all the reasons therefor.

[Footnote 2 will be renumbered as footnote 3. No amendments to paragraphs .A1–.A5.]

.A6

The ~~restriction of the use of the~~ ***alert that restricts the use of the*** reporting accountant's written report referred to in paragraph .14*f* is not intended to preclude distribution of the report to the continuing accountant.

[No amendments to paragraphs .A7–.A8.]

Section 920, *Letters for Underwriters and Certain Other Requesting Parties*

[No amendments to paragraphs .01–.31.]

~~**.32**~~

~~The auditor should not mention in a comfort letter reports issued in accordance with section 265, *Communicating Internal Control Related Matters Identified in an Audit*, or any restricted use reports issued to the entity in connection with procedures performed on the entity's internal control over financial reporting in accordance with AT section 501, *An Examination of*~~

~~*an Entity's Internal Control Over Financial Reporting That Is Integrated With an Audit of Its Financial Statements.*~~

.33

~~The auditor should not refer to, or attach, any restricted use report to the comfort letter.~~ ***The auditor should not mention, refer to, or attach to the comfort letter any report or other auditor's written communication that includes an alert that restricts the use of the auditor's written communication, in accordance with section 905,* Alert That Restricts the Use of the Auditor's Written Communication, *or any restricted use reports issued in accordance with Statements on Standards for Attestation Engagements or Statements on Standards for Accounting and Review Services*** ~~to the comfort letter~~. (Ref: par. .A34)

[No amendments to paragraphs .34–.75 and .A1–.A33.]

.A34

An example of a***n auditor's written communication that includes an alert that restricts the use of the auditor's written communication that is not permitted to be mentioned, referred to, or attached to the comfort letter is an auditor's written communication issued in accordance with section 265,* Communicating Internal Control Related Matters Identified in an Audit. *Examples of*** restricted use report***s*** that ~~is~~ ***are*** not permitted to be ***mentioned,*** referred to, or attached to the comfort letter ~~is~~ ***include*** a report on agreed-upon procedures ***and any restricted use report issued in connection with procedures performed on the entity's internal control over financial reporting, in accordance with AT section 501,* An Examination of an Entity's Internal Control Over Financial Reporting That Is Integrated With an Audit of Its Financial Statements**.

[No amendments to paragraphs .A35–.A93.]

Section 935, *Compliance Audits*

[No amendments to paragraphs .01–.29.]

Report on Compliance Only

.30

The auditor's report on compliance should be in writing and include the following elements:

a. A title that includes the word *independent*.

b. An addressee appropriate for the circumstances of the engagement.

c. An introductory paragraph that includes the following:

   i. Identification of the one or more government programs covered by the compliance audit or reference to a separate schedule containing that information

   ii. Identification of the applicable compliance requirements or a reference to where they can be found

   iii. Identification of the period covered by the report

d. A section with the heading "Management's Responsibility" that includes a statement that compliance with the applicable compliance requirements is the responsibility of the entity's management. If the document containing the auditor's report contains a separate statement by management about its responsibility for the applicable compliance requirements, the auditor's report should not include a reference to such statement by management.

e. A section with the heading "Auditor's Responsibility" that includes the following statements:

i. A statement that the auditor's responsibility is to express an opinion on the entity's compliance with the applicable compliance requirements based on the compliance audit

ii. A statement that the compliance audit was conducted in accordance with auditing standards generally accepted in the United States of America, the standards applicable to financial audits contained in *Government Auditing Standards*, and the governmental audit requirement

iii. A statement that the compliance audit included examining, on a test basis, evidence about the entity's compliance with those requirements and performing such other procedures as the auditor considered necessary in the circumstances

iv. A statement that the auditor believes the compliance audit provides a reasonable basis for the auditor's opinion

v. A statement that the compliance audit does not provide a legal determination of the entity's compliance

f. If noncompliance results in a modified opinion, a section with an appropriate heading, indicating the basis for the modified opinion that includes a description of such noncompliance, or a reference to a description of such noncompliance in an accompanying schedule.[5] (Ref: par. .A34)

g. A section with the heading "Opinion" that includes the auditor's opinion, at the level specified by the governmental audit requirement, on whether the entity complied, in all material respects, with the applicable compliance requirements.

h. If other noncompliance that is required to be reported by the governmental audit requirement is identified (that is, noncompliance that does not result in a modified opinion), an other-matter paragraph[6] that includes a description of such noncompliance or a reference to a description of such noncompliance in an accompanying schedule. (Ref: par. .A34)

i. If the criteria used to evaluate compliance are

i. established or determined by contractual agreement or regulatory provisions that are developed solely for the parties to the agreement or regulatory agency responsible for the provisions or

ii. available only to the specified parties,

~~a separate paragraph at the end of the report that includes (1) a statement indicating that the report is intended solely for the information and use of the specified parties, (2) an identification of the specified parties to whom use is restricted, and (3) a statement that the report is not intended to be and should not be used by anyone other than the specified parties. (Ref: par. .A33)~~ ***an alert describing the purpose of the auditor's report and that the report is not suitable for any other purpose, as required by section 905,* Alert That Restricts the Use of the Auditor's Written Communication.**[7]

j. The manual or printed signature of the auditor's firm.

k. The city and state where the auditor practices.

l. The date of the auditor's report.

[Revised October 2011 to reflect conforming changes necessary due to the issuance of SAS No. 123.]

[Footnotes 7–17 will be renumbered as footnotes 8–18.]

Combined Report on Compliance and Internal Control Over Compliance

.31

If the governmental audit requirement requires the auditor to report on internal control over compliance and the auditor combines the auditor's report on compliance with a report on internal control over compliance, the following should be added to the report elements listed in paragraph .30, in a section with the heading "Internal Control Over Compliance" that appears before the section required by paragraph .30*i*, if any:

a. A statement that management is responsible for establishing and maintaining effective internal control over compliance with the requirements of laws, regulations, rules, and provisions of contracts or grant agreements applicable to government programs.

b. A statement that in planning and performing the compliance audit, the auditor considered the entity's internal control over compliance with the applicable compliance requirements to determine the auditing procedures for the purpose of expressing an opinion on compliance, but not for the purpose of expressing an opinion on the effectiveness of internal control over compliance.

c. A statement that the auditor is not expressing an opinion on internal control over compliance.

d. A statement that the auditor's consideration of the entity's internal control over compliance was not designed to identify all deficiencies in internal control that might be significant deficiencies or material weaknesses in internal control over compliance.

e. The definition of *deficiency in internal control over compliance* and *material weakness in internal control over compliance*.

f. A description of any identified material weaknesses in internal control over compliance or a reference to an accompanying schedule containing such a description.

g. If significant deficiencies in internal control over compliance were identified, the definition of *significant deficiency in internal control over compliance* and a description of the deficiencies or a reference to an accompanying schedule containing such a description.

h. If no material weaknesses in internal control over compliance were identified, a statement to that effect.

i. The ~~restricted use paragraph~~ ***alert*** described in paragraph .30*i*. The ~~restricted use paragraph~~ ***alert*** should be included in all combined reports on the entity's compliance and internal control over compliance.

A combined report on compliance and internal control over compliance is presented in the exhibit, "Illustrative Combined Report on Compliance With Applicable Requirements and Internal Control Over Compliance—*(Unmodified Opinion on Compliance; No Material Weaknesses or Significant Deficiencies in Internal Control Over Compliance Identified).*"

[No amendments to paragraphs .32–.43 and paragraphs .A1–.A32.]

~~.A33~~

~~Nothing precludes the auditor from restricting the use of any report to intended users.[fn 16]~~ (Ref: par. .30*n*)

[No amendments to paragraphs .A34–.A42.]

Amended Footnotes

Section 260, *The Auditor's Communication With Those Charged With Governance*

[1] ~~Paragraph .07 of section 905, *Restricting the Use of an Auditor's Report*. Statement on Auditing Standards (SAS) No. 87, *Restricting the Use of an Auditor's Report*, is currently effective and codified as AU section 532. SAS No. 87 has been included in section 905, as designated by SAS No. 122, *Statements on Auditing Standards: Clarification and Recodification*, and will be superseded when it is redrafted for clarity and convergence as part of the Clarification and Convergence project of the Auditing Standards Board. Until such time, section 905 has been conformed to reflect updated section and paragraph cross references but has not otherwise been subjected to a comprehensive review or revision.~~ ***Paragraphs .06c and .07 of section 905,* Alert That Restricts the Use of the Auditor's Written Communication.**

Section 265, *Communicating Internal Control Related Matters Identified in an Audit*

[2,‡] ~~Statement on Auditing Standards (SAS) No. 87, *Restricting the Use of an Auditor's Report*, is currently effective and codified as AU section 532. SAS No. 87 has been included in section 905, as designated by SAS No. 122, *Statements on Auditing Standards: Clarification and Recodification*, and will be superseded when it is redrafted for clarity and convergence as part of the Clarification and Convergence project of the Auditing Standards Board. Until such time, section 905 has been conformed to reflect updated section and paragraph cross references but has not otherwise been subjected to a comprehensive review or revision.~~ ***Paragraphs .06c, .07, and .11 of section 905,* Alert That Restricts the Use of the Auditor's Written Communication.**

~~[‡] Statement on Auditing Standards (SAS) No. 87, *Restricting the Use of an Auditor's Report*, is currently effective and codified as AU section 532. SAS No. 87 has been included in section 905, as designated by SAS No. 122, *Statements on Auditing Standards: Clarification and Recodification*, and will be superseded when it is redrafted for clarity and convergence as part of the Clarification and Convergence project of the Auditing Standards Board. Until such time, section 905 has been conformed to reflect updated section and paragraph cross references but has not otherwise been subjected to a comprehensive review or revision.~~

[9] ***Paragraph .08 of section 905,* Alert That Restricts the Use of the Auditor's Written Communication.**

[1] ***When the engagement is also performed in accordance with* Government Auditing Standards, *the alert required by paragraph .14*d *may read as follows: "The purpose of this communication is solely to describe the scope of our testing of internal control over financial reporting and the results of that testing. This communication is an***

integral part of an audit performed in accordance with* Government Auditing Standards *in considering the Company's internal control over financial reporting. Accordingly, this communication is not suitable for any other purpose." The AICPA Audit Guide Government Auditing Standards* and Circular A-133 Audits *provides additional interpretative guidance, including illustrative reports.

[1] ***When the engagement is also performed in accordance with* Government Auditing Standards, *the alert required by paragraph .14*d *may read as follows: "The purpose of this communication is solely to describe the scope of our testing of internal control over financial reporting and the results of that testing. This communication is an integral part of an audit performed in accordance with* Government Auditing Standards *in considering the Organization's internal control over financial reporting. Accordingly, this communication is not suitable for any other purpose." The AICPA Audit Guide Government Auditing Standards* and Circular A-133 Audits *provides additional interpretative guidance, including illustrative reports.***

Section 725, *Supplementary Information in Relation to the Financial Statements as a Whole*

‡ ~~SAS No. 87, *Restricting the Use of an Auditor's Report*, is currently effective and codified as AU section 532. SAS No. 87 has been included in section 905, as designated by SAS No. 122, *Statements on Auditing Standards: Clarification and Recodification*, and will be superseded when it is redrafted for clarity and convergence as part of the Clarification and Convergence Project of the Auditing Standards Board. Until such time, section 905 has been conformed to reflect updated section and paragraph cross references but has not otherwise been subjected to a comprehensive review or revision. [Footnote added, October 2011, to reflect conforming changes necessary due to the issuance of SAS No. 122.]~~

Section 800, *Special Considerations—Audits of Financial Statements Prepared in Accordance With Special Purpose Frameworks*

[9] Paragraph .08 of section 706.

[10] See ***paragraphs .06*a–b *and .07 of*** section 905, ~~*Restricting the Use of an Auditor's Report*~~ **Alert That Restricts the Use of the Auditor's Written Communication**. ~~SAS No. 87, *Restricting the Use of an Auditor's Report*, is currently effective and codified as AU section 532. SAS No. 87 has been included in section 905, as designated by SAS No. 122, *Statements on Auditing Standards: Clarification and Recodification*, and will be superseded when it is redrafted for clarity and convergence as part of the Clarification and Convergence project of the Auditing Standards Board. Until such time, section 905 has been conformed to reflect updated section and paragraph cross references but has not otherwise been subjected to a comprehensive review or revision.~~

‡ ~~SAS No. 87, *Restricting the Use of an Auditor's Report*, is currently effective and codified as AU section 532. SAS No. 87 has been included in section 905, as designated by SAS No. 122, *Statements on Auditing Standards: Clarification and Recodification*, and will be superseded when it is redrafted for clarity and convergence as part of the Clarification and~~

~~Convergence project of the Auditing Standards Board. Until such time, section 905 has been conformed to reflect updated section and paragraph cross references but has not otherwise been subjected to a comprehensive review or revision.~~

[18] Paragraph .21.

[19] Paragraph .18*b*.

[20] Paragraphs .19 and .21.

[21] Paragraphs .20–.21.

Section 806, *Reporting on Compliance With Aspects of Contractual Agreements or Regulatory Requirements in Connection With Audited Financial Statements*

[1] See section 705, Modifications to the Opinion in the Independent Auditor's Report.

~~2,~~ [2] ~~See section 905, *Restricting the Use of an Auditor's Report*. SAS No. 87, *Restricting the Use of an Auditor's Report*, is currently effective and codified as AU section 532. SAS No. 87 has been included in section 905, as designated by SAS No. 122, *Statements on Auditing Standards: Clarification and Recodification*, and will be superseded when it is redrafted for clarity and convergence as part of the Clarification and Convergence project of the Auditing Standards Board. Until such time, section 905 has been conformed to reflect updated section and paragraph cross references but has not otherwise been subjected to a comprehensive review or revision.~~ ***Paragraphs .06c, .07, and .11 of section 905,* Alert That Restricts the Use of the Auditor's Written Communication.**

[3] Paragraph .41 of section 700, *Forming an Opinion and Reporting on Financial Statements*.

[4] See section 706, *Emphasis-of-Matter Paragraphs and Other-Matter Paragraphs in the Independent Auditor's Report*, for guidance on other-matter paragraphs.

[5] See footnote 2.

[9] See footnote 2.

[1] The subtitle "Report on the Financial Statements" is unnecessary in circumstances when the second subtitle "Report on Other Legal and Regulatory Requirements" is not applicable.

[2] In circumstances when the auditor also has responsibility to express an opinion on the effectiveness of internal control in conjunction with the audit of the financial statements, this sentence would be worded as follows: "In making those risk assessments, the auditor considers internal control relevant to the entity's preparation and fair presentation of the financial statements in order to design audit procedures that are appropriate in the circumstances." In addition, the next sentence "Accordingly, we express no such opinion," would not be included.

[3] When the engagement is also performed in accordance with* Government Auditing Standards, *the alert may read as follows: "The purpose of the communication related to compliance with the afore-

mentioned [compliance requirements] described in the Other Matter paragraph [or, Report on Compliance] is solely to describe the scope of our testing of compliance and the results of that testing. This communication is an integral part of an audit performed in accordance with* Government Auditing Standards *in considering ABC Company's compliance. Accordingly, this communication is not suitable for any other purpose." The AICPA Audit Guide Government Auditing Standards* and Circular A-133 Audits *provides additional interpretative guidance, including illustrative reports.

Section 915, *Reports on Application of Requirements of an Applicable Financial Reporting Framework*

[2] ***See paragraphs .06*a–b *and .07 of section 905,* Alert That Restricts the Use of the Auditor's Written Communication.**

Section 935, *Compliance Audits*

[5] Paragraph .17 of section 705, *Modifications to the Opinion in the Independent Auditor's Report*. [Footnote added, October 2011, to reflect conforming changes necessary due to the issuance of SAS No. 123.]

[6] Paragraph .08 of section 706, *Emphasis-of-Matter Paragraphs and Other-Matter Paragraphs in the Independent Auditor's Report*. [Footnote added, October 2011, to reflect conforming changes necessary due to the issuance of SAS No. 123.]

[7] ***See paragraphs .06*a–b, *.11, and .A11 of section 905,* Alert That Restricts the Use of the Auditor's Written Communication.**

[16] ~~Footnote 4 of section 905, *Restricting the Use of an Auditor's Report*. Statement on Auditing Standards (SAS) No. 87, Restricting the Use of an Auditor's Report, is currently effective and codified as AU section 532. SAS No. 87 has been included in section 905, as designated by SAS No. 122, Statements on Auditing Standards: Clarification and Recodification, and will be superseded when it is redrafted for clarity and convergence as part of the Clarification and Convergence Project of the Auditing Standards Board. Until such time, section 905 has been conformed to reflect updated section and paragraph cross references, but has not otherwise been subjected to a comprehensive review or revision. [Footnote renumbered and revised, October 2011, to reflect conforming changes necessary due to the issuance of SAS No. 122. Footnote renumbered, October 2011, to reflect conforming changes necessary due to the issuance of SAS No. 123.]~~

AU-C Section 910 *

Financial Statements Prepared in Accordance With a Financial Reporting Framework Generally Accepted in Another Country

Source: SAS No. 124.

Effective for audits of financial statements for periods ending on or after December 15, 2012.

Introduction

Scope of This Section

.01 This section addresses circumstances in which an auditor practicing in the United States is engaged to report on financial statements that have been prepared in accordance with a financial reporting framework generally accepted in another country not adopted by a body designated by the Council of the AICPA (Council) to establish generally accepted accounting principles (GAAP) (hereinafter referred to as a financial reporting framework generally accepted in another country) when such audited financial statements are intended for use outside the United States. This section is not intended to preclude the use of such audited financial statements in the United States.

.02 Pursuant to Rule 202, *Compliance With Standards* (ET sec. 202 par. .01), and Rule 203, *Accounting Principles* (ET sec. 203 par. .01), the Council designates the bodies to establish GAAP. This section does not apply to financial statements prepared in accordance with financial reporting frameworks established by the bodies designated by the Council. Section 700, *Forming an Opinion and Reporting on Financial Statements*, applies to engagements to report on such financial statements, including financial statements prepared in accordance with International Financial Reporting Standards (IFRS) as issued by the International Accounting Standards Board (IASB).

.03 This section is applicable to engagements to report on financial statements prepared in accordance with a jurisdictional variation of IFRS such that the entity's financial statements do not contain an explicit and unreserved statement in an appropriate note to the financial statements that its financial statements are in compliance with IFRS as promulgated by the IASB.

.04 This section does not apply to engagements to report on financial statements of a U.S. subsidiary of a foreign registrant parent company that are presented in the parent company's filing with the U.S. Securities and Exchange Commission when the subsidiary's financial statements have been prepared in accordance with a financial reporting framework used by the parent company and audited in accordance with auditing standards generally accepted in the United States of America (GAAS).

---

* This section has been codified using an "AU-C" identifier instead of an "AU" identifier. "AU-C" is a temporary identifier to avoid confusion with references to existing "AU" sections, which will remain in AICPA *Professional Standards* through 2013. The "AU-C" identifier will revert to "AU" in 2014, by which time substantially all engagements for which the "AU" sections were still effective are expected to be completed.

Effective Date

.05 This section is effective for audits of financial statements for periods ending on or after December 15, 2012.

Objective

.06 The objective of the auditor, when engaged to report on financial statements prepared in accordance with a financial reporting framework generally accepted in another country, when such audited financial statements are intended for use outside the United States, is to address appropriately the special considerations that are relevant to

a. the acceptance of the engagement,

b. the planning and performance of the engagement, and

c. forming an opinion and reporting on the financial statements.

Requirements

Considerations When Accepting the Engagement (Ref: par. .A1)

.07 Section 210, *Terms of Engagement,* requires the auditor, as part of establishing whether the preconditions for an audit are present prior to accepting the engagement, to determine the acceptability of the financial reporting framework applied in the preparation of the financial statements.[1] In an audit of financial statements prepared in accordance with a financial reporting framework generally accepted in another country, the auditor should obtain an understanding of

a. The purpose for which the financial statements are prepared and whether the financial reporting framework applied in the preparation of the financial statements is a fair presentation framework.

b. The intended users of the financial statements.

c. The steps taken by management to determine that the applicable financial reporting framework is acceptable in the circumstances.

.08 When the auditor plans to use the form and content of the auditor's report of another country, the auditor should obtain an understanding of the applicable legal responsibilities involved. (Ref: par. .A8)

Performance (Ref: par. .A2–.A3)

.09 When auditing financial statements prepared in accordance with a financial reporting framework generally accepted in another country that are intended for use only outside the United States, the auditor should comply with GAAS, except for requirements related to the form and content of the report in the situation described in paragraph .12. The auditor should determine whether the application of GAAS requires special consideration in the circumstances of the engagement.

.10 Section 315, *Understanding the Entity and Its Environment and Assessing the Risks of Material Misstatements,* requires the auditor to obtain an

---

[1] See paragraph .06 of section 210, *Terms of Engagement*.

understanding of the entity's selection and application of accounting policies.[2] When reporting on financial statements prepared in accordance with a financial reporting framework generally accepted in another country, the auditor should obtain an understanding of such framework.

Application of Auditing Standards of Another Country

.11 If the auditor is engaged to audit financial statements prepared in accordance with a financial reporting framework generally accepted in another country, and the agreed-upon terms of engagement require the auditor to apply either the auditing standards of that country or International Standards on Auditing (ISAs), the auditor should obtain an understanding of and apply those relevant auditing standards, as well as GAAS, except for requirements related to the form and content of the report in the situation described in paragraph .12. (Ref: par. .A4–.A6)

Reporting

Reporting—Use Only Outside the United States

.12 If the auditor is reporting on financial statements prepared in accordance with a financial reporting framework generally accepted in another country that are intended for use only outside the United States, the auditor should report using either

a. a U.S. form of report that reflects that the financial statements being reported on have been prepared in accordance with a financial reporting framework generally accepted in another country, including (Ref: par. .A7)
   i. the elements required by section 700 and
   ii. a statement that refers to the note to the financial statements that describes the basis of presentation of the financial statements on which the auditor is reporting, including identification of the country of origin of the accounting principles, or

b. the report form and content of the other country (or, if applicable, as set forth in the ISAs), provided that
   i. such a report would be issued by auditors in the other country in similar circumstances,
   ii. the auditor understands and has obtained sufficient appropriate audit evidence to support the statements contained in such a report, and
   iii. the auditor has complied with the reporting standards of that country and identifies the other country in the report. (Ref: par. .A8–.A9)

Reporting—Use in the United States

.13 If financial statements prepared in accordance with a financial reporting framework generally accepted in another country also are intended for use in the United States, the auditor should report using the U.S. form of report.[3]

---

[2] See paragraph .12(c) of section 315, *Understanding the Entity and Its Environment and Assessing the Risks of Material Misstatement.*

[3] See section 700, *Forming an Opinion and Reporting on Financial Statements.*

In addition, the auditor should include in the auditor's report an emphasis-of-matter paragraph[4] that

a. identifies the financial reporting framework used in the preparation of the financial statements,

b. refers to the note to the financial statements that describes that framework, and

c. indicates that such framework differs from accounting principles generally accepted in the United States of America. (Ref: par. .A7 and .A10)

Application and Other Explanatory Material

Considerations When Accepting the Engagement (Ref: par. .07–.08)

.A1 In obtaining an understanding of the purpose for which the financial statements are prepared and of the intended users, the auditor may consider whether the intended users are likely to be familiar with the applicable financial reporting framework. For example, if the financial statements are to be used in the United States in addition to the other country(ies) for which they are intended, the auditor may consider whether intended users within the United States deal directly with the entity and whether the financial statements are to be used in a manner that permits such users to discuss with the entity differences from accounting and reporting practices in the United States and their significance. Accordingly, an auditor may conclude that financial statements prepared in accordance with a financial reporting framework generally accepted in another country are not appropriate for use in a private placement memorandum to be distributed widely in the United States.

Performance (Ref: par. .09–.10)

.A2 The accounting principles used to prepare financial statements in accordance with a financial reporting framework generally accepted in another country may differ from those used to prepare financial statements in accordance with accounting principles generally accepted in the United States of America, and such differences may affect the auditor's risk assessment and design of further audit procedures. For example, the financial reporting framework generally accepted in another country may require that certain assets be revalued to adjust for the effects of inflation—in which case, the auditor may find it necessary to perform procedures to test the revaluation adjustments. As another example, a particular country's financial reporting framework may not require or permit recognition of deferred taxes; consequently, procedures for testing deferred tax balances would not be applicable.

.A3 An understanding of the financial reporting framework generally accepted in another country may be obtained by reading the statutes or professional literature, or codifications thereof, which establish or describe the financial reporting framework generally accepted in the other country. Often, the application of accounting principles to a particular situation requires practical experience, and accordingly, the auditor may consult with persons having expertise in applying the financial reporting framework of the other country.

---

[4] See section 706, *Emphasis-of-Matter Paragraphs and Other-Matter Paragraphs in the Independent Auditor's Report*.

Application of Auditing Standards of Another Country (Ref: par. .11)

.A4 Applying either the auditing standards of another country or the ISAs may require the auditor to perform procedures in addition to those procedures required by GAAS.

.A5 An understanding of the auditing standards of another country or the ISAs may be obtained by reading the statutes or professional literature, or codifications thereof, which establish or describe such standards.

.A6 Statutes or professional literature, or codifications thereof, however, may not include a complete description of the auditing practices in another country. The auditor may consult with persons having expertise in, including practical experience in applying, the auditing standards of the other country or the ISAs, as relevant.

Reporting (Ref: par. .08 and .12–.13)

.A7 The exhibit "Illustrations of Auditor's Reports on Financial Statements Prepared in Accordance With a Financial Reporting Framework Generally Accepted in Another Country" contains illustrations of auditor's reports on financial statements incorporating the elements required by paragraphs .12–.13.

Reporting—Use Only Outside the United States (Ref: par. .08 and .12)

.A8 Even when the form and content of the auditor's report used in another country appears similar to that used in the United States, the report may convey a different meaning and entail different legal responsibilities for the auditor due to custom or culture. Issuing a report of another country may require the auditor to report on statutory compliance or otherwise require understanding of local laws and regulations. When issuing the auditor's report of another country, the auditor is required by paragraph .08 to obtain an understanding of applicable legal responsibilities, in addition to the auditing standards and the financial reporting framework generally accepted in the other country, as required by paragraphs .07 and .10–.11. Accordingly, depending on the nature and extent of the auditor's knowledge and experience, the auditor may consult with persons having expertise in the audit reporting practices of the other country and associated legal responsibilities to obtain the understanding needed to issue that country's report.

.A9 An entity that prepares financial statements in accordance with GAAP also may prepare financial statements in accordance with a financial reporting framework generally accepted in another country for use outside the United States (for example, financial statements prepared in accordance with a jurisdictional variation of IFRS such that the entity's financial statements do not contain an explicit and unreserved statement of compliance with IFRS as issued by the IASB). In such circumstances, the auditor may report on the financial statements that are in accordance with a financial reporting framework generally accepted in another country by reporting in accordance with paragraph .12. The auditor may include in one or both of the reports a statement that another report has been issued on the financial statements for the entity that have been prepared in accordance with a financial reporting framework generally accepted in another country. The auditor's statement may also reference any note disclosure in the financial statements that describes significant differences between the accounting principles used and GAAP. An example of such a statement, which may be included in an emphasis-of-matter paragraph, is as follows:

We also have reported separately on the financial statements of ABC Company for the same period presented in accordance with [*specify the financial reporting framework generally accepted*] in [*name of country*]. (The significant differences between the [*specify the financial reporting framework generally accepted*] in [*name of country*] and accounting principles generally accepted in the United States of America are summarized in Note X.)

Reporting—Use in the United States (Ref: par. .13)

.A10 When reporting on financial statements prepared in accordance with a financial reporting framework generally accepted in another country that will be used in the United States and outside the United States, the auditor may issue two reports: one of the reports described in paragraph .12 for use outside the United States and the U.S. form of report with an emphasis-of-matter paragraph, as described in paragraph .13, for use in the United States.

.A11

Exhibit—Illustrations of Auditor's Reports on Financial Statements Prepared in Accordance With a Financial Reporting Framework Generally Accepted in Another Country (Ref: par. .A7)

Illustration 1—U.S. Form of Independent Auditor's Report to Report on Financial Statements Prepared in Accordance With a Financial Reporting Framework Generally Accepted in Another Country That Are Intended for Use Only Outside the United States

Illustration 2—U.S. Form of Independent Auditor's Report To Report on Financial Statements Prepared in Accordance With a Financial Reporting Framework Generally Accepted in Another Country That Also Are Intended for Use in the United States

Illustration 1—U.S. Form of Independent Auditor's Report to Report on Financial Statements Prepared in Accordance With a Financial Reporting Framework Generally Accepted in Another Country That Are Intended for Use Only Outside the United States

Independent Auditor's Report

[Appropriate Addressee]

We have audited the accompanying financial statements of ABC Company, which comprise the balance sheet as of December 31, 20X1, and the related statements of income, changes in stockholders' equity, and cash flows for the year then ended, and the related notes to the financial statements, which, as described in note X to the financial statements, have been prepared on the basis of [specify the financial reporting framework generally accepted] in [name of country].

Management's Responsibility for the Financial Statements

Management is responsible for the preparation and fair presentation of these financial statements in accordance with [specify the financial reporting framework generally accepted] in [name of country]; this includes the design, implementation, and maintenance of internal control relevant to the preparation and fair presentation of financial statements that are free from material misstatement, whether due to fraud or error.

Auditor's Responsibility

Our responsibility is to express an opinion on these financial statements based on our audit. We conducted our audit in accordance with auditing standards generally accepted in the United States of America (and [in name of country]). Those standards require that we plan and perform the audit to obtain reasonable assurance about whether the financial statements are free from material misstatement.

An audit involves performing procedures to obtain audit evidence about the amounts and disclosures in the financial statements. The procedures selected depend on the auditor's judgment, including the assessment of the risks of material misstatement of the financial statements, whether due to fraud or error. In making those risk assessments, the auditor considers internal control relevant to the entity's preparation and fair presentation of the financial statements in order to design audit procedures that are appropriate in the circumstances, but not for the purpose of expressing an opinion on the effectiveness of the entity's internal control. Accordingly, we express no such opinion. An audit also includes evaluating the appropriateness of accounting policies used and the reasonableness of significant accounting estimates made by management, as well as evaluating the overall presentation of the financial statements.

We believe that the audit evidence we have obtained is sufficient and appropriate to provide a basis for our audit opinion.

Opinion

In our opinion, the financial statements referred to above present fairly, in all material respects, the financial position of ABC Company as of December 31, 20X1, and the results of its operations and its cash flows for the year then ended in accordance with [*specify the financial reporting framework generally accepted*] in [*name of country*].

[*Auditor's signature*]

[*Auditor's city and state*]

[*Date of the auditor's report*]

Illustration 2—U.S. Form of Independent Auditor's Report To Report on Financial Statements Prepared in Accordance With a Financial Reporting Framework Generally Accepted in Another Country That Also Are Intended for Use in the United States

Independent Auditor's Report

[*Appropriate Addressee*]

We have audited the accompanying financial statements of ABC Company, which comprise the balance sheet as of December 31, 20X1, and the related statements of income, changes in stockholders' equity, and cash flows for the year then ended, and the related notes to the financial statements, which, as described in note X to the financial statements, have been prepared on the basis of [*specify the financial reporting framework generally accepted*] in [*name of country*].

Management's Responsibility for the Financial Statements

Management is responsible for the preparation and fair presentation of these financial statements in accordance with [*specify the financial reporting framework generally accepted*] in [*name of country*]; this includes the design, implementation, and maintenance of internal control relevant to the preparation and fair presentation of financial statements that are free from material misstatement, whether due to fraud or error.

Auditor's Responsibility

Our responsibility is to express an opinion on these financial statements based on our audit. We conducted our audit in accordance with auditing standards generally accepted in the United States of America (and [*in name of country*]). Those standards require that we plan and perform the audit to obtain reasonable assurance about whether the financial statements are free from material misstatement.

An audit involves performing procedures to obtain audit evidence about the amounts and disclosures in the financial statements. The procedures selected depend on the auditor's judgment, including the assessment of the risks of material misstatement of the financial statements, whether due to fraud or error. In making those risk assessments, the auditor considers internal control relevant to the entity's preparation and fair presentation of the financial statements in order to design audit procedures that are appropriate in the circumstances, but not for the purpose of expressing an opinion on the effectiveness of the entity's internal control. Accordingly, we express no such opinion. An audit also includes evaluating the appropriateness of accounting policies used and the reasonableness of significant accounting estimates made by management, as well as evaluating the overall presentation of the financial statements.

We believe that the audit evidence we have obtained is sufficient and appropriate to provide a basis for our audit opinion.

Opinion

In our opinion, the financial statements referred to above present fairly, in all material respects, the financial position of ABC Company as of December 31, 20X1, and the results of its operations and its cash flows for the year then ended in accordance with [*specify the financial reporting framework generally accepted*] in [*name of country*].

Emphasis of Matter

As discussed in Note X to the financial statements, the Company prepares its financial statements in accordance with [*specify the financial reporting framework generally accepted*] in [*name of country*], which differ(s) from accounting principles generally accepted in the United States of America. Our opinion is not modified with respect to this matter.

[*Auditor's signature*]

[*Auditor's city and state*]

[*Date of the auditor's report*]

AU-C Section 915 *

Reports on Application of Requirements of an Applicable Financial Reporting Framework

Source: SAS No. 122; SAS No. 123; SAS No. 125.

Effective for engagements that end on or after December 15, 2012.

Introduction

Scope of This Section

.01 This section addresses the reporting accountant's responsibilities when requested to issue a written report on

a. the application of the requirements of an applicable financial reporting framework to a specific transaction or

b. the type of report that may be issued on a specific entity's financial statements. (Ref: par. .A1)

.02 This section also applies to oral advice provided by the reporting accountant

a. that the reporting accountant concludes is intended to be used by a principal to the transaction as an important factor considered in reaching a decision on the application of the requirements of an applicable financial reporting framework to a specific transaction or

b. on the type of report that may be issued on a specific entity's financial statements.

.03 Differing interpretations may exist concerning whether and, if so, how existing accounting policies in an applicable financial reporting framework apply to new transactions or how new accounting policies in an applicable financial reporting framework apply to existing transactions. Management and others may consult with accountants on the application of the requirements of an applicable financial reporting framework to those transactions or to increase their knowledge of specific financial reporting issues. Such consultations may provide relevant information and insights not otherwise available.

.04 This section does not apply to

a. a continuing accountant with respect to the specific entity whose financial statements the continuing accountant has been engaged to report on,

b. engagements either to assist in litigation involving accounting or auditing matters or to provide expert testimony in connection with such litigation, or

c. professional advice provided to another accountant in public practice.

---

* This section has been codified using an "AU-C" identifier instead of an "AU" identifier. "AU-C" is a temporary identifier to avoid confusion with references to existing "AU" sections, which will remain in AICPA *Professional Standards* through 2013. The "AU-C" identifier will revert to "AU" in 2014, by which time substantially all engagements for which the "AU" sections were still effective are expected to be completed.

.05 This section also does not apply to communications such as position papers prepared by an accountant for the purpose of presenting views on an issue involving the application of the requirements of an applicable financial reporting framework, provided that these communications are not intended to provide guidance on the application of these requirements to a specific transaction. Position papers include newsletters, articles, speeches, and texts thereof; lectures and other forms of public presentations; and letters for the public record to professional and governmental standards-setting bodies.

Effective Date

.06 This section is effective for engagements that end on or after December 15, 2012.

Objective

.07 The objective of the reporting accountant, when engaged to issue a written report or provide oral advice on the application of the requirements of an applicable financial reporting framework to a specific transaction or on the type of report that may be issued on a specific entity's financial statements, is to address appropriately

a. the acceptance of the engagement.

b. the planning and performance of the engagement.

c. reporting on the specific transaction or type of report.

Definitions

.08 For purposes of this section, the following terms have the meanings attributed as follows:

Continuing accountant. An accountant who has been engaged to report on the financial statements of a specific entity or entities of which the specific entity is a component.

Hypothetical transaction. A transaction or financial reporting issue that does not involve facts or circumstances of a specific entity.

Reporting accountant. An accountant, other than a continuing accountant, in the practice of public accounting, as described in ET section 92, *Definitions*, who prepares a written report or provides oral advice on the application of the requirements of an applicable financial reporting framework to a specific transaction or on the type of report that may be issued on a specific entity's financial statements.[1] (A reporting accountant who is also engaged to provide accounting and reporting advice to a specific entity on a recurring basis is commonly referred to as an advisory accountant.) (Ref: par. .A4)

Specific transaction. A completed or proposed transaction or group of related transactions or a financial reporting issue involving facts and circumstances of a specific entity.

Written report. Any written communication that provides a conclusion on the appropriate application of the requirements of an applicable financial reporting framework to a specific transaction

[1] Paragraph .29 of ET section 92, *Definitions*.

or on the type of report that may be issued on a specific entity's financial statements.

Requirements

Engagement Acceptance

.09 In determining whether to accept the engagement, the reporting accountant should consider

a. the circumstances under which the written report or oral advice is requested,

b. the purpose of the request, and

c. the intended use of the written report or oral advice.

For purposes of this section, the reporting accountant is not required to be independent of the entity.

.10 The reporting accountant should accept an engagement to issue a written report on the application of the requirements of an applicable financial reporting framework to a specific transaction only when the transaction involves facts or circumstances of a specific entity. The reporting accountant should not accept an engagement to issue a written report on hypothetical transactions.

.11 If the reporting accountant has determined in accordance with paragraphs .09–.10 that it is appropriate to accept an engagement to be performed in accordance with this section, the reporting accountant should establish an understanding with the requesting party that

a. responsibility for the proper accounting treatment rests with management, who is expected to consult with its continuing accountant;

b. management acknowledges that the reporting accountant may need to consult with the continuing accountant and that, upon request, management will authorize the continuing accountant to respond fully to the reporting accountant's inquiries; and

c. management will notify those charged with governance and the continuing accountant concerning the nature of the engagement.

If management refuses to agree to authorize the continuing accountant to respond fully to the reporting accountant's inquiries, the reporting accountant should inquire about the reasons and consider the implications of that refusal when determining whether to accept the engagement.

Engagement Planning and Performance

.12 The reporting accountant should

a. obtain an understanding of the form and substance of the specific transaction(s) or the conditions relevant to the type of report that may be issued on a specific entity's financial statements;

b. review the relevant requirements of the applicable financial reporting framework, if appropriate;

c. consult with other professionals, experts, or regulatory authorities, if appropriate;

d. perform research or other procedures, as appropriate, to identify and consider existing creditable precedents or analogies;

e. except as provided in paragraph .13, request permission from the entity's management to consult with the continuing accountant and request the entity's management to authorize the continuing accountant to respond fully to the reporting accountant's inquiries; and

f. except as provided in paragraph .13, consult with the continuing accountant to determine the available facts relevant to forming a conclusion. (Ref: par. .A2–.A3)

Consulting With the Continuing Accountant

.13 The reporting accountant should consult with the continuing accountant to determine whether the reporting accountant has obtained the available facts relevant to form a conclusion, unless

a. the reporting accountant is engaged to issue a written report or provide oral advice on the application of the requirements of an applicable financial reporting framework to a specific transaction, as described in paragraphs .01*a* and .02*a*, and

b. the reporting accountant is engaged to provide recurring accounting and reporting advice (for example, bookkeeping or assistance in formulating accounting positions in selected matters, which are services commonly performed by an advisory accountant) and

  i. does not believe that a second opinion is being requested,

  ii. has full access to management, and

  iii. believes that the relevant information has been obtained in order to issue a written report or provide oral advice regarding the application of the requirements of an applicable financial reporting framework to an entity's specific transaction.

If the reporting accountant determines in accordance with the preceding *a–b* that it is not necessary to consult with the continuing accountant, the reporting accountant should document the rationale for not consulting. (Ref: par. .A2–.A4)

Written Report (Ref: par. .A5–.A7)

.14 The reporting accountant's written report should be addressed to the requesting party (for example, management or those charged with governance) and should include the following:

a. A brief description of the nature of the engagement and a statement that the engagement was performed in accordance with this section.

b. Identification of the specific entity; a description of the specific transaction(s), if applicable; a statement of the relevant facts, circumstances, and assumptions; and a statement about the source of such information.

c. A statement describing the appropriate application of the requirements of an applicable financial reporting framework (including the country of origin) to the specific transaction or type of report that may be issued on the entity's financial statements and, if appropriate, a description of the reasons for the reporting accountant's conclusion.

d. A statement that the responsibility for the proper accounting treatment rests with the preparers of the financial statements, who should consult with their continuing accountant.

e. A statement that any difference in the facts, circumstances, or assumptions presented may change the report.

f. An alert that restricts the use of the report solely to the specified parties, as required by section 905, *Alert That Restricts the Use of the Auditor's Written Communication.*[2]

g. If the reporting accountant is not independent of the entity, a statement indicating the reporting accountant's lack of independence. The reporting accountant is neither required to provide, nor precluded from providing, the reasons for the lack of independence; however, if the reporting accountant chooses to provide the reasons for the lack of independence, the reporting accountant should include all the reasons therefor.

[As amended, December 2011, effective for the auditor's written communications issued on or after December 15, 2012, by SAS No. 125.]

Application and Other Explanatory Material

Scope of This Section (Ref: par. .01b)

.A1 Examples of the types of reports or illustrative report wording that a reporting accountant may provide include the following:

- A report expressing a modified opinion versus a report expressing an unmodified opinion
- A report prepared in accordance with auditing standards generally accepted in the United States of America versus a report prepared in accordance with international auditing standards
- Wording that might be included in a modified opinion

Engagement Planning and Performance

.A2 The responsibilities of an entity's continuing accountant to respond to inquiries by the reporting accountant are the same as the responsibilities of a predecessor auditor to respond to inquiries by the auditor. Section 210, *Terms of Engagement*, addresses the responsibilities of a predecessor auditor.[3] (Ref: par. .12*f*–.13)

.A3 The continuing accountant may provide information related to the form and substance of the specific transaction that is not otherwise available to the reporting accountant regarding, for example, the following:

- How management has applied the requirements of an applicable financial reporting framework to similar transactions
- Whether the method of accounting recommended by the continuing accountant is disputed by management

---

[2] See paragraphs .06*a–b* and .07 of section 905, *Alert That Restricts the Use of the Auditor's Written Communication*. [Footnote added, effective for the auditor's written communications issued on or after December 15, 2012, by SAS No. 125.]

[3] Paragraph .A30 of section 210, *Terms of Engagement*. [Footnote renumbered, effective for the auditor's written communications issued on or after December 15, 2012, by SAS No. 125.]

- The continuing accountant's conclusion on the application of the requirements of an applicable financial reporting framework to the specific transaction or the type of report that may be issued on the entity's financial statements (Ref: par. .12*f*–.13)

.A4 When determining whether the criteria in paragraph .13 are satisfied such that consultation with the continuing accountant is not necessary, the reporting accountant may consider the following:

- The nature of the engagement
- Whether the reporting accountant believes that full knowledge of the form and substance of the transaction has been obtained
- How management has applied the requirements of the applicable financial reporting framework to similar transactions in the past
- Whether management has discussed the method of accounting with the continuing accountant

A recurring engagement for a reporting accountant may constitute the effective outsourcing of certain controllership or other financial reporting functions or involve financial reporting advisory services. Such an engagement may allow the reporting accountant to have complete access to management. (Ref: par. .08 and .13)

Written Report (Ref: par. .14)

.A5 Although the reporting requirements in paragraph .14 only apply to written reports, reporting accountants may find the requirements useful when providing oral advice.

.A6 The alert that restricts the use of the reporting accountant's written report referred to in paragraph .14*f* is not intended to preclude distribution of the report to the continuing accountant. [As amended, effective for the auditor's written communications issued on or after December 15, 2012, by SAS No. 125.]

.A7 The exhibit "Illustrative Written Report to the Requesting Entity" provides an example of a written report to the requesting party.

.A8

Exhibit—Illustrative Written Report to the Requesting Party

The following is an illustration of the reporting accountant's written report to the requesting party (for example, management or those charged with governance) on the application of the requirements of accounting principles generally accepted in the United States of America to a specific transaction.

Introduction

We have been engaged to report on the appropriate application of the requirements of accounting principles generally accepted in the United States of America to the specific transaction described below. This report is being issued to ABC Company for assistance in evaluating accounting policies for the described specific transaction. Our engagement has been conducted in accordance with Statement on Auditing Standards No. 122 section 915, *Reports on Application of Requirements of an Applicable Financial Reporting Framework.*

Description of Transaction

The facts, circumstances, and assumptions relevant to the specific transaction as provided to us by the management of ABC Company are as follows:

[*Text discussing the facts, circumstances, and assumptions relevant to the specific transaction*]

Appropriate Accounting Principles

[*Text discussing accounting principles generally accepted in the United States of America and how they apply to the described transaction*]

Concluding Comments

The ultimate responsibility for the decision on the appropriate application of the requirements of accounting principles generally accepted in the United States of America for an actual transaction rests with the preparers of financial statements, who should consult with their continuing accountant. Our conclusion on the appropriate application of the requirements of accounting principles generally accepted in the United States of America for the described specific transaction is based solely on the facts provided to us as previously described; should these facts and circumstances differ, our conclusion may change.

Restricted Use

This report is intended solely for the information and use of those charged with governance and management of ABC Company and is not intended to be and should not be used by anyone other than these specified parties.

AU-C Section 920 *

Letters for Underwriters and Certain Other Requesting Parties

Source: SAS No. 122; SAS No. 125.

Effective for comfort letters issued on or after December 15, 2012.

Introduction

Scope of This Section

.01 This section addresses the auditor's responsibilities when engaged to issue letters (commonly referred to as *comfort letters*) to requesting parties in connection with a nonissuer entity's financial statements included in registration statements filed with the Securities and Exchange Commission (SEC) under the Securities Act of 1933 (the 1933 Act) (for example, inclusion of the nonissuer entity's financial statements as required by either Rule 3-05 or 3-09 of Regulation S-X) or included in other securities offerings.

.02 Auditors' services include audits or reviews of financial statements included in securities offerings. In connection with the securities offerings, auditors are often requested to issue comfort letters to certain requesting parties. The auditor is not required by generally accepted auditing standards (GAAS) to accept an engagement to issue a comfort letter.

.03 The service of providing letters for underwriters developed following the passing of the 1933 Act. Section 11 of the 1933 Act provides that underwriters, among others, could be liable if any part of a registration statement contains material omissions or misstatements. The 1933 Act also provides for an affirmative defense for underwriters if it can be demonstrated that, after a reasonable investigation, the underwriter has reasonable grounds to believe that no material omissions or misstatements existed in a securities offering. An auditor issuing a comfort letter is one of a number of procedures that may be used to establish that an underwriter has conducted a reasonable investigation. Consequently, underwriters may request auditors to assist them in developing a record of reasonable investigation.

.04 The subjects that may be covered in a comfort letter include

- the independence of the auditor.
- whether the audited financial statements included in the securities offering comply regarding form, in all material respects, with the applicable accounting requirements of the 1933 Act and the related rules and regulations adopted by the SEC.

---

* This section has been codified using an "AU-C" identifier instead of an "AU" identifier. "AU-C" is a temporary identifier to avoid confusion with references to existing "AU" sections, which will remain in AICPA *Professional Standards* through 2013. The "AU-C" identifier will revert to "AU" in 2014, by which time substantially all engagements for which the "AU" sections were still effective are expected to be completed.

- unaudited financial statements, condensed interim financial information, capsule financial information, pro forma financial information, financial forecasts, management's discussion and analysis (MD&A), and changes in selected financial statement items during a period subsequent to the date and period of the latest financial statements included in the securities offering.
- tables, statistics, and other financial information included in the securities offering.
- negative assurance about whether certain nonfinancial statement information included in the securities offering complies regarding form, in all material respects, with Regulation S-K.[1]

Effective Date

.05 This section is effective for comfort letters issued on or after December 15, 2012.

Objectives

.06 The objectives of the auditor, when engaged to issue a letter to a requesting party in connection with an entity's financial statements included in a securities offering, are to

a. address appropriately the acceptance of the engagement and the scope of services; and

b. issue a letter with the appropriate form and content.

Definitions

.07 For purposes of this section, the following terms have the meanings attributed as follows:

Capsule financial information. Unaudited summarized interim financial information for periods subsequent to the periods covered by the audited financial statements or unaudited interim financial information included in the securities offering. Capsule financial information may be presented in narrative or tabular form and is often provided for the most recent interim period and for the corresponding period of the prior year.

Change period. The period ending on the cut-off date and ordinarily beginning, for balance sheet items, immediately after the date of the latest balance sheet in the securities offering and, for income statement items, immediately after the latest period for which such items are presented in the securities offering.

Closing date. The date on which the issuer of the securities or selling security holder delivers the securities to the underwriter in exchange for the proceeds of the offering.

Comfort letter. A letter issued by an auditor in accordance with this section to requesting parties in connection with an entity's financial statements included in a securities offering.

---

[1] Regulation S-K, "Standard Instructions for Filing Forms Under Securities Act of 1933, Securities Exchange Act of 1934 and Energy Policy and Conservation Act of 1975."

Comparison date and comparison period. The date as of which, and period for which, data at the cut-off date and data for the change period are to be compared.

Cut-off date. The date through which certain procedures described in the comfort letter are to relate.

Effective date. The date on which the securities offering becomes effective.

Entity. The party whose financial statements are the subject of the engagement.

Negative assurance. A statement that, based on the procedures performed, nothing has come to the auditor's attention that caused the auditor to believe that specified matters do not meet specified criteria (for example, that nothing came to the auditor's attention that caused the auditor to believe that any material modifications should be made to the unaudited interim financial information for it to be in accordance with generally accepted accounting principles).

Requesting party. One of the following specified parties requesting a comfort letter, which has negotiated an agreement with the entity:

- An underwriter
- Other parties that are conducting a review process that is, or will be, substantially consistent with the due diligence process performed when the securities offering is, or if the securities offering was, being registered pursuant to the 1933 Act, as follows:
  - — A selling shareholder, sales agent, or other party with a statutory due diligence defense under Section 11 of the 1933 Act
  - — A broker-dealer or other financial intermediary acting as principal or agent in a securities offering in connection with the following types of securities offerings:
- Foreign offerings, including Regulation S, Eurodollar, and other offshore offerings
- Transactions that are exempt from the registration requirements of Section 5 of the 1933 Act, including those pursuant to Regulation A, Regulation D, and Rule 144A
- Offerings of securities issued or backed by governmental, municipal, banking, tax-exempt, or other entities that are exempt from registration under the 1933 Act
  - — The buyer or seller in connection with acquisition transactions in which there is an exchange of stock (Ref: par. .A1)

Securities offerings. One of the following types of securities offerings:

- Registration of securities with the SEC under the 1933 Act
- Foreign offerings, including Regulation S, Eurodollar, and other offshore offerings

- Transactions that are exempt from the registration requirements of Section 5 of the 1933 Act, including those pursuant to Regulation A, Regulation D, and Rule 144A
- Offerings of securities issued or backed by governmental, municipal, banking, tax-exempt, or other entities that are exempt from registration under the 1933 Act
- Acquisition transactions in which there is an exchange of stock

Underwriter. As defined in the 1933 Act

> any person who has purchased from an issuer with a view to, or offers or sells for an issuer in connection with, the distribution of any security, or participates or has a direct or indirect participation in any such undertaking, or participates or has a participation in the direct or indirect underwriting of any such undertaking; but such term shall not include a person whose interest is limited to a commission from an underwriter or dealer not in excess of the usual and customary distributors' or sellers' commission. As used in this paragraph, the term "issuer" shall include, in addition to an issuer, any person directly or indirectly controlling or controlled by the issuer, or any person under direct or indirect common control with the issuer.

Except when the context otherwise requires, the word *underwriter*, as used in this section, refers to the managing, or lead, underwriter, who typically negotiates the underwriting agreement or purchase agreement (hereafter referred to as the *underwriting agreement*) for a group of underwriters whose exact composition is not determined until shortly before a securities offering becomes effective.

.08 References in this section to information that is *included* in a document are to be read to also encompass information that is *incorporated by reference* in that document.

Requirements

Engagement Acceptance

.09 The auditor should determine whether to accept an engagement to issue a comfort letter in connection with financial statements included in a securities offering. The auditor is not required to accept such an engagement.

.10 The auditor should provide a comfort letter in connection with financial statements included in a securities offering only to

a. underwriters.

b. other parties meeting the definition of a *requesting party* in paragraph .07.

.11 The auditor should request the requesting party to provide either

a. a written opinion from external legal counsel that the requesting party has a statutory due diligence defense under Section 11 of the 1933 Act; or

b. a representation letter that

   i. is addressed to the auditor;

   ii. contains the statement, "The review process applied to the information relating to the issuer, is, or will be, substantially consistent with the due diligence process that we would perform if this securities offering were being registered pursuant to the Securities Act of 1933. We are knowledgeable with respect to that due diligence process."; and (Ref: par. .A3–.A4)

iii. is signed by the requesting party.

.12 If a requesting party, other than an underwriter, requests a comfort letter but does not provide the legal opinion or representation letter described in paragraph .11, the auditor should not provide negative assurance on the financial statements as a whole, or on any of the specified elements, accounts, or items thereof. In such circumstances, the comfort letter should include the following statements: (Ref: par. .A5)

a. It should be understood that we have no responsibility for establishing (and did not establish) the scope and nature of the procedures enumerated in the preceding paragraphs; rather, the procedures enumerated therein are those that the requesting party asked us to perform. Accordingly, we make no representations regarding questions of legal interpretation or regarding the sufficiency for your purposes of the procedures enumerated in the preceding paragraphs; also, such procedures would not necessarily reveal any material misstatement of the amounts or percentages previously listed as set forth in the [*offering circular*]. Further, we have addressed ourselves solely to the foregoing data and make no representations regarding the adequacy of disclosures or whether any material facts have been omitted. This letter relates only to the financial statement items previously specified and does not extend to any financial statement of the company as a whole. (Ref: par. .A6)

b. The foregoing procedures do not constitute an audit conducted in accordance with generally accepted auditing standards. Had we performed additional procedures or had we conducted an audit or a review of the company's [*give dates of any interim financial statements*] consolidated financial statements in accordance with auditing standards generally accepted in the United States of America, other matters might have come to our attention that would have been reported to you.

c. These procedures should not be taken to supplant any additional inquiries or procedures that you would undertake in your consideration of the proposed offering.

d. This letter is solely for your information and to assist you in your inquiries in connection with the offering of the securities covered by the [*offering circular*]. It is not to be used, circulated, quoted, or otherwise referred to for any other purpose, including but not limited to, the registration, purchase, or sale of securities, nor is it to be filed with or referred to in whole or in part in the offering document or any other document, except that reference may be made to it in any list of closing documents pertaining to the offering of the securities covered by the offering document.

e. We have no responsibility to update this letter for events and circumstances occurring after [*cut-off date*].

.13 The auditor should not provide a comfort letter to any parties other than a requesting party as defined in this section. (Ref: par. .A7)

.14 When issuing a letter in accordance with this section, the auditor should not circumvent the requirements of this section by issuing any additional letters or reports to a requesting party in connection with the securities offering in which the auditor comments on items for which commenting is otherwise precluded by this section.

Agreeing Upon the Scope of Services

.15 The auditor should obtain an understanding of the specific matters to be addressed in the comfort letter. (Ref: par. .A8)

.16 The auditor should ask to meet with the requesting party and the entity to discuss the procedures to be followed in connection with an engagement to issue a comfort letter. (Ref: par. .A9–.A10)

.17 The auditor should clearly state in any discussion of procedures that the auditor cannot provide any assurance regarding the sufficiency of the procedures for the requesting party's purposes. (Ref: par. .A11–.A14)

.18 The auditor should provide a draft of the form of the letter the auditor expects to furnish. To the extent possible, the draft should deal with all matters to be covered in the final letter and should use exactly the same terms as those to be used in the final letter, subject to the understanding that the comments in the final letter cannot be determined until the procedures underlying it have been performed. The draft letter should be identified as a draft to avoid giving the impression that the procedures described therein have been performed. (Ref: par. .A15)

.19 In both the draft and final forms of the comfort letter, the auditor should clearly describe the procedures performed by the auditor. The auditor should not state or imply that the auditor is carrying out such procedures as the auditor considers necessary because such statements or implications may lead to misunderstanding about the responsibility for the sufficiency of the procedures for the requesting party purposes.

.20 If the auditor has been unable to have a discussion with the requesting party about the auditor's planned procedures, the auditor should describe in the draft letter those procedures specified in the draft underwriting agreement that the auditor is willing to perform. (Ref: par. .A16–.A17)

.21 When the comfort letter relates to group financial statements, the auditor of the group financial statements should read the comfort letters of the component auditors reporting on significant components. The auditor should state in the comfort letter that

a. reading the component auditors' letters was one of the procedures followed, and

b. the procedures, other than reading the component auditors' letters, performed by the auditor of the group financial statements, relate solely to entities audited by the auditor of the group financial statements and to the group financial statements. (Ref: par. .A18)

.22 When comfort letters are requested from more than one auditor, the requirements of this section apply to each auditor. (Ref: par. .A19)

.23 In competitive bidding situations in which legal counsel for the requesting party acts as the requesting party's representative prior to opening and acceptance of the bid, the auditor should carry out the discussions and other communications required by this section with the legal counsel until the requesting party is selected. In such circumstances, the auditor should not agree to provide a comfort letter addressed to the entity, legal counsel, or a nonspecific addressee, such as "any or all underwriters to be selected." If the auditor agrees to provide a draft comfort letter, the draft comfort letter should include a legend describing the letter's purpose and limitations. (Ref: par. .A20–.A23)

Format and Contents of Comfort Letters

Dating

.24 The letter should state that the inquiries and other procedures described in the letter did not cover the period from the cut-off date to the date of the letter. (Ref: par. .A24–.A25)

.25 When an additional letter, dated at or shortly before the closing date, is requested, the auditor should carry out the specified procedures and inquiries as of the cut-off date for each letter. The subsequent letter should relate only to information in the securities offering as most recently amended. (Ref: par. .A26)

Addressee

.26 The letter should be addressed only to the requesting party, or both the requesting party and the entity, and should not be provided to any other parties. (Ref: par. .A27)

Introductory Paragraph

.27 The letter should contain an introductory paragraph that identifies the financial statements and the securities offering.

Auditor's Report

.28 The auditor should, in the comfort letter, make reference to, but not repeat, the report on the audited financial statements included in the securities offering. (Ref: par. .A28)

.29 When the auditor's report on the audited financial statements included in the securities offering contains an emphasis-of-matter or other-matter paragraph addressing matters other than consistency of application of accounting policies,[2] the auditor should refer to that fact in the comfort letter and discuss the subject matter of the paragraph. In those instances in which the SEC accepts a modified opinion on historical financial statements, the auditor should refer to the modification in the opening paragraph of the comfort letter and discuss the subject matter of the modification. (Ref: par. .A29–.A30)

.30 The auditor should not provide negative assurance regarding the auditor's report or regarding financial statements that have been audited and are reported on in the securities offering by other auditors. (Ref: par. .A31)

.31 In the introductory paragraph of the comfort letter, if the auditor refers to reports that the auditor has previously issued other than the report on the audited financial statements included in the securities offering, the auditor should not repeat the reports in the comfort letter or otherwise imply that the auditor is reporting as of the date of the comfort letter or assuming responsibility for the sufficiency of the procedures for the requesting party's purposes. (Ref: par. .A32–.A33)

[.32] [Paragraph deleted, effective for the auditor's written communications issued on or after December 15, 2012, by SAS No. 125.]

---

[2] See section 706, *Emphasis-of-Matter Paragraphs and Other-Matter Paragraphs in the Independent Auditor's Report.*

.33 The auditor should not mention, refer to, or attach to the comfort letter any report or other auditor's written communication that includes an alert that restricts the use of the auditor's written communication, in accordance with section 905, *Alert That Restricts the Use of the Auditor's Written Communication*, or any restricted use reports issued in accordance with Statements on Standards for Attestation Engagements or Statements on Standards for Accounting and Review Services. (Ref: par. .A34) [As amended, effective for the auditor's written communications issued on or after December 15, 2012, by SAS No. 125.]

Representations

.34 The auditor should refer in the comfort letter to the requesting party's representations when the representation letter described in paragraph .11 has been provided. (Ref: par. .A35)

Independence

.35 The auditor should state in the comfort letter that the auditor is independent, or the date through which the auditor was independent, with respect to the entity, and identify the applicable independence rules. (Ref: par. .A36–.A38)

Compliance With SEC Requirements

.36 If the auditor is requested to include an opinion in the comfort letter on whether the financial statements covered by the auditor's report comply as to form with the pertinent accounting requirements adopted by the SEC, the auditor's opinion should refer to compliance as to form, in all material respects, with the applicable accounting requirements of the 1933 Act and the related rules and regulations adopted by the SEC. (Ref: par. .A39–.A41)

.37 Certain financial statements may be incorporated in a registration statement under the 1933 Act by reference to filings under the Securities Exchange Act of 1934 (the 1934 Act). If the auditor is requested to include an opinion in the comfort letter on whether the financial statements covered by the auditor's report comply as to form with the pertinent accounting requirements adopted by the SEC, the auditor's opinion should refer to whether the audited financial statements incorporated by reference in the registration statement comply as to form, in all material respects, with the applicable accounting requirements of the 1934 Act and the related rules and regulations adopted by the SEC. However, the auditor should not opine on compliance with the provisions of the 1934 Act regarding internal control over financial reporting.

.38 If the auditor has been requested to include an opinion in the comfort letter on whether the financial statements covered by the auditor's report comply as to form with the pertinent accounting requirements adopted by the SEC, and a material departure from the pertinent rules and regulations adopted by the SEC exists, the auditor should disclose the departure in the comfort letter. (Ref: par. .A42)

.39 The auditor should express an opinion on compliance as to form with requirements under the rules and regulations adopted by the SEC only with respect to those rules and regulations applicable to the form and content of financial statements that the auditor has audited. When the financial statements or financial statement schedules have not been audited, the auditor is limited to providing negative assurance on compliance as to form.

.40 The auditor should not comment in a comfort letter on compliance as to form of MD&A with rules and regulations adopted by the SEC. (Ref: par. .A43)

Commenting in a Comfort Letter on Information Other Than Audited Financial Statements

General

.41 When commenting in a comfort letter on information other than audited financial statements, the auditor should

a. describe the procedures performed by the auditor, as required by paragraph .19. (Ref: par. .A44–.A46)

b. describe the criteria specified by the requesting party.

c. state that the procedures performed with respect to interim periods may not disclose matters of significance regarding certain matters about which negative assurance is requested. (Ref: par. .A47–.A48)

.42 The auditor should not, in the comfort letter

a. make any statements, or imply, that the auditor has applied procedures that the auditor determined to be necessary or sufficient for the requesting party's purposes.

b. use terms of uncertain meaning (such as *general review*, *limited review*, *reconcile*, *check*, or *test*) in describing the work unless the procedures encompassed by these terms are described in the comfort letter.

c. make a statement that nothing else has come to the auditor's attention that would be of interest to the requesting party as a result of carrying out the specified procedures. (Ref: par. .A49)

.43 When the report on the audited financial statements in the securities offering is a modified report, the auditor should consider the effect on providing negative assurance in the comfort letter regarding subsequent interim financial information included in the securities offering or regarding an absence of specified subsequent changes. The auditor should also follow the requirements of paragraph .29. (Ref: par. .A50)

Knowledge of Internal Control

.44 The auditor should obtain an understanding of the entity's internal control over financial reporting for both annual and interim periods when commenting in a comfort letter on

a. unaudited interim financial information, including unaudited condensed interim financial information;

b. capsule financial information;

c. a financial forecast when historical financial statements provide a basis for one or more significant assumptions for the forecast; or

d. subsequent changes in specified financial statement items. (Ref: par. .A51)

Unaudited Interim Financial Information

.45 The auditor should provide negative assurance on unaudited interim financial information included in the securities offering only if the auditor has conducted a review of the interim financial information in accordance with GAAS applicable to reviews of interim financial information. If the auditor has not conducted a review in accordance with GAAS applicable to reviews of interim financial information, the auditor is limited to reporting procedures performed and findings obtained. (Ref: par. .A52)

.46 The negative assurance provided regarding such unaudited interim information should be about whether

a. any material modifications should be made to the unaudited interim financial information for it to be in accordance with the applicable financial reporting framework, and

b. the unaudited interim financial information complies as to form in all material respects with the applicable accounting requirements of the 1933 Act and the related rules and regulations adopted by the SEC, if applicable.

.47 If the auditor states in the comfort letter that the auditor has performed a review of the unaudited interim financial information, the auditor should attach the review report to the letter unless the review report is already included in the securities offering. (Ref: par. .A53)

.48 The auditor should specifically identify, in the comfort letter, any unaudited interim financial information and should state that the auditor has not audited the interim financial information in accordance with GAAS and does not express an opinion concerning such information. (Ref: par. .A54–.A55)

.49 When the auditor is requested by the requesting party to provide negative assurance on the unaudited interim financial information, or information extracted therefrom, for a monthly period ending after the latest financial statements included in the securities offering, the requirements in paragraphs .45–.48 apply. In such a circumstance, a copy of the unaudited interim financial information should be attached to the comfort letter.

Capsule Financial Information

.50 The auditor should not provide negative assurance regarding whether the selected capsule financial information is in accordance with the applicable financial reporting framework unless

a. the auditor has performed a review of the financial statements underlying the capsule financial information in accordance with GAAS applicable to reviews of interim financial information, and

b. the selected capsule financial information is in accordance with minimum disclosure requirements of the applicable financial reporting framework for interim financial information.

If these conditions have not been met, the auditor is limited to reporting procedures performed and findings obtained. (Ref: par. .A56)

.51 The auditor should not provide negative assurance on selected capsule financial information regarding whether the dollar amounts were determined on a basis substantially consistent with that of the corresponding amounts in the audited financial statements unless the auditor has performed a review of the financial statements underlying the capsule financial information in accordance with GAAS applicable to reviews of interim financial information. Otherwise, the auditor is limited to reporting procedures performed and findings obtained. (Ref: par. .A57)

Pro Forma Financial Information

.52 The auditor should not comment in a comfort letter on pro forma financial information unless the auditor has an appropriate level of knowledge of the accounting and financial reporting practices of the entity. (Ref: par. .A58)

.53 The auditor should not provide negative assurance in a comfort letter on pro forma financial information, including negative assurance on

- the application of pro forma adjustments to historical amounts,
- the compilation of pro forma financial information, or
- whether the pro forma financial information complies as to form in all material respects with the applicable accounting requirements of Rule 11-02 of Regulation S-X,[3]

unless the auditor has obtained the required knowledge described in paragraph .52 and has performed

a. an audit of the annual financial statements, or

b. a review, in accordance with GAAS applicable to reviews of interim financial information,

of the interim financial information of the entity (or, in the case of a business combination, of a significant constituent part of the combined entity) to which the pro forma adjustments were applied. If these conditions are not met, the auditor is limited to reporting procedures performed and findings obtained. (Ref: par. .A59)

Financial Forecasts

.54 When performing procedures agreed to with the requesting party on a financial forecast and commenting thereon in a comfort letter, the auditor should

a. obtain an understanding of the entity's internal control over financial reporting for both annual and interim periods, as required by paragraph .44;

b. perform procedures required by AT section 301, *Financial Forecasts and Projections*, for reporting on the compilation of a forecast;[4]

c. issue a report on the compilation of prospective financial information in accordance with AT section 301 and attach the report thereon to the comfort letter;[5] and

d. perform additional procedures as requested by the requesting party and report the findings in the comfort letter. (Ref: par. .A60–.A61)

.55 The auditor should not provide negative assurance on the results of procedures performed on a financial forecast.

.56 The auditor should not provide negative assurance with respect to compliance of the financial forecast with Rule 11-03 of Regulation S-X unless the auditor has performed an examination of the financial forecast in accordance with AT section 301.

---

[3] Regulation S-X, "Form and Content of and Requirements for Financial Statements, Securities Act of 1933, Securities Exchange Act of 1934, Public Utility Holding Company Act of 1935, Investment Company Act of 1940, and Energy Policy and Conservation Act of 1975."

[4] Paragraph .69 of AT section 301, *Financial Forecasts and Projections*.

[5] Paragraphs .18–.19 of AT section 301.

.57 If the financial forecast is included in the securities offering, the auditor should not issue a comfort letter unless the financial forecast is accompanied by an indication that the auditor has not examined the financial forecast and, therefore, does not express an opinion on it. (Ref: par. .A62)

Subsequent Changes

.58 The auditor should base comments regarding subsequent changes in specified financial statement items solely on the limited procedures performed with respect to the change period as determined by the requesting party. (Ref: par. .A63–.A65)

.59 The auditor should provide negative assurance in the comfort letter regarding subsequent changes in specified financial statement items only as of a date less than 135 days from the end of the most recent period for which the auditor has performed an audit or a review. (Ref: par. .A66)

.60 When the requesting party requests negative assurance regarding subsequent changes in specified financial statement items as of a date 135 days or more from the end of the most recent period for which the auditor has performed an audit or a review, the auditor is limited to reporting procedures performed and findings obtained.

.61 In commenting on subsequent changes, the auditor should not characterize subsequent changes using ambiguous terms, such as referring to the change as "adverse." The auditor should note in the comfort letter if there has been a change in the application of the requirements of the applicable financial reporting framework. (Ref: par. .A67–.A68)

.62 The auditor should comment only on the occurrence of subsequent changes in specified financial statement items that are not disclosed in the securities offering. Accordingly, the auditor should include the phrase *except for changes, increases, or decreases that the securities offering discloses have occurred or may occur* in the comfort letter when it has come to the auditor's attention that a change, increase, or decrease has occurred during the change period, and the amount of such change, increase, or decrease is disclosed in the securities offering. This phrase need not be included in the letter when no changes, increases, or decreases in the specified financial statement items are disclosed in the securities offering. (Ref: par. .A69–.A70)

.63 The auditor should identify in the comfort letter in both draft and final form the dates as of which, and periods for which, data at the cut-off date and data for the change period are to be compared, whether or not specified in the underwriting agreement. (Ref: par. .A71–.A72)

.64 If the requesting party requests the use of a change period or periods other than those described in paragraph .07, the auditor should explain to the requesting party the implications of using an earlier date. If the requesting party, nonetheless, requests the use of a change period or periods other than those described in paragraph .07, the auditor is permitted to use the period or periods requested. (Ref: par. .A73)

Tables, Statistics, and Other Financial Information

.65 The auditor should not comment in a comfort letter on tables, statistics, and other financial information appearing in the securities offering unless the information

a. is expressed in dollars (or percentages derived from such dollar amounts) and has been obtained from accounting records that are subject to internal control over financial reporting, or *b.* has been derived directly from such accounting records by analysis or computation. (Ref: par. .A74)

.66 The auditor should not comment in a comfort letter on quantitative information that has been obtained from accounting records unless the information is subject to the same controls over financial reporting as the dollar amounts.

.67 The auditor should not comment in a comfort letter on tables, statistics, and other financial information relating to an unaudited period unless the auditor has

a. performed an audit of the entity's financial statements for a period including, or immediately prior to, the unaudited period or completed an audit for a later period, or

b. otherwise obtained knowledge of the entity's internal control over financial reporting.

.68 The auditor should not use the term *presents fairly* in comments concerning tables, statistics, and other financial information (Ref: par. .A75) and should not comment on

a. information subject to legal interpretation, such as beneficial share ownership;

b. nonfinancial data presented in MD&A, unless the auditor has conducted an examination or review of MD&A in accordance with AT section 701, *Management's Discussion and Analysis*; or (Ref: par. .A76)

c. matters merely because the auditor is capable of reading, counting, measuring, or performing other functions that might be applicable.

.69 The auditor's comments in the comfort letter concerning tables, statistics, and other financial information included in the securities offering should include

a. a clear identification of the specific information commented on;

b. a description of the procedures performed; and

c. the findings, expressed in terms of agreement between items compared. (Ref: par. .A77–.A78)

.70 With respect to the acceptability of methods of allocation used in deriving the figures commented on, the auditor should comment only to the extent to which such allocation is made in, or can be derived directly by analysis or computation from, the entity's accounting records. Such comments, if made, should make clear that

a. such allocations may be, to a substantial extent, arbitrary.

b. the method of allocation used is not the only acceptable method.

c. other acceptable methods of allocation might produce significantly different results.

.71 The comfort letter should state that the auditor makes no representations regarding

a. any matter of legal interpretation;

b. the completeness or adequacy of disclosure; and

c. the adequacy of the procedures followed, and that such procedures would not necessarily disclose material misstatements or omissions in the information to which the comments relate. (Ref: par. .A79–.A80)

Compliance as to Form With Regulation S-K

.72 The auditor should not provide negative assurance about whether certain financial information in registration statements, included because of specific requirements of Regulation S-K, is in conformity with the disclosure requirements of Regulation S-K unless the following conditions are met:

a. The information is derived, directly or by analysis or computation, from the accounting records subject to internal control over financial reporting.

b. The information is capable of evaluation against reasonable criteria that have been established by the SEC. (Ref: par. .A81 and .A84–.A87)

.73 The auditor should not express an opinion on conformity with the disclosure requirements of Regulation S-K. (Ref: par. .A82–.A83)

Concluding Paragraph

.74 The comfort letter should include a concluding paragraph restricting the use of the comfort letter for the information of the addressees and to assist the requesting parties in connection with the securities offering. (Ref: par. .A88)

Disclosure of Subsequently Discovered Matters

.75 The auditor should inform the entity when the auditor has discovered matters that require mention in the final comfort letter but were not mentioned in the draft letter that has been furnished to the requesting party. If the entity decides that disclosure will not be made in the securities offering, the auditor should inform the entity that the matters will be mentioned in the comfort letter and should recommend that the requesting party be informed promptly. (Ref: par. .A89–.A90)

Application and Other Explanatory Material

Definitions (Ref: par. .07)

.A1 An example of a comfort letter in connection with an acquisition transaction in which there is an exchange of stock is a cross-comfort letter related to a typical Form S-4 or merger proxy situation. An auditor's report on a preliminary investigation in connection with a proposed transaction (for example, a merger, an acquisition, or a financing) is not covered by this section; the guidance in AT section 201, *Agreed-Upon Procedures Engagements*, may apply to such engagements.

Engagement Acceptance (Ref: par. .09–.13)

.A2 An attorney's letter indicating that a party "may" be deemed to be an underwriter or has liability substantially equivalent to that of an underwriter under the securities laws would not meet this requirement.

.A3 What is "substantially consistent" may vary from situation to situation and may not be the same as that done in a registered offering of the same securities for the same issuer. Whether the procedures being, or to be, followed will be "substantially consistent" is determined by the requesting party on a case-by-case basis.

.A4 Exhibit A, "Illustration of Representation Letter From Requesting Party," contains illustrative wording for a representation letter when the requesting party is not an underwriter.

.A5 Exhibit B, "Examples of Comfort Letters," contains examples of comfort letters. Example Q, "Letter to a Requesting Party That Has Not Provided the Legal Opinion or the Representation Letter Required by Paragraph .11," of this exhibit provides an example of a comfort letter issued to a requesting party that has not provided the representation letter described in paragraph .11.

.A6 Interpretation No. 2, "Responding to Requests for Reports on Matters Relating to Solvency," of AT section 101, *Attest Engagements* (AT sec. 9101 par. .23–.33), contains guidance on additional statements to be included if this comfort letter is requested in connection with a secured debt offering.

.A7 Although the auditor is not permitted to provide a comfort letter other than to requesting parties, the auditor, instead, may provide a report on agreed-upon procedures. AT section 201 provides guidance on such reports.

Agreeing Upon the Scope of Services (Ref: par. .15–.23)

.A8 The underwriting agreement may specify the matters to be addressed in the comfort letter. If the underwriting agreement or draft underwriting agreement is not available or does not specify the matters to be addressed, the understanding of the scope of the comfort letter may be obtained from a description furnished by the entity or requesting party. Obtaining this understanding as early as possible, and before the auditor provides a draft of the form of the letter the auditor expects to furnish, assists the auditor in determining whether the auditor will be able to furnish a letter in acceptable form.

.A9 If the requesting party refuses to meet together with the entity, the auditor may consider the implications in determining whether to accept the engagement.

.A10 During this meeting, the auditor may describe procedures that are frequently followed. Exhibit B provides examples of comfort letters that include these procedures. Because of the auditor's knowledge of the entity, such a meeting may assist the requesting party in reaching a decision about procedures to be followed by the auditor.

.A11 When financial information in a securities offering has not been audited in accordance with GAAS and, accordingly, is not covered by an auditor's opinion, the nature of the comments that the auditor can properly make with respect to that financial information is limited. As noted in paragraph .03, obtaining a comfort letter from an auditor is one procedure used by a requesting party to establish that the requesting party has conducted a "reasonable investigation," as a defense against possible claims under Section 11 of the 1933 Act. What constitutes a reasonable investigation of unaudited financial information sufficient to satisfy a requesting party's purposes is a matter of legal interpretation. Consequently, only the requesting party can determine what is sufficient for the requesting party's purposes.

.A12 The assistance that the auditor can provide by way of a comfort letter is subject to limitations. One limitation is that auditors can properly comment in their professional capacity only on matters to which their professional expertise is relevant. Another limitation is that procedures contemplated in a comfort letter, which do not constitute an audit of financial statements, do not provide the auditor with a basis for expressing an opinion. Such limited procedures may bring to the auditor's attention significant findings or issues affecting the financial information, but they do not provide assurance that the auditor will become aware of any or all significant findings or issues that would be disclosed in an audit. Accordingly, a risk exists that the auditor may have provided negative assurance on the absence of conditions or matters that may prove to have existed.

.A13 Comfort letters are not required under the 1933 Act, and copies are not filed with the SEC. Nonetheless, it is a common condition of an underwriting agreement in connection with the offering for sale of securities registered with the SEC under the 1933 Act that the auditor is to furnish a comfort letter. Some underwriters do not make the receipt of a comfort letter a condition of the underwriting agreement but, nevertheless, ask for such a letter.

.A14 Exhibit B, example A-1, "Typical Comfort Letter for a 1933 Act Offering," provides an illustration of an appropriate way of expressing that the auditor cannot provide any assurance regarding the sufficiency of the procedures for the requesting party's purposes.[6]

.A15 By providing a draft letter early in the process, the auditor has the opportunity to clearly show the requesting party what they may expect to receive from the auditor. Thus, the requesting party has the opportunity to discuss further with the auditor the procedures that the auditor expects to perform and to request any additional procedures that the requesting party may desire. If the additional procedures pertain to matters relevant to the auditor's professional competence and the auditor is willing to perform them, a revised draft may be prepared.

.A16 Acceptance by the requesting party of the draft comfort letter (and subsequently by acceptance of the comfort letter in final form) is an indication to the auditor that the requesting party considers the procedures described to be sufficient for the requesting party's purposes. Clearly describing the procedures to be followed by the auditor in the comfort letter avoids misunderstanding about the basis on which the auditor's comments have been made and assists the requesting party in deciding whether the procedures performed are sufficient for the requesting party's purposes.

.A17 The following is an example of a paragraph that may be placed on the draft letter for identification and explanation of its purposes and limitations.

> This draft is furnished solely for the purpose of indicating the form of letter that we would expect to be able to furnish [*name of requesting party*] in response to their request, the matters expected to be covered in the letter, and the nature of the procedures that we would expect to carry out with respect to such matters. Based on our discussions with [*name of requesting party*], it is our understanding that the procedures outlined in this draft letter are those they wish us to follow. Unless [*name of requesting party*] informs us otherwise, we shall assume that there are no additional procedures they wish us to follow. The text of the letter itself will depend, of course, on the results of the procedures, which we would not expect to complete until shortly before the letter is given and in no event before the cut-off date indicated therein.

If the auditor has not had any discussions with the requesting party about the auditor's planned procedures, the second sentence in this paragraph would be revised as follows: "In the absence of any discussions with [*name of requesting party*], we have set out in this draft letter those procedures referred to in the draft underwriting agreement (of which we have been furnished a copy) that we are willing to follow."

---

[6] Paragraph 4 of example A-1, "Typical Comfort Letter for a 1933 Act Offering," in exhibit B, "Examples of Comfort Letters."

.A18 Situations may exist in which more than one auditor is involved in the audit of the financial statements of a business and in which the reports of more than one auditor appear in the registration statement. For example, certain significant divisions, branches, or subsidiaries may be audited by component auditors.

.A19 Comfort letters are requested occasionally from more than one auditor, for example, in connection with securities offerings to be used in the subsequent sale of shares issued in recently effected mergers and from predecessor auditors. In such circumstances, it is the entity's responsibility, at the earliest practicable date, to inform any other auditors who may be involved about any letter that may be requested of them and arrange for them to receive a draft of the underwriting agreement so that they may make arrangements at an early date for the preparation of a draft of their letter and for the performance of their procedures. The entity or requesting party is also responsible for arranging for a copy of the comfort letters of component auditors in draft and final form to be provided to the auditor of the group financial statements.

.A20 In certain circumstances, regulations under the 1933 Act permit companies to register a designated amount of securities for continuous or delayed offerings during an extended period by filing one "shelf" registration statement. At the effective date of a shelf registration statement, the registrant may not yet have selected an underwriter. An entity or the legal counsel designated to represent the underwriting group may, however, ask the auditor to issue a comfort letter at the effective date of a shelf registration statement to expedite the due diligence activities of the underwriter when subsequently designated and to avoid later corrections of financial information included in an effective prospectus. However, as stated in paragraph .A11, only the underwriter can determine the procedures that will be sufficient for the underwriter's purposes.

.A21 The auditor may agree to furnish the entity or legal counsel for the underwriting group with a draft comfort letter describing the procedures that the auditor has performed and the comments that the auditor is willing to express as a result of those procedures.

.A22 The following is an example of a legend describing the letter's purpose and limitations.

> This draft describes the procedures that we have performed and represents a letter we would be prepared to sign if the managing underwriter had been chosen and requested such a letter. The text of the final letter will depend, of course, on whether the managing underwriter who is selected requests that these and other procedures be performed to meet his or her needs and whether the managing underwriter requests that any of the procedures be updated to the date of issuance of the signed letter.

.A23 A signed comfort letter may be issued to the underwriter selected for the portion of the issue then being offered when the underwriting agreement for an offering is signed and on each closing date.

Format and Contents of Comfort Letters

Dating (Ref: par. .24–.25)

.A24 The letter ordinarily is dated on, or shortly after, the underwriting agreement is signed.

.A25 The underwriting agreement ordinarily specifies the date, often referred to as the *cut-off date*, to which certain procedures described in the letter are to relate, for example, a date five days before the date of the letter. A factor in considering whether to accept the engagement is whether the period between the cut-off date and the date of the letter provides sufficient time to allow the auditor to perform the procedures and prepare the letter.

.A26 Comments included in an earlier letter that relate to information in the securities offering as most recently amended may be incorporated by reference in a subsequent letter. Exhibit B, example C, "Letter Reaffirming Comments in Example A as of a Later Date," provides an example of such reference.

Addressee (Ref: par. .26)

.A27 An example of an appropriate form of address for this purpose is "The Blank Company and XYZ & Company, as Representative of the Several Underwriters." Copies of a comfort letter addressed in accordance with the requirements in paragraph .26 may be provided to the auditor of the group financial statements when a comfort letter related to a component included in group financial statements is issued by a component auditor.

Auditor's Report (Ref: par. .28–.33)

.A28 The requesting party occasionally requests that the auditor repeat in the comfort letter the report on the audited financial statements included in the registration statement. Because of the significance of the date of the auditor's report, the auditor is not permitted to agree to this request.

.A29 Examples of matters addressed in emphasis-of-matter or other-matter paragraphs in the auditor's report that do not affect the opinion on the basic financial statements are

- interim financial information accompanying or included in the notes to audited financial statements,[7] or
- required supplementary information described in section 730, *Required Supplementary Information*.[8]

.A30 A requesting party may request that the auditor comment in the comfort letter on

- unaudited interim financial information required by item 302(a) of Regulation S-K, or
- required supplementary information.

Section 930, *Interim Financial Information*, applies to unaudited interim financial information, and section 730 applies to required supplementary information. These sections require the auditor to modify the auditor's report on the audited financial statements to refer to such information when

- the scope of the procedures with regard to the information was restricted, or
- when the information appears not to be presented in accordance with the applicable financial reporting framework or, for required supplementary information, applicable guidelines.

Such modifications of the auditor's report in the registration statement would ordinarily be referred to in the opening paragraph of the comfort letter (see also paragraph .43). Additional comments on such unaudited information are,

---

[7] Paragraphs .40–.41 of section 930, *Interim Financial Information*.

[8] Paragraphs .07–.09 of section 730, *Required Supplementary Information*.

therefore, unnecessary. However, if the requesting party requests that the auditor perform procedures with regard to such information in addition to those procedures performed in connection with the review or audit as prescribed by section 930 and section 730, the auditor may do so and report the findings.

.A31 The requesting party occasionally requests negative assurance regarding the auditor's report. Because auditors have a statutory responsibility with respect to their opinion as of the effective date of a securities offering and because the additional significance, if any, of negative assurance is unclear and such assurance may, therefore, give rise to misunderstanding, the auditor is not permitted to provide such negative assurance.

.A32 In the introductory paragraph of the comfort letter, the auditor may refer to the fact that the auditor has issued reports on

- summary financial statements that are derived from audited financial statements.[9]
- interim financial information.[10]
- pro forma financial information.[11]
- a financial forecast.[12]
- MD&A.[13]

.A33 If the reports are not included in the securities offering, they may be attached to the comfort letter.

.A34 An example of an auditor's written communication that includes an alert that restricts the use of the auditor's written communication that is not permitted to be mentioned, referred to, or attached to the comfort letter is an auditor's written communication issued in accordance with section 265, *Communicating Internal Control Related Matters Identified in an Audit*. Examples of restricted use reports that are not permitted to be mentioned, referred to, or attached to the comfort letter include a report on agreed-upon procedures and any restricted use report issued in connection with procedures performed on the entity's internal control over financial reporting, in accordance with AT section 501, *An Examination of an Entity's Internal Control Over Financial Reporting That Is Integrated With an Audit of Its Financial Statements*. [As amended, effective for the auditor's written communications issued on or after December 15, 2012, by SAS No. 125.]

Representations (Ref: par. .34)

.A35 Exhibit B, example A-2, "Typical Comfort Letter for a Non-1933 Act Offering When the Required Representation Letter Has Been Obtained," contains a reference to the requesting party's representations.

Independence (Ref: par. .35)

.A36 Exhibit B, example A-1 contains an illustration of an appropriate statement confirming the auditor's independence under SEC rules and regulations in conjunction with SEC filings.

---

[9] See section 810, *Engagements to Report on Summary Financial Statements.*

[10] See section 930.

[11] See AT section 401, *Reporting on Pro Forma Financial Information* .

[12] See AT section 301.

[13] See AT section 701, *Management's Discussion and Analysis* .

.A37 Exhibit B, example A-2 includes an illustration of an appropriate statement confirming the auditor's independence in conjunction with a securities offering when the auditor is independent under AICPA standards.

.A38 The auditors for previously nonaffiliated entities recently acquired by the registrant would not be required to have been independent with respect to the entity whose shares are being registered. Exhibit B, example B, "Letter When a Short-Form Registration Statement Is Filed Incorporating Previously Filed Form 8-K by Reference," includes an illustration of an appropriate statement concerning the auditor's independence in such a case.

Compliance With SEC Requirements (Ref: par. .36–.40)

.A39 Although the guidance in this section generally addresses comfort letters issued in connection with securities offerings registered pursuant to the 1933 Act, it also provides guidance on comfort letters issued in other securities transactions. However, the guidance that specifically refers to compliance of the information commented on with SEC rules and regulations, such as compliance with Regulation S-X or S-K, generally applies only to comfort letters issued in connection with securities offerings registered pursuant to the 1933 Act.

.A40 The phrase *rules and regulations adopted by the SEC* is used because auditors are not expected to be familiar with, or express opinions on compliance with, informal positions of the SEC staff.

.A41 An illustration of an appropriate opinion regarding compliance as to form with pertinent accounting requirements adopted by the SEC is as follows:

> In our opinion [*include phrase* except as disclosed in the registration statement *if applicable*], the [*identify the financial statements and financial statement schedules*] audited by us and included in the registration statement comply as to form in all material respects with the applicable accounting requirements of the 1933 Act and the related rules and regulations adopted by the SEC.

.A42 Exhibit B, example K, "Alternate Wording When the SEC Has Agreed to a Departure From Its Accounting Requirements," illustrates an appropriate manner of disclosing a material departure from the pertinent rules and regulations adopted by the SEC.

.A43 The auditor may agree to examine or review MD&A in accordance with AT section 701.

Commenting in a Comfort Letter on Information Other Than Audited Financial Statements

General (Ref: par. .41–.43)

.A44 Comments included in the letter will often concern

- unaudited interim financial information.
- capsule financial information.
- pro forma financial information.
- financial forecasts.
- subsequent changes in specified financial statement items.

When the auditor has been requested to provide negative assurance on interim financial information or capsule financial information, the procedures involved in a review performed in accordance with GAAS applicable to reviews of interim financial information need not be specified.

.A45 Exhibit B, example A-1 contains an illustration of how the procedures performed by the auditor may be described.[14]

.A46 If the auditor states that the auditor has performed a review in accordance with GAAS applicable to reviews of interim financial information, this does not imply that those procedures are sufficient for the requesting party's purposes. The requesting party may ask the auditor to perform additional procedures. For example, the requesting party may request that the auditor apply additional procedures and specify items of financial information to be reviewed and the materiality level for changes in those items that would necessitate further inquiry by the auditor.

.A47 The procedures performed with respect to interim periods may not disclose subsequent changes in the specified financial statement items, inconsistencies in the application of the applicable financial reporting framework, instances of noncompliance as to form with accounting requirements of the SEC, or other matters about which negative assurance is requested.

.A48 An illustration of an appropriate manner of noting the limitations of procedures performed is shown in example A-1 of exhibit B.[15]

.A49 Because there is no way for the auditor to anticipate other matters that would be of interest to a requesting party, the auditor is precluded, in accordance with paragraph .42, from making a statement that nothing else has come to the auditor's attention that would be of interest to the requesting party.

.A50 Exhibit B, example I, "Alternate Wording When Auditor's Report on Audited Financial Statements Contains an Emphasis-of-Matter Paragraph," contains an illustration of alternate wording when the auditor's report on audited financial statements is a modified report.

Knowledge of Internal Control (Ref: par. .44)

.A51 The auditor may have obtained a sufficient understanding of an entity's internal control over financial reporting for both annual and interim periods through performing an audit on the entity's financial statements for one or more periods.

Unaudited Interim Financial Information (Ref: par. .45–.49)

.A52 The SEC requirements specify condensed financial statements. However, the requirements in paragraphs .45–.49 also apply to complete financial statements. For purposes of this section, interim financial statements may be for a 12-month period ending on a date other than the entity's normal year-end.

.A53 The auditor may, but is not required to, state in the comfort letter that the auditor has performed a review of interim financial information in accordance with GAAS applicable to reviews of interim financial information, and has issued a report on the review.

.A54 Exhibit B, example A-1 provides an illustration of a description related to the procedures specified for a review in accordance with GAAS applicable to reviews of interim financial information.[16] Exhibit B, example O, "Alternate Wording When the Procedures That the Requesting Party Has Requested the Auditor to Perform on Interim Financial Information Are Less Than a Review in Accordance With Generally Accepted Auditing Standards Applicable

---

[14] Paragraph 4 of example A-1 in exhibit B.

[15] See the last three sentences in paragraph 4 of example A-1 in exhibit B.

[16] Paragraphs 4*a* and 5*a* of example A-1 in exhibit B.

to Reviews of Interim Financial Information," provides an illustration of alternate wording when the procedures that the requesting party has requested the auditor to perform on interim financial information are less than a review in accordance with GAAS applicable to reviews of interim financial information.

.A55 Exhibit B, example A-1 includes an illustration of an appropriate manner of making clear that the auditor is not expressing an opinion on unaudited interim financial information.[17]

Capsule Financial Information (Ref: par. .50–.51)

.A56 In some securities offerings, supplementary capsule financial information comprising unaudited summarized interim financial information for subsequent periods accompanies the information shown in the audited financial statements or unaudited interim financial information. This capsule financial information (either in narrative or tabular form) often is provided for the most recent interim period and for the corresponding period of the prior year.

.A57 The requesting party may ask the auditor to provide negative assurance with respect to the unaudited interim financial information, or unaudited condensed interim financial information that underlie the capsule financial information, and ask the auditor to state that the capsule financial information agrees with amounts set forth in such financial information. Exhibit B, example L, "Alternate Wording When Recent Earnings Data Are Presented in Capsule Form," provides an illustration of the auditor's comments in these circumstances.[18]

Pro Forma Financial Information (Ref: par. .52–.53)

.A58 An appropriate level of knowledge of the accounting and financial reporting practices of the entity may be obtained by the auditor auditing or reviewing, in accordance with GAAS, historical financial statements of the entity (or, in the case of a business combination, of a significant constituent part of the combined entity) for the most recent annual or interim period for which the pro forma financial information is presented.

.A59 Exhibit B, example D, "Comments on Pro Forma Financial Information," provides an illustration of wording regarding procedures performed on pro forma financial information.

Financial Forecasts (Ref: par. .54–.57)

.A60 When an entity's securities are subject to regulation by the SEC and the auditor agrees to perform a compilation of a financial forecast, the SEC's views regarding independence are relevant. Independence may be deemed to be impaired when services include preparation or assembly of financial forecasts.

.A61 Exhibit B, example E, "Comments on a Financial Forecast," provides illustrations of appropriate wording describing procedures performed on a financial forecast.

.A62 The attestation standards that apply to financial forecasts provide for examinations or compilations of financial forecasts but not reviews. If a compilation report on the financial forecast has been issued in connection with the comfort letter, the report need not be included in the securities offering.

---

[17] Paragraph 3 of example A-1 in exhibit B.

[18] Paragraphs 4*b* and 5*b* of example L, "Alternate Wording When Recent Earnings Data Are Presented in Capsule Form," in exhibit B.

Subsequent Changes (Ref: par. .58–.64)

.A63 Comments regarding subsequent changes typically relate to whether, during the change period, there has been any

- change in capital stock;
- increase in long-term debt; or
- decreases in other specified financial statement items.

These comments might also address such matters as subsequent changes in the amounts of

- net current assets or stockholders' equity attributable to the entity.
- net sales and the income before continuing operations and of net income or net income attributable to the entity.

.A64 Procedures may include

- reading minutes and discussing with those charged with governance those meetings for which minutes have not been approved, and
- making inquiries of entity officials relating to the whole of the change period and obtaining appropriate written representations of the entity officials to support the answers to the inquiries.

.A65 Exhibit B, example A-1 provides an illustration of a description of procedures related to subsequent changes.[19]

.A66 Examples of the application of the requirements of paragraph .59 are as follows:

- When the auditor has audited the December 31, 20X0 financial statements, the auditor may provide negative assurance about changes in specified financial statement items as of any date through May 14, 20X1 (134 days subsequent to December 31).
- When the auditor has audited the December 31, 20X0 financial statements and has also conducted a review of the interim financial information as of and for the quarter ended March 31, 20X1, in accordance with GAAS applicable to reviews of interim financial information, the auditor may provide negative assurance about changes in specified financial statement items as of any date through August 12, 20X1 (134 days subsequent to March 31).

.A67 An appropriate manner of expressing negative assurance regarding subsequent changes is shown in exhibit B, in example A-1 if there has been no decrease, and in example M, "Alternate Wording When Auditors Are Aware of a Decrease in a Specified Financial Statement Item," if there has been a decrease.[20] Exhibit B, example O provides an illustration of reporting procedures performed and findings obtained when the procedures that the requesting party has requested the auditor to perform on interim financial information are less than a review performed in accordance with GAAS applicable to reviews of interim financial information.

.A68 In commenting on subsequent changes, the auditor may use terms such as *change*, *increase*, or *decrease*. Terms such as *adverse* are not clearly understood and may cause the comments on subsequent changes to be ambiguous.

---

[19] Paragraph 6 of example A-1 in exhibit B.

[20] Paragraphs 5*b* and 6 of example A-1 in exhibit B.

.A69 The comparison for the change period relates to the entire period and not to portions of that period. A decrease during one part of the period may be offset by an equal or larger increase in another part of the period; however, because no decrease for the period as a whole existed, the comfort letter would not report the decrease occurring during one part of the period.

.A70 When more than one auditor is involved, the auditor of the group financial statements may comment that there were no decreases in the consolidated financial statement items, when appropriate, despite the possibility that decreases have been mentioned in a comfort letter issued by a component auditor. Exhibit B, example J, "Alternate Wording When More Than One Auditor Is Involved," contains an illustration of wording when more than one auditor is involved.

.A71 The underwriting agreement usually specifies the dates as of which, and periods for which, data at the cut-off date and data for the change period are to be compared. For balance sheet items, the comparison date is normally that of the latest balance sheet included in the securities offering (that is, immediately prior to the beginning of the change period). For income statement items, the comparison period or periods might be, but are not limited to, the corresponding period of the preceding year or a period of corresponding length immediately preceding the change period.

.A72 The reasons for identifying the date and period used for comparison are to avoid misunderstandings about the matters being compared, and so that the requesting party can determine whether the comparison period is suitable for the requesting party's purposes.

.A73 The requesting party occasionally requests that the change period begin immediately after the date of the latest audited balance sheet (which is, ordinarily, also the closing date of the latest audited statement of income) in the securities offering, even though the securities offering includes a more recent unaudited balance sheet and statement of income. The use of the earlier date may defeat the requesting party's purpose because it is possible that an increase in one of the items referred to in paragraph .A63 occurring between the dates of the latest audited and unaudited balance sheets included in the securities offering might more than offset a decrease occurring after the latter date. A similar situation might arise in the comparison of income statement items. In these circumstances, the decrease occurring after the date of the latest unaudited interim financial statements included in the securities offering would not be reported in the comfort letter.

Tables, Statistics, and Other Financial Information (Ref: par. .65–.71)

.A74 Other financial information appearing in the securities offering does not include financial information that is covered by the auditor's opinion on the financial statements.

.A75 Because the term *presents fairly*, when used by independent auditors, ordinarily relates to presentations of financial statements, the use of the term in commenting on other types of information may be misleading.

.A76 When the auditor has conducted an examination or a review of MD&A in accordance with AT section 701, the auditor may agree to trace nonfinancial data presented outside MD&A to similar data included in the MD&A presentation. When the auditor does not perform a review or an examination of MD&A or does not attach or refer to a report on MD&A, the auditor may perform procedures agreed to with the requesting party with respect to items in MD&A subject to internal control over financial reporting.

.A77 Options for describing the procedures performed and the findings obtained include

- describing them individually for each item of specific information commented on.
- grouping or summarizing some or all of the descriptions, as long as
  - — the procedures and findings are adequately described,
  - — the applicability of the descriptions to items in the securities offering is clear, and
  - — the descriptions do not imply that the auditor assumes responsibility for the adequacy of the procedures.
- presenting a matrix listing the financial information and common procedures employed and indicating the procedures applied to the specific items.
- identifying procedures performed with specified symbols and identifying items to which those procedures have been applied directly on a copy of the prospectus, which is attached to the comfort letter.

.A78 Exhibit B, examples F, "Comments on Tables, Statistics, and Other Financial Information—Complete Description of Procedures and Findings," G, "Comments on Tables, Statistics, and Other Financial Information—Summarized Description of Procedures and Findings Regarding Tables, Statistics, and Other Financial Information," and H, "Comments on Tables, Statistics, and Other Financial Information: Descriptions of Procedures and Findings Regarding Tables, Statistics, and Other Financial Information—Attached Securities Offering (or Selected Pages) Identifies Items to Which Procedures Were Applied Through the Use of Designated Symbols," provide illustrations of appropriate ways of expressing comments on tables, statistics, and other financial information.

.A79 Except with respect to requirements for financial statements and certain Regulation S-K items discussed in paragraph .72, the question of what constitutes appropriate information for compliance with the requirements of a particular item of the securities offering form is a matter of legal interpretation outside the competence of auditors.

.A80 Exhibit B, example F contains an illustration of an appropriate way of stating the limitations regarding the sufficiency of the auditor's procedures.[21]

Compliance as to Form With Regulation S-K (Ref: par. .72–.73)

.A81 The following are the disclosure requirements of Regulation S-K that generally meet the criteria in paragraph .72:

- Item 301, "Selected Financial Data"
- Item 302, "Supplementary Financial Information"
- Item 402, "Executive Compensation"
- Item 503(d), "Ratio of Earnings to Fixed Charges"

.A82 Because information relevant to Regulation S-K disclosure requirements other than those noted previously is generally not derived from the accounting records subject to internal control over financial reporting, it is not

---

[21] Paragraph 9 of example F, "Comments on Tables, Statistics, and Other Financial Information—Complete Description of Procedures and Findings," in exhibit B.

appropriate for the auditor to comment on conformity of this information with Regulation S-K.

.A83 The auditor's inability to comment on conformity with Regulation S-K does not preclude the auditor from performing procedures and reporting findings with respect to this information.

.A84 Item 305, "Quantitative and Qualitative Disclosures About Market Risk," of Regulation S-K does not meet the criteria in paragraph .65 for the auditor to provide comments on the Item 305 qualitative disclosures because the disclosures are not derived from the accounting records but are descriptive and hypothetical or forward-looking in nature.

.A85 Item 305 does not meet the criteria in paragraph .72 for the auditor to provide negative assurance on conformity with Item 305. Although some information needed to comply with Item 305 is derived from the accounting records, registrants must also provide a substantial amount of information that is not derived from accounting records subject to internal control over financial reporting.

.A86 Item 305 requires quantitative disclosures that may be presented in the form of a tabular presentation, sensitivity analysis, or value-at-risk disclosures. The auditor may perform limited procedures related to tabular presentations to the extent that such information is derived from the accounting records subject to internal control over financial reporting.

.A87 The appendix, "Commenting in a Comfort Letter on Quantitative Disclosures About Market Risk Made in Accordance With Item 305 of Regulation S-K," provides guidance on providing comments on Item 305 quantitative disclosures and examples of very simplified procedures, findings, and limitations related to Item 305 tabular presentation disclosures.

Concluding Paragraph (Ref: par. .74)

.A88 An illustration of an appropriate concluding paragraph is shown in exhibit B, examples A-1, A-2, and B.

Disclosure of Subsequently Discovered Matters (Ref: par. .75)

.A89 Subsequently discovered matters may include changes in specified items not disclosed in the securities offering, as discussed in paragraph .62.

.A90 The auditor's participation in the meeting may be helpful when the entity and requesting party discuss such matters.

.A91

Appendix—Commenting in a Comfort Letter on Quantitative Disclosures About Market Risk Made in Accordance With Item 305 of Regulation S-K

.A91-1 Regulation S-K, Item 305, Quantitative and Qualitative Disclosures About Market Risk, requires certain quantitative and qualitative disclosures with respect to derivative financial instruments, generally as defined in Financial Accounting Standards Board *Accounting Standards Codification*™ glossary.

.A91-2 In addition to qualitative (that is, descriptive) disclosures, Item 305 requires quantitative disclosures that may be presented in the form of a tabular presentation, sensitivity analysis, or value-at-risk disclosures. Disclosures generally include a combination of historical and fair value data and the hypothetical effects on such data of assumed changes in interest rates, foreign currency exchange rates, commodity prices, and other relevant market rates. The quantitative and qualitative information required by Item 305 are disclosed outside the financial statements and related notes thereto.

.A91-3 Item 305 does not meet the criteria in paragraph .65 for the auditor to provide comments on the Item 305 qualitative disclosures because the disclosures are descriptive and are not derived from the accounting records because they are hypothetical or forward-looking in nature.

.A91-4 Although some information needed to comply with Item 305 is derived from the accounting records, registrants must also provide a substantial amount of information that is not derived from accounting records subject to internal control over financial reporting. As a result, Item 305 does not meet the criteria in paragraph .72 for the auditor to provide negative assurance on conformity with Item 305 of Regulation S-K.

.A91-5 The three alternative forms of quantitative disclosures under Item 305 reflect hypothetical effects on market risk sensitive instruments and result in differing presentations. The forward-looking information used to prepare these presentations may be substantially removed from the accounting records that are subject to internal control over financial reporting. Further, paragraph .68 also states that the auditor should not comment on matters merely because the auditor is capable of reading, counting, measuring, or performing other functions that might be applicable. Accordingly, an auditor's ability to comment on these disclosures is largely dependent upon the degree to which the forward-looking information used to prepare these disclosures is linked to such accounting records.

.A91-6 The tabular presentation includes the fair values of market risk sensitive instruments and contract terms to determine the future cash flows from those instruments that are categorized by expected maturity dates. This approach may require the use of yield curves and implied forward rates to determine expected maturity dates, as well as assumptions regarding prepayments and weighted average interest rates.

.A91-7 The term *sensitivity analysis* describes a general class of models that are designed to assess the risk of loss in market risk sensitive instruments, based upon hypothetical changes in market rates or prices. Sensitivity analysis does not refer to any one, specific model and may include duration analysis or other "sensitivity" measures. The disclosures are dependent upon assumptions about theoretical future market conditions and, therefore, are not derived from the accounting records.

.A91-8 The term *value at risk* describes a general class of models that provide a probabilistic assessment of the risk of loss in market risk sensitive instruments over a selected period of time, with a selected likelihood of occurrences based upon selected confidence intervals. Value-at-risk disclosures are extremely aggregated and, in addition to the assumptions made for sensitivity analyses, may include additional assumptions regarding correlation between asset classes and future market volatilities. As a result, these disclosures are not derived from the accounting records.

.A91-9 Of the three disclosure alternatives, the tabular presentation contains the most limited number of assumptions and least complex mathematical calculations. Furthermore, certain information, such as contractual terms, included in a tabular presentation is derived from the accounting records. Accordingly, auditors may perform limited procedures related to tabular presentations to the extent that such information is derived from the accounting records subject to internal control over financial reporting.

.A91-10 The modeling techniques and underlying assumptions utilized for sensitivity analysis and value-at-risk disclosures generally will be highly complex. The resultant disclosures may be substantially different from the basic historical financial input derived directly from the accounting records. Due to the hypothetical and forward-looking nature of these disclosures and the potentially limited usefulness of any procedures that may be performed, sensitivity analysis or value-at-risk disclosures do not meet the criteria in paragraph .65 for the auditor to agree to make any comments or perform any procedures related to sensitivity analysis or value-at-risk disclosures.

.A91-11 When performing procedures related to tabular presentation disclosures, the auditor is required by paragraph .65 to consider whether the entity's documentation of its contractual positions in derivatives, commodities, and other financial instruments is subject to internal control over financial reporting and whether it provides a complete record of the entity's market risk sensitive instruments. In addition, the auditor is not permitted to express positive or negative assurance about the reasonableness of the assumptions underlying the disclosures.

.A91-12 Item 305 requires registrants to stratify financial instruments according to market risk category, that is, interest rate risk, foreign exchange risk, and equity price risk. Item 305 stipulates that if an instrument is at risk in more than one category, the instrument should be included in the disclosures for each applicable category. The stratifications and the company's determination of market risk categories are not derived from the company's accounting records. Accordingly, the auditor is not permitted to provide any findings that the company's stratifications are complete or comply as to form with Item 305 requirements and should disclaim with respect to the company's determination of market risk categories.

.A91-13 Item 305 encourages registrants to provide quantitative and qualitative information about market risk in terms of, among other things, the magnitude of actual past market movements and estimates of possible near-term market movements. As market data is not derived from the company's accounting records, the auditor is not permitted to agree to perform any procedures related to such market data.

.A91-14 Further, the auditor may need to utilize a specialist in performing procedures related to those disclosures.

.A91-15 The following examples, based on example H, "Comments on Tables, Statistics, and Other Financial Information: Descriptions of Procedures and Findings Regarding Tables, Statistics, and Other Financial Information—Attached Securities Offering (or Selected Pages) Identifies Items to Which Procedures Were Applied Through the Use of Designated Symbols," of exhibit B, "Examples of Comfort Letters," provide very simplified procedures, findings, and limitations related to Item 305 tabular presentation disclosures. In practice, the procedures generally will be substantially more complex.

Symbol	*Procedures and Findings*
√	Compared with a schedule prepared by the Company from its accounting records. We (*a*) compared the amounts on the schedule to corresponding amounts appearing in the accounting records and found such amounts to be in agreement, and (*b*) determined that the schedule was mathematically correct. However, we make no comment as to the appropriateness or completeness of the Company's classification of its market-risk-sensitive instruments into market risk categories, nor as to its determination of the expected maturity dates or amounts. (Note: This is an example of procedures related to tabular presentations of face amounts, carrying amounts, fair values, and notional amounts, which stratify such amounts as to interest rate risk.)
⊗	Compared with a schedule prepared by the Company from its accounting records to calculate weighted average fixed interest rates and weighted average fixed pay and receive rates and found such percentages to be in agreement. We (*a*) compared the amounts on the schedule to corresponding amounts appearing in the accounting records and found such amounts to be in agreement, and (*b*) determined that the schedule was mathematically correct. However, we make no comment as to the appropriateness of the Company's methodology in calculating weighted average fixed rates. (*Note*: It may be necessary to provide a more complete description of the procedures performed in other circumstances.) We make no comment as to the appropriateness or completeness of the Company's determination of the Regulation S-K requirements for quantitative and qualitative disclosures about market risks or with respect to the reasonableness of the assumptions underlying the disclosures.

[*The following is an extract from a registration statement that illustrates how an auditor can document procedures performed on a tabular presentation of market risk disclosures made in accordance with Item 305 of Regulation S-K.*]

INTEREST RATE SENSITIVITY

The following table provides information about the Company's derivative financial instruments and other financial instruments that are sensitive to changes in interest rates, including interest rate swaps and debt obligations. For debt obligations, the table presents principal cash flows and related weighted average interest rates by expected maturity dates. For interest rate swaps, the table presents notional amounts and weighted average interest rates by expected maturity dates. Notional amounts are used to calculate the contractual payments to be exchanged under the contract. Weighted average variable rates are based on implied forward rates in the yield curve at the reporting date. The information is presented in U.S. dollar equivalents, which is the Company's reporting currency. The instrument's actual cash flows are denominated in both U.S. dollars ($US) and German deutschmarks (DM), as indicated in parentheses.

	Expected maturity dates						
	20X2[1]	*20X3*[1]	*20X4*[1]	*20X5*[1]	*Thereafter*[1]	*Total*	*Fair Value*
Liabilities							
Long-Term Debt:	*($US equivalent in millions)*						
Fixed Rate ($US)	$XXX	$XXX	$XXX	$XXX	$XXX	$XXX ✓	$XXX ✓
Average interest rate	XX%	XX%	XX%	XX%	XX%	XX% ⊗	
Fixed Rate (DM)	XXX	XXX	XXX	XXX	XXX	XXX ✓	XXX ✓
Average interest rate	XX%	XX%	XX%	XX%	XX%	XX% ⊗	
Variable Rate ($US)	XXX	XXX	XXX	XXX	XXX	XXX ✓	XXX ✓
Average interest rate	XX%	XX%	XX%	XX%	XX%	XX%[1]	
Interest Rate Derivatives	*($US equivalent in millions)*						
Interest Rate Swaps:							
Variable to fixed ($US)	$XXX	$XXX	$XXX	$XXX	$XXX	$XXX ✓	$XXX ✓
Average pay rate-fixed	XX%	XX%	XX%	XX%	XX%	XX% ⊗	
Average receive rate-variable	XX%	XX%	XX%	XX%	XX%	XX%[1]	
Fixed to Variable ($US)	XXX	XXX	XXX	XXX	XXX	XXX ✓	XXX ✓
Average pay rate-variable	XX%	XX%	XX%	XX%	XX%	XX%[1]	
Average receive rate-fixed	XX%	XX%	XX%	XX%	XX%	XX% ⊗	

[1] Because these disclosures include either management's expectations of future cash flows or the use of implied forward rates applied to such expected cash flows, such information does not meet the criteria of paragraph .65. Accordingly, the auditor is not permitted to express findings on amounts in these columns.

.A92

Exhibit A—Illustration of Representation Letter From Requesting Party (Ref: par. .A4)

The following is an example of a letter from a nonunderwriter when the securities offering is not being registered under the Securities Act of 1933.

[*Date*]

Dear ABC Accountants:

[*Name of requesting party*], as principal or agent, in the placement of [*identify securities*] to be issued by [*name of issuer*], will be reviewing certain information relating to [*issuer*] that will be included (incorporated by reference) in the document [*if appropriate, identify the document*], which may be delivered to investors and utilized by them as a basis for their investment decision. This review process, applied to the information relating to the issuer, is (will be) substantially consistent with the due diligence review process that an underwriter would perform if this placement [*issuance*] of securities were being registered pursuant to the Securities Act of 1933 (the Act). We are knowledgeable with respect to the due diligence review process that would be performed if this placement of securities were being registered pursuant to the Act. We hereby request that you deliver to us a "comfort" letter concerning the financial statements of the issuer and certain statistical and other data included in the offering document. We will contact you to identify the procedures we wish you to follow and the form we wish the comfort letter to take.

Very truly yours,

[*Name of Requesting Party*]

.A93

Exhibit B—Examples of Comfort Letters

Introduction

.A93-1 The contents of comfort letters vary depending on the extent of the information in the securities offering and the wishes of the requesting party. Shelf registration statements may have several closing dates and different underwriters. Descriptions of procedures and findings regarding interim financial statements, tables, statistics, or other financial information that is incorporated by reference from previous Securities Exchange Act of 1934 filings may have to be repeated in several comfort letters. To avoid restating these descriptions in each comfort letter, the auditor may initially issue the comments in a format (such as an appendix) that can be referred to in, and attached to, subsequently issued comfort letters.

.A93-2 A typical comfort letter includes

a. a statement regarding the independence of the auditor. (Ref: par. .15)

b. if applicable, an opinion regarding whether the audited financial statements included (incorporated by reference) in the securities offering comply as to form in all material respects with the applicable accounting requirements of the Securities Act of 1933 (the 1933 Act) and related rules and regulations adopted by the Securities and Exchange Commission (SEC). (Ref: par. .16–.20)

c. negative assurance on whether

   i. if applicable, the unaudited interim financial information included (incorporated by reference) in the registration statement (Ref: par. .25–.26) complies as to form in all material respects with the applicable accounting requirements of the 1933 Act and the related rules and regulations adopted by the SEC.

   ii. any material modifications should be made to the unaudited financial information included (incorporated by reference) in the securities offering for them to be in conformity with the applicable financial reporting framework.

d. negative assurance on whether, during a specified period following the date of the latest financial statements in the securities offering and prospectus, there has been any change in capital stock, increase in long-term debt, or any decrease in other specified financial statement items. (Ref: par. .38–.44)

Example A-1 contains a typical comfort letter for a 1933 Act offering and example A-2 contains a typical comfort letter for a non-1933 Act offering. Letters that cover some of the items may be developed by omitting inapplicable portions of these examples. Examples B, D–O, and R contain additional or alternate wording for examples A-1 or A-2, as applicable, for various scenarios.

Although the illustrations in this exhibit describe procedures that may be followed by auditors as a basis for their comments, this section does not necessarily prescribe such procedures.

Example A—Typical Comfort Letters

Example A-1—Typical Comfort Letter for a 1933 Act Offering

.A93-3 Example A-1 is an example of a letter that the auditor of a nonissuer may provide when a registrant is including the nonissuer's financial statements in the securities offering to be filed with the SEC. Appropriate modifications would be made if additional financial information is covered by the comfort letter. Example A-1 assumes the following circumstances:

- The prospectus includes audited consolidated balance sheets as of December 31, 20X5 and 20X4, and audited consolidated statements of income, stockholders' equity, and cash flows for each year in the three-year period ended December 31, 20X5. Note that the example assumes all the net income is attributable to the company. If that were not the case, the references to net income would be modified, or additional references would be included as appropriate.
- The prospectus also includes an unaudited condensed consolidated balance sheet as of March 31, 20X6, and unaudited condensed consolidated statements of income, stockholders' equity, and cash flows for the three-month periods ended March 31, 20X6 and 20X5, reviewed in accordance with generally accepted auditing standards applicable to reviews of interim financial information but not previously reported on by the auditor. The example also assumes that the auditor has not previously reported on the interim financial information. If the auditor has previously reported on the interim financial information, that fact may be referred to in the introductory paragraph of the comfort letter as follows:

  > Also, we have reviewed the unaudited condensed consolidated financial statements as of March 31, 20X6 and 20X5, and for the three-month periods then ended, as indicated in our report dated May 15, 20X6, which is included (incorporated by reference) in the registration statement.

  The cut-off date is June 23, 20X6, and the letter is dated June 28, 20X6. The effective date is June 28, 20X6.
- The auditors are reporting independence under the SEC rules and regulations. If the auditors were not required to be independent under the SEC rules and regulations in conjunction with an SEC filing, paragraph 1 in example A-1 would be replaced with paragraph 1 in example A-2.

The auditor may agree to comment in the comfort letter on whether the interim financial information complies as to form in all material respects with the applicable accounting requirements of the rules and regulations adopted by the SEC.

The example also assumes that there has been no change in the application of a requirement of generally accepted accounting principles during the interim period. If there has been such a change, a reference to that change would be included in paragraph 5 of example A-1.

Each of the comments in the letter is in response to a requirement of the underwriting agreement. For purposes of example A-1, the income statement items of the current interim period are to be compared with those of the corresponding period of the preceding year.

June 28, 20X6

[*Addressee*]

Dear Ladies and Gentlemen:

We have audited the consolidated financial statements of The Nonissuer Company, Inc. (the company) and subsidiaries, which comprise the consolidated balance sheets as of December 31, 20X5 and 20X4, and the related consolidated statements of income, changes in stockholders' equity, and cash flows for each of the years in the three-year period ended December 31, 20X5, and the related notes to the consolidated financial statements, all included in The Issuer Company's (the registrant) registration statement (no. 33-00000) on Form S-1 filed by the registrant under the Securities Act of 1933 (the Act); our report with respect thereto is also included in that registration statement. The registration statement, as amended on June 28, 20X6, is herein referred to as the registration statement.

In connection with the registration statement—

1. We are independent certified public accountants with respect to the company within the meaning of the 1933 Act and the applicable rules and regulations thereunder adopted by the SEC.

2. In our opinion [*include the phrase* except as disclosed in the registration statement *if applicable*], the consolidated financial statements audited by us and included in the registration statement comply as to form in all material respects with the applicable accounting requirements of the Act and the related rules and regulations adopted by the SEC.

3. We have not audited any financial statements of the company as of any date or for any period subsequent to December 31, 20X5; although, we have conducted an audit for the year ended December 31, 20X5, the purpose (and, therefore, the scope) of the audit was to enable us to express our opinion on the consolidated financial statements as of December 31, 20X5, and for the year then ended, but not on the financial statements for any interim period within that year. Therefore, we are unable to and do not express any opinion on the unaudited condensed consolidated balance sheet as of March 31, 20X6, and the unaudited condensed consolidated statements of income, stockholders' equity, and cash flows for the three-month periods ended March 31, 20X6 and 20X5, included in the registration statement, or on the financial position, results of operations, or cash flows as of any date or for any period subsequent to December 31, 20X5.

4. For purposes of this letter we have read the 20X6 minutes of meetings of the stockholders, the board of directors, and [*include other appropriate committees, if any*] of the company and its subsidiaries as set forth in the minute books at June 23, 20X6, officials of the company having advised us that the minutes of all such meetings through that date were set forth therein and having discussed with us the unapproved minutes of meetings held

on [*dates*]; we have carried out other procedures to June 23, 20X6, as follows (our work did not extend to the period from June 24, 20X6 to June 28, 20X6, inclusive):

a. With respect to the three-month periods ended March 31, 20X6 and 20X5, we have—

(i) Performed the procedures specified for a review in accordance with auditing standards generally accepted in the United States of America applicable to reviews of interim financial information, on the unaudited condensed consolidated balance sheet as of March 31, 20X6, and the unaudited condensed consolidated statements of income, stockholders' equity, and cash flows for the three-month periods ended March 31, 20X6 and 20X5, included in the registration statement.

(ii) Inquired of certain officials of the company who have responsibility for financial and accounting matters whether the unaudited condensed consolidated financial statements referred to in *a*(i) comply as to form in all material respects with the applicable accounting requirements of the Act and the related rules and regulations adopted by the SEC.

b. With respect to the period from April 1, 20X6 to May 31, 20X6, we have—

(i) Read the unaudited consolidated financial statements of the company and subsidiaries for April and May of both 20X5 and 20X6 furnished us by the company, officials of the company having advised us that no such financial statements as of any date or for any period subsequent to May 31, 20X6, were available. [*If applicable:* The financial information for April and May of both 20X5 and 20X6 is incomplete in that it omits the statements of cash flows and other disclosures.]

(ii) Inquired of certain officials of the company who have responsibility for financial and accounting matters whether the unaudited consolidated financial statements referred to in *b*(i) are stated on a basis substantially consistent with that of the audited consolidated financial statements included in the registration statement.

The foregoing procedures do not constitute an audit conducted in accordance with generally accepted auditing standards. Also, they would not necessarily reveal matters of significance with respect to the comments in the following paragraph. Accordingly, we make no representations regarding the sufficiency of the foregoing procedures for your purposes.

5. Nothing came to our attention as a result of the foregoing procedures, however, that caused us to believe that—

a.

(i) Any material modifications should be made to the unaudited condensed consolidated financial statements described in 4*a*(i), included in the registration statement, for them to be in conformity with generally accepted accounting principles.[1]

(ii) The unaudited condensed consolidated financial statements described in 4*a*(i) do not comply as to form in all material respects with the applicable accounting requirements of the Act and the related rules and regulations adopted by the SEC.

b.

(i) At May 31, 20X6, there was any change in the capital stock, increase in long-term debt, or decrease in consolidated net current assets or stockholders' equity of the consolidated companies as compared with amounts shown in the March 31, 20X6 unaudited condensed consolidated balance sheet included in the registration statement, or

(ii) for the period from April 1, 20X6 to May 31, 20X6, there were any decreases, as compared to the corresponding period in the preceding year, in consolidated net sales or in income before extraordinary items or of net income, except in all instances for changes, increases, or decreases that the registration statement discloses have occurred or may occur.

6. As mentioned in 4*b*, company officials have advised us that no consolidated financial statements as of any date or for any period subsequent to May 31, 20X6 are available; accordingly, the procedures carried out by us with respect to changes in financial statement items after May 31, 20X6 have, of necessity, been even more limited than those with respect to the periods referred to in 4. We have inquired of certain officials of the company who have responsibility for financial and accounting matters whether (*a*) at June 23, 20X6, there was any change in the capital stock, increase in long-term debt, or any decreases in consolidated net current assets or stockholders' equity of the consolidated companies as compared with amounts shown on the March 31, 20X6, unaudited condensed consolidated balance sheet included in the registration statement, or (*b*) for the period from April 1, 20X6 to June 23, 20X6, there were any decreases, as compared with the corresponding period in the preceding year, in consolidated net sales, or in income before extraordinary items or of net income. On the basis of these inquiries and our reading of the minutes as described in 4, nothing came to our attention that caused us to believe that there was any such change, increase, or decrease, except in all instances for changes, increases, or decreases that the registration statement discloses have occurred or may occur.

---

[1] Section 930, *Interim Financial Information*, does not require the auditor to modify the report on a review of interim financial information for a lack of consistency in the application of accounting policies provided that the interim financial information appropriately discloses such matters.

7. This letter is solely for the information of the addressees and to assist the underwriters in conducting and documenting their investigation of the affairs of the company in connection with the offering of the securities covered by the registration statement, and it is not to be used, circulated, quoted, or otherwise referred to within or without the underwriting group for any other purpose, including but not limited to the registration, purchase, or sale of securities, nor is it to be filed with or referred to in whole or in part in the registration statement or any other document, except that reference may be made to it in the underwriting agreement or in any list of closing documents pertaining to the offering of the securities covered by the registration statement.

Example A-2—Typical Comfort Letter for a Non-1933 Act Offering When the Required Representation Letter Has Been Obtained

.A93-4 Example A-2 is applicable when a comfort letter is issued in a non-1933 Act offering. Example A-2 assumes the following:

- The offerer is not an SEC registrant.
- The requesting party has given the auditor a representation letter as required by paragraph .10 and described in paragraph .11.
- Interim financial information is included in the offering document, and the auditor has performed review procedures in accordance with generally accepted auditing standards applicable to reviews of interim financial information.
- The auditor did not perform an audit of the effectiveness of internal control over financial reporting in any period.
- There has not been a change in the application of a requirement of generally accepted accounting principles during the interim period. If there has been such a change, a reference to that change would be included in paragraph 4 of example A-2.

The cut-off date is June 23, 20X6, and the letter is dated June 28, 20X6.

Each of the comments in the letter is in response to a request from the requesting party. For purposes of example A-2, the income statement items of the current interim period are to be compared with those of the corresponding period of the preceding year.

June 28, 20X6

[*Addressee*]

Dear Ladies and Gentlemen:

We have audited the consolidated financial statements of The Nonissuer Company, Inc. (the company) and subsidiaries, which comprise the consolidated balance sheets as of December 31, 20X5 and 20X4, and the related consolidated statements of income, changes in stockholders' equity, and cash flows for each of the years in the three-year period ended December 31, 20X5, and the related notes to the consolidated financial statements, all included [*or incorporated by reference*] in the offering memorandum for $30,000,000 of Senior Debt due May 30, 20Z6. Our report with respect thereto is included in the offering memorandum. This offering memorandum, dated June 28, 20X6, is herein referred to as the Offering Memorandum.

This letter is being furnished in reliance upon your representation to us that—

a. You are knowledgeable with respect to the due diligence review process that would be performed if this placement of securities were being registered pursuant to the Securities Act of 1933 (the Act).

b. In connection with the offering of Senior Debt, the review process you have performed is substantially consistent with the due diligence review process that you would have performed if this placement of securities were being registered pursuant to the Act.

In connection with the Offering Memorandum—

1. We are independent certified public accountants with respect to the company under Rule 101 of the AICPA's Code of Professional Conduct and its interpretations and rulings.

2. We have not audited any financial statements of the company as of any date or for any period subsequent to December 31, 20X5; although, we have conducted an audit for the year ended December 31, 20X5, the purpose (and, therefore, the scope) of the audit was to enable us to express our opinion on the consolidated financial statements as of December 31, 20X5, and for the year then ended, but not on the financial statements for any interim period within that year. Therefore, we are unable to and do not express any opinion on the unaudited condensed consolidated balance sheet as of March 31, 20X6, and the unaudited condensed consolidated statements of income, of cash flows, and of changes in stockholders' equity for the three-month periods ended March 31, 20X5 and 20X6, included in the Offering Memorandum, or on the financial position, results of operations, or cash flows as of any date or for any period subsequent to December 31, 20X5.

3. For purposes of this letter, we have read the 20X6 minutes of meetings of the stockholders, the board of directors, and [*include other appropriate committees, if any*] of the company and its subsidiaries as set forth in the minute books at June 23, 20X6, officials of the company having advised us that the minutes of all such meetings through that date were set forth therein and having discussed with us the unapproved minutes of meetings held on [*dates*]; we have carried out other procedures to June 23, 20X6, as follows (our work did not extend to the period from June 24, 20X6 to June 28, 20X6, inclusive):

    a. With respect to the three-month periods ended March 31, 20X6 and 20X5, we have—

    (i) Performed the procedures specified for a review in accordance with auditing standards generally accepted in the United States of America applicable to reviews of interim financial information, on the unaudited condensed consolidated balance sheet as of March 31, 20X6, and unaudited condensed consolidated statements of income, stockholders' equity, and cash flows for the three-month periods ended March 31, 20X6 and 20X5, included in the Offering Memorandum.

    b. With respect to the period from April 1, 20X6 to May 31, 20X6, we have—

(i) Read the unaudited consolidated financial statements of the company and subsidiaries for April and May of both 20X5 and 20X6 furnished us by the company, officials of the company having advised us that no such financial statements as of any date or for any period subsequent to May 31, 20X6, were available. [*If applicable:* The financial information for April and May of both 20X5 and 20X6 is incomplete in that it omits the statement of cash flows and other disclosures.]

(ii) Inquired of certain officials of the company who have responsibility for financial and accounting matters whether the unaudited consolidated financial statements referred to in *b*(i) are stated on a basis substantially consistent with that of the audited consolidated financial statements included in the Offering Memorandum.

The foregoing procedures do not constitute an audit conducted in accordance with generally accepted auditing standards. Also, they would not necessarily reveal matters of significance with respect to the comments in the following paragraph. Accordingly, we make no representations regarding the sufficiency of the foregoing procedures for your purposes.

4. Nothing came to our attention as a result of the foregoing procedures, however, that caused us to believe that—

a.

(i) Any material modifications should be made to the unaudited condensed consolidated financial statements described in 3*a*(i), included in the Offering Memorandum, for them to be in conformity with generally accepted accounting principles.[2]

b.

(i) At May 31, 20X6, there was any change in the capital stock, increase in long-term debt, or decrease in consolidated net current assets or stockholders' equity of the consolidated companies as compared with amounts shown in the March 31, 20X6 unaudited condensed consolidated balance sheet included in the Offering Memorandum, or

(ii) for the period from April 1, 20X6 to May 31, 20X6, there were any decreases, as compared to the corresponding period in the preceding year, in consolidated net sales, or in income before extraordinary items or of net income, except in all instances for changes, increases, or decreases that the Offering Memorandum discloses have occurred or may occur.

5. As mentioned in 3*b*, company officials have advised us that no consolidated financial statements as of any date or for any period subsequent to May 31, 20X6 are available; accordingly, the

---

[2] Section 930 does not require the auditor to modify the report on a review of interim financial information for a lack of consistency in the application of accounting policies provided that the interim financial information appropriately discloses such matters.

procedures carried out by us with respect to changes in financial statement items after May 31, 20X6, have, of necessity, been even more limited than those with respect to the periods referred to in 3. We have inquired of certain officials of the company who have responsibility for financial and accounting matters whether (*a*) at June 23, 20X6, there was any change in the capital stock, increase in long-term debt, or any decreases in consolidated net current assets or stockholders' equity of the consolidated companies as compared with amounts shown on the March 31, 20X6 unaudited condensed consolidated balance sheet included in the Offering Memorandum, or (*b*) for the period from April 1, 20X6 to June 23, 20X6, there were any decreases, as compared with the corresponding period in the preceding year, in consolidated net sales or in income before extraordinary items or of net income. On the basis of these inquiries and our reading of the minutes as described in 3, nothing came to our attention that caused us to believe that there was any such change, increase, or decrease, except in all instances for changes, increases, or decreases that the Offering Memorandum discloses have occurred or may occur.

6. This letter is solely for the information of the addressees and to assist the requesting party in conducting and documenting their investigation of the affairs of the company in connection with the offering of the securities covered by the Offering Memorandum, and it is not to be used, circulated, quoted, or otherwise referred to for any purpose, including but not limited to the registration, purchase, or sale of securities, nor is it to be filed with or referred to in whole or in part in the Offering Memorandum or any other document, except that reference may be made to it in the Purchase Contract or in any list of closing documents pertaining to the offering of the securities covered by the Offering Memorandum.

Example B—Letter When a Short-Form Registration Statement Is Filed Incorporating Previously Filed Form 8-K by Reference

.A93-5 Example B is an example of modifications to the letter that the auditor of a nonissuer may provide when a registrant has acquired the nonissuer, and the registrant uses a short-form registration statement (for example, Form S-3), which incorporates a previously filed Form 8-K that includes the nonpublic company's financial statements. The auditor was independent of the nonissuer but is not independent with respect to the registrant.

June 28, 20X6

[*Addressee*]

Dear Ladies and Gentlemen:

We have audited the consolidated financial statements of The Nonissuer Company, Inc. (the company) and subsidiaries, which comprise the consolidated balance sheets as of December 31, 20X5 and 20X4, and the related consolidated statements of income, changes in stockholders' equity, and cash flows for each of the years in the three-year period ended December 31, 20X5, and the related notes to the consolidated financial statements, all included in The Issuer Company's (the registrant) current report on Form 8-K dated May 15, 20X6, and incorporated by reference in the registration statement (no. 33-00000) on Form S-3 filed by the registrant under the Securities Act of 1933 (the Act); our report with respect thereto is also incorporated by reference in that registration statement. The registration statement, as amended on June 28, 20X6, is herein referred to as the registration statement.

In connection with the registration statement—

1. As of [*insert date of the auditor's most recent report on the financial statements of the entity*] and during the period covered by the financial statements on which we reported, we were independent certified public accountants with respect to the company under Rule 101 of the AICPA's Code of Professional Conduct and its interpretations and rulings.
2. In our opinion, the consolidated financial statements audited by us and incorporated by reference in the registration statement comply as to form in all material respects with the applicable accounting requirements of the Act and the Securities Exchange Act of 1934 and the related rules and regulations adopted by the SEC.
3. We have not audited any financial statements of the company as of any date or for any period subsequent to December 31, 20X5; although we have conducted an audit for the year ended December 31, 20X5, the purpose (and, therefore, the scope) of the audit was to enable us to express our opinion on the consolidated financial statements as of December 31, 20X5, and for the year then ended, but not on the consolidated financial statements for any interim period within that year. Therefore, we are unable to, and do not express any opinion on, the unaudited condensed consolidated balance sheet as of March 31, 20X6, and the unaudited condensed consolidated statements of income, stockholders' equity, and cash flows for the three-month periods ended March 31, 20X6 and 20X5, included in the registrant's current report on Form 8-K dated May 15, 20X6, incorporated by reference in the registration statement, or on the financial position, results of operations, or cash flows as of any date or for any period subsequent to December 31, 20X5.
4. For purposes of this letter, we have read the 20X6 minutes of the meetings of the stockholders, the board of directors, and [*include other appropriate committees, if any*] of the company and its subsidiaries as set forth in the minute books at June 23, 20X6, officials of the company having advised us that the minutes of all such meetings through that date were set forth therein, and having discussed with us the unapproved minutes of meetings held on [*dates*]; we have carried out other procedures to June 23, 20X6, as follows (our work did not extend to the period from June 24, 20X6 to June 28, 20X6, inclusive):

   With respect to the three-month periods ended March 31, 20X6 and 20X5, we have—

   (i) Performed a review in accordance with auditing standards generally accepted in the United States of America applicable to reviews of interim financial information on the unaudited condensed consolidated balance sheet as of March 31, 20X6, and the unaudited condensed consolidated statements of income, stockholders' equity, and cash flows for the three-month periods ended March 31, 20X6 and 20X5, included in the registrant's current report on Form 8-K dated May 15, 20X6, incorporated by reference in the registration statement.

(ii) Inquired of certain officials of the company who have responsibility for financial and accounting matters whether the unaudited condensed consolidated financial statements referred to in (i) comply as to form in all material respects with the applicable accounting requirements of the Securities Exchange Act of 1934 and the related rules and regulations adopted by the SEC.

The foregoing procedures do not constitute an audit conducted in accordance with generally accepted auditing standards. Also, they would not necessarily reveal matters of significance with respect to the comments in the following paragraph. Accordingly, we make no representations about the sufficiency of the foregoing procedures for your purposes.

5. Nothing came to our attention as a result of the foregoing procedures, however, that caused us to believe that—

(i) Any material modifications should be made to the unaudited condensed consolidated financial statements described in 4(i), incorporated by reference in the registration statement, for them to be in conformity with generally accepted accounting principles.

(ii) The unaudited condensed consolidated financial statements described in 4(i) do not comply as to form in all material respects with the applicable accounting requirements of the Securities Exchange Act of 1934 and the related rules and regulations adopted by the SEC.

6. This letter is solely for the information of the addressees and to assist the underwriters in conducting and documenting their investigation of the affairs of the company in connection with the offering of the securities covered by the registration statement, and for use of the auditors of the registrant in furnishing their letter to the underwriters, and it is not to be used, circulated, quoted, or otherwise referred to within the underwriting group for any other purpose, including but not limited to the registration, purchase, or sale of securities, nor is it to be filed with or referred to, in whole or in part, in the registration statement or any other document, except that reference may be made to it in the underwriting agreement or any list of closing documents pertaining to the offering of the securities covered by the registration statement.

Example C—Letter Reaffirming Comments in Example A-1 as of a Later Date

.A93-6 If more than one comfort letter is requested, the later letter may, in appropriate situations, refer to information appearing in the earlier letter without repeating such information (see paragraph .25 of this section and paragraph .A93-1 of this exhibit). Example C reaffirms and updates the information in example A-1.

July 25, 20X6

[*Addressee*]

Dear Ladies and Gentlemen:

We refer to our letter of June 28, 20X6, relating to the registration statement (no. 33-00000) of The Nonissuer Company, Inc. (the company). We reaffirm as of the date hereof (and as though made on the date hereof) all statements made in that letter except that, for the purposes of this letter

a. The registration statement to which this letter relates is as amended on July 13, 20X6 [*effective date*].

b. The reading of minutes described in paragraph 4 of that letter has been carried out through July 20, 20X6 [*the new cut-off date*].

c. The procedures and inquiries covered in paragraph 4 of that letter were carried out to July 20, 20X6 [*the new cut-off date*] (our work did not extend to the period from July 21, 20X6 to July 25, 20X6 [*date of letter*], inclusive).

d. The period covered in paragraph 4*b* of that letter is changed to the period from April 1, 20X6 to June 30, 20X6, officials of the company having advised us that no such financial statements as of any date or for any period subsequent to June 30, 20X6, were available.

e. The references to May 31, 20X6 in paragraph 5*b* of that letter are changed to June 30, 20X6.

f. The references to May 31, 20X6 and June 23, 20X6 in paragraph 6 of that letter are changed to June 30, 20X6 and July 20, 20X6, respectively.

This letter is solely for the information of the addressees and to assist the underwriters in conducting and documenting their investigation of the affairs of the company in connection with the offering of the securities covered by the registration statement, and it is not to be used, circulated, quoted, or otherwise referred to within or without the underwriting group for any other purpose, including but not limited to the registration, purchase, or sale of securities, nor is it to be filed with or referred to, in whole or in part, in the registration statement or any other document, except that reference may be made to it in the underwriting agreement or any list of closing documents pertaining to the offering of the securities covered by the registration statement.

Example D—Comments on Pro Forma Financial Information

.A93-7 Example D is applicable when the auditor is asked to provide negative assurance on (*a*) whether the pro forma financial information included in a registration statement complies as to form in all material respects with the applicable accounting requirements of Rule 11-02 of Regulation S-X, and (*b*) the application of pro forma adjustments to historical amounts in the compilation of the pro forma financial information (see paragraphs .52–.53). The material in this example is intended to be inserted between paragraphs 6 and 7 in example A-1. The example assumes that the auditor has not previously reported on the pro forma financial information. If the auditor did previously report on the pro forma financial information, they may refer in the introductory paragraph of the comfort letter to the fact that they have issued a report, and the report may be attached to the comfort letter (see paragraph .A32–.A33). Therefore, in that circumstance, the procedures in 6*b*(i) and 6*c* ordinarily would not be performed, and the auditor would not separately comment on the application of pro forma adjustments to historical financial information because that assurance is encompassed in the auditors' report on pro forma financial information. The auditor may, however, agree to comment on compliance as to form with the applicable accounting requirements of Rule 11-02 of Regulation S-X.

6. At your request, we have—
   a. Read the unaudited pro forma condensed consolidated balance sheet as of March 31, 20X6, and the unaudited pro forma condensed consolidated statements of income for the year ended December 31, 20X5, and the three-month period ended March 31, 20X6, included in the registration statement.
   b. Inquired of certain officials of the company who have responsibility for financial and accounting matters about
      (i) the basis for their determination of the pro forma adjustments and
      (ii) whether the unaudited pro forma condensed consolidated financial statements referred to in 6*a* comply as to form in all material respects with the applicable accounting requirements of Rule 11-02 of Regulation S-X.
   c. Proved the arithmetic accuracy of the application of the pro forma adjustments to the historical amounts in the unaudited pro forma condensed consolidated financial statements.

   The foregoing procedures are substantially less in scope than an examination, the objective of which is the expression of an opinion on management's assumptions, the pro forma adjustments, and the application of those adjustments to historical financial information. Accordingly, we do not express such an opinion. The foregoing procedures would not necessarily reveal matters of significance with respect to the comments in the following paragraph. Accordingly, we make no representation about the sufficiency of such procedures for your purposes.

7. Nothing came to our attention as a result of the procedures specified in paragraph 6, however, that caused us to believe that the unaudited pro forma condensed consolidated financial statements referred to in 6*a* included in the registration statement have not been properly compiled on the pro forma bases described in the notes thereto. Had we performed additional procedures or had we made an examination of the pro forma condensed consolidated financial statements, other matters might have come to our attention that would have been reported to you.

Example E—Comments on a Financial Forecast

.A93-8 Example E is applicable when an auditor is asked to comment on a financial forecast (see paragraph .54). The material in this example is intended to be inserted between paragraphs 6 and 7 in example A-1 and 5 and 6 in example A-2. The example assumes that the auditor has previously reported on the compilation of the financial forecast and that the report is attached to the letter (see paragraph .A33 and example O).

7. At your request, we performed the following procedure with respect to the forecasted consolidated balance sheet and consolidated statements of income and cash flows as of December 31, 20X6, and for the year then ending. With respect to forecasted rental income, we compared the occupancy statistics about expected demand for rental of the housing units to statistics for existing comparable properties and found them to be the same.

8. Because the procedure described above does not constitute an examination of prospective financial statements in accordance with standards promulgated by the American Institute of Certified Public Accountants, we do not express an opinion on whether the prospective financial statements are presented in conformity with AICPA presentation guidelines or on whether the underlying assumptions provide a reasonable basis for the presentation.

Had we performed additional procedures or had we made an examination of the forecast in accordance with standards promulgated by the AICPA, matters might have come to our attention that would have been reported to you. Furthermore, there will usually be differences between the forecasted and actual results because events and circumstances frequently do not occur as expected, and those differences may be material.

Example F—Comments on Tables, Statistics, and Other Financial Information—Complete Description of Procedures and Findings

.A93-9 Example F is applicable when the auditor is asked to comment on tables, statistics, or other compilations of information appearing in a registration statement (paragraphs .65–.71). Each of the comments is in response to a specific request. The paragraphs in example F are intended to follow paragraph 6 in example A-1 or paragraph 5 in example A-2.

In some cases, the auditor may choose to combine in one paragraph the substance of paragraphs 6 and 8 shown as follows. This may be done by expanding the identification of items in paragraph 8 to provide the identification information included in paragraph 6. In such cases, the introductory sentences in paragraphs 6 and 8 and the text of paragraph 7 might be combined as follows: "For purposes of this letter, we have also read the following information and have performed the additional procedures stated below with respect to such information. Our audit of the consolidated financial statements. . ."

6. For purposes of this letter, we have also read the following, set forth in the securities offering on the indicated pages.

Item	*Page*	*Description*
a	4	"Capitalization." The amounts under the captions "Amount Outstanding as of May 31, 20X6" and "As Adjusted." The related notes, except the following in Note 2: "See Transactions With Interested Persons." From the proceeds of this offering the company intends to prepay $900,000 on these notes, pro rata. See "Use of Proceeds."
b	13	"History and Business—Sales and Marketing." The table following the first paragraph.
c	33	"Selected Financial Data."

7. Our audit of the consolidated financial statements for the periods referred to in the introductory paragraph of this letter comprised audit tests and procedures deemed necessary for the purpose of expressing an opinion on such financial statements as a whole. For none of the periods referred to therein, or any other period, did we perform audit tests for the purpose of expressing an opinion on individual balances of accounts or summaries of selected transactions such as those enumerated above, and, accordingly, we express no opinion thereon.

8. However, for purposes of this letter, we have performed the following additional procedures, which were applied as indicated with respect to the items enumerated above.

Item in 6	*Procedures and Findings*
a	We compared the amounts and numbers of shares listed under the caption, "Amount Outstanding as of May 31, 20X6," with the balances in the appropriate accounts in the company's general ledger and found them to be in agreement. We compared the amounts and numbers of shares listed under the caption, "Amount Outstanding as of May 31, 20X6," adjusted for the issuance of the debentures to be offered by means of the securities offering and for the proposed use of a portion of the proceeds thereof to prepay portions of certain notes, as described under "Use of Proceeds," with the amounts and numbers of shares shown under the caption, "As Adjusted," and found such amounts and numbers of shares to be in agreement. (However, we make no comments regarding the reasonableness of the "Use of Proceeds" or whether such use will actually take place.)
b	We compared the amounts of military sales, commercial sales, and total sales shown in the securities offering with the balances in the appropriate accounts in the company's accounting records for the respective fiscal years and for the unaudited interim periods and found them to be in agreement. We proved the arithmetic accuracy of the percentages of such amounts of military sales and commercial sales to total sales for the respective fiscal years and for the unaudited interim periods. We compared such computed percentages with the corresponding percentages appearing in the registration statement and found them to be in agreement.
c	We compared the amounts of net sales and income from continuing operations for the years ended December 31, 20X5, 20X4, and 20X3, with the respective amounts in the consolidated financial statements on pages 27 and 28 and the amounts for the years ended December 31, 20X2 and 20X1, with the respective amounts in the consolidated financial statements for 20X2 and 20X1 and found them to be in agreement. We compared the amounts of total assets, long-term obligations, and redeemable preferred stock at December 31, 20X5 and 20X4, with the respective amounts in the consolidated financial statements on pages 27 and 28 and the amounts at December 31, 20X3, 20X2, and 20X1, with the corresponding amounts in the consolidated financial statements for 20X3, 20X2, and 20X1 and found them to be in agreement. We compared the information included under the heading "Selected Financial Data" with the disclosure requirements of Item 301 of Regulation S-K. We also inquired of certain officials of the company who have responsibility for financial and accounting matters whether this information conforms in all material respects with the disclosure requirements of Item 301 of Regulation S-K. Nothing came to our attention

Item in 6	*Procedures and Findings*
	as a result of the foregoing procedures that caused us to believe that this information does not conform in all material respects with the disclosure requirements of Item 301 of Regulation S-K.

9. It should be understood that we make no representations regarding questions of legal interpretation or regarding the sufficiency for your purposes of the procedures enumerated in the preceding paragraph; also, such procedures would not necessarily reveal any material misstatement of the amounts or percentages listed above. Further, we have addressed ourselves solely to the foregoing data as set forth in the registration statement and make no representations regarding the adequacy of disclosure or regarding whether any material facts have been omitted.

Example G—Comments on Tables, Statistics, and Other Financial Information—Summarized Description of Procedures and Findings Regarding Tables, Statistics, and Other Financial Information

.A93-10 Example G illustrates, in paragraph 8*a*, a method of summarizing the descriptions of procedures and findings regarding tables, statistics, and other financial information in order to avoid repetition in the comfort letter. Each of the comments is in response to a specific request. The paragraphs in example G are intended to follow paragraph 6 in example A-1 or paragraph 5 in example A-2.

Other methods of summarizing the descriptions may also be appropriately used. For example, the letter may present a matrix listing the financial information and common procedures employed and indicating the procedures applied to specific items.

6. For purposes of this letter, we have also read the following, set forth in the registration statement on the indicated pages.

Item	*Page*	*Description*
a	4	"Capitalization." The amounts under the captions "Amount Outstanding as of May 31, 20X6" and "As Adjusted." The related notes, except the following in Note 2: "See Transactions With Interested Persons." From the proceeds of this offering the company intends to prepay $900,000 on these notes, pro rata. See "Use of Proceeds."
b	13	"History and Business—Sales and Marketing." The table following the first paragraph.
c	33	"Selected Financial Data."

7. Our audit of the consolidated financial statements for the periods referred to in the introductory paragraph of this letter comprised audit tests and procedures deemed necessary for the purpose of expressing an opinion on such financial statements as a whole. For none of the periods referred to therein, or any other period, did we perform audit tests for the purpose of expressing an opinion on individual balances of accounts or summaries of selected transactions, such as those enumerated above, and, accordingly, we express no opinion thereon.

8. However, for purposes of this letter and with respect to the items enumerated in 6 above—

   a. Except for item 6*a*, we have (i) compared the dollar amounts either with the amounts in the audited consolidated financial statements described in the introductory paragraph of this letter or, for prior years, included in the company's accounting records, or with amounts in the unaudited consolidated financial statements described in paragraph 3 to the extent such amounts are included in or can be derived from such statements and found them to be in agreement; (ii) compared the amounts of military sales, commercial sales, and total sales with amounts in the company's accounting records and found them to be in agreement; (iii) compared other dollar amounts with amounts shown in analyses prepared by the company and found them to be in agreement; and (iv) proved the arithmetic accuracy of the percentages based on the data in the above-mentioned financial statements, accounting records, and analyses.

   We compared the information in item 6*c* with the disclosure requirements of Item 301 of Regulation S-K. We also inquired of certain officials of the company who have responsibility for financial and accounting matters whether this information conforms in all material respects with the disclosure requirements of Item 301 of Regulation S-K. Nothing came to our attention as a result of the foregoing procedures that caused us to believe that this information does not conform in all material respects with the disclosure requirements of Item 301 of Regulation S-K.

   b. With respect to item 6*a*, we compared the amounts and numbers of shares listed under the caption "Amount Outstanding as of May 31, 20X6" with the balances in the appropriate accounts in the company's general ledger at May 31, 20X6, and found them to be in agreement. We compared the amounts and numbers of shares listed under the caption "Amount Outstanding as of May 31, 20X6," adjusted for the issuance of the debentures to be offered by means of the securities offering and for the proposed use of a portion of the proceeds thereof to prepay portions of certain notes, as described under "Use of Proceeds," with the amounts and numbers of shares shown under the caption, "As Adjusted" and found such amounts and numbers of shares to be in agreement. (However, we make no comments regarding the reasonableness of "Use of Proceeds" or whether such use will actually take place.)

9. It should be understood that we make no representations regarding questions of legal interpretation or regarding the sufficiency for your purposes of the procedures enumerated in the preceding paragraph; also, such procedures would not necessarily reveal any material misstatement of the amounts or percentages listed above. Further, we have addressed ourselves solely to the foregoing data as set forth in the registration statement and make no representations regarding the adequacy of disclosure or regarding whether any material facts have been omitted.

Example H—Comments on Tables, Statistics, and Other Financial Information: Descriptions of Procedures and Findings Regarding Tables, Statistics, and Other Financial Information—Attached Securities Offering (or Selected Pages) Identifies Items to Which Procedures Were Applied Through the Use of Designated Symbols

.A93-11 This example illustrates an alternate format, which could facilitate reporting when the auditor is requested to perform procedures on numerous statistics included in a securities offering. Each of the comments is in response to a specific request. The paragraph in example H is intended to follow paragraph 6 in example A-1 or paragraph 5 in example A-2.

7. For purposes of this letter, we have also read the items identified by you on the attached copy of the registration statement and have performed the following procedures, which were applied as indicated with respect to the symbols explained below:

   ✓

   Compared the amount with ABC Company's financial statements for the period indicated included in the securities offering and found them to be in agreement.

8. Our audit of the consolidated financial statements for the periods referred to in the introductory paragraph of this letter comprised audit tests and procedures deemed necessary for the purpose of expressing an opinion on such financial statements as a whole. For none of the periods referred to therein, nor any other period, did we perform audit tests for the purpose of expressing an opinion on individual balances of accounts or summaries of selected transactions, such as those enumerated above, and, accordingly, we express no opinion thereon.

9. It should be understood that we make no representations regarding questions of legal interpretation or regarding the sufficiency for your purposes of the procedures enumerated in the preceding paragraph; also, such procedures would not necessarily reveal any material misstatement of the amounts or percentages listed above. Further, we have addressed ourselves solely to the foregoing data as set forth in the registration statement and make no representations regarding the adequacy of disclosure or regarding whether any material facts have been omitted.

   [*The following is an extract from a securities offering that illustrates how an auditor can document procedures performed on numerous statistics included in the securities offering.*]

Summary Financial Information of ABC Company (In thousands)

	ABC Company Year Ended December 31,		
Income statement data	*20X3*	*20X4*	*20X5*
Revenue from home sales	$104,110✓	$115,837✓	$131,032✓
Gross profit from sales	23,774✓	17,099✓	22,407✓
Income from home building net of tax	7,029✓	1,000✓	3,425✓

Example I—Alternate Wording When Auditor's Report on Audited Financial Statements Contains an Emphasis-of-Matter Paragraph

.A93-12 Example I is applicable when the auditor's report on the audited financial statements included in the securities offering contains an emphasis-of-matter paragraph regarding a matter that would also affect the unaudited condensed consolidated interim financial statements included in the securities offering. The introductory paragraph would be revised as follows:

> Our reports with respect thereto (which contain an emphasis-of-matter paragraph that describes a lawsuit to which the Company is a defendant, discussed in note 8 to the consolidated financial statements), are also included in the securities offering.

The matter described in the emphasis-of-matter paragraph would also be evaluated to determine whether it also requires mention in the comments on the unaudited condensed consolidated interim financial information (paragraph 5*b* of example A-1). If it is concluded that mention of such a matter in the comments on unaudited condensed consolidated financial statements is appropriate, a sentence would be added at the end of paragraph 5*b* in example A-1 and paragraph 4*b* of example A-2:

> Reference should be made to the introductory paragraph of this letter, which states that our audit report covering the consolidated financial statements as of and for the year ended December 31, 20X5, includes an emphasis-of-matter paragraph that describes a lawsuit to which the company is a defendant, discussed in note 8 to the consolidated financial statements.

Example J—Alternate Wording When More Than One Auditor Is Involved

.A93-13 Example J applies when more than one auditor is involved in the audit of the financial statements of a business, and the group engagement team has obtained a copy of the comfort letter of the component auditors (see paragraph .21). Example J consists of an addition to paragraph 4, a substitution for the applicable part of paragraph 5, and an addition to paragraph 6 of example A-1 and paragraph 3, 4, and 5 of example A-2, respectively.

> [4]*c*. We have read the letter dated ______ of [*the other auditors*] with regard to [*the related company*].
>
> 5. Nothing came to our attention as a result of the foregoing procedures (which, so far as [*the related company*] is concerned, consisted solely of reading the letter referred to in 4*c*), however, that caused us to believe that . . .
>
> 6. . . . On the basis of these inquiries and our reading of the minutes and the letter dated ______ of [*the other auditors*] with regard to [*the related company*], as described in 4, nothing came to our attention that caused us to believe that there was any such change, increase, or decrease, except in all instances for changes, increases, or decreases that the registration statement discloses have occurred or may occur.

Example K—Alternate Wording When the SEC Has Agreed to a Departure From Its Accounting Requirements

.A93-14 Example K is applicable when (*a*) there is a departure from the applicable accounting requirements of the 1933 Act and the related rules and regulations adopted by the SEC, and (*b*) representatives of the SEC have agreed to the departure. Paragraph 2 of example A-1 would be revised to read as follows:

2. In our opinion [*include the phrase* except as disclosed in the registration statement *if applicable*], the consolidated financial statements and financial statement schedules audited by us and included (incorporated by reference) in the registration statement comply as to form in all material respects with the applicable accounting requirements of the Act and the related rules and regulations adopted by the SEC; however, as agreed to by representatives of the SEC, separate financial statements and financial statement schedules of ABC Company (an equity investee) as required by Rule 3-09 of Regulation S-X have been omitted.

Example L—Alternate Wording When Recent Earnings Data Are Presented in Capsule Form

.A93-15 Example L is applicable when (*a*) the statement of income in the securities offering is supplemented by later information regarding sales and earnings (capsule financial information), (*b*) the auditor is asked to comment on that information (paragraphs .50–.51), and (*c*) the auditor has conducted a review in accordance with generally accepted auditing standards applicable to reviews of interim financial information of the financial statements from which the capsule financial information is derived. The same facts exist as in example A-1, except for the following:

- Sales and net income (no extraordinary items) share for the six-month periods ended June 30, 20X6 and 20X5 (both unaudited), are included in capsule form more limited than that specified by Financial Accounting Standards Board *Accounting Standards Codification* 270, *Interim Reporting*.
- No financial statements later than those for June 20X6 are available.
- The letter is dated July 25, 20X6, and the cut-off date is July 20, 20X6.

Paragraphs 4, 5, and 6 of example A-1 would be revised to read as follows:

4. For purposes of this letter, we have read the 20X6 minutes of the meetings of the stockholders, the board of directors, and [*include other appropriate committees, if any*] of the company and its subsidiaries as set forth in the minute books at July 20, 20X6, officials of the company having advised us that the minutes of all such meetings through that date were set forth therein and discussed with us the unapproved minutes of meetings held on [*dates*]; we have carried out other procedures to July 20, 20X6, as follows (our work did not extend to the period from July 21, 20X6 to July 25, 20X6, inclusive):

   a. With respect to the three-month periods ended March 31, 20X6 and 20X5, we have—

(i) Performed the procedures specified for a review in accordance with auditing standards generally accepted in the United States of America applicable to reviews of interim financial information, on the unaudited condensed consolidated balance sheet as of March 31, 20X6, and the unaudited condensed consolidated statements of income, stockholders' equity, and cash flows for the three-month periods ended March 31, 20X6 and 20X5, included in the registration statement.

(ii) Inquired of certain officials of the company who have responsibility for financial and accounting matters whether the unaudited condensed consolidated financial statements referred to in *a*(i) comply as to form in all material respects with the applicable accounting requirements of the Act and the related rules and regulations adopted by the SEC.

b. With respect to the six-month periods ended June 30, 20X6 and 20X5, we have—

(i) Read the unaudited amounts for sales, net income, and earnings per share for the six-month periods ended June 30, 20X6 and 20X5, as set forth in paragraph [*identify location*].

(ii) Performed the procedures specified for a review in accordance with auditing standards generally accepted in the United States of America, applicable to reviews of interim financial information, on the unaudited condensed consolidated balance sheet as of June 30, 20X6 and the unaudited condensed consolidated statements of income, stockholders' equity, and cash flows for the six-month periods ended June 30, 20X6 and 20X5, from which the unaudited amounts referred to in *b*(i) are derived.

(iii) Inquired of certain officials of the company who have responsibility for financial and accounting matters whether the unaudited amounts referred to in *b*(i) are stated on a basis substantially consistent with that of the corresponding amounts in the audited consolidated statements of income.

The foregoing procedures do not constitute an audit conducted in accordance with generally accepted auditing standards. Also, they would not necessarily reveal matters of significance with respect to the comments in the following paragraph. Accordingly, we make no representations regarding the sufficiency of the foregoing procedures for your purposes.

5. Nothing came to our attention as a result of the foregoing procedures, however, that caused us to believe that—

a.

(i) Any material modifications should be made to the unaudited condensed consolidated financial statements described in 4*a*(i), included in the registration statement, for them to be in conformity with generally accepted accounting principles.

(ii) The unaudited condensed consolidated financial statements described in 4*a*(i) do not comply as to form in all material respects with the applicable accounting requirements of the Act and the related rules and regulations adopted by the SEC.

b.

(i) The unaudited amounts for sales and net income for the six-month periods ended June 30, 20X6 and 20X5, referred to in 4*b*(i) do not agree with the amounts set forth in the unaudited condensed consolidated financial statements for those same periods.

(ii) The unaudited amounts referred to in 4*b*(i) were not determined on a basis substantially consistent with that of the corresponding amounts in the audited consolidated statements of income.

c. At June 30, 20X6, there was any change in the capital stock, increase in long-term debt, or any decreases in consolidated net current assets or stockholders' equity of the consolidated companies as compared with amounts shown in the March 31, 20X6, unaudited condensed consolidated balance sheet included in the registration statement, except in all instances for changes, increases, or decreases that the registration statement discloses have occurred or may occur.

6. Company officials have advised us that no consolidated financial statements as of any date or for any period subsequent to June 30, 20X6 are available; accordingly, the procedures carried out by us with respect to changes in financial statement items after June 30, 20X6 have, of necessity, been even more limited than those with respect to the periods referred to in 4. We have inquired of certain officials of the company who have responsibility for financial and accounting matters whether (*a*) at July 20, 20X6, there was any change in the capital stock, increase in long-term debt, or any decreases in consolidated net current assets or stockholders' equity of the consolidated companies as compared with amounts shown on the March 31, 20X6, unaudited condensed consolidated balance sheet included in the registration statement; or (*b*) for the period from July 1, 20X6 to July 20, 20X6, there were any decreases, as compared with the corresponding period in the preceding year, in consolidated net sales, or in income before extraordinary items or of net income. On the basis of these inquiries and our reading of the minutes as described in 4, nothing came to our attention that caused us to believe that there was any such change, increase, or decrease, except in all instances for changes, increases, or decreases that the registration statement discloses have occurred or may occur.

Example M—Alternate Wording When Auditors Are Aware of a Decrease in a Specified Financial Statement Item

.A93-16 Example M covers a situation in which auditors are aware of a decrease in a financial statement item on which they are requested to comment (see paragraphs .58–.64). The same facts exist as in example A-1, except for the decrease covered in the following change in paragraph 5*b*.

b. (i) At May 31, 20X6, there was any change in the capital stock, increase in long-term debt, or any decrease in consolidated stockholders' equity of the consolidated companies as compared with amounts shown in the March 31, 20X6 unaudited condensed consolidated balance sheet included in the registration statement, or

(ii) for the period from April 1, 20X6 to May 31, 20X6, there were any decreases, as compared with the corresponding period in the preceding year, in consolidated net sales, or income before extraordinary items or of net income, except in all instances for changes, increases, or decreases that the registration statement discloses have occurred or may occur and except that the unaudited consolidated balance sheet as of May 31, 20X6, which we were furnished by the company, showed a decrease from March 31, 20X6 in consolidated net current assets as follows (in thousands of dollars):

	Current Assets	*Current Liabilities*	*Net Current Assets*
March 31, 20X6	$4,251	$1,356	$2,895
May 31, 20X6	3,986	1,732	2,254

6. As mentioned in 4*b*, company officials have advised us that no consolidated financial statements as of any date or for any period subsequent to May 31, 20X6, are available; accordingly, the procedures carried out by us with respect to changes in financial statement items after May 31, 20X6, have, of necessity, been even more limited than those with respect to the periods referred to in 4. We have inquired of certain officials of the company who have responsibility for financial and accounting matters whether (*a*) at June 23, 20X6, there was any change in the capital stock, increase in long-term debt, or any decreases in consolidated net current assets or stockholders' equity of the consolidated companies as compared with amounts shown on the March 31, 20X6, unaudited condensed consolidated balance sheet included in the registration statement; or (*b*) for the period from April 1, 20X6 to June 23, 20X6, there were any decreases, as compared with the corresponding period in the preceding year, in consolidated net sales or in income before extraordinary items or of net income. On the basis of these inquiries and our reading of the minutes as described in 4, nothing came to our attention that caused us to believe that there was any such change, increase, or decrease, except in all instances for changes, increases, or decreases that the registration statement discloses have occurred or may occur and except as described in the following sentence: We have been informed by officials of the company that there continues to be

a decrease in net current assets that is estimated to be approximately the same amount as set forth in 5*b* [*or whatever other disclosure fits the circumstances*].

Example N—Alternate Wording of the Letter for Companies That Are Permitted to Present Interim Earnings Data for a 12-Month Period

.A93-17 Certain types of companies are permitted to include earnings data for a 12-month period to the date of the latest balance sheet furnished in lieu of earnings data for both the interim period between the end of the latest fiscal year and the date of the latest balance sheet and the corresponding period of the preceding fiscal year. The following would be substituted for the applicable part of paragraph 3 of example A-1.

3. ...was to enable us to express our opinion on the financial statements as of December 31, 20X5, and for the year then ended, but not on the financial statements for any period included in part within that year. Therefore, we are unable to, and do not express any opinion on, the unaudited condensed consolidated balance sheet as of March 31, 20X6, and the related unaudited condensed consolidated statements of income, stockholders' equity, and cash flows for the 12 months then ended included in the securities offering.

Example O—Alternate Wording When the Procedures That the Requesting Party Has Requested the Auditor to Perform on Interim Financial Information Are Less Than a Review in Accordance With Generally Accepted Auditing Standards Applicable to Reviews of Interim Financial Information

.A93-18 The example assumes that the requesting party has asked the auditor to perform specified procedures on the interim financial information and report thereon in the comfort letter. The letter is dated June 28, 20X6; procedures were performed through June 23, 20X6, the cut-off date. Because a review in accordance with generally accepted auditing standards applicable to reviews of interim financial information was not performed on the interim financial information as of March 31, 20X6, and for the quarter then ended, the auditor is limited to reporting procedures performed and findings obtained on the interim financial information. The following would be substituted for paragraph 4*a* of example A-1. Example O assumes there has not been a change in the application of a requirement of generally accepted accounting principles during the interim period. If there has been such a change, a reference to that change would be included in subparagraph *a*(ii) that follows.

4. For purposes of this letter, we have read the 20X6 minutes of meetings of the stockholders, the board of directors, and [*include other appropriate committees, if any*] of the company and its subsidiaries as set forth in the minute books at June 23, 20X6, officials of the company having advised us that the minutes of all such meetings through that date were set forth therein and having discussed with us the unapproved minutes of meetings held on [*dates*]; we have carried out other procedures to June 23, 20X6,

as follows (our work did not extend to the period from June 24, 20X6 to June 28, 20X6, inclusive):

a. With respect to the three-month periods ended March 31, 20X6 and 20X5, we have—

(i) Read the unaudited condensed consolidated balance sheet as of March 31, 20X6, and the unaudited condensed consolidated statements of income, stockholders' equity, and cash flows for the three-month periods ended March 31, 20X6 and 20X5, included in the registration statement, and agreed the amounts included therein with the company's accounting records as of March 31, 20X6 and 20X5, and for the three-month periods then ended.

(ii) Inquired of certain officials of the company who have responsibility for financial and accounting matters whether the unaudited condensed consolidated financial statements referred to in *a*(i): (1) are in conformity with generally accepted accounting principles applied on a basis substantially consistent with that of the audited consolidated financial statements included in the registration statement, and (2) comply as to form, in all material respects, with the applicable accounting requirements of the Act and the related rules and regulations adopted by the SEC. Those officials stated that the unaudited condensed consolidated financial statements (1) are in conformity with generally accepted accounting principles applied on a basis substantially consistent with that of the audited consolidated financial statements, and (2) comply as to form, in all material respects, with the applicable accounting requirements of the Act and the related rules and regulations adopted by the SEC.

Example P—Intentionally Omitted (See example A-2)[3]

Example Q—Letter to a Requesting Party That Has Not Provided the Legal Opinion or the Representation Letter Required by Paragraph .11

.A93-19 This example illustrates the letter to be provided in accordance with paragraph .11 in which the auditor does not provide negative assurance. This example assumes that these procedures are being performed at the request of the placement agent on information included in an offering circular in connection with a private placement of unsecured notes. The letter is dated June 30, 20X6; procedures were performed through June 25, 20X6, the cut-off date. The

[3] Example P, "A Typical Comfort Letter in a Non-1933 Act Offering, Including the Required Underwriter Representations," in AU section 634, *Letters for Underwriters and Certain Other Requesting Parties*, was moved to example A-2, "Typical Comfort Letter for a Non-1933 Act Offering When the Required Representation Letter Has Been Obtained," in this section when AU section 634 was redrafted for clarity, and is intentionally blank to retain the letters assigned to the other examples.

statements in paragraphs 4–8 of the example are illustrative of the statements required to be included by paragraph .12.

This example may also be used in connection with a filing under the 1933 Act when a party other than a named underwriter (for example, a selling shareholder) has not provided the auditor with the representation letter described in paragraph .11. In such a situation, this example may be modified to include the auditor's comments on independence and compliance as to form of the audited financial statements and financial statements schedules with the applicable accounting requirements of the 1933 Act and the related rules and regulations adopted by the SEC. Paragraph 1*a*(ii) may include an inquiry, and the response of company officials, on compliance as to form of the unaudited condensed interim financial statements.

June 30, 20X6

[*Addressee*]

Dear Ladies and Gentlemen:

We have audited the consolidated financial statements of The Nonissuer Company, Inc. (the company) and subsidiaries, which comprise the consolidated balance sheets as of December 31, 20X5 and 20X4, and the related consolidated statements of income, changes in stockholders' equity, and cash flows for each of the years in the three-year period ended December 31, 20X5, and the related notes to the consolidated financial statements, all included in the offering circular for $30,000,000 of notes due June 30, 20Z6. Our report with respect thereto is included in the offering circular. The offering circular dated June 30, 20X6, is herein referred to as the offering circular.

We are independent certified public accountants with respect to the company under Rule 101 of the AICPA's Code of Professional Conduct and its interpretations and rulings.

We have not audited any financial statements of the company as of any date or for any period subsequent to December 31, 20X5; although, we have conducted an audit for the year ended December 31, 20X5, the purpose (and, therefore, the scope) of the audit was to enable us to express our opinion on the consolidated financial statements as of December 31, 20X5, and for the year then ended, but not on the financial statements for any interim period within that year. Therefore, we are unable to, and do not express any opinion on, the unaudited condensed consolidated balance sheet as of March 31, 20X6, and the unaudited condensed consolidated statements of income, stockholders' equity, and cash flows for the three-month periods ended March 31, 20X6 and 20X5, included in the offering circular, or on the financial position, results of operations, or cash flows as of any date or for any period subsequent to December 31, 20X5.

1. At your request, we have read the 20X6 minutes of meetings of the stockholders, the board of directors, and [*include other appropriate committees, if any*] of the company as set forth in the minute books at June 25, 20X6, officials of the company having advised us that the minutes of all such meetings through that date were set forth therein and having discussed with us the unapproved minutes of meetings held on [*dates*]; we have carried out other procedures to June 25, 20X6, as follows (our work did not extend to the period from June 26, 20X6 to June 30, 20X6, inclusive):

   a. With respect to the three-month periods ended March 31, 20X6 and 20X5, we have—

(i) Read the unaudited condensed consolidated balance sheet as of March 31, 20X6, and the unaudited condensed consolidated statements of income, stockholders' equity, and cash flows of the company for the three-month periods ended March 31, 20X6 and 20X5, included in the offering circular, and agreed the amounts included therein with the company's accounting records as of March 31, 20X6 and 20X5, and for the three-month periods then ended.

(ii) Inquired of certain officials of the company who have responsibility for financial and accounting matters whether the unaudited condensed consolidated financial statements referred to in *a*(i) are in conformity with generally accepted accounting principles applied on a basis substantially consistent with that of the audited consolidated financial statements included in the offering circular. Those officials stated that the unaudited condensed consolidated financial statements are in conformity with generally accepted accounting principles applied on a basis substantially consistent with that of the audited consolidated financial statements.

b. With respect to the period from April 1, 20X6 to May 31, 20X6, we have—

(i) Read the unaudited condensed consolidated financial statements of the company for April and May of both 20X5 and 20X6, furnished us by the company, and agreed the amounts included therein with the company's accounting records. Officials of the company have advised us that no financial statements as of any date or for any period subsequent to May 31, 20X6 were available. [*if applicable:* The financial information for April and May of both 20X5 and 20X6 is incomplete in that it omits the statements of cash flows and other disclosures.]

(ii) Inquired of certain officials of the company who have responsibility for financial and accounting matters whether (1) the unaudited condensed consolidated financial statements referred to in *b*(i) are stated on a basis substantially consistent with that of the audited consolidated financial statements included in the offering circular, (2) at May 31, 20X6, there was any change in the capital stock, increase in long-term debt, or any decrease in consolidated net current assets or stockholders' equity of the consolidated companies as compared with amounts shown in the March 31, 20X6, unaudited condensed consolidated balance sheet included in the offering circular, and (3) for the period from April 1, 20X6 to May 31, 20X6, there were any decreases, as compared with the corresponding period in the preceding year, in consolidated net sales, or in income before extraordinary items or of net income.

Those officials stated that (1) the unaudited condensed consolidated financial statements referred to in *b*(ii) are stated on a basis substantially consistent with that of the audited consolidated financial statements included in the offering circular, (2) at May 31, 20X6, there was no change in the capital stock, no increase in long-term debt, and no decrease in consolidated net current assets or stockholders' equity of the consolidated companies as compared with amounts shown in the March 31, 20X6, unaudited condensed consolidated balance sheet included in the offering circular, and (3) there were no decreases for the period from April 1, 20X6 to May 31, 20X6, as compared with the corresponding period in the preceding year, in consolidated net sales, or in income before extraordinary items or of net income.

c. As mentioned in 1*b*, company officials have advised us that no financial statements as of any date or for any period subsequent to May 31, 20X6, are available; accordingly, the procedures carried out by us with respect to changes in financial statement items after May 31, 20X6, have, of necessity, been even more limited than those with respect to the periods referred to in 1*a* and 1*b*. We have inquired of certain officials of the company who have responsibility for financial and accounting matters whether (i) at June 25, 20X6, there was any change in the capital stock, increase in long-term debt, or any decreases in consolidated net current assets or stockholders' equity of the consolidated companies as compared with amounts shown on the March 31, 20X6, unaudited condensed consolidated balance sheet included in the offering circular or (ii) for the period from April 1, 20X6 to June 25, 20X6, there were any decreases, as compared with the corresponding period in the preceding year, in consolidated net sales or in income before extraordinary items or of net income.

Those officials referred to above stated that (i) at June 25, 20X6, there was no change in the capital stock, no increase in long-term debt, and no decreases in consolidated net current assets or stockholders' equity of the consolidated companies as compared with amounts shown on the March 31, 20X6, unaudited condensed consolidated balance sheet, and (ii) there were no decreases for the period from April 1, 20X6 to June 25, 20X6, as compared with the corresponding period in the preceding year, in consolidated net sales or in income before extraordinary items or of net income.

2. For purposes of this letter, we have also read the items identified by you on the attached copy of the offering circular and have performed the following procedures, which were applied as indicated with respect to the symbols explained below:

Compared the amount with the company's financial statements for the period indicated and found them to be in agreement.

Compared the amount with the company's financial statements for the period indicated included in the offering circular and found them to be in agreement.

Compared with a schedule or report prepared by the company and found them to be in agreement.

3. Our audit of the consolidated financial statements for the periods referred to in the introductory paragraph of this letter comprised audit tests and procedures deemed necessary for the purpose of expressing an opinion on such financial statements as a whole. For none of the periods referred to therein, nor for any other period, did we perform audit tests for the purpose of expressing an opinion on individual balances of accounts or summaries of selected transactions, such as those enumerated above, and, accordingly, we express no opinion thereon.
4. It should be understood that we have no responsibility for establishing (and did not establish) the scope and nature of the procedures enumerated in paragraphs 1–3 above; rather, the procedures enumerated therein are those the requesting party asked us to perform. Accordingly, we make no representations regarding questions of legal interpretation[4] or regarding the sufficiency for your purposes of the procedures enumerated in the preceding paragraphs; also, such procedures would not necessarily reveal any material misstatement of the amounts or percentages listed above as set forth in the offering circular. Further, we have addressed ourselves solely to the foregoing data and make no representations regarding the adequacy of disclosures or whether any material facts have been omitted. This letter relates only to the financial statement items specified above and does not extend to any financial statement of the company as a whole.
5. The foregoing procedures do not constitute an audit conducted in accordance with generally accepted auditing standards. Had we performed additional procedures or had we conducted an audit or a review of the company's March 31, April 30, or May 31, 20X6 and 20X5 condensed consolidated financial statements in accordance with generally accepted auditing standards, other matters might have come to our attention that would have been reported to you.
6. These procedures should not be taken to supplant any additional inquiries or procedures that you would undertake in your consideration of the proposed offering.

[4] Paragraph .A6 of this section.

7. This letter is solely for your information and to assist you in your inquiries in connection with the offering of the securities covered by the offering circular, and it is not to be used, circulated, quoted, or otherwise referred to for any other purpose, including but not limited to the registration, purchase, or sale of securities, nor is it to be filed with or referred to, in whole or in part, in the offering circular or any other document, except that reference may be made to it in any list of closing documents pertaining to the offering of the securities covered by the offering document.
8. We have no responsibility to update this letter for events and circumstances occurring after June 25, 20X6.

Example R—Alternate Wording When Reference to Examination of Annual Management's Discussion and Analysis and Review of Interim Management's Discussion and Analysis Is Made

.A93-20 This example is applicable when the auditor is making reference to an examination of annual MD&A and a review of interim MD&A. The same facts exist as in example A-1, except for the following:

- The auditor has examined the company's Management's Discussion and Analysis (MD&A) for the year ended December 31, 20X5, in accordance with AT section 701, *Management's Discussion and Analysis*.
- The auditor has also performed reviews of the company's unaudited condensed consolidated financial statements in accordance with generally accepted auditing standards applicable to reviews of interim financial information and the company's MD&A for the three-month period ended March 31, 20X6, in accordance with AT section 701.
- The accountant's reports on the examination and review of MD&A have been previously issued, but not distributed publicly; none of these reports is included in the securities offering. In this example, the auditor has elected to attach the previously issued reports to the comfort letter (see paragraph .A33).

Appropriate modifications would be made to the opening paragraph of the comfort letter if the auditor has performed a review of the company's annual MD&A.

The following would be substituted for the first paragraph of example A-1.

> We have audited the consolidated financial statements of The Nonissuer Company, Inc. (the company) and subsidiaries, which comprise the consolidated balance sheets as of December 31, 20X5 and 20X4, and the related consolidated statements of income, changes in stockholders' equity, and cash flows for each of the years in the three-year period ended December 31, 20X5, the related notes to the consolidated financial statements, and the related financial statement schedules, all included in The Issuer Company's (the registrant) registration statement (no. 33-00000) on Form S-1 filed by the registrant under the Securities Act of 1933 (the Act); our reports with respect thereto are also included in that registration statement. The registration statement, as amended on June 28, 20X6, is herein referred to as the registration statement. Also, we have examined the company's Management's Discussion and Analysis (MD&A) for the year ended December 31, 20X5, included in the registration statement, as indicated in our report dated March 28, 20X6; our report with respect thereto is attached. We

have also reviewed the unaudited condensed consolidated financial statements as of March 31, 20X6 and 20X5, and for the three-month periods then ended, included in the registration statement, as indicated in our report dated May 15, 20X6, and have also reviewed the company's MD&A for the three-month period ended March 31, 20X6, included in the registration statement, as indicated in our report dated May 15, 20X6; our reports with respect thereto are attached.

The following paragraph would be added after paragraph 3 of example A-1:

4. We have not examined any MD&A of the company as of or for any period subsequent to December 31, 20X5; although we have made an examination of the company's MD&A for the year ended December 31, 20X5, included in the registration statement, the purpose (and, therefore, the scope) of the examination was to enable us to express our opinion on such MD&A, but not on the MD&A for any interim period within that year. Therefore, we are unable to and do not express any opinion on the MD&A for the three-month period ended March 31, 20X6, included in the registration statement, or for any period subsequent to March 31, 20X6.

AU-C Section 925 *

Filings With the U.S. Securities and Exchange Commission Under the Securities Act of 1933

Source: SAS No. 122.

Effective for filings under the Securities Act of 1933 that include audited financial statements for periods ending on or after December 15, 2012.

Introduction

Scope of This Section (Ref: par. .A1)

.01 This section addresses the auditor's responsibilities in connection with financial statements of a nonissuer included or incorporated by reference in a registration statement filed with the U.S. Securities and Exchange Commission (SEC) under the Securities Act of 1933, as amended. Exhibit A, "Background," provides background information on certain liability provisions of Section 11 of the Securities Act of 1933, including Section 11(b)(3)(B).

Effective Date

.02 This section is effective for filings under the Securities Act of 1933 that include audited financial statements for periods ending on or after December 15, 2012.

Objective

.03 The objective of the auditor, in connection with audited financial statements of a nonissuer that are separately included or incorporated by reference in a registration statement filed under the Securities Act of 1933, is to perform specified procedures at or shortly before the effective date of the registration statement to sustain the burden of proof that the auditor has performed a reasonable investigation, as referred to in Section 11(b)(3)(B) of the Securities Act of 1933.

Definitions

.04 For purposes of this section, the following terms have the meanings attributed as follows:

Auditor's consent. A statement signed and dated by the auditor that indicates that the auditor consents to the use of the auditor's report, and other references to the auditor, in a registration statement filed under the Securities Act of 1933.

Awareness letter. A letter signed and dated by the auditor to acknowledge the auditor's awareness that the auditor's review

---

* This section has been codified using an "AU-C" identifier instead of an "AU" identifier. "AU-C" is a temporary identifier to avoid confusion with references to existing "AU" sections, which will remain in AICPA *Professional Standards* through 2013. The "AU-C" identifier will revert to "AU" in 2014, by which time substantially all engagements for which the "AU" sections were still effective are expected to be completed.

report on unaudited interim financial information is being used in a registration statement filed under the Securities Act of 1933. This letter is not considered to be part of the registration statement and is also commonly referred to as an *acknowledgment letter*.

Effective date of the registration statement. The date on which the registration statement filed under the Securities Act of 1933 becomes effective for purposes of evaluating the auditor's liability under Section 11 of the Securities Act of 1933. (Ref: par. .A2 and .A14)

.05 References to *included* or *the inclusion of* in a registration statement in this section means *included* or *incorporated by reference* in a registration statement filed under the Securities Act of 1933.

Requirements

Effective Date of the Registration Statement (Ref: par. .A3)

.06 Because the effective date of a registration statement filed under the Securities Act of 1933 may not necessarily coincide with the filing date, the auditor should request management to keep the auditor advised of the progress of the registration proceedings through the effective date of the registration statement.

The Prospectus and Other Information (Ref: par. .A4–.A8)

.07 When the auditor's report on audited financial statements is included in a registration statement filed under the Securities Act of 1933, the auditor should perform the procedures described in section 720, *Other Information in Documents Containing Audited Financial Statements*, on the prospectus and pertinent portions of the registration statement (including material that is incorporated by reference).

.08 In connection with the procedures required by paragraph .07, the auditor should determine that the auditor's name is not being used in a way that indicates that the auditor's responsibility is greater than the auditor intends.

Subsequent Events Procedures (Ref: par. .A9–.A11)

.09 When the most recent separate financial statements of the entity and related auditor's report are included in the registration statement, the auditor should perform the following procedures described in section 560, *Subsequent Events and Subsequently Discovered Facts*, at or shortly before the effective date of the registration statement:[1]

a. Audit procedures designed to identify events occurring between the date of the auditor's report and the effective date of the registration statement that require adjustment to, or disclosure in, the financial statements. Such procedures, which take into account the auditor's risk assessment in determining the nature and extent of such audit procedures, should include

   i. obtaining an understanding of any procedures that management has established to ensure that such events are identified.

---

[1] Paragraphs .09–.10 of section 560, *Subsequent Events and Subsequently Discovered Facts*.

ii. inquiring of management and, when appropriate, those charged with governance about whether any such events have occurred that might affect the financial statements.

iii. reading minutes, if any, of the meetings of the entity's owners, management, and those charged with governance that have been held after the date of the financial statements and inquiring about matters discussed at any such meetings for which minutes are not yet available.

iv. reading the entity's latest subsequent interim financial statements, if any.

b. Obtain updated written representations from management at or shortly before the effective date of the registration statement, about whether

i. any information has come to management's attention that would cause management to believe that any of the previous representations should be modified.

ii. any events have occurred subsequent to the date of the financial statements that would require adjustment to, or disclosure in, those financial statements.

.10 When the auditor has audited the most recent period for which separate audited financial statements of the entity are included in the registration statement and

a. the entity has been acquired by another entity,

b. the acquirer's audited financial statements included in the registration statement reflect a period that includes the date of acquisition, and

c. the auditor is a predecessor auditor because the auditor is not the continuing auditor of the entity,

the auditor may be unable to perform all of the procedures in paragraph .09. In such circumstances, the auditor should obtain written representations from management and the successor auditor as described in section 560 at or shortly before the effective date of the registration statement.[2]

.11 If a predecessor auditor audited the entity's separate financial statements for a prior period included in the registration statement but has not audited the entity's separate financial statements for the most recent audited period for which the entity's audited financial statements are included in the registration statement, then the predecessor auditor should perform the following procedures described in section 560 through a date at or shortly before the effective date of the registration statement:[3]

a. Read the financial statements of the subsequent period to be presented on a comparative basis

b. Compare the prior period financial statements that the predecessor auditor reported on with the financial statements of the subsequent period to be presented on a comparative basis

c. Obtain written representations from management at or shortly before the effective date

---

[2] Paragraph .19*c–d* of section 560.

[3] Paragraph .19 of section 560.

d. Obtain a representation letter from the successor auditor stating whether the successor auditor's audit revealed any matters that, in the successor auditor's opinion, might have a material effect on, or require disclosure in, the financial statements reported on by the predecessor auditor

.12 If the auditor becomes aware of subsequently discovered facts, the auditor should not provide the auditor's consent until the auditor's consideration of subsequently discovered facts, including the effect on the auditor's report on the financial statements, has been satisfactorily completed in accordance with section 560.[4] If management does not revise the audited financial statements in circumstances in which the auditor believes they need to be revised, then the auditor should determine whether to withhold the auditor's consent (and the awareness letter, if applicable). (Ref: par. .A11)

Unaudited Annual Financial Statements or Unaudited Interim Financial Information

.13 If the auditor concludes, based on known facts, that unaudited annual financial statements or unaudited interim financial information included in a registration statement filed under the Securities Act of 1933 is not in conformity with the requirements of the applicable financial reporting framework, then the auditor should request that management revise the unaudited annual financial statements or unaudited interim financial information appropriately.

.14 If management does not revise the unaudited annual financial statements or unaudited interim financial information appropriately and

a. the auditor has reported on a review of the unaudited annual financial statements or unaudited interim financial information,

b. the auditor's review report is included in the registration statement, and

c. the subsequently discovered facts are such that they would have affected the report had they been known to the auditor at the date of the report,

the auditor should perform the applicable procedures described in section 560.[5]

.15 If management does not revise the unaudited annual financial statements or unaudited interim financial information appropriately and

a. the auditor has not reported on a review of the unaudited annual financial statements or unaudited interim financial information or

b. the auditor's review report is not included in the registration statement,

the auditor should modify the report on the audited financial statements to describe the departure from the requirements of the applicable financial reporting framework contained in the unaudited annual financial statements or unaudited interim financial information, as described in section 930, *Interim Financial Information*.[6]

.16 Additionally, the auditor should determine whether to withhold the auditor's consent (and the awareness letter, if applicable). (Ref: par. .A11)

---

[4] Paragraphs .15–.18 of section 560.

[5] Paragraphs .14 and .17–.18 of section 560.

[6] Paragraph .35 of section 930, *Interim Financial Information*.

Application and Other Explanatory Material

Scope of This Section (Ref: par. .01)

.A1 This section is written from the perspective of a registration statement filed under the Securities Act of 1933. The liability provisions under the Securities Act of 1933 differ from those (Section 10[b] and Rule 10[b][5], in particular) under the Securities Exchange Act of 1934.

Definitions

Effective Date of the Registration Statement (Ref: par. .04)

.A2 Exhibit A describes the process commonly referred to as *shelf registration*. Exhibit A also provides additional guidance about the effective date of a registration statement, including situations in which a posteffective amendment is made or a prospectus supplement is filed.[7] Both of these situations may create a new effective date. Exhibit A also discusses the auditor's liability under Section 11 of the Securities Act of 1933 with regard to these situations.

Effective Date of the Registration Statement (Ref: par. .06)

.A3 Requesting management to keep the auditor advised of the progress of the registration proceedings through the effective date is important so that the auditor's consideration of events occurring after the date of the auditor's report up to the effective date, or as close thereto as reasonable and practicable, can be completed by the effective date of the registration statement. Generally, the filing date of a registration statement will precede the effective date. In addition to performing the procedures required by this section at or shortly before the effective date, the auditor may also perform some or all of the procedures in this section at or shortly before the filing date.

The Prospectus and Other Information (Ref: par. .07–.08)

.A4 The reading of the entire prospectus (including any supplemental prospectuses and documents incorporated by reference—such as forms 10-K, 10-Q, and 8-K) assists the auditor in fulfilling the auditor's statutory responsibilities to perform a reasonable investigation, as described in Section 11(c) of the Securities Act of 1933.

References to the Auditor as an Expert in Connection With a Securities Act of 1933 Registration Statement

.A5 The requirements in paragraphs .07–.08 assist the auditor in determining that the references to the auditor in the Securities Act of 1933 registration statement are appropriate. For example, management's disclosure in the "experts" section cannot imply that the financial statements have been prepared by the auditor or that the financial statements are not the direct representations of management.

.A6 The SEC does not require an entity to include an auditor's review report on unaudited interim financial information in the registration statement unless the registration statement states that the unaudited interim financial information has been reviewed by an independent auditor. If the registration

---

[7] Paragraphs 8–12 of exhibit A, "Background."

statement includes the auditor's review report on interim financial information, then the requirements in paragraphs .07–.08 assist the auditor in determining that the issuer discloses the fact that an interim review report is not a report on, or a part of, the registration statement prepared or certified by the auditor, within the meaning of Section 7 and Section 11 of the Securities Act of 1933, and that the auditor's liability under Section 11 does not extend to the auditor's review report.

.A7 The auditor is not considered an expert with respect to the auditor's review report on interim financial information and, therefore, it is important that this fact is clearly described. For example, the disclosures relating to the auditor's report on the audited financial statements may be included under a heading titled "Experts," and the disclosures in paragraph .A6 would then be included under a heading titled "Independent Auditors." Alternatively, the disclosures described in paragraph .A6 may be included under an "experts" section together with language stating the fact that an interim review report is not a report on, or a part of, the registration statement prepared or certified by the auditor, within the meaning of Section 7 and Section 11 of the Securities Act of 1933, and that the auditor's liability under Section 11 does not extend to the auditor's review report.

.A8 Exhibit A describes the disclosures relating to the auditor's report on the audited financial statements. Exhibit B, "Illustrative Disclosures and Reports," provides an illustration of this disclosure.

Subsequent Events Procedures (Ref: par. .09–.12)

.A9 An example of the conditions described in paragraphs .09–.11 would be a situation in which an issuer recently acquired a nonissuer that is considered significant to the issuer based on quantitative thresholds specified in the SEC's rules and regulations. In this case, the issuer's registration statement may need to include the separate audited financial statements of the acquired nonissuer for one or more periods.

.A10 In addition to the procedures required by paragraph .09, the auditor may consider it necessary and appropriate to inquire of, or extend previous oral or written inquiries to, the entity's legal counsel concerning litigation, claims, and assessments, as described in section 501, *Audit Evidence—Specific Considerations for Selected Items*.

.A11 In making the determination whether to withhold the auditor's consent, the auditor may consider it appropriate to obtain legal advice. (Ref: par. .12 and .16)

Exhibits

.A12 Exhibit A provides detailed background guidance on the following: (Ref: par. .04)

- The liability provisions of Section 11 of the Securities Act of 1933
- The auditor's consent and awareness letter
- The effective date of the registration statement
- References to the auditor as an expert in connection with a Securities Act of 1933 registration statement
- References to the auditor as an expert in a document other than a Securities Act of 1933 registration statement

- Letters similar to a consent prepared in connection with a document that is not a Securities Act of 1933 registration statement

.A13 Exhibit B provides illustrative disclosures and reports.

.A14

Exhibit A—Background

Exhibit A is intended to provide limited background information only.

Exhibit A is not intended to be, and does not constitute, a comprehensive or complete discussion of the liability provisions of the Securities Act of 1933, as amended. Exhibit A is not legal advice and reading it as such is inappropriate. Auditors are advised to consult with their legal counsel regarding the information provided in Exhibit A and the entire content of Section 11 of the Securities Act of 1933.

1. When an auditor's report is included in a registration statement filed under the Securities Act of 1933, the auditor's responsibility, generally, is in substance no different from that involved in other types of reporting. However, the nature and extent of this responsibility are specified in some detail in the applicable statutes and the related rules and regulations.

Liability Provisions of Section 11 of the Securities Act of 1933

2. Liability under the Securities Act of 1933 is defined in several sections of that act. One important section for auditors is Section 11.

3. Section 11(a) imposes civil liability on a number of parties that are involved in a registration statement filed under the Securities Act of 1933. One of the parties specifically mentioned in Section 11(a) is an auditor who has consented to the use of the auditor's report on audited financial statements in connection with a registration statement filed under the Securities Act of 1933 (Section 11[a][4]).

4. Section 11(b)(3)(B) of the Securities Act of 1933 provides that the auditor is not liable under Section 11(a) if the auditor

> sustain[s] the burden of proof . . . that . . . as regards any part of the registration statement purporting to be made upon his authority as an expert or purporting to be a copy of or extract from a report or valuation of himself as an expert, (i) he had, after reasonable investigation, reasonable ground to believe and did believe, at the time such part of the registration statement became effective, that the statements therein were true and that there was no omission to state a material fact required to be stated therein or necessary to make the statements therein not misleading, or (ii) such part of the registration statement did not fairly represent his statement as an expert or was not a fair copy of or extract from his report or valuation as an expert.

5. Section 11(c) of the Securities Act of 1933 indicates that for the purpose of determining what constitutes reasonable investigation and reasonable ground to believe, "the standard of reasonableness shall be that required of a prudent man in the management of his own property."

Auditor's Consent and Awareness Letter

6. Section 7 of the Securities Act of 1933 requires an issuer to provide the consent of any auditor whose report on audited financial statements is included in a Securities Act of 1933 registration statement. The issuer's responsibility to file the auditor's consent is further discussed in Rule 436 of the Securities Act of 1933.

7. Rule 436(c) of the Securities Act of 1933 indicates that an auditor's report based on a review of interim financial information is not a report within the meaning of Section 11. Thus, the auditor does not have a similar statutory responsibility for such reports as of the effective date of the registration statement. Accordingly, the auditor's consent would not refer to the auditor's report on interim financial statements. However, the issuer is required to file an awareness letter from an auditor if the auditor's review report on interim financial information is included in a registration statement filed under the Securities Act of 1933.

Effective Date of the Registration Statement

8. The information in a registration statement filed under the Securities Act of 1933 is evaluated as of its effective date. Accordingly, the auditor who has consented to the inclusion of the auditor's report on audited financial statements in such a registration statement has a statutory responsibility that is determined in light of the circumstances on that date. The effective date for purposes of evaluating liability under Section 11 may be different for different parties. For instance, the effective date for determining liability under Section 11 for the issuer or for an underwriter may be later than the effective date for determining Section 11 liability for the auditor.

9. Certain Securities Act of 1933 rules and forms (for example, Rule 415 and Form S-3) permit issuers to register offerings of securities to be offered and sold on a delayed or continuous basis. This process is commonly referred to as *shelf registration*.

10. The prospectus included in a shelf registration statement at the time it becomes effective is commonly referred to as a *base prospectus*. Many issuers follow a "bare bones" approach to preparing the base prospectus by relying entirely on the documents incorporated by reference (for example, forms 10-K, 10-Q, and 8-K) to provide most, if not all, of the issuer-related disclosures. The base prospectus also generally omits information relating to the specific amount of each security to be offered and pricing information. That information is typically provided through a prospectus supplement filed pursuant to Rule 424(b) of the Securities Act of 1933 at the time the securities are sold (commonly referred to as *taken off the shelf* or a *shelf takedown*).

11. At the time of filing a shelf registration statement, the issuer undertakes to update the prospectus for a number of items. The issuer's undertakings are set forth in Item 512 of Regulation S-K. Information omitted from the base prospectus, as well as the information that the issuer has undertaken to provide at a later date, may be conveyed to investors

- by a posteffective amendment to the registration statement,
- by a prospectus supplement filed pursuant to Rule 424(b) of the Securities Act of 1933, or
- through the incorporation by reference of the information from a report filed under the Securities Exchange Act of 1934 (for example, Form 10-K or Form 8-K).

12. As previously discussed, liability under Section 11 of the Securities Act of 1933 is assessed based on the information included in the registration statement as of its effective date. As also previously noted, the effective date for purposes of evaluating liability under Section 11 as it relates to the auditor may differ from the effective date as it relates to other parties (for example, the issuer or any underwriters). From the auditor's perspective, the effective date in connection with a Securities Act of 1933 registration statement is the latest of the following:

- The date the original registration statement (for example, on Form S-3) becomes effective
- The effective date of any posteffective amendment
- The filing date of a prospectus supplement if the filing of the prospectus supplement creates a new effective date for the auditor (for example, the prospectus supplement may contain new or revised audited financial statements or other information about which the auditor is an expert and for which a new consent is required, as described in Rule 430B[f][3] of the Securities Act of 1933)
- The filing date of any report (for example, under the Securities Exchange Act of 1934) that includes or amends audited financial statements and is incorporated by reference into the already effective registration statement

For example, assume an issuer with an already effective shelf registration statement on Form S-3 acquires a private company, and the issuer is required to file the acquired company's audited financial statements pursuant to the requirements of Form 8-K. In this case, the issuer will be required to file an auditor's consent from the acquired company's auditor as an exhibit to Form 8-K. The guidance in this section is applicable to the acquired company's auditor in connection with providing the auditor's consent to the issuer.

References to the Auditor as an Expert in Connection With a Securities Act of 1933 Registration Statement

13. Although not required, most Securities Act of 1933 registration statements relating to underwritten offerings contain a section titled "Experts." This section can be defined as management's disclosure in a Securities Act of 1933 registration statement that states that audited financial statements are included in the registration statement in reliance upon the auditor's report on the audited financial statements. The "experts" section also typically indicates that the auditor's report on the audited financial statements has been given on the auditor's authority as an expert in accounting and auditing.

14. Exhibit B, "Illustrative Disclosures and Reports," provides an example of a typical "experts" section.

15. As with all sections of the registration statement, the disclosures in the "experts" section are the issuer's responsibility. However, Rule 436(b) of the Securities Act of 1933 requires the issuer to file an auditor's consent to being named as an expert.

References to the Auditor as an Expert in a Document Other Than a Securities Act of 1933 Registration Statement

16. The term *expert* has a specific statutory meaning under the Securities Act of 1933. Outside the Securities Act of 1933 context, the term *expert* is typically undefined. Accordingly, except as described in paragraph 18 of this exhibit, when an issuer wishes to make reference to the auditor's role in an offering document in connection with a securities offering that is not registered under the Securities Act of 1933, the caption to that section of the document would generally be titled "Independent Auditors" (or something similar) rather than "Experts," with no reference to the auditor as an expert anywhere in the document.

17. Exhibit B provides an example of a typical description of the auditor's role when an issuer wishes to make reference to the auditor in an offering document in connection with a securities offering that is not registered under the Securities Act of 1933.

18. There may be situations in which the term *expert* is sufficiently defined such that the auditor may agree to be referred to as an expert outside the context of a registration statement filed under the Securities Act of 1933. For example, if the term *expert* is defined under applicable state law, the auditor may agree to be named as an expert in an offering document in an intrastate securities offering. The auditor may also agree to be named as an expert, as that term is used by the Office of Thrift Supervision (OTS), in securities offering documents that are subject to the jurisdiction of the OTS. An understanding of any auditor liability provisions that may be included in the applicable federal or state statutes is an important consideration.

Letters Similar to Consents Prepared in Connection With a Document That Is Not a Securities Act of 1933 Registration Statement

19. When an auditor's report is used in connection with an offering transaction that is not registered under the Securities Act of 1933, it is not usually necessary for the auditor to provide any type of written consent. If the auditor is asked to provide a written consent for use in connection with a document other than a Securities Act of 1933 registration statement, then the auditor may provide a letter indicating that the auditor agrees to the inclusion of the auditor's report on the audited financial statements in the offering materials. This letter would typically not be included in the offering materials.

20. Exhibit B provides an example of language the auditor might use to indicate that the auditor agrees to the inclusion of the auditor's report on the audited financial statements in the offering materials when the auditor's report is used in connection with an offering transaction that is not registered under the Securities Act of 1933.

.A15

Exhibit B—Illustrative Disclosures and Reports

The following is an example of a typical "experts" section in a registration statement filed under the Securities Act of 1933:

Experts

The consolidated balance sheets of Company X as of December 31, 20X2 and 20X1, and the related consolidated statements of income and comprehensive income, changes in stockholders' equity, and cash flows for each of the three years in the period ended December 31, 20X2, included in this prospectus, have been so included in reliance on the report of ABC & Co, independent auditors, given on the authority of that firm as experts in auditing and accounting.

The following is an example of a disclosure for a registration statement filed under the Securities Act of 1933 that includes the auditor's review report on unaudited interim financial information when such disclosure is included in a separate section. This disclosure may also be included under a section titled "Experts":

Independent Auditors

With respect to the unaudited interim financial information of Company X for the three-month periods ended March 31, 20X3 and 20X2, included in this prospectus, ABC & Co. has reported that they have applied limited procedures in accordance with professional standards for a review of such information. However, their separate report dated May XX, 20X3, included herein, states that they did not audit and they do not express an opinion on that interim financial information. Accordingly, the degree of reliance on their report on such information should be restricted in light of the limited nature of the review procedures applied. ABC & Co. is not subject to the liability provisions of section 11 of the Securities Act of 1933 for their report on the unaudited interim financial information because that report is not a "report" or a "part" of the registration statement prepared or certified by the accountants within the meaning of Sections 7 and 11 of the Act.

The following is an example of a typical description of the auditor's role when an issuer wishes to make reference to the auditor in an offering document prepared in connection with a securities offering that is not registered under the Securities Act of 1933:

Independent Auditors

The financial statements of Company X as of December 31, 20X2 and for the year then ended, included in this offering circular, have been audited by ABC & Co., independent auditors, as stated in their report appearing herein.

Although generally not necessary, the following is an example of language the auditor might use indicating that the auditor agrees to the inclusion of the auditor's report on the audited financial statements in offering materials prepared in connection with a securities offering that is not registered under the Securities Act of 1933:

We agree to the inclusion in the offering circular of our report, dated February 5, 20X3, on our audit of the financial statements of Company X.

AU-C Section 930 *

Interim Financial Information

Source: SAS No. 122.

Effective for reviews of interim financial information for interim periods of fiscal years beginning on or after December 15, 2012.

Introduction

Scope of This Section

.01 This section addresses the auditor's responsibilities when engaged to review interim financial information under the conditions specified in this section. The term *auditor* is used throughout this section, not because the auditor is performing an audit but because the scope of this section is limited to a review of interim financial information performed by an auditor of the financial statements of the entity.

.02 This section applies to a review of interim financial information when

a. the entity's latest annual financial statements have been audited by the auditor or a predecessor auditor;

b. the auditor either

  i. has been engaged to audit the entity's current year financial statements or

  ii. audited the entity's latest annual financial statements, and in situations in which it is expected that the current year financial statements will be audited, the engagement of another auditor to audit the current year financial statements is not effective prior to the beginning of the period covered by the review; (Ref: par. .A1)

c. the entity prepares its interim financial information in accordance with the same financial reporting framework as that used to prepare the annual financial statements; and

d. all of the following conditions are met if the interim financial information is condensed:

  i. The condensed interim financial information purports to be prepared in accordance with an appropriate financial reporting framework, which includes appropriate form and content of interim financial information. (Ref: par. .A2)

  ii. The condensed interim financial information includes a note that the financial information does not represent complete financial statements and is to be read in conjunction with the entity's latest audited annual financial statements.

---

* This section has been codified using an "AU-C" identifier instead of an "AU" identifier. "AU-C" is a temporary identifier to avoid confusion with references to existing "AU" sections, which will remain in AICPA *Professional Standards* through 2013. The "AU-C" identifier will revert to "AU" in 2014, by which time substantially all engagements for which the "AU" sections were still effective are expected to be completed.

iii. The condensed interim financial information accompanies the entity's latest audited annual financial statements, or such audited annual financial statements are made readily available by the entity. (Ref: par. .A3)

Statements on Standards for Accounting and Review Services provide guidance for review engagements for which this section is not applicable.

.03 An auditor may find this section, adapted as necessary in the circumstances, useful when that auditor has not been engaged to perform a review of interim financial information but has nonetheless decided to perform review procedures on such financial information (for example, in connection with the inclusion of the auditor's report on the annual financial statements in an unregistered securities offering document).

Effective Date

.04 This section is effective for reviews of interim financial information for interim periods of fiscal years beginning on or after December 15, 2012.

Objective

.05 The objective of the auditor when performing an engagement to review interim financial information is to obtain a basis for reporting whether the auditor is aware of any material modifications that should be made to the interim financial information for it to be in accordance with the applicable financial reporting framework through performing limited procedures. (Ref: par. .A4–.A5)

Definition

.06 For purposes of this section, the following term has the meaning attributed as follows:

Interim financial information. Financial information prepared and presented in accordance with an applicable financial reporting framework that comprises either a complete or condensed set of financial statements covering a period or periods less than one full year or covering a 12-month period ending on a date other than the entity's fiscal year end.

Requirements

Acceptance

.07 Before accepting an engagement to review an entity's interim financial information for a new client, the auditor should follow the procedures for initial engagements required by section 210, *Terms of Engagement*.[1]

.08 Before accepting an engagement to perform a review of interim financial information, the auditor should

a. determine whether the financial reporting framework to be applied in the preparation of the interim financial information is acceptable and

[1] Paragraphs .11–.12 of section 210, *Terms of Engagement*.

b. obtain the agreement of management that it acknowledges and understands its responsibility

i. for the preparation and fair presentation of the interim financial information in accordance with the applicable financial reporting framework;

ii. for the design, implementation, and maintenance of internal control sufficient to provide a reasonable basis for the preparation and fair presentation of interim financial information in accordance with the applicable financial reporting framework;

iii. to provide the auditor with

(1) access to all information of which management is aware that is relevant to the preparation and fair presentation of the interim financial information, such as records, documentation, and other matters;

(2) additional information that the auditor may request from management for the purpose of the review; and

(3) unrestricted access to persons within the entity of whom the auditor determines it necessary to make inquiries;[2] and

iv. to include the auditor's review report in any document containing interim financial information that indicates that such information has been reviewed by the entity's auditor.

.09 The auditor should not accept an engagement to review interim financial information if

a. the auditor has determined that the financial reporting framework to be applied in the preparation of the interim financial information is unacceptable.

b. the agreement referred to in paragraph .08*b* has not been obtained.

Agreement on Engagement Terms

.10 The auditor should agree upon the terms of the engagement with management or those charged with governance, as appropriate. The agreed-upon terms of the engagement should be recorded in an engagement letter or other suitable form of written agreement and should include the following: (Ref: par. .A6)

a. The objectives and scope of the engagement

b. The responsibilities of management set forth in paragraph .08*b*

c. The responsibilities of the auditor

d. The limitations of a review engagement

e. Identification of the applicable financial reporting framework for the preparation of the interim financial information

---

[2] Paragraph .06 of section 210.

Procedures for a Review of Interim Financial Information

Understanding the Entity and Its Environment, Including Its Internal Control

.11 To plan and conduct the engagement, the auditor should have an understanding of the entity and its environment, including its internal control as it relates to the preparation and fair presentation of both annual and interim financial information, sufficient to be able to

a. identify the types of potential material misstatements in the interim financial information and consider the likelihood of their occurrence.

b. select the inquiries and analytical procedures that will provide the auditor with a basis for reporting whether the auditor is aware of any material modifications that should be made to the interim financial information for it to be in accordance with the applicable financial reporting framework.

.12 To update or, in the case of an auditor who has not yet performed an audit of the entity's annual financial statements, obtain the understanding required by paragraph .11, the auditor should perform the following procedures: (Ref: par. .A7–.A8)

a. Read available documentation of the preceding year's audit and of reviews of the prior interim period(s) of the current year and the corresponding interim period(s) of the prior year to the extent necessary, based on the auditor's judgment, to enable the auditor to identify matters that may affect the current period interim financial information. (Ref: par. .A9–.A10) In reading such documents, the auditor should specifically consider the nature of any

i. corrected material misstatements;

ii. matters identified in any summary of uncorrected misstatements;

iii. identified risks of material misstatement due to fraud, including the risk of management override of controls; and

iv. significant financial accounting and reporting matters that may be of continuing significance, such as significant deficiencies and material weaknesses.

b. Read the most recent annual and comparable prior interim period financial information.

c. Consider the results of any audit procedures performed with respect to the current year's financial statements.

d. Inquire of management about changes in the entity's business activities.

e. Inquire of management about the identity of, and nature of transactions with, related parties.

f. Inquire of management about whether significant changes in internal control, as it relates to the preparation and fair presentation of interim financial information, have occurred subsequent to the preceding annual audit or prior review of interim financial information, including changes in the entity's policies, procedures, and personnel, as well as the nature and extent of such changes.

Analytical Procedures, Inquiries, and Other Review Procedures

Analytical Procedures

.13 The auditor should apply analytical procedures to the interim financial information to identify and provide a basis for inquiry about the relationships and individual items that appear to be unusual and that may indicate a material misstatement. Such analytical procedures should include the following: (Ref: par. .A11–.A13)

a. Comparing the interim financial information with comparable information for the immediately preceding interim period, if applicable, and with the corresponding period(s) in the previous year, giving consideration to knowledge about changes in the entity's business and specific transactions

b. Considering plausible relationships among both financial and, when relevant, nonfinancial information (Ref: par. .A14)

c. Comparing recorded amounts or ratios developed from recorded amounts to expectations developed by the auditor through identifying and using relationships that are reasonably expected to exist, based on the auditor's understanding of the entity and the industry in which the entity operates

d. Comparing disaggregated revenue data (Ref: par. .A15)

Inquiries and Other Review Procedures

.14 The auditor should make the following inquiries and perform the following other review procedures when conducting a review of interim financial information:

a. Read the available minutes of meetings of stockholders, directors, and appropriate committees and inquire about matters dealt with at meetings for which minutes are not available to identify matters that may affect the interim financial information. (Ref: par. .A16)

b. Obtain reports from component auditors, if any, related to reviews performed of the interim financial information of significant components of the reporting entity, including its investees, or inquire of those auditors if reports have not been issued. (Ref: par. .A17)

c. Inquire of management about

i. whether the interim financial information has been prepared and fairly presented in accordance with the applicable financial reporting framework consistently applied.

ii. unusual or complex situations that may have an effect on the interim financial information. (Ref: par. .A18)

iii. significant transactions occurring or recognized in the interim period, particularly those in the last several days of the interim period.

iv. the status of uncorrected misstatements identified during the previous audit and interim review (that is, whether adjustments had been recorded subsequent to the periods covered by the prior audit or interim review and, if so, the amounts recorded and period in which such adjustments were recorded).

v. matters about which questions have arisen in the course of applying the review procedures.

vi. events subsequent to the date of the interim financial information that could have a material effect on the fair presentation of such information.

vii. its knowledge of any fraud or suspected fraud affecting the entity involving (1) management, (2) employees who have significant roles in internal control, or (3) others when the fraud could have a material effect on the financial information.

viii. whether management is aware of allegations of fraud or suspected fraud affecting the entity communicated by employees, former employees, regulators, or others.

ix. significant journal entries and other adjustments.

x. communications from regulatory agencies.

xi. significant deficiencies and material weaknesses in the design or operation of internal control as it relates to the preparation and fair presentation of both annual and interim financial information.

xii. changes in related parties or significant new related party transactions.

d. Obtain evidence that the interim financial information agrees or reconciles with the accounting records. In addition, the auditor should inquire of management about the reliability of the records to which the interim financial information was compared or reconciled. (Ref: par. .A19)

e. Read the interim financial information to consider whether, based on the results of the review procedures performed and other information that has come to the auditor's attention, the information to be reported is in accordance with the applicable financial reporting framework.

f. Read other information in documents containing the interim financial information to consider whether such information or the manner of its presentation is materially inconsistent with the interim financial information. If the auditor concludes that a material inconsistency exists or becomes aware of information that the auditor believes is a material misstatement of fact, the auditor should take action based on the auditor's professional judgment. (Ref: par. .A20–.A21)

Inquiry Concerning Litigation, Claims, and Assessments

.15 If information comes to the auditor's attention regarding litigation, claims, or assessments that leads the auditor to question whether the interim financial information has been prepared, in all material respects, in accordance with the applicable financial reporting framework, and the auditor believes that the entity's internal or external legal counsel may have relevant information, the auditor should inquire of such legal counsel concerning litigation, claims, and assessments. (Ref: par. .A22)

Inquiry Concerning an Entity's Ability to Continue as a Going Concern

.16 If (*a*) conditions or events that may indicate substantial doubt about an entity's ability to continue as a going concern existed at the date of prior period financial statements, regardless of whether the substantial doubt was alleviated by the auditor's consideration of management's plans, or (*b*) in the course of performing review procedures on the current period interim financial information, the auditor becomes aware of conditions or events that might be indicative of the entity's possible inability to continue as a going concern, the auditor should

a. inquire of management about its plans for dealing with the adverse effects of the conditions and events, and (Ref: par. .A23)

b. consider the adequacy of the disclosure about such matters in the interim financial information. (Ref: par. .A24)

Consideration of Management's Responses and Extension of Interim Review Procedures

.17 The auditor should consider the reasonableness and consistency of management's responses in light of the results of other review procedures and the auditor's knowledge of the entity's business and its internal control. However, the auditor is not required to corroborate management's responses with other evidence.

.18 When a matter comes to the auditor's attention that leads the auditor to question whether the interim financial information has been prepared in accordance with the applicable financial reporting framework in all material respects, the auditor should make additional inquiries of management or others or perform other procedures to provide a basis for reporting whether the auditor is aware of any material modifications that should be made to the interim financial information. (Ref: par. .A25)

Evaluating the Results of Interim Review Procedures

.19 The auditor should accumulate misstatements, including inadequate disclosure, identified by the auditor in performing the review procedures or brought to the auditor's attention during the performance of the review. (Ref: par. .A26)

.20 The auditor should evaluate, individually and in the aggregate, misstatements, including inadequate disclosure, accumulated in accordance with paragraph .19 to determine whether material modification should be made to the interim financial information for it to be in accordance with the applicable financial reporting framework. (Ref: par. .A27–.A28)

Written Representations From Management

.21 For all interim financial information presented and for all periods covered by the review, the auditor should request management to provide written representations, as of the date of the auditor's review report (Ref: par. .A29–.A30)

a. that management has fulfilled its responsibility for the preparation and fair presentation of the interim financial information, in accordance with the applicable financial reporting framework, as set out in the terms of the engagement.

b. that management acknowledges its responsibility for designing, implementing, and maintaining internal control relevant to the preparation and fair presentation of interim financial statements, including its responsibility to prevent and detect fraud.

c. that management has disclosed to the auditor all significant deficiencies and material weaknesses in the design or operation of internal control of which management is aware as it relates to the preparation and fair presentation of both annual and interim financial information.

d. that management has provided the auditor with all relevant information and access, as agreed upon in the terms of the engagement.

e. that all transactions have been recorded and are reflected in the interim financial information.

f. that management has disclosed to the auditor the results of its assessment of the risk that the interim financial information may be materially misstated as a result of fraud.

g. that management has disclosed to the auditor its knowledge of fraud or suspected fraud affecting the entity involving

  i. management,

  ii. employees who have significant roles in internal control, or

  iii. others when the fraud could have a material effect on the interim financial information.

h. that management has disclosed to the auditor its knowledge of any allegations of fraud or suspected fraud affecting the entity's interim financial information communicated by employees, former employees, regulators, or others.

i. that management has disclosed to the auditor all known instances of noncompliance or suspected noncompliance with laws and regulations whose effects should be considered when preparing interim financial information.

j. about whether management believes that the effects of uncorrected misstatements are immaterial, individually and in the aggregate, to the interim financial information as a whole. A summary of such items should be included in, or attached to, the written representation. (Ref: par. .A31)

k. that management has disclosed to the auditor all known actual or possible litigation and claims whose effects should be considered when preparing the interim financial information, and it has appropriately accounted for and disclosed such litigation and claims in accordance with the applicable financial reporting framework.

l. about whether management believes that significant assumptions used by it in making accounting estimates are reasonable.

m. that management has disclosed to the auditor the identity of the entity's related parties and all the related party relationships and transactions of which it is aware, and it has appropriately accounted for and disclosed such relationships and transactions.

n. that all events occurring subsequent to the date of the interim financial information and for which the applicable financial reporting framework requires adjustment or disclosure have been adjusted or disclosed.

.22 If the auditor has concerns about the reliability of the representations or if management does not provide the requested written representations, the auditor should take appropriate action. When management does not provide the written representations described in paragraph .21*a*–*e*, the auditor should withdraw from the engagement to review the interim financial information. (Ref: par. .A32)

Communications With Management and Those Charged With Governance

Matters Affecting the Completion of the Review

.23 If the auditor cannot complete the review, the auditor should communicate to the appropriate level of management and those charged with governance

a. the reason why the review cannot be completed;

b. that an incomplete review does not provide a basis for reporting and, accordingly, that the auditor is precluded from issuing a review report; and

c. any material modifications of which the auditor has become aware that should be made to the interim financial information for it to be in accordance with the applicable financial reporting framework, in accordance with paragraphs .24–.26. (Ref: par. .A33)

.24 The auditor should communicate to the appropriate level of management, as soon as practicable, matters that come to the auditor's attention during the conduct of the review that cause the auditor to believe that

a. material modification should be made to the interim financial information for it to be in accordance with the applicable financial reporting framework, or

b. the entity issued the interim financial information before the completion of the review.

.25 If, in the auditor's judgment, management does not respond appropriately to the auditor's communication within a reasonable period of time, the auditor should inform those charged with governance of the matters as soon as practicable.

.26 If, in the auditor's judgment, those charged with governance do not respond appropriately to the auditor's communication within a reasonable period of time, the auditor should consider whether to withdraw (*a*) from the engagement to review the interim financial information and (*b*) if applicable, from serving as the entity's auditor. (Ref: par. .A34)

Other Matters

.27 If the auditor becomes aware that fraud may have occurred, the auditor should communicate the matter as soon as practicable to the appropriate level of management. If the fraud involves senior management or results in a material misstatement of the interim financial information, the auditor should communicate the matter directly to those charged with governance. If the auditor becomes aware of matters involving identified or suspected noncompliance with laws and regulations whose effects should be considered when preparing interim financial information, the auditor should communicate the matters to those charged with governance, other than when the matters are clearly inconsequential.

.28 The auditor should communicate relevant matters of governance interest arising from the review of interim financial information to those charged with governance, including the following:

a. Significant deficiencies or material weaknesses in internal control as it relates to the preparation and fair presentation of annual and interim financial information (Ref: par. .A35)

b. Any of the matters described in section 260, *The Auditor's Communication With Those Charged With Governance*, that have been identified, as they relate to the interim financial information (Ref: par. .A36–.A38)

The Auditor's Report on a Review of Interim Financial Information

Form of the Auditor's Review Report

.29 The auditor's review report should be in writing. (Ref: par. .A39)

.30 The written review report should include the following: (Ref: par. .A40–.A41)

a. A title that includes the word *independent* to clearly indicate that it is the report of an independent auditor.

b. An addressee as appropriate for the circumstances of the engagement.

c. An introductory paragraph that

  i. identifies the entity whose interim financial information has been reviewed,

  ii. states that the interim financial information identified in the report was reviewed,

  iii. identifies the interim financial information, and

  iv. specifies the date or period covered by each financial statement comprising the interim financial information.

d. A section with the heading "Management's Responsibility for the Financial Statements" that includes an explanation that management is responsible for the preparation and fair presentation of the interim financial information in accordance with the applicable financial reporting framework; this responsibility includes the design, implementation, and maintenance of internal control sufficient to provide a reasonable basis for the preparation and fair presentation of interim financial information in accordance with the applicable financial reporting framework.

e. A section with the heading "Auditor's Responsibility" that includes the following statements:

  i. The auditor's responsibility is to conduct the review of interim financial information in accordance with auditing standards generally accepted in the United States of America applicable to reviews of interim financial information.

  ii. A review of interim financial information consists principally of applying analytical procedures and making inquiries of persons responsible for financial and accounting matters.

  iii. A review of interim financial information is substantially less in scope than an audit conducted in accordance with auditing standards generally accepted in the United States of America, the objective of which is an expression of an opinion regarding the financial information as a whole, and accordingly, no such opinion is expressed.

f. A concluding section with an appropriate heading that includes a statement about whether the auditor is aware of any material modifications that should be made to the accompanying interim financial information for it to be in accordance with the applicable financial reporting framework and that identifies the country of origin of those accounting principles, if applicable.

g. The manual or printed signature of the auditor's firm.

h. The city and state where the auditor practices.

i. The date of the review report, which should be dated as of the date of completion of the review procedures.

.31 The auditor should determine that management has clearly marked as unaudited each page of the interim financial information accompanying the review report.

Comparative Interim Financial Information That Has Not Been Reviewed Presented With Reviewed Interim Financial Information

.32 If an auditor is engaged to perform a review of the most recent interim period in accordance with this section, and such financial information will be presented in comparative form with interim financial information of a prior period that has not been reviewed, such interim financial information should be accompanied by an indication in the auditor's review report that the auditor has not reviewed the prior period interim financial information and that the auditor assumes no responsibility for it. (Ref: par. .A42)

Interim Financial Information Presented With Condensed Balance Sheet Information for the Most Recent Year End

.33 When a condensed balance sheet derived from audited financial statements is presented on a comparative basis with the interim financial information, the auditor should report on the condensed balance sheet only when the auditor audited the financial statements from which the condensed balance sheet was derived. The auditor should compare the condensed balance sheet with the related information in the audited financial statements to determine whether the condensed balance sheet agrees with, or can be recalculated from, the related information in the audited financial statements. The auditor's report on the interim financial information should include a paragraph addressing the condensed balance sheet that

a. identifies the condensed balance sheet on which the auditor is reporting.

b. identifies the audited financial statements from which the condensed balance sheet was derived and indicates that such financial statements are not separately presented.

c. refers to the auditor's report on the audited financial statements, the date of that report, and the type of opinion expressed and, if the opinion is modified, the basis for the modification.

d. describes the nature of any emphasis-of-matter paragraph or other-matter paragraph included in the auditor's report.

e. includes an opinion about whether the condensed balance sheet is consistent, in all material respects, in relation to the audited financial statements from which it has been derived. (Ref: par. .A43)

Modification of the Auditor's Review Report

.34 When the interim financial information has not been prepared in accordance with the applicable financial reporting framework in all material respects, the auditor should consider whether modification of the auditor's review report on the interim financial information is sufficient to address the departure from the applicable financial reporting framework. (Ref: par. .A44–.A47)

.35 If the auditor concludes that modification of the standard review report is sufficient to address the departure, the auditor should modify the review report. The modification should describe the nature of the departure and, if practicable, should state the effects on the interim financial information. If the departure is due to inadequate disclosure, the auditor should, if practicable, include the information in the report that the auditor believes is necessary for adequate disclosure in accordance with the applicable financial reporting framework. (Ref: par. .A48)

.36 If the auditor believes that modification of the review report is not sufficient to address the deficiencies in the interim financial information, the auditor should withdraw from the review engagement and provide no further services with respect to such interim financial information.

Subsequent Discovery of Facts Existing at the Date of the Auditor's Review Report

.37 If, subsequent to the date of the auditor's review report, the auditor becomes aware that facts existed at the date of the review report that might have affected the auditor's review report had the auditor then been aware of those matters, the auditor should apply the requirements and guidance, adapted as necessary, in section 560, *Subsequent Events and Subsequently Discovered Facts*.

Other Considerations

.38 If management does not include the auditor's review report in a report, document, or written communication containing the reviewed interim financial information that indicates that such information has been reviewed by the entity's auditor, despite having agreed in the terms of the engagement to do so, the auditor should perform the following procedures:

- Request that management amend the report, document, or written communication to include the auditor's review report and reissue the report, document, or written communication
- If management does not comply with the request to amend and reissue the report, document, or written communication, request that the auditor's name not be associated with the interim financial information or referred to in the report, document, or written communication because the auditor will not permit either the use of the auditor's name or reference to the auditor unless the auditor's review report is included with the reviewed interim financial information in these circumstances
- Communicate management's noncompliance with the requests to those charged with governance
- When appropriate, recommend that the entity consult with its legal counsel about the application of relevant laws and regulations to the circumstances
- Consider what other actions might be appropriate (Ref: par. .A49)

.39 If the auditor has issued a modified review report due to a departure from the applicable financial reporting framework, and management issues the interim financial information without including the review report in the document containing the interim financial information, the auditor should determine the appropriate course of action in the circumstances, including whether to withdraw from the engagement to audit the annual financial statements.

Interim Financial Information Accompanying Audited Financial Statements

.40 The auditor should include an other-matter paragraph in the auditor's report on the audited financial statements when all the following conditions exist:

a. The interim financial information that has been reviewed in accordance with this section is included in a document containing audited financial statements.

b. The interim financial information accompanying audited financial statements does not appear to be presented in accordance with the applicable financial reporting framework.

c. The auditor's separate review report, which refers to the departure from the applicable financial reporting framework, is not presented with the interim financial information.

.41 The auditor is required by section 700, *Forming an Opinion and Reporting on Financial Statements*, to address in the auditor's report on the audited financial statements information that is not required by the applicable financial reporting framework but is nevertheless presented as part of the basic financial statements if it cannot be clearly differentiated.[3] When the interim financial information included in a note to the financial statements, including information that has been reviewed in accordance with this section, is not appropriately marked as unaudited, the auditor should, in the auditor's report on the audited financial statements, disclaim an opinion on the interim financial information. (Ref: par. .A50–.A51)

Documentation

.42 The auditor should prepare documentation in connection with a review of interim financial information that will enable an experienced auditor, having no previous connection to the review, to understand

a. the nature, timing, and extent of the review procedures performed;

b. the results of the review procedures performed and the evidence obtained; and

c. significant findings or issues arising during the review, the conclusions reached thereon, and significant professional judgments made in reaching those conclusions.

.43 The documentation should include the communications required by this section, whether written or oral. (Ref: par. .A52–.A53)

---

[3] Paragraph .58 of section 700, *Forming an Opinion and Reporting on Financial Statements.*

Application and Other Explanatory Material

Scope of This Section (Ref: par. .02)

.A1 The ability to apply this section even when the auditor does not expect to be engaged to audit the current year financial statements provides for appropriate transitions between the predecessor auditor and the auditor of the current year financial statements.

.A2 Appropriate financial reporting frameworks for condensed interim financial information may include, for example, Financial Accounting Standards Board (FASB) *Accounting Standards Codification* (ASC) 270, *Interim Reporting*, and Article 10 of Securities and Exchange Commission (SEC) Regulation S-X, with respect to accounting principles generally accepted in the United States of America, or International Accounting Standard 34, *Interim Financial Reporting*, with respect to International Financial Reporting Standards issued by the International Accounting Standards Board. FASB ASC 270 outlines the application of U.S. generally accepted accounting principles (GAAP) to the determination of income when interim financial information is presented, provides for the use of estimated effective income tax rates, and specifies certain disclosure requirements for condensed interim financial information issued by public companies and may be adapted by nonissuers as a fair presentation framework for condensed interim financial information. In addition to FASB ASC 270, other FASB ASC topics also include disclosure requirements for interim financial information.

The Meaning of Readily Available (Ref: par. .02d(iii))

.A3 Audited financial statements are deemed to be readily available if a third-party user can obtain the financial statements without any further action by the entity (for example, financial statements on an entity's website may be considered readily available, but being available upon request is not considered readily available).

Objective (Ref: par. .05)

.A4 The objective of a review of interim financial information differs significantly from that of an audit conducted in accordance with auditing standards generally accepted in the United States of America. A review of interim financial information does not provide a basis for expressing an opinion about whether the interim financial information is presented fairly, in all material respects, in accordance with the applicable financial reporting framework.

.A5 A review, in contrast to an audit, is not designed to provide the auditor with a basis for obtaining reasonable assurance that the interim financial information is free from material misstatement. A review consists principally of performing analytical procedures and making inquiries of persons responsible for financial and accounting matters and does not contemplate (*a*) tests of accounting records through inspection, observation, or confirmation; (*b*) tests of controls to evaluate their effectiveness; (*c*) the obtainment of corroborating evidence in response to inquiries; or (*d*) the performance of certain other procedures ordinarily performed in an audit. A review may bring to the auditor's attention significant findings or issues affecting the interim financial information, but it does not provide assurance that the auditor will become aware of all significant findings or issues that would be identified in an audit.

Acceptance

Agreement on Engagement Terms (Ref: par. .10)

.A6 The engagement letter or other suitable form of written agreement documenting the agreed-upon terms of the engagement with the entity regarding a review of interim financial information may use the following wording to include the information necessary to meet the requirements of paragraph .10:

Objectives and scope of the engagement

- The objective of a review of interim financial information is to provide the auditor with a basis for reporting whether the auditor is aware of any material modifications that should be made to the interim financial information for it to be in accordance with the applicable financial reporting framework.
- A review includes obtaining sufficient knowledge of the entity's business and internal control, as it relates to the preparation and fair presentation of both annual and interim financial information, to enable the auditor to
  - — identify the types of potential material misstatements in the interim financial information and consider the likelihood of their occurrence.
  - — select the inquiries and analytical procedures that will provide the auditor with a basis for reporting whether the auditor is aware of any material modifications that should be made to the interim financial information for it to conform with the applicable financial reporting framework.

Management's responsibilities

- Management is responsible for the following:
  - — Preparing and presenting the interim financial information in accordance with the applicable financial reporting framework.
  - — Designing, implementing, and maintaining internal control sufficient to provide a reasonable basis for the preparation and fair presentation of interim financial information in accordance with the applicable financial reporting framework.
  - — Providing the auditor with (*a*) access to all information of which management is aware that is relevant to the preparation and fair presentation of the interim financial information, such as records, documentation, and other matters; (*b*) additional information that the auditor may request from management for the purpose of the review; and (*c*) unrestricted access to persons within the entity of whom the auditor determines it necessary to make inquiries.
  - — Including the auditor's review report in any document containing interim financial information that indicates that such information has been reviewed by the entity's auditor.
  - — Identifying and ensuring that the entity complies with the laws and regulations applicable to its activities.

— Providing the auditor, at the conclusion of the engagement, with a letter confirming certain representations made during the review.

— Adjusting the interim financial information to correct material misstatements. Although a review of interim financial information is not designed to provide the auditor with reasonable assurance that the interim financial information is free from material misstatement, management nonetheless is responsible for affirming in its representation letter to the auditor that the effects of any uncorrected misstatements aggregated by the auditor during the current engagement and pertaining to the current year period(s) under review are immaterial, both individually and in the aggregate, to the interim financial information as a whole.

The auditor's responsibilities

- The auditor is responsible for conducting the review in accordance with auditing standards generally accepted in the United States of America applicable to reviews of interim financial information. A review of interim financial information consists principally of performing analytical procedures and making inquiries of persons responsible for financial and accounting matters. It is substantially less in scope than an audit conducted in accordance with auditing standards generally accepted in the United States of America, the objective of which is the expression of an opinion regarding the financial information as a whole. Accordingly, the auditor will not express an opinion on the interim financial information.

Limitations of the engagement

- A review does not provide a basis for expressing an opinion about whether the interim financial information is presented fairly, in all material respects, in accordance with the applicable financial reporting framework.
- A review does not provide the auditor with a basis for obtaining reasonable assurance that the auditor will become aware of all significant findings or issues that would be identified in an audit.
- A review is not designed to provide the auditor with a basis for obtaining reasonable assurance on internal control or to identify significant deficiencies or material weaknesses in internal control; however, the auditor is responsible for communicating to management and those charged with governance any significant deficiencies or material weaknesses in internal control that the auditor identifies during the performance of review procedures.

Procedures for a Review of Interim Financial Information

Understanding the Entity and Its Environment, Including Its Internal Control (Ref: par. .11–.12)

.A7 As required by section 315, *Understanding the Entity and Its Environment and Assessing the Risks of Material Misstatement*, the auditor who has audited the entity's financial statements for one or more annual periods would have obtained an understanding of the entity and its environment, including its internal control as it relates to the preparation and fair presentation of annual financial information, that was sufficient to conduct the audit. Internal control over the preparation and fair presentation of interim financial information may differ from internal control over the preparation and fair presentation of annual financial statements because certain accounting principles and practices used for interim financial information may differ from those used for the preparation of annual financial statements (for example, the use of estimated effective income tax rates for the preparation of interim financial information).

.A8 The auditor is unable to complete the review if the entity's internal control appears to contain deficiencies so significant that it would be impracticable for the auditor to effectively perform review procedures that would achieve the objective stated in paragraph .05. Paragraph .23 addresses the auditor's responsibilities when the review cannot be completed.

.A9 In an initial review of interim financial information, when performing the procedures for a new client required by paragraph .07, the auditor also may consider requesting access to review the predecessor auditor's documentation related to reviews of an interim period or interim periods in the prior year. However, the inquiries made and analytical procedures performed, or other procedures performed in the initial review, and the conclusions reached are solely the responsibility of the auditor. Therefore, the auditor is not permitted to make reference to the report or work of the predecessor auditor as the basis, in part, for the auditor's own report.

.A10 If the predecessor auditor does not respond to the auditor's inquiries or does not allow the auditor to review the predecessor auditor's documentation, the auditor may inquire why and use alternative procedures to obtain the understanding required by paragraph .11.

Analytical Procedures, Inquiries, and Other Review Procedures

Analytical Procedures (Ref: par. .13)

.A11 Procedures for conducting a review of interim financial information generally are limited to analytical procedures, inquiries, and other procedures that address significant accounting and disclosure matters relating to the interim financial information. The auditor's understanding of the entity and its environment, including its internal control, the results of the risk assessments relating to the preceding audit, and the auditor's consideration of materiality as it relates to the interim financial information, influences the nature and extent of the inquiries made and analytical procedures performed. For example, if the auditor becomes aware of a significant change in the entity's control activities at a particular location, the auditor may consider the following procedures:

- Making additional inquiries, such as whether management monitored the changes and considered whether they were operating as intended
- Employing analytical procedures with a more precise expectation

.A12 Examples of analytical procedures that an auditor may consider performing when conducting a review of interim financial information are contained in appendix A, "Analytical Procedures the Auditor May Consider Performing When Conducting a Review of Interim Financial Information." The auditor also may find the guidance in section 520, *Analytical Procedures*, useful in conducting a review of interim financial information.

.A13 Expectations developed by the auditor in performing analytical procedures in connection with a review of interim financial information ordinarily are less precise than those developed in an audit. Also, in a review, the auditor is not required to corroborate management's responses with other evidence.

.A14 In considering plausible relationships, the auditor may consider information developed and used by the entity (for example, analyses prepared for management or those charged with governance).

.A15 To compare disaggregated revenue data, the auditor may compare, for example, revenue reported by month and product line or operating segment during the current interim period with that of comparable prior periods.

Inquiries and Other Review Procedures (Ref: par. .14)

.A16 Many of the inquiries and review procedures can be performed before, or simultaneously with, the entity's preparation of the interim financial information. For example, the auditor may update the understanding of the entity's internal control and begin reading applicable minutes before the end of an interim period. Performing some of the review procedures earlier in the interim period also permits early identification and consideration of significant findings and issues affecting the interim financial information. In addition, when the auditor performing the review of interim financial information is also engaged to perform an audit of the annual financial statements of the entity, certain auditing procedures associated with the annual audit of the financial statements may be performed concurrently with the review of interim financial information. For example, information gained from reading the minutes of meetings of the board of directors in connection with the review also may be relevant to the annual audit. Also, there may be significant or unusual transactions occurring during an interim period (for example, business combinations, restructurings, or significant revenue transactions) for which the procedures that would need to be performed for purposes of the audit of the annual financial statements could be performed, to the extent practicable, at the time of the review of the interim period in which the transactions are first recorded.

.A17 The auditor may find the guidance in section 600, *Special Considerations—Audits of Group Financial Statements (Including the Work of Component Auditors)*, useful in conducting a review of interim financial information for an entity that prepares group financial statements.

.A18 Examples of unusual or complex situations about which the auditor may inquire of management are contained in appendix B, "Unusual or Complex Situations to Be Considered by the Auditor When Conducting a Review of Interim Financial Information."

.A19 To obtain evidence that the interim financial information agrees or reconciles with the accounting records, the auditor may compare the interim financial information to (*a*) the accounting records, such as the general ledger; (*b*) a consolidating schedule derived from the accounting records; or (*c*) other supporting data in the entity's records.

.A20 The auditor may find the guidance in section 720, *Other Information in Documents Containing Audited Financial Statements*, in considering other information included in documents containing interim financial information.

.A21 The auditor may request component auditors involved in the engagement, if any, to read the other information.

Inquiry Concerning Litigation, Claims, and Assessments (Ref: par. .15)

.A22 A review of interim financial information does not contemplate obtaining corroborating evidence for responses to inquiries, such as those concerning litigation, claims, and assessments. Consequently, the auditor is not required to send an inquiry letter to an entity's legal counsel concerning litigation, claims, and assessments.

Inquiry Concerning an Entity's Ability to Continue as a Going Concern (Ref: par. .16)

.A23 A review of interim financial information is not designed to identify conditions or events that may indicate substantial doubt about an entity's ability to continue as a going concern. However, conditions or events that may cast substantial doubt on the entity's ability to continue as a going concern may have existed at the date of the prior period financial statements or may be identified as a result of inquiries of management or in the course of performing other review procedures. When performing a review engagement, the auditor is not required to obtain evidence in support of the information that mitigates the effects of the conditions and events.

.A24 Section 570, *The Auditor's Consideration of an Entity's Ability to Continue as a Going Concern*, may provide useful guidance to the auditor when considering whether there is adequate and appropriate disclosure in the interim financial information about the entity's possible inability to continue as a going concern.[4] When

a. conditions or events exist as of the interim reporting date covered by the review that might be indicative of the entity's possible inability to continue as a going concern, or

b. the auditor's report for the prior year end contained an emphasis-of-matter paragraph indicating the existence of substantial doubt about the entity's ability to continue as a going concern, and the conditions that raised such doubt continued to exist as of the interim reporting date covered by the review,

the auditor is not required to modify the report if there is adequate and appropriate disclosure about these conditions or events in the interim financial information. However, if the auditor determines that the disclosure about the entity's possible inability to continue as a going concern is inadequate, resulting in a departure from the applicable financial reporting framework, the auditor is required by paragraph .34 to modify the report.

Consideration of Management's Responses and Extension of Interim Review Procedures (Ref: par. .18)

.A25 The auditor's interim review procedures may lead the auditor to make additional inquiries, such as questioning whether, for example, a significant sales transaction is recorded in accordance with the applicable financial reporting framework. Additional procedures that the auditor may perform to resolve such questions include discussing the terms of the transaction with senior sales and accounting personnel, reading the sales contract, or both.

Evaluating the Results of Interim Review Procedures (Ref: par. .19–.20)

.A26 The auditor may designate an amount below which misstatements would be clearly trivial and would not need to be accumulated because the auditor expects that the accumulation of such amounts would not have a material effect on the interim financial information.[5]

---

[4] Paragraph .12 of section 570, *The Auditor's Consideration of an Entity's Ability to Continue as a Going Concern*. [Footnote revised, August 2012, to reflect conforming changes necessary due to the issuance of SAS No. 126.]

[5] Paragraph .A2 of section 450, *Evaluation of Misstatements Identified During the Audit*.

.A27 As noted in paragraph .A2, appropriate financial reporting frameworks for interim financial information may include, for example, FASB ASC 270 and Article 10 of SEC Regulation S-X. FASB ASC 270 describes the applicability of GAAP to interim financial information and indicates the types of disclosures necessary to report on a meaningful basis for a period of less than one full year. FASB ASC 270-10-45-16 provides guidance on assessing materiality in interim periods. For example, it states that in determining materiality for the purpose of reporting the correction of an error, amounts shall be related to the estimated income for the full fiscal year and also to the effect on the trend of earnings. Further, Rule 10-01(a)(5) of SEC Regulation S-X states the following:

> The interim financial information shall include disclosures either on the face of the financial statements or in accompanying footnotes sufficient so as to make the interim information presented not misleading. Registrants may presume that users of the interim financial information have read or have access to the audited financial statements for the preceding fiscal year and that the adequacy of additional disclosure needed for a fair presentation, except in regard to material contingencies may be determined in that context. Accordingly, footnote disclosure which would substantially duplicate the disclosure contained in the most recent annual report to security holders or latest audited financial statements, such as a statement of significant accounting policies and practices, details of accounts which have not changed significantly in amount or composition since the end of the most recently completed fiscal year, and detailed disclosures prescribed by Rule 4-08 of this Regulation, may be omitted. However, disclosure shall be provided where events subsequent to the end of the most recent fiscal year have occurred which have a material impact on the registrant. Disclosures should encompass for example, significant changes since the end of the most recently completed fiscal year in such items as: accounting principles and practices; estimates inherent in the preparation of the financial statements; status of long-term contracts; capitalization including significant new borrowings or modification of existing financing arrangements; and the reporting entity resulting from business combinations or dispositions. Notwithstanding the above, where material contingencies exist, disclosure of such matters shall be provided even though a significant change since year end may not have occurred.

.A28 Considerations that may affect the evaluation of whether uncorrected misstatements, individually or in the aggregate, are material include the following:

- The nature, cause (if known), and amount of the misstatements
- Whether the misstatements originated in the preceding year or interim periods of the current year
- Materiality judgments made in conjunction with the current or prior year's annual audit
- The potential effect of the misstatements on future interim or annual periods
- The appropriateness of offsetting a misstatement of an estimated amount with a misstatement of an item capable of precise measurement
- Recognition that an accumulation of immaterial misstatements in the balance sheet could contribute to material misstatements in future periods

Section 450, *Evaluation of Misstatements Identified During the Audit*, provides guidance regarding qualitative considerations in evaluating whether misstatements are material.

Written Representations From Management (Ref: par. .21–.22)

.A29 Exhibit A, "Illustrative Management Representation Letters for a Review of Interim Financial Information," contains illustrative representation letters for engagements to review interim financial information.

.A30 The auditor may request additional representations regarding matters specific to the entity's business or industry.

.A31 If no uncorrected misstatements were identified, the representation regarding uncorrected misstatements is not relevant and, accordingly, is not required.

.A32 Appropriate action when management does not provide one or more requested written representations or when the auditor has concerns about the reliability of the representations may include

- discussing the matter with management and, when relevant, those charged with governance;
- reevaluating the integrity of management and evaluating the effect that this may have on the reliability of representations (oral or written) and evidence in general; and
- considering whether to withdraw from the engagement to review the interim financial information and, if applicable, as the entity's auditor.

Communications With Management and Those Charged With Governance

Matters Affecting the Completion of the Review (Ref: par. .23–.26)

.A33 When an auditor is unable to perform the procedures that the auditor considers necessary to achieve the objective of a review of interim financial information, or management does not provide the auditor with the written representations that the auditor believes are necessary, the review will be incomplete.

.A34 The auditor may seek legal advice when considering whether to withdraw from the engagement to review the interim financial information and as the entity's auditor.

Other Matters (Ref: par. .27–.28)

.A35 Section 265, *Communicating Internal Control Related Matters Identified in an Audit*, provides guidance on identifying and communicating deficiencies in internal control.

.A36 As a result of performing the review of the interim financial information, the auditor may become aware of matters that, in the opinion of the auditor, are both significant and relevant to those charged with governance in overseeing the financial reporting and disclosure process. Examples of such matters include the following:

- A change in a significant accounting policy affecting the interim financial information
- Adjustments that either individually or in the aggregate could have a significant effect on the entity's financial reporting process
- Uncorrected misstatements aggregated by the auditor that were determined by management to be immaterial, both individually

and in the aggregate, to the interim financial information as a whole

.A37 The objective of a review of interim financial information differs significantly from that of an audit. Therefore, any communication that the auditor may make about the quality, not just the acceptability, of the entity's accounting principles as applied to its interim financial reporting generally is limited to the effect of significant events, transactions, and changes in accounting estimates that the auditor considered when conducting the review of interim financial information. Further, interim review procedures do not provide assurance that the auditor will become aware of all matters that might affect the auditor's judgments about the quality of the entity's accounting principles that would be identified as a result of an audit.

.A38 The communications required by paragraphs .23–.28 may be oral or written. The communications are most helpful when made on a sufficiently timely basis to enable management or those charged with governance to take appropriate action.

The Auditor's Report on a Review of Interim Financial Information

Form of the Auditor's Review Report (Ref: par. .29–.30)

.A39 Entities may be required by third parties to engage auditors to perform a review of interim financial information, but such third parties may choose to not require that a written auditor's review report on such information be provided to users of the entity's interim financial information. For example, entities that trade unregistered private equity securities on electronic trading platforms, often referred to as private equity exchanges, may be required to provide financial and other information to the qualified investors on the exchange's website. The ongoing reporting requirements of these exchanges are substantially similar to the reporting required of issuers, wherein entities trading securities on such exchanges are required to engage auditors to review their interim financial information but are not required to include written review reports with interim financial information provided to qualified investors. Nonetheless, in accordance with paragraph .29, the auditor's report on the review of the interim financial information is required to be in writing.

.A40 Reporting considerations related to the dating of reports or subsequent events encountered during a review are similar to those encountered in an audit of financial statements. Sections 560 and 700 provide guidance on these issues.

.A41 Exhibit B, "Illustrations of Auditor's Review Reports on Interim Financial Information," contains illustrations of review reports.

Comparative Interim Financial Information That Has Not Been Reviewed Presented With Reviewed Interim Financial Information (Ref: par. .32)

.A42 The indication that the auditor has not reviewed the prior period interim financial information and that the auditor assumes no responsibility for it may be worded, for example, as follows:

> The accompanying [*describe the interim financial information or statements*] of ABC Company and subsidiaries as of September 30, 20X1, and for the three-month period then ended were not reviewed by us, and accordingly, we do not express any form of assurance on it.

Interim Financial Information Presented With Condensed Balance Sheet Information for the Most Recent Year End (Ref: par. .33)

.A43 Because interim financial reporting is intended to be an update to year-end reporting, condensed balance sheet information as of the most recent year end often is presented for comparative purposes with the corresponding information as of the latest interim period. Appendix B includes an illustration of a review report on comparative interim financial information that includes a condensed balance sheet derived from audited financial statements.

Modification of the Auditor's Review Report (Ref: par. .34–.35)

.A44 Departures from the applicable financial reporting framework include inadequate disclosure and changes in accounting policies that are not in accordance with the applicable financial reporting framework.

.A45 Section 700 addresses the reporting requirements when the circumstances contemplated by Rule 203, *Accounting Principles* (ET sec. 203 par. .01), of the AICPA Code of Professional Conduct are present.

.A46 If the interim financial information adequately discloses the existence of substantial doubt about the entity's ability to continue as a going concern (see paragraph .16) or a lack of consistency in the application of accounting principles affecting the interim financial information, the auditor may, but is not required to, include an emphasis-of-matter paragraph in the auditor's review report.

.A47 Exhibit C, "Illustrations of Example Modifications to the Auditor's Review Report Due to Departures From the Applicable Financial Reporting Framework," contains illustrative examples of paragraphs modifying the auditor's review report.

.A48 The information necessary for adequate disclosure is influenced by the form and context in which the interim financial information is presented. For example, the disclosures considered necessary for interim financial information presented in accordance with the minimum disclosure requirements of FASB ASC 270-10-50-1, which is applicable to condensed financial statements of public companies, are considerably less extensive than those necessary for annual financial statements that present financial position, results of operations, and cash flows in accordance with the applicable financial reporting framework. FASB ASC 270-10-50-3 states that a presumption exists that users of summarized interim financial data will have read the latest published annual report, including the financial disclosures required by GAAP and management's commentary concerning the annual financial results, and that the summarized interim data will be viewed in that context.

Other Considerations (Ref: par. .38)

.A49 The auditor may seek legal advice in considering what actions, if any, may be appropriate in these circumstances.

Interim Financial Information Accompanying Audited Financial Statements (Ref: par. .40–.41)

.A50 Interim financial information may accompany audited financial statements. If management chooses or is required to present interim financial information in a note to the audited financial statements, management is responsible for clearly marking the information as unaudited in the note.

.A51 Because the interim financial information has not been audited and is not required for the audited financial statements to be fairly stated in accordance with the applicable financial reporting framework, the auditor ordinarily need not modify the auditor's report on the audited financial statements to refer to the interim financial information accompanying the audited financial statements, including when the auditor has performed a review in accordance with this section.

Documentation (Ref: par. .42–.43)

.A52 The auditor may find the guidance in section 230, *Audit Documentation*, useful in determining the form and content of the review documentation, including guidance on the timing of the final assembly of the engagement documentation.

.A53 Examples of findings or issues that, in the auditor's judgment, are significant include the results of review procedures that indicate that the interim financial information could be materially misstated, including actions taken to address such findings, and the basis for the final conclusions reached.

.A54

Appendix A—Analytical Procedures the Auditor May Consider Performing When Conducting a Review of Interim Financial Information (Ref: par. .A12)

Analytical procedures are designed to identify relationships and individual items that appear to be unusual and that may reflect a material misstatement of the interim financial information. Examples of analytical procedures that an auditor may consider performing in a review of interim financial information include the following:

- Comparing current interim financial information with the interim financial information of the immediately preceding interim period, the interim financial information of the corresponding interim period of the preceding financial year, and the most recent audited annual financial statements.
- Comparing current interim financial information with anticipated results, such as budgets or forecasts (for example, comparing tax balances and the relationship between the provision for income taxes and pretax income in the current interim financial information with corresponding information in (*a*) budgets, using expected rates, and (*b*) financial information for prior periods). Caution is necessary when comparing and evaluating current interim financial information with budgets, forecasts, or other anticipated results because of the inherent lack of precision in estimating the future and the susceptibility of such information to manipulation and misstatement by management to reflect desired interim results.
- Comparing current interim financial information with relevant nonfinancial information.
- Comparing ratios and indicators for the current interim period with expectations based on prior periods (for example, performing gross profit analysis by product line and operating segment using elements of the current interim financial information and comparing the results with corresponding information for prior periods). Examples of key ratios and indicators are the current ratio, receivable turnover or days sales outstanding, inventory turnover, depreciation to average fixed assets, debt to equity, gross profit percentage, net income percentage, and plant operating rates.
- Comparing ratios and indicators for the current interim period with those of entities in the same industry.
- Comparing relationships among elements in the current interim financial information with corresponding relationships in the interim financial information of prior periods (for example, expense by type as a percentage of sales, assets by type as a percentage of total assets, and percentage of change in sales to percentage of change in receivables).
- Comparing disaggregated data. The following are examples of how data may be disaggregated:

— By period (for example, interim financial information items disaggregated into quarterly, monthly, or weekly amounts)

— By product line or operating segment

— By location (for example, subsidiary, division, or branch)

Analytical procedures may include such statistical techniques as trend analysis or regression analysis and may be performed manually or with the use of computer-assisted techniques.

.A55

Appendix B—Unusual or Complex Situations to Be Considered by the Auditor When Conducting a Review of Interim Financial Information (Ref: par. .A18)

The following are examples of situations about which the auditor may inquire of management:

- Business combinations
- New or complex revenue recognition methods
- Impairment of assets
- Disposal of a segment of a business
- Use of derivative instruments and hedging activities
- Sales and transfers that may call into question the classification of investments in securities, including management's intent and ability with respect to the remaining securities classified as held to maturity
- Adoption of new stock compensation plans or changes to existing plans
- Restructuring charges taken in the current and prior quarters
- Significant, unusual, or infrequently occurring transactions
- Changes in litigation or contingencies
- Changes in major contracts with customers or suppliers
- Application of new accounting principles
- Changes in accounting principles or the methods of applying them
- Trends and developments affecting accounting estimates, such as allowances for bad debts and excess or obsolete inventories, provisions for warranties and employee benefits, and realization of unearned income and deferred charges
- Compliance with debt covenants
- Changes in related parties or significant new related party transactions
- Material off-balance-sheet transactions, special purpose entities, and other equity investments
- Unique terms for debt or capital stock that could affect classification

.A56

Exhibit A—Illustrative Management Representation Letters for a Review of Interim Financial Information (Ref: par. .A29)

The following management representation letters, which relate to a review of interim financial information, are presented for illustrative purposes only.

Illustration 1—Short Form Representation Letter for a Review of Interim Financial Information

Illustration 2—Detailed Representation Letter for a Review of Interim Financial Information

It is assumed in these illustrations that the applicable financial reporting framework is accounting principles generally accepted in the United States of America, that no conditions or events exist that might be indicative of the entity's possible inability to continue as a going concern, and that no exceptions exist to the requested written representations. If circumstances differ from these assumptions, the representations would need to be modified to reflect the actual circumstances.

Illustration 1—Short Form Representation Letter for a Review of Interim Financial Information

This representation letter is to be used in conjunction with the representation letter for the audit of the financial statements of the prior year. Management confirms the representations made in the representation letter for the audit of the financial statements of the prior year end, as they apply to the interim financial information, and makes additional representations that may be needed for the interim financial information.

[*Date*]

To [*Independent Auditor*]:

This representation letter is provided in connection with your review of the [*consolidated*] balance sheet as of June 30, 20X1 and the related [*consolidated*] statements of income, changes in equity, and cash flows for the six-month period then ended of ABC Company for the purpose of reporting whether any material modifications should be made to the [*consolidated*] interim financial information for it to be in accordance with accounting principles generally accepted in the United States of America (U.S. GAAP) [*including, if appropriate, an indication as to the appropriate form and content of interim financial information (for example, Article 10 of SEC Regulation S-X)*].

We confirm that [*, to the best of our knowledge and belief, having made such inquiries as we considered necessary for the purpose of appropriately informing ourselves*] [*as of (date of auditor's review report),*]:

Interim Financial Information

1. We have fulfilled our responsibilities, as set out in the terms of the engagement letter dated [*insert date*] for the preparation and fair presentation of interim financial information in accordance with U.S. GAAP; in particular the interim financial information is presented in accordance therewith.
2. We acknowledge our responsibility for the design, implementation, and maintenance of internal control relevant to the preparation and fair presentation of interim financial information that is free from material misstatement, whether due to fraud or error.
3. The interim financial information has been adjusted or includes disclosures for all events subsequent to the date of the interim financial information for which U.S. GAAP requires adjustment or disclosure.
4. The effects of uncorrected misstatements are immaterial, both individually and in the aggregate, to the interim financial information as a whole. A list of the uncorrected misstatements is attached to the representation letter.

   [*Any other matters that the auditor may consider appropriate*]

Information Provided

5. We have provided you with:
   - Access to all information of which we are aware that is relevant to the preparation and fair presentation of the interim financial information such as records, documentation, and other matters;
   - Minutes of the meetings of stockholders, directors, and committees of directors, or summaries of actions of recent meetings for which minutes have not yet been prepared;
   - Additional information that you have requested from us for the purpose of the review; and
   - Unrestricted access to persons within the entity of whom you determined it necessary to make inquiries.
6. We have disclosed to you all significant deficiencies or material weaknesses in the design or operation of internal control of which we are aware, as it relates to the preparation and fair presentation of both annual and interim financial information.
7. We have disclosed to you the results of our assessment of the risk that the interim financial information may be materially misstated as a result of fraud.
8. We have [*no knowledge of any*] [*disclosed to you all information of which we are aware in relation to*] fraud or suspected fraud that affects the entity and involves:
   - Management;
   - Employees who have significant roles in internal control; or
   - Others when the fraud could have a material effect on the interim financial information.
9. We have [*no knowledge of any*] [*disclosed to you all information in relation to*] allegations of fraud, or suspected fraud, affecting

the entity's interim financial information communicated by employees, former employees, analysts, regulators, or others.

10. We have disclosed to you the identity of the entity's related parties and all the related party relationships and transactions of which we are aware.

[*Any other matters that the auditor may consider necessary*]

11. We have reviewed our representation letter to you dated [*date of representation letter relating to most recent audit*] with respect to the audited consolidated financial statements as of and for the year ended [*prior year-end date*]. We believe that representations [*references to applicable representations*] within that representation letter do not apply to the interim financial information referred to above. We now confirm those representations [*references to applicable representations*], as they apply to the interim financial information referred to above, and incorporate them herein, with the following changes:

[*Indicate any changes.*]

12. [*Add any representations related to new accounting or auditing standards that are being implemented for the first time.*]

____

[*Name of Chief Executive Officer and Title*]

____

[*Name of Chief Financial Officer and Title*]

____

[*Name of Chief Accounting Officer and Title*]

Illustration 2—Detailed Representation Letter for a Review of Interim Financial Information

This representation letter is similar in detail to the management representation letter used for the audit of the financial statements of the prior year and, thus, need not refer to the written management representations received in the most recent audit.

[*Date*]

To [*Independent Auditor*]:

This representation letter is provided in connection with your review of the [*consolidated*] balance sheet as of June 30, 20X1 and the related [*consolidated*] statements of income, changes in equity, and cash flows for the six-month period then ended of ABC Company for the purpose of reporting whether any material modifications should be made to the [*consolidated*] interim financial information for it to be in accordance with accounting principles generally accepted in the United States of America (U.S. GAAP) [*including, if appropriate, an indication as to the appropriate form and content of interim financial information (for example, Article 10 of SEC Regulation S-X)*].

We confirm that [*, to the best of our knowledge and belief, having made such inquiries as we considered necessary for the purpose of appropriately informing ourselves*] [*as of (date of auditor's review report),*]:

Interim Financial Information

1. We have fulfilled our responsibilities, as set out in the terms of the engagement letter dated [*insert date*] for the preparation and fair presentation of the interim financial information in accordance with U.S. GAAP; in particular the interim financial information is presented in accordance therewith.
2. We acknowledge our responsibility for the design, implementation, and maintenance of internal control relevant to the preparation and fair presentation of interim financial information that is free from material misstatement, whether due to fraud or error.
3. Significant assumptions used by us in making accounting estimates, including those measured at fair value, are reasonable.
4. Related party relationships and transactions have been appropriately accounted for and disclosed in accordance with the requirements of U.S. GAAP.
5. The interim financial information has been adjusted or includes disclosures for all events subsequent to the date of the interim financial information for which U.S. GAAP requires adjustment or disclosure.
6. The effects of uncorrected misstatements are immaterial, both individually and in the aggregate, to the interim financial information as a whole. A list of the uncorrected misstatements is attached to the representation letter.

[*Any other matters that the auditor may consider appropriate*]

Information Provided

7. We have provided you with:

   - Access to all information of which we are aware that is relevant to the preparation and fair presentation of the interim financial information such as records, documentation, and other matters;
   - Minutes of the meetings of stockholders, directors, and committees of directors, or summaries of actions of recent meetings for which minutes have not yet been prepared;
   - Additional information that you have requested from us for the purpose of the review; and
   - Unrestricted access to persons within the entity of whom you determined it necessary to make inquiries.

8. All transactions have been recorded in the accounting records and are reflected in the interim financial information.
9. We have disclosed to you all significant deficiencies or material weaknesses in the design or operation of internal control of which we are aware, as it relates to the preparation and fair presentation of both annual and interim financial information.
10. We have disclosed to you the results of our assessment of the risk that the interim financial information may be materially misstated as a result of fraud.
11. We have [*no knowledge of any*] [*disclosed to you all information of which we are aware in relation to*] fraud or suspected fraud that affects the entity and involves:

- Management;
- Employees who have significant roles in internal control; or
- Others when the fraud could have a material effect on the interim financial information.

12. We have [*no knowledge of any*][*disclosed to you all information in relation to*] allegations of fraud, or suspected fraud, affecting the entity's interim financial information communicated by employees, former employees, analysts, regulators, or others.
13. We have disclosed to you all known instances of non-compliance or suspected non-compliance with laws and regulations whose effects should be considered when preparing interim financial information.
14. There have been no communications from regulatory agencies concerning noncompliance with or deficiencies in financial reporting practices.
15. We have disclosed to you the identity of the entity's related parties and all the related party relationships and transactions of which we are aware.

[*Any other matters that the auditor may consider necessary*]

____

[*Name of Chief Executive Officer and Title*]

____

[*Name of Chief Financial Officer and Title*]

____

[*Name of Chief Accounting Officer and Title*]

.A57

Exhibit B—Illustrations of Auditor's Review Reports on Interim Financial Information (Ref: par. .A41)

Illustration 1—A Review Report on Interim Financial Information

Circumstances include the following:

- A review of interim financial information presented as a complete set of financial statements, including disclosures

Independent Auditor's Review Report

[*Appropriate Addressee*]

Report on the Financial Statements

We have reviewed the accompanying [*describe the interim financial information or statements reviewed*] of ABC Company and subsidiaries as of September 30, 20X1, and for the three-month and nine-month periods then ended.

Management's Responsibility

The Company's management is responsible for the preparation and fair presentation of the interim financial information in accordance with [*identify the applicable financial reporting framework; for example, accounting principles generally accepted in the United States of America*]; this responsibility includes the design, implementation, and maintenance of internal control sufficient to provide a reasonable basis for the preparation and fair presentation of interim financial information in accordance with [*identify the applicable financial reporting framework; for example, accounting principles generally accepted in the United States of America*].

Auditor's Responsibility

Our responsibility is to conduct our review in accordance with auditing standards generally accepted in the United States of America applicable to reviews of interim financial information. A review of interim financial information consists principally of applying analytical procedures and making inquiries of persons responsible for financial and accounting matters. It is substantially less in scope than an audit conducted in accordance with auditing standards generally accepted in the United States of America, the objective of which is the expression of an opinion regarding the financial information. Accordingly, we do not express such an opinion.

Conclusion

Based on our review, we are not aware of any material modifications that should be made to the accompanying interim financial information for it to be in accordance with [*identify the applicable financial reporting framework; for example, accounting principles generally accepted in the United States of America*].

[*Auditor's signature*]

[*Auditor's city and state*]

[*Date of the auditor's report*]

Illustration 2—A Review Report on Condensed Comparative Interim Financial Information

The following is an example of a review report on a condensed balance sheet as of March 31, 20X1; the related condensed statements of income and cash flows for the three-month periods ended March 31, 20X1 and 20X0; and a condensed balance sheet derived from audited financial statements as of December 31, 20X0. If the auditor's report on the preceding year-end financial statements was other than unmodified or included an emphasis-of-matter paragraph because of a going concern matter or an inconsistency in the application of accounting principles, the last paragraph of the illustrative report would be appropriately modified.

Independent Auditor's Review Report

[*Appropriate Addressee*]

Report on the Financial Statements

We have reviewed the condensed consolidated financial statements of ABC Company and subsidiaries, which comprise the balance sheet as of March 31, 20X1, and the related condensed consolidated statements of income and cash flows for the three-month periods ended March 31, 20X1 and 20X0.

Management's Responsibility

The Company's management is responsible for the preparation and fair presentation of the condensed financial information in accordance with [*identify the applicable financial reporting framework; for example, accounting principles generally accepted in the United States of America*]; this responsibility includes the design, implementation, and maintenance of internal control sufficient to provide a reasonable basis for the preparation and fair presentation of interim financial information in accordance with [*identify the applicable financial reporting framework; for example, accounting principles generally accepted in the United States of America*].

Auditor's Responsibility

Our responsibility is to conduct our reviews in accordance with auditing standards generally accepted in the United States of America applicable to reviews of interim financial information. A review of interim financial information consists principally of applying analytical procedures and making inquiries of persons responsible for financial and accounting matters. It is substantially less in scope than an audit conducted in accordance with auditing standards generally accepted in the United States of America, the objective of which is the expression of an opinion regarding the financial information. Accordingly, we do not express such an opinion.

Conclusion

Based on our reviews, we are not aware of any material modifications that should be made to the condensed financial information referred to above for it to be in accordance with [*identify the applicable financial reporting framework; for example, accounting principles generally accepted in the United States of America*].

Report on Condensed Balance Sheet as of [Date]

We have previously audited, in accordance with auditing standards generally accepted in the United States of America, the consolidated balance sheet as of December 31, 20X0, and the related consolidated statements of income, changes in stockholders' equity, and cash flows for the year then ended (not presented herein); and we expressed an unmodified audit opinion on those audited consolidated financial statements in our report dated February 15, 20X1. In our opinion, the accompanying condensed consolidated balance sheet of ABC Company and subsidiaries as of December 31, 20X0, is consistent, in all material respects, with the audited consolidated financial statements from which it has been derived.

[*Auditor's signature*]

[*Auditor's city and state*]

[*Date of the auditor's report*]

Illustration 3—A Review Report That Refers to a Component Auditor's Review Report on the Interim Financial Information of a Significant Component of a Reporting Entity

Circumstances include the following:

- A review of interim financial information presented as a complete set of financial statements, including disclosures.
- The auditor is making reference to another auditor's review report on the interim financial information of a significant component of a reporting entity.

Independent Auditor's Review Report

[*Appropriate Addressee*]

Report on the Financial Statements

We have reviewed the accompanying [*describe the interim financial information or statements reviewed*] of ABC Company and subsidiaries as of September 30, 20X1, and for the three-month and nine-month periods then ended.

Management's Responsibility

The Company's management is responsible for the preparation and fair presentation of the interim financial information in accordance with [*identify the applicable financial reporting framework; for example, accounting principles generally accepted in the United States of America*]; this responsibility includes the design, implementation, and maintenance of internal control sufficient to provide a reasonable basis for the preparation and fair presentation of interim financial information in accordance with [*identify the applicable financial reporting framework; for example, accounting principles generally accepted in the United States of America*].

Auditor's Responsibility

Our responsibility is to conduct our review in accordance with auditing standards generally accepted in the United States of America applicable to reviews of interim financial information. A review of interim financial information consists principally of applying analytical procedures and making inquiries of persons responsible for financial and accounting matters. It is substantially less in scope than an audit conducted in accordance with auditing standards generally accepted in the United States of America, the objective of which is the expression of an opinion regarding the financial information. Accordingly, we do not express such an opinion.

We were furnished with the report of other auditors on their review of the interim financial information of DEF subsidiary, whose total assets as of September 30, 20X1, and whose revenues for the three-month and nine-month periods then ended, constituted 15 percent, 20 percent, and 22 percent, respectively, of the related consolidated totals.

Conclusion

Based on our review and the review report of other auditors, we are not aware of any material modifications that should be made to the accompanying interim financial information for it to be in accordance with [*identify the applicable financial reporting framework; for example, accounting principles generally accepted in the United States of America*].

[*Auditor's signature*]

[*Auditor's city and state*]

[*Date of the auditor's report*]

Illustration 4—A Review Report on Comparative Interim Financial Information When the Prior Period Was Reviewed by Another Auditor

Circumstances include the following:

- A review of interim financial information presented as a complete set of financial statements, including disclosures as of March 31, 20X1, and for the three-month period then ended.
- Comparative information is presented for the balance sheet as of December 31, 20X0, and for the statements of income and cash flows for the comparable interim period.
- The December 31, 20X0, financial statements were audited, and the March 31, 20X0, interim financial information was reviewed, by another auditor.

Independent Auditor's Review Report

[*Appropriate Addressee*]

Report on the Financial Statements

We have reviewed the accompanying [*describe the interim financial information or statements reviewed*] of ABC Company and subsidiaries as of March 31, 20X1, and for the three-month period then ended. The consolidated statements of income and cash flows of ABC Company and subsidiaries for the three-month period ended March 31, 20X0, were reviewed by other auditors whose report dated June 1, 20X0, stated that based on their review, they were not aware of any material modifications that should be made to those statements in order for them to be in conformity with [*identify the applicable financial reporting framework; for example, accounting principles generally accepted in the United States of America*]. The consolidated balance sheet of the Company as of December 31, 20X0, and the related consolidated statements of income, changes in stockholders' equity, and cash flows for the year then ended (not presented herein), were audited by other auditors whose report dated March 15, 20X1, expressed an unmodified opinion on that statement.

Management's Responsibility

The Company's management is responsible for the preparation and fair presentation of the interim financial information in accordance with [*identify the applicable financial reporting framework; for example, accounting principles generally accepted in the United States of America*]; this responsibility includes the design, implementation, and maintenance of internal control sufficient to provide a reasonable basis for the preparation and fair presentation of interim financial information in accordance with [*identify the applicable financial reporting framework; for example, accounting principles generally accepted in the United States of America*].

Auditor's Responsibility

Our responsibility is to conduct our review in accordance with auditing standards generally accepted in the United States of America applicable to reviews of interim financial information. A review of interim financial information consists principally of applying analytical procedures and making inquiries of persons responsible for financial and accounting matters. It is substantially less in scope than an audit conducted in accordance with auditing standards generally accepted in the United States of America, the objective of which is the expression of an opinion regarding the financial information. Accordingly, we do not express such an opinion.

Conclusion

Based on our review, we are not aware of any material modifications that should be made to the accompanying interim financial information as of and for the three months ended March 31, 20X1, for it to be in accordance with [*identify the applicable financial reporting framework; for example, accounting principles generally accepted in the United States of America*].

[*Auditor's signature*]

[*Auditor's city and state*]

[*Date of the auditor's report*]

.A58

Exhibit C—Illustrations of Example Modifications to the Auditor's Review Report Due to Departures From the Applicable Financial Reporting Framework (Ref: par. .A47)

Illustration 1—Modification Due to a Departure From the Applicable Financial Reporting Framework

The following is an example of a modification of the auditor's review report due to a departure from the applicable financial reporting framework:

[*Basis for Modification Paragraph*]

Based on information furnished to us by management, we believe that the Company has excluded from property and debt in the accompanying balance sheet certain lease obligations that we believe should be capitalized to be in accordance with [*identify the applicable financial reporting framework; for example, accounting principles generally accepted in the United States of America*]. This information indicates that if these lease obligations were capitalized at September 30, 20X1, property would be increased by $____, long-term debt would be increased by $____, and net income would be increased (decreased) by $______ and $______, respectively, for the three-month and nine-month periods then ended.

[*Conclusion*]

Based on our review, with the exception of the matter(s) described in the preceding paragraph(s), we are not aware of any material modifications that should be made to the accompanying interim financial information for it to be in accordance with [*identify the applicable financial reporting framework; for example, accounting principles generally accepted in the United States of America*].

Illustration 2—Modification Due to Inadequate Disclosure

The following is an example of a modification of the auditor's review report due to inadequate disclosure:

[*Basis for Modification Paragraph*]

Management has informed us that the Company is presently defending a claim regarding [*describe the nature of the loss contingency*] and that the extent of the Company's liability, if any, and the effect on the accompanying interim financial information is not determinable at this time. The interim financial information fails to disclose these matters, which we believe are required to be disclosed in accordance with [*identify the applicable financial reporting framework; for example, accounting principles generally accepted in the United States of America*].

[*Conclusion*]

Based on our review, with the exception of the matter(s) described in the preceding paragraph(s), we are not aware of any material modifications that should be made to the accompanying interim financial information for it to be in accordance with [*identify the applicable financial reporting framework; for example, accounting principles generally accepted in the United States of America*].

Illustration 3—Emphasis-of-Matter Paragraph When a Going Concern Emphasis-of-Matter Paragraph Was Included in the Prior Year's Audit Report, and Conditions Giving Rise to the Emphasis-of-Matter Paragraph Continue to Exist

The following is an example of an emphasis-of-matter paragraph when a going concern emphasis-of-matter paragraph was included in the prior year's audit report, and conditions giving rise to the emphasis-of-matter paragraph continue to exist:

[*Emphasis-of-Matter Paragraph*]

Note 4 of the Company's audited financial statements as of December 31, 20X1, and for the year then ended, discloses that the Company was unable to renew its line of credit or obtain alternative financing at December 31, 20X1. Our auditor's report on those financial statements includes an emphasis-of-matter paragraph referring to the matters in note 4 of those financial statements and indicating that these matters raised substantial doubt about the Company's ability to continue as a going concern. As indicated in note 3 of the Company's unaudited interim financial information as of March 31, 20X2, and for the three months then ended, the Company was still unable to renew its line of credit or obtain alternative financing as of March 31, 20X2. The accompanying interim financial information does not include any adjustments that might result from the outcome of this uncertainty.

Illustration 4—Emphasis-of-Matter Paragraph When a Going Concern Emphasis-of-Matter Paragraph Was Not Included in the Prior Year's Audit Report, and Conditions or Events Exist as of the Interim Reporting Date Covered by the Review That Might Be Indicative of the Entity's Possible Inability to Continue as a Going Concern

The following is an example of an emphasis-of-matter paragraph when a going concern emphasis-of-matter paragraph was not included in the prior year's audit report, and conditions or events exist as of the interim reporting date covered by the review that might be indicative of the entity's possible inability to continue as a going concern:

[*Emphasis-of-Matter Paragraph*]

As indicated in note 3, certain conditions indicate that the Company may be unable to continue as a going concern. The accompanying interim financial information does not include any adjustments that might result from the outcome of this uncertainty.

AU-C Section 935

Compliance Audits

(Supersedes SAS No. 74.)

Source: SAS No. 117; SAS No. 122; SAS No. 123; SAS No. 125.

Effective for compliance audits for fiscal periods ending on or after June 15, 2010. Earlier application is permitted.

NOTE

To address practice issues, Statement on Auditing Standards (SAS) No. 117, *Compliance Audits*, was issued in December 2009 as a SAS resulting from the Clarification and Convergence Project of the Auditing Standards Board, and is effective for compliance audits for fiscal periods ending on or after June 15, 2010.

SAS No. 117 was originally codified as AU section 801. SAS No. 122, *Statement on Auditing Standards: Clarification and Recodification*, redesignates AU section 801 as section 935, but does not supersede SAS No. 117.

This section contains conforming changes necessary in specific paragraphs and footnotes due to the issuance of SAS No. 122.

Introduction and Applicability

.01 Governments frequently establish governmental audit requirements for entities to undergo an audit of their compliance with applicable compliance requirements. This section is applicable when an auditor is engaged, or required by law or regulation, to perform a compliance audit in accordance with all of the following:

- Generally accepted auditing standards (GAAS)
- The standards for financial audits under *Government Auditing Standards*
- A governmental audit requirement that requires an auditor to express an opinion on compliance (Ref: par. .A1–.A2)

.02 This section addresses the application of GAAS to a compliance audit. Compliance audits usually are performed in conjunction with a financial statement audit. This section does not apply to the financial statement audit component of such engagements. Although certain AU-C sections are not applicable to a compliance audit, as identified in the appendix "AU-C Sections That Are Not Applicable to Compliance Audits," all AU-C sections other than this section are applicable to the audit of financial statements performed in conjunction with a compliance audit. [Revised, October 2011, to reflect conforming changes necessary due to the issuance of SAS No. 122.]

.03 This section is not applicable when the governmental audit requirement calls for an examination, in accordance with Statements on Standards for Attestation Engagements, of an entity's compliance with specified requirements or an examination of an entity's internal control over compliance. AT section 601, *Compliance Attestation*, is applicable to these engagements. If the entity is required to undergo a compliance audit and an examination of internal control over compliance, this section is applicable to performing and reporting on the compliance audit, and AT section 601 is applicable to performing and reporting on the examination of internal control over compliance. (Ref: par. .A2)

.04 AU-C sections 200–800 address audits of financial statements, as well as other kinds of engagements. Generally, these AU-C sections can be adapted to the objectives of a compliance audit. However, those AU-C sections, or portions thereof, identified in the appendix cannot be adapted to a compliance audit because they address the matters that are not applicable to a compliance audit. [Revised, October 2011, to reflect conforming changes necessary due to the issuance of SAS No. 122.]

.05 Except for the AU-C sections that are listed in the appendix as not applicable to a compliance audit, all of the other AU-C sections are applicable to a compliance audit. However, the auditor is not required, in planning and performing a compliance audit, to make a literal translation of each procedure that might be performed in a financial statement audit, but rather to obtain sufficient appropriate audit evidence to support the auditor's opinion on compliance. [Revised, October 2011, to reflect conforming changes necessary due to the issuance of SAS No. 122.]

.06 Some AU-C sections can be adapted and applied to a compliance audit with relative ease, for example, by simply replacing the word *misstatement* with the word *noncompliance*. Other AU-C sections are more difficult to adapt and apply and entail additional modification. For that reason, this section provides more specific guidance on how to adapt and apply certain AU-C sections to a compliance audit. [Revised, October 2011, to reflect conforming changes necessary due to the issuance of SAS No. 122.]

.07 *Government Auditing Standards* and governmental audit requirements contain certain standards and requirements that are supplementary to those in GAAS, as well as guidance on how to apply those standards and requirements.

Management's Responsibilities

.08 A compliance audit is based on the premise that management is responsible for the entity's compliance with compliance requirements. Management's responsibility for the entity's compliance with compliance requirements includes the following:

a. Identifying the entity's government programs and understanding and complying with the compliance requirements

b. Establishing and maintaining effective controls that provide reasonable assurance that the entity administers government programs in compliance with the compliance requirements

c. Evaluating and monitoring the entity's compliance with the compliance requirements

d. Taking corrective action when instances of noncompliance are identified, including corrective action on audit findings of the compliance audit

Effective Date

.09 The provisions of this section are effective for compliance audits for fiscal periods ending on or after June 15, 2010. Earlier application is permitted.

Objectives (Ref: par. .A3)

.10 The auditor's objectives in a compliance audit are to

a. obtain sufficient appropriate audit evidence to form an opinion and report at the level specified in the governmental audit requirement on whether the entity complied in all material respects with the applicable compliance requirements; and

b. identify audit and reporting requirements specified in the governmental audit requirement that are supplementary to GAAS and *Government Auditing Standards*, if any, and perform procedures to address those requirements.

Definitions

.11 For purposes of adapting GAAS to a compliance audit, the following terms have the meanings attributed as follows:

Applicable compliance requirements. Compliance requirements that are subject to the compliance audit.

Audit findings. The matters that are required to be reported by the auditor in accordance with the governmental audit requirement.

Audit risk of noncompliance. The risk that the auditor expresses an inappropriate audit opinion on the entity's compliance when material noncompliance exists. Audit risk of noncompliance is a function of the risks of material noncompliance and detection risk of noncompliance.

Compliance audit. A program-specific audit or an organization-wide audit of an entity's compliance with applicable compliance requirements.

Compliance requirements. Laws, regulations, rules, and provisions of contracts or grant agreements applicable to government programs with which the entity is required to comply.

Deficiency in internal control over compliance. A deficiency in internal control over compliance exists when the design or operation of a control over compliance does not allow management or employees, in the normal course of performing their assigned functions, to prevent, or detect and correct, noncompliance on a timely basis. A deficiency in *design* exists when (*a*) a control necessary to meet the control objective is missing, or (*b*) an existing control is not properly designed so that, even if the control operates as designed, the control objective would not be met. A deficiency in *operation* exists when a properly designed control does not operate as designed or the person performing the control does not possess the necessary authority or competence to perform the control effectively.

Detection risk of noncompliance. The risk that the procedures performed by the auditor to reduce audit risk of noncompliance to an acceptably low level will not detect noncompliance that exists and that could be material, either individually or when aggregated with other instances of noncompliance.

Government Auditing Standards. Standards and guidance issued by the Comptroller General of the United States, U.S. Government Accountability Office for financial audits, attestation engagements, and performance audits. *Government Auditing Standards* also is known as generally accepted government auditing standards (GAGAS) or the Yellow Book.

Government program. The means by which governmental entities achieve their objectives. For example, one of the objectives of the U.S. Department of Agriculture is to provide nutrition to individuals in need. Examples of government programs designed to achieve that objective are the Supplemental Nutrition Assistance Program and the National School Lunch Program. Government programs that are relevant to this section are those in which a grantor or pass-through entity provides an award to another entity, usually in the form of a grant, contract, or other agreement. Not all government programs provide cash assistance; sometimes noncash assistance is provided (for example, a loan guarantee, commodities, or property).

Governmental audit requirement. A government requirement established by law, regulation, rule, or provision of contracts or grant agreements requiring that an entity undergo an audit of its compliance with applicable compliance requirements related to one or more government programs that the entity administers. (Ref: par. .A4)

Grantor. A government agency from which funding for the government program originates.

Known questioned costs. Questioned costs specifically identified by the auditor. Known questioned costs are a subset of likely questioned costs.

Likely questioned costs. The auditor's best estimate of total questioned costs, not just the known questioned costs. Likely questioned costs are developed by extrapolating from audit evidence obtained, for example, by projecting known questioned costs identified in an audit sample to the entire population from which the sample was drawn.

Material noncompliance. In the absence of a definition of material noncompliance in the governmental audit requirement, a failure to follow compliance requirements or a violation of prohibitions included in the applicable compliance requirements that results in noncompliance that is quantitatively or qualitatively material, either individually or when aggregated with other noncompliance, to the affected government program.

Material weakness in internal control over compliance. A deficiency, or combination of deficiencies, in internal control over compliance, such that there is a reasonable possibility that material noncompliance with a compliance requirement will not be prevented, or detected and corrected, on a timely basis. In this section, a reasonable possibility exists when the likelihood of the event is either reasonably possible or probable as defined as follows:

Reasonably possible. The chance of the future event or events occurring is more than remote but less than likely.

Remote. The chance of the future event or events occurring is slight.

Probable. The future event or events are likely to occur.

Organization-wide audit. An audit of an entity's financial statements and an audit of its compliance with the applicable compliance requirements as they relate to one or more government programs that the entity administers.

Pass-through entity. An entity that receives an award from a grantor or other entity and distributes all or part of it to another entity to administer a government program.

Program-specific audit. An audit of an entity's compliance with applicable compliance requirements as they relate to one government program that the entity administers. The compliance audit portion of a program-specific audit is performed in conjunction with either an audit of the entity's or the program's financial statements.

Questioned costs. Costs that are questioned by the auditor because (1) of a violation or possible violation of the applicable compliance requirements, (2) the costs are not supported by adequate documentation, or (3) the incurred costs appear unreasonable and do not reflect the actions that a prudent person would take in the circumstances.

Risk of material noncompliance. The risk that material noncompliance exists prior to the audit. This consists of two components, described as follows:

Inherent risk of noncompliance. The susceptibility of a compliance requirement to noncompliance that could be material, either individually or when aggregated with other instances of noncompliance, before consideration of any related controls over compliance.

Control risk of noncompliance. The risk that noncompliance with a compliance requirement that could occur and that could be material, either individually or when aggregated with other instances of noncompliance, will not be prevented, or detected and corrected, on a timely basis by the entity's internal control over compliance.

Significant deficiency in internal control over compliance. A deficiency, or a combination of deficiencies, in internal control over compliance that is less severe than a material weakness in internal control over compliance, yet important enough to merit attention by those charged with governance.

[Revised, October 2011, to reflect conforming changes necessary due to the issuance of SAS No. 122.]

Requirements

Adapting and Applying the AU-C Sections to a Compliance Audit (Ref: par. .A5 and .A38)

.12 When performing a compliance audit, the auditor, using professional judgment, should adapt and apply the AU-C sections to the objectives of a compliance audit, except for the AU-C sections listed in the appendix. [Revised, October 2011, to reflect conforming changes necessary due to the issuance of SAS No. 122.]

Establishing Materiality Levels (Ref: par. .A6–.A8)

.13 The auditor should establish and apply materiality levels for the compliance audit based on the governmental audit requirement.

Identifying Government Programs and Applicable Compliance Requirements (Ref: par. .A9–.A11)

.14 As discussed in paragraph .08, a compliance audit is based on the premise that management is responsible for identifying the entity's government programs and understanding and complying with the compliance requirements. The auditor should determine which of those government programs and compliance requirements to test (that is, the applicable compliance requirements) in accordance with the governmental audit requirement.

Performing Risk Assessment Procedures (Ref: par. .A12–.A15)

.15 For each of the government programs and applicable compliance requirements selected for testing, the auditor should perform risk assessment procedures to obtain a sufficient understanding of the applicable compliance requirements and the entity's internal control over compliance with the applicable compliance requirements.[1]

.16 In performing risk assessment procedures, the auditor should inquire of management about whether there are findings and recommendations in reports or other written communications resulting from previous audits, attestation engagements, and internal or external monitoring that directly relate to the objectives of the compliance audit. The auditor should gain an understanding of management's response to findings and recommendations that could have a material effect on the entity's compliance with the applicable compliance requirements (for example, taking corrective action). The auditor should use this information to assess risk and determine the nature, timing, and extent of the audit procedures for the compliance audit, including determining the extent to which testing the implementation of any corrective actions is applicable to the audit objectives.

Assessing the Risks of Material Noncompliance (Ref: par. .A16–.A18)

.17 The auditor should assess the risks of material noncompliance whether due to fraud or error for each applicable compliance requirement and should

---

[1] Paragraphs .03–.12*b* and .12*d*–.25 of section 315, *Understanding the Entity and Its Environment and Assessing the Risks of Material Misstatement*. [Footnote revised, October 2011, to reflect conforming changes necessary due to the issuance of SAS No. 122.]

consider whether any of those risks are pervasive to the entity's compliance because they may affect the entity's compliance with many compliance requirements.[2]

Performing Further Audit Procedures in Response to Assessed Risks

.18 If the auditor identifies risks of material noncompliance that are pervasive to the entity's compliance, the auditor should develop an overall response to such risks. (Ref: par. .A19)

.19 The auditor should design and perform further audit procedures, including tests of details (which may include tests of transactions) to obtain sufficient appropriate audit evidence about the entity's compliance with each of the applicable compliance requirements in response to the assessed risks of material noncompliance. Risk assessment procedures, tests of controls, and analytical procedures alone are not sufficient to address a risk of material noncompliance. (Ref: par. .A20–.A23)

.20 The auditor should design and perform further audit procedures in response to the assessed risks of material noncompliance. These procedures should include performing tests of controls over compliance if

- the auditor's risk assessment includes an expectation of the operating effectiveness of controls over compliance related to the applicable compliance requirements;
- substantive procedures alone do not provide sufficient appropriate audit evidence; or
- such tests of controls over compliance are required by the governmental audit requirement.

If any of the conditions in this paragraph are met, the auditor should test the operating effectiveness of controls over each applicable compliance requirement to which the conditions apply in each compliance audit. (Ref: par. .A24–.A25)

Supplementary Audit Requirements

.21 The auditor should determine whether audit requirements are specified in the governmental audit requirement that are supplementary to GAAS and *Government Auditing Standards* and perform procedures to address those requirements, if any. (Ref: par. .A26)

.22 In instances where audit guidance provided by a governmental agency for the performance of compliance audits has not been updated for, or otherwise conflicts with, current GAAS or *Government Auditing Standards,* the auditor should comply with the most current applicable GAAS and *Government Auditing Standards* instead of the outdated or conflicting guidance. (Ref: par. .A27)

Written Representations

.23 The auditor should request from management written representations[3] that are tailored to the entity and the governmental audit requirement: (Ref: par. .A28)

---

[2] Paragraphs .28–.32 of section 315. [Footnote revised, October 2011, to reflect conforming changes necessary due to the issuance of SAS No. 122.]

[3] See section 580, *Written Representations*. [Footnote revised, October 2011, to reflect conforming changes necessary due to the issuance of SAS No. 122.]

a. acknowledging management's responsibility for understanding and complying with the compliance requirements;

b. acknowledging management's responsibility for establishing and maintaining controls that provide reasonable assurance that the entity administers government programs in accordance with the compliance requirements;

c. stating that management has identified and disclosed to the auditor all of its government programs and related activities subject to the governmental audit requirement;

d. stating that management has made available to the auditor all contracts and grant agreements, including amendments, if any, and any other correspondence relevant to the programs and related activities subject to the governmental audit requirement;

e. stating that management has disclosed to the auditor all known noncompliance with the applicable compliance requirements or stating that there was no such noncompliance;

f. stating whether management believes that the entity has complied with the applicable compliance requirements (except for noncompliance it has disclosed to the auditor);

g. stating that management has made available to the auditor all documentation related to compliance with the applicable compliance requirements;

h. identifying management's interpretation of any applicable compliance requirements that are subject to varying interpretations;

i. stating that management has disclosed to the auditor any communications from grantors and pass-through entities concerning possible noncompliance with the applicable compliance requirements, including communications received from the end of the period covered by the compliance audit to the date of the auditor's report;

j. stating that management has disclosed to the auditor the findings received and related corrective actions taken for previous audits, attestation engagements, and internal or external monitoring that directly relate to the objectives of the compliance audit, including findings received and corrective actions taken from the end of the period covered by the compliance audit to the date of the auditor's report;

k. stating that management has disclosed to the auditor all known noncompliance with the applicable compliance requirements subsequent to the period covered by the auditor's report or stating that there were no such known instances; and

l. stating that management is responsible for taking corrective action on audit findings of the compliance audit.

.24 If the auditor determines that it is necessary to obtain additional representations related to the entity's compliance with the applicable compliance requirements, the auditor should request such additional representations.

Subsequent Events

.25 The auditor should perform audit procedures up to the date of the auditor's report to obtain sufficient appropriate audit evidence that all subsequent events related to the entity's compliance during the period covered by the auditor's report on compliance have been identified. (Ref: par. .A29)

.26 The auditor should take into account the auditor's risk assessment in determining the nature and extent of such audit procedures, which should include, but are not limited to, inquiring of management about and considering

- relevant internal auditors' reports issued during the subsequent period.
- other auditors' reports identifying noncompliance that were issued during the subsequent period.
- reports from grantors and pass-through entities on the entity's noncompliance that were issued during the subsequent period.
- information about the entity's noncompliance obtained through other professional engagements performed for that entity.

.27 The auditor has no obligation to perform any audit procedures related to the entity's compliance during the period subsequent to the period covered by the auditor's report. However, if before the report release date, the auditor becomes aware of noncompliance in the period subsequent to the period covered by the auditor's report that is of such a nature and significance that its disclosure is needed to prevent report users from being misled, the auditor should discuss the matter with management and, if appropriate, those charged with governance, and should include an other-matter paragraph in the auditor's report describing the nature of the noncompliance. (Ref: par. .A30) [Revised, October 2011, to reflect conforming changes necessary due to the issuance of SAS No. 122.]

Evaluating the Sufficiency and Appropriateness of the Audit Evidence and Forming an Opinion (Ref: par. .A31–.A32)

.28 The auditor should evaluate the sufficiency and appropriateness of the audit evidence obtained.[4]

.29 The auditor should form an opinion, at the level specified by the governmental audit requirement, on whether the entity complied in all material respects with the applicable compliance requirements, and report appropriately. In forming an opinion, the auditor should evaluate likely questioned costs, not just known questioned costs, as well as other material noncompliance that, by its nature, may not result in questioned costs.

Reporting

Report on Compliance Only

.30 The auditor's report on compliance should be in writing and include the following elements:

a. A title that includes the word *independent*.

b. An addressee appropriate for the circumstances of the engagement.

c. An introductory paragraph that includes the following:

 i. Identification of the one or more government programs covered by the compliance audit or reference to a separate schedule containing that information

---

[4] Paragraphs .27–.29 of section 330, *Performing Audit Procedures in Response to Assessed Risks and Evaluating the Audit Evidence Obtained.* [Footnote revised, October 2011, to reflect conforming changes necessary due to the issuance of SAS No. 122.]

ii. Identification of the applicable compliance requirements or a reference to where they can be found

iii. Identification of the period covered by the report

d. A section with the heading "Management's Responsibility" that includes a statement that compliance with the applicable compliance requirements is the responsibility of the entity's management. If the document containing the auditor's report contains a separate statement by management about its responsibility for the applicable compliance requirements, the auditor's report should not include a reference to such statement by management.

e. A section with the heading "Auditor's Responsibility" that includes the following statements:

i. A statement that the auditor's responsibility is to express an opinion on the entity's compliance with the applicable compliance requirements based on the compliance audit

ii. A statement that the compliance audit was conducted in accordance with auditing standards generally accepted in the United States of America, the standards applicable to financial audits contained in *Government Auditing Standards*, and the governmental audit requirement

iii. A statement that the compliance audit included examining, on a test basis, evidence about the entity's compliance with those requirements and performing such other procedures as the auditor considered necessary in the circumstances

iv. A statement that the auditor believes the compliance audit provides a reasonable basis for the auditor's opinion

v. A statement that the compliance audit does not provide a legal determination of the entity's compliance

f. If noncompliance results in a modified opinion, a section with an appropriate heading, indicating the basis for the modified opinion that includes a description of such noncompliance, or a reference to a description of such noncompliance in an accompanying schedule.[5] (Ref: par. .A34)

g. A section with the heading "Opinion" that includes the auditor's opinion, at the level specified by the governmental audit requirement, on whether the entity complied, in all material respects, with the applicable compliance requirements.

h. If other noncompliance that is required to be reported by the governmental audit requirement is identified (that is, noncompliance that does not result in a modified opinion), an other-matter paragraph[6] that includes a description of such noncompliance or a reference to a description of such noncompliance in an accompanying schedule. (Ref: par. .A34)

---

[5] Paragraph .17 of section 705, *Modifications to the Opinion in the Independent Auditor's Report*. [Footnote added, October 2011, to reflect conforming changes necessary due to the issuance of SAS No. 123.]

[6] Paragraph .08 of section 706, *Emphasis-of-Matter Paragraphs and Other-Matter Paragraphs in the Independent Auditor's Report*. [Footnote added, October 2011, to reflect conforming changes necessary due to the issuance of SAS No. 123.]

i. If the criteria used to evaluate compliance are

  i. established or determined by contractual agreement or regulatory provisions that are developed solely for the parties to the agreement or regulatory agency responsible for the provisions or

  ii. available only to the specified parties,

an alert describing the purpose of the auditor's report and that the report is not suitable for any other purpose, as required by section 905, *Alert That Restricts the Use of the Auditor's Written Communication*.[7]

j. The manual or printed signature of the auditor's firm.

k. The city and state where the auditor practices.

l. The date of the auditor's report.

[Revised, October 2011, to reflect conforming changes necessary due to the issuance of SAS No. 123. As amended, effective for the auditor's written communications issued on or after December 15, 2012, by SAS No. 125.]

Combined Report on Compliance and Internal Control Over Compliance

.31 If the governmental audit requirement requires the auditor to report on internal control over compliance and the auditor combines the auditor's report on compliance with a report on internal control over compliance, the following should be added to the report elements listed in paragraph .30 in a section with the heading "Internal Control Over Compliance" that appears before the section required by paragraph 30*i*, if any:

a. A statement that management is responsible for establishing and maintaining effective internal control over compliance with the requirements of laws, regulations, rules, and provisions of contracts or grant agreements applicable to government programs.

b. A statement that in planning and performing the compliance audit, the auditor considered the entity's internal control over compliance with the applicable compliance requirements to determine the auditing procedures for the purpose of expressing an opinion on compliance, but not for the purpose of expressing an opinion on the effectiveness of internal control over compliance.

c. A statement that the auditor is not expressing an opinion on internal control over compliance.

d. A statement that the auditor's consideration of the entity's internal control over compliance was not designed to identify all deficiencies in internal control that might be significant deficiencies or material weaknesses in internal control over compliance.

e. The definition of *deficiency in internal control over compliance* and *material weakness in internal control over compliance*.

f. A description of any identified material weaknesses in internal control over compliance or a reference to an accompanying schedule containing such a description.

---

[7] See paragraphs .06*a–b*, .11, and .A11 of section 905, *Alert That Restricts the Use of the Auditor's Written Communication*. [Footnote added, effective for the auditor's written communications issued on or after December 15, 2012, by SAS No. 125.]

g. If significant deficiencies in internal control over compliance were identified, the definition of *significant deficiency in internal control over compliance* and a description of the deficiencies or a reference to an accompanying schedule containing such a description.

h. If no material weaknesses in internal control over compliance were identified, a statement to that effect.

i. The alert described in paragraph .30*i*. The alert should be included in all combined reports on the entity's compliance and internal control over compliance.

A combined report on compliance and internal control over compliance is presented in the exhibit "Illustrative Combined Report on Compliance With Applicable Requirements and Internal Control Over Compliance—(Unmodified Opinion on Compliance; No Material Weaknesses or Significant Deficiencies in Internal Control Over Compliance Identified)." [Revised, October 2011, to reflect conforming changes necessary due to the issuance of SAS No. 123. As amended, effective for the auditor's written communications issued on or after December 15, 2012, by SAS No. 125.]

Separate Report on Internal Control Over Compliance

.32 If the governmental audit requirement requires the auditor to report on internal control over compliance and the auditor chooses to issue a separate report on internal control over compliance, the auditor should include in that separate report the elements in paragraph .31*a–i* and the following additional elements:

a. A title that includes the word *independent*

b. A statement that the auditor audited the entity's compliance with applicable compliance requirements pertaining to [*identify the government program(s) and the period audited*] and a reference to the auditor's report on compliance

c. A statement that the compliance audit was conducted in accordance with auditing standards generally accepted in the United States of America, the standards applicable to financial audits contained in *Government Auditing Standards*, and the governmental audit requirement

d. The manual or printed signature of the auditor's firm

e. The date of the auditor's report

.33 The auditor should report noncompliance as well as other matters that are required to be reported by the governmental audit requirement in the manner specified by the governmental audit requirement. If the other matters required to be reported by the governmental audit requirement are not appropriate for the auditor to report on, the auditor should follow paragraph .38. (Ref: par. .A34)

.34 The auditor should modify the auditor's opinion on compliance in accordance with section 705, *Modifications to the Opinion in the Independent Auditor's Report*, if any of the following conditions exist:

a. The compliance audit identifies noncompliance with the applicable compliance requirements that the auditor believes has a material effect on the entity's compliance.

b. A restriction on the scope of the compliance audit.

[Revised, October 2011, to reflect conforming changes necessary due to the issuance of SAS No. 122.]

.35 The auditor should modify the report described in paragraphs .30 and .32 when the auditor makes reference to the report of another auditor as the basis, in part, for the auditor's report.

.36 In the absence of a governmental audit requirement to report on internal control over compliance, the auditor should, nevertheless, communicate in writing to management and those charged with governance identified significant deficiencies and material weakness in internal control over compliance.[8] (Ref: par. .A35–.A36)

.37 The auditor also should communicate to those charged with governance of the auditor's responsibilities under GAAS, *Government Auditing Standards*, and the governmental audit requirement, an overview of the planned scope and timing of the compliance audit, and significant findings from the compliance audit.[9] [Revised, October 2011, to reflect conforming changes necessary due to the issuance of SAS No. 122.]

.38 Printed forms, schedules, or reports designed or adopted by government agencies with which they are to be filed sometimes contain prescribed wording. If a printed form, schedule, or report requires the auditor to make a statement that the auditor has no basis to make, the auditor should accordingly reword the form, schedule, or report or attach an appropriately worded separate report. (Ref: par. .A37)

Documentation (Ref: par. .A38)

.39 The auditor should document the risk assessment procedures performed, including those related to gaining an understanding of internal control over compliance.[10]

.40 The auditor should document the auditor's responses to the assessed risks of material noncompliance, the procedures performed to test compliance with the applicable compliance requirements, and the results of those procedures, including any tests of controls over compliance.[11]

.41 The auditor should document materiality levels and the basis on which they were determined.

.42 The auditor should document how the auditor complied with the specific governmental audit requirements that are supplementary to GAAS and *Government Auditing Standards*.

---

[8] See section 265, *Communicating Internal Control Related Matters Identified in an Audit*. [Footnote revised, October 2011, to reflect conforming changes necessary due to the issuance of SAS No. 122. Footnote renumbered, October 2011, to reflect conforming changes necessary due to the issuance of SAS No. 123. Footnote renumbered, effective for the auditor's written communications issued on or after December 15, 2012, by SAS No. 125.]

[9] See section 260, *The Auditor's Communication With Those Charged With Governance*. [Footnote revised, October 2011, to reflect conforming changes necessary due to the issuance of SAS No. 122. Footnote renumbered, October 2011, to reflect conforming changes necessary due to the issuance of SAS No. 123. Footnote renumbered, effective for the auditor's written communications issued on or after December 15, 2012, by SAS No. 125.]

[10] Paragraph .33*a*–*b* and .33*d* of section 315. [Footnote revised, October 2011, to reflect conforming changes necessary due to the issuance of SAS No. 122. Footnote renumbered, October 2011, to reflect conforming changes necessary due to the issuance of SAS No. 123. Footnote renumbered, effective for the auditor's written communications issued on or after December 15, 2012, by SAS No. 125.]

[11] Paragraph .30 of section 330. [Footnote revised, October 2011, to reflect conforming changes necessary due to the issuance of SAS No. 122. Footnote renumbered, October 2011, to reflect conforming changes necessary due to the issuance of SAS No. 123. Footnote renumbered, effective for the auditor's written communications issued on or after December 15, 2012, by SAS No. 125.]

Reissuance of the Compliance Report (Ref: par. .A39–.A40)

.43 If an auditor reissues the auditor's report, the reissued report should include an other-matter paragraph stating that the report is replacing a previously issued report and describing the reasons why the report is being reissued, and any changes from the previously issued report. If additional procedures are performed to obtain sufficient appropriate audit evidence for all of the government programs being reported on, the auditor's report date should be updated to reflect the date the auditor obtained sufficient appropriate audit evidence regarding the events that caused the auditor to perform the new procedures. If, however, additional procedures are performed to obtain sufficient appropriate audit evidence for only some of the government programs being reported on, the auditor should dual date the report with the updated report date reflecting the date the auditor obtained sufficient appropriate audit evidence regarding the government programs affected by the circumstances and referencing the government programs for which additional audit procedures have been performed. Reissuance of an auditor-prepared document required by the governmental audit requirement that is incorporated by reference into the auditor's report is considered to be a reissuance of the report. [Revised, October 2011, to reflect conforming changes necessary due to the issuance of SAS No. 122.]

Application and Other Explanatory Material

Introduction and Applicability

.A1 An example of an engagement to which this section is applicable is an audit performed in accordance with the provisions of Office of Management and Budget (OMB) Circular A-133, *Audits of States, Local Governments and Non-Profit Organizations*. This section is applicable because OMB Circular A-133 is a governmental audit requirement that requires the auditor to perform a compliance audit in accordance with both GAAS and *Government Auditing Standards* and to express an opinion on compliance. Another example is a department specific requirement such as the U.S. Department of Housing and Urban Development *Audit Requirements Related to Entities Such As Public Housing Agencies, Nonprofit and For-Profit Housing Projects, and Certain Lenders*. An example of an engagement to which this section is not applicable is an engagement performed to satisfy a law or regulation requiring the entity to have an auditor determine whether the entity has spent transportation excise tax monies in accordance with the specific purposes outlined in the law or regulation, but not requiring that the audit be performed in accordance with both GAAS and *Government Auditing Standards*. Such an engagement could be performed under AT section 601; AT section 101, *Attest Engagements*; or AT section 201, *Agreed-Upon Procedures Engagements*, depending on the requirements of the government. Law or regulation will not always indicate which standards to follow. In such cases, professional judgment will be needed to determine, based on the circumstances, the appropriate standards to follow. (Ref: par. .01) [Revised, October 2011, to reflect conforming changes necessary due to the issuance of SAS No. 122.]

.A2 An example of a governmental audit requirement that calls for an examination of an entity's compliance with specified requirements in accordance with AT section 601 is the U.S. Department of Education's audit guide *Audits of Federal Student Financial Assistance Programs at Participating Institutions and Institution Servicers*. (Ref: par. .01 and .03)

Objectives

.A3 Most governmental audit requirements specify that the auditor's opinion on compliance is at the program level. However, some governmental audit requirements may specify a different level (for example, at the applicable compliance requirement level). (Ref: par. .10) [Revised, October 2011, to reflect conforming changes necessary due to the issuance of SAS No. 122.]

Definitions

Governmental Audit Requirement

.A4 Governmental audit requirements also may set forth specific supplementary requirements of the compliance audit (for example, procedures to be performed by the auditor, documentation requirements, the form of reporting, and continuing professional education requirements with which the auditor is required to comply. (Ref: par. .11) [Revised, October 2011, to reflect conforming changes necessary due to the issuance of SAS No. 122.]

Adapting and Applying the AU-C Sections to a Compliance Audit (Ref: par. .12)

.A5 AU-C sections often identify audit procedures and contain examples that are specific to a financial statement audit. The auditor is not expected to adapt or apply all such procedures to the compliance audit, only those that, in the auditor's professional judgment, are relevant and necessary to meet the objectives of the compliance audit. [Revised, October 2011, to reflect conforming changes necessary due to the issuance of SAS No. 122.]

Establishing Materiality Levels (Ref: par. .13)

.A6 In a compliance audit, the auditor's purpose for establishing materiality levels is to

- *a.* determine the nature and extent of risk assessment procedures.
- *b.* identify and assess the risks of material noncompliance.
- *c.* determine the nature, timing, and extent of further audit procedures.
- *d.* evaluate whether the entity complied with the applicable compliance requirements.
- *e.* report findings of noncompliance and other matters required to be reported by the governmental audit requirement.

.A7 Generally, for all of the purposes identified in paragraph .A6, the auditor's consideration of materiality is in relation to the government program taken as a whole. However, the governmental audit requirement may specify a different level of materiality for one or more of these purposes. For example, for purposes of reporting findings of noncompliance, OMB Circular A-133 requires that noncompliance that is material in relation to one of the 14 types of compliance requirements identified in the OMB *Compliance Supplement* (*Compliance Supplement*) be reported. (See paragraph .A10 for further information about the *Compliance Supplement*.)

.A8 Because the governmental audit requirement usually is established by the grantors and the auditor's report on compliance is primarily for their use, the auditor's determination of materiality usually is influenced by the needs of the grantors. However, in a compliance audit, the auditor's judgment about matters that are material to users of the auditor's report also is based on consideration of the needs of users as a group, including grantors.

Identifying Government Programs and Applicable Compliance Requirements (Ref: par. .14)

.A9 Some governmental audit requirements specifically identify the applicable compliance requirements. Other governmental audit requirements provide a framework for the auditor to determine the applicable compliance requirements. For example, the *Compliance Supplement* provides such a framework for OMB Circular A-133 audits.

.A10 The following are some of the sources an auditor may consult when identifying and obtaining an understanding of the applicable compliance requirements:

a. The *Compliance Supplement*, which is issued by OMB, and used in OMB Circular A-133 audits, contains the compliance requirements that typically are applicable to federal government programs, as well as suggested audit procedures when compliance requirements are applicable and have a direct and material effect on the entity's compliance. Part 7 of the *Compliance Supplement* provides guidance for identifying compliance requirements for programs not included therein.

b. The applicable program-specific audit guide issued by the grantor agency, which contains the compliance requirements pertaining to the government program and suggested audit procedures to test for compliance with the applicable compliance requirements.

.A11 The following are procedures the auditor may perform to identify and obtain an understanding of the applicable compliance requirements if the *Compliance Supplement* or a program-specific audit guide is not applicable:

a. Reading laws, regulations, rules, and provisions of contracts or grant agreements that pertain to the government program

b. Making inquiries of management and other knowledgeable entity personnel (for example, the chief financial officer, internal auditors, legal counsel, compliance officers, or grant or contract administrators)

c. Making inquiries of appropriate individuals outside the entity, such as

  i. the office of the federal, state, or local program official or auditor, or other appropriate audit oversight organizations or regulators, about the laws and regulations applicable to entities within their jurisdiction, including statutes and uniform reporting requirements

  ii. a third-party specialist, such as an attorney

d. Reading the minutes of meetings of the governing board of the entity being audited

e. Reading audit documentation about the applicable compliance requirements prepared during prior years' audits or other engagements

f. Discussing the applicable compliance requirements with auditors who performed prior years' audits or other engagements

The procedures listed in this paragraph also may assist the auditor in obtaining a further understanding of the applicable compliance requirements even when the *Compliance Supplement* or program-specific audit guide is applicable.

Performing Risk Assessment Procedures (Ref: par. .15–.16)

.A12 Obtaining an understanding of the government program, the applicable compliance requirements, and the entity's internal control over compliance establishes a frame of reference within which the auditor plans the compliance audit and exercises professional judgment about assessing risks of material noncompliance and responding to those risks throughout the compliance audit.

.A13 The nature and extent of the risk assessment procedures the auditor performs may vary from entity to entity and are influenced by factors such as the following:

- The newness and complexity of the applicable compliance requirements
- The auditor's knowledge of the entity's internal control over compliance with the applicable compliance requirements obtained in previous audits or other professional engagements
- The nature of the applicable compliance requirements
- The services provided by the entity and how they are affected by external factors
- The level of oversight by the grantor or pass-through entity
- How management addresses findings

.A14 Performing risk assessment procedures to obtain an understanding of the entity's internal control over compliance includes an evaluation of the design of controls and whether the controls have been implemented. Internal control consists of the following five interrelated components: the control environment, the entity's risk assessment, information and communication systems, control activities, and monitoring.[12] Section 315, *Understanding the Entity and Its Environment and Assessing the Risks of Material Misstatement*, contains a detailed discussion of these components.[13] [Revised, October 2011, to reflect conforming changes necessary due to the issuance of SAS No. 122.]

.A15 The auditor's procedures described in paragraph .16, related to understanding how management has responded to findings and recommendations that could have a material effect on the entity's compliance with the applicable compliance requirements, are performed to assist the auditor in understanding whether management responded appropriately to such findings. Examples of external monitoring include regulatory reviews, program reviews by government agencies or pass-through entities, and grantor reviews. Examples of internal monitoring include reports prepared by the internal audit function and internal quality assessments.

---

[12] [Footnote deleted, October 2011, to reflect conforming changes necessary due to the issuance of SAS No. 122. Footnote renumbered, October 2011, to reflect conforming changes necessary due to the issuance of SAS No. 123. Footnote renumbered, effective for the auditor's written communications issued on or after December 15, 2012, by SAS No. 125.]

[13] Paragraphs .15–.25 and appendix B, "Internal Control Components," of section 315. [Footnote added, October 2011, to reflect conforming changes necessary due to the issuance of SAS No. 122. Footnote renumbered, October 2011, to reflect conforming changes necessary due to the issuance of SAS No. 123. Footnote renumbered, effective for the auditor's written communications issued on or after December 15, 2012, by SAS No. 125.]

Assessing the Risks of Material Noncompliance (Ref: par. .17)

.A16 Factors the auditor may consider in assessing the risks of material noncompliance are as follows:

- The complexity of the applicable compliance requirements
- The susceptibility of the applicable compliance requirements to noncompliance
- The length of time the entity has been subject to the applicable compliance requirements
- The auditor's observations about how the entity has complied with the applicable compliance requirements in prior years
- The potential effect on the entity of noncompliance with the applicable compliance requirements
- The degree of judgment involved in adhering to the compliance requirements
- The auditor's assessment of the risks of material misstatement in the financial statement audit

.A17 In assessing the risks of material noncompliance, the auditor may evaluate inherent risk of noncompliance and control risk of noncompliance individually or in combination.

.A18 Examples of situations in which there may be a risk of material noncompliance that is pervasive to the entity's noncompliance are as follows:

- An entity that is experiencing financial difficulty and for which there is an increased risk that grant funds will be diverted for unauthorized purposes
- An entity that has a history of poor recordkeeping for its government programs

Performing Further Audit Procedures in Response to Assessed Risks

.A19 Section 330, *Performing Audit Procedures in Response to Assessed Risks and Evaluating the Audit Evidence Obtained*, provides guidance that may be adapted when developing an overall response to the risks of material noncompliance.[14] (Ref: par. .18) [Revised, October 2011, to reflect conforming changes necessary due to the issuance of SAS No. 122.]

.A20 A compliance audit includes designing procedures to detect both intentional and unintentional material noncompliance. The auditor can obtain reasonable, but not absolute, assurance about the entity's compliance because of factors such as the need for judgment, the use of sampling, the inherent limitations of internal control over compliance with applicable compliance requirements, and the fact that much of the evidence available to the auditor is persuasive rather than conclusive in nature. Also, procedures that are effective for detecting noncompliance that is unintentional may be ineffective for detecting noncompliance that is intentional and concealed through collusion between

---

[14] Paragraphs .A1–.A3 of section 330. [Footnote added, October 2011, to reflect conforming changes necessary due to the issuance of SAS No. 122. Footnote renumbered, October 2011, to reflect conforming changes necessary due to the issuance of SAS No. 123. Footnote renumbered, effective for the auditor's written communications issued on or after December 15, 2012, by SAS No. 125.]

entity personnel and a third party or among management or employees of the entity. Therefore, the subsequent discovery that material noncompliance with applicable compliance requirements exists does not, in and of itself, evidence inadequate planning, performance, or judgment on the part of the auditor. (Ref: par. .19)

.A21 An auditor may decide to use audit sampling to obtain sufficient appropriate audit evidence in a compliance audit. Section 530, *Audit Sampling*, discusses the factors to be considered in planning, designing, and evaluating audit samples, including sampling for tests of controls. In addition, the AICPA Audit Guide Government Auditing Standards *and Circular A-133 Audits* contains guidance on sampling in the context of a compliance audit. (Ref: par. .19) [Revised, October 2011, to reflect conforming changes necessary due to the issuance of SAS No. 122.]

.A22 To test for compliance with applicable laws and regulations, tests of details (including tests of transactions) may be performed in the following areas:

- Grant disbursements or expenditures
- Eligibility files
- Cost allocation plans
- Periodic reports filed with grantor agencies (Ref: par. .19)

.A23 The use of analytical procedures to gather substantive evidence is generally less effective in a compliance audit than it is in a financial statement audit. However, substantive analytical procedures may contribute some evidence when performed in addition to tests of transactions and other auditing procedures necessary to provide the auditor with sufficient appropriate audit evidence. (Ref: par. .19)

.A24 Section 330 provides guidance related to designing and performing further audit procedures in response to the assessed risks of material noncompliance.[15] Section 330, which also addresses the use of audit evidence about the operating effectiveness of controls obtained in prior audits, are not applicable to a compliance audit.[16] (Ref: par. .20) [Revised, October 2011, to reflect conforming changes necessary due to the issuance of SAS No. 122.]

.A25 Some governmental audit requirements, for example, OMB Circular A-133, require tests of the operating effectiveness of controls identified as likely to be effective, even if the auditor believes that such testing would be inefficient. (Ref: par. .20)

Supplementary Audit Requirements

.A26 Examples of supplementary audit requirements are the requirements in OMB Circular A-133 for the auditor to

- perform specified procedures to identify major programs.

---

[15] Paragraphs .06–.12, .15–.18, and .22–.25 of section 330. [Footnote added, October 2011, to reflect conforming changes necessary due to the issuance of SAS No. 122. Footnote renumbered, October 2011, to reflect conforming changes necessary due to the issuance of SAS No. 123. Footnote renumbered, effective for the auditor's written communications issued on or after December 15, 2012, by SAS No. 125.]

[16] Paragraph .13–.14 of section 330. [Footnote added, October 2011, to reflect conforming changes necessary due to the issuance of SAS No. 122. Footnote renumbered, October 2011, to reflect conforming changes necessary due to the issuance of SAS No. 123. Footnote renumbered, effective for the auditor's written communications issued on or after December 15, 2012, by SAS No. 125.]

- follow up on prior audit findings and perform procedures to assess the reasonableness of the summary schedule of prior audit findings. (Ref: par. .21)

.A27 When there is conflicting guidance, the auditor may decide to consult with the government agency responsible for establishing audit guidance or that provides the funding. (Ref: par. .22)

Written Representations

.A28 In some cases, management may include qualifying language in the written representations to the effect that representations are made to the best of management's knowledge and belief. However, such qualifying language is not appropriate for the representations in paragraph .23*a–b* and .23*l*. (Ref: par. .23)

Subsequent Events

.A29 Two types of subsequent events may occur. The first type consists of events that provide additional evidence with respect to conditions that existed at the end of the reporting period that affect the entity's compliance during the reporting period. The second type consists of events of noncompliance that did not exist at the end of the reporting period but arose subsequent to the reporting period. (Ref: par. .25)

.A30 An example of a matter of noncompliance that may occur subsequent to the period being audited but before the report release date that may warrant disclosure to prevent report users from being misled is the discovery of noncompliance in the subsequent period of such magnitude that it caused the grantor to stop funding the program. (Ref: par. .27)

Evaluating the Sufficiency and Appropriateness of the Audit Evidence and Forming an Opinion (Ref: par. .28–.29)

.A31 In determining whether an entity has materially complied with the applicable compliance requirements, the auditor may consider the following factors:

a. The frequency of noncompliance with the applicable compliance requirements identified during the compliance audit

b. The nature of the noncompliance with the applicable compliance requirements identified

c. The adequacy of the entity's system for monitoring compliance with the applicable compliance requirements and the possible effect of any noncompliance on the entity

d. Whether any identified noncompliance with the applicable compliance requirements resulted in likely questioned costs that are material to the government program

.A32 The auditor's evaluation of whether the entity materially complied with applicable compliance requirements includes consideration of noncompliance identified by the auditor, regardless of whether the entity corrected the noncompliance after the auditor brought it to management's attention.

Reporting

[.A33] [Paragraph deleted, effective for the auditor's written communications issued on or after December 15, 2012, by SAS No. 125.][17]

.A34 If the report is a matter of public record or available for public inspection, removing personally identifiable information in the compliance audit report and findings of noncompliance will reduce the likelihood of sensitive information being disclosed. (Ref: par. .30*l–m* and .33)

.A35 When the auditor communicates significant deficiencies or material weaknesses in internal control over compliance to management and those charged with governance, *Government Auditing Standards* also requires the auditor to obtain a response from the responsible officials, preferably in writing, concerning their views on the findings, conclusions, and recommendations included in the auditor's report on internal control over compliance and include a copy of any written response in the auditor's report.[18] (Ref: par. .36)

.A36 If such a written response is included in a document containing the auditor's written communication to management and those charged with governance concerning identified significant deficiencies or material weaknesses in internal control over compliance, the auditor may add a paragraph to the auditor's written communication disclaiming an opinion on such information. Following is an example of such a paragraph: (Ref: par. .36)

> ABC Agency's written response to the significant deficiencies [*and material weaknesses*] in internal control over compliance identified in our compliance audit was not subjected to the auditing procedures applied in the compliance audit of ABC Agency's compliance and, accordingly, we express no opinion on it.

.A37 If the auditor is submitting a reworded form, schedule, or report or appropriately worded separate report, the auditor may include a separate communication to the agency explaining why the auditor's report was modified. (Ref: par. .38)

Documentation (Ref: par. .12 and .39–.42)

.A38 The auditor is not expected to prepare specific documentation of how the auditor adapted and applied each of the applicable AU-C sections to the objectives of a compliance audit. The documentation of the audit strategy, audit plan, and work performed cumulatively demonstrate whether the auditor has complied with the requirement in paragraph .12. [Revised, October 2011, to reflect conforming changes necessary due to the issuance of SAS No. 122.]

Reissuance of the Compliance Report (Ref: par. .43)

.A39 The following are examples of situations in which the auditor might reissue the compliance report:

- A quality control review performed by a governmental agency indicates that the auditor did not test an applicable compliance requirement.

---

[17] [Footnote deleted and renumbered, effective for the auditor's written communications issued on or after December 15, 2012, by SAS No. 125.]

18 See the "Reporting Views of Responsibilities Officials" section of *Government Auditing Standards*. [Footnote renumbered and revised, October 2011, to reflect conforming changes necessary due to the issuance of SAS No. 122. Footnote renumbered, October 2011, to reflect conforming changes necessary due to the issuance of SAS No. 123. Footnote renumbered, effective for the auditor's written communications issued on or after December 15, 2012, by SAS No. 125.]

- The discovery subsequent to the date of the compliance report that the entity had another government program that was required to be tested.

.A40 An example of an auditor-prepared document required by a governmental audit requirement that is incorporated by reference in the auditor's report is the schedule of findings and questioned costs in a compliance audit under OMB Circular A-133.

.A41

Appendix—AU-C Sections That Are Not Applicable to Compliance Audits[1]

The following AU-C sections and individually enumerated requirement paragraphs of specific AU-C sections are not applicable to a compliance audit performed under this section either because *(a)* they are not relevant to a compliance audit environment, *(b)* the procedures and guidance would not contribute to meeting the objectives of a compliance audit, or *(c)* the subject matter is specifically covered in this section. Where the table in this appendix specifies individual requirement paragraphs rather than an entire AU-C section, the application and other explanatory material paragraphs related to such requirement paragraphs also do not apply. However, an auditor may apply these AU-C sections and paragraphs if the auditor believes doing so will provide appropriate audit evidence in the specific circumstances to support the auditor's opinion on compliance.

AU-C Section	*Paragraphs Not Applicable to Compliance Audits*
210, *Terms of Engagement*	Paragraphs .06*a* and .08*a*
240, *Consideration of Fraud in a Financial Statement Audit*	Paragraphs .26 and .32*b*
250, *Consideration of Laws and Regulations in an Audit of Financial Statements*	All
315, *Understanding the Entity and Its Environment and Assessing the Risks of Material Misstatement*	Paragraphs .12*c*, .26–.27, and .33*c*
330, *Performing Audit Procedures in Response to Assessed Risks and Evaluating the Audit Evidence Obtained*	Paragraphs .13–.14, .19–.21, .26, and .31–.32
501, *Audit Evidence—Specific Considerations for Selected Items*	All
505, *External Confirmations*	All
510, *Opening Balances—Initial Audit Engagements, Including Reaudit Engagements*	Paragraphs .06, .08–.13, and .15–.17
540, *Auditing Accounting Estimates, Including Fair Value Accounting Estimates, and Related Disclosures*	All
550, *Related Parties*	All
560, *Subsequent Events and Subsequently Discovered Facts*	Paragraphs .09–.11 and .19–.20
570, *The Auditor's Consideration of an Entity's Ability to Continue as a Going Concern*	All

(continued)

[1] [Footnote deleted, October 2011, to reflect conforming changes necessary due to the issuance of SAS No. 122.]

AU-C Section	*Paragraphs Not Applicable to Compliance Audits*
600, *Special Considerations—Audits of Group Financial Statements (Including the Work of Component Auditors)*	Paragraphs .25*a*, .38, .40*c*, .54, and .55*c*
700, *Forming an Opinion and Reporting on Financial Statements*	Paragraphs .14–.18, .21–.41, and .44–.58
705, *Modifications to the Opinion in the Independent Auditor's Report*	Paragraphs .18–.20
706, *Emphasis-of-Matter Paragraphs and Other-Matter Paragraphs in the Independent Auditor's Report*	Paragraphs .06–.07
708, *Consistency of Financial Statements*	All
720, *Other Information in Documents Containing Audited Financial Statements*	All
725, *Supplementary Information in Relation to the Financial Statements as a Whole*	All
730, *Required Supplementary Information*	All
800, *Special Considerations—Audits of Financial Statements Prepared in Accordance With Special Purpose Frameworks*	All
805, *Special Considerations—Audits of Single Financial Statements and Specific Elements, Accounts, or Items of a Financial Statement*	All
806, *Reporting on Compliance With Aspects of Contractual Agreements or Regulatory Requirements in Connection With Audited Financial Statements*	All
810, *Engagements to Report on Summary Financial Statements*	All
910, *Financial Statements Prepared in Accordance With a Financial Reporting Framework Generally Accepted in Another Country*	All
915, *Reports on Application of Requirements of an Applicable Financial Reporting Framework*	All
920, *Letters for Underwriters and Certain Other Requesting Parties*	All
925, *Filings With the U.S. Securities and Exchange Commission Under the Securities Act of 1933*	All
930, *Interim Financial Information*	All

[Revised, January 2011, to reflect conforming changes necessary due to the issuance of SAS Nos. 118–120. Revised, October 2011, to reflect conforming changes necessary due to the issuance of SAS Nos. 122 and 123. Revised, August 2012, to reflect conforming changes necessary due to the issuance of SAS No. 126.]

.A42

Exhibit—Illustrative Combined Report on Compliance With Applicable Requirements and Internal Control Over Compliance—*(Unmodified Opinion on Compliance; No Material Weaknesses or Significant Deficiencies in Internal Control Over Compliance Identified)*

The following is an illustrative combined report on compliance with applicable requirements and internal control over compliance that contains the elements in paragraphs .30–.31. This illustrative report contains an unmodified opinion on compliance with no material weaknesses or significant deficiencies in internal control over compliance identified. The AICPA Audit Guide Government Auditing Standards *and Circular A-133 Audits* contains illustrative language for other types of reports, including reports containing qualified or adverse opinions on compliance with either material weaknesses in internal control over compliance, significant deficiencies in internal control over compliance, or both identified.

Independent Auditor's Report

[*Addressee*]

Compliance

We have audited Example Entity's compliance with the [*identify the applicable compliance requirements or refer to the document that describes the applicable compliance requirements*] applicable to Example Entity's [*identify the government program(s) audited or refer to a separate schedule that identifies the program(s)*] for the year ended June 30, 20X1.

Management's Responsibility

Compliance with the requirements referred to above is the responsibility of Example Entity's management.

Auditor's Responsibility

Our responsibility is to express an opinion on Example Entity's compliance based on our audit.

We conducted our audit of compliance in accordance with auditing standards generally accepted in the United States of America; the standards applicable to financial audits contained in *Government Auditing Standards*[1] issued by the Comptroller General of the United States; and [*insert the name of the governmental audit requirement or program-specific audit guide*]. Those standards and [*insert the name of the governmental audit requirement or program-specific audit guide*] require that we plan and perform the audit to obtain reasonable assurance about whether noncompliance with the compliance requirements referred to above that could have a material effect on [*identify the government program(s) audited or refer to a separate schedule that identifies the program(s)*] occurred. An audit includes examining, on a test basis, evidence about Example Entity's compliance with those requirements and performing such other procedures as we considered necessary in the circumstances. We believe that our

[1] The standards applicable to financial audits are in chapters 1–5 of *Government Auditing Standards.*

audit provides a reasonable basis for our opinion. Our audit does not provide a legal determination of Example Entity's compliance with those requirements.

Opinion

In our opinion, Example Entity complied, in all material respects, with the compliance requirements referred to above that are applicable to [*identify the government program(s) audited*] for the year ended June 30, 20X1.

Internal Control Over Compliance

Management of Example Entity is responsible for establishing and maintaining effective internal control over compliance with the compliance requirements referred to above. In planning and performing our audit, we considered Example Entity's internal control over compliance to determine the auditing procedures for the purpose of expressing our opinion on compliance, but not for the purpose of expressing an opinion on the effectiveness of internal control over compliance. Accordingly, we do not express an opinion on the effectiveness of Example Entity's internal control over compliance.

A *deficiency in internal control over compliance* exists when the design or operation of a control does not allow management or employees, in the normal course of performing their assigned functions, to prevent, or detect and correct, noncompliance on a timely basis. A *material weakness* in internal control over compliance is a deficiency, or combination of deficiencies in internal control over compliance, such that there is a reasonable possibility that material noncompliance with a compliance requirement will not be prevented, or detected and corrected, on a timely basis.

Our consideration of internal control over compliance was for the limited purpose described in the first paragraph of this section and was not designed to identify all deficiencies in internal control that might be deficiencies, significant deficiencies, or material weaknesses in internal control over compliance. We did not identify any deficiencies in internal control over compliance that we consider to be material weaknesses, as defined above.

This report is intended solely for the information and use of management, [*identify the body or individuals charged with governance*], others within the entity, [*identify the legislative or regulatory body*] and [*identify the grantor agency(ies)*] and is not intended to be and should not be used by anyone other than these specified parties.

[*Signature*]

[*Date*]

[Revised, October 2011, to reflect conforming changes necessary due to the issuance of SAS No. 122.]

AU-C Exhibits

TABLE OF CONTENTS

AU-C Exhibit A

List of AU-C Sections Designated by SAS No. 122, Statements on Auditing Standards: Clarification and Recodification, *Cross Referenced to List of AU Sections*

Part I—AU-C Section to AU Section Cross References

*AU-C Sections Designated by SAS No. 122**		*AU Sections Superseded by SAS No. 122 (SAS Nos. 1–121 except SAS Nos. 51, 59, 65, 87, and 117–120)*		
AU-C Section	*Title*	*AU Section*	*Title*	*Paragraph*
Preface	*Principles Underlying an Audit Conducted in Accordance With Generally Accepted Auditing Standards*			
200–299	**General Principles and Responsibilities**			
200	*Overall Objectives of the Independent Auditor and the Conduct of an Audit in Accordance With Generally Accepted Auditing Standards*	110	*Responsibilities and Functions of the Independent Auditor*	All
		120	*Defining Professional Requirements in Statements on Auditing Standards*	All
		150	*Generally Accepted Auditing Standards*	All
		201	*Nature of the General Standards*	All
		210	*Training and Proficiency of the Independent Auditor*	All
		220	*Independence*	All
		230	*Due Professional Care in the Performance of Work*	All
210	*Terms of Engagement*	311	*Planning and Supervision*	.08–.10
		315	*Communications Between Predecessor and Successor Auditors*	.03–.10 and .14

(continued)

* Statement on Auditing Standards (SAS) No. 122, *Statements on Auditing Standards: Clarification and Recodification*, contains "AU-C" section numbers instead of "AU" section numbers. "AU-C" is a temporary identifier to avoid confusion with references to existing "AU" sections, which remain effective through 2013. The "AU-C" identifier will revert to "AU" in 2014, by which time SAS No. 122 becomes fully effective for all engagements.

AU-C Sections Designated by SAS No. 122		*AU Sections Superseded by SAS No. 122 (SAS Nos. 1–121 except SAS Nos. 51, 59, 65, 87, and 117–120)*		
AU-C Section	*Title*	*AU Section*	*Title*	*Paragraph*
220	*Quality Control for an Engagement Conducted in Accordance With Generally Accepted Auditing Standards*	161	*The Relationship of Generally Accepted Auditing Standards to Quality Control Standards*	All
230	*Audit Documentation*	339	*Audit Documentation*	All
240	*Consideration of Fraud in a Financial Statement Audit*	316	*Consideration of Fraud in a Financial Statement Audit*	All
250	*Consideration of Laws and Regulations in an Audit of Financial Statements*	317	*Illegal Acts by Clients*	All
260	*The Auditor's Communication With Those Charged With Governance*	380	*The Auditor's Communication With Those Charged With Governance*	All
265	*Communicating Internal Control Related Matters Identified in an Audit*	325	*Communicating Internal Control Related Matters Identified in an Audit*	All
300–499	**Risk Assessment and Response to Assessed Risks**			
300	*Planning an Audit*	311	*Planning and Supervision*	All except .08–.10
315	*Understanding the Entity and Its Environment and Assessing the Risks of Material Misstatement*	314	*Understanding the Entity and Its Environment and Assessing the Risks of Material Misstatement*	All
320	*Materiality in Planning and Performing an Audit*	312[1]	*Audit Risk and Materiality in Conducting an Audit*	All
330	*Performing Audit Procedures in Response to Assessed Risks and Evaluating the Audit Evidence Obtained*	318	*Performing Audit Procedures in Response to Assessed Risks and Evaluating the Audit Evidence Obtained*	All
402	*Audit Considerations Relating to an Entity Using a Service Organization*	324[2]	*Service Organizations*	All
450	*Evaluation of Misstatements Identified During the Audit*	312[3]	*Audit Risk and Materiality in Conducting an Audit*	All
500–599	**Audit Evidence**			
500	*Audit Evidence*	326	*Audit Evidence*	All

[1] AU-C section 450, *Evaluation of Misstatements Identified During the Audit*, also supersedes AU section 312, *Audit Risk and Materiality in Conducting an Audit*.

[2] Statement on Standards for Attestation Engagements No. 16, *Reporting on Controls at a Service Organization* (AT sec. 801), also supersedes AU section 324, *Service Organizations*.

[3] AU-C section 320, *Materiality in Planning and Performing an Audit*, also supersedes AU section 312.

AU-C Sections Designated by SAS No. 122		*AU Sections Superseded by SAS No. 122 (SAS Nos. 1–121 except SAS Nos. 51, 59, 65, 87, and 117–120)*		
AU-C Section	*Title*	*AU Section*	*Title*	*Paragraph*
501	*Audit Evidence—Specific Considerations for Selected Items*	331	*Inventories*	All
		332	*Auditing Derivative Instruments, Hedging Activities, and Investments in Securities*	All
		337	*Inquiry of a Client's Lawyer Concerning Litigation, Claims, and Assessments*	All except AU 337B[4]
		901[5]	*Public Warehouses—Controls and Auditing Procedures for Goods Held*	All
505	*External Confirmations*	330	*The Confirmation Process*	All
510	*Opening Balances—Initial Audit Engagements, Including Reaudit Engagements*	315	*Communications Between Predecessor and Successor Auditors*	All except .03–.10 and .14
520	*Analytical Procedures*	329	*Analytical Procedures*	All
530	*Audit Sampling*	350	*Audit Sampling*	All
540	*Auditing Accounting Estimates, Including Fair Value Accounting Estimates, and Related Disclosures*	328	*Auditing Fair Value Measurements and Disclosures*	All
		342	*Auditing Accounting Estimates*	All
550	*Related Parties*	334	*Related Parties*	All
560	*Subsequent Events and Subsequently Discovered Facts*	508	*Reports on Audited Financial Statements*	.71–.73
		530	*Dating of the Independent Auditor's Report*	.03–.08
		560	*Subsequent Events*	All
		561	*Subsequent Discovery of Facts Existing at the Date of the Auditor's Report*	All
570[6]	*The Auditor's Consideration of an Entity's Ability to Continue as a Going Concern*	341	*The Auditor's Consideration of an Entity's Ability to Continue as a Going Concern*	All

(continued)

---

[4] AU-C section 501, *Audit Evidence—Specific Considerations for Selected Items*, withdraws AU section 337B, *Exhibit I—Excerpts From Financial Accounting Standards Board* Accounting Standards Codification *450, Contingencies*.

[5] AU-C section 501 withdraws AU section 901, *Public Warehouses—Controls and Auditing Procedures for Goods Held*.

[6] In July 2012, SAS No. 126, *The Auditor's Consideration of the Entity's Ability to Continue as a Going Concern* (Redrafted) (sec. 570), was issued. The Auditing Standards Board (ASB) moved forward with the clarity redraft of AU section 341, *The Auditor's Consideration of the Entity's Ability*

(continued)

AU-C Sections Designated by SAS No. 122		*AU Sections Superseded by SAS No. 122 (SAS Nos. 1–121 except SAS Nos. 51, 59, 65, 87, and 117–120)*		
AU-C Section	*Title*	*AU Section*	*Title*	*Paragraph*
580	*Written Representations*	333	*Management Representations*	All
585	*Consideration of Omitted Procedures After the Report Release Date*	390	*Consideration of Omitted Procedures After the Report Date*	All
600–699	**Using the Work of Others**			
600	*Special Considerations—Audits of Group Financial Statements (Including the Work of Component Auditors)*	508	*Reports on Audited Financial Statements*	.12–.13
		543	*Part of Audit Performed by Other Independent Auditors*	All
610[7]	*The Auditor's Consideration of the Internal Audit Function in an Audit of Financial Statements*	322	*The Auditor's Consideration of the Internal Audit Function in an Audit of Financial Statements*	All
620	*Using the Work of an Auditor's Specialist*	336	*Using the Work of a Specialist*	All
700–799	**Audit Conclusions and Reporting**			
700	*Forming an Opinion and Reporting on Financial Statements*	410	*Adherence to Generally Accepted Accounting Principles*	All
		530	*Dating of the Independent Auditor's Report*	.01–.02
		508	*Reports on Audited Financial Statements*	.01–.11, .14–.15, .19–.32, .35–.52, .58–.70, and .74–.76[8]

(footnote continued)

to Continue as a Going Concern, in order to be consistent with the format of the other clarified SASs that were recently issued as SAS Nos. 122–125. However, the ASB has decided to delay convergence with International Standard on Auditing (ISA) 570, *Going Concern*, pending the Financial Accounting Standards Board's anticipated development of accounting guidance addressing going concern.

[7] SAS No. 65, *The Auditor's Consideration of the Internal Audit Function in an Audit of Financial Statements*, is currently effective and codified as AU section 322. SAS No. 122 redesignates AU section 322 as AU-C section 610, which will be superseded when it is redrafted for clarity and convergence with ISA 610 (Revised), *Using the Work of Internal Auditors*, as part of the Clarification and Convergence Project of the ASB. Until such time, AU-C section 610 has been conformed to reflect updated section and paragraph cross references, but has not otherwise been subjected to a comprehensive review or revision.

[8] AU-C section 705, *Modifications to the Opinion in the Independent Auditor's Report*, and AU-C section 706, *Emphasis-of-Matter Paragraphs and Other-Matter Paragraphs in the Independent Auditor's Report*, also supersede paragraphs .01–.11, .14–.15, .19–.32, .35–.52, .58–.70, and .74–.76 of AU section 508, *Reports on Audited Financial Statements*.

AU-C Sections Designated by SAS No. 122		AU Sections Superseded by SAS No. 122 (SAS Nos. 1–121 except SAS Nos. 51, 59, 65, 87, and 117–120)		
AU-C Section	*Title*	*AU Section*	*Title*	*Paragraph*
705	*Modifications to the Opinion in the Independent Auditor's Report*	431	*Adequacy of Disclosure in Financial Statements*	All
		508	*Reports on Audited Financial Statements*	.01–.11, .14–.15, .19–.32, .35–.52, .58–.70, and .74–.76[9]
706	*Emphasis-of-Matter Paragraphs and Other-Matter Paragraphs in the Independent Auditor's Report*	508	*Reports on Audited Financial Statements*	.01–.11, .14–.15, .19–.32, .35–.52, .58–.70, and .74–.76[10]
708	*Consistency of Financial Statements*	420	*Consistency of Application of Generally Accepted Accounting Principles*	All
		508	*Reports on Audited Financial Statements*	.16–.18 and .53–.57
720[11]	*Other Information in Documents Containing Audited Financial Statements*	550	*Other Information in Documents Containing Audited Financial Statements*	All
725[12]	*Supplementary Information in Relation to the Financial Statements as a Whole*	551	*Supplementary Information in Relation to the Financial Statements as a Whole*	All
730[13]	*Required Supplementary Information*	558	*Required Supplementary Information*	All

(continued)

[9] AU-C section 700, *Forming an Opinion and Reporting on Financial Statements*, and AU-C section 706 also supersede paragraphs paragraphs .01–.11, .14–.15, .19–.32, .35–.52, .58–.70, and .74–.76 of AU section 508.

[10] AU-C section 700 and AU-C section 705 also supersede paragraphs .01–.11, .14–.15, .19–.32, .35–.52, .58–.70, and .74–.76 of AU section 508.

[11] To address practice issues, SAS No. 118, *Other Information in Documents Containing Audited Financial Statements*, was issued in February 2010 as a SAS resulting from the Clarification and Convergence Project of the ASB, and is effective for audits of financial statements for periods beginning on or after December 15, 2010. SAS No. 118 was originally codified as AU section 550. SAS No. 122 redesignates AU section 550 as AU-C section 720 but does not supersede SAS No. 118. AU-C section 720 contains conforming changes necessary due to the issuance of SAS No. 122.

[12] To address practice issues, SAS No. 119, *Supplementary Information in Relation to the Financial Statements as a Whole*, was issued in February 2010 as a SAS resulting from the Clarification and Convergence Project of the ASB, and is effective for audits of financial statements for periods beginning on or after December 15, 2010. SAS No. 119 was originally codified as AU section 551. SAS No. 122 redesignates AU section 551 as AU-C section 725 but does not supersede SAS No. 119. AU-C section 725 contains conforming changes necessary due to the issuance of SAS No. 122.

[13] To address practice issues, SAS No. 120, *Required Supplementary Information*, was issued in February 2010 as a SAS resulting from the Clarification and Convergence Project of the ASB, and is effective for audits of financial statements for periods beginning on or after December 15, 2010. SAS No. 120 was originally codified as AU section 558. SAS No. 122 redesignates AU section 558 as AU-C section 730 but does not supersede SAS No. 120. AU-C section 730 contains conforming changes necessary due to the issuance of SAS No. 122.

AU-C Sections Designated by SAS No. 122		AU Sections Superseded by SAS No. 122 (SAS Nos. 1–121 except SAS Nos. 51, 59, 65, 87, and 117–120)		
AU-C Section	*Title*	*AU Section*	*Title*	*Paragraph*
800–899	**Special Considerations**			
800	*Special Considerations—Audits of Financial Statements Prepared in Accordance With Special Purpose Frameworks*	544	*Lack of Conformity With Generally Accepted Accounting Principles*	All
		623	*Special Reports*	.01–.10 and .22–.34
805	*Special Considerations—Audits of Single Financial Statements and Specific Elements, Accounts, or Items of a Financial Statement*	508	*Reports on Audited Financial Statements*	.33–.34
		623	*Special Reports*	.11–.18
806	*Reporting on Compliance With Aspects of Contractual Agreements or Regulatory Requirements in Connection With Audited Financial Statements*	623	*Special Reports*	.19–.21
810	*Engagements to Report on Summary Financial Statements*	552	*Reporting on Condensed Financial Statements and Selected Financial Data*	All
900–999	**Special Considerations in the United States**			
905	*Alert That Restricts the Use of the Auditor's Written Communication*	532	*Restricting the Use of an Auditor's Report*	All
910	*Financial Statements Prepared in Accordance With a Financial Reporting Framework Generally Accepted in Another Country*	534	*Reporting on Financial Statements Prepared for Use in Other Countries*	All
915	*Reports on Application of Requirements of an Applicable Financial Reporting Framework*	625	*Reports on the Application of Accounting Principles*	All
920	*Letters for Underwriters and Certain Other Requesting Parties*	634	*Letters for Underwriters and Certain Other Requesting Parties*	All
925	*Filings With the U.S. Securities and Exchange Commission Under the Securities Act of 1933*	711	*Filings Under Federal Securities Statutes*	All
930	*Interim Financial Information*	722	*Interim Financial Information*	All

AU-C Sections Designated by SAS No. 122		*AU Sections Superseded by SAS No. 122 (SAS Nos. 1–121 except SAS Nos. 51, 59, 65, 87, and 117–120)*		
AU-C Section	*Title*	*AU Section*	*Title*	*Paragraph*
935[14]	*Compliance Audits*	801	*Compliance Audits*	All
		504[15]	*Association With Financial Statements*	All

[14] To address practice issues, SAS No. 117, *Compliance Audits*, was issued in December 2009 as a SAS resulting from the Clarification and Convergence Project of the ASB, and is effective for compliance audits for fiscal periods ending on or after June 15, 2010. SAS No. 117 was originally codified as AU section 801. SAS No. 122 redesignates AU section 801 as AU-C section 935 but does not supersede SAS No. 117. AU-C section 935 contains conforming changes necessary due to the issuance of SAS No. 122.

[15] The ASB has withdrawn AU section 504, *Association With Financial Statements*, and addressed its content in AU-C section 200, *Overall Objectives of the Independent Auditor and the Conduct of an Audit in Accordance With Generally Accepted Auditing Standards*, AU-C section 230, *Audit Documentation*, AU-C section 260, *The Auditor's Communication With Those Charged With Governance*, AU-C section 705, and AU-C section 915, *Reports on Application of Requirements of an Applicable Financial Reporting Framework*, and through proposed amendments to Statements on Standards for Accounting and Review Services to the extent needed.

Part II—AU Section to AU-C Section Cross References

AU Sections Superseded by SAS No. 122 (SAS Nos. 1–121 except SAS Nos. 51, 59, 65, 87, and 117–120)			*AU-C Sections Designated by SAS No. 122* *	
AU Section	*Title*	*Paragraph*	*AU-C Section*	*Title*
100	**Introduction**			
110	*Responsibilities and Functions of the Independent Auditor*	All	200	*Overall Objectives of the Independent Auditor and the Conduct of an Audit in Accordance With Generally Accepted Auditing Standards*
120	*Defining Professional Requirements in Statements on Auditing Standards*	All		
150	*Generally Accepted Auditing Standards*	All		
161	*The Relationship of Generally Accepted Auditing Standards to Quality Control Standards*	All	220	*Quality Control for an Engagement Conducted in Accordance With Generally Accepted Auditing Standards*
200	**The General Standards**			
201	*Nature of the General Standards*	All	200	*Overall Objectives of the Independent Auditor and the Conduct of an Audit in Accordance With Generally Accepted Auditing Standards*
210	*Training and Proficiency of the Independent Auditor*	All		
220	*Independence*	All		
230	*Due Professional Care in the Performance of Work*	All		
300	**The Standards of Field Work**			
311	*Planning and Supervision*	All except .08–.10	300	*Planning an Audit*
		.08–.10	210	*Terms of Engagement*
312	*Audit Risk and Materiality in Conducting an Audit*	All	320	*Materiality in Planning and Performing an Audit*
			450	*Evaluation of Misstatements Identified During the Audit*
314	*Understanding the Entity and Its Environment and Assessing the Risks of Material Misstatement*	All	315	*Understanding the Entity and Its Environment and Assessing the Risks of Material Misstatement*
315	*Communications Between Predecessor and Successor Auditors*	All except .03–.10 and .14	510	*Opening Balances—Initial Audit Engagements, Including Reaudit Engagements*
		.03–.10 and .14	210	*Terms of Engagement*

* Statement on Auditing Standards (SAS) No. 122, *Statements on Auditing Standards: Clarification and Recodification*, contains "AU-C" section numbers instead of "AU" section numbers. "AU-C" is a temporary identifier to avoid confusion with references to existing "AU" sections, which remain effective through 2013. The "AU-C" identifier will revert to "AU" in 2014, by which time SAS No. 122 becomes fully effective for all engagements.

AU Sections Superseded by SAS No. 122 (SAS Nos. 1–121 except SAS Nos. 51, 59, 65, 87, and 117–120)			*AU-C Sections Designated by SAS No. 122*	
AU Section	*Title*	*Paragraph*	*AU-C Section*	*Title*
316	*Consideration of Fraud in a Financial Statement Audit*	All	240	*Consideration of Fraud in a Financial Statement Audit*
317	*Illegal Acts by Clients*	All	250	*Consideration of Laws and Regulations in an Audit of Financial Statements*
318	*Performing Audit Procedures in Response to Assessed Risks and Evaluating the Audit Evidence Obtained*	All	330	*Performing Audit Procedures in Response to Assessed Risks and Evaluating the Audit Evidence Obtained*
322	*The Auditor's Consideration of the Internal Audit Function in an Audit of Financial Statements*	All	610[1]	*The Auditor's Consideration of the Internal Audit Function in an Audit of Financial Statements*
324[2]	*Service Organizations*	All	402	*Audit Considerations Relating to an Entity Using a Service Organization*
325	*Communicating Internal Control Related Matters Identified in an Audit*	All	265	*Communicating Internal Control Related Matters Identified in an Audit*
326	*Audit Evidence*	All	500	*Audit Evidence*
328	*Auditing Fair Value Measurements and Disclosures*	All	540	*Auditing Accounting Estimates, Including Fair Value Accounting Estimates, and Related Disclosures*
329	*Analytical Procedures*	All	520	*Analytical Procedures*
330	*The Confirmation Process*	All	505	*External Confirmations*
331	*Inventories*	All	501	*Audit Evidence—Specific Considerations for Selected Items*
332	*Auditing Derivative Instruments, Hedging Activities, and Investments in Securities*	All		
333	*Management Representations*	All	580	*Written Representations*
334	*Related Parties*	All	550	*Related Parties*
336	*Using the Work of a Specialist*	All	620	*Using the Work of an Auditor's Specialist*

(continued)

[1] Statement on Auditing Standards (SAS) No. 65, *The Auditor's Consideration of the Internal Audit Function in an Audit of Financial Statements*, is currently effective and codified as AU section 322. SAS No. 122 redesignates AU section 322 as AU-C section 610, which will be superseded when it is redrafted for clarity and convergence with International Standard on Auditing (ISA) 610 (Revised), *Using the Work of Internal Auditors*, as part of the Clarification and Convergence Project of the Auditing Standards Board (ASB). Until such time, AU-C section 610 has been conformed to reflect updated section and paragraph cross references, but has not otherwise been subjected to a comprehensive review or revision.

[2] AU section 324, *Service Organizations*, is also superseded by Statement on Standards for Attestation Engagements No. 16, *Reporting on Controls at a Service Organization* (AT sec. 801).

AU Sections Superseded by SAS No. 122 (SAS Nos. 1–121 except SAS Nos. 51, 59, 65, 87, and 117–120)			*AU-C Sections Designated by SAS No. 122*	
AU Section	*Title*	*Paragraph*	*AU-C Section*	*Title*
337	*Inquiry of a Client's Lawyer Concerning Litigation, Claims, and Assessments*	All except AU 337B[3]	501	*Audit Evidence—Specific Considerations for Selected Items*
339	*Audit Documentation*	All	230	*Audit Documentation*
341	*The Auditor's Consideration of an Entity's Ability to Continue as a Going Concern*	All	570[4]	*The Auditor's Consideration of an Entity's Ability to Continue as a Going Concern*
342	*Auditing Accounting Estimates*	All	540	*Auditing Accounting Estimates, Including Fair Value Accounting Estimates, and Related Disclosures*
350	*Audit Sampling*	All	530	*Audit Sampling*
380	*The Auditor's Communication With Those Charged With Governance*	All	260	*The Auditor's Communication With Those Charged With Governance*
390	*Consideration of Omitted Procedures After the Report Date*	All	585	*Consideration of Omitted Procedures After the Report Release Date*
400	**The First, Second, and Third Standards of Reporting**			
410	*Adherence to Generally Accepted Accounting Principles*	All	700	*Forming an Opinion and Reporting on Financial Statements*
420	*Consistency of Application of Generally Accepted Accounting Principles*	All	708	*Consistency of Financial Statements*
431	*Adequacy of Disclosure in Financial Statements*	All	705	*Modifications to the Opinion in the Independent Auditor's Report*
500	**The Fourth Standard of Reporting**			
504[5]	*Association With Financial Statements*	All		

[3] AU section 337B, *Exhibit I—Excerpts From Financial Accounting Standards Board* Accounting Standards Codification *450, Contingencies*, is withdrawn by AU-C section 501, *Audit Evidence—Specific Considerations for Selected Items.*

[4] In July 2012, SAS No. 126, *The Auditor's Consideration of the Entity's Ability to Continue as a Going Concern* (Redrafted) (sec. 570), was issued. The Auditing Standards Board (ASB) moved forward with the clarity redraft of AU section 341, *The Auditor's Consideration of the Entity's Ability to Continue as a Going Concern*, in order to be consistent with the format of the other clarified SASs that were recently issued as SAS Nos. 122–125. However, the ASB has decided to delay convergence with ISA 570, *Going Concern*, pending the Financial Accounting Standards Board's anticipated development of accounting guidance addressing going concern.

[5] The ASB has withdrawn AU section 504, *Association With Financial Statements*, and addressed its content in AU-C section 200, *Overall Objectives of the Independent Auditor and the Conduct of an Audit in Accordance With Generally Accepted Auditing Standards*, AU-C section 230,

(continued)

AU Sections Superseded by SAS No. 122 (SAS Nos. 1–121 except SAS Nos. 51, 59, 65, 87, and 117–120)			*AU-C Sections Designated by SAS No. 122*	
AU Section	*Title*	*Paragraph*	*AU-C Section*	*Title*
508	*Reports on Audited Financial Statements*	.01–.11, .14–.15, .19–.32, .35–.52, .58–.70, and .74–.76	700	*Forming an Opinion and Reporting on Financial Statements*
			705	*Modifications to the Opinion in the Independent Auditor's Report*
			706	*Emphasis-of-Matter Paragraphs and Other-Matter Paragraphs in the Independent Auditor's Report*
		.12–.13	600	*Special Considerations—Audits of Group Financial Statements (Including the Work of Component Auditors)*
		.16–.18 and .53–.57	708	*Consistency of Financial Statements*
		.33–.34	805	*Special Considerations—Audits of Single Financial Statements and Specific Elements, Accounts, or Items of a Financial Statement*
		.71–.73	560	*Subsequent Events and Subsequently Discovered Facts*
530	*Dating of the Independent Auditor's Report*	.01–.02	700	*Forming an Opinion and Reporting on Financial Statements*
		.03–.08	560	*Subsequent Events and Subsequently Discovered Facts*
532	*Restricting the Use of an Auditor's Report*	All	905	*Alert That Restricts the Use of the Auditor's Written Communication*
534	*Reporting on Financial Statements Prepared for Use in Other Countries*	All	910	*Financial Statements Prepared in Accordance With a Financial Reporting Framework Generally Accepted in Another Country*
543	*Part of Audit Performed by Other Independent Auditors*	All	600	*Special Considerations—Audits of Group Financial Statements (Including the Work of Component Auditors)*

(continued)

(footnote continued)

Audit Documentation, AU-C section 260, *The Auditor's Communication With Those Charged With Governance*, AU-C section 705, *Modifications to the Opinion in the Independent Auditor's Report*, and AU-C section 915, *Reports on Application of Requirements of an Applicable Financial Reporting Framework*, and through proposed amendments to Statements on Standards for Accounting and Review Services to the extent needed.

AU Sections Superseded by SAS No. 122 (SAS Nos. 1–121 except SAS Nos. 51, 59, 65, 87, and 117–120)			AU-C Sections Designated by SAS No. 122	
AU Section	*Title*	*Paragraph*	*AU-C Section*	*Title*
544	*Lack of Conformity With Generally Accepted Accounting Principles*	All	800	*Special Considerations—Audits of Financial Statements Prepared in Accordance With Special Purpose Frameworks*
550	*Other Information in Documents Containing Audited Financial Statements*	All	720[6]	*Other Information in Documents Containing Audited Financial Statements*
551	*Supplementary Information in Relation to the Financial Statements as a Whole*	All	725[7]	*Supplementary Information in Relation to the Financial Statements as a Whole*
552	*Reporting on Condensed Financial Statements and Selected Financial Data*	All	810	*Engagements to Report on Summary Financial Statements*
558	*Required Supplementary Information*	All	730[8]	*Required Supplementary Information*
560	*Subsequent Events*	All	560	*Subsequent Events and Subsequently Discovered Facts*
561	*Subsequent Discovery of Facts Existing at the Date of the Auditor's Report*	All	560	*Subsequent Events and Subsequently Discovered Facts*

[6] To address practice issues, SAS No. 118, *Other Information in Documents Containing Audited Financial Statements*, was issued in February 2010 as a SAS resulting from the Clarification and Convergence Project of the ASB, and is effective for audits of financial statements for periods beginning on or after December 15, 2010. SAS No. 118 was originally codified as AU section 550. SAS No. 122 redesignates AU section 550 as AU-C section 720 but does not supersede SAS No. 118. AU-C section 720 contains conforming changes necessary due to the issuance of SAS No. 122.

[7] To address practice issues, SAS No. 119, *Supplementary Information in Relation to the Financial Statements as a Whole*, was issued in February 2010 as a SAS resulting from the Clarification and Convergence Project of the ASB, and is effective for audits of financial statements for periods beginning on or after December 15, 2010. SAS No. 119 was originally codified as AU section 551. SAS No. 122 redesignates AU section 551 as AU-C section 725 but does not supersede SAS No. 119. AU-C section 725 contains conforming changes necessary due to the issuance of SAS No. 122.

[8] To address practice issues, SAS No. 120, *Required Supplementary Information*, was issued in February 2010 as a SAS resulting from the Clarification and Convergence Project of the ASB, and is effective for audits of financial statements for periods beginning on or after December 15, 2010. SAS No. 120 was originally codified as AU section 558. SAS No. 122 redesignates AU section 558 as AU-C section 730 but does not supersede SAS No. 120. AU-C section 730 contains conforming changes necessary due to the issuance of SAS No. 122.

AU Sections Superseded by SAS No. 122 (SAS Nos. 1–121 except SAS Nos. 51, 59, 65, 87, and 117–120)			*AU-C Sections Designated by SAS No. 122*	
AU Section	*Title*	*Paragraph*	*AU-C Section*	*Title*
600	**Other Types of Reports**			
623	*Special Reports*	.01–.10 and .22–.34	800	*Special Considerations—Audits of Financial Statements Prepared in Accordance With Special Purpose Frameworks*
		.11–.18	805	*Special Considerations—Audits of Single Financial Statements and Specific Elements, Accounts, or Items of a Financial Statement*
		.19–.21	806	*Reporting on Compliance With Aspects of Contractual Agreements or Regulatory Requirements in Connection With Audited Financial Statements*
625	*Reports on the Application of Accounting Principles*	All	915	*Reports on Application of Requirements of an Applicable Financial Reporting Framework*
634	*Letters for Underwriters and Certain Other Requesting Parties*	All	920	*Letters for Underwriters and Certain Other Requesting Parties*
700	**Special Topics**			
711	*Filings Under Federal Securities Statutes*	All	925	*Filings With the U.S. Securities and Exchange Commission Under the Securities Act of 1933*
722	*Interim Financial Information*	All	930	*Interim Financial Information*
800	**Compliance Auditing**			
801	*Compliance Audits*	All	935[9]	*Compliance Audits*

(continued)

[9] To address practice issues, SAS No. 117, *Compliance Audits*, was issued in December 2009 as a SAS resulting from the Clarification and Convergence Project of the ASB, and is effective for compliance audits for fiscal periods ending on or after June 15, 2010. SAS No. 117 was originally codified as AU section 801. SAS No. 122 redesignates AU section 801 as AU-C section 935 but does not supersede SAS No. 117. AU-C section 935 contains conforming changes necessary due to the issuance of SAS No. 122.

AU Sections Superseded by SAS No. 122 (SAS Nos. 1–121 except SAS Nos. 51, 59, 65, 87, and 117–120)			*AU-C Sections Designated by SAS No. 122*	
AU Section	*Title*	*Paragraph*	*AU-C Section*	*Title*
900	**Special Reports of the Committee on Auditing Procedure**			
901[10]	*Public Warehouses—Controls and Auditing Procedures for Goods Held*	All	501	*Audit Evidence—Specific Considerations for Selected Items*

[10] AU section 901, *Public Warehouses—Controls and Auditing Procedures for Goods Held,* is withdrawn by AU-C section 501.

AU-C Exhibit B

Retained Interpretations

Auditing interpretations of generally accepted auditing standards (GAAS) are *interpretive publications*, as defined in section 200, *Overall Objectives of the Independent Auditor and the Conduct of an Audit in Accordance With Generally Accepted Auditing Standards.* Section 200 requires the auditor to consider applicable interpretive publications in planning and performing the audit. Interpretive publications are not auditing standards. Interpretive publications are recommendations on the application of GAAS in specific circumstances, including engagements for entities in specialized industries. An interpretive publication is issued under the authority of the Auditing Standards Board (ASB) after all ASB members have been provided an opportunity to consider and comment on whether the proposed interpretive publication is consistent with GAAS. Auditing interpretations of GAAS are included in AU-C sections.

All auditing interpretations corresponding to a Statement on Auditing Standards (SAS) have been considered in the development of a clarified SAS and incorporated accordingly, and have been withdrawn by the ASB except for the following interpretations that the ASB has retained and revised to reflect the issuance of AU-C sections. The effective date of the revised interpretations aligns with the effective date of the corresponding clarified SAS:

Former Interpretations			*Revised Interpretations*		
AU Section	*Interpretation No.*	*Title*	*AU-C Section**	*Interpretation No.*	*Title*
9325 par. .04–.06	2	Communication of Significant Deficiencies and Material Weaknesses Prior to the Completion of the Compliance Audit for Participants in Office of Management and Budget Single Audit Pilot Project	9265 par. .01–.03	1	Communication of Significant Deficiencies and Material Weaknesses Prior to the Completion of the Compliance Audit for Participants in Office of Management and Budget Single Audit Pilot Project

(continued)

* Statement on Auditing Standards (SAS) No. 122, *Statements on Auditing Standards: Clarification and Recodification*, contains "AU-C" section numbers instead of "AU" section numbers. "AU-C" is a temporary identifier to avoid confusion with references to existing "AU" sections, which remain effective through 2013. The "AU-C" identifier will revert to "AU" in 2014, by which time SAS No. 122 becomes fully effective for all engagements.

Former Interpretations			*Revised Interpretations*		
AU Section	*Interpretation No.*	*Title*	*AU-C Section*	*Interpretation No.*	*Title*
9325 par. .07–.10	3	Communication of Significant Deficiencies and Material Weaknesses Prior to the Completion of the Compliance Audit for Auditors That Are Not Participants in Office of Management and Budget Pilot Project	9265 par. .04–.07	2	Communication of Significant Deficiencies and Material Weaknesses Prior to the Completion of the Compliance Audit for Auditors That Are Not Participants in Office of Management and Budget Pilot Project
9325 par. .11–.13	4	Appropriateness of Identifying No Significant Deficiencies or No Material Weaknesses in an Interim Communication	9265 par. .08–.10	3	Appropriateness of Identifying No Significant Deficiencies or No Material Weaknesses in an Interim Communication
9326 par. .06–.23	2	The Effect of an Inability to Obtain Audit Evidence Relating to Income Tax Accruals	9500 par. .01–.22	1	The Effect of an Inability to Obtain Audit Evidence Relating to Income Tax Accruals
9336 par. .01–.21	1	The Use of Legal Interpretations As Audit Evidence to Support Management's Assertion That a Transfer of Financial Assets Has Met the Isolation Criterion in Paragraphs 7–14 of Financial Accounting Standards Board *Accounting Standards Codification* 860-10-40	9620 par. .01–.21	1	The Use of Legal Interpretations as Audit Evidence to Support Management's Assertion That a Transfer of Financial Assets Has Met the Isolation Criterion in Paragraphs 7–14 of Financial Accounting Standards Board *Accounting Standards Codification* 860-10-40
9508 par. .33–[.38]	8	Reporting on Financial Statements Prepared on a Liquidation Basis of Accounting	9700 par. .01–.05	1	Reporting on Financial Statements Prepared on a Liquidation Basis of Accounting
9551 par. .01–.04	1	Dating the Auditor's Report on Supplementary Information	9725 par. .01–.04	1	Dating the Auditor's Report on Supplementary Information

AU-C Appendixes

TABLE OF CONTENTS

AU-C Appendix A
Historical Background

In 1917, the American Institute of Certified Public Accountants, then known as the American Institute of Accountants, at the request of the Federal Trade Commission, prepared "a memorandum on balance-sheet audits," which the Federal Trade Commission approved and transmitted to the Federal Reserve Board.

The Federal Reserve Board, after giving the memorandum its provisional endorsement, published it in the *Federal Reserve Bulletin* of April 1917; reprints were widely disseminated for the consideration of "banks, bankers, banking associations; merchants, manufacturers, and associations of manufacturers; auditors, accountants, and associations of accountants" in pamphlet form with the title of "Uniform Accounting: a Tentative Proposal Submitted by the Federal Reserve Board."

In 1918, it was reissued under the same sponsorship, with a new title "Approved Methods for the Preparation of Balance-Sheet Statements." There was practically no change from 1917 except that, as indicated by the respective titles and corresponding change in the preface, instead of the objective of "a uniform system of accounting to be adopted by manufacturing and merchandising concerns," the new objective was "the preparation of balance-sheet statements" for the same businesses.

In 1929, a special committee of the Institute undertook revision of the earlier pamphlet in the light of the experience of the past decade; again under the auspices of the Federal Reserve Board, the revised pamphlet was issued in 1929 as "Verification of Financial Statements."

The preface of the 1929 pamphlet spoke of its predecessors as having been criticized, on the one hand, by some accountants for being "more comprehensive than their conception of the so-called balance-sheet audit," and, on the other hand, by other accountants because "the procedure would not bring out all the desired information." This recognition of opposing views evidenced the growing realization of the impracticability of uniform procedures to fit the variety of situations encountered in practice. Of significance is the appearance in the opening paragraph of "General Instructions" in the 1929 publication of the statement:

> The extent of the verification will be determined by the conditions in each concern. In some cases, the auditor may find it necessary to verify a substantial portion or all of the transactions recorded upon the books. In others, where the system of internal check is good, tests only may suffice. The responsibility for the extent of the work required must be assumed by the auditor.

Between 1932 and 1934, there was correspondence, dealing with both accounting and auditing matters, between the Institute's special committee on cooperation with stock exchanges and the committee on stock list of the New York Stock Exchange. The views expressed were an important development in the recognition of the position of accountancy in finance and business. The series of letters was published in 1934 under the title *Audits of Corporate Accounts*.

In 1936, a committee of the Institute prepared and published a further revision of the earlier pamphlets under the title of "Examination of Financial Statements by Independent Public Accountants." The Institute availed itself of the views of persons outside the ranks of the profession whose opinions would be helpful, but the authority behind and responsibility for the publication of the pamphlet rested wholly with the Institute as the authoritative representative of a profession that had by that time become well established in the business community.

In the 1936 revision, aside from the very briefly noted "Modifications of Program for Larger or Smaller Companies," the detailed procedures were restrictively stated to be an "outline of examination of financial statements of a small or moderate size company." Moreover, the nature and extent of such examinations were based on the purpose of the examination, the required detail to be reported on, the type of business, and, most important of all, the system of internal control; variations in the extent of the examination were specifically related to "the size of the organization and the personnel employed" and were said to be "essentially a matter of judgment which must be exercised by the accountant."

It is possible from the foregoing narrative to trace the development of the profession's view of an audit based on the experience of three decades. The succession of titles is illustrative. The earliest ambition for "uniform accounting" was quickly realized to be unattainable, and the same listed procedures were related instead to "balance-sheet statements." Then, with the gradually greater emphasis on periodic earnings, the earlier restrictive consideration of the balance sheet was superseded in the 1929 title, "Verification of Financial Statements," by according the income statement at least equal status. When in turn the 1936 revision was undertaken, there was a growing realization that, with the complexity of modern business and the need of the independent auditor to rely on testing, such a word as "verification" was not an accurate portrayal of the independent auditor's function. Accordingly, the bulletin of that year was stated to cover an "examination" of financial statements.

Statements on Auditing Procedure

The Committee on Auditing Procedure had its beginning on January 30, 1939, when the executive committee of the Institute authorized the appointment of a small committee "to examine into auditing procedure and other related questions in the light of recent public discussion."

On May 9 of that year, the report "Extensions of Auditing Procedure" of this special committee was adopted by the Council of the Institute and authority given for its publication and distribution, and in the same year the bylaws were amended to create a standing Committee on Auditing Procedure.

In 1941, the executive committee authorized the issuance to Institute members, in pamphlet form, of the Statements on Auditing Procedure, prepared by the Committee on Auditing Procedure, previously published only in *The Journal of Accountancy*.

The Statements on Auditing Procedure were designed to guide the independent auditor in the exercise of his judgment in the application of auditing procedures. In no sense were they intended to take the place of auditing textbooks; by their very nature textbooks must deal in a general way with the description of procedures and refinement of detail rather than the variety of circumstances encountered in practice that require the independent auditor to exercise his judgment.

Largely to meet this need, the Institute began the series of Statements on Auditing Procedure. The first of these presented the report of the original special committee, as modified and approved, at the Institute's annual meeting on September 19, 1939, and issued under the title of "Extensions of Auditing Procedure."

Statement No. 1 presented conclusions drawn from the experience and tradition of the profession which largely furnished the foundation for the Committee's present structural outline of auditing standards; the other Statements on Auditing Procedure appropriately fit into that structural outline.

The "Codification of Statements on Auditing Procedure" was issued by the Committee on Auditing Procedure in 1951 to consolidate the features of the first 24 pronouncements, which were of continuing usefulness.

When the Securities and Exchange Commission (SEC) adopted the requirement that a representation on compliance with generally accepted auditing standards be included in the independent auditor's report on financial statements filed with the SEC, it became apparent that a pronouncement was needed to define these standards. Accordingly, the Committee on Auditing Procedure undertook a special study of auditing standards (as distinguished from auditing procedures) and submitted a report that was published in October 1947 under the title "Tentative Statement of Auditing Standards—Their Generally Accepted Significance and Scope." The recommendations of this brochure ceased to be tentative when, at the September 1948 meeting, the membership of the Institute approved the summarized statement of auditing standards.

In 1954 the tentative brochure was replaced by the booklet *Generally Accepted Auditing Standards—Their Significance and Scope*, which was issued as a special report of the Committee on Auditing Procedure. This pronouncement also gave recognition to the approval of Statement on Auditing Procedure No. 23 (Revised), *Clarification of Accountant's Report When Opinion Is Omitted* (1949) and the issuance of the codification (1951).

Statement on Auditing Procedure No. 33 was issued in 1963 as a consolidation of, and a replacement for, the following pronouncements of the Committee on Auditing Procedure: *Internal Control* (1949), *Generally Accepted Auditing Standards* (1954), *Codification of Statements on Auditing Procedure* (1951), and Statements on Auditing Procedure Nos. 25–32, which were issued between 1951 and 1963. Statement No. 33 was a codification of earlier committee pronouncements that the committee believed to be of continuing interest to the independent auditor.

Statements on Auditing Standards

After issuance of Statement on Auditing Procedure No. 33, 21 additional Statements on Auditing Procedure, Nos. 34–54, were issued by the Committee on Auditing Procedure. In November 1972, these pronouncements were codified in Statement on Auditing Standards (SAS) No. 1, *Codification of Auditing Standards and Procedures*. Also, in 1972, the name of the committee was changed to the Auditing Standards Executive Committee to recognize its role as the AICPA's senior technical committee charged with interpreting generally accepted auditing standards.

The Auditing Standards Executive Committee issued 22 additional statements through No. 23. These statements were incorporated in this publication, which provides a continuous codification of SASs.

Creation of the Auditing Standards Board

As a result of the recommendations of the Commission on Auditors' Responsibilities, an independent study group appointed by the AICPA, a special committee was formed to study the structure of the AICPA's auditing standard-setting activity. In May 1978, the AICPA Council adopted the recommendations of that committee to restructure the Committee. Accordingly, in October 1978 the Auditing Standards Board (ASB) was formed as the successor to prior senior technical committees on auditing matters. The ASB was given the following charge:

> The AICPA Auditing Standards Board shall be responsible for the promulgation of auditing standards and procedures to be observed by members of the AICPA in accordance with the Institute's rules of conduct.
>
> The board shall be alert to new opportunities for auditors to serve the public, both by the assumption of new responsibilities and by improved ways of meeting old ones, and shall as expeditiously as possible develop standards and procedures that will enable the auditor to assume those responsibilities.
>
> Auditing standards and procedures promulgated by the board shall—
>
> *a.* Define the nature and extent of the auditor's responsibilities.
>
> *b.* Provide guidance to the auditor in carrying out his duties, enabling him to express an opinion on the reliability of the representations on which he is reporting.
>
> *c.* Make special provision, where appropriate, to meet the needs of small enterprises.
>
> *d.* Have regard to the costs which they impose on society in relation to the benefits reasonably expected to be derived from the audit function.
>
> The Auditing Standards Board shall provide auditors with all possible guidance in the implementation of its pronouncements, by means of interpretations of its statements, by the issuance of guidelines, and by any other means available to it.

Changes Created by Sarbanes-Oxley Act of 2002

AICPA members who perform auditing and other related professional services have been required to comply with SASs promulgated by the AICPA ASB. These standards constitute what is known as generally accepted auditing standards (GAAS). Prior to Sarbanes-Oxley, the ASB's auditing standards have applied to audits of all entities. However, as a result of the passage of the Sarbanes-Oxley Act of 2002, auditing rules and related professional practice standards to be used in the performance of and reporting on audits of the financial statements of public companies (or issuers) are to be established by the Public Company Accounting Oversight Board (PCAOB). Accordingly, public accounting firms auditing issuers are now required to be registered with the PCAOB and to adhere to all PCAOB rules and standards in those audits. In 2003, the PCAOB adopted the then-existing Audit and Attest Standards as its interim auditing standards.

The preparation and issuance of audit reports for those entities not subject to the Sarbanes-Oxley Act or the rules of the SEC (hereinafter referred to as nonissuers) continue to be governed by GAAS promulgated by the ASB.

The Reconstituted ASB

In February 2004, the AICPA's Board of Directors unanimously recommended that the AICPA's Governing Council take the following action at its meeting in May 2004:

- Designate the PCAOB as a body with the authority to promulgate auditing and related attestation standards, quality control, ethics, independence, and other standards relating to the preparation and issuance of audit reports for issuers.
- Amend the ASB's current designation to recognize the ASB as a body with the authority to promulgate auditing, attestation, and quality control standards relating to the preparation and issuance of audit reports for non-issuers only.

As a result of this action, the ASB was reconstituted and its jurisdiction amended by AICPA Council to recognize the ASB as a body with the authority to promulgate auditing, attestation and quality control standards relating to the preparation and issuance of audit and attestation reports for nonissuers.

U.S. Auditing Standards—AICPA (Clarified)

In October 2011, the ASB issued SAS No. 122, *Statements on Auditing Standards: Clarification and Recodification*, which was the culmination of a multi-year Clarity Project to clarify the SASs and converge them with the International Standards on Auditing. Beginning with SAS No. 122, all new SASs are now included in the section *U.S. Auditing Standards—AICPA (Clarified)*. SAS No. 122 is effective for audits of financial statements for periods ending on or after December 15, 2012. Refer to individual AU-C sections for specific effective date language.

AU-C Appendix B

Substantive Differences Between the International Standards on Auditing and Generally Accepted Auditing Standards

> ***Note:*** This appendix refers to the new AU-C sections. For a complete listing of how the AU-C sections map to the extant AU sections, see AU-C exhibit A.

200–299	**GENERAL PRINCIPLES AND RESPONSIBILITIES**
ISA 200	Overall Objectives of the Independent Auditor and the Conduct of an Audit in Accordance with International Standards on Auditing
ISA 210	Agreeing the Terms of Audit Engagements
ISA 220	Quality Control for an Audit of Financial Statements
ISA 230	Audit Documentation
ISA 240	The Auditor's Responsibilities Relating to Fraud in an Audit of Financial Statements
ISA 250	Consideration of Laws and Regulations in an Audit of Financial Statements
ISA 260	Communication with Those Charged with Governance
ISA 265	Communicating Deficiencies in Internal Control to Those Charged with Governance and Management
300–499	**RISK ASSESSMENT AND RESPONSE TO ASSESSED RISKS**
ISA 300	Planning an Audit of Financial Statements
ISA 315	Identifying and Assessing the Risks of Material Misstatement through Understanding the Entity and Its Environment
ISA 320	Materiality in Planning and Performing an Audit
ISA 330	The Auditor's Responses to Assessed Risks
ISA 402	Audit Considerations Relating to an Entity Using a Service Organization
ISA 450	Evaluation of Misstatements Identified during the Audit
500–599	**AUDIT EVIDENCE**
ISA 500	Audit Evidence
ISA 501	Audit Evidence—Specific Considerations for Selected Items
ISA 505	External Confirmations
ISA 510	Initial Audit Engagements—Opening Balances
ISA 520	Analytical Procedures
ISA 530	Audit Sampling
ISA 540	Auditing Accounting Estimates, Including Fair Value Accounting Estimates, and Related Disclosures

(continued)

ISA 550	Related Parties
ISA 560	Subsequent Events
ISA 570	Going Concern (Not Converged)*
ISA 580	Written Representations
600–699	**USING THE WORK OF OTHERS**
ISA 600	Special Considerations—Audits of Group Financial Statements (Including the Work of Component Auditors)
ISA 610	Using the Work of Internal Auditors (Not Converged)†
ISA 620	Using the Work of an Auditor's Expert
700–799	**AUDIT CONCLUSIONS AND REPORTING**
ISA 700	Forming an Opinion and Reporting on Financial Statements
ISA 705	Modifications to the Opinion in the Independent Auditor's Report
ISA 706	Emphasis of Matter Paragraphs and Other Matter Paragraphs in the Independent Auditor's Report
ISA 710	Comparative Information—Corresponding Figures and Comparative Financial Statements
ISA 720	The Auditor's Responsibilities Relating to Other Information in Documents Containing Audited Financial Statements
800–899	**SPECIALIZED AREAS**
ISA 800	Special Considerations—Audits of Financial Statements Prepared in Accordance with Special Purpose Frameworks
ISA 805	Special Considerations—Audits of Single Financial Statements and Specific Elements, Accounts or Items of a Financial Statement
ISA 810	Engagements to Report on Summary Financial Statements

This analysis was prepared by the AICPA Audit and Attest Standards staff to highlight substantive differences between the Statements on Auditing Standards and International Standards on Auditing, and the rationales therefore. This analysis is not authoritative and is prepared for informational purposes only. It has not been acted on, or reviewed by, the Auditing Standards Board.

* In July 2012, Statement on Auditing Standards (SAS) No. 126, *The Auditor's Consideration of the Entity's Ability to Continue as a Going Concern* (sec. 570), was issued. The Auditing Standards Board (ASB) moved forward with the clarity redraft of AU section 341, *The Auditor's Consideration of the Entity's Ability to Continue as a Going Concern*, in order to be consistent with the format of the other clarified SASs that were recently issued as SAS Nos. 122–125. However, the ASB has decided to delay convergence with International Standard on Auditing 570, *Going Concern*, pending the Financial Accounting Standards Board's anticipated development of accounting guidance addressing going concern.

† SAS No. 65, *The Auditor's Consideration of the Internal Audit Function in an Audit of Financial Statements*, is currently effective and codified as former AU section 322. SAS No. 65 has been included in new section 610, as designated by SAS No. 122, *Statements on Auditing Standards: Clarification and Recodification*, and will be superseded when it is redrafted for clarity and convergence with International Standard on Auditing 610 (Revised), *Using the Work of Internal Auditors*, as part of the Clarification and Convergence project of the Auditing Standards Board. Until such time, new section 610 has been conformed to reflect updated section and paragraph cross references but has not otherwise been subjected to a comprehensive review or revision.

Statements on Auditing Standards (SASs) are issued by the Auditing Standards Board (ASB), the senior committee of the AICPA designated to issue pronouncements on auditing matter for nonissuers.[1] Rule 202, *Compliance With Standards* (ET sec. 202 par. .01), of the AICPA Code of Professional Conduct requires an AICPA member who performs an audit of a nonissuer to comply with standards promulgated by the ASB.

In 2007, the ASB began a project to clarify its standards to make them easier to read, understand, and apply, and to converge its standards with those developed by the International Auditing and Assurance Standards Board (IAASB) of the International Federation of Accountants (IFAC). Accordingly, the ASB established clarity drafting conventions and has revised all its SASs in accordance with those conventions, using corresponding International Standards on Auditing (ISAs) as a base. Each clarified SAS differs from its corresponding ISA only where the ASB believes compelling reasons exist for the differences. As described in this appendix, nearly all ISA requirements are also requirements of auditing standards generally accepted in the United States of America (GAAS). However, GAAS contain additional requirements that address issues specific to the United States of America or retain current practices.

An AICPA member practicing in the United States of America may be engaged to audit the financial statements of a nonissuer in accordance with the ISAs. In those circumstances where the auditor's report states that the audit was conducted in accordance with the ISAs, the U.S. auditor should comply with both the ISAs and, as required by the AICPA Code of Professional Conduct, GAAS. An engagement of this nature is normally conducted by performing an audit in accordance with GAAS plus performing any additional procedures required by the ISAs.

The purpose of this appendix is to assist the U.S. auditor in planning and performing an engagement in accordance with the ISAs. This document provides a brief description of how each ISA differs from the comparable U.S. standard. However, to fully understand how the ISA might affect the nature, timing, and extent of the procedures performed in an engagement in accordance with GAAS, the auditor should consider the ISAs in their entirety by considering the standards together with the related guidance included in the ISAs. In performing an audit in accordance with the ISAs, the auditor also needs to comply with IFAC's Code of Ethics.

This analysis compares the ISAs included in the 2010 edition of the *Handbook of International Quality Control, Auditing, Review, Other Assurance, and Related Services Pronouncements*, to the AICPA's *Professional Standards*. References to GAAS are made to the relevant AU sections. This analysis describes the differences in terms of

a. differences in language,

b. requirements in the ISAs not in GAAS,

c. requirements in GAAS not in the ISAs,

d. differences between requirements, and

e. the placement of certain requirements within GAAS.

---

[1] The term *issuer* means an issuer (as defined in Section 3 of the Securities Exchange Act of 1934 (15 U.S.C. 78c)), the securities of which are registered under Section 12 of that act (15 U.S.C. 78l), or that is required to file reports under Section 15(d) (15 U.S.C. 78o(d)), or that files or has filed a registration statement that has not yet become effective under the Securities Act of 1933 (15 U.S.C. 77a et seq.), and that it has not withdrawn. The term *nonissuer* refers to any entity not subject to the Sarbanes-Oxley Act or the rules of the Securities and Exchange Commission.

General

In converging with the ISAs, the ASB has made various changes to the language of the ISAs throughout the SASs. Such changes have been made to use terms applicable in the United States and to make the SASs easier to read and apply in the United States. The ASB believes that such changes do not create differences between the application of the ISAs and the application of GAAS. Selected changes are described in the analysis that follows.

ISA 200, *Overall Objectives of the Independent Auditor and the Conduct of an Audit in Accordance with International Standards on Auditing,* Compared to Section 200, *Overall Objectives of the Independent Auditor and the Conduct of an Audit in Accordance With Generally Accepted Auditing Standards*

Requirements in the ISAs Not in GAAS

The ISAs provide for reporting on financial statements that are prepared in accordance with fair presentation financial reporting frameworks and compliance financial reporting frameworks. In the ISAs, compliance frameworks do not necessarily require fair presentation. GAAS address reporting on financial statements that are prepared in accordance with fair presentation frameworks only, because the ASB believes that fair presentation frameworks are the only financial reporting frameworks used in the United States.

Requirements in GAAS Not in the ISAs

GAAS, as described in paragraph .25 of section 200, contain two categories of professional requirements: unconditional requirements and presumptively mandatory requirements. Paragraph .25 of section 200 describes the auditor's obligation to comply with (1) an unconditional requirement in all cases where such requirement is relevant, and (2) a presumptively mandatory requirement in all cases where such a requirement is relevant except in rare circumstances. The ISAs contain only one category of professional requirements, with which paragraphs 22–23 of ISA 200 require the auditor to comply when such requirements are relevant except in rare circumstances. The ASB retained two categories of professional requirements so as not to create unnecessary differences with the application of the auditing standards promulgated by the Public Company Accounting Oversight Board (PCAOB), which contain the same two categories of professional requirements as described in section 200.

Paragraphs .27–.28 of section 200 contain requirements relating to interpretive publications and other auditing publications. The ISAs do not address interpretive publications or other auditing publications.

ISA 210, *Agreeing the Terms of Audit Engagements,* Compared to Section 210, *Terms of Engagement*

Requirements in the ISAs Not in GAAS

Paragraphs 11–12 of ISA 210 contain requirements relating to situations when law or regulation prescribes management's responsibilities. Paragraph 18 of

ISA 210 contains requirements relating to situations when law or regulation supplements financial reporting standards established by an authorized or recognized standards-setting organization. The ASB believes that these situations are not applicable to nonissuers in the United States and, accordingly, such requirements are not included in GAAS.

Requirements in GAAS Not in the ISAs

Paragraphs .11–.12 of section 210 address the auditor's communications with predecessor auditors in initial audit or reaudit engagements. ISA 210 does not contain these requirements. The ASB believes these requirements and related application material are appropriate for inclusion in GAAS.

Paragraph 13 of ISA 210 requires that for recurring audits, the auditor should assess whether there is a need to remind the entity of the existing terms of the engagement. Paragraph .13 of section 210 requires the auditor to remind the entity of the existing terms of the engagement and to document the reminder. The ASB believes that it is important to review the terms of the engagement with the entity each year.

Placement of Certain Requirements Within GAAS

Paragraphs 19–20 of ISA 210 contain requirements relating to situations when the financial reporting framework is prescribed by law or regulation. These requirements are addressed in section 800, *Special Considerations—Audits of Financial Statements Prepared in Accordance With Special Purpose Frameworks*. The different placement of these requirements does not create differences between the ISAs as a whole and GAAS as a whole.

ISA 220, *Quality Control for an Audit of Financial Statements*, Compared to Section 220, *Quality Control for an Engagement Conducted in Accordance With Generally Accepted Auditing Standards*

Requirements in the ISAs Not in GAAS

Paragraph 21 of ISA 220 contains requirements relating to audits of listed entities. Such requirements are not applicable to audits of nonissuers in the United States and, accordingly, such requirements are not included in GAAS.

Differences Between Requirements

Paragraph .21 of section 220 requires that when an engagement quality control review is performed, the engagement quality control review be completed before the engagement partner releases the auditor's report. Paragraph 19 of ISA 220 requires that the quality control review be completed before the engagement partner dates the auditor's report. The ASB believes that an engagement quality control review is an independent review of the engagement team's significant judgments, including the date selected by the engagement team to date the report. As noted in the application material to section 220, when the engagement quality control review results in additional procedures being performed, the date of the report would be changed.

ISA 230, *Audit Documentation*, Compared to Section 230, *Audit Documentation*

Requirements in GAAS Not in the ISAs

Paragraph .10 of section 230 requires the auditor to include abstracts or copies of significant contracts or agreements in documentation of auditing procedures related to inspection of those significant contracts or agreements. ISA 230 does not require the auditor to include abstracts or copies of the entity's records. Paragraph A3 of ISA 230 (which is application material relating to the requirement in paragraph 8 of ISA 230, which corresponds to paragraph .08 in section 230) states, "the auditor may include abstracts or copies of the entity's records (for example, significant and specific contracts and agreements) as part of audit documentation."

When performing auditing procedures related to inspection of significant contracts or agreements, the ASB believes that, in the context of the preparation of audit documentation that is sufficient to enable an experienced auditor to understand the audit evidence obtained, it is important to include abstracts or copies of such contracts or agreements. Further, the PCAOB standards include a requirement that documentation of auditing procedures related to the inspection of significant contracts or agreements should include abstracts or copies of the documents.[2] The ASB does not want to create a difference with PCAOB standards in this regard.

Differences Between Requirements

Paragraph 14 of ISA 230 requires the auditor to assemble the audit documentation in an audit file and complete the administrative process of assembling the final audit file on a timely basis after the date of the auditor's report, and the related application and other explanatory material indicates that an appropriate time limit within which to complete the assembly of the final audit file is ordinarily not more than 60 days after the date of the auditor's report. Paragraph .16 of section 230 requires the auditor to assemble the audit documentation in an audit file and complete the administrative process of assembling the final audit file on a timely basis, no later than 60 days following the report release date. The auditor is required by paragraph .15 of section 230 to document the report release date in the audit documentation.

Paragraph 15 of ISA 230 requires that after the assembly of the final audit file has been completed, the auditor not delete or discard audit documentation of any nature before the end of its retention period. Paragraph A23 of ISA 230 states, "the retention period for audit engagements is ordinarily no shorter than five years from the date of the auditor's report, or, if later, the date of the group auditor's report." Paragraph .17 of section 230 requires that after the documentation completion date, the auditor not delete or discard audit documentation before the end of the specified retention period, and goes on to state that "such retention period, however, should not be shorter than five years from the report release date."

The ASB believes that it is appropriate to be consistent with the standards of the PCAOB in relation to the date from which the documentation completion

---

[2] Paragraph 10 of PCAOB Auditing Standard No. 3, *Audit Documentation* (AICPA, *PCAOB Standards and Related Rules*, Auditing Standards).

and retention periods are measured.[3] Notwithstanding that the documentation completion period is measured from the same date in GAAS and in the PCAOB standard, the ASB continues to believe that a 60-day period is appropriate for GAAS as opposed to the 45-day period in the PCAOB standard.

ISA 240, *The Auditor's Responsibilities Relating to Fraud in an Audit of Financial Statements*, Compared to Section 240, *Consideration of Fraud in a Financial Statement Audit*

Differences in Language

Paragraph 11 of ISA 240 and paragraph .11 of section 240 define *fraud*. However, the definition of fraud in paragraph .11 of section 240 was revised by changing the words "to obtain illegal or unjust advantage" to "results in a misstatement in financial statements that are the subject of an audit." The ASB believes that (*a*) the definition in ISA 240 is too broad and could inappropriately expose auditors to additional liability in the United States, and (*b*) the meaning of *unjust* could be interpreted very broadly and subjectively in its application and could imply a scope well beyond the intent of the standard. The ASB believes that the change in the definition does not create significant differences between the application of ISA 240 and the application of section 240.

Requirements in GAAS Not in the ISAs

Section 240 contains requirements, consistent with requirements of SAS No. 99, *Consideration of Fraud in a Financial Statement Audit*, as amended, that have been expanded from the requirements of ISA 240, or elevated from application material in ISA 240, as follows:

- The requirement in paragraph 14 of ISA 240 for the auditor to investigate inconsistent responses to auditor inquiries of management or those charged with governance has been expanded in paragraph .14 of section 240 to also include responses that are otherwise unsatisfactory (for example, vague or implausible responses).
- The requirement in paragraph 15 of ISA 240 that requires members of the engagement team to discuss the susceptibility of the entity's financial statements to material misstatements has been expanded in paragraph .15 of section 240 to include additional discussion items from application and other explanatory material in ISA 240 to requirements in section 240. These include a required brainstorming session focused very specifically on, among other things, internal and external fraud factors and the possibility of management override of controls. In addition, section 240 further clarifies the requirement for participation of key engagement team members and the engagement partner in the discussion and brainstorming sessions. Lastly, section 240 requires appropriate communication throughout the audit among the engagement team members. Several of these discussion items have been elevated from paragraphs A10–A11 of ISA 240.

---

[3] Paragraphs 14–15 of PCAOB Auditing Standard No. 3.

- The requirement in paragraph 44 of ISA 240 to document the significant decisions reached during the discussion among the engagement team regarding fraud-related matters has been expanded in paragraph .43 of section 240 to also require documenting how and when the discussion occurred and the audit team members who participated.
- Procedures elevated from paragraph A18 of ISA 240 to requirements in paragraph .19 of section 240, related to making inquiries of internal audit as part of performing risk assessment procedures, include determining (*a*) whether internal audit has performed any procedures to identify or detect fraud during the year, and (*b*) whether management has satisfactorily responded to any findings resulting from these inquiries.
- The requirement in paragraph 34 of ISA 240 to evaluate whether the results of analytical procedures at or near the end of the reporting period indicate a previously unrecognized risk of material misstatement due to fraud has been expanded in paragraph .34 of section 240 to include the accumulated results of auditing procedures, including analytical procedures performed as substantive tests or when forming an overall conclusion. Section 240 also specifically requires performance of analytical procedures relating to revenue accounts through the end of the reporting period, in light of the generally higher risk of financial statement fraud involving revenue.
- The requirements in paragraph 32(a) of ISA 240 address designing and performing auditing procedures to test the appropriateness of journal entries. In addition to essential guidance about addressing the risk of possible management override of controls, included in paragraph .32*a* of section 240 are requirements to
  - — obtain an understanding of the entity's financial reporting process and controls over journal entries and other adjustments, and determine whether such controls are suitably designed and have been implemented.
  - — consider fraud risk factors, the nature and complexity of accounts, and entries processed outside the normal course of business, elevated from the application and other explanatory material contained in paragraph A43 of ISA 240 in order to emphasize the importance of these considerations.
  - — include identification and testing of specific journal entries regardless of controls.
- The requirement for the auditor to design and perform auditing procedures to review accounting estimates for biases and evaluate whether the circumstances producing the bias, if any, represent a risk of material misstatement due to fraud, in paragraph 32(b) of ISA 240, has been expanded in paragraph .32*b* of section 240 to include those estimates that are based on highly sensitive assumptions.

ISA 250, *Consideration of Laws and Regulations in an Audit of Financial Statements*, Compared to Section 250, *Consideration of Laws and Regulations in an Audit of Financial Statements*

Differences in Language

Changes to the language of section 250 include:

- In paragraphs .10*a* and .13, changing the phrase "compliance with the provisions of those laws and regulations generally recognized to have a direct and material effect on the determination of material amounts and disclosures in the financial statements" to the phrase "material amounts and disclosures in the financial statements that are determined by the provisions of those laws and regulations generally recognized to have a direct effect on their determination." This change was made to address the ASB's concerns that the language in ISA 250 expanded the auditor's responsibility to encompass all aspects of those laws and regulations described in paragraph .06*a* of section 250, as opposed to focusing on the amounts and disclosures included in the financial statements. The ASB has discussed this issue with the IAASB, and the wording in section 250 reflects the intent of ISA 250. The IAASB made subsequent changes to the application material in ISA 250 to make this clear.
- In paragraphs .10*b* and .14, changing "to help identify" to "that may identify." The ASB believes that the wording of section 250 better conveys the intent of ISA 250.
- In paragraph .18, adding the phrase "(at a level above those involved with the suspected noncompliance, if possible)."

Such changes have been made to make section 250 easier to read and apply. The ASB believes that such changes do not create differences between the application of ISA 250 and the application of section 250.

Placement of Certain Requirements Within GAAS

Paragraph 16 of ISA 250 requires the auditor to request management and, when appropriate, those charged with governance to provide written representations regarding identified or suspected instances of noncompliance with relevant laws and regulations. The ASB believes this requirement is more appropriately placed in section 580, *Written Representations*. The placement of these requirements does not create differences between the ISAs as a whole and GAAS as a whole.

ISA 260, *Communication with Those Charged with Governance*, Compared to Section 260, *The Auditor's Communication With Those Charged With Governance*

Differences in Language

Changes to the language of section 260 from ISA 260 include

- in paragraph .12, requiring that the auditor communicate with those charged with governance "the auditor's views about qualitative aspects of the entity's significant accounting practices" compared with the requirement in paragraph 16 of ISA 260 that the auditor communicate with those charged with governance "the auditor's views about significant qualitative aspects of the entity's accounting practices." The ASB believes that the wording of section 260 better conveys the intent of ISA 260.
- in paragraph .16, changing the language in ISA 260 from "Written communications need not include all matters that arose during the course of the audit" to "This communication need not include matters that arose during the course of the audit that were communicated with those charged with governance and satisfactorily resolved."

Such changes have been made to make section 260 easier to read and apply. The ASB believes that such changes do not create differences between the application of ISA 260 and the application of section 260.

Requirements in the ISAs Not in GAAS

Paragraphs 13 and 16 of ISA 260 require the auditor to communicate certain matters regarding independence in the case of listed entities. These requirements are not applicable to the audits of nonissuers in the United States and, therefore, are not included in section 260.

Requirements in GAAS Not in the ISAs

Paragraph .12*a* of section 260 requires the auditor, when applicable, to determine that those charged with governance are informed about the process used by management in formulating particularly sensitive accounting estimates and about the basis for the auditor's conclusions regarding the reasonableness of those estimates.

Paragraph .14*a* and *c* of section 260 require, when not all of those charged with governance are involved in managing the entity, the auditor to communicate (*a*) material, corrected misstatements that were brought to the attention of management as a result of audit procedures, and (*b*) the auditor's views about significant matters that were the subject of management's consultations with other accountants on accounting or auditing matters when the auditor is aware that such consultation has occurred. Paragraph .12*c* of section 260 requires the auditor to communicate disagreements with management, if any. ISA 260 does not require communication of these matters. The ASB believes that it is important for these matters to be communicated to those charged with governance of nonissuers in the United States.

Paragraph .17 of section 260 requires the auditor, when communicating matters in accordance with section 260 in writing, to indicate in the communication that it is intended solely for the information and use of those charged with governance and, if appropriate, management and is not intended to be, and should not be, used by anyone other than these specified parties. ISA 260 does not require this indication, nor does it prohibit it. The ASB believes that this communication meets the criteria for a by-product report under SAS No. 87, *Restricting the Use of an Auditor's Report*.[‡]

[‡] SAS No. 87, *Restricting the Use of an Auditor's Report*, is currently effective and codified as former AU section 532. SAS No. 87 has been included in new section 905, as designated by SAS

(continued)

Placement of Certain Requirements Within GAAS

Consistent with requirements in paragraphs 12–13 of ISA 450, *Evaluation of Misstatements Identified during the Audit*, paragraph .13 of section 260 contains a requirement for the auditor to communicate certain matters regarding uncorrected misstatements. The ASB believes that this communication with those charged with governance is more appropriately placed in section 260. Paragraph 12(c)(i) of ISA 260 requires the auditor to communicate material weaknesses in internal control identified during an audit to those charged with governance. The ASB believes this requirement is more appropriately placed in section 265, *Communicating Internal Control Related Matters Identified in an Audit.* The placement of these requirements does not create differences between the ISAs as a whole and GAAS as a whole.

ISA 265, *Communicating Deficiencies in Internal Control to Those Charged with Governance and Management,* Compared to Section 265, *Communicating Internal Control Related Matters Identified in an Audit*

Differences in Language

Section 265 includes and defines the term *material weakness*, whereas ISA 265 does not.

The definition *of material weakness*, along with the definitions of *deficiency in internal control* and *significant deficiency in internal control* have been modified to align with the definitions of these terms in Statement on Standards for Attestation Engagements No. 15, *An Examination of an Entity's Internal Control Over Financial Reporting That Is Integrated With an Audit of Its Financial Statements* (AT sec. 501). These terms and definitions are consistent with those used in the standards of the PCAOB. The ASB believes that consistency between its standards and those of the PCAOB in the use and definition of these terms is essential in the United States due to legal and regulatory requirements, including those pertaining to the evaluation of the effectiveness of an entity's internal control over financial reporting.

The ASB believes that the definitions are consistent with the intent of ISA 265 and that the modifications do not create differences between the application of ISA 265 and the application of section 265.

Requirements in GAAS Not in the ISAs

Section 265 requires the auditor to evaluate each deficiency to determine, on the basis of the audit work performed, whether, individually or in combination, the deficiencies constitute significant deficiencies or material weaknesses. ISA 265 does not explicitly refer to the auditor's evaluation of each deficiency in

---

(footnote continued)

No. 122, *Statements on Auditing Standards: Clarification and Recodification*, and will be superseded when it is redrafted for clarity and convergence as part of the Clarification and Convergence project of the Auditing Standards Board. Until such time, new section 905 has been conformed to reflect updated section and paragraph cross references but has not otherwise been subjected to a comprehensive review or revision.

making this determination. The ASB believes that the requirement in section 265 is consistent with the intent of ISA 265.

Section 265 requires the auditor to communicate significant deficiencies and material weaknesses to management and those charged with governance. Because ISA 265 does not include or define the term *material weakness*, ISA 265 does not contain a requirement to separately identify or communicate material weaknesses.

Section 265 includes an additional requirement for the auditor to consider, if the auditor determines that a deficiency, or a combination of deficiencies, in internal control is not a material weakness, whether prudent officials, having knowledge of the same facts and circumstances, would likely reach the same conclusion (paragraph .10).

Section 265 explicitly requires the auditor to document the communication of other deficiencies in internal control that are communicated orally to management (paragraph .12*b*).

Paragraphs 9–10 of ISA 265 require the auditor to communicate to those charged with governance and management on a timely basis. Paragraph .13 of section 265 requires the communication to be made no later than 60 days following the report release date. ISA 265 recognizes in paragraph A13 that the written communication of significant deficiencies forms part of the final audit file and is subject to the overriding requirement for the auditor to complete the assembly of the final audit file on a timely basis. ISA 230 states that an appropriate time limit within which to complete the assembly of the final audit file is ordinarily not more than 60 days after the date of the auditor's report.

In addition to the required elements of the written communication identified in paragraph 11 of ISA 265, paragraph .14 of section 265 requires that the following additional items/elements be included in the written communication:

- The definition of *material weakness* and, when relevant, the definition of *significant deficiency*
- An explanation that the auditor is not expressing an opinion on the effectiveness of internal control
- An explanation that the auditor's consideration of internal control was not designed to identify all deficiencies in internal control that might be material weaknesses or significant deficiencies
- A statement restricting the use of the communication to management, those charged with governance, others within the organization, and any governmental authority to which the auditor is required to report

Paragraph .15 of section 265 includes reporting requirements when the auditor issues a written communication stating that no material weaknesses were identified during the audit of the financial statements. Paragraph .16 of section 265 prohibits the issuance of a written communication stating that no significant deficiencies were identified during the audit. ISA 265 does not address the issuance of communications indicating no material weaknesses or no significant deficiencies.

ISA 300, *Planning an Audit of Financial Statements*, Compared to Section 300, *Planning an Audit*

Requirements in GAAS Not in the ISAs

Paragraph .12 of section 300 contains requirements regarding the auditor's obligations for determining the extent of involvement of professionals possessing specialized skills. ISA 300 does not contain these requirements. The ASB believes these requirements, and the related application material, are necessary for the auditor's consideration of the need for specialized skills and knowledge in the audit.

ISA 315, *Identifying and Assessing the Risks of Material Misstatement through Understanding the Entity and Its Environment*, Compared to Section 315, *Understanding the Entity and Its Environment and Assessing the Risks of Material Misstatement*

Differences in Language

Paragraph .10 of section 315 uses different wording than paragraph 9 of ISA 315 to describe the auditor's requirement regarding the relevance of information obtained. Paragraphs .19 and .25 of section 315 include additional modifiers to conform to the comparable auditing standard issued by the Public Company Accounting Oversight Board.

Both ISA 240 and section 240 contain requirements for the auditor to consider the risks of material misstatement due to fraud. Paragraph .09 of section 315 contains a specific requirement for the auditor to consider the results of the assessment of the risk of material misstatement due to fraud during planning, whereas ISA 315 does not. In addition, certain requirements in paragraphs .21 and .33 of section 315 contain more specificity than do the equivalent requirements in ISA 315.

These differences do not create differences between the application of ISA 315 and the application of section 315.

ISA 320, *Materiality in Planning and Performing an Audit*, Compared to Section 320, *Materiality in Planning and Performing an Audit*

There are no differences between the application of ISA 320 and the application of section 320.

ISA 330, *The Auditor's Responses to Assessed Risks*, Compared to Section 330, *Performing Audit Procedures in Response to Assessed Risks and Evaluating the Audit Evidence Obtained*

Requirements in GAAS Not in the ISAs

Paragraph .20 of section 330 includes a requirement to confirm accounts receivable unless certain conditions exist. This requirement is not in the ISAs. The ASB believes it is appropriate to retain the requirement in paragraph 34 of SAS No. 67, *The Confirmation Process*.

Differences Between Requirements

To be consistent with the wording of the comparable requirements in the comparable auditing standard issued by the PCAOB, the requirement in paragraph .07 of section 330 has been modified with the words "relevant" and "material," and the requirement in paragraph .10 of section 330 has been expanded to specifically include addressing, when applicable, whether the person performing the control possesses the necessary authority and competence to perform the control effectively. The ASB believes these differences do not create differences between the application of ISA 330 and the application of section 330.

Placement of Certain Requirements Within GAAS

Paragraph .25 of section 330 includes a requirement for the auditor addressing the means of selecting items for testing. This requirement is in the ISAs in ISA 500, *Audit Evidence*. The ASB believes this requirement is more appropriately placed in section 330. The placement of this requirement does not create a difference between the ISAs as a whole and GAAS as a whole.

ISA 402, *Audit Considerations Relating to an Entity Using a Service Organization*, Compared to Section 402, *Audit Considerations Relating to an Entity Using a Service Organization*

Differences in Language

The definitions of *Report on a description of a service organization's system and the suitability of the design of controls (type 1 report)* and *Report on a description of a service organization's system and the suitability of the design and operating effectiveness of controls* (*type 2 report*), in paragraph .08 of section 402, indicate that management's written assertion is an element of these reports. This is consistent with the definitions of these terms in International Standard on Assurance Engagements 3402, *Assurance Reports on Controls at a Service Organization*. The definitions of these terms in paragraph 8 of ISA 402 do not include management's written assertion as an element of the reports. The ASB believes that the definitions are consistent with the intent of ISA 402 and that the modifications do not create differences between the application of ISA 402 and the application of section 402.

ISA 450, *Evaluation of Misstatements Identified during the Audit*, Compared to Section 450, *Evaluation of Misstatements Identified During the Audit*

Placement of Certain Requirements Within GAAS

Paragraphs 12–13 of ISA 450 require the auditor to communicate certain matters regarding uncorrected misstatements to those charged with governance. The ASB believes that the requirements for this communication are more appropriately placed in section 260.

Paragraph 14 of ISA 450 requires the auditor to request written representations from management and, where appropriate, those charged with governance regarding uncorrected misstatements. The ASB believes this requirement is more appropriately placed in section 580.

The placement of these requirements does not create differences between the ISAs as a whole and GAAS as a whole.

ISA 500, *Audit Evidence*, Compared to Section 500, *Audit Evidence*

Placement of Certain Requirements Within GAAS

Paragraph 10 of ISA 500 includes a requirement for the auditor addressing the means of selecting items for testing. The ASB believes this requirement is more appropriately placed in section 330. The placement of this requirement does not create a difference between the ISAs as a whole and GAAS as a whole.

ISA 501, *Audit Evidence—Specific Considerations for Selected Items*, Compared to Section 501, *Audit Evidence—Specific Considerations for Selected Items*

Requirements in GAAS Not in the ISAs

Section 501 contains specific requirements relating to auditing investments in securities and derivative instruments that are not in ISA 501. The ASB concluded that it was appropriate to retain these specific requirements of SAS No. 92, *Auditing Derivatives Instruments, Hedging Activities, and Investments in Securities*.

SAS No. 12, *Inquiry of a Client's Lawyer Concerning Litigation, Claims, and Assessments*, is based on the premise that the applicable financial reporting framework complies with Financial Accounting Standards Board *Accounting Standards Codification* 450, *Contingencies*. In addition, the audit inquiry letters required under SAS No. 12 have been subjected to the provisions of the 1975 agreement between the AICPA and the American Bar Association (ABA treaty). Consequently, section 501 contains specific requirements relating to litigation, claims and assessments consistent with the requirements of SAS No. 12 that are not contained in ISA 501. The ASB decided to retain such content in section 501 because it is particular to the U.S. environment and continues to be relevant in practice.

Placement of Certain Requirements Within GAAS

Paragraph 12 of ISA 501 requires the auditor to request written representations from management and, where appropriate, those charged with governance regarding litigation and claims. The ASB believes this requirement is more appropriately placed in section 580. The placement of these requirements does not create differences between the ISAs as a whole and GAAS as a whole.

ISA 505, *External Confirmations*, Compared to Section 505, *External Confirmations*

Differences in Language

The definition of *external confirmation* has been expanded to include an example of a medium through which a response may be obtained. The example—direct access by the auditor to information held by a third party—addresses a situation that is increasingly common. The ASB believes that the inclusion of this concept clarifies the definition and is consistent with the intent of the definition in ISA 505.

ISA 510, *Initial Audit Engagements—Opening Balances*, Compared to Section 510, *Opening Balances—Initial Audit Engagements, Including Reaudit Engagements*

Requirements in GAAS Not in the ISAs

Paragraph .07 of section 510 carries forward a requirement from paragraph 11 of SAS No. 84, *Communications Between Predecessor and Successor Auditors*, as amended, which states that the auditor, when the prior period financial statements were audited by a predecessor auditor, should request management to authorize the predecessor auditor to allow a review of the predecessor auditor's audit documentation and to respond fully to inquiries by the auditor. Other requirements related to reviewing the predecessor auditor's audit documentation do not differ between ISA 510 and section 510.

Paragraph .13 of section 510 incorporates requirements from paragraph 22 of SAS No. 84, as amended, concerning the auditor's response when management refuses to inform the predecessor auditor that the prior period financial statements may need revision or if the auditor is not satisfied with the resolution of the matter. The ASB believes it is important to address this situation.

Paragraph .14 of section 510 incorporates a requirement from paragraph 13 of SAS No. 84, as amended, that states that the auditor should not make reference to the report or work of the predecessor auditor as the basis, in part, for the successor auditor's own opinion. The ASB believes this requirement is necessary in the United States to clearly distinguish this situation from the circumstances in section 600, *Special Considerations—Audits of Group Financial Statements (Including the Work of Component Auditors)*, in which the auditor determines to make reference to the audit of a component auditor in the auditor's report on the group financial statements.

Differences Between Requirements

Paragraph 6(c) of ISA 510 requires the auditor to perform one or more of three identified procedures, in addition to the procedures required in paragraph

6(a–b) of ISA 510, to obtain sufficient appropriate audit evidence about whether the opening balances contain misstatements that materially affect the current period's financial statements. Two of the three procedures are (*a*) reviewing the predecessor auditor's audit documentation to obtain evidence regarding opening balances, and (*b*) evaluating whether audit procedures performed in the current audit provide evidence relevant to the opening balances. The ASB does not believe that either of these procedures, on its own, provides sufficient evidence regarding opening balances, and accordingly, the ASB has redrafted paragraph .08*c* of section 510 to require the auditor to evaluate whether audit procedures performed in the current period provide evidence relevant to the opening balances and also to perform one or both of the other procedures identified in paragraph .08*c*(i–ii) of section 510.

ISA 520, *Analytical Procedures*, Compared to Section 520, *Analytical Procedures*

Differences in Language

The ASB has made various changes to the language throughout section 520 in comparison with ISA 520. The changes to section 520 include the following:

- In paragraph .05*c*, adding the parenthetical "(taking into account whether substantive analytical procedures are to be performed alone or in combination with tests of details)" to clarify that the auditor can use as audit evidence a substantive analytical procedure that is less precise than performance materiality when such analytical procedure is combined with other substantive audit procedures.
- In paragraph .05*d*, adding "compare the recorded amounts, or ratios developed from recorded amounts, with the expectations." The ASB is of the understanding that such procedure is presumed in ISA 520.

Such changes have been made to make section 520 easier to read and apply. The ASB believes that the changes made do not create differences between the application of ISA 520 and the application of section 520.

Requirements in GAAS Not in the ISAs

Section 520 includes specific documentation requirements, in paragraph .08, which ISA 520 does not. Such requirements are contained in SAS No. 56, *Analytical Procedures*, as amended, which section 520 supersedes, and the ASB believes that the requirements are appropriate and should be retained.

ISA 530, *Audit Sampling*, Compared to Section 530, *Audit Sampling*

Differences in Language

The definition of *audit sampling* in paragraph 5 of ISA 530 was revised in section 530 because the ASB believes that the ISA 530 wording defining audit sampling to require the auditor to select items such that "each item has a chance of selection" is too imprecise to be meaningful. The definition was revised to (*a*) focus on conclusions about the population, and (*b*) include the fundamental concept of representativeness. Paragraph .08 of section 530, which establishes a requirement with respect to the selection of items in a population, reflects the revised definition of *audit sampling*.

The wording in paragraph .13 of section 530 was broadened from the wording in paragraph 14 of ISA 530 to better encompass the related application material.

Requirements in the ISAs Not in GAAS

The requirement in paragraph 13 of ISA 530 that addresses the issue of anomalies is not included in section 530. The ASB expressed concerns about terms used in paragraph 13 of ISA 530, such as "in the extremely rare circumstances" and "a high degree of certainty." These terms are not used in GAAS and the ASB believes these terms would not be consistently interpreted in practice. The ASB also believes that the deletion from section 530 of the option to consider a misstatement an anomaly will enhance audit quality because misstatements identified by the auditor during audit sampling will be treated in the same manner as any other misstatement identified by the auditor and, thus, will prevent the misuse of anomalies.

Paragraph 14 of ISA 530 requires, for tests of details, the projection of misstatements found in a sample to the population. The ASB believes that projection of misstatements is also relevant to tests of controls and tests of compliance, and accordingly, has broadened the requirement in paragraph .14 of section 530 to project the results of audit sampling to also include tests of controls and tests of compliance.

Other

The appendixes of ISA 530 were not been included in section 530 because the guidance contained therein is covered by the AICPA Audit Guide *Audit Sampling*.

ISA 540, *Auditing Accounting Estimates, Including Fair Value Accounting Estimates, and Related Disclosures*, Compared to Section 540, *Auditing Accounting Estimates, Including Fair Value Accounting Estimates, and Related Disclosures*

Placement of Certain Requirements Within GAAS

Paragraph 22 of ISA 540 requires the auditor to obtain written representations from management and, when appropriate, those charged with governance about whether management and, when appropriate, those charged with governance believe significant assumptions used in making accounting estimates are reasonable. The ASB believes this requirement is more appropriately placed in section 580. The placement of this requirement does not create a difference between the ISAs as a whole and GAAS as a whole.

ISA 550, *Related Parties*, Compared to Section 550, *Related Parties*

Requirements in GAAS Not in the ISAs

ISA 550 distinguishes between fair presentation and compliance frameworks and between financial reporting frameworks that contain related party requirements and financial reporting frameworks that have minimal or no related party requirements. However, the ASB believes that fair presentation frameworks are the only financial reporting framework used in the United States. Further, to achieve fair presentation, disclosures related to related parties, such as those required by generally accepted accounting principles (GAAP), are necessary and, accordingly, section 550 defines *related party* as "a party as defined in GAAP." Thus, section 550 does not refer to applicable financial reporting frameworks; the applicability, objectives, and requirements of section 550 are the same regardless of the applicable financial reporting framework.

Placement of Certain Requirements Within GAAS

Paragraph 26 of ISA 550 requires the auditor to request that management and, when appropriate, those charged with governance, provide written representations regarding related party transactions. The ASB believes this requirement is more appropriately placed in section 580. The placement of this requirement does not create a difference between the ISAs as a whole and GAAS as a whole.

ISA 560, *Subsequent Events*, Compared to Section 560, *Subsequent Events and Subsequently Discovered Facts*

Differences in Language

Paragraph 5 of ISA 560 defines *subsequent events* to include both events occurring between the date of the financial statements and the date of the auditor's report and facts that become known to the auditor after the date of the auditor's report. Section 560 includes separate definitions for *subsequent events* and *subsequently discovered facts* to clearly distinguish the auditor's responsibilities for each. The definition of *subsequently discovered facts* was also expanded to use language that is consistent with language in the objectives and requirements of ISA 560 (paragraphs 4(b) and 14) but that is not specifically included in the definition in ISA 560.

Paragraph 5 of ISA 560 further defines *the date the financial statements are issued*, which is the date the auditor's report and audited financial statements are made available to third parties. This term was deleted from section 560 because the applicable financial reporting framework may define the financial statement issuance date. In addition, because GAAS define the report release date, the ASB believes the definition could cause confusion with respect to the release versus the issuance of the auditor's report. Although the definition was deleted, the requirements in section 560 were modified to use terms that are well understood in the United States and to be consistent with the intent of the requirements in ISA 560.

Paragraph 12 of ISA 560 permits the auditor to dual date the auditor's report when law or regulation does not prohibit management from restricting the revision of the financial statements to the effects of the subsequent event or events causing that revision and those responsible for approving the financial statements are not prohibited from restricting their approval to that revision. In the United States, no such prohibition by law or regulation exists. Accordingly, paragraph .13*b* of section 560 omits the reference to law or regulation.

Because the date of the auditor's report and the report release date are within the auditor's control, the requirements in paragraphs .12–.18 of section 560 were restructured with reference to the report release date in lieu of reference to the date that the financial statements were issued. Similar changes were made to the related application and other explanatory material.

Paragraph 15(b) of ISA 560 requires the auditor to review the steps taken by management to ensure that anyone in receipt of the previously issued financial statements, together with the auditor's report thereon, is informed of the situation. Paragraphs .16*b* and .17*b* of section 560 require the auditor to determine whether management's steps are timely and appropriate. The ASB believes this is consistent with the intent of the requirements of ISA 560.

The ASB believes these changes do not create differences between the application of ISA 560 and the application of section 560.

Requirements in the ISAs Not in GAAS

Certain requirements in ISA 560 also require the auditor to provide the auditor's report or a new or revised auditor's report. These references were eliminated from the requirements in section 560 because the ASB believes that it is not necessary to require the auditor to provide the auditor's report.

Paragraph 12(b) of ISA 560, which is an optional form of dual dating, was not included in section 560 because it is uncommon in the United States to provide a new or revised auditor's report that includes a statement in an emphasis-of-matter paragraph that conveys that the auditor's procedures on subsequent events are restricted solely to the revision of the financial statements, as described in the relevant note to the financial statements.

Requirements in GAAS Not in the ISAs

Section 560 includes an additional objective in paragraph .06, requirements in paragraphs .19–.20, and application and other explanatory material in paragraphs .A27–.A30 related to a predecessor auditor's responsibilities when reissuing the auditor's report on previously issued financial statements that are to be presented on a comparative basis with audited financial statements of a subsequent period. ISA 560 does not include such requirements.

Paragraph 9 of ISA 560 requires the auditor to request that management and, when appropriate, those charged with governance provide written representations regarding subsequent events. This requirement is included in paragraph .18 of section 580. However, if the financial statements are subsequently revised, paragraph .13*a–b* of section 560 include additional requirements for the auditor to request management to provide certain representations when the auditor either dates the auditor's report as of a later date or includes an additional date limited to the revision (that is, dual dates the auditor's report for that revision). These representations are not included in ISA 560.

Placement of Certain Requirements Within GAAS

Paragraph 5 of ISA 560 defines *the date of approval of the financial statements*. This definition was deleted from the definitions of section 560 because the ASB did not believe it was necessary to its application and because the term is described in paragraph .A41 of section 700, *Forming an Opinion and Reporting on Financial Statements*.

Paragraphs 11(b)(ii) and 15(c)(i) of ISA 560 require that the new auditor's report not be dated earlier than the date of approval of the revised financial statements. This requirement is not included in section 560 because the requirements for dating the report are addressed in section 700.

As noted in the preceding section, the requirement in paragraph 9 of ISA 560 regarding written representations has been moved to section 580.

Paragraph 16 of ISA 560 requires the auditor to include in the new or revised auditor's report an emphasis-of-matter paragraph or other-matter paragraph in situations when the financial statements are revised after the financial statements have been issued. Paragraph 16 of ISA 710, *Comparative Information—Corresponding Figures and Comparative Financial Statements*, includes a similar requirement related to comparative financial statements and the auditor's opinion on prior period financial statements, when reporting on prior period financial statements in connection with the current period's audit, differs from the opinion previously expressed. Requirements have been placed in paragraph .16*c* of section 560 and paragraphs .13–.14 of section 708, *Consistency of Financial Statements*, that when considered together, achieve the intent of the requirements in paragraph 16 of ISA 560 and paragraph 16 of ISA 710.

The ASB believes such placements do not create differences between the ISAs as a whole and GAAS as a whole.

ISA 580, *Written Representations*, Compared to Section 580, *Written Representations*

Differences in Language

Paragraph 8 of ISA 580 describes management's responsibility in the case of a fair presentation framework. The ASB believes that all the acceptable financial reporting frameworks in the United States are fair presentation frameworks, and, thus, the requirements of section 580 reflect this perspective.

Requirements in the ISAs Not in GAAS

Paragraph 15 of ISA 580 contains a requirement related to situations in which law or regulation requires management to make written public statements about its responsibilities. The ASB believes that these situations are not applicable to nonissuers in the United States and, accordingly, such requirements are not included in section 580.

Differences Between Requirements

Paragraph 14 of ISA 580 requires that the date of the written representations be as near as practicable to, but not after, the date of the auditor's report on the financial statements. Paragraph .20 of section 580 requires that the date of the written representations be as of the date of the auditor's report, which is consistent with SAS No. 85, *Management Representations*, as amended. Paragraph .A27 of section 580 states that, occasionally, circumstances may prevent management from signing the representation letter and returning it to the auditor on the date of the auditor's report. In these circumstances, the auditor may accept management's oral confirmation, on or before the date of the representations, that management has reviewed the final representation letter and will sign the representation letter without exception as providing sufficient appropriate audit evidence for the auditor to date the report. However, possession of the signed management representation letter prior to releasing the auditor's report is necessary because paragraph .21 of section 580 requires that the representations be in the form of a written letter from management.

Placement of Certain Requirements Within GAAS

The following ISAs contain requirements for requesting written representations:

- Paragraph 39 of ISA 240
- Paragraph 16 of ISA 250
- Paragraph 14 of ISA 450
- Paragraph 12 of ISA 501
- Paragraph 22 of ISA 540
- Paragraph 26 of ISA 550
- Paragraph 9 of ISA 560

Such requirements have been included in paragraphs .12–.19 of section 580. The ASB believes these requirements, which relate to representations that would be obtained for every audit engagement, are more appropriately placed in section 580. The placement of these requirements does not create differences between the ISAs as a whole and GAAS as a whole.

ISA 600, *Special Considerations—Audits of Group Financial Statements (Including the Work of Component Auditors)*, Compared to Section 600, *Special Considerations—Audits of Group Financial Statements (Including the Work of Component Auditors)*

Differences in Language

All the requirements in ISA 600 are addressed to either the group engagement partner or the group engagement team. In section 600, requirements that, in the circumstances, may be appropriately fulfilled by the firm are addressed to the auditor of the group financial statements. These requirements, in paragraphs .16 and .29, relate to engagement acceptance and modification of the auditor's opinion on the group financial statements. The ASB believes that this does not create a substantive difference between the requirements of ISA 600 and the requirements of section 600.

Requirements in the ISAs Not in GAAS

ISA 600 does not permit the auditor's report on the group financial statements to make reference to a component auditor unless required by law or regulation to include such reference. Section 600, consistent with SAS No. 1 section 543,

Part of Audit Performed by Other Independent Auditors, as amended, permits the auditor, in the auditor's report on the group financial statements, to make reference to the audit of a component auditor.

The ASB believes that the ability to make reference to the report of another auditor is appropriate in the United States for several reasons. No compelling practice issues suggest a need to change an approach that has always been permitted by GAAS in the United States. The size, complexity, and diversity of some audits, in particular the audit of the federal government in which withdrawing from the engagement or disclaiming an opinion are not viable options, make eliminating the option to make reference to a component auditor problematic. In addition, the ASB believes that there will be considerable practical problems with access issues, particularly with equity investments, under the approach in ISA 600. The ASB believes that there is no difference in the effectiveness of the audit in either approach when the audits are conducted in accordance with GAAS. Accordingly, section 600 contains requirements and application and other explanatory material relating to making reference to the report of another auditor that are not in ISA 600, which results in substantive differences in the wording of the objectives, requirements, and application material between ISA 600 and section 600. A group audit conducted in accordance with GAAS when the group engagement partner determines to make reference to the audit performed by a component auditor would not comply with the ISAs. As such, in an audit conducted under both GAAS and the ISAs, the auditor of the group financial statements would need to assume responsibility for the work of all component auditors and, therefore, plan the audit accordingly to comply with both sets of standards.

When no reference is made to a component auditor in the auditor's report on the group financial statements, no substantive differences exist between the requirements ISA 600 and the requirements of section 600.

ISA 620, *Using the Work of an Auditor's Expert*, Compared to Section 620, *Using the Work of an Auditor's Specialist*

Differences in Language

Paragraph 12(b) of ISA 620 requires the auditor to evaluate the significant assumptions and methods of the auditor's specialist. The ASB expanded the wording of this requirement to more clearly articulate the auditor's responsibility in this regard. The ASB believes this does not create a difference between the application of ISA 620 and the application of section 620.

Requirements in the ISAs Not in GAAS

Paragraph 14 of ISA 620 contains a conditional requirement regarding the auditor's reference to the auditor's specialist in the auditor's report when such reference is required by law or regulation. Because such reference is not required by law or regulation in the United States, such requirement is not included in section 620.

ISA 700, *Forming an Opinion and Reporting on Financial Statements*, Compared to Section 700, *Forming an Opinion and Reporting on Financial Statements*

Requirements in the ISAs Not in GAAS

Compliance Framework

Paragraphs 7(b), 19, and 36 of ISA 700 discuss financial statements prepared in accordance with a compliance framework. GAAS do not include any references to compliance frameworks because the ASB believes that all financial reporting frameworks used in the United States are fair presentation frameworks. Accordingly, section 700 is written in the context of a complete set of general purpose financial statements prepared in accordance with a fair presentation framework.

Definitions

Paragraph 7(b) of ISA 700 defines *fair presentation framework*. Section 700 does not include this definition because fair presentation framework is already defined section 200, *Overall Objectives of the Independent Auditor and the Conduct of an Audit in Accordance With Generally Accepted Auditing Standards*. As noted previously, section 700 does not include any references to compliance frameworks; therefore, there is no need to emphasize the differences between a fair presentation framework and a compliance framework in section 700.

Use of True and Fair View

Paragraphs 27, 32, and 35(b) of ISA 700 indicate that the description in the auditor's report can refer either to the preparation and fair presentation of the financial statements or the preparation of financial statements that give a true and fair view. GAAS do not include any references to "true and fair view" because such wording has not historically been used in the United States; GAAS continues to require the use of "present fairly, in all material respects" in the auditor's opinion. The ASB believes this does not result in a difference in the application of the ISAs and the application of GAAS.

Introductory Paragraph

Paragraph 23(d) of ISA 700 requires the introductory paragraph in the auditor's report to refer to the summary of significant accounting policies and other explanatory information. Section 700 does not include this requirement because the ASB believes the notes to the financial statements are an integral part of the financial statements, and specific notes need not be identified in the introductory paragraph. Because the notes to the financial statements are an integral part of the financial statements, the ASB has included a reference to the related notes to the financial statements in the illustrative auditor's reports in the exhibit, "Illustrations of Auditor's Reports on Financial Statements," of section 700. The ASB believes this does not create a difference between the application of ISA 700 and the application of section 700.

Paragraph 24 of ISA 700 requires the report to use a term that is appropriate in the context of the legal framework in the relevant jurisdiction when the auditor's report discusses management's responsibilities. Section 700 does not include this requirement because the ASB believes this paragraph relates to jurisdictions where the structure of the boards and corporate law are different than in the United States. In the United States, the ASB believes reference to management is sufficient. The ASB believes this does not create a difference between the application of ISA 700 and the application of section 700.

Auditor's Responsibility

Paragraph 30 of ISA 700 requires the auditor's report to include in the "Auditor's Responsibilities" section a statement that the auditing standards require that the auditor comply with ethical requirements. Paragraph .31 of section 700 does not contain this requirement because in the United States, auditors must comply with the ethical standards contained in the AICPA Code of Professional Conduct. Accordingly, the ASB believes that the title indicating that it is the report of an independent auditor affirms that the auditor has met the ethical requirements and, therefore, need not make an additional reference in the auditor's report. Further, the ASB was mindful to minimize the differences between the PCAOB form of the auditor's report and section 700. The ASB believes a reference to ethical requirements in one report and not the other would cause confusion in the United States and that such differentiation between the two reports is not necessary.

Information Presented in the Financial Statements

Paragraph 46 of ISA 700 contains requirements when supplementary information that is not required by the applicable financial reporting framework is presented with the audited financial statements. If such supplementary information is not clearly differentiated from the audited financial statements, ISA 700 requires the auditor to ask management to change how the unaudited supplementary information is presented and if management refuses to do so, the auditor should explain in the auditor's report that such supplementary information has not been audited. In the United States, section 725, *Supplementary Information in Relation to the Financial Statements as a Whole*, addresses the auditor's responsibility when engaged to report on supplementary information. At the present time, no ISAs exist that correspond to section 725. GAAS do not include the requirement for the auditor to ask management to change how the unaudited supplementary information is presented when the supplementary information is not clearly differentiated from the audited financial statements.

Requirements in GAAS Not in the ISAs

Management's Responsibilities

Paragraph .28 of section 700 adds a requirement that the description of management's responsibilities for the financial statements in the auditor's report should not be referenced to a separate statement by management about such responsibilities if such a statement is included in a document containing the auditor's report.

Paragraph .41 of section 700 includes a requirement that sufficient appropriate audit evidence includes evidence that the audit documentation has been reviewed.

ISA 700 does not contain these requirements, which the ASB believes are appropriate for inclusion in GAAS to retain existing requirements.

Differences Between Requirements

Management's Responsibilities

Paragraph 26 of ISA 700 requires the report to describe management's responsibilities for the preparation of the financial statements. The description should include an explanation that management is responsible for the preparation of the financial statements in accordance with the applicable financial reporting framework and for such internal control as it determines is necessary to enable the preparation of financial statements that are free from material misstatement, whether due to fraud or error. Section 700 requires the auditor's report to state that this responsibility includes the design, implementation, and maintenance of internal control relevant to the preparation and fair presentation of the financial statements. The ASB believes section 700 better conveys management's responsibility in the United States.

Auditor's Report for Audits Conducted in Accordance With Both Auditing Standards of a Specific Jurisdiction and ISAs

Paragraphs 44–45 of ISA 700 contain requirements when an auditor is required to conduct an audit in accordance with the auditing standards of a specific jurisdiction but may additionally have complied with the ISAs in the conduct of the audit. Paragraphs .42–.43 of section 700 have been revised to reflect reporting conventions in the United States.

The ASB believes these differences do not create a difference between the application of ISA 700 and the application of section 700.

Placement of Certain Requirements Within GAAS

Comparative Financial Statements

Section 700 addresses comparative financial statements and comparative information, which are not addressed in ISA 700 but are addressed in ISA 710, *Comparative Information—Corresponding Figures and Comparative Financial Statements.* See the section "ISA 710, *Comparative Information—Corresponding Figures and Comparative Financial Statements*, Compared to Section 700, *Forming an Opinion and Reporting on Financial Statements*," following for a comparison of the requirements of section 700 and the requirements of ISA 710. ISA 710 addresses reporting in other jurisdictions that are not common to the United States, including corresponding figures that are not covered by the auditor's report. For simplicity, the ASB decided to include those requirements and application material that apply in the United States in section 700 rather than have a separate AU section.

Auditor's Report Prescribed by Law or Regulation

Paragraph 43 of ISA 700 discusses the auditor's report prescribed by law or regulation. Section 700 does not contain this section because it does not pertain to general purpose financial statements in the United States. Auditor's reports prescribed by law or regulation are addressed in section 800.

The ASB believes that the placement of these requirements does not create differences between the application of the ISAs as a whole and the application of GAAS as a whole.

ISA 705, *Modifications to the Opinion in the Independent Auditor's Report*, Compared to Section 705, *Modifications to the Opinion in the Independent Auditor's Report*

Requirements in the ISAs Not in GAAS

Compliance Framework

GAAS do not include any references to compliance frameworks because the ASB believes that all financial reporting frameworks used in the United States are fair presentation frameworks. Accordingly, the reference to compliance frameworks in paragraph 23(b) of ISA 705 has not been included in paragraph .25 of section 705.

Use of True and Fair View

GAAS do not include any references to "true and fair view" because such wording has not historically been used in the United States; GAAS continues to require the use of "present fairly, in all material respects" in the auditor's opinion. Accordingly, the references to "true and fair view" in paragraphs 23(a) and 24(a) of ISA 705 are not included in paragraphs .24–.25 of section 705. The ASB believes this does not result in a difference in the application of the ISAs and the application of GAAS.

Multiple Uncertainties

Paragraph 10 of ISA 705 requires the auditor to disclaim an opinion when, in extremely rare circumstances involving multiple uncertainties, the auditor concludes that, notwithstanding having obtained sufficient appropriate audit evidence regarding each of the individual uncertainties, it is not possible to form an opinion on the financial statements due to the potential interaction of the uncertainties and their possible cumulative effect on the financial statements. Section 705 does not include this requirement because the ASB believes that a disclaimer of opinion is appropriate only when the auditor is not able to obtain sufficient appropriate audit evidence. The ASB believes the guidance in paragraph 30 of SAS No. 58, *Reports on Audited Financial Statements*, as amended, is appropriate in these circumstances; therefore, paragraph .A13 of section 705 includes this guidance.

Differences Between Requirements

Management-Imposed Scope Limitation

Paragraph 13(b)(i) of ISA 705 requires the auditor to withdraw from the audit when the auditor is unable to obtain sufficient appropriate audit evidence, and the auditor concludes that the possible effects on the financial statements of undetected misstatements, if any, could be both material and pervasive so that a qualification of the opinion would be inadequate to communicate the gravity of the situation. Paragraph .13 of section 705 changes this requirement so that the auditor should consider withdrawal from the engagement under such circumstances. The ASB believes that in the United States, the auditor should not be required to withdraw from an engagement but, rather, should consider whether to withdraw or disclaim an opinion on the financial statements. The

ASB believes this does not create differences between the application of ISA 705 and the application of section 705.

ISA 706, *Emphasis of Matter Paragraphs and Other Matter Paragraphs in the Independent Auditor's Report*, Compared to Section 706, *Emphasis-of-Matter Paragraphs and Other-Matter Paragraphs in the Independent Auditor's Report*

There are no substantive differences between ISA 706 and section 706.

ISA 710, *Comparative Information—Corresponding Figures and Comparative Financial Statements*, Compared to Section 700, *Forming an Opinion and Reporting on Financial Statements*

Differences in Language

The definitions of *comparative information* and *comparative financial statements* in paragraph 6(a) and (c) of ISA 710 have been revised to reflect U.S. conventions.

Requirements in the ISAs Not in GAAS

ISA 710 addresses reporting in other jurisdictions that are not common in the United States, including corresponding figures that are not covered by the auditor's report. GAAS do not include any references to corresponding figures because these are not common in the United States.

Requirements in GAAS Not in the ISAs

Comparative Information

Paragraph .45 of section 700 requires that when expressing an opinion on all periods presented, the auditor should update the report on the individual financial statements of one or more prior periods presented on a comparative basis with those of the current period. The auditor's report on comparative financial statements should not be dated earlier than the date on which the auditor has obtained sufficient appropriate audit evidence on which to support the opinion for the most recent audit.

Paragraph .47 of section 700 contains a requirement that if comparative information is presented, and the entity requests the auditor to express an opinion on all periods presented, the auditor should consider whether the information included for the prior period contains sufficient detail to constitute a fair presentation in accordance with the applicable financial reporting framework.

Audit Procedures

Paragraph .48 of section 700 contains a requirement that the audit procedures in paragraphs .49–.51 of section 700 should apply regardless of whether comparative financial statements or comparative information is presented for the prior period.

Prior Period Financial Statements

Paragraph .53 of section 700 includes requirements on what to disclose in an other-matter paragraph when reporting on prior period financial statements in connection with the current period's audit, and the auditor's opinion on such prior period financial statements differs from the opinion the auditor previously expressed.

Paragraph .54 of section 700 adds "and the predecessor auditor's report on the prior period's financial statements is not reissued" to the requirement. This was added to clarify that if the report was reissued, section 560 would apply. In addition, a requirement was added to include in the other-matter paragraph the nature of any emphasis-of-matter paragraph or other-matter paragraph included in the predecessor auditor's report, if any.

Prior Period Financial Statements Not Audited

Paragraphs .56–.57 of section 700 include requirements on how to report when prior period financial statements were not audited, reviewed, or compiled, to better clarify what is covered in section 700 related to comparative financial statements and comparative information.

ISA 710 does not contain these requirements. The ASB believes these requirements and related application material are appropriate for inclusion in GAAS.

Placement of Certain Requirements Within GAAS

ISA 710 addresses reporting in other jurisdictions that are not common to the United States, including corresponding figures that are not covered by the auditor's report. For simplicity, the ASB decided to include certain requirements and application material for comparative financial statements and comparative information in section 700 rather than having a separate AU section. The ASB believes that the requirements in section 700 related to comparative financial statements and comparative information are consistent with the intent of ISA 710 and that the placement of these requirements does not create differences between the application of the ISAs as a whole and the application of GAAS as a whole.

ISA 720, *The Auditor's Responsibilities Relating to Other Information in Documents Containing Audited Financial Statements*, Compared to Section 720, *Other Information in Documents Containing Audited Financial Statements*

Differences in Language

The ASB has made various changes to the language throughout section 720, in comparison with ISA 720. The changes to section 720 include the following:

- In paragraph .01, clarifying that "auditor's opinion" is the opinion on the financial statements.
- In paragraph .02, adding clarifying language that documents containing audited financial statements refer to "annual reports of governments and organizations for charitable or philanthropic purposes that are available to the public" and that section 720 also applies to "other documents to which the auditor, at management's request, devotes attention."

- In paragraph .05, deleting the phrase "either by law, regulation or custom" from the definition of *other information* to avoid confusion with required supplementary information.
- In paragraph .12, adding the phrase "other-matter" to clarify the report modification.
- In paragraph .17, adding the wording "by the entity in determining whether such matter is a material misstatement of fact" to clarify that the advice is received by the entity.

Such changes have been made to make section 720 easier to read and apply. The ASB believes that such changes do not create differences between the application of ISA 720 and the application of section 720.

Differences Between Requirements

Section 720 clarifies that the auditor's objective is to respond appropriately (in paragraph .04), and the requirement is to read the other information (in paragraph .06) when the auditor becomes aware that documents containing audited financial statements and the auditor's report thereon include other information that could undermine the credibility of those financial statements and the auditor's report. The objective in ISA 720 and the corresponding requirement are not specifically limited to documents of which the auditor is aware. However, ISA 720 states that "documents containing audited financial statements" refers to annual reports (or similar documents) that are issued to owners (or similar stakeholders) containing audited financial statements and the auditor's report thereon. ISA 720 further states that it may be applied, adapted as necessary in the circumstances, to other documents containing audited financial statements. The ASB believes that the language added to section 720 limiting the auditor's responsibilities clarifies the intent of the objective and the requirement in ISA 720 and is appropriate in the U.S. legal environment.

Section 720 applies the requirement in paragraph .07 for the auditor to make appropriate arrangements with management or those charged with governance to obtain the other information, and the requirements in paragraphs .10–.15 regarding the auditor's identification of material inconsistencies, to the report release date, but ISA 720 applies the corresponding requirements to the date of the auditor's report. The ASB determined that the report release date, as defined in GAAS, is more appropriate in the U.S. environment.

ISA 800, *Special Considerations—Audits of Financial Statements Prepared in Accordance with Special Purpose Frameworks*, Compared to Section 800, *Special Considerations—Audits of Financial Statements Prepared in Accordance With Special Purpose Frameworks*

Differences in Language

Definitions

Paragraph 6 of ISA 800 defines a *special purpose framework* as a financial reporting framework (a fair presentation framework or a compliance framework) designed to meet the financial information needs of specific users. Section 800 defines a special purpose framework as one of the following bases of accounting: cash, tax, regulatory, and contractual bases of accounting, all of which are fair presentation frameworks in the United States.

Considerations When Planning and Performing the Audit

Paragraph 9 of ISA 800 requires the auditor to determine whether application of the ISAs requires special consideration in the circumstances of the engagement. However, paragraph .12 of section 800 requires the auditor to adapt all AU sections relevant to the audit as necessary in the circumstances of the engagement. The ASB believes that the requirement in section 800 is consistent with the intent of ISA 800 and that such changes do not create differences between the application of ISA 800 and the application of section 800.

Requirements in GAAS Not in the ISAs

Considerations When Accepting the Engagement

Paragraph .11 of section 800 includes a requirement for the auditor, when accepting the engagement, to obtain the agreement of management that it acknowledges and understands its responsibility to include all informative disclosures, including specified disclosures, that are appropriate for the special purpose framework used to prepare the entity's financial statements.

Description of the Applicable Financial Reporting Framework

Paragraph .15 of section 800 includes a requirement for the auditor to evaluate whether the financial statements are suitably titled, include a summary of significant accounting policies, and adequately describe how the special purpose framework differs from GAAP.

Fair Presentation

If the special purpose financial statements contain items that are the same as, or similar to, those in financial statements prepared in accordance with GAAP, paragraph .17 of section 800 includes a requirement for the auditor to evaluate whether the financial statements include informative disclosures similar to those required by GAAP. Paragraph .17 of section 800 also requires the auditor to evaluate whether additional disclosures, beyond those specifically required by the framework, related to matters that are not specifically identified on the face of the financial statements or other disclosures may be necessary for the financial statements to achieve fair presentation.

Restricting the Use of the Auditor's Report

Paragraph .20 of section 800 requires the auditor's report to include an other-matter paragraph that restricts the use of the auditor's report to those within the entity, the parties to the contract or agreement, or the regulatory agencies to whose jurisdiction the entity is subject when the special purpose financial statements are prepared in accordance with a contractual or regulatory basis of accounting, except for the circumstances described in paragraph .21 of section 800. In accordance with paragraph .21 of section 800, the other-matter paragraph is not required when the special purpose financial statements are prepared in accordance with a regulatory basis of accounting and the special purpose financial statements together with the auditor's report are intended for general use. In this circumstance, the auditor is required to express an opinion on whether the financial statements are prepared in accordance with GAAP and, in a separate paragraph, an opinion on whether the financial statements are prepared in accordance with the special purpose framework.

Auditor's Report Prescribed by Law or Regulation

Paragraphs .22–.23 of section 800 include requirements when the auditor is required by law or regulation to use a specific layout, form, or wording of the auditor's report.

These requirements are not included in ISA 800.

Differences Between Requirements

Auditor's Report

Paragraph 13 of ISA 800 requires the auditor's report to describe the purpose for which the financial statements are prepared and, if necessary, the intended users, or refer to a note in the special purpose financial statements that contains that information. Section 800 does not require this description when the special purpose financial statements are prepared in accordance with the cash or tax basis of accounting.

Alerting Readers That the Financial Statements Are Prepared in Accordance With a Special Purpose Framework

Paragraph 14 of ISA 800 requires the auditor's report to include an emphasis-of-matter paragraph alerting users of the auditor's report that the financial statements are prepared in accordance with a special purpose framework and that, as a result, the financial statements may not be suitable for another purpose. Section 800 does not require the auditor's report to state that the "financial statements may not be suitable for another purpose." However, paragraph .19*c* of section 800 requires the emphasis-of-matter paragraph to state that the special purpose framework is a basis of accounting other than GAAP. In accordance with paragraph .21 of section 800, the emphasis-of-matter paragraph is not required when the special purpose financial statements are prepared in accordance with a regulatory basis of accounting and the special purpose financial statements together with the auditor's report are intended for general use.

ISA 805, *Special Considerations—Audits of Single Financial Statements and Specific Elements, Accounts or Items of a Financial Statement*, Compared to Section 805, *Special Considerations—Audits of Single Financial Statements and Specific Elements, Accounts, or Items of a Financial Statement*

Requirements in the ISAs Not in GAAS

Form of Opinion

Paragraph 9 of ISA 805 requires the auditor to consider whether the expected form of opinion is appropriate in the circumstances. This requirement was not included in section 805 because the circumstances to which it relates are not applicable in the United States.

Requirements in GAAS Not in the ISAs

Considerations When Accepting the Engagement and Planning and Performing the Audit

Paragraph .10 of section 805 requires the auditor to obtain an understanding of (*a*) the purpose for which the single financial statement or specific element of a financial statement is prepared, (*b*) the intended users, and (*c*) the steps taken by management to determine that the application of the financial reporting framework is acceptable in the circumstances. The ASB believes this requirement is necessary in determining the acceptability of the financial reporting framework that is applicable to a single financial statement or a specific element of a financial statement.

Paragraph .09 of section 805 requires the auditor to determine whether the auditor will be able to perform procedures on interrelated items as a consideration when accepting the engagement. Paragraph .13 of section 805 includes a requirement for the auditor to perform procedures on interrelated items as necessary to meet the objective of the audit. In the case of an audit of a specific element that is, or is based upon, the entity's stockholders' equity or net income (or the equivalents thereto), paragraph .13 of section 805 further requires the auditor to perform procedures necessary to obtain sufficient appropriate audit evidence about financial position, or financial position and results of operations, respectively, because of the interrelationship between the element and the balance sheet accounts and the income statement accounts.

Materiality

Paragraph .14 of section 805 requires the auditor to determine materiality for the single financial statement being reported on, and in the case of an audit of one or more specific elements of a financial statement, materiality for each individual element reported on.

Reporting on an Incomplete Presentation but One That Is Otherwise in Accordance With GAAP

When the auditor reports on an incomplete presentation but one that is otherwise in accordance with GAAP, paragraph .24 of section 805 requires the auditor to include an emphasis-of-matter paragraph in the auditor's report, alerting users as to the purpose of the presentation and that the presentation is incomplete. ISA 805 does not address reporting on incomplete presentations that are otherwise in accordance with the applicable financial reporting framework.

ISA 805 does not contain these requirements.

Differences Between Requirements

Reporting on the Entity's Complete Set of Financial Statements and a Single Financial Statement or a Specific Element of Those Financial Statements

Paragraph 12 of ISA 805 requires the auditor to express a separate opinion for each engagement when undertaking an engagement to report on a single financial statement or a specific element of a financial statement in conjunction with an engagement to audit the entity's complete set of financial statements. Paragraph .16 of section 805 requires that the separate opinions be in separate auditor's reports and that the report on a specific element include certain information about the auditor's report on the entity's complete set of financial statements.

Paragraph .20 of section 805 address the case of an audit of a specific element of a financial statement when the opinion in the auditor's report on an entity's complete set of financial statements is modified and the modification of the auditor's opinion is relevant to the audit of the specific element. In such cases, the auditor is required to express either an adverse opinion or disclaim an opinion on the specific element, depending on the reasons for the modification of the auditor's opinion on the complete set of financial statements. ISA 805 does not specifically require an adverse opinion or disclaimer of opinion in such circumstances.

Paragraph 16 of ISA 805 addresses situations when the auditor concludes that it is necessary to express an adverse opinion or disclaim an opinion on the entity's complete set of financial statements as a whole, but in the context of a separate audit of a specific element that is included in those financial statements, the auditor nevertheless considers it appropriate to express an unmodified opinion on that element. In addition to the matters in ISA 805, paragraph .21 of section 805 precludes such reporting when the specific element is, or is based upon, the entity's stockholders' equity or net income (or the equivalent thereto).

ISA 810, *Engagements to Report on Summary Financial Statements*, Compared to Section 810, *Engagements to Report on Summary Financial Statements*

Differences in Language

Paragraph .05 of section 810 includes more specificity than is in paragraph 3 of ISA 810, including an objective to perform the procedures necessary as the basis for the auditor's opinion on the summary financial statements, and a description of the opinion. The ASB believes that these changes do not create differences between the intent of ISA 810 and the intent of section 810.

Paragraph 6(b)(ii) of ISA 810 requires that management make the audited financial statements available to the intended users of the summary financial statements without undue difficulty. Section 810 requires in paragraph .09*b*(ii) that management make the audited financial statements readily available. This is not a substantive difference between ISA 810 and the section 810. The terminology in section 810 aligns with section 930, *Interim Financial Information*.

If the summary financial statements contain comparatives that were reported on by another auditor, both ISA 810 and section 810 require the auditor's report on the summary financial statements to contain certain matters. Such matters are included directly in paragraph .23 of section 810 and incorporated in paragraph 22 of ISA 810 by reference to ISA 710.

Requirements in the ISAs Not in GAAS

Paragraphs 6–7 of ISA 810 include requirements pertaining to (*a*) criteria established by law or regulation, (*b*) situations in which law or regulation does not require the audited financial statements to be made available, and (*c*) accepting the engagement when required by law or regulation to do so. These requirements were not included in section 810 because they are not applicable to the United States.

Paragraph 9 of ISA 810 permits the use of two different phrases when opining on summary financial statements. Paragraph .14 of section 810 only includes one of these phrases, which is consistent with existing practice.

Paragraphs 10–11 of ISA 810 address situations when regulation prescribes the wording of the opinion on the summary financial statements in terms that are different from those described in ISA 810. These requirements were not included in section 810 as they are not applicable in the United States.

Paragraph 15 of ISA 810 requires the auditor to evaluate the appropriateness of using a different addressee, if the addressee of the summary financial statements is not the same as the addressee of the auditor's report on the audited financial statements. Section 810 does not include this requirement because the ASB believes having different addressees is never appropriate.

Requirements in GAAS Not in the ISAs

Paragraph 6(a) of ISA 810 requires the auditor to determine whether the applied criteria are acceptable. The requirement in paragraph .09*a* of section 810 was expanded to clarify what constitutes acceptable criteria.

Paragraph .09*b*(iii) of section 810 requires the auditor to obtain the agreement of management that it acknowledges and understands its responsibility to provide the auditor with written representations, as described in paragraph .12 of section 810. ISA 810 does not include such a requirement.

Paragraphs .12–.13 of section 810 include requirements for the auditor to request management to provide written representations related to the summary financial statements. Such representations are necessary in the United States, particularly in situations when the auditor's report on the summary financial statements is dated later than the auditor's report on the audited financial statements. ISA 810 does not include any requirements for written representations.

Paragraph .16 of section 810 was expanded to require the auditor to withdraw from the engagement to report on the summary financial statements when withdrawal is possible under applicable law or regulation and when the auditor's report on the audited financial statements contains an adverse opinion or a disclaimer of opinion. Paragraph .16*d* of section 810 further clarifies the reporting elements when the auditor issues a report on the summary financial statements in those situations when it is not possible to withdraw from the engagement.

Paragraph .17*e*(i–ii) of section 810 includes additional elements for the auditor's report on the summary financial statements with regard to the nature of the procedures that were performed by the auditor on the summary financial statements, including that the auditor did not perform audit procedures regarding the audited financial statements after the date of the report on those financial statements if the date of the auditor's report on the summary financial statements is later than the date of the auditor's report on the audited financial statements.

Paragraph .24 of section 810 includes an additional reporting requirement if the summary financial statements contain comparatives that were not reported on by the auditor or another auditor.

Paragraph .27 of section 810 includes additional requirements related to other information, which require the auditor to discuss the matter with management if the auditor identifies a material inconsistency and to consider appropriate further action in the circumstances if the auditor identifies a material inconsistency or becomes aware of an apparent material misstatement of fact.

Differences Between Requirements

Paragraph 17 of ISA 810 addresses the reporting elements when the auditor's report on the audited financial statements contains a qualified opinion, an emphasis-of-matter paragraph, or an other-matter paragraph. In ISA 810, the requirement in this paragraph only applies when the auditor expresses an unmodified opinion on the summary financial statements. In section 810, the requirement in paragraph .20 applies when the auditor expresses either an unmodified opinion or an adverse opinion on the summary financial statements.

Section 810, in paragraph .21, eliminated the reference to the restriction on distribution of the auditor's report in paragraph 20 of ISA 810. In the United States, use of an auditor's report is restricted, not its distribution. An auditor is not responsible for controlling management's distribution of restricted-use reports.

AU-C Appendix C

[*Reserved.*]

AU-C Appendix D

AICPA Audit and Accounting Guides and Statements of Position

Audit and Accounting Guides

Airlines

Analytical Procedures

Assessing and Responding to Audit Risk in a Financial Statement Audit

Audit Sampling

Auditing Derivative Instruments, Hedging Activities, and Investments in Securities

Auditing Revenue in Certain Industries

Brokers and Dealers in Securities

Compilation and Review Engagements

Construction Contractors

Depository and Lending Institutions: Banks and Savings Institutions, Credit Unions, Finance Companies and Mortgage Companies

Employee Benefit Plans

Entities With Oil and Gas Producing Activities

Gaming

Government Auditing Standards *and Circular A-133 Audits*

Health Care Entities

Investment Companies

Life and Health Insurance Entities

Not-for-Profit Entities

Property and Liability Insurance Entities

Prospective Financial Information

Reporting on Controls at a Service Organization Relevant to Security, Availability, Processing Integrity, Confidentiality, or Privacy (SOC 2)

Service Organizations: Applying SSAE No. 16, Reporting on Controls at a Service Organization *(SOC 1)*

State and Local Governments

Statements of Position—Auditing and Attestation

Auditing Property / Casualty Insurance Entities' Statutory Financial Statements— Applying Certain Requirements of the NAIC Annual Statement Instructions	*10/92*
Guidance to Practitioners in Conducting and Reporting on an Agreed-Upon Procedures Engagement to Assist Management in Evaluating the Effectiveness of Its Corporate Compliance Program	*5/99*
Auditing Health Care Third-Party Revenues and Related Receivables	*3/00*
Performing Agreed-Upon Procedures Engagements That Address Internal Control Over Derivative Transactions as Required by the New York State Insurance Law	*6/01*
Performing Agreed-Upon Procedures Engagements That Address Annual Claims Prompt Payment Reports as Required by the New Jersey Administrative Code	*5/02*
Attest Engagements on Greenhouse Gas Emissions Information	*9/03*
Auditing the Statement of Social Insurance	*11/04*
Attestation Engagements That Address Specified Compliance Control Objectives and Related Controls at Entities That Provide Services to Investment Companies, Investment Advisers, or Other Service Providers	*10/07*
Performing Agreed-Upon Procedures Engagements That Address the Completeness, Accuracy, or Consistency of XBRL-Tagged Data	*4/09*
Reporting Pursuant to the Global Investment Performance Standards	*10/12*

AU-C Appendix E

*Schedule of Changes in Statements on Auditing Standards**

Section	*Paragraph*	*Changes*	*Date of Change*
200	.03	Added by SAS No. 123.	October 2011
200	.15	Added by SAS No. 123.	October 2011
200	.A17	Amended by SAS No. 123.	October 2011
200	.A18	Added by SAS No. 123.	October 2011
230	.19	Added by SAS No. 123.	October 2011
260	.12	Amended by SAS No. 123.	October 2011
260	.17	Amended by SAS No. 125.	December 2011
260	.A27	Added by SAS No. 123.	October 2011
265	.14	Amended by SAS No. 125.	December 2011
265	.A32	Amended by SAS No. 125.	December 2011
265	.A38–.A39	Amended by SAS No. 125.	December 2011
570		Superseded by SAS No. 126.	June 2012
600	.25	Amended by SAS No. 127.	January 2013
600	.26	Added by SAS No. 127.	January 2013
600	.28	Amended by SAS No. 127.	January 2013
600	.32	Amended by SAS No. 127.	January 2013
600	.50	Amended by SAS No. 127.	January 2013
600	.A53	Amended by SAS No. 127.	January 2013
600	.A54–.A56	Added by SAS No. 127.	January 2013
600	.A57	Amended by SAS No. 127.	January 2013
600	.A60	Amended by SAS No. 127.	January 2013
600	.A97	Amended by SAS No. 127.	January 2013
705	.16	Added by SAS No. 123.	October 2011
705	.A19	Added by SAS No. 123.	October 2011
720	.10	Amended by SAS No. 123.	October 2011
720	.11	Added by SAS No. 123.	October 2011
720	.A4	Amended by SAS No. 123.	October 2011
725	.A16	Amended by SAS No. 125.	December 2011
800	.01	Amended by SAS No. 127.	January 2013
800	.07	Amended by SAS No. 127.	January 2013
800	.11	Amended by SAS No. 127.	January 2013
800	.18	Amended by SAS No. 127.	January 2013

(continued)

* This table lists changes to AU-C sections only. These changes are the result of Statements on Auditing Standards (SASs) issued after SAS No. 122, *Statements on Auditing Standards: Clarification and Recodification*, which was issued in October 2011. Refer to AU appendix E for the pre-SAS No. 122 schedule of changes for AU sections.

Section	*Paragraph*	*Changes*	*Date of Change*
800	.20	Amended by SAS No. 125.	December 2011
800	.20	Amended by SAS No. 127.	January 2013
800	.A4–.A5	Amended by SAS No. 127.	January 2013
800	.A8	Amended by SAS No. 127.	January 2013
800	.A24	Amended by SAS No. 127.	January 2013
800	.A26–.A27	Amended by SAS No. 125.	December 2011
800	.A33	Amended by SAS No. 125.	December 2011
800	.A33	Amended by SAS No. 127.	January 2013
806	.12–.13	Amended by SAS No. 125.	December 2011
806	.A6–.A8	Amended by SAS No. 125.	December 2011
905		Superseded by SAS No. 125.	December 2011
910		Superseded by SAS No. 124.	October 2011
915	.09	Amended by SAS No. 123.	October 2011
915	.14	Amended by SAS No. 123.	October 2011
915	.14	Amended by SAS No. 125.	December 2011
915	.A6	Amended by SAS No. 125.	December 2011
920	.32	Deleted by SAS No. 125.	December 2011
920	.33	Amended by SAS No. 125.	December 2011
920	.A34	Amended by SAS No. 125.	December 2011
935	.30–.31	Amended by SAS No. 123.	October 2011
935	.30–.31	Amended by SAS No. 125.	December 2011
935	.A33	Deleted by SAS No. 125.	December 2011
935	.A41	Amended by SAS No. 123.	October 2011

AU-C Appendix F
Other Auditing Publications

This listing identifies *other auditing publications* published by the AICPA that have been reviewed by the AICPA Audit and Attest Standards staff and are therefore presumed to be appropriate as defined in section 200, *Overall Objectives of the Independent Auditor and the Conduct of an Audit in Accordance With Generally Accepted Auditing Standards.* Products may be obtained through www.cpa2biz.com.

AICPA *Technical Practice Aids* Accounting and Auditing Publications Technical Questions and Answers (TISs)

(available in hard copy)

- TIS section 8000, *Audit Field Work*
- TIS section 9000, *Auditors' Reports*

Current AICPA Audit Risk Alerts

Communicating Internal Control Related Matters in an Audit—Understanding SAS No. 115

Compilation and Review Developments

Employee Benefit Plans Industry Developments

Financial Institutions Industry Developments: Including Depository and Lending Institutions and Brokers and Dealers in Securities

General Accounting and Auditing Developments

Government Auditing Standards *and Circular A-133 Developments*

Health Care Industry Developments

Independence and Ethics Developments

Insurance Industry Developments

Investment Companies Industry Developments

Not-for-Profit Entities Industry Developments

Real Estate and Construction Industry Developments

State and Local Governmental Developments

Understanding the Clarified Auditing Standards

Understanding the New Auditing Standards Related to Risk Assessment

Understanding the Responsibilities of Auditors for Audits of Group Financial Statements

Other Publications

2011 Yellow Book Independence—Nonaudit Services Documentation

Alternative Investments—Audit Considerations (available for download at www.aicpa.org/interestareas/frc/auditattest/fieldwork/pages/alternative_investments.aspx)

Audits of Futures Commission Merchants, Introducing Brokers, and Commodity Pools

Applying OCBOA in State and Local Governmental Financial Statements

Documenting and Testing Compliance and Internal Control Over Compliance in a Single Audit

Establishing and Maintaining a System of Quality Control for a CPA Firm's Accounting and Auditing Practice

Preparing and Reporting on Cash- and Tax-Basis Financial Statements

Using an SSAE No. 16 Service Auditor's Report (SOC 1 Report) in Audits of Employee Benefit Plans

---

AU-C TOPICAL INDEX

References are to AU-C section and paragraph numbers.
Section numbers in the 9000 series refer to interpretations.

A

References are to AU-C section and paragraph numbers.

B

C

References are to AU-C section and paragraph numbers.

References are to AU-C section and paragraph numbers.

References are to AU-C section and paragraph numbers.

P

Q

R

S

References are to AU-C section and paragraph numbers.

References are to AU-C section and paragraph numbers.

AT Section

STATEMENTS ON STANDARDS FOR ATTESTATION ENGAGEMENTS

CONTENTS

AT CROSS-REFERENCES TO SSAEs

Statements on Standards for Attestation Engagements*

No.	*Date Issued*	*Title*	*Section*
1	Mar. 1986	Attestation Standards [Revised and recodified by SSAE No. 10; see AT sections 101, 301, and 401]	
1	Dec. 1987	Attest Services Related to MAS Engagements [Revised and recodified by SSAE No. 10; see AT sections 101, 301, and 401]	
1	Oct. 1985	Financial Forecasts and Projections [Revised and recodified by SSAE No. 10; see AT sections 101, 301, and 401]	
1	Sept. 1988	Reporting on Pro Forma Financial Information [Revised and recodified by SSAE No. 10; see AT sections 101, 301, and 401]	
2	May 1993	Reporting on an Entity's Internal Control Over Financial Reporting [Revised and recodified by SSAE No. 10; subsequently superseded by SSAE No. 15, see AT section 501]	
3	Dec. 1993	Compliance Attestation [Revised and recodified by SSAE No. 10; see AT section 601]	
4	Sept. 1995	Agreed-Upon Procedures Engagements [Revised and recodified by SSAE No. 10; see AT section 201]	
5	Nov. 1995	Amendment to Statement on Standards for Attestation Engagements No. 1, *Attestation Standards* [Revised and recodified by SSAE No. 10; see AT section 101]	
6	Dec. 1995	Reporting on an Entity's Internal Control Over Financial Reporting: An Amendment to Statement on Standards for Attestation Engagements No. 2 [Revised and recodified by SSAE No. 10]	
7	Oct. 1997	Establishing an Understanding With the Client [Revised and recodified by SSAE No. 10; see AT section 101]	

(continued)

* Pronouncements in effect are indicated in **boldface** type.

Statements on Standards for Attestation Engagements—continued

No.	*Date Issued*	*Title*	*Section*
8	Mar. 1998	Management's Discussion and Analysis [Revised and recodified by SSAE No. 10; see AT section 701]	
9	Jan. 1999	Amendments to Statement on Standards for Attestation Engagements Nos. 1, 2, and 3 [Revised and recodified by SSAE No. 10; see AT sections 101 and 601]	
10	**Jan. 2001**	**Attestation Standards: Revision and Recodification**[1]	
11	**Jan. 2002**	**Attest Documentation**[2]	
12	**Sept. 2002**	**Amendment to Statement on Standards for Attestation Engagements No. 10, *Attestation Standards: Revision and Recodification*** [3]	
13	**Dec. 2005**	**Defining Professional Requirements in Statements on Standards for Attestation Engagements**	20
14	**Nov. 2006**	**SSAE Hierarchy**	50
15	**Sept. 2008**	**An Examination of an Entity's Internal Control Over Financial Reporting That Is Integrated With an Audit of Its Financial Statements**	501
16	**April 2010**	**Reporting on Controls at a Service Organization**	801
17	**Dec. 2010**	**Reporting on Compiled Prospective Financial Statements When the Practitioner's Independence Is Impaired** [4]	

[1] SSAE No. 10 has been integrated within AT sections 101, 201, 301, 401, 601, and 701.

[2] SSAE No. 11 has been integrated within AT sections 101.100–[.108], 201[.27–.30], 301[.17], and 301[.32].

[3] SSAE No. 12 has been integrated within AT sections 101.17–.18.

[4] SSAE No. 17 has been integrated within AT section 301.23.

Sources of Sections in Current Text

AT Section	*Contents*	*Source*
20	Defining Professional Requirements in Statements on Standards for Attestation Engagements	SSAE No. 13
50	SSAE Hierarchy	SSAE No. 14
101	Attest Engagements	SSAE No. 10
201	Agreed-Upon Procedures Engagements	SSAE No. 10
301	Financial Forecasts and Projections	SSAE No. 10
401	Reporting on Pro Forma Financial Information	SSAE No. 10
501	An Examination of an Entity's Internal Control Over Financial Reporting That Is Integrated With an Audit of Its Financial Statements	SSAE No. 15
601	Compliance Attestation	SSAE No. 10
701	Management's Discussion and Analysis	SSAE No. 10
801	Reporting on Controls at a Service Organization	SSAE No. 16

ATTESTATION STANDARDS

Introduction

The accompanying "attestation standards" provide guidance and establish a broad framework for a variety of attest services increasingly demanded of the accounting profession. The standards and related interpretive commentary are designed to provide professional guidelines that will enhance both consistency and quality in the performance of such services.

For years, attest services generally were limited to expressing a positive opinion on historical financial statements on the basis of an audit in accordance with generally accepted auditing standards (GAAS). However, certified public accountants increasingly have been requested to provide, and have been providing, assurance on representations other than historical financial statements and in forms other than the positive opinion. In responding to these needs, certified public accountants have been able to generally apply the basic concepts underlying GAAS to these attest services. As the range of attest services has grown, however, it has become increasingly difficult to do so.

Consequently, the main objective of adopting these attestation standards and the related interpretive commentary is to provide a general framework for and set reasonable boundaries around the attest function. As such, the standards and commentary (*a*) provide useful and necessary guidance to certified public accountants engaged to perform new and evolving attest services and (*b*) guide AICPA standard-setting bodies in establishing, if deemed necessary, interpretive standards for such services.

The attestation standards are a natural extension of the ten generally accepted auditing standards. Like the auditing standards, the attestation standards deal with the need for technical competence, independence in mental attitude, due professional care, adequate planning and supervision, sufficient evidence, and appropriate reporting; however, they are much broader in scope. (The eleven attestation standards are listed below.) Such standards apply to a growing array of attest services. These services include, for example, reports on descriptions of systems of internal control; on descriptions of computer software; on compliance with statutory, regulatory, and contractual requirements; on investment performance statistics; and on information supplementary to financial statements. Thus, the standards have been developed to be responsive to a changing environment and the demands of society.

These attestation standards apply only to attest services rendered by a certified public accountant in the practice of public accounting—that is, a practitioner as defined in footnote 1 of paragraph .01.

The attestation standards do not supersede any of the existing standards in Statements on Auditing Standards (SASs) and Statements on Standards for Accounting and Review Services (SSARSs). Therefore, the practitioner who is engaged to perform an engagement subject to these existing standards should follow such standards.

Attestation Standards

General Standards

1. The practitioner must have adequate technical training and proficiency to perform in the attestation engagement.
2. The practitioner must have adequate knowledge of the subject matter.
3. The practitioner must have reason to believe that the subject matter is capable of evaluation against criteria that are suitable and available to users.
4. The practitioner must maintain independence in mental attitude in all matters relating to the engagement.
5. The practitioner must exercise due professional care in the planning and performance of the engagement and the preparation of the report.

Standards of Fieldwork

1. The practitioner must adequately plan the work and must properly supervise any assistants.
2. The practitioner must obtain sufficient evidence to provide a reasonable basis for the conclusion that is expressed in the report.

Standards of Reporting

1. The practitioner must identify the subject matter or the assertion being reported on and state the character of the engagement in the report.
2. The practitioner must state the practitioner's conclusion about the subject matter or the assertion in relation to the criteria against which the subject matter was evaluated.
3. The practitioner must state all of the practitioner's significant reservations about the engagement, the subject matter, and, if applicable, the assertion related thereto in the report.
4. The practitioner must state in the report that the report is intended solely for the information and use of the specified parties under the following circumstances:
   - When the criteria used to evaluate the subject matter are determined by the practitioner to be appropriate only for a limited number of parties who either participated in their establishment or can be presumed to have an adequate understanding of the criteria
   - When the criteria used to evaluate the subject matter are available only to specified parties
   - When reporting on subject matter and a written assertion has not been provided by the responsible party
   - When the report is on an attestation engagement to apply agreed-upon procedures to the subject matter

[As amended, effective for attest reports issued on or after June 30, 1999, by SSAE No. 9. As amended, effective when the subject matter or assertion is as of or for a period ending on or after June 1, 2001, by SSAE No. 10. Revised, December 2006, to reflect conforming changes necessary due to the issuance of SSAE No. 14.]

Introduction

AT Section
STATEMENTS ON STANDARDS FOR ATTESTATION ENGAGEMENTS

The following is a Codification of currently effective Statements on Standards for Attestation Engagements ("SSAEs") and related Attestation Interpretations. Statements on Standards for Attestation Engagements are issued by senior committees of the AICPA designated to issue pronouncements on attestation matters. Rule 202, Compliance With Standards, *of the AICPA Code of Professional Conduct requires an AICPA member who performs an attest engagement (a practitioner) to comply with such pronouncements. A practitioner is required to comply with an unconditional requirement in all cases in which the circumstances exist to which the unconditional requirement applies. A practitioner is also required to comply with a presumptively mandatory requirement in all cases in which the circumstances exist to which the presumptively mandatory requirement applies; however, in rare circumstances, the practitioner may depart from a presumptively mandatory requirement provided the practitioner documents his or her justification for the departure and how the alternative procedures performed in the circumstances were sufficient to achieve the objectives of the presumptively mandatory requirement.*

Attestation Interpretations are recommendations on the application of SSAEs in specific circumstances, including engagements for entities in specialized industries, issued under the authority of AICPA senior committees. An interpretation is not as authoritative as a pronouncement; however, if a practitioner does not apply an attestation interpretation, the practitioner should be prepared to explain how he or she complied with the SSAE provisions addressed by such attestation interpretation. The specific terms used to define professional requirements in the SSAEs are not intended to apply to interpretations because interpretations are not attestation standards. It is the Auditing Standards Board's intention to make conforming changes to the interpretations over the next several years to remove any language that would imply a professional requirement where none exists.

TABLE OF CONTENTS

AT Section 20

Defining Professional Requirements in Statements on Standards for Attestation Engagements

Source: SSAE No. 13.

Effective December 2005.

Introduction

.01 This section sets forth the meaning of certain terms used in Statements on Standards for Attestation Engagements (SSAEs) issued by the Auditing Standards Board in describing the professional requirements imposed on practitioners.

Professional Requirements

.02 SSAEs contain professional requirements together with related guidance in the form of explanatory material. Practitioners have a responsibility to consider the entire text of an SSAE in carrying out their work on an engagement and in understanding and applying the professional requirements of the relevant SSAEs.

.03 Not every paragraph of an SSAE carries a professional requirement that the practitioner is expected to fulfill. Rather, the professional requirements are communicated by the language and the meaning of the words used in the SSAEs.

.04 SSAEs use two categories of professional requirements, identified by specific terms, to describe the degree of responsibility they impose on practitioners, as follows:

- *Unconditional requirements.* The practitioner is required to comply with an unconditional requirement in all cases in which the circumstances exist to which the unconditional requirement applies. SSAEs use the words *must* or *is required* to indicate an unconditional requirement.

- *Presumptively mandatory requirements.* The practitioner is also required to comply with a presumptively mandatory requirement in all cases in which the circumstances exist to which the presumptively mandatory requirement applies; however, in rare circumstances, the practitioner may depart from a presumptively mandatory requirement provided the practitioner documents his or her justification for the departure and how the alternative procedures performed in the circumstances were sufficient to achieve the objectives of the presumptively mandatory requirement. SSAEs use the word *should* to indicate a presumptively mandatory requirement.

If an SSAE provides that a procedure or action is one that the practitioner "should consider," the consideration of the procedure or action is presumptively required, whereas carrying out the procedure or action is not. The professional requirements of an SSAE are to be understood and applied in the context of the explanatory material that provides guidance for their application.

Explanatory Material

.05 Explanatory material is defined as the text within an SSAE (excluding any related appendixes or interpretations[1]) that may:

- Provide further explanation and guidance on the professional requirements; or
- Identify and describe other procedures or actions relating to the activities of the practitioner.

.06 Explanatory material that provides further explanation and guidance on the professional requirements is intended to be descriptive rather than imperative. That is, it explains the objective of the professional requirements (where not otherwise self-evident); it explains why the practitioner might consider or employ particular procedures, depending on the circumstances; and it provides additional information for the practitioner to consider in exercising professional judgment in performing the engagement.

.07 Explanatory material that identifies and describes other procedures or actions relating to the activities of the practitioner is not intended to impose a professional requirement for the practitioner to perform the suggested procedures or actions. Rather, these procedures or actions require the practitioner's attention and understanding; how and whether the practitioner carries out such procedures or actions in the engagement depends on the exercise of professional judgment in the circumstances consistent with the objective of the standard. The words *may*, *might*, and *could* are used to describe these actions and procedures.

Application

.08 The provisions of this section are effective upon issuance.[2]

---

[1] Interpretive publications differ from explanatory material. Interpretive publications, for example, interpretations of the Statements on Standards for Attestation Engagements (SSAEs), appendixes to the SSAEs and AICPA auditing Statements of Position, are issued under the authority of the Auditing Standards Board (ASB). In contrast, explanatory material is always contained within the standards sections of the SSAE and is meant to be more descriptive in nature.

[2] The specific terms used to define professional requirements in this attestation standard are not intended to apply to any interpretive publications issued under the authority of the ASB, for example, interpretations of the SSAEs, or appendixes to the SSAEs, since interpretive publications are not attestation standards. (See footnote 1.) It is the ASB's intention to make conforming changes to the interpretive publications over the next several years to remove any language that would imply a professional requirement where none exists. It is the ASB's intention that such language would only be used in the standards sections of the SSAEs.

AT Section 50

SSAE Hierarchy

Source: SSAE No. 14.

Effective when the subject matter or assertion is as of or for a period ending on or after December 15, 2006.

.01 A practitioner plans, conducts, and reports the results of an attestation engagement in accordance with attestation standards. Attestation standards provide a measure of quality and the objectives to be achieved in the attestation engagement. Attestation procedures differ from attestation standards. Attestation procedures are acts that the practitioner performs during the course of the attestation engagement to comply with the attestation standards.

Attestation Standards

.02 The general, fieldwork, and reporting standards (the 11 attestation standards) approved and adopted by the membership of the AICPA, as amended by the AICPA Auditing Standards Board (ASB), are as follows:

General Standards

1. The practitioner must have adequate technical training and proficiency to perform the attestation engagement.
2. The practitioner must have adequate knowledge of the subject matter.
3. The practitioner must have reason to believe that the subject matter is capable of evaluation against criteria that are suitable and available to users.
4. The practitioner must maintain independence in mental attitude in all matters relating to the engagement.
5. The practitioner must exercise due professional care in the planning and performance of the engagement and the preparation of the report.

Standards of Fieldwork

1. The practitioner must adequately plan the work and must properly supervise any assistants.
2. The practitioner must obtain sufficient evidence to provide a reasonable basis for the conclusion that is expressed in the report.

Standards of Reporting[1]

1. The practitioner must identify the subject matter or the assertion being reported on and state the character of the engagement in the report.
2. The practitioner must state the practitioner's conclusion about the subject matter or the assertion in relation to the criteria against which the subject matter was evaluated in the report.
3. The practitioner must state all of the practitioner's significant reservations about the engagement, the subject matter, and, if applicable, the assertion related thereto in the report.

---

[1] The reporting standards apply only when the practitioner issues a report.

4. The practitioner must state in the report that the report is intended solely for the information and use of the specified parties under the following circumstances:
   - When the criteria used to evaluate the subject matter are determined by the practitioner to be appropriate only for a limited number of parties who either participated in their establishment or can be presumed to have an adequate understanding of the criteria.
   - When the criteria used to evaluate the subject matter are available only to specified parties.
   - When reporting on subject matter and a written assertion has not been provided by the responsible party.
   - When the report is on an attestation engagement to apply agreed-upon procedures to the subject matter.

Footnote 1 is also to be added to the heading *Standards of Reporting* preceding paragraph .63 of section 101, *Attest Engagements*.

.03 Statements on Standards for Attestation Engagements (SSAEs) are issued by senior committees of the AICPA designated to issue pronouncements on attestation matters. Rule 202, *Compliance With Standards* (ET sec. 201 par. .01), of the AICPA Code of Professional Conduct requires an AICPA member who performs an attestation engagement (the practitioner) to comply with such pronouncements.[2] SSAEs are developed and issued through a due process that includes deliberation in meetings open to the public, public exposure of proposed SSAEs, and a formal vote. The SSAEs are codified within the framework of the 11 attestation standards.

.04 The nature of the 11 attestation standards and the SSAEs requires the practitioner to exercise professional judgment in applying them. When, in rare circumstances, the practitioner departs from a presumptively mandatory requirement, the practitioner must document in the working papers his or her justification for the departure and how the alternative procedures performed in the circumstances were sufficient to achieve the objectives of the presumptively mandatory requirement.[3]

Attestation Interpretations[4]

.05 Attestation interpretations consist of Interpretations of the SSAEs, appendixes to the SSAEs, attestation guidance included in AICPA Audit and Accounting Guides, and AICPA attestation Statements of Position. Attestation interpretations are recommendations on the application of SSAEs in specific circumstances, including engagements for entities in specialized industries, issued under the authority of the AICPA senior committees.

.06 The practitioner should be aware of and consider attestation interpretations applicable to the attestation engagement. If the practitioner does not apply the attestation guidance included in an applicable attestation interpretation, the practitioner should be prepared to explain how he or she complied with the SSAE provisions addressed by such attestation guidance.

---

[2] In certain engagements, the practitioner also may be subject to other attestation requirements, such as *Government Auditing Standards* issued by the comptroller general of the United States.

[3] The term *presumptively mandatory requirement* is defined in section 20, *Defining Professional Requirements in Statements on Standards for Attestation Engagements*.

[4] Appendixes to Statements on Standards for Attestation Engagements (SSAEs) referred to in paragraph .05 of this section do not include previously issued appendixes to original pronouncements that, when adopted, modified other SSAEs.

Other Attestation Publications

.07 Other attestation publications include AICPA attestation publications not referred to above; attestation articles in the *Journal of Accountancy* and other professional journals; attestation articles in the AICPA *CPA Letter*; continuing professional education programs and other instruction materials, textbooks, guide books, attest programs, and checklists; and other attestation publications from state CPA societies, other organizations, and individuals.[5] Other attestation publications have no authoritative status; however, they may help the practitioner understand and apply the SSAEs.

.08 A practitioner may apply the attestation guidance included in an other attestation publication if he or she is satisfied that, in his or her judgment, it is both relevant to the circumstances of the attestation engagement, and appropriate. In determining whether an other attestation publication is appropriate, the practitioner may wish to consider the degree to which the publication is recognized as being helpful in understanding and applying SSAEs and the degree to which the issuer or author is recognized as an authority in attestation matters. Other attestation publications published by the AICPA that have been reviewed by the AICPA Audit and Attest Standards Staff are presumed to be appropriate.

.09 This section is effective when the subject matter or assertion is as of or for a period ending on or after December 15, 2006.

---

[5] The practitioner is not expected to be aware of the full body of other attestation publications.

AT Section 101

Attest Engagements

Source: SSAE No. 10; SSAE No. 11; SSAE No. 12; SSAE No. 14.

See section 9101 for interpretations of this section.

Effective when the subject matter or assertion is as of or for a period ending on or after June 1, 2001, unless otherwise indicated.

Applicability

.01 This section applies to engagements, except for those services discussed in paragraph .04, in which a certified public accountant in the practice of public accounting[1] (hereinafter referred to as a *practitioner*) is engaged to issue or does issue an examination, a review, or an agreed-upon procedures report on subject matter, or an assertion about the subject matter (hereafter referred to as *the assertion*), that is the responsibility of another party.[2]

.02 This section establishes a framework for attest[3] engagements performed by practitioners and for the ongoing development of related standards. For certain subject matter, specific attestation standards have been developed to provide additional requirements for engagement performance and reporting.

.03 When a practitioner undertakes an attest engagement for the benefit of a government body or agency and agrees to follow specified government standards, guides, procedures, statutes, rules, and regulations, the practitioner is obliged to follow those governmental requirements as well as the applicable attestation standards.

.04 Professional services provided by practitioners that are not covered by this SSAE include the following:

a. Services performed in accordance with Statements on Auditing Standards (SASs)

b. Services performed in accordance with Statements on Standards for Accounting and Review Services (SSARSs)

c. Services performed in accordance with the Statement on Standards for Consulting Services (SSCS), such as engagements in which the practitioner's role is solely to assist the client (for example, acting as the company accountant in preparing information other than financial statements), or engagements in which a practitioner is engaged to testify as an expert witness in accounting, auditing, taxation, or other matters, given certain stipulated facts

---

1 For a definition of the term *practice of public accounting*, see ET section 92, *Definitions*, paragraph .29.

2 See paragraph .02 of section 301, *Financial Forecasts and Projections*, for additional guidance on applicability when engaged to provide an attest service on a financial forecast or projection.

3 The term *attest* and its variants, such as *attesting* and *attestation,* are used in a number of state accountancy laws, and in regulations issued by state boards of accountancy under such laws, for different purposes and with different meanings from those intended by this section. Consequently, the definition of *attest engagements* set out in paragraph .01, and the attendant meaning of *attest* and *attestation* as used throughout the section, should not be understood as defining these terms and similar terms, as they are used in any law or regulation, nor as embodying a common understanding of the terms which may also be reflected in such laws or regulations.

d. Engagements in which the practitioner is engaged to advocate a client's position—for example, tax matters being reviewed by the Internal Revenue Service

e. Tax engagements in which a practitioner is engaged to prepare tax returns or provide tax advice

.05 An attest engagement may be part of a larger engagement, for example, a feasibility study or business acquisition study may also include an examination of prospective financial information. In such circumstances, these standards apply only to the attest portion of the engagement.

.06 Any professional service resulting in the expression of assurance must be performed under AICPA professional standards that provide for the expression of such assurance. Reports issued by a practitioner in connection with other professional standards should be written to be clearly distinguishable from and not to be confused with attest reports. For example, a practitioner performing an engagement which is intended solely to assist an organization in improving its controls over the privacy of client data should not issue a report as a result of that engagement expressing assurance as to the effectiveness of such controls. Additionally, a report that merely excludes the words, " ...was conducted in accordance with attestation standards established by the American Institute of Certified Public Accountants..." but is otherwise similar to an examination, a review or an agreed-upon procedures attest report may be inferred to be an attest report.

Definitions and Underlying Concepts

Subject Matter

.07 The subject matter of an attest engagement may take many forms, including the following:

a. Historical or prospective performance or condition (for example, historical or prospective financial information, performance measurements, and backlog data)

b. Physical characteristics (for example, narrative descriptions, square footage of facilities)

c. Historical events (for example, the price of a market basket of goods on a certain date)

d. Analyses (for example, break-even analyses)

e. Systems and processes (for example, internal control)

f. Behavior (for example, corporate governance, compliance with laws and regulations, and human resource practices)

The subject matter may be as of a point in time or for a period of time.

Assertion

.08 An assertion is any declaration or set of declarations about whether the subject matter is based on or in conformity with the criteria selected.

.09 A practitioner may report on a written assertion or may report directly on the subject matter. In either case, the practitioner should ordinarily obtain a written assertion in an examination or a review engagement. A written assertion may be presented to a practitioner in a number of ways, such as in a narrative description, within a schedule, or as part of a representation letter appropriately identifying what is being presented and the point in time or period of time covered.

.10 When a written assertion has not been obtained, a practitioner may still report on the subject matter; however, the form of the report will vary depending on the circumstances and its use should be restricted.[4] In this section, see paragraphs .58 and .60 on gathering sufficient evidence and paragraphs .73–.75 and .78–.80 for reporting guidance.

Responsible Party

.11 The *responsible party* is defined as the person or persons, either as individuals or representatives of the entity, responsible for the subject matter. If the nature of the subject matter is such that no such party exists, a party who has a reasonable basis for making a written assertion about the subject matter may provide such an assertion (hereinafter referred to as the *responsible party*).

.12 The practitioner may be engaged to gather information to enable the responsible party to evaluate the subject matter in connection with providing a written assertion. Regardless of the procedures performed by the practitioner, the responsible party must accept responsibility for its assertion and the subject matter and must not base its assertion solely on the practitioner's procedures.[5]

.13 Because the practitioner's role in an attest engagement is that of an *attester*, the practitioner should not take on the role of the responsible party in an attest engagement. Therefore, the need to clearly identify a responsible party is a prerequisite for an attest engagement. A practitioner may accept an engagement to perform an examination, a review or an agreed-upon procedures engagement on subject matter or an assertion related thereto provided that one of the following conditions is met.

a. The party wishing to engage the practitioner is responsible for the subject matter, or has a reasonable basis for providing a written assertion about the subject matter if the nature of the subject matter is such that a responsible party does not otherwise exist.

b. The party wishing to engage the practitioner is not responsible for the subject matter but is able to provide the practitioner, or have a third party who is responsible for the subject matter provide the practitioner, with evidence of the third party's responsibility for the subject matter.

.14 The practitioner should obtain written acknowledgment or other evidence of the responsible party's responsibility for the subject matter, or the written assertion, as it relates to the objective of the engagement. The responsible party can acknowledge that responsibility in a number of ways, for example, in an engagement letter, a representation letter, or the presentation of the subject matter, including the notes thereto, or the written assertion. If the practitioner is not able to directly obtain written acknowledgment, the practitioner should obtain other evidence of the responsible party's responsibility for the subject matter (for example, by reference to legislation, a regulation, or a contract).

---

[4] When the practitioner is unable to perform the inquiry and analytical or other procedures that he or she considers necessary to achieve the limited assurance contemplated by a review, or when the client is the responsible party and does not provide the practitioner with a written assertion, the review will be incomplete. A review that is incomplete is not an adequate basis for issuing a review report and, accordingly, the practitioner should withdraw from the engagement.

[5] See paragraph .112 regarding the practitioner's assistance in developing subject matter or criteria.

Applicability to Agreed-Upon Procedures Engagements

.15 An agreed-upon procedures attest engagement is one in which a practitioner is engaged to issue a report of findings based on specific procedures performed on subject matter. The general, fieldwork, and reporting standards for attest engagements set forth in this section are applicable to agreed-upon procedures engagements. Because the application of these standards to agreed-upon procedures engagements is discussed in section 201, *Agreed-Upon Procedures Engagements*, such engagements are not discussed further in this section.

The Relationship of Attestation Standards to Quality Control Standards

.16 The practitioner is responsible for compliance with the American Institute of Certified Public Accountants' (AICPA's) Statements on Standards for Attestation Engagements (SSAEs) in an attest engagement. Rule 202, *Compliance With Standards*, of the Code of Professional Conduct (ET sec. 202 par. .01), requires members to comply with such standards when conducting professional services.

.17 A firm of practitioners has a responsibility to adopt a system of quality control in the conduct of a firm's attest practice.[6] Thus, a firm should establish quality control policies and procedures to provide it with reasonable assurance that its personnel comply with the attestation standards in its attest engagements. The nature and extent of a firm's quality control policies and procedures depend on factors such as its size, the degree of operating autonomy allowed its personnel and its practice offices, the nature of its practice, its organization, and appropriate cost-benefit considerations. [As amended, effective September 2002, by SSAE No. 12.]

.18 Attestation standards relate to the conduct of individual attest engagements; quality control standards relate to the conduct of a firm's attest practice as a whole. Thus, attestation standards and quality control standards are related and the quality control policies and procedures that a firm adopts may affect both the conduct of individual attest engagements and the conduct of a firm's attest practice as a whole. However, deficiencies in or instances of noncompliance with a firm's quality control policies and procedures do not, in and of themselves, indicate that a particular engagement was not performed in accordance with attestation standards. [As amended, effective September 2002, by SSAE No. 12.]

General Standards

Training and Proficiency

.19 The first general standard is—*The practitioner must have adequate technical training and proficiency to perform the attestation engagement.* [As amended, effective when the subject matter or assertion is as of or for a period ending on or after December 15, 2006, by SSAE No. 14.]

---

[6] The elements of a system of quality control are identified in Statement on Quality Control Standards (SQCS) No. 8, *A Firm's System of Quality Control* (QC sec. 10). A system of quality control consists of policies designed to provide the firm with reasonable assurance that the firm and its personnel comply with professional standards and applicable legal and regulatory requirements and that reports issued by the firm are appropriate in the circumstances, and the procedures necessary to implement and monitor compliance with those policies. [As amended, effective September 2002, by SSAE No. 12. Footnote amended due to the issuance of SQCS No. 7, December 2008.]

.20 Performing attest services is different from preparing and presenting subject matter or an assertion. The latter involves collecting, classifying, summarizing, and communicating information; this usually entails reducing a mass of detailed data to a manageable and understandable form. On the other hand, performing attest services involves gathering evidence to support the subject matter or the assertion and objectively assessing the measurements and communications of the responsible party. Thus, attest services are analytical, critical, investigative, and are concerned with the basis and support for the subject matter or the assertion.

Adequate Knowledge of Subject Matter

.21 The second general standard is—*The practitioner must have adequate knowledge of the subject matter.* [As amended, effective when the subject matter or assertion is as of or for a period ending on or after December 15, 2006, by SSAE No. 14.]

.22 A practitioner may obtain adequate knowledge of the subject matter through formal or continuing education, including self-study, or through practical experience. However, this standard does not necessarily require a practitioner to personally acquire all of the necessary knowledge in the subject matter to be qualified to express a conclusion. This knowledge requirement may be met, in part, through the use of one or more specialists on a particular attest engagement if the practitioner has sufficient knowledge of the subject matter (*a*) to communicate to the specialist the objectives of the work and (*b*) to evaluate the specialist's work to determine if the objectives were achieved.

Suitability and Availability of Criteria

.23 The third general standard is—*The practitioner must have reason to believe that the subject matter is capable of evaluation against criteria that are suitable and available to users.* [As amended, effective when the subject matter or assertion is as of or for a period ending on or after December 15, 2006, by SSAE No. 14.]

Suitability of Criteria

.24 Criteria are the standards or benchmarks used to measure and present the subject matter and against which the practitioner evaluates the subject matter.* Suitable criteria must have each of the following attributes:

- *Objectivity*—Criteria should be free from bias.
- *Measurability*—Criteria should permit reasonably consistent measurements, qualitative or quantitative, of subject matter.
- *Completeness*—Criteria should be sufficiently complete so that those relevant factors that would alter a conclusion about subject matter are not omitted.
- *Relevance*—Criteria should be relevant to the subject matter.

.25 Criteria that are established or developed by groups composed of experts that follow due process procedures, including exposure of the proposed

* An example of suitable criteria are the Trust Services criteria developed by the AICPA's Assurance Services Executive Committee. These criteria may be used when the subject matter of the engagement is the security, availability, or processing integrity of a system, or the confidentiality or privacy of the information processed or stored by that system. The Trust Services criteria are presented in TSP sections 100 and 200 of the AICPA's *Technical Practice Aids.* [Footnote added by the Assurance Services Executive Committee, January 2003. Footnote revised, May 2006, to reflect conforming changes necessary due to the issuance of Generally Accepted Privacy Principles.]

criteria for public comment, ordinarily should be considered suitable. Criteria promulgated by a body designated by the AICPA Governing Council under the AICPA Code of Professional Conduct are, by definition, considered to be suitable.

.26 Criteria may be established or developed by the client, the responsible party, industry associations, or other groups that do not follow due process procedures or do not as clearly represent the public interest. To determine whether these criteria are suitable, the practitioner should evaluate them based on the attributes described in paragraph .24.

.27 Regardless of who establishes or develops the criteria, the responsible party or the client is responsible for selecting the criteria and the client is responsible for determining that such criteria are appropriate for its purposes.

.28 The use of suitable criteria does not presume that all persons or groups would be expected to select the same criteria in evaluating the same subject matter. There may be more than one set of suitable criteria for a given subject matter. For example, in an engagement to express assurance about customer satisfaction, a responsible party may select as a criterion for customer satisfaction that all customer complaints are resolved to the satisfaction of the customer. In other cases, another responsible party may select a different criterion, such as the number of repeat purchases in the three months following the initial purchase.

.29 In evaluating the measurability attribute as described in paragraph .24, the practitioner should consider whether the criteria are sufficiently precise to permit people having competence in and using the same measurement criterion to be able to ordinarily obtain materially similar measurements. Consequently, practitioners should not perform an engagement when the criteria are so subjective or vague that reasonably consistent measurements, qualitative or quantitative, of subject matter cannot ordinarily be obtained. However, practitioners will not always reach the same conclusion because such evaluations often require the exercise of considerable professional judgment.

.30 For the purpose of assessing whether the use of particular criteria can be expected to yield reasonably consistent measurement and evaluation, consideration should be given to the nature of the subject matter. For example, *soft information*, such as forecasts or projections, would be expected to have a wider range of reasonable estimates than *hard* data, such as the calculated investment performance of a defined portfolio of managed investment products.

.31 Some criteria may be appropriate for only a limited number of parties who either participated in their establishment or can be presumed to have an adequate understanding of the criteria. For instance, criteria set forth in a lease agreement for override payments may be appropriate only for reporting to the parties to the agreement because of the likelihood that such criteria would be misunderstood or misinterpreted by parties other than those who have specifically agreed to the criteria. Such criteria can be agreed upon directly by the parties or through a designated representative. If a practitioner determines that such criteria are appropriate only for a limited number of parties, the use of the report should be restricted to those specified parties who either participated in their establishment or can be presumed to have an adequate understanding of the criteria.

.32 The third general standard in paragraph .23 applies equally regardless of the level of the attest service to be provided. Consequently, it is inappropriate to perform a review engagement if the practitioner concludes that an examination cannot be performed because competent persons using the same criteria would not be able to obtain materially similar evaluations.

Availability of Criteria

.33 The criteria should be available to users in one or more of the following ways:

a. Available publicly

b. Available to all users through inclusion in a clear manner in the presentation of the subject matter or in the assertion

c. Available to all users through inclusion in a clear manner in the practitioner's report

d. Well understood by most users, although not formally available (for example, "The distance between points A and B is twenty feet;" the criterion of distance measured in feet is considered to be well understood)

e. Available only to specified parties; for example, terms of a contract or criteria issued by an industry association that are available only to those in the industry

.34 If criteria are only available to specified parties, the practitioner's report should be restricted to those parties who have access to the criteria as described in paragraphs .78 and .80.

Independence

.35 The fourth general standard is—*The practitioner must maintain independence in mental attitude in all matters relating to the engagement.*[7] [As amended, effective when the subject matter or assertion is as of or for a period ending on or after December 15, 2006, by SSAE No. 14.]

.36 The practitioner should maintain the intellectual honesty and impartiality necessary to reach an unbiased conclusion about the subject matter or the assertion. This is a cornerstone of the attest function.

.37 In the final analysis, independence in mental attitude means objective consideration of facts, unbiased judgments, and honest neutrality on the part of the practitioner in forming and expressing conclusions. It implies not the attitude of an advocate or an adversary but an impartiality that recognizes an obligation for fairness. Independence in mental attitude presumes an undeviating concern for an unbiased conclusion about the subject matter or an assertion no matter what the subject matter or the assertion may be.

.38 The profession has established, through the AICPA's Code of Professional Conduct, precepts to guard against the *presumption* of loss of independence. Presumption is stressed because the possession of intrinsic independence is a matter of personal quality rather than of rules that formulate certain objective tests. Insofar as these precepts have been incorporated in the profession's code, they have the force of professional law for the independent practitioner.

---

[7] The practitioner performing an attest engagement should be independent pursuant to Rule 101, *Independence*, of the Code of Professional Conduct (ET sec. 101 par. .01). Interpretation No. 11, " Modified Application of Rule 101 for Engagements Performed in Accordance With Statements on Standards for Attestation Engagements," of Rule 101 (ET sec. 101 par. .13) provides guidance about its application to certain attest engagements. [Footnote revised, December 2012, to reflect conforming changes necessary due to the revision of Ethics Interpretation 101-11.]

Due Professional Care

.39 The fifth general standard is—*The practitioner must exercise due professional care in the planning and performance of the engagement and the preparation of the report.* [As amended, effective when the subject matter or assertion is as of or for a period ending on or after December 15, 2006, by SSAE No. 14.]

.40 Due professional care imposes a responsibility on each practitioner involved with the engagement to observe each of the attestation standards. Exercise of due professional care requires critical review at every level of supervision of the work done and the judgment exercised by those assisting in the engagement, including the preparation of the report.

.41 *Cooley on Torts*, a legal treatise, describes the obligation for due care as follows:

> Every man who offers his services to another and is employed assumes the duty to exercise in the employment such skill as he possesses with reasonable care and diligence. In all these employments where peculiar skill is requisite, if one offers his services, he is understood as holding himself out to the public as possessing the degree of skill commonly possessed by others in the same employment, and if his pretentions are unfounded, he commits a species of fraud upon every man who employs him in reliance on his public profession. But no man, whether skilled or unskilled, undertakes that the task he assumes shall be performed successfully, and without fault or error; he undertakes for good faith and integrity, but not for infallibility, and he is liable to his employer for negligence, bad faith, or dishonesty, but not for losses consequent upon mere errors of judgment.[8]

Standards of Fieldwork

Planning and Supervision

.42 The first standard of fieldwork is—*The practitioner must adequately plan the work and must properly supervise any assistants.* [As amended, effective when the subject matter or assertion is as of or for a period ending on or after December 15, 2006, by SSAE No. 14.]

.43 Proper planning and supervision contribute to the effectiveness of attest procedures. Proper planning directly influences the selection of appropriate procedures and the timeliness of their application, and proper supervision helps ensure that planned procedures are appropriately applied.

.44 Planning an attest engagement involves developing an overall strategy for the expected conduct and scope of the engagement. To develop such a strategy, practitioners need to have sufficient knowledge to enable them to understand adequately the events, transactions, and practices that, in their judgment, have a significant effect on the subject matter or the assertion.

.45 Factors to be considered by the practitioner in planning an attest engagement include the following:

a. The criteria to be used

[8] D. Haggard, *Cooley on Torts*, 472 (4th ed., 1932).

b. Preliminary judgments about attestation risk[9] and materiality for attest purposes

c. The nature of the subject matter or the items within the assertion that are likely to require revision or adjustment

d. Conditions that may require extension or modification of attest procedures

e. The nature of the report expected to be issued

.46 The practitioner should establish an understanding with the client regarding the services to be performed for each engagement.[10] Such an understanding reduces the risk that either the practitioner or the client may misinterpret the needs or expectations of the other party. For example, it reduces the risk that the client may inappropriately rely on the practitioner to protect the entity against certain risks or to perform certain functions that are the client's responsibility. The understanding should include the objectives of the engagement, management's responsibilities, the practitioner's responsibilities, and limitations of the engagement. The practitioner should document the understanding in the working papers, preferably through a written communication with the client. If the practitioner believes an understanding with the client has not been established, he or she should decline to accept or perform the engagement.

.47 The nature, extent, and timing of planning will vary with the nature and complexity of the subject matter or the assertion and the practitioner's prior experience with management. As part of the planning process, the practitioner should consider the nature, extent, and timing of the work to be performed to accomplish the objectives of the attest engagement. Nevertheless, as the attest engagement progresses, changed conditions may make it necessary to modify planned procedures.

.48 Supervision involves directing the efforts of assistants who participate in accomplishing the objectives of the attest engagement and determining whether those objectives were accomplished. Elements of supervision include instructing assistants, staying informed of significant problems encountered, reviewing the work performed, and dealing with differences of opinion among personnel. The extent of supervision appropriate in a given instance depends on many factors, including the nature and complexity of the subject matter and the qualifications of the persons performing the work.

.49 Assistants should be informed of their responsibilities, including the objectives of the procedures that they are to perform and matters that may affect the nature, extent, and timing of such procedures. The practitioner with final responsibility for the engagement should direct assistants to bring to his or her attention significant questions raised during the attest engagement so that their significance may be assessed.

.50 The work performed by each assistant should be reviewed to determine whether it was adequately performed and to evaluate whether the results are consistent with the conclusion to be presented in the practitioner's report.

---

[9] *Attestation risk* is the risk that the practitioner may unknowingly fail to appropriately modify his or her attest report on the subject matter or an assertion that is materially misstated. It consists of (*a*) the risk (consisting of *inherent risk* and *control risk*) that the subject matter or assertion contains deviations or misstatements that could be material and (*b*) the risk that the practitioner will not detect such deviations or misstatements (*detection risk*).

[10] See paragraph 29 of SQCS No. 8. [Footnote amended due to the issuance of SQCS No. 7, December 2008. Footnote revised, December 2012, due to the issuance of SQCS No. 8.]

Obtaining Sufficient Evidence

.51 The second standard of fieldwork is—*The practitioner must obtain sufficient evidence to provide a reasonable basis for the conclusion that is expressed in the report.* [As amended, effective when the subject matter or assertion is as of or for a period ending on or after December 15, 2006, by SSAE No. 14.]

.52 Selecting and applying procedures that will accumulate evidence that is sufficient in the circumstances to provide a reasonable basis for the level of assurance to be expressed in the attest report requires the careful exercise of professional judgment. A broad array of available procedures may be applied in an attest engagement. In establishing a proper combination of procedures to appropriately restrict attestation risk, the practitioner should consider the following presumptions, bearing in mind that they are not mutually exclusive and may be subject to important exceptions.

a. Evidence obtained from independent sources outside an entity provides greater assurance about the subject matter or the assertion than evidence secured solely from within the entity.

b. Information obtained from the independent attester's direct personal knowledge (such as through physical examination, observation, computation, operating tests, or inspection) is more persuasive than information obtained indirectly.

c. The more effective the controls over the subject matter, the more assurance they provide about the subject matter or the assertion.

.53 Thus, in the hierarchy of available attest procedures, those that involve search and verification (for example, inspection, confirmation, or observation), particularly when using independent sources outside the entity, are generally more effective in restricting attestation risk than those involving internal inquiries and comparisons of internal information (for example, analytical procedures and discussions with individuals responsible for the subject matter or the assertion). On the other hand, the latter are generally less costly to apply.

.54 In an attest engagement designed to provide a high level of assurance (referred to as an *examination*), the practitioner's objective is to accumulate sufficient evidence to restrict attestation risk to a level that is, in the practitioner's professional judgment, appropriately low for the high level of assurance that may be imparted by his or her report. In such an engagement, a practitioner should select from all available procedures—that is, procedures that assess inherent and control risk and restrict detection risk—any combination that can restrict attestation risk to such an appropriately low level.

.55 In an attest engagement designed to provide a moderate level of assurance (referred to as a *review*), the objective is to accumulate sufficient evidence to restrict attestation risk to a moderate level. To accomplish this, the types of procedures performed generally are limited to inquiries and analytical procedures (rather than also including search and verification procedures).

.56 Nevertheless, there will be circumstances in which inquiry and analytical procedures (*a*) cannot be performed, (*b*) are deemed less efficient than other procedures, or (*c*) yield evidence indicating that the subject matter or the assertion may be incomplete or inaccurate. In the first circumstance, the practitioner should perform other procedures that he or she believes can provide him or her with a level of assurance equivalent to that which inquiries and analytical procedures would have provided. In the second circumstance, the practitioner may perform other procedures that he or she believes would be more efficient to provide him or her with a level of assurance equivalent to that which inquiries and analytical procedures would provide. In the third circumstance, the practitioner should perform additional procedures.

.57 The extent to which attestation procedures will be performed should be based on the level of assurance to be provided and the practitioner's consideration of (*a*) the nature and materiality of the information to be tested to the subject matter or the assertion taken as a whole, (*b*) the likelihood of misstatements, (*c*) knowledge obtained during current and previous engagements, (*d*) the responsible party's competence in the subject matter, (*e*) the extent to which the information is affected by the asserter's judgment, and (*f*) inadequacies in the responsible party's underlying data.

.58 As part of the attestation procedures, the practitioner considers the written assertion ordinarily provided by the responsible party. If a written assertion cannot be obtained from the responsible party, the practitioner should consider the effects on his or her ability to obtain sufficient evidence to form a conclusion about the subject matter. When the practitioner's client is the responsible party, a failure to obtain a written assertion should result in the practitioner concluding that a scope limitation exists.[11] When the practitioner's client is not the responsible party and a written assertion is not provided, the practitioner may be able to conclude that he or she has sufficient evidence to form a conclusion about the subject matter.

Representation Letter

.59 During an attest engagement, the responsible party makes many representations to the practitioner, both oral and written, in response to specific inquiries or through the presentation of subject matter or an assertion. Such representations from the responsible party are part of the evidential matter the practitioner obtains.

.60 Written representations from the responsible party ordinarily confirm representations explicitly or implicitly given to the practitioner, indicate and document the continuing appropriateness of such representations, and reduce the possibility of misunderstanding concerning the matters that are the subject of the representations. Accordingly, in an examination or a review engagement, a practitioner should consider obtaining a representation letter from the responsible party. Examples of matters that might appear in such a representation letter include the following:[12]

a. A statement acknowledging responsibility for the subject matter and, when applicable, the assertion

b. A statement acknowledging responsibility for selecting the criteria, where applicable

---

[11] When the client is the responsible party, it is presumed that the client will be capable of providing the practitioner with a written assertion regarding the subject matter. Failure to provide the written assertion in this circumstance is a client-imposed limitation on the practitioner's evidence-gathering efforts. In an examination, the practitioner should modify the report for the scope limitation. In a review engagement, such a scope limitation results in an incomplete review and the practitioner should withdraw from the engagement.

[12] Specific written representations will depend on the circumstances of the engagement (for example, whether the client is the responsible party) and the nature of the subject matter and the criteria. For example, when the client is not the responsible party but has selected the criteria, the practitioner might obtain the representation regarding responsibility for selection of the criteria from the client rather than the responsible party (see paragraph .61).

c. A statement acknowledging responsibility for determining that such criteria are appropriate for its purposes, where the responsible party is the client

d. The assertion about the subject matter based on the criteria selected

e. A statement that all known matters contradicting the assertion and any communication from regulatory agencies affecting the subject matter or the assertion have been disclosed to the practitioner

f. Availability of all records relevant to the subject matter

g. A statement that any known events subsequent to the period (or point in time) of the subject matter being reported on that would have a material effect on the subject matter (or, if applicable, the assertion) have been disclosed to the practitioner

h. Other matters as the practitioner deems appropriate

.61 When the client is not the responsible party, the practitioner should consider obtaining a letter of written representations from the client as part of the attest engagement. Examples of matters that might appear in such a representation letter include the following:

a. A statement that any known events subsequent to the period (or point in time) of the subject matter being reported on that would have a material effect on the subject matter (or, if applicable, the assertion) have been disclosed to the practitioner

b. A statement acknowledging the client's responsibility for selecting the criteria, where applicable

c. A statement acknowledging the client's responsibility for determining that such criteria are appropriate for its purposes

d. Other matters as the practitioner deems appropriate

.62 If the responsible party or the client refuses to furnish all written representations that the practitioner deems necessary, the practitioner should consider the effects of such a refusal on his or her ability to issue a conclusion about the subject matter. If the practitioner believes that the representation letter is necessary to obtain sufficient evidence to issue a report, the responsible party's or the client's refusal to furnish such evidence in the form of written representations constitutes a limitation on the scope of an examination sufficient to preclude an unqualified opinion and is ordinarily sufficient to cause the practitioner to disclaim an opinion or withdraw from an examination engagement. However, based on the nature of the representations not obtained or the circumstances of the refusal, the practitioner may conclude, in an examination engagement, that a qualified opinion is appropriate. Further, the practitioner should consider the effects of the refusal on his or her ability to rely on other representations. When a scope limitation exists in a review engagement, the practitioner should withdraw from the engagement. (See paragraph .75.)

Standards of Reporting[13]

.63 The first standard of reporting is—*The practitioner must identify the subject matter or the assertion being reported on and state the character of the engagement in the report.* [As amended, effective when the subject matter or assertion is as of or for a period ending on or after December 15, 2006, by SSAE No. 14.]

---

[13] The reporting standards apply only when the practitioner issues a report. [Footnote added, effective when the subject matter or assertion is as of or for a period ending on or after December 15, 2006, by SSAE No. 14.]

.64 The practitioner who accepts an attest engagement should issue a report on the subject matter or the assertion or withdraw from the attest engagement. If the practitioner is reporting on the assertion, the assertion should be bound with or accompany the practitioner's report or the assertion should be clearly stated in the practitioner's report.[14]

.65 The statement of the character of an attest engagement includes the following two elements: (*a*) a description of the nature and scope of the work performed and (*b*) a reference to the professional standards governing the engagement. The terms *examination* and *review* should be used to describe engagements to provide, respectively, a high level and a moderate level of assurance. The reference to professional standards should be accomplished by referring to "attestation standards established by the American Institute of Certified Public Accountants."

.66 The second standard of reporting is—*The practitioner must state the practitioner's conclusion about the subject matter or the assertion in relation to the criteria against which the subject matter was evaluated in the report.* However, if conditions exist that, individually or in combination, result in one or more material misstatements or deviations from the criteria, the practitioner should modify the report and, to most effectively communicate with the reader of the report, should ordinarily express his or her conclusion directly on the subject matter,[15] not on the assertion. [As amended, effective when the subject matter or assertion is as of or for a period ending on or after December 15, 2006, by SSAE No. 14.]

.67 The practitioner should consider the concept of materiality in applying this standard. In expressing a conclusion, the practitioner should consider an omission or a misstatement to be material if the omission or misstatement—individually or when aggregated with others—is such that a reasonable person would be influenced by the omission or misstatement. The practitioner should consider both qualitative and quantitative aspects of omissions and misstatements.

.68 The term *general use* applies to attest reports that are not restricted to specified parties. General-use attest reports should be limited to two levels of assurance: one based on a restriction of attestation risk to an appropriately low level (an *examination*) and the other based on a restriction of attestation risk to a moderate level (a *review*). In an engagement to achieve a high level of assurance (an *examination*), the practitioner's conclusion should be expressed in the form of an opinion. When attestation risk has been restricted only to a moderate level (a *review*), the conclusion should be expressed in the form of negative assurance.

.69 A practitioner may report on subject matter or an assertion at multiple dates or covering multiple periods during which criteria have changed (for example, a report on comparative information). In those circumstances, the practitioner should determine whether the criteria are clearly stated or described for each of the dates or periods, and whether the changes have been adequately disclosed.

---

[14] The use of a "hot link" within the practitioner's report to management's assertion, such as might be used in a WebTrust[SM] report, would meet this requirement. [Footnote renumbered by the issuance of SSAE No. 14, November 2006.]

[15] Specific standards may require that the practitioner express his or her conclusion directly on the subject matter. For example, if management states in its assertion that a material weakness exists in the entity's internal control over financial reporting, the practitioner should state his or her opinion directly on the effectiveness of internal control, not on management's assertion related thereto. [Footnote renumbered by the issuance of SSAE No. 14, November 2006.]

.70 If the criteria used for the subject matter for the current date or period differ from those criteria used for the subject matter for a preceding date or period and the subject matter for the prior date or period is not presented, the practitioner should consider whether the changes in criteria are likely to be significant to users of the report. If so, the practitioner should determine whether the criteria are clearly stated or described and the fact that the criteria have changed is disclosed. (See paragraphs .76–.77.)

.71 The third standard of reporting is—*The practitioner must state all of the practitioner's significant reservations about the engagement, the subject matter, and, if applicable, the assertion related thereto in the report.* [As amended, effective when the subject matter or assertion is as of or for a period ending on or after December 15, 2006, by SSAE No. 14.]

.72 *Reservations about the engagement* refers to any unresolved problem that the practitioner had in complying with these attestation standards, interpretive standards, or the specific procedures agreed to by the specified parties. The practitioner should not express an unqualified conclusion unless the engagement has been conducted in accordance with the attestation standards. Such standards will not have been complied with if the practitioner has been unable to apply all the procedures that he or she considers necessary in the circumstances.

.73 Restrictions on the scope of an engagement, whether imposed by the client or by such other circumstances as the timing of the work or the inability to obtain sufficient evidence, may require the practitioner to qualify the assurance provided, to disclaim any assurance, or to withdraw from the engagement. For example, if the practitioner's client is the responsible party, a failure to obtain a written assertion should result in the practitioner concluding that a scope limitation exists. (See paragraph .58.)

.74 The practitioner's decision to provide a qualified opinion, to disclaim an opinion, or to withdraw because of a scope limitation in an examination engagement depends on an assessment of the effect of the omitted procedure(s) on his or her ability to express assurance. This assessment will be affected by the nature and magnitude of the potential effects of the matters in question, and by their significance to the subject matter or the assertion. If the potential effects are pervasive to the subject matter or the assertion, a disclaimer or withdrawal is more likely to be appropriate. When restrictions that significantly limit the scope of the engagement are imposed by the client or the responsible party, the practitioner generally should disclaim an opinion or withdraw from the engagement. The reasons for a qualification or disclaimer should be described in the practitioner's report.

.75 In a review engagement, when the practitioner is unable to perform the inquiry and analytical or other procedures he or she considers necessary to achieve the limited assurance contemplated by a review, or when the client is the responsible party and does not provide the practitioner with a written assertion, the review will be incomplete. A review that is incomplete is not an adequate basis for issuing a review report and, accordingly, the practitioner should withdraw from the engagement.

.76 *Reservations about the subject matter or the assertion* refers to any unresolved reservation about the assertion or about the conformity of the subject matter with the criteria, including the adequacy of the disclosure of material matters. They can result in either a qualified or an adverse opinion, depending on the materiality of the departure from the criteria against which the subject matter or the assertion was evaluated, or a modified conclusion in a review engagement.

.77 Reservations about the subject matter or the assertion may relate to the measurement, form, arrangement, content, or underlying judgments and assumptions applicable to the subject matter or the assertion and its appended notes, including, for example, the terminology used, the amount of detail given, the classification of items, and the bases of amounts set forth. The practitioner considers whether a particular reservation should affect the report given the circumstances and facts of which he or she is aware at the time.

.78 The fourth standard of reporting is—*The practitioner must state in the report that the report is intended solely for the information and use of the specified parties under the following circumstances:*

- *When the criteria used to evaluate the subject matter are determined by the practitioner to be appropriate only for a limited number of parties who either participated in their establishment or can be presumed to have an adequate understanding of the criteria*
- *When the criteria used to evaluate the subject matter are available only to specified parties*
- *When reporting on subject matter and a written assertion has not been provided by the responsible party*
- *When the report is on an attestation engagement to apply agreed-upon procedures to the subject matter*

[As amended, effective when the subject matter or assertion is as of or for a period ending on or after December 15, 2006, by SSAE No. 14.]

.79 The need for restriction on the use of a report may result from a number of circumstances, including the purpose of the report, the criteria used in preparation of the subject matter, the extent to which the procedures performed are known or understood, and the potential for the report to be misunderstood when taken out of the context in which it was intended to be used. A practitioner should consider informing his or her client that restricted-use reports are not intended for distribution to nonspecified parties, regardless of whether they are included in a document containing a separate general-use report.[16,17] However, a practitioner is not responsible for controlling a client's distribution of restricted-use reports. Accordingly, a restricted-use report should alert readers to the restriction on the use of the report by indicating that the report is not intended to be and should not be used by anyone other than the specified parties.

.80 An attest report that is restricted as to use should contain a separate paragraph at the end of the report that includes the following elements:

a. A statement indicating that the report is intended solely for the information and use of the specified parties

---

[16] In some cases, restricted-use reports filed with regulatory agencies are required by law or regulation to be made available to the public as a matter of public record. Also, a regulatory agency as part of its oversight responsibility for an entity may require access to restricted-use reports in which they are not named as a specified party. [Footnote renumbered by the issuance of SSAE No. 14, November 2006.]

[17] This section does not preclude the practitioner, in connection with establishing the terms of the engagement, from reaching an understanding with the client that the intended use of the report will be restricted, and from obtaining the client's agreement that the client and the specified parties will not distribute the report to parties other than those identified in the report. [Footnote renumbered by the issuance of SSAE No. 14, November 2006.]

b. An identification of the specified parties to whom use is restricted

c. A statement that the report is not intended to be and should not be used by anyone other than the specified parties

An example of such a paragraph is the following.

> This report is intended solely for the information and use of [*the specified parties*] and is not intended to be and should not be used by anyone other than these specified parties.

.81 Other attestation standards may specify situations that require restricted reports such as the following:

a. A review report on management's discussion and analysis

b. A report on prospective financial information when the report is intended for use by the responsible party alone, or by the responsible party and third parties with whom the responsible party is negotiating directly, as described in paragraph .10 of section 301, *Financial Forecasts and Projections*.

Furthermore, nothing in this section precludes a practitioner from restricting the use of any report.

.82 If a practitioner issues a single combined report covering both (*a*) subject matter or presentations that require a restriction on use to specified parties and (*b*) subject matter or presentations that ordinarily do not require such a restriction, the use of such a single combined report should be restricted to the specified parties.

.83 In some instances, a separate restricted-use report may be included in a document that also contains a general-use report. The inclusion of a separate restricted-use report in a document that contains a general-use report does not affect the intended use of either report. The restricted-use report remains restricted as to use, and the general-use report continues to be for general use.

Examination Reports

.84 When expressing an opinion, the practitioner should clearly state whether, in his or her opinion, (*a*) the subject matter is based on (or in conformity with) the criteria in all material respects or (*b*) the assertion is presented (or fairly stated), in all material respects, based on the criteria. Reports expressing an opinion may be qualified or modified for some aspect of the subject matter, the assertion or the engagement (see the third reporting standard). However, as stated in paragraph .66, if conditions exist that, individually or in combination, result in one or more material misstatements or deviations from the criteria, the practitioner should modify the report and, to most effectively communicate with the reader of the report, should ordinarily express his or her conclusion directly on the subject matter, not on the assertion. In addition, such reports may emphasize certain matters relating to the attest engagement, the subject matter, or the assertion. The form of the practitioner's report will depend on whether the practitioner opines on the subject matter or the assertion.

.85 The practitioner's examination report on subject matter should include the following:

a. A title that includes the word *independent*

b. An identification of the subject matter and the responsible party

c. A statement that the subject matter is the responsibility of the responsible party *d.* A statement that the practitioner's responsibility is to express an opinion on the subject matter based on his or her examination

e. A statement that the examination was conducted in accordance with attestation standards established by the American Institute of Certified Public Accountants, and, accordingly, included procedures that the practitioner considered necessary in the circumstances

f. A statement that the practitioner believes the examination provides a reasonable basis for his or her opinion

g. The practitioner's opinion on whether the subject matter is based on (or in conformity with) the criteria in all material respects

h. A statement restricting the use of the report to specified parties under the following circumstances (see paragraphs .78–.83):

(1) When the criteria used to evaluate the subject matter are determined by the practitioner to be appropriate only for a limited number of parties who either participated in their establishment or can be presumed to have an adequate understanding of the criteria

(2) When the criteria used to evaluate the subject matter are available only to the specified parties

(3) When a written assertion has not been provided by the responsible party (The practitioner should also include a statement to that effect in the introductory paragraph of the report.)

i. The manual or printed signature of the practitioner's firm

j. The date of the examination report

Appendix A [paragraph .114], *Examination Reports*, includes a standard examination report on subject matter. (See example 1.)

.86 The practitioner's examination report on an assertion should include the following:

a. A title that includes the word *independent*

b. An identification of the assertion and the responsible party (When the assertion does not accompany the practitioner's report, the first paragraph of the report should also contain a statement of the assertion.)

c. A statement that the assertion is the responsibility of the responsible party

d. A statement that the practitioner's responsibility is to express an opinion on the assertion based on his or her examination

e. A statement that the examination was conducted in accordance with attestation standards established by the American Institute of Certified Public Accountants, and, accordingly, included procedures that the practitioner considered necessary in the circumstances

f. A statement that the practitioner believes the examination provides a reasonable basis for his or her opinion

g. The practitioner's opinion on whether the assertion is presented (or fairly stated), in all material respects, based on the criteria (However, see paragraph .66.)

h. A statement restricting the use of the report to specified parties under the following circumstances (see paragraphs .78–.83):

(1) When the criteria used to evaluate the subject matter are determined by the practitioner to be appropriate only for a limited number of parties who either participated in their establishment

or can be presumed to have an adequate understanding of the criteria

(2) When the criteria used to evaluate the subject matter are available only to the specified parties

i. The manual or printed signature of the practitioner's firm

j. The date of the examination report

Appendix A [paragraph .114] includes a standard examination report on an assertion. (See example 2.)

.87 Nothing precludes the practitioner from examining an assertion but opining directly on the subject matter. (See Appendix A [paragraph .114], example 3.)

Review Reports

.88 In a review report, the practitioner's conclusion should state whether any information came to the practitioner's attention on the basis of the work performed that indicates that (*a*) the subject matter is not based on (or in conformity with) the criteria or (*b*) the assertion is not presented (or fairly stated) in all material respects based on the criteria. (As discussed more fully in the commentary to the third reporting standard, if the subject matter or the assertion is not modified to correct for any such information that comes to the practitioner's attention, such information should be described in the practitioner's report.)

.89 The practitioner's review report on subject matter should include the following:

a. A title that includes the word *independent*

b. An identification of the subject matter and the responsible party

c. A statement that the subject matter is the responsibility of the responsible party

d. A statement that the review was conducted in accordance with attestation standards established by the American Institute of Certified Public Accountants

e. A statement that a review is substantially less in scope than an examination, the objective of which is an expression of opinion on the subject matter, and accordingly, no such opinion is expressed

f. A statement about whether the practitioner is aware of any material modifications that should be made to the subject matter in order for it to be based on (or in conformity with), in all material respects, the criteria, other than those modifications, if any, indicated in his or her report

g. A statement restricting the use of the report to specified parties under the following circumstances (see paragraphs .78–.83):

(1) When the criteria used to evaluate the subject matter are determined by the practitioner to be appropriate only for a limited number of parties who either participated in their establishment or can be presumed to have an adequate understanding of the criteria

(2) When the criteria used to evaluate the subject matter are available only to the specified parties

(3) When a written assertion has not been provided by the responsible party and the responsible party is not the client (The practitioner should also include a statement to that effect in the introductory paragraph of the report.)

h. The manual or printed signature of the practitioner's firm

i. The date of the review report

Appendix B [paragraph .115] *Review Reports*, includes a standard review report on subject matter. (See example 1.) Appendix B [paragraph .115] also includes a review report on subject matter that is the responsibility of a party other than client; the report is restricted as to use because a written assertion has not been provided by the responsible party. (See example 2.)

.90 The practitioner's review report on an assertion should include the following:

a. A title that includes the word *independent*

b. An identification of the assertion and the responsible party (When the assertion does not accompany the practitioner's report, the first paragraph of the report should also contain a statement of the assertion.)

c. A statement that the assertion is the responsibility of the responsible party

d. A statement that the review was conducted in accordance with attestation standards established by the American Institute of Certified Public Accountants

e. A statement that a review is substantially less in scope than an examination, the objective of which is an expression of opinion on the assertion, and accordingly, no such opinion is expressed

f. A statement about whether the practitioner is aware of any material modifications that should be made to the assertion in order for it to be presented (or fairly stated), in all material respects, based on (or in conformity with) the criteria, other than those modifications, if any, indicated in his or her report (However, see paragraph .66.)

g. A statement restricting the use of the report to specified parties under the following circumstances (see paragraphs .78–.83):

(1) When the criteria used to evaluate the subject matter are determined by the practitioner to be appropriate only for a limited number of parties who either participated in their establishment or can be presumed to have an adequate understanding of the criteria

(2) When the criteria used to evaluate the subject matter are available only to the specified parties

h. The manual or printed signature of the practitioner's firm

i. The date of the review report

Appendix B [paragraph .115] includes a review report on an assertion that is restricted as to use because the criteria are available only to the specified parties. (See example 3.)

Other Information in a Client-Prepared Document Containing the Practitioner's Attest Report[18]

.91 A client may publish various documents that contain information (hereinafter referred to as *other information*) in addition to the practitioner's attest report on subject matter (or on an assertion related thereto). Paragraphs .92–.94 provide guidance to the practitioner when the other information is contained in (*a*) annual reports to holders of securities or beneficial interests, annual reports of organizations for charitable or philanthropic purposes distributed to the public, and annual reports filed with regulatory authorities under the Securities Exchange Act of 1934 or (*b*) other documents to which the practitioner, at the client's request, devotes attention. These paragraphs are not applicable when an attest report appears in a registration statement filed under the Securities Act of 1933. (See AU-C section 920, *Letters for Underwriters and Certain Other Requesting Parties*, and AU-C section 925, *Filings With the U.S. Securities and Exchange Commission Under the Securities Act of 1933*.) Also, these paragraphs are not applicable to other information on which the practitioner or another practitioner is engaged to issue an opinion. [Revised, December 2012, to reflect conforming changes necessary due to the issuance of SAS Nos. 122–126.]

.92 The practitioner's responsibility with respect to other information in such a document does not extend beyond the information identified in his or her report, and the practitioner has no obligation to perform any procedures to corroborate any other information contained in the document. However, the practitioner should read the other information not covered by the practitioner's report or by the report of the other practitioner and consider whether it, or the manner of its presentation, is materially inconsistent with the information appearing in the practitioner's report. If the practitioner believes that the other information is inconsistent with the information appearing in the practitioner's report, he or she should consider whether the practitioner's report requires revision. If the practitioner concludes that the report does not require revision, he or she should request the client to revise the other information. If the other information is not revised to eliminate the material inconsistency, the practitioner should consider other actions, such as revising his or her report to include an explanatory paragraph describing the material inconsistency, withholding the use of his or her report in the document, or withdrawing from the engagement.

.93 If, while reading the other information for the reasons set forth in paragraph .92, the practitioner becomes aware of information that he or she believes is a material misstatement of fact that is not a material inconsistency as described in paragraph .92, he or she should discuss the matter with the client. In connection with this discussion, the practitioner should consider that he or she may not have the expertise to assess the validity of the statement, that there may be no standards by which to assess its presentation, and that there may be valid differences of judgment or opinion. If the practitioner concludes he or she has a valid basis for concern, the practitioner should propose that the client consult with some other party whose advice may be useful, such as the entity's legal counsel.

---

[18] Such guidance pertains only to other information in a client-prepared document. The practitioner has no responsibility to read information contained in documents of nonclients. Further, the practitioner is not required to read information contained in electronic sites, or to consider the consistency of other information in electronic sites with the original documents since electronic sites are a means of distributing information and are not "documents" as that term is used in this section. Practitioners may be asked by their clients to render attest services with respect to information in electronic sites, in which case, other attest standards may apply to those services. [Footnote renumbered by the issuance of SSAE No. 14, November 2006.]

.94 If, after discussing the matter, the practitioner concludes that a material misstatement of fact remains, the action taken will depend on his or her judgment in the circumstances. The practitioner should consider steps such as notifying the client's management and audit committee in writing of his or her views concerning the information and consulting his or her legal counsel about further action appropriate in the circumstances.[19]

Consideration of Subsequent Events in an Attest Engagement

.95 Events or transactions sometimes occur subsequent to the point in time or period of time of the subject matter being tested but prior to the date of the practitioner's report that have a material effect on the subject matter and therefore require adjustment or disclosure in the presentation of the subject matter or assertion. These occurrences are referred to as *subsequent events*. In performing an attest engagement, a practitioner should consider information about subsequent events that comes to his or her attention. Two types of subsequent events require consideration by the practitioner.

.96 The first type consists of events that provide additional information with respect to conditions that existed at the point in time or during the period of time of the subject matter being tested. This information should be used by the practitioner in considering whether the subject matter is presented in conformity with the criteria and may affect the presentation of the subject matter, the assertion, or the practitioner's report.

.97 The second type consists of those events that provide information with respect to conditions that arose subsequent to the point in time or period of time of the subject matter being tested that are of such a nature and significance that their disclosure is necessary to keep the subject matter from being misleading. This type of information will not normally affect the practitioner's report if the information is appropriately disclosed.

.98 While the practitioner has no responsibility to detect subsequent events, the practitioner should inquire of the responsible party (and his or her client if the client is not the responsible party) as to whether they are aware of any subsequent events, through the date of the practitioner's report, that would have a material effect on the subject matter or assertion.[20] If the practitioner has decided to obtain a representation letter, the letter ordinarily would include a representation concerning subsequent events. (See paragraphs .60–.61.)

.99 The practitioner has no responsibility to keep informed of events subsequent to the date of his or her report; however, the practitioner may later become aware of conditions that existed at that date that might have affected the practitioner's report had he or she been aware of them. In such circumstances, the practitioner may wish to consider the guidance in AU-C section

---

[19] If the client does not have an audit committee, the practitioner should communicate with individuals whose authority and responsibility are equivalent to those of an audit committee, such as the board of directors, the board of trustees, an owner in a owner-managed entity, or those who engaged the practitioner. [Footnote renumbered by the issuance of Statement on SSAE No. 14, November 2006.]

[20] For certain subject matter, specific subsequent event standards have been developed to provide additional requirements for engagement performance and reporting. Additionally, a practitioner engaged to examine the design or effectiveness of internal control over items not covered by section 501, *An Examination of an Entity's Internal Control Over Financial Reporting That Is Integrated With an Audit of Its Financial Statements*, or section 601, *Compliance Attestation*, should consider the subsequent events guidance set forth in paragraphs .129–.134 of section 501 and paragraphs .50–.52 of section 601. [Footnote renumbered by the issuance of SSAE No. 14, November 2006.]

560, *Subsequent Events and Subsequently Discovered Facts*. [Revised, December 2012, to reflect conforming changes necessary due to the issuance of SAS Nos. 122–126.]

Attest Documentation[21]

.100 The practitioner should prepare and maintain attest documentation, the form and content of which should be designed to meet the circumstances of the particular attest engagement.[22] Attest documentation is the principal record of attest procedures applied, information obtained, and conclusions or findings reached by the practitioner in the engagement. The quantity, type, and content of attest documentation are matters of the practitioner's professional judgment. [As amended, effective for attest engagements when the subject matter or assertion is as of or for a period ending on or after December 15, 2002, by SSAE No. 11.]

.101 Attest documentation serves mainly to:

a. Provide the principal support for the practitioner's report, including the representation regarding observance of the standards of fieldwork, which is implicit in the reference in the report to attestation standards.[23]

b. Aid the practitioner in the conduct and supervision of the attest engagement.

For examinations of prospective financial statements, attest documentation ordinarily should indicate that the process by which the entity develops its prospective financial statements was considered in determining the scope of the examination. [Paragraph added, effective for attest engagements when the subject matter or assertion is as of or for a period ending on or after December 15, 2002, by SSAE No. 11.]

.102 Examples of attest documentation are work programs, analyses, memoranda, letters of confirmation and representation, abstracts or copies of entity documents, and schedules or commentaries prepared or obtained by the practitioner. Attest documentation may be in paper form, electronic form, or other media. [Paragraph renumbered and amended, effective for attest engagements when the subject matter or assertion is as of or for a period ending on or after December 15, 2002, by SSAE No. 11.]

.103 Attest documentation should be sufficient to (*a*) enable members of the engagement team with supervision and review responsibilities to understand the nature, timing, extent, and results of attest procedures performed,

---

[21] *Attest documentation* also may be referred to as *working papers*. [Footnote added, effective for attest engagements when the subject matter or assertion is as of or for a period ending on or after December 15, 2002, by SSAE No. 11. Footnote renumbered by the issuance of SSAE No. 14, November 2006.]

[22] [Footnote renumbered and deleted by the issuance of SSAE No. 11, January 2002. Footnote subsequently renumbered by the issuance of SSAE No. 14, November 2006.]

[23] However, there is no intention to imply that the practitioner would be precluded from supporting his or her report by other means in addition to attest documentation. [Footnote added, effective for attest engagements when the subject matter or assertion is as of or for a period ending on or after December 15, 2002, by SSAE No. 11. Footnote renumbered by the issuance of SSAE No. 14, November 2006.]

and the information obtained[24] and (*b*) indicate the engagement team member(s) who performed and reviewed the work. [Paragraph added, effective for attest engagements when the subject matter or assertion is as of or for a period ending on or after December 15, 2002, by SSAE No. 11.]

.104 Attest documentation is the property of the practitioner, and some states recognize this right of ownership in their statutes. The practitioner should adopt reasonable procedures to retain attest documentation for a period of time sufficient to meet the needs of his or her practice and to satisfy any applicable legal or regulatory requirements for records retention.[25, [26]] [Paragraph renumbered and amended, effective for attest engagements when the subject matter or assertion is as of or for a period ending on or after December 15, 2002, by SSAE No. 11.]

.105 The practitioner has an ethical, and in some situations a legal, obligation to maintain the confidentiality of client information or information of the responsible party.[27] Because attest documentation often contains confidential information, the practitioner should adopt reasonable procedures to maintain the confidentiality of that information.[†] [Paragraph added, effective for attest engagements when the subject matter or assertion is as of or for a period ending on or after December 15, 2002, by SSAE No. 11.]

.106 The practitioner also should adopt reasonable procedures to prevent unauthorized access to attest documentation. [Paragraph added, effective for attest engagements when the subject matter or assertion is as of or for a period ending on or after December 15, 2002, by SSAE No. 11.]

.107 Certain attest documentation may sometimes serve as a useful reference source for the client, but it should not be regarded as a part of, or a substitute for, the client's records. [Paragraph renumbered and amended, effective for attest engagements when the subject matter or assertion is as of or for a period ending on or after December 15, 2002, by SSAE No. 11.]

[.108] [Paragraph renumbered and deleted by the issuance of SSAE No. 11, January 2002.]

---

[24] A firm of practitioners has a responsibility to adopt a system of quality control policies and procedures to provide the firm with reasonable assurance that its personnel comply with applicable professional standards, including attestation standards, and the firm's standards of quality in conducting individual attest engagements. Review of attest documentation and discussions with engagement team members are among the procedures a firm performs when monitoring compliance with the quality control policies and procedures that it has established. (Also, see paragraphs .17–.18.) [Footnote added, effective for attest engagements when the subject matter or assertion is as of or for a period ending on or after December 15, 2002, by SSAE No. 11. Footnote renumbered by the issuance of SSAE No. 14, November 2006.]

[25] The procedures should enable the practitioner to access electronic attest documentation throughout the retention period. [Footnote added, effective for attest engagements when the subject matter or assertion is as of or for a period ending on or after December 15, 2002, by SSAE No. 11. Footnote renumbered by the issuance of SSAE No. 14, November 2006.]

[[26]] [Footnote renumbered and deleted by the issuance of SSAE No. 11, January 2002. Footnote subsequently renumbered by the issuance of SSAE No. 14, November 2006.]

[27] Also, see Rule 301, *Confidential Client Information*, of the AICPA's Code of Professional Conduct (ET sec. 301 par. .01). [Footnote added, effective for attest engagements when the subject matter or assertion is as of or for a period ending on or after December 15, 2002, by SSAE No. 11. Footnote renumbered by the issuance of SSAE No. 14, November 2006.]

[†] ***Note:*** See Interpretation No. 4, "Providing Access to or Copies of Attest Documentation to a Regulator," of section 101 (sec. 9101 par. .43–.46).

Attest Services Related to Consulting Service Engagements

Attest Services as Part of a Consulting Service Engagement

.109 When a practitioner provides an attest service (as defined in this section) as part of a consulting service engagement, this SSAE applies only to the attest service. The SSCS applies to the balance of the consulting service engagement. [Paragraph renumbered by the issuance of SSAE No. 11, January 2002.]

.110 When the practitioner determines that an attest service is to be provided as part of a consulting service engagement, the practitioner should inform the client of the relevant differences between the two types of services and obtain concurrence that the attest service is to be performed in accordance with the appropriate professional requirements. The practitioner should take such actions because the professional requirements for an attest service differ from those for a consulting service engagement. [Paragraph renumbered by the issuance of SSAE No. 11, January 2002.]

.111 The practitioner should issue separate reports on the attest engagement and the consulting service engagement and, if presented in a common binder, the report on the attest engagement or service should be clearly identified and segregated from the report on the consulting service engagement. [Paragraph renumbered by the issuance of SSAE No. 11, January 2002.]

Subject Matter, Assertions, Criteria, and Evidence

.112 An attest service may involve subject matter, an assertion, criteria, or evidential matter developed during a concurrent or prior consulting service engagement. Subject matter or an assertion developed with the practitioner's advice and assistance as the result of such consulting services engagement may be the subject of an attest engagement, provided the responsible party accepts and acknowledges responsibility for the subject matter or assertion. (See paragraph .12.) Criteria developed with the practitioner's assistance may be used to evaluate subject matter in an attest engagement, provided such criteria meet the requirements of this section. Relevant information obtained in the course of a concurrent or prior consulting service engagement may be used as evidential matter in an attest engagement, provided the information satisfies the requirements of this section. [Paragraph renumbered by the issuance of SSAE No. 11, January 2002.]

Effective Date

.113 This section is effective when the subject matter or assertion is as of or for a period ending on or after June 1, 2001. Early application is permitted. [Paragraph renumbered by the issuance of SSAE No. 11, January 2002.]

.114

Appendix A

Examination Reports

Example 1

This is a standard examination report on subject matter for general use. This report pertains to subject matter for which suitable criteria exist and are available to all users through inclusion in a clear manner in the presentation of the subject matter. (See paragraphs .78–.83 for guidance on restricting the use of the report when criteria are available only to specified parties; see Example 4 for an illustration of such a report.) A written assertion has been obtained from the responsible party.

Independent Accountant's Report

> We have examined the [*identify the subject matter—for example, the accompanying schedule of investment returns of XYZ Company for the year ended December 31, 20XX*]. XYZ Company's management is responsible for the schedule of investment returns. Our responsibility is to express an opinion based on our examination.
>
> Our examination was conducted in accordance with attestation standards established by the American Institute of Certified Public Accountants and, accordingly, included examining, on a test basis, evidence supporting [*identify the subject matter—for example, XYZ Company's schedule of investment returns*] and performing such other procedures as we considered necessary in the circumstances. We believe that our examination provides a reasonable basis for our opinion.
>
> [*Additional paragraph(s) may be added to emphasize certain matters relating to the attest engagement or the subject matter.*]
>
> In our opinion, the schedule referred to above presents, in all material respects, [*identify the subject matter—for example, the investment returns of XYZ Company for the year ended December 31, 20XX*] based on [*identify criteria—for example, the ABC criteria set forth in Note 1*].
>
> [*Signature*]
>
> [*Date*]

Example 2

This report is a standard examination report on an assertion for general use. The report pertains to subject matter for which suitable criteria exist and are available to all users through inclusion in a clear manner in the presentation of the subject matter. (See paragraphs .78–.83 for guidance on restricting the use of the report when criteria are available only to specified parties.) A written assertion has been obtained from the responsible party.

Independent Accountant's Report

> We have examined management's assertion that [*identify the assertion—for example, the accompanying schedule of investment returns of XYZ Company for the year ended December 31, 20XX is presented in accordance with ABC criteria set forth in Note 1*]. XYZ Company's management is responsible for the assertion. Our responsibility is to express an opinion on the assertion based on our examination.

Our examination was conducted in accordance with attestation standards established by the American Institute of Certified Public Accountants and, accordingly, included examining, on a test basis, evidence supporting management's assertion and performing such other procedures as we considered necessary in the circumstances. We believe that our examination provides a reasonable basis for our opinion.

[*Additional paragraph(s) may be added to emphasize certain matters relating to the attest engagement or the assertion.*]

In our opinion, management's assertion referred to above is fairly stated, in all material respects, based on [*identify established or stated criteria—for example, the ABC criteria set forth in Note 1*].

[*Signature*]

[*Date*]

Example 3

This is an examination report for general use; the introductory paragraph states the practitioner has examined management's assertion but the practitioner opines directly on the subject matter (see paragraph .87). The report pertains to subject matter for which suitable criteria exist and are available to all users through inclusion in a clear manner in the presentation of the subject matter. (See paragraphs .78–.83 for guidance on restricting the use of the report when criteria are available only to specified parties.) A written assertion has been obtained from the responsible party.

Independent Accountant's Report

We have examined management's assertion that [*identify the assertion—for example, the accompanying schedule of investment returns of XYZ Company for the year ended December 31, 20XX is presented in accordance with the ABC criteria set forth in Note 1*]. XYZ Company's management is responsible for the assertion. Our responsibility is to express an opinion based on our examination.

Our examination was conducted in accordance with attestation standards established by the American Institute of Certified Public Accountants and, accordingly, included examining, on a test basis, evidence supporting [*identify the subject matter—for example, XYZ Company's schedule of investment returns*] and performing such other procedures as we considered necessary in the circumstances. We believe that our examination provides a reasonable basis for our opinion.

[*Additional paragraph(s) may be added to emphasize certain matters relating to the attest engagement or the assertion.*]

In our opinion, the schedule referred to above, presents, in all material respects, [*identify the subject matter—for example, the investment returns of XYZ Company for the year ended December 31, 20XX*] based on [*identify criteria—for example, the ABC criteria set forth in Note 1*].

[*Signature*]

[*Date*]

Example 4

This is an examination report on subject matter. Although suitable criteria exist, use of the report is restricted because the criteria are available only to specified parties. (See paragraph .34.) A written assertion has been obtained from the responsible party.

Independent Accountant's Report

We have examined the accompanying schedule of investment returns of XYZ Company for the year ended December 31, 20XX. XYZ Company's management is responsible for the schedule of investment returns. Our responsibility is to express an opinion based on our examination.

Our examination was conducted in accordance with attestation standards established by the American Institute of Certified Public Accountants and, accordingly, included examining, on a test basis, evidence supporting [*identify the subject matter—for example, XYZ Company's schedule of investment returns*] and performing such other procedures as we considered necessary in the circumstances. We believe that our examination provides a reasonable basis for our opinion.

[*Additional paragraph(s) may be added to emphasize certain matters relating to the attest engagement or the assertion.*]

In our opinion, the schedule referred to above, presents, in all material respects, [*identify the subject matter—for example, the investment returns of XYZ Company for the year ended December 31, 20XX*] based on the ABC criteria referred to in the investment management agreement between XYZ Company and DEF Investment Managers, Ltd., dated November 15, 20X1.

This report is intended solely for the information and use of XYZ Company and [*identify other specified parties—for example, DEF Investment Managers, Ltd.*] and is not intended to be and should not be used by anyone other than these specified parties.

[*Signature*]

[*Date*]

Example 5

This is an examination report with a qualified opinion because conditions exist that, individually or in combination, result in one or more material misstatements or deviations from the criteria; the report is for general use. The report pertains to subject matter for which suitable criteria exist and are available to all users through inclusion in a clear manner in the presentation of the subject matter. (See paragraphs .78–.83 for guidance on restricting the use of the report when criteria are available only to specified parties.) A written assertion has been obtained from the responsible party.

Independent Accountant's Report

We have examined the accompanying schedule of investment returns of XYZ Company for the year ended December 31, 20XX. XYZ Company's management is responsible for the schedule of investment returns. Our responsibility is to express an opinion based on our examination.

Our examination was conducted in accordance with attestation standards established by the American Institute of Certified Public Accountants and, accordingly, included examining, on a test basis, evidence supporting [*identify the subject matter—for example, XYZ Company's schedule of investment returns*] and performing such other procedures as we considered necessary in the circumstances. We believe that our examination provides a reasonable basis for our opinion.

Our examination disclosed the following [*describe condition(s) that, individually or in the aggregate, resulted in a material misstatement or deviation from the criteria*].

In our opinion, except for the material misstatement [*or deviation from the criteria*] described in the preceding paragraph, the schedule referred to above, presents, in all material respects, [*identify the subject matter—for example, the investment returns of XYZ Company for the year ended December 31, 20XX*] based on [*identify criteria—for example, the ABC criteria set forth in Note 1*].

[*Signature*]

[*Date*]

Example 6

This is an examination report that contains a disclaimer of opinion because of a scope restriction. (See paragraph .74 for reporting guidance when there is a scope restriction.) The report pertains to subject matter for which suitable criteria exist and are available to all users through inclusion in a clear manner in the presentation of the subject matter.

Independent Accountant's Report

We were engaged to examine the accompanying schedule of investment returns of XYZ Company for the year ended December 31, 20XX. XYZ Company's management is responsible for the schedule of investment returns.

[*Scope paragraph should be omitted.*]

[*Include paragraph to describe scope restrictions.*]

Because of the restriction on the scope of our examination discussed in the preceding paragraph, the scope of our work was not sufficient to enable us to express, and we do not express, an opinion on whether the schedule referred to above presents, in all material respects, [*identify the subject matter—for example, the investment returns of XYZ Company for the year ended December 31, 20XX*] based on [*identify criteria—for example, the ABC criteria set forth in Note 1*].

[*Signature*]

[*Date*]

Example 7

This is an examination report on subject matter that is the responsibility of a party other than the client. The report is restricted as to use since a written assertion has not been provided by the responsible party. (See paragraph .78.) The subject matter pertains to criteria that are suitable and are available to the client.

Independent Accountant's Report

To the Board of Directors

DEF Company:

We have examined the [*identify the subject matter—for example, the accompanying schedule of investment returns of XYZ Company for the year ended December 31, 20XX*]. XYZ Company's management is responsible for the schedule of investment returns. XYZ management did not provide us a written assertion about their schedule of investment returns for the year ended December 31, 20XX. Our responsibility is to express an opinion based on our examination.

Our examination was conducted in accordance with attestation standards established by the American Institute of Certified Public Accountants and, accordingly, included examining, on a test basis, evidence supporting [*identify the subject matter—for example, XYZ Company's schedule of investment returns*] and performing such other procedures as we considered necessary in the circumstances. We believe that our examination provides a reasonable basis for our opinion.

[*Additional paragraph(s) may be added to emphasize certain matters relating to the attest engagement or the subject matter.*]

In our opinion, the schedule referred to above presents, in all material respects, [*identify the subject matter—for example, the investment returns of XYZ Company for the year ended December 31, 20XX*] based on [*identify criteria—for example, the ABC criteria set forth in Note 1*].

This report is intended solely for the information and use of the management and board of directors of DEF Company and is not intended to be and should not be used by anyone other than these specified parties.

[*Signature*]

[*Date*]

[Paragraph renumbered by the issuance of SSAE No. 11, January 2002.]

.115

Appendix B

Review Reports

Example 1

This is a standard review report on subject matter for general use. The report pertains to subject matter for which suitable criteria exist and are available to all users through inclusion in a clear manner in the presentation of the subject matter. (See paragraphs .78–.83 for guidance on restricting the use of the report when criteria are available only to specified parties.) A written assertion has been obtained from the responsible party.

Independent Accountant's Report

We have reviewed the [*identify the subject matter—for example, the accompanying schedule of investment returns of XYZ Company for the year ended December 31, 20XX*]. XYZ Company's management is responsible for the schedule of investment returns.

Our review was conducted in accordance with attestation standards established by the American Institute of Certified Public Accountants. A review is substantially less in scope than an examination, the objective of which is the expression of an opinion on [*identify the subject matter—for example, XYZ Company's schedule of investment returns*]. Accordingly, we do not express such an opinion.

[*Additional paragraph(s) may be added to emphasize certain matters relating to the attest engagement or the subject matter.*]

Based on our review, nothing came to our attention that caused us to believe that the [*identify the subject matter—for example, schedule of investment returns of XYZ Company for the year ended December 31, 20XX*] is not presented, in all material respects, in conformity with [*identify the criteria—for example, the ABC criteria set forth in Note 1*].

[*Signature*]

[*Date*]

Example 2

This is a review report on subject matter that is the responsibility of a party other than the client. This review report is restricted as to use since a written assertion has not been provided by the responsible party. (See paragraph .78.) The subject matter pertains to criteria that are suitable and are available to the client.

Independent Accountant's Report

To the Board of Directors

DEF Company:

We have reviewed [*identify the subject matter—for example, the accompanying schedule of investment returns of XYZ Company for the year ended December 31, 20XX*]. XYZ Company's management is responsible for the schedule of investment returns. XYZ Company's management did not provide us a written assertion about their schedule of investment returns for the year ended December 31, 20XX.

Our review was conducted in accordance with attestation standards established by the American Institute of Certified Public Accountants. A review is substantially less in scope than an examination, the objective of which is the expression of an opinion on [*identify the subject matter—for example, XYZ Company's schedule of investment returns*]. Accordingly, we do not express such an opinion.

[*Additional paragraph(s) may be added to emphasize certain matters relating to the attest engagement or the subject matter.*]

Based on our review, nothing came to our attention that caused us to believe that [*identify the subject matter—for example, the schedule of investment returns of XYZ Company for the year ended December 31, 20XX*] is not presented, in all material respects, in conformity with [*identify the criteria—for example, the ABC criteria set forth in Note 1*].

This report is intended solely for the information and use of the management and board of directors of DEF Company and is not intended to be and should not be used by anyone other than these specified parties.

[*Signature*]

[*Date*]

Example 3

This is a review report on an assertion. Although suitable criteria exist for the subject matter, the report is restricted as to use since the criteria are available only to specified parties; if the criteria are available as described in paragraph .33(*a*)–(*d*), the paragraph restricting the use of the report would be omitted. A written assertion has been obtained from the responsible party.

Independent Accountant's Report

We have reviewed management's assertion that [*identify the assertion—for example, the accompanying schedule of investment returns of XYZ Company for the year ended December 31, 20XX is presented in accordance with the ABC criteria referred to in Note 1*]. XYZ Company's management is responsible for the assertion.

Our review was conducted in accordance with attestation standards established by the American Institute of Certified Public Accountants. A review is substantially less in scope than an examination, the objective of which is the expression of an opinion on management's assertion. Accordingly, we do not express such an opinion.

[*Additional paragraph(s) may be added to emphasize certain matters relating to the attest engagement or the assertion.*]

Based on our review, nothing came to our attention that caused us to believe that management's assertion referred to above is not fairly stated, in all material respects, based on [*identify the criteria—for example, the ABC criteria referred to in the investment management agreement between XYZ Company and DEF Investment Managers, Ltd., dated November 15, 20X1*].

This report is intended solely for the information and use of XYZ Company and [*identify other specified parties—for example, DEF Investment Managers, Ltd.*] and is not intended to be and should not be used by anyone other than these specified parties.

[*Signature*]

[*Date*]

[Paragraph renumbered by the issuance of SSAE No. 11, January 2002.]

AT Section 9101

Attest Engagements: Attest Engagements Interpretations of Section 101

1. Defense Industry Questionnaire on Business Ethics and Conduct[1]

.01 *Question*—Certain defense contractors have made a commitment to adopt and implement six principles of business ethics and conduct contained in the *Defense Industry Initiatives on Business Ethics and Conduct* (initiatives). One of those principles concerns defense contractors' public accountability for their commitment to the initiatives. That public accountability begins by the contractor completing an annual *Public Accountability Questionnaire* (questionnaire).

.02 Each of the participating signatory companies (signatories) completes a questionnaire concerning certain policies, procedures, and programs that were to have been in place during the reporting period. The public accountability process requires signatories to perform internal audits and to provide officer certifications as to whether the responses to the questionnaire are current and accurate.

.03 Alternatively, a defense contractor may request its independent public accountant (practitioner) to examine or review its responses to the questionnaire for the purpose of expressing a conclusion about the appropriateness of those responses in a report. Would such an engagement be an attest engagement under section 101, *Attest Engagements*?

.04 *Interpretation*—Section 101 states that the attestation standards apply when a CPA in the practice of public accounting is engaged to issue or does issue an examination, a review, or an agreed-upon procedures report on subject matter, or an assertion about the subject matter that is the responsibility of another party. When a practitioner is engaged by a defense contractor to provide an examination or a review report on the contractor's written responses to the questionnaire, such an engagement involves subject matter that is the responsibility of the defense contractor. Consequently, section 101 applies to such engagements.

.05 *Question*—Paragraph .23 of section 101 specifies that "the practitioner must have reason to believe that the subject matter is capable of evaluation against criteria that are suitable and available to users." What are the criteria against which such subject matter is to be evaluated and are such criteria suitable and available?

.06 *Interpretation*—The criteria for evaluating the defense contractor's responses are set forth primarily in the questionnaire and the instructions thereto. The suitability of those criteria should be evaluated by assessing whether the criteria meet the characteristics discussed in paragraph .24 of section 101.

.07 The criteria set forth in the questionnaire and its instructions will, when properly followed, be suitable. Although these should provide suitable

---

[1] Information regarding the Defense Industry Initiative on Business Ethics and Conduct (DII) is available at DII's website www.dii.org.

criteria, the questionnaire and its instructions are not generally available. Therefore, the practitioner's report should normally be restricted. The availability requirement can be met if the defense contractor attaches the criteria to the presentation.

.08 *Question*—What is the nature of the procedures that should be applied to the questionnaire responses?

.09 *Interpretation*—The objective of the procedures performed in either an examination or a review engagement is to obtain evidential matter that the defense contractor has designed and placed in operation policies and programs in a manner that supports the signatory's responses to each of the questions on the questionnaire and that the policies and programs operated during the period covered by the questionnaire. The objective does not include providing assurance about whether the defense contractor's policies and programs operated effectively to ensure compliance with the defense contractor's code of business ethics and conduct on the part of individual employees or about whether the defense contractor and its employees have complied with federal procurement laws. In an examination, the evidential matter should be sufficient to limit attestation risk to a level that is appropriately low for the high degree of assurance imparted by an examination report. In a review, this evidential matter should be sufficient to limit attestation risk to a moderate level.

.10 Examination procedures include obtaining evidential matter by reading relevant policies and programs, making inquiries of appropriate defense contractor personnel, inspecting documents and records, confirming defense contractor assertions with its employees or others, and observing activities. In an examination it will be necessary for a practitioner's procedures to go beyond simply reading relevant policies and programs and making inquiries of appropriate defense contractor personnel. Alternatively, review procedures are generally limited to reading relevant policies and procedures and making inquiries of appropriate defense contractor personnel. When applying examination or review procedures, the practitioner should assess the appropriateness (including the comprehensiveness) of the policies and programs supporting the signatory's responses to each of the questions on the questionnaire.

.11 A particular defense contractor's policies and programs may vary from those of other defense contractors. As a result, evidential matter obtained from the procedures performed cannot be evaluated solely on a quantitative basis. Consequently, it is not practicable to establish only quantitative guidelines for determining the nature or extent of the evidential matter that is necessary to provide the assurance required in either an examination or a review. The qualitative aspects should also be considered.

.12 In determining the nature, timing, and extent of examination or review procedures, the practitioner should consider information obtained in the performance of other services for the defense contractor, for example, the audit of the defense contractor's financial statements. For multi-location defense contractors, whether policies and programs operated during the period should be evaluated for both the defense contractor's headquarters and for selected defense contracting locations. The practitioner may consider using the work of the defense contractor's internal auditors. AU-C section 610, *The Auditor's Consideration of the Internal Audit Function in an Audit of Financial Statements*, may be useful in that consideration.

.13 Examination procedures, and in some instances review procedures, may require access to information involving specific instances of actual or alleged noncompliance with laws. An inability to obtain access to such information because of restrictions imposed by a defense contractor (for example, to protect attorney-client privilege) may constitute a scope limitation. Paragraphs .73–.75 of section 101 provide guidance in such situations. The practitioner should assess the effect of the inability to obtain access to such information on his or her ability to form a conclusion about whether the related policy or program operated during the period. If the defense contractor's reasons for not permitting access to the information are reasonable (for example, the information is the subject of litigation or a governmental investigation) and have been approved by an executive officer of the defense contractor, the occurrences of restricted access to information are few in number, and the practitioner has access to other information about that specific instance or about other instances that is sufficient to permit a conclusion to be formed about whether the related policy or program operated during the period, the practitioner ordinarily would conclude that it is not necessary to disclaim assurance.

.14 If the practitioner's scope of work has been restricted with respect to one or more questions, the practitioner should consider the implications of that restriction on the practitioner's ability to form a conclusion about other questions. In addition, as the nature or number of questions on which the defense contractor has imposed scope limitations increases in significance, the practitioner should consider whether to withdraw from the engagement.

.15 *Question*—What is the form of report that should be issued to meet the requirements of section 101?

.16 *Interpretation*—The standards of reporting in section 101 provide guidance about report content and wording and the circumstances that may require report modification. Appendix A and appendix B provide illustrative reports appropriate for various circumstances. Paragraph .66 of section 101 permits the practitioner to report directly on the subject matter or on management's assertion. In either case, the practitioner should ordinarily obtain a written assertion. An illustrative defense contractor assertion is also presented in appendix A and appendix B.

.17 The engagements addressed in this interpretation do not include providing assurance about whether the defense contractor's policies and programs operated effectively to ensure compliance with the defense contractor's code of business ethics and conduct on the part of individual employees or about whether the defense contractor and its employees have complied with federal procurement laws. The practitioner's report should explicitly disclaim an opinion on the extent of such compliance.

.18 Because variations in individual performance and interpretation will affect the operation of the defense contractor's policies and programs during the period, adherence to all such policies and programs in every case may not be possible. In determining whether a reservation about a response in the questionnaire is sufficiently significant to result in an opinion modified for an exception to that response, the practitioner should consider the nature, causes, patterns, and pervasiveness of the instances in which the policies and programs did not operate as designed and their implications for that response in the questionnaire.

.19 When scope limitations have precluded the practitioner from forming an opinion on the responses to one or more questions, the practitioner's report should describe all such scope restrictions. If the defense contractor imposed such a scope limitation after the practitioner had begun performing procedures, that fact should be stated in the report.

.20 A defense contractor may request the practitioner to communicate to management, the board of directors, or one of its committees, either orally or in writing, conditions noted that do not constitute significant reservations about the answers to the questionnaire but that might nevertheless be of value to management. Agreed-upon arrangements between the practitioner and the defense contractor to communicate conditions noted may include, for example, the reporting of matters of less significance than those contemplated by the criteria, the existence of conditions specified by the defense contractor, the results of further investigation of matters noted to identify underlying causes, or suggestions for improvements in various policies or programs. Under these arrangements, the practitioner may be requested to visit specific locations, assess the effectiveness of specific policies or programs, or undertake specific procedures not otherwise planned. In addition, the practitioner is not precluded from communicating matters believed to be of value, even if no specific request has been made.

.21

Appendix A

Illustrative Defense Contractor Assertions and Examination Reports

Defense Industry Questionnaire on Business Ethics and Conduct

Illustration 1: Unqualified Opinion; General-Use Report; Criteria Attached to the Presentation

Defense Contractor Assertion

Statement of Responses to the Defense Industry Questionnaire on *Business Ethics and Conduct for the period from _______ to _______.*

The affirmative responses in the accompanying *Questionnaire on Business Ethics and Conduct with Responses by the XYZ Company for the period from _______ to _______* are based on policies and programs in operation for that period and are appropriately presented in conformity with the criteria set forth in the *Defense Industry Initiatives on Business Ethics and Conduct*, including the Questionnaire.

Attachments:

Defense Industry Initiatives on Business Ethics and Conduct

Instructions and Questionnaire on Business Ethics and Conduct with Responses by the XYZ Company for the period from _______ to _______.

Examination Report

Independent Accountant's Report

To the Board of Directors of the XYZ Company

We have examined the XYZ Company's *Statement of Responses to the Defense Industry Questionnaire on Business Ethics and Conduct for the period from _______ to _______*, and the Questionnaire and responses attached thereto. XYZ Company's management is responsible for its responses to the Questionnaire. Our responsibility is to express an opinion based on our examination.

Our examination was conducted in accordance with attestation standards established by the American Institute of Certified Public Accountants and, accordingly, included examining, on a test basis, evidence as to whether XYZ Company had policies and programs in operation during that period that support the affirmative responses to the *Questionnaire* and performing such other procedures as we considered necessary in the circumstances. We believe that our examination provides a reasonable basis for our opinion. Our examination procedures were not designed, however, to evaluate whether the aforementioned policies and programs operated effectively to ensure compliance with the Company's *Code of Business Ethics and Conduct* on the part of individual employees or to evaluate the extent to which the Company or its employees have complied with federal procurement laws, and we do not express an opinion or any other form of assurance thereon.

In our opinion, the affirmative responses in the Questionnaire accompanying the *Statement of Responses to the Defense Industry Questionnaire on Business Ethics and Conduct for the period from _______ to _______* referred to above are appropriately presented in conformity with the criteria set forth in the *Defense Industry Initiatives on Business Ethics and Conduct*, including the Questionnaire.

Illustration 2: Unqualified Opinion; Report Modified for Negative Responses to Defense Contractor Assertion; Use of the Report is Restricted Because Criteria are Available Only to Specified Parties

Defense Contractor Assertion

Statement of Responses to the Defense Industry Questionnaire on *Business Ethics and Conduct for the period from _______ to _______.*

The affirmative responses in the accompanying *Questionnaire on Business Ethics and Conduct with Responses by the XYZ Company for the period from _______ to _______* are based on policies and programs in operation for that period and are appropriately presented in conformity with the criteria set forth in the *Defense Industry Initiatives on Business Ethics and Conduct*, including the Questionnaire. Negative responses indicate that the Company did not have policies and programs in operation during that period with respect to those areas.

Attachments: None

(The responses could include an explanation of negative responses if the defense contractor so desired.)

Examination Report

Independent Accountant's Report

To the Board of Directors of the XYZ Company

We have examined the XYZ Company's *Statement of Responses to the Defense Industry Questionnaire on Business Ethics and Conduct for the period from _______ to _______.* XYZ Company's management is responsible for its responses to the Questionnaire. Our responsibility is to express an opinion based on our examination.

[*Standard Scope Paragraph*]

In our opinion, the affirmative responses in the Questionnaire referred to above are appropriately presented in conformity with the criteria set forth in the *Defense Industry Initiatives on Business Ethics and Conduct*, including the Questionnaire. The negative responses to Questions _______ and _______ in the Questionnaire indicate that the Company did not have policies and programs in operation during the period with respect to those areas.

This report is intended solely for the information and use of the XYZ Company and [*identify other specified parties—for example,* the Defense Industry Initiative] and is not intended to be and should not be used by anyone other than these specified parties.

Illustration 3: Opinion Modified for Exception on Certain Response

Defense Contractor Assertion

Statement of Responses to the Defense Industry Questionnaire on *Business Ethics and Conduct for the period from ______ to ______*.

The affirmative responses in the accompanying *Questionnaire on Business Ethics and Conduct with Responses by the XYZ Company for the period from ______ to ______*, are based on policies and programs in operation for that period and are appropriately presented in conformity with the criteria set forth in the *Defense Industry Initiatives on Business Ethics and Conduct*, including the Questionnaire.

Attachments:

Defense Industry Initiatives on Business Ethics and Conduct

Questionnaire on Business Ethics and Conduct with Responses by the XYZ Company for the period from ______ to ______.

Examination Report

Independent Accountant's Report

To the Board of Directors of the XYZ Company

[*Standard Introductory and Scope Paragraphs*]

Management believes that an appropriate mechanism exists for informing employees of the results of any follow-up into their charges of violations of the Company's Code of Business Ethics and Conduct, and has accordingly answered Question 12 in the affirmative. That mechanism consists principally of distributing newspaper articles and press releases of violations of federal procurement laws that have been voluntarily reported to the appropriate governmental agencies. We do not believe that such a mechanism is sufficient, inasmuch as it does not provide follow-up information on violations reported by employees that are not deemed reportable to a governmental agency. Consequently, in our opinion, the affirmative response to Question 12 in the Questionnaire is not appropriately presented in conformity with the criteria set forth in the *Defense Industry Initiatives on Business Ethics and Conduct*, including the Questionnaire.

In our opinion, except for the response to Question 12 as discussed in the preceding paragraph, the affirmative responses in the Questionnaire accompanying the *Statement of Responses to the Defense Industry Questionnaire on Business Ethics and Conduct for the period from ______ to ______* referred to above are appropriately presented in conformity with the criteria set forth in the Defense Industry Initiatives on Business Ethics and Conduct, including the Questionnaire.

Illustration 4: Opinion Modified for Exception on a Certain Response; Report also Modified for Negative Responses

Defense Contractor Assertion

Statement of Responses to the *Defense Industry Questionnaire on Business Ethics and Conduct for the period from ______ to ______.*

The affirmative responses in the accompanying *Questionnaire on Business Ethics and Conduct with Responses by the XYZ Company for the period from _______ to _______* are based on policies and programs in operation for that period and are appropriately presented in conformity with the criteria set forth in the *Defense Industry Initiatives on Business Ethics and Conduct*, including the Questionnaire. Negative responses indicate that the Company did not have policies and programs in operation during that period with respect to those areas.

Attachments:

Defense Industry Initiatives on Business Ethics and Conduct

Questionnaire on Business Ethics and Conduct with Responses by the XYZ Company for the period from _______ to _______.

(The responses could include an explanation of negative responses if the defense contractor so desired.)

Examination Report

Independent Accountant's Report

To the Board of Directors of the XYZ Company

[*Standard Introductory and Scope Paragraphs*]

Management believes that an appropriate mechanism exists for letting employees know of the results of any follow-up into their charges of violations of the Company's Code of Business Ethics and Conduct, and has accordingly answered Question 12 in the affirmative. That mechanism consists principally of distributing newspaper articles and press releases of violations of federal procurement laws that have been voluntarily reported to the appropriate governmental agencies. We do not believe that such a mechanism is sufficient, inasmuch as it does not provide follow-up information on violations reported by employees that are not deemed reportable to a governmental agency. Consequently, in our opinion, the affirmative response to Question 12 in the Questionnaire is not appropriately presented in conformity with the criteria set forth in the Defense Industry Initiatives on Business Ethics and Conduct, including the Questionnaire.

In our opinion, except for the response to Question 12 as discussed in the preceding paragraph, the affirmative responses in the Questionnaire accompanying the *Statement of Responses to the Defense Industry Questionnaire on Business Ethics and Conduct for the period from _______ to _______* referred to above are appropriately presented in conformity with the criteria set forth in the *Defense Industry Initiatives on Business Ethics and Conduct*, including the Questionnaire. The negative responses to Questions _______ and _______ in the Questionnaire indicate that the Company did not have policies and programs in operation during the period with respect to those areas.

Illustration 5: Opinion Disclaimed on Certain Responses Because of Scope Restrictions Imposed by Client

Defense Contractor Assertion

Statement of Responses to the Defense Industry Questionnaire on *Business Ethics and Conduct for the period from _______ to _______.*

The affirmative responses in the accompanying *Questionnaire on Business Ethics and Conduct with Responses by the XYZ Company for the period from _______ to _______* are based on policies and programs in operation for that period and are appropriately presented in conformity with the criteria set forth in the *Defense Industry Initiatives on Business Ethics and Conduct*, including the Questionnaire.

Attachments:

Defense Industry Initiatives on Business Ethics and Conduct

Questionnaire on Business Ethics and Conduct with Responses by the XYZ Company for the period from _______ to _______.

Examination Report

Independent Accountant's Report

To the Board of Directors of the XYZ Company

[*Standard Introductory Paragraph*]

Except as described below, our examination was conducted in accordance with attestation standards established by the American Institute of Certified Public Accountants and, accordingly, included examining, on a test basis, evidence as to whether XYZ Company had policies and programs in operation during that period that support the affirmative responses to the *Questionnaire*. We believe that our examination provides a reasonable basis for our opinion. Our examination procedures were not designed, however, to evaluate whether the aforementioned policies and programs operated effectively to ensure compliance with the Company's *Code of Business Ethics and Conduct* on the part of individual employees or to evaluate the extent to which the Company or its employees have complied with federal procurement laws, and we do not express an opinion or any other form of assurance thereon.

We were not permitted to read relevant documents and files or interview appropriate employees to determine that the affirmative answers to Questions 6, 7, and 8 are appropriate. The nature of those questions precluded us from satisfying ourselves as to the appropriateness of those answers by means of other examination procedures.

In our opinion, the affirmative responses to Questions 1 through 5 and 9 through 17 in the Questionnaire accompanying the *Statement of Responses to the Defense Industry Questionnaire on Business Ethics and Conduct for the period from _______ to _______* referred to above are appropriately presented in conformity with the criteria set forth in the *Defense Industry Initiatives on Business Ethics and Conduct*, including the Questionnaire. Because of the matters discussed in the preceding paragraph, the scope of our work was not sufficient to express, and we do not express, an opinion on the appropriateness of the affirmative responses to Questions 6, 7, and 8 in the Questionnaire.

.22

Appendix B

Illustrative Defense Contractor Assertion and Review Report; Use of Report Is Restricted Because Criteria Are Available Only To Specified Parties

Defense Industry Questionnaire on Business Ethics and Conduct

Defense Contractor Assertion

Statement of Responses to the Defense Industry Questionnaire on *Business Ethics and Conduct for the period from ______ to ______.*

The affirmative responses in the accompanying *Questionnaire on Business Ethics and Conduct with Responses by the XYZ Company for the period from ______ to ______* are based on policies and programs in operation during that period and are appropriately presented in conformity with the criteria set forth in the *Defense Industry Initiatives on Business Ethics and Conduct*, including the Questionnaire.

Attachments: None

Review Report

Independent Accountant's Report

To the Board of Directors of the XYZ Company

We have reviewed the XYZ Company's *Statement of Responses to the Defense Industry Questionnaire on Business Ethics and Conduct for the period from ______ to ______.* XYZ Company's management is responsible for the Statement of Responses to the Defense Industry Questionnaire on Business Ethics.

Our review was conducted in accordance with attestation standards established by the American Institute of Certified Public Accountants. A review is substantially less in scope than an examination, the objective of which is the expression of an opinion on the affirmative responses in the Questionnaire. Accordingly, we do not express such an opinion. Additionally, our review was not designed to evaluate whether the aforementioned policies and programs operated effectively to ensure compliance with the Company's *Code of Business Ethics and Conduct* on the part of individual employees or to evaluate the extent to which the Company or its employees have complied with federal procurement laws and we do not express an opinion or any other form of assurance thereon.

Based on our review, nothing came to our attention that caused us to believe that the affirmative responses in the Questionnaire referred to above are not appropriately presented in conformity with the criteria set forth in the *Defense Industry Initiatives on Business Ethics and Conduct*, including the Questionnaire.

This report is intended solely for the information and use of the XYZ Company and [*identify other specified parties—for example,* the Defense Industry Initiative] and is not intended to be and should not be used by anyone other than these specified parties.

[Issue Date: August 1987; Amended: February 1989; Modified: May 1989; Revised: January 2001; November 2006; Revised: December 2012.]

2. Responding to Requests for Reports on Matters Relating to Solvency

.23 *Question*—Lenders, as a requisite to the closing of certain secured financings in connection with leveraged buyouts, recapitalizations and certain other financial transactions, have sometimes requested written assurance from an accountant regarding the prospective borrower's solvency and related matters.[2] The lender is concerned that such financings not be considered to include a fraudulent conveyance or transfer under the Federal Bankruptcy Code[3] or the relevant state fraudulent conveyance or transfer statute.[4] If the financing is subsequently determined to have included a fraudulent conveyance or transfer, repayment obligations and security interests may be set aside or subordinated to the claims of other creditors.

.24 May a practitioner provide assurance concerning *matters relating to solvency* as hereinafter defined?

.25 *Interpretation*—No. For reasons set forth subsequently, a practitioner should not provide any form of assurance, through examination, review, or agreed-upon procedures engagements, that an entity

- is not insolvent at the time the debt is incurred or would not be rendered insolvent thereby.
- does not have unreasonably small capital.
- has the ability to pay its debts as they mature.

---

[2] Although this interpretation describes requests from secured lenders and summarizes the potential effects of fraudulent conveyance or transfer laws upon such lenders, the interpretation is not limited to requests from lenders. All requests for assurance on matters relating to solvency are governed by this interpretation.

[3] Section 548 of the Federal Bankruptcy Code defines *fraudulent transfers and obligations* as follows:

> The trustee may avoid any transfer of an interest of the debtor in property or any obligation incurred by the debtor, that was made or incurred on or within one year before the date of the filing of the petition, if the debtor voluntarily or involuntarily—
>
> (1) made such transfer or incurred such obligation with actual intent to hinder, delay, or defraud any entity to which the debtor was or became, on or after the date that such transfer occurred or such obligation was incurred, indebted; or
>
> (2)(A) received less than a reasonably equivalent value in exchange for such transfer or obligation; and
>
> (2)(B)(i) was insolvent on the date that such transfer was made or such obligation was incurred, or became insolvent as a result of such transfer or obligation;
>
> (2)(B)(ii) was engaged in business or a transaction, or was about to engage in business or a transaction, for which any property remaining with the debtor was an unreasonably small capital; or
>
> (2)(B)(iii) intended to incur, or believed that the debtor would incur, debts that would be beyond the debtor's ability to pay as such debts matured. (Bankruptcy Law Reporter, 3 vols. [Chicago: Commerce Clearing House, 1986], vol. 1, 1339).

[4] State fraudulent conveyance or transfer statutes such as the Uniform Fraudulent Conveyance Act and the Uniform Fraudulent Transfer Act reflect substantially similar provisions. These state laws may be employed absent a declaration of bankruptcy or by a bankruptcy trustee under Section 544(1) of the Federal Bankruptcy Code. Although the statute of limitations varies from state to state, in some states financing transactions may be vulnerable to challenge for up to six years from closing.

In the context of particular transactions other terms are sometimes used or defined by the parties as equivalents of or substitutes for the terms listed above (for example, *fair salable value of assets exceeds liabilities*). These terms, and those matters listed previously, are hereinafter referred to as *matters relating to solvency*. The prohibition extends to providing assurance concerning all such terms.

.26 The third general attestation standard states that the practitioner must have reason to believe that the subject matter is capable of evaluation against criteria that are suitable and available to users. Suitable criteria must have each of the following attributes:

- *Objectivity*—Criteria should be free from bias.
- *Measurability*—Criteria should permit reasonably consistent measurements, qualitative or quantitative, of subject matter.
- *Completeness*—Criteria should be sufficiently complete so those relevant factors that would alter a conclusion about subject matter are not omitted.
- *Relevance*—Criteria should be relevant to the subject matter.

In addition, the second general attestation standard states that the practitioner must have adequate knowledge of the subject matter.

.27 The matters relating to solvency mentioned in paragraph .23 are subject to legal interpretation under, and varying legal definition in, the Federal Bankruptcy Code and various state fraudulent conveyance and transfer statutes. Because these matters are not clearly defined in an accounting sense, and are therefore subject to varying interpretations, they do not provide the practitioner with suitable criteria required to evaluate the subject matter or an assertion under the third general attestation standard. In addition, lenders are concerned with legal issues on matters relating to solvency and the practitioner is generally unable to evaluate or provide assurance on these matters of legal interpretation. Therefore, practitioners are precluded from giving any form of assurance on matters relating to solvency or any financial presentation of matters relating to solvency.

.28 Under existing AICPA standards, the practitioner may provide a client with various professional services that may be useful to the client in connection with a financing. These services include the following:

- Audit of historical financial statements
- Review of historical financial information (a review in accordance with AU-C section 930, *Interim Financial Information*, of interim financial information, or in accordance with AR section 90, *Review of Financial Statements*)
- Examination or review of pro forma financial information (section 401, *Reporting on Pro Forma Financial Information*)
- Examination or compilation of prospective financial information (section 301, *Financial Forecasts and Projections*)

.29 In addition, under existing AICPA attestation standards (section 201, *Agreed-Upon Procedures Engagements*), the practitioner can provide the client and lender with an agreed-upon procedures report. In such an engagement, a client and lender may request that specified procedures be applied to various financial presentations, such as historical financial information, pro forma financial information, and prospective financial information, which can be useful to a client or lender in connection with a financing.

.30 The practitioner should be aware that certain of the services described in paragraph .28 require that the practitioner have an appropriate level of knowledge of the entity's accounting and financial reporting practices and its internal control. This has ordinarily been obtained by the practitioner auditing historical financial statements of the entity for the most recent annual period or by otherwise obtaining an equivalent knowledge base. When considering acceptance of an engagement relating to a financing, the practitioner should consider whether he or she can perform these services without an equivalent knowledge base.

.31 A report on agreed-upon procedures should not provide any assurances on matters relating to solvency or any financial presentation of matters relating to solvency (for example, fair salable value of assets less liabilities or fair salable value of assets less liabilities, contingent liabilities, and other commitments). A practitioner's report on the results of applying agreed-upon procedures should contain the report elements set forth in paragraph .31 of section 201 (or paragraph .55 of section 301 if applying agreed upon procedures to prospective financial information). The practitioner's report on the results of applying agreed-upon procedures should state that

- the service has been requested in connection with a financing (no reference should be made to any solvency provisions in the financing agreement).
- no representations are provided regarding questions of legal interpretation.
- no assurance is provided concerning the borrower's (*a*) solvency, (*b*) adequacy of capital, or (*c*) ability to pay its debts.
- the procedures should not be taken to supplant any additional inquiries and procedures that the lender should undertake in its consideration of the proposed financing.
- where applicable, an audit of recent historical financial statements has previously been performed and that no audit of any historical financial statements for a subsequent period has been performed. In addition, if any services have been performed pursuant to paragraph .28, they may be referred to.

.32 The report ordinarily is dated at or shortly before the closing date. The financing agreement ordinarily specifies the date, often referred to as the cutoff date, to which the report is to relate (for example, a date three business days before the date of the report). The report should state that the inquiries and other procedures carried out in connection with the report did not cover the period from the cutoff date to the date of the report.

.33 The practitioner might consider furnishing the client with a draft of the agreed-upon procedures report. The draft report should deal with all matters expected to be covered in the terms expected to be used in the final report. The draft report should be identified as a draft in order to avoid giving the impression that the procedures described therein have been performed. This practice of furnishing a draft report at an early point permits the practitioner to make clear to the client and lender what they may expect the accountant to furnish and gives them an opportunity to change the financing agreement or the agreed-upon procedures if they so desire.

[Issue Date: May 1988; Amended: February 1993;
Revised: January 2001; November 2006; Revised: December 2012.]

3. Applicability of Attestation Standards to Litigation Services

.34 *Question*—Paragraph .04 of section 101 provides an example of a litigation service provided by practitioners that would not be considered an attest engagement as defined by section 101. When does section 101 not apply to litigation service engagements?

.35 *Interpretation*—Section 101 does not apply to litigation services that involve pending or potential formal legal or regulatory proceedings before a *trier of fact*[5] in connection with the resolution of a dispute between two or more parties in any of the following circumstances when the

a. practitioner has not been engaged to issue and does not issue an examination, a review, or an agreed-upon procedures report on subject matter, or an assertion about the subject matter that is the responsibility of another party.

b. service comprises being an expert witness.

c. service comprises being a trier of fact or acting on behalf of one.

d. practitioner's work under the rules of the proceedings is subject to detailed analysis and challenge by each party to the dispute.

e. practitioner is engaged by an attorney to do work that will be protected by the attorney's work product privilege and such work is not intended to be used for other purposes.

When performing such litigation services, the practitioner should comply with Rule 201, *General Standards* (ET sec. 201 par. .01) of the AICPA Code of Professional Conduct.

.36 *Question*—When does section 101 apply to litigation service engagements?

.37 *Interpretation*—Section 101 applies to litigation service engagements only when the practitioner is engaged to issue or does issue an examination, a review, or an agreed-upon procedures report on subject matter, or an assertion about the subject matter, that is the responsibility of another party.

.38 *Question*—Paragraph .04(*c*) of section 101 provides the following example of litigation service engagements that are not considered attest engagements: "Services performed in accordance with the Statement on Standards for Consulting Services, such as.... engagements in which a practitioner is engaged to testify as an expert witness in accounting, auditing, taxation, or other matters, given certain stipulated facts."

What does the term *stipulated facts* as used in paragraph .04(*c*) of section 101 mean?

.39 *Interpretation*—The term *stipulated facts* as used in paragraph .04(*c*) of section 101 means facts or assumptions that are specified by one or more parties to a dispute to serve as the basis for the development of an expert opinion. It is not used in its typical legal sense of facts agreed to by all parties involved in a dispute.

.40 *Question*—Does Interpretation No. 2, "Responding to Requests for Reports on Matters Relating to Solvency," of section 101 (par. .23–.33), prohibit a practitioner from providing expert testimony, as described in paragraph .04(*c*) of section 101 before a trier of fact on matters relating to solvency?

---

[5] A *trier of fact* in this section means a court, regulatory body, or government authority; their agents; a grand jury; or an arbitrator or mediator of the dispute.

.41 *Interpretation*—No. Matters relating to solvency mentioned in paragraph .25 are subject to legal interpretation under, and varying legal definition in, the Federal Bankruptcy Code and various state fraudulent conveyance and transfer statutes. Because these matters are not clearly defined in an accounting sense, and therefore subject to varying interpretations, they do not provide the practitioner with the suitable criteria required to evaluate the assertion. Thus, Interpretation No. 2 (par. .23–.33) prohibits a practitioner from providing any form of assurance in reporting upon examination, review, or agreed-upon procedures engagements about matters relating to solvency (as defined in paragraph .25).

.42 However, a practitioner who is involved with pending or potential formal legal or regulatory proceedings before a trier of fact in connection with the resolution of a dispute between two or more parties may provide an expert opinion or consulting advice about matters relating to solvency. The prohibition in paragraphs .23–.33 does not apply in such engagements because as part of the legal or regulatory proceedings, each party to the dispute has the opportunity to analyze and challenge the legal definition and interpretation of the matters relating to solvency and the criteria the practitioner uses to evaluate matters related to solvency. Such services are not intended to be used by others who do not have the opportunity to analyze and challenge such definitions and interpretations.

[Issue Date: July 1990; Revised: January 2001.]

4. Providing Access to or Copies of Attest Documentation to a Regulator

.43 *Question*—Interpretation No. 1, "Providing Access to or Copies of Audit Documentation to a Regulator," of AU-C section 230, *Audit Documentation* (AU-C sec. 9230 par .01–.15), contains guidance relating to providing access to or copies of audit documentation to a regulator. Is this guidance applicable to an attest engagement when a regulator requests access to or copies of the attest documentation?

.44 *Interpretation*—Yes. The guidance in Interpretation No. 1 (AU sec. 9230 par .01–.15) is applicable in these circumstances; however, the letter to a regulator should be tailored to meet the individual engagement characteristics or the purpose of the regulatory request, for example, a quality control review. Illustrative letters for an examination engagement performed in accordance with section 601, *Compliance Attestation*, and an agreed-upon procedures engagement performed in accordance with section 201, follow.

.45 Illustrative letter for examination engagement:

Illustrative Letter to Regulator [6]

[Date]

[Name and Address of Regulatory Agency]

Your representatives have requested access to our attest documentation in connection with our engagement to examine (*identify the subject matter examined*

[6] The practitioner should appropriately modify this letter when the engagement has been conducted in accordance with Statements on Standards for Attestation Engagements (SSAE) and also in accordance with additional attest requirements specified by a regulatory agency (for example, the requirements specified in *Government Auditing Standards* issued by the Comptroller General of the United States).

or restate management's assertion). It is our understanding that the purpose of your request is (*state purpose*: for example, "to facilitate your regulatory examination").[7]

Our examination was conducted in accordance with attestation standards[8] established by the American Institute of Certified Public Accountants, the objective of which is to form an opinion as to whether the subject matter (or management's assertion) is fairly stated, in all material respects, based on (*identify criteria*). Under these standards, we have the responsibility to plan and perform our examination to provide a reasonable basis for our opinion and to exercise due professional care in the performance of our examination. Our examination is subject to the inherent risk that material noncompliance, if it exists, would not be detected. In addition, our examination does not address the possibility that material noncompliance may occur in the future. Also, our use of professional judgment and the assessments of attestation risk and materiality for the purpose of our examination means that matters may have existed that would have been assessed differently by you. Our examination does not provide a legal determination on (*name of entity*)'s compliance with specified requirements.

The attest documentation was prepared for the purpose of providing the principal support for our opinion on (*name of entity*)'s compliance and to aid in the performance and supervision of our examination. The attest documentation is the principal record of attest procedures performed, information obtained, and conclusions reached in the examination. The procedures that we performed were limited to those we considered necessary under attestation standards[9] established by the American Institute of Certified Public Accountants to provide us with reasonable basis for our opinion. Accordingly, we make no representation as to the sufficiency or appropriateness, for your purposes, of either the procedures or information in our attest documentation. In addition, any notations, comments, and individual conclusions appearing on any of the attest documentation do not stand alone and should not be read as an opinion on any part of management's assertion or the related subject matter.

Our examination was conducted for the purpose stated above and was not planned or performed in contemplation of your (*state purpose*: for example, "regulatory examination"). Therefore, items of possible interest to you may not have been specifically addressed. Accordingly, our examination, and the attest documentation prepared in connection therewith, should not supplant other inquiries and procedures that should be undertaken by the (*name of regulatory agency*) for the purpose of monitoring and regulating (*name of entity*). In addition, we have not performed any procedures since the date of our report with respect to the subject matter (*or management's assertion related thereto*), and significant events or circumstances may have occurred since that date.

The attest documentation constitutes and reflects work performed or information obtained by us in the course of our examination. The documents contain trade secrets and confidential commercial and financial information of our firm and (*name of entity*) that is privileged and confidential, and we expressly reserve all rights with respect to disclosures to third parties. Accordingly, we request confidential treatment under the Freedom of Information Act or similar laws and regulations when requests are made for the attest documentation or

---

[7] If the practitioner is not required by law, regulation, or engagement contract to provide a regulator access to the attest documentation but otherwise intends to provide such access (see Interpretation No. 1, "Providing Access to or Copies of Audit Documentation to a Regulator," of AU-C section 230, *Audit Documentation* [AU-C sec. 9230 par. .11–.15]), the letter should include a statement that: "Management of (*name of entity*) has authorized us to provide you access to our attest documentation for (*state purpose*)." [Footnote revised, December 2012, to reflect conforming changes necessary due to the issuance of SAS Nos. 122–126.]

[8] Refer to footnote 6.

[9] Refer to footnote 6.

information contained therein or any documents created by the (*name of regulatory agency*) containing information derived there from. We further request that written notice be given to our firm before distribution of the information in the attest documentation (or copies thereof) to others, including other governmental agencies, except when such distribution is required by law or regulation.[10]

[*If it is expected that copies will be requested, add the following*:

Any copies of our attest documentation we agree to provide you will contain a legend "Confidential Treatment Requested by (*name of practitioner, address, telephone number*)."]

[*Firm signature*]

.46 Example letter for agreed-upon procedures engagements:

Illustrative Letter to Regulator[11]

[*Date*]

[*Name and Address of Regulatory Agency*]

Your representatives have requested access to our attest documentation in connection with our engagement to perform agreed-upon procedures on (*identify the subject matter or management's assertion*). It is our understanding that the purpose of your request is (*state purpose:* for example, "to facilitate your regulatory examinations").[12]

Our agreed-upon procedures engagement was conducted in accordance with attestation standards[13] established by the American Institute of Certified Public Accountants. Under these standards, we have the responsibility to perform the agreed-upon procedures to provide a reasonable basis for the findings expressed in our report. We were not engaged to, and did not, perform an examination, the objective of which would be to form an opinion on (*identify the subject matter or management's assertion*). Our engagement is subject to the inherent risk that material misstatement of (*identify the subject matter or management's assertion*), if it exists, would not be detected. (*The practitioner may add the following:* "In addition, our engagement does not address the possibility that material misstatement of (*identify the subject matter or management's assertion*) may occur in the future.") The procedures that we performed were limited to those agreed to by the specified users, and the sufficiency of these procedures is solely the responsibility of the specified users of the report. Further, our engagement does not provide a legal determination on (*name of entity*)'s compliance with specified requirements.

The attest documentation was prepared to document agreed-upon procedures applied, information obtained, and findings reached in the engagement. Accordingly, we make no representation, for your purposes, as to the sufficiency

---

[10] This illustrative paragraph may not in and of itself be sufficient to gain confidential treatment under the rules and regulations of certain regulatory agencies. The practitioner should consider tailoring this paragraph to the circumstances after consulting the regulations of each applicable regulatory agency and, if necessary, consult with legal counsel regarding the specific procedures and requirements necessary to gain confidential treatment.

[11] The practitioner should appropriately modify this letter when the engagement has been conducted in accordance with the SSAEs and also in accordance with additional attest requirements specified by a regulatory agency (for example, the requirements specified in *Government Auditing Standards* issued by the Comptroller General of the United States).

[12] If the practitioner is not required by law, regulation or engagement contract to provide a regulator access to the attest documentation but otherwise intends to provide such access (see Interpretation No. 1 of AU-C section 230) the letter should include a statement that: "Management of (*name of entity*) has authorized us to provide you access to our attest documentation for (*state purpose*)." [Footnote revised, December 2012, to reflect conforming changes necessary due to the issuance of SAS Nos. 122–126.]

[13] Refer to footnote 6.

or appropriateness of the information in our attest documentation. In addition, any notations, comments, and individual findings appearing on any of the attest documentation should not be read as an opinion on management's assertion or the related subject matter, or any part thereof.

Our engagement was performed for the purpose stated above and was not performed in contemplation of your (*state purpose*: for example, "regulatory examination"). Therefore, items of possible interest to you may not have been specifically addressed. Accordingly, our engagement, and the attest documentation prepared in connection therewith, should not supplant other inquiries and procedures that should be undertaken by the (*name of regulatory agency*) for the purpose of monitoring and regulating (*name of client*). In addition, we have not performed any procedures since the date of our report with respect to the subject matter or management's assertion related thereto, and significant events or circumstances may have occurred since that date.

The attest documentation constitutes and reflects procedures performed or information obtained by us in the course of our engagement. The documents contain trade secrets and confidential commercial and financial information of our firm and (*name of client*) that is privileged and confidential, and we expressly reserve all rights with respect to disclosures to third parties. Accordingly, we request confidential treatment under the Freedom of Information Act or similar laws and regulations when requests are made for the attest documentation or information contained therein or any documents created by the (*name of regulatory agency*) containing information derived therefrom. We further request that written notice be given to our firm before distribution of the information in the attest documentation (or copies thereof) to others, including other governmental agencies, except when such distribution is required by law or regulation.[14]

[*If it is expected that copies will be requested, add the following:*

Any copies of our attest documentation we agree to provide you will contain a legend "Confidential Treatment Requested by (*name of practitioner, address, telephone number*)."]

[*Firm signature*]

[Issue Date: May 1996; Revised: January 2001; January 2002; Revised: December 2012.]

5. Attest Engagements on Financial Information[15] Included in eXtensible Business Reporting Language Instance Documents

.47 *Question*—What is eXtensible Business Reporting Language (XBRL) and an XBRL Instance Document?

.48 *Interpretation*—XBRL, the business reporting aspect of the Extensible Markup Language (XML), is a freely licensable open technology standard, which makes it possible to store and transfer data along with the complex hierarchies, data processing rules, and descriptions that enable analysis and

---

[14] This illustrative paragraph may not in and of itself be sufficient to gain confidential treatment under the rules and regulations of certain regulatory agencies. The practitioner should consider tailoring this paragraph to the circumstances after consulting the regulations of each applicable regulatory agency and, if necessary, consult with legal counsel regarding the specific procedures and requirements necessary to gain confidential treatment.

[15] Financial information includes data presented in audited or reviewed financial statements or other financial information (for example, management discussion and analysis).

distribution.[16] An entity may make its financial information available in the form of an XBRL Instance Document (instance document). An *instance document* is essentially a machine-readable format of financial information (that is, a computer can read the data, search for information, or perform calculations). Through the XBRL tagging process, a mapping of the financial information is created that enables a user to extract specific information, facilitating analysis. For example, XBRL would enable a user to use a software tool to automatically extract certain financial line items and automatically import those amounts into a worksheet calculating financial ratios.

.49 The instance document consists of various data points and their corresponding XBRL tags (that describe the financial information) and may include references to other items such as a PDF (Adobe Acrobat) version of financial information. Hence, an instance document is a stand-alone document that may be published using a website, e-mail, and other electronic distribution means.

.50 *Question*—What are the practitioner's considerations when the practitioner has been engaged to examine and report on whether the instance document accurately reflects the financial information?

.51 *Interpretation*—The third general attestation standard states that the practitioner shall perform the engagement only if he or she has reason to believe that the subject matter is capable of evaluation against criteria that are suitable and available to users. Two related criteria, XBRL taxonomies and XBRL International Technical Specifications, meet the available and suitable attributes under the attestation standards because a panel of experts developed the criteria and followed due process procedures that included exposure of the proposed criteria for public comment. The entity has the ability to extend the XBRL taxonomy by creating its own entity extension taxonomy. The entity may also create one or more custom entity taxonomies (for example, for a unique industry that is not yet represented by an XBRL taxonomy). Because neither the XBRL entity extension nor the custom taxonomy typically undergoes due process procedures when developed, the practitioner should evaluate whether the XBRL entity extension or custom taxonomy represents suitable and available criteria as described in paragraphs .24–.34 of section 101.

.52 The practitioner should perform procedures he or she believes are necessary to obtain sufficient evidential matter to form an opinion. Example procedures the practitioner should consider performing include the following:

- Compare the rendered[17] instance document to the financial information.
- Trace and agree the instance document's tagged information to the financial information.
- Test that the financial information is appropriately tagged and included in the instance document.
- Test for consistency of tagging (for example, an entity may use one taxonomy tag for one year and then switch to a different tag for the same financial information the following year. In this case, the financial information for both years should use the same tag).

---

[16] The eXtensible Business Reporting Language (XBRL) tags and their relationship to other XBRL tags are represented in a taxonomy. The XBRL taxonomy is needed for a full rendering of the XBRL Instance Document.

[17] A rendered instance document converts the machine-readable format to a human readable version through a software tool.

- Test that the entity extension or custom taxonomy meets the XBRL International Technical Specification (for example, through the use of a validation tool).

.53 When the client is the responsible party, the client will provide the practitioner with a written assertion regarding the subject matter. An example of a written assertion follows:

> We assert that the accompanying XBRL Instance Document accurately reflects the data presented in the financial statements of XYZ Company as of December 31, 20XX, and for the year then ended in conformity with [*identify the criteria—for example, specify XBRL taxonomy, such as "XBRL U.S. Consumer and Industrial Taxonomy," and where applicable, the company extension taxonomy, such as "XYZ Company's extension taxonomy" and the XBRL International Technical Specifications (specify version)*].

.54 The practitioner should identify in his or her report whether the underlying financial information has been audited or reviewed, and should refer to the report of such audit or review.[18] If the underlying information has not been audited or reviewed, the practitioner should disclaim an opinion on the underlying information. Any information in the Instance Document that is not covered by the practitioner's report should clearly be identified as such.

.55 Report Examples

Example 1: Reporting on the Subject Matter

<u>Independent Accountant's Report</u>

> We have examined the accompanying XBRL Instance Document of XYZ Company, which reflects the data presented in the financial statements of XYZ Company as of December 31, 20XX, and for the year then ended [*optional to include the location of the financial statements, such as "included in the Company's Form 10-K for the year ended December 31, 20XX"*]. XYZ Company's management is responsible for the XBRL Instance Document. Our responsibility is to express an opinion based on our examination.
>
> Our examination was conducted in accordance with attestation standards established by the American Institute of Certified Public Accountants and, accordingly, included examining, on a test basis, evidence supporting the XBRL Instance Document and performing such other procedures as we considered necessary in the circumstances. We believe that our examination provides a reasonable basis for our opinion.
>
> In our opinion, the XBRL Instance Document of XYZ Company referred to above accurately reflects, in all material respects, the data presented in the financial statements in conformity with [*identify the criteria—for example, specific XBRL taxonomy, such as the "XBRL U.S. Consumer and Industrial Taxonomy," and where applicable, the company extension taxonomy, such as "XYZ Company's extension taxonomy," and the XBRL International Technical Specifications 2.0*].
>
> We have also audited, in accordance with auditing standards generally accepted in the United States of America, the financial statements of XYZ Company as of December 31, 20XX, and for the year then ended, and in our report dated

[18] When no audit or review report has been issued, no reference to a report is required.

[*Month*] XX, 20XX, we expressed an unqualified opinion on those financial statements.[19,20]

[*Signature*]

[*Date*]

Example 2: Reporting on Management's Assertions

Independent Accountant's Report

We have examined management's assertion that [*identify the assertion—for example, the accompanying XBRL Instance Document accurately reflects the data presented in the financial statements of XYZ Company as of December 31, 20XX, and for the year then ended in conformity with (identify the criteria—for example, specific XBRL taxonomy, such as the "XBRL U.S. Consumer and Industrial Taxonomy," and where applicable, the company extension taxonomy, such as "XYZ Company's extension taxonomy," and the XBRL International Technical Specifications 2.0)*]. XYZ Company's management is responsible for the assertion. Our responsibility is to express an opinion on the assertion based on our examination.

We have also audited, in accordance with auditing standards generally accepted in the United States of America, the financial statements of XYZ Company, which comprise the balance sheet as of December 31, 20XX, and the related statements of income, changes in stockholders' equity, and cash flows, for the year then ended, and the related notes to the financial statements. In our report dated [*Month*] XX, 20XX, we expressed an unmodified opinion on those financial statements.

Our examination was conducted in accordance with attestation standards established by the American Institute of Certified Public Accountants and, accordingly, included examining, on a test basis, evidence supporting the XBRL Instance Document and performing such other procedures as we considered necessary in the circumstances. We believe that our examination provides a reasonable basis for our opinion.

In our opinion, management's assertion referred to above is fairly stated, in all material respects, in conformity with [*identify the criteria—for example, specific XBRL taxonomy, such as the "XBRL U.S. Consumer and Industrial Taxonomy," and where applicable, the company extension taxonomy, such as "XYZ Company's extension taxonomy," and the XBRL International Technical Specifications 2.0*].

[*Signature*]

[*Date*]

[Issue Date: September 2003; Revised: December 2012.]

---

[19] If the financial statements have been reviewed, the sentence would read: "We have also reviewed, in accordance with [*standards established by the American Institute of Certified Public Accountants*] [*Statements on Standards for Accounting and Review Services issued by the American Institute of Certified Public Accountants*], the financial statements of XYZ Company as of March 31, 20XX, and for the three months then ended, the objective of which was the expression of limited assurance on such financial statements, and issued our report thereon dated [*Month*] XX, 20XX, [*describe any modifications of such report*]."

If the financial information has not been audited or reviewed, no reference to a report is required. The sentence would read: "We were not engaged to and did not conduct an audit or review of the [*identify information*], the objectives of which would have been the expression of an opinion or limited assurance on such [*identify information*]. Accordingly, we do not express an opinion or any other assurance on [*it*] [*them*]."

[20] If the audit opinion on the related financial statements is other than unqualified, the practitioner should disclose that fact, and any substantive reasons therefore.

6. Reporting on Attestation Engagements Performed in Accordance With *Government Auditing Standards*[21]

.56 *Question*—Chapter 5, "Standards for Attestation Engagements," of the 2011 revision of *Government Auditing Standards* (commonly referred to as the Yellow Book) sets forth additional fieldwork and reporting standards for attestation engagements performed pursuant to generally accepted government auditing standards (GAGAS). Practitioners performing attestation engagements under GAGAS are also required to follow the general standards set forth in chapter 3, "General Standards," of the Yellow Book, as well as the guidance and requirements in chapters 1, "Government Auditing: Foundation and Ethical Principles," and 2, "Standards for Use and Application of GAGAS." For examination attestation engagements performed pursuant to GAGAS, paragraph 5.18 of the Yellow Book prescribes additional reporting standards[22] that go beyond the standards of reporting set forth in paragraphs .63–.90 of section 101. When a practitioner performs an attestation examination in accordance with GAGAS, how should the report be modified?

.57 *Interpretation*—The practitioner should modify the scope paragraph of the attestation report to indicate that the examination or review was "conducted in accordance with attestation standards established by the American Institute of Certified Public Accountants and the standards applicable to attestation engagements contained in *Government Auditing Standards* issued by the Comptroller General of the United States."

.58 Additionally, GAGAS require the practitioner's attestation report to disclose any matters (often referred to as findings) that are set forth in paragraphs 5.20–.26 of the revised Yellow Book. Paragraphs 5.27–.28 of the revised Yellow Book set forth the presentation requirements that the practitioner should use, to the extent possible, in reporting a finding. The following illustration is a standard examination report modified to make reference to a schedule of findings when any of the matters set forth in paragraphs 5.20–.26 have been identified. This report pertains to subject matter for which suitable criteria exist and are available to all users through inclusion in a clear manner in the presentation of the subject matter. A written assertion has been obtained from the responsible party. Although the following illustrative report modifications would comply with the Yellow Book requirement, this illustration is not intended to preclude a practitioner from complying with these additional Yellow Book reporting requirements in other ways. In this illustrative report, the practitioner is reporting on the subject matter.

Independent Accountant's Report

We have examined [*identify the subject matter—for example, the accompanying schedule of performance measures of XYZ Agency for the year ended December*

---

[21] Although separate interpretations for other AT sections have not been issued to deal with attestation engagements performed in accordance with *Government Auditing Standards*, a practitioner may use this guidance to help him or her appropriately modify an attest report pursuant to other AT sections.

[22] Paragraph 5.18 of the Yellow Book sets forth the additional reporting requirements: (*a*) reporting auditors' compliance with generally accepted government auditing standards, (*b*) reporting deficiencies in internal control, fraud, noncompliance with provisions of laws, regulations, contracts, and grant agreements, and abuse, (*c*) reporting views of responsible officials, (*d*) reporting confidential or sensitive information, and (*e*) distributing reports. [Footnote revised, January 2008, to reflect conforming changes necessary due to the issuance of the 2007 revised *Government Auditing Standards*. Footnote revised, December 2012, to reflect conforming changes necessary due to the issuance of the 2011 revision of *Government Auditing Standards*.]

31, 20XX].[23] XYZ Agency's management is responsible for the [*identify the subject matter—for example, schedule of performance measures*]. Our responsibility is to express an opinion based on our examination.

Our examination was conducted in accordance with attestation standards established by the American Institute of Certified Public Accountants and the standards applicable to attestation engagements contained in *Government Auditing Standards* issued by the Comptroller General of the United States and, accordingly, included examining, on a test basis, evidence supporting [*identify the subject matter—for example, XYZ Agency's schedule of performance measures*] and performing such other procedures as we considered necessary in the circumstances. We believe that our examination provides a reasonable basis for our opinion.

[*Additional paragraph(s) may be added to emphasize certain matters relating to the attest engagement or the subject matter.*]

In our opinion, the schedule referred to above presents, in all material respects, [*identify the subject matter—for example, the performance measures of XYZ Agency for the year ended December 31, 20XX*], in conformity with [*identify criteria—for example, the criteria set forth in Note 1*].

[*When any of the matters set forth in paragraphs 5.20–.26 of the Yellow Book have been identified the following paragraph would be added.*]

In accordance with *Government Auditing Standards*, we are required to report all deficiencies that are considered to be significant deficiencies or material weaknesses in internal control; fraud and noncompliance with provisions of laws or regulations that have a material effect on [*identify the subject matter—for example, XYZ Agency's schedule of performance measures*]; and any other instances that warrant the attention of those charged with governance; noncompliance with provisions of contracts or grant agreements, and abuse that has a material effect on the subject matter.[24] We are also required to obtain and report the views of responsible officials concerning the findings, conclusions, and recommendations, as well as any planned corrective actions. We performed our examination to express an opinion on whether [*identify the subject matter—for example, XYZ Agency's schedule of performance measures*] is presented in accordance with the criteria described above and not for the purpose of expressing an opinion on the internal control over [*identify the subject matter—for example, reporting of performance measures*] or on compliance and other matters; accordingly, we express no such opinions. Our examination disclosed certain findings that are required to be reported under *Government Auditing Standards* and

[23] If the practitioner is reporting on an assertion about the subject matter, the practitioner would identify the assertion rather than the subject matter, for example, "management's assertion that the accompanying schedule presents the performance measures of XYZ Agency for the year ended December 31, 20XX in conformity with the criteria in Note 1." [Footnote added, December 2012, to reflect conforming changes necessary due to the issuance of the 2011 revision of *Government Auditing Standards*.]

[24] Note that paragraph 5.25 of *Government Auditing Standards* states that when auditors detect instances of noncompliance with provisions of contracts or grant agreements, or abuse that have an effect on the subject matter or an assertion about the subject matter that is less than material but warrant the attention of those charged with governance, they should communicate those findings in writing to entity officials. When auditors detect any instances of fraud, noncompliance with provisions of laws, regulations, contracts, or grant agreements, or abuse that do not warrant the attention of those charged with governance, the auditors' determination of whether and how to communicate such instances to audited entity officials is a matter of professional judgment. [Footnote added, January 2008, to reflect conforming changes necessary due to the issuance of the 2007 revised *Government Auditing Standards*. Footnote renumbered and revised, December 2012, to reflect conforming changes necessary due to the issuance of the 2011 revision of *Government Auditing Standards*.]

those findings, along with the views of responsible officials, are described in the attached Schedule of Findings.[25]

[*Signature*]

[*Date*]

[25] [Footnote renumbered and deleted to reflect conforming changes necessary due to the issuance of the 2007 revised *Government Auditing Standards*. Footnote renumbered, December 2012, to reflect conforming changes necessary due to the issuance of the 2011 revision of *Government Auditing Standards*.]

Illustrative Schedule of Findings

XYZ Agency
Schedule of Findings[26]
Year Ended December 31, 20XX

Finding No. 1

Criteria

Condition

Cause

Effect or Potential Effect

Management's Response

Finding No. 2

Criteria

Condition

Cause

Effect or Potential Effect

Management's Response

[Issue Date: December 2004; Revised: January 2008; Revised: December 2012.]

[26] Refer to paragraphs 5.11–.15 of the Yellow Book regarding the content of the schedule of findings. [Footnote renumbered and revised: January 2008, to reflect conforming changes necessary due to the issuance of the 2007 revised *Government Auditing Standards*. Footnote renumbered and revised, December 2012, to reflect conforming changes necessary due to the issuance of the 2011 revision of *Government Auditing Standards*.]

7. Reporting on the Design of Internal Control

.59 *Question*—A practitioner may be asked to report on the suitability[27] of the design of an entity's internal control over financial reporting (internal control) for preventing or detecting and correcting material misstatements of the entity's financial statements on a timely basis. Such requests may be made by, for example,

- an entity applying for a government grant or contract that is required to submit a written preaward survey by management about the suitability of the design of the entity's internal control or a portion of the entity's internal control, together with a practitioner's report thereon.
- a new casino applying for a license to operate that is required by a regulatory agency to submit a practitioner's report on whether the entity's internal control *that it plans to implement* is suitably designed to provide reasonable assurance that the control objectives specified in the regulatory agency's regulations would be achieved. (In this situation the casino would not yet have begun operations, and audited financial statements or financial data relevant to the period covered by the engagement may not exist.)

May a practitioner report on the suitability of the design of an entity's internal control based on the risk assessment procedures the auditor performs to obtain a sufficient understanding of the entity and its environment, including its internal control, in an audit of the entity's financial statements?

.60 *Interpretation*—No. In a financial statement audit, the purpose of the auditor's understanding of the entity and its environment, including its internal control, is to enable the auditor to assess the risk of material misstatement of the financial statements whether due to error or fraud, and to design the nature, timing, and extent of further audit procedures. The understanding obtained in a financial statement audit does not provide the practitioner with a sufficient basis to report on the suitability of the design of an entity's internal control or any portion thereof.

.61 *Question*—How may a practitioner report on the suitability of the design of an entity's internal control or a portion thereof?

.62 *Interpretation*—The practitioner may perform an examination under section 101, or apply agreed-upon procedures under section 201, to management's written assertion about the suitability of the design of the entity's internal control. Footnote 4 of section 501, *An Examination of an Entity's Internal Control Over Financial Reporting That is Integrated With an Audit of Its Financial Statements*, states that although section 501 does not directly apply when an auditor is engaged to examine the suitability of design of an entity's internal control, it may be useful in planning and performing such engagements. Paragraphs .57–.59 of section 501 discuss how the auditor evaluates the design effectiveness of controls.

.63 When the engagement involves the application of agreed-upon procedures to a written assertion about the suitability of the design of an entity's internal control over compliance with specified requirements, the practitioner should also follow the provisions of paragraphs .09 and .11–.29 of section 601.

---

[27] In this interpretation, the *suitability of the design of internal control* means the same thing as the *design effectiveness of an entity's internal control.* [Footnote renumbered, December 2012, to reflect conforming changes necessary due to the issuance of the 2011 revision of *Government Auditing Standards.*]

.64 The following is an illustrative report a practitioner may issue when reporting on the suitability of the design of an entity's internal control that has been implemented. The report may be modified, as appropriate, to fit the particular circumstances.

Independent Accountant's Report

[*Introductory paragraph*]

We have examined the suitability of the design of W Company's internal control over financial reporting to prevent or detect and correct material misstatements in its financial statements on a timely basis as of December 31, 20XX, based on [*identify criteria*].[28] W Company's management is responsible for the suitable design of internal control over financial reporting. Our responsibility is to express an opinion on the design of internal control based on our examination.

[*Scope paragraph*]

Our examination was conducted in accordance with attestation standards established by the American Institute of Certified Public Accountants and, accordingly, included obtaining an understanding of internal control over financial reporting, evaluating the design of internal control, and performing such other procedures as we considered necessary in the circumstances. We believe that our examination provides a reasonable basis for our opinion. We were not engaged to examine and report on the operating effectiveness of W Company's internal control over financial reporting as of December 31, 20XX, and, accordingly, we express no opinion on operating effectiveness.

[*Inherent limitations paragraph*]

Because of its inherent limitations, internal control over financial reporting may not prevent or detect and correct misstatements. Also, projections of any evaluation of effectiveness to future periods are subject to the risk that controls may become inadequate because of changes in conditions, or that the degree of compliance with the policies or procedures may deteriorate.

[*Opinion paragraph*]

In our opinion, W Company's internal control over financial reporting was suitably designed, in all material respects, to prevent or detect and correct material misstatements in the financial statements on a timely basis as of December 31, 20XX, based on [*identify criteria*].

[*Signature*]

[*Date*]

.65 When reporting on the suitability of the design of an entity's internal control that has not yet been implemented, the practitioner would be unable to confirm that the controls have been implemented and should disclose that information in the practitioner's report. In those circumstances, the practitioner should modify (1) the scope paragraph of the illustrative report in paragraph .64 to inform readers that the controls identified in the report have not yet been implemented and (2) the inherent limitations paragraph to reflect the related risk. Following are modified illustrative report paragraphs for use when controls have not yet been implemented. (New language is shown in boldface italics. Deleted language is shown in strikethrough.)

---

[28] This report assumes that the control criteria are both suitable and available to users as discussed in paragraphs .23–.33 of section 101. Therefore, the use of this report is not restricted. [Footnote renumbered, December 2012, to reflect conforming changes necessary due to the issuance of the 2011 revision of *Government Auditing Standards*.]

Our examination was conducted in accordance with attestation standards established by the American Institute of Certified Public Accountants and, accordingly, included obtaining an understanding of internal control over financial reporting, evaluating the design of internal control, and performing such other procedures as we considered necessary in the circumstances. We believe that our examination provides a reasonable basis for our opinion. ***Because operations had not begun as of December 31, 20XX, we could not confirm that the specified controls were implemented. Accordingly, our report solely addresses the suitability of the design of the Company's internal control and does not address whether the controls were implemented. Furthermore, because the specified controls have not yet been implemented, we were unable to test, and did not test,*** the operating effectiveness of W Company's internal control over financial reporting as of December 31, 20XX, and, accordingly, we express no opinion on operating effectiveness.

[*Inherent limitations paragraph*]

Because of its inherent limitations, internal control over financial reporting may not prevent or detect and correct misstatements. Also, projections of any evaluation of effectiveness to future periods are subject to the risk that controls ***may not be implemented as intended when operations begin or*** may become inadequate because of changes in conditions~~, or that the degree of compliance with the policies or procedures may deteriorate~~.

.66 *Question*—A practitioner may be asked to sign a prescribed form developed by the party to whom the form is to be submitted regarding the design of an entity's internal control. What are the practitioner's responsibilities when requested to sign such a form if it includes language that is not consistent with the practitioner's function or responsibility or with the reporting requirements of professional standards?

.67 *Interpretation*—Paragraphs .22–.23 of AU-C section 800, *Special Considerations—Audits of Financial Statements Prepared in Accordance With Special Purpose Frameworks*, address such situations in the context of an audit of financial statements and indicate that the auditor should either reword the prescribed form of report or attach an appropriately worded separate report that conforms with the auditor's function or responsibility and professional standards. When reporting on the suitability of the design of an entity's internal control under section 101, the practitioner's report should contain all of the elements in either paragraphs .85 or .86, as applicable, which can be accomplished by either rewording the prescribed form of report or attaching an appropriately worded separate report in place of the prescribed form.

.68 *Question*—An entity may be required to submit a practitioner's report about an entity's *ability* to establish suitably designed internal control (or its assertion thereon). May a practitioner issue such a report based on (*a*) the risk assessment procedures related to existing internal control that the auditor performs in an audit of an entity's financial statements or (*b*) the performance of an attest engagement?

.69 *Interpretation*—No. Neither the risk assessment procedures the auditor performs in an audit of an entity's financial statements nor the performance of an attest engagement provide the practitioner with a basis for issuing a report on the *ability* of an entity to establish suitably designed internal control. There are no suitable criteria for evaluating an entity's ability to establish suitably designed internal control. The requesting party may be willing to accept a report of the practitioner on a consulting service. The practitioner may include in the consulting service report *a.* a statement that the practitioner is unable to perform an attest engagement that addresses the entity's ability to establish suitably designed internal control because there are no suitable criteria for evaluating the entity's ability to do so;

b. a description of the nature and scope of the practitioner's services; and

c. the practitioner's findings.

The practitioner may refer to the guidance in CS section 100, *Consulting Services: Definitions and Standards.*

[Issue Date: December 2008; Revised: December 2012.]

8. Including a Description of Tests of Controls or Other Procedures, and the Results Thereof, in an Examination Report

.70 *Question*—Section 801, *Reporting on Controls at a Service Organization*, addresses examination engagements undertaken by a service auditor to report on controls at organizations that provide services to user entities when those controls are likely to be relevant to user entities' internal control over financial reporting (ICFR). For a type 2 report resulting from such an examination engagement, section 801 provides for a separate section of the report that includes a description of the service auditor's tests of controls likely to be relevant to user entities' ICFR and the results of those tests. This information is intended for user auditors who may need detailed information about the results of such tests of controls to determine how the results affect a particular user entity's financial statements.

.71 Paragraph .02 of section 801 refers the practitioner to section 101, when a practitioner is engaged to examine and report on controls at a service organization other than those likely to be relevant to user entities' ICFR (for example, controls at a service provider that are relevant to user entities' compliance with laws or regulations or controls at a service provider that are relevant to the privacy of user entities' information).[29] If a practitioner performs an examination engagement under section 101, may the practitioner's examination report include, in a separate section, a description of tests of controls or other procedures performed in support of the practitioner's opinion resulting from such an engagement?

.72 *Interpretation*—Nothing in section 101 precludes a practitioner from including in a separate section of his or her examination report a description of tests of controls or other procedures performed and the results thereof. However, in some cases, such a description may overshadow the practitioner's overall opinion or may cause report users to misunderstand the opinion. Therefore, the circumstances of the particular engagement are relevant to the practitioner's consideration regarding whether to include a description of tests of controls or other procedures performed, and the results thereof, in a separate section of the practitioner's examination report. In determining whether to include such a description in the practitioner's examination report, the following considerations are relevant:

---

[29] As indicated in paragraph A2 of section 801, *Reporting on Controls at a Service Organization*, paragraph .02 of section 801 is not intended to permit a report that combines reporting on a service organization's controls likely to be relevant to user entities' internal control over financial reporting (ICFR) with reporting on controls that are not likely to be relevant to user entities' ICFR. [Footnote renumbered, December 2012, to reflect conforming changes necessary due to the issuance of the 2011 revision of *Government Auditing Standards*.]

- Whether there has been a request for such information and whether the specified parties making the request have an appropriate business need or reasonable basis for requesting the information (for example, the specified parties are required to maintain and monitor controls that either encompass or are dependent on controls that are the subject of the examination and, therefore, need information about the tests of controls to enable them to have a basis for concluding that they have met the requirements applicable to them)
- Whether the specified parties have an understanding of the nature and subject matter of the engagement and experience in using the information in such reports
- Whether including such a description in the examination report is likely to cause report users to misunderstand the opinion
- Whether the practitioner's tests of controls or other procedures performed directly relate to the subject matter of the engagement

Paragraph .79 of section 101 states, "The need for restriction on the use of a report may result from a number of circumstances, including the purpose of the report, the criteria used in preparation of the subject matter, the extent to which the procedures performed are known or understood, and the potential for the report to be misunderstood when taken out of the context in which it was intended to be used." The addition of a description of tests of controls or other procedures performed, and the results thereof, in a separate section of an examination report may increase the need for use of the report to be restricted to specified parties.

[Issue Date: July 2010.]

AT Section 201

Agreed-Upon Procedures Engagements

Source: SSAE No. 10; SSAE No. 11.

Effective when the subject matter or assertion is as of or for a period ending on or after June 1, 2001, unless otherwise indicated.

Introduction and Applicability

.01 This section sets forth attestation standards and provides guidance to a practitioner concerning performance and reporting in all agreed-upon procedures engagements, except as noted in paragraph .02. A practitioner also should refer to the following sections of this Statement on Standards for Attestation Engagements (SSAE), which provide additional guidance for certain types of agreed-upon procedures engagements:

a. Section 301, *Financial Forecasts and Projections*
b. Section 601, *Compliance Attestation*

.02 This section does not apply to the following:[1]

a. Situations in which an auditor reports on specified compliance requirements based solely on an audit of financial statements, as addressed in AU-C section 806, *Reporting on Compliance With Aspects of Contractual Agreements or Regulatory Requirements in Connection With Audited Financial Statements*

b. Engagements for which the objective is to report in accordance with AU-C section 935, *Compliance Audits*, unless the terms of the engagement specify that the engagement be performed pursuant to SSAEs

c. Engagements covered by AU-C section 920, *Letters for Underwriters and Certain Other Requesting Parties*

d. Certain professional services that would not be considered as falling under this section as described in paragraph .04 of section 101, *Attest Engagements*

[Revised, December 2010, to reflect conforming changes necessary due to the issuance of SAS No. 117. Revised, August 2011, to reflect conforming changes necessary due to the issuance of SSAE No. 16. Revised, December 2012, to reflect conforming changes necessary due to the issuance of SAS Nos. 122–126.]

Agreed-Upon Procedures Engagements

.03 An agreed-upon procedures engagement is one in which a practitioner is engaged by a client to issue a report of findings based on specific procedures performed on subject matter. The client engages the practitioner to assist specified parties in evaluating subject matter or an assertion as a result of a need

---

[1] Interpretation No. 2, "Responding to Requests for Reports on Matters Relating to Solvency," of section 101, *Attest Engagements* (sec. 9101 par. .23–.33), prohibits the performance of any attest engagements concerning matters of solvency or insolvency.

or needs of the specified parties.[2] Because the specified parties require that findings be independently derived, the services of a practitioner are obtained to perform procedures and report his or her findings. The specified parties and the practitioner agree upon the procedures to be performed by the practitioner that the specified parties believe are appropriate. Because the needs of the specified parties may vary widely, the nature, timing, and extent of the agreed-upon procedures may vary as well; consequently, the specified parties assume responsibility for the sufficiency of the procedures since they best understand their own needs. In an engagement performed under this section, the practitioner does not perform an examination or a review, as discussed in section 101, and does not provide an opinion or negative assurance.[3] (See paragraph .24.) Instead, the practitioner's report on agreed-upon procedures should be in the form of procedures and findings. (See paragraph .31.)

.04 As a consequence of the role of the specified parties in agreeing upon the procedures performed or to be performed, a practitioner's report on such engagements should clearly indicate that its use is restricted to those specified parties.[4] Those specified parties, including the client, are hereinafter referred to as *specified parties*.

Standards

.05 The general, fieldwork, and reporting standards for attestation engagements as established in section 50, *SSAE Hierarchy*, together with interpretive guidance regarding their application as addressed throughout this section, should be followed by the practitioner in performing and reporting on agreed-upon procedures engagements. [Revised, November 2006, to reflect conforming changes necessary due to the issuance of SSAE No. 14.]

Conditions for Engagement Performance

.06 The practitioner may perform an agreed-upon procedures attest engagement provided that—

a. The practitioner is independent.

b. One of the following conditions is met.

(1) The party wishing to engage the practitioner is responsible for the subject matter, or has a reasonable basis for providing a written assertion about the subject matter when the nature of the subject matter is such that a responsible party does not otherwise exist.

(2) The party wishing to engage the practitioner is not responsible for the subject matter but is able to provide the practitioner, or have a third party who is responsible for the subject matter provide the practitioner with evidence of the third party's responsibility for the subject matter.

---

[2] See paragraphs .08–.09 for a discussion of subject matter and assertion.

[3] For guidance on expressing an opinion on specified elements, accounts, or items of a financial statement based on an audit, see AU-C section 805, *Special Considerations—Audits of Single Financial Statements and Specific Elements, Accounts, or Items of a Financial Statement*. [Footnote revised, December 2012, to reflect conforming changes necessary due to the issuance of SAS Nos. 122–126.]

[4] See paragraphs .78–.83 of section 101 for additional guidance regarding restricted-use reports.

c. The practitioner and the specified parties agree upon the procedures performed or to be performed by the practitioner.

d. The specified parties take responsibility for the sufficiency of the agreed-upon procedures for their purposes.

e. The specific subject matter to which the procedures are to be applied is subject to reasonably consistent measurement.

f. Criteria to be used in the determination of findings are agreed upon between the practitioner and the specified parties.

g. The procedures to be applied to the specific subject matter are expected to result in reasonably consistent findings using the criteria.

h. Evidential matter related to the specific subject matter to which the procedures are applied is expected to exist to provide a reasonable basis for expressing the findings in the practitioner's report.

i. Where applicable, the practitioner and the specified parties agree on any materiality limits for reporting purposes. (See paragraph .25.)

j. Use of the report is restricted to the specified parties.

k. For agreed-upon procedures engagements on prospective financial information, the prospective financial statements include a summary of significant assumptions. (See paragraph .52 of section 301.)

Agreement on and Sufficiency of Procedures

.07 To satisfy the requirements that the practitioner and the specified parties agree upon the procedures performed or to be performed and that the specified parties take responsibility for the sufficiency of the agreed-upon procedures for their purposes, ordinarily the practitioner should communicate directly with and obtain affirmative acknowledgment from each of the specified parties. For example, this may be accomplished by meeting with the specified parties or by distributing a draft of the anticipated report or a copy of an engagement letter to the specified parties and obtaining their agreement. If the practitioner is not able to communicate directly with all of the specified parties, the practitioner may satisfy these requirements by applying any one or more of the following or similar procedures.

- Compare the procedures to be applied to written requirements of the specified parties.
- Discuss the procedures to be applied with appropriate representatives of the specified parties involved.
- Review relevant contracts with or correspondence from the specified parties.

The practitioner should not report on an engagement when specified parties do not agree upon the procedures performed or to be performed and do not take responsibility for the sufficiency of the procedures for their purposes. (See paragraph .36 for guidance on satisfying these requirements when the practitioner is requested to add other parties as specified parties after the date of completion of the agreed-upon procedures.)

Subject Matter and Related Assertions

.08 The subject matter of an agreed-upon procedures engagement may take many different forms and may be at a point in time or covering a period of time. In an agreed-upon procedures engagement, it is the specific subject matter to which the agreed-upon procedures are to be applied using the criteria selected. Even though the procedures are agreed upon between the practitioner and the specified parties, the subject matter and the criteria must meet the conditions set forth in the third general standard. (See paragraphs .23–.24 of section 101.) The criteria against which the specific subject matter needs to be measured may be recited within the procedures enumerated or referred to in the practitioner's report.

.09 An assertion is any declaration or set of declarations about whether the subject matter is based on or in conformity with the criteria selected. A written assertion is generally not required in an agreed-upon procedures engagement unless specifically required by another attest standard (for example, see paragraph .11 of section 601). If, however, the practitioner requests the responsible party to provide an assertion, the assertion may be presented in a representation letter or another written communication from the responsible party, such as in a statement, narrative description, or schedule appropriately identifying what is being presented and the point in time or the period of time covered.

Establishing an Understanding With the Client

.10 The practitioner should establish an understanding with the client regarding the services to be performed. When the practitioner documents the understanding through a written communication with the client (an *engagement letter*), such communication should be addressed to the client, and in some circumstances also to all specified parties. Matters that might be included in such an understanding include the following:

- The nature of the engagement
- Identification of the subject matter (or the assertion related thereto), the responsible party, and the criteria to be used
- Identification of specified parties (See paragraph .36.)
- Specified parties' acknowledgment of their responsibility for the sufficiency of the procedures
- Responsibilities of the practitioner (See paragraphs .12–.14 and .40.)
- Reference to attestation standards established by the American Institute of Certified Public Accountants (AICPA)
- Agreement on procedures by enumerating (or referring to) the procedures (See paragraphs .15–.18.)
- Disclaimers expected to be included in the practitioner's report
- Use restrictions
- Assistance to be provided to the practitioner (See paragraphs .22–.23.)
- Involvement of a specialist (See paragraphs .19–.21.)
- Agreed-upon materiality limits (See paragraph .25.)

Nature, Timing, and Extent of Procedures

Responsibility of the Specified Parties

.11 Specified parties are responsible for the sufficiency (nature, timing, and extent) of the agreed-upon procedures because they best understand their own needs. The specified parties assume the risk that such procedures might be insufficient for their purposes. In addition, the specified parties assume the risk that they might misunderstand or otherwise inappropriately use findings properly reported by the practitioner.

Practitioner's Responsibility

.12 The responsibility of the practitioner is to carry out the procedures and report the findings in accordance with the general, fieldwork, and reporting standards as discussed and interpreted in this section. The practitioner assumes the risk that misapplication of the procedures may result in inappropriate findings being reported. Furthermore, the practitioner assumes the risk that appropriate findings may not be reported or may be reported inaccurately. The practitioner's risks can be reduced through adequate planning and supervision and due professional care in performing the procedures, determining the findings, and preparing the report.

.13 The practitioner should have adequate knowledge in the specific subject matter to which the agreed-upon procedures are to be applied. He or she may obtain such knowledge through formal or continuing education, practical experience, or consultation with others.[5]

.14 The practitioner has no responsibility to determine the differences between the agreed-upon procedures to be performed and the procedures that the practitioner would have determined to be necessary had he or she been engaged to perform another form of attest engagement. The procedures that the practitioner agrees to perform pursuant to an agreed-upon procedures engagement may be more or less extensive than the procedures that the practitioner would determine to be necessary had he or she been engaged to perform another form of engagement.

Procedures to Be Performed

.15 The procedures that the practitioner and specified parties agree upon may be as limited or as extensive as the specified parties desire. However, mere reading of an assertion or specified information about the subject matter does not constitute a procedure sufficient to permit a practitioner to report on the results of applying agreed-upon procedures. In some circumstances, the procedures agreed upon evolve or are modified over the course of the engagement. In general, there is flexibility in determining the procedures as long as the specified parties acknowledge responsibility for the sufficiency of such procedures for their purposes. Matters that should be agreed upon include the nature, timing, and extent of the procedures.

---

[5] Paragraphs .19–.20 of section 601 provide guidance about obtaining an understanding of certain requirements in an agreed-upon procedures engagement on compliance.

.16 The practitioner should not agree to perform procedures that are overly subjective and thus possibly open to varying interpretations. Terms of uncertain meaning (such as general review, limited review, check, or test) should not be used in describing the procedures unless such terms are defined within the agreed-upon procedures. The practitioner should obtain evidential matter from applying the agreed-upon procedures to provide a reasonable basis for the finding or findings expressed in his or her report, but need not perform additional procedures outside the scope of the engagement to gather additional evidential matter.

.17 Examples of appropriate procedures include the following:

- Execution of a sampling application after agreeing on relevant parameters
- Inspection of specified documents evidencing certain types of transactions or detailed attributes thereof
- Confirmation of specific information with third parties
- Comparison of documents, schedules, or analyses with certain specified attributes
- Performance of specific procedures on work performed by others (including the work of internal auditors—see paragraphs .22–.23)
- Performance of mathematical computations

.18 Examples of inappropriate procedures include the following:

- Mere reading of the work performed by others solely to describe their findings
- Evaluating the competency or objectivity of another party
- Obtaining an understanding about a particular subject
- Interpreting documents outside the scope of the practitioner's professional expertise

Involvement of a Specialist[6]

.19 The practitioner's education and experience enable him or her to be knowledgeable about business matters in general, but he or she is not expected to have the expertise of a person trained for or qualified to engage in the practice of another profession or occupation. In certain circumstances, it may be appropriate to involve a specialist to assist the practitioner in the performance of one or more procedures. The following are examples.

- An attorney might provide assistance concerning the interpretation of legal terminology involving laws, regulations, rules, contracts, or grants.
- A medical specialist might provide assistance in understanding the characteristics of diagnosis codes documented in patient medical records.
- An environmental engineer might provide assistance in interpreting environmental remedial action regulatory directives that may affect

---

[6] A *specialist* is a person (or firm) possessing skill or knowledge in a particular field other than the attest function. As used herein, a specialist does not include a person employed by the practitioner's firm who participates in the attest engagement.

the agreed-upon procedures applied to an environmental liabilities account in a financial statement.

- A geologist might provide assistance in distinguishing between varying physical characteristics of a generic minerals group related to information to which the agreed-upon procedures are applied.

.20 The practitioner and the specified parties should explicitly agree to the involvement of the specialist in assisting a practitioner in the performance of an agreed-upon procedures engagement. This agreement may be reached when obtaining agreement on the procedures performed or to be performed and acknowledgment of responsibility for the sufficiency of the procedures, as discussed in paragraph .07. The practitioner's report should describe the nature of the assistance provided by the specialist.

.21 A practitioner may agree to apply procedures to the report or work product of a specialist that does not constitute assistance by the specialist to the practitioner in an agreed-upon procedures engagement. For example, the practitioner may make reference to information contained in a report of a specialist in describing an agreed-upon procedure. However, it is inappropriate for the practitioner to agree to merely read the specialist's report solely to describe or repeat the findings, or to take responsibility for all or a portion of any procedures performed by a specialist or the specialist's work product.

Internal Auditors and Other Personnel

.22 The agreed-upon procedures to be enumerated or referred to in the practitioner's report are to be performed entirely by the practitioner except as discussed in paragraphs .19–.21.[7] However, internal auditors or other personnel may prepare schedules and accumulate data or provide other information for the practitioner's use in performing the agreed-upon procedures. Also, internal auditors may perform and report separately on procedures that they have carried out. Such procedures may be similar to those that a practitioner may perform under this section.

.23 A practitioner may agree to perform procedures on information documented in the working papers of internal auditors. For example, the practitioner may agree to—

- Repeat all or some of the procedures.
- Determine whether the internal auditors' working papers contain documentation of procedures performed and whether the findings documented in the working papers are presented in a report by the internal auditors.

However, it is inappropriate for the practitioner to—

- Agree to merely read the internal auditors' report solely to describe or repeat their findings.
- Take responsibility for all or a portion of any procedures performed by internal auditors by reporting those findings as the practitioner's own.
- Report in any manner that implies shared responsibility for the procedures with the internal auditors.

---

[7] AU-C section 610, *The Auditor's Consideration of the Internal Audit Function in an Audit of Financial Statements*, does not apply to agreed-upon procedures engagements. [Footnote revised, December 2012, to reflect conforming changes necessary due to the issuance of SAS Nos. 122–126.]

Findings

.24 A practitioner should present the results of applying agreed-upon procedures to specific subject matter in the form of findings. The practitioner should not provide negative assurance about whether the subject matter or the assertion is fairly stated based on the criteria. For example, the practitioner should not include a statement in his or her report that "nothing came to my attention that caused me to believe that the [*identify subject matter*] is not presented based on [or the assertion is not fairly stated based on] [*identify criteria*]."

.25 The practitioner should report all findings from application of the agreed-upon procedures. The concept of materiality does not apply to findings to be reported in an agreed-upon procedures engagement unless the definition of materiality is agreed to by the specified parties. Any agreed-upon materiality limits should be described in the practitioner's report.

.26 The practitioner should avoid vague or ambiguous language in reporting findings. Examples of appropriate and inappropriate descriptions of findings resulting from the application of certain agreed-upon procedures follow.

Procedures Agreed Upon	***Appropriate Description of Findings***	***Inappropriate Description of Findings***
Inspect the shipment dates for a sample (agreed-upon) of specified shipping documents, and determine whether any such dates were subsequent to December 31, 20XX.	No shipment dates shown on the sample of shipping documents were subsequent to December 31, 20XX.	Nothing came to my attention as a result of applying that procedure.
Calculate the number of blocks of streets paved during the year ended September 30, 20XX, shown on contractors' certificates of project completion; compare the resultant number to the number in an identified chart of performance statistics.	The number of blocks of streets paved in the chart of performance statistics was Y blocks more than the number calculated from the contractors' certificates of project completion.	The number of blocks of streets paved approximated the number of blocks included in the chart of performance statistics.
Calculate the rate of return on a specified investment (according to an agreed-upon formula) and verify that the resultant percentage agrees to the percentage in an identified schedule.	No exceptions were found as a result of applying the procedure.	The resultant percentage approximated the predetermined percentage in the identified schedule.

Procedures Agreed Upon	*Appropriate Description of Findings*	*Inappropriate Description of Findings*
Inspect the quality standards classification codes in identified performance test documents for products produced during a specified period; compare such codes to those shown in an identified computer printout.	All classification codes inspected in the identified documents were the same as those shown in the computer printout except for the following: [*List all exceptions.*]	All classification codes appeared to comply with such performance documents.
Trace all outstanding checks appearing on a bank reconciliation as of a certain date to checks cleared in the bank statement of the subsequent month.	All outstanding checks appearing on the bank reconciliation were cleared in the subsequent month's bank statement except for the following: [*List all exceptions.*]	Nothing came to my attention as a result of applying the procedure.
Compare the amounts of the invoices included in the "over ninety days" column shown in an identified schedule of aged accounts receivable of a specific customer as of a certain date to the amount and invoice date shown on the outstanding invoice and determine whether or not the invoice dates precede the date indicated on the schedule by more than ninety days.	All outstanding invoice amounts agreed with the amounts shown on the schedule in the "over ninety days" column, and the dates shown on such invoices preceded the date indicated on the schedule by more than ninety days.	The outstanding invoice amounts agreed within approximation of the amounts shown on the schedule in the "over ninety days" column, and nothing came to our attention that the dates shown on such invoices preceded the date indicated on the schedule by more than ninety days.

Working Papers

[.27–.30] [Paragraphs deleted by the issuance of SSAE No. 11, January 2002.][8–9]

[8–9] [Footnotes deleted by the issuance of SSAE No. 11, January 2002.]

Reporting

Required Elements

.31 The practitioner's report on agreed-upon procedures should be in the form of procedures and findings. The practitioner's report should contain the following elements:

a. A title that includes the word *independent*

b. Identification of the specified parties (See paragraph .36.)

c. Identification of the subject matter[10] (or the written assertion related thereto) and the character of the engagement

d. Identification of the responsible party

e. A statement that the subject matter is the responsibility of the responsible party

f. A statement that the procedures performed were those agreed to by the specified parties identified in the report

g. A statement that the agreed-upon procedures engagement was conducted in accordance with attestation standards established by the AICPA

h. A statement that the sufficiency of the procedures is solely the responsibility of the specified parties and a disclaimer of responsibility for the sufficiency of those procedures

i. A list of the procedures performed (or reference thereto) and related findings (The practitioner should not provide negative assurance—see paragraph .24.)

j. Where applicable, a description of any agreed-upon materiality limits (See paragraph .25.)

k. A statement that the practitioner was not engaged to and did not conduct an examination [11, 12] of the subject matter, the objective of which would be the expression of an opinion, a disclaimer of opinion on the subject matter, and a statement that if the practitioner had performed

---

[10] In some agreed-upon procedures engagements, the practitioner may be asked to apply agreed-upon procedures to more than one subject matter or assertion. In these engagements, the practitioner may issue one report that refers to all subject matter covered or assertions presented. (For example, see paragraph .28 of section 601.)

[11] If the practitioner also wishes to refer to a review, alternate wording would be as follows.

> A statement that the practitioner was not engaged to and did not conduct an examination or a review of the subject matter, the objectives of which would be the expression of an opinion or limited assurance, a disclaimer of opinion on the subject matter, and a statement that if the practitioner had performed additional procedures, other matters might have come to his or her attention that would have been reported.

[12] If the subject matter consists of elements, accounts, or items of a financial statement, this statement may be worded as follows.

> We were not engaged to and did not conduct an audit [*or a review*], the objective of which would be the expression of an opinion [*or limited assurance*] on the [*identify elements, accounts, or items of a financial statement*]. Accordingly, we do not express such an opinion [*or limited assurance*].

Alternatively, the wording may be the following.

> These agreed-upon procedures do not constitute an audit [*or a review*] of financial statements or any part thereof, the objective of which is the expression of opinion [or limited assurance] on the financial statements or a part thereof.

additional procedures, other matters might have come to his or her attention that would have been reported[13]

l. A statement of restrictions on the use of the report because it is intended to be used solely by the specified parties[14]

m. Where applicable, reservations or restrictions concerning procedures or findings as discussed in paragraphs .33, .35, and .39–.40

n. For an agreed-upon procedures engagement on prospective financial information, all items included in paragraph .55 of section 301

o. Where applicable, a description of the nature of the assistance provided by a specialist as discussed in paragraphs .19–.21

p. The manual or printed signature of the practitioner's firm

q. The date of the report

Illustrative Report

.32 The following is an illustration of an agreed-upon procedures report.

Independent Accountant's Report
on Applying Agreed-Upon Procedures

To the Audit Committees and Managements of ABC Inc. and XYZ Fund:

We have performed the procedures enumerated below, which were agreed to by the audit committees and managements of ABC Inc. and XYZ Fund, solely to assist you in evaluating the accompanying Statement of Investment Performance Statistics of XYZ Fund (prepared in accordance with the criteria specified therein) for the year ended December 31, 20X1. XYZ Fund's management is responsible for the statement of investment performance statistics. This agreed-upon procedures engagement was conducted in accordance with attestation standards established by the American Institute of Certified Public Accountants. The sufficiency of these procedures is solely the responsibility of those parties specified in this report. Consequently, we make no representation regarding the sufficiency of the procedures described below either for the purpose for which this report has been requested or for any other purpose.

[*Include paragraphs to enumerate procedures and findings.*]

We were not engaged to and did not conduct an examination, the objective of which would be the expression of an opinion on the accompanying Statement of Investment Performance Statistics of XYZ Fund. Accordingly, we do not express such an opinion. Had we performed additional procedures, other matters might have come to our attention that would have been reported to you.

This report is intended solely for the information and use of the audit committees and managements of ABC Inc. and XYZ Fund,[15] and is not intended to be and should not be used by anyone other than these specified parties.

[*Signature*]

[*Date*]

---

[13] [Footnote deleted, December 2012, to reflect conforming changes necessary due to the issuance of SSARS No. 19 and SAS Nos. 122–126.]

[14] The purpose of the restriction on the use of the practitioner's report on applying agreed-upon procedures is to restrict its use to only those parties that have agreed upon the procedures performed and taken responsibility for the sufficiency of the procedures. Paragraph .36 describes the process for adding parties who were not originally contemplated in the agreed-upon procedures engagement.

[15] The report may list the specified parties or refer the reader to the specified parties listed elsewhere in the report.

Explanatory Language

.33 The practitioner also may include explanatory language about matters such as the following:

- Disclosure of stipulated facts, assumptions, or interpretations (including the source thereof) used in the application of agreed-upon procedures (For example, see paragraph .26 of section 601.)
- Description of the condition of records, controls, or data to which the procedures were applied
- Explanation that the practitioner has no responsibility to update his or her report
- Explanation of sampling risk

Dating of Report

.34 The date of completion of the agreed-upon procedures should be used as the date of the practitioner's report.

Restrictions on the Performance of Procedures

.35 When circumstances impose restrictions on the performance of the agreed-upon procedures, the practitioner should attempt to obtain agreement from the specified parties for modification of the agreed-upon procedures. When such agreement cannot be obtained (for example, when the agreed-upon procedures are published by a regulatory agency that will not modify the procedures), the practitioner should describe any restrictions on the performance of procedures in his or her report or withdraw from the engagement.

Adding Specified Parties (Nonparticipant Parties)

.36 Subsequent to the completion of the agreed-upon procedures engagement, a practitioner may be requested to consider the addition of another party as a specified party (*a nonparticipant party*). The practitioner may agree to add a nonparticipant party as a specified party, based on consideration of such factors as the identity of the nonparticipant party and the intended use of the report.[16] If the practitioner does agree to add the nonparticipant party, he or she should obtain affirmative acknowledgment, normally in writing, from the nonparticipant party agreeing to the procedures performed and of its taking responsibility for the sufficiency of the procedures. If the nonparticipant party is added after the practitioner has issued his or her report, the report may be reissued or the practitioner may provide other written acknowledgment that the nonparticipant party has been added as a specified party. If the report is reissued, the report date should not be changed. If the practitioner provides written acknowledgment that the nonparticipant party has been added as a specified party, such written acknowledgment ordinarily should state that no procedures have been performed subsequent to the date of the report.

---

[16] When considering whether to add a nonparticipant party, the guidance in paragraphs .A27–.A28 of AU-C section 560, *Subsequent Events and Subsequently Discovered Facts*, may be helpful. [Footnote revised, December 2012, to reflect conforming changes necessary due to the issuance of SAS Nos. 122–126.]

Written Representations

.37 A practitioner may find a representation letter to be a useful and practical means of obtaining representations from the responsible party. The need for such a letter may depend on the nature of the engagement and the specified parties. For example, paragraph .68 of section 601 requires a practitioner to obtain written representations from the responsible party in an agreed-upon procedures engagement related to compliance with specified requirements.

.38 Examples of matters that might appear in a representation letter from the responsible party include the following:

a. A statement acknowledging responsibility for the subject matter and, when applicable, the assertion

b. A statement acknowledging responsibility for selecting the criteria and for determining that such criteria are appropriate for their purposes

c. The assertion about the subject matter based on the criteria selected

d. A statement that all known matters contradicting the subject matter or the assertion and any communication from regulatory agencies affecting the subject matter or the assertion has been disclosed to the practitioner

e. Availability of all records relevant to the subject matter and the agreed-upon procedures

f. Other matters as the practitioner deems appropriate

.39 The responsible party's refusal to furnish written representations determined by the practitioner to be appropriate for the engagement constitutes a limitation on the performance of the engagement. In such circumstances, the practitioner should do one of the following.

a. Disclose in his or her report the inability to obtain representations from the responsible party.

b. Withdraw from the engagement.[17]

c. Change the engagement to another form of engagement.

Knowledge of Matters Outside Agreed-Upon Procedures

.40 The practitioner need not perform procedures beyond the agreed-upon procedures. However, in connection with the application of agreed-upon procedures, if matters come to the practitioner's attention by other means that significantly contradict the subject matter (or written assertion related thereto) referred to in the practitioner's report, the practitioner should include this matter in his or her report.[18] For example, if, during the course of applying

---

[17] For an agreed-upon procedures engagement performed pursuant to section 601, management's refusal to furnish all required representations also constitutes a limitation on the scope of the engagement that requires the practitioner to withdraw from the engagement.

[18] If the practitioner has performed (or has been engaged to perform) an audit of the entity's financial statements to which an element, account, or item of a financial statement relates and the auditor's report on such financial statements includes a departure from a standard report (see AU-C section 805, *Special Considerations—Audits of Single Financial Statements and Specific Elements, Accounts, or Items of a Financial Statement*), he or she should consider including a reference to the auditor's report and the departure from the standard report in his or her agreed-upon procedures report. [Footnote revised, December 2012, to reflect conforming changes necessary due to the issuance of SAS Nos. 122–126.]

agreed-upon procedures regarding an entity's internal control, the practitioner becomes aware of a material weakness by means other than performance of the agreed-upon procedure, the practitioner should include this matter in his or her report.

Change to an Agreed-Upon Procedures Engagement From Another Form of Engagement

.41 A practitioner who has been engaged to perform another form of attest engagement or a nonattest service engagement may, before the engagement's completion, be requested to change the engagement to an agreed-upon procedures engagement under this section. A request to change the engagement may result from a change in circumstances affecting the client's requirements, a misunderstanding about the nature of the original services or the alternative services originally available, or a restriction on the performance of the original engagement, whether imposed by the client or caused by circumstances.

.42 Before a practitioner who was engaged to perform another form of engagement agrees to change the engagement to an agreed-upon procedures engagement, he or she should consider the following:

a. The possibility that certain procedures performed as part of another type of engagement are not appropriate for inclusion in an agreed-upon procedures engagement

b. The reason given for the request, particularly the implications of a restriction on the scope of the original engagement or the matters to be reported

c. The additional effort required to complete the original engagement

d. If applicable, the reasons for changing from a general-use report to a restricted-use report

.43 If the specified parties acknowledge agreement to the procedures performed or to be performed and assume responsibility for the sufficiency of the procedures to be included in the agreed-upon procedures engagement, either of the following would be considered a reasonable basis for requesting a change in the engagement—

a. A change in circumstances that requires another form of engagement

b. A misunderstanding concerning the nature of the original engagement or the available alternatives

.44 In all circumstances, if the original engagement procedures are substantially complete or the effort to complete such procedures is relatively insignificant, the practitioner should consider the propriety of accepting a change in the engagement.

.45 If the practitioner concludes, based on his or her professional judgment, that there is reasonable justification to change the engagement, and provided he or she complies with the standards applicable to agreed-upon procedures engagements, the practitioner should issue an appropriate agreed-upon procedures report. The report should not include reference to either the original engagement or performance limitations that resulted in the changed engagement. (See paragraph .40.)

Combined Reports Covering Both Restricted-Use and General-Use Subject Matter or Presentations

.46 When a practitioner performs services pursuant to an engagement to apply agreed-upon procedures to specific subject matter as part of or in addition to another form of service, this section applies only to those services described herein; other Standards would apply to the other services. Other services may include an audit, review, or compilation of a financial statement, another attest service performed pursuant to the SSAEs, or a nonattest service.[19] Reports on applying agreed-upon procedures to specific subject matter may be combined with reports on such other services, provided the types of services can be clearly distinguished and the applicable Standards for each service are followed. See paragraphs .82–.83 of section 101 regarding restricting the use of the combined report.

Effective Date

.47 This section is effective when the subject matter or assertion is as of or for a period ending on or after June 1, 2001. Early application is permitted.

---

[19] See paragraphs .105–.107 of section 101 for requirements relating to attest services provided as part of a consulting service engagement.

.48

Appendix

Additional Illustrative Reports

The following are additional illustrations of reporting on applying agreed-upon procedures to elements, accounts, or items of a financial statement.

1. Report in Connection With a Proposed Acquisition

Independent Accountant's Report
on Applying Agreed-Upon Procedures

To the Board of Directors and Management of X Company:

We have performed the procedures enumerated below, which were agreed to by the Board of Directors and Management of X Company, solely to assist you in connection with the proposed acquisition of Y Company as of December 31, 20XX. Y Company is responsible for its cash and accounts receivable records. This agreed-upon procedures engagement was conducted in accordance with attestation standards established by the American Institute of Certified Public Accountants. The sufficiency of these procedures is solely the responsibility of the parties specified in this report. Consequently, we make no representation regarding the sufficiency of the procedures described below either for the purpose for which this report has been requested or for any other purpose.

The procedures and the associated findings are as follows:

Cash

1. We obtained confirmation of the cash on deposit from the following banks, and we agreed the confirmed balance to the amount shown on the bank reconciliations maintained by Y Company. We mathematically checked the bank reconciliations and compared the resultant cash balances per book to the respective general ledger account balances.

Bank	*General Ledger Account Balances as of December 31, 20XX*
ABC National Bank	$ 5,000
DEF State Bank	3,776
XYZ Trust Company regular account	86,912
XYZ Trust Company payroll account	5,000
	$110,688

We found no exceptions as a result of the procedures.

Accounts Receivable

2. We added the individual customer account balances shown in an aged trial balance of accounts receivable (identified as Exhibit A) and compared the resultant total with the balance in the general ledger account.

   We found no difference.

3. We compared the individual customer account balances shown in the aged trial balance of accounts receivable (Exhibit A) as of

December 31, 19XX, to the balances shown in the accounts receivable subsidiary ledger.

We found no exceptions as a result of the comparisons.

4. We traced the aging (according to invoice dates) for 50 customer account balances shown in Exhibit A to the details of outstanding invoices in the accounts receivable subsidiary ledger. The balances selected for tracing were determined by starting at the eighth item and selecting every fifteenth item thereafter.

   We found no exceptions in the aging of the amounts of the 50 customer account balances selected. The sample size traced was 9.8 percent of the aggregate amount of the customer account balances.

5. We mailed confirmations directly to the customers representing the 150 largest customer account balances selected from the accounts receivable trial balance, and we received responses as indicated below. We also traced the items constituting the outstanding customer account balance to invoices and supporting shipping documents for customers from which there was no reply. As agreed, any individual differences in a customer account balance of less than $300 were to be considered minor, and no further procedures were performed.

   Of the 150 customer balances confirmed, we received responses from 140 customers; 10 customers did not reply. No exceptions were identified in 120 of the confirmations received. The differences disclosed in the remaining 20 confirmation replies were either minor in amount (as defined above) or were reconciled to the customer account balance without proposed adjustment thereto. A summary of the confirmation results according to the respective aging categories is as follows.

Accounts Receivable
December 31, 20XX

Aging Categories	*Customer Account Balances*	*Confirmations Requested*	*Confirmations Received*
Current	$156,000	$ 76,000	$ 65,000
Past due:			
Less than one month:	60,000	30,000	19,000
One to three months	36,000	18,000	10,000
Over three months	48,000	48,000	8,000
	$300,000	$172,000	$102,000

We were not engaged to and did not conduct an audit, the objective of which would be the expression of an opinion on cash and accounts receivable. Accordingly, we do not express such an opinion. Had we performed additional procedures, other matters might have come to our attention that would have been reported to you.

This report is intended solely for the information and use of the board of directors and management of X Company and is not intended to be and should not be used by anyone other than these specified parties.

[*Signature*]

[*Date*]

2. Report in Connection With Claims of Creditors

Independent Accountant's Report
on Applying Agreed-Upon Procedures

To the Trustee of XYZ Company:

We have performed the procedures described below, which were agreed to by the Trustee of XYZ Company, with respect to the claims of creditors solely to assist you in determining the validity of claims of XYZ Company as of May 31, 20XX, as set forth in the accompanying Schedule A. XYZ Company is responsible for maintaining records of claims submitted by creditors of XYZ Company. This agreed-upon procedures engagement was conducted in accordance with attestation standards established by the American Institute of Certified Public Accountants. The sufficiency of these procedures is solely the responsibility of the party specified in this report. Consequently, we make no representation regarding the sufficiency of the procedures described below either for the purpose for which this report has been requested or for any other purpose.

The procedures and associated findings are as follows:

1. Compare the total of the trial balance of accounts payable at May 31, 20XX, prepared by XYZ Company, to the balance in the related general ledger account.

   The total of the accounts payable trial balance agreed with the balance in the related general ledger account.

2. Compare the amounts for claims received from creditors (as shown in claim documents provided by XYZ Company) to the respective amounts shown in the trial balance of accounts payable. Using the data included in the claims documents and in XYZ Company's accounts payable detail records, reconcile any differences found to the accounts payable trial balance.

   All differences noted are presented in column 3 of Schedule A. Except for those amounts shown in column 4 of Schedule A, all such differences were reconciled.

3. Obtain the documentation submitted by creditors in support of the amounts claimed and compare it to the following documentation in XYZ Company's files: invoices, receiving reports, and other evidence of receipt of goods or services.

   No exceptions were found as a result of these comparisons.

We were not engaged to and did not conduct an audit, the objective of which would be the expression of an opinion on the claims of creditors set forth in the accompanying Schedule A. Accordingly, we do not express such an opinion. Had we performed additional procedures, other matters might have come to our attention that would have been reported to you.

This report is intended solely for the information and use of the Trustee of XYZ Company and is not intended to be and should not be used by anyone other than this specified party.

[*Signature*]

[*Date*]

AT Section 301

Financial Forecasts and Projections

Source: SSAE No. 10; SSAE No. 11; SSAE No. 17.

Effective when the date of the practitioner's report is on or after June 1, 2001, unless otherwise indicated.

Introduction

.01 This section sets forth standards and provides guidance to practitioners who are engaged to issue or do issue examination (paragraphs .29–.50), compilation (paragraphs .12–.28), or agreed-upon procedures reports (paragraphs .51–.56) on prospective financial statements.

.02 Whenever a practitioner (*a*) submits, to his or her client or others, prospective financial statements that he or she has assembled, or assisted in assembling, that are or reasonably might be expected to be used by another (third) party[1] or (*b*) reports on prospective financial statements that are, or reasonably might be expected to be used by another (third) party, the practitioner should perform one of the engagements described in the preceding paragraph. In deciding whether the prospective financial statements are or reasonably might be expected to be used by a third party, the practitioner may rely on either the written or oral representation of the responsible party, unless information comes to his or her attention that contradicts the responsible party's representation. If such third-party use of the prospective financial statements is not reasonably expected, the provisions of this section are not applicable unless the practitioner has been engaged to examine, compile, or apply agreed-upon procedures to the prospective financial statements.

.03 This section also provides standards for a practitioner who is engaged to examine, compile, or apply agreed-upon procedures to partial presentations. A partial presentation is a presentation of prospective financial information that excludes one or more of the items required for prospective financial statements as described in appendix A [paragraph .68], "Minimum Presentation Guidelines."

.04 The practitioner who has been engaged to or does compile, examine, or apply agreed-upon procedures to a partial presentation should perform the engagement in accordance with the guidance in paragraphs .12–.28 for compilations, .29–.50 for examinations, and .51–.56 for agreed-upon procedures, respectively, modified to reflect the nature of the presentation as discussed in paragraphs .03 and .57–.58.

.05 This section does not provide standards or procedures for engagements involving prospective financial statements used solely in connection with litigation support services. A practitioner may, however, look to these standards because they provide helpful guidance for many aspects of such engagements and may be referred to as useful guidance in such engagements. Litigation support services are engagements involving pending or potential formal legal proceedings before a trier of fact in connection with the resolution

---

[1] However, paragraph .59 permits an exception to this for certain types of budgets.

of a dispute between two or more parties, for example, when a practitioner acts as an expert witness. This exception is provided because, among other things, the practitioner's work in such proceedings is ordinarily subject to detailed analysis and challenge by each party to the dispute. This exception does not apply, however, if either of the following occur.

a. The practitioner is specifically engaged to issue or does issue an examination, a compilation, or an agreed-upon procedures report on prospective financial statements.

b. The prospective financial statements are for use by third parties who, under the rules of the proceedings, do not have the opportunity for analysis and challenge by each party to a dispute in a legal proceeding.

For example, creditors may not have such opportunities when prospective financial statements are submitted to them to secure their agreement to a plan of reorganization.

.06 In reporting on prospective financial statements, the practitioner may be called on to assist the responsible party in identifying assumptions, gathering information, or assembling the statements.[2] The responsible party is nonetheless responsible for the preparation and presentation of the prospective financial statements because the prospective financial statements are dependent on the actions, plans, and assumptions of the responsible party, and only it can take responsibility for the assumptions. Accordingly, the practitioner's engagement should not be characterized in his or her report or in the document containing his or her report as including "preparation" of the prospective financial statements. A practitioner may be engaged to prepare a financial analysis of a potential project where the engagement includes obtaining the information, making appropriate assumptions, and assembling the presentation. Such an analysis is not and should not be characterized as a forecast or projection and would not be appropriate for general use. However, if the responsible party reviewed and adopted the assumptions and presentation, or based its assumptions and presentation on the analysis, the practitioner could perform one of the engagements described in this section and issue a report appropriate for general use.

.07 The concept of materiality affects the application of this section to prospective financial statements as materiality affects the application of generally accepted auditing standards (GAAS) to historical financial statements. Materiality is a concept that is judged in light of the expected range of reasonableness of the information; therefore, users should not expect prospective information (information about events that have not yet occurred) to be as precise as historical information.

Definitions

.08 For the purposes of this section the following definitions apply.

a. *Prospective financial statements*—Either financial forecasts or financial projections including the summaries of significant assumptions and accounting policies. Although prospective financial statements may cover a period that has partially expired, statements for periods that have completely expired are not considered to be prospective

[2] Some of these services may not be appropriate if the practitioner is to be named as the person reporting on an examination in a filing with the Securities and Exchange Commission (SEC). SEC Release Nos. 33-5992 and 34-15305, "Disclosure of Projections of Future Economic Performance," state that for prospective financial statements filed with the commission, "a person should not be named as an outside reviewer if he actively assisted in the preparation of the projection."

financial statements. Pro forma financial statements and partial presentations are not considered to be prospective financial statements.[3]

b. *Partial presentation*—A presentation of prospective financial information that excludes one or more of the items required for prospective financial statements as described in appendix A (paragraph .68), "Minimum Presentation Guidelines." Partial presentations are not ordinarily appropriate for general use; accordingly, partial presentations should be restricted for use by specified parties who will be negotiating directly with the responsible party.

c. *Financial forecast*—Prospective financial statements that present, to the best of the responsible party's knowledge and belief, an entity's expected financial position, results of operations, and cash flows. A financial forecast is based on the responsible party's assumptions reflecting the conditions it expects to exist and the course of action it expects to take. A financial forecast may be expressed in specific monetary amounts as a single point estimate of forecasted results or as a range, where the responsible party selects key assumptions to form a range within which it reasonably expects, to the best of its knowledge and belief, the item or items subject to the assumptions to actually fall. When a forecast contains a range, the range is not selected in a biased or misleading manner, for example, a range in which one end is significantly less expected than the other. Minimum presentation guidelines for prospective financial statements are set forth in appendix A (paragraph .68).

d. *Financial projection*—Prospective financial statements that present, to the best of the responsible party's knowledge and belief, given one or more hypothetical assumptions, an entity's expected financial position, results of operations, and cash flows. A financial projection is sometimes prepared to present one or more hypothetical courses of action for evaluation, as in response to a question such as, "What would happen if . . . ?" A financial projection is based on the responsible party's assumptions reflecting conditions it expects would exist and the course of action it expects would be taken, given one or more hypothetical assumptions. A projection, like a forecast, may contain a range. Minimum presentation guidelines for prospective financial statements are set forth in appendix A (paragraph .68).

e. *Entity*—Any unit, existing or to be formed, for which financial statements could be prepared in accordance with generally accepted accounting principles (GAAP) or a special purpose framework.[4] For example, an entity can be an individual, partnership, corporation, trust, estate, association, or governmental unit.

f. *Hypothetical assumption*—An assumption used in a financial projection to present a condition or course of action that is not necessarily expected to occur, but is consistent with the purpose of the projection.

---

[3] The objective of pro forma financial information is to show what the significant effects on the historical financial information might have been had a consummated or proposed transaction (or event) occurred at an earlier date. Although the transaction in question may be prospective, this section does not apply to such presentations because they are essentially historical financial statements and do not purport to be prospective financial statements. See section 401, *Reporting on Pro Forma Financial Information*.

[4] AU-C section 800, *Special Considerations—Audits of Financial Statements Prepared in Accordance With Special Purpose Frameworks*, defines a *special purpose framework* as a cash, tax, regulatory, or contractual basis of accounting (commonly referred to as *comprehensive bases of accounting other than GAAP*). [Footnote revised, December 2012, to reflect conforming changes necessary due to the issuance of SAS Nos. 122–126.]

g. *Responsible party*—The person or persons who are responsible for the assumptions underlying the prospective financial statements. The responsible party usually is management, but it can be persons outside of the entity who do not currently have the authority to direct operations (for example, a party considering acquiring the entity).

h. *Assembly*—The manual or computer processing of mathematical or other clerical functions related to the presentation of the prospective financial statements. Assembly does not refer to the mere reproduction and collation of such statements or to the responsible party's use of the practitioner's computer processing hardware or software.

i. *Key factors*—The significant matters on which an entity's future results are expected to depend. Such factors are basic to the entity's operations and thus encompass matters that affect, among other things, the entity's sales, production, service, and financing activities. Key factors serve as a foundation for prospective financial statements and are the bases for the assumptions.

[Revised, December 2012, to reflect conforming changes necessary due to the issuance of SAS Nos. 122–126.]

Uses of Prospective Financial Statements

.09 Prospective financial statements are for either *general use* or *limited use*. *General use* of prospective financial statements refers to the use of the statements by persons with whom the responsible party is not negotiating directly, for example, in an offering statement of an entity's debt or equity interests. Because recipients of prospective financial statements distributed for general use are unable to ask the responsible party directly about the presentation, the presentation most useful to them is one that portrays, to the best of the responsible party's knowledge and belief, the expected results. Thus, only a financial forecast is appropriate for general use.

.10 *Limited use* of prospective financial statements refers to the use of prospective financial statements by the responsible party alone or by the responsible party and third parties with whom the responsible party is negotiating directly. Examples include use in negotiations for a bank loan, submission to a regulatory agency, and use solely within the entity. Third-party recipients of prospective financial statements intended for limited use can ask questions of the responsible party and negotiate terms directly with it. Any type of prospective financial statements that would be useful in the circumstances would normally be appropriate for limited use. Thus, the presentation may be a financial forecast or a financial projection.

.11 Because a financial projection is not appropriate for general use, a practitioner should not consent to the use of his or her name in conjunction with a financial projection that he or she believes will be distributed to those who will not be negotiating directly with the responsible party, for example, in an offering statement of an entity's debt or equity interests, unless the projection is used to supplement a financial forecast.

Compilation of Prospective Financial Statements

.12 A compilation of prospective financial statements is a professional service that involves the following:

a. Assembling, to the extent necessary, the prospective financial statements based on the responsible party's assumptions *b.* Performing the required compilation procedures,[5] including reading the prospective financial statements with their summaries of significant assumptions and accounting policies, and considering whether they appear to be presented in conformity with AICPA presentation guidelines[6] and not obviously inappropriate

c. Issuing a compilation report

.13 A compilation is not intended to provide assurance on the prospective financial statements or the assumptions underlying such statements. Because of the limited nature of the practitioner's procedures, a compilation does not provide assurance that the practitioner will become aware of significant matters that might be disclosed by more extensive procedures, for example, those performed in an examination of prospective financial statements.

.14 The summary of significant assumptions is essential to the reader's understanding of prospective financial statements. Accordingly, the practitioner should not compile prospective financial statements that exclude disclosure of the summary of significant assumptions. Also, the practitioner should not compile a financial projection that excludes either (*a*) an identification of the hypothetical assumptions or (*b*) a description of the limitations on the usefulness of the presentation.

.15 The following standards apply to a compilation of prospective financial statements and to the resulting report.

a. The compilation should be performed by a person or persons having adequate technical training and proficiency to compile prospective financial statements.

b. Due professional care should be exercised in the performance of the compilation and the preparation of the report.

c. The work should be adequately planned, and assistants, if any, should be properly supervised.

d. Applicable compilation procedures should be performed as a basis for reporting on the compiled prospective financial statements. (See appendix B [paragraph .69], "Training and Proficiency, Planning and Procedures Applicable to Compilations," for the procedures to be performed.)

e. The report based on the practitioner's compilation of prospective financial statements should conform to the applicable guidance in paragraphs .18–.28.

.16 The practitioner should consider, after applying the procedures specified in paragraph .69, whether representations or other information he or she has received appear to be obviously inappropriate, incomplete, or otherwise misleading, and if so, the practitioner should attempt to obtain additional or revised information. If he or she does not receive such information, the practitioner should ordinarily withdraw from the compilation engagement.[7] (Note that the

---

[5] See appendix B (paragraph .69), subparagraph 5, for the required procedures.

[6] AICPA presentation guidelines are detailed in AICPA Guide *Prospective Financial Information*.

[7] The practitioner need not withdraw from the engagement if the effect of such information on the prospective financial statement does not appear to be material.

omission of disclosures, other than those relating to significant assumptions, would not require the practitioner to withdraw. See paragraph .26.)

Working Papers

[.17] [Paragraph deleted by the issuance of SSAE No. 11, January 2002.]

Reports on Compiled Prospective Financial Statements

.18 The practitioner's standard report on a compilation of prospective financial statements should include the following:

a. An identification of the prospective financial statements presented by the responsible party

b. A statement that the practitioner has compiled the prospective financial statements in accordance with attestation standards established by the American Institute of Certified Public Accountants

c. A statement that a compilation is limited in scope and does not enable the practitioner to express an opinion or any other form of assurance on the prospective financial statements or the assumptions

d. A caveat that the prospective results may not be achieved

e. A statement that the practitioner assumes no responsibility to update the report for events and circumstances occurring after the date of the report

f. The manual or printed signature of the practitioner's firm

g. The date of the compilation report

.19 The following is the form of the practitioner's standard report on the compilation of a forecast that does not contain a range.[8]

> We have compiled the accompanying forecasted balance sheet, statements of income, retained earnings, and cash flows of XYZ Company as of December 31, 20XX, and for the year then ending, in accordance with attestation standards established by the American Institute of Certified Public Accountants.[9]
>
> A compilation is limited to presenting in the form of a forecast information that is the representation of management[10] and does not include evaluation of the support for the assumptions underlying the forecast. We have not examined the forecast and, accordingly, do not express an opinion or any other form of

---

[8] The forms of reports provided in this section are appropriate whether the presentation is based on GAAP or on a special purpose framework. [Footnote revised, December 2012, to reflect conforming changes necessary due to the issuance of SAS Nos. 122–126.]

[9] When the presentation is summarized as discussed in appendix A (paragraph .68), this sentence might read, "We have compiled the accompanying summarized forecast of XYZ Company as of December 31, 20XX, and for the year then ending in accordance with attestation standards established by the American Institute of Certified Public Accountants."

[10] If the responsible party is other than management, the references to management in the standard reports provided in this section should be changed to refer to the party who assumes responsibility for the assumptions.

assurance on the accompanying statements or assumptions. Furthermore, there will usually be differences between the forecasted and actual results, because events and circumstances frequently do not occur as expected, and those differences may be material. We have no responsibility to update this report for events and circumstances occurring after the date of this report.

[*Signature*]

[*Date*]

.20 When the presentation is a projection, the practitioner's compilation report should include the report elements set forth in paragraph .18. Additionally, the report should include a statement describing the special purpose for which the projection was prepared as well as a separate paragraph that restricts the use of the report because it is intended to be used solely by the specified parties. The following is the form of the practitioner's standard report on a compilation of a projection that does not contain a range.

We have compiled the accompanying projected balance sheet, statements of income, retained earnings, and cash flows of XYZ Company as of December 31, 20XX, and for the year then ending, in accordance with attestation standards established by the American Institute of Certified Public Accountants.[11] The accompanying projection was prepared for [*state special purpose, for example, "the purpose of negotiating a loan to expand XYZ Company's plant"*].

A compilation is limited to presenting in the form of a projection information that is the representation of management and does not include evaluation of the support for the assumptions underlying the projection. We have not examined the projection and, accordingly, do not express an opinion or any other form of assurance on the accompanying statements or assumptions. Furthermore, even if [*describe hypothetical assumption, for example, "the loan is granted and the plant is expanded,"*] there will usually be differences between the projected and actual results, because events and circumstances frequently do not occur as expected, and those differences may be material. We have no responsibility to update this report for events and circumstances occurring after the date of this report.

The accompanying projection and this report are intended solely for the information and use of [*identify specified parties, for example, "XYZ Company and DEF Bank"*] and is not intended to be and should not be used by anyone other than these specified parties.

[*Signature*]

[*Date*]

.21 When the prospective financial statements contain a range, the practitioner's standard report should also include a separate paragraph that states that the responsible party has elected to portray the expected results of one or more assumptions as a range. The following is an example of the separate paragraph to be added to the practitioner's report when he or she compiles prospective financial statements, in this case a forecast, that contain a range.

As described in the summary of significant assumptions, management of XYZ Company has elected to portray forecasted [*describe financial statement element*

---

[11] When the presentation is summarized as discussed in appendix A (paragraph .68), this sentence might read as follows.

We have compiled the accompanying summarized projection of XYZ Company as of December 31, 20XX, and for the year then ending in accordance with attestation standards established by the American Institute of Certified Public Accountants.

or elements for which the expected results of one or more assumptions fall within a range, and identify the assumptions expected to fall within a range, for example, "revenue at the amounts of $X,XXX and $Y,YYY, which is predicated upon occupancy rates of XX percent and YY percent of available apartments,"] rather than as a single point estimate. Accordingly, the accompanying forecast presents forecasted financial position, results of operations, and cash flows [*describe one or more assumptions expected to fall within a range, for example, "at such occupancy rates."*] However, there is no assurance that the actual results will fall within the range of [*describe one or more assumptions expected to fall within a range, for example, "occupancy rates"*] presented.

.22 The date of completion of the practitioner's compilation procedures should be used as the date of the report.

.23 A practitioner may compile prospective financial statements for an entity with respect to which he or she is not independent.[12] In such circumstances, the practitioner's report should be modified to indicate his or her lack of independence in a separate paragraph of the practitioner's report. An example of such a disclosure would be

We are not independent with respect to XYZ Company.

The practitioner is not precluded from disclosing a description about the reason(s) that his or her independence is impaired. The following are examples of descriptions the practitioner may use:

a. We are not independent with respect to XYZ Company as of and for the year ended [*or ending, as applicable*] December 31, 20XX, because a member of the engagement team had a direct financial interest in XYZ Company.

b. We are not independent with respect to XYZ Company as of and for the year ended [*or ending, as applicable*] December 31, 20XX, because an immediate family member of one of the members of the engagement team was employed by XYZ Company.

c. We are not independent with respect to XYZ Company as of and for the year ended [*or ending, as applicable*] December 31, 20XX, because we performed certain accounting services (the practitioner may include a specific description of those services) that impaired our independence.

If the accountant elects to disclose a description about the reasons his or her independence is impaired, the accountant should ensure that all reasons are included in the description.

[As amended, effective for compilations of prospective financial statements for periods ending on or after December 15, 2010, by SSAE No. 17.]

.24 Prospective financial statements may be included in a document that also contains historical financial statements and the practitioner's report thereon.[13] In addition, the historical financial statements that appear in the document may be summarized and presented with the prospective financial statements for comparative purposes.[14] An example of the reference to the prac-

---

[12] In making a judgment about whether he or she is independent, the practitioner should be guided by the AICPA Code of Professional Conduct. [Footnote amended, effective for compilations of prospective financial statements for periods ending on or after December 15, 2010, by SSAE No. 17.]

[13] Footnote revised, November 2002, to reflect conforming changes necessary due to the issuance of SSARS No. 9. Footnote deleted, December 2012, to reflect conforming changes necessary due to the issuance of SSARS No. 19 and SAS Nos. 122–126.]

[14] AU-C section 810, *Engagements to Report on Summary Financial Statements*, addresses the auditor's responsibilities relating to an engagement to report separately on summary financial

(continued)

titioner's report on the historical financial statements when he or she audited, reviewed, or compiled those statements is presented below.

[*Concluding sentence of last paragraph*]

> The historical financial statements for the year ended December 31, 20XX, [*from which the historical data are derived*] and our report thereon are set forth on pages XX-XX of this document.

.25 In some circumstances, a practitioner may wish to expand his or her report to emphasize a matter regarding the prospective financial statements. Such information may be presented in a separate paragraph of the practitioner's report. However, the practitioner should exercise care that emphasizing such a matter does not give the impression that he or she is expressing assurance or expanding the degree of responsibility he or she is taking with respect to such information.[15] For example, the practitioner should not include statements in his or her compilation report about the mathematical accuracy of the statements or their conformity with presentation guidelines.

Modifications of the Standard Compilation Report

.26 An entity may request a practitioner to compile prospective financial statements that contain presentation deficiencies or omit disclosures other than those relating to significant assumptions. The practitioner may compile such prospective financial statements provided the deficiency or omission is clearly indicated in his or her report and is not, to his or her knowledge, undertaken with the intention of misleading those who might reasonably be expected to use such statements.

.27 Notwithstanding the preceding, if the compiled prospective financial statements are prepared in accordance with a special purpose financial reporting framework and do not include disclosure of the framework used, the framework should be disclosed in the practitioner's report. [Revised, December 2012, to reflect conforming changes necessary due to the issuance of SAS Nos. 122–126.]

.28 The following is an example of a paragraph that should be added to a report on compiled prospective financial statements, in this case a financial forecast, in which the summary of significant accounting policies has been omitted.

> Management has elected to omit the summary of significant accounting policies required by the guidelines for presentation of a forecast established by the American Institute of Certified Public Accountants. If the omitted disclosures were included in the forecast, they might influence the user's conclusions about the Company's financial position, results of operations, and cash flows for the forecast period. Accordingly, this forecast is not designed for those who are not informed about such matters.

Examination of Prospective Financial Statements

.29 An examination of prospective financial statements is a professional service that involves—

(footnote continued)

statements derived from financial statements audited in accordance with generally accepted auditing standards by the same auditor. [Footnote revised, December 2012, to reflect conforming changes necessary due to the issuance of SAS Nos. 122–126.]

[15] However, the practitioner may provide assurance on tax matters in order to comply with the requirements of regulations governing practice before the Internal Revenue Service (IRS) contained in 31 CFR pt. 10 (Treasury Department Circular No. 230).

a. Evaluating the preparation of the prospective financial statements.

b. Evaluating the support underlying the assumptions.

c. Evaluating the presentation of the prospective financial statements for conformity with AICPA presentation guidelines.[16]

d. Issuing an examination report.

.30 As a result of his or her examination, the practitioner has a basis for reporting on whether, in his or her opinion—

a. The prospective financial statements are presented in conformity with AICPA guidelines.

b. The assumptions provide a reasonable basis for the responsible party's forecast, or whether the assumptions provide a reasonable basis for the responsible party's projection given the hypothetical assumptions.

.31 The practitioner should follow the general, fieldwork, and reporting standards for attestation engagements established in section 50, *SSAE Hierarchy*, and further explained in section 101, *Attest Engagements*, in performing an examination of prospective financial statements and reporting thereon. (See paragraph .70 for standards concerning such technical training and proficiency, planning the examination engagement, and the types of procedures a practitioner should perform to obtain sufficient evidence for his or her examination report.) [Revised, November 2006, to reflect conforming changes necessary due to the issuance of SSAE No. 14.]

Working Papers

[.32] [Paragraph deleted by the issuance of SSAE No. 11, January 2002.]

Reports on Examined Prospective Financial Statements

.33 The practitioner's standard report on an examination of prospective financial statements should include the following:

a. A title that includes the word *independent*

b. An identification of the prospective financial statements presented

c. An identification of the responsible party and a statement that the prospective financial statements are the responsibility of the responsible party

d. A statement that the practitioner's responsibility is to express an opinion on the prospective financial statements based on his or her examination

e. A statement that the examination of the prospective financial statements was conducted in accordance with attestation standards established by the American Institute of Certified Public Accountants and, accordingly, included such procedures as the practitioner considered necessary in the circumstances

f. A statement that the practitioner believes that the examination provides a reasonable basis for his or her opinion

---

[16] AICPA presentation guidelines are detailed in AICPA Guide *Prospective Financial Information*.

g. The practitioner's opinion that the prospective financial statements are presented in conformity with AICPA presentation guidelines and that the underlying assumptions provide a reasonable basis for the forecast or a reasonable basis for the projection given the hypothetical assumptions[17]

h. A caveat that the prospective results may not be achieved

i. A statement that the practitioner assumes no responsibility to update the report for events and circumstances occurring after the date of the report

j. The manual or printed signature of the practitioner's firm

k. The date of the examination report

.34 The following is the form of the practitioner's standard report on an examination of a forecast that does not contain a range.

Independent Accountant's Report

We have examined the accompanying forecasted balance sheet, statements of income, retained earnings, and cash flows of XYZ Company as of December 31, 20XX, and for the year then ending.[18] XYZ Company's management is responsible for the forecast. Our responsibility is to express an opinion on the forecast based on our examination.

Our examination was conducted in accordance with attestation standards established by the American Institute of Certified Public Accountants and, accordingly, included such procedures as we considered necessary to evaluate both the assumptions used by management and the preparation and presentation of the forecast. We believe that our examination provides a reasonable basis for our opinion.

In our opinion, the accompanying forecast is presented in conformity with guidelines for presentation of a forecast established by the American Institute of Certified Public Accountants, and the underlying assumptions provide a reasonable basis for management's forecast. However, there will usually be differences between the forecasted and actual results, because events and circumstances frequently do not occur as expected, and those differences may be material. We have no responsibility to update this report for events and circumstances occurring after the date of this report.

[*Signature*]

[*Date*]

.35 When a practitioner examines a projection, his or her opinion regarding the assumptions should be conditioned on the hypothetical assumptions; that is, he or she should express an opinion on whether the assumptions provide a reasonable basis for the projection given the hypothetical assumptions. The practitioner's examination report on a projection should include the report elements set forth in paragraph .33. Additionally, the report should include a statement describing the special purpose for which the projection was prepared as well a separate paragraph that restricts the use of the report because it is

---

[17] The practitioner's report need not comment on the consistency of the application of accounting principles as long as the presentation of any change in accounting principles is in conformity with AICPA presentation guidelines as detailed in AICPA Guide *Prospective Financial Information*.

[18] When the presentation is summarized as discussed in appendix A (paragraph .68), this sentence might read, "We have examined the accompanying summarized forecast of XYZ Company as of December 31, 20XX, and for the year then ending."

intended to be used solely by specified parties. The following is the form of the practitioner's standard report on an examination of a projection that does not contain a range.

Independent Accountant's Report

We have examined the accompanying projected balance sheet, statements of income, retained earnings, and cash flows of XYZ Company as of December 31, 20XX, and for the year then ending.[19] XYZ Company's management is responsible for the projection, which was prepared for [*state special purpose, for example, "the purpose of negotiating a loan to expand XYZ Company's plant"*]. Our responsibility is to express an opinion on the projection based on our examination.

Our examination was conducted in accordance with attestation standards established by the American Institute of Certified Public Accountants and, accordingly, included such procedures as we considered necessary to evaluate both the assumptions used by management and the preparation and presentation of the projection. We believe that our examination provides a reasonable basis for our opinion.

In our opinion, the accompanying projection is presented in conformity with guidelines for presentation of a projection established by the American Institute of Certified Public Accountants, and the underlying assumptions provide a reasonable basis for management's projection [*describe the hypothetical assumption, for example, "assuming the granting of the requested loan for the purpose of expanding XYZ Company's plant as described in the summary of significant assumptions."*] However, even if [*describe hypothetical assumption, for example, "the loan is granted and the plant is expanded,"*], there will usually be differences between the projected and actual results, because events and circumstances frequently do not occur as expected, and those differences may be material. We have no responsibility to update this report for events and circumstances occurring after the date of this report.

The accompanying projection and this report are intended solely for the information and use of [*identify specified parties, for example, "XYZ Company and DEF National Bank"*] and is not intended to be and should not be used by anyone other than these specified parties.

[*Signature*]

[*Date*]

.36 When the prospective financial statements contain a range, the practitioner's standard report should also include a separate paragraph that states that the responsible party has elected to portray the expected results of one or more assumptions as a range. The following is an example of the separate paragraph to be added to the practitioner's report when he or she examines prospective financial statements, in this case a forecast, that contain a range.

As described in the summary of significant assumptions, management of XYZ Company has elected to portray forecasted [*describe financial statement element or elements for which the expected results of one or more assumptions fall within a range, and identify assumptions expected to fall within a range, for example, "revenue at the amounts of $X,XXX and $Y,YYY, which is predicated upon occupancy rates of XX percent and YY percent of available apartments,"*] rather than as a single point estimate. Accordingly, the accompanying forecast presents forecasted financial position, results of operations, and cash flows [*de-*

[19] When the presentation is summarized as discussed in appendix A (paragraph .68), this sentence might read, "We have examined the accompanying summarized projection of XYZ Company as of December 31, 20XX, and for the year then ending."

> *scribe one or more assumptions expected to fall within a range, for example, "at such occupancy rates."*] However, there is no assurance that the actual results will fall within the range of [*describe one or more assumptions expected to fall within a range, for example, "occupancy rates"*] presented.

.37 The date of completion of the practitioner's examination procedures should be used as the date of the report.

Modifications to the Practitioner's Opinion[20]

.38 The following circumstances result in the following types of modified practitioner's report involving the practitioner's opinion.

a. If, in the practitioner's opinion, the prospective financial statements depart from AICPA presentation guidelines, he or she should express a qualified opinion (see paragraph .39) or an adverse opinion. (See paragraph .41.)[21] However, if the presentation departs from the presentation guidelines because it fails to disclose assumptions that appear to be significant, the practitioner should express an adverse opinion. (See paragraphs .41–.42.)

b. If the practitioner believes that one or more significant assumptions do not provide a reasonable basis for the forecast, or a reasonable basis for the projection given the hypothetical assumptions, he or she should express an adverse opinion. (See paragraph .41.)

c. If the practitioner's examination is affected by conditions that preclude application of one or more procedures he or she considers necessary in the circumstances, he or she should disclaim an opinion and describe the scope limitation in his or her report. (See paragraph .43.)

.39 *Qualified Opinion.* In a qualified opinion, the practitioner should state, in a separate paragraph, all substantive reasons for modifying his or her opinion and describe the departure from AICPA presentation guidelines. His or her opinion should include the words "except" or "exception" as the qualifying language and should refer to the separate explanatory paragraph. The following is an example of an examination report on a forecast that is at variance with AICPA guidelines for presentation of a financial forecast.

Independent Accountant's Report

> We have examined the accompanying forecasted balance sheet, statements of income, retained earnings, and cash flows of XYZ Company as of December 31, 20XX, and for the year then ending. XYZ Company's management is responsible for the forecast. Our responsibility is to express an opinion on the forecast based on our examination.
>
> Our examination was conducted in accordance with attestation standards established by the American Institute of Certified Public Accountants and, accordingly, included such procedures as we considered necessary to evaluate both the assumptions used by management and the preparation and presentation of the forecast. We believe that our examination provides a reasonable basis for our opinion.

---

[20] Paragraphs .38–.44 describe circumstances in which the practitioner's standard report on prospective financial statements may require modification. The guidance for modifying the practitioner's standard report is generally applicable to partial presentations. Also, depending on the nature of the presentation, the practitioner may decide to disclose that the partial presentation is not intended to be a presentation of financial position, results of operations, or cash flows. Illustrative reports on partial presentations may be found in AICPA Guide *Prospective Financial Information*.

[21] However, the practitioner may issue the standard examination report on a financial forecast filed with the SEC that meets the presentation requirements of article XI of Regulation S-X.

The forecast does not disclose significant accounting policies. Disclosure of such policies is required by guidelines for presentation of a forecast established by the American Institute of Certified Public Accountants.

In our opinion, except for the omission of the disclosure of the significant accounting policies as discussed in the preceding paragraph, the accompanying forecast is presented in conformity with guidelines for a presentation of a forecast established by the American Institute of Certified Public Accountants and the underlying assumptions provide a reasonable basis for management's forecast. However, there will usually be differences between the forecasted and actual results, because events and circumstances frequently do not occur as expected, and those differences may be material. We have no responsibility to update this report for events and circumstances occurring after the date of this report.

[*Signature*]

[*Date*]

.40 Because of the nature, sensitivity, and interrelationship of prospective information, a reader would find a practitioner's report qualified for a measurement departure,[22] the reasonableness of the underlying assumptions, or a scope limitation difficult to interpret. Accordingly, the practitioner should not express his or her opinion about these items with language such as "except for . . ." or "subject to the effects of. . . ." Rather, when a measurement departure, an unreasonable assumption, or a limitation on the scope of the practitioner's examination has led him or her to conclude that he or she cannot issue an unqualified opinion, he or she should issue the appropriate type of modified opinion described in paragraphs .41–.44.

.41 *Adverse Opinion.* In an adverse opinion the practitioner should state, in a separate paragraph, all of the substantive reasons for his or her adverse opinion. His or her opinion should state that the presentation is not in conformity with presentation guidelines and should refer to the explanatory paragraph. When applicable, his or her opinion paragraph should also state that, in the practitioner's opinion, the assumptions do not provide a reasonable basis for the prospective financial statements. An example of an adverse opinion on an examination of prospective financial statements is set forth below. In this case, a financial forecast was examined and the practitioner's opinion was that a significant assumption was unreasonable. The example should be revised as appropriate for a different type of presentation or if the adverse opinion is issued because the statements do not conform to the presentation guidelines.

Independent Accountant's Report

We have examined the accompanying forecasted balance sheet, statements of income, retained earnings, and cash flows of XYZ Company as of December 31, 20XX, and for the year then ending. XYZ Company's management is responsible for the forecast. Our responsibility is to express an opinion on the forecast based on our examination.

Our examination was conducted in accordance with attestation standards established by the American Institute of Certified Public Accountants and, accordingly, included such procedures as we considered necessary to evaluate

[22] An example of a measurement departure is the failure to capitalize a capital lease in a forecast where the historical financial statements for the prospective period are expected to be presented in accordance with GAAP.

both the assumptions used by management and the preparation and presentation of the forecast. We believe that our examination provides a reasonable basis for our opinion.

As discussed under the caption "Sales" in the summary of significant forecast assumptions, the forecasted sales include, among other things, revenue from the Company's federal defense contracts continuing at the current level. The Company's present federal defense contracts will expire in March 20XX. No new contracts have been signed and no negotiations are under way for new federal defense contracts. Furthermore, the federal government has entered into contracts with another company to supply the items being manufactured under the Company's present contracts.

In our opinion, the accompanying forecast is not presented in conformity with guidelines for presentation of a financial forecast established by the American Institute of Certified Public Accountants because management's assumptions, as discussed in the preceding paragraph, do not provide a reasonable basis for management's forecast. We have no responsibility to update this report for events or circumstances occurring after the date of this report.

[*Signature*]

[*Date*]

.42 If the presentation, including the summary of significant assumptions, fails to disclose assumptions that, at the time, appear to be significant, the practitioner should describe the assumptions in his or her report and express an adverse opinion. The practitioner should not examine a presentation that omits all disclosures of assumptions. Also, the practitioner should not examine a financial projection that omits (*a*) an identification of the hypothetical assumptions or (*b*) a description of the limitations on the usefulness of the presentation.

.43 *Disclaimer of Opinion.* In a disclaimer of opinion, the practitioner's report should indicate, in a separate paragraph, the respects in which the examination did not comply with standards for an examination. The practitioner should state that the scope of the examination was not sufficient to enable him or her to express an opinion with respect to the presentation or the underlying assumptions, and his or her disclaimer of opinion should include a direct reference to the explanatory paragraph. The following is an example of a report on an examination of prospective financial statements, in this case a financial forecast, for which a significant assumption could not be evaluated.

Independent Accountant's Report

We were engaged to examine the accompanying forecasted balance sheet, statements of income, retained earnings, and cash flows of XYZ Company as of December 31, 20XX, and for the year then ending. XYZ Company's management is responsible for the forecast.

As discussed under the caption "Income From Investee" in the summary of significant forecast assumptions, the forecast includes income from an equity investee constituting 23 percent of forecasted net income, which is management's estimate of the Company's share of the investee's income to be accrued for 20XX. The investee has not prepared a forecast for the year ending December 31, 20XX, and we were therefore unable to obtain suitable support for this assumption.

Because, as described in the preceding paragraph, we are unable to evaluate management's assumption regarding income from an equity investee and other assumptions that depend thereon, the scope of our work was not sufficient to express, and we do not express, an opinion with respect to the presentation of or the assumptions underlying the accompanying forecast. We have no responsibility to update this report for events and circumstances occurring after the date of this report.

[*Signature*]

[*Date*]

.44 When there is a scope limitation and the practitioner also believes there are material departures from the presentation guidelines, those departures should be described in the practitioner's report.

Other Modifications to the Standard Examination Report

.45 The circumstances described below, although not necessarily resulting in modifications to the practitioner's opinion, would result in the following types of modifications to the standard examination report.

.46 *Emphasis of a Matter.* In some circumstances, the practitioner may wish to emphasize a matter regarding the prospective financial statements but nevertheless intends to express an unqualified opinion. The practitioner may present other information and comments he or she wishes to include, such as explanatory comments or other informative material, in a separate paragraph of his or her report.

.47 *Evaluation Based in Part on a Report of Another Practitioner.* When more than one practitioner is involved in the examination, the guidance provided for that situation in connection with examinations of historical financial statements is generally applicable. When the principal practitioner decides to refer to the report of another practitioner as a basis, in part, for his or her own opinion, he or she should disclose that fact in stating the scope of the examination and should refer to the report of the other practitioner in expressing his or her opinion. Such a reference indicates the division of responsibility for the performance of the examination.

.48 *Comparative Historical Financial Information.* Prospective financial statements may be included in a document that also contains historical financial statements and a practitioner's report thereon.[23] In addition, the historical financial statements that appear in the document may be summarized and presented with the prospective financial statements for comparative purposes.[24] An example of the reference to the practitioner's report on the historical financial statements when he or she audited, reviewed, or compiled those statements is presented in paragraph .24.

.49 *Reporting When the Examination Is Part of a Larger Engagement.* When the practitioner's examination of prospective financial statements is part of a larger engagement, for example, a financial feasibility study or business acquisition study, it is appropriate to expand the report on the examination of the prospective financial statements to describe the entire engagement.

---

[23] [Footnote revised, November 2002, to reflect conforming changes necessary due to the issuance of SSARS No. 9. Footnote deleted, December 2012, to reflect conforming changes necessary due to the issuance of SAS Nos. 122–126.]

[24] AU-C section 810, *Engagements to Report on Summary Financial Statements,* addresses the auditor's responsibilities relating to an engagement to report separately on summary financial statements derived from financial statements audited in accordance with GAAS by the same auditor. [Footnote revised, December 2012, to reflect conforming changes necessary due to the issuance of SAS Nos. 122–126.]

.50 The following is a report that might be issued when a practitioner chooses to expand his or her report on a financial feasibility study.[25]

Independent Accountant's Report

a. The Board of Directors
Example Hospital
Example, Texas

b. We have prepared a financial feasibility study of Example Hospital's (the Hospital's) plans to expand and renovate its facilities. The study was undertaken to evaluate the ability of the Hospital to meet its operating expenses, working capital needs, and other financial requirements, including the debt service requirements associated with the proposed $25,000,000 [*legal title of bonds*] issue, at an assumed average annual interest rate of 10.0 percent during the five years ending December 31, 20X6.

c. The proposed capital improvements program (the Program) consists of a new two-level addition, which is to provide fifty additional medical-surgical beds, increasing the complement to 275 beds. In addition, various administrative and support service areas in the present facilities are to be remodeled. The Hospital administration anticipates that construction is to begin June 30, 20X2, and to be completed by December 31, 20X3.

d. The estimated total cost of the Program is approximately $30,000,000. It is assumed that the $25,000,000 of revenue bonds that the Example Hospital Finance Authority proposes to issue would be the primary source of funds for the Program. The responsibility for payment of debt service on the bonds is solely that of the Hospital. Other necessary funds to finance the Program are assumed to be provided from the Hospital's funds, from a local fund drive, and from interest earned on funds held by the bond trustee during the construction period.

e. Our procedures included analysis of the following:

- Program history, objectives, timing, and financing
- The future demand for the Hospital's services, including consideration of the following:
  - Economic and demographic characteristics of the Hospital's defined service area
  - Locations, capacities, and competitive information pertaining to other existing and planned area hospitals
  - Physician support for the Hospital and its programs
  - Historical utilization levels
- Planning agency applications and approvals
- Construction and equipment costs, debt service requirements, and estimated financing costs
- Staffing patterns and other operating considerations

---

[25] Although the entity referred to in the report is a hospital, the form of report is also applicable to other entities such as hotels or stadiums. Also, although the illustrated report format and language should not be departed from in any significant way, the language used should be tailored to fit the circumstances that are unique to a particular engagement (for example, the description of the proposed capital improvement program, paragraph *c*; the proposed financing of the program, paragraphs *b* and *d*; the specific procedures applied by the practitioner, paragraph *e*; and any explanatory comments included in emphasis-of-a-matter paragraphs, paragraph *i*, which deals with general matter; and paragraph *j*, which deals with specific matters).

- Third-party reimbursement policy and history
- Revenue/expense/volume relationships

f. We also participated in gathering other information, assisted management in identifying and formulating its assumptions, and assembled the accompanying financial forecast based on those assumptions.

g. The accompanying financial forecast for the annual periods ending December 31, 20X2, through 20X6, is based on assumptions that were provided by or reviewed with and approved by management. The financial forecast includes the following:

- Balance sheets
- Statements of operations
- Statements of cash flows
- Statements of changes in net assets

h. We have examined the financial forecast. Example Hospital's management is responsible for the forecast. Our responsibility is to express an opinion on the forecast based on our examination. Our examination was conducted in accordance with attestation standards established by the American Institute of Certified Public Accountants and, accordingly, included such procedures as we considered necessary to evaluate both the assumptions used by management and the preparation and presentation of the forecast. We believe that our examination provides a reasonable basis for our opinion.

i. Legislation and regulations at all levels of government have affected and may continue to affect revenues and expenses of hospitals. The financial forecast is based on legislation and regulations currently in effect. If future legislation or regulations related to hospital operations are enacted, such legislation or regulations could have a material effect on future operations.

j. The interest rate, principal payments, Program costs, and other financing assumptions are described in the section entitled "Summary of Significant Forecast Assumptions and Rationale." If actual interest rates, principal payments, and funding requirements are different from those assumed, the amount of the bond issue and debt service requirements would need to be adjusted accordingly from those indicated in the forecast. If such interest rates, principal payments, and funding requirements are lower than those assumed, such adjustments would not adversely affect the forecast.

k. Our conclusions are presented below.

- In our opinion, the accompanying financial forecast is presented in conformity with guidelines for presentation of a financial forecast established by the American Institute of Certified Public Accountants.
- In our opinion, the underlying assumptions provide a reasonable basis for management's forecast. However, there will usually be differences between the forecasted and actual results, because events and circumstances frequently do not occur as expected, and those differences may be material.

- The accompanying financial forecast indicates that sufficient funds could be generated to meet the Hospital's operating expenses, working capital needs, and other financial requirements, including the debt service requirements associated with the proposed $25,000,000 bond issue, during the forecast periods. However, the achievement of any financial forecast is dependent on future events, the occurrence of which cannot be assured.

l. We have no responsibility to update this report for events and circumstances occurring after the date of this report.

[*Signature*]

[*Date*]

Applying Agreed-Upon Procedures to Prospective Financial Statements

.51 The practitioner who accepts an engagement to apply agreed-upon procedures to prospective financial statements should follow the general, fieldwork, and reporting standards for attest engagements established in section 50, *SSAE Hierarchy*, and the guidance set forth herein and in section 201, *Agreed-Upon Procedures Engagements*. [Revised, November 2006, to reflect conforming changes necessary due to the issuance of SSAE No. 14.]

.52 A practitioner may perform an agreed-upon procedures attest engagement on prospective financial statements[26] provided the following conditions are met.

a. The practitioner is independent.

b. The practitioner and the specified parties agree upon the procedures performed or to be performed by the practitioner.

c. The specified parties take responsibility for the sufficiency of the agreed-upon procedures for their purposes.

d. The prospective financial statements include a summary of significant assumptions.

e. The prospective financial statements to which the procedures are to be applied are subject to reasonably consistent evaluation against criteria that are suitable and available to the specified parties.

f. Criteria to be used in the determination of findings are agreed upon between the practitioner and the specified parties.[27]

g. The procedures to be applied to the prospective financial statements are expected to result in reasonably consistent findings using the criteria.

h. Evidential matter related to the prospective financial statements to which the procedures are applied is expected to exist to provide a reasonable basis for expressing the findings in the practitioner's report.

---

[26] Practitioners should follow the guidance in AU-C section 920, *Letters for Underwriters and Certain Other Requesting Parties*, when requested to perform agreed-upon procedures on a forecast and report thereon in a letter for an underwriter. [Footnote revised, December 2012, to reflect conforming changes necessary due to the issuance of SAS Nos. 122–126.]

[27] For example, accounting principles and other presentation criteria as discussed in chapter 8, "Presentation Guidelines," of AICPA Guide *Prospective Financial Information*.

i. Where applicable, the practitioner and the specified users agree on any agreed-upon materiality limits for reporting purposes. (See paragraph .25 of section 201.)

j. Use of the report is to be restricted to the specified parties.[28]

.53 Generally, the practitioner's procedures may be as limited or as extensive as the specified parties desire, as long as the specified parties take responsibility for their sufficiency. However, mere reading of prospective financial statements does not constitute a procedure sufficient to permit a practitioner to report on the results of applying agreed-upon procedures to such statements. (See paragraph .15 of section 201.)

.54 To satisfy the requirements that the practitioner and the specified parties agree upon the procedures performed or to be performed and that the specified parties take responsibility for the sufficiency of the agreed-upon procedures for their purposes, ordinarily the practitioner should communicate directly with and obtain affirmative acknowledgment from each of the specified parties. For example, this may be accomplished by meeting with the specified parties or by distributing a draft of the anticipated report or a copy of an engagement letter to the specified parties and obtaining their agreement. If the practitioner is not able to communicate directly with all of the specified parties, the practitioner may satisfy these requirements by applying any one or more of the following or similar procedures:

- Compare the procedures to be applied to written requirements of the specified parties.
- Discuss the procedures to be applied with appropriate representatives of the specified parties involved.
- Review relevant contracts with or correspondence from the specified parties.

The practitioner should not report on an engagement when specified parties do not agree upon the procedures performed or to be performed and do not take responsibility for the sufficiency of the procedures for their purposes. (See paragraph .36 of section 201 for guidance on satisfying these requirements when the practitioner is requested to add other parties as specified parties after the date of completion of the agreed-upon procedures.)

Reports on the Results of Applying Agreed-Upon Procedures

.55 The practitioner's report on the results of applying agreed-upon procedures should be in the form of procedures and findings. The practitioner's report should contain the following elements:

a. A title that includes the word *independent*

b. Identification of the specified parties

c. Reference to the prospective financial statements covered by the practitioner's report and the character of the engagement

d. A statement that the procedures performed were those agreed to by the specified parties identified in the report

---

[28] In some cases, restricted-use reports filed with regulatory agencies are required by law or regulation to be made available to the public as a matter of public record. Also, a regulatory agency as part of its oversight responsibility for an entity may require access to restricted-use reports in which they are not named as a specified party. (See paragraph .79 of section 101.)

e. Identification of the responsible party and a statement that the prospective financial statements are the responsibility of the responsible party

f. A statement that the agreed-upon procedures engagement was conducted in accordance with attestation standards established by the American Institute of Certified Public Accountants

g. A statement that the sufficiency of the procedures is solely the responsibility of the specified parties and a disclaimer of responsibility for the sufficiency of those procedures

h. A list of the procedures performed (or reference thereto) and related findings (The practitioner should not provide negative assurance—see paragraph .24 of section 201.)

i. Where applicable, a description of any agreed-upon materiality limits (See paragraph .25 of section 201.)

j. A statement that the practitioner was not engaged to and did not conduct an examination of prospective financial statements; a disclaimer of opinion on whether the presentation of the prospective financial statements is in conformity with AICPA presentation guidelines and on whether the underlying assumptions provide a reasonable basis for the forecast, or a reasonable basis for the projection given the hypothetical assumptions; and a statement that if the practitioner had performed additional procedures, other matters might have come to his or her attention that would have been reported

k. A statement of restrictions on the use of the report because it is intended to be used solely by the specified parties

l. Where applicable, reservations or restrictions concerning procedures or findings as discussed in paragraphs .33, .35, and .39–.40 of section 201

m. A caveat that the prospective results may not be achieved

n. A statement that the practitioner assumes no responsibility to update the report for events and circumstances occurring after the date of the report

o. Where applicable, a description of the nature of the assistance provided by a specialist as discussed in paragraphs .19–.21 of section 201

p. The manual or printed signature of the practitioner's firm

q. The date of the report

.56 The following illustrates a report on applying agreed-upon procedures to the prospective financial statements. (See section 201.)

Independent Accountant's Report
on Applying Agreed-Upon Procedures

Board of Directors—XYZ Corporation

Board of Directors—ABC Company

At your request, we have performed certain agreed-upon procedures, as enumerated below, with respect to the forecasted balance sheet and the related forecasted statements of income, retained earnings, and cash flows of DEF Company, a subsidiary of ABC Company, as of December 31, 20XX, and for the year then ending. These procedures, which were agreed to by the Boards of

Directors of XYZ Corporation and ABC Company, were performed solely to assist you in evaluating the forecast in connection with the proposed sale of DEF Company to XYZ Corporation. DEF Company's management is responsible for the forecast.

This agreed-upon procedures engagement was conducted in accordance with attestation standards established by the American Institute of Certified Public Accountants. The sufficiency of these procedures is solely the responsibility of the specified parties. Consequently, we make no representation regarding the sufficiency of the procedures described below either for the purpose for which this report has been requested or for any other purpose.

[*Include paragraphs to enumerate procedures and findings.*]

We were not engaged to and did not conduct an examination, the objective of which would be the expression of an opinion on the accompanying prospective financial statements. Accordingly, we do not express an opinion on whether the prospective financial statements are presented in conformity with AICPA presentation guidelines or on whether the underlying assumptions provide a reasonable basis for the presentation. Had we performed additional procedures, other matters might have come to our attention that would have been reported to you. Furthermore, there will usually be differences between the forecasted and actual results, because events and circumstances frequently do not occur as expected, and those differences may be material. We have no responsibility to update this report for events and circumstances occurring after the date of this report.

This report is intended solely for the information and use of the Boards of Directors of ABC Company and XYZ Corporation and is not intended to be and should not be used by anyone other than these specified parties.

[*Signature*]

[*Date*]

Partial Presentations

.57 The practitioner's procedures on a partial presentation may be affected by the nature of the information presented. Many elements of prospective financial statements are interrelated. The practitioner should give appropriate consideration to whether key factors affecting elements, accounts, or items that are interrelated with those in the partial presentation he or she has been engaged to examine or compile have been considered, including key factors that may not necessarily be obvious to the partial presentation (for example, productive capacity relative to a sales forecast), and whether all significant assumptions have been disclosed. The practitioner may find it necessary for the scope of the examination or compilation of some partial presentations to be similar to that for the examination or compilation of a presentation of prospective financial statements. For example, the scope of a practitioner's procedures when he or she examines forecasted results of operations would likely be similar to that of procedures used for the examination of prospective financial statements since the practitioner would most likely need to consider the interrelationships of all accounts in the examination of results of operations.

.58 Because partial presentations are generally appropriate only for limited use, reports on partial presentations of both forecasted and projected information should include a description of any limitations on the usefulness of the presentation.

Other Information

.59 When a practitioner's compilation, review, or audit report on historical financial statements is included in a practitioner-submitted document containing prospective financial statements, the practitioner should either examine, compile, or apply agreed-upon procedures to the prospective financial statements and report accordingly, unless the following occur.

a. The prospective financial statements are labeled as a "budget."

b. The budget does not extend beyond the end of the current fiscal year.

c. The budget is presented with interim historical financial statements for the current year.

In such circumstances, the practitioner need not examine, compile, or apply agreed-upon procedures to the budget; however, he or she should report on it and—

a. Indicate that he or she did not examine or compile the budget.

b. Disclaim an opinion or any other form of assurance on the budget.

In addition, the budgeted information may omit the summaries of significant assumptions and accounting policies required by the guidelines for presentation of prospective financial statements established by the AICPA, provided such omission is not, to the practitioner's knowledge, undertaken with the intention of misleading those who might reasonably be expected to use such budgeted information, and is disclosed in the practitioner's report. The following is the form of the standard paragraphs to be added to the practitioner's report in this circumstance when the summaries of significant assumptions and accounting policies have been omitted.

> The accompanying budgeted balance sheet, statements of income, retained earnings, and cash flows of XYZ Company as of December 31, 20XX, and for the six months then ending, have not been compiled or examined by us, and, accordingly, we do not express an opinion or any other form of assurance on them.
>
> Management has elected to omit the summaries of significant assumptions and accounting policies required under established guidelines for presentation of prospective financial statements. If the omitted summaries were included in the budgeted information, they might influence the user's conclusions about the company's budgeted information. Accordingly, this budgeted information is not designed for those who are not informed about such matters.

.60 When the practitioner's compilation, review, or audit report on historical financial statements is included in a client-prepared document containing prospective financial statements, the practitioner should not consent to the use of his or her name in the document unless:

a. He or she has examined, compiled, or applied agreed-upon procedures to the prospective financial statements and his or her report accompanies them.

b. The prospective financial statements are accompanied by an indication by the responsible party or the practitioner that the practitioner has not performed such a service on the prospective financial statements and that the practitioner assumes no responsibility for them.

c. Another practitioner has examined, compiled, or applied agreed-upon procedures to the prospective financial statements and his or her report is included in the document.

In addition, if the practitioner has audited the historical financial statements and the prospective financial statements that he or she did not examine, compile, or apply agreed-upon procedures to are included in a document containing the audited historical financial statements and the auditor's report thereon,[29] he or she should refer to AU-C section 720, *Other Information in Documents Containing Audited Financial Statements*. [Revised, December 2010, to reflect conforming changes necessary due to the issuance of SAS Nos. 118–120. Revised, December 2012, to reflect conforming changes necessary due to the issuance of SAS Nos. 122–126.]

.61 The practitioner whose report on prospective financial statements is included in a client-prepared document containing historical financial statements should not consent to the use of his or her name in the document unless:

a. He or she has compiled, reviewed, or audited the historical financial statements and his or her report accompanies them.

b. The historical financial statements are accompanied by an indication by the responsible party or the practitioner that the practitioner has not performed such a service on the historical financial statements and that the practitioner assumes no responsibility for them.

c. Another practitioner has compiled, reviewed, or audited the historical financial statements and his or her report is included in the document.

.62 An entity may publish various documents that contain information other than historical financial statements in addition to the compiled or examined prospective financial statements and the practitioner's report thereon. The practitioner's responsibility with respect to information in such a document does not extend beyond the financial information identified in the report, and he or she has no obligation to perform any procedures to corroborate other information contained in the document. However, the practitioner should read the other information and consider whether such information, or the manner of its presentation, is materially inconsistent with the information, or manner of its presentation, appearing in the prospective financial statements.

.63 If the practitioner examines prospective financial statements included in a document containing inconsistent information, he or she might not be able to conclude that there is adequate support for each significant assumption. The practitioner should consider whether the prospective financial statements, his or her report, or both require revision. Depending on the conclusion he or she reaches, the practitioner should consider other actions that may be appropriate, such as issuing an adverse opinion, disclaiming an opinion because of a scope limitation, withholding the use of his or her report in the document, or withdrawing from the engagement.

.64 If the practitioner compiles the prospective financial statements included in the document containing inconsistent information, he or she should attempt to obtain additional or revised information. If he or she does not receive

---

[29] AU-C section 720 applies only to such prospective financial statements contained in annual reports (or similar documents) that are issued to owners (or similar stakeholders) and annual reports of governments and organizations for charitable or philanthropic purposes that are available to the public that contain audited financial statements and the auditor's report thereon. AU-C section 720 also may be applied, adapted as necessary in the circumstances, to other documents to which the auditor, at management's request, devotes attention. AU-C section 720 does not apply when the historical financial statements and report appear in a registration statement filed under the Securities Act of 1933 (in which case, see AU-C section 925, *Filings With the U.S. Securities and Exchange Commission Under the Securities Act of 1933*). [Footnote revised, December 2010, to reflect conforming changes necessary due to the issuance of SAS Nos. 118–120. Footnote revised, December 2012, to reflect conforming changes necessary due to the issuance of SAS Nos. 122–126.]

such information, the practitioner should withhold the use of his or her report or withdraw from the compilation engagement.

.65 If, while reading the other information appearing in the document containing the examined or compiled prospective financial statements, as described in the preceding paragraphs, the practitioner becomes aware of information that he or she believes is a material misstatement of fact that is not an inconsistent statement, he or she should discuss the matter with the responsible party. In connection with this discussion, the practitioner should consider that he or she may not have the expertise to assess the validity of the statement made, that there may be no standards by which to assess its presentation, and that there may be valid differences of judgment or opinion. If the practitioner concludes that he or she has a valid basis for concern, he or she should propose that the responsible party consult with some other party whose advice might be useful, such as the entity's legal counsel.

.66 If, after discussing the matter as described in paragraph .65, the practitioner concludes that a material misstatement of fact remains, the action he or she takes will depend on his or her judgment in the particular circumstances. The practitioner should consider steps such as notifying the responsible party in writing of his or her views concerning the information and consulting his or her legal counsel about further appropriate action in the circumstances.

Effective Date

.67 This section is effective when the date of the practitioner's report is on or after June 1, 2001. Early application is permitted.

.68

Appendix A

Minimum Presentation Guidelines*

1. Prospective information presented in the format of historical financial statements facilitates comparisons with financial position, results of operations, and cash flows of prior periods, as well as those actually achieved for the prospective period. Accordingly, prospective financial statements preferably should be in the format of the historical financial statements that would be issued for the period(s) covered unless there is an agreement between the responsible party and potential users specifying another format. Prospective financial statements may take the form of complete basic financial statements[1] or may be limited to the following minimum items (where such items would be presented for historical financial statements for the period).[2]

a. Sales or gross revenues

b. Gross profit or cost of sales

c. Unusual or infrequently occurring items

d. Provision for income taxes

e. Discontinued operations or extraordinary items

f. Income from continuing operations

g. Net income

h. Basic and diluted earnings per share

i. Significant changes in financial position[3]

j. A description of what the responsible party intends the prospective financial statements to present, a statement that the assumptions are based on the responsible party's judgment at the time the prospective information was prepared, and a caveat that the prospective results may not be achieved

---

* ***Note:*** This appendix describes the minimum items that constitute a presentation of a financial forecast or a financial projection, as specified in AICPA Guide *Prospective Financial Information*. Complete presentation guidelines for entities that choose to issue prospective financial statements, together with illustrative presentations, are included in the Guide. The guide also prescribes presentation guidelines for partial presentations.

[1] The details of each statement may be summarized or condensed so that only the major items in each are presented. The usual footnotes associated with historical financial statements need not be included as such. However, significant assumptions and accounting policies should be disclosed.

[2] Similar types of financial information should be presented for entities for which these terms do not describe operations. Further, similar items should be presented if a comprehensive basis of accounting other than GAAP is used to present the prospective financial statements. For example, if the cash basis were used, item a would be cash receipts.

[3] The responsible party should disclose significant cash flows and other significant changes in balance sheet accounts during the period. However, neither a balance sheet nor a statement of cash flows, as described in Financial Accounting Standards Board (FASB) *Accounting Standards Codification* (ASC) 230, *Statement of Cash Flows*, is required. Furthermore, none of the specific captions or disclosures required by FASB ASC 230 is required. Significant changes disclosed will depend on the circumstances; however, such disclosures will often include cash flows from operations. See AICPA Guide *Prospective Financial Information* exhibits 9-2 and 9-6 for illustrations of alternate methods of presenting significant cash flows. [Footnote revised, June 2009, to reflect conforming changes necessary due to the issuance of FASB ASC.]

k. Summary of significant assumptions

l. Summary of significant accounting policies

2. A presentation that omits one or more of the applicable minimum items *a–i* is a partial presentation, which would not ordinarily be appropriate for general use. If an omitted applicable minimum item is derivable from the information presented, the presentation would not be deemed to be a partial presentation. A presentation that contains the applicable minimum items *a–i*, but omits items *j–l*, is subject to all of the provisions of this section applicable to complete presentations.

.69

Appendix B

Training and Proficiency, Planning, and Procedures Applicable to Compilations

Training and Proficiency

1. The practitioner should be familiar with the guidelines for the preparation and presentation of prospective financial statements. The guidelines are contained in AICPA Guide *Prospective Financial Information*.

2. The practitioner should possess or obtain a level of knowledge of the industry and the accounting principles and practices of the industry in which the entity operates or will operate that will enable him or her to compile prospective financial statements that are in appropriate form for an entity operating in that industry.

Planning the Compilation Engagement

3. To compile the prospective financial statements of an existing entity, the practitioner should obtain a general knowledge of the nature of the entity's business transactions and the key factors upon which its future financial results appear to depend. He or she should also obtain an understanding of the accounting principles and practices of the entity to determine whether they are comparable to those used within the industry in which the entity operates.

4. To compile the prospective financial statements of a proposed entity, the practitioner should obtain knowledge of the proposed operations and the key factors upon which its future results appear to depend and that have affected the performance of entities in the same industry.

Compilation Procedures

5. In a compilation of prospective financial statements the practitioner should perform the following, where applicable.

a. Establish an understanding with the client regarding the services to be performed. The understanding should include the objectives of the engagement, the client's responsibilities, the practitioner's responsibilities, and limitations of the engagement. The practitioner should document the understanding in the working papers, preferably through a written communication with the client. If the practitioner believes an understanding with the client has not been established, he or she should decline to accept or perform the engagement.

b. Inquire about the accounting principles used in the preparation of the prospective financial statements.

(1) For existing entities, compare the accounting principles used to those used in the preparation of previous historical financial statements and inquire whether such principles are the same as those expected to be used in the historical financial statements covering the prospective period.

(2) For entities to be formed or entities formed that have not commenced operations, compare specialized industry accounting principles used, if any, to those typically used in the industry. Inquire whether the accounting principles used for the prospective financial statements are those that are expected to be used when or if the entity commences operations.

c. Ask how the responsible party identifies the key factors and develops its assumptions.

d. List, or obtain a list of the responsible party's significant assumptions providing the basis for the prospective financial statements and consider whether there are any obvious omissions in light of the key factors upon which the prospective results of the entity appear to depend.

e. Consider whether there appear to be any obvious internal inconsistencies in the assumptions.

f. Perform or test the mathematical accuracy of the computations that translate the assumptions into prospective financial statements.

g. Read the prospective financial statements, including the summary of significant assumptions, and consider whether—

(1) The statements, including the disclosures of assumptions and accounting policies, appear to be not presented in conformity with the AICPA presentation guidelines for prospective financial statements.[1]

(2) The statements, including the summary of significant assumptions, appear to be not obviously inappropriate in relation to the practitioner's knowledge of the entity and its industry and, for the following:

(a) Financial forecast, the expected conditions and course of action in the prospective period

(b) Financial projection, the purpose of the presentation

h. If a significant part of the prospective period has expired, inquire about the results of operations or significant portions of the operations (such as sales volume), and significant changes in financial position, and consider their effect in relation to the prospective financial statements. If historical financial statements have been prepared for the expired portion of the period, the practitioner should read such statements and consider those results in relation to the prospective financial statements.

i. Confirm his or her understanding of the statements (including assumptions) by obtaining written representations from the responsible party. Because the amounts reflected in the statements are not supported by historical books and records but rather by assumptions, the practitioner should obtain representations in which the responsible party indicates its responsibility for the assumptions. The representations should be signed by the responsible party at the highest

---

[1] Presentation guidelines for entities that issue prospective financial statements are set forth and illustrated in AICPA Guide *Prospective Financial Information*.

level of authority who the practitioner believes is responsible for and knowledgeable, directly or through others, about matters covered by the representations.

(1) For a *financial forecast*, the representations should include the responsible party's assertion that the financial forecast presents, to the best of its knowledge and belief, the expected financial position, results of operations, and cash flows for the forecast period and that the forecast reflects the responsible party's judgment, based on present circumstances, of the expected conditions and its expected course of action. The representations should also include a statement that the forecast is presented in conformity with guidelines for presentation of a forecast established by the American Institute of Certified Public Accountants. The representations should also include a statement that the assumptions on which the forecast is based are reasonable. If the forecast contains a range, the representation should also include a statement that, to the best of the responsible party's knowledge and belief, the item or items subject to the assumption are expected to actually fall within the range and that the range was not selected in a biased or misleading manner.

(2) For a *financial projection*, the representations should include the responsible party's assertion that the financial projection presents, to the best of its knowledge and belief, the expected financial position, results of operations, and cash flows for the projection period given the hypothetical assumptions, and that the projection reflects its judgment, based on present circumstances, of expected conditions and its expected course of action given the occurrence of the hypothetical events. The representations should also (*i*) identify the hypothetical assumptions and describe the limitations on the usefulness of the presentation, (*ii*) state that the assumptions are appropriate, (*iii*) indicate if the hypothetical assumptions are improbable, and (*iv*) if the projection contains a range, include a statement that, to the best of the responsible party's knowledge and belief, given the hypothetical assumptions, the item or items subject to the assumption are expected to actually fall within the range and that the range was not selected in a biased or misleading manner. The representations should also include a statement that the projection is presented in conformity with guidelines for presentation of a projection established by the American Institute of Certified Public Accountants.

j. Consider, after applying the preceding procedures, whether he or she has received representations or other information that appears to be obviously inappropriate, incomplete, or otherwise misleading and, if so, attempt to obtain additional or revised information. If he or she does not receive such information, the practitioner should ordinarily withdraw from the compilation engagement.[2] (Note that the omission of disclosures, other than those relating to significant assumptions, would not require the practitioner to withdraw; see paragraph .26.)

---

[2] The practitioner need not withdraw from the engagement if the effect of such information on the prospective financial statements does not appear to be material.

.70

Appendix C

Training and Proficiency, Planning, and Procedures Applicable to Examinations

Training and Proficiency

1. The practitioner should be familiar with the guidelines for the preparation and presentation of prospective financial statements. The guidelines are contained in AICPA Guide *Prospective Financial Information*.

2. The practitioner should possess or obtain a level of knowledge of the industry and the accounting principles and practices of the industry in which the entity operates or will operate that will enable him or her to examine prospective financial statements that are in appropriate form for an entity operating in that industry.

Planning an Examination Engagement

3. Planning the examination engagement involves developing an overall strategy for the expected scope and conduct of the engagement. To develop such a strategy, the practitioner needs to have sufficient knowledge to enable him or her to adequately understand the events, transactions, and practices that, in his or her judgment, may have a significant effect on the prospective financial statements.

4. Factors to be considered by the practitioner in planning the examination include the following:

a. The accounting principles to be used and the type of presentation

b. The anticipated level of attestation risk related to the prospective financial statements[1]

c. Preliminary judgments about materiality levels

d. Items within the prospective financial statements that are likely to require revision or adjustment

e. Conditions that may require extension or modification of the practitioner's examination procedures

f. Knowledge of the entity's business and its industry

g. The responsible party's experience in preparing prospective financial statements

h. The length of the period covered by the prospective financial statements

i. The process by which the responsible party develops its prospective financial statements

---

[1] *Attestation* risk is the risk that the practitioner may unknowingly fail to appropriately modify his or her examination report on prospective financial statements that are materially misstated, that is, that are not presented in conformity with AICPA presentation guidelines or have assumptions that do not provide a reasonable basis for management's forecast, or management's projection given the hypothetical assumptions. It consists of (*a*) the risk (consisting of *inherent risk* and *control risk*) that the prospective financial statements contain errors that could be material and (*b*) the risk (*detection risk*) that the practitioner will not detect such errors.

5. The practitioner should obtain knowledge of the entity's business, accounting principles, and the key factors upon which its future financial results appear to depend. The practitioner should focus on areas such as the following:

a. The availability and cost of resources needed to operate (Principal items usually include raw materials, labor, short-term and long-term financing, and plant and equipment.)

b. The nature and condition of markets in which the entity sells its goods or services, including final consumer markets if the entity sells to intermediate markets

c. Factors specific to the industry, including competitive conditions, sensitivity to economic conditions, accounting policies, specific regulatory requirements, and technology

d. Patterns of past performance for the entity or comparable entities, including trends in revenue and costs, turnover of assets, uses and capacities of physical facilities, and management policies

Examination Procedures

6. The practitioner should establish an understanding with the responsible party regarding the services to be performed. The understanding should include the objectives of the engagement, the responsible party's responsibilities, the practitioner's responsibilities, and limitations of the engagement. The practitioner should document the understanding in the working papers, preferably through a written communication with the responsible party. If the practitioner believes an understanding with the responsible party has not been established, he or she should decline to accept or perform the engagement. If the responsible party is different than the client, the practitioner should establish the understanding with both the client and the responsible party, and the understanding also should include the client's responsibilities.

7. The practitioner's objective in an examination of prospective financial statements is to accumulate sufficient evidence to restrict attestation risk to a level that is, in his or her professional judgment, appropriate for the level of assurance that may be imparted by his or her examination report. In a report on an examination of prospective financial statements, the practitioner provides assurance only about whether the prospective financial statements are presented in conformity with AICPA presentation guidelines and whether the assumptions provide a reasonable basis for management's forecast, or a reasonable basis for management's projection given the hypothetical assumptions. He or she does not provide assurance about the achievability of the prospective results because events and circumstances frequently do not occur as expected and achievement of the prospective results is dependent on the actions, plans, and assumptions of the responsible party.

8. In his or her examination of prospective financial statements, the practitioner should select from all available procedures—that is, procedures that assess inherent and control risk and restrict detection risk—any combination that can restrict attestation risk to such an appropriate level. The extent to which examination procedures will be performed should be based on the practitioner's consideration of the following:

a. The nature and materiality of the information to the prospective financial statements taken as a whole

b. The likelihood of misstatements

c. Knowledge obtained during current and previous engagements

d. The responsible party's competence with respect to prospective financial statements

e. The extent to which the prospective financial statements are affected by the responsible party's judgment, for example, its judgment in selecting the assumptions used to prepare the prospective financial statements

f. The adequacy of the responsible party's underlying data

9. The practitioner should perform those procedures he or she considers necessary in the circumstances to report on whether the assumptions provide a reasonable basis for the following.

a. *Financial forecast.* The practitioner can form an opinion that the assumptions provide a reasonable basis for the forecast if the responsible party represents that the presentation reflects, to the best of its knowledge and belief, its estimate of expected financial position, results of operations, and cash flows for the prospective period[2] and the practitioner concludes, based on his or her examination, (*i*) that the responsible party has explicitly identified all factors expected to materially affect the operations of the entity during the prospective period and has developed appropriate assumptions with respect to such factors[3] and (*ii*) that the assumptions are suitably supported.

b. *Financial projection given the hypothetical assumptions.* The practitioner can form an opinion that the assumptions provide a reasonable basis for the financial projection given the hypothetical assumptions if the responsible party represents that the presentation reflects, to the best of its knowledge and belief, expected financial position, results of operations, and cash flows for the prospective period given the hypothetical assumptions[4] and the practitioner concludes, based on his or her examination, that:

(1) The responsible party has explicitly identified all factors that would materially affect the operations of the entity during the prospective period if the hypothetical assumptions were to materialize and has developed appropriate assumptions with respect to such factors and

(2) The other assumptions are suitably supported given the hypothetical assumptions. However, as the number and significance of the hypothetical assumptions increase, the practitioner may not be able to satisfy himself or herself about the presentation as a whole by obtaining support for the remaining assumptions.

10. The practitioner should evaluate the support for the assumptions.

a. *Financial forecast*—The practitioner can conclude that assumptions are suitably supported if the preponderance of information supports each significant assumption.

---

[2] If the forecast contains a range, the representation should also include a statement that, to the best of the responsible party's knowledge and belief, the item or items subject to the assumption are expected to actually fall within the range and that the range was not selected in a biased or misleading manner.

[3] An attempt to list all assumptions is inherently not feasible. Frequently, basic assumptions that have enormous potential impact are considered to be implicit, such as conditions of peace and absence of natural disasters.

[4] If the projection contains a range, the representation should also include a statement that, to the best of the responsible party's knowledge and belief, given the hypothetical assumptions, the item or items subject to the assumption are expected to actually fall within the range and that the range was not selected in a biased or misleading manner.

b. *Financial projection*—In evaluating support for assumptions other than hypothetical assumptions, the practitioner can conclude that they are suitably supported if the preponderance of information supports each significant assumption given the hypothetical assumptions. The practitioner need not obtain support for the hypothetical assumptions, although he or she should consider whether they are consistent with the purpose of the presentation.

11. In evaluating the support for assumptions, the practitioner should consider—

a. Whether sufficient pertinent sources of information about the assumptions have been considered. Examples of external sources the practitioner might consider are government publications, industry publications, economic forecasts, existing or proposed legislation, and reports of changing technology. Examples of internal sources are budgets, labor agreements, patents, royalty agreements and records, sales backlog records, debt agreements, and actions of the board of directors involving entity plans.

b. Whether the assumptions are consistent with the sources from which they are derived.

c. Whether the assumptions are consistent with each other.

d. Whether the historical financial information and other data used in developing the assumptions are sufficiently reliable for that purpose. Reliability can be assessed by inquiry and analytical or other procedures, some of which may have been completed in past audits or reviews of the historical financial statements. If historical financial statements have been prepared for an expired part of the prospective period, the practitioner should consider the historical data in relation to the prospective results for the same period, where applicable. If the prospective financial statements incorporate such historical financial results and that period is significant to the presentation, the practitioner should make a review of the historical information in conformity with the applicable standards for a review.[5]

e. Whether the historical financial information and other data used in developing the assumptions are comparable over the periods specified or whether the effects of any lack of comparability were considered in developing the assumptions.

f. Whether the logical arguments or theory, considered with the data supporting the assumptions, are reasonable.

12. In evaluating the preparation and presentation of the prospective financial statements, the practitioner should perform procedures that will provide reasonable assurance as to the following.

---

[5] If the entity is an issuer, the practitioner should perform the procedures in paragraphs .13–.19 of AU section 722, *Interim Financial Information* (AICPA, *PCAOB Standards and Related Rules*, Interim Standards). If the entity is a nonissuer, the practitioner should perform the procedures in AR section 90, *Review of Financial Statements*, or in AU-C section 930, *Interim Financial Information*, when the review of interim financial information meets the provisions of that section. [Footnote revised, November 2002, to reflect conforming changes necessary due to the issuance of SAS No. 100 and SSARS No. 9. Footnote revised, May 2004, to reflect the conforming changes necessary due to the issuance of SSARS No. 10. Footnote revised, December 2012, to reflect conforming changes necessary due to the issuance of SAS Nos. 122–126 and SSARS No. 19.]

a. The presentation reflects the identified assumptions.

b. The computations made to translate the assumptions into prospective amounts are mathematically accurate.

c. The assumptions are internally consistent.

d. Accounting principles used in the—

(1) Financial forecast are consistent with the accounting principles expected to be used in the historical financial statements covering the prospective period and those used in the most recent historical financial statements, if any.

(2) Financial projection are consistent with the accounting principles expected to be used in the prospective period and those used in the most recent historical financial statements, if any, or that they are consistent with the purpose of the presentation.[6]

e. The presentation of the prospective financial statements follows the AICPA guidelines applicable for such statements.[7]

f. The assumptions have been adequately disclosed based on AICPA presentation guidelines for prospective financial statements.

13. The practitioner should consider whether the prospective financial statements, including related disclosures, should be revised because of any of the following:

a. Mathematical errors

b. Unreasonable or internally inconsistent assumptions

c. Inappropriate or incomplete presentation

d. Inadequate disclosure

14. The practitioner should obtain written representations from the responsible party acknowledging its responsibility for both the presentation and the underlying assumptions. The representations should be signed by the responsible party at the highest level of authority who the practitioner believes is responsible for and knowledgeable, directly or through others in the organization, about the matters covered by the representations. Paragraph .69, subparagraph 5*i* describes the specific representations to be obtained for a financial forecast and a financial projection. See paragraph .43 for guidance on the form of report to be rendered if the practitioner is not able to obtain the required representations.

[6] The accounting principles used in a financial projection need not be those expected to be used in the historical financial statements for the prospective period if use of different principles is consistent with the purpose of the presentation.

[7] Presentation guidelines for entities that issue prospective financial statements are set forth and illustrated in AICPA Guide *Prospective Financial Information*.

AT Section 401

Reporting on Pro Forma Financial Information

Source: SSAE No. 10.

Effective when the presentation of pro forma financial information is as of or for a period ending on or after June 1, 2001. Earlier application is permitted.

Introduction

.01 This section provides guidance to a practitioner who is engaged to issue or does issue an examination or a review report on pro forma financial information. Such an engagement should comply with the general and fieldwork standards established in section 50, *SSAE Hierarchy*, and the specific performance and reporting standards set forth in this section.[1] [Revised, November 2006, to reflect conforming changes necessary due to the issuance of SSAE No. 14.]

.02 When pro forma financial information is presented outside the basic financial statements but within the same document, and the practitioner is not engaged to report on the pro forma financial information, the practitioner's responsibilities are described in AU-C section 720, *Other Information in Documents Containing Audited Financial Statements*, and AU-C section 925, *Filings With the U.S. Securities and Exchange Commission Under the Securities Act of 1933*. [Revised, December 2012, to reflect conforming changes necessary due to the issuance of SAS Nos. 122–126.]

.03 This section does not apply in those circumstances when, for purposes of a more meaningful presentation, a transaction consummated after the balance-sheet date is reflected in the historical financial statements (such as a revision of debt maturities or a revision of earnings per share calculations for a stock split).[2]

Presentation of Pro Forma Financial Information

.04 The objective of pro forma financial information is to show what the significant effects on historical financial information might have been had a consummated or proposed transaction (or event) occurred at an earlier date. Pro forma financial information is commonly used to show the effects of transactions such as the following:

- Business combination
- Change in capitalization

---

[1] Paragraph .10 of AU-C section 920, *Letters for Underwriters and Certain Other Requesting Parties*, identifies certain parties who may request a letter. When one of those parties requests a letter or asks the practitioner to perform agreed-upon procedures on pro forma financial information in connection with an offering, the practitioner should follow the guidance in paragraphs .10, .13, .44, and .52–.53 of AU-C section 920. [Footnote revised, December 2012, to reflect conforming changes necessary due to the issuance of SAS Nos. 122–126.]

[2] In certain circumstances, generally accepted accounting principles may require the presentation of pro forma financial information in the financial statements or the accompanying notes. That information includes, for example, pro forma financial information required by Financial Accounting Standards Board (FASB) *Accounting Standards Codification* (ASC) 805, *Business Combinations*, or FASB ASC 250, *Accounting Changes and Error Corrections*. [Footnote revised, June 2009, to reflect conforming changes necessary due to the issuance of FASB ASC. Footnote revised, December 2012, to reflect conforming changes necessary due to the issuance of SAS Nos. 122–126.]

- Disposition of a significant portion of the business
- Change in the form of business organization or status as an autonomous entity
- Proposed sale of securities and the application of the proceeds

.05 This objective is achieved primarily by applying pro forma adjustments to historical financial information. Pro forma adjustments should be based on management's assumptions and give effect to all significant effects directly attributable to the transaction (or event).

.06 Pro forma financial information should be labeled as such to distinguish it from historical financial information. This presentation should describe the transaction (or event) that is reflected in the pro forma financial information, the source of the historical financial information on which it is based, the significant assumptions used in developing the pro forma adjustments, and any significant uncertainties about those assumptions. The presentation also should indicate that the pro forma financial information should be read in conjunction with related historical financial information and that the pro forma financial information is not necessarily indicative of the results (such as financial position and results of operations, as applicable) that would have been attained had the transaction (or event) actually taken place earlier.[3]

Conditions for Reporting

.07 The practitioner may agree to report on an examination or a review of pro forma financial information if the following conditions are met.

a. The document that contains the pro forma financial information includes (or incorporates by reference) complete historical financial statements of the entity for the most recent year (or for the preceding year if financial statements for the most recent year are not yet available) and, if pro forma financial information is presented for an interim period, the document also includes (or incorporates by reference) historical interim financial information for that period (which may be presented in condensed form).[4] In the case of a business combination, the document should include (or incorporate by reference) the appropriate historical financial information for the significant constituent parts of the combined entity.

b. The historical financial statements of the entity (or, in the case of a business combination, of each significant constituent part of the combined entity) on which the pro forma financial information is based have been audited or reviewed.[5] The practitioner's attestation risk

---

[3] For further guidance on the presentation of pro forma financial information included in filings with the Securities and Exchange Commission (SEC), see Article 11 of Regulation S-X.

[4] For pro forma financial information included in an SEC Form 8-K, historical financial information previously included in an SEC filing would meet this requirement. Interim historical financial information may be presented as a column in the pro forma financial information.

[5] The practitioner's audit or review report should be included (or incorporated by reference) in the document containing the pro forma financial information. For issuers, the review may be that as defined in AU section 722, *Interim Financial Information* (AICPA, *PCAOB Standards and Related Rules*, Interim Standards). For nonissuers, the review may be that as defined in AR section 90, *Review of Financial Statements*, or in AU-C section 930, *Interim Financial Information*, when the review of interim financial information meets the provisions of that section. [Footnote revised, November 2002, to reflect conforming changes necessary due to the issuance of SAS No. 100. Footnote revised, December 2012, to reflect conforming changes necessary due to the issuance of SAS Nos. 122–126 and SSARS No. 19.]

relating to the pro forma financial information is affected by the scope of the engagement providing the practitioner with assurance about the underlying historical financial information to which the pro forma adjustments are applied. Therefore, the level of assurance given by the practitioner on the pro forma financial information, as of a particular date or for a particular period, should be limited to the level of assurance provided on the historical financial statements (or, in the case of a business combination, the lowest level of assurance provided on the underlying historical financial statements of any significant constituent part of the combined entity). For example, if the underlying historical financial statements of each constituent part of the combined entity have been audited at year-end and reviewed at an interim date, the practitioner may perform an examination or a review of the pro forma financial information at year-end but is limited to performing a review of the pro forma financial information at the interim date.

c. The practitioner who is reporting on the pro forma financial information should have an appropriate level of knowledge of the accounting and financial reporting practices of each significant constituent part of the combined entity. This would ordinarily have been obtained by the practitioner auditing or reviewing historical financial statements of each entity for the most recent annual or interim period for which the pro forma financial information is presented. If another practitioner has performed such an audit or a review, the need, by a practitioner reporting on the pro forma financial information, for an understanding of the entity's accounting and financial reporting practices is not diminished, and that practitioner should consider whether, under the particular circumstances, he or she can acquire sufficient knowledge of these matters to perform the procedures necessary to report on the pro forma financial information.

Practitioner's Objective

.08 The objective of the practitioner's examination procedures applied to pro forma financial information is to provide reasonable assurance as to whether—

- Management's assumptions provide a reasonable basis for presenting the significant effects directly attributable to the underlying transaction (or event).
- The related pro forma adjustments give appropriate effect to those assumptions.
- The pro forma column reflects the proper application of those adjustments to the historical financial statements.

.09 The objective of the practitioner's review procedures applied to pro forma financial information is to provide negative assurance as to whether any information came to the practitioner's attention to cause him or her to believe that—

- Management's assumptions do not provide a reasonable basis for presenting the significant effects directly attributable to the underlying transaction (or event).
- The related pro forma adjustments do not give appropriate effect to those assumptions.

- The pro forma column does not reflect the proper application of those adjustments to the historical financial statements.

Procedures

.10 Other than the procedures applied to the historical financial statements,[6] the procedures the practitioner should apply to the assumptions and pro forma adjustments for either an examination or a review engagement are as follows.

a. Obtain an understanding of the underlying transaction (or event), for example, by reading relevant contracts and minutes of meetings of the board of directors and by making inquiries of appropriate officials of the entity, and, in cases, of the entity acquired or to be acquired.

b. Obtain a level of knowledge of each constituent part of the combined entity in a business combination that will enable the practitioner to perform the required procedures. Procedures to obtain this knowledge may include communicating with other practitioners who have audited or reviewed the historical financial information on which the pro forma financial information is based. Matters that may be considered include accounting principles and financial reporting practices followed, transactions between the entities, and material contingencies.

c. Discuss with management their assumptions regarding the effects of the transaction (or event).

d. Evaluate whether pro forma adjustments are included for all significant effects directly attributable to the transaction (or event).

e. Obtain sufficient evidence in support of such adjustments. The evidence required to support the level of assurance given is a matter of professional judgment. The practitioner typically would obtain more evidence in an examination engagement than in a review engagement. Examples of evidence that the practitioner might consider obtaining are purchase, merger or exchange agreements, appraisal reports, debt agreements, employment agreements, actions of the board of directors, and existing or proposed legislation or regulatory actions.

f. Evaluate whether management's assumptions that underlie the pro forma adjustments are presented in a sufficiently clear and comprehensive manner. Also, evaluate whether the pro forma adjustments are consistent with each other and with the data used to develop them.

g. Determine that computations of pro forma adjustments are mathematically correct and that the pro forma column reflects the proper application of those adjustments to the historical financial statements.

h. Obtain written representations from management concerning their—

- Responsibility for the assumptions used in determining the pro forma adjustments

---

[6] See paragraph .07*b*.

- Assertion that the assumptions provide a reasonable basis for presenting all of the significant effects directly attributable to the transaction (or event), that the related pro forma adjustments give appropriate effect to those assumptions, and that the pro forma column reflects the proper application of those adjustments to the historical financial statements

- Assertion that the significant effects directly attributable to the transaction (or event) are appropriately disclosed in the pro forma financial information

i. Read the pro forma financial information and evaluate whether—

- The underlying transaction (or event), the pro forma adjustments, the significant assumptions and the significant uncertainties, if any, about those assumptions have been appropriately described.

- The source of the historical financial information on which the pro forma financial information is based has been appropriately identified.

Reporting on Pro Forma Financial Information

.11 The practitioner's report on pro forma financial information should be dated as of the completion of the appropriate procedures. The practitioner's report on pro forma financial information may be added to the practitioner's report on historical financial information, or it may appear separately. If the reports are combined and the date of completion of the procedures for the examination or review of the pro forma financial information is after the date of completion of the fieldwork for the audit or review of the historical financial information, the combined report should be dual-dated. (For example, "February 15, 20X2, except for the paragraphs regarding pro forma financial information as to which the date is March 20, 20X2.")

.12 A practitioner's examination report on pro forma financial information should include the following:

a. A title that includes the word *independent*

b. An identification of the pro forma financial information

c. A reference to the financial statements from which the historical financial information is derived and a statement that such financial statements were audited (The report on pro forma financial information should refer to any modification in the practitioner's report on the historical financial information.)

d. An identification of the responsible party and a statement that the responsible party is responsible for the pro forma financial information

e. A statement that the practitioner's responsibility is to express an opinion on the pro forma financial information based on his or her examination *f.* A statement that the examination of the pro forma financial information was conducted in accordance with attestation standards established by the American Institute of Certified Public Accountants and, accordingly, included such procedures as the practitioner considered necessary in the circumstances

g. A statement that the practitioner believes that the examination provides a reasonable basis for his or her opinion

h. A separate paragraph explaining the objective of pro forma financial information and its limitations

i. The practitioner's opinion as to whether management's assumptions provide a reasonable basis for presenting the significant effects directly attributable to the transaction (or event), whether the related pro forma adjustments give appropriate effect to those assumptions, and whether the pro forma column reflects the proper application of those adjustments to the historical financial statements (see paragraphs .18 and .20)

j. The manual or printed signature of the practitioner's firm

k. The date of the examination report

.13 A practitioner's review report on pro forma financial information should include the following:

a. A title that includes the word *independent*

b. An identification of the pro forma financial information

c. A reference to the financial statements from which the historical financial information is derived and a statement as to whether such financial statements were audited or reviewed (The report on pro forma financial information should refer to any modification in the practitioner's report on the historical financial information.)

d. An identification of the responsible party and a statement that the responsible party is responsible for the pro forma financial information

e. A statement that the review of the pro forma financial information was conducted in accordance with attestation standards established by the American Institute of Certified Public Accountants

f. A statement that a review is substantially less in scope than an examination, the objective of which is the expression of an opinion on the pro forma financial information and, accordingly, the practitioner does not express such an opinion

g. A separate paragraph explaining the objective of pro forma financial information and its limitations

h. The practitioner's conclusion as to whether any information came to the practitioner's attention to cause him or her to believe that management's assumptions do not provide a reasonable basis for presenting the significant effects directly attributable to the transaction (or event), or that the related pro forma adjustments do not give appropriate effect to those assumptions, or that the pro forma column does not reflect the proper application of those adjustments to the historical financial statements (See paragraphs .19–.20.)

i. The manual or printed signature of the practitioner's firm

j. The date of the review report

.14 Nothing precludes the practitioner from restricting the use of the report (see paragraphs .78–.83 of section 101).

.15 Because a pooling-of-interests business combination is accounted for by combining historical amounts retroactively, pro forma adjustments for a proposed transaction generally affect only the equity section of the pro forma condensed balance sheet. Further, because of the requirements of Financial Accounting Standards Board *Accounting Standards Codification* 805, *Business Combinations*, a business combination effected as a pooling of interests would not ordinarily involve a choice of assumptions by management. Accordingly, a report on a proposed pooling transaction need not address management's assumptions unless the pro forma financial information includes adjustments to conform the accounting principles of the combining entities. (See paragraph .21.) [Revised, June 2009, to reflect conforming changes necessary due to the issuance of FASB ASC.]

.16 Restrictions on the scope of the engagement (see paragraphs .73–.75 of section 101), reservations about the propriety of the assumptions and the conformity of the presentation with those assumptions (including adequate disclosure of significant matters), or other reservations may require the practitioner to qualify the opinion, disclaim an opinion, or withdraw from the engagement.[7] The practitioner should disclose all substantive reasons for any report modifications. Uncertainty as to whether the transaction (or event) will be consummated would not ordinarily require a report modification. (See paragraph .22.)

Effective Date

.17 This section is effective when the presentation of pro forma financial information is as of or for a period ending on or after June 1, 2001. Early application is permitted.

[7] See paragraphs .76–.77 of section 101.

.18

Appendix A

Report on Examination of Pro Forma Financial Information

Independent Accountant's Report

We have examined the pro forma adjustments reflecting the transaction [*or event*] described in Note 1 and the application of those adjustments to the historical amounts in [*the assembly of*][8] the accompanying pro forma financial condensed balance sheet of X Company as of December 31, 20X1, and the pro forma condensed statement of income for the year then ended. The historical condensed financial statements are derived from the historical financial statements of X Company, which were audited by us, and of Y Company, which were audited by other accountants,[9] appearing elsewhere herein [*or incorporated by reference*].[10] Such pro forma adjustments are based upon management's assumptions described in Note 2. X Company's management is responsible for the pro forma financial information. Our responsibility is to express an opinion on the pro forma financial information based on our examination.

Our examination was conducted in accordance with attestation standards established by the American Institute of Certified Public Accountants and, accordingly, included such procedures as we considered necessary in the circumstances. We believe that our examination provides a reasonable basis for our opinion.

The objective of this pro forma financial information is to show what the significant effects on the historical financial information might have been had the transaction [*or event*] occurred at an earlier date. However, the pro forma condensed financial statements are not necessarily indicative of the results of operations or related effects on financial position that would have been attained had the above-mentioned transaction [*or event*] actually occurred earlier.

[*Additional paragraph(s) may be added to emphasize certain matters relating to the attest engagement or the subject matter.*]

In our opinion, management's assumptions provide a reasonable basis for presenting the significant effects directly attributable to the above-mentioned transaction [*or event*] described in Note 1, the related pro forma adjustments give appropriate effect to those assumptions, and the pro forma column reflects the proper application of those adjustments to the historical financial statement amounts in the pro forma condensed balance sheet as of December 31, 20X1, and the pro forma condensed statement of income for the year then ended.

[*Signature*]

[*Date*]

---

[8] This wording is appropriate when one column of pro forma financial information is presented without separate columns of historical financial information and pro forma adjustments.

[9] If either accountant's report includes an explanatory paragraph or is other than unqualified, that fact should be referred to within this report.

[10] If the option in footnote 4 to paragraph .07*a* is followed, the report should be appropriately modified.

.19

Appendix B

Report on Review of Pro Forma Financial Information

Independent Accountant's Report

We have reviewed the pro forma adjustments reflecting the transaction [*or event*] described in Note 1 and the application of those adjustments to the historical amounts in [*the assembly of*][11] the accompanying pro forma condensed balance sheet of X Company as of March 31, 20X2, and the pro forma condensed statement of income for the three months then ended. These historical condensed financial statements are derived from the historical unaudited financial statements of X Company, which were reviewed by us, and of Y Company, which were reviewed by other accountants,[12, 13] appearing elsewhere herein [*or incorporated by reference*].[14] Such pro forma adjustments are based on management's assumptions as described in Note 2. X Company's management is responsible for the pro forma financial information.

Our review was conducted in accordance with attestation standards established by the American Institute of Certified Public Accountants. A review is substantially less in scope than an examination, the objective of which is the expression of an opinion on management's assumptions, the pro forma adjustments and the application of those adjustments to historical financial information. Accordingly, we do not express such an opinion.

The objective of this pro forma financial information is to show what the significant effects on the historical financial information might have been had the transaction [*or event*] occurred at an earlier date. However, the pro forma condensed financial statements are not necessarily indicative of the results of operations or related effects on financial position that would have been attained had the above-mentioned transaction [*or event*] actually occurred earlier.

[*Additional paragraph(s) may be added to emphasize certain matters relating to the attest engagement or the subject matter.*]

Based on our review, nothing came to our attention that caused us to believe that management's assumptions do not provide a reasonable basis for presenting the significant effects directly attributable to the above-mentioned transaction [*or event*] described in Note 1, that the related pro forma adjustments do not give

---

[11] This wording is appropriate when one column of pro forma financial information is presented without separate columns of historical financial information and pro forma adjustments.

[12] If either accountant's report includes an explanatory paragraph or is modified, that fact should be referred to within this report.

[13] Where one set of historical financial statements is audited and the other set is reviewed, wording similar to the following would be appropriate:

> The historical condensed financial statements are derived from the historical financial statements of X Company, which were audited by us, and of Y Company, which were reviewed by other accountants, appearing elsewhere herein [*or incorporated by reference*].

[14] If the option in footnote 4 to paragraph .07*a* is followed, the report should be appropriately modified.

appropriate effect to those assumptions, or that the pro forma column does not reflect the proper application of those adjustments to the historical financial statement amounts in the pro forma condensed balance sheet as of March 31, 20X2, and the pro forma condensed statement of income for the three months then ended.

[*Signature*]

[*Date*]

.20

Appendix C

Report on Examination of Pro Forma Financial Information at Year-End With a Review of Pro Forma Financial Information for a Subsequent Interim Date

Independent Accountant's Report

We have examined the pro forma adjustments reflecting the transaction [*or event*] described in Note 1 and the application of those adjustments to the historical amounts in [*the assembly of*][15] the accompanying pro forma financial condensed balance sheet of X Company as of December 31, 20X1, and the pro forma condensed statement of income for the year then ended. The historical condensed financial statements are derived from the historical financial statements of X Company, which were audited by us, and of Y Company, which were audited by other accountants,[16] appearing elsewhere herein [*or incorporated by reference*].[17] Such pro forma adjustments are based upon management's assumptions described in Note 2. X Company's management is responsible for the pro forma financial information. Our responsibility is to express an opinion on the pro forma financial information based on our examination.

Our examination was conducted in accordance with attestation standards established by the American Institute of Certified Public Accountants and, accordingly, included such procedures as we considered necessary in the circumstances. We believe that our examination provides a reasonable basis for our opinion.

In addition, we have reviewed the pro forma adjustments and the application of those adjustments to the historical amounts in [*the assembly of*] the accompanying pro forma condensed balance sheet of X Company as of March 31, 20X2, and the pro forma condensed statement of income for the three months then ended. The historical condensed financial statements are derived from the historical financial statements of X Company, which were reviewed by us, and of Y Company, which were reviewed by other accountants,[18] appearing elsewhere herein [*or incorporated by reference*].[19] Such pro forma adjustments are based upon management's assumptions as described in Note 2. Our review

---

[15] This wording is appropriate when one column of pro forma financial information is presented without separate columns of historical financial information and pro forma adjustments.

[16] If either accountant's report includes an explanatory paragraph or is other than unqualified, that fact should be referred to within this report.

[17] If the option in footnote 4 to paragraph .07*a* is followed, the report should be appropriately modified.

[18] Where one set of historical financial statements is audited and the other set is reviewed, wording similar to the following would be appropriate:

> The historical condensed financial statements are derived from the historical financial statements of X Company, which were audited by us, and of Y Company, which were reviewed by other accountants, appearing elsewhere herein [*or incorporated by reference*].

[19] If the option in footnote 4 to paragraph .07*a* is followed, the report should be appropriately modified.

was conducted in accordance with attestation standards established by the American Institute of Certified Public Accountants. A review is substantially less in scope than an examination, the objective of which is the expression of an opinion on management's assumptions, the pro forma adjustments, and the application of those adjustments to historical financial information. Accordingly, we do not express such an opinion on the pro forma adjustments or the application of such adjustments to the pro forma condensed balance sheet as of March 31, 20X2, and the pro forma condensed statement of income for the three months then ended.

The objective of this pro forma financial information is to show what the significant effects on the historical financial information might have been had the transactions [*or event*] occurred at an earlier date. However, the pro forma condensed financial statements are not necessarily indicative of the results of operations or related effects on financial position that would have been attained had the above-mentioned transaction [*or event*] actually occurred earlier.

[*Additional paragraph(s) may be added to emphasize certain matters relating to the attest engagements or the subject matter.*]

In our opinion, management's assumptions provide a reasonable basis for presenting the significant effects directly attributable to the above-mentioned transaction [*or event*] described in Note 1, the related pro forma adjustments give appropriate effect to those assumptions, and the pro forma column reflects the proper application of those adjustments to the historical financial statement amounts in the pro forma condensed balance sheet as of December 31, 20X1, and the pro forma condensed statement of income for the year then ended.

Based on our review, nothing came to our attention that caused us to believe that management's assumptions do not provide a reasonable basis for presenting the significant effects directly attributable to the above-mentioned transaction [*or event*] described in Note 1, that the related pro forma adjustments do not give appropriate effect to those assumptions, or that the pro forma column does not reflect the proper application of those adjustments to the historical financial statement amounts in the pro forma condensed balance sheet as of March 31, 20X2, and the pro forma condensed statement of income for the three months then ended.

[*Signature*]

[*Date*]

.21

Appendix D

Report on Examination of Pro Forma Financial Information Giving Effect to a Business Combination to Be Accounted for as a Pooling of Interests[20]

Independent Accountant's Report

We have examined the pro forma adjustments reflecting the proposed business combination to be accounted for as a pooling of interests described in Note 1 and the application of those adjustments to the historical amounts in the accompanying pro forma condensed balance sheet of X Company as of December 31, 20X1, and the pro forma condensed statements of income for each of three years in the period then ended. These historical condensed financial statements are derived from the historical financial statements of X Company, which were audited by us,[21] and of Y Company, which were audited by other accountants, appearing elsewhere herein [*or incorporated by reference*].[22] Such pro forma adjustments are based upon management's assumptions described in Note 2. X Company's management is responsible for the pro forma financial information. Our responsibility is to express an opinion on the pro forma financial information based on our examination.

Our examination was conducted in accordance with attestation standards established by the American Institute of Certified Public Accountants and, accordingly, included such procedures as we considered necessary in the circumstances. We believe that our examination provides a reasonable basis for our opinion.

The objective of this pro forma financial information is to show what the significant effects on the historical financial information might have been had the transactions [*or event*] occurred at an earlier date.

[*Additional paragraph(s) may be added to emphasize certain matters relating to the attest engagement or the subject matter.*]

In our opinion, the accompanying condensed pro forma financial statements of X Company as of December 31, 20X1, and for each of the three years in the period then ended give appropriate effect to the pro forma adjustments necessary to reflect the proposed business combination on a pooling of interests basis as described in Note 1 and the pro forma column reflects the proper application of those adjustments to the historical financial statements.

[*Signature*]

[*Date*]

---

[20] See paragraph .15 for a discussion of the form of the opinion on pro forma financial information in a pooling of interests business combination.

[21] If either accountant's report includes an explanatory paragraph or is other than unqualified, that fact should be referred to within this report.

[22] If the option in footnote 4 to paragraph .07*a* is followed, the report should be appropriately modified.

.22

Appendix E

Other Example Reports

An example of a report qualified because of a scope limitation follows.

Independent Accountant's Report

We have examined the pro forma adjustments reflecting the transaction [*or event*] described in Note 1 and the application of those adjustments to the historical amounts in [*the assembly of*][23] the accompanying pro forma condensed balance sheet of X Company as of December 31, 20X1, and the pro forma condensed statement of income for the year then ended. The historical condensed financial statements are derived from the historical financial statements of X Company, which were audited by us, and of Y Company, which were audited by other accountants,[24] appearing elsewhere herein [*or incorporated by reference*].[25] Such pro forma adjustments are based upon management's assumptions described in Note 2. X Company's management is responsible for the pro forma financial information. Our responsibility is to express an opinion on the pro forma financial information based on our examination.

Except as described below, our examination was conducted in accordance with attestation standards established by the American Institute of Certified Public Accountants and, accordingly, included such procedures as we considered necessary in the circumstances. We believe that our examination provides a reasonable basis for our opinion.

We are unable to perform the examination procedures we considered necessary with respect to assumptions relating to the proposed loan described in Adjustment E in Note 2.

[*Same paragraph as third paragraph in examination report in paragraph .18*]

In our opinion, except for the effects of such changes, if any, as might have been determined to be necessary had we been able to satisfy ourselves as to the assumptions relating to the proposed loan, management's assumptions provide a reasonable basis for presenting the significant effects directly attributable to the above-mentioned transaction [*or event*] described in Note 1, the related pro forma adjustments give appropriate effect to those assumptions, and the pro forma column reflects the proper application of those adjustments to the historical financial statement amounts in the pro forma condensed balance sheet as of December 31, 20X1, and the pro forma condensed statement of income for the year then ended.

[*Signature*]

[*Date*]

---

[23] This wording is appropriate when one column of pro forma financial information is presented without separate columns of historical financial information and pro forma adjustments.

[24] If either accountant's report includes an explanatory paragraph or is other than unqualified, that fact should be referred to within this report.

[25] If the option in footnote 4 to paragraph .07*a* is followed, the report should be appropriately modified.

An example of a report qualified for reservations about the propriety of assumptions on an acquisition transaction follows:

[*Same first three paragraphs as examination report in paragraph .18*]

As discussed in Note 2 to the pro forma financial statements, the pro forma adjustments reflect management's assumption that X Division of the acquired company will be sold. The net assets of this division are reflected at their historical carrying amount; generally accepted accounting principles require these net assets to be recorded at estimated net realizable value.

In our opinion, except for inappropriate valuation of the net assets of X Division, management's assumptions described in Note 2 provide a reasonable basis for presenting the significant effects directly attributable to the above-mentioned transaction [*or event*] described in Note 1, the related pro forma adjustments give appropriate effect to those assumptions, and the pro forma column reflects the proper application of those adjustments to the historical financial statement amounts in the pro forma condensed balance sheet as of December 31, 20X1, and the pro forma condensed statement of income for the year then ended.

[*Signature*]

[*Date*]

An example of a disclaimer of opinion because of a scope limitation follows:

<u>Independent Accountant's Report</u>

We were engaged to examine the pro forma adjustments reflecting the transaction [*or event*] described in Note 1 and the application of those adjustments to the historical amounts in [*the assembly of*][26] the accompanying pro forma financial condensed balance sheet of X Company as of December 31, 20X1, and the pro forma condensed statement of income for the year then ended. The historical condensed financial statements are derived from the historical financial statements of X Company, which were audited by us, and of Y Company, which were audited by other accountants,[27] appearing elsewhere herein [*or incorporated by reference*].[28] Such pro forma adjustments are based upon management's assumptions described in Note 2. X Company's management is responsible for the pro forma financial information.

As discussed in Note 2 to the pro forma financial statements, the pro forma adjustments reflect management's assumptions that the elimination of duplicate facilities would have resulted in a 30 percent reduction in operating costs. Management could not supply us with sufficient evidence to support this assertion.

[*Same paragraph as third paragraph in examination report in paragraph .18*]

Since we were unable to evaluate management's assumptions regarding the reduction in operating costs and other assumptions related thereto, the scope of our work was not sufficient to express and, therefore, we do not express an

---

[26] This wording is appropriate when one column of pro forma financial information is presented without separate columns of historical financial information and pro forma adjustments.

[27] If either accountant's report includes an explanatory paragraph or is other than unqualified, that fact should be referred to within this report.

[28] If the option in footnote 4 to paragraph .07*a* is followed, the report should be appropriately modified.

opinion on the pro forma adjustments, management's underlying assumptions regarding those adjustments and the application of those adjustments to the historical financial statement amounts in the pro forma condensed financial statement amounts in the pro forma condensed balance sheet as of December 31, 20X1, and the pro forma condensed statement of income for the year then ended.

[*Signature*]

[*Date*]

AT Section 501

An Examination of an Entity's Internal Control Over Financial Reporting That Is Integrated With an Audit of Its Financial Statements

Source: SSAE No. 15.

See section 9501 for interpretations of this section.

Effective when the subject matter or assertion is as of or for a period ending on or after December 15, 2008. Earlier application is permitted.

Applicability

.01 This section establishes requirements and provides guidance that applies when a practitioner[1] is engaged to perform an examination of the design and operating effectiveness of an entity's internal control over financial reporting (*examination of internal control*)[2] that is integrated with an audit of financial statements (*integrated audit*).[3]

.02 Ordinarily, the auditor will be engaged to examine the effectiveness of the entity's internal control over financial reporting (hereinafter referred to as *internal control*) as of the end of the entity's fiscal year; however, management may select a different date. If the auditor is engaged to examine the effectiveness of an entity's internal control at a date different from the end of the entity's fiscal year, the examination should, nevertheless, be integrated with a financial statement audit (see paragraphs .18–.19).

.03 An auditor may be engaged to examine the effectiveness of an entity's internal control for a period of time. In that circumstance, the guidance in this section should be modified accordingly, and the examination of internal control should be integrated with an audit of financial statements that covers the same period of time.

.04 This section does not provide guidance for the following:

a. Engagements to examine the suitability of design of an entity's internal control. Such engagements may be developed and performed under section 101, *Attest Engagements* [4]

---

[1] In this section, the *practitioner* is referred to as the *auditor* because the examination of internal control is integrated with an audit of financial statements, and an examination provides the same level of assurance as an audit.

[2] In this section, the phrase *examination of internal control* means an engagement to report directly on internal control or on management's assertion thereon. The performance guidance in this section applies equally to either reporting alternative.

[3] Certain regulatory bodies require the examination of internal control and the audit of the financial statements to be performed by the same auditor. There are difficulties inherent in integrating the examination of internal control and the audit of the financial statements to meet the requirements of this section when the audit of the financial statements is performed by a different auditor. In such circumstances, the requirements of this section, nevertheless, apply.

[4] Although this section does not apply when an auditor is engaged to examine the suitability of design of an entity's internal control, it may be useful in planning and performing such engagements.

b. Engagements to examine controls over the effectiveness and efficiency of operations. Such engagements may be developed and performed under section 101.

c. Engagements to examine controls over compliance with laws and regulations. See section 601, *Compliance Attestation*.

d. Engagements to report on controls at a service organization. See section 801, *Reporting on Controls at a Service Organization*.

e. Engagements to perform agreed-upon procedures on controls. See section 201, *Agreed-Upon Procedures Engagements*.

.05 The auditor may be requested to perform certain nonattest services related to the entity's internal control in addition to the examination of internal control. The auditor should determine whether to perform such nonattest services after considering relevant ethical requirements.

.06 An auditor should not accept an engagement to review an entity's internal control or a written assertion thereon.

Definitions and Underlying Concepts

.07 For purposes of this section, the terms listed below are defined as follows:

Control objective. The aim or purpose of specified controls. Control objectives ordinarily address the risks that the controls are intended to mitigate. In the context of internal control, a control objective generally relates to a relevant assertion for a significant account or disclosure and addresses the risk that the controls in a specific area will not provide reasonable assurance that a misstatement or omission in that relevant assertion is prevented, or detected and corrected on a timely basis.

Deficiency. A deficiency in internal control exists when the design or operation of a control does not allow management or employees, in the normal course of performing their assigned functions, to prevent, or detect and correct misstatements on a timely basis. A deficiency in design exists when (*a*) a control necessary to meet the control objective is missing or (*b*) an existing control is not properly designed so that, even if the control operates as designed, the control objective would not be met. A deficiency in operation exists when a properly designed control does not operate as designed, or when the person performing the control does not possess the necessary authority or competence to perform the control effectively.

Detective control. A control that has the objective of detecting and correcting errors or fraud that has already occurred that could result in a misstatement of the financial statements.

Financial statements and related disclosures. An entity's financial statements and notes to the financial statements as presented in accordance with the applicable financial reporting framework.[5] References to financial statements and related disclosures do not extend to the preparation

[5] The *applicable financial reporting framework* is defined in paragraph .14 of AU-C section 200, *Overall Objectives of the Independent Auditor and the Conduct of an Audit in Accordance With Generally Accepted Auditing Standards*, as "the financial reporting framework adopted by management and, when appropriate, those charged with governance in the preparation and fair presentation of the financial statements that is acceptable in view of the nature of the entity and the objective of the financial statements, or that is required by law or regulation." Paragraph .A31 of AU-C section 700, *Forming an Opinion and Reporting on Financial Statements*, provides the following examples

(continued)

of other financial information presented outside an entity's basic financial statements and notes.

Internal control over financial reporting.[6] A process effected by those charged with governance,[7] management, and other personnel, designed to provide reasonable assurance regarding the preparation of reliable financial statements in accordance with the applicable financial reporting framework and includes those policies and procedures that[8]

i. pertain to the maintenance of records that, in reasonable detail, accurately and fairly reflect the transactions and dispositions of the assets of the entity;
ii. provide reasonable assurance that transactions are recorded as necessary to permit preparation of financial statements in accordance with the applicable financial reporting framework, and that receipts and expenditures of the entity are being made only in accordance with authorizations of management and those charged with governance; and
iii. provide reasonable assurance regarding prevention, or timely detection and correction of unauthorized acquisition, use, or disposition of the entity's assets that could have a material effect on the financial statements.

Internal control has inherent limitations. Internal control is a process that involves human diligence and compliance and is subject to lapses in judgment and breakdowns resulting from human failures. Internal control also can be circumvented by collusion or improper management override. Because of such limitations, there is a risk that material misstatements will not be prevented, or detected and corrected on a timely basis by internal control. However, these inherent limitations are known aspects of the financial reporting process.

Management's assertion. Management's conclusion about the effectiveness of the entity's internal control that is included in management's report on internal control.

(footnote continued)

of applicable financial reporting frameworks: accounting principles generally accepted in the United States of America (or U.S. generally accepted accounting principles), International Financial Reporting Standards promulgated by the International Accounting Standards Board (IASB), and *International Financial Reporting Standard for Small and Medium-Sized Entities* promulgated by the IASB. [Footnote revised, December 2012, to reflect conforming changes necessary due to the issuance of SAS Nos. 122–126.]

[6] For insured depository institutions (IDIs) subject to the internal control reporting requirements of Section 112 of the Federal Deposit Insurance Corporation Improvement Act (FDICIA), internal control includes controls over the preparation of the IDI's financial statements and related disclosures in accordance with GAAP and with the instructions to the *Consolidated Financial Statements for Bank Holding Companies*. Internal control also includes controls over the preparation of the IDI's financial statements and related disclosures in accordance with GAAP and controls over the preparation of schedules equivalent to the basic financial statements in accordance with the Federal Financial Institutions Examination Council Instructions for Consolidated Reports of Condition and Income (call report instructions) or with the Office of Thrift Supervision Instructions for Thrift Financial Reports (TFR instructions).

[7] The term *those charged with governance* is defined in paragraph .06 of AU-C section 260, *The Auditor's Communication With Those Charged With Governance*, as "the person(s) or organization(s) (for example, a corporate trustee) with responsibility for overseeing the strategic direction of the entity and the obligations related to the accountability of the entity. This includes overseeing the financial reporting process. Those charged with governance may include management personnel; for example, executive members of a governance board or an owner-manager." [Footnote revised, December 2012, to reflect conforming changes necessary due to the issuance of SAS Nos. 122–126.]

[8] The auditor's procedures performed as part of the integrated audit are not part of an entity's internal control.

Material weakness. A deficiency, or a combination of deficiencies, in internal control such that there is a reasonable possibility[9] that a material misstatement of the entity's financial statements will not be prevented, or detected and corrected on a timely basis.

Preventive control. A control that has the objective of preventing errors or fraud that could result in a misstatement of the financial statements.

Relevant assertion. A financial statement assertion[10] that has a reasonable possibility of containing a misstatement or misstatements that would cause the financial statements to be materially misstated. The determination of whether an assertion is a relevant assertion is made without regard to the effect of controls.

Significant account or disclosure. An account balance or disclosure that has a reasonable possibility that it could contain a misstatement that, individually or when aggregated with others, has a material effect on the financial statements, considering the risks of both overstatement and understatement. The determination of whether an account balance or disclosure is a significant account or disclosure is made without regard to the effect of controls.

Significant account or disclosure. An account balance or disclosure that has a reasonable possibility that it could contain a misstatement that, individually or when aggregated with others, has a material effect on the financial statements, considering the risks of both overstatement and understatement. The determination of whether an account balance or disclosure is a significant account or disclosure is made without regard to the effect of controls.

Significant deficiency. A deficiency, or a combination of deficiencies, in internal control that is less severe than a material weakness, yet important enough to merit attention by those charged with governance.

.08 Effective internal control provides reasonable assurance regarding the reliability of financial reporting and the preparation of financial statements for external purposes. If one or more material weaknesses exist, the entity's internal control cannot be considered effective.

.09 The auditor's objective in an examination of internal control is to form an opinion on the effectiveness of the entity's internal control. Because an entity's internal control cannot be considered effective if one or more material weaknesses exist, to form a basis for expressing an opinion, the auditor should plan and perform the examination to obtain sufficient appropriate evidence to obtain reasonable assurance[11] about whether material weaknesses exist as of

---

[9] A reasonable possibility exists when the chance of the future event or events occurring is more than remote. [Footnote revised, June 2009, to reflect conforming changes necessary due to the issuance of FASB ASC. Footnote revised, December 2012, to reflect conforming changes necessary due to the issuance of SAS Nos. 122–126.]

[10] The financial statement assertions are described in paragraph .A114 of AU-C section 315, *Understanding the Entity and Its Environment and Assessing the Risks of Material Misstatement*. The auditor may use the financial statement assertions as they are described in AU-C section 315 or may express them differently, provided that all aspects described in AU-C section 315 have been covered. [Footnote revised, December 2012, to reflect conforming changes necessary due to the issuance of SAS Nos. 122–126.]

[11] The high, but not absolute, level of assurance that is intended to be obtained by the auditor is expressed in the auditor's report as obtaining reasonable assurance about whether effective internal control over financial reporting was maintained in all material respects as of the date specified in management's assertion. See paragraph .54 of section 101, *Attest Engagements*, and AU-C section 200. [Footnote revised, December 2012, to reflect conforming changes necessary due to the issuance of SAS Nos. 122–126.].

the date specified in management's assertion. A material weakness in internal control may exist even when financial statements are not materially misstated. The auditor is not required to search for deficiencies that, individually or in combination, are less severe than a material weakness.

.10 An auditor engaged to perform an examination of internal control should comply with the general, fieldwork, and reporting standards in section 101, and the specific performance and reporting requirements set forth in this section. In this section, the subject matter is the effectiveness of internal control, and the responsible party usually is management of the entity. Accordingly, the term *management* is used in this section to refer to the responsible party.

.11 The auditor should use the same suitable and available control criteria[12] to perform his or her examination of internal control as management uses for its evaluation of the effectiveness of the entity's internal control.

.12 An auditor may perform an examination of internal control only if the following conditions are met:

a. Management accepts responsibility for the effectiveness of the entity's internal control.

b. Management evaluates the effectiveness of the entity's internal control using suitable and available criteria.

c. Management supports its assertion about the effectiveness of the entity's internal control with sufficient appropriate evidence (see discussion beginning at paragraph .14).

d. Management provides its assertion about the effectiveness of the entity's internal control in a report that accompanies the auditor's report (see paragraph .95).

.13 Management's refusal to furnish a written assertion should cause the auditor to withdraw from the engagement. However, if law or regulation does not allow the auditor to withdraw from the engagement and management refuses to furnish a written assertion, the auditor should disclaim an opinion on internal control.[13]

Evidence Supporting Management's Assertion

.14 Management is responsible for identifying and documenting the controls and the control objectives that they were designed to achieve. Such documentation serves as a basis for management's assertion. Documentation of the design of controls, including changes to those controls, is evidence that controls upon which management's assertion is based are

- identified.

---

[12] According to paragraph .23 of section 101 "[t]he third general attestation standard is—*The auditor must have reason to believe that the subject matter is capable of evaluation against criteria that are suitable and available to users.*" The Committee of Sponsoring Organizations of the Treadway Commission's (COSO) report *Internal Control—Integrated Framework* provides suitable and available criteria against which management may evaluate and report on the effectiveness of the entity's internal control. *Internal Control—Integrated Framework* describes an entity's internal control as consisting of five components: control environment, risk assessment, information and communication, control activities, and monitoring. See AU-C section 315 for a discussion of these components. If management selects another framework, see paragraphs .23–.34 of section 101 for guidance on evaluating the suitability and availability of criteria. [Footnote revised, December 2012, to reflect conforming changes necessary due to the issuance of SAS Nos. 122–126.]

[13] See paragraphs .117–.121 when disclaiming an opinion, including the requirement for the auditor's report to include a description of any material weaknesses identified.

- capable of being communicated to those responsible for their performance.
- capable of being monitored and evaluated by the entity.

.15 Management's documentation may take various forms, for example, entity policy manuals, accounting manuals, narrative memoranda, flowcharts, decision tables, procedural write-ups, or completed questionnaires. No one, particular form of documentation is prescribed, and the extent of documentation may vary depending upon the size and complexity of the entity and the entity's monitoring activities.

.16 Management's monitoring activities also may provide evidence of the design and operating effectiveness of internal control in support of management's assertion. Monitoring of controls is a process to assess the effectiveness of internal control performance over time. It involves assessing the effectiveness of controls on a timely basis, identifying and reporting deficiencies to appropriate individuals within the organization, and taking necessary corrective actions. Management accomplishes monitoring of controls through ongoing activities, separate evaluations, or a combination of the two.

.17 Ongoing monitoring activities are often built into the normal recurring activities of an entity and include regular management and supervisory activities. The greater the degree and effectiveness of ongoing monitoring, the less need for separate evaluations. Usually, some combination of ongoing monitoring and separate evaluations will ensure that internal control maintains its effectiveness over time.

Integrating the Examination With the Financial Statement Audit

.18 The examination of internal control should be integrated with an audit of financial statements. Although the objectives of the engagements are not the same, the auditor should plan and perform the integrated audit to achieve the objectives of both engagements simultaneously. The auditor should design tests of controls

- to obtain sufficient appropriate evidence to support the auditor's opinion on internal control as of the period-end; and
- to obtain sufficient appropriate evidence to support the auditor's control risk assessments for purposes of the audit of financial statements.

.19 The date specified in management's assertion (the as-of date of the examination) should correspond to the balance sheet date (or period ending date) of the period covered by the financial statements (see paragraph .02).

.20 Obtaining sufficient appropriate evidence to support the operating effectiveness of controls for purposes of the financial statement audit ordinarily allows the auditor to modify the substantive procedures that otherwise would have been necessary to opine on the financial statements. (Integration is described further beginning at paragraph .159.)

.21 In some circumstances, particularly in some audits of smaller, less complex entities, the auditor might choose not to test the operating effectiveness of controls for purposes of the audit of the financial statements. In such circumstances, the auditor's tests of the operating effectiveness of controls would be performed principally for the purpose of supporting his or her opinion on whether the entity's internal control is effective as of period-end. The auditor should consider the results of the financial statement auditing procedures in determining his or her risk assessments and the testing necessary to conclude on the operating effectiveness of a control.

Planning the Examination

.22 The auditor should plan the examination of internal control. Evaluating whether the following matters are important to the entity's financial statements and internal control and, if so, how they may affect the auditor's procedures, may assist the auditor in planning the examination:

- Knowledge of the entity's internal control obtained during other engagements performed by the auditor or, if applicable, during a review of a predecessor auditor's working papers
- Matters affecting the industry in which the entity operates, such as financial reporting practices, economic conditions, laws and regulations, and technological changes
- Matters relating to the entity's business, including its organization, operating characteristics, and capital structure
- The extent of recent changes, if any, in the entity, its operations, or its internal control
- The auditor's preliminary judgments about materiality, risk, and other factors relating to the determination of material weaknesses
- Deficiencies previously communicated to those charged with governance or management
- Legal or regulatory matters of which the entity is aware
- The type and extent of available evidence related to the effectiveness of the entity's internal control
- Preliminary judgments about the effectiveness of internal control
- Public information about the entity relevant to the evaluation of the likelihood of material financial statement misstatements and the effectiveness of the entity's internal control
- Knowledge about risks related to the entity evaluated as part of the auditor's client acceptance and retention evaluation
- The relative complexity of the entity's operations

Role of Risk Assessment

.23 Risk assessment underlies the entire examination process described by this section, including the determination of significant accounts and disclosures and relevant assertions, the selection of controls to test, and the determination of the evidence necessary to conclude on the effectiveness of a given control. When performing an examination of internal control that is integrated with an audit of financial statements, the same risk assessment process supports both engagements.[14]

.24 The auditor should focus more attention on the areas of highest risk. A direct relationship exists between the degree of risk that a material weakness could exist in a particular area of the entity's internal control and the amount

[14] The risk assessment procedures performed in connection with a financial statement audit are described in AU-C section 315. [Footnote revised, December 2012, to reflect conforming changes necessary due to the issuance of SAS Nos. 122–126.]

of attention that would be devoted to that area. In addition, an entity's internal control is less likely to prevent, or detect and correct a misstatement caused by fraud than a misstatement caused by error. It is not necessary to test controls that, even if deficient, would not present a reasonable possibility of material misstatement to the financial statements.

Scaling the Examination

.25 The size and complexity of the entity, its business processes, and business units may affect the way in which the entity achieves many of its control objectives. Many smaller entities have less complex operations. Additionally, some larger, complex entities may have less complex units or processes. Factors that might indicate less complex operations include fewer business lines; less complex business processes and financial reporting systems; more centralized accounting functions; extensive involvement by senior management in the day-to-day activities of the business; and fewer levels of management, each with a wide span of control. Accordingly, a smaller, less complex entity, or even a larger, less complex entity might achieve its control objectives differently from a more complex entity.

.26 The size and complexity of the organization, its business processes, and business units also may affect the auditor's risk assessment and the determination of the necessary procedures and the controls necessary to address those risks. Scaling is most effective as a natural extension of the risk-based approach and applicable to examinations of all entities.

Addressing the Risk of Fraud

.27 When planning and performing the examination of internal control, the auditor should incorporate the results of the fraud risk assessment performed in the financial statement audit. As part of identifying and testing entity-level controls, as discussed beginning at paragraph .37, and selecting other controls to test, as discussed beginning at paragraph .54, the auditor should evaluate whether the entity's controls sufficiently address identified risks of material misstatement due to fraud[15] and the risk of management override of other controls. Controls that might address these risks include

- controls over significant, unusual transactions, particularly those that result in late or unusual journal entries;
- controls over journal entries and adjustments made in the period-end financial reporting process;
- controls over related party transactions;
- controls related to significant management estimates; and
- controls that mitigate incentives for, and pressures on, management to falsify or inappropriately manage financial results.

.28 If the auditor identifies deficiencies in controls designed to prevent, or detect and correct misstatements caused by fraud during the examination of internal control, he or she should take into account those deficiencies when developing his or her response to risks of material misstatement during the

---

[15] See paragraphs .25–.27 of AU-C section 240, *Consideration of Fraud in a Financial Statement Audit*, regarding the auditor's identification and assessment of the risks of material misstatement due to fraud. [Footnote revised, December 2012, to reflect conforming changes necessary due to the issuance of SAS Nos. 122–126.]

financial statement audit, as provided in paragraphs .28–.33 of AU-C section 240, *Consideration of Fraud in a Financial Statement Audit*. [Revised, December 2012, to reflect conforming changes necessary due to the issuance of SAS Nos. 122–126.]

Using the Work of Others

.29 The auditor should evaluate the extent to which he or she will use the work of others to reduce the work the auditor might otherwise perform himself or herself.

.30 AU-C section 610, *The Auditor's Consideration of the Internal Audit Function in an Audit of Financial Statements*, applies in an integrated audit. For purposes of the examination of internal control, however, the auditor may use the work performed by, or receive direct assistance from, internal auditors, entity personnel (in addition to internal auditors), and third parties working under the direction of management or those charged with governance that provide evidence about the effectiveness of internal control. In an integrated audit, the auditor also may use this work to obtain evidence supporting the assessment of control risk for purposes of the financial statement audit. [Revised, December 2012, to reflect conforming changes necessary due to the issuance of SAS Nos. 122–126.]

.31 The auditor should obtain an understanding of the work of others sufficient to identify those activities related to the effectiveness of internal control that are relevant to planning the examination of internal control. The extent of the procedures necessary to obtain this understanding will vary, depending on the nature of those activities.

.32 The auditor should assess the competence and objectivity of the persons whose work the auditor plans to use to determine the extent to which the auditor may use their work. The higher the degree of competence and objectivity, the greater use the auditor may make of the work. The auditor should apply paragraphs .09–.11 of AU-C section 610 to assess the competence and objectivity of internal auditors. The auditor should apply the principles underlying those paragraphs to assess the competence and objectivity of persons other than internal auditors whose work the auditor plans to use. [Revised, December 2012, to reflect conforming changes necessary due to the issuance of SAS Nos. 122–126.]

.33 For purposes of using the work of others, competence means the attainment and maintenance of a level of understanding, knowledge, and skills that enables that person to perform ably the tasks assigned to them, and objectivity means the ability to perform those tasks impartially and with intellectual honesty. To assess competence, the auditor should evaluate factors about the person's qualifications and ability to perform the work that the auditor plans to use. To assess objectivity, the auditor should evaluate whether factors are present that either inhibit or promote a person's ability to perform with the necessary degree of objectivity the work that the auditor plans to use. The effect of the work of others on the auditor's work also depends on the relationship between the risk associated with a control and the competence and objectivity of those who performed the work. As the risk associated with a control decreases, the necessary level of competence and objectivity decreases as well. In higher risk areas (for example, controls that address specific fraud risks), use of the work of others would be limited, if it could be used at all.

.34 The extent to which the auditor may use the work of others also depends, in part, on the risk associated with the control being tested (see paragraph .62). As the risk associated with a control increases, the need for the auditor to perform his or her own work on the control increases.

Materiality

.35 In planning and performing the examination of internal control, the auditor should use the same materiality used in planning and performing the audit of the entity's financial statements.[16]

Using a Top-Down Approach

.36 The auditor should use a top-down approach[17] to the examination of internal control to select the controls to test. A top-down approach involves

- beginning at the financial statement level;
- using the auditor's understanding of the overall risks to internal control;
- focusing on entity-level controls;
- working down to significant accounts and disclosures and their relevant assertions;
- directing attention to accounts, disclosures, and assertions that present a reasonable possibility of material misstatement to the financial statements and related disclosures;
- verifying the auditor's understanding of the risks in the entity's processes; and
- selecting controls for testing that sufficiently address the assessed risk of material misstatement to each relevant assertion.

Identifying Entity-Level Controls

.37 The auditor should test those entity-level controls that are important to his or her conclusion about whether the entity has effective internal control. The auditor's evaluation of entity-level controls can result in increasing or decreasing the testing that he or she otherwise would have performed on other controls.

.38 Entity-level controls include

- controls related to the control environment;
- controls over management override;[18]
- the entity's risk assessment process;
- centralized processing and controls, including shared service environments;

---

[16] See AU-C section 320, *Audit Risk and Materiality in Planning and Performing an Audit*, which provides additional explanation of materiality. [Footnote revised, December 2012, to reflect conforming changes necessary due to the issuance of SAS Nos. 122–126.]

[17] The top-down approach describes the auditor's sequential thought process in identifying risks and the controls to test, not necessarily the order in which the auditor will perform the examination procedures.

[18] Controls over management override are important to effective internal control for all entities and may be particularly important at smaller, less complex entities because of the increased involvement of senior management in performing controls and in the period-end financial reporting process. For smaller, less complex entities, the controls that address the risk of management override might be different from those at a larger entity. For example, a smaller, less complex entity might rely on more detailed oversight by those charged with governance that focuses on the risk of management override.

- controls to monitor results of operations;
- controls to monitor other controls, including activities of the internal audit function, those charged with governance, and self-assessment programs;
- controls over the period-end financial reporting process; and
- programs and controls that address significant business control and risk management practices.

.39 Entity-level controls vary in nature and precision:

- Some entity-level controls, such as certain control environment controls, have an important but indirect effect on the likelihood that a misstatement will be prevented, or detected and corrected on a timely basis. These controls might affect the other controls that the auditor selects for testing and the nature, timing, and extent of procedures the auditor performs on other controls.
- Some entity-level controls monitor the effectiveness of other controls. Such controls might be designed to identify possible breakdowns in lower level controls, but not at a level of precision that would, by themselves, sufficiently address the assessed risk that material misstatements to a relevant assertion will be prevented, or detected and corrected on a timely basis. These controls, when operating effectively, might allow the auditor to reduce the testing of other controls.
- Some entity-level controls might be designed to operate at a level of precision that would adequately prevent, or detect and correct on a timely basis misstatements to one or more relevant assertions. If an entity-level control sufficiently addresses the assessed risk of material misstatement, the auditor need not test additional controls relating to that risk.

Control Environment

.40 Because of its importance to effective internal control, the auditor should evaluate the control environment at the entity. When evaluating the control environment, the auditor should apply paragraphs .A71–.A80 of AU-C section 315, *Understanding the Entity and Its Environment and Assessing the Risks of Material Misstatement*. As part of evaluating the control environment, the auditor should assess

- whether management's philosophy and operating style promote effective internal control;
- whether sound integrity and ethical values, particularly of top management, are developed and understood; and
- whether those charged with governance understand and exercise oversight responsibility over financial reporting and internal control.

[Revised, December 2012, to reflect conforming changes necessary due to the issuance of SAS Nos. 122–126.]

Period-End Financial Reporting Process

.41 Because of its importance to financial reporting and to the integrated audit, the auditor should evaluate the period-end financial reporting process.[19] The period-end financial reporting process includes the following:

- Procedures used to enter transaction totals into the general ledger

---

[19] Because the annual period-end financial reporting process normally occurs after the as-of date of management's assertion, those controls usually cannot be tested until after the as-of date.

- Procedures related to the selection and application of accounting policies
- Procedures used to initiate, authorize, record, and process journal entries in the general ledger
- Procedures used to record recurring and nonrecurring adjustments to the financial statements
- Procedures for preparing financial statements and related disclosures

.42 As part of evaluating the period-end financial reporting process, the auditor should assess

- the inputs, procedures performed, and outputs of the processes the entity uses to produce its financial statements;
- the extent of IT involvement in the period-end financial reporting process;
- who participates from management;
- the locations involved in the period-end financial reporting process;
- the types of adjusting and consolidating entries; and
- the nature and extent of the oversight of the process by management and those charged with governance.

Identifying Significant Accounts and Disclosures and Their Relevant Assertions

.43 The auditor should identify significant accounts and disclosures and their relevant assertions. To identify significant accounts and disclosures and their relevant assertions, the auditor should evaluate the qualitative and quantitative risk factors related to the financial statement line items and disclosures. Risk factors relevant to the identification of significant accounts and disclosures and their relevant assertions include

- size and composition of the account;
- susceptibility to misstatement due to errors or fraud;
- volume of activity, complexity, and homogeneity of the individual transactions processed through the account or reflected in the disclosure;
- nature of the account, class of transactions, or disclosure;
- accounting and reporting complexities associated with the account, class of transactions, or disclosure;
- exposure to losses in the account;
- possibility of significant contingent liabilities arising from the activities reflected in the account or disclosure;
- existence of related party transactions in the account; and
- changes from the prior period in the account, class of transactions, or disclosure characteristics.

.44 As part of identifying significant accounts and disclosures and their relevant assertions, the auditor also should determine the likely sources of potential misstatements that would cause the financial statements to be materially misstated. The auditor might determine the likely sources of potential misstatements by asking himself or herself "what could go wrong?" within a given significant account or disclosure.

.45 The risk factors that the auditor should evaluate in the identification of significant accounts and disclosures and their relevant assertions are the same in the examination of internal control as in the audit of the financial statements; accordingly, significant accounts and disclosures and their relevant assertions are the same in an integrated audit.[20]

.46 The components of a potential significant account or disclosure might be subject to significantly different risks. If so, different controls might be necessary to adequately address those risks.

.47 When an entity has multiple locations or business units, the auditor should identify significant accounts and disclosures and their relevant assertions based on the consolidated financial statements.

Understanding Likely Sources of Misstatement

.48 To further understand the likely sources of potential misstatements, and as a part of selecting the controls to test, the auditor should achieve the following objectives:

- Understand the flow of transactions related to the relevant assertions, including how these transactions are initiated, authorized, processed, and recorded
- Identify the points within the entity's processes at which a misstatement, including a misstatement due to fraud, could arise that, individually or in combination with other misstatements, would be material (for example, points at which information is initiated, transferred, or otherwise modified)
- Identify the controls that management has implemented to address these potential misstatements
- Identify the controls that management has implemented over the prevention, or timely detection and correction of unauthorized acquisition, use, or disposition of the entity's assets that could result in a material misstatement of the financial statements

.49 Because of the degree of judgment required, the auditor should either perform the procedures that achieve the objectives in paragraph .48 himself or herself or supervise the work of others who provide direct assistance to the auditor, as described in AU-C section 610. [Revised, December 2012, to reflect conforming changes necessary due to the issuance of SAS Nos. 122–126.]

.50 The auditor also should understand how IT affects the entity's flow of transactions. The auditor should apply paragraphs .A54–.A60 of AU-C section 315, which discuss the effect of IT on internal control and the risks to assess. [Revised, December 2012, to reflect conforming changes necessary due to the issuance of SAS Nos. 122–126.]

.51 The identification of risks and controls within IT is not a separate evaluation. Instead, it is an integral part of the top-down approach used to identify likely sources of misstatement and the controls to test, as well as to assess risk and allocate audit effort.

Performing Walkthroughs

.52 Performing walkthroughs will frequently be the most effective way of achieving the objectives in paragraph .48. A walkthrough involves following

---

[20] The risk assessment procedures performed in connection with a financial statement audit are described in AU-C section 315. [Footnote revised, December 2012, to reflect conforming changes necessary due to the issuance of SAS No. 122–126.]

a transaction from origination through the entity's processes, including information systems, until it is reflected in the entity's financial records, using the same documents and IT that entity personnel use. Walkthrough procedures may include a combination of inquiry, observation, inspection of relevant documentation, recalculation, and control reperformance.

.53 A walkthrough includes questioning the entity's personnel about their understanding of what is required by the entity's prescribed procedures and controls at the points at which important processing procedures occur. These probing questions, combined with the other walkthrough procedures, allow the auditor to gain a sufficient understanding of the process and to be able to identify important points at which a necessary control is missing or not designed effectively. Additionally, probing questions that go beyond a narrow focus on the single transaction used as the basis for the walkthrough may provide an understanding of the different types of significant transactions handled by the process.

Selecting Controls to Test

.54 The auditor should test those controls that are important to the auditor's conclusion about whether the entity's controls sufficiently address the assessed risk of material misstatement to each relevant assertion.

.55 There might be more than one control that addresses the assessed risk of material misstatement to a particular relevant assertion; conversely, one control might address the assessed risk of material misstatement to more than one relevant assertion. It may not be necessary to test all controls related to a relevant assertion nor necessary to test redundant controls, unless redundancy is, itself, a control objective.

.56 The decision concerning whether a control would be selected for testing depends on which controls, individually or in combination, sufficiently address the assessed risk of material misstatement to a given relevant assertion rather than on how the control is labeled (for example, entity-level control, transaction-level control, control activity, monitoring control, preventive control, or detective control).

Testing Controls

Evaluating Design Effectiveness

.57 The auditor should evaluate the design effectiveness of controls by determining whether the entity's controls, if they are applied as prescribed by persons possessing the necessary authority and competence to perform the control effectively, satisfy the entity's control objectives, and can effectively prevent, or detect and correct misstatements caused by errors or fraud that could result in material misstatements in the financial statements.

.58 A smaller, less complex entity might achieve its control objectives in a different manner from a larger, more complex organization. For example, a smaller, less complex entity might have fewer employees in the accounting function, limiting opportunities to segregate duties and leading the entity to implement alternative controls to achieve its control objectives. In such circumstances, the auditor should evaluate whether those alternative controls are effective.

.59 Procedures performed to evaluate design effectiveness may include a mix of inquiry of appropriate personnel, observation of the entity's operations, and inspection of relevant documentation. Walkthroughs that include these procedures ordinarily are sufficient to evaluate design effectiveness.

Testing Operating Effectiveness

.60 The auditor should test the operating effectiveness of a control by determining whether the control is operating as designed and whether the person performing the control possesses the necessary authority and competence to perform the control effectively.[21]

.61 Procedures performed to test operating effectiveness may include a mix of inquiry of appropriate personnel, observation of the entity's operations, inspection of relevant documentation, recalculation, and reperformance of the control.

Relationship of Risk to the Evidence to Be Obtained

.62 For each control selected for testing, the evidence necessary to persuade the auditor that the control is effective depends upon the risk associated with the control. The risk associated with a control consists of the risk that the control might not be effective and, if not effective, the risk that a material weakness exists. As the risk associated with the control being tested increases, the evidence that the auditor should obtain also increases.

.63 Although the auditor should obtain evidence about the effectiveness of controls for each relevant assertion, he or she is not responsible for obtaining sufficient appropriate evidence to support an opinion about the effectiveness of each individual control. Rather, the auditor's objective is to express an opinion on the entity's internal control overall. This allows the auditor to vary the evidence obtained regarding the effectiveness of individual controls selected for testing based on the risk associated with the individual control.

.64 Factors that affect the risk associated with a control may include

- the nature and materiality of misstatements that the control is intended to prevent, or detect and correct;
- the inherent risk associated with the related account(s) and assertion(s);
- whether there have been changes in the volume or nature of transactions that might adversely affect control design or operating effectiveness;
- whether the account has a history of errors;
- the effectiveness of entity-level controls, especially controls that monitor other controls;
- the nature of the control and the frequency with which it operates;
- the degree to which the control relies on the effectiveness of other controls (for example, the control environment or IT general controls);
- the competence of the personnel who perform the control or monitor its performance and whether there have been changes in key personnel who perform the control or monitor its performance;

---

[21] In some situations, particularly in smaller, less complex entities, an entity might use a third party to provide assistance with certain financial reporting functions. When assessing the competence of personnel responsible for an entity's financial reporting and associated controls, the auditor may take into account the combined competence of entity personnel and other parties that assist with functions related to financial reporting.

- whether the control relies on performance by an individual or is automated (that is, an automated control would generally be expected to be lower risk if relevant IT general controls are effective);[22] and
- the complexity of the control and the significance of the judgments that would be made in connection with its operation.[23]

.65 When the auditor identifies control deviations, he or she should determine the effect of the deviations on his or her assessment of the risk associated with the control being tested and the evidence to be obtained, as well as on the operating effectiveness of the control.

.66 Because effective internal control cannot and does not provide absolute assurance of achieving the entity's control objectives, an individual control does not necessarily have to operate without any deviation to be considered effective.

.67 The evidence provided by the auditor's tests of the effectiveness of controls depends upon the mix of the nature, timing, and extent of the auditor's procedures. Further, for an individual control, different combinations of the nature, timing, and extent of testing may provide sufficient appropriate evidence in relation to the risk associated with the control.

.68 Walkthroughs may include a combination of inquiry of appropriate personnel, observation of the entity's operations, inspection of relevant documentation, recalculation, and reperformance of the control and might provide sufficient appropriate evidence of operating effectiveness, depending on the risk associated with the control being tested, the specific procedures performed as part of the walkthrough, and the results of those procedures.

Nature of Tests of Controls

.69 Some types of tests, by their nature, produce greater evidence of the effectiveness of controls than other tests. The following tests that the auditor might perform are presented in order of the evidence that they ordinarily would produce, from least to most: inquiry, observation, inspection of relevant documentation, recalculation, and reperformance of a control. Inquiry alone, however, does not provide sufficient appropriate evidence to support a conclusion about the effectiveness of a control.

.70 The nature of the tests of effectiveness that will provide sufficient appropriate evidence depends, to a large degree, on the nature of the control to be tested, including whether the operation of the control results in documentary evidence of its operation. Documentary evidence of the operation of some controls, such as management's philosophy and operating style, might not exist.

.71 A smaller, less complex entity or unit might have less formal documentation regarding the operation of its controls. In those situations, testing controls through inquiry combined with other procedures, such as observation of activities, inspection of less formal documentation, recalculation, or reperformance of certain controls, might provide sufficient appropriate evidence about whether the control is effective.

---

[22] A smaller, less complex entity or business unit with simple business processes and centralized accounting operations might have relatively simple information systems that make greater use of off-the-shelf packaged software without modification. In the areas in which off-the-shelf software is used, the auditor's testing of IT controls might focus on the application controls built into the prepackaged software that management relies on to achieve its control objectives and the IT general controls that are important to the effective operation of those application controls.

[23] Generally, a conclusion that a control is not operating effectively can be supported by less evidence than is necessary to support a conclusion that a control is operating effectively.

Timing and Extent of Tests of Controls

.72 Testing controls over a longer period of time provides more evidence of the effectiveness of controls than testing over a shorter period of time. Further, testing performed closer to the date of management's assertion provides more evidence than testing performed earlier in the year. The auditor should balance performing the tests of controls closer to the as-of date with the need to test controls over a sufficient period of time to obtain sufficient appropriate evidence of operating effectiveness.

.73 Prior to the date specified in management's assertion, management might implement changes to the entity's controls to make them more effective or efficient or to address deficiencies. If the auditor determines that the new controls achieve the related objectives of the control criteria and have been in effect for a sufficient period to permit the auditor to assess their design and operating effectiveness by performing tests of controls, he or she will not need to test the design and operating effectiveness of the superseded controls for purposes of expressing an opinion on internal control. If the operating effectiveness of the superseded controls is important to the auditor's control risk assessment in the financial statement audit, the auditor should test the design and operating effectiveness of those superseded controls, as appropriate. (Integration is discussed beginning at paragraph .159.)

.74 The more extensively a control is tested, the greater the evidence obtained from that test.

Rollforward Procedures

.75 When the auditor reports on the effectiveness of controls as of a specific date and obtains evidence about the operating effectiveness of controls at an interim date, he or she should determine what additional evidence concerning the operation of the controls for the remaining period is necessary.

.76 The additional evidence that is necessary to update the results of testing from an interim date to the entity's period-end depends on the following factors:[24]

- The specific control tested prior to the as-of date, including the risks associated with the control, the nature of the control, and the results of those tests
- The sufficiency of the evidence of operating effectiveness obtained at an interim date
- The length of the remaining period
- The possibility that there have been any significant changes in internal control subsequent to the interim date

Special Considerations for Subsequent Years' Examinations

.77 In subsequent years' examinations, the auditor should incorporate knowledge obtained during past examinations he or she performed of the entity's internal control into the decision making process for determining the nature, timing, and extent of testing necessary. This decision making process is described in paragraphs .62–.76.

---

[24] In some circumstances, such as when evaluation of these factors indicates a low risk that the controls are no longer effective during the rollforward period, inquiry alone might be sufficient as a rollforward procedure.

.78 Factors that affect the risk associated with a control in subsequent years' examinations include those in paragraph .64 and the following:

- The nature, timing, and extent of procedures performed in previous examinations
- The results of the previous years' testing of the control
- Whether there have been changes in the control or the process in which it operates since the previous examination

.79 After taking into account the risk factors identified in paragraphs .64 and .78, the additional information available in subsequent years' examinations might permit the auditor to assess the risk as lower than in the initial year. This, in turn, might permit the auditor to reduce testing in subsequent years.

.80 The auditor also may use a benchmarking strategy for automated application controls in subsequent years' examinations. Benchmarking is described further beginning at paragraph .153.

.81 In addition, the auditor should vary the nature, timing, and extent of testing of controls from period to period to introduce unpredictability into the testing and respond to changes in circumstances. For this reason, the auditor might test controls at a different interim period, increase or reduce the number and types of tests performed, or change the combination of procedures used.

Evaluating Identified Deficiencies

.82 The auditor should evaluate the severity of each deficiency to determine whether the deficiency, individually or in combination, is a material weakness as of the date of management's assertion.

.83 The severity of a deficiency depends on

- the magnitude of the potential misstatement resulting from the deficiency or deficiencies; and
- whether there is a reasonable possibility that the entity's controls will fail to prevent, or detect and correct a misstatement of an account balance or disclosure.

The severity of a deficiency does not depend on whether a misstatement actually occurred.

.84 Factors that affect the magnitude of the misstatement that might result from a deficiency or deficiencies include, but are not limited to, the following:

- The financial statement amounts or total of transactions exposed to the deficiency
- The volume of activity (in the current period or expected in future periods) in the account or class of transactions exposed to the deficiency

.85 In evaluating the magnitude of the potential misstatement, the maximum amount by which an account balance or total of transactions can be overstated is generally the recorded amount, whereas understatements could be larger.

.86 Risk factors affect whether there is a reasonable possibility that a deficiency, or a combination of deficiencies, will result in a misstatement of an account balance or disclosure. The factors include, but are not limited to, the following:

- The nature of the financial statement accounts, classes of transactions, disclosures, and assertions involved

- The susceptibility of the related asset or liability to loss or fraud
- The subjectivity, complexity, or extent of judgment required to determine the amount involved
- The interaction or relationship of the control with other controls
- The interaction among the deficiencies
- The possible future consequences of the deficiency

.87 The evaluation of whether a deficiency presents a reasonable possibility of misstatement may be made without quantifying the probability of occurrence as a specific percentage or range. Also, in many cases, the probability of a small misstatement will be greater than the probability of a large misstatement.

.88 Multiple deficiencies that affect the same significant account or disclosure, relevant assertion, or component of internal control increase the likelihood of material misstatement and may, in combination, constitute a material weakness, even though such deficiencies individually may be less severe. Therefore, the auditor should determine whether deficiencies that affect the same significant account or disclosure, relevant assertion, or component of internal control collectively result in a material weakness.

.89 Multiple deficiencies that affect the same significant account or disclosure, relevant assertion, or component of internal control also may collectively result in a significant deficiency.

.90 A compensating control can limit the severity of a deficiency and prevent it from being a material weakness. Although compensating controls can mitigate the effects of a deficiency, they do not eliminate the deficiency. The auditor should evaluate the effect of compensating controls when determining whether a deficiency or combination of deficiencies is a material weakness. To have a mitigating effect, the compensating control should operate at a level of precision that would prevent, or detect and correct a material misstatement. The auditor should test the operating effectiveness of compensating controls.

Indicators of Material Weaknesses

.91 Indicators of material weaknesses in internal control include

- identification of fraud, whether or not material, on the part of senior management;
- restatement of previously issued financial statements to reflect the correction of a material misstatement due to error or fraud;
- identification by the auditor of a material misstatement of financial statements under audit in circumstances that indicate that the misstatement would not have been detected and corrected by the entity's internal control; and
- ineffective oversight of the entity's financial reporting and internal control by those charged with governance.

.92 If the auditor determines that a deficiency, or a combination of deficiencies, is not a material weakness, he or she should consider whether prudent officials, having knowledge of the same facts and circumstances, would likely reach the same conclusion.

Concluding Procedures

Forming an Opinion

.93 The auditor should form an opinion on the effectiveness of internal control by evaluating evidence obtained from all sources, including the auditor's testing of controls, misstatements detected during the financial statement audit, and any identified deficiencies.

.94 As part of this evaluation, the auditor should review reports issued during the year by internal audit (or similar functions) that address controls related to internal control and evaluate deficiencies identified in those reports.

.95 After forming an opinion on the effectiveness of the entity's internal control, the auditor should evaluate management's report to determine whether it appropriately contains the following:

- A statement regarding management's responsibility for internal control
- A description of the subject matter of the examination (for example, controls over the preparation of the entity's financial statements in accordance with generally accepted accounting principles [GAAP])
- An identification of the criteria against which internal control is measured (for example, criteria established in the Committee of Sponsoring Organizations of the Treadway Commission's *Internal Control—Integrated Framework*)
- Management's assertion about the effectiveness of internal control
- A description of the material weaknesses, if any
- The date as of which management's assertion is made

.96 If the auditor determines that any required element of management's report is incomplete or improperly presented, the auditor should request management to revise its report. If management does not revise its report, the auditor should apply paragraph .116. If management refuses to furnish a report, the auditor should apply paragraph .13.

Obtaining Written Representations

.97 In an examination of internal control, the auditor should obtain written representations from management

a. acknowledging management's responsibility for establishing and maintaining effective internal control;

b. stating that management has performed an evaluation of the effectiveness of the entity's internal control and specifying the control criteria;

c. stating that management did not use the auditor's procedures performed during the integrated audit as part of the basis for management's assertion;

d. stating management's assertion about the effectiveness of the entity's internal control based on the control criteria as of a specified date;

e. stating that management has disclosed to the auditor all deficiencies in the design or operation of internal control, including separately disclosing to the auditor all such deficiencies that it believes to be significant deficiencies or material weaknesses in internal control;

f. describing any fraud resulting in a material misstatement to the entity's financial statements and any other fraud that does not result in a material misstatement to the entity's financial statements, but involves senior management or management or other employees who have a significant role in the entity's internal control;

g. stating whether the significant deficiencies and material weaknesses identified and communicated to management and those charged with governance during previous engagements pursuant to paragraph .100 have been resolved and specifically identifying any that have not; and

h. stating whether there were, subsequent to the date being reported on, any changes in internal control or other factors that might significantly affect internal control, including any corrective actions taken by management with regard to significant deficiencies and material weaknesses.

.98 The failure to obtain written representations from management, including management's refusal to furnish them, constitutes a limitation on the scope of the examination.[25] The auditor should evaluate the effects of management's refusal on his or her ability to rely on other representations, such as those obtained in the audit of the entity's financial statements.

.99 The auditor should apply AU-C section 580, *Written Representations*, as it relates to matters such as who should sign the letter, the period to be covered by the letter, and when to obtain an updated letter. [Revised, December 2012, to reflect conforming changes necessary due to the issuance of SAS Nos. 122–126.]

Communicating Certain Matters

.100 Deficiencies identified during the integrated audit that, upon evaluation, are considered significant deficiencies or material weaknesses should be communicated, in writing, to management and those charged with governance as a part of each integrated audit, including significant deficiencies and material weaknesses that were previously communicated to management and those charged with governance and have not yet been remediated. Significant deficiencies and material weaknesses that previously were communicated and have not yet been remediated may be communicated, in writing, by referring to the previously issued written communication and the date of that communication.

.101 If the auditor concludes that the oversight of the entity's financial reporting and internal control by the audit committee (or similar subgroups with different names) is ineffective, the auditor should communicate that conclusion, in writing, to the board of directors or other similar governing body if one exists.

.102 The written communications referred to in paragraphs .100–.101 should be made by the report release date,[26] which is the date the auditor grants the entity permission to use the auditor's report. For a governmental entity, the auditor is not required to make the written communications by the report release date, if such written communications would be publicly available prior to management's report on internal control, the entity's financial statements, and the auditor's report thereon. In that circumstance, the written communications should be made as soon as practicable, but no later than 60 days following the report release date.

---

[25] See paragraph .117 when the scope of the engagement has been restricted.

[26] See paragraph .A2 of AU-C section 230, *Audit Documentation*, for additional guidance related to the report release date. [Footnote revised, December 2012, to reflect conforming changes necessary due to the issuance of SAS Nos. 122–126.]

.103 Because of the importance of timely communication, the auditor may choose to communicate significant matters during the course of the integrated audit. If the communication is made during the integrated audit, the form of interim communication would be affected by the relative significance of the identified deficiencies and the urgency for corrective follow-up action. Such early communication is not required to be in writing. However, regardless of how the early communication is delivered, the auditor should communicate all significant deficiencies and material weaknesses in writing to management and those charged with governance in accordance with paragraphs .100–.102, even if the significant deficiencies or material weaknesses were remediated during the examination.

.104 The auditor also should communicate to management, in writing, all deficiencies (those deficiencies that are not material weaknesses or significant deficiencies) identified during the integrated audit on a timely basis, but no later than 60 days following the report release date, and inform those charged with governance when such a communication was made. In making the written communication referred to in this paragraph, the auditor is not required to communicate those deficiencies that are not material weaknesses or significant deficiencies that were included in previous written communications, whether those communications were made by the auditor, internal auditors, or others within the organization.

.105 The auditor is not required to perform procedures that are sufficient to identify all deficiencies; rather, the auditor communicates deficiencies of which he or she is aware.

.106 Because the integrated audit does not provide the auditor with assurance that he or she has identified all deficiencies less severe than a material weakness, the auditor should not issue a report stating that no such deficiencies were identified during the integrated audit. Also, because the auditor's objective in an examination of internal control is to form an opinion on the effectiveness of the entity's internal control, the auditor should not issue a report indicating that no material weaknesses were identified during the integrated audit.

Reporting on Internal Control

.107 The auditor's report on the examination of internal control should include the following elements:[27]

a. A title that includes the word *independent*

b. A statement that management is responsible for maintaining effective internal control and for evaluating the effectiveness of internal control

c. An identification of management's assertion on internal control that accompanies the auditor's report, including a reference to management's report

d. A statement that the auditor's responsibility is to express an opinion on the entity's internal control (or on management's assertion)[28] based on his or her examination[29]

e. A statement that the examination was conducted in accordance with attestation standards established by the American Institute of Certified Public Accountants

---

[27] Report modifications are discussed further beginning at paragraph .115.

[28] The auditor may report directly on the entity's internal control or on management's written assertion, except as described in paragraph .112.

[29] Because the examination of internal control is integrated with the audit of the financial statements and an examination provides the same level of assurance as an audit, the auditor may refer to the examination of internal control as an audit in his or her report or other communications.

f. A statement that such standards require that the auditor plan and perform the examination to obtain reasonable assurance about whether effective internal control was maintained in all material respects

g. A statement that an examination includes obtaining an understanding of internal control, assessing the risk that a material weakness exists, testing and evaluating the design and operating effectiveness of internal control based on the assessed risk, and performing such other procedures as the auditor considers necessary in the circumstances

h. A statement that the auditor believes the examination provides a reasonable basis for his or her opinion

i. A definition of internal control (the auditor should use the same description of the entity's internal control as management uses in its report)

j. A paragraph stating that, because of inherent limitations, internal control may not prevent, or detect and correct misstatements and that projections of any evaluation of effectiveness to future periods are subject to the risk that controls may become inadequate because of changes in conditions, or that the degree of compliance with the policies or procedures may deteriorate

k. The auditor's opinion on whether the entity maintained, in all material respects, effective internal control as of the specified date, based on the control criteria; or, the auditor's opinion on whether management's assertion about the effectiveness of the entity's internal control as of the specified date is fairly stated, in all material respects, based on the control criteria

l. The manual or printed signature of the auditor's firm

m. The date of the report

Separate or Combined Reports

.108 The auditor may choose to issue a combined report (that is, one report containing both an opinion on the financial statements and an opinion on internal control) or separate reports on the entity's financial statements and on internal control.

.109 If the auditor issues a separate report on internal control, he or she should add the following paragraph to the auditor's report on the financial statements:

> We also have examined [*or audited*][30] in accordance with attestation standards established by the American Institute of Certified Public Accountants, [*company name*]'s internal control over financial reporting as of December 31, 20X8, based on [*identify control criteria*] and our report dated [*date of report, which should be the same as the date of the report on the financial statements*] expressed [*include nature of opinion*].

The auditor also should add the following paragraph to the report on internal control:

> We also have audited, in accordance with auditing standards generally accepted in the United States of America, the [*identify financial statements*] of [*company name*] and our report dated [*date of report, which should be the same as the date of the report on internal control*] expressed [*include nature of opinion*].

---

[30] See footnote 29.

Report Date

.110 The auditor should date the report no earlier than the date on which the auditor has obtained sufficient appropriate evidence to support the auditor's opinion. Because the examination of internal control is integrated with the audit of the financial statements, the dates of the reports should be the same.

Adverse Opinions

.111 Paragraphs .82–.92 describe the evaluation of deficiencies. If there are deficiencies that, individually or in combination, result in one or more material weaknesses as of the date specified in management's assertion, the auditor should express an adverse opinion on the entity's internal control, unless there is a restriction on the scope of the engagement.[31]

.112 When internal control is not effective because one or more material weaknesses exist, the auditor is prohibited from expressing an opinion on management's assertion and should report directly on the effectiveness of internal control. In addition, the auditor's report should include

- the definition of a material weakness.
- a statement that one or more material weaknesses have been identified and an identification of the material weaknesses described in management's assertion. The auditor's report need only refer to the material weaknesses described in management's report and need not include a description of each material weakness, provided each material weakness is included and fairly presented in all material respects in management's report, as described in the following paragraph.

.113 If one or more material weaknesses have not been included in management's report accompanying the auditor's report, the auditor's report should be modified to state that one or more material weaknesses have been identified but not included in management's report. Additionally, the auditor's report should include a description of each material weakness not included in management's report, which should provide the users of the report with specific information about the nature of each material weakness and its actual and potential effect on the presentation of the entity's financial statements issued during the existence of the weakness. In this case, the auditor also should communicate, in writing, to those charged with governance that one or more material weaknesses were not disclosed or identified as a material weakness in management's report. If one or more material weaknesses have been included in management's report but the auditor concludes that the disclosure of such material weaknesses is not fairly presented in all material respects, the auditor's report should describe this conclusion as well as the information necessary to fairly describe each material weakness.

.114 The auditor should determine the effect an adverse opinion on internal control has on his or her opinion on the financial statements. Additionally, the auditor should disclose whether his or her opinion on the financial statements was affected by the material weaknesses.[32]

---

[31] See paragraph .117 when the scope of the engagement has been restricted.

[32] If the auditor issues a separate report on internal control in this circumstance, the disclosure required by this paragraph may be combined with the report language described in paragraph .109. The auditor may present the combined language either as a separate paragraph or as part of the paragraph that identifies the material weakness.

Report Modifications

.115 The auditor should modify his or her report if any of the following conditions exist:

a. Elements of management's report are incomplete or improperly presented.

b. There is a restriction on the scope of the engagement.

c. The auditor decides to refer to the report of a component auditor as the basis, in part, for the auditor's own report.

d. There is other information contained in management's report.

[Revised, December 2012, to reflect conforming changes necessary due to the issuance of SAS Nos. 122–126.]

Elements of Management's Report Are Incomplete or Improperly Presented

.116 If the auditor determines that any required element of management's report (see paragraph .95) is incomplete or improperly presented and management does not revise its report, the auditor should modify his or her report to include an explanatory paragraph describing the reasons for this determination. If the auditor determines that the required disclosure about one or more material weaknesses is not fairly presented in all material respects, the auditor should apply paragraph .113.

Scope Limitations

.117 The auditor may express an opinion on the entity's internal control only if the auditor has been able to apply the procedures necessary in the circumstances. If there are restrictions on the scope of the engagement, the auditor should withdraw from the engagement or disclaim an opinion.

.118 When disclaiming an opinion because of a scope limitation, the auditor should state that he or she does not express an opinion on the effectiveness of internal control and, in a separate paragraph or paragraphs, the substantive reasons for the disclaimer. The auditor should not identify the procedures that were performed nor include the statements describing the characteristics of an examination of internal control (paragraph .107[d–h]); to do so might overshadow the disclaimer.

.119 When the auditor plans to disclaim an opinion and the limited procedures performed by the auditor caused the auditor to conclude that one or more material weaknesses exist, the auditor's report also should include

- the definition of a material weakness.
- a description of any material weaknesses identified in the entity's internal control. This description should address the requirements in paragraph .112 and should provide the users of the report with specific information about the nature of any material weakness and its actual and potential effect on the presentation of the entity's financial statements issued during the existence of the weakness. The auditor also should apply the requirements in paragraph .114.

.120 The auditor may issue a report disclaiming an opinion on internal control as soon as the auditor concludes that a scope limitation will prevent the auditor from obtaining the reasonable assurance necessary to express an opinion.[33] The auditor is not required to perform any additional work prior to issuing a disclaimer when the auditor concludes that he or she will not be able to obtain sufficient appropriate evidence to express an opinion.

.121 If the auditor concludes that he or she cannot express an opinion because there has been a limitation on the scope of the examination, the auditor should communicate, in writing, to management and those charged with governance that the examination of internal control cannot be satisfactorily completed.

Opinion Based, in Part, on the Report of a Component Auditor

.122 When an entity is composed of one or more components (for example, subsidiaries, divisions, or branches), and another auditor has examined the internal control of one or more of the components, the auditor should determine whether it is appropriate to serve as the auditor of the group's internal control and use the work and reports of the component auditor as a basis, in part, for the auditor's opinion. The auditor considering whether to serve as the auditor of the group's internal control may have performed all but a relatively minor portion of the work, or the component auditor may have performed significant parts of the examination. In the latter case, the auditor should decide whether the auditor's own involvement is sufficient to enable the auditor to serve as the auditor of the group's internal control and to report on internal control as such. In deciding this question, the auditor should consider, among other things, the materiality of the portion of internal control the auditor has examined in comparison with the portion examined by the component auditor, the extent of the auditor's knowledge of overall internal control, and the importance of the components examined by the auditor in relation to the group as a whole. [Revised, December 2012, to reflect conforming changes necessary due to the issuance of SAS Nos. 122–126.]

.123 If the auditor decides that it is appropriate to serve as the auditor of the group's internal control, the auditor should then decide whether to make reference in his or her report on the group's internal control to the examination of internal control performed by the component auditor. If the auditor decides to assume responsibility for the work of the component auditor insofar as that work relates to the expression of an opinion on the group's internal control taken as a whole, no reference should be made to the component auditor's work or report. On the other hand, if the auditor decides not to assume responsibility, the auditor's report should make reference to the examination of the component auditor and should clearly indicate the division of responsibility between the auditor and the component auditor in expressing an opinion on the group's internal control. Regardless of the auditor's decision, the auditor remains responsible for the performance of his or her own work and report. [Revised, December 2012, to reflect conforming changes necessary due to the issuance of SAS Nos. 122–126.]

.124 The decision about whether to make reference to a component auditor in the report on the examination of internal control might differ from the corresponding decision as it relates to the audit of the financial statements. For example, the audit report on the financial statements may make reference to

---

[33] In this case, in following paragraph .110 regarding dating the report, the report date is the date that the auditor has obtained sufficient appropriate evidence to support the representations in the report.

the audit of a significant equity investment performed by a component auditor[34] but the report on internal control might not make a similar reference because management's assertion ordinarily would not extend to controls at the equity method investee.[35] [Revised, December 2012, to reflect conforming changes necessary due to the issuance of SAS Nos. 122–126.]

.125 When the auditor of the group's internal control decides to make reference to the report of the component auditor as a basis, in part, for the auditor's opinion on the group's internal control, the auditor should refer to the report of the component auditor when describing the scope of the examination and when expressing the opinion. Whether the component auditor's opinion is expressed on management's assertion or on internal control does not affect the determination of whether the opinion of the auditor of the group's internal control is expressed on management's assertion or on internal control. [Revised, December 2012, to reflect conforming changes necessary due to the issuance of SAS Nos. 122–126.]

Management's Report Contains Additional Information

.126 Management's report accompanying the auditor's report may contain information in addition to the elements described in paragraph .95 that are subject to the auditor's evaluation.[36] If management's report could reasonably be viewed by users of the report as including such additional information, the auditor should disclaim an opinion on the information.

.127 The auditor may use the following sample language as the last paragraph of the auditor's report to disclaim an opinion on such additional information:

> We do not express an opinion or any other form of assurance on [*describe additional information, such as management's cost-benefit statement*].

.128 If the auditor believes that management's additional information contains a material misstatement of fact, he or she should apply the guidance in paragraphs .92–.94 of section 101 and take appropriate action. If the auditor concludes that a material misstatement of fact remains, the auditor should notify management and those charged with governance, in writing, of the auditor's views concerning the information. AU-C section 250, *Consideration of Laws and Regulations in an Audit of Financial Statements*, also may require the auditor to take additional action. [Revised, December 2012, to reflect conforming changes necessary due to the issuance of SAS Nos. 122–126.]

---

[34] AU-C section 600, *Special Considerations—Audits of Group Financial Statements (Including the Work of Component Auditors*, addresses special considerations that apply to group audits, in particular those that involve component auditors. [Footnote added, December 2012, to reflect conforming changes necessary due to the issuance of SAS Nos. 122–126.]

[35] See paragraph .140 for further discussion of the evaluation of the controls for an equity method investment. [Footnote renumbered, December 2012, to reflect conforming changes necessary due to the issuance of SAS Nos. 122–126.]

[36] An entity may publish various documents that contain information in addition to management's report and the auditor's report on internal control. Paragraphs .91–.94 of section 101 provide guidance to the auditor in these circumstances. If management makes the types of disclosures described in paragraph .126 outside its report and includes them elsewhere within a document that includes the auditor's report, the auditor would not need to disclaim an opinion on such information. However, in that situation, the auditor's responsibilities are the same as those described in paragraph .128, if the auditor believes that the additional information contains a material misstatement of fact. [Footnote renumbered, December 2012, to reflect conforming changes necessary due to the issuance of SAS Nos. 122–126.]

Subsequent Events

.129 Changes in internal control or other factors that might significantly affect internal control might occur subsequent to the date as of which internal control is being examined but before the date of the auditor's report. The auditor should inquire of management whether there were any such changes or factors and obtain written representations from management relating to such matters, as described in paragraph .97.

.130 To obtain additional information about changes in internal control or other factors that might significantly affect the effectiveness of the entity's internal control, the auditor should inquire about and examine, for this subsequent period, the following:

- Relevant internal audit (or similar functions, such as loan review in a financial institution) reports issued during the subsequent period
- Independent auditor reports (if other than the auditor's) of deficiencies
- Regulatory agency reports on the entity's internal control
- Information about the effectiveness of the entity's internal control obtained through other engagements

.131 The auditor might inquire about and examine other documents for the subsequent period. AU-C section 560, *Subsequent Events and Subsequently Discovered Facts*, establishes requirements and provides guidance on subsequent events for a financial statement audit that also may be helpful to the auditor performing an examination of internal control. [Revised, December 2012, to reflect conforming changes necessary due to the issuance of SAS Nos. 122–126.]

.132 If, subsequent to the date as of which internal control is being examined but before the date of the auditor's report, the auditor obtains knowledge about a material weakness that existed as of the date specified in management's assertion, the auditor should report directly on internal control and issue an adverse opinion, as required by paragraph .111. The auditor should also follow paragraph .116 if management's assertion states that internal control is effective. If the auditor is unable to determine the effect of the matter on the effectiveness of the entity's internal control as of the date specified in management's assertion, the auditor should disclaim an opinion. As described in paragraph .126, the auditor should disclaim an opinion on management's disclosures about corrective actions taken by the entity, if any.

.133 The auditor may obtain knowledge about conditions that did not exist at the date specified in management's assertion but arose subsequent to that date and before the release of the auditor's report. If a subsequent event of this type has a material effect on the entity's internal control, the auditor should include in his or her report an explanatory paragraph describing the event and its effects or directing the reader's attention to the event and its effects as disclosed in management's report.

.134 The auditor has no responsibility to keep informed of events subsequent to the date of his or her report; however, after the release of the report on internal control, the auditor may become aware of conditions that existed at the report date that might have affected the auditor's opinion had he or she been aware of them. The evaluation of such subsequent information is similar to the evaluation of facts discovered subsequent to the date of the report on an audit of financial statements, as described in AU-C section 560. [Revised, December 2012, to reflect conforming changes necessary due to the issuance of SAS Nos. 122–126.]

Special Topics

Entities With Multiple Locations

.135 In determining the locations or business units at which to perform tests of controls, the auditor should assess the risk of material misstatement to the financial statements associated with the location or business unit and correlate the amount of attention devoted to the location or business unit with the degree of risk. The auditor may eliminate from further consideration locations or business units that, individually or when aggregated with others, do not present a reasonable possibility of material misstatement to the entity's consolidated financial statements.

.136 In assessing and responding to risk, the auditor should test controls over specific risks that present a reasonable possibility of material misstatement to the entity's consolidated financial statements. In lower risk locations or business units, the auditor first might evaluate whether testing entity-level controls, including controls in place to provide assurance that appropriate controls exist throughout the organization, provides the auditor with sufficient appropriate evidence.

.137 In determining the locations or business units at which to perform tests of controls, the auditor may take into account work performed by others on behalf of management. For example, if the internal auditors' planned procedures include relevant audit work at various locations, the auditor may coordinate work with the internal auditors and reduce the number of locations or business units at which the auditor would otherwise need to perform examination procedures.

.138 In applying the requirement in paragraph .81 regarding special considerations for subsequent years' examinations, the auditor should vary the nature, timing, and extent of testing of controls at locations or business units from year to year.

Special Situations

.139 The scope of the examination should include entities that are acquired on or before the date of management's assertion and operations that are accounted for as discontinued operations on the date of management's assertion that are reported in accordance with the applicable financial reporting framework in the entity's financial statements.

.140 For equity method investments, the scope of the examination should include controls over the reporting in accordance with the applicable financial reporting framework, in the entity's financial statements, of the entity's portion of the investees' income or loss, the investment balance, adjustments to the income or loss and investment balance, and related disclosures. The examination ordinarily would not extend to controls at the equity method investee.

.141 In situations in which a regulator allows management to limit its assertion by excluding certain entities, the auditor may limit the examination in the same manner. In these situations, the auditor's opinion would not be affected by a scope limitation. However, the auditor should include, either in an additional explanatory paragraph or as part of the scope paragraph in his or her report, a disclosure similar to management's regarding the exclusion of an entity from the scope of both management's assertion and the auditor's examination of internal control. Additionally, the auditor should evaluate the reasonableness of management's conclusion that the situation meets the criteria of the regulator's allowed exclusion and the appropriateness of any required disclosure related to such a limitation. If the auditor believes that management's disclosure about the limitation requires modification, the auditor should communicate the matter to the appropriate level of management. If, in the auditor's judgment, management does not respond appropriately to the auditor's communication within a reasonable period of time, the auditor should inform those charged with governance of the matter as soon as practicable. If management and those charged with governance do not respond appropriately, the auditor should modify his or her report on the examination of internal control to include an explanatory paragraph describing the reasons why the auditor believes management's disclosure requires modification.

Use of Service Organizations

.142 AU-C section 402 [37] addresses an auditor's responsibility for obtaining sufficient appropriate audit evidence in an audit of the financial statements of an entity that uses one or more service organizations (a user entity). Services provided by a service organization are relevant to the audit of a user entity's financial statements when those services and the controls over them affect the user entity's information system. The auditor may apply the relevant concepts described in AU-C section 402 to the examination of internal control. [Revised, December 2012, to reflect conforming changes necessary due to the issuance of SAS Nos. 122–126.]

.143 Paragraph .03 of AU-C section 402 identifies the situations in which a service organization's services and controls over them are part of a user entity's information system. If the service organization's services are part of the user entity's information system, as described therein, then they are part of the user entity's internal control. When the service organization's services are part of the user entity's internal control, the auditor should consider the activities of the service organization when determining the evidence required to support his or her opinion. [Revised, December 2012, to reflect conforming changes necessary due to the issuance of SAS Nos. 122–126.]

.144 The auditor should perform the procedures in paragraphs .09–.19 of AU-C section 402 with respect to the activities performed by the service organization. These procedures include

a. obtaining an understanding of the how the user entity uses the services of the service organization in its operations,

b. evaluating the design and implementation of relevant controls at the user entity that relate to the services provided by the service organization), and

c. obtaining evidence that controls at the service organization that are relevant to the auditor's opinion on internal control are operating effectively.

[Revised, December 2012, to reflect conforming changes necessary due to the issuance of SAS Nos. 122–126.]

.145 Evidence that the controls that are relevant to the auditor's opinion on internal control are operating effectively may be obtained by following the

[37] AU-C section 402, *Audit Considerations Relating to an Entity Using a Service Organization*, contains the requirements and application guidance for auditors of the financial statements of entities that use a service organization (user auditors). [Footnote added, August 2011, to reflect conforming changes necessary due to the issuance of SSAE No. 16. Footnote renumbered and revised, December 2012, to reflect conforming changes necessary due to the issuance of SAS Nos. 122–126.]

procedures described in paragraphs .16–.17 of AU-C section 402. These procedures include one or more of the following:

a. Obtaining and reading a service auditor's report on management's description of a service organization's system and the suitability of the design and operating effectiveness of controls, which includes a description of the service auditor's tests of controls and results (a type 2 report),[38] if available

b. Performing appropriate tests of controls at the service organization

c. Using another auditor to perform tests of controls at the service organization on behalf of the auditor

[Revised, August 2011, to reflect conforming changes necessary due to the issuance of SSAE No. 16. Revised, December 2012, to reflect conforming changes necessary due to the issuance of SAS Nos. 122–126.]

.146 If the auditor plans to use a type 2 report as audit evidence that controls are operating effectively, the auditor should determine whether the type 2 report provides sufficient appropriate audit evidence about the effectiveness of the controls to support his or her opinion on internal control by evaluating[39]

- the time period covered by the tests of controls and its relation to the as-of date of management's assertion.
- the scope of the services auditor's work and the services and processes covered, the controls tested, and the tests that were performed and the way in which tested controls relate to the entity's controls.
- the results of those tests of controls and the service auditor's opinion on the operating effectiveness of the controls.

[Revised, August 2011, to reflect conforming changes necessary due to the issuance of SSAE No. 16. Revised, December 2012, to reflect conforming changes necessary due to the issuance of SAS Nos. 122–126.]

.147 If the service auditor's type 2 report contains a statement indicating that the control objectives stated in the description can be achieved only if complementary user entity controls are suitably designed and operating effectively, along with the controls at the service organization, the auditor should determine whether the entity has designed and implemented such controls and, if so, should test their operating effectiveness. [Revised, August 2011, to reflect conforming changes necessary due to the issuance of SSAE No. 16. Revised, December 2012, to reflect conforming changes necessary due to the issuance of SAS Nos. 122–126.]

.148 In determining whether the type 2 service auditor's report provides sufficient appropriate evidence to support the auditor's opinion on internal control, the auditor should be satisfied regarding the following:

---

[38] A report on management's description of a service organization's system and the suitability of the design of controls (a type 1 report) does not include a description of the service auditor's tests of controls and results of those tests or the service auditor's opinion on the operating effectiveness of controls and therefore does not provide evidence of the operating effectiveness of controls. Type 1 and type 2 reports are defined in paragraph .07 of section 801, *Reporting on Controls at a Service Organization*. [Footnote revised and renumbered, August 2011, to reflect conforming changes necessary due to the issuance of SSAE No. 16. Footnote renumbered, December 2012, to reflect conforming changes necessary due to the issuance of SAS Nos. 122–126.]

[39] These factors are similar to factors the auditor would consider in determining whether the report provides sufficient appropriate evidence to support the auditor's assessed level of control risk in an audit of the financial statements, as described in paragraph .A32 of AU-C section 402. [Footnote renumbered, August 2011, to reflect conforming changes necessary due to the issuance of SSAE No. 16. Footnote renumbered and revised, December 2012, to reflect conforming changes necessary due to the issuance of SAS Nos. 122–126.]

- The service auditor's professional competence and independence from the service organization. Appropriate sources of information concerning the service auditor's professional competence and independence are discussed in paragraphs .A21–.A22 of AU-C section 402.
- The adequacy of the standards under which the type 2 report was issued.

[Revised, August 2011, to reflect conforming changes necessary due to the issuance of SSAE No. 16. Revised, December 2012, to reflect conforming changes necessary due to the issuance of SAS Nos. 122–126.]

.149 When a significant period of time has elapsed between the time period covered by the tests of controls in the service auditor's report and the date specified in management's assertion, additional procedures should be performed. The auditor should inquire of management to determine whether management has identified any changes in the service organization's controls subsequent to the period covered by the service auditor's report (such as changes communicated to management from the service organization, changes in personnel at the service organization with whom management interacts, changes in reports or other data received from the service organization, changes in contracts or service level agreements with the service organization, or errors identified in the service organization's processing). If management has identified such changes, the auditor should evaluate the effect of such changes on the effectiveness of the entity's internal control. The auditor also should evaluate whether the results of other procedures he or she performed indicate that there have been changes in the controls at the service organization.

.150 As risk increases, the need for the auditor to obtain additional evidence increases. Accordingly, the auditor should determine whether to obtain additional evidence about the operating effectiveness of controls at the service organization based on the procedures performed by management or the auditor and the results of those procedures and on an evaluation of the following risk factors:

- The elapsed time between the time period covered by the tests of controls in the service auditor's report and the date specified in management's assertion
- The significance of the activities of the service organization
- Whether there are errors that have been identified in the service organization's processing
- The nature and significance of any changes in the service organization's controls identified by management or the auditor

.151 If the auditor concludes that additional evidence about the operating effectiveness of controls at the service organization is required, the auditor's additional procedures might include

- evaluating procedures performed by management and the results of those procedures.
- contacting the service organization, through the user entity, to obtain specific information.
- requesting that a service auditor be engaged to perform procedures that will supply the necessary information.
- visiting the service organization and performing such procedures.

.152 The auditor should not refer to the service auditor's report when expressing an opinion on internal control.

Benchmarking of Automated Controls

.153 Entirely automated application controls are generally less susceptible to breakdowns due to human failure. This feature may allow the auditor to use a benchmarking strategy.

.154 If general controls over program changes, access to programs, and computer operations are effective and continue to be tested, and if the auditor verifies that the automated application control has not changed since the auditor established a baseline (that is, last tested the application control), the auditor may conclude that the automated application control continues to be effective without repeating the prior year's specific tests of the operation of the automated application control. The nature and extent of the evidence that the auditor should obtain to verify that the control has not changed may vary depending on the circumstances, including the strength of the entity's program change controls.

.155 The consistent and effective functioning of the automated application controls may be dependent upon the related files, tables, data, and parameters. For example, an automated application for calculating interest income might be dependent on the continued integrity of a rate table used by the automated calculation.

.156 To determine whether to use a benchmarking strategy, the auditor should assess the following risk factors. As these factors indicate lower risk, the control being evaluated might be well-suited for benchmarking. As these factors indicate increased risk, the control being evaluated is less suited for benchmarking. These factors are

- the extent to which the application control can be matched to a defined program within an application.
- the extent to which the application is stable (that is, there are few changes from period to period).
- the availability and reliability of a report of the compilation dates of the programs placed in production. (This information may be used as evidence that controls within the program have not changed.)

.157 Benchmarking automated application controls can be especially effective for entities using purchased software when the possibility of program changes is remote (for example, when the vendor does not allow access or modification to the source code).

.158 After a period of time, the length of which depends upon the circumstances, the baseline of the operation of an automated application control should be reestablished. To determine when to reestablish a baseline, the auditor should evaluate the following factors:

- The effectiveness of the IT control environment, including controls over application and system software acquisition and maintenance, access controls, and computer operations.
- The auditor's understanding of the nature of changes, if any, on the specific programs that contain the controls.
- The nature and timing of other related tests.
- The consequences of errors associated with the application control that was benchmarked.
- Whether the control is sensitive to other business factors that may have changed. For example, an automated control may have been

designed with the assumption that only positive amounts will exist in a file. Such a control would no longer be effective if negative amounts (credits) begin to be posted to the account.

Integration With the Financial Statement Audit

Tests of Controls in an Examination of Internal Control

.159 The objective of the tests of controls in an examination of internal control is to obtain evidence about the effectiveness of controls to support the auditor's opinion on the entity's internal control. The auditor's opinion relates to the effectiveness of the entity's internal control as of a point in time and taken as a whole.

.160 To express an opinion on internal control as of a point in time, the auditor should obtain evidence that internal control has operated effectively for a sufficient period of time, which may be less than the entire period (ordinarily one year) covered by the entity's financial statements. To express an opinion on internal control taken as a whole, the auditor should obtain evidence about the effectiveness of selected controls over all relevant assertions. This entails testing the design and operating effectiveness of controls ordinarily not tested when expressing an opinion only on the financial statements.

.161 When concluding on the effectiveness of internal control for purposes of expressing an opinion on internal control, the auditor should incorporate the results of any additional tests of controls performed to achieve the objective related to expressing an opinion on the financial statements, as discussed in the following section.

Tests of Controls in an Audit of Financial Statements

.162 To express an opinion on the financial statements, the auditor ordinarily performs tests of controls and substantive procedures. Tests of controls are performed when the auditor's risk assessment includes an expectation of the operating effectiveness of controls or when substantive procedures alone do not provide sufficient appropriate audit evidence at the relevant assertion level.[40] Tests of controls are designed to obtain sufficient appropriate audit evidence that the controls are operating effectively throughout the period of reliance.[41] However, the auditor is not required to test controls for all relevant assertions and, for a variety of reasons, the auditor may choose not to do so.

.163 When concluding on the effectiveness of controls for the purpose of the financial statement audit, the auditor also should evaluate the results of any additional tests of controls performed by the auditor to achieve the objective related to expressing an opinion on the entity's internal control, as discussed in paragraph .160. Consideration of these results may cause the auditor to alter the nature, timing, and extent of substantive procedures and to plan and perform further tests of controls, particularly in response to identified deficiencies.

---

[40] See paragraph .18 of AU-C section 330, *Performing Audit Procedures in Response to Assessed Risks and Evaluating the Audit Evidence Obtained*. [Footnote renumbered, August 2011, to reflect conforming changes necessary due to the issuance of SSAE No. 16. Footnote renumbered and revised, December 2012, to reflect conforming changes necessary due to the issuance of SAS Nos. 122–126.]

[41] See paragraph .A31 of AU-C section 330. [Footnote renumbered, August 2011, to reflect conforming changes necessary due to the issuance of SSAE No. 16. Footnote renumbered and revised, December 2012, to reflect conforming changes necessary due to the issuance of SAS Nos. 122–126.]

Effect of Tests of Controls on Substantive Procedures

.164 If, during the examination of internal control, the auditor identifies a deficiency, he or she should determine the effect of the deficiency, if any, on the nature, timing, and extent of substantive procedures to be performed to reduce audit risk in the audit of the financial statements to an appropriately low level.

.165 Regardless of the assessed risk of material misstatement in connection with the audit of the financial statements, the auditor should perform substantive procedures for all relevant assertions related to each material class of transactions, account balance, and disclosure.[42] Performing procedures to express an opinion on internal control does not diminish this requirement. [Footnote renumbered, August 2011, to reflect conforming changes necessary due to the issuance of SSAE No. 16.]

Effect of Substantive Procedures on Conclusions About the Operating Effectiveness of Controls

.166 In an examination of internal control, the auditor should evaluate the effect of the findings of the substantive procedures performed in the audit of financial statements on the effectiveness of internal control. This evaluation should include, at a minimum

- the risk assessments in connection with the selection and application of substantive procedures, especially those related to fraud.
- findings with respect to illegal acts and related party transactions.
- indications of management bias in making accounting estimates and in selecting accounting principles.
- misstatements detected by substantive procedures. The extent of such misstatements might alter the auditor's judgment about the effectiveness of controls.

.167 To obtain evidence about whether a selected control is effective, the control should be tested directly; the operating effectiveness of a control cannot be inferred from the absence of misstatements detected by substantive procedures. The absence of misstatements detected by substantive procedures, however, may affect the auditor's risk assessments in determining the testing necessary to conclude on the operating effectiveness of a control.

Effective Date

.168 This section is effective for integrated audits for periods ending on or after December 15, 2008. Earlier implementation is permitted.

---

[42] See paragraphs .18 and .A45 of AU-C section 330. [Footnote renumbered, August 2011, to reflect conforming changes necessary due to the issuance of SSAE No. 16. Footnote renumbered and revised, December 2012, to reflect conforming changes necessary due to the issuance of SAS Nos. 122–126.]

.169

Exhibit A—Illustrative Reports

1. The following illustrate the report elements described in this section. These illustrative reports refer to an examination; however, the auditor may refer to the examination of internal control as an audit.[1]

2. Report modifications are discussed beginning at paragraph .115 of this section.

Example 1: Unqualified Opinion on Internal Control

3. The following is an illustrative report expressing an unqualified opinion directly on internal control.

Independent Auditor's Report

[*Introductory paragraph*]

We have examined W Company's internal control over financial reporting as of December 31, 20XX, based on [*identify criteria*].[2] W Company's management is responsible for maintaining effective internal control over financial reporting, and for its assertion about the effectiveness of internal control over financial reporting, included in the accompanying [*title of management's report*]. Our responsibility is to express an opinion on W Company's internal control over financial reporting based on our examination.

[*Scope paragraph*]

We conducted our examination in accordance with attestation standards established by the American Institute of Certified Public Accountants. Those standards require that we plan and perform the examination to obtain reasonable assurance about whether effective internal control over financial reporting was maintained in all material respects. Our examination included obtaining an understanding of internal control over financial reporting, assessing the risk that a material weakness exists, and testing and evaluating the design and operating effectiveness of internal control based on the assessed risk. Our examination also included performing such other procedures as we considered necessary in the circumstances. We believe that our examination provides a reasonable basis for our opinion.

[*Definition paragraph*]

An entity's internal control over financial reporting is a process effected by those charged with governance, management, and other personnel, designed to provide reasonable assurance regarding the preparation of reliable financial statements in accordance with [*applicable financial reporting framework, such as accounting principles generally accepted in the United States of America*]. An entity's internal control over financial reporting includes those policies and procedures that (1) pertain to the maintenance of records that, in reasonable detail, accurately and fairly reflect the transactions and dispositions of the assets of the entity; (2) provide reasonable assurance that transactions are recorded as

---

[1] Because the examination of internal control is integrated with the audit of the financial statements and an examination provides the same level of assurance as an audit, the auditor may refer to the examination of internal control as an audit in his or her report or other communications.

[2] For example, the following may be used to identify the criteria: "criteria established in *Internal Control—Integrated Framework* issued by the Committee of Sponsoring Organizations of the Treadway Commission (COSO)."

necessary to permit preparation of financial statements in accordance with [*applicable financial reporting framework, such as accounting principles generally accepted in the United States of America*], and that receipts and expenditures of the entity are being made only in accordance with authorizations of management and those charged with governance; and (3) provide reasonable assurance regarding prevention, or timely detection and correction of unauthorized acquisition, use, or disposition of the entity's assets that could have a material effect on the financial statements.

[*Inherent limitations paragraph*]

Because of its inherent limitations, internal control over financial reporting may not prevent, or detect and correct misstatements. Also, projections of any evaluation of effectiveness to future periods are subject to the risk that controls may become inadequate because of changes in conditions, or that the degree of compliance with the policies or procedures may deteriorate.

[*Opinion paragraph*]

In our opinion, W Company maintained, in all material respects, effective internal control over financial reporting as of December 31, 20XX, based on [*identify criteria*].

[*Audit of financial statements paragraph*]

We also have audited, in accordance with auditing standards generally accepted in the United States of America, the [*identify financial statements*] of W Company and our report dated [*date of report, which should be the same as the date of the report on the examination of internal control*] expressed [*include nature of opinion*].

[*Signature*]

[*Date*]

Example 2: Unqualified Opinion on Management's Assertion

4. The following is an illustrative report expressing an unqualified opinion on management's assertion.

<u>Independent Auditor's Report</u>

[*Introductory paragraph*]

We have examined management's assertion, included in the accompanying [*title of management report*], that W Company maintained effective internal control over financial reporting as of December 31, 20XX based on [*identify criteria*].[3] W Company's management is responsible for maintaining effective internal control over financial reporting, and for its assertion about the effectiveness of internal control over financial reporting, included in the accompanying [*title of management's report*]. Our responsibility is to express an opinion on management's assertion based on our examination.

[*Scope paragraph*]

We conducted our examination in accordance with attestation standards established by the American Institute of Certified Public Accountants. Those standards require that we plan and perform the examination to obtain reasonable

---

[3] See footnote 2 of this exhibit.

assurance about whether effective internal control over financial reporting was maintained in all material respects. Our examination included obtaining an understanding of internal control over financial reporting, assessing the risk that a material weakness exists, and testing and evaluating the design and operating effectiveness of internal control based on the assessed risk. Our examination also included performing such other procedures as we considered necessary in the circumstances. We believe that our examination provides a reasonable basis for our opinion.

[*Definition paragraph*]

An entity's internal control over financial reporting is a process effected by those charged with governance, management, and other personnel, designed to provide reasonable assurance regarding the preparation of reliable financial statements in accordance with [*applicable financial reporting framework, such as accounting principles generally accepted in the United States of America*]. An entity's internal control over financial reporting includes those policies and procedures that (1) pertain to the maintenance of records that, in reasonable detail, accurately and fairly reflect the transactions and dispositions of the assets of the entity; (2) provide reasonable assurance that transactions are recorded as necessary to permit preparation of financial statements in accordance with [*applicable financial reporting framework, such as accounting principles generally accepted in the United States of America*], and that receipts and expenditures of the entity are being made only in accordance with authorizations of management and those charged with governance; and (3) provide reasonable assurance regarding prevention, or timely detection and correction of unauthorized acquisition, use, or disposition of the entity's assets that could have a material effect on the financial statements.

[*Inherent limitations paragraph*]

Because of its inherent limitations, internal control over financial reporting may not prevent, or detect and correct misstatements. Also, projections of any evaluation of effectiveness to future periods are subject to the risk that controls may become inadequate because of changes in conditions, or that the degree of compliance with the policies or procedures may deteriorate.

[*Opinion paragraph*]

In our opinion, management's assertion that W Company maintained effective internal control over financial reporting as of December 31, 20XX is fairly stated, in all material respects, based on [*identify criteria*].

[*Audit of financial statements paragraph*]

We also have audited, in accordance with auditing standards generally accepted in the United States of America, the [*identify financial statements*] of W Company and our report dated [*date of report, which should be the same as the date of the report on the examination of internal control*] expressed [*include nature of opinion*].

[*Signature*]

[*Date*]

Example 3: Adverse Opinion on Internal Control

5. The following is an illustrative report expressing an adverse opinion on internal control. In this example, the opinion on the financial statements is not affected by the adverse opinion on internal control.

Independent Auditor's Report

[*Introductory paragraph*]

We have examined W Company's internal control over financial reporting as of December 31, 20XX, based on [*identify criteria*].[4] W Company's management is responsible for maintaining effective internal control over financial reporting, and for its assertion about the effectiveness of internal control over financial reporting, included in the accompanying [*title of management's report*]. Our responsibility is to express an opinion on W Company's internal control over financial reporting based on our examination.

[*Scope paragraph*]

We conducted our examination in accordance with attestation standards established by the American Institute of Certified Public Accountants. Those standards require that we plan and perform the examination to obtain reasonable assurance about whether effective internal control over financial reporting was maintained in all material respects. Our examination included obtaining an understanding of internal control over financial reporting, assessing the risk that a material weakness exists, and testing and evaluating the design and operating effectiveness of internal control based on the assessed risk. Our examination also included performing such other procedures as we considered necessary in the circumstances. We believe that our examination provides a reasonable basis for our opinion.

[*Definition paragraph*]

An entity's internal control over financial reporting is a process effected by those charged with governance, management, and other personnel, designed to provide reasonable assurance regarding the preparation of reliable financial statements in accordance with [*applicable financial reporting framework, such as accounting principles generally accepted in the United States of America*]. An entity's internal control over financial reporting includes those policies and procedures that (1) pertain to the maintenance of records that, in reasonable detail, accurately and fairly reflect the transactions and dispositions of the assets of the entity; (2) provide reasonable assurance that transactions are recorded as necessary to permit preparation of financial statements in accordance with [*applicable financial reporting framework, such as accounting principles generally accepted in the United States of America*], and that receipts and expenditures of the entity are being made only in accordance with authorizations of management and those charged with governance; and (3) provide reasonable assurance regarding prevention, or timely detection and correction of unauthorized acquisition, use, or disposition of the entity's assets that could have a material effect on the financial statements.

[*Inherent limitations paragraph*]

Because of its inherent limitations, internal control over financial reporting may not prevent, or detect and correct misstatements. Also, projections of any evaluation of effectiveness to future periods are subject to the risk that controls may become inadequate because of changes in conditions, or that the degree of compliance with the policies or procedures may deteriorate.

[*Explanatory paragraph*]

A material weakness is a deficiency, or a combination of deficiencies, in internal control over financial reporting, such that there is a reasonable possibility

---

[4] See footnote 2 of this exhibit.

that a material misstatement of the entity's financial statements will not be prevented, or detected and corrected on a timely basis. The following material weakness has been identified and included in the accompanying [*title of management's report*].

[*Identify the material weakness described in management's report.*][5]

[*Opinion paragraph*]

In our opinion, because of the effect of the material weakness described above on the achievement of the objectives of the control criteria, W Company has not maintained effective internal control over financial reporting as of December 31, 20XX, based on [*identify criteria*].

[*Audit of financial statements paragraph*]

We also have audited, in accordance with auditing standards generally accepted in the United States of America, the [*identify financial statements*] of W Company. We considered the material weakness identified above in determining the nature, timing, and extent of audit tests applied in our audit of the 20XX financial statements, and this report does not affect our report dated [*date of report, which should be the same as the date of the report on the examination of internal control*], which expressed [*include nature of opinion*].

[*Signature*]

[*Date*]

Example 4: Disclaimer of Opinion on Internal Control

6. The following is an illustrative report expressing a disclaimer of opinion on internal control. In this example, the auditor is applying paragraph .119 of this section because a material weakness was identified during the limited procedures performed by the auditor.

Independent Auditor's Report

[*Introductory paragraph*]

We were engaged to examine W Company's internal control over financial reporting as of December 31, 20XX, based on [*identify criteria*].[6] W Company's management is responsible for maintaining effective internal control over financial reporting, and for its assertion about the effectiveness of internal control over financial reporting, included in the accompanying [*title of management's report*].

[*Paragraph that describes the substantive reasons for the scope limitation*] Accordingly, we were unable to perform auditing procedures necessary to form an opinion on W Company's internal control over financial reporting as of December 31, 20XX.

[*Definition paragraph*]

An entity's internal control over financial reporting is a process effected by those charged with governance, management, and other personnel, designed

---

[5] See paragraphs .111–.114 of this section for specific reporting requirements. The auditor's report need only refer to the material weaknesses described in management's report and need not include a description of each material weakness, provided each material weakness is included and fairly presented in all material respects in management's report.

[6] See footnote 2 of this exhibit.

to provide reasonable assurance regarding the preparation of reliable financial statements in accordance with [*applicable financial reporting framework, such as accounting principles generally accepted in the United States of America*]. An entity's internal control over financial reporting includes those policies and procedures that (1) pertain to the maintenance of records that, in reasonable detail, accurately and fairly reflect the transactions and dispositions of the assets of the entity; (2) provide reasonable assurance that transactions are recorded as necessary to permit preparation of financial statements in accordance with [*applicable financial reporting framework, such as accounting principles generally accepted in the United States of America*], and that receipts and expenditures of the entity are being made only in accordance with authorizations of management and those charged with governance; and (3) provide reasonable assurance regarding prevention, or timely detection and correction of unauthorized acquisition, use, or disposition of the entity's assets that could have a material effect on the financial statements.

[*Inherent limitations paragraph*]

Because of its inherent limitations, internal control over financial reporting may not prevent, or detect and correct misstatements. Also, projections of any evaluation of effectiveness to future periods are subject to the risk that controls may become inadequate because of changes in conditions, or that the degree of compliance with the policies or procedures may deteriorate.

[*Explanatory paragraph*]

A material weakness is a deficiency, or a combination of deficiencies, in internal control over financial reporting, such that there is a reasonable possibility that a material misstatement of the entity's financial statements will not be prevented, or detected and corrected on a timely basis. If one or more material weaknesses exist, an entity's internal control over financial reporting cannot be considered effective. The following material weakness has been identified and included in the accompanying [*title of management's report*].

[*Identify the material weakness described in management's report and include a description of the material weakness, including its nature and its actual and potential effect on the presentation of the entity's financial statements issued during the existence of the material weakness.*]

[*Opinion paragraph*]

Because of the limitation on the scope of our audit described in the second paragraph, the scope of our work was not sufficient to enable us to express, and we do not express, an opinion on the effectiveness W Company's internal control over financial reporting.

[*Audit of financial statements paragraph*]

We have audited, in accordance with auditing standards generally accepted in the United States of America, the [*identify financial statements*] of W Company and our report dated [*date of report*] expressed [*include nature of opinion*]. We considered the material weakness identified above in determining the nature, timing, and extent of audit tests applied in our audit of the 20XX financial statements, and this report does not affect such report on the financial statements.

[*Signature*]

[*Date*]

Example 5: Unqualified Opinion on Internal Control Based, in Part, on the Report of Another Auditor

7. The following is an illustrative report expressing an unqualified opinion on internal control when the auditor decides to refer to the report of another auditor as the basis, in part, for the auditor's own report.

Independent Auditor's Report

[*Introductory paragraph*]

We have examined W Company's internal control over financial reporting as of December 31, 20XX, based on [*identify criteria*].[7] W Company's management is responsible for maintaining effective internal control over financial reporting, and for its assertion about the effectiveness of internal control over financial reporting, included in the accompanying [*title of management's report*]. Our responsibility is to express an opinion on W Company's internal control over financial reporting based on our examination. We did not examine the effectiveness of internal control over financial reporting of B Company, a wholly owned subsidiary, whose financial statements reflect total assets and revenues constituting 20 percent and 30 percent, respectively, of the related consolidated financial statement amounts as of and for the year ended December 31, 20XX. The effectiveness of B Company's internal control over financial reporting was examined by other auditors whose report has been furnished to us, and our opinion, insofar as it relates to the effectiveness of B Company's internal control over financial reporting, is based solely on the report of the other auditors.

[*Scope paragraph*]

We conducted our examination in accordance with attestation standards established by the American Institute of Certified Public Accountants. Those standards require that we plan and perform the examination to obtain reasonable assurance about whether effective internal control over financial reporting was maintained in all material respects. Our examination included obtaining an understanding of internal control over financial reporting, assessing the risk that a material weakness exists, and testing and evaluating the design and operating effectiveness of internal control based on the assessed risk. Our examination also included performing such other procedures as we considered necessary in the circumstances. We believe that our examination and the report of the other auditors provide a reasonable basis for our opinion.

[*Definition paragraph*]

An entity's internal control over financial reporting is a process effected by those charged with governance, management, and other personnel, designed to provide reasonable assurance regarding the preparation of reliable financial statements in accordance with [*applicable financial reporting framework, such as accounting principles generally accepted in the United States of America*]. An entity's internal control over financial reporting includes those policies and procedures that (1) pertain to the maintenance of records that, in reasonable detail, accurately and fairly reflect the transactions and dispositions of the assets of the entity; (2) provide reasonable assurance that transactions are recorded as necessary to permit preparation of financial statements in accordance with [*applicable financial reporting framework, such as accounting principles generally accepted in the United States of America*], and that receipts and expenditures of the entity are being made only in accordance with authorizations of management and those charged with governance; and (3) provide reasonable assurance

---

[7] See footnote 2 of this exhibit.

regarding prevention, or timely detection and correction of unauthorized acquisition, use, or disposition of the entity's assets that could have a material effect on the financial statements.

[*Inherent limitations paragraph*]

Because of its inherent limitations, internal control over financial reporting may not prevent, or detect and correct misstatements. Also, projections of any evaluation of effectiveness to future periods are subject to the risk that controls may become inadequate because of changes in conditions, or that the degree of compliance with the policies or procedures may deteriorate.

[*Opinion paragraph*]

In our opinion, based on our examination and the report of the other auditors, W Company maintained, in all material respects, effective internal control over financial reporting as of December 31, 20XX, based on [*identify criteria*].[8]

[*Audit of financial statements paragraph*]

We also have audited, in accordance with auditing standards generally accepted in the United States of America, the [*identify financial statements*] of W Company and our report dated [*date of report, which should be the same as the date of the report on the examination of internal control*] expressed [*include nature of opinion*].

[*Signature*]

[*Date*]

Example 6: Combined Report Expressing an Unqualified Opinion on Internal Control and an Unmodified Opinion on the Financial Statements

8. The following is an illustrative combined report expressing an unqualified opinion directly on internal control and an unmodified opinion on the financial statements. This report refers to the examination of internal control as an audit.[9]

<u>Independent Auditor's Report</u>

[*Appropriate Addressee*]

We have audited the financial statements of W Company, which comprise the balance sheet as of December 31, 20XX, and the related statements of income, changes in stockholder's equity, and cash flows for the year then ended, and the related notes to the financial statements. We also have audited W Company's internal control over financial reporting as of December 31, 20XX, based on [*identify criteria*].[10]

Management's Responsibility

W. Company's management is responsible for the preparation and fair presentation of these financial statements in accordance with accounting principles generally accepted in the United States of America, for maintaining internal control over financial reporting including the design, implementation, and maintenance of controls relevant to the preparation and fair presentation of these financial statements that are free from material misstatement, whether

---

[8] As discussed in paragraph .125 of this section, whether the other auditor's opinion is expressed on management's assertion or on internal control does not affect the determination of whether the principal auditor's opinion is expressed on management's assertion or on internal control.

[9] See footnote 1 of this exhibit.

[10] See footnote 2 of this exhibit.

due to error of fraud, and for its assertion about the effectiveness of internal control over financial reporting, included in the accompanying [*title of management's report*].

Auditor's Responsibility

Our responsibility is to express an opinion on these financial statements and an opinion on W Company's internal control over financial reporting based on our audits. We conducted our audit of the financial statements in accordance with auditing standards generally accepted in the United States of America and our audit of internal control over financial reporting in accordance with attestation standards established by the American Institute of Certified Public Accountants. Those standards require that we plan and perform the audits to obtain reasonable assurance about whether the financial statements are free of material misstatement and whether effective internal control over financial reporting was maintained in all material respects.

An audit of financial statements involves performing procedures to obtain audit evidence about the amounts and disclosures in the financial statements. The procedures selected depend on the auditor's judgment, including assessment of the risks of material misstatement of the financial statements, whether due to fraud or error. In making those risk assessments, the auditor considers internal control relevant to the entity's preparation and fair presentation of the financial statements in order to design audit procedures that are appropriate in the circumstances. An audit of internal control over financial reporting involves obtaining an understanding of internal control over financial reporting, assessing the risk that a material weakness exists, and testing and evaluating the design and operating effectiveness of internal control based on the assessed risk. Our audits also included performing such other procedures as we considered necessary in the circumstances.

We believe that the audit evidence we obtained is sufficient and appropriate to provide a basis for our audit opinions.

Definitions and Inherent Limitations of Internal Control

An entity's internal control over financial reporting is a process effected by those charged with governance, management, and other personnel, designed to provide reasonable assurance regarding the preparation of reliable financial statements in accordance with [*applicable financial reporting framework, such as accounting principles generally accepted in the United States of America*]. An entity's internal control over financial reporting includes those policies and procedures that (1) pertain to the maintenance of records that, in reasonable detail, accurately and fairly reflect the transactions and dispositions of the assets of the entity; (2) provide reasonable assurance that transactions are recorded as necessary to permit preparation of financial statements in accordance with [*applicable financial reporting framework, such as accounting principles generally accepted in the United States of America*], and that receipts and expenditures of the entity are being made only in accordance with authorizations of management and those charged with governance; and (3) provide reasonable assurance regarding prevention, or timely detection and correction of unauthorized acquisition, use, or disposition of the entity's assets that could have a material effect on the financial statements.

Because of its inherent limitations, internal control over financial reporting may not prevent, or detect and correct misstatements. Also, projections of any evaluation of effectiveness to future periods are subject to the risk that controls may become inadequate because of changes in conditions, or that the degree of compliance with the policies or procedures may deteriorate.

Opinion

In our opinion, the financial statements referred to above present fairly, in all material respects, the financial position of W Company as of December 31, 20XX, and the results of its operations and its cash flows for the year then ended in accordance with accounting principles generally accepted in the United States of America. Also in our opinion, W Company maintained, in all material respects, effective internal control over financial reporting as of December 31, 20XX, based on [*identify criteria*].

[*Auditor's signature*]

[*Auditor's city and state*]

[*Date of the auditor's report*]

[Revised, December 2012, to reflect conforming changes necessary due to the issuance of SAS Nos. 122–126.]

.170

Exhibit B—Illustrative Communication of Significant Deficiencies and Material Weaknesses

1. The following is an illustrative written communication of significant deficiencies and material weaknesses.

In connection with our audit of W Company's (the "Company") financial statements as of December 31, 20XX and for the year then ended, and our audit of the Company's internal control over financial reporting as of December 31, 20XX ("integrated audit"), the standards established by the American Institute of Certified Public Accountants require that we advise you of the following internal control matters identified during our integrated audit.

Our responsibility is to plan and perform our integrated audit to obtain reasonable assurance about whether the financial statements are free of material misstatement, whether caused by error or fraud, and whether effective internal control over financial reporting was maintained in all material respects (that is, whether material weaknesses exist as of the date specified in management's assertion). The integrated audit is not designed to detect deficiencies that, individually or in combination, are less severe than a material weakness. However, we are responsible for communicating to management and those charged with governance significant deficiencies and material weaknesses identified during the integrated audit. We are also responsible for communicating to management deficiencies that are of a lesser magnitude than a significant deficiency, unless previously communicated, and inform those charged with governance when such a communication was made.

A deficiency in internal control over financial reporting exists when the design or operation of a control does not allow management or employees, in the normal course of performing their assigned functions, to prevent, or detect and correct misstatements on a timely basis. [*A material weakness is a deficiency, or a combination of deficiencies, in internal control over financial reporting, such that there is a reasonable possibility that a material misstatement of the Company's financial statements will not be prevented, or detected and corrected on a timely basis. We believe the following deficiencies constitute material weaknesses:*]

[*Describe the material weaknesses that were identified during the integrated audit. The auditor may separately identify those material weaknesses that exist as of the date of management's assertion by referring to the auditor's report.*]

[*A significant deficiency is a deficiency, or a combination of deficiencies, in internal control over financial reporting that is less severe than a material weakness, yet important enough to merit attention by those charged with governance. We consider the following deficiencies to be significant deficiencies:*]

[*Describe the significant deficiencies that were identified during the integrated audit.*]

This communication is intended solely for the information and use of management, [*identify the body or individuals charged with governance*], others within the organization, and [*identify any specified governmental authorities*] and is not intended to be and should not be used by anyone other than these specified parties.

.171

Exhibit C—Reporting Under Section 112 of the Federal Deposit Insurance Corporation Improvement Act (FDICIA)

1. In Financial Institution Letter (FIL) 86-94, *Additional Guidance Concerning Annual Audits, Audit Committees and Reporting Requirements*, issued December 23, 1994, the Federal Deposit Insurance Corporation (FDIC) provided guidance on the meaning of the term *financial reporting* for purposes of compliance by insured depository institutions (IDIs) with Section 112 of the Federal Deposit Insurance Corporation Improvement Act (FDICIA) (Section 36 of the Federal Deposit Insurance Act, 12.U.S.C. 1831m), and its implementing regulation, 12 CFR Part 363. The FDIC indicated that financial reporting, at a minimum, includes financial statements prepared in accordance with generally accepted accounting principles (GAAP) and the schedules equivalent to the basic financial statements that are included in the IDI's appropriate regulatory report (for example, Schedules RC, RI, and RI-A in the Consolidated Reports of Condition and Income [Call Report]). Accordingly, to comply with FDICIA and Part 363, management of the IDI (or a parent holding company)[1] and the auditor should identify and test controls over the preparation of GAAP-based financial statements as well as the schedules equivalent to the basic financial statements that are included in the IDI's (or its holding company's) appropriate regulatory report. Further, both management and the auditor should include in their report on the IDI's (or its holding company's) internal control a specific description indicating that the scope of internal control included controls over the preparation of the IDI's (or its holding company's) GAAP-based financial statements as well as the schedules equivalent to the basic financial statements that are included in the IDI's (or its holding company's) appropriate regulatory report.

2. In accordance with paragraph .107 of this section, the auditor's report should include a definition of internal control (the auditor should use the same description of the entity's internal control as management uses in its report). The following is an illustrative definition paragraph that may be used when an IDI that is a bank (which is not subject to Section 404 of the Sarbanes-Oxley Act of 2002) elects to report on controls for FDICIA purposes at the bank holding company level:

> An entity's internal control over financial reporting is a process effected by those charged with governance, management, and other personnel, designed to provide reasonable assurance regarding the preparation of reliable financial statements in accordance with accounting principles generally accepted in the United States of America. Because management's assessment and our examination were conducted to meet the reporting requirements of Section 112 of the Federal Deposit Insurance Corporation Improvement Act (FDICIA), our examination of [*Holding Company's*] internal control over financial reporting included controls over the preparation of financial statements in accordance with accounting principles generally accepted in the United States of America and with the instructions to the Consolidated Financial Statements for Bank

---

[1] See Financial Institution Letter (FIL) 86-94 for further discussion of reporting at the holding company level for Federal Deposit Insurance Corporation Improvement Act purposes and the application of holding company reporting as it relates to controls over the preparation of "regulatory reports."

Holding Companies (Form FR Y-9C).[2] An entity's internal control over financial reporting includes those policies and procedures that (1) pertain to the maintenance of records that, in reasonable detail, accurately and fairly reflect the transactions and dispositions of the assets of the entity; (2) provide reasonable assurance that transactions are recorded as necessary to permit preparation of financial statements in accordance with accounting principles generally accepted in the United States of America, and that receipts and expenditures of the entity are being made only in accordance with authorizations of management and those charged with governance; and (3) provide reasonable assurance regarding prevention, or timely detection and correction of unauthorized acquisition, use, or disposition of the entity's assets that could have a material effect on the financial statements.

[2] This sentence would be modified if the insured depository institution (IDI) reports at the institution level rather than at the bank holding company level to refer to the Federal Financial Institutions Examination Council Instructions for Consolidated Reports of Condition and Income or the Office of Thrift Supervision Instructions for Thrift Financial Reports instead of to the Form FR Y-9C. This sentence would also be modified if the IDI reports at a holding company level and employs another approach to reporting on controls over the preparation of regulatory reports as permitted by FIL 86-94.

.172

Exhibit D—Illustrative Management Report

1. The following is an illustrative management report containing the reporting elements described in paragraph .95 of this section:

Management's Report on Internal Control Over Financial Reporting

W Company's internal control over financial reporting is a process effected by those charged with governance, management, and other personnel, designed to provide reasonable assurance regarding the preparation of reliable financial statements in accordance with [*applicable financial reporting framework, such as accounting principles generally accepted in the United States of America*]. An entity's internal control over financial reporting includes those policies and procedures that (1) pertain to the maintenance of records that, in reasonable detail, accurately and fairly reflect the transactions and dispositions of the assets of the entity; (2) provide reasonable assurance that transactions are recorded as necessary to permit preparation of financial statements in accordance with [*applicable financial reporting framework, such as accounting principles generally accepted in the United States of America*], and that receipts and expenditures of the entity are being made only in accordance with authorizations of management and those charged with governance; and (3) provide reasonable assurance regarding prevention, or timely detection and correction of unauthorized acquisition, use, or disposition of the entity's assets that could have a material effect on the financial statements.

Management is responsible for establishing and maintaining effective internal control over financial reporting. Management assessed the effectiveness of W Company's internal control over financial reporting as of December 31, 20XX, based on the framework set forth by the Committee of Sponsoring Organizations of the Treadway Commission in *Internal Control—Integrated Framework*. Based on that assessment, management concluded that, as of December 31, 20XX, W Company's internal control over financial reporting is effective based on the criteria established in *Internal Control—Integrated Framework*.

W Company

Report signers, if applicable

Date

AT Section 9501

An Examination of an Entity's Internal Control Over Financial Reporting That Is Integrated With an Audit of Its Financial Statements: Attest Engagements Interpretations of Section 501

1. Reporting Under Section 112 of the Federal Deposit Insurance Corporation Improvement Act

.01 *Question*—For purposes of compliance by insured depository institutions (IDIs) with Section 112 of the Federal Deposit Insurance Corporation Improvement Act (FDICIA) (Section 36, Independent Annual Audits of Insured Depository Institutions, of the Federal Deposit Insurance Act [*Banks and Banking, U.S. Code* Title 12, Section 1831m]) and its implementing regulation, Title 12 U.S. *Code of Federal Regulations* (CFR) Part 363, an IDI that is a subsidiary of a holding company may use the consolidated holding company's financial statements to satisfy the audited financial statements requirement of 12 CFR 363, provided certain criteria are met.[1] For some IDIs, however, an examination of internal control over financial reporting is required at the IDI level. Paragraph .18 of section 501, *An Examination of an Entity's Internal Control Over Financial Reporting That Is Integrated With an Audit of Its Financial Statements*, requires that an examination of internal control over financial reporting (internal control) be integrated with an audit of financial statements. For IDIs that require an examination of internal control at the IDI level, can the auditor meet the integrated audit requirement when the IDI does not prepare financial statements for external distribution? If so, how can the auditor report on the effectiveness of the IDI's internal control over financial reporting?

.02 *Interpretation*—To comply with the integrated audit requirement in section 501, when the IDI uses the consolidated holding company's financial statements to satisfy the audited financial statements requirement of 12 CFR 363, the auditor would be required to perform procedures necessary to obtain sufficient appropriate audit evidence to enable the auditor to express an opinion on the IDI's financial statements and on its internal control over financial reporting. When the IDI does not prepare financial statements for external distribution, "financial statements" for this purpose may consist of the IDI's financial information in a reporting package or equivalent schedules and analyses that include the IDI information necessary for the preparation of the holding company's consolidated financial statements, including disclosures. The measurement of materiality is determined based on the IDI's financial information rather than the consolidated holding company's financial statements.[2] If the

---

[1] Refer to Section 36 of the Federal Deposit Insurance Act (FDI Act), Section 363.1: Scope and Definitions, for the requirements pertaining to compliance by subsidiaries of holding companies.

[2] See paragraph .10 of AU-C section 320, *Materiality in Planning and Performing an Audit*. [Footnote revised, December 2012, to reflect conforming changes necessary due to the issuance of SAS Nos. 122–126.]

auditor is unable to apply the procedures necessary to obtain sufficient appropriate audit evidence with respect to the IDI's financial information, the auditor is required by paragraph .117 of section 501 to withdraw from the engagement or disclaim an opinion on the effectiveness of the IDI's internal control over financial reporting.

.03 As indicated in exhibit C, "Reporting Under Section 112 of the Federal Deposit Insurance Corporation Improvement Act (FDICIA)," of section 501, the FDIC indicated that financial reporting, at a minimum, includes financial statements prepared in accordance with generally accepted accounting principles (GAAP) and the schedules equivalent to the basic financial statements that are included in the IDI's appropriate regulatory report (for example, Schedules RC, RI, and RI-A in the Consolidated Reports of Condition and Income [call report]). When the IDI does not prepare financial statements for external distribution, the auditor is, nevertheless, required by paragraph .41 of section 501 to evaluate the IDI's period-end financial reporting process. This process includes, among other things, the IDI's procedures for preparing financial information for purposes of the consolidated holding company's financial statements, which are prepared in accordance with GAAP, and the schedules equivalent to the basic financial statements that are included in the IDI's appropriate regulatory report.

.04 The period-end financial reporting process may occur either at the IDI or the holding company, or both. The organizational structure, including where the controls relevant to the IDI's financial information operate, may affect how the auditor evaluates this process. For example,

a. when the period-end financial reporting process occurs at the holding company and the IDI comprises substantially all of the consolidated total assets, there may be no distinguishable difference between the IDI's and its holding company's process for purposes of the integrated audit. This is because the auditor's risk assessment, including the determination of significant accounts and disclosures and relevant assertions, the selection of controls to test, and the determination of the evidence necessary to conclude on the effectiveness of a given control, would likely be the same for the IDI and the holding company.[3] In this circumstance, the period-end financial reporting process of the holding company would be, in effect, the period-end financial reporting process of the IDI and, therefore, would be included in the scope of the integrated audit of the IDI.

b. when the period-end financial reporting process occurs at the holding company and the IDI does not comprise substantially all of the consolidated total assets, the IDI's financial reporting process may be sufficient for the auditor to meet the requirement in paragraph .41 of section 501, if the necessary GAAP information is prepared by the IDI or the holding company, and the process can be evaluated by the auditor. The auditor may determine that the IDI's preparation of the IDI's appropriate regulatory report, together with other financial information at the IDI level that is incorporated into the consolidated holding company's financial statements, is sufficient for this purpose. In this circumstance, both the period-end financial reporting process of the holding company, as it relates to the financial information of the IDI, and the period-end financial reporting process of the IDI, with respect to the preparation of the schedules equivalent to the basic financial statements that are

[3] See paragraph .23 of section 501, *An Examination of an Entity's Internal Control Over Financial Reporting That Is Integrated With an Audit of Its Financial Statements.*

included in the IDI's appropriate regulatory report, would be included in the scope of the integrated audit of the IDI.

.05 The illustrative reports in exhibit A, "Illustrative Reports," of section 501 may be used to report on the effectiveness of the IDI's internal control over financial reporting. Because 12 CFR 363 does not require the auditor to issue a separate auditor's report on the IDI's financial statements, the requirement in paragraph .109 of section 501 to add a paragraph to the internal control report that references the financial statement audit will not apply when the auditor does not issue a separate auditor's report on the IDI's financial statements. In accordance with paragraph .107 of section 501, the auditor's report on internal control is required to include a definition of *internal control* that uses the same description of internal control as management uses in its report. The following is an illustrative definition paragraph that may be used when an IDI that is not subject to Section 404 of the Sarbanes-Oxley Act of 2002 elects to report on controls for FDICIA purposes at the IDI level, and the IDI uses the consolidated holding company's financial statements to satisfy the audited financial statements requirement of 12 CFR 363:

> An entity's internal control over financial reporting is a process effected by those charged with governance, management, and other personnel, designed to provide reasonable assurance regarding the preparation of reliable financial statements in accordance with generally accepted accounting principles. Because management's assessment and our examination were conducted to meet the reporting requirements of Section 112 of the Federal Deposit Insurance Corporation Improvement Act (FDICIA), our examination of [*IDI's*] internal control over financial reporting included controls over the preparation of financial information for purposes of [*consolidated holding company's*] financial statements in accordance with accounting principles generally accepted in the United States of America and controls over the preparation of schedules equivalent to basic financial statements in accordance with the Federal Financial Institutions Examination Council Instructions for Consolidated Reports of Condition and Income (call report instructions). An entity's internal control over financial reporting includes those policies and procedures that (1) pertain to the maintenance of records that, in reasonable detail, accurately and fairly reflect the transactions and dispositions of the assets of the entity; (2) provide reasonable assurance that transactions are recorded as necessary to permit preparation of financial statements in accordance with generally accepted accounting principles, and that receipts and expenditures of the entity are being made only in accordance with authorizations of management and those charged with governance; and (3) provide reasonable assurance regarding prevention, or timely detection and correction of unauthorized acquisition, use, or disposition of the entity's assets that could have a material effect on the financial statements.

.06 Management may evaluate and report on the effectiveness of the IDI's internal control based on the Committee of Sponsoring Organizations of the Treadway Commission's (COSO) report, *Internal Control—Integrated Framework*. Because COSO establishes control objectives relating to the preparation of reliable "published" financial statements, the COSO criteria, as modified for purposes of reporting under Section 112 of FDICIA, is appropriate only for the IDI and its regulatory agencies. Accordingly, the report is required to be restricted as to use.[4] An example of such a restriction is as follows:

---

[4] Paragraph .78 of section 101, *Attest Engagements*, requires the report to be restricted as to use "when the criteria used to evaluate the subject matter are determined by the practitioner to be appropriate only for a limited number of parties who either participated in their establishment or can

(continued)

.07 Likewise, the auditor's report and management's assertion refer to the modified COSO criteria. For example, the following may be used to identify the criteria: "criteria established in *Internal Control—Integrated Framework* issued by the Committee of Sponsoring Organizations of the Treadway Commission (COSO) as modified for the express purpose of meeting the regulatory requirements of Section 112 of the Federal Deposit Insurance Corporation Improvement Act (FDICIA)."

[Issue Date: September 2010.]

(footnote continued)

be presumed to have an adequate understanding of the criteria." Although reports on internal control issued in accordance with this interpretation are required to be restricted as to use, Section 36 of the FDI Act and Title 12 U.S. *Code of Federal Regulations* Part 363 require that these reports be available for public inspection.

AT Section 601

Compliance Attestation

Source: SSAE No. 10.

Effective when the subject matter or assertion is as of or for a period ending on or after June 1, 2001. Earlier application is permitted.

Introduction and Applicability

.01 This section provides guidance for engagements related to either (*a*) an entity's compliance with requirements of specified laws, regulations, rules, contracts, or grants or (*b*) the effectiveness of an entity's internal control over compliance with specified requirements.[1] Compliance requirements may be either financial or nonfinancial in nature. An attest engagement conducted in accordance with this section should comply with the general, fieldwork, and reporting standards established in section 50, *SSAE Hierarchy*, and the specific standards set forth in this section. [Revised, November 2006, to reflect conforming changes necessary due to the issuance of SSAE No. 14.]

.02 This section does not—

a. Affect the auditor's responsibility in an audit of financial statements performed in accordance with generally accepted auditing standards (GAAS).

b. Apply to situations in which an auditor reports on specified compliance requirements based solely on an audit of financial statements, as addressed in AU-C section 806, *Reporting on Compliance With Aspects of Contractual Agreements or Regulatory Requirements in Connection With Audited Financial Statements*.

c. Apply to engagements for which the objective is to report in accordance with AU-C section 935, *Compliance Audits*, unless the terms of the engagement specify an attest report under this section.

d. Apply to engagements covered by AU-C section 920, *Letters for Underwriters and Certain Other Requesting Parties*.

e. Apply to the report that encompasses internal control over compliance for a broker or dealer in securities as required by rule 17a-5 of the Securities Exchange Act of 1934 (the 1934 Act).[2]

[Revised, December 2010, to reflect conforming changes necessary due to the issuance of SAS No. 117. Revised, December 2012, to reflect conforming changes necessary due to the issuance of SAS Nos. 122–126.]

---

[1] Throughout this section—

a. An entity's compliance with requirements of specified laws, regulations, rules, contracts, or grants is referred to as *compliance with specified requirements*.

b. An entity's internal control over compliance with specified requirements is referred to as its *internal control over compliance*. The internal control addressed in this section may include parts of but is not the same as internal control over financial reporting.

[2] An example of this report is contained in AICPA Audit and Accounting Guide *Brokers and Dealers in Securities*.

.03 A report issued in accordance with the provisions of this section does not provide a legal determination of an entity's compliance with specified requirements. However, such a report may be useful to legal counsel or others in making such determinations.

Scope of Services

.04 The practitioner may be engaged to perform agreed-upon procedures to assist users in evaluating the following subject matter (or assertions related thereto)—

a. The entity's compliance with specified requirements

b. The effectiveness of the entity's internal control over compliance[3]

c. Both the entity's compliance with specified requirements and the effectiveness of the entity's internal control over compliance

The practitioner also may be engaged to examine the entity's compliance with specified requirements or a written assertion thereon.

.05 An important consideration in determining the type of engagement to be performed is expectations by users of the practitioner's report. Since the users decide the procedures to be performed in an agreed-upon procedures engagement, it often will be in the best interests of the practitioner and users (including the client) to have an agreed-upon procedures engagement rather than an examination engagement. When deciding whether to accept an examination engagement, the practitioner should consider the risks discussed in paragraphs .31–.35.

.06 A practitioner may be engaged to examine the effectiveness of the entity's internal control over compliance or an assertion thereon. However, in accordance with section 50, the practitioner cannot accept an engagement unless he or she has reason to believe that the subject matter is capable of reasonably consistent evaluation against criteria that are suitable and available to users.[4] If a practitioner determines that such criteria do exist for internal

---

[3] An entity's internal control over compliance is the process by which management obtains reasonable assurance of compliance with specified requirements. Although the comprehensive internal control may include a wide variety of objectives and related policies and procedures, only some of these may be relevant to an entity's compliance with specified requirements. (See footnote 1*b*.) The components of internal control over compliance vary based on the nature of the compliance requirements. For example, internal control over compliance with a capital requirement would generally include accounting procedures, whereas internal control over compliance with a requirement to practice nondiscriminatory hiring may not include accounting procedures.

[4] Criteria issued by regulatory agencies and other groups composed of experts that follow due-process procedures, including exposure of the proposed criteria for public comment, ordinarily should be considered suitable criteria for this purpose. For example, the Committee of Sponsoring Organizations (COSO) of the Treadway Commission's Report, *Internal Control—Integrated Framework*, provides suitable criteria against which management may evaluate and report on the effectiveness of the entity's internal control. However, more detailed criteria relative to specific compliance requirements may have to be developed and an appropriate threshold for measuring the severity of control deficiencies needs to be developed in order to apply the concepts of the COSO report to internal control over compliance.

Criteria established by a regulatory agency that does not follow such due-process procedures also may be considered suitable criteria for use by the regulatory agency. The practitioner should determine whether such criteria are suitable for general use reporting by evaluating them against the attributes in paragraph .24 of section 101. If the practitioner determines that such criteria are suitable for general use reporting, those criteria should also be available to users as discussed in paragraph .33 of section 101.

If the practitioner concludes that the criteria are appropriate only for a limited number of parties or are available only to specified parties, the practitioner's report shall state that the use of the report is restricted to those parties specified in the report. (See paragraphs .30, .34, and .78–.83 of section 101.)

control over compliance, he or she should perform the engagement in accordance with section 101, *Attest Engagements*. Additionally, section 501, *An Examination of an Entity's Internal Control Over Financial Reporting That Is Integrated With an Audit of Its Financial Statements*, may be helpful to a practitioner in such an engagement. [Revised, November 2006, to reflect conforming changes necessary due to the issuance of SSAE No. 14.]

.07 A practitioner should not accept an engagement to perform a review, as defined in paragraph .55 of section 101, of an entity's compliance with specified requirements or about the effectiveness of an entity's internal control over compliance or an assertion thereon.

.08 The practitioner may be engaged to provide other types of services in connection with the entity's compliance with specified requirements or the entity's internal control over compliance. For example, management may engage the practitioner to provide recommendations on how to improve the entity's compliance or related internal control. A practitioner engaged to provide such nonattest services should refer to the guidance in CS section 100, *Consulting Services: Definitions and Standards*.

Conditions for Engagement Performance

.09 A practitioner may perform an agreed-upon procedures engagement related to an entity's compliance with specified requirements or the effectiveness of internal control over compliance if the following conditions are met.

a. The responsible party accepts responsibility for the entity's compliance with specified requirements and the effectiveness of the entity's internal control over compliance.

b. The responsible party evaluates the entity's compliance with specified requirements or the effectiveness of the entity's internal control over compliance.

See also section 201, *Agreed-Upon Procedures Engagements*.

.10 A practitioner may perform an examination engagement related to an entity's compliance with specified requirements if the following conditions are met.

a. The responsible party accepts responsibility for the entity's compliance with specified requirements and the effectiveness of the entity's internal control over compliance.

b. The responsible party evaluates the entity's compliance with specified requirements.

c. Sufficient evidential matter exists or could be developed to support management's evaluation.

.11 As part of engagement performance, the practitioner should obtain from the responsible party a written assertion about compliance with specified requirements or internal control over compliance. The responsible party may present its written assertion in either of the following:

a. A separate report that will accompany the practitioner's report

b. A representation letter to the practitioner

.12 The responsible party's written assertion about compliance with specified requirements or internal control over compliance may take many forms. Throughout this section, for example, the phrase "responsible party's assertion that W Company complied with [*specify compliance requirement*] as of [*date*]," illustrates such an assertion. Other phrases may also be used. However, a practitioner should not accept an assertion that is so subjective (for example, "very effective" internal control over compliance) that people having competence in and using the same or similar criteria would not ordinarily be able to arrive at similar conclusions.

.13 Regardless of whether the practitioner's client is the responsible party, the responsible party's refusal to furnish a written assertion as part of an examination engagement should cause the practitioner to withdraw from the engagement. However, an exception is provided if an examination of an entity's compliance with specified requirements is required by law or regulation. In that instance, the practitioner should disclaim an opinion on compliance unless he or she obtains evidential matter that warrants expressing an adverse opinion. If the practitioner expresses an adverse opinion and the responsible party does not provide an assertion, the practitioner's report should be restricted as to use. (See paragraphs .78–.81 of section 101.) If, as part of an agreed-upon procedures engagement, the practitioner's client is the responsible party, a refusal by that party to provide an assertion requires the practitioner to withdraw from the engagement. However, withdrawal is not required if the engagement is required by law or regulation. If, in an agreed-upon procedures engagement, the practitioner's client is not the responsible party, the practitioner is not required to withdraw but should consider the effects of the responsible party's refusal on the engagement and his or her report.

.14 Additionally, at the beginning of the engagement, the practitioner may want to consider discussing with the client and the responsible party the need for the responsible party to provide the practitioner with a written representation letter at the conclusion of the examination engagement or an agreed-upon procedures engagement in which the client is the responsible party. In that letter, the responsible party will be asked to provide, among other possible items, an acknowledgment of their responsibility for establishing and maintaining effective internal control over compliance and their assertion stating their evaluation of the entity's compliance with specified requirements. The responsible party's refusal to furnish these representations (see paragraphs .68–.70) will constitute a limitation on the scope of the engagement.

Responsible Party

.15 The responsible party is responsible for ensuring that the entity complies with the requirements applicable to its activities. That responsibility encompasses the following.

a. Identify applicable compliance requirements.

b. Establish and maintain internal control to provide reasonable assurance that the entity complies with those requirements.

c. Evaluate and monitor the entity's compliance.

d. Specify reports that satisfy legal, regulatory, or contractual requirements.

The responsible party's evaluation may include documentation such as accounting or statistical data, entity policy manuals, accounting manuals, narrative memoranda, procedural write-ups, flowcharts, completed questionnaires, or internal auditors' reports. The form and extent of documentation will vary depending on the nature of the compliance requirements and the size and complexity of the entity. The responsible party may engage the practitioner to gather information to assist it in evaluating the entity's compliance. Regardless of the procedures performed by the practitioner, the responsible party must accept responsibility for its assertion and must not base such assertion solely on the practitioner's procedures.

Agreed-Upon Procedures Engagement

.16 The objective of the practitioner's agreed-upon procedures is to present specific findings to assist users in evaluating an entity's compliance with specified requirements or the effectiveness of an entity's internal control over compliance based on procedures agreed upon by the users of the report. A practitioner engaged to perform agreed-upon procedures on an entity's compliance with specified requirements or about the effectiveness of an entity's internal control over compliance should follow the guidance set forth herein and in section 201.

.17 The practitioner's procedures generally may be as limited or as extensive as the specified users desire, as long as the specified users (*a*) agree upon the procedures performed or to be performed and (*b*) take responsibility for the sufficiency of the agreed-upon procedures for their purposes. (See paragraph .15 of section 201.)

.18 To satisfy the requirements that the practitioner and the specified users agree upon the procedures performed or to be performed and that the specified users take responsibility for the sufficiency of the agreed-upon procedures for their purposes, ordinarily the practitioner should communicate directly with and obtain affirmative acknowledgment from each of the specified users. For example, this may be accomplished by meeting with the specified users or by distributing a draft of the anticipated report or a copy of an engagement letter to the specified users and obtaining their agreement. If the practitioner is not able to communicate directly with all of the specified users, the practitioner may satisfy these requirements by applying any one or more of the following or similar procedures.

- Compare the procedures to be applied to written requirements of the specified users.
- Discuss the procedures to be applied with appropriate representatives of the specified users involved.
- Review relevant contracts with or correspondence from the specified users.

The practitioner should not report on an engagement when specified users do not agree upon the procedures performed or to be performed and do not take responsibility for the sufficiency of the procedures for their purposes. See paragraph .36 of section 201 for guidance on satisfying these requirements when the practitioner is requested to add other parties as specified parties after the date of completion of the agreed-upon procedures.

.19 In an engagement to perform agreed-upon procedures on an entity's compliance with specified requirements or about the effectiveness of an entity's internal control over compliance, the practitioner is required to perform only the procedures that have been agreed to by users.[5] However, prior to performing such procedures, the practitioner should obtain an understanding of the specified compliance requirements, as discussed in paragraph .20. (See section 201.)

.20 To obtain an understanding of the specified compliance requirements, a practitioner should consider the following:

a. Laws, regulations, rules, contracts, and grants that pertain to the specified compliance requirements, including published requirements

b. Knowledge about the specified compliance requirements obtained through prior engagements and regulatory reports

c. Knowledge about the specified compliance requirements obtained through discussions with appropriate individuals within the entity (for example, the chief financial officer, internal auditors, legal counsel, compliance officer, or grant or contract administrators)

d. Knowledge about the specified compliance requirements obtained through discussions with appropriate individuals outside the entity (for example, a regulator or a third-party specialist)

.21 When circumstances impose restrictions on the scope of an agreed-upon procedures engagement, the practitioner should attempt to obtain agreement from the users for modification of the agreed-upon procedures. When such agreement cannot be obtained (for example, when the agreed-upon procedures are published by a regulatory agency that will not modify the procedures), the practitioner should describe such restrictions in his or her report or withdraw from the engagement.

.22 The practitioner has no obligation to perform procedures beyond the agreed-upon procedures. However, if noncompliance comes to the practitioner's attention by other means, such information ordinarily should be included in his or her report.

.23 The practitioner may become aware of noncompliance that occurs subsequent to the period addressed by the practitioner's report but before the date of the practitioner's report. The practitioner should consider including information regarding such noncompliance in his or her report. However, the practitioner has no responsibility to perform procedures to detect such noncompliance other than obtaining the responsible party's representation about noncompliance in the subsequent period, as described in paragraph .68.

.24 The practitioner's report on agreed-upon procedures on an entity's compliance with specified requirements (or the effectiveness of an entity's internal control over compliance) should be in the form of procedures and findings. The practitioner's report should contain the following elements:

a. A title that includes the word *independent*

b. Identification of the specified parties

c. Identification of the subject matter of the engagement (or management's assertion thereon), including the period or point in time addressed and a reference to the character of the engagement[6]

---

[5] AU-C section 610, *The Auditor's Consideration of the Internal Audit Function in an Audit of Financial Statements*, does not apply to agreed-upon procedures engagements. [Footnote revised, December 2012, to reflect conforming changes necessary due to the issuance of SAS Nos. 122–126.]

[6] Generally, management's assertion about compliance with specified requirements will address a *period* of time, whereas an assertion about internal control over compliance will address a *point* in time.

d. An identification of the responsible party

e. A statement that the subject matter is the responsibility of the responsible party

f. A statement that the procedures, which were agreed to by the specified parties identified in the report, were performed to assist the specified parties in evaluating the entity's compliance with specified requirements or the effectiveness of its internal control over compliance

g. A statement that the agreed-upon procedures engagement was conducted in accordance with attestation standards established by the American Institute of Certified Public Accountants

h. A statement that the sufficiency of the procedures is solely the responsibility of the specified parties and a disclaimer of responsibility for the sufficiency of those procedures

i. A list of the procedures performed (or reference thereto) and related findings (The practitioner should not provide negative assurance. See paragraph .24 of section 201.)

j. Where applicable, a description of any agreed-upon materiality limits (See paragraph .25 of section 201.)

k. A statement that the practitioner was not engaged to and did not conduct an examination of the entity's compliance with specified requirements (or the effectiveness of an entity's internal control over compliance), a disclaimer of opinion thereon, and a statement that if the practitioner had performed additional procedures, other matters might have come to his or her attention that would have been reported

l. A statement restricting the use of the report to the specified parties

m. Where applicable, reservations or restrictions concerning procedures or findings as discussed in paragraphs .33, .35, and .39–.40 of section 201

n. Where applicable, a description of the nature of the assistance provided by the specialist as discussed in paragraphs .19–.21 of section 201

o. The manual or printed signature of the practitioner's firm

p. The date of the report

.25 The following is an illustration of an agreed-upon procedures report on an entity's compliance with specified requirements in which the procedures and findings are enumerated rather than referenced.

Independent Accountant's Report on Applying Agreed-Upon Procedures

We have performed the procedures enumerated below, which were agreed to by [*list specified parties*], solely to assist the specified parties in evaluating [*name of entity*]'s compliance with [*list specified requirements*] during the [*period*] ended [*date*].[7] Management is responsible for [*name of entity*]'s compliance with those requirements. This agreed-upon procedures engagement

[7] If the agreed-upon procedures have been published by a third-party user (for example, a regulator in regulatory policies or a lender in a debt agreement), this sentence might begin, "We have performed the procedures included in [*title of publication or other document*] and enumerated below, which were agreed to by [*list specified parties*], solely to assist the specified parties in evaluating ...."

was conducted in accordance with attestation standards established by the American Institute of Certified Public Accountants. The sufficiency of these procedures is solely the responsibility of those parties specified in this report. Consequently, we make no representation regarding the sufficiency of the procedures described below either for the purpose for which this report has been requested or for any other purpose.

[*Include paragraphs to enumerate procedures and findings.*]

We were not engaged to and did not conduct an examination, the objective of which would be the expression of an opinion on compliance. Accordingly, we do not express such an opinion. Had we performed additional procedures, other matters might have come to our attention that would have been reported to you.

This report is intended solely for the information and use of [*list or refer to specified parties*] and is not intended to be and should not be used by anyone other than these specified parties.

[*Signature*]

[*Date*]

.26 Evaluating compliance with certain requirements may require interpretation of the laws, regulations, rules, contracts, or grants that establish those requirements. In such situations, the practitioner should consider whether he or she is provided with the suitable criteria required to evaluate an assertion under the third general attestation standard. If these interpretations are significant, the practitioner may include a paragraph stating the description and the source of interpretations made by the entity's management. An example of such a paragraph, which should precede the procedures and findings paragraph(s), follows.

We have been informed that, under [*name of entity*]'s interpretation of [*identify the compliance requirement*], [*explain the nature and source of the relevant interpretation*].

.27 The following is an illustration of an agreed-upon procedures report on the effectiveness of an entity's internal control over compliance in which the procedures and findings are enumerated rather than referenced.

<u>Independent Accountant's Report on Applying Agreed-Upon Procedures</u>

We have performed the procedures enumerated below, which were agreed to by [*list specified parties*], solely to assist the specified parties in evaluating the effectiveness of [*name of entity*]'s internal control over compliance with [*list specified requirements*] as of [*date*].[8] Management is responsible for [*name of entity*]'s internal control over compliance with those requirements. This agreed-upon procedures engagement was conducted in accordance with attestation standards established by the American Institute of Certified Public Accountants. The sufficiency of these procedures is solely the responsibility of those parties specified in this report. Consequently, we make no representation regarding the sufficiency of the procedures described below either for the purpose for which this report has been requested or for any other purpose.

---

[8] If the agreed-upon procedures have been published by a third-party user (for example, a regulator in regulatory policies or a lender in a debt agreement), this sentence might begin, "We have performed the procedures included in [*title of publication or other document*] and enumerated below, which were agreed to by [*list specified parties*], solely to assist the specified parties in evaluating the effectiveness of [*name of entity*]'s internal control over compliance ...."

[*Include paragraphs to enumerate procedures and findings.*]

We were not engaged to and did not conduct an examination, the objective of which would be the expression of an opinion on the effectiveness of internal control over compliance. Accordingly, we do not express such an opinion. Had we performed additional procedures, other matters might have come to our attention that would have been reported to you.

This report is intended solely for the information and use of [*list or refer to specified parties*] and is not intended to be and should not be used by anyone other than these specified parties.

[*Signature*]

[*Date*]

.28 In some agreed-upon procedures engagements, procedures may relate to both compliance with specified requirements and the effectiveness of internal control over compliance. In these engagements, the practitioner may issue one report that addresses both. For example, the first sentence of the introductory paragraph would state the following.

We have performed the procedures enumerated below, which were agreed to by [*list users of report*], solely to assist the users in evaluating [*name of entity*]'s compliance with [*list specified requirements*] during the [*period*] ended [*date*] and the effectiveness of [*name of entity*]'s internal control over compliance with the aforementioned compliance requirements as of [*date*].

.29 The date of completion of the agreed-upon procedures should be used as the date of the practitioner's report.

Examination Engagement

.30 The objective of the practitioner's examination procedures applied to an entity's compliance with specified requirements is to express an opinion on an entity's compliance (or assertion related thereto), based on the specified criteria. To express such an opinion, the practitioner accumulates sufficient evidence about the entity's compliance with specified requirements, thereby restricting attestation risk to an appropriately low level.

Attestation Risk

.31 In an engagement to examine compliance with specified requirements, the practitioner seeks to obtain reasonable assurance that the entity complied, in all material respects, based on the specified criteria. This includes designing the examination to detect both intentional and unintentional material noncompliance. Absolute assurance is not attainable because of factors such as the need for judgment, the use of sampling, and the inherent limitations of internal control over compliance and because much of the evidence available to the practitioner is persuasive rather than conclusive in nature. Also, procedures that are effective for detecting noncompliance that is unintentional may be ineffective for detecting noncompliance that is intentional and concealed through collusion between personnel of the entity and a third party or among management or employees of the entity. Therefore, the subsequent discovery that material noncompliance exists does not, in and of itself, evidence inadequate planning, performance, or judgment on the part of the practitioner.

.32 Attestation risk is the risk that the practitioner may unknowingly fail to modify appropriately his or her opinion. It is composed of inherent risk, control risk, and detection risk. For purposes of a compliance examination, these components are defined as follows:

a. *Inherent risk*—The risk that material noncompliance with specified requirements could occur, assuming there are no related controls
b. *Control risk*—The risk that material noncompliance that could occur will not be prevented or detected on a timely basis by the entity's controls
c. *Detection risk*—The risk that the practitioner's procedures will lead him or her to conclude that material noncompliance does not exist when, in fact, such noncompliance does exist

Inherent Risk

.33 In assessing inherent risk, the practitioner should consider factors affecting risk similar to those an auditor would consider when planning an audit of financial statements. Such factors are discussed in paragraph .A75 of AU-C section 240, *Consideration of Fraud in a Financial Statement Audit*. In addition, the practitioner should consider factors relevant to compliance engagements, such as the following:

- The complexity of the specified compliance requirements
- The length of time the entity has been subject to the specified compliance requirements
- Prior experience with the entity's compliance
- The potential impact of noncompliance

[Revised, January 2004, to reflect conforming changes necessary due to the issuance of SAS No. 99. Revised, December 2012, to reflect conforming changes necessary due to the issuance of SAS Nos. 122–126.]

Control Risk

.34 The practitioner should assess control risk as discussed in paragraphs .45–.46. Assessing control risk contributes to the practitioner's evaluation of the risk that material noncompliance exists. The process of assessing control risk (together with assessing inherent risk) provides evidential matter about the risk that such noncompliance may exist. The practitioner uses this evidential matter as part of the reasonable basis for his or her opinion.

Detection Risk

.35 In determining an acceptable level of detection risk, the practitioner assesses inherent risk and control risk and considers the extent to which he or she seeks to restrict attestation risk. As assessed inherent risk or control risk decreases, the acceptable level of detection risk increases. Accordingly, the practitioner may alter the nature, timing, and extent of compliance tests performed based on the assessments of inherent risk and control risk.

Materiality

.36 In an examination of an entity's compliance with specified requirements, the practitioner's consideration of materiality differs from that of an audit of financial statements in accordance with GAAS. In an examination of an entity's compliance with specified requirements, the practitioner's consideration of materiality is affected by (*a*) the nature of the compliance requirements, which may or may not be quantifiable in monetary terms, (*b*) the nature and frequency of noncompliance identified with appropriate consideration of sampling risk, and (*c*) qualitative considerations, including the needs and expectations of the report's users.

.37 In a number of situations, the terms of the engagement may provide for a supplemental report of all or certain noncompliance discovered. Such terms should not change the practitioner's judgments about materiality in planning and performing the engagement or in forming an opinion on an entity's compliance with specified requirements or on the responsible party's assertion about such compliance.

Performing an Examination Engagement

.38 The practitioner should exercise (*a*) due care in planning, performing, and evaluating the results of his or her examination procedures and (*b*) the proper degree of professional skepticism to achieve reasonable assurance that material noncompliance will be detected.

.39 In an examination of the entity's compliance with specified requirements, the practitioner should—

a. Obtain an understanding of the specified compliance requirements. (See paragraph .40.)

b. Plan the engagement. (See paragraphs .41–.44.)

c. Consider relevant portions of the entity's internal control over compliance. (See paragraphs .45–.47.)

d. Obtain sufficient evidence including testing compliance with specified requirements. (See paragraphs .48–.49.)

e. Consider subsequent events. (See paragraphs .50–.52.)

f. Form an opinion about whether the entity complied, in all material respects, with specified requirements (or whether the responsible party's assertion about such compliance is fairly stated in all material respects), based on the specified criteria. (See paragraph .53.)

Obtaining an Understanding of the Specified Compliance Requirements

.40 A practitioner should obtain an understanding of the specified compliance requirements. To obtain such an understanding, a practitioner should consider the following:

a. Laws, regulations, rules, contracts, and grants that pertain to the specified compliance requirements, including published requirements

b. Knowledge about the specified compliance requirements obtained through prior engagements and regulatory reports

c. Knowledge about the specified compliance requirements obtained through discussions with appropriate individuals within the entity (for example, the chief financial officer, internal auditors, legal counsel, compliance officer, or grant or contract administrators)

d. Knowledge about the specified compliance requirements obtained through discussions with appropriate individuals outside the entity (for example, a regulator or third-party specialist)

Planning the Engagement

General Considerations

.41 Planning an engagement to examine an entity's compliance with specified requirements involves developing an overall strategy for the expected conduct and scope of the engagement. The practitioner should consider the planning matters discussed in paragraphs .42–.47 of section 101.

Multiple Components

.42 In an engagement to examine an entity's compliance with specified requirements when the entity has operations in several components (for example, locations, branches, subsidiaries, or programs), the practitioner may determine that it is not necessary to test compliance with requirements at every component. In making such a determination and in selecting the components to be tested, the practitioner should consider factors such as the following:

a. The degree to which the specified compliance requirements apply at the component level

b. Judgments about materiality

c. The degree of centralization of records

d. The effectiveness of the control environment, particularly management's direct control over the exercise of authority delegated to others and its ability to supervise activities at various locations effectively

e. The nature and extent of operations conducted at the various components

f. The similarity of operations over compliance for different components

Using the Work of a Specialist

.43 In some compliance engagements, the nature of the specified compliance requirements may require specialized skill or knowledge in a particular field other than accounting or auditing. In such cases, the practitioner may use the work of a specialist and should follow the relevant performance and reporting guidance in AU-C section 620, *Using the Work of an Auditor's Specialist*. [Revised, December 2012, to reflect conforming changes necessary due to the issuance of SAS Nos. 122–126.]

Internal Audit Function

.44 Another factor the practitioner should consider when planning the engagement is whether the entity has an internal audit function and the extent to which internal auditors are involved in monitoring compliance with the specified requirements. A practitioner should consider the guidance in AU-C section 610, *The Auditor's Consideration of the Internal Audit Function in an Audit of Financial Statements*, when addressing the competence and objectivity of internal auditors, the nature, timing, and extent of work to be performed, and other related matters. [Revised, December 2012, to reflect conforming changes necessary due to the issuance of SAS Nos. 122–126.]

Consideration of Internal Control Over Compliance

.45 The practitioner should obtain an understanding of relevant portions of internal control over compliance sufficient to plan the engagement and to assess control risk for compliance with specified requirements. In planning the examination, such knowledge should be used to identify types of potential noncompliance, to consider factors that affect the risk of material noncompliance, and to design appropriate tests of compliance.

.46 A practitioner generally obtains an understanding of the design of specific controls by performing the following:

a. Inquiries of appropriate management, supervisory, and staff personnel

b. Inspection of the entity's documents

c. Observation of the entity's activities and operations

The nature and extent of procedures a practitioner performs vary from entity to entity and are influenced by factors such as the following:

- The newness and complexity of the specified requirements
- The practitioner's knowledge of internal control over compliance obtained in previous professional engagements
- The nature of the specified compliance requirements
- An understanding of the industry in which the entity operates
- Judgments about materiality

When seeking to assess control risk below the maximum, the practitioner should perform tests of controls to obtain evidence to support the assessed level of control risk.

.47 During the course of an examination engagement, the practitioner may become aware of significant deficiencies or material weaknesses in the design or operation of internal control over compliance that could adversely affect the entity's ability to comply with specified requirements. A practitioner's responsibility to communicate these deficiencies in an examination of an entity's compliance with specified requirements is similar to the auditor's responsibility described in AU-C section 265, *Communicating Internal Control Related Matters Identified in an Audit*. If, in a multiple-party arrangement, the practitioner's client is not the responsible party, the practitioner has no responsibility to communicate significant deficiencies or material weaknesses to the responsible party. For example, if the practitioner is engaged by his or her client to examine the compliance of another entity, the practitioner has no obligation to communicate any significant deficiencies or material weaknesses that he or she becomes aware of to the other entity. However, the practitioner is not precluded from making such a communication. [Revised, May 2006, to reflect conforming changes necessary due to the issuance of SAS No. 112. Revised, January 2010, to reflect conforming changes necessary due to the issuance of SAS No. 115. Revised, December 2012, to reflect conforming changes necessary due to the issuance of SAS Nos. 122–126.]

Obtaining Sufficient Evidence

.48 The practitioner should apply procedures to provide reasonable assurance of detecting material noncompliance. Determining these procedures and evaluating the sufficiency of the evidence obtained are matters of professional judgment. When exercising such judgment, practitioners should consider the guidance contained in paragraphs .51–.54 of section 101 and AU-C section 530, *Audit Sampling*. [Revised, December 2012, to reflect conforming changes necessary due to the issuance of SAS Nos. 122–126.]

.49 For engagements involving compliance with regulatory requirements, the practitioner's procedures should include reviewing reports of significant examinations and related communications between regulatory agencies and the entity and, when appropriate, making inquiries of the regulatory agencies, including inquiries about examinations in progress.

Consideration of Subsequent Events

.50 The practitioner's consideration of subsequent events in an examination of an entity's compliance with specified requirements is similar to the auditor's consideration of subsequent events in a financial statement audit, as outlined in AU-C section 560, *Subsequent Events and Subsequently Discovered Facts*. The practitioner should consider information about such events that comes to his or her attention after the end of the period addressed by the practitioner's report and prior to the issuance of his or her report. [Revised, December 2012, to reflect conforming changes necessary due to the issuance of SAS Nos. 122–126.]

.51 Two types of subsequent events require consideration by the responsible party and evaluation by the practitioner. The first consists of events that provide additional information about the entity's compliance during the period addressed by the practitioner's report and may affect the practitioner's report. For the period from the end of the reporting period (or point in time) to the date of the practitioner's report, the practitioner should perform procedures to identify such events that provide additional information about compliance during the reporting period. Such procedures should include but may not be limited to inquiring about and considering the following information:

- Relevant internal auditors' reports issued during the subsequent period
- Other practitioners' reports identifying noncompliance, issued during the subsequent period
- Regulatory agencies' reports on the entity's noncompliance, issued during the subsequent period
- Information about the entity's noncompliance, obtained through other professional engagements for that entity

.52 The second type consists of noncompliance that occurs subsequent to the period being reported on but before the date of the practitioner's report. The practitioner has no responsibility to detect such noncompliance. However, should the practitioner become aware of such noncompliance, it may be of such a nature and significance that disclosure of it is required to keep users from being misled. In such cases, the practitioner should include in his or her report an explanatory paragraph describing the nature of the noncompliance.

Forming an Opinion

.53 In evaluating whether the entity has complied in all material respects (or whether the responsible party's assertion about such compliance is stated fairly in all material respects), the practitioner should consider (*a*) the nature and frequency of the noncompliance identified and (*b*) whether such noncompliance is material relative to the nature of the compliance requirements, as discussed in paragraph .36.

Reporting

.54 The practitioner may examine and report directly on an entity's compliance (see paragraphs .55–56) or he or she may examine and report on the responsible party's written assertion (see paragraphs .57–.58 and .61), except as described in paragraph .64.

.55 The practitioner's examination report on compliance, which is ordinarily addressed to the entity, should include the following:

a. A title that includes the word *independent*

b. Identification of the specified compliance requirements, including the period covered, and of the responsible party[9]

c. A statement that compliance with the specified requirements is the responsibility of the entity's management

d. A statement that the practitioner's responsibility is to express an opinion on the entity's compliance with those requirements based on his or her examination

e. A statement that the examination was conducted in accordance with attestation standards established by the American Institute of Certified Public Accountants and, accordingly, included examining, on a test basis, evidence about the entity's compliance with those requirements and performing such other procedures as the practitioner considered necessary in the circumstances

f. A statement that the practitioner believes the examination provides a reasonable basis for his or her opinion

g. A statement that the examination does not provide a legal determination on the entity's compliance

h. The practitioner's opinion on whether the entity complied, in all material respects, with specified requirements based on the specified criteria[10] (See paragraph .64 for reporting on material noncompliance.)

i. A statement restricting the use of the report to the specified parties (see the fourth reporting standard)[11] under the following circumstances (See also paragraph .13.):

- When the criteria used to evaluate compliance are determined by the practitioner to be appropriate only for a limited number of parties who either participated in their establishment or can be presumed to have an adequate understanding of the criteria.
- When the criteria used to evaluate compliance are available only to the specified parties

j. The manual or printed signature of the practitioner's firm

k. The date of the examination report

.56 The following is the form of report a practitioner should use when he or she is expressing an opinion on an entity's compliance with specified requirements during a period of time.

---

[9] A practitioner also may be engaged to report on an entity's compliance with specified requirements as of point in time. In this case, the illustrative reports in this section should be adapted as appropriate.

[10] Frequently, criteria will be contained in the compliance requirements, in which case it is not necessary to repeat the criteria in the practitioner's report; however, if the criteria are not included in the compliance requirement, the practitioner's report should identify the criteria. For example, if a compliance requirement is to "maintain $25,000 in capital," it would not be necessary to identify the $25,000 in the report; however, if the requirement is to "maintain adequate capital," the practitioner should identify the criteria used to define *adequate.*

[11] In certain situations, however, criteria that have been specified by management and other report users may be suitable for general use.

Independent Accountant's Report

[Introductory paragraph]

We have examined [*name of entity*]'s compliance with [*list specified compliance requirements*] during the [*period*] ended [*date*]. Management is responsible for [*name of entity*]'s compliance with those requirements. Our responsibility is to express an opinion on [*name of entity*]'s compliance based on our examination.

[Scope paragraph]

Our examination was conducted in accordance with attestation standards established by the American Institute of Certified Public Accountants and, accordingly, included examining, on a test basis, evidence about [*name of entity*]'s compliance with those requirements and performing such other procedures as we considered necessary in the circumstances. We believe that our examination provides a reasonable basis for our opinion. Our examination does not provide a legal determination on [*name of entity*]'s compliance with specified requirements.

[Opinion paragraph]

In our opinion, [*name of entity*] complied, in all material respects, with the aforementioned requirements for the year ended December 31, 20XX.[12]

[Signature]

[Date]

.57 The practitioner's examination report on an entity's assertion about compliance with specified requirements, which is ordinarily addressed to the entity, should include the following:

a. A title that includes the word *independent*

b. Identification of the responsible party's assertion about the entity's compliance with specified requirements, including the period covered by the responsible party's assertion, and of the responsible party (When the responsible party's assertion does not accompany the practitioner's report, the first paragraph of the report should also contain a statement of the responsible party's assertion.)[13]

c. A statement that compliance with the requirements is the responsibility of the entity's management

d. A statement that the practitioner's responsibility is to express an opinion on the responsible party's assertion on the entity's compliance with those requirements based on his or her examination

e. A statement that the examination was conducted in accordance with attestation standards established by the American Institute of Certified Public Accountants and, accordingly, included examining, on a test basis, evidence about the entity's compliance with those requirements and performing such other procedures as the practitioner considered necessary in the circumstances

[12] If it is necessary to identify criteria (see footnote 10), the criteria should be identified in the opinion paragraph (for example, "... in all material respects, based on the criteria set forth in Attachment 1").

[13] A practitioner also may be engaged to report on the responsible party's assertion about an entity's compliance with specified requirements as of a point in time. In this case, the illustrative reports in this section should be adapted as appropriate.

f. A statement that the practitioner believes the examination provides a reasonable basis for his or her opinion

g. A statement that the examination does not provide a legal determination on the entity's compliance

h. The practitioner's opinion on whether the responsible party's assertion about compliance with specified requirements is fairly stated in all material respects based on the specified criteria[14] (See paragraph .64 for reporting on material noncompliance.)

i. A statement restricting the use of the report to the specified parties (see the fourth reporting standard)[15, 16] under the following circumstances:

- When the criteria used to evaluate compliance are determined by the practitioner to be appropriate only for a limited number of parties who either participated in their establishment or can be presumed to have an adequate understanding of the criteria

- When the criteria used to evaluate compliance are available only to the specified parties

j. The manual or printed signature of the practitioner's firm

k. The date of the examination report

.58 The following is the form of report that a practitioner should use when expressing an opinion on management's assertion about compliance with specified requirements.

<u>Independent Accountant's Report</u>

[*Introductory paragraph*]

We have examined management's assertion, included in the accompanying [*title of management report*], that [*name of entity*] complied with [*list specified compliance requirements*] during the [*period*] ended [*date*].[17, 18] Management is responsible for [*name of entity*]'s compliance with those requirements. Our responsibility is to express an opinion on management's assertion about [*name of entity*]'s compliance based on our examination.

[*Standard scope paragraph*]

[*Opinion paragraph*]

---

[14] Frequently, criteria will be contained in the compliance requirements, in which case it is not necessary to repeat the criteria in the practitioner's report; however, if the criteria are not included in the compliance requirement, the practitioner's report should identify the criteria. For example, if a compliance requirement is to "maintain $25,000 in capital," it would not be necessary to identify the $25,000 in the report; however, if the requirement is to "maintain adequate capital," the practitioner should identify the criteria used to define *adequate*.

[15] Although a practitioner's report may be appropriate for general use, the practitioner is not precluded from restricting the use of the report.

[16] In certain situations, however, criteria that have been specified by management and other report users may be suitable for general use.

[17] The practitioner should identify the management report examined by reference to the report title used by management in its report. Further, he or she should use the same description of compliance requirements as management uses in its report.

[18] If management's assertion is stated in the practitioner's report and does not accompany the practitioner's report, the phrase "included in the accompanying [*title of management report*]" would be omitted.

In our opinion, management's assertion that [*name of entity*] complied with the aforementioned requirements during the [*period*] ended [*date*] is fairly stated, in all material respects.[19]

[*Signature*]

[*Date*]

.59 Evaluating compliance with certain requirements may require interpretation of the laws, regulations, rules, contracts, or grants that establish those requirements. In such situations, the practitioner should consider whether he or she is provided with the suitable criteria required to evaluate compliance under the third general attestation standard. If these interpretations are significant, the practitioner may include a paragraph stating the description and the source of interpretations made by the entity's management. The following is an example of such a paragraph, which should directly follow the scope paragraph:

We have been informed that, under [*name of entity*]'s interpretation of [*identify the compliance requirement*], [*explain the source and nature of the relevant interpretation*].

.60 The date of completion of the examination procedures should be used as the date of the practitioner's report.

.61 Nothing precludes the practitioner from examining an assertion but opining directly on compliance.

.62 Paragraphs .78–.83 of section 101 provide guidance on restricting the use of an attest report. Nothing in this section precludes the practitioner from restricting the use of the report. For example, if the practitioner is asked by a client to examine another entity's compliance with certain regulations, he or she may want to restrict the use of the report to the client since the practitioner has no control over how the report may be used by the other entity.

Report Modifications

.63 The practitioner should modify the standard report described in paragraphs .55 and .57, if any of the following conditions exist.

- There is material noncompliance with specified requirements (paragraphs .64–.67).
- There is a restriction on the scope of the engagement.[20]
- The practitioner decides to refer to the report of another practitioner as the basis, in part, for the practitioner's report.[21]

Material Noncompliance

.64 When an examination of an entity's compliance with specified requirements discloses noncompliance with the applicable requirements that the practitioner believes have a material effect on the entity's compliance, the practitioner should modify the report and, to most effectively communicate with the reader of the report, should state his or her opinion on the entity's specified compliance requirements, not on the responsible party's assertion.

---

[19] If it is necessary to identify criteria (see footnote 10), the criteria should be identified in the opinion paragraph (for example, "...in all material respects, based on the criteria set forth in Attachment 1").

[20] The practitioner should refer to paragraphs .73–.74 of section 101 for guidance on scope restrictions.

[21] The practitioner should refer to paragraphs .122–.125 of section 501 for guidance on an opinion based in part on the report of another practitioner and adapt such guidance to the standard reports in this section.

.65 The following is the form of report, modified with explanatory language, that a practitioner should use when he or she has concluded that a qualified opinion is appropriate under the circumstances. It has been assumed that the practitioner has determined that the specified compliance requirements are both suitable for general use and available to users as discussed in paragraphs .23–.33 of section 101, and, therefore, that a restricted use paragraph is not required.

Independent Accountant's Report

[*Introductory paragraph*]

We have examined [*name of entity*]'s compliance with [*list specified compliance requirements*] for the [*period*] ended [*date*]. Management is responsible for compliance with those requirements. Our responsibility is to express an opinion on [*name of entity*]'s compliance based on our examination.

[*Standard scope paragraph*]

[*Explanatory paragraph*]

Our examination disclosed the following material noncompliance with [*type of compliance requirement*] applicable to [*name of entity*] during the [*period*] ended [*date*]. [*Describe noncompliance.*]

[*Opinion paragraph*]

In our opinion, except for the material noncompliance described in the third paragraph, [*name of entity*] complied, in all material respects, with the aforementioned requirements for the [*period*] ended [*date*].

[*Signature*]

[*Date*]

.66 The following is the form of report, modified with explanatory language, that a practitioner should use when he or she concludes that an adverse opinion is appropriate in the circumstances. The practitioner has determined that the specified compliance requirements are both suitable for general use and available to users as discussed in paragraphs .23–.33 of section 101.

Independent Accountant's Report

[*Introductory paragraph*]

We have examined [*name of entity*]'s compliance with [*list specified compliance requirements*] for the [*period*] ended [*date*]. Management is responsible for compliance with those requirements. Our responsibility is to express an opinion on [*name of entity*]'s compliance based on our examination.

[*Standard scope paragraph*]

[*Explanatory paragraph*]

Our examination disclosed the following material noncompliance with [*type of compliance requirement*] applicable to [*name of entity*] during the [*period*] ended [*date*]. [*Describe noncompliance.*]

[*Opinion paragraph*]

In our opinion, because of the effect of the noncompliance described in the third paragraph, [*name of entity*] has not complied with the aforementioned requirements for the [*period*] ended [*date*].

[*Signature*]

[*Date*]

.67 If the practitioner's report on his or her examination of the entity's compliance with specified requirements is included in a document that also includes his or her audit report on the entity's financial statements, the following sentence should be included in the paragraph of an examination report that describes material noncompliance.

> These conditions were considered in determining the nature, timing, and extent of audit tests applied in our audit of the 20XX financial statements, and this report does not affect our report dated [*date of report*] on those financial statements.

The practitioner also may include the preceding sentence when the two reports are not included within the same document.

Representation Letter

.68 In an examination engagement or an agreed-upon procedures engagement, the practitioner should obtain written representations from the responsible party—[22]

a. Acknowledging the responsible party's responsibility for complying with the specified requirements.

b. Acknowledging the responsible party's responsibility for establishing and maintaining effective internal control over compliance.

c. Stating that the responsible party has performed an evaluation of (1) the entity's compliance with specified requirements or (2) the entity's controls for ensuring compliance and detecting noncompliance with requirements, as applicable.

d. Stating the responsible party's assertion about the entity's compliance with the specified requirements or about the effectiveness of internal control over compliance, as applicable, based on the stated or established criteria.

e. Stating that the responsible party has disclosed to the practitioner all known noncompliance.

f. State that the responsible party has made available all documentation related to compliance with the specified requirements.

g. Stating the responsible party's interpretation of any compliance requirements that have varying interpretations.

h. State that the responsible party has disclosed any communications from regulatory agencies, internal auditors, and other practitioners concerning possible noncompliance with the specified requirements, including communications received between the end of the period addressed in the written assertion and the date of the practitioner's report.

i. Stating that the responsible party has disclosed any known noncompliance occurring subsequent to the period for which, or date as of which, the responsible party selects to make its assertion.

---

[22] Paragraph .21 of AU-C section 580, *Written Representations*, states that the written representations should be in the form of a representation letter addressed to the auditor. [Footnote revised, December 2012, to reflect conforming changes necessary due to the issuance of SAS Nos. 122–126.]

.69 The responsible party's refusal to furnish all appropriate written representations in an examination engagement constitutes a limitation on the scope of the engagement sufficient to preclude an unqualified opinion and is ordinarily sufficient to cause the practitioner to disclaim an opinion or withdraw from the engagement. However, based on the nature of the representations not obtained or the circumstances of the refusal, the practitioner may conclude in an examination engagement that a qualified opinion is appropriate. When the practitioner is performing agreed-upon procedures and the practitioner's client is the responsible party, the responsible party's refusal to furnish all appropriate written representations constitutes a limitation on the scope of the engagement sufficient to cause the practitioner to withdraw. When the practitioner's client is not the responsible party, the practitioner is not required to withdraw but should consider the effects of the responsible party's refusal on his or her report. Further, the practitioner should consider the effects of the responsible party's refusal on his or her ability to rely on other representations of the responsible party.

.70 When the practitioner's client is not the responsible party, the practitioner may also want to obtain written representations from the client. For example, when a practitioner's client has entered into a contract with a third party (responsible party) and the practitioner is engaged to examine the responsible party's compliance with that contract, the practitioner may want to obtain written representations from his or her client as to their knowledge of any noncompliance.

Other Information in a Client-Prepared Document Containing Management's Assertion About the Entity's Compliance With Specified Requirements or the Effectiveness of the Internal Control Over Compliance

.71 An entity may publish various documents that contain information (referred to as *other information*) in addition to the practitioner's attest report on either (*a*) the entity's compliance with specified requirements or (*b*) the effectiveness of the entity's internal control over compliance or written assertion thereon. Paragraphs .91–.94 of section 101 provide guidance to the practitioner if the other information is contained in either of the following:

a. Annual reports to holders of securities or beneficial interests, annual reports of organizations for charitable or philanthropic purposes distributed to the public, and annual reports filed with regulatory authorities under the 1934 Act

b. Other documents to which the practitioner, at the client's request, devotes attention

Effective Date

.72 This section is effective when the subject matter or assertion is as of or for a period ending on or after June 1, 2001. Early application is permitted.

AT Section 701

Management's Discussion and Analysis

Source: SSAE No. 10.

Effective when management's discussion and analysis is for a period ending on or after June 1, 2001. Earlier application is permitted.

General

.01 This section sets forth attestation standards and provides guidance to a practitioner concerning the performance of an attest engagement[1] with respect to management's discussion and analysis (MD&A) prepared pursuant to the rules and regulations adopted by the Securities and Exchange Commission (SEC), which are presented in annual reports to shareholders and in other documents.[2]

Applicability

.02 This section is applicable to the following levels of service when a practitioner is engaged by (*a*) a public[3] entity that prepares MD&A in accordance with the rules and regulations adopted by the SEC (see paragraph .04) or (*b*) a nonpublic entity that prepares an MD&A presentation and whose management provides a written assertion that the presentation has been prepared using the rules and regulations adopted by the SEC:[4]

- An examination of an MD&A presentation
- A review of an MD&A presentation for an annual period, an interim period, or a combined annual and interim period[5]

---

[1] Paragraph .01 of section 101, *Attest Engagements*, defines an attest engagement as one in which a practitioner "is engaged to issue or does issue an examination, a review, or an agreed-upon procedures report on subject matter, or an assertion about the subject matter (hereafter referred to as the *assertion*), that is the responsibility of another party."

[2] Because this section provides guidance specific to attest engagements concerning MD&A presentations, a practitioner should not perform a compliance attestation engagement under section 601, *Compliance Attestation*, with respect to an MD&A presentation.

[3] For purposes of this section, a public entity is any entity (*a*) whose securities trade in a public market either on a stock exchange (domestic or foreign) or in the over-the-counter (OTC) market, including securities quoted only locally or regionally, (*b*) that makes a filing with a regulatory agency in preparation for the sale of any class of its securities in a public market, or (*c*) a subsidiary, corporate joint venture, or other entity controlled by an entity covered by (*a*) or (*b*).

[4] Such assertion may be made by any of the following:
(*a*) Including a statement in the body of the MD&A presentation that it has been prepared using the rules and regulations adopted by the SEC.
(*b*) Providing a separate written assertion to accompany the MD&A presentation.
(*c*) Providing a written assertion in a representation letter to the practitioner.

[5] As discussed in paragraph .85*k*, a review report is not intended to be filed with the SEC as a report under the Securities Act of 1933 (the 1993 Act) or the Securities Exchange Act of 1934 (the 1934 Act) and, accordingly, the review report should contain a statement of restrictions on the use of the report to specified parties if the entity is (*a*) a public entity or (*b*) a nonpublic entity that is making or has made an offering of securities and it appears that the securities may subsequently be registered or subject to a filing with the SEC or other regulatory agency.

A practitioner[6] engaged to examine or review MD&A and report thereon should comply with the general, fieldwork, and reporting standards established in section 50, *SSAE Hierarchy*, and the specific standards set forth in this section. A practitioner engaged to perform agreed-upon procedures on MD&A should follow the guidance set forth in section 201, Agreed-Upon Procedures Engagements.[7] [Revised, November 2006, to reflect conforming changes necessary due to the issuance of SSAE No. 14.]

.03 This section does not—

a. Change the auditor's responsibility in an audit of financial statements performed in accordance with generally accepted auditing standards (GAAS).

b. Apply to situations in which the practitioner is requested to provide management with recommendations to improve the MD&A rather than to provide assurance. A practitioner engaged to provide such nonattest services should refer to CS section 100, *Consulting Services: Definitions and Standards*.

c. Apply to situations in which the practitioner is engaged to provide attest services with respect to an MD&A presentation that is prepared based on criteria other than the rules and regulations adopted by the SEC. A practitioner engaged to perform an examination or a review based upon such criteria should refer to the guidance in section 101, or to section 201 if engaged to perform an agreed-upon procedures engagement.[8]

.04 The requirements for MD&A have changed periodically since the first requirement was adopted by the SEC in 1974. As of the date of issuance of this SSAE, the rules and regulations for MD&A adopted by the SEC are found in Item 303 of Regulation S-K, as interpreted by Financial Reporting Release (FRR) No. 36, *Management's Discussion and Analysis of Financial Condition and Results of Operations; Certain Investment Company Disclosures* (Chapter 5 of the "Codification of Financial Reporting Policies"); Item 303 of Regulation S-B for small business issuers; and Item 9 of Form 20-F for Foreign Private Issuers.[9] Item 303 of Regulation S-K, as interpreted by FRR No. 36, Item 303 of Regulation S-B for small business issuers, and Item 9 of Form 20-F for Foreign Private Issuers, provide the relevant rules and regulations adopted by the SEC

---

[6] In this section, the terms *practitioner* or *accountant* generally refer to a person engaged to perform an attest service on MD&A. The term *accountant* may also refer to a person engaged to review financial statements. The term *auditor* refers to a person engaged to audit financial statements. As this section includes certain requirements for the practitioner to have audited or performed a review of financial statements in accordance with AU-C section 930, *Interim Financial Information*, the terms *auditor, practitioner*, or *accountant* may refer, in this section, to the same person. [Footnote revised, December 2012, to reflect conforming changes necessary due to the issuance of SAS Nos. 122–126.]

[7] Practitioners should follow guidance in AU-C section 920, *Letters for Underwriters and Certain Other Requesting Parties*, when requested to perform agreed-upon procedures on MD&A and report thereon in a letter for an underwriter. [Footnote revised, December 2012, to reflect conforming changes necessary due to the issuance of SAS Nos. 122–126.]

[8] The guidance in this section may be helpful when performing an engagement to provide attest services with respect to an MD&A presentation that is based on criteria other than the rules and regulations adopted by the SEC. Such other criteria would have to be suitable and available as discussed in paragraphs .23–.33 of section 101.

[9] The SEC staff from time to time issues guidance related to the SEC's adopted requirements; for example, Staff Accounting Bulletins (SABs), Staff Legal Bulletins, and speeches. Although such guidance may provide additional information with respect to the adopted requirements for MD&A, the practitioner should not be expected to attest to assertions on compliance with such guidance. The practitioner may find it helpful to also familiarize himself or herself with material contained on the SEC's website www.sec.gov that provides further information with respect to the SEC's views concerning MD&A disclosures.

that meet the definition of suitable criteria in paragraphs .23–.32 of section 101. The practitioner should consider whether the SEC has adopted additional rules and regulations with respect to MD&A subsequent to the issuance of this section.

Conditions for Engagement Performance

Examination

.05 The practitioner's objective in an engagement to examine MD&A is to express an opinion on the MD&A presentation taken as a whole by reporting whether—

a. The presentation includes, in all material respects, the required elements of the rules and regulations adopted by the SEC.[10]

b. The historical financial amounts have been accurately derived, in all material respects, from the entity's financial statements.[11]

c. The underlying information, determinations, estimates, and assumptions of the entity provide a reasonable basis for the disclosures contained therein.[12]

.06 A practitioner may accept an engagement to examine MD&A of a public or nonpublic entity, provided the practitioner audits, in accordance with GAAS,[13] the financial statements for at least the latest period to which the MD&A presentation relates and the financial statements for the other periods covered by the MD&A presentation have been audited by the practitioner or a predecessor auditor. A base knowledge of the entity and its operations gained through an audit of the historical financial statements and knowledge about the industry and the environment is necessary to provide the practitioner with sufficient knowledge to properly evaluate the results of the procedures performed in connection with the examination.

.07 If a predecessor auditor has audited the financial statements for a prior period covered by the MD&A presentation, the practitioner (the successor auditor) should also consider whether, under the particular circumstances, he or she can acquire sufficient knowledge of the business and of the entity's accounting and financial reporting practices for such period so that he or she would be able to—

a. Identify types of potential material misstatements in MD&A and consider the likelihood of their occurrence.

---

[10] The required elements as of the date of issuance of this SSAE include a discussion of the entity's financial condition, changes in financial condition, and results of operations, including a discussion of liquidity and capital resources.

[11] Whether historical financial amounts are accurately derived from the financial statements includes both amounts that are derived from the face of the financial statements (which includes the notes to the financial statements) and financial statement schedules and those that are derived from underlying records supporting elements, accounts, or items included in the financial statements.

[12] Whether the underlying information, determinations, estimates, and assumptions of the entity provide a reasonable basis for the disclosures contained therein requires consideration of management's interpretation of the disclosure criteria for MD&A, management's determinations as to the relevancy of information to be included, and estimates and assumptions made by management that affect reported information.

[13] Restrictions on the scope of the audit of the financial statements will not necessarily preclude the practitioner from accepting an engagement to examine MD&A. Note that the SEC will generally not accept an auditor's report that is modified for a scope limitation. The practitioner should consider the nature and magnitude of the scope limitation and the form of the auditor's report in assessing whether an examination of MD&A could be performed.

b. Perform the procedures that will provide the practitioner with a basis for expressing an opinion as to whether the MD&A presentation includes, in all material respects, the required elements of the rules and regulations adopted by the SEC.

c. Perform the procedures that will provide the practitioner with a basis for expressing an opinion on the MD&A presentation with respect to whether the historical financial amounts have been accurately derived, in all material respects, from the entity's financial statements for such period.

d. Perform the procedures that will provide the practitioner with a basis for expressing an opinion as to whether the underlying information, determinations, estimates, and assumptions of the entity provide a reasonable basis for the disclosures contained therein.

Refer to paragraphs .99–.101 for guidance regarding the review of the predecessor auditor's working papers.

Review

.08 The objective of a review of MD&A is to report whether any information came to the practitioner's attention to cause him or her to believe that—

a. The MD&A presentation does not include, in all material respects, the required elements of the rules and regulations adopted by the SEC.

b. The historical financial amounts included therein have not been accurately derived, in all material respects, from the entity's financial statements.

c. The underlying information, determinations, estimates, and assumptions of the entity do not provide a reasonable basis for the disclosures contained therein.

A review consists principally of applying analytical procedures and making inquiries of persons responsible for financial, accounting, and operational matters. A review ordinarily does not contemplate (*a*) tests of accounting records through inspection, observation, or confirmation, (*b*) obtaining corroborating evidential matter in response to inquiries, or (*c*) the application of certain other procedures ordinarily performed during an examination of MD&A. A review may bring to the practitioner's attention significant matters affecting the MD&A, but it does not provide assurance that the practitioner will become aware of all significant matters that would be disclosed in an examination.

.09 A practitioner may accept an engagement to review the MD&A presentation of a public entity for an annual period provided the practitioner has audited, in accordance with GAAS, the financial statements for at least the latest annual period to which the MD&A presentation relates and the financial statements for the other periods covered by the MD&A presentation have been audited by the practitioner or a predecessor auditor.[14] A base knowledge of the entity and its operations gained through an audit of the historical financial

---

[14] As discussed in paragraph .85*k*, a review report is not intended to be filed with the SEC as a report under the 1933 Act or the 1934 Act and, accordingly, the review report should contain a statement of restrictions on the use of the report to specified parties if the entity is (*a*) a public entity or (*b*) a nonpublic entity that is making or has made an offering of securities and it appears that the securities may subsequently be registered or subject to a filing with the SEC or other regulatory agency.

statements and knowledge about the industry and the environment is necessary to provide the practitioner with sufficient knowledge to properly evaluate the results of the procedures performed in connection with the review.

.10 If a predecessor auditor has audited the financial statements for a prior period covered by the MD&A presentation, the practitioner should also consider whether, under the particular circumstances, he or she can acquire sufficient knowledge of the business and of the entity's accounting and financial reporting practices for such period so he or she would be able to—

a. Identify types of potential material misstatements in the MD&A and consider the likelihood of their occurrence.

b. Perform the procedures that will provide the practitioner with a basis for reporting whether any information has come to the practitioner's attention to cause him or her to believe any of the following.

(1) The MD&A presentation does not include, in all material respects, the required elements of the rules and regulations adopted by the SEC.

(2) The historical financial amounts included therein have not been accurately derived, in all material respects, from the entity's financial statements for such period.

(3) The underlying information, determinations, estimates, and assumptions of the entity do not provide a reasonable basis for the disclosures contained therein.

.11 A practitioner may accept an engagement to review the MD&A presentation of a public entity for an interim period provided that both of the following conditions are met.

a. The practitioner performs either (*1*) a review of the historical financial statements for the related comparative interim periods and issues a review report thereon in accordance with AU-C section 930, *Interim Financial Information*, or (*2*) an audit of the interim financial statements.

b. The MD&A presentation for the most recent fiscal year has been or will be examined or reviewed by either the practitioner or a predecessor auditor.

[Revised, December 2012, to reflect conforming changes necessary due to the issuance of SAS Nos. 122–126.]

.12 If a predecessor auditor examined or reviewed the MD&A presentation of a public entity for the most recent fiscal year, the practitioner should not accept an engagement to review the MD&A presentation for an interim period unless he or she can acquire sufficient knowledge of the business and of the entity's accounting and financial reporting practices for the interim period to perform the procedures described in paragraph .10.

.13 If a nonpublic entity chooses to prepare MD&A, the practitioner should not accept an engagement to perform a review of such MD&A for an annual period under this section unless both of the following conditions are met.

a. The annual financial statements for the periods covered by the MD&A presentation have been or will be audited and the practitioner has audited or will audit the most recent year (refer to paragraph .07 if the financial statements for prior years were audited by a predecessor auditor).

b. Management will provide a written assertion that the presentation has been prepared using the rules and regulations adopted by the SEC as the criteria. (See paragraph .02.)

.14 A practitioner may accept an engagement to review the MD&A presentation of a nonpublic entity for an interim period provided that all of the following conditions are met.

a. The practitioner performs one of the following:

(1) A review of the historical financial statements for the related interim periods under the Statements on Standards for Accounting and Review Services (SSARSs) and issues a review report thereon

(2) A review of the condensed interim financial information for the related interim periods under AU-C section 930 and issues a review report thereon, and such interim financial information is accompanied by complete annual financial statements for the most recent fiscal year that have been audited

(3) An audit of the interim financial statements

b. The MD&A presentation for the most recent fiscal year has been or will be examined or reviewed.

c. Management will provide a written assertion stating that the presentation has been prepared using the rules and regulations adopted by the SEC as the criteria. (See paragraph .02.)

[Revised, December 2012, to reflect conforming changes necessary due to the issuance of SAS Nos. 122–126.]

Engagement Acceptance Considerations

.15 In determining whether to accept an engagement, the practitioner should consider whether management (and others engaged by management to assist them, such as legal counsel) has the appropriate knowledge of the rules and regulations adopted by the SEC to prepare MD&A.

Responsibilities of Management

.16 Management is responsible for the preparation of the entity's MD&A pursuant to the rules and regulations adopted by the SEC. The preparation of MD&A in conformity with the rules and regulations adopted by the SEC requires management to interpret the criteria, accurately derive the historical amounts from the entity's books and records, make determinations as to the relevancy of information to be included, and make estimates and assumptions that affect reported information.

.17 An entity should not name the practitioner in a client-prepared document as having examined or reviewed MD&A unless the MD&A presentation and related practitioner's report and the related financial statements and auditor's (or accountant's review) report are included in the document (or, in the case of a public entity, incorporated by reference to such information filed with a regulatory agency). If such a statement is made in a document that does not include (or incorporate by reference) such information, the practitioner should request that neither his or her name nor reference to the practitioner be made with respect to the MD&A information, or that such document be revised to include the required presentations and reports. If the client does not comply, the practitioner should advise the client that he or she does not consent to either the use of his or her name or the reference to the practitioner, and he or she should consider what other actions might be appropriate.[15]

Obtaining an Understanding of the SEC Rules and Regulations and Management's Methodology for the Preparation of MD&A

.18 The practitioner should obtain an understanding of the rules and regulations adopted by the SEC for MD&A. (Refer to paragraph .04.)

.19 The practitioner should inquire of management regarding the method of preparing MD&A, including matters such as the sources of the information, how the information is gathered, how management evaluates the types of factors having a material effect on financial condition (including liquidity and capital resources), results of operations, and cash flows, and whether there have been any changes in the procedures from the prior year.

Timing of Procedures

.20 Proper planning by the practitioner contributes to the effectiveness of the attest procedures in an examination or a review of MD&A. Performing some of the work in conjunction with the audit of the historical financial statements or the review of interim financial statements may permit the work to be carried out in a more efficient manner and to be completed at an earlier date. When performing an examination or a review of MD&A, the practitioner may consider the results of tests of controls, analytical procedures,[16] and substantive tests performed in a financial statement audit or analytical procedures and inquiries made in a review of financial statements or interim financial information.

Materiality

.21 The practitioner should consider the concept of materiality in planning and performing the engagement. The objective of an examination or a review is to report on the MD&A presentation taken as a whole and not on the individual amounts and disclosures contained therein. In the context of an MD&A presentation, the concept of materiality encompasses both material omissions (for example, the omission of trends, events, and uncertainties that are currently known to management that are reasonably likely to have material effects on the entity's financial condition, results of operations, liquidity, or capital resources) and material misstatements in MD&A, both of which are referred to herein as a misstatement. Assessing the significance of a misstatement of some items in MD&A may be more dependent upon qualitative than

---

[15] In considering what other actions, if any, may be appropriate in these circumstances, the practitioner may wish to consult his or her legal counsel.

[16] AU-C section 520, *Analytical Procedures*, defines analytical procedures as "evaluations of financial information through analysis of plausible relationships among both financial and nonfinancial data. Analytical procedures also encompass such investigation, as is necessary, of identified fluctuations or relationships that are inconsistent with other relevant information or that differ from expected values by a significant amount." In applying analytical procedures to MD&A, the practitioner develops expectations of matters that would be discussed in MD&A by identifying and using plausible relationships that are reasonably expected to exist based on the practitioner's understanding of the client and of the industry in which the client operates, and the knowledge of relationships among the various financial elements gained through the audit of financial statements or review of interim financial information. Refer to AU-C section 520 for further discussion of analytical procedures. [Footnote revised, December 2012, to reflect conforming changes necessary due to the issuance of SAS Nos. 122–126.]

quantitative considerations. Qualitative aspects of materiality relate to the relevance and reliability of the information presented (for example, qualitative aspects of materiality are considered in assessing whether the underlying information, determinations, estimates, and assumptions of the entity provide a reasonable basis for the disclosures in the MD&A). Furthermore, quantitative information is often more meaningful when accompanied by qualitative disclosures. For example, quantitative information about market risk-sensitive instruments is more meaningful when accompanied by qualitative information about an entity's market risk exposures and how those exposures are managed. Materiality is also a concept that is judged in light of the expected range of reasonableness of the information; therefore, users should not expect prospective information (information about events that have not yet occurred) to be as precise as historical information.

.22 In expressing an opinion, or providing the limited assurance of a review engagement, on the presentation, the practitioner should consider the omission or misstatement of an individual assertion (see paragraph .34) to be material if the magnitude of the omission or misstatement—individually or when aggregated with other omissions or misstatements—is such that a reasonable person using the MD&A presentation would be influenced by the inclusion or correction of the individual assertion. The relative rather than absolute size of an omission or misstatement may determine whether it is material in a given situation.

Inclusion of Pro Forma Financial Information

.23 Management may include pro forma financial information with respect to a business combination or other transactions in MD&A. The practitioner should consider the guidance in paragraph .10 of section 401, *Reporting on Pro Forma Financial Information*, when performing procedures with respect to such information, even if management indicates in MD&A that certain information has been derived from unaudited financial statements. For example, in an examination of MD&A, the practitioner's procedures would ordinarily include obtaining an understanding of the underlying transaction or event, discussing with management their assumptions, obtaining sufficient evidence in support of the adjustments, and other procedures for the purpose of expressing an opinion on the MD&A presentation taken as a whole and not for expressing an opinion on (or providing the limited assurance of a review of) the pro forma financial information included therein under section 401.

Inclusion of External Information

.24 An entity may also include in its MD&A information external to the entity, such as the rating of its debt by certain rating agencies or comparisons with statistics from a trade association. Such external information should also be subjected to the practitioner's examination or review procedures. For example, in an examination, the practitioner might compare information concerning the statistics of a trade organization to a published source; however, the practitioner would not be expected to test the underlying support for the trade association's calculation of such statistics.

Inclusion of Forward-Looking Information

.25 An entity may include certain forward-looking disclosures in the MD&A presentation, including cautionary language concerning the achievability of the matters disclosed. Although any forward-looking disclosures that are included in the MD&A presentation should be subjected to the practitioner's examination or review, such information is subjected to testing only for the purpose of expressing an opinion that the underlying information, determinations, estimates, and assumptions provide a reasonable basis for the disclosures contained therein or providing the limited assurance of a review on the MD&A presentation taken as a whole. The practitioner may consider the guidance in section 301, *Financial Forecasts and Projections*, when performing procedures with respect to forward-looking information. The practitioner may also consider whether meaningful cautionary language has been included with the forward-looking information.

.26 Section 27A of the Securities Act of 1933 (the 1933 Act) and Section 21E of the Securities Exchange Act of 1934 (the 1934 Act) provide a safe harbor from liability in private litigation with respect to forward-looking statements that include or make reference to meaningful cautionary language. However, such sections also include exclusions from safe harbor protection in certain situations. Whether an entity's forward-looking statements and the practitioner's report thereon qualify for safe harbor protection is a legal matter.

Inclusion of Voluntary Information

.27 An entity may voluntarily include other information in the MD&A presentation that is not required by the rules and regulations adopted by the SEC for MD&A. When the entity includes in MD&A additional information required by other rules and regulations of the SEC (for example, Item 305 of Regulation S-K, *Quantitative and Qualitative Disclosures About Market Risk*), the practitioner should also consider such other rules and regulations in subjecting such information to his or her examination or review procedures.[17]

Examination Engagement

.28 To express an opinion about whether (*a*) the presentation includes, in all material respects, the required elements of the rules and regulations adopted by the SEC, (*b*) the historical financial amounts have been accurately derived, in all material respects, from the entity's financial statements, and (*c*) the underlying information, determinations, estimates, and assumptions of the entity provide a reasonable basis for the disclosures contained therein, the practitioner seeks to obtain reasonable assurance by accumulating sufficient evidence in support of the disclosures and assumptions, thereby restricting attestation risk to an appropriately low level.

Attestation Risk

.29 In an engagement to examine MD&A, the practitioner plans and performs the examination to obtain reasonable assurance of detecting both intentional and unintentional misstatements that are material to the MD&A presentation taken as a whole. Absolute assurance is not attainable because of factors such as the need for judgment regarding the areas to be tested and the nature, timing, and extent of tests to be performed; the concept of selective testing of the data; and the inherent limitations of the controls applicable to the preparation of MD&A. The practitioner exercises professional judgment in

---

[17] To the extent that the voluntary information includes forward-looking information, refer to paragraphs .25–.26.

assessing the significant determinations made by management as to the relevancy of information to be included, and the estimates and assumptions that affect reported information. As a result of these factors, in the great majority of cases, the practitioner has to rely on evidence that is persuasive rather than convincing. Also, procedures may be ineffective for detecting an intentional misstatement that is concealed through collusion among client personnel and third parties or among management or employees of the client. Therefore, the subsequent discovery that a material misstatement exists in the MD&A does not, in and of itself, evidence (*a*) failure to obtain reasonable assurance; (*b*) inadequate planning, performance, or judgment on the part of the practitioner; (*c*) the absence of due professional care; or (*d*) a failure to comply with this section.

.30 Factors to be considered by the practitioner in planning an examination of MD&A include (*a*) the anticipated level of attestation risk related to assertions embodied in the MD&A presentation, (*b*) preliminary judgments about materiality for attest purposes, (*c*) the items within the MD&A presentation that are likely to require revision or adjustment, and (*d*) conditions that may require extension or modification of attest procedures. For purposes of an engagement to examine MD&A, the components of attestation risk are defined as follows.

a. *Inherent risk* is the susceptibility of an assertion within MD&A to a material misstatement, assuming that there are no related controls. (See paragraphs .34–.38.)

b. *Control risk* is the risk that a material misstatement that could occur in an assertion within MD&A will not be prevented or detected on a timely basis by the entity's controls; some control risk will always exist because of the inherent limitations of any internal control.

c. *Detection risk* is the risk that the practitioner will not detect a material misstatement that exists in an assertion within MD&A.

Inherent Risk

.31 The level of inherent risk varies with the nature of the assertion. For example, the inherent risk concerning financial information included in the MD&A presentation may be low, whereas the inherent risk concerning the completeness of the disclosure of the entity's risks or liquidity may be high.

Control Risk

.32 The practitioner should assess control risk as discussed in paragraphs .53–.57. Assessing control risk contributes to the practitioner's evaluation of the risk that material misstatement in the MD&A exists. In the process of assessing control risk (together with assessing inherent risk), the practitioner may obtain evidential matter about the risk that such misstatement may exist. The practitioner uses this evidential matter as part of the reasonable basis for his or her opinion on the MD&A presentation taken as a whole.

Detection Risk

.33 In determining an acceptable level of detection risk, the practitioner assesses inherent risk and control risk, and considers the extent to which he or she seeks to restrict attestation risk. As assessed inherent risk or control risk decreases, the acceptable level of detection risk increases. Accordingly, the practitioner may alter the nature, timing, and extent of tests performed based on the assessments of inherent risk and control risk.

Nature of Assertions

.34 Assertions are representations by management that are embodied in the MD&A presentation. They can be either explicit or implicit and can be classified according to the following broad categories:

a. Occurrence

b. Consistency with the financial statements

c. Completeness

d. Presentation and disclosure

.35 Assertions about occurrence address whether reported transactions or events have occurred during a given period. Assertions about consistency with the financial statements address whether—

a. Reported transactions, events, and explanations are consistent with the financial statements.

b. Historical financial amounts have been accurately derived from the financial statements and related records.

c. Nonfinancial data have been accurately derived from related records.

.36 Assertions about completeness address whether descriptions of transactions and events necessary to obtain an understanding of the entity's financial condition (including liquidity and capital resources), changes in financial condition, results of operations, and material commitments for capital resources are included in MD&A; and whether known events, transactions, conditions, trends, demands, commitments, or uncertainties that will result in or are reasonably likely to result in material changes to these items are appropriately described in the MD&A presentation.

.37 For example, if management asserts that the reason for an increase in revenues is a price increase in the current year, they are explicitly asserting that both an increase in revenues and a price increase have occurred in the current year, and implicitly asserting that any historical financial amounts included are consistent with the financial statements for such period. They are also implicitly asserting that the explanation for the increase in revenues is complete; that there are no other significant reasons for the increase in revenues.

.38 Assertions about presentation and disclosure address whether information included in the MD&A presentation is properly classified, described, and disclosed. For example, management asserts that any forward-looking information included in MD&A is properly classified as being based on management's present assessment and includes an appropriate description of the expected results. To further disclose the nature of such information, management may also include a statement that actual results in the future may differ materially from management's present assessment. (See paragraphs .25–.26.)

.39 The auditor of the underlying financial statements is responsible for designing and performing audit procedures to obtain sufficient appropriate audit evidence to be able to draw reasonable conclusions on which to base the auditor's opinion, as discussed in AU-C section 500, *Audit Evidence*. Although procedures designed to achieve the practitioner's objective of forming an opinion on the MD&A presentation taken as a whole may test certain assertions embodied in the underlying financial statements, the practitioner is not expected to test the underlying financial statement assertions in an examination of MD&A. For example, the practitioner is not expected to test the completeness of revenues or the existence of inventory when testing the assertions in MD&A concerning an increase in revenues or an increase in inventory levels; assurance related to completeness of revenues or for existence of inventory would be obtained as part of the audit. The practitioner is, however, responsible for testing the completeness of the explanation for the increase in revenues or the increase in inventory levels. [Revised, December 2012, to reflect conforming changes necessary due to the issuance of SAS Nos. 122–126.]

Performing an Examination Engagement

.40 The practitioner should exercise (*a*) due professional care in planning, performing, and evaluating the results of his or her examination procedures and (*b*) the proper degree of professional skepticism to obtain reasonable assurance that material misstatements will be detected.

.41 In an examination of MD&A, the practitioner should perform the following.

a. Obtain an understanding of the rules and regulations adopted by the SEC for MD&A and management's method of preparing MD&A. (See paragraphs .18–.19.)

b. Plan the engagement. (See paragraphs .42–.48.)

c. Consider relevant portions of the entity's internal control applicable to the preparation of MD&A. (See paragraphs .49–.58.)

d. Obtain sufficient evidence, including testing completeness. (See paragraphs .59–.64.)

e. Consider the effect of events subsequent to the balance-sheet date. (See paragraphs .65–.66.)

f. Obtain written representations from management concerning its responsibility for MD&A, completeness of minutes, events subsequent to the balance-sheet date, and other matters about which the practitioner believes written representations are appropriate. (See paragraphs .110–.112.)

g. Form an opinion about whether the MD&A presentation includes, in all material respects, the required elements of the rules and regulations adopted by the SEC, whether the historical financial amounts included therein have been accurately derived, in all material respects, from the entity's financial statements, and whether the underlying information, determinations, estimates, and assumptions of the entity provide a reasonable basis for the disclosures contained in the MD&A. (See paragraph .67.)

Planning the Engagement

General Considerations

.42 Planning an engagement to examine MD&A involves developing an overall strategy for the expected scope and performance of the engagement. When developing an overall strategy for the engagement, the practitioner should consider factors such as the following:

- Matters affecting the industry in which the entity operates, such as financial reporting practices, economic conditions, laws and regulations, and technological changes
- Knowledge of the entity's internal control applicable to the preparation of MD&A obtained during the audit of the financial statements and the extent of recent changes, if any
- Matters relating to the entity's business, including its organization, operating characteristics, capital structure, and distribution methods
- The types of relevant information that management reports to external analysts (for example, press releases and presentations to lenders and rating agencies, if any, concerning past and future performance)
- How the entity analyzes actual performance compared to budgets and the types of information provided in documents submitted to the board of directors for purposes of the entity's day-to-day operations and long-range planning
- The extent of management's knowledge of and experience with the rules and regulations adopted by the SEC for MD&A
- If the entity is a nonpublic entity, the intended use of the MD&A presentation
- Preliminary judgments about (*a*) materiality, (*b*) inherent risk at the individual assertion level, and (*c*) factors (for example, matters identified during the audit or review of the historical financial statements) relating to significant deficiencies in internal control applicable to the preparation of MD&A (See paragraph .58.)
- The fraud risk factors or other conditions identified during the audit of the most recent annual financial statements and the practitioner's response to such risk factors
- The type and extent of evidential matter supporting management's assertions and disclosures in the MD&A presentation
- The nature of complex or subjective matters potentially material to the MD&A presentation that may require special skill or knowledge and whether such matters may require using the work of a specialist to obtain sufficient evidential matter (See paragraph .47.)
- The presence of an internal audit function (See paragraph .48.)

.43 In planning an engagement when MD&A has not previously been examined, the practitioner should consider the degree to which the entity has information available for such prior periods and the continuity of the entity's personnel and their ability to respond to inquiries with respect to such periods. In addition, the practitioner should obtain an understanding of the entity's internal control in prior years applicable to the preparation of MD&A.

Consideration of Audit Results

.44 The practitioner should also consider the results of the audits of the financial statements for the periods covered by the MD&A presentation on the examination engagement, such as matters relating to the following:

- The availability and condition of the entity's records
- The nature and magnitude of audit adjustments

- Misstatements[18] that were not corrected in the financial statements that may affect MD&A disclosures (for example, misclassifications between financial statement line items)

[Revised, December 2012, to reflect conforming changes necessary due to the issuance of SAS Nos. 122–126.]

.45 The practitioner should also consider the possible impact on the scope of the examination engagement of any modification or contemplated modification of the auditor's report, including matters addressed in explanatory language. For example, if the auditor has modified the auditor's report to include a going-concern uncertainty explanatory paragraph, the practitioner would consider such a matter in assessing attestation risk.

Multiple Components

.46 In an engagement to examine MD&A, if the entity has operations in several components (for example, locations, branches, subsidiaries, or programs), the practitioner examining the group's MD&A should determine the components to which procedures should be applied. In making such a determination and in selecting the components to be tested, the practitioner examining the group's MD&A should consider factors such as the following:

- The relative importance of each component to the applicable disclosure in the group's MD&A
- The degree of centralization of records
- The effectiveness of controls, particularly those that affect group management's direct control over the exercise of authority delegated to others and its ability to supervise activities at various locations effectively
- The nature and extent of operations conducted at the various components
- The similarity of operations and internal control for different components

The practitioner examining the group's MD&A should consider whether the audit base of the components is consistent with the components that are disclosed in MD&A Accordingly, it may be desirable for the practitioner examining the group's MD&A to coordinate the audit work with the components that will be disclosed. [Revised, December 2012, to reflect conforming changes necessary due to the issuance of SAS Nos. 122–126.]

Using the Work of a Specialist

.47 In some engagements to examine MD&A, the nature of complex or subjective matters potentially material to the MD&A presentation may require specialized skill or knowledge in a particular field other than accounting or auditing. For example, the entity may include information concerning plant production capacity, which would ordinarily be determined by an engineer. In such cases, the practitioner may use the work of a specialist and should consider the relevant guidance in AU-C section 620, *Using the Work of an Auditor's Specialist*. An auditor's specialist may be either an auditor's internal specialist (for example, a partner of the auditor's firm) or an external specialist. [Revised,

---

[18] Refer to paragraphs .05–.06 and .11–.13 of AU-C section 320, *Materiality in Planning and Performing an Audit*, and paragraph .10 of AU-C section 450, *Evaluation of Misstatements Identified During the Audit*. [Footnote revised, December 2012, to reflect conforming changes necessary due to the issuance of SAS Nos. 122–126.]

December 2012, to reflect conforming changes necessary due to the issuance of SAS Nos. 122–126.]

Internal Audit Function

.48 Another factor the practitioner should consider when planning the engagement is whether the entity has an internal audit function and the extent to which internal auditors are involved in directly testing the MD&A presentation, in monitoring the entity's internal control applicable to the preparation of MD&A, or in testing the underlying records supporting disclosures in the MD&A. A practitioner should consider the guidance in AU-C section 570, *The Auditor's Consideration of the Internal Audit Function in an Audit of Financial Statements*, when addressing the competence and objectivity of internal auditors; the nature, timing, and extent of work to be performed; and other related matters. [Revised, December 2012, to reflect conforming changes necessary due to the issuance of SAS Nos. 122–126.]

Consideration of Internal Control Applicable to the Preparation of MD&A

.49 The practitioner should obtain an understanding of the entity's internal control applicable to the preparation of MD&A sufficient to plan the engagement and to assess control risk. Generally, controls that are relevant to an examination pertain to the entity's objective of preparing MD&A in conformity with the rules and regulations adopted by the SEC, and may include controls within the control environment, risk assessment, information and communication, control activities, and monitoring components.

.50 The controls relating to operations and compliance objectives may be relevant to an examination if they pertain to data the practitioner evaluates or uses in applying examination procedures. For example, controls over the gathering of information, which are different from financial statement controls, and controls relating to nonfinancial data that are included in the MD&A presentation, may be relevant to an examination engagement.

.51 In planning the examination, knowledge of such controls should be used to identify types of potential misstatement (including types of potential material omissions), to consider factors that affect the risk of material misstatement and to design appropriate tests.

.52 A practitioner generally obtains an understanding of the design of the entity's internal control applicable to the preparation of MD&A by making inquiries of appropriate management, supervisory, and staff personnel; by inspection of the entity's documents; and by observation of the entity's relevant activities, including controls over matters discussed, nonfinancial data included, and management evaluation of the reasonableness of information included. The nature and extent of procedures a practitioner performs vary from entity to entity and are influenced by factors such as the entity's complexity, the length of time that the entity has prepared MD&A pursuant to the rules and regulations adopted by the SEC, the practitioner's knowledge of the entity's controls obtained in audits and previous professional engagements, and judgments about materiality.

.53 After obtaining an understanding of the entity's internal control applicable to the preparation of MD&A, the practitioner assesses control risk for the assertions embodied in the MD&A presentation. (Refer to paragraphs .34–.39.) The practitioner may assess control risk at the maximum level (the greatest probability that a material misstatement that could occur in an assertion will not be prevented or detected on a timely basis by an entity's controls) because the practitioner believes controls are unlikely to pertain to an assertion, are unlikely to be effective, or because evaluating their effectiveness would be inefficient. Alternatively, the practitioner may obtain evidential matter about the effectiveness of both the design and operation of a control that supports a lower assessed level of control risk. Such evidential matter may be obtained from tests of controls planned and performed concurrently with obtaining the understanding of the internal control or from procedures performed to obtain the understanding that were not specifically planned as tests of controls.

.54 After obtaining the understanding and assessing control risk, the practitioner may desire to seek a further reduction in the assessed level of control risk for certain assertions. In such cases, the practitioner considers whether evidential matter sufficient to support a further reduction is likely to be available and whether performing additional tests of controls to obtain such evidential matter would be efficient.

.55 When seeking to assess control risk below the maximum for controls over financial and nonfinancial data, the practitioner should perform tests of controls to obtain evidence to support the assessed level of control risk. For example, the practitioner may perform tests of controls directed toward the effectiveness of the design or operation of internal control over the accumulation of the number of units sold for a manufacturing company, average interest rates earned and paid for a financial institution, or average net sales per square foot for a retail entity.

.56 The practitioner uses the knowledge provided by the understanding of internal control applicable to the preparation of MD&A and the assessed level of control risk in determining the nature, timing, and extent of substantive tests for the MD&A assertions.

.57 The practitioner should document the understanding of the internal control components obtained to plan the examination and the assessment of control risk. The form and extent of this documentation is influenced by the size and complexity of the entity, as well as the nature of the entity's controls applicable to the preparation of MD&A.

.58 During the course of an engagement to examine MD&A, the practitioner may become aware of control deficiencies in the design or operation of controls applicable to the preparation of MD&A that could adversely affect the entity's ability to prepare MD&A in accordance with the rules and regulations adopted by the SEC. The practitioner should consider the implications of such control deficiencies on his or her ability to rely on management's explanations and on comparisons to summary accounting records. A practitioner's responsibility to communicate these control deficiencies in an examination of MD&A is similar to the auditor's responsibility described in AU-C section 265, *Communicating Internal Control Related Matters Identified in an Audit*, and AU-C section 260, *The Auditor's Communication With Those Charged With Governance*. [Revised, March 2006, to reflect conforming changes necessary due to the issuance of SAS No. 112. Revised, January 2010, to reflect conforming changes necessary due to the issuance of SAS No. 115. Revised, December 2012, to reflect conforming changes necessary due to the issuance of SAS Nos. 122–126.]

Obtaining Sufficient Evidence

.59 The practitioner should apply procedures to obtain reasonable assurance of detecting material misstatements. In an audit of historical financial statements, the practitioner will have applied audit procedures to some of the information included in the MD&A. However, because the objective of those audit procedures is to have a reasonable basis for expressing an opinion on the financial statements taken as a whole rather than on the MD&A, certain additional examination procedures should be performed as discussed in paragraphs .60–.64. Determining these procedures and evaluating the sufficiency of the evidence obtained are matters of professional judgment.

.60 The practitioner ordinarily should apply the following procedures.

a. Read the MD&A and compare the content for consistency with the audited financial statements; compare financial amounts to the audited financial statements or related accounting records and analyses; recompute the increases, decreases, and percentages disclosed.

b. Compare nonfinancial amounts to the audited financial statements, if applicable, or to other records. (Refer to paragraphs .62–.64.)

c. Consider whether the explanations in MD&A are consistent with the information obtained during the audit; investigate further those explanations that cannot be substantiated by information in the audit working papers through inquiry (including inquiry of officers and other executives having responsibility for operational areas) and inspection of client records.

d. Examine internally generated documents (for example, variance analyses, sales analyses, wage cost analyses, sales or service pricing sheets, and business plans or programs) and externally generated documents (for example, correspondence, contracts, or loan agreements) in support of the existence, occurrence, or expected occurrence of events, transactions, conditions, trends, demands, commitments, and uncertainties disclosed in the MD&A.

e. Obtain available prospective financial information (for example, budgets; sales forecasts; forecasts of labor, overhead, and materials costs; capital expenditure requests; and financial forecasts and projections) and compare such information to forward-looking MD&A disclosures. Inquire of management as to the procedures used to prepare the prospective financial information. Evaluate whether the underlying information, determinations, estimates, and assumptions of the entity provide a reasonable basis for the MD&A disclosures of events, transactions, conditions, trends, demands, commitments, or uncertainties.[19]

f. Consider obtaining available prospective financial information relating to prior periods and comparing actual results with forecasted and projected amounts.

g. Make inquiries of officers and other executives having responsibility for operational areas (such as sales, marketing, and production) and financial and accounting matters, as to their plans and expectations for the future that could affect the entity's liquidity and capital resources.

h. Consider obtaining external information concerning industry trends, inflation, and changing prices and comparing the related MD&A disclosures to such information.

i. Compare the information in MD&A with the rules and regulations adopted by the SEC and consider whether the presentation includes the required elements of such rules and regulations.

---

[19] Refer to paragraph .26 for a discussion concerning the safe harbor rules for forward-looking statements.

j. Read the minutes of meetings to date of the board of directors and other significant committees to identify matters that may affect MD&A; consider whether such matters are appropriately addressed in MD&A.

k. Inquire of officers as to the entity's prior experience with the SEC and the extent of comments received upon review of documents by the SEC; read correspondence between the entity and the SEC with respect to such review, if any.

l. Obtain public communications (for example, press releases and quarterly reports) and the related supporting documentation dealing with historical and future results; consider whether MD&A is consistent with such communications.

m. Consider obtaining other types of publicly available information (for example, analyst reports and news articles); compare the MD&A presentation with such information.

Testing Completeness

.61 The practitioner should design procedures to test the presentation for completeness, including tests of the completeness of explanations that relate to historical disclosures as discussed in paragraphs .36–.37. The practitioner should also consider whether the MD&A discloses matters that could significantly impact future financial condition and results of operations of the entity by considering information that he or she obtained through the following:

a. Audit of the financial statements

b. Inquiries of the entity's officers and other executives directed to current events, conditions, economic changes, commitments and uncertainties, within both the entity and its industry

c. Other information obtained through procedures such as those listed in paragraphs .60 and .65–.66

As discussed in paragraph .31, the inherent risk concerning the completeness of disclosures may be high; if it is, the practitioner may extend the procedures (for example, by making additional inquiries of management or by examining additional internally generated documents).

Nonfinancial Data

.62 Management may include nonfinancial data (such as units produced; the number of units sold, locations, or customers; plant utilization; or square footage) in the MD&A. The practitioner should consider whether the definitions used by management for such nonfinancial data are reasonable for the particular disclosure in the MD&A and whether there are suitable criteria (for example, industry standards with respect to square footage for retail operations), as discussed in paragraphs .23–.32 of section 101.

.63 In some situations, the nonfinancial data or the controls over the nonfinancial data may have been tested by the practitioner in conjunction with the financial statement audit; however, the practitioner's consideration of the nature of the procedures to apply to nonfinancial data in an examination of MD&A is based on the concept of materiality with respect to the MD&A presentation. The practitioner should consider whether industry standards exist for the nonfinancial data or whether there are different methods of measurement that may be used, and, if such methods could result in significantly different results, whether the method of measurement selected by management is reasonable and consistent between periods covered by the MD&A presentation. For example, the number of customers reported by management could vary depending on whether management defines a customer as a subsidiary or "ship to" location of a company rather than the company itself.

.64 In testing nonfinancial data included in the MD&A, the practitioner may seek to assess control risk below the maximum for controls over such nonfinancial data, as discussed in paragraph .55. The practitioner weighs the increase in effort of the examination associated with the additional tests of controls that is necessary to obtain evidential matter against the resulting decrease in examination effort associated with the reduced substantive tests. For those nonfinancial assertions for which the practitioner performs additional tests of controls, the practitioner determines the assessed level of control risk that the results of those tests will support. This assessed level of control risk is used in determining the appropriate detection risk to accept for those nonfinancial assertions and, accordingly, in determining the nature, timing, and extent of substantive tests for such assertions.

Consideration of the Effect of Events Subsequent to the Balance-Sheet Date

.65 As there is an expectation by the SEC that MD&A considers events through a date at or near the filing date,[20] the practitioner should consider information about events[21] that comes to his or her attention after the end of the period addressed by MD&A and prior to the issuance of his or her report that may have a material effect on the entity's financial condition (including liquidity and capital resources), changes in financial condition, results of operations, and material commitments for capital resources. Events or matters that should be disclosed in MD&A include those that—[22]

- Are reasonably expected to have a material favorable or unfavorable impact on net sales or revenues or income from continuing operations.
- Are reasonably likely to result in the entity's liquidity increasing or decreasing in any material way.
- Will have a material effect on the entity's capital resources.
- Would cause reported financial information not to be necessarily indicative of future operating results or of future financial condition.

The practitioner should consider whether events identified during the examination of the MD&A presentation or the audit of the related financial statements require adjustment to or disclosure in the MD&A presentation. When MD&A will be included or incorporated by reference in a 1933 Act document that is filed with the SEC, the practitioner's procedures should extend up to the filing

---

[20] A registration statement under the 1933 Act speaks as of its effective date.

[21] Such events are only referred to as *subsequent events* in relation to an MD&A presentation if they occur after the MD&A presentation has been issued. The annual MD&A presentation ordinarily would not be updated for subsequent events if an MD&A presentation for a subsequent interim period has been issued or the event has been reported through a filing on Form 8-K.

[22] The practitioner should refer to the rules and regulations adopted by the SEC for other examples of events that should be disclosed.

date or as close to it as is reasonable and practicable in the circumstances.[23] If a public entity's MD&A presentation is to be included only in a filing under the 1934 Act (for example, Forms 10-K or 10-KSB), the practitioner's responsibility to consider subsequent events does not extend beyond the date of the report on MD&A. Paragraphs .94–.98 provide guidance when the practitioner is engaged subsequent to the filing of the MD&A presentation.

.66 In an examination of MD&A, the practitioner's fieldwork ordinarily extends beyond the date of the auditor's report on the related financial statements.[24] Accordingly, the practitioner generally should—

a. Read available minutes of meetings of stockholders, the board of directors, and other appropriate committees; as to meetings for which minutes are not available, inquire about matters dealt with at such meetings.

b. Read the latest available interim financial statements for periods subsequent to the date of the auditor's report, compare them with the financial statements for the periods covered by the MD&A, and inquire of and discuss with officers and other executives having responsibility for operational, financial, and accounting matters (limited where appropriate to major locations) matters such as the following:

- Whether interim financial statements have been prepared on the same basis as the audited financial statements
- Whether there were any significant changes in the entity's operations, liquidity, or capital resources in the subsequent period
- The current status of items in the financial statements for which the MD&A has been prepared that were accounted for on the basis of tentative, preliminary, or inconclusive data
- Whether any unusual adjustments were made during the period from the balance-sheet date to the date of inquiry

c. Make inquiries of members of senior management as to the current status of matters concerning litigation, claims, and assessments identified during the audit of the financial statements and of any new matters or unfavorable developments. Consider obtaining updated legal letters from legal counsel.[25]

d. Consider whether there have been any changes in economic conditions or in the industry that could have a significant effect on the entity.

---

[23] Additionally, if the practitioner's report on MD&A is included or incorporated by reference in a 1933 Act document, the practitioner should extend his or her procedures with respect to subsequent events from the date of his or her report on MD&A up to the effective date or as close thereto as is reasonable and practicable in the circumstances.

[24] Undertaking an engagement to examine MD&A does not extend the auditor's responsibility to update the subsequent events review procedures for the financial statements beyond the date of the auditor's report. However, see AU-C section 560, *Events and Subsequently Discovered Facts*. Also, see AU-C section 925, *Filings With the U.S. Securities and Exchange Commission Under the Securities Act of 1933*, as to an auditor's responsibility when his or her report is included in a registration statement filed under the 1933 Act. [Footnote revised, December 2012, to reflect conforming changes necessary due to the issuance of SAS Nos. 122–126.]

[25] See paragraphs .16–.24 of AU-C section 501, *Audit Evidence—Specific Considerations for Selected Items*, for guidance concerning obtaining legal letters. [Footnote revised, December 2012, to reflect conforming changes necessary due to the issuance of SAS Nos. 122–126.]

e. Obtain written representations from appropriate officials as to whether any events occurred subsequent to the latest balance-sheet date that would require disclosure in the MD&A. (See paragraphs .110–.112.)

f. Make such additional inquiries or perform such other procedures as considered necessary and appropriate to address questions that arise in carrying out the foregoing procedures, inquiries, and discussions.

Forming an Opinion

.67 The practitioner should consider the concept of materiality discussed in paragraphs .21–.22, and the impact of any modification of the auditor's report on the historical financial statements in forming an opinion on the examination of MD&A, including the practitioner's ability to evaluate the results of inquiries and other procedures.

Reporting

.68 In order for the practitioner to issue a report on an examination of MD&A, the financial statements for the periods covered by the MD&A presentation and the related auditor's report(s) should accompany the MD&A presentation (or, with respect to a public entity, be incorporated in the document containing the MD&A by reference to information filed with a regulatory agency). In addition, if the entity is a nonpublic entity, one of the following conditions should be met.

a. A statement should be included in the body of the MD&A presentation that it has been prepared using the rules and regulations adopted by the SEC.

b. A separate written assertion should accompany the MD&A presentation or such assertion should be included in a representation letter obtained from the entity.

.69 The practitioner's report on an examination of MD&A should include the following:

a. A title that includes the word *independent*

b. An identification of the MD&A presentation, including the period covered

c. A statement that management is responsible for the preparation of the MD&A pursuant to the rules and regulations adopted by the SEC, and a statement that the practitioner's responsibility is to express an opinion on the presentation based on his or her examination

d. A reference to the auditor's report on the related financial statements, and if the report was other than a standard report, the substantive reasons therefor

e. A statement that the examination was conducted in accordance with attestation standards established by the AICPA and a description of the scope of an examination of MD&A

f. A statement that the practitioner believes the examination provides a reasonable basis for his or her opinion *g.* A paragraph stating that—

(1) The preparation of MD&A requires management to interpret the criteria, make determinations as to the relevancy of information to be included, and make estimates and assumptions that affect reported information

(2) Actual results in the future may differ materially from management's present assessment of information regarding the estimated future impact of transactions and events that have occurred or are expected to occur, expected sources of liquidity and capital resources, operating trends, commitments, and uncertainties

h. If the entity is a nonpublic entity, a statement that, although the entity is not subject to the rules and regulations of the SEC, the MD&A presentation is intended to be a presentation in accordance with the rules and regulations adopted by the SEC

i. The practitioner's opinion on whether—

(1) The presentation includes, in all material respects, the required elements of the rules and regulations adopted by the SEC

(2) The historical financial amounts have been accurately derived, in all material respects, from the entity's financial statements

(3) The underlying information, determinations, estimates, and assumptions of the entity provide a reasonable basis for the disclosures contained therein

j. The manual or printed signature of the practitioner's firm

k. The date of the examination report

Appendix A [paragraph .114], "Examination Reports," includes a standard examination report. (See Example 1.)

Dating

.70 The practitioner's report on the examination of MD&A should be dated as of the completion of the practitioner's examination procedures. That date should not precede the date of the auditor's report on the latest historical financial statements covered by the MD&A.

Report Modifications

.71 The practitioner should modify the standard report described in paragraph .69, if any of the following conditions exist.

- The presentation excludes a material required element under the rules and regulations adopted by the SEC. (See paragraph .72.)
- The historical financial amounts have not been accurately derived, in all material respects, from the entity's financial statements. (See paragraph .72.)
- The underlying information, determinations, estimates, and assumptions used by management do not provide the entity with a reasonable basis for the disclosure in the MD&A. (See paragraph .72.)
- There is a restriction on the scope of the engagement. (See paragraph .73.)

- The practitioner decides to refer to the report of another practitioner as the basis in part for his or her report. (See paragraph .74.)
- The practitioner is engaged to examine the MD&A presentation after it has been filed with the SEC or other regulatory agency. (See paragraphs .94–.98.)

.72 The practitioner should express a qualified or an adverse opinion if (*a*) the MD&A presentation excludes a material required element, (*b*) historical financial amounts have not been accurately derived in all material respects, or (*c*) the underlying information, determinations, estimates, and assumptions of the entity do not provide a reasonable basis for the disclosures; for example, if there is a lack of consistency between management's method of measuring nonfinancial data between periods covered by the MD&A presentation. The basis for such opinion should be stated in the practitioner's report. Appendix A [paragraph .114] includes several examples of such modifications. (See Example 2.) Also refer to paragraph .107 for required communications with the audit committee.

.73 If the practitioner is unable to perform the procedures he or she considers necessary in the circumstances, the practitioner should modify the report or withdraw from the engagement. If the practitioner modifies the report, he or she should describe the limitation on the scope of the examination in an explanatory paragraph and qualify his or her opinion, or disclaim an opinion. However, limitations on the ability of the practitioner to perform necessary procedures could also arise because of the lack of adequate support for a significant representation in the MD&A. That circumstance may result in a conclusion that the unsupported representation constitutes a material misstatement of fact and, accordingly, the practitioner may qualify his or her opinion or express an adverse opinion, as described in paragraph .72.

Reference to Report of Another Practitioner

.74 If another practitioner examined the MD&A presentation of a component (refer to paragraph .46), the practitioner examining the group's MD&A may decide to make reference to such report of the component practitioner as a basis for his or her opinion on the group's consolidated MD&A presentation. The practitioner examining the group's MD&A should disclose this fact in the introductory paragraph of the report and should refer to the report of the component practitioner in expressing an opinion on the group's consolidated MD&A presentation. These references indicate (1) that the practitioner examining the group's MD&A is not taking responsibility for the work of the component practitioner, and (2) the source of the examination evidence with respect to those components for which reference to the examination of component practitioners is made. Appendix A [paragraph .114] provides an example of a report for such a situation. (See example 3.) Refer to paragraph .105 for guidance when the other practitioner does not issue a report. [Revised, December 2012, to reflect conforming changes necessary due to the issuance of SAS Nos. 122–126.]

Emphasis of a Matter

.75 In a number of circumstances, the practitioner may wish to emphasize a matter regarding the MD&A presentation. For example, he or she may wish to emphasize that the entity has included information beyond the required elements of the rules and regulations adopted by the SEC. Such explanatory comments should be presented in a separate paragraph of the practitioner's report.

Review Engagement

.76 The objective of a review engagement, including a review of MD&A for an interim period, is to accumulate sufficient evidence to provide the practitioner with a basis for reporting whether any information came to the practitioner's attention to cause him or her to believe that (*a*) the MD&A presentation does not include, in all material respects, the required elements of the rules and regulations adopted by the SEC, (*b*) the historical financial amounts included therein have not been accurately derived, in all material respects, from the entity's financial statements, or (*c*) the underlying information, determinations, estimates, and assumptions of the entity do not provide a reasonable basis for the disclosures contained therein. MD&A for an interim period may be a freestanding presentation or it may be combined with the MD&A presentation for the most recent fiscal year. Procedures for conducting a review of MD&A generally are limited to inquiries and analytical procedures, rather than also including search and verification procedures, concerning factors that have a material effect on financial condition, including liquidity and capital resources, results of operations, and cash flows. In a review engagement, the practitioner should—

a. Obtain an understanding of the rules and regulations adopted by the SEC for MD&A and management's method of preparing MD&A. (See paragraphs .18–.19.)

b. Plan the engagement. (See paragraph .77.)

c. Consider relevant portions of the entity's internal control applicable to the preparation of the MD&A. (See paragraph .78.)

d. Apply analytical procedures and make inquiries of management and others. (See paragraphs .79–.80.)

e. Consider the effect of events subsequent to the balance-sheet date. The practitioner's consideration of such events in a review of MD&A is similar to the practitioner's consideration in an examination. (See paragraphs .65–.66.)

f. Obtain written representations from management concerning its responsibility for MD&A, completeness of minutes, events subsequent to the balance-sheet date, and other matters about which the practitioner believes written representations are appropriate. (See paragraph .110.)

g. Form a conclusion as to whether any information came to the practitioner's attention that causes him or her to believe any of the following.

(1) The MD&A presentation does not include, in all material respects, the required elements of the rules and regulations adopted by the SEC.

(2) The historical financial amounts included therein have not been accurately derived, in all material respects, from the entity's financial statements.

(3) The underlying information, determinations, estimates, and assumptions of the entity do not provide a reasonable basis for the disclosures contained therein.

Planning the Engagement

.77 Planning an engagement to review MD&A involves developing an overall strategy for the analytical procedures and inquiries to be performed. When developing an overall strategy for the review engagement, the practitioner should consider factors such as the following:

- Matters affecting the industry in which the entity operates, such as financial reporting practices, economic conditions, laws and regulations, and technological changes
- Matters relating to the entity's business, including its organization, operating characteristics, capital structure, and distribution methods
- The types of relevant information that management reports to external analysts (for example, press releases or presentations to lenders and rating agencies concerning past and future performance)
- The extent of management's knowledge of and experience with the rules and regulations adopted by the SEC for MD&A
- If the entity is a nonpublic entity, the intended use of the MD&A presentation
- Matters identified during the audit or review of the historical financial statements relating to MD&A reporting, including knowledge of the entity's internal control applicable to the preparation of MD&A and the extent of recent changes, if any
- Matters identified during prior engagements to examine or review MD&A
- Preliminary judgments about materiality
- The nature of complex or subjective matters potentially material to the MD&A that may require special skill or knowledge
- The presence of an internal audit function and the extent to which internal auditors are involved in directly testing the MD&A presentation or underlying records

Consideration of Internal Control Applicable to the Preparation of MD&A

.78 To perform a review of MD&A, the practitioner needs to have sufficient knowledge of the entity's internal control applicable to the preparation of MD&A to—

- Identify types of potential misstatements in MD&A, including types of material omissions, and consider the likelihood of their occurrence.
- Select the inquiries and analytical procedures that will provide a basis for reporting whether any information causes the practitioner to believe the following.
  - — The MD&A presentation does not include, in all material respects, the required elements of the rules and regulations adopted by the SEC, or the historical financial amounts included therein have not been accurately derived, in all material respects, from the entity's financial statements.
  - — The underlying information, determinations, estimates, and assumptions of the entity do not provide a reasonable basis for the disclosures contained therein.

Application of Analytical Procedures and Inquiries

.79 The practitioner ordinarily would not obtain corroborating evidential matter of management's responses to the practitioner's inquiries in performing a review of MD&A. The practitioner should, however, consider the consistency of management's responses in light of the results of other inquiries and the application of analytical procedures. The practitioner ordinarily should apply the following analytical procedures and inquiries.

a. Read the MD&A presentation and compare the content for consistency with the audited financial statements (or reviewed interim financial information if MD&A includes interim information); compare financial amounts to the audited or reviewed financial statements or related accounting records and analyses; recompute the increases, decreases, and percentages disclosed.

b. Compare nonfinancial amounts to the audited (or reviewed) financial statements, if applicable, or to other records. (Refer to paragraph .80.)

c. Consider whether the explanations in MD&A are consistent with the information obtained during the audit or the review of interim financial information; make further inquiries of officers and other executives having responsibility for operational areas as necessary.

d. Obtain available prospective financial information (for example, budgets; sales forecasts; forecasts of labor, overhead, and materials costs; capital expenditure requests; and financial forecasts and projections) and compare such information to forward-looking MD&A disclosures. Inquire of management as to the procedures used to prepare the prospective financial information. Consider whether information came to the practitioner's attention that causes him or her to believe that the underlying information, determinations, estimates, and assumptions of the entity do not provide a reasonable basis for the disclosures of trends, demands, commitments, events, or uncertainties.[26]

e. Make inquiries of officers and other executives having responsibility for operational areas (such as sales, marketing, and production) and financial and accounting matters, as to any plans and expectations for the future that could affect the entity's liquidity and capital resources.

f. Compare the information in MD&A with the rules and regulations adopted by the SEC and consider whether the presentation includes the required elements of such rules and regulations.

g. Read the minutes of meetings to date of the board of directors and other significant committees to identify actions that may affect MD&A; consider whether such matters are appropriately addressed in the MD&A presentation.

h. Inquire of officers as to the entity's prior experience with the SEC and the extent of comments received upon review of documents by the SEC; read correspondence between the entity and the SEC with respect to such review, if any.

i. Inquire of management regarding the nature of public communications (for example, press releases and quarterly reports) dealing with historical and future results and consider whether the MD&A presentation is consistent with such communications.

---

[26] Refer to paragraph .26 for a discussion concerning the safe harbor rules for forward-looking statements.

.80 If nonfinancial data are included in the MD&A presentation, the practitioner should inquire as to the nature of the records from which such information was derived and observe the existence of such records, but need not perform other tests of such records beyond analytical procedures and inquiries of individuals responsible for maintaining them. The practitioner should consider whether such nonfinancial data are relevant to users of the MD&A presentation and whether such data are clearly defined in the MD&A presentation. The practitioner should make inquiries regarding whether the definition of the nonfinancial data was consistently applied during the periods reported.

.81 However, if the practitioner becomes aware that the presentation may be incomplete or contain inaccuracies, or is otherwise unsatisfactory, the practitioner should perform the additional procedures he or she deems necessary to achieve the limited assurance contemplated by a review engagement.

Reporting

.82 In order for the practitioner to issue a report on a review of MD&A for an annual period, the financial statements for the periods covered by the MD&A presentation and the related auditor's report(s) should accompany the MD&A presentation (or with respect to a public entity be incorporated in the document containing the MD&A by reference to information filed with a regulatory agency).

.83 If the MD&A presentation relates to an interim period and the entity is a public entity, the financial statements for the interim periods covered by the MD&A presentation and the related accountant's review report(s) should accompany the MD&A presentation, or be incorporated in the document containing the MD&A by reference to information filed with a regulatory agency. The comparative financial statements for the most recent annual period and the related MD&A should accompany the MD&A presentation for the interim period, or be incorporated by reference to information filed with a regulatory agency. Generally, the requirement for inclusion of the annual financial statements and related MD&A is satisfied by a public entity that has met its reporting responsibility for filing its annual financial statements and MD&A in its annual report on Form 10-K.

.84 If the MD&A presentation relates to an interim period and the entity is a nonpublic entity, the following documents should accompany the interim MD&A presentation in order for the practitioner to issue a review report:

a. The MD&A presentation for the most recent fiscal year and related accountant's examination or review report(s)

b. The financial statements for the periods covered by the respective MD&A presentations (most recent fiscal year and interim periods and the related auditor's report(s) and accountant's review report(s))

In addition, one of the following conditions should be met.

- A statement should be included in the body of the MD&A presentation that it has been prepared using the rules and regulations adopted by the SEC.
- A separate written assertion should accompany the MD&A presentation or such assertion should be included in a representation letter obtained from the entity.

.85 The practitioner's report on a review of MD&A should include the following:

a. A title that includes the word *independent*

b. An identification of the MD&A presentation, including the period covered

c. A statement that management is responsible for the preparation of the MD&A pursuant to the rules and regulations adopted by the SEC

d. A reference to the auditor's report on the related financial statements, and, if the report was other than a standard report, the substantive reasons therefor

e. A statement that the review was conducted in accordance with attestation standards established by the AICPA

f. A description of the procedures for a review of MD&A

g. A statement that a review of MD&A is substantially less in scope than an examination, the objective of which is an expression of opinion regarding the MD&A presentation, and accordingly, no such opinion is expressed

h. A paragraph stating that—

(1) The preparation of MD&A requires management to interpret the criteria, make determinations as to the relevancy of information to be included, and make estimates and assumptions that affect reported information

(2) Actual results in the future may differ materially from management's present assessment of information regarding the estimated future impact of transactions and events that have occurred or are expected to occur, expected sources of liquidity and capital resources, operating trends, commitments, and uncertainties

i. If the entity is a nonpublic entity, a statement that although the entity is not subject to the rules and regulations of the SEC, the MD&A presentation is intended to be a presentation in accordance with the rules and regulations adopted by the SEC

j. A statement about whether any information came to the practitioner's attention that caused him or her to believe that—

(1) The MD&A presentation does not include, in all material respects, the required elements of the rules and regulations adopted by the SEC

(2) The historical financial amounts included therein have not been accurately derived, in all material respects, from the entity's financial statements

(3) The underlying information, determinations, estimates, and assumptions of the entity do not provide a reasonable basis for the disclosures contained therein

k. If the entity is a public entity as defined in paragraph .02, or a nonpublic entity that is making or has made an offering of securities and it appears that the securities may subsequently be registered or subject to a filing with the SEC or other regulatory agency (for example, certain offerings of securities under Rule 144A of the 1933 Act that purport to conform to Regulation S-K), a statement of restrictions on the use of the report to specified parties, because it is not intended to be filed with the SEC as a report under the 1933 Act or the 1934 Act.

l. The manual or printed signature of the practitioner's firm

m. The date of the review report

Appendix B [paragraph .115], "Review Reports," provides examples of a standard review report for an annual and interim period.

Dating

.86 The practitioner's report on the review of MD&A should be dated as of the completion of the practitioner's review procedures. That date should not precede the date of the accountant's report on the latest historical financial statements covered by the MD&A.

Report Modifications

.87 The practitioner should modify the standard review report described in paragraph .86 if any of the following conditions exist.

- The presentation excludes a material required element of the rules and regulations adopted by the SEC. (See paragraph .89.)
- The historical financial amounts have not been accurately derived, in all material respects, from the entity's financial statements. (See paragraph .89.)
- The underlying information, determinations, estimates, and assumptions used by management do not provide the entity with a reasonable basis for the disclosures in the MD&A. (See paragraph .89.)
- The practitioner decides to refer to the report of another practitioner as the basis, in part, for his or her report. (See paragraph .90.)
- The practitioner is engaged to review the MD&A presentation after it has been filed with the SEC or other regulatory agency. (See paragraphs .94–.98.)

.88 When the practitioner is unable to perform the inquiry and analytical procedures he or she considers necessary to achieve the limited assurance provided by a review, or the client does not provide the practitioner with a representation letter, the review will be incomplete. A review that is incomplete is not an adequate basis for issuing a review report. If the practitioner is unable to complete a review because of a scope limitation, the practitioner should consider the implications of that limitation with respect to possible misstatements of the MD&A presentation. In those circumstances, the practitioner should also refer to paragraphs .107–.109 for guidance concerning communications with the audit committee.

.89 If the practitioner becomes aware that the MD&A is materially misstated, the practitioner should modify the review report to describe the nature of the misstatement. Appendix B [paragraph .115] contains an example of such a modification of the accountant's report. (See Example 3.)

.90 If another practitioner reviewed or examined the MD&A for a material component, the practitioner may decide to make reference to such report of the other practitioner in reporting on the consolidated MD&A presentation. Such reference indicates a division of responsibility for performance of the review.

Emphasis of a Matter

.91 In some circumstances, the practitioner may wish to emphasize a matter regarding the MD&A presentation. For example, he or she may wish to emphasize that the entity has included information beyond the required elements of the rules and regulations adopted by the SEC. Such explanatory comments should be presented in a separate paragraph of the practitioner's report.

Combined Examination and Review Report on MD&A

.92 A practitioner may be engaged both to examine an MD&A presentation as of the most recent fiscal year-end and to review a separate MD&A presentation for a subsequent interim period. If the examination and review are completed at the same time, a combined report may be issued. Appendix C [paragraph .116], "Combined Reports," contains an example of a combined report on an examination of an annual MD&A presentation and the review of a separate MD&A presentation for an interim period. (See Example 1.)

.93 If an entity prepares a combined MD&A presentation for annual and interim periods in which there is a discussion of liquidity and capital resources only as of the most recent interim period but not as of the most recent annual period, the practitioner is limited to performing the highest level of service that is provided with respect to the historical financial statements for any of the periods covered by the MD&A presentation. For example, if the annual financial statements have been audited and the interim financial statements have been reviewed, the practitioner may be engaged to perform a review of the combined MD&A presentation. Appendix C [paragraph .116] contains an example of a review report on a combined MD&A presentation for annual and interim periods. (See Example 2.)

When Practitioner Is Engaged Subsequent to the Filing of MD&A

.94 Management's responsibility for updating an MD&A presentation for events occurring subsequent to the issuance of MD&A depends on whether the entity is a public or nonpublic entity. A public entity is required to report significant subsequent events in a Form 8-K or Form 10-Q, or in a registration statement; therefore, a public company would ordinarily not modify its MD&A presentation once it is filed with the SEC (or other regulatory agency).

.95 Therefore, if the practitioner is engaged to examine (or review) an MD&A presentation of a public entity that has already been filed with the SEC (or other regulatory agency), the practitioner should consider whether material subsequent events are appropriately disclosed in a Form 8-K or 10-Q, or a registration statement that includes or incorporates by reference such MD&A presentation. Refer to paragraphs .65–.66 for guidance concerning consideration of events up to the filing date when the practitioner's report on MD&A will be included (or incorporated by reference) in a 1933 Act document filed with the SEC that will require a consent.

.96 If subsequent events of a public entity are appropriately disclosed in a Form 8-K or 10-Q, or in a registration statement, or if there have been no material subsequent events, the practitioner should add the following paragraph to his or her examination or review report following the opinion or concluding paragraph, respectively.

> The accompanying Management's Discussion and Analysis does not consider events that have occurred subsequent to Month XX, 20X6, the date as of which it was filed with the Securities and Exchange Commission.

.97 If there has been a material subsequent event that has not been disclosed in a manner described in paragraph .95 and if the practitioner determines that it is appropriate to issue a report even though the MD&A presentation has not been updated for such material subsequent event (for example, because the filing of the Form 10-Q that will disclose such events has not yet occurred), the practitioner should express a qualified or an adverse opinion (or appropriately modify the review report) on the MD&A presentation. As discussed in paragraph .107, if such material subsequent event is not appropriately disclosed, the practitioner should evaluate (*a*) whether to resign from the engagement related to the MD&A presentation and (*b*) whether to remain as the entity's auditor or stand for re-election to audit the entity's financial statements.

.98 Because a nonpublic entity is not subject to the filing requirements of the SEC, an MD&A presentation of a nonpublic entity should be updated for material subsequent events through the date of the practitioner's report.

When a Predecessor Auditor Has Audited Prior Period Financial Statements

.99 If a predecessor auditor has audited the financial statements for a prior period covered by the MD&A, the need by the practitioner reporting on the MD&A for an understanding of the business and the entity's accounting and financial reporting practices for such prior period, as discussed in paragraph .07, is not diminished and the practitioner should apply the appropriate procedures. In applying the appropriate procedures, the practitioner may consider reviewing the predecessor auditor's working papers with respect to audits of financial statements and examinations or reviews of MD&A presentations for such prior periods.

.100 Information that may be obtained from the audit or attest working papers of the predecessor auditor will not provide a sufficient basis in itself for the practitioner to express an opinion with respect to the MD&A disclosures for such prior periods. If the practitioner has audited the current year, the results of such audit may be considered in planning and performing the examination of MD&A and may provide evidential matter that is useful in performing the examination, including with respect to matters disclosed for prior periods. For example, an increase in salaries expense may be the result of an acquisition in the last half of the prior year. Auditing procedures applied to payroll expense in the current year that validate the increase as a result of the acquisition may provide evidential matter with respect to the increase in salaries expense in the prior year attributed to the acquisition.

.101 In addition to the procedures described in paragraphs .49–.66, the practitioner will need to make inquiries of the predecessor auditor and management as to audit adjustments proposed by the predecessor auditor that were not recorded in the financial statements.

Communications Between Predecessor and Successor Auditors

.102 If the practitioner is appointed as the successor auditor, he or she follows the guidance AU-C section 210, *Terms of Engagement*, in considering whether or not to accept the engagement. If, at the time of the appointment as auditor, the practitioner is also being engaged to examine or review MD&A, the practitioner should also make specific inquiries of the predecessor auditor regarding MD&A. [Revised, December 2012, to reflect conforming changes necessary due to the issuance of SAS Nos. 122–126.]

.103 The practitioner's examination may be facilitated by (*a*) making specific inquiries of the predecessor regarding matters that the successor believes may affect the conduct of the examination (or review), such as areas that required an inordinate amount of time or problems that arose from the condition of the records, and (*b*) if the predecessor previously examined or reviewed MD&A, reviewing the predecessor's working papers for the predecessor's examination or review engagement.

.104 If, subsequent to his or her engagement to audit the financial statements, the practitioner is requested to examine MD&A, the practitioner should request the client to authorize the predecessor auditor to allow a review of the predecessor's audit working papers related to the financial statement periods included in the MD&A presentation. Although the practitioner may previously have had access to the predecessor auditor's working papers in connection with the successor's audit of the financial statements, ordinarily the predecessor auditor should permit the practitioner to review those audit working papers relating to matters that are disclosed or that would likely be disclosed in MD&A.

Another Auditor Audits a Significant Part of the Financial Statements

.105 When one or more component auditors audits a significant part of a group's financial statements, the practitioner[27] may request that the component auditor perform procedures with respect to the MD&A or the practitioner may perform the procedures directly with respect to such component(s).[28] Unless the component auditor issues an examination or review report on a separate MD&A presentation of such component(s) (see paragraph .74), the practitioner examining the group's MD&A should not make reference to the work of the component practitioner on MD&A in his or her report on MD&A[29] Accordingly, if the practitioner examining the group's MD&A has requested such component auditor to perform procedures, the practitioner examining the group's MD&A should perform those procedures that he or she considers necessary to take responsibility for the work of the other auditor. Such procedures may include one or more of the following:

a. Visiting the component auditor and discussing the procedures followed and the results thereof.

---

[27] The practitioner serving as auditor of the group's financial statements is presumed to have an audit base for purposes of examining or reviewing the consolidated MD&A presentation. [Footnote revised, December 2012, to reflect conforming changes necessary due to the issuance of SAS Nos. 122–126.]

[28] The practitioner should consider whether he or she has sufficient industry expertise with respect to a subsidiary audited by a component auditor to take sole responsibility for the group's consolidated MD&A presentation. [Footnote revised, December 2012, to reflect conforming changes necessary due to the issuance of SAS Nos. 122–126.]

[29] This does not preclude the practitioner from referring to the component auditor's report on the financial statements in his or her report on the group's MD&A. [Footnote revised, December 2012, to reflect conforming changes necessary due to the issuance of SAS Nos. 122–126.]

b. Reviewing the working papers of the component auditor with respect to the component.

c. Participating in discussions with the component's management regarding matters that may affect the preparation of the component's MD&A.

d. Making supplemental tests with respect to such component.

The determination of the extent of the procedures to be applied by the practitioner examining the group's MD&A rests with that practitioner alone in the exercise of his or her professional judgment and in no way constitutes a reflection on the adequacy of the component auditor's work. Because the practitioner examining the group's MD&A in this case assumes responsibility for his or her opinion on the MD&A presentation without making reference to the procedures performed by the other auditor, the judgment of the practitioner examining the group's MD&A should govern as to the extent of procedures to be undertaken. [Revised, December 2012, to reflect conforming changes necessary due to the issuance of SAS Nos. 122–126.]

Responsibility for Other Information in Documents Containing MD&A

.106 A client may publish annual reports containing MD&A and other documents to which the practitioner, at the client's request, devotes attention. See paragraphs .91–.94 of section 101 for pertinent guidance in these circumstances. See Appendix D of this section [paragraph .117], "Comparison of Activities Performed Under SAS No. 8, *Other Information in Documents Containing Audited Financial Statements*, Versus a Review or an Examination Attest Engagement." The guidance in AU-C section 925, *Filings With the U.S. Securities and Exchange Commission Under the Securities Act of 1933*, is pertinent when the practitioner's report on MD&A is included in a registration statement, proxy statement, or periodic report filed under the federal securities statutes. [Revised, December 2012, to reflect conforming changes necessary due to the issuance of SAS Nos. 122–126.]

Communications With the Audit Committee

.107 If the practitioner concludes that the MD&A presentation contains material inconsistencies with other information included in the document containing the MD&A presentation or with the historical financial statements,[30] material omissions, or material misstatements of fact, and management refuses to take corrective action, the practitioner should inform the audit committee or others with equivalent authority and responsibility. If the MD&A is not revised, the practitioner should evaluate (*a*) whether to resign from the engagement related to the MD&A, and (*b*) whether to remain as the entity's auditor or stand for re-election to audit the entity's financial statements. The practitioner may wish to consult with his or her attorney when making these evaluations.

.108 If the practitioner is engaged after the MD&A presentation has been filed with the SEC (or other regulatory agency), and becomes aware that such MD&A presentation on file with the SEC (or other regulatory agency) has not been revised for a matter for which the practitioner has or would qualify his or her opinion, the practitioner should discuss such matter with the audit commit-

---

[30] See AU-C section 720, *Information in Documents Containing Audited Financial Statements*, for guidance on the impact of material inconsistencies or material misstatements of fact on the auditor's report on the related historical financial statements. [Footnote revised, December 2012, to reflect conforming changes necessary due to the issuance of SAS Nos. 122–126.]

tee and request that the MD&A presentation be revised. If the audit committee fails to take appropriate action, the practitioner should consider whether to resign as the independent auditor of the company. The practitioner may consider paragraphs .21–.23 and .27 of AU-C section 250, *Consideration of Laws and Regulations in an Audit of Financial Statements*, concerning communication with the audit committee and other considerations. [Revised, December 2012, to reflect conforming changes necessary due to the issuance of SAS Nos. 122–126.]

.109 If, as a result of performing an examination or a review of MD&A, the practitioner has determined that there is evidence that fraud may exist, that matter should be brought to the attention of an appropriate level of management. This is generally appropriate even if the matter might be considered clearly inconsequential. If the matter relates to the audited financial statements, the practitioner should consider the guidance in AU-C section 240, *Consideration of Fraud in a Financial Statement Audit*, concerning communication responsibilities, and the effect on the auditor's report on the financial statements. [Revised, December 2012, to reflect conforming changes necessary due to the issuance of SAS Nos. 122–126.]

Obtaining Written Representations

.110 In an examination or a review engagement, the practitioner should obtain written representations from management.[31] The specific written representations obtained by the practitioner will depend on the circumstances of the engagement and the nature of the MD&A presentation. Specific representations should relate to the following matters:

a. Management's acknowledgment of its responsibility for the preparation of MD&A and management's assertion that the MD&A presentation has been prepared in accordance with the rules and regulations adopted by the SEC for MD&A[32]

b. A statement that the historical financial amounts included in MD&A have been accurately derived from the entity's financial statements

c. Management's belief that the underlying information, determinations, estimates, and assumptions of the entity provide a reasonable basis for the disclosures contained in the MD&A

d. A statement that management has made available all significant documentation related to compliance with SEC rules and regulations for MD&A

e. Completeness and availability of all minutes of meetings of stockholders, directors, and committees of directors

f. For a public entity, whether any communications from the SEC were received concerning noncompliance with or deficiencies in MD&A reporting practices

---

[31] Paragraph .21 of AU-C section 580, *Written Representations*, requires that written representations be in the form of a representation letter addressed to the auditor. Paragraph .09*b* of AU-C section 925 requires the auditor to obtain updated written representations from management at or shortly before the effective date of the registration statement, about (*a*) whether any information has come to management's attention that would cause management to believe that any of the previous representations should be modified, and (*b*) whether any events have occurred subsequent to the date of the financial statements that would require adjustment to, or disclosure in, those financial statements. (See paragraph .65.) [Footnote revised, December 2012, to reflect conforming changes necessary due to the issuance of SAS Nos. 122–126.]

[32] Management should specify the SEC rules (for example, Item 303 of Regulation S-K, Item 303 of Regulation S-B, or Item 9 of Form 20-F). For nonpublic entities, the practitioner also obtains a written assertion that the presentation has been prepared using the rules and regulations adopted by the SEC. (See paragraph .02.)

g. Whether any events occurred subsequent to the latest balance-sheet date that would require disclosure in the MD&A

h. If forward-looking information is included, a statement that—

- The forward-looking information is based on management's best estimate of expected events and operations, and is consistent with budgets, forecasts, or operating plans prepared for such periods
- The accounting principles expected to be used for the forward-looking information are consistent with the principles used in preparing the historical financial statements
- Management has provided the latest version of such budgets, forecasts, or operating plans, and has informed the practitioner of any anticipated changes or modifications to such information that could affect the disclosures contained in the MD&A presentation

i. If voluntary information is included that is subject to the rules and regulations adopted by the SEC (for example, information required by Item 305, *Quantitative and Qualitative Disclosures About Market Risk*), a statement that such voluntary information has been prepared in accordance with the related rules and regulations adopted by the SEC for such information

j. If pro forma information is included, a statement that—

- Management is responsible for the assumptions used in determining the pro forma adjustments
- Management believes that the assumptions provide a reasonable basis for presenting all the significant effects directly attributable to the transaction or event, that the related pro forma adjustments give appropriate effect to those assumptions, and that the pro forma column reflects the proper application of those adjustments to the historical financial statements
- Management believes that the significant effects directly attributable to the transaction or event are appropriately disclosed in the pro forma financial information

.111 In an examination, management's refusal to furnish written representations constitutes a limitation on the scope of the engagement sufficient to preclude an unqualified opinion and is ordinarily sufficient to cause a practitioner to disclaim an opinion or withdraw from the examination engagement. However, based on the nature of the representations not obtained or the circumstances of the refusal, the practitioner may conclude that a qualified opinion is appropriate in an examination engagement. In a review engagement, management's refusal to furnish written representations constitutes a limitation of the scope of the engagement sufficient to require withdrawal from the review engagement. Further, the practitioner should consider the effects of the refusal on his or her ability to rely on other management representations.

.112 If the practitioner is precluded from performing procedures he or she considers necessary in the circumstances with respect to a matter that is material to the MD&A presentation, even though management has given representations concerning the matter, there is a limitation on the scope of the engagement, and the practitioner should qualify his or her opinion or disclaim an opinion in an examination engagement, or withdraw from a review engagement.

Effective Date

.113 This section is effective when management's discussion and analysis is for a period ending on or after June 1, 2001. Early application is permitted.

.114

Appendix A

Examination Reports

Example 1: Standard Examination Report

1. The following is an illustration of a standard examination report.

Independent Accountant's Report

[*Introductory paragraph*]

We have examined XYZ Company's Management's Discussion and Analysis taken as a whole, included [*incorporated by reference*] in the Company's [*insert description of registration statement or document*]. Management is responsible for the preparation of the Company's Management's Discussion and Analysis pursuant to the rules and regulations adopted by the Securities and Exchange Commission. Our responsibility is to express an opinion on the presentation based on our examination. We have audited, in accordance with auditing standards generally accepted in the United States of America, the financial statements of XYZ Company, which comprise the balance sheets as of December 31, 20X5 and 20X4, and the related statements of income, changes in stockholder's equity, and cash flows for each of the years in the three-year period ended December 31, 20X5, and the related notes to the financial statements. In our report dated [*Month*] XX, 20X6, we expressed an unmodified opinion on those financial statements.[33]

[*Scope paragraph*]

Our examination of Management's Discussion and Analysis was conducted in accordance with attestation standards established by the American Institute of Certified Public Accountants and, accordingly, included examining, on a test basis, evidence supporting the historical amounts and disclosures in the presentation. An examination also includes assessing the significant determinations made by management as to the relevancy of information to be included and the estimates and assumptions that affect reported information. We believe that our examination provides a reasonable basis for our opinion.

---

[33] If prior financial statements were audited by other auditors, this sentence would be replaced by the following.

> We have audited, in accordance with auditing standards generally accepted in the United States of America, the financial statements of XYZ Company, which comprise the balance sheet as of December 31, 20X5, and the related statement of income, changes in stockholder's equity, and cash flows for the year then ended, and the related notes to the financial statements. In our report dated [*Month*] XX, 20X6, we expressed an unmodified opinion on those financial statements. The financial statements of XYZ Company; which comprise the balance sheet as of December 31, 20X4, and the related statement of income, changes in stockholder's equity, and cash flows for each of the years in the two-year period then ended, and the notes to the financial statements; were audited by other auditors, whose report dated [*Month*] XX, 20X5, expressed an unmodified opinion on those financial statements.

If the practitioner's opinion on the financial statements is based on the report of component auditors, this sentence would be replaced by the following:

> We have audited, in accordance with auditing standards generally accepted in the United States of America, the financial statements of XYZ Company which comprise the balance sheets as of December 31, 20X5 and 20X4, and the related statements of income, changes in stockholders' equity, and cash flows for each of the years in the three-year period ended December 31, 20X5, and the notes to the financial statements. In our report dated [*Month*] XX, 20X6, we expressed an unmodified opinion on those financial statements based on our audits and the report of component auditors.

Refer to Example 3 if the practitioner's opinion on MD&A is based on the report of another practitioner on a component of the entity. [Footnote revised, December 2012, to reflect conforming changes necessary due to the issuance of SAS Nos. 122–126.]

[*Explanatory paragraph*][34]

The preparation of Management's Discussion and Analysis requires management to interpret the criteria, make determinations as to the relevancy of information to be included, and make estimates and assumptions that affect reported information. Management's Discussion and Analysis includes information regarding the estimated future impact of transactions and events that have occurred or are expected to occur, expected sources of liquidity and capital resources, operating trends, commitments, and uncertainties. Actual results in the future may differ materially from management's present assessment of this information because events and circumstances frequently do not occur as expected.

[*Opinion paragraph*]

In our opinion, the Company's presentation of Management's Discussion and Analysis includes, in all material respects, the required elements of the rules and regulations adopted by the Securities and Exchange Commission; the historical financial amounts included therein have been accurately derived, in all material respects, from the Company's financial statements; and the underlying information, determinations, estimates, and assumptions of the Company provide a reasonable basis for the disclosures contained therein.

[*Signature*]

[*Date*]

Example 2: Modifications to Examination Report for a Qualified Opinion

2. An example of a modification of an examination report for a qualified opinion due to a material omission described in paragraph .72 follows.

[*Additional explanatory paragraph preceding the opinion paragraph*]

Based on information furnished to us by management, we believe that the Company has excluded a discussion of the significant capital outlay required for its plans to expand into the telecommunications industry and the possible effects on the Company's financial condition, liquidity, and capital resources.

[*Opinion paragraph*]

In our opinion, except for the omission of the matter described in the preceding paragraph, the Company's presentation of Management's Discussion and Analysis includes, in all material respects, the required elements of the rules and regulations adopted by the Securities and Exchange Commission; the historical financial amounts included therein have been accurately derived, in all material respects, from the Company's financial statements; and the underlying information, determinations, estimates, and assumptions of the Company provide a reasonable basis for the disclosures contained therein.

3. An example of a modification of an examination report for a qualified opinion when overly subjective assertions are included in MD&A follows.

[*Additional explanatory paragraph preceding the opinion paragraph*]

Based on information furnished to us by management, we believe that the underlying information, determinations, estimates, and assumptions used by

---

[34] The following sentence should be added to the beginning of the explanatory paragraph if the entity is a nonpublic entity, as discussed in paragraph .69*h*:

Although XYZ Company is not subject to the rules and regulations of the Securities and Exchange Commission, the accompanying Management's Discussion and Analysis is intended to be a presentation in accordance with the rules and regulations adopted by the Securities and Exchange Commission.

management do not provide the Company with a reasonable basis for the disclosure concerning [*describe*] in the Company's Management's Discussion and Analysis.

[*Opinion paragraph*]

In our opinion, except for the disclosure regarding [*describe*] discussed in the preceding paragraph, the Company's presentation of Management's Discussion and Analysis includes, in all material respects, the required elements of the rules and regulations adopted by the Securities and Exchange Commission; the historical financial amounts included therein have been accurately derived, in all material respects, from the Company's financial statements; and the underlying information, determinations, estimates, and assumptions of the Company provide a reasonable basis for the disclosures contained therein.

Example 3: Examination Report With Reference to the Report of Another Practitioner

4. The following is an illustration of an examination report indicating a division of responsibility with another practitioner, who has examined a separate MD&A presentation of a wholly-owned subsidiary, when the practitioner reporting is serving as the auditor of the related group's consolidated financial statements.

Independent Accountant's Report

[*Introductory paragraphs*]

We have examined XYZ Company's Management's Discussion and Analysis taken as a whole, included [*incorporated by reference*] in the Company's [*insert description of registration statement or document*]. Management is responsible for the preparation of the Company's Management's Discussion and Analysis pursuant to the rules and regulations adopted by the Securities and Exchange Commission. Our responsibility is to express an opinion on the presentation based on our examination. We did not examine Management's Discussion and Analysis of ABC Corporation, a wholly-owned subsidiary, included in ABC Corporation's [*insert description of registration statement or document*]. Such Management's Discussion and Analysis was examined by other accountants, whose report has been furnished to us, and our opinion, insofar as it relates to information included for ABC Corporation, is based solely on the report of the other accountants.

We have audited, in accordance with auditing standards generally accepted in the United States of America, the consolidated financial statements of XYZ Company, which comprise the consolidated balance sheets as of December 31, 20X5 and 20X4, and the related consolidated statements of income, changes in stockholders' equity, and cash flows, for each of the years in the three-year period ended December 31, 20X5. In our report dated [*Month*] XX, 20X6, we expressed an unmodified opinion on those financial statements based on our audits and the report of other auditors.

[*Scope paragraph*]

Our examination of Management's Discussion and Analysis was conducted in accordance with attestation standards established by the American Institute of Certified Public Accountants and, accordingly, included examining, on a test basis, evidence supporting the historical amounts and disclosures in the presentation. An examination also includes assessing the significant determinations made by management as to the relevancy of information to be included and the estimates and assumptions that affect reported information. We believe that our examination and the report of other accountants provide a reasonable basis for our opinion.

[*Explanatory paragraph*][35]

The preparation of Management's Discussion and Analysis requires management to interpret the criteria, make determinations as to the relevancy of information to be included, and make estimates and assumptions that affect reported information. Management's Discussion and Analysis includes information regarding the estimated future impact of transactions and events that have occurred or are expected to occur, expected sources of liquidity and capital resources, operating trends, commitments, and uncertainties. Actual results in the future may differ materially from management's present assessment of this information because events and circumstances frequently do not occur as expected.

[*Opinion paragraph*]

In our opinion, based on our examination and the report of other accountants, the Company's presentation of Management's Discussion and Analysis included [*incorporated by reference*] in the Company's [*insert description of registration statement or document*] includes, in all material respects, the required elements of the rules and regulations adopted by the Securities and Exchange Commission; the historical financial amounts included therein have been accurately derived, in all material respects, from the Company's financial statements; and the underlying information, determinations, estimates, and assumptions of the Company provide a reasonable basis for the disclosures contained therein.

[*Signature*]

[*Date*]

[Revised, December 2012, to reflect conforming changes necessary due to the issuance of SAS Nos. 122–126.]

---

[35] The following sentence should be added to the beginning of the explanatory paragraph if the entity is a nonpublic entity, as discussed in paragraph .69*h*.

Although XYZ Company is not subject to the rules and regulations of the Securities and Exchange Commission, the accompanying Management's Discussion and Analysis is intended to be a presentation in accordance with the rules and regulations adopted by the Securities and Exchange Commission.

.115

Appendix B

Review Reports

Example 1: Standard Review Report on an Annual MD&A Presentation

1. The following is an illustration of a standard review report on an annual MD&A presentation.

Independent Accountant's Report

[*Introductory paragraph*]

We have reviewed XYZ Company's Management's Discussion and Analysis taken as a whole, included [*incorporated by reference*] in the Company's [*insert description of registration statement or document*]. Management is responsible for the preparation of the Company's Management's Discussion and Analysis pursuant to the rules and regulations adopted by the Securities and Exchange Commission. We have audited, in accordance with auditing standards generally accepted in the United States of America, the financial statements of XYZ Company, which comprise the balance sheets as of December 31, 20X5 and 20X4, and the related statements of income, changes in stockholders' equity, and cash flows for each of the years in the three-year period ended December 31, 20X5. In our report dated [*Month*] XX, 20X6, we expressed an unqualified opinion on those financial statements.

[*Scope paragraph*]

We conducted our review of Management's Discussion and Analysis in accordance with attestation standards established by the American Institute of Certified Public Accountants. A review of Management's Discussion and Analysis consists principally of applying analytical procedures and making inquiries of persons responsible for financial, accounting, and operational matters. It is substantially less in scope than an examination, the objective of which is the expression of an opinion on the presentation. Accordingly, we do not express such an opinion.

[*Explanatory paragraph*][36]

The preparation of Management's Discussion and Analysis requires management to interpret the criteria, make determinations as to the relevancy of information to be included, and make estimates and assumptions that affect reported information. Management's Discussion and Analysis includes information regarding the estimated future impact of transactions and events that have occurred or are expected to occur, expected sources of liquidity and capital resources, operating trends, commitments, and uncertainties. Actual results in the future may differ materially from management's present assessment of this information because events and circumstances frequently do not occur as expected.

[*Concluding paragraph*]

---

[36] The following sentence should be added to the beginning of the explanatory paragraph if the entity is a nonpublic entity, as discussed in paragraph .85*i*.

Although XYZ Company is not subject to the rules and regulations of the Securities and Exchange Commission, the accompanying Management's Discussion and Analysis is intended to be a presentation in accordance with the rules and regulations adopted by the Securities and Exchange Commission.

Based on our review, nothing came to our attention that caused us to believe that the Company's presentation of Management's Discussion and Analysis does not include, in all material respects, the required elements of the rules and regulations adopted by the Securities and Exchange Commission, that the historical financial amounts included therein have not been accurately derived, in all material respects, from the Company's financial statements, or that the underlying information, determinations, estimates and assumptions of the Company do not provide a reasonable basis for the disclosures contained therein.

[*Restricted use paragraph*][37]

This report is intended solely for the information and use of [*list or refer to specified parties*] and is not intended to be and should not be used by anyone other than the specified parties.

[*Signature*]

[*Date*]

Example 2: Standard Review Report on an Interim MD&A Presentation

2. The following is an illustration of a standard review report on an MD&A presentation for an interim period.

Independent Accountant's Report

[*Introductory paragraph*]

We have reviewed XYZ Company's Management's Discussion and Analysis taken as a whole included in the Company's [*insert description of registration statement or document*]. Management is responsible for the preparation of the Company's Management's Discussion and Analysis pursuant to the rules and regulations adopted by the Securities and Exchange Commission. We have reviewed, in accordance with standards established by the American Institute of Certified Public Accountants, the interim financial information of XYZ Company as of June 30, 20X6 and 20X5, and for the three-month and six-month periods then ended, and have issued our report thereon dated July XX, 20X6.

[*Scope paragraph*]

We conducted our review of Management's Discussion and Analysis in accordance with attestation standards established by the American Institute of Certified Public Accountants. A review of Management's Discussion and Analysis consists principally of applying analytical procedures and making inquiries of persons responsible for financial, accounting, and operational matters. It is substantially less in scope than an examination, the objective of which is the expression of an opinion on the presentation. Accordingly, we do not express such an opinion.

[*Explanatory paragraph*][38]

---

[37] This paragraph may be omitted for certain nonpublic entities. (Refer to paragraph .85*k*.)

[38] The following sentence should be added to the beginning of the explanatory paragraph if the entity is a nonpublic entity, as discussed in paragraph .85*i*.

Although XYZ Company is not subject to the rules and regulations of the Securities and Exchange Commission, the accompanying Management's Discussion and Analysis is intended to be a presentation in accordance with the rules and regulations adopted by the Securities and Exchange Commission.

The preparation of Management's Discussion and Analysis requires management to interpret the criteria, make determinations as to the relevancy of information to be included, and make estimates and assumptions that affect reported information. Management's Discussion and Analysis includes information regarding the estimated future impact of transactions and events that have occurred or are expected to occur, expected sources of liquidity and capital resources, operating trends, commitments, and uncertainties. Actual results in the future may differ materially from management's present assessment of this information because events and circumstances frequently do not occur as expected.

[*Concluding paragraph*]

Based on our review, nothing came to our attention that caused us to believe that the Company's presentation of Management's Discussion and Analysis does not include, in all material respects, the required elements of the rules and regulations adopted by the Securities and Exchange Commission, that the historical financial amounts included therein have not been accurately derived, in all material respects, from the Company's financial statements, or that the underlying information, determinations, estimates, and assumptions of the Company do not provide a reasonable basis for the disclosures contained therein.

[*Restricted use paragraph*][39]

This report is intended solely for the information and use of [*list or refer to specified parties*] and is not intended to be and should not be used by anyone other than the specified parties.

[*Signature*]

[*Date*]

Example 3: Modification to Review Report for a Material Misstatement

3. An example of a modification of the accountant's report when MD&A is materially misstated, as discussed in paragraph .89, follows.

[*Additional explanatory paragraph preceding the concluding paragraph*]

Based on information furnished to us by management, we believe that the Company has excluded a discussion of the significant capital outlay required for its plans to expand into the telecommunications industry and the possible effects on the Company's financial condition, liquidity, and capital resources.

[*Concluding paragraph*]

Based on our review, with the exception of the matter described in the preceding paragraph, nothing came to our attention that caused us to believe that the Company's presentation of Management's Discussion and Analysis does not include, in all material respects, the required elements of the rules and regulations adopted by the Securities and Exchange Commission, that the historical financial amounts included therein have not been accurately derived, in all material respects, from the Company's financial statements, or that the underlying information, determinations, estimates and assumptions of the Company do not provide a reasonable basis for the disclosures contained therein.

[Revised, December 2012, to reflect conforming changes necessary due to the issuance of SAS Nos. 122–126.]

---

[39] This paragraph may be omitted for certain nonpublic entities. (Refer to paragraph .85*k*.)

.116

Appendix C

Combined Reports

Example 1: Combined Examination and Review Report on MD&A

1. An example of a combined report on an examination of an annual MD&A presentation and the review of MD&A for an interim period discussed in paragraph .92 follows.

<u>Independent Accountant's Report</u>

[Introductory paragraph]

We have examined XYZ Company's Management's Discussion and Analysis taken as a whole for the three-year period ended December 31, 20X5, included [*incorporated by reference*] in the Company's [*insert description of registration statement or document*]. Management is responsible for the preparation of the Company's Management's Discussion and Analysis pursuant to the rules and regulations adopted by the Securities and Exchange Commission. Our responsibility is to express an opinion on the annual presentation based on our examination. We have audited, in accordance with auditing standards generally accepted in the United States of America, the financial statements of XYZ Company as of December 31, 20X5 and 20X4, and for each of the years in the three-year period ended December 31, 19X5, and in our report dated [*Month*] XX, 20X6, we expressed an unqualified opinion on those financial statements.

[Scope paragraph]

Our examination of Management's Discussion and Analysis was conducted in accordance with attestation standards established by the American Institute of Certified Public Accountants and, accordingly, included examining, on a test basis, evidence supporting the historical amounts and disclosures in the presentation. An examination also includes assessing the significant determinations made by management as to the relevancy of information to be included and the estimates and assumptions that affect reported information. We believe that our examination provides a reasonable basis for our opinion.

[Explanatory paragraph][40]

The preparation of Management's Discussion and Analysis requires management to interpret the criteria, make determinations as to the relevancy of information to be included, and make estimates and assumptions that affect reported information. Management's Discussion and Analysis includes information regarding the estimated future impact of transactions and events that have occurred or are expected to occur, expected sources of liquidity and capital resources, operating trends, commitments, and uncertainties. Actual results in

[40] The following sentence should be added to the beginning of the explanatory paragraph if the entity is a nonpublic entity, as discussed in paragraph .69*h*.

Although XYZ Company is not subject to the rules and regulations of the Securities and Exchange Commission, the accompanying Management's Discussion and Analysis is intended to be a presentation in accordance with the rules and regulations adopted by the Securities and Exchange Commission.

the future may differ materially from management's present assessment of this information because events and circumstances frequently do not occur as expected.

[*Opinion paragraph*]

In our opinion, the Company's presentation of Management's Discussion and Analysis for the three-year period ended December 31, 20X5, includes, in all material respects, the required elements of the rules and regulations adopted by the Securities and Exchange Commission; the historical financial amounts included therein have been accurately derived, in all material respects, from the Company's financial statements; and the underlying information, determinations, estimates, and assumptions of the Company provide a reasonable basis for the disclosures contained therein.

[*Paragraphs on interims*]

We have also reviewed XYZ Company's Management's Discussion and Analysis taken as a whole for the six-month period ended June 30, 20X6 included [*incorporated by reference*] in the Company's [*insert description of registration statement or document*]. We have reviewed, in accordance with standards established by the American Institute of Certified Public Accountants, the interim financial information of XYZ Company as of June 30, 20X6 and 20X5, and for the six-month periods then ended, and have issued our report thereon dated July XX, 20X6.

We conducted our review of Management's Discussion and Analysis in accordance with attestation standards established by the American Institute of Certified Public Accountants. A review of Management's Discussion and Analysis consists principally of applying analytical procedures and making inquiries of persons responsible for financial, accounting, and operational matters. It is substantially less in scope than an examination, the objective of which is the expression of an opinion on the presentation. Accordingly, we do not express such an opinion.

Based on our review, nothing came to our attention that caused us to believe that the Company's presentation of Management's Discussion and Analysis for the six-month period ended June 30, 20X6, does not include, in all material respects, the required elements of the rules and regulations adopted by the Securities and Exchange Commission, that the historical financial amounts included therein have not been accurately derived, in all material respects, from the Company's unaudited interim financial statements, or that the underlying information, determinations, estimates, and assumptions of the Company do not provide a reasonable basis for the disclosures contained therein.

[*Restricted use paragraph*][41]

This report is intended solely for the information and use of [*list or refer to specified parties*] and is not intended to be and should not be used by anyone other than the specified parties.

[*Signature*]

[*Date*]

Example 2: Review Report on a Combined Annual and Interim MD&A Presentation

2. An example of a review report on a combined MD&A presentation for annual and interim periods follows.

---

[41] This paragraph may be omitted for certain nonpublic entities. (Refer to paragraph .85*k*.)

Independent Accountant's Report

[*Introductory paragraph*]

We have reviewed XYZ Company's Management's Discussion and Analysis taken as a whole included [*incorporated by reference*] in the Company's [*insert description of registration statement or document*]. Management is responsible for the preparation of the Company's Management's Discussion and Analysis pursuant to the rules and regulations adopted by the Securities and Exchange Commission. We have audited, in accordance with auditing standards generally accepted in the United States of America, the financial statements of XYZ Company as of December 31, 20X5 and 20X4, and for each of the years in the three-year period ended December 31, 20X5, and in our report dated [*Month*] XX, 20X6, we expressed an unqualified opinion on those financial statements. We have reviewed, in accordance with standards established by the American Institute of Certified Public Accountants, the interim financial information of XYZ Company as of June 30, 20X6 and 20X5, and for the six-month periods then ended, and have issued our report thereon dated July XX, 20X6.

[*Scope paragraph*]

We conducted our review of Management's Discussion and Analysis in accordance with attestation standards established by the American Institute of Certified Public Accountants. A review of Management's Discussion and Analysis consists principally of applying analytical procedures and making inquiries of persons responsible for financial, accounting, and operational matters. It is substantially less in scope than an examination, the objective of which is the expression of an opinion on the presentation. Accordingly, we do not express such an opinion.

[*Explanatory paragraph*][42]

The preparation of Management's Discussion and Analysis requires management to interpret the criteria, make determinations as to the relevancy of information to be included, and make estimates and assumptions that affect reported information. Management's Discussion and Analysis includes information regarding the estimated future impact of transactions and events that have occurred or are expected to occur, expected sources of liquidity and capital resources, operating trends, commitments, and uncertainties. Actual results in the future may differ materially from management's present assessment of this information because events and circumstances frequently do not occur as expected.

[*Concluding paragraph*]

Based on our review, nothing came to our attention that caused us to believe that the Company's presentation of Management's Discussion and Analysis does not include, in all material respects, the required elements of the rules and regulations adopted by the Securities and Exchange Commission, that the historical financial amounts included therein have not been accurately derived, in all material respects, from the Company's financial statements, or that the underlying information, determinations, estimates, and assumptions of the Company do not provide a reasonable basis for the disclosures contained therein.

[*Restricted use paragraph*][43]

---

[42] The following sentence should be added to the beginning of the explanatory paragraph if the entity is a nonpublic entity, as discussed in paragraph .69*h*.

Although XYZ Company is not subject to the rules and regulations of the Securities and Exchange Commission, the accompanying Management's Discussion and Analysis is intended to be a presentation in accordance with the rules and regulations adopted by the Securities and Exchange Commission.

[43] This paragraph may be omitted for certain nonpublic entities. (Refer to paragraph .85*k*.)

This report is intended solely for the information and use of [*list or refer to specified parties*] and is not intended to be and should not be used by anyone other than the specified parties.

[*Signature*]

[*Date*]

.117

Appendix D

Comparison of Activities Performed Under SAS No. 118, *Other Information in Documents Containing Audited Financial Statements* [AU-C Section 720], Versus a Review or an Examination Attest Engagement*

Activities	*SAS No. 118 (AU-C Section 720)*	*Review*	*Examination*
Obtain an understanding of SEC rules and regulations and management's methodology for the preparation of Management's Discussion and Analysis (MD&A).	Not applicable (N/A)—Auditor is only required to read the information in the MD&A in order to identify material inconsistencies, if any, with the audited financial statements.	Obtain an understanding of the rules and regulations adopted by the SEC for MD&A. Inquire of management regarding the method of preparing MD&A.	Same as for a review.
Plan the engagement.	N/A	Develop an overall strategy for the analytical procedures and inquiries to be performed to provide negative assurance.	Develop an overall strategy for the expected scope and performance of the engagement to obtain reasonable assurance to express an opinion.
Consider internal control.	N/A	Consider relevant portions of the entity's internal control applicable to the preparation of MD&A to identify the types of potential misstatements and to select the inquiries and analytical procedures; no testing of controls would be performed.	Obtain an understanding of internal control applicable to the preparation of MD&A sufficient to plan the engagement and to assess control risk; controls may be tested by performing inquiries of client personnel, inspection of documents, and observation of relevant activities.

* Refer to AU-C section 720, *Other Information in Documents Containing Audited Financial Statements*. [Footnote revised, December 2012, to reflect conforming changes necessary due to the issuance of SAS Nos. 122–126.]

(continued)

Activities	*SAS No. 118 (AU-C Section 720)*	*Review*	*Examination*
Test assertions.	N/A	Apply the following analytical procedures and make inquiries of management and others; no corroborating evidential matter is obtained: • Read the MD&A and compare the content for consistency with the financial statements; compare financial amounts to the financial statements or related accounting records and analyses; recompute increases, decreases and percentages disclosed. • Compare nonfinancial amounts to the financial statements or other records. • Consider whether MD&A explanations are consistent with information obtained during the audit or review of financial statements; make further inquiries, as necessary. (Note: Such additional inquiries may result in a decision to perform other procedures or detail tests.) • Compare information in MD&A with the rules and regulations adopted by the SEC. • Obtain and read available prospective financial information; inquire of management as to the procedures used to prepare such information; consider whether information came to the practitioner's attention that causes him or her to believe that the underlying information, determinations, estimates, and assumptions do not provide a reasonable basis for the MD&A disclosures.	Apply the following analytical and corroborative procedures to obtain reasonable assurance of detecting material misstatements: • Read the MD&A and compare the content for consistency with the financial statements; compare financial amounts to the financial statements or related accounting records and analyses; recompute increases, decreases and percentages disclosed. • Compare nonfinancial amounts to the financial statements or other records; perform tests on other records based on the concept of materiality. • Consider whether explanations are consistent with the information obtained during the audit of financial statements; investigate further explanations that cannot be substantiated by information in the audit working papers through inquiry and inspection of client records. • Examine internally and externally generated documents in support of the existence, occurrence, or expected occurrence of events, transactions, conditions, trends, demands, commitments, and uncertainties disclosed in MD&A. • Compare information in MD&A with the rules and regulations adopted by the SEC.

Activities	*SAS No. 118 (AU-C Section 720)*	*Review*	*Examination*
Test assertions. (*continued*)		• Obtain public communications and minutes of meetings for comparison with disclosures in MD&A. • Make inquiries of the officers or executives with responsibility for operational areas and financial and accounting matters as to their plans and expectations for the future. • Inquire as to prior experience with the SEC and the extent of comments received; read correspondence. • Consider whether there are any additional matters that should be disclosed in the MD&A based on the results of the preceding procedures and knowledge obtained during the audit or review of the financial statements.	• Obtain and read available prospective financial information; inquire of management as to the procedures used to prepare such information; evaluate whether the underlying information, determinations, estimates, and assumptions provide a reasonable basis for the MD&A disclosures. • Obtain public communications and minutes of meetings; consider obtaining other types of publicly available information for comparison with the disclosures in MD&A. • Make inquiries of the officers or executives with responsibility for operational areas and financial and accounting matters as to their plans and expectations for the future. • Inquire as to prior experience with the SEC and the extent of comments received; read correspondence. • Test completeness by considering the results of the preceding procedures and knowledge obtained during the audit of the financial statements, and whether such matters are appropriately disclosed in the MD&A; extend procedures if the inherent risk relating to completeness of disclosures is high.

(continued)

Activities	*SAS No. 118 (AU-C Section 720)*	*Review*	*Examination*
Consider the effect of events subsequent to the balance-sheet date.	Yes	Yes	Yes
Obtain written representations from management.	Yes	Yes	Yes
Form a conclusion and report.	The auditor has no reporting responsibility with respect to MD&A unless the auditor concludes that there is a material inconsistency in the MD&A that has not been eliminated. In such a situation, the auditor may add an other matter paragraph to the auditor's report on the audited financial statements describing the material inconsistency or withhold the auditor's report. If, while reading the MD&A, the auditor becomes aware of an apparent material misstatement of fact, the auditor should discuss such matter with management and take other actions based on management's response.	Form a conclusion based on the results of the preceding procedures and report in the form of negative assurance.	Form an opinion based on the results of the preceding procedures and report conclusion by expressing an opinion.

[Revised, December 2010, to reflect conforming changes necessary due to the issuance of SAS Nos. 118–120. Revised, December 2012, to reflect conforming changes necessary due to the issuance of SAS Nos. 122–126.]

AT Section 801

Reporting on Controls at a Service Organization

(Supersedes the guidance for service auditors in Statement on Auditing Standards No. 70, *Service Organizations*, as amended.)

Source: SSAE No. 16.

Effective for service auditors' reports for periods ending on or after June 15, 2011. Earlier implementation is permitted.

Introduction

Scope of This Section

.01 This section addresses examination engagements undertaken by a service auditor to report on controls at organizations that provide services to user entities when those controls are likely to be relevant to user entities' internal control over financial reporting. It complements AU-C section 402, *Audit Considerations Relating to an Entity Using a Service Organization*, in that reports prepared in accordance with this section may provide appropriate evidence under AU-C section 402. (Ref: par. .A1) [Revised, December 2012, to reflect conforming changes necessary due to the issuance of SAS Nos. 122–126.]

.02 The focus of this section is on controls at service organizations likely to be relevant to user entities' internal control over financial reporting. The guidance herein also may be helpful to a practitioner performing an engagement under section 101, *Attest Engagements*, to report on controls at a service organization

a. other than those that are likely to be relevant to user entities' internal control over financial reporting (for example, controls that affect user entities' compliance with specified requirements of laws, regulations, rules, contracts, or grants, or controls that affect user entities' production or quality control). Section 601, *Compliance Attestation*, is applicable if a practitioner is reporting on an entity's own compliance with specified requirements or on its controls over compliance with specified requirements. (Ref: par. .A2–.A3)

b. when management of the service organization is not responsible for the design of the system (for example, when the system has been designed by the user entity or the design is stipulated in a contract between the user entity and the service organization). (Ref: par. .A4)

.03 In addition to performing an examination of a service organization's controls, a service auditor may be engaged to (*a*) examine and report on a user entity's transactions or balances maintained by a service organization, or (*b*) perform and report the results of agreed upon procedures related to the controls of a service organization or to transactions or balances of a user entity maintained by a service organization. However, these engagements are not addressed in this section.

.04 The requirements and application material in this section are based on the premise that management of the service organization (also referred to as management) will provide the service auditor with a written assertion that is included in or attached to management's description of the service organization's system. Paragraph .10 of this section addresses the circumstance in which management refuses to provide such a written assertion. Section 101 indicates that when performing an attestation engagement, a practitioner may report directly on the subject matter or on management's assertion. For engagements conducted under this section, the service auditor is required to report directly on the subject matter.

Effective Date

.05 This section is effective for service auditors' reports for periods ending on or after June 15, 2011. Earlier implementation is permitted.

Objectives

.06 The objectives of the service auditor are to

a. obtain reasonable assurance about whether, in all material respects, based on suitable criteria,

  i. management's description of the service organization's system fairly presents the system that was designed and implemented throughout the specified period (or in the case of a type 1 report, as of a specified date).

  ii. the controls related to the control objectives stated in management's description of the service organization's system were suitably designed throughout the specified period (or in the case of a type 1 report, as of a specified date).

  iii. when included in the scope of the engagement, the controls operated effectively to provide reasonable assurance that the control objectives stated in management's description of the service organization's system were achieved throughout the specified period.

b. report on the matters in 6(a) in accordance with the service auditor's findings.

Definitions

.07 For purposes of this section, the following terms have the meanings attributed in the subsequent text:

Carve-out method. Method of addressing the services provided by a subservice organization whereby management's description of the service organization's system identifies the nature of the services performed by the subservice organization and excludes from the description and from the scope of the service auditor's engagement, the subservice organization's relevant control objectives and related controls. Management's description of the service organization's system and the scope of the service auditor's engagement include controls at the service organization that monitor the effectiveness of controls at the subservice organization, which may include management of the service organization's review of a service auditor's report on controls at the subservice organization.

Complementary user entity controls. Controls that management of the service organization assumes, in the design of the service provided by the service organization, will be implemented by user entities, and which, if necessary to achieve the control objectives stated in management's description of the service organization's system, are identified as such in that description.

Control objectives. The aim or purpose of specified controls at the service organization. Control objectives address the risks that controls are intended to mitigate.

Controls at a service organization. The policies and procedures at a service organization likely to be relevant to user entities' internal control over financial reporting. These policies and procedures are designed, implemented, and documented by the service organization to provide reasonable assurance about the achievement of the control objectives relevant to the services covered by the service auditor's report. (Ref: par. .A5)

Controls at a subservice organization. The policies and procedures at a subservice organization likely to be relevant to internal control over financial reporting of user entities of the service organization. These policies and procedures are designed, implemented, and documented by a subservice organization to provide reasonable assurance about the achievement of control objectives that are relevant to the services covered by the service auditor's report.

Criteria. The standards or benchmarks used to measure and present the subject matter and against which the service auditor evaluates the subject matter. (Ref: par. .A6)

Inclusive method. Method of addressing the services provided by a subservice organization whereby management's description of the service organization's system includes a description of the nature of the services provided by the subservice organization as well as the subservice organization's relevant control objectives and related controls. (Ref: par. .A7–.A9)

Internal audit function. The service organization's internal auditors and others, for example, members of a compliance or risk department, who perform activities similar to those performed by internal auditors. (Ref: par. .A10)

Report on management's description of a service organization's system and the suitability of the design of controls (referred to in this section as a *type 1 report*). A report that comprises the following:

a. Management's description of the service organization's system.

b. A written assertion by management of the service organization about whether, in all material respects, and based on suitable criteria,

   i. management's description of the service organization's system fairly presents the service organization's system that was designed and implemented as of a specified date.

   ii. the controls related to the control objectives stated in management's description of the service organization's system were suitably designed to achieve those control objectives as of the specified date.

c. A service auditor's report that expresses an opinion on the matters in (b)(i)–(b)(ii).

Report on management's description of a service organization's system and the suitability of the design and operating effectiveness of controls (referred to in this section as a *type 2 report*). A report that comprises the following:

a. Management's description of the service organization's system.

b. A written assertion by management of the service organization about whether in all material respects, and based on suitable criteria,

i. management's description of the service organization's system fairly presents the service organization's system that was designed and implemented throughout the specified period.

ii. the controls related to the control objectives stated in management's description of the service organization's system were suitably designed throughout the specified period to achieve those control objectives.

iii. the controls related to the control objectives stated in management's description of the service organization's system operated effectively throughout the specified period to achieve those control objectives.

c. A service auditor's report that

i. expresses an opinion on the matters in (b)(i)–(b)(iii).

ii. includes a description of the tests of controls and the results thereof.

Service auditor. A practitioner who reports on controls at a service organization.

Service organization. An organization or segment of an organization that provides services to user entities, which are likely to be relevant to those user entities' internal control over financial reporting.

Service organization's assertion. A written assertion about the matters referred to in part (b) of the definition of *Report on management's description of a service organization's system and the suitability of the design and operating effectiveness of controls*, for a type 2 report; and, for a type 1 report, the matters referred to in part (b) of the definition of *Report on management's description of a service organization's system and the suitability of the design of controls*.

Service organization's system. The policies and procedures designed, implemented, and documented, by management of the service organization to provide user entities with the services covered by the service auditor's report. Management's description of the service organization's system identifies the services covered, the period to which the description relates (or in the case of a type 1 report, the date to which the description relates), the control objectives specified by management or an outside party, the party specifying the control objectives (if not specified by management), and the related controls. (Ref: par. .A11)

Subservice organization. A service organization used by another service organization to perform some of the services provided to user entities that are likely to be relevant to those user entities' internal control over financial reporting.

Test of controls. A procedure designed to evaluate the operating effectiveness of controls in achieving the control objectives stated in management's description of the service organization's system.

User auditor. An auditor who audits and reports on the financial statements of a user entity.

User entity. An entity that uses a service organization.

Requirements

Management and Those Charged With Governance

.08 When this section requires the service auditor to inquire of, request representations from, communicate with, or otherwise interact with management of the service organization, the service auditor should determine the appropriate person(s) within the service organization's management or governance structure with whom to interact. This should include consideration of which person(s) have the appropriate responsibilities for and knowledge of the matters concerned. (Ref: par. .A12)

Acceptance and Continuance

.09 A service auditor should accept or continue an engagement to report on controls at a service organization only if (Ref: par. .A13)

a. the service auditor has the capabilities and competence to perform the engagement. (Ref: par. .A14–.A15)

b. the service auditor's preliminary knowledge of the engagement circumstances indicates that

  i. the criteria to be used will be suitable and available to the intended user entities and their auditors;

  ii. the service auditor will have access to sufficient appropriate evidence to the extent necessary; and

  iii. the scope of the engagement and management's description of the service organization's system will not be so limited that they are unlikely to be useful to user entities and their auditors.

c. management agrees to the terms of the engagement by acknowledging and accepting its responsibility for the following:

  i. Preparing its description of the service organization's system and its assertion, including the completeness, accuracy, and method of presentation of the description and assertion. (Ref: par. .A16)

  ii. Having a reasonable basis for its assertion. (Ref: par. .A17)

  iii. Selecting the criteria to be used and stating them in the assertion.

  iv. Specifying the control objectives, stating them in the description of the service organization's system, and, if the control objectives are specified by law, regulation, or another party (for example, a user group or a professional body), identifying in the description the party specifying the control objectives.

v. Identifying the risks that threaten the achievement of the control objectives stated in the description and designing, implementing, and documenting controls that are suitably designed and operating effectively to provide reasonable assurance that the control objectives stated in the description of the service organization's system will be achieved. (Ref: par. .A18)

vi. Providing the service auditor with

(1) access to all information, such as records and documentation, including service level agreements, of which management is aware that is relevant to the description of the service organization's system and the assertion;

(2) additional information that the service auditor may request from management for the purpose of the examination engagement;

(3) unrestricted access to personnel within the service organization from whom the service auditor determines it is necessary to obtain evidence relevant to the service auditor's engagement; and

(4) written representations at the conclusion of the engagement.

vii. Providing a written assertion that will be included in, or attached to management's description of the service organization's system, and provided to user entities.

.10 If management will not provide the service auditor with a written assertion, the service auditor should not circumvent the requirement to obtain an assertion by performing a service auditor's engagement under section 101. (Ref: par. .A19)

.11 Management's subsequent refusal to provide a written assertion represents a scope limitation and consequently, the service auditor should withdraw from the engagement. If law or regulation does not allow the service auditor to withdraw from the engagement, the service auditor should disclaim an opinion.

Request to Change the Scope of the Engagement

.12 If management requests a change in the scope of the engagement before the completion of the engagement, the service auditor should be satisfied, before agreeing to the change, that a reasonable justification for the change exists. (Ref: par. .A20–.A21)

Assessing the Suitability of the Criteria (Ref: par. .A6 and .A22–.A23)

.13 As required by paragraph .23 of section 101, the service auditor should assess whether management has used suitable criteria

a. in preparing its description of the service organization's system;

b. in evaluating whether controls were suitably designed to achieve the control objectives stated in the description; and

c. in the case of a type 2 report, in evaluating whether controls operated effectively throughout the specified period to achieve the control objectives stated in the description of the service organization's system.

.14 In assessing the suitability of the criteria to evaluate whether management's description of the service organization's system is fairly presented, the service auditor should determine if the criteria include, at a minimum,

a. whether management's description of the service organization's system presents how the service organization's system was designed and implemented, including the following information about the service organization's system, if applicable:

i. The types of services provided including, as appropriate, the classes of transactions processed.

ii. The procedures, within both automated and manual systems, by which services are provided, including, as appropriate, procedures by which transactions are initiated, authorized, recorded, processed, corrected as necessary, and transferred to the reports and other information prepared for user entities.

iii. The related accounting records, whether electronic or manual, and supporting information involved in initiating, authorizing, recording, processing, and reporting transactions; this includes the correction of incorrect information and how information is transferred to the reports and other information prepared for user entities.

iv. How the service organization's system captures and addresses significant events and conditions other than transactions.

v. The process used to prepare reports and other information for user entities.

vi. The specified control objectives and controls designed to achieve those objectives, including as applicable, complementary user entity controls contemplated in the design of the service organization's controls.

vii. Other aspects of the service organization's control environment, risk assessment process, information and communication systems (including the related business processes), control activities, and monitoring controls that are relevant to the services provided. (Ref: par. A17 and .A24)

b. in the case of a type 2 report, whether management's description of the service organization's system includes relevant details of changes to the service organization's system during the period covered by the description. (Ref: par. .A44)

c. whether management's description of the service organization's system does not omit or distort information relevant to the service organization's system, while acknowledging that management's description of the service organization's system is prepared to meet the common needs of a broad range of user entities and their user auditors, and may not, therefore, include every aspect of the service organization's system that each individual user entity and its user auditor may consider important in its own particular environment.

.15 In assessing the suitability of the criteria to evaluate whether the controls are suitably designed, the service auditor should determine if the criteria include, at a minimum, whether *a.* the risks that threaten the achievement of the control objectives stated in management's description of the service organization's system have been identified by management.

b. the controls identified in management's description of the service organization's system would, if operating as described, provide reasonable assurance that those risks would not prevent the control objectives stated in the description from being achieved.

.16 In assessing the suitability of the criteria to evaluate whether controls operated effectively to provide reasonable assurance that the control objectives stated in management's description of the service organization's system were achieved, the service auditor should determine if the criteria include, at a minimum, whether the controls were consistently applied as designed throughout the specified period, including whether manual controls were applied by individuals who have the appropriate competence and authority.

Materiality

.17 When planning and performing the engagement, the service auditor should evaluate materiality with respect to the fair presentation of management's description of the service organization's system, the suitability of the design of controls to achieve the related control objectives stated in the description and, in the case of a type 2 report, the operating effectiveness of the controls to achieve the related control objectives stated in the description. (Ref: par. .A25–.A27)

Obtaining an Understanding of the Service Organization's System (Ref: par. .A28–.A30)

.18 The service auditor should obtain an understanding of the service organization's system, including controls that are included in the scope of the engagement.

Obtaining Evidence Regarding Management's Description of the Service Organization's System (Ref: par. .A26 and .A31–.A35)

.19 The service auditor should obtain and read management's description of the service organization's system and should evaluate whether those aspects of the description that are included in the scope of the engagement are presented fairly, including whether

a. the control objectives stated in management's description of the service organization's system are reasonable in the circumstances. (Ref: par. .A34)

b. controls identified in management's description of the service organization's system were implemented. (Ref: par. .A35)

c. complementary user entity controls, if any, are adequately described. (Ref: par. .A32)

d. services performed by a subservice organization, if any, are adequately described, including whether the inclusive method or the carve-out method has been used in relation to them.

.20 The service auditor should determine through inquiries made in combination with other procedures whether the service organization's system has been implemented. Such other procedures should include observation and inspection of records and other documentation of the manner in which the service organization's system operates and controls are applied. (Ref: par. .A35)

Obtaining Evidence Regarding the Design of Controls (Ref: par .A26 and .A36–.A39)

.21 The service auditor should determine which of the controls at the service organization are necessary to achieve the control objectives stated in management's description of the service organization's system and should assess whether those controls were suitably designed to achieve the control objectives by

a. identifying the risks that threaten the achievement of the control objectives stated in management's description of the service organization's system, and (Ref: par. .A36)

b. evaluating the linkage of the controls identified in management's description of the service organization's system with those risks.

Obtaining Evidence Regarding the Operating Effectiveness of Controls (Ref: par. .A26 and .A40–.A45)

Assessing Operating Effectiveness

.22 When performing a type 2 engagement, the service auditor should test those controls that the service auditor has determined are necessary to achieve the control objectives stated in management's description of the service organization's system and should assess their operating effectiveness throughout the period. Evidence obtained in prior engagements about the satisfactory operation of controls in prior periods does not provide a basis for a reduction in testing, even if it is supplemented with evidence obtained during the current period. (Ref: par. .A40–.A44)

.23 When performing a type 2 engagement, the service auditor should inquire about changes in the service organization's controls that were implemented during the period covered by the service auditor's report. If the service auditor believes the changes would be considered significant by user entities and their auditors, the service auditor should determine whether those changes are included in management's description of the service organization's system. If such changes are not included in the description, the service auditor should describe the changes in the service auditor's report and determine the effect on the service auditor's report. If the superseded controls are relevant to the achievement of the control objectives stated in the description, the service auditor should, if possible, test the superseded controls before the change. If the service auditor cannot test superseded controls relevant to the achievement of the control objectives stated in the description, the service auditor should determine the effect on the service auditor's report. (Ref: par. .A42(c) and .A45)

.24 When designing and performing tests of controls, the service auditor should

a. perform other procedures in combination with inquiry to obtain evidence about the following:

i. How the control was applied.

ii. The consistency with which the control was applied.

iii. By whom or by what means the control was applied.

b. determine whether the controls to be tested depend on other controls, and if so, whether it is necessary to obtain evidence supporting the operating effectiveness of those other controls.

c. determine an effective method for selecting the items to be tested to meet the objectives of the procedure.

.25 When determining the extent of tests of controls and whether sampling is appropriate, the service auditor should consider the characteristics of the population of the controls to be tested, including the nature of the controls, the frequency of their application (for example, monthly, daily, many times per day), and the expected rate of deviation. AU-C section 530, *Audit Sampling*, addresses the auditor's use of statistical and nonstatistical sampling when designing and selecting the audit sample, performing tests of controls and tests of details, and evaluating the results from the sample. If the service auditor determines that sampling is appropriate, the service auditor should apply AU-C section 530. [Revised, December 2012, to reflect conforming changes necessary due to the issuance of SAS Nos. 122–126.]

Nature and Cause of Deviations

.26 The service auditor should investigate the nature and cause of any deviations identified, and should determine whether

a. identified deviations are within the expected rate of deviation and are acceptable. If so, the testing that has been performed provides an appropriate basis for concluding that the control operated effectively throughout the specified period.

b. additional testing of the control or of other controls is necessary to reach a conclusion about whether the controls related to the control objectives stated in management's description of the service organization's system operated effectively throughout the specified period.

c. the testing that has been performed provides an appropriate basis for concluding that the control did not operate effectively throughout the specified period.

.27 If, as a result of performing the procedures in paragraph .26, the service auditor becomes aware that any identified deviations have resulted from intentional acts by service organization personnel, the service auditor should assess the risk that management's description of the service organization's system is not fairly presented, the controls are not suitably designed, and in a type 2 engagement, the controls are not operating effectively. (Ref: par. .A31)

Using the Work of the Internal Audit Function

Obtaining an Understanding of the Internal Audit Function (Ref: par. .A46–.A47)

.28 If the service organization has an internal audit function, the service auditor should obtain an understanding of the nature of the responsibilities of the internal audit function and of the activities performed in order to determine whether the internal audit function is likely to be relevant to the engagement.

Planning to Use the Work of the Internal Audit Function

.29 When the service auditor intends to use the work of the internal audit function, the service auditor should determine whether the work of the internal audit function is likely to be adequate for the purposes of the engagement by evaluating the following:

a. The objectivity and technical competence of the members of the internal audit function

b. Whether the work of the internal audit function is likely to be carried out with due professional care

c. Whether it is likely that effective communication will occur between the internal audit function and the service auditor, including consideration of the effect of any constraints or restrictions placed on the internal audit function by the service organization

.30 If the service auditor determines that the work of the internal audit function is likely to be adequate for the purposes of the engagement, in determining the planned effect of the work of the internal audit function on the nature, timing, or extent of the service auditor's procedures, the service auditor should evaluate the following:

a. The nature and scope of specific work performed, or to be performed, by the internal audit function

b. The significance of that work to the service auditor's conclusions

c. The degree of subjectivity involved in the evaluation of the evidence gathered in support of those conclusions

Using the Work of the Internal Audit Function (Ref: par. .A48)

.31 In order for the service auditor to use specific work of the internal audit function, the service auditor should evaluate and perform procedures on that work to determine its adequacy for the service auditor's purposes.

.32 To determine the adequacy of specific work performed by the internal audit function for the service auditor's purposes, the service auditor should evaluate whether

a. the work was performed by members of the internal audit function having adequate technical training and proficiency;

b. the work was properly supervised, reviewed, and documented;

c. sufficient appropriate evidence was obtained to enable the internal audit function to draw reasonable conclusions;

d. conclusions reached are appropriate in the circumstances and any reports prepared by the internal audit function are consistent with the results of the work performed; and

e. exceptions relevant to the engagement or unusual matters disclosed by the internal audit function are properly resolved.

Effect on the Service Auditor's Report

.33 If the work of the internal audit function has been used, the service auditor should not make reference to that work in the service auditor's opinion. Notwithstanding its degree of autonomy and objectivity, the internal audit function is not independent of the service organization. The service auditor has sole responsibility for the opinion expressed in the service auditor's report and, accordingly, that responsibility is not reduced by the service auditor's use of the work of the internal audit function. (Ref: par. .A49)

.34 In the case of a type 2 report, if the work of the internal audit function has been used in performing tests of controls, that part of the service auditor's report that describes the service auditor's tests of controls and results thereof should include a description of the internal auditor's work and of the service auditor's procedures with respect to that work. (Ref: par. .A50)

Direct Assistance

.35 When the service auditor uses members of the service organization's internal audit function to provide direct assistance, the service auditor should adapt and apply the requirements in paragraph .27 of AU-C section 610, *The Auditor's Consideration of the Internal Audit Function in an Audit of Financial Statements*. [Revised, December 2012, to reflect conforming changes necessary due to the issuance of SAS Nos. 122–126.]

Written Representations (Ref: par. .A51–.A55)

.36 The service auditor should request management to provide written representations that

a. reaffirm its assertion included in or attached to the description of the service organization's system;

b. it has provided the service auditor with all relevant information and access agreed to; and [1]

c. it has disclosed to the service auditor any of the following of which it is aware:

i. Instances of noncompliance with laws and regulations or uncorrected errors attributable to the service organization that may affect one or more user entities.

ii. Knowledge of any actual, suspected, or alleged intentional acts by management or the service organization's employees, that could adversely affect the fairness of the presentation of management's description of the service organization's system or the completeness or achievement of the control objectives stated in the description.

iii. Design deficiencies in controls.

iv. Instances when controls have not operated as described.

v. Any events subsequent to the period covered by management's description of the service organization's system up to the date of the service auditor's report that could have a significant effect on management's assertion.

.37 If a service organization uses a subservice organization and management's description of the service organization's system uses the inclusive method, the service auditor also should obtain the written representations identified in paragraph .36 from management of the subservice organization.

.38 The written representations should be in the form of a representation letter addressed to the service auditor and should be as of the same date as the date of the service auditor's report.

.39 If management does not provide one or more of the written representations requested by the service auditor, the service auditor should do the following:

a. Discuss the matter with management

---

[1] See paragraph .09(c)(vi)(1).

b. Evaluate the effect of such refusal on the service auditor's assessment of the integrity of management and evaluate the effect that this may have on the reliability of management's representations and evidence in general

c. Take appropriate actions, which may include disclaiming an opinion or withdrawing from the engagement

If management refuses to provide the representations in paragraphs .36(a)–.36(b) of this section, the service auditor should disclaim an opinion or withdraw from the engagement.

Other Information (Ref: par. .A56–.A57)

.40 The service auditor should read other information, if any, included in a document containing management's description of the service organization's system and the service auditor's report to identify material inconsistencies, if any, with that description. While reading the other information for the purpose of identifying material inconsistencies, the service auditor may become aware of an apparent misstatement of fact in the other information.

.41 If the service auditor becomes aware of a material inconsistency or an apparent misstatement of fact in the other information, the service auditor should discuss the matter with management. If the service auditor concludes that there is a material inconsistency or a misstatement of fact in the other information that management refuses to correct, the service auditor should take further appropriate action.[2]

Subsequent Events

.42 The service auditor should inquire whether management is aware of any events subsequent to the period covered by management's description of the service organization's system up to the date of the service auditor's report that could have a significant effect on management's assertion. If the service auditor becomes aware, through inquiry or otherwise, of such an event, or any other event that is of such a nature and significance that its disclosure is necessary to prevent users of a type 1 or type 2 report from being misled, and information about that event is not disclosed by management in its description, the service auditor should disclose such event in the service auditor's report.

.43 The service auditor has no responsibility to keep informed of events subsequent to the date of the service auditor's report; however, after the release of the service auditor's report, the service auditor may become aware of conditions that existed at the report date that might have affected management's assertion and the service auditor's report had the service auditor been aware of them. The evaluation of such subsequent information is similar to the evaluation of facts discovered subsequent to the date of the report on an audit of financial statements, as described in AU-C section 560, *Subsequent Events and Subsequently Discovered Facts*, and therefore, the service auditor should adapt and apply AU-C section 560. [Revised, December 2012, to reflect conforming changes necessary due to the issuance of SAS Nos. 122–126.]

Documentation (Ref: par. .A58)

.44 The service auditor should prepare documentation that is sufficient to enable an experienced service auditor, having no previous connection with the engagement, to understand the following:

---

[2] See paragraphs .91–.94 of section 101, *Attest Engagements*.

a. The nature, timing, and extent of the procedures performed to comply with this section and with applicable legal and regulatory requirements

b. The results of the procedures performed and the evidence obtained

c. Significant findings or issues arising during the engagement, the conclusions reached thereon, and significant professional judgments made in reaching those conclusions

.45 In documenting the nature, timing, and extent of procedures performed, the service auditor should record the following:

a. Identifying characteristics of the specific items or matters being tested

b. Who performed the work and the date such work was completed

c. Who reviewed the work performed and the date and extent of such review

.46 If the service auditor uses specific work of the internal audit function, the service auditor should document the conclusions reached regarding the evaluation of the adequacy of the work of the internal audit function and the procedures performed by the service auditor on that work.

.47 The service auditor should document discussions of significant findings or issues with management and others, including the nature of the significant findings or issues, when the discussions took place, and with whom.

.48 If the service auditor has identified information that is inconsistent with the service auditor's final conclusion regarding a significant finding or issue, the service auditor should document how the service auditor addressed the inconsistency.

.49 The service auditor should assemble the engagement documentation in an engagement file and complete the administrative process of assembling the final engagement file on a timely basis, no later than 60 days following the service auditor's report release date.

.50 After the assembly of the final engagement file has been completed, the service auditor should not delete or discard documentation before the end of its retention period.

.51 If the service auditor finds it necessary to modify existing engagement documentation or add new documentation after the assembly of the final engagement file has been completed, the service auditor should, regardless of the nature of the modifications or additions, document the following:

a. The specific reasons for making them

b. When and by whom they were made and reviewed

Preparing the Service Auditor's Report

Content of the Service Auditor's Report (Ref: par. .A59)

.52 A service auditor's type 2 report should include the following elements:

a. A title that includes the word *independent*.

b. An addressee.

c. Identification of

i. management's description of the service organization's system and the function performed by the system.

ii. any parts of management's description of the service organization's system that are not covered by the service auditor's report. (Ref: par. .A56)

iii. any information included in a document containing the service auditor's report that is not covered by the service auditor's report. (Ref: par. .A56)

iv. the criteria.

v. any services performed by a subservice organization and whether the carve-out method or the inclusive method was used in relation to them. Depending on which method is used, the following should be included:

(1) If the carve-out method was used, a statement that management's description of the service organization's system excludes the control objectives and related controls at relevant subservice organizations, and that the service auditor's procedures do not extend to the subservice organization.

(2) If the inclusive method was used, a statement that management's description of the service organization's system includes the subservice organization's specified control objectives and related controls, and that the service auditor's procedures included procedures related to the subservice organization.

d. If management's description of the service organization's system refers to the need for complementary user entity controls, a statement that the service auditor has not evaluated the suitability of the design or operating effectiveness of complementary user entity controls, and that the control objectives stated in the description can be achieved only if complementary user entity controls are suitably designed and operating effectively, along with the controls at the service organization.

e. A reference to management's assertion and a statement that management is responsible for (Ref: par. .A60)

i. preparing the description of the service organization's system and the assertion, including the completeness, accuracy, and method of presentation of the description and assertion;

ii. providing the services covered by the description of the service organization's system;

iii. specifying the control objectives unless the control objectives are specified by law, regulation, or another party, and stating them in the description of the service organization's system;

iv. identifying the risks that threaten the achievement of the control objectives;

v. selecting the criteria; and

vi. designing, implementing, and documenting controls that are suitably designed and operating effectively to achieve the related control objectives stated in the description of the service organization's system.

f. A statement that the service auditor's responsibility is to express an opinion on the fairness of the presentation of management's description of the service organization's system and on the suitability of the design and operating effectiveness of the controls to achieve the related control objectives stated in the description, based on the service auditor's examination.

g. A statement that the examination was conducted in accordance with attestation standards established by the American Institute of Certified Public Accountants and that those standards require the service auditor to plan and perform the examination to obtain reasonable assurance about whether management's description of the service organization's system is fairly presented and the controls are suitably designed and operating effectively throughout the specified period to achieve the related control objectives.

h. A statement that an examination of management's description of a service organization's system and the suitability of the design and operating effectiveness of the service organization's controls to achieve the related control objectives stated in the description involves performing procedures to obtain evidence about the fairness of the presentation of the description and the suitability of the design and operating effectiveness of those controls to achieve the related control objectives stated in the description.

i. A statement that the examination included assessing the risks that management's description of the service organization's system is not fairly presented and that the controls were not suitably designed or operating effectively to achieve the related control objectives.

j. A statement that the examination also included testing the operating effectiveness of those controls that the service auditor considers necessary to provide reasonable assurance that the related control objectives stated in management's description of the service organization's system were achieved.

k. A statement that an examination engagement of this type also includes evaluating the overall presentation of management's description of the service organization's system and suitability of the control objectives stated in the description.

l. A statement that the service auditor believes the examination provides a reasonable basis for his or her opinion.

m. A statement about the inherent limitations of controls, including the risk of projecting to future periods any evaluation of the fairness of the presentation of management's description of the service organization's system or conclusions about the suitability of the design or operating effectiveness of controls.

n. The service auditor's opinion on whether, in all material respects, based on the criteria described in management's assertion,

   i. management's description of the service organization's system fairly presents the service organization's system that was designed and implemented throughout the specified period.

   ii. the controls related to the control objectives stated in management's description of the service organization's system were suitably designed to provide reasonable assurance that those control objectives would be achieved if the controls operated effectively throughout the specified period.

iii. the controls the service auditor tested, which were those necessary to provide reasonable assurance that the control objectives stated in management's description of the service organization's system were achieved, operated effectively throughout the specified period.

iv. if the application of complementary user entity controls is necessary to achieve the related control objectives stated in management's description of the service organization's system, a reference to this condition.

o. A reference to a description of the service auditor's tests of controls and the results thereof, that includes

i. identification of the controls that were tested, whether the items tested represent all or a selection of the items in the population, and the nature of the tests in sufficient detail to enable user auditors to determine the effect of such tests on their risk assessments. (Ref: par. .A50)

ii. if deviations have been identified in the operation of controls included in the description, the extent of testing performed by the service auditor that led to the identification of the deviations (including the number of items tested), and the number and nature of the deviations noted (even if, on the basis of tests performed, the service auditor concludes that the related control objective was achieved). (Ref: par. .A65)

p. A statement restricting the use of the service auditor's report to management of the service organization, user entities of the service organization's system during some or all of the period covered by the service auditor's report, and the independent auditors of such user entities. (Ref: par. .A61–.A64)

q. The date of the service auditor's report.

r. The name of the service auditor and the city and state where the service auditor maintains the office that has responsibility for the engagement.

.53 A service auditor's type 1 report should include the following elements:

a. A title that includes the word *independent*.

b. An addressee.

c. Identification of

i. management's description of the service organization's system and the function performed by the system.

ii. any parts of management's description of the service organization's system that are not covered by the service auditor's report. (Ref: par. .A56)

iii. any information included in a document containing the service auditor report that is not covered by the service auditor's report. (Ref: par. .A56)

iv. the criteria.

v. any services performed by a subservice organization and whether the carve-out method or the inclusive method was used in relation to them. Depending on which method is used, the following should be included:

(1) If the carve-out method was used, a statement that management's description of the service organization's system excludes the control objectives and related controls at relevant subservice organizations, and that the service auditor's procedures do not extend to the subservice organization.

(2) If the inclusive method was used, a statement that management's description of the service organization's system includes the subservice organization's specified control objectives and related controls, and that the service auditor's procedures included procedures related to the subservice organization.

d. If management's description of the service organization's system refers to the need for complementary user entity controls, a statement that the service auditor has not evaluated the suitability of the design or operating effectiveness of complementary user entity controls, and that the control objectives stated in the description can be achieved only if complementary user entity controls are suitably designed and operating effectively, along with the controls at the service organization.

e. A reference to management's assertion and a statement that management is responsible for (Ref: par. .A60)

i. preparing the description of the service organization's system and assertion, including the completeness, accuracy, and method of presentation of the description and assertion;

ii. providing the services covered by the description of the service organization's system;

iii. specifying the control objectives, unless the control objectives are specified by law, regulation, or another party, and stating them in the description of the service organization's system;

iv. identifying the risks that threaten the achievement of the control objectives,

v. selecting the criteria; and

vi. designing, implementing, and documenting controls that are suitably designed and operating effectively to achieve the related control objectives stated in the description of the service organization's system.

f. A statement that the service auditor's responsibility is to express an opinion on the fairness of the presentation of management's description of the service organization's system and on the suitability of the design of the controls to achieve the related control objectives stated in the description, based on the service auditor's examination.

g. A statement that the examination was conducted in accordance with attestation standards established by the American Institute of Certified Public Accountants, and that those standards require the service auditor to plan and perform the examination to obtain reasonable assurance about whether management's description of the service organization's system is fairly presented and the controls are suitably designed as of the specified date to achieve the related control objectives.

h. A statement that the service auditor has not performed any procedures regarding the operating effectiveness of controls and, therefore, expresses no opinion thereon.

i. A statement that an examination of management's description of a service organization's system and the suitability of the design of the service organization's controls to achieve the related control objectives stated in the description involves performing procedures to obtain evidence about the fairness of the presentation of the description and the suitability of the design of those controls to achieve the related control objectives stated in the description.

j. A statement that the examination included assessing the risks that management's description of the service organization's system is not fairly presented and that the controls were not suitably designed to achieve the related control objectives.

k. A statement that an examination engagement of this type also includes evaluating the overall presentation of management's description of the service organization's system and suitability of the control objectives stated in the description.

l. A statement that the service auditor believes the examination provides a reasonable basis for his or her opinion.

m. A statement about the inherent limitations of controls, including the risk of projecting to future periods any evaluation of the fairness of the presentation of management's description of the service organization's system or conclusions about the suitability of the design of the controls to achieve the related control objectives.

n. The service auditor's opinion on whether, in all material respects, based on the criteria described in management's assertion,

    i. management's description of the service organization's system fairly presents the service organization's system that was designed and implemented as of the specified date.

    ii. the controls related to the control objectives stated in management's description of the service organization's system were suitably designed to provide reasonable assurance that those control objectives would be achieved if the controls operated effectively as of the specified date.

    iii. if the application of complementary user entity controls is necessary to achieve the related control objectives stated in management's description of the service organization's system, a reference to this condition.

o. A statement restricting the use of the service auditor's report to management of the service organization, user entities of the service organization's system as of the end of the period covered by the service auditor's report, and the independent auditors of such user entities. (Ref: par. .A61–.A64)

p. The date of the service auditor's report.

q. The name of the service auditor and the city and state where the service auditor maintains the office that has responsibility for the engagement.

Report Date

.54 The service auditor should date the service auditor's report no earlier than the date on which the service auditor has obtained sufficient appropriate evidence to support the service auditor's opinion.

Modified Opinions (Ref: par. .A66)

.55 The service auditor's opinion should be modified and the service auditor's report should contain a clear description of all the reasons for the modification, if the service auditor concludes that

a. management's description of the service organization's system is not fairly presented, in all material respects;

b. the controls are not suitably designed to provide reasonable assurance that the control objectives stated in management's description of the service organization's system would be achieved if the controls operated as described;

c. in the case of a type 2 report, the controls did not operate effectively throughout the specified period to achieve the related control objectives stated in management's description of the service organization's system; or

d. the service auditor is unable to obtain sufficient appropriate evidence

.56 If the service auditor plans to disclaim an opinion because of the inability to obtain sufficient appropriate evidence, and, based on the limited procedures performed, has concluded that,

a. certain aspects of management's description of the service organization's system are not fairly presented, in all material respects;

b. certain controls were not suitably designed to provide reasonable assurance that the control objectives stated in management's description of the service organization's system would be achieved if the controls operated as described; or

c. in the case of a type 2 report, certain controls did not operate effectively throughout the specified period to achieve the related control objectives stated in management's description of the service organization's system,

the service auditor should identify these findings in his or her report.

.57 If the service auditor plans to disclaim an opinion, the service auditor should not identify the procedures that were performed nor include statements describing the characteristics of a service auditor's engagement in the service auditor's report; to do so might overshadow the disclaimer.

Other Communication Responsibilities

.58 If the service auditor becomes aware of incidents of noncompliance with laws and regulations, fraud, or uncorrected errors attributable to management or other service organization personnel that are not clearly trivial and that may affect one or more user entities, the service auditor should determine the effect of such incidents on management's description of the service organization's system, the achievement of the control objectives, and the service auditor's report.

Additionally, the service auditor should determine whether this information has been communicated appropriately to affected user entities. If the information has not been so communicated, and management of the service organization is unwilling to do so, the service auditor should take appropriate action. (Ref: par. .A67)

Application and Other Explanatory Material

Scope of This Section

.A1 *Internal control* is a process designed to provide reasonable assurance regarding the achievement of objectives related to the reliability of financial reporting, effectiveness and efficiency of operations, and compliance with applicable laws and regulations. Controls related to a service organization's operations and compliance objectives may be relevant to a user entity's internal control over financial reporting. Such controls may pertain to assertions about presentation and disclosure relating to account balances, classes of transactions or disclosures, or may pertain to evidence that the user auditor evaluates or uses in applying auditing procedures. For example, a payroll processing service organization's controls related to the timely remittance of payroll deductions to government authorities may be relevant to a user entity because late remittances could incur interest and penalties that would result in a liability for the user entity. Similarly, a service organization's controls over the acceptability of investment transactions from a regulatory perspective may be considered relevant to a user entity's presentation and disclosure of transactions and account balances in its financial statements. (Ref: par. .01)

.A2 Paragraph .02 of this section refers to other engagements that the practitioner may perform and report on under section 101 to report on controls at a service organization. Paragraph .02 is not, however, intended to

- provide for the alteration of the definitions of *service organization* and *service organization's system* in paragraph .07 to permit reports issued under this section to include in the description of the service organization's system aspects of their services (including relevant control objectives and related controls) not likely to be relevant to user entities' internal control over financial reporting, or
- permit a report to be issued that combines reporting under this section on a service organization's controls that are likely to be relevant to user entities' internal control over financial reporting, with reporting under section 101 on controls that are not likely to be relevant to user entities' internal control over financial reporting. (Ref: par. .02(a))

.A3 When a service auditor conducts an engagement under section 101 to report on controls at a service organization other than those controls likely to be relevant to user entities' internal control over financial reporting, and the service auditor intends to use the guidance in this section in planning and performing that engagement, the service auditor may encounter issues that differ significantly from those associated with engagements to report on a service organization's controls likely to be relevant to user entities' internal control over financial reporting. For example,

- identification of suitable and available criteria, as prescribed in paragraphs .23–.34 of section 101, for evaluating the fairness of presentation of management's description of the service organization's system and the suitability of the design and the operating effectiveness of the controls.
- identification of appropriate control objectives, and the basis for evaluating the reasonableness of the control objectives in the circumstances of the particular engagement.

- identification of the intended users of the report and the manner in which they intend to use the report.
- relevance and appropriateness of the definitions in paragraph .07 of this section, many of which specifically relate to internal control over financial reporting.
- application of references to auditing standards (AU-C sections) that are intended to provide the service auditor with guidance relevant to internal control over financial reporting.
- application of the concept of materiality in the circumstances of the particular engagement.
- developing the language to be used in the practitioner's report, including addressing paragraphs .84–.87 of section 101, which identify the elements to be included in an examination report. (Ref: par. .02(a))

.A4 When management of the service organization is not responsible for the design of the system, it is unlikely that management of the service organization will be in a position to assert that the system is suitably designed. Controls cannot operate effectively unless they are suitably designed. Because of the inextricable link between the suitability of the design of controls and their operating effectiveness, the absence of an assertion with respect to the suitability of design will likely preclude the service auditor from opining on the operating effectiveness of controls. As an alternative, the practitioner may perform tests of controls in either an agreed-upon procedures engagement under section 201, *Agreed Upon Procedures Engagements*, or an examination of the operating effectiveness of the controls under section 101. (Ref: par. .02(b))

Definitions

Controls at a Service Organization (Ref: par. .07)

.A5 The policies and procedures referred to in the definition of *controls at a service organization* in paragraph .07 include aspects of user entities' information systems maintained by the service organization and may also include aspects of one or more of the other components of internal control at a service organization. For example, the definition of *controls at a service organization* may include aspects of the service organization's control environment, monitoring, and control activities when they relate to the services provided. Such definition does not, however, include controls at a service organization that are not related to the achievement of the control objectives stated in management's description of the service organization's system; for example, controls related to the preparation of the service organization's own financial statements.

Criteria (Ref: par. .07 and .14–.16)

.A6 For the purposes of engagements performed in accordance with this section, criteria need to be available to user entities and their auditors to enable them to understand the basis for the service organization's assertion about the fair presentation of management's description of the service organization's system, the suitability of the design of controls that address control objectives stated in the description of the system and, in the case of a type 2 report, the operating effectiveness of such controls. Information about suitable criteria is provided in paragraphs .23–.34 of section 101. Paragraphs .14–.16 of this section discuss the criteria for evaluating the fairness of the presentation of management's description of the service organization's system and the suitability of the design and operating effectiveness of the controls.

Inclusive Method (Ref: par. .07)

.A7 As indicated in the definition of *inclusive method* in paragraph .07, a service organization that uses a subservice organization presents management's description of the service organization's system to include a description of the services provided by the subservice organization as well as the subservice organization's relevant control objectives and related controls. When the inclusive method is used, the requirements of this section also apply to the services provided by the subservice organization, including the requirement to obtain management's acknowledgement and acceptance of responsibility for the matters in paragraph .09(c)(i)–(vii) as they relate to the subservice organization.

.A8 Performing procedures at the subservice organization entails coordination and communication between the service organization, the subservice organization, and the service auditor. The inclusive method generally is feasible if, for example, the service organization and the subservice organization are related, or if the contract between the service organization and the subservice organization provides for issuance of a service auditor's report. If the service auditor is unable to obtain an assertion from the subservice organization regarding management's description of the service organization's system provided, including the relevant control objectives and related controls at the subservice organization, the service auditor is unable to use the inclusive method but may instead use the carve-out method.

.A9 There may be instances when the service organization's controls, such as monitoring controls, permit the service organization to include in its assertion the relevant aspects of the subservice organization's system, including the relevant control objectives and related controls of the subservice organization. In such instances, the service auditor is basing his or her opinion solely on the controls at the service organization, and hence, the inclusive method is not applicable.

Internal Audit Function (Ref: par. .07)

.A10 The "others" referenced in the definition of *internal audit function* may be individuals who perform activities similar to those performed by internal auditors and include service organization personnel (in addition to internal auditors), and third parties working under the direction of management or those charged with governance.

Service Organization's System (Ref: par. .07)

.A11 The policies and procedures referred to in the definition of *service organization's system* refer to the guidelines and activities for providing transaction processing and other services to user entities and include the infrastructure, software, people, and data that support the policies and procedures.

Management and Those Charged With Governance (Ref: par. .08)

.A12 Management and governance structures vary by entity, reflecting influences such as size and ownership characteristics. Such diversity means that it is not possible for this section to specify for all engagements the person(s) with whom the service auditor is to interact regarding particular matters. For example, the service organization may be a segment of an organization and not a separate legal entity. In such cases, identifying the appropriate management personnel or those charged with governance from whom to request written representations may require the exercise of professional judgment.

Acceptance and Continuance

.A13 If one or more of the conditions in paragraph .09 are not met and the service auditor is nevertheless required by law or regulation to accept or continue an engagement to report on controls at a service organization, the service auditor is required, in accordance with the requirements in paragraphs .55–.56, to determine the effect on the service auditor's report of one or more of such conditions not being met. (Ref: par. .09)

Capabilities and Competence to Perform the Engagement (Ref: par. .09a)

.A14 Relevant capabilities and competence to perform the engagement include matters such as the following:

- Knowledge of the relevant industry
- An understanding of information technology and systems
- Experience in evaluating risks as they relate to the suitable design of controls
- Experience in the design and execution of tests of controls and the evaluation of the results

.A15 In performing a service auditor's engagement, the service auditor need not be independent of each user entity. (Ref: par. .09a)

Management's Responsibility for Documenting the Service Organization's System (Ref: par. .09(c)(i))

.A16 Management of the service organization is responsible for documenting the service organization's system. No one particular form of documentation is prescribed and the extent of documentation may vary depending on the size and complexity of the service organization and its monitoring activities.

Reasonable Basis for Management's Assertion (Ref: par. .07, definition of service organization's system; par. .09(c)(ii) and .14(a)(vii))

.A17 Management's monitoring activities may provide evidence of the design and operating effectiveness of controls in support of management's assertion. *Monitoring of controls* is a process to assess the effectiveness of internal control performance over time. It involves assessing the effectiveness of controls on a timely basis, identifying and reporting deficiencies to appropriate individuals within the service organization, and taking necessary corrective actions. Management accomplishes monitoring of controls through ongoing activities, separate evaluations, or a combination of the two. Ongoing monitoring activities are often built into the normal recurring activities of an entity and include regular management and supervisory activities. Internal auditors or personnel performing similar functions may contribute to the monitoring of a service organization's activities. Monitoring activities may also include using information communicated by external parties, such as customer complaints and regulator comments, which may indicate problems or highlight areas in need of improvement. The greater the degree and effectiveness of ongoing monitoring, the less need for separate evaluations. Usually, some combination of ongoing monitoring and separate evaluations will ensure that internal control maintains its effectiveness over time. The service auditor's report on controls is not a substitute for the service organization's own processes to provide a reasonable basis for its assertion.

Identification of Risks (Ref: par. .09(c)(v))

.A18 Control objectives relate to risks that controls seek to mitigate. For example, the risk that a transaction is recorded at the wrong amount or in the wrong period can be expressed as a control objective that transactions are recorded at the correct amount and in the correct period. Management is responsible for identifying the risks that threaten achievement of the control objectives stated in management's description of the service organization's system. Management may have a formal or informal process for identifying relevant risks. A formal process may include estimating the significance of identified risks, assessing the likelihood of their occurrence, and deciding about actions to address them. However, because control objectives relate to risks that controls seek to mitigate, thoughtful identification by management of control objectives when designing, implementing, and documenting the service organization's system may itself comprise an informal process for identifying relevant risks.

Management's Refusal to Provide a Written Assertion

.A19 A recent change in service organization management or the appointment of the service auditor by a party other than management are examples of situations that may cause management to be unwilling to provide the service auditor with a written assertion. However, other members of management may be in a position to, and will agree to, sign the assertion so that the service auditor can meet the requirement of paragraph .09(c)(vii). (Ref: par. .10)

Request to Change the Scope of the Engagement (Ref: par. .12)

.A20 A request to change the scope of the engagement may not have a reasonable justification if, for example, the request is made

- to exclude certain control objectives at the service organization from the scope of the engagement because of the likelihood that the service auditor's opinion would be modified with respect to those control objectives.
- to prevent the disclosure of deviations identified at a subservice organization by requesting a change from the inclusive method to the carve-out method.

.A21 A request to change the scope of the engagement may have a reasonable justification when, for example, the request is made to exclude from the engagement a subservice organization because the service organization cannot arrange for access by the service auditor, and the method used for addressing the services provided by that subservice organization is changed from the inclusive method to the carve-out method.

Assessing the Suitability of the Criteria (Ref: par. .13–.16)

.A22 Section 101 requires a practitioner, among other things, to determine whether the subject matter is capable of evaluation against criteria that are suitable and available to users. As indicated in paragraph .27 of section 101, regardless of who establishes or develops the criteria, management is responsible for selecting the criteria and for determining whether the criteria are appropriate. The subject matter is the underlying condition of interest to intended users of an attestation report. The following table identifies the subject matter and minimum criteria for each of the opinions in type 2 and type 1 reports.

	Subject Matter	*Criteria*	*Comment*
Opinion on the fair presentation of management's description of the service organization's system (type 1 and type 2 reports).	Management's description of the service organization's system that is likely to be relevant to user entities' internal control over financial reporting and is covered by the service auditor's report, and management's assertion about whether the description is fairly presented.	Management's description of the service organization's system is fairly presented if it *a.* presents how the service organization's system was designed and implemented including, as appropriate, the matters identified in paragraph .14(a) and, in the case of a type 2 report, includes relevant details of changes to the service organization's system during the period covered by the description. *b.* does not omit or distort information relevant to the service organization's system, while acknowledging that management's description of the service organization's system is prepared to meet the common needs of a broad range of user entities and may not, therefore, include every aspect of the service organization's system that each individual user entity may consider important in its own particular environment.	The specific wording of the criteria for this opinion may need to be tailored to be consistent with criteria established by, for example, law, regulation, user groups, or a professional body. Criteria for evaluating management's description of the service organization's system are provided in paragraph .14. Paragraphs .19–.20 and .A31–.A33 offer further guidance on determining whether these criteria are met.

(continued)

	Subject Matter	*Criteria*	*Comment*	
Opinion on suitability of design and operating effectiveness (type 2 reports).	The design and operating effectiveness of the controls that are necessary to achieve the control objectives stated in management's description of the service organization's system.	The controls are suitably designed and operating effectively to achieve the control objectives stated in management's description of the service organization's system if *a.* management has identified the risks that threaten the achievement of the control objectives stated in management's description of the service organization's system. *b.* the controls identified in management's description of the service organization's system would, if operating as described, provide reasonable assurance that those risks would not prevent the control objectives stated in the description from being achieved. *c.* the controls were consistently applied as designed throughout the specified period. This includes whether manual controls were applied by individuals who have the appropriate competence and authority.	When the criteria for this opinion are met, controls will have provided reasonable assurance that the related control objectives stated in management's description of the service organization's system were achieved throughout the specified period.	The control objectives stated in management's description of the service organization's system are part of the criteria for these opinions. The control objectives stated in the description will differ from engagement to engagement. If the service auditor concludes that the control objectives stated in the description are not fairly presented, then those control objectives would not be suitable as part of the criteria for forming an opinion on the design and operating effectiveness of the controls.

	Subject Matter	Criteria	Comment
Opinion on suitability of design (type 1 reports).	The suitability of the design of the controls necessary to achieve the control objectives stated in management's description of the service organization's system and relevant to the services covered by the service auditor's report.	The controls are suitably designed to achieve the control objectives stated in management's description of the service organization's system if *a.* management has identified the risks that threaten the achievement of the control objectives stated in its description of the service organization's system. *b.* the controls identified in management's description of the service organization's system would, if operating as described, provide reasonable assurance that those risks would not prevent the control objectives stated in the description from being achieved.	Meeting these criteria does not, of itself, provide any assurance that the control objectives stated in management's description of the service organization's system were achieved because no evidence has been obtained about the operating effectiveness of the controls.

.A23 Paragraph .14(a) identifies a number of elements that are included in management's description of the service organization's system as appropriate. These elements may not be appropriate if the system being described is not a system that processes transactions; for example, if the system relates to general controls over the hosting of an IT application but not the controls embedded in the application itself. (Ref: par. .14)

.A24 The requirement to include in management's description of the service organization's system "other aspects of the service organization's control environment, risk assessment process, information and communication systems (including the related business processes), control activities, and monitoring controls, that are relevant to the services provided" is also applicable to the internal control components of subservice organizations used by the service organization when the inclusive method is used. See AU-C section 315, *Understanding the Entity and Its Environment and Assessing the Risks of Material Misstatement*, for a discussion of these components. (Ref: par. .14(a)(vii)) [Revised, December 2012, to reflect conforming changes necessary due to the issuance of SAS Nos. 122–126.]

Materiality (Ref: par. .17)

.A25 In an engagement to report on controls at a service organization, the concept of materiality relates to the information being reported on, not the financial statements of user entities. The service auditor plans and performs procedures to determine whether management's description of the service organization's system is fairly presented, in all material respects; whether controls at the service organization are suitably designed in all material respects to achieve the control objectives stated in the description; and in the case of a type 2 report, whether controls at the service organization operated effectively throughout the specified period in all material respects to achieve the control objectives stated in the description. The concept of materiality takes into account that the service auditor's report provides information about the service organization's system to meet the common information needs of a broad range of user entities and their auditors who have an understanding of the manner in which the system is being used by a particular user entity for financial reporting.

.A26 Materiality with respect to the fair presentation of management's description of the service organization's system and with respect to the design of controls primarily includes the consideration of qualitative factors; for example, whether

- management's description of the service organization's system includes the significant aspects of the processing of significant transactions.
- management's description of the service organization's system omits or distorts relevant information.
- the controls have the ability, as designed, to provide reasonable assurance that the control objectives stated in management's description of the service organization's system would be achieved.

Materiality with respect to the operating effectiveness of controls includes the consideration of both quantitative and qualitative factors; for example, the tolerable rate and observed rate of deviation (a quantitative matter) and the nature and cause of any observed deviations (a qualitative matter).

.A27 The concept of materiality is not applied when disclosing, in the description of the tests of controls, the results of those tests when deviations have been identified. This is because, in the particular circumstances of a specific user entity or user auditor, a deviation may have significance beyond whether or not, in the opinion of the service auditor, it prevents a control from operating effectively. For example, the control to which the deviation relates may be particularly significant in preventing a certain type of error that may be material in the particular circumstances of a user entity's financial statements.

Obtaining an Understanding of the Service Organization's System (Ref: par. .18)

.A28 Obtaining an understanding of the service organization's system, including related controls, assists the service auditor in the following:

- Identifying the boundaries of the system and how it interfaces with other systems
- Assessing whether management's description of the service organization's system fairly presents the service organization's system that has been designed and implemented
- Determining which controls are necessary to achieve the control objectives stated in management's description of the service organization's system, whether controls were suitably designed to achieve those control objectives, and, in the case of a type 2 report, whether controls were operating effectively throughout the period to achieve those control objectives

.A29 Management's description of the service organization's system includes "aspects of the service organization's control environment, risk assessment process, information and communication systems (including relevant business processes), control activities and monitoring activities that are relevant to the services provided." Although aspects of the service organization's control environment, risk assessment process, and monitoring activities may not be presented in the description in the context of control objectives, they may nevertheless be necessary to achieve the specified control objectives stated in the description. Likewise, deficiencies in these controls may have an effect on the service auditor's assessment of whether the controls, taken as a whole, were suitably designed or operating effectively to achieve the specified control objectives. See AU-C section 315 for a discussion of these components of internal control. [Revised, December 2012, to reflect conforming changes necessary due to the issuance of SAS Nos. 122–126.]

.A30 The service auditor's procedures to obtain the understanding referred to in paragraph .A28 may include the following:

- Inquiring of management and others within the service organization who, in the service auditor's judgment, may have relevant information
- Observing operations and inspecting documents, reports, and printed and electronic records of transaction processing
- Inspecting a selection of agreements between the service organization and user entities to identify their common terms
- Reperforming the application of a control

One or more of the preceding procedures may be accomplished through the performance of a walkthrough.

Obtaining Evidence Regarding Management's Description of the Service Organization's System (Ref: par. .19–.20)

.A31 In a service auditor's examination engagement, the service auditor plans and performs the engagement to obtain reasonable assurance of detecting errors or omissions in management's description of the service organization's system and instances in which control objectives were not achieved. Absolute assurance is not attainable because of factors such as the need for judgment, the use of sampling, and the inherent limitations of controls at the service organization that affect whether the description is fairly presented and the controls are suitably designed and operating effectively to achieve the control objectives, and because much of the evidence available to the service auditor is persuasive rather than conclusive in nature. Also, procedures that are effective for detecting unintentional errors or omissions in the description, and instances in which control objectives were not achieved, may be ineffective for detecting intentional errors or omissions in the description and instances in which the control objectives were not achieved that are concealed through collusion between service organization personnel and a third party or among management or employees of the service organization. Therefore, the subsequent discovery of the existence of material omissions or errors in the description or instances in which control objectives were not achieved does not, in and of itself, evidence inadequate planning, performance, or judgment on the part of the service auditor. (Ref: par. .27)

.A32 Considering the following questions may assist the service auditor in determining whether management's description of the service organization's system is fairly presented, in all material respects:

- Does management's description address the major aspects of the service provided and included in the scope of the engagement that could reasonably be expected to be relevant to the common needs of a broad range of user auditors in planning their audits of user entities' financial statements?

- Is the description prepared at a level of detail that could reasonably be expected to provide a broad range of user auditors with sufficient information to obtain an understanding of internal control in accordance with AU-C section 315? The description need not address every aspect of the service organization's processing or the services provided to user entities and need not be so detailed that it would potentially enable a reader to compromise security or other controls at the service organization.
- Is the description prepared in a manner that does not omit or distort information that might affect the decisions of a broad range of user auditors; for example, does the description contain any significant omissions or inaccuracies regarding processing of which the service auditor is aware?
- Does the description include relevant details of changes to the service organization's system during the period covered by the description when the description covers a period of time?
- Have the controls identified in the description actually been implemented?
- Are complementary user entity controls, if any, adequately described? In most cases, the control objectives stated in the description are worded so that they are capable of being achieved through the effective operation of controls implemented by the service organization alone. In some cases, however, the control objectives stated in the description cannot be achieved by the service organization alone because their achievement requires particular controls to be implemented by user entities. This may be the case when, for example, the control objectives are specified by a regulatory authority. When the description does include complementary user entity controls, the description separately identifies those controls along with the specific control objectives that cannot be achieved by the service organization alone. (Ref: par. .19(c))
- If the inclusive method has been used, does the description separately identify controls at the service organization and controls at the subservice organization? If the carve-out method is used, does the description identify the functions that are performed by the subservice organization? When the carve-out method is used, the description need not describe the detailed processing or controls at the subservice organization.

[Revised, December 2012, to reflect conforming changes necessary due to the issuance of SAS Nos. 122–126.]

.A33 The service auditor's procedures to evaluate the fair presentation of management's description of the service organization's system may include the following:

- Considering the nature of the user entities and how the services provided by the service organization are likely to affect them; for example, the predominant types of user entities, and whether the user entities are regulated by government agencies
- Reading contracts with user entities to gain an understanding of the service organization's contractual obligations

- Observing procedures performed by service organization personnel
- Reviewing the service organization's policy and procedure manuals and other documentation of the system; for example, flowcharts and narratives
- Performing walkthroughs of transactions through the service organization's system

.A34 Paragraph .19(a) requires the service auditor to evaluate whether the control objectives stated in management's description of the service organization's system are reasonable in the circumstances. Considering the following questions may assist the service auditor in this evaluation:

- Have the control objectives stated in the description been specified by the service organization or by outside parties, such as regulatory authorities, a user group, a professional body, or others?
- Do the control objectives stated in the description and specified by the service organization relate to the types of assertions commonly embodied in the broad range of user entities' financial statements to which controls at the service organization could reasonably be expected to relate (for example, assertions about existence and accuracy that are affected by access controls that prevent or detect unauthorized access to the system)? Although the service auditor ordinarily will not be able to determine how controls at a service organization specifically relate to the assertions embodied in individual user entities' financial statements, the service auditor's understanding of the nature of the service organization's system, including controls, and the services being provided is used to identify the types of assertions to which those controls are likely to relate.
- Are the control objectives stated in the description and specified by the service organization complete? Although a complete set of control objectives can provide a broad range of user auditors with a framework to assess the effect of controls at the service organization on assertions commonly embodied in user entities' financial statements, the service auditor ordinarily will not be able to determine how controls at a service organization specifically relate to the assertions embodied in individual user entities' financial statements and cannot, therefore, determine whether control objectives are complete from the viewpoint of individual user entities or user auditors. It is the responsibility of individual user entities or user auditors to assess whether the service organization's description addresses the particular control objectives that are relevant to their needs. If the control objectives are specified by an outside party, including control objectives specified by law or regulation, the outside party is responsible for their completeness and reasonableness. (Ref: par. .19(a))

.A35 The service auditor's procedures to determine whether the system described by the service organization has been implemented may be similar to, and performed in conjunction with, procedures to obtain an understanding of that system. Other procedures that the service auditor may use in combination with inquiry of management and other service organization personnel include observation, inspection of records and other documentation, as well as reperformance of the manner in which transactions are processed through the system and controls are applied. (Ref: par. .19(b) and .20)

Obtaining Evidence Regarding the Design of Controls (Ref: par. .21)

.A36 The risks and control objectives identified in paragraph .21(a) encompass intentional and unintentional acts that threaten the achievement of the control objectives. (Ref: par. .21(a))

.A37 From the viewpoint of a user auditor, a control is suitably designed to achieve the control objectives stated in management's description of the service organization's system if individually or in combination with other controls, it would, when complied with satisfactorily, provide reasonable assurance that material misstatements are prevented, or detected and corrected. A service auditor, however, is not aware of the circumstances at individual user entities that would affect whether or not a misstatement resulting from a control deficiency is material to those user entities. Therefore, from the viewpoint of a service auditor, a control is suitably designed if individually or in combination with other controls, it would, when complied with satisfactorily, provide reasonable assurance that the control objective(s) stated in the description of the service organization's system are achieved.

.A38 A service auditor may consider using flowcharts, questionnaires, or decision tables to facilitate understanding the design of the controls.

.A39 Controls may consist of a number of activities directed at the achievement of various control objectives. Consequently, if the service auditor evaluates certain activities as being ineffective in achieving a particular control objective, the existence of other activities may allow the service auditor to conclude that controls related to the control objective are suitably designed to achieve the control objective.

Obtaining Evidence Regarding the Operating Effectiveness of Controls (Ref: par. .22–.27)

.A40 From the viewpoint of a user auditor, a control is operating effectively if individually or in combination with other controls, it provides reasonable assurance that material misstatements whether due to fraud or error are prevented, or detected and corrected. A service auditor, however, is not aware of the circumstances at individual user entities that would affect whether or not a misstatement resulting from a control deviation is material to those user entities. Therefore, from the viewpoint of a service auditor, a control is operating effectively if individually or in combination with other controls, it provides reasonable assurance that the control objectives stated in management's description of the service organization's system are achieved. Similarly, a service auditor is not in a position to determine whether any observed control deviation would result in a material misstatement from the viewpoint of an individual user entity. (Ref: par. .22)

.A41 Obtaining an understanding of controls sufficient to opine on the suitability of their design is not sufficient evidence regarding their operating effectiveness unless some automation provides for the consistent operation of the controls as they were designed and implemented. For example, obtaining information about the implementation of a manual control at a point in time does not provide evidence about operation of the control at other times. However, because of the inherent consistency of IT processing, performing procedures to determine the design of an automated control and whether it has been implemented may serve as evidence of that control's operating effectiveness, depending on the service auditor's assessment and testing of controls such as those over program changes. (Ref: par. .22)

.A42 A type 2 report that covers a period that is less than six months is unlikely to be useful to user entities and their auditors. If management's description of the service organization's system covers a period that is less than six months, the description may describe the reasons for the shorter period and the service auditor's report may include that information as well. Circumstances that may result in a report covering a period of less than six months include the following:

- The service auditor was engaged close to the date by which the report on controls is to be issued, and controls cannot be tested for operating effectiveness for a six month period.
- The service organization or a particular system or application has been in operation for less than six months.
- Significant changes have been made to the controls, and it is not practicable either to wait six months before issuing a report or to issue a report covering the system both before and after the changes. (Ref: par. .23)

.A43 Evidence about the satisfactory operation of controls in prior periods does not provide evidence of the operating effectiveness of controls during the current period. The service auditor expresses an opinion on the effectiveness of controls throughout each period; therefore, sufficient appropriate evidence about the operating effectiveness of controls throughout the current period is required for the service auditor to express that opinion for the current period. Knowledge of deviations observed in prior engagements may, however, lead the service auditor to increase the extent of testing during the current period. (Ref: par. .22)

.A44 Determining the effect of changes in the service organization's controls that were implemented during the period covered by the service auditor's report involves gathering information about the nature and extent of such changes, how they affect processing at the service organization, and how they might affect assertions in the user entities' financial statements. (Ref: par. .14(b) and .23)

.A45 Certain controls may not leave evidence of their operation that can be tested at a later date and, accordingly, the service auditor may find it appropriate to test the operating effectiveness of such controls at various times throughout the reporting period. (Ref: par. .22)

Using the Work of an Internal Audit Function

Obtaining an Understanding of the Internal Audit Function (Ref: par. .28)

.A46 An internal audit function may be responsible for providing analyses, evaluations, assurances, recommendations, and other information to management and those charged with governance. An internal audit function at a service organization may perform activities related to the service organization's internal control or activities related to the services and systems, including controls that the service organization provides to user entities.

.A47 The scope and objectives of an internal audit function vary widely and depend on the size and structure of the service organization and the requirements of management and those charged with governance. Internal audit function activities may include one or more of the following:

- Monitoring the service organization's internal control or the application processing systems. This may include controls relevant to the services provided to user entities. The internal audit function may be assigned specific responsibility for reviewing controls, monitoring their operation, and recommending improvements thereto.
- Examination of financial and operating information. The internal audit function may be assigned to review the means by which the service organization identifies, measures, classifies, and reports financial and operating information; to make inquiries about specific matters; and to perform other procedures including detailed testing of transactions, balances, and procedures.
- Evaluation of the economy, efficiency, and effectiveness of operating activities including nonfinancial activities of the service organization.
- Evaluation of compliance with laws, regulations, and other external requirements and with management policies, directives, and other internal requirements.

Using the Work of the Internal Audit Function (Ref: par .31–.32)

.A48 The nature, timing, and extent of the service auditor's procedures on specific work of the internal auditors will depend on the service auditor's assessment of the significance of that work to the service auditor's conclusions (for example, the significance of the risks that the controls tend to mitigate), the evaluation of the internal audit function, and the evaluation of the specific work of the internal auditors. Such procedures may include the following:

- Examination of items already examined by the internal auditors
- Examination of other similar items
- Observation of procedures performed by the internal auditors

Effect on the Service Auditor's Report (Ref: par. .33–.34)

.A49 The responsibility to report on management's description of the service organization's system and the suitability of the design and operating effectiveness of controls rests solely with the service auditor and cannot be shared with the internal audit function. Therefore, the judgments about the significance of deviations in the design or operating effectiveness of controls, the sufficiency of tests performed, the evaluation of identified deficiencies, and other matters affecting the service auditor's report are those of the service auditor. In making judgments about the extent of the effect of the work of the internal audit function on the service auditor's procedures, the service auditor may determine, based on risk associated with the controls and the significance of the judgments relating to them, that the service auditor will perform the work relating to some or all of the controls rather than using the work performed by the internal audit function.

.A50 In the case of a type 2 report, when the work of the internal audit function has been used in performing tests of controls, the service auditor's description of that work and of the service auditor's procedures with respect to that work may be presented in a number of ways, for example, (Ref: par. .34 and .52(o)(i))

- by including introductory material to the description of tests of controls indicating that certain work of the internal audit function was used in performing tests of controls.

- attribution of individual tests to internal audit.

Written Representations (Ref: par. .36–.39)

.A51 Written representations reaffirming the service organization's assertion about the effective operation of controls may be based on ongoing monitoring activities, separate evaluations, or a combination of the two. (Ref: par. .A12)

.A52 In certain circumstances, a service auditor may obtain written representations from parties in addition to management of the service organization, such as those charged with governance.

.A53 The written representations required by paragraph .36 are separate from and in addition to the assertion included in or attached to management's description of the service organization's system required by paragraph .09(c)(vii).

.A54 If the service auditor is unable to obtain written representations regarding relevant control objectives and related controls at the subservice organization, management of the service organization would be unable to use the inclusive method but could use the carve-out method.

.A55 In addition to the written representations required by paragraph .36, the service auditor may consider it necessary to request other written representations.

Other Information

.A56 The "other information" referred to in paragraphs .40–.41 may be the following:

- Information provided by the service organization and included in a section of the service auditor's type 1 or type 2 report, or
- Information outside the service auditor's type 1 or type 2 report included in a document that contains the service auditor's report. This other information may be provided by the service organization or by another party. (Ref: par. .40, .52(c)(ii)–(iii), and .53(c)(ii)–(iii))

.A57 If other information included in a document containing management's description of the service organization's system and the service auditor's report contains future-oriented information that cannot be reasonably substantiated, the service auditor may request that the information be removed or revised. (Ref: par. .41)

Documentation

.A58 Paragraph 57 of Statement on Quality Control Standards No. 8, *A Firm's System of Quality Control*, requires the firm to establish policies and procedures that address engagement performance, supervision responsibilities, and review responsibilities. The requirement to document who reviewed the work performed and the extent of the review, in accordance with the firm's policies and procedures addressing review responsibilities, does not imply a need for each specific working paper to include evidence of review. The requirement, however, means documenting what work was reviewed, who reviewed such work, and when it was reviewed. (Ref: par. .44)

Preparing the Service Auditor's Report

Content of the Service Auditor's Report (Ref: par. .52–.53)

.A59 Examples of service auditors' reports are presented in appendixes A–C and illustrative assertions by management of the service organization are presented in exhibit A.

.A60 The service organization's assertion may be presented in management's description of the service organization's system or may be attached to the description. (Ref: par. .52(e) and .53(e))

Use of the Service Auditor's Report (Ref: par. .52(p) and .53(o))

.A61 Paragraph .79 of section 101 requires that the use of a practitioner's report be restricted to specified parties when the criteria used to evaluate or measure the subject matter are available only to specified parties or appropriate only for a limited number of parties who either participated in their establishment or can be presumed to have an adequate understanding of the criteria. The criteria used for engagements to report on controls at a service organization are relevant only for the purpose of providing information about the service organization's system, including controls, to those who have an understanding of how the system is used for financial reporting by user entities and, accordingly, the service auditor's report states that the report and the description of tests of controls are intended only for use by management of the service organization, user entities of the service organization ("during some or all of the period covered by the report" for a type 2 report, and "as of the ending date of the period covered by the report" for a type 1 report), and their user auditors. (The illustrative service auditor's reports in appendix A illustrate language for a paragraph restricting the use of a service auditor's report.)

.A62 Paragraph .79 of section 101 indicates that the need for restriction on the use of a report may result from a number of circumstances, including the potential for the report to be misunderstood when taken out of the context in which it was intended to be used, and the extent to which the procedures performed are known or understood.

.A63 Although a service auditor is not responsible for controlling a service organization's distribution of a service auditor's report, a service auditor may inform the service organization of the following:

- A service auditor's type 1 report is not intended for distribution to parties other than the service organization, user entities of the service organization's system as of the end of the period covered by the service auditor's report, and their user auditors.
- A service auditor's type 2 report is not intended for distribution to parties other than the service organization, user entities of the service organization's system during some or all of the period covered by the service auditor's report, and their user auditors.

.A64 A user entity is also considered a user entity of the service organization's subservice organizations if controls at subservice organizations are relevant to internal control over financial reporting of the user entity. In such case, the user entity is referred to as an indirect or downstream user entity of the subservice organization. Consequently, an indirect or downstream user entity may be included in the group to whom use of the service auditor's report is restricted if controls at the service organization are relevant to internal control over financial reporting of such indirect or downstream user entity.

Description of the Service Auditor's Tests of Controls and the Results Thereof (Ref: par. .52(o)(ii))

.A65 In describing the service auditor's tests of controls for a type 2 report, it assists readers if the service auditor's report includes information about causative factors for identified deviations, to the extent the service auditor has identified such factors.

Modified Opinions (Ref: par. .55–.57)

.A66 Examples of elements of modified service auditor's reports are presented in appendix B.

Other Communication Responsibilities (Ref: par. .58)

.A67 Actions that a service auditor may take when he or she becomes aware of noncompliance with laws and regulations, fraud, or uncorrected errors at the service organization (after giving additional consideration to instances in which the service organization has not appropriately communicated this information to affected user entities, and the service organization is unwilling to do so) include the following:

- Obtaining legal advice about the consequences of different courses of action
- Communicating with those charged with governance of the service organization
- Disclaiming an opinion, modifying the service auditor's opinion, or adding an emphasis paragraph
- Communicating with third parties, for example, a regulator, when required to do so
- Withdrawing from the engagement

.A68

Appendix A: Illustrative Service Auditor's Reports

The following illustrative reports are for guidance only and are not intended to be exhaustive or applicable to all situations.

Example 1: Type 2 Service Auditor's Report

Independent Service Auditor's Report on a Description of a Service Organization's System and the Suitability of the Design and Operating Effectiveness of Controls

To: XYZ Service Organization

Scope

We have examined XYZ Service Organization's description of its [*type or name of*] system for processing user entities' transactions [*or identification of the function performed by the system*] throughout the period [*date*] to [*date*] (description) and the suitability of the design and operating effectiveness of controls to achieve the related control objectives stated in the description.

Service organization's responsibilities

On page XX of the description, XYZ Service Organization has provided an assertion about the fairness of the presentation of the description and suitability of the design and operating effectiveness of the controls to achieve the related control objectives stated in the description. XYZ Service Organization is responsible for preparing the description and for the assertion, including the completeness, accuracy, and method of presentation of the description and the assertion, providing the services covered by the description, specifying the control objectives and stating them in the description, identifying the risks that threaten the achievement of the control objectives, selecting the criteria, and designing, implementing, and documenting controls to achieve the related control objectives stated in the description.

Service auditor's responsibilities

Our responsibility is to express an opinion on the fairness of the presentation of the description and on the suitability of the design and operating effectiveness of the controls to achieve the related control objectives stated in the description, based on our examination. We conducted our examination in accordance with attestation standards established by the American Institute of Certified Public Accountants. Those standards require that we plan and perform our examination to obtain reasonable assurance about whether, in all material respects, the description is fairly presented and the controls were suitably designed and operating effectively to achieve the related control objectives stated in the description throughout the period [*date*] to [*date*].

An examination of a description of a service organization's system and the suitability of the design and operating effectiveness of the service organization's controls to achieve the related control objectives stated in the description involves performing procedures to obtain evidence about the fairness of the presentation of the description and the suitability of the design and operating effectiveness of those controls to achieve the related control objectives stated in the description. Our procedures included assessing the risks that the description is not fairly presented and that the controls were not suitably designed or operating effectively to achieve the related control objectives stated in the description. Our procedures also included testing the operating effectiveness of those controls that we consider necessary to provide reasonable assurance that the related control objectives stated in the description were achieved. An examination engagement of this type also includes evaluating the overall presentation of the description and the suitability of the control objectives stated therein, and the suitability of the criteria specified by the service organization and described at page *[aa]*. We believe that the evidence we obtained is sufficient and appropriate to provide a reasonable basis for our opinion.

Inherent limitations

Because of their nature, controls at a service organization may not prevent, or detect and correct, all errors or omissions in processing or reporting transactions [*or identification of the function performed by the system*]. Also, the projection to the future of any evaluation of the fairness of the presentation of the description, or conclusions about the suitability of the design or operating effectiveness of the controls to achieve the related control objectives is subject to the risk that controls at a service organization may become inadequate or fail.

Opinion

In our opinion, in all material respects, based on the criteria described in XYZ Service Organization's assertion on page [*aa*],

a. the description fairly presents the [*type or name of*] system that was designed and implemented throughout the period [*date*] to [*date*].

b. the controls related to the control objectives stated in the description were suitably designed to provide reasonable assurance that the control objectives would be achieved if the controls operated effectively throughout the period [*date*] to [*date*].

c. the controls tested, which were those necessary to provide reasonable assurance that the control objectives stated in the description were achieved, operated effectively throughout the period [*date*] to [*date*].

Description of tests of controls

The specific controls tested and the nature, timing, and results of those tests are listed on pages [*yy–zz*].

Restricted use

This report, including the description of tests of controls and results thereof on pages [*yy–zz*], is intended solely for the information and use of XYZ Service Organization, user entities of XYZ Service Organization's [*type or name of*] system during some or all of the period [*date*] to [*date*], and the independent auditors of such user entities, who have a sufficient understanding to consider it, along with other information including information about controls implemented by user entities themselves, when assessing the risks of material misstatements of user entities' financial statements. This report is not intended to be and should not be used by anyone other than these specified parties.

[*Service auditor's signature*]

[*Date of the service auditor's report*]

[*Service auditor's city and state*]

Following is a modification of the scope paragraph in a type 2 service auditor's report if the description refers to the need for complementary user entity controls. (New language is shown in boldface italics):

> We have examined XYZ Service Organization's description of its [*type or name of*] system for processing user entities' transactions [*or identification of the function performed by the system*] throughout the period [*date*] to [*date*] (description) and the suitability of the design and operating effectiveness of controls to achieve the related control objectives stated in the description. ***The description indicates that certain control objectives specified in the description can be achieved only if complementary user entity controls contemplated in the design of XYZ Service Organization's controls are suitably designed and operating effectively, along with related controls at the service organization. We have not evaluated the suitability of the design or operating effectiveness of such complementary user entity controls.***

Following is a modification of the applicable subparagraphs of the opinion paragraph of a type 2 service auditor's report if the application of complementary user entity controls is necessary to achieve the related control objectives stated in the description of the service organization's system (New language is shown in boldface italics):

b. The controls related to the control objectives stated in the description were suitably designed to provide reasonable assurance that those control objectives would be achieved if the controls operated effectively throughout the period [*date*] to [*date*] ***and user entities applied the complementary user entity controls contemplated in the design of XYZ Service Organization's controls throughout the period [date] to [date]***.

c. The controls tested, which ***together with the complementary user entity controls referred to in the scope paragraph of this report, if operating effectively,*** were those necessary to provide reasonable assurance that the control objectives stated in the description were achieved, operated effectively throughout the period [*date*] to [*date*].

Following is a modification of the paragraph that describes the responsibilities of management of the service organization for use in a type 2 service auditor's report when the control objectives have been specified by an outside party. (New language is shown in boldface italics):

> On page XX of the description, XYZ Service Organization has provided an assertion about the fairness of the presentation of the description and suitability of the design and operating effectiveness of the controls to achieve the related control objectives stated in the description. XYZ Service Organization is responsible for preparing the description and for its assertion], including the completeness, accuracy, and method of presentation of the description and assertion, providing the services covered by the description, selecting the criteria, and designing, implementing, and documenting controls to achieve the related control objectives stated in the description. ***The control objectives have been specified by [name of party specifying the control objectives] and are stated on page [aa] of the description***.

Example 2: Type 1 Service Auditor's Report

Independent Service Auditor's Report on a Description of a Service Organization's System and the Suitability of the Design of Controls

To: XYZ Service Organization

Scope

We have examined XYZ Service Organization's description of its [*type or name of*] system for processing user entities' transactions [*or identification of the function performed by the system*] as of [*date*], and the suitability of the design of controls to achieve the related control objectives stated in the description.

Service organization's responsibilities

On page XX of the description, XYZ Service Organization has provided an assertion about the fairness of the presentation of the description and suitability of the design of the controls to achieve the related control objectives stated in the description. XYZ Service Organization is responsible for preparing the description and for its assertion, including the completeness, accuracy, and method of presentation of the description and the assertion, providing the services covered by the description, specifying the control objectives and stating them in the description, identifying the risks that threaten the achievement of the control objectives, selecting the criteria, and designing, implementing, and documenting controls to achieve the related control objectives stated in the description.

Service auditor's responsibilities

Our responsibility is to express an opinion on the fairness of the presentation of the description and on the suitability of the design of the controls to achieve the related control objectives stated in the description, based on our examination. We conducted our examination in accordance with attestation standards established by the American Institute of Certified Public Accountants. Those standards require that we plan and perform our examination to obtain reasonable assurance, in all material respects, about whether the description is fairly presented and the controls were suitably designed to achieve the related control objectives stated in the description as of [*date*].

An examination of a description of a service organization's system and the suitability of the design of the service organization's controls to achieve the related control objectives stated in the description involves performing procedures to obtain evidence about the fairness of the presentation of the description of the system and the suitability of the design of the controls to achieve the related control objectives stated in the description. Our procedures included assessing the risks that the description is not fairly presented and that the controls were not suitably designed to achieve the related control objectives stated in the description. An examination engagement of this type also includes evaluating the overall presentation of the description and the suitability of the control objectives stated therein, and the suitability of the criteria specified by the service organization and described at page *[aa]*.

We did not perform any procedures regarding the operating effectiveness of the controls stated in the description and, accordingly, do not express an opinion thereon.

We believe that the evidence we obtained is sufficient and appropriate to provide a reasonable basis for our opinion.

Inherent limitations

Because of their nature, controls at a service organization may not prevent, or detect and correct, all errors or omissions in processing or reporting transactions [*or identification of the function performed by the system*]. The projection to the future of any evaluation of the fairness of the presentation of the description, or any conclusions about the suitability of the design of the controls to achieve the related control objectives is subject to the risk that controls at a service organization may become ineffective or fail.

Opinion

In our opinion, in all material respects, based on the criteria described in XYZ Service Organization's assertion,

a. the description fairly presents the [*type or name of*] system that was designed and implemented as of [*date*], and

b. the controls related to the control objectives stated in the description were suitably designed to provide reasonable assurance that the control objectives would be achieved if the controls operated effectively as of [*date*].

Restricted use

This report is intended solely for the information and use of XYZ Service Organization, user entities of XYZ Service Organization's [*type or name of*] system as of [*date*], and the independent auditors of such user entities, who have a sufficient understanding to consider it, along with other information including information about controls implemented by user entities themselves, when obtaining an understanding of user entities information and communication systems relevant to financial reporting. This report is not intended to be and should not be used by anyone other than these specified parties.

[*Service auditor's signature*]

[*Date of the service auditor's report*]

[*Service auditor's city and state*]

Following is a modification of the scope paragraph in a type 1 report if the description of the service organization's system refers to the need for complementary user entity controls. (New language is shown in boldface italics)

> We have examined XYZ Service Organization's description of its [type or name of] system (description) made available to user entities of the system for processing their transactions [or identification of the function performed by the system] as of [date], and the suitability of the design of controls to achieve the related control objectives stated in the description. ***The description indicates that certain complementary user entity controls must be suitably designed and implemented at user entities for related controls at the service organization to be considered suitably designed to achieve the related control objectives. We have not evaluated the suitability of the design or operating effectiveness of such complementary user entity controls.***

Following is a modification of the applicable subparagraph in the opinion paragraph of a type 1 report if the application of complementary user entity controls is necessary to achieve the related control objectives stated in management's description of the service organization's system (New language is shown in boldface italics):

> *b.* The controls related to the control objectives stated in the description were suitably designed to provide reasonable assurance that those control objectives would be achieved if the controls operated effectively as of [*date*] ***and user entities applied the complementary user entity controls contemplated in the design of XYZ Service Organization's controls as of [date].***

Following is a modification of the paragraph that describes management of XYZ Service Organization's responsibilities to be used in a type 1 report when the control objectives have been specified by an outside party. (New language is shown in boldface italics):

> On page XX of the description, XYZ Service Organization has provided an assertion about the fairness of the presentation of the description and suitability of the design of the controls to achieve the related control objectives stated in the description. XYZ Service Organization is responsible for preparing the description and assertion, including the completeness, accuracy, and method of presentation of the description and assertion, providing the services covered by the description, selecting the criteria, and designing, implementing, and documenting controls to achieve the related control objectives stated in the description. ***The control objectives have been specified by [name of party specifying the control objectives] and are stated on page [aa] of the description.***

.A69

Appendix B: Illustrative Modified Service Auditor's Reports

The following examples of modified service auditor's reports are for guidance only and are not intended to be exhaustive or applicable to all situations. They are based on the illustrative reports in appendix A.

Example 1: Qualified Opinion for a Type 2 Report—The Description of the Service Organization's System is Not Fairly Presented in All Material Respects

The following is an illustrative paragraph describing the basis for the qualified opinion. The paragraph would be inserted before the modified opinion paragraph. All other report paragraphs are unchanged.

Basis for qualified opinion

The accompanying description states on page [*mn*] that XYZ Service Organization uses operator identification numbers and passwords to prevent unauthorized access to the system. Based on inquiries of staff personnel and observation of activities, we have determined that operator identification numbers and passwords are employed in applications A and B but are not required to access the system in applications C and D.

Opinion

In our opinion, except for the matter described in the preceding paragraph, and based on the criteria described in XYZ Service Organization's assertion on page *[aa]*, in all material respects. . .

Example 2: Qualified Opinion—The Controls are Not Suitably Designed to Provide Reasonable Assurance That the Control Objectives Stated in the Description of the Service Organization's System Would be Achieved if the Controls Operated Effectively

The following is an illustrative paragraph describing the basis for the qualified opinion. The paragraph would be inserted before the modified opinion paragraph. All other report paragraphs are unchanged.

Basis for qualified opinion

As discussed on page [*mn*] of the accompanying description, from time to time, XYZ Service Organization makes changes in application programs to correct deficiencies or to enhance capabilities. The procedures followed in determining whether to make changes, in designing the changes, and in implementing them do not include review and approval by authorized individuals who are independent from those involved in making the changes. There also are no specified requirements to test such changes or provide test results to an authorized reviewer prior to implementing the changes. As a result the controls are not suitably designed to achieve the control objective, "Controls provide reasonable assurance that changes to existing applications are authorized, tested, approved, properly implemented, and documented."

Opinion

In our opinion, except for the matter described in the preceding paragraph, and based on the criteria described in XYZ Service Organization's assertion on page *[aa]*, in all material respects. . .

Example 3: Qualified Opinion for a Type 2 Report—The Controls Did Not Operate Effectively Throughout the Specified Period to Achieve the Control Objectives Stated in the Description of the Service Organization's System

The following is an illustrative paragraph describing the basis for the qualified opinion. The paragraph would be inserted before the modified opinion paragraph. All other report paragraphs are unchanged.

Basis for qualified opinion

XYZ Service Organization states in its description that it has automated controls in place to reconcile loan payments received with the various output reports. However, as noted on page [*mn*] of the description of tests of controls and results thereof, this control was not operating effectively throughout the period [*date*] to [*date*] due to a programming error. This resulted in the nonachievement of the control objective, "Controls provide reasonable assurance that loan payments received are properly recorded" throughout the period January 1, 20X1, to April 30, 20X1. XYZ Service Organization implemented a change to the program performing the calculation as of May 1, 20X1, and our tests indicate that it was operating effectively throughout the period May 1, 20X1, to December 31, 20X1.

Opinion

In our opinion, except for the matter described in the preceding paragraph, and based on the criteria described in XYZ Service Organization's assertion on page [*aa*], in all material respects. . . .

Example 4: Qualified Opinion—The Service Auditor is Unable to Obtain Sufficient Appropriate Evidence

The following is an illustrative paragraph describing the basis for the qualified opinion. The paragraph would be inserted before the modified opinion paragraph. All other report paragraphs are unchanged.

Basis for qualified opinion

XYZ Service Organization states in its description that it has automated controls in place to reconcile loan payments received with the output generated. However, electronic records of the performance of this reconciliation for the period from [*date*] to [*date*] were deleted as a result of a computer processing error and, therefore, we were unable to test the operation of this control for that period. Consequently, we were unable to determine whether the control objective, "Controls provide reasonable assurance that loan payments received are properly recorded" was achieved throughout the period [*date*] to [*date*].

Opinion

In our opinion, except for the matter described in the preceding paragraph, and based on the criteria described in XYZ Service Organization's assertion on page [*aa*], in all material respects. . .

.A70

Appendix C: Illustrative Report Paragraphs for Service Organizations That Use a Subservice Organization

Following are modifications of the illustrative type 2 report in example 1 of appendix A for use in engagements in which the service organization uses a subservice organization. (New language is shown in boldface italics; deleted language is shown by strikethrough.)

Example 1: Carve-Out Method

Scope

We have examined XYZ Service Organization's description of its system for processing user entities' transactions [*or identification of the function performed by the system*] throughout the period [*date*] to [*date*] (description) and the suitability of the design and operating effectiveness of controls to achieve the related control objectives stated in the description.

XYZ Service Organization uses a computer processing service organization for all of its computerized application processing. The description on pages [bb–cc] includes only the controls and related control objectives of XYZ Service Organization and excludes the control objectives and related controls of the computer processing service organization. Our examination did not extend to controls of the computer processing service organization.

All other report paragraphs are unchanged.

Example 2: Inclusive Method

Scope

We have examined XYZ Service Organization's ***and ABC Subservice Organization's*** description of ~~its~~ ***their*** [*type or name of*] system for processing user entities' transactions [*or identification of the function performed by the system*] throughout the period [*date*] to [*date*] (description) and the suitability of the design and operating effectiveness of ***XYZ Service Organization's and ABC Subservice Organization's*** controls to achieve the related control objectives stated in the description. ***ABC Subservice Organization is an independent service organization that provides computer processing services to XYZ Service Organization. XYZ Service Organization's description includes a description of ABC Subservice Organization's*** **[type or name of]** ***system used by XYZ Service Organization to process transactions for its user entities, as well as relevant control objectives and controls of ABC Subservice Organization.***

XYZ Service Organization's responsibilities

On page XX of the description, XYZ Service Organization ***and ABC Subservice Organization*** ~~has~~ ***have*** provided ~~an~~ ***their*** assertion***s*** about the fairness of the presentation of the description and suitability of the design and operating effectiveness of the controls to achieve the related control objectives stated in the description. XYZ Service Organization ***and ABC Subservice Organization are*** ~~is~~ responsible for preparing the description and assertion***s***, including the completeness, accuracy, and method of presentation of the description and assertion***s***, providing the services covered by the description, specifying the control objectives and stating them in the description, identifying the risks that threaten the achievement of the control objectives, selecting the criteria, and designing, implementing, and documenting controls to achieve the related control objectives stated in the description.

Inherent limitations

Because of their nature, controls at a service organization ***or subservice organization*** may not prevent, or detect and correct, all errors or omissions in processing or reporting transactions. Also, the projection to the future of any evaluation of the fairness of the presentation of the description or any conclusions about the suitability of the design or operating effectiveness of the controls to achieve the related control objectives is subject to the risk that controls at a service organization ***or subservice organization*** may become ineffective or fail.

Opinion

In our opinion, in all material respects, based on the criteria specified in XYZ Service Organization**'s and ABC Subservice Organization's** assertions on page [*aa*],

a. the description fairly presents ***XYZ Service Organization's*** ~~the~~ [*type or name of*] system ***and ABC Subservice Organization's [type or name of] system used by XYZ Service Organization to process transactions for its user entities [or identification of the function performed by the service organization's system]*** that ***were*** ~~was~~ designed and implemented throughout the period [*date*] to [*date*].

b. the controls related to the control objectives ***of XYZ Service Organization and ABC Subservice Organization*** stated in the description were suitably designed to provide reasonable assurance that the control objectives would be achieved if the controls operated effectively throughout the period [*date*] to [*date*].

c. the controls ***of XYZ Service Organization and ABC Subservice Organization that*** we tested, which were those necessary to provide reasonable assurance that the control objectives stated in the description were achieved, operated effectively throughout the period [*date*] to [*date*].

All other report paragraphs are unchanged.

.A71

Exhibit A: Illustrative Assertions by Management of a Service Organization

The assertion by management of the service organization may be included in management's description of the service organization's system or may be attached to the description. The following illustrative assertions are intended for assertions that are included in the description.

The following illustrative management assertions are for guidance only and are not intended to be exhaustive or applicable to all situations.

Example 1: Assertion by Management of a Service Organization for a Type 2 Report

XYZ Service Organization's Assertion

We have prepared the description of XYZ Service Organization's [*type or name of*] system (description) for user entities of the system during some or all of the period [*date*] to [*date*], and their user auditors who have a sufficient understanding to consider it, along with other information, including information about controls implemented by user entities of the system themselves, when assessing the risks of material misstatements of user entities' financial statements. We confirm, to the best of our knowledge and belief, that

a. the description fairly presents the [*type or name of*] system made available to user entities of the system during some or all of the period [*date*] to [*date*] for processing their transactions [*or identification of the function performed by the system*]. The criteria we used in making this assertion were that the description

i. presents how the system made available to user entities of the system was designed and implemented to process relevant transactions, including

(1) the classes of transactions processed.

(2) the procedures, within both automated and manual systems, by which those transactions are initiated, authorized, recorded, processed, corrected as necessary, and transferred to the reports presented to user entities of the system.

(3) the related accounting records, supporting information, and specific accounts that are used to initiate, authorize, record, process, and report transactions; this includes the correction of incorrect information and how information is transferred to the reports presented to user entities of the system.

(4) how the system captures and addresses significant events and conditions, other than transactions.

(5) the process used to prepare reports or other information provided to user entities' of the system.

(6) specified control objectives and controls designed to achieve those objectives.

(7) other aspects of our control environment, risk assessment process, information and communication systems (including the related business processes), control activities, and monitoring controls that are relevant to processing and reporting transactions of user entities of the system.

ii. does not omit or distort information relevant to the scope of the [*type or name of*] system, while acknowledging that the description is prepared to meet the common needs of a broad range of user entities of the system and the independent auditors of those user entities, and may not, therefore, include every aspect of the [*type or name of*] system that each individual user entity of the system and its auditor may consider important in its own particular environment.

b. the description includes relevant details of changes to the service organization's system during the period covered by the description when the description covers a period of time.

c. the controls related to the control objectives stated in the description were suitably designed and operated effectively throughout the period [*date*] to [*date*] to achieve those control objectives. The criteria we used in making this assertion were that

i. the risks that threaten the achievement of the control objectives stated in the description have been identified by the service organization;

ii. the controls identified in the description would, if operating as described, provide reasonable assurance that those risks would not prevent the control objectives stated in the description from being achieved; and

iii. the controls were consistently applied as designed, including whether manual controls were applied by individuals who have the appropriate competence and authority.

Example 2: Assertion by Management of a Service Organization for a Type 1 Report

XYZ Service Organization's Assertion

We have prepared the description of XYZ Service Organization's [*type or name of*] system (description) for user entities of the system as of [*date*], and their user auditors who have a sufficient understanding to consider it, along with other information including information about controls implemented by user entities themselves, when obtaining an understanding of user entities' information and communication systems relevant to financial reporting. We confirm, to the best of our knowledge and belief, that

a. the description fairly presents the [*type or name of*] system made available to user entities of the system as of [*date*] for processing their transactions [*or identification of the function performed by the system*]. The criteria we used in making this assertion were that the description

i. presents how the system made available to user entities of the system was designed and implemented to process relevant transactions, including

(1) the classes of transactions processed.

(2) the procedures, within both automated and manual systems, by which those transactions are initiated, authorized, recorded, processed, corrected as necessary, and transferred to the reports presented to user entities of the system.

(3) the related accounting records, supporting information, and specific accounts that are used to initiate, authorize, record, process, and report transactions; this includes the correction of incorrect information and how information is transferred to the reports provided to user entities of the system.

(4) how the system captures and addresses significant events and conditions, other than transactions.

(5) the process used to prepare reports or other information provided to user entities of the system.

(6) specified control objectives and controls designed to achieve those objectives.

(7) other aspects of our control environment, risk assessment process, information and communication systems (including the related business processes), control activities, and monitoring controls that are relevant to processing and reporting transactions of user entities of the system.

ii. does not omit or distort information relevant to the scope of the [*type or name of*] system, while acknowledging that the description is prepared to meet the common needs of a broad range of user entities of the system and the independent auditors of those user entities, and may not, therefore, include every aspect of the [*type or name of*] system that each individual user entity of the system and its auditor may consider important in its own particular environment.

b. the controls related to the control objectives stated in the description were suitably designed as of [*date*] to achieve those control objectives. The criteria we used in making this assertion were that

i. the risks that threaten the achievement of the control objectives stated in the description have been identified by the service organization.

ii. the controls identified in the description would, if operating as described, provide reasonable assurance that those risks would not prevent the control objectives stated in the description from being achieved.

.A72

Exhibit B: Comparison of Requirements of Section 801, *Reporting On Controls at a Service Organization*, With Requirements of International Standard on Assurance Engagements 3402, *Assurance Reports on Controls at a Service Organization*

This analysis was prepared by the AICPA Audit and Attest Standards staff to highlight substantive differences between section 801, *Reporting on Controls at a Service Organization*, and International Standard on Assurance Engagements (ISAE) 3402, *Assurance Reports on Controls at a Service Organization*, and to explain the rationale for those differences. This analysis is not authoritative and is prepared for informational purposes only.

1. Intentional Acts by Service Organization Personnel

Paragraph .26 of this section requires the service auditor to investigate the nature and cause of any deviations identified, as does paragraph 28 of ISAE 3402. Paragraph .27 of this section indicates that if the service auditor becomes aware that the deviations resulted from intentional acts by service organization personnel, the service auditor should assess the risk that the description of the service organization's system is not fairly presented and that the controls are not suitably designed or operating effectively. The ISAE does not contain the requirement included in paragraph .27 of this section. The Auditing Standards Board (ASB) believes that information about intentional acts affects the nature, timing, and extent of the service auditor's procedures. Therefore, paragraph .27 provides follow-up action for the service auditor when he or she obtains information about intentional acts as a result of performing the procedures in paragraph .26 of this section.

Paragraph .36(c)(ii) of this section, which is not included in ISAE 3402, also requires the service auditor to request written representations from management that it has disclosed to the service auditor knowledge of any actual, suspected, or alleged intentional acts by management or the service organization's employees, of which it is aware, that could adversely affect the fairness of the presentation of management's description of the service organization's system or the completeness or achievement of the control objectives stated in the description.

2. Anomalies

Paragraph 29 of ISAE 3402 contains a requirement that enables a service auditor to conclude that a deviation identified in tests of controls involving sampling is not representative of the population from which the sample was drawn. This section does not include this requirement because of concerns about use of terms such as, "in the extremely rare circumstances" and "a high degree of certainty." These terms are not used in U.S professional standards and the ASB believes their introduction in this section could have unintended consequences. The ASB also believes that the deletion of this requirement will enhance examination quality because deviations identified by the service auditor in tests of controls involving sampling will be treated in the same manner as any other deviation identified by the practitioner, rather than as an anomaly.

3. Direct Assistance

Paragraph .35 of this section requires the service auditor to adapt and apply the requirements in paragraph .27 of AU-C section 610, *The Auditor's Consideration of the Internal Audit Function in an Audit of Financial Statements*, when the service auditor uses members of the service organization's internal audit function to provide direct assistance. Because AU-C section 610 provides for an auditor to use the work of the internal audit function in a direct assistance capacity, paragraph .35 of this section also provides for this. The International Standards on Auditing and the ISAEs do not provide for use of the internal audit function for direct assistance.

4. Subsequent Events

With respect to events that occur subsequent to the period covered by the description of the service organization's system up to the date of the service auditor's report, paragraph .42 of this section requires the service auditor to disclose in the service auditor's report, if not disclosed by management in its description, any event that is of such a nature and significance that its disclosure is necessary to prevent users of a type 1 or type 2 report from being misled. The ASB believes that information about such events could be important to user entities and their auditors. ISAE 3402 limits the types of subsequent events that would need to be disclosed in the service auditor's report to those that could have a significant effect on the service auditor's report.

Paragraph .43 of this section requires the service auditor to adapt and apply the guidance in AU-C section 560, *Subsequent Events and Subsequently Discovered Facts*, if, after the release of the service auditor's report, the service auditor becomes aware of conditions that existed at the report date that might have affected management's assertion and the service auditor's report had the service auditor been aware of them. The ISAE does not include a similar requirement. The ASB believes that, by analogy, AU-C section 560 provides needed guidance to a service auditor by presenting the various circumstances that could occur during the subsequent events period and the actions a service auditor should take.

5. Statement Restricting Use of the Service Auditor's Report

This section requires the service auditor's report to include a statement restricting the use of the report to management of the service organization, user entities of the service organization's system, and user auditors. The ASB believes that the unambiguous language in the restricted use statement prevents misunderstanding regarding who the report is intended for. Paragraphs .A61–.A62 of this section explain the reasons for restricting the use of the report. ISAE 3402 requires the service auditor's report to include a statement indicating that the report is intended only for user entities and their auditors, However, the ISAE does not require the inclusion of a statement restricting the use of the report to specified parties, although it does not prohibit the inclusion of restricted use language in the report.

6. Documentation Completion

Paragraph 50 of the ISAE requires the service auditor to assemble the documentation in an engagement file and complete the administrative process of assembling the final engagement file on a timely basis after the date of the service auditor's assurance report. Paragraph .49 of this section also requires the service auditor to assemble the engagement documentation in an engagement file and complete the administrative process of assembling the final engagement file on a timely basis, but also indicates that a timely basis is no later than 60 days following the service auditor's report release date. The ASB made this change to parallel the definition of *documentation completion date* in paragraph .06 of AU-C section 230, *Audit Documentation*.

7. Engagement Acceptance and Continuance

Paragraph .09 of this section establishes conditions for the acceptance and continuance of an engagement to report on controls at a service organization. One of the conditions is that management acknowledge and accept responsibility for providing the service auditor with written representations at the conclusion of the engagement. ISAE 3402 does not include this requirement as a condition of engagement acceptance and continuance.

8. Disclaimer of Opinion

If management does not provide the service auditor with certain written representations, paragraph 40 of ISAE 3402 requires the service auditor, after discussing the matter with management, to disclaim an opinion. In the same circumstances, paragraph .39 of this section requires the service auditor to take appropriate action, which may include disclaiming an opinion or withdrawing from the engagement.

Paragraphs .56–.57 of this section contain certain incremental requirements when the service auditor plans to disclaim an opinion.

9. Elements of the Section 801 Report That Are Not Required in the ISAE 3402 Report

Paragraphs .52–.53 of this section contain certain requirements regarding the content of the service auditor's report, which are incremental to those in ISAE 3402. These incremental requirements are included in paragraphs .52(c)(iii); .52(e)(iv); .52(i); and .52(k) for type 2 reports, and in paragraphs .53(c)(iii); .53(e)(iv); .53(j); and .53(k) for type 1 reports.

[Revised, December 2012, to reflect conforming changes necessary due to the issuance of SAS Nos. 122–126.]

AT TOPICAL INDEX

References are to AT section and paragraph numbers.

A

References are to AT section and paragraph numbers.

References are to AT section and paragraph numbers.

L

M

References are to AT section and paragraph numbers.

S

T

References are to AT section and paragraph numbers.